MY DAD HAD THAT CAR

THAT CAR

A NOSTALGIC LOOK AT

THE AMERICAN AUTOMOBILE

1920–1990

MY DAD HAD THAT CAR

A NOSTALGIC LOOK AT

THE AMERICAN AUTOMOBILE

1920–1990

TAD BURNESS

WITH COMMENTARY BY **MATT STONE**

BLACK DOG
& LEVENTHAL
PUBLISHERS
NEW YORK

DEDICATION

First, we dedicate this book in loving memory of Tad Burness and his great love for nostalgia and all things car-related. Even though your residence is now in Heaven, your legacy and memories live on in your family, friends, and readers of this new book.

Second and most importantly, we dedicate this book to the glory of God because we know that "Every good and perfect gift is from above and comes down from the Father." (James 1:17a)

—Sandra Burness & Tammy Rimack

Copyright © 1986, 1990 by Tad Burness
Cover design by James Iacobelli
Cover art © Tad Burness
Cover copyright © 2017 by Hachette Book Group, Inc.

Black Dog & Leventhal Publishers
Hachette Book Group
1290 Avenue of the Americas
New York, NY 10104
www.hachettebookgroup.com
www.blackdogandleventhal.com

Originally published under the name *Monstrous American Car Spotter's Guide 1920–1980* and *American Car Spotter's Guide 1981–1990* by Motorbooks International in the United States.

First Edition: May 2017

Black Dog & Leventhal Publishers is an imprint of Hachette Books, a division of Hachette Book Group. The Black Dog & Leventhal Publishers name and logo are trademarks of Hachette Book Group, Inc.

The publisher is not responsible for websites (or their content) that are not owned by the publisher.

The Hachette Speakers Bureau provides a wide range of authors for speaking events. To find out more, go to www.HachetteSpeakersBureau.com or call (866) 376-6591.

Library of Congress Control Number: 2016956753

ISBNs: 978-0-316-43091-3 (hardcover); 978-0-316-50695-3 (ebook); 978-0-316-50692-2 (Mobipocket); 978-0-316-50694-6 (PDF)

Printed in China

IM

10 9 8 7 6

CONTENTS

Foreword by Matt Stone vii

Part One: Ace to Yellow Cab 1920–1939 1

Part Two: Airway to Willys 1940–1965 285

Part Three: American Motors to Thunderbird 1966–1980.....................641

Part Four: American Car Spotter's Guide 1981–1990.........................1071

Index..1355

FOREWORD
My Dad Had That Car

By the time I was ten years old, I could identify nearly every car on the road–by year, make, model, and possibly engine spec. Remember, there was no Google back then. I learned it all the old fashioned way:, from my father (a serious car guy), from the pages of *Motor Trend* and *Road & Track* magazines, and by making my dad take me to every new car dealership on Holt Boulevard in Ontario, California, each fall, when all the "next year's" models premiered. We cruised the lots and I collected sales brochures (some of which I still have).

Mostly I just paid attention to what was on the road, often with my camera around my neck to snap my own photos. What I didn't have was the late Tad Burness's original *Monstrous American Car Spotter's Guide*. Think of a single book, as large as any Webster's dictionary, with more than 1,000 pages and 10,000 illustrations of every American car, make, and model from 1920–1980. It weighed more than most notebook computers do these days.

Mr. Burness hit upon a somewhat magical format with this encyclopedic collection of copious illustrations combined with a surprising amount of detailed information about these many thousands of cars. Now a professional automotive writer and book author, it is my honor to assist in the freshening, updating, and republishing Mr. Burness's original "Google on paper" guidebook to nearly every American car built from 1920 to 1990. (The original volume only went through 1980s, with a subsequent version that came along later, extending the window of coverage through 1990.) I find it interesting that these wonderful books, first published in 1970, grew out of Mr. Burness's own scrapbooks

which he assembled to share with his friends at car club meetings. These imaginative books have been out of print for more than a decade, and now—combined into one even more massive volume and wearing a new name—it's back! I hope you missed this storehouse of information and charming presentation as I have.

The effort necessary to create or procure the more than 10,000 photos and illustrations in the original *Spotter's Guide* was considerable, particularly so in the time before computerized assistance. The table of contents and chapter openers will help you zero in on the specific make or model you may initially be most interested in, but the fun way to enjoy this amazing material is to start at the beginning with Ace, produced from 1920–1922 in Ypsilanti, Michigan, then slowly browse through page by page, year by year, make by model, and I promise you that nearly every page will surprise and delight you. You'll discover car brands you've never heard of and models you've never seen, produced in places you never dreamt built cars.

Why did Mr. Burness decide only to include American cars? We're not sure, as he doesn't explain this motivation in any of his text, but perhaps this is what interested him the most or that gathering solid information and enough photos and illustrations from around the (pre-Internet) world would have been too arduous an undertaking. Mr. Burness covers American cars up and down the spectrum, from the smallest, least expensive, or prestigious, up to the largest, most powerful, and most costly makes.

You may be surprised to know that Illinois was once a hotbed of automotive production–plus Indiana and New Jersey. They even built cars in my car buddy Bill Thornley's current hometown of Fullerton, California (that of course would be the Balboa brand of automobiles, produced from 1923–1925, running a powerful 100 horsepower, 178-cubic-inch supercharged Kessler straight-8 engine). You'll see the car brands that did and didn't survive the Great Depression and World War II, and all the rest that succeeded or failed of their own accord.

While you won't find pages of specifications tables, there are a surprising number of factoids and interesting sidenotes on every page, some of which you won't find on the Internet. I'll bet you didn't know that Briggs & Stratton, of Milwaukee, the company that may have made the single-cylinder engine in your lawn mower, also produced cars from 1919–1923. The illustrations will show you they were little more than a buckboard with bicycle-type spoke wheels and fenders. Given that the text is spare and space is at a premium on these highly illustrated pages, Mr. Burness did a lot of abbreviating, such as "C.I.D." for "Cubic Inches Displacement," "WB" for "Wheelbase," and "F.O.B." for "Freight on Board," which was a common descriptor of giving price information for what the vehicle cost prior to shipping from its factory (such as "$895 Freight on Board, Detroit"—in other words, the price quote doesn't include shipping).

With this book, I assure you an enjoyable and nostalgic walk through American automotive history and design. The illustrations are detailed and delightful, and many of the photographs are the carmaker's own advertising, sales brochure, or public relations still shots. The images are black and white, which lends a wonderful archival quality to the presentation.

And if you're talking about a 1934 Ford 3-window coupe, a 1946 Ford Tudor, a 1952 Ford Customline V-8, or a 1963 Lincoln Continental hardtop sedan, 1983 Mustang GT Turbo, then yeah—*My Dad Had That Car*!

This is the kind of visual, written, and graphics information that hooked me on cars back in the 1960s, and I'm sure will equally ignite or reinvigorate your passion for collector cars. I'm privileged to be a part of the rebirth of Tad Burness's great original work and vision.

Enjoy.

Matt Stone
January, 2017

MY DAD HAD THAT CAR

PART ONE

1920–1939
ACE TO YELLOW CAB

CONTENTS

Body Key 4
Tire Key 4
Ace 5
Allen 5
AMCO 5
American 5
American Steamer 6
Anderson........................6
Apperson 7
Argonne Four 7
Auburn..........................8
Austin 4 13
Balboa 13
Bay State 13
Beggs 13
Bell..............................14
Biddle............................14
Birch 14
Birmingham 14
Bour-Davis......................14
Brewster 15
Brewster-Ford..................15
Briggs and Stratton..........15
Briscoe 15
Brooke-Spacke..................15
Brooks Steamer 15
Bryan Steamer 16
Buick............................16
Bush..............................25
Cadillac..........................26
Cardway..........................35
Case 35
Chalmers........................35
Chandler........................36
Checker..........................39
Chevrolet 39
Chrysler 50
Cleveland Six..................64
Climber..........................65
Coats 65
Cole Aero-Eight 65
Columbia Six 66
Comet 66
Commonwealth 66
Continental…..................66

Cord..............................67
Courier..........................68
Crane-Simplex 68
Crawford 68
Crosley 68
Crow-Elkhart 68
Cunningham....................68
Dagmar..........................69
Daniels 69
Davis 69
Delling Steam..................70
DeSoto 70
Detroit Air-Cooled..........75
Detroit Electric 75
Detroit Steam..................75
DeVaux 75
Diana 75
Dixie Flyer 75
Doble Steam....................76
Dodge 76
Dorris............................86
Dort 86
Driggs 86
Duesenberg 87
Dupont 88
Durant 89
Dymaxion 90
Eagle 90
Earl 90
Elcar 90
Elgin 91
Erskine 91
Essex 92
Falcon 97
Falcon-Knight 97
Fargo 97
Ferris 97
Flint 97
Ford 99
Fox 105
Franklin 106
Gardner..........................110
Gearless Steam 111
Geronimo........................111
Globe 111

Graham-Paige................112
Graham 113
Grant 6 116
Gray 116
Gray Light Car................116
Halladay 117
Handley-Knight 117
Hanson 6 117
Harris 6 117
Haynes 117
H.C.S. 119
Heine-Velox 119
Hertz............................119
Holmes 119
Hudson 120
Huffman 127
Hupmobile....................128
Innes 136
Jackson 136
Jaeger 136
Jewett 137
Jones 6 139
Jordan 139
Julian 141
Kelsey 141
Kenworthy 141
King 141
Kissel 142
Kleiber 144
Kline Kar........................144
Lafayette........................144
Lasalle 147
Leach 151
Leon Rubay....................151
Lexington 151
Liberty Six......................151
Lincoln..........................152
Locomobile 162
Lorraine 164
Maibohm 164
Marmon 164
Marquette 168
Masterbilt 6....................168
Maxwell 169
MacDonald 170

McFarlan........................170
Mercer 170
Mercury 170
Mercury 171
Meteor 171
Milburn 171
Miller 171
Mitchell 171
Monitor 171
Monroe 171
Moon 172
Moore 173
Morriss-London 173
Nash..............................173
National 184
Nelson 184
Noma 6 184
Oakland 185
Ogren 190
Oldsmobile 190
Overland 199
Owen Magnetic..............202
Packard 203
Paige..............................215
Pan 218
Parenti 218
Paterson 6 218
Peerless 218
Peters 222
Phianna 222
Piedmont 222
Pierce-Arrow 222
Pilot 226
Plymouth 227
Pontiac 232
Porter 239
Premier 239
R&V Knight 240
Rauch & Lang................240
Reo 240
Revere 247
Richelieu 247
Rickenbacker..................247
Roamer 247
Rockne 6 248

Rollin 248
Rolls-Royce 248
Roosevelt........................249
Rugby 249
Ruxton 249
Saxon 249
Sayers (S&S) 250
Schuler 250
Scripps-Booth 250
Severin 250
Shaw 250
Sheridan 250
Singer............................251
Skelton 4........................251
Standard Eight 251
Stanley 251
Stanwood 6 251
Star................................252
Stearns-Knight 254
Stephens 255
Sterling-Knight 255
Stevens-Duryea 255
Stout Scarab 255
Studebaker 256
Stutz 263
Templar..........................266
Terraplane 266
Texan 268
Tulsa 4 268
Velie 268
Viking............................271
Waltham 272
Wasp 272
Westcott 272
Whippet..........................273
White 275
Wills Sainte Claire..........275
Willys 276
Willys-Knight..................279
Windsor 8 284
Winther 6 284
Winton 6 284
Yellow Cab 284

Tad Burness began his mammoth *Car Spotter's Guide* at 1920, which makes a lot of sense because the American automobile industry by then was crystalizing and had begun to mature. Additionally, the cars got more interesting.

General Motors, the international automotive and transportation powerhouse we now know, was founded in 1908, so it was still somewhat embryonic prior to World War I. And the world wars each catalyzed considerable development in terms of the automobile, primarily because of the need to engineer ever-stronger and more reliable engines to power military vehicles of all stripes, including ships, smaller boats, tanks, and such during wartime. So the newer, faster, tougher engine technology developed for military use by car companies trickled down into consumer automobiles once the war was over, when the big factories resumed production of cars and trucks. The variety of technologies born of war—metallurgy, electrical systems, cooling systems, carburetors and ignitions, advancements in tires, aerodynamics, and so on— all spurred the design and mechanical advancement of the automobile. While many historians and enthusiasts alike justifiably revel in the birth and very early development of automobiles and the motorized transportation industry, Mr. Burness chose 1920 as the launching point for his famous guides.

I find it interesting that "Part One, 1920–1939" begins and ends with two carmaker brands that are no longer with us, Ace and Yellow Cab. Ace cars, as a division of the Apex Motor Corporation, were produced only from 1920–1922 in Ypsilanti, Michigan, not far from Detroit, which would of course, become known as The Motor City and remains to most people the epicenter of American car design, production, legend, and lore. You may not recognize Yellow Cab (proper noun) as a *brand* of car, although anyone that's ever spent any time in a major city immediately identifies a yellow cab (lower case) as a taxi. The Yellow Cab Company of Chicago (not to be confused with the similarly named Yellow Taxicab Co.) was founded by John D. Hertz (of today's Hertz Corporation's worldwide retail car rental network) in 1914. Its specially designed taxicabs were powered by a 4-cylinder Continental engine equipped with a purpose-built taxicab body supplied by the Racine Body Co., of Racine, Wisconsin.

Everyone has their favorite brands and models, but the car business often revolved, watched, and studied the progress (and occasional lack thereof) of Ford. At the beginning of the 1920s, Ford was still producing the Model T, which Henry Ford I held onto well past its prime; true, it's the car that put America on wheels and really made production line assembly methods viable for carmakers, but the beloved Tin Lizzie's reign was largely over by the mid-20s. Something new was needed, that of course was the Model A, which came to market for 1928 with a conventional manual transmission and foot pedal set up (instead of the Model T's fussy pedal arrangement and steering wheel–mounted throttle), plus twice the horsepower of the Model T.

The Model A in its many body style variations put Ford back in the spotlight, but the times and vehicle development were advancing quickly, and it wasn't long before Ford was again ready to move the ball downfield in 1932. Prior to that time, V-8 engines were only found in large, expensive, luxury automobiles, but Ford created the ultimate example of automotive trickle-down economics beginning in 1932 with the birth of the world-changing Ford "Flathead" V-8; available in a popularly priced car and truck lineup. The flathead promised and delivered nearly 100 horsepower, smoothness, strong low-end torque, reliability, and luxury car prestige never before offered in a Ford or any of its competitors.

A lot changed in December, 1929, with the stock market crash and the beginning of the Great Depression. Many carmakers folded their factory tents during the 1930s, and those still in business wrapped up the decade preparing for yet another world war. Please enjoy this deeply illustrated walk through the automotive 1920s and 30s.

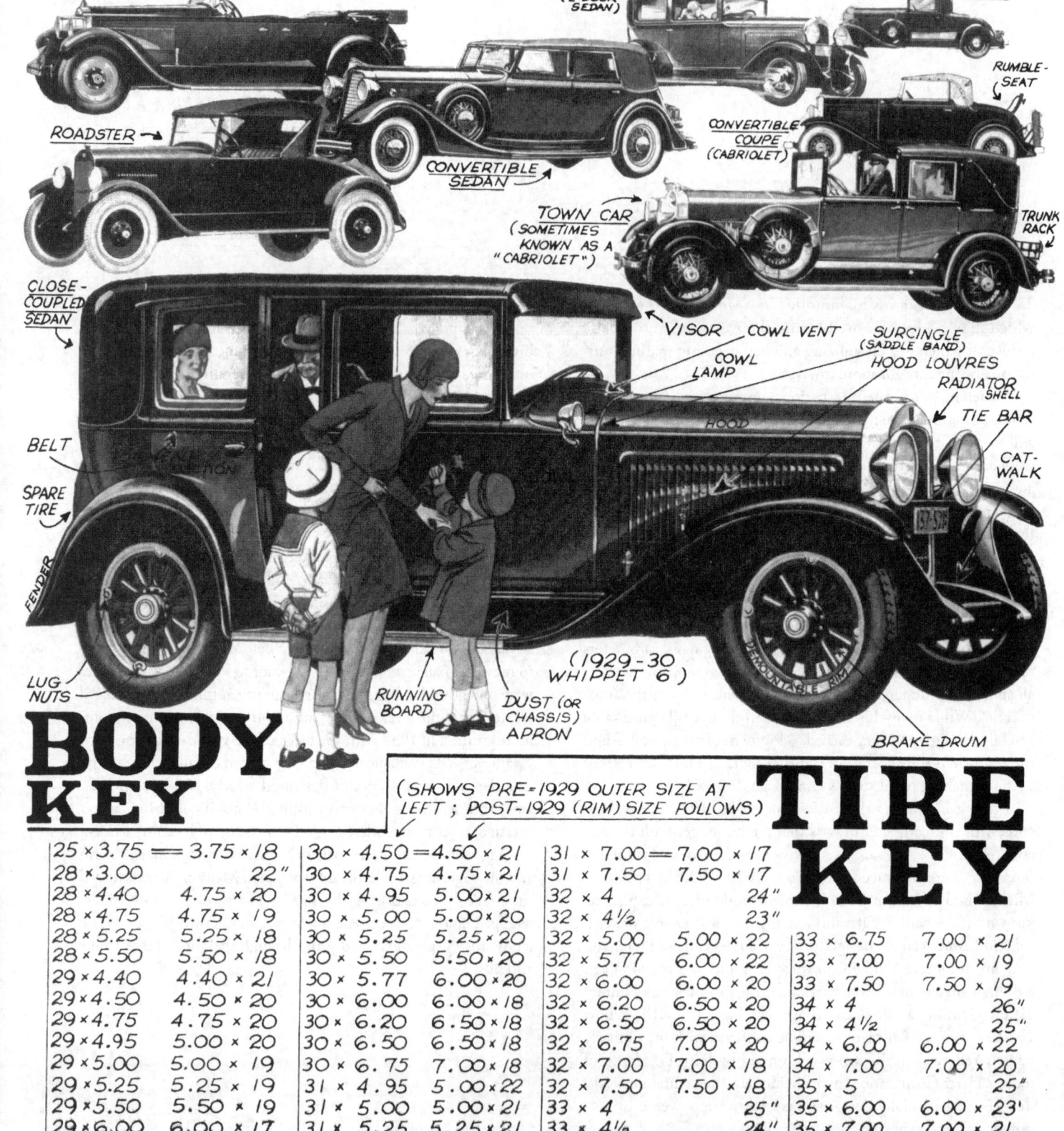

TOURING CAR OR PHAETON

COACH (2-DOOR SEDAN)

COUPE

ROADSTER

CONVERTIBLE SEDAN

CONVERTIBLE COUPE (CABRIOLET)

RUMBLE-SEAT

TOWN CAR (SOMETIMES KNOWN AS A "CABRIOLET")

TRUNK RACK

CLOSE-COUPLED SEDAN

VISOR COWL VENT SURCINGLE (SADDLE BAND)
COWL LAMP HOOD LOUVRES
RADIATOR SHELL
TIE BAR
CAT-WALK

BELT

SPARE TIRE

FENDER

LUG NUTS

RUNNING BOARD

DUST (OR CHASSIS) APRON

(1929-30 WHIPPET 6)

BRAKE DRUM

BODY KEY

TIRE KEY

(SHOWS PRE-1929 OUTER SIZE AT LEFT; POST-1929 (RIM) SIZE FOLLOWS)

25 × 3.75 = 3.75 × 18	30 × 4.50 = 4.50 × 21	31 × 7.00 = 7.00 × 17				
28 × 3.00 — 22"	30 × 4.75 — 4.75 × 21	31 × 7.50 — 7.50 × 17				
28 × 4.40 — 4.75 × 20	30 × 4.95 — 5.00 × 21	32 × 4 — 24"				
28 × 4.75 — 4.75 × 19	30 × 5.00 — 5.00 × 20	32 × 4½ — 23"				
28 × 5.25 — 5.25 × 18	30 × 5.25 — 5.25 × 20	32 × 5.00 — 5.00 × 22	33 × 6.75 — 7.00 × 21			
28 × 5.50 — 5.50 × 18	30 × 5.50 — 5.50 × 20	32 × 5.77 — 6.00 × 22	33 × 7.00 — 7.00 × 19			
29 × 4.40 — 4.40 × 21	30 × 5.77 — 6.00 × 20	32 × 6.00 — 6.00 × 20	33 × 7.50 — 7.50 × 19			
29 × 4.50 — 4.50 × 20	30 × 6.00 — 6.00 × 18	32 × 6.20 — 6.50 × 20	34 × 4 — 26"			
29 × 4.75 — 4.75 × 20	30 × 6.20 — 6.50 × 18	32 × 6.50 — 6.50 × 20	34 × 4½ — 25"			
29 × 4.95 — 5.00 × 20	30 × 6.50 — 6.50 × 18	32 × 6.75 — 7.00 × 20	34 × 6.00 — 6.00 × 22			
29 × 5.00 — 5.00 × 19	30 × 6.75 — 7.00 × 18	32 × 7.00 — 7.00 × 18	34 × 7.00 — 7.00 × 20			
29 × 5.25 — 5.25 × 19	31 × 4.95 — 5.00 × 22	32 × 7.50 — 7.50 × 18	35 × 5 — 25"			
29 × 5.50 — 5.50 × 19	31 × 5.00 — 5.00 × 21	33 × 4 — 25"	35 × 6.00 — 6.00 × 23"			
29 × 6.00 — 6.00 × 17	31 × 5.25 — 5.25 × 21	33 × 4½ — 24"	35 × 7.00 — 7.00 × 21			
29 × 6.50 — 6.50 × 17	31 × 6.00 — 6.00 × 19	33 × 5.77 — 6.00 × 23	36 × 4 — 28"			
	31 × 6.20 — 6.50 × 19	33 × 6.00 — 6.00 × 21	36 × 4½ — 27"			
30 × 3.00 — 24"	31 × 6.50 — 6.50 × 19	33 × 6.20 — 6.50 × 21	37 × 5 — 27"			
30 × 3½ — 23"	31 × 6.75 — 7.00 × 19	33 × 6.50 — 6.50 × 21	38 × 4½ — 29"			

ACE
(1920–1922)

('21)
MODEL L (6 CYL.)

APEX MOTOR CORP., YPSILANTI, MICH.
USED 4-CYL. GRAY-BELL OR
6-CYL. HERSCHELL-SPILLMAN
AND CONTINENTAL ENGINES.

BECAME A PART OF AMERICAN
MOTOR TRUCK CO., NEWARK, OHIO.

(1914–1922) ALLEN

ALLEN MOTOR CO.,
FOSTORIA, OHIO

(MODEL "43" ALL-NEW FOR 1920)
110" W.B., 4-CYL., 192.4 C.I.D.
4.63 GEAR RATIO
32 × 4" TIRES

20-22 MODEL "43"

AMCO (1920)

AMERICAN MOTORS, INC., N.Y.C.
with 4 CYL. G.B. and S. ENGINE
DESIGNED FOR EXPORT ONLY
RIGHT HAND DRIVE AVAILABLE
114" wheelbase

AMERICAN

AMERICAN MOTORS CORPORATION
Factory and General Offices: Plainfield, N.J.
AMERICAN SOUTHERN MOTORS CORPORATION,
Greensboro, N.C.

(1916–1924)

20

(DRUM HEADLIGHTS
and NICKEL TRIM IN '23)

WITH HERSCHELL-SPILLMAN
6-CYL. ENGINE

(NO RADICAL
CHANGES FOR 1920,
BUT COLUMBIA
REAR AXLE IS NEW.)

AMERICAN STEAMER

22 (ONLY MODEL YEAR)

(1922 -1924) AMERICAN STEAM TRUCK CO., CHICAGO and ELGIN, ILL.

2 - CYLINDER COMPOUND ENGINE

ANDERSON 6
(1916 – 1926)
ANDERSON MOTOR CO., ROCK HILL, S.C.

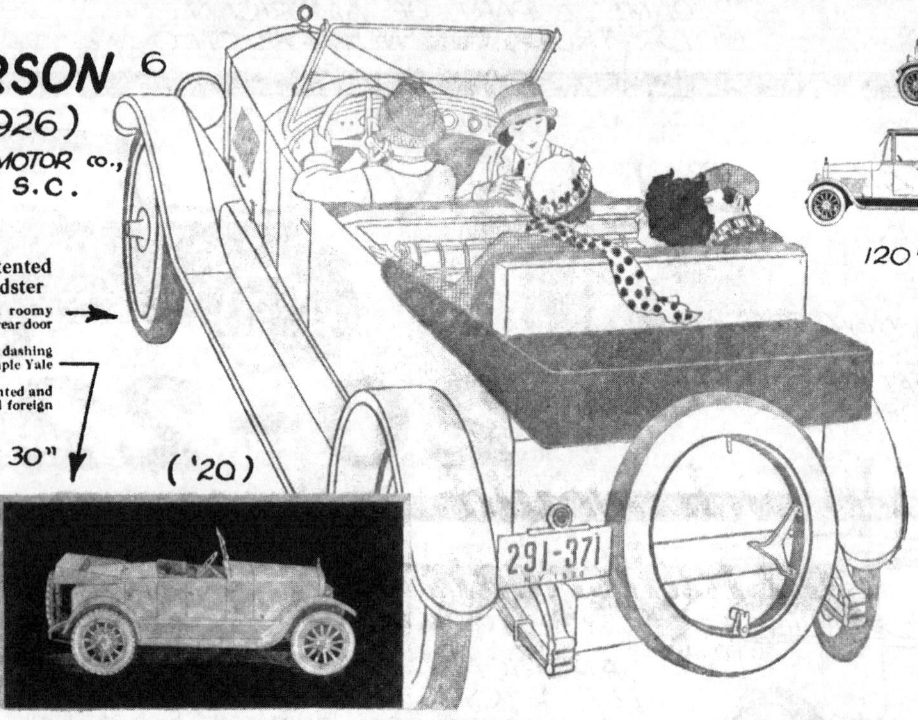

The Anderson Patented Convertible Roadster

With tonneau open—a roomy touring car for five, with rear door and complete top.
With tonneau closed—a dashing roadster for two, with ample Yale lock luggage space.
Protected by patents granted and pending in the U. S. and foreign countries.

1920 "SERIES 30" HAS A NEW "7-R" CONTINENTAL ENGINE (6 CYLS., 224 C.I.D.) 4.50 GEAR RATIO

('20)

291-371

20 120" W.B.(THROUGH '22) 55 H.P. @ 2600 RPM

2 SERIES IN 1923 :
"41" = 114 " W.B. 195.6 C.I.D. "6-Y" CONTINENTAL ENGINE
"50" = 122 " W.B. 242.1 C.I.D. CONTINENTAL ENGINE

21 "J" SPT. TOUR. "SERIES 40" (SAME SPECS. AS '20, CONT'D. 1922)

23 4.62 GEAR RATIO ←"50"

"41" AND "50" SERIES CONTINUED, WITH 4.75 and 4.50 GEAR RATIOS

24 "41" WHEELBASE NOW 115"

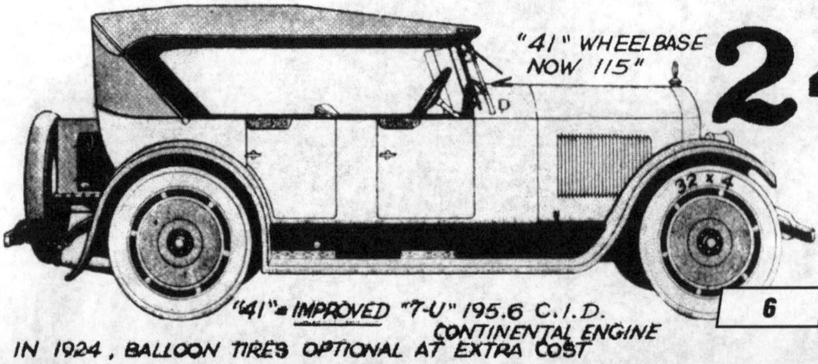

"41"= IMPROVED "7-U" 195.6 C.I.D. CONTINENTAL ENGINE
IN 1924, BALLOON TIRES OPTIONAL AT EXTRA COST

'25 "41" HAS 49 H.P. @ 2500 RPM

'25 "50" HAS 56 H.P. @ 2300 RPM "8-R" CONT. ENG. **24-26**

APPERSON BROS. AUTOMOBILE CO. (1902-1926)
Kokomo, Indiana

APPERSON

331.8 C.I.D. V-8

THE EIGHT WITH EIGHTY LESS PARTS

STANDARD MODEL

130" WHEELBASES (8-CYL., THROUGH '26)

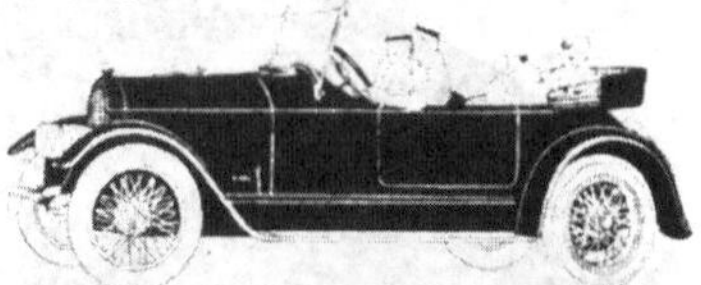

"ANNIVERSARY"

4.25 GEAR RATIOS

34 × 4 1/2

33 × 4

20   "ANNIVERSARY" MODEL (NOTE DIFFERENT RADIATOR DESIGN)

1922 = FIRST YEAR WITH SQUARE-BACK AND SQUARE-EDGED BODIES. DRUM HEADLIGHTS ON LATER MODELS OF "BEVERLY" SPORTSTER.

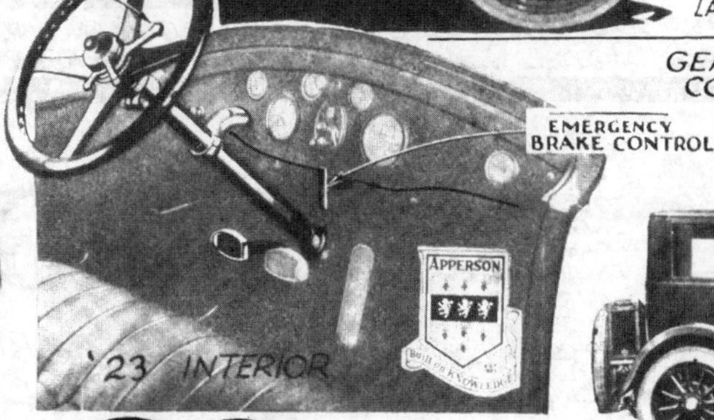

GEARSHIFT and HAND-BRAKE CONTROLS MOVED AWAY FROM FLOOR in 1923.

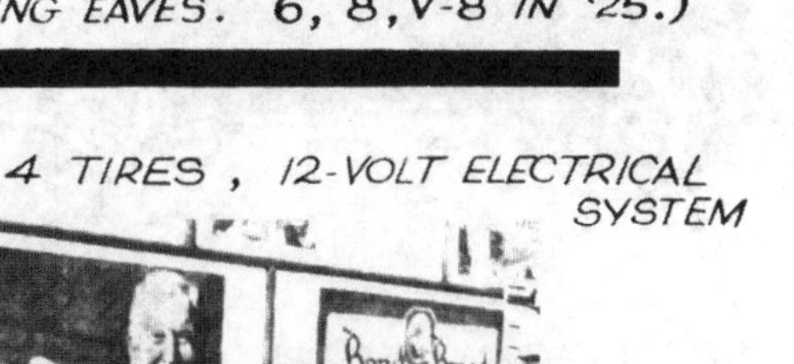

THE SELECTOR

EMERGENCY BRAKE CONTROL

'23 INTERIOR

('24)(6)

APPERSON

BALLOON TIRES AND 4-WHEEL BRAKES OPTIONAL

21 331.8 C.I.D. V-8 AVAILABLE THROUGH '25; (REPLACED BY LYCOMING 276 C.I.D., 65-H.P. STRAIGHT-8 FOR '25-26)

23 NEW 207.1 C.I.D. SIX ALSO AVAIL. '25 CLOSED CARS SIMILAR, BUT HAVE VENTILATING EAVES. 6, 8, V-8 IN '25.)

ARGONNE FOUR

ARGONNE MOTOR CAR CO., JERSEY CITY, N.J. (1919* – 1920)

*(ALL CARS 1920 MODELS)

128" WHEELBASE, 32 × 4 TIRES, 12-VOLT ELECTRICAL SYSTEM

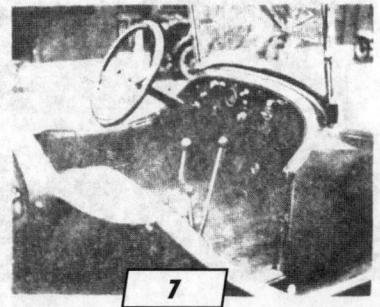

DUESENBERG-DESIGNED "OWN" 4-CYL. ENGINE

(3 3/4" × 5 1/8" BORE + STROKE)

AUBURN Beauty·SIX

AUBURN AUTOMOBILE COMPANY, Auburn, Indiana

(1900 – 1937)*

*–1936 MODEL IS
FINAL AUBURN

"BEAUTY SIX"
DESIGNATION
RETAINED THROUGH
1922.

BLACK HARD-RUBBER (METAL-BOUND)
OUTSIDE DOOR HANDLES REPLACE BRIGHT METAL
TYPE IN 1922.

(DRUM HEADLIGHTS IN 1922)

19-22

33 × 4

"6-39" HAS 120" W.B., 224 C.I.D. 6-CYL. CONTINENTAL ENGINE, 4.66 GEAR RATIO
(1920) "6-51" IS 1922 MODEL WITH 121" W.B., 5.00 GEAR RATIO; "8-R" REPLACES "7-R"
CONTINENTAL ENGINE IN
LATER MODELS.

NEW MODELS ON JAN. 1, 1923, BUT "6-51"
STILL AVAILABLE UNTIL 3-23.

"6-43" HAS 114" W.B.,
195.6 C.I.D. CONTINENTAL "6-Y"
ENGINE   31 × 4 TIRES
SAME SIZE "7-U" CONTINENTAL
ENGINE IN 1924, STARTS
9-1-23.

"6-63" HAS 122" W.B.,
248.9 C.I.D. AUBURN O.H.V.
ENGINE.* 32 × 4½ TIRES
*– Weidely spec.

23-24

"6-43"
AND
"6-63"
(6 CYL.)

EARLIEST 1925 MODELS
(9-24 TO 12-24) (8 CYL.)
SIMILAR IN STYLE.
(6 CYL. CONTINUED)

"6-43"

4.63 GEAR RATIO ('24)
"6-43" (1924) FIRST YEAR
WITH CHAIN CHECKS ON
DOORS.

"6-43" "ENGLISH COACH"
OFFERED '24 - EARLY '25.

8

"SPORT CAR" ("6-63")

AUBURN

8-88 ROADSTER

21-171
OHIO-1926

COMPLETELY
RESTYLED
EARLY IN 1925.

25-27

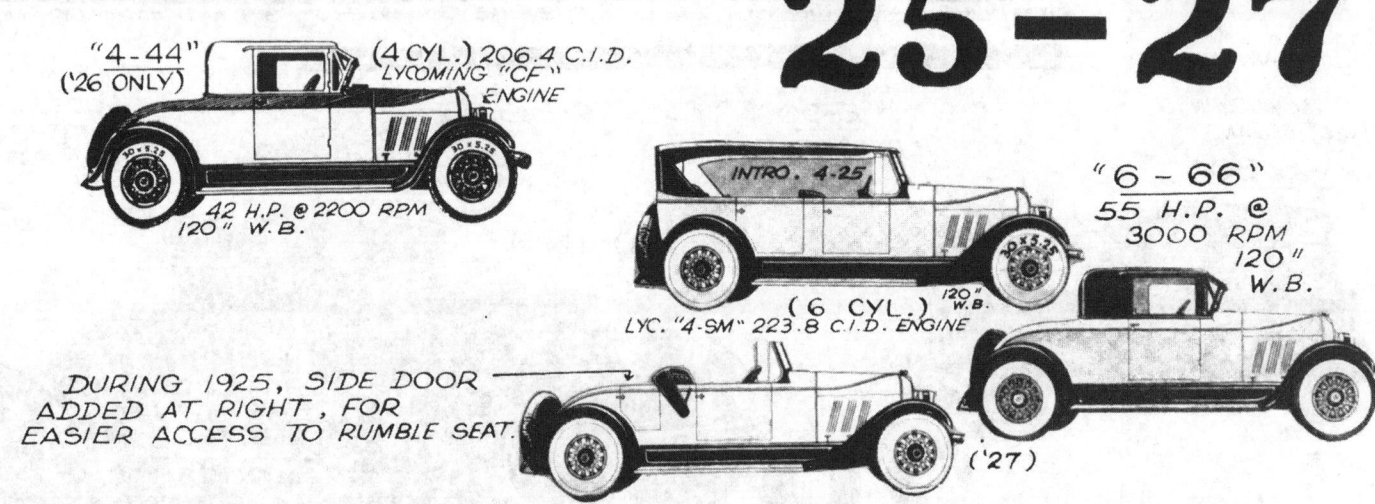

"4-44"
('26 ONLY)   (4 CYL.) 206.4 C.I.D.
LYCOMING "CF"
ENGINE

42 H.P. @ 2200 RPM
120" W.B.

INTRO. 4-25

"6-66"
55 H.P. @
3000 RPM
120"
W.B.

(6 CYL.) 120" W.B.
LYC. "4-SM" 223.8 C.I.D. ENGINE

DURING 1925, SIDE DOOR
ADDED AT RIGHT, FOR
EASIER ACCESS TO RUMBLE SEAT.

('27)

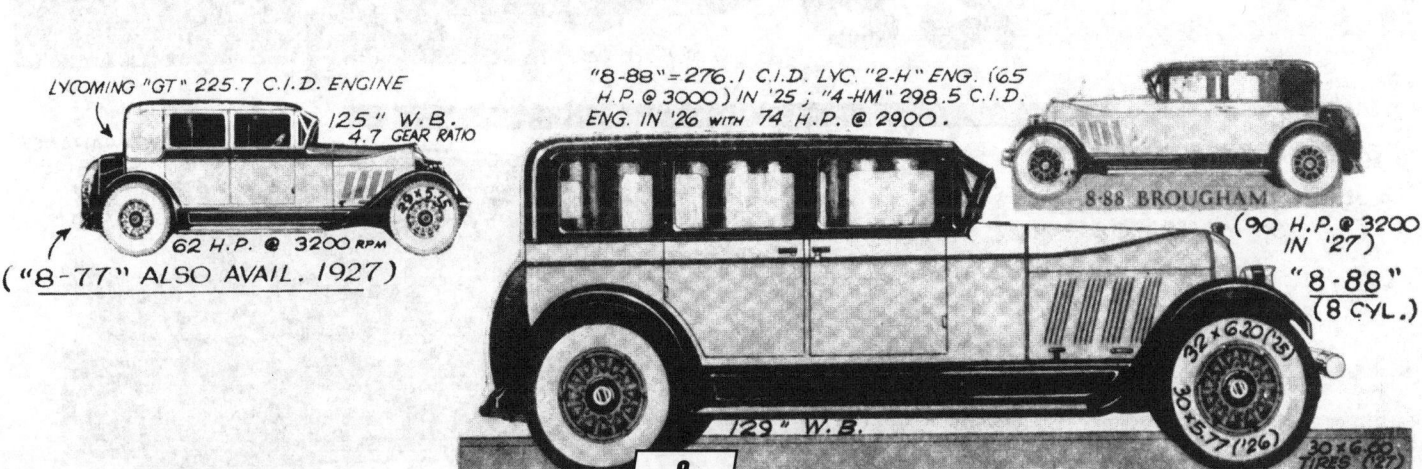

LYCOMING "GT" 225.7 C.I.D. ENGINE

125" W.B.
4.7 GEAR RATIO

62 H.P. @ 3200 RPM

("8-77" ALSO AVAIL. 1927)

"8-88" = 276.1 C.I.D. LYC. "2-H" ENG. (65
H.P. @ 3000) IN '25; "4-HM" 298.5 C.I.D.
ENG. IN '26 WITH 74 H.P. @ 2900.

8-88 BROUGHAM

(90 H.P. @ 3200
IN '27)

"8-88"
(8 CYL.)

129" W.B.

32 x 6.20 ('25)
30 x 5.77 ('26)
30 x 6.00
TIRES ('27)

9

AUBURN

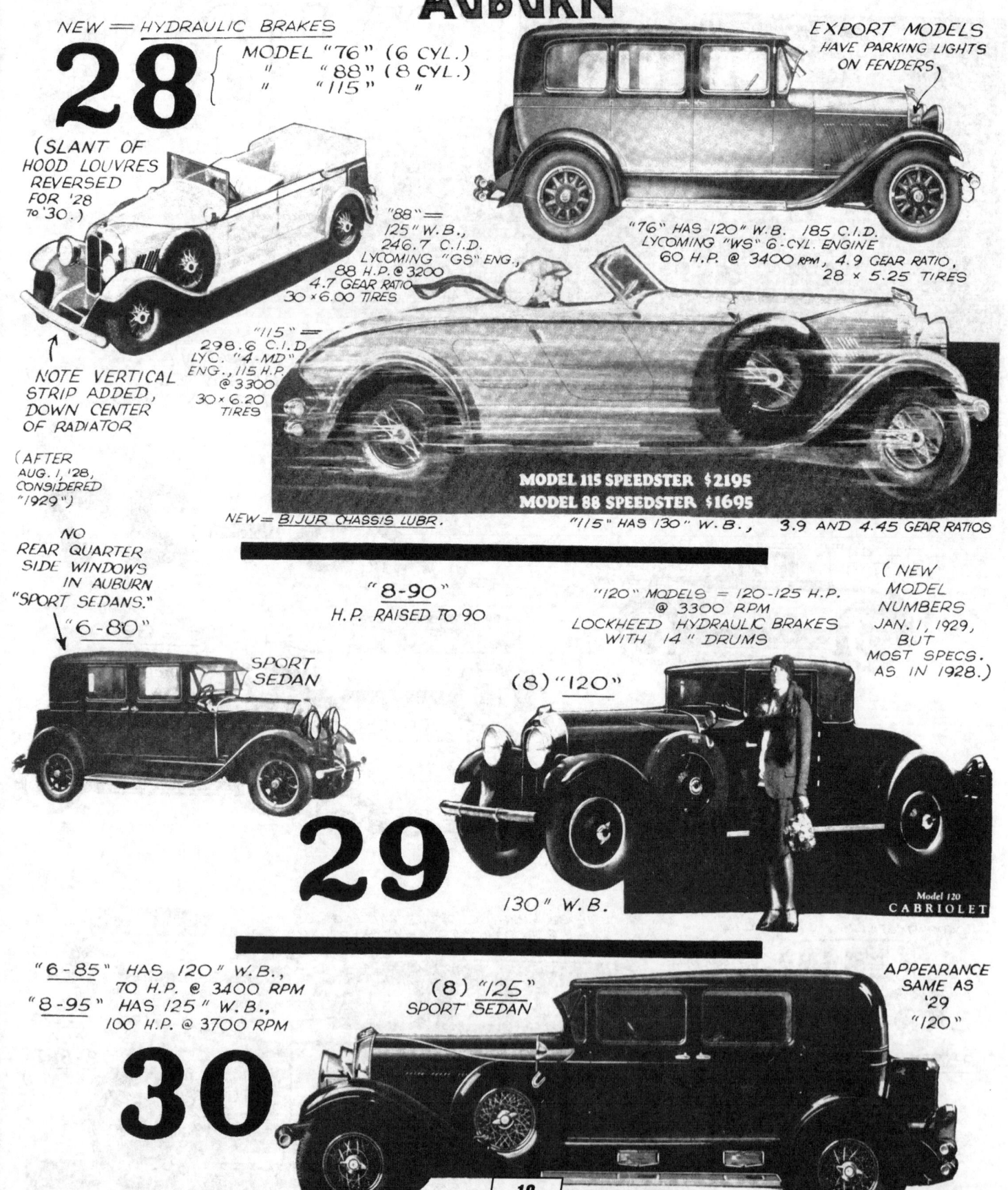

NEW = HYDRAULIC BRAKES

28
- MODEL "76" (6 CYL.)
- " "88" (8 CYL.)
- " "115" "

(SLANT OF HOOD LOUVRES REVERSED FOR '28 TO '30.)

NOTE VERTICAL STRIP ADDED, DOWN CENTER OF RADIATOR

(AFTER AUG. 1, '28, CONSIDERED "1929")

EXPORT MODELS HAVE PARKING LIGHTS ON FENDERS

"88" = 125" W.B., 246.7 C.I.D. LYCOMING "GS" ENG., 88 H.P. @ 3200 4.7 GEAR RATIO 30 × 6.00 TIRES

"115" = 298.6 C.I.D. LYC. "4-MD" ENG., 115 H.P. @ 3300 30 × 6.20 TIRES

"76" HAS 120" W.B. 185 C.I.D. LYCOMING "WS" 6-CYL. ENGINE 60 H.P. @ 3400 RPM, 4.9 GEAR RATIO, 28 × 5.25 TIRES

MODEL 115 SPEEDSTER $2195
MODEL 88 SPEEDSTER $1695

NEW = BIJUR CHASSIS LUBR.

"115" HAS 130" W.B., 3.9 AND 4.45 GEAR RATIOS

NO REAR QUARTER SIDE WINDOWS IN AUBURN "SPORT SEDANS."

"6-80"

"8-90" H.P. RAISED TO 90

"120" MODELS = 120-125 H.P. @ 3300 RPM LOCKHEED HYDRAULIC BRAKES WITH 14" DRUMS

(NEW MODEL NUMBERS JAN. 1, 1929, BUT MOST SPECS. AS IN 1928.)

SPORT SEDAN

(8) "120"

29

130" W.B.

Model 120 CABRIOLET

"6-85" HAS 120" W.B., 70 H.P. @ 3400 RPM
"8-95" HAS 125" W.B., 100 H.P. @ 3700 RPM

(8) "125" SPORT SEDAN

APPEARANCE SAME AS '29 "120"

30

10 125 H.P. @ 3600 RPM

COMPLETELY RESTYLED FOR 1931 !

AUBURN

4.45 GEAR RATIO

126" W.B.
286.6 C.I.D. LYCOMING "GU"
STRAIGHT-8 ENGINE.
98 H.P. @ 3400 RPM
(THROUGH '32)

2-DOOR BROUGHAM

31-32

"8-98" ONLY MODEL AVAILABLE IN 1931. IN 1932, A CHOICE OF "8-100" OR "12-160." "A" AFTER '32 MODEL NO. DENOTES CUSTOM SERIES WITH "DUAL RATIO" 2-SPEED DIFFERENTIAL.

"8-100" HAS **4.7** GEAR RATIO, 127 OR 136" W.B.

6.00 × 17 TIRES IN 1932

V-12 LYCOMING "BB" 391 C.I.D. ENGINE
160 H.P. @ 3400 RPM   132" W.B.
4 TO 1 GEAR RATIO

V-12 HAS "12" ON BUMPER

V-12 (1932)

33

8

SPEEDSTER

V-12 "SALON" SERIES

11

AUBURN

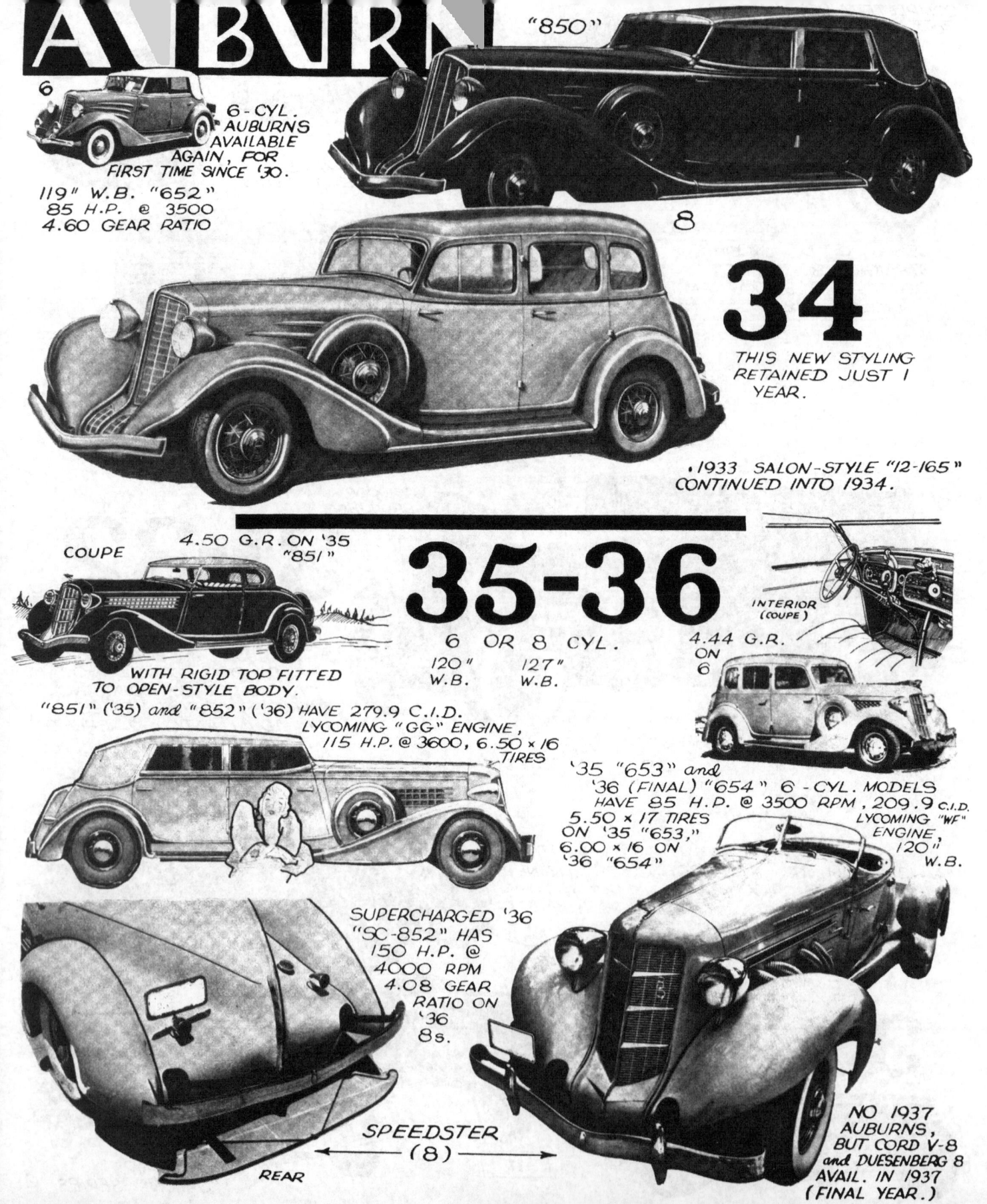

"850"

6 - CYL. AUBURNS AVAILABLE AGAIN, FOR FIRST TIME SINCE '30.

119" W.B. "652"
85 H.P. @ 3500
4.60 GEAR RATIO

8

34

THIS NEW STYLING RETAINED JUST 1 YEAR.

• 1933 SALON-STYLE "12-165" CONTINUED INTO 1934.

35-36

COUPE

4.50 G.R. ON '35 "851"

INTERIOR (COUPE)

6 OR 8 CYL.
120" 127"
W.B. W.B.

4.44 G.R. ON 6

WITH RIGID TOP FITTED TO OPEN-STYLE BODY.

"851" ('35) and "852" ('36) HAVE 279.9 C.I.D. LYCOMING "GG" ENGINE, 115 H.P. @ 3600, 6.50 × 16 TIRES

'35 "653" and '36 (FINAL) "654" 6 - CYL. MODELS HAVE 85 H.P. @ 3500 RPM, 209.9 C.I.D. LYCOMING "WF" ENGINE, 120" W.B.
5.50 × 17 TIRES ON '35 "653,"
6.00 × 16 ON '36 "654"

SUPERCHARGED '36 "SC-852" HAS 150 H.P. @ 4000 RPM 4.08 GEAR RATIO ON '36 8s.

REAR

SPEEDSTER ← (8) →

NO 1937 AUBURNS, BUT CORD V-8 and DUESENBERG 8 AVAIL. IN 1937 (FINAL YEAR.)

AUSTIN 4

(BLT. 1930-1941 AT BUTLER, PA.)

"BANTAM" CAR

(SLANTING WINDSHIELD *and* VERTICAL HOOD LOUVRES INTRODUCED FOR '33.)

V-WINDSHIELD ON ROADSTER SINCE '31

75" W.B. (THROUGH '41)

33-34

"2-75" SERIES

(1935 HAS SLANTING LOUVRES)
13 H.P. @ 3200 RPM (1932 THROUGH '36)

30-32

12½ H.P. @ 3000 RPM (THROUGH '31)

4 CYLS., 45.6 C.I.D.
5.25 GEAR RATIO (THROUGH '41)
3.75 × 18 TIRES (THROUGH '36)

39

"62"

37

38

"60"

20 H.P. @ 4000 RPM (THROUGH '39)

(DURING '39, HOOD LOUVRES SHORTENED, THEN ELIMINATED.)

Bantam

BALBOA

BALBOA MOTOR CORP. FULLERTON, CALIF.

(1923 - 1925)

KESSLER STRAIGHT-8 ENGINE   178 C.I.D.
SUPERCHARGED   100 H.P. @ 4000 RPM

BAY STATE

R. H. LONG CO., FRAMINGHAM, MASS.

(1922 - 1924)

(CONTINENTAL 6-CYL. ENGINE)

BEGGS

20

BEGGS MOTOR CAR CO., KANSAS CITY, MO.
(1918 - 1923)
6-CYL. CONTINENTAL ENGINE

120" WHEELBASE

BELL

BELL MOTOR CAR CO., YORK, PA.
(1915-1921)

20-21

BIDDLE

BIDDLE MOTOR CAR
CO., PHILADELPHIA, PA.
(1915-1923)

121" W.B., 32 × 4" TIRES
4-CYLINDER DUESENBERG OR
BUDA ENGINE

4.5 GEAR RATIO

BIRCH (1917-1923)

"SUPER 4" **20**

BIRCH MOTOR CARS, INC., CHICAGO
(SOLD BY MAIL ORDER, 4 and 6 CYL.)

BIRMINGHAM

BIRMINGHAM MOTORS, JAMESTOWN, N.Y.
(1920 - 1924)

6 - CYL. CONTINENTAL "7-R" engine
124" W.B., 32 × 4 TIRES

WILSON BODY, MADE OF "HASKELITE"
PLYWOOD, COVERED WITH DUPONT FABRIKOID

22

(ONLY YEAR MODEL
IN
PRODUCTION)

4 - WHEEL
INDEPENDENT
SUSPENSION

BOUR - DAVIS (1915-1922)

BUILT AT CHICAGO, ILL.; SHREVEPORT, LA.; also DETROIT
(COMPANY CHANGED LOCATIONS, KNOWN AS BOUR-DAVIS CO.
AND ALSO AS LOUISIANA MOTOR CAR CO.)

125" WHEELBASE

20

NEW FOR 1920:
WESTINGHOUSE STARTING + LIGHTING,
13-DISC CLUTCH, AND NEW CARBURETOR.

224 C.I.D. CONTINENTAL
ENGINE, 4.75 GEAR RATIO

BREWSTER

21

(BREWSTER-KNIGHT)

BREWSTER + CO.,
LONG ISLAND
CITY, N.Y.

(1915 - 1925)

"41" TOWN LANDAULETTE

4-CYL. KNIGHT
ENGINE **24**

6-PASS
DOUBLE ENCL.
DRIVE

BREWSTER - FORD

(CUSTOM BODY ON FORD V-8 CHASSIS)

SPRINGFIELD
MFG. CO.,
SPRINGFIELD,
MASS.

(1934
TO
1936)

BRIGGS AND STRATTON

← I-CYLINDER
AIR COOLED ENGINE

BRIGGS AND STRATTON,
MILWAUKEE, WIS.

(1919 — 1923)

B R I S C O E

BRISCOE MOTOR CORP., JACKSON, MICH.

(1914 - 1921)   (109" W.B.)

NEW "BEVEL-
LINE" STYLING
FOR 1920.

20-21

"4-34"

4 CYLS.

LATE '21 = NAME
CHANGED TO EARL

4.18 GEAR RATIO, 31 × 4 TIRES

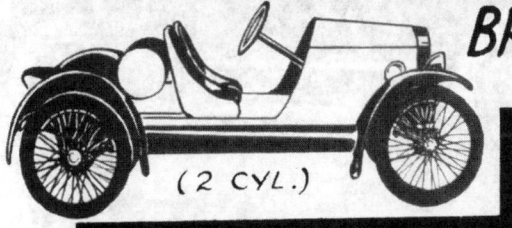

(2 CYL.)

BROOKE-SPACKE

(1920 — 1921)

SPACKE MACHINE and TOOL CO.,
INDIANAPOLIS, INDIANA
(1921 = MORE COMPLETE BODY)

BROOKS STEAMER

26

MFD. IN CANADA,
1923 - 1926.
OPERATIONS
MOVED TO
BUFFALO,
N.Y., 1926.

(FABRIC-COVERED
BODY)

BRYAN STEAMER

BRYAN STEAM MOTORS, PERU, INDIANA
(1918 – 1923)   (TOURING CARS ONLY)

BUICK

BUICK MOTOR COMPANY, FLINT, MICHIGAN
Division of General Motors Corporation
Canadian Factories: McLaughlin-Buick, Oshawa, Ontario

ESTABLISHED 1903; A G.M. PRODUCT SINCE 1908.

4.0 GEAR RATIO

6 CYLINDERS OVERHEAD VALVES (241.6 C.I.D. THROUGH '23)

19-20
21-22

1922 CLOSED CARS HAVE HEATER.

1922 SIX and NEW FOUR AVAILABLE AUGUST, 1921.

4.08 G.R. ('21)

33 x 4

1922 GEAR RATIOS — 4.66 (4, THROUGH '23) 4.60 ; 4.90 (6)

TRUNK DETAILS

23

NEW COWL VENT

BUICK 4 HAS 170 C.I.D., 35 H.P.

"4-36" COUPE

"4-38" TOURING SEDAN → (2-DOOR COACH)

'23 HAS DRUM-TYPE LAMPS; ALUMINUM HOOD BEADING ON 6.

"6-45"

4

6

31 x 4

32 x 4

4.40 G.R. (6)

7-PASS.

"6-54"

"6-50"

BUICK

4 (FINAL 4-CYL. BUICK)

NEW 4-WHEEL BRAKES (FRONT BRAKE DETAILS)

"4-37" SEDAN

24

NEW STYLING, NEW RADIATOR DESIGN

"4-34" ROADSTER

"4-33" 4-PASS. COUPE

"4-35" TOURING

PAINTED RADIATOR SHELL ON 4-CYL. MODELS

$\frac{4}{6}$

6

HAS LONGER HOOD AND NICKEL-PLATED RADIATOR

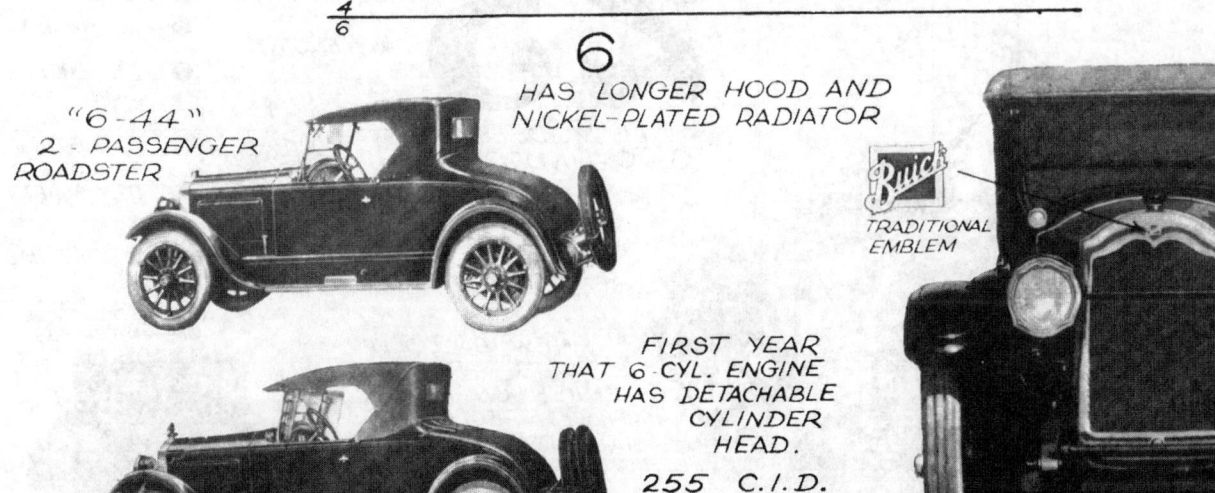

"6-44" 2-PASSENGER ROADSTER

Buick

TRADITIONAL EMBLEM

FIRST YEAR THAT 6-CYL. ENGINE HAS DETACHABLE CYLINDER HEAD. 255 C.I.D. 65 H.P. @ 2600 RPM

"6-54" SPORT ROADSTER

"6-45"
5-PASS. TOURING

BUICK
24
(CONT'D.)

"DOUBLE
SERVICE"
5-PASS. SEDAN
"6-41"

A LOW-
PRICED
SEDAN
WITH
SQUARE-
EDGED
REAR
PANELS.

"6-49" 7-PASS.
TOURING

"6-47"
5-PASS. SEDAN

"6-55" 4-PASS.
SPORT TOURING

"6-50"
7-PASS. SEDAN

"6-48"
4-PASS. COUPE

"6-51"
BROUGHAM

(EARLIEST '24
BROUGHAM HAS SEMI-
RECTANGULAR-STYLE
REAR QUARTER
WINDOWS
INSTEAD OF
OVAL AS
ILLUSTRATED.)

25

ALL MODELS
6-CYLINDERS

WITH
"SEALED
CHASSIS"

MASTER 6
255 C.I.D.
70 H.P.
@ 2800 RPM

'25 CLOSED
BODIES HAVE
1-PIECE
WINDSHIELD

STANDARD 6
190.8 C.I.D.
50 H.P.
@ 2800
RPM

Here are the vital points at which Buick engineering
provides this extra protection:

❶ = FAN HUB   ❺ = CLUTCH

❷ = ENGINE   ❻ = TRANSMISSION

                       ❼ = UNIVERSAL
                            JOINT

❸ = STARTER-   ❽ = TORQUE TUBE
     GENERATOR   (ENCLOSING
     (IN 1 UNIT)   DRIVESHAFT)

❹ = FLYWHEEL   ❾ = DIFFERENTIAL

NEW BALLOON
TIRES. DUCO
FINISH ON ALL
MODELS BEGINNING
JANUARY, 1925.

(32 × 5.77 TIRES
ON MASTER 6)

2-DOOR COACHES
AVAILABLE AFTER NOV., '24.

"6-48"
4-PASS. COUPE
(MASTER 6)   WITH NEW
OVAL QUARTER WINDOWS)

BUICK

STANDARD 6
207.1 C.I.D.
60 H.P. @ 2800 RPM
114 3/8" W.B.

MASTER 6
274.2 C.I.D.
75 H.P. @ 2800 RPM
120" or 128" W.B.

CLOSED CARS WITH
NEW DOUBLE-BEAD
BELT MOLDINGS.

PUROLATOR OIL FILTER
ON ALL MODELS.

"54-C" COUNTRY CLUB
COUPE

26

(INTRODUCED AUG. 1, 1925)

MASTER 6

"27" SEDAN

"48"
4-PASS.
COUPE

STANDARD 6

31 × 5.25 TIRES ON STANDARD,
33 × 6.00 " ON MASTER (THROUGH '28)

WHEN BETTER AUTOMOBILES ARE BUILT — BUICK WILL BUILD THEM

"128" HAS INSIDE
WATER TEMPERATURE
GAUGE AND
ORNAMENTAL
RADIATOR
CAP.

(STARTS AUG. 1, 1926)

27

"115" ═ 63 H.P.

"120," "128" ═ 77 H.P.

ONE-PIECE WINDSHIELD
ON OPEN CARS

SERIES #
INDICATES
WHEELBASE,"
EXCEPT "115"
HAS 114½" W.B.

19

BUICK

ASSIST CORD

"115," "120" and "128" SERIES AGAIN

(MINOR RESTYLING)

28

(MODELS AND SPECS. SIMILAR TO 1927)

"115" has 31 × 5.25 TIRES, 5.1 G.R.
"120" and "128" have 33 × 6.00 TIRES, 4.9 G.R.

UPPER RADIATOR PAN IS DEEPER FOR 1928.

NEW BOWL-SHAPED HEADLIGHTS

IGNITION AND STEERING LOCK

NEW RADIATOR MASCOT

WATER TEMP. GAUGE ON ALL 1928 MODELS.

STANDARD GEARSHIFT PATTERN ADOPTED.

LANDAUS WITH NEW STYLE QUARTER WINDOWS

The Silver Anniversary **BUICK**

29 (COMPLETELY RESTYLED)

(INTRODUCED SATURDAY, JULY 28, 1928)

4.9 GEAR RATIO ("116;") 4.8 ON OTHERS

SILVER ANNIVERSARY BUICK—FIVE PASSENGER SEDAN

EARLY TYPE HUB CAP (PLAINER STYLE)

29½ MODELS HAVE COLORFUL HUB CAPS OF NEW DESIGN (RED and BLACK, ON SILVER.)

"51" CLOSE-COUPLED SEDAN

BECAUSE OF ITS ODD, BULGING SIDE-PANELS, THE 1929 MODEL WAS SOON NICKNAMED "THE PREGNANT BUICK."

239.1 C.I.D., 74 H.P. @ 2800 OR 309.6 C.I.D. WITH 90½ H.P. @ 2800

new FUEL PUMP ON ALL '29 BUICKS.

"26"

"54-CC"

"20" SERIES   116" W.B.
40   "   121   "
50   "   129   "
30 x 5.50 OR
32 x 6.50 TIRES

NEW DASH HAS BLACK CIRCULAR GAUGES IN A ROW.

BUICK
(COMPLETELY RESTYLED)
('30 MODEL INTRO. JULY, 1929)

1930 – 6 CYL.
1931 – 8 CYL.

new "ROAD-SHOCK ELIMINATOR"
new NON-GLARE WINDSHIELD (SLANTED 7°)

VALVE-IN-HEAD
Buick
MOTOR CARS

5.50 OR 6.50 × 19 TIRES

1930 INSTRUMENT PANEL

3 SERIES FOR '30 →	"40"	118" W.B.	80½ H.P.
	50	124	98
	60	132	"

NEW STRAIGHT-8 1931 ENGINES REPLACE ALL 1930 SIXES

30-31

1931 MODEL HAS ALL-NEW INSTRUMENT PANEL. →

FINAL BUICK ROADSTER

4 1931 BASIC MODEL SERIES

"50"	114" W.B.	77 H.P.	220.7 C.I.D.
60	118	90	272.6
80	124	104	344.8
90	132	"	"

TIRES = 5.25 × 18 (50,)
5.50 × 19 (60,)
OR 6.50 × 19 (80 and 90 SERIES)

1931 HAS SYNCHRO-MESH TRANSMISSION.

WINGED "8" → ON RADIATOR CAP OF 1931 MODEL.

22

32 BUICK
with WIZARD CONTROL

NEW STYLE
SWEEP-HAND
SPEEDOMETER

SPEEDOMETER

DASH GAUGES
MOVED TO LEFT SIDE

DETAILS OF
FRONT
END

"50" HAS
230.4 C.I.D.,
78 H.P. @
3200 RPM,
114" W.B.
5.50 × 18 TIRES

"60" HAS
272.5 C.I.D.,
90 H.P. @
3000 RPM,
118" W.B.
6.00 × 18 TIRES

"80" AND "90" HAVE
344.7 C.I.D.,
104 H.P. @ 2900 RPM,
126" AND 134" W.B.
7.00 × 18 TIRES

H.P. INCREASED '33
(@ 3200 RPM)
TO 86 ("50,")
97 ("60,")
113 ("80", "90")

NEW 6.00 × 17, 6.50 × 17, 7.00 × 17 TIRE SIZES ('33 ONLY)

WHEELBASES OF 119, 127, 130, 138"

33

BUICK

NEW 16" WHEELS ON ALL.

INTERIOR →

93, 88, 100 or

88 TO 116 H.P. @ 3200 RPM

233, 235.3, 278.1 or 344.8 C.I.D.; 4.33, 4.8, 4.7 or 4.36 G.R.

"AUTOMATIC STARTING"

'34

34-35

"40," "50," "60" and "90" SERIES ("40" STARTS 5-34)

117", 119", 128", 136" W.B.

6.50 × 16, 7.00 × 15, 7.00 × 16 or 7.50 × 16 TIRES (THROUGH '39) 4.44, 3.9, 4.22 or 4.55 G.R.

"40" HAS 233 C.I.D. (AS SINCE '34) OTHERS HAVE 320.2 C.I.D.
"40" HAS 93 H.P. OTHERS HAVE 120 (@ 3200 RPM)

ROADMASTER

The ROADMASTER, series 80 six-passenger Sedan

118," 122," 131" and 138" WHEELBASES

36

STARTING 1936, NAMES GIVEN TO MODELS

"40" = SPECIAL
"60" = CENTURY
"80" = ROADMASTER
"90" = LIMITED

← INTERIOR

The BUICK LIMITED, Series 90 four door six passenger

BUICK

"SPECIAL" has 100 H.P. @ 248 C.I.D. 3200 RPM (THROUGH '49)

320.2 C.I.D. ON OTHERS (TO '52, EXCEPT "SUPER," WHICH STARTS '40.)

1937

37

130 H.P. @ 3400 RPM ON "CENTURY 60" and up.

7.50 x 16

"LIMITED"

4.4, 3.9, 4.22 (1937 WHEELBASES: 122", 126", 131", 138") OR 4.62 G.R.

SPECIAL ══ 122" W.B. 107 H.P. @ 3400 RPM

CENTURY ══ 126" W.B. 141 H.P. @ 3600 RPM, AS ON LARGER MODELS.

ROADMASTER = 133" W.B.

LIMITED ══ 140" W.B.

(SAME FIGURES THROUGH '40, EXCEPT "SPECIAL" W.B.)

4.44, 3.9, 4.18 OR 4.56 G.R. (THROUGH '39)

"LIMITED"

SINCLAIR

"ROADMASTER"

1938

38

DELCO-REMY IGN. (SINCE '27) FISHER BODIES, AS BEFORE

← DASH

39

DIRECTIONAL SIGNALS

"SPECIAL" WHEELBASE SHORTENED TO 120."

"LIMITEDS" have OLDER STYLE BODIES.

BUICK EIGHT

1939

BUSH
(1916 - 1924)

BUSH MOTOR CO., CHICAGO

4 OR 6 CYLS.

LYCOMING, R, OR CONTINENTAL ENGINES

('19-20)

"E.C. 4" has 192.4 C.I.D. LYCOMING ENGINE. "E.C. 6" has 230.1 C.I.D. RUTENBER ENGINE. BOTH have 116" W.B., 33 x 4 TIRES ('21 SPECIFICATIONS)

25

CADILLAC

DIVISION OF GENERAL MOTORS CORPORATION

(ESTABLISHED 1902 ; JOINED G.M. 1909)

V-8 ENGINE

20-21

TYPE 59

314.4 C.I.D. (1915 THROUGH '27)
60 H.P. @ 2700 RPM (TO '23)
125" OR 132" W.B. (THROUGH '21)

4-PASS. ('21)

35 x 5" TIRES IN 1920; 34 x 4½" 1921.

4.44 GEAR RATIO

'21 IS FINAL MODEL with TILTING STEER. WHEEL.

TRADITIONAL EMBLEM AND MOTTO

Standard of the World

4.5 and 2 OTHER GEAR RATIOS

STEERING-COLUMN QUADRANT REPLACED BY SMALLER FINGER-GRIPS FOR SPARK and THROTTLE CONTROLS. SUPPLEMENTARY TRANSMISSION LOCK.

22-23

TYPE 61

WITH AMES CUSTOM BODY ('23) (MOST BODIES BY FISHER, BUT IN CALIFORNIA, CUSTOM BODIES ARE AVAILABLE BY DON LEE.)

VICTORIA COUPE CONTINUED, with DOORS HINGED at REAR. NEW FOR 1922 IS 5-PASS. COUPE (ILLUSTRATED,) with DOORS HINGED AT FRONT, AND with LONGER CAB SECTION.

new '22 TYPE 61 STEERING WHEEL RIM, SPOKES, and HORN BUTTON are all made of WALNUT! LARGER COWL VENT.

RADIATOR IS HIGHER FOR 1922.

132" W.B. only OPTIONAL GEAR RATIOS

33 x 5 TIRES (THROUGH '25)

NEW '22 "61" has DELCO SWITCHES AT CENTER OF DASH

new BAUSCH and LOMB OPTICAL LENSES

INTERIOR

SPEEDOMETER AND CLOCK

CADILLAC

V-63

STANDARD OF THE WORLD

5 - PASSENGER SEDAN

NEW 5-PASS. LANDAU →

STANDARD OF THE WORLD

THE NEW V-63 SUBURBAN

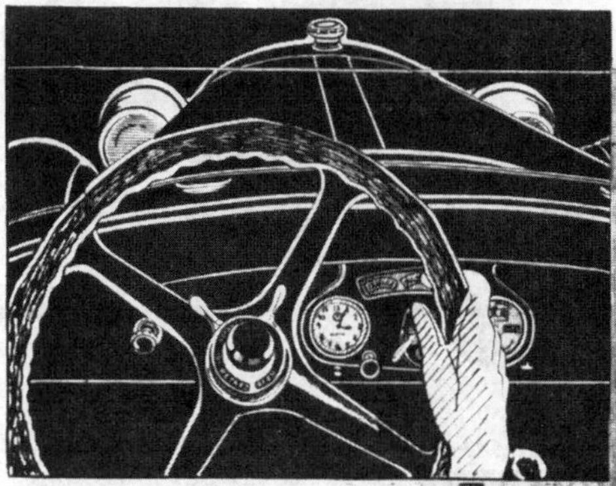

DASH

24
NEW "V-63"

AS FITTED WITH DUAL SPARE TIRES

INTERNAL-EXPANDING FRONT-WHEEL BRAKES (EXTERNAL-CONTRACTING ON REAR WHEELS.)

72 H.P. @ 3000 RPM (THROUGH '25)

132" WHEELBASE

CADILLAC

25
V-63

COACH INTRO. JAN., 1925

STANDARD W.B. == 132"
* CUSTOM BUILT LINE " == 138"
* - aluminum bodies

4.91 GEAR RATIO

FROM 1926 TO 1935, MODEL NUMBER INDICATES DISPL. OF ENGINE, (EXCEPT FOR FRACTION-OF-INCH DIFFERENCES.)

26

33 × 6.75 BALLOON TIRES (THROUGH '27)

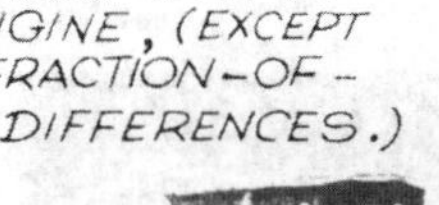

"314" (INTRO. 7-30-25)
(314.4 C.I.D.)
87 H.P. @ 3000 RPM
(THROUGH '27)

VERTICAL RADIATOR SHUTTERS

S T A N D A R D · O F · T H E · WORLD

(CUSTOM ROADSTER ON 132" W.B.)

HORN IS UNDER LEFT HEADLAMP

SINCE 1-26, CUSTOM CLOSED MODELS HAVE THIS TYPE OF WINDSHIELD.

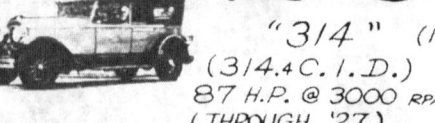
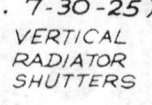

50 BODY STYLES AND TYPES; 500 COLOR AND UPHOLSTERY COMBINATIONS!

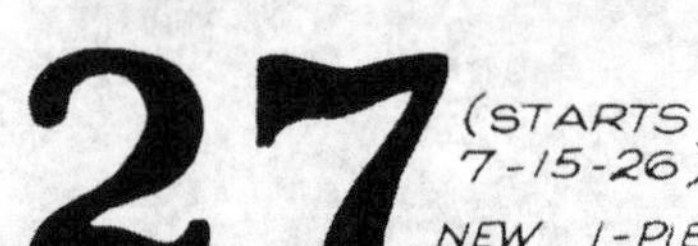

4.91 GEAR RATIO

27 (STARTS 7-15-26)

"314"

NEW 1-PIECE FRONT FENDERS

BATTERY and TOOL BOX CONCEALED BEHIND DUST SHIELD

7-PASS. CUSTOM SUBURBAN

28

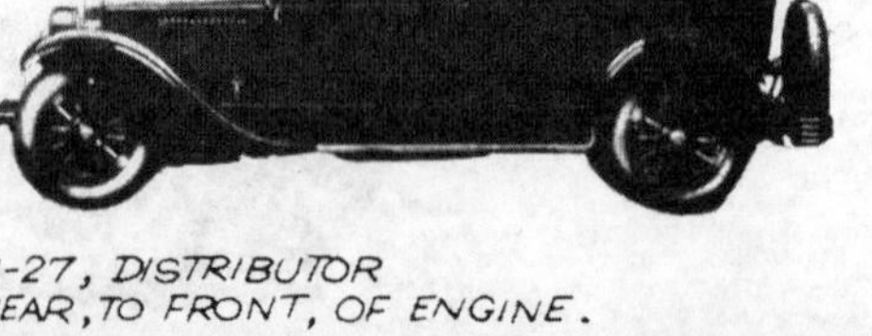

LIGHT SWITCH ON STEERING QUADRANT

STARTING 1-27, DISTRIBUTOR MOVED, FROM REAR, TO FRONT, OF ENGINE.

CADILLAC

DIVISION OF GENERAL MOTORS

28

"341"
(-A)

4.75 GEAR RATIO

90 H.P. @ 3000

32 × 6.75 TIRES

SMALL CIRCULAR GAUGES, FRAMED INDIVIDUALLY

140" WHEELBASE
(THROUGH '29)

29

"341-B"

New Adjustable Front Seats

SYNCHRO-MESH TRANSMISSION (NEW)

FISHER OR FLEETWOOD BODIES

7.00 × 20 TIRES

new FUEL PUMP INTRODUCED

H.P. RAISED TO 95 DURING 1929.

PARKING LIGHTS MOVED TO FRONT FENDERS

7-PASSENGER IMPERIAL

30

'30 has SLANTED, NON-GLARE WINDSHIELD

7.00 × 19 TIRES ON ALL 1930 MODELS

V-8

7-PASS.

VACUUM TANK RETURNS (SOME MODELS)

5.08 GEAR RATIO

"353" (V-8) 95 H.P. @ 3000 RPM (THROUGH '31)

new FULL-LENGTH ROW OF HOOD LOUVRES (V-8)
V-8 CONTINUES 140" W.B.

V-16 INTERIOR

"452" (V-16)
452 C.I.D. (THROUGH '37)

SIXTEEN CYLINDERS

(NEW)

185 H.P. @ 3400 RPM

VACUUM BOOSTER BRAKES

4.39 GEAR RATIO

V-16 has VACUUM FUEL FEED

V-16 HAS 148" WHEELBASE
(THROUGH '31)

CADILLAC

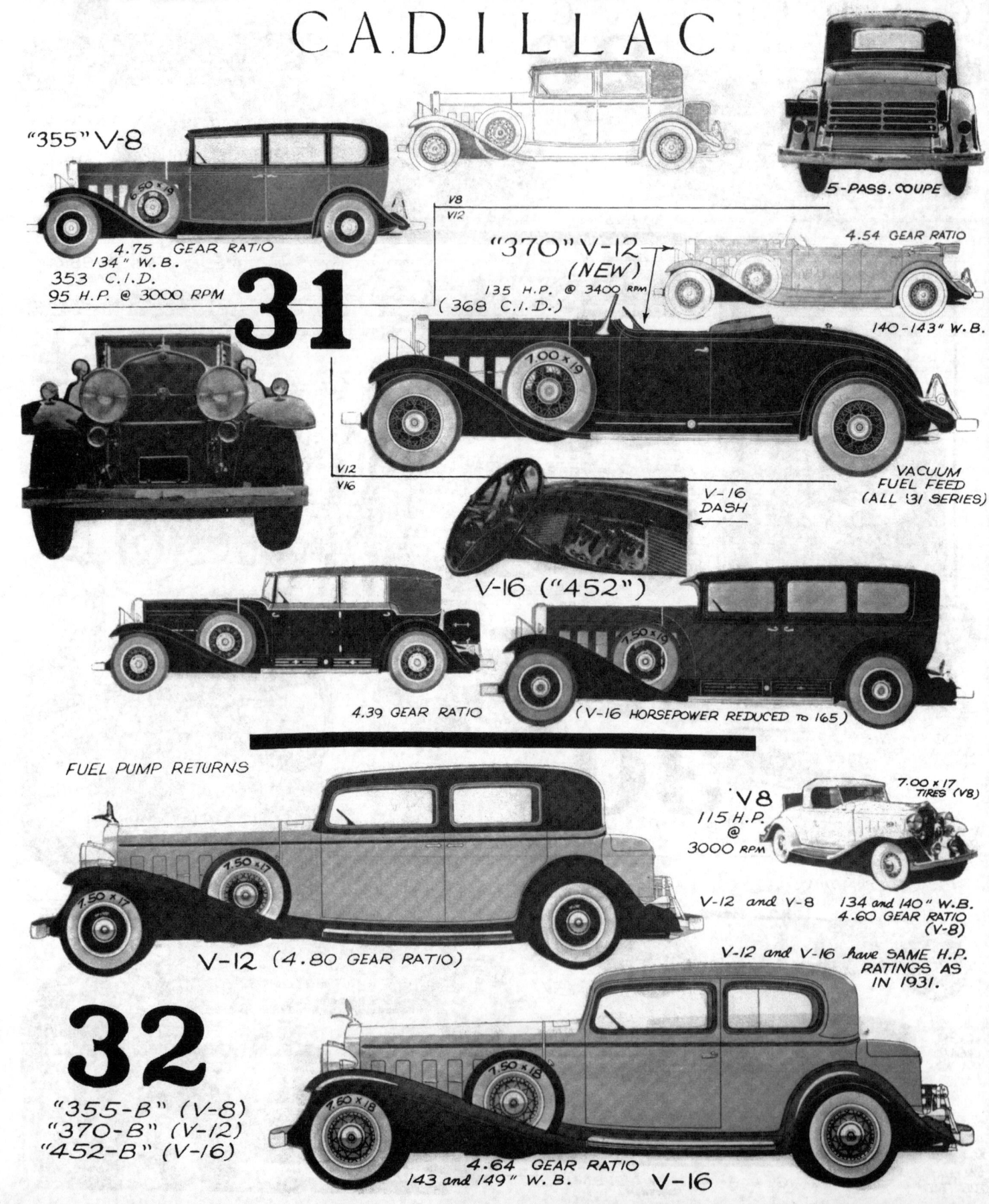

"355" V-8

4.75 GEAR RATIO
134" W.B.
353 C.I.D.
95 H.P. @ 3000 RPM

5-PASS. COUPE

4.54 GEAR RATIO

"370" V-12
(NEW)
135 H.P. @ 3400 RPM
(368 C.I.D.)

140-143" W.B.

31

V8
V12

7.00 x 19

V12
V16

VACUUM
FUEL FEED
(ALL '31 SERIES)

V-16
DASH

V-16 ("452")

7.50 x 19

4.39 GEAR RATIO

(V-16 HORSEPOWER REDUCED TO 165)

FUEL PUMP RETURNS

7.50 x 17

V8
115 H.P.
@
3000 RPM

7.00 x 17
TIRES (V8)

V-12 and V-8   134 and 140" W.B.
4.60 GEAR RATIO
(V-8)

V-12 (4.80 GEAR RATIO)

V-12 and V-16 have SAME H.P.
RATINGS AS
IN 1931.

32

"355-B" (V-8)
"370-B" (V-12)
"452-B" (V-16)

7.50 x 18

7.50 x 18

4.64 GEAR RATIO
143 and 149" W.B.   V-16

CADILLAC

33

7.00×17" TIRES ON V-8
(THROUGH '35)

"355-C" (V-8)
"370-C" (V-12)
"452 C" (V-16)

SAME H.P.
RATINGS AS
IN 1932.

V-12

V-12

7.50×17 TIRES
on V-12 and V-16
(THROUGH '35)

V-16 ENGINE

CHICAGO WORLD'S
FAIR SHOW CAR

V-16

V-8	SERIES	10 = 128" W.B.	4.60 G.R.	130 H.P. @ 3400 RPM
"	"	20 = 136" "	"	
"	"	30 = 146" "	4.80 G.R.	
V-12	SERIES	40 = 146" "	4.80 G.R.	150 H.P. @ 3600 RPM
V-16	SERIES	60 = 154" "	4.64 G.R.	185 H.P. @ 3800 RPM

(V-8)

8J1888

34

"355-D" (V-8)
"370-D" (V-12)
"452-D" (V-16)

TEARDROP
HOOD LOUVRES ON V-16

CADILLAC

7.50 × 17 TIRES (V-16) (ALSO V-12)

V-16

(SOLID BUMPERS MORE TYPICAL DURING '35.)

V-8

35
(INTRO. JAN., 1935)

1935 INTERIOR
(PLAIN UPHOLSTERY REPLACES PLAITED)

"355-E" (V-8) "370-E"(V-12)
"16-62" (V-16)

7.00 × 17 TIRES (V-8)

TWO V-8s FOR 1936 : "60" HAS 322 C.I.D. ENGINE
(125 H.P. @ 3400 RPM) (USED IN La SALLE, 1937-1940;)
"70" and "75" HAVE 346 C.I.D. ENGINE
(135 H.P. @ 3400 RPM)

60

85

90

FLEETWOOD V-12

"60," "70," "75" (V-8)   "80," "85"(V-12) "90"(V-16)

(HYDRAULIC BRAKES ON V-8 and V-12)

36
(STARTS OCT., 1935)

CADILLAC

60
(V-8)

(FINAL V-12 CADILLAC)
85

"60" NOW SHARES 346 C.I.D.
V-8 ENGINE WITH "70" and "75."

37
(STARTS OCT., 1936)

FLEETWOOD V 8·12·16

FINAL YEAR FOR OVERHEAD VALVES IN
V-16 ENGINE

V-16 HAS HYDRAULIC
VACUUM BOOSTER BRAKES, RETAINS TEARDROP HOOD LOUVRES, 154"
W.B., 7.50 x 17 TIRES

V-8

V-16 (L-HEAD)
4.31
G.R.

38
(STARTS OCT., 1937)

V-16 HAS NEW ENGINE OF 431 C.I.D.,
175 H.P. @ 3600 RPM

CADILLAC

38 (CONT'D.)

"75" RATED AT 140 H.P.
WHILE OTHER V-8 MODELS
RATED AT 135.

"60 - SPECIAL" = (WITHOUT RUNNING BOARDS)
HAS ITS OWN
UNIQUE STYLING.

127" W.B. ON "60-S" (THROUGH '40)

"SUNSHINE ROOF," NEW TO U.S.A.
IN '38, AVAILABLE ON SOME '39
MODELS OF CADILLAC, LA SALLE,
BUICK AND OLDSMOBILE.

60-SPECIAL
(FRONT
DETAILS)

FLEETWOOD V·8 and 16

126" W.B.
ON "61,"
141" W.B.
ON "75"
and V-16

V-16

(V-16
DISCONTINUED
DURING 1940)
185 H.P. @ 3600 RPM
FOR 1939-1940 V-16s.

39
(STARTS OCT., 1938)

75

WITH 6-CYL. CONTINENTAL ENGINE

CARDWAY
(1923—1925)
(REPORTEDLY, ONLY 6 BUILT)

FREDERICK CARDWAY, N.Y.C.

CASE (1910 TO 1927)
J.I.C. CASE CO., RACINE, WIS.

('20)

NEW 126" W.B.

MODEL V

NEW BODIES FOR 1920, AND NEW 1-PIECE FRONT SEAT IN TOURING. 6 CYL. CONTINENTAL ENGINE (303.1 C.I.D.) RAYFIELD CARB., DELCO IGNITION, AND NEW ALEMITE LUBRICATION SYSTEM.

132" W.B.

SCHEB. CARB. ('26 ON)

'25 "J.I.C."
122" WB   4.9 G.R.
6 CYL. (241.6 CID)
56 H.P. @ 2300

'25 "Y"
132" WB   4.45 G.R.
6 CYL. (234.8 CID;
331.3 IN '26-'27)
70 H.P. @ 2400
34 x 7.30 TIRES ('26-7)
FEW CHANGES THR. '27.

32 x 4½

('24) MODEL "Y"

(REPLACES MODEL "W," AUG. 1, '23)
(MODEL "X" ALSO)
(LIKE "JIC") "JAY EYE CEE" 6
(122" W.B.)

('25)
(HYDRAULIC BRAKES)

CHALMERS (1908-1924)
CHALMERS MOTOR CAR CO., DETROIT, MICH.
CHALMERS MOTOR CO. OF CANADA, LTD., WINDSOR, ONTARIO
32 x 4 OR   33 x 4½ TIRES

"35-C"
(5-PASS.)

224 C.I.D., 6 CYL.
117 and 122" W.B.

20-21

4.75 and 5.18 GEAR RATIOS

REMY IGN.

22-23

KNOWN AS "NEW SERIES" ('22)
"IMPROVED"   ('23)

32 x 4

5.12 GEAR RATIO

(MOST OTHER SPECS. SAME AS 1920)

STROMBERG CARB. (THROUGH '25)

23½

24
(PRODUCED DURING LATTER MONTHS OF 1923.)

HYDRAULIC BRAKES AVAILABLE
5.10 GEAR RATIO

REPLACED BY CHRYSLER

NEW AUTO-LITE IGN.

NEW RIBBED WHEELS

THE CHANDLER MOTOR CAR COMPANY
Export Department, 1819 Broadway, New York City

CLEVELAND
Cable Address, "Chenmotor"

CHANDLER

(1913-1929)

20

6 CYLINDERS
288.6 C.I.D.
THROUGH '28

RAYFIELD
CARB.

4.40
GEAR RATIO
THROUGH '22

123" W.B.
(THROUGH
1926)

7-PASS. SEDAN

CHANDLER SIX
Famous For Its Marvelous Motor

21

The Chandler Dispatch

The Royal Dispatch, a new short model of utmost distinction and ultra-smart style

FIRST YEAR
WITH VISOR,
COWL LIGHTS,
COWL VENT,
DRUM-TYPE
HEADLIGHTS.

22

(NEW BODY
LINES)

ROYAL
DISPATCH HAS
34 × 4½ TIRES

CYLINDERS NOW CAST
EN BLOC (1923)

METROPOLITAN
5-PASS. SEDAN (NEW)

STARTS
6-22

NEW 32 × 4 TIRES *
and STROMBERG CARBURETOR
NEW 4.45 GEAR RATIO

23

The New Pike's Peak Motor

Built by Chandler

* = 33 × 4½ ON
CLOSED CARS, ROYAL DISP.

CHANDLER
CAR OF THE YEAR

with the TRAFFIC TRANSMISSION

(The Traffic Transmission is built complete in the Chandler plant under Campbell patents.)

24

NEW CONSTANT-MESH TRANSMISSION ELIMINATES CLASHING AND DOUBLE-CLUTCHING.

ALUMINUM BEAD BETWEEN HOOD and COWL

32 × 4 OR 33 × 4½ TIRES (BALLOONS OPTIONAL)

MODEL 32-A ("SS")

ALL OPEN MODELS HAVE ALUMINUM KICK PADS ON RUNNING BOARDS.

"CHUMMY" (5-PASSENGER)

7-PASS. TOURING

25

"33" and "33-A"

49 H.P. @ 2100 RPM
4-WHEEL BRAKES OPTIONAL
OVERALL HEIGHT OF CLOSED CARS REDUCED TO LESS THAN 6 FEET.

SCHEBLER CARBURETOR
33 × 6 TIRES

COACH IMPERIAL

at exactly Touring Car price

Body by Fisher

$1595

The Greatest Success in Ten Years of Succeeding

CHANDLER

26

MODEL "SS-35"
55 H.P. @ 2800 RPM

NEW VERTICAL RADIATOR STRIPS

7-PASS. SEDAN

20TH CENTURY SEDAN

The New Royal Eight BY CHANDLER

314 C.I.D.   80 H.P. @ 3000 RPM
124" W.B.

27½

27

STANDARD 6

TILLOTSON CARBURETOR ON STD. 6. SCHEBLER ON OTHERS.

BIG 6

METROPOLITAN SEDAN
(EARLY '27 TYPE)

STANDARD 6
MODEL "31" (108½" W.B.)
180.2 C.I.D., 45 H.P.
BIG 6 "35" (124" W.B.)
289 C.I.D., 55 H.P. @ 2100 RPM
SPECIAL 6 "43" = 218.6 C.I.D., 60 H.P. @ 2600 RPM
115" W.B.

SPECIAL 6   (ALSO "BIG 6")

1928

EARLY SERIES (DRUM HEADLIGHTS)

28
(JOINS HUPMOBILE)

ROYAL 8

28½

196 C.I.D.
45 H.P. @ 2600 RPM

195.5 C.I.D.
"6-65"
55 H.P. @ 3000

"BIG 6" CONT'D. FROM 1928, 331.3 C.I.D. 83 H.P.

29

ROYAL 8 "75"

38

CHANDLER'S FINAL CARS

"85" = LARGER 8

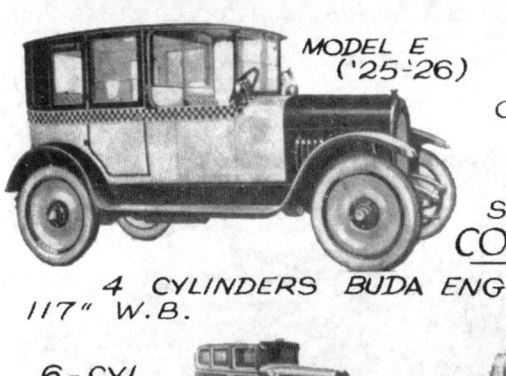

MODEL E ('25-'26)

CHECKER

MODEL F ('26 '27)

CHECKER CAB MFG. CO., KALAMAZOO, MICH. (SINCE 1923)

SUCCEEDS THE COMMONWEALTH CAR

4 CYLINDERS BUDA ENG. 117" W.B.

6-CYL. MODEL G IN '27-'28

5.09 G.R.

MODEL K ('29-'30)

4.9 G.R. (K)

127" W.B., 7.00 x 18 TIRES MANY VARIATIONS ON EACH MODEL!

VARIETY OF MODEL M (INTRO. 1931) 122" W.B.

6.50 x 18 TIRES

MODEL M 126" W.B. ('32) (VARIATION)

HAS 228.1 C.I.D. BUDA 6-CYL. "JC-214" ENG.

MODEL T ('33) (NEW PORTHOLES IN HOOD DOORS)

MODEL Y ('36 - '39)

NO PRIVATE CARS AVAIL. UNTIL 1959.

30 x 3½ OR 31 x 4 TIRES

26 H.P. @ 1800 RPM

"490"

CHEVROLET

(ESTABLISHED NOV., 1911; JOINED G.M. MAY, 1918.)

ASSEMBLY AT FLINT, MICH. (MAIN PLANT)

Chevrolet Motor Co., Detroit, Michigan
Division of General Motors Corporation

"FB" 110" W.B.

"490" has 4-CYL. ENGINE 170.9 C.I.D.

102" W.B.

3.63 G.R.

GRAVITY FUEL FEED

"490" SEDAN

20-21

(FB 50)

37 H.P. @ 2000 RPM

"FB" HAS 4-CYL., 224.3 C.I.D. ENGINE

4.62 G.R.

VACUUM FUEL FEED

'22 MODEL IS FIRST "490" WITH HAND-OPERATED EMERGENCY BRAKE

LOWER WINDSHIELD

"490" (32 H.P.)

STEEL FELLOE WHEELS

FRONT SEAT CUSHION LOWERED 4½" TO PROVIDE HIGHER SEAT BACK.

SHORTER STEERING COLUMN.

22

GYPSY-TYPE SIDE CURTAINS

GAS TANK ENLARGED TO 10 GALLONS.

3.66 G.R.

MODEL "FB 42" SEDAN
32 x 4 TIRES ADOPTED DURING '22 (FB)

CHEVROLET

SUPERIOR" (B)

WHEELBASE INCREASED TO 103" ON ALL.

(759 AIR-COOLED SERIES C, M CHEVROLETS ALSO BLT., JAN., '23 TO MAY, '23. RECALLED BY FACTORY, JUNE '23. 4 CYL., 134.7 C.I.D., 4.44 G.R.)

23

1923 4-Passenger Sedanette

3.77 G.R. (THROUGH '24)

EARLY "B" TYPE (9-23 TO 1-24)

CURVED FRONT AXLE AND CABLE-OPERATED BRAKES.

24

"SUPERIOR" NAME CONT'D. THROUGH '26.

(24½)

26 H.P. @ 2000 RPM (THROUGH '27)

FINAL YEAR WITH CONE CLUTCH

24½ DE LUXE (NICKEL TRIM)

LATER ("F") TYPE has STRAIGHT FRONT AXLE and BRAKE RODS.

29 x 4.40 BALLOON TIRES (CLOSED MODELS)

8-25: new KLAXON HORN, new STEER. WHEEL with CORRUGATED WALNUT FINISH RIM

1-PC. "VV" (VERTICAL VENTILATING) WINDSHIELD (ON CLOSED CARS.)

3.82 G.R. (THROUGH '31)

25

(K)

INTRO. 1-3-25

NEW RADIATOR DESIGN

30 x 3½ TIRES ON OPEN MODELS

for Economical Transportation

CHEVROLET

26
(V)

AIR CLEANER INTRODUCED

(INTERIOR)

NEW TIE-BAR BETWEEN HEADLIGHTS
29 x 4.40 TIRES (THROUGH '27)

GENERATOR MOVED FROM RIGHT TO LEFT SIDE OF ENGINE ('26.)

FROM '23 TO '26, CHEVROLET CARS BLT. SEPT. or LATER ARE SOMETIMES CLASSIFIED AS FOLLOWING YEAR'S MODEL, THOUGH ACTUAL MODEL CHANGE (DURING THESE YEARS) OCCURS IN JANUARY.

COACH HAS GREEN CORDUROY UPHOLSTERY. SEDAN HAS BLUE CORDUROY. BROWN "PLUSH" IN COUPE.

new SPARE TIRE CARRIER

TOURING CAR

('27½)

IMPERIAL LANDAU (INTRODUCED MAY, 1927)

CO-INCIDENTAL STEERING and IGNITION LOCK

new "BULLET" HEADLIGHTS

NEW RADIATOR DESIGN

27
(AA)
"CAPITOL"

new AC OIL FILTER, AC AIR CLEANER

ROADSTER

new 1-PC. FULL-CROWN FENDERS

41

CHEVROLET
for Economical Transportation

57376 A 28

(FINAL 4-CYL. MODEL)

28

(AB)
"NATIONAL"

Bigger and Better

HORSEPOWER
INCREASED TO
35 @ 2200 RPM

WHEELBASE INCREASED
TO 107"

NEW RADIATOR
DESIGN AGAIN

INTERIOR

CHEVROLET
for Economical Transportation

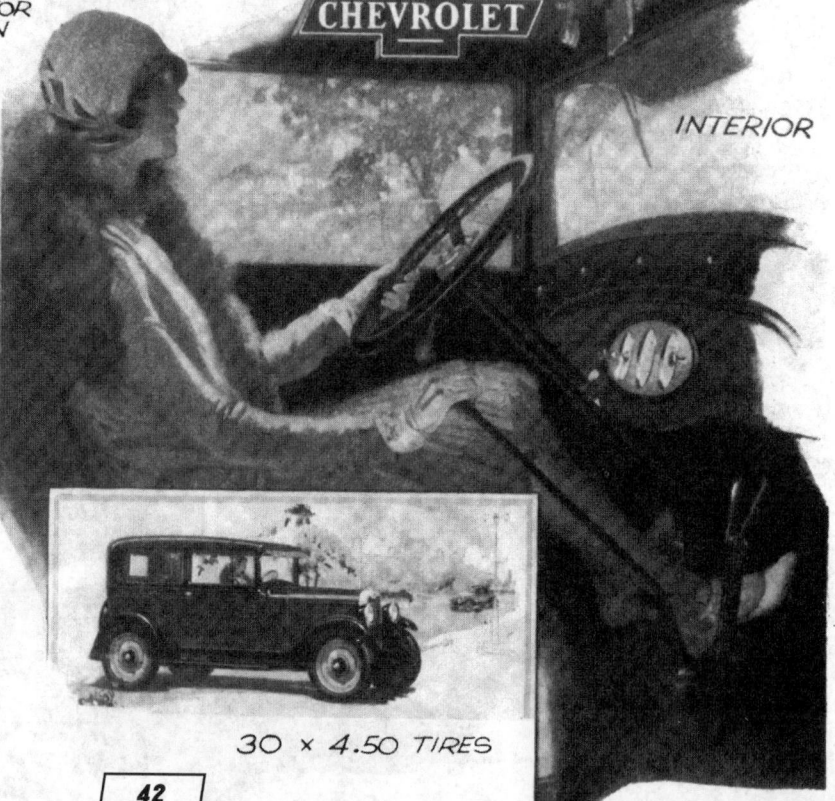

4 - WHEEL BRAKES

30 × 4.50 TIRES

NEW CHEVROLET SIX

(6 - CYLINDER CHEVROLETS ONLY = 1929 THROUGH 1954.)

ALL - NEW 1929 ENGINE →

29

(AC) "INTERNATIONAL"

COMPLETELY RESTYLED

new FUEL PUMP

193.9 C.I.D.

46 H.P. @ 2600 RPM

FISHER BODIES, AS BEFORE

'29 DASH HAS 3 UPRIGHT OVALS WITHIN HORIZONTAL OVAL PANEL. ('30 DASH HAS SMALL CIRCULAR INSTRUMENTS.)

CHEVROLET
for Economical Transportation

1929 IS FINAL CHEVROLET WITH FUEL GAUGE LOCATED OUTSIDE, ON TANK.

4.50 × 20" TIRES

3.81 G.R.= (ACCORDING TO CERTAIN SOURCES ; 3.82 OTHERWISE.)

43

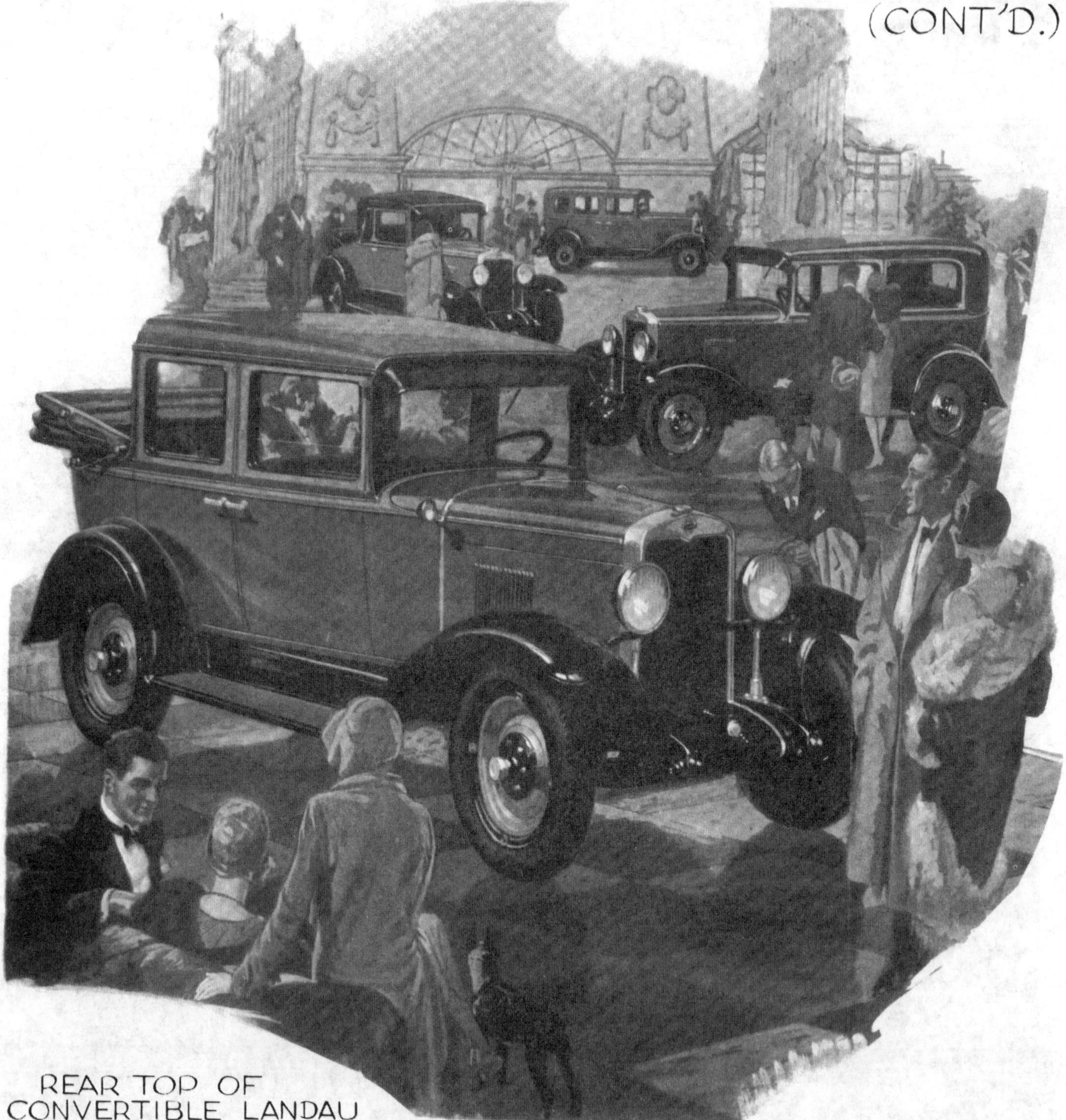

REAR TOP OF
CONVERTIBLE LANDAU
CAN BE FOLDED

for Economical Transportation

CHEVROLET

30
"UNIVERSAL" (AD)

New Dash Gasoline Gauge

NEW DARK-FACED, CIRCULAR GAUGES

The Chevrolet Special Sedan is a de luxe creation in every sense of the word. Standard equipment includes six wire wheels with fender wells, bumpers front and rear, robe rail, dome light, silk assist cords, etc.

THE ROADSTER

THE SPORT ROADSTER

50 H.P.
@
2600 RPM

THE COUPE

THE SPORT COUPE

THE SEDAN

(CABRIOLET SUSPENDED FOR 1930; RE-INTRODUCED JANUARY, 1931.)

THE PHAETON

4.75 × 19" TIRES (THROUGH '31) AND NEW, SLIGHTLY SLANTED NON-GLARE WINDSHIELD →

THE CLUB SEDAN

(30½ MODEL HAS *Landau Irons*.)

45

THE COACH

CHEVROLET

31 NEW 109" WHEELBASE

STANDARD '31s DO NOT HAVE THE NEW RADIATOR STONE GUARD.

2 NEW BODY TYPES IN '31 →

(AE) "INDEPENDENCE"

THE STANDARD COACH

DASH ('31)

HORN BUTTON — OIL PRESSURE GAUGE / SPEEDOMETER / CHOKE BUTTON — THROTTLE BUTTON / GASOLINE GAUGE — AMMETER — WATER TEMPERATURE INDICATOR — SPARK BUTTON — LIGHTING SWITCH — GEARSHIFT LEVER — IGNITION — CLUTCH PEDAL — BRAKE PEDAL — HEAD LAMP DIMMER SWITCH — ACCELERATOR — STARTING PEDAL — HAND BRAKE LEVER — ACCELERATOR FOOT REST

'32 HAS NEW SYNCHRO-MESH TRANSMISSION

DASH ('32)

FREE WHEELING BUTTON — HORN BUTTON — OIL PRESSURE GAUGE / SPEEDOMETER / CHOKE BUTTON — HEAT CONTROL BUTTON — THROTTLE BUTTON / GASOLINE GAUGE — AMMETER — WATER TEMPERATURE — SPARK BUTTON — LIGHTING SWITCH — GEARSHIFT LEVER — IGNITION — CLUTCH PEDAL — BRAKE PEDAL — HEAD LAMP DIMMER SWITCH — ACCELERATOR — STARTING PEDAL — HAND BRAKE — ACCELERATOR FOOT REST

"CONFEDERATE" (BA)

32

60 H.P. @ 3000 RPM

"FREE WHEELING" (New)

4.1 G.R.

46

5.25 × 18" TIRES

THE SPORT ROADSTER

107" W.B.
4.3 GEAR RATIO

5.25 × 17" TIRES

CHEVROLET

33

MASTER and EAGLE "CA"

STARTS 12-32

206.8 C.I.D. 65 H.P. @ 2800 RPM

181 C.I.D. 60 H.P. @ 3000 RPM

5.25 × 18" TIRES

STANDARD "CC"
(WITH HOOD LOUVRES)
STARTS 3-33

DASH

(110" W.B.)
ACCELERATOR CONTROLS STARTER

4.11 GEAR RATIO
(THROUGH '36)

NEW "KNEE ACTION" INDEPENDENT FRONT WHEEL SUSPENSION (WITH FRONT COIL SPRINGS) ON "MASTER" (DA) SERIES.

CHEVROLET MASTER SIX COUPE

CHEVROLET MASTER SIX SPORT COUPE

34

"STANDARD" (DC)
SERIES INTRODUCED LATE
(SPRING, 1934) WITH 107" W.B.,
5.25 × 17" TIRES,
181 C.I.D. ENGINE WITH
60 H.P. @ 3000 RPM

"MASTER" HAS 112" W.B.,
5.50 × 17" TIRES,
206.8 C.I.D. ENGINE
WITH 80 H.P. @ 3300 RPM

DASH

47

CHEVROLET

"STANDARD" MODEL (EC) RESEMBLES 1934 BUT HAS PAINTED HEADLIGHT SHELLS. DASH GAUGES MOVED TO CENTER.

"MASTER" (EA and ED)

"ED" SERIES AVAIL. W/O "KNEE ACTION"

35

(ALL MODELS NOW HAVE THE 80-H.P. "BLUE FLAME" ENGINE.)

3-WINDOW SPORT COUPE WITH RUMBLE SEAT

(5-WINDOW BUSINESS COUPE ALSO AVAILABLE) NEW 113" W.B. (MASTER) (STD. RETAINS 107" W.B.)

H.P. REDUCED TO 79 @ 3200 RPM, FOR '36

"EXPEDITER" COUPE AVAIL. WITH PICKUP BOX

(FC)
STANDARD ⟹ 109" W.B.
MASTER ⟹ 113" W.B.
(FA and FD)
"KNEE ACTION" OPTIONAL (FA)

36

'36 DASH

NEW 216.5 C.I.D. 1937 ENGINE (85 H.P. @ 3200 RPM)

37

NEW STYLING ALSO

"GB" ⟹ MASTER (3.73 G.R.)
"GA" ⟹ MASTER DE LUXE WITH "KNEE ACTION" (4.22 G.R.)

112¼" W.B. ON ALL (THROUGH 1939)

6.00 × 16" IS NOW THE TIRE SIZE ON ALL MODELS.

'37 DASH

48

(1937 GEAR RATIOS CONTINUED THROUGH '39)

CHEVROLET

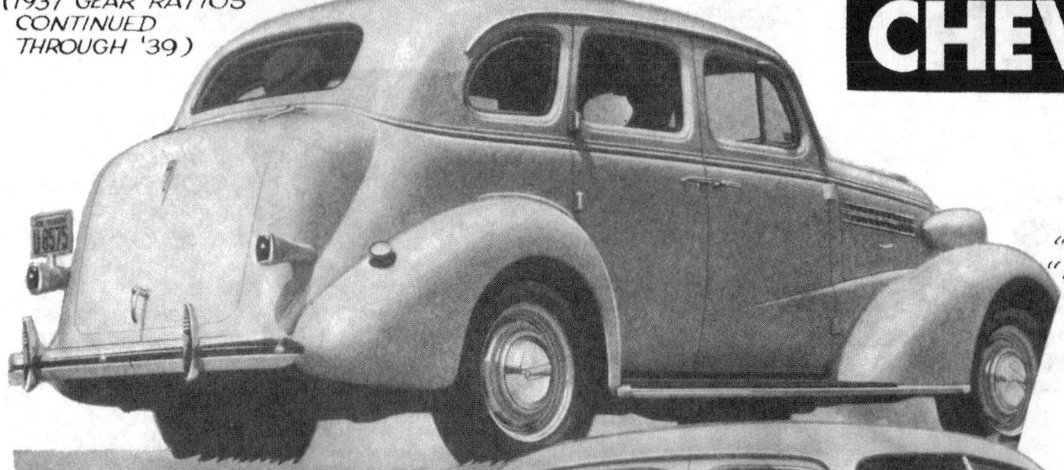

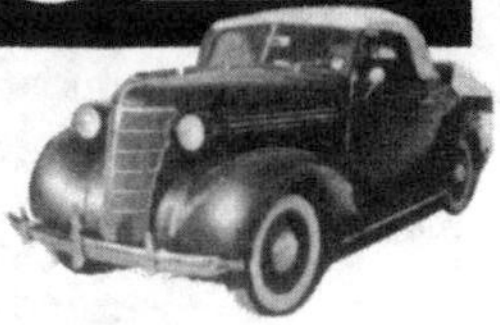

"HB" = MASTER
"HA" = MASTER DE LUXE

38

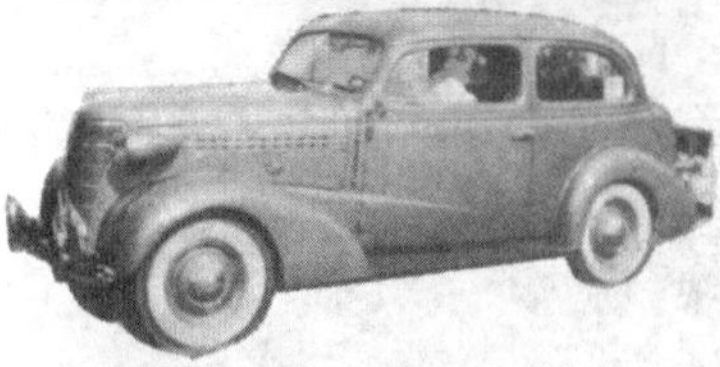

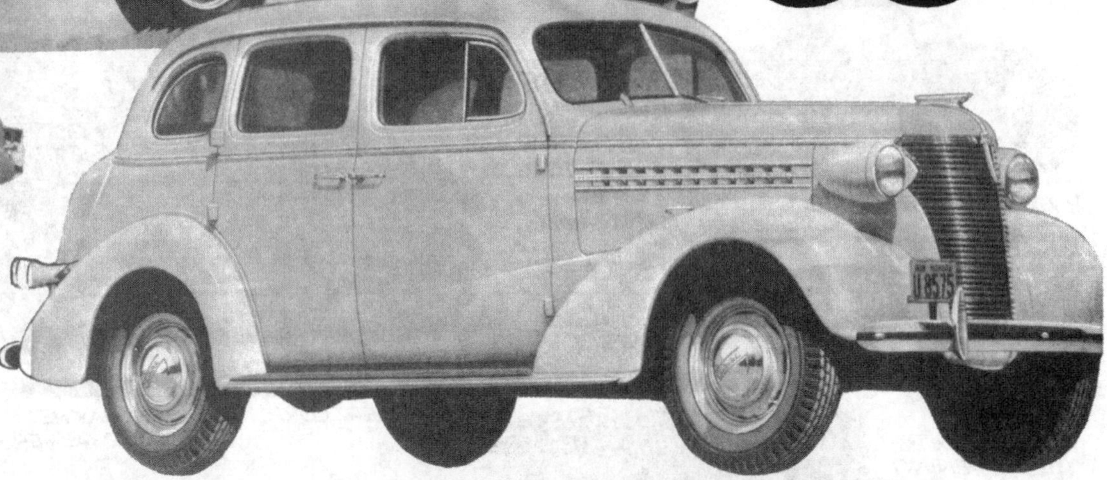

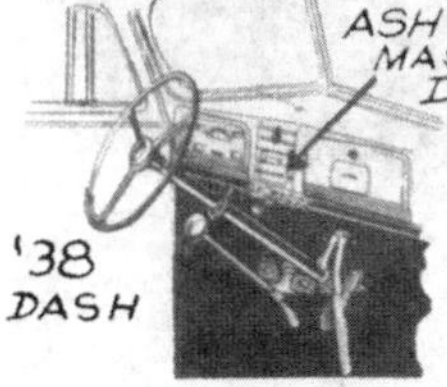

ASH TRAY IN MASTER DE LUXE MODELS

'38 DASH

CHROME TRIM, GRILLE AND OUTSIDE DOOR HANDLES HAVE DECORATIVE VERMILLION-RED STRIPES IN HORIZONTAL GROOVES.

"JB" = MASTER
"JA" = MASTER DE LUXE
85 H.P. @ 3200 RPM, AS BEFORE.

FISHER BODIES, AS BEFORE

NEW STEERING COLUMN GEARSHIFT CONTROL IS OPTIONAL. HAND BRAKE LEVER HUNG AT LEFT, BELOW DASH.

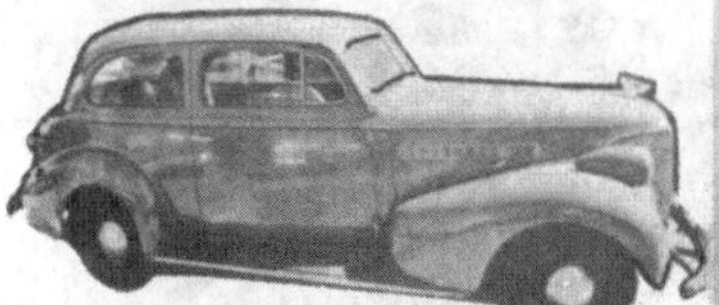

THE MASTER DE LUXE FOUR-PASSENGER COUPE

39

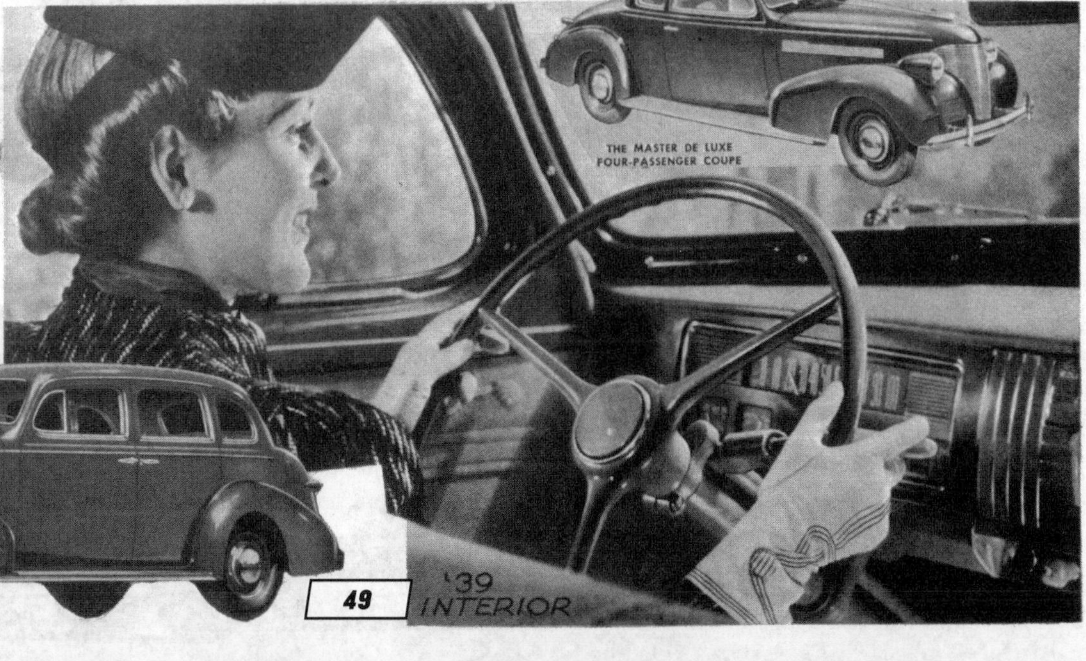

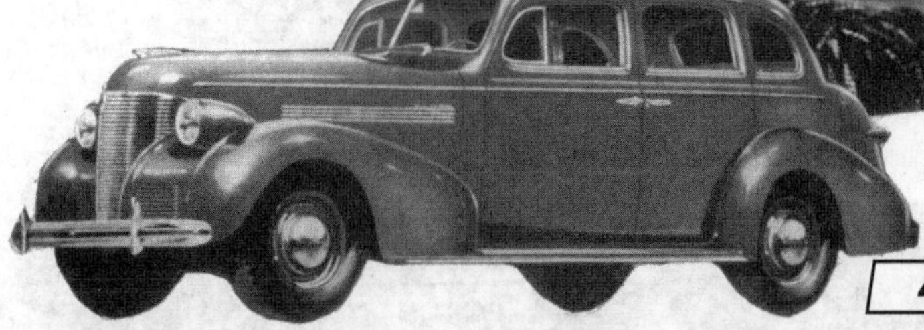

'39 INTERIOR

CHRYSLER (DETROIT)

(REPLACES '24 CHALMERS 12-23 INTRO. 1-24)

IMPERIAL SEDAN

NEW HIGH-COMPRESSION (4.6 TO 1) ENGINE

OPEN CARS CAPABLE OF 70 M.P.H.

PHAETON

BROUGHAM

24
(MODEL B)
6 CYL.
201.5 C.I.D.
68 H.P.
@
3200 RPM

112 3/4" W.B.

29 × 4.50 TIRES

Roadster

HYDRAULIC BRAKES

DASH

(CHRYSLER CORP. REPLACES MAXWELL-CHALMERS)

NEW ROYAL COUPE HAS OPENING REAR WINDOW, RUMBLE SEAT

Six (B)
25
(TO 7-25)

IMPERIAL

GEAR-SHIFT LEVER LONGER FOR 1925.

30 × 5.77 TIRES

ROADSTER HAS WIDER DOORS FOR 1925.

COACH

50

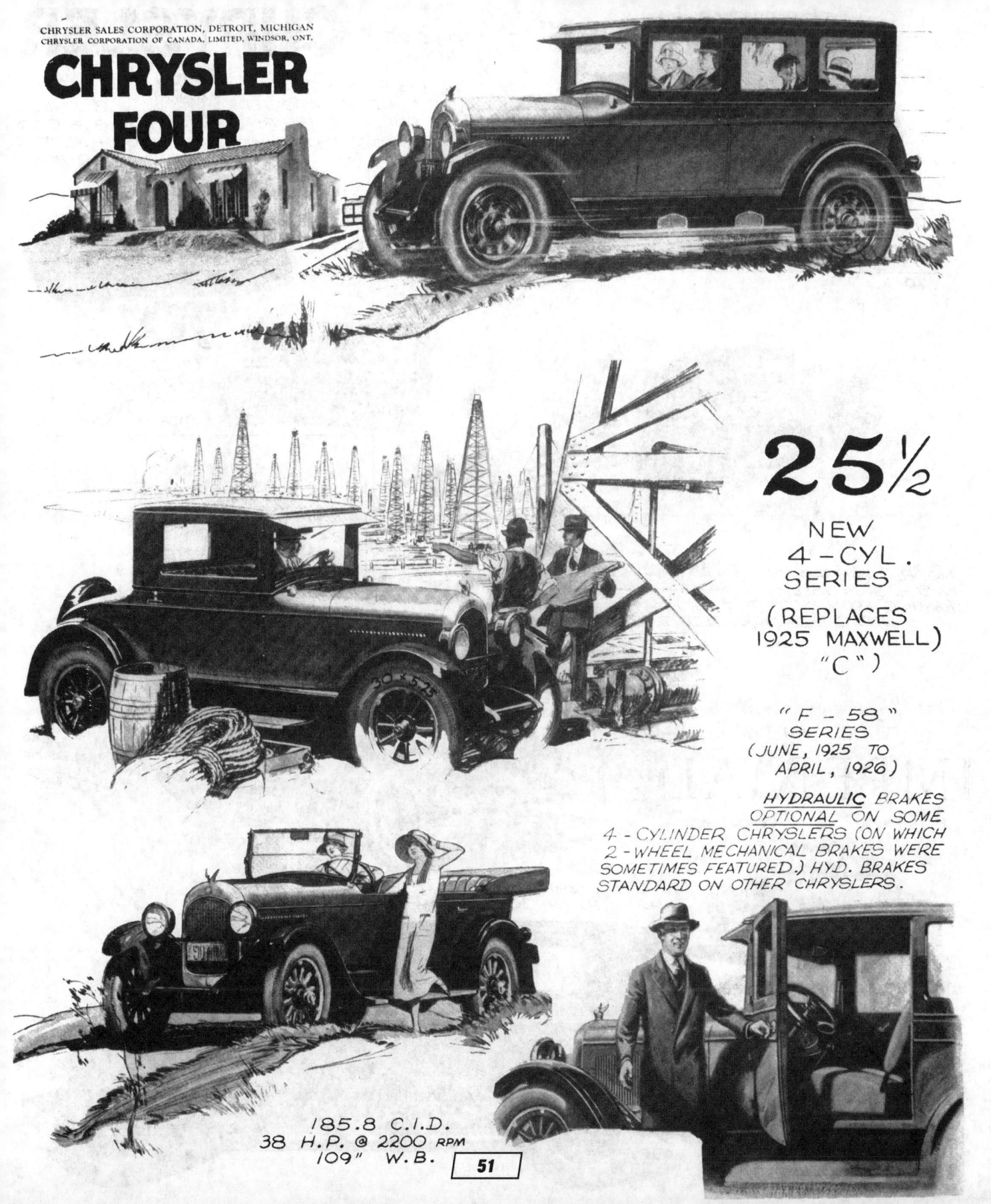

CHRYSLER SALES CORPORATION, DETROIT, MICHIGAN
CHRYSLER CORPORATION OF CANADA, LIMITED, WINDSOR, ONT.

CHRYSLER FOUR

25½

NEW
4 - CYL.
SERIES

(REPLACES
1925 MAXWELL)
"C")

" F - 58 "
SERIES
(JUNE, 1925 TO
APRIL, 1926)

HYDRAULIC BRACKES
OPTIONAL ON SOME
4 - CYLINDER CHRYSLERS (ON WHICH
2 - WHEEL MECHANICAL BRAKES WERE
SOMETIMES FEATURED.) HYD. BRAKES
STANDARD ON OTHER CHRYSLERS.

185.8 C.I.D.
38 H.P. @ 2200 RPM
109" W.B.

CHRYSLER

"58" (F) 30 × 5.25 TIRES 4-CYL.

(FEDCO SERIAL NUMBERS ADOPTED DURING 1925, FOR 1926 SEASON; CONT'D. TO EARLY 1930.)

6-CYL. 2/8.6 C.I.D. 68 H.P. @ 3000 RPM

58/70

"70" (G)

(7-25 TO 9-26)

DASH →

"70" Royal Sedan,

30 × 5.77 TIRES

26

MODEL NUMBERS OF 1926–30 CHRYSLERS (RANGING FROM "50" TO "80,") INDICATED GUARANTEED TOP SPEED.

70/80

The Imperial 2-passenger Coupe

The New
IMPERIAL
(E-80)

The Imperial 2-4-passenger Roadster

6 CYL., 288.7 C.I.D. 92 H.P. @ 3000 RPM

120, 127, 133" WHEELBASES

The Imperial Phaeton

The Imperial 7-passenger Sedan

(STARTS DEC., 1925)

52

CHRYSLER
"50 - 60 - 70 - 80"
CHRYSLER MODEL NUMBERS MEAN MILES PER HOUR

LEATHER UPH. IN COUPE →

"50"
(I)
(7-26 TO 7-27)

106" W.B.   4 CYL.
170.3 C.I.D., 38 H.P. @ 2200 RPM

ALL-STEEL Budd BODIES AVAILABLE ON SOME "50" MODELS.

"50" DASH ↑

"60"
(H)

109" W.B.

(6-26 TO 6-27)
6 CYL., 180.2 C.I.D.
54 H.P. @ 3000 RPM

"60" DASH ↓

27

STARTING 8-26 BUDD-MICHELIN DISC WHEELS AVAIL. ON ALL SERIES of EARLY '27 CHRYSLERS.

28 x 5.25

AS-100

60
70

FINER 70
(G)
(9-26 TO 10-27)

NEW CO-INCIDENTAL LOCK
68 H.P. @ 3000 RPM

DASH

30 x 6.00 TIRES

112 3/4" W.B.

4-PASS. COUPE (NEW) →

70
80

IMPERIAL "80"
(E)

FRANK QUAIL

NEW 30 x 6.75 TIRES

SAME SPECS. AS 1926

877-500

FRANK QUAIL

53

CHRYSLER

"52" IS FINAL 4-CYL. MODEL WHICH SOMETIMES OFFERS 2-WHEEL MECHANICAL BRAKES.

"52" CHRYSLER BODIES HAVE COMPOSITE WOOD INNER FRAMEWORK, AS ON MOST OTHER PRE-1930 CHRYSLERS.

DASH ("52")

MODEL "52" IS FINAL 4-CYLINDER CHRYSLER, WITH 170.3 C.I.D., 45 H.P. @ 2800 RPM, 106" W.B.

PRODUCED JULY, 1927 TO JUNE, 1928. REPLACED BY THE CHRYSLER-PLYMOUTH CAR. (SEE: "PLYMOUTH")

"52" HAS 4.7 GEAR RATIO

"52" (I)

28

"62" HAS 4.6 GEAR RATIO
28 × 5.25 TIRES

52
62

CHRYSLER "RED HEAD" ENGINES (WITH HIGH-COMPRESSION CYLINDER HEAD) REQUIRED ETHYL GASOLINE WHEN NEW.)

"62" (M)

"52" AND "62" INSTRUMENTS FRAMED SEPERATELY IN INDIVIDUAL PANES.

"62" GIVES 54 H.P. @ 3200 RPM WITH STANDARD 5.2-COMPRESSION "SILVER DOME" HEAD. 6.2-COMPRESSION "RED HEAD" GIVES 60 H.P.

Great New Chrysler "62" Coupe (with rumble seat), $1245

(108 3/4" W.B.)

(JUNE, 1927 TO JUNE, 1928)

54

DASH
(MACHINE-TURNED METAL PANEL)

CHRYSLER

Two-Passenger Coupe

Four-Passenger Coupe

Crown Sedan

1928 IS FINAL YEAR THAT CHRYSLER USES ANY FISHER BODIES.

(COWL LIGHTS, AFTER JAN., 1928)

"72" and "80" INSTRUMENTS BEHIND LONG GLASS PANEL.

D = DIETRICH BODY
L = LE BARON "

Royal Sedan, $1595

(118 3/4" W. B.)
30 x 6.00 TIRES

28
(CONT'D.)

"72" GIVES 75 H.P. @ 3200 RPM WITH STD. 5.1-COMPRESSION HEAD. 6.2-COMPRESSION "Red Head" GIVES 85 H.P.

ILLUSTRIOUS NEW "72"
TOWN CABRIOLET
BODY BY LE BARON

"72" HAS 4.3 GEAR RATIO

"72" (J)
(7-27 TO 6-28)

NEW 248.9 C.I.D. ENGINE

CLOSE-COUPLED SEDAN $1695

EARLY MODEL

LATE MODEL

LATE "72" ROADSTER HAS COWL LIGHTS, NEW WINDSHIELD, NEW SIDE MOULDING.

72/80

NEW 309.6 C.I.D. ENGINE
112 H.P. @ 3000 RPM WITH "Red Head" 6 TO 1 COMPR.
(STD. HEAD = 100 H.P.) 4.75 COMPR.

IMPERIAL "80" HAS 4.08 GEAR RATIO

(11-27 TO 6-28) **Imperial "80"**

L "80" (L-80)

136" W. B.

New 112 h.p. Imperial "80" Town Sedan, $2995

RT. DOOR FOR RUMBLE SEAT

30 x 6.75 TIRES

INSTRUMENT PANEL

NO RADIATOR EMBLEM ON '28 "80."

Locke Touralette

CHRYSLER

65 H.P. @ 3200 RPM   195.6 C.I.D.

65 (P)

5-WINDOW COUPE HAS RUMBLE SEAT

5.2 STD. COMPR.
6.0 - COMPR. "Red Head"
GIVES 70 H.P.

"75" VICTORIA COUPE (RARE!)

112 3/4" W.B.
5.50 x 18 TIRES
(IGNITION KEY-HOLE REPLACES SWITCH)

(6-28 TO 6-29)

(3-WINDOW BUSINESS COUPE ALSO IN "65" SERIES.)

65 75

"65" INSTRUMENT PANEL ARRANGEMENT GENERALLY SIMILAR TO "62" BUT HAS "WOODGRAIN" TRIM ABOVE.

6.00 x 18 TIRES

"75" (P)
(R)

FEDCO I.D. PLATE

ALL GAUGES BEHIND LONG GLASS PANEL
DARK-FACED GAUGES ON SOME EARLY "75" MODELS;
LIGHT-FACED ON LATER MODELS.

ROYAL SEDAN

INTERIOR

(6-28 TO 6-29)
121" W.B.
FIRST CHRYSLER TO FEATURE BUILT-IN RADIATOR SHUTTERS.

REAR

(SAME ENGINE SPECS. AS LATE "72")

(HIGH-COMPRESSION "Red Head" OPTIONAL THROUGH 1933, AND OPTIONAL ALUMINUM HEAD FROM 1934 THROUGH 1941.)

29

75

(TO 1928)

(1930 IMPERIAL 6 SIMILAR TO 1929, BUT HAS 4-SPEED "Multi-Range" TRANSMISSION AND SMOOTH, NON-CORRUGATED BUMPERS.)

7.00 x 18 TIRES ('29 and '30)

IMPERIAL

'29-30 IMPERIAL HAS SAME SPECS. AS '28 MODEL

(SIDE DOOR FOR RUMBLE SEAT)

IMPERIAL CHRYSLER

(L)
(STARTS OCTOBER, 1928)

EARLIEST MODEL HAS NO LOWER COWL MOLDING.

Custom Roadster

New Imperial 7-passenger Sedan illustrated. Also available in 5-passenger Sedan.

CHRYSLER 30

SOME "66" MODELS WITH SPLIT GROUP OF HOOD LOUVRES DURING 1930

3-SPEED TRANS. ON "66"

WOOD WHEELS STANDARD. (WIRE WHEELS OPTIONAL)

(ALL 6-CYL. MODELS)

new FUEL PUMP INTRODUCED (ON ALL BUT THE IMPERIAL 6.)

DASH (EXPORT MODEL)

68 H.P. @ 3000 RPM

5.50 x 18 TIRES

NEW "66" (7-29 TO 5-30)

(CC)

218.6 C.I.D. ("66" and EARLY "70")

112 ¾" W.B.

66
70

= HOOD "PENNON" LOUVRES ON 70 (and 77) BLT. BEF. 1-30.

116 9/16" W.B.

"70" DASH

EARLY MODEL

CHRYSLER BLDG. (N.Y.) BUILT 1929-30 (77 STORIES)

5.50 x 18 TIRES

EARLY 70 (and 77) HAS PARK. LIGHTS HUNG FROM VISOR (CLOSED CARS)

4 The chromium plated sconce-type parking lights, metal cadet visor, tandem windshield cleaner, and the chromium window archi-traves are new features of design.

MULTI-RANGE 4-SPEED TRANS.

NEW "70" (V)

75 H.P. @ 3200 RPM

LATE MODEL 11-29 = "77" ENGINE USED

70
77

70
77

5. The concave moulding on the Roadster and Phaeton reflect originality of design.

93 H.P. @ 3200 RPM

268.9 C.I.D.

NEW "77" (W)

LATER "70" AND "77" has VERTICAL HOOD LOUVRES.

124 9/16" W.B.

77 IMPERIAL

1. The Futura Design Instrument Panel, designed by Chrysler, executed by Cartier (Paris-New York.)

1930 "IMPERIAL" RESEMBLES ILLUSTRATED 1929 STYLE. DIFFERENCES LISTED IN '29 IMPERIAL SECTION. (6-CYLINDER IMPERIAL DISCONTINUED IN JUNE, 1930.)

CHRYSLER

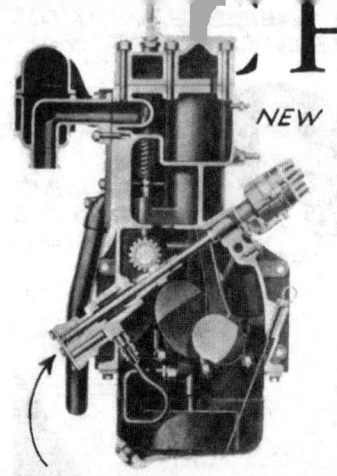

NEW 195.6 C.I.D. ENGINE

ACCESSORY SHAFT IS INCLINED AND THE OIL PUMP IS EXTERNALLY MOUNTED ON THE LEFT SIDE OF THE ENGINE

30½ SIX

MODEL "CJ" (STARTS MARCH, 1930)

UPPER RADIATOR TANK MATCHES CORE ON "CJ" SERIES (LATEST MODEL CJ CONSIDERED "EARLY '31")

BUSINESS COUPE (SIDEMOUNT SPARE TIRES OPTIONAL)

"Royal" RUMBLE-SEAT COUPE ALSO AVAILABLE.

FIRST CHRYSLER 6-CYL. ENGINE TO HAVE 4 MAIN BEARINGS INSTEAD OF 7.

(DE SOTO INTRODUCED WITH A 4-BEARING 6 FOR 1929. DODGE OFFERED ONE FOR LATER '30 SEASON.)

has FUEL PUMP

109" W.B.

"CJs" BUILT AFTER JULY 20, 1930 SOMETIMES CONSIDERED "EARLY 1931" MODELS.

62 H.P. @ 3200 RPM
4.7 GEAR RATIO
4.75/5.00 x 19 TIRES

AS ON OTHER PRE-1931 CHRYSLER CORP. CARS, WOOD WHEELS WERE STANDARD EQUIPMENT. (WIRE WHEELS OPTIONAL) STEEL BODY FRAME

FEDCO I.D. PLATE ON EARLIEST MODELS, BISECTING GRAIN STRIP.

≫ CONVERTIBLE COUPE ≪

THE "CJ" SIX WAS THE FIRST CHRYSLER SINCE 1925 WHICH DID NOT BEAR A "TOP SPEED" MODEL NO. (TOP SPEED OF "CJ" = 62.)

ROADSTER, TOURING CAR, ALSO AVAIL. IN THIS "CJ" SERIES.

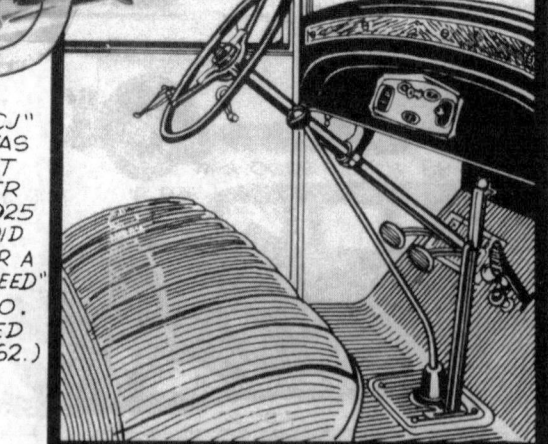

(LATE MODEL "CJ" INTERIOR HAD POSITION OF KEY and SPEEDOMETER REVERSED.)

CHRYSLER

1931 "CM" SIX BEGINS JAN., 1931. 8-CYL. '31 MODELS INTRODUCED JULY, 1930.

217.8 C.I.D. 78 H.P. @ 3400 RPM

116 3/8" W.B. 5.25 × 19 TIRES

Six Sedan—$895

SIX (CM)

(NEW STYLING) V-GRILLE

← EARLY 6 SEDAN = (NO VISOR)

WIRE WHEELS STANDARD ON '31 SIX.

31 6 70 8

"70" (6 CYL.) (TO MAY, 1931)

"70" Business Coupe—$1245

"70" Royal Coupe—$1295

268.9 C.I.D. 93 H.P. @ 3200 RPM

"70" Brougham—$1245

WIRE WHEELS OPTIONAL

70 8

"70" Royal Sedan—$1295

116 9/16" W.B. 5.50 × 18 TIRES

EIGHT (CD) (7-30 TO 4-31)

EARLY "CD" HAS 240.3 C.I.D. AND 80 H.P. @ 3400 RPM. (LATER "CD" HAS 260.8 C.I.D. AND 88 H.P. @ 3400 RPM, AS OF JAN., 1931.)

CHRYSLER EIGHT SPORT ROADSTER

SEDAN

124" W.B. 5.50 × 18 TIRES

(REPLACED BY DE LUXE 8s, SPRING, '31)

CHRYSLER'S FIRST 8s (1930 DE SOTO AND DODGE OFFERED A STRAIGHT-8 ENGINE PRIOR TO CHRYSLER.)

EIGHT COUPE $1495/F. O. B. FACTORY

8 DLX. 8

Roadster—$1545

Convertible Coupe—$1585

De Luxe Eight

(CD DELUXE) (4-31 TO 11-31)

282.1 C.I.D. 100 H.P. @ 3400 RPM

124" W.B.

Eight De Luxe Five-Passenger Coupe—$1565

(INTERIOR)

CHRYSLER

DUAL-COWL PHAETON
(BODY BY LE BARON)

(7-30 TO 10-31)

IMPERIAL EIGHT (CG)

VICTORIA
(CUSTOM BODY BY WATERHOUSE)

145" WHEELBASES ON 1931 IMPERIALS

(BODY BY LE BARON)

SEDAN

ROADSTER

31 (CONT'D.)

CLOSE-COUPLED SEDAN
384.8 C.I.D., 125 H.P. @ 3200 RPM (THROUGH '32)

FUEL PUMP ON ALL MODELS.

5.50 × 18 TIRES
224 C.I.D.
82 H.P. @ 3400

Chrysler Six Sedan

116 3/8" W.B. (CI)
(12-31 TO 11-32)

6/8

SIX 32

'32 MODELS HAVE "FLOATING POWER" FLEXIBLE ENGINE MOUNTS, AUTOMATIC CLUTCH, FREE-WHEELING.

DASH

100 H.P. @ 3400 RPM (CP)

298.7 C.I.D.
125" W.B.

EIGHT (CP)
(12-31 TO 11-32)
298.7 C.I.D., 100 H.P. @ 3400 RPM

6.50 × 17 TIRES

Chrysler Eight Sedan

IMPERIAL EIGHT.

7.00 × 17 TIRES

LENGTHENED HOOD WITH VENT DOORS

135" W.B. (CH)
Imperial Eight Sedan

7.50 × 17 TIRES

146" W.B. (CL)
Imperial Custom Eight Close-Coupled Sedan

CHRYSLER SIX SEDAN $785
(CO)

Chrysler

CHRYSLER ROADSTER IS
DISCONTINUED IN 1933.

6

SIX (CO) HAS 116½" W.B.,→
224 C.I.D., 83
OR 89 H.P. @
3400 RPM

(CT)
ROYAL 8
273.8 C.I.D.
90 H.P. @ 3400 RPM

119½"
W.B.

(12-32 TO 12-33)

33

IMPERIAL 8 (CQ)
298.7 C.I.D.
100 OR 108 H.P.
@ 3400 RPM, WITH
5.2-COMPRESSION
"SILVER DOME" OR
6.2-COMPRESSION
"RED HEAD"

126" W.B.

HIGH-COMPRESSION "RED HEAD"
ENGINES AVAILABLE ON CHRYSLERS
OF 1928 THROUGH 1933.

(CUSTOM IMPERIAL "CL"
SERIES RUNS FROM
2-33 TO 12-33.)

146" W.B.
384.8 C.I.D.
125 OR
135 H.P.
@
3200

Custom
IMPERIAL
8
(CL)

(CL)
INTERIOR

FOR 1934,
"AIRFLOW" BODIES ON ALL 8s

122 H.P. @ 3400
RPM

34

130
H.P.
@
3400
RPM

AIRFLOW 8 (CU)
298.7
C.I.D.

128" W.B.
AIRFLOW IMPERIAL (CV)
323.5 C.I.D.

241.6 C.I.D.
93 H.P. @
3400
RPM

6 (CA, CB)
117" W.B., 121"
WB

122¹³/₁₆

61

CW = 150 H.P.
146½" W.B.

(CX)

1934 CHRYSLER AIRFLOW CUSTOM IMPERIAL CW)

(C-6)=6
(CZ)=8

AIRSTREAM *Chrysler*

35

AIRFLOW 8 (C-1, C-2, C-3, CW)

H.P. RANGE = 93 (6) TO 150 (CW IMPERIAL AIRFLOW)

36

(C-7 REAR)

(C-8)

INTERIORS

(C-10)

BEAUTIFUL NEW AIRFLOWS

NEW SIX (C-7)
DeLUXE EIGHT (C-8)

NOTE DIFFERENCES IN HOOD
LOUVRE DESIGNS

8 CYL.
AIRFLOWS
(C-9, C-10, C-11, CW)

Chrysler

ROYAL 6 (C-16)

AIRFLOW 8 (C-17)

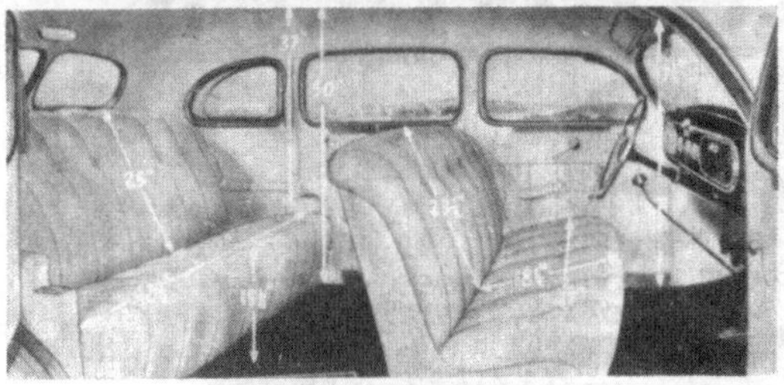

37

C-15 CUSTOM IMPERIAL NO LONGER AN "AIRFLOW"

IMPERIAL 8 (C-14) ↗

ROYAL 6 (C-18)
119" W.B. (THROUGH '39)
241.5 C.I.D. (THROUGH '41)
95 H.P. @ 3600 RPM

38

RICH NEW INTERIORS!

110 - H.P.
NEW YORK SPECIAL
and IMPERIAL (C-19)
8

Custom
130-H.P. IMPERIAL 8
(C-20)
323.5 C.I.D.
('34-50)

LIGHT-COLORED
STEERING
WHEEL

144" W.B.
(THROUGH '39)

NEW V-WINDSHIELD, "WATERFALL" LOWER GRILLE, SUNKEN HEADLIGHTS FOR 1939

ROYAL 6 (and Windsor)
(C-22)

100 H.P.
@
3600

39

NEW YORKER 8
and Saratoga 8 (C-23)
" Imperial 8

(C-24)

Custom Imperial 8

CLEVELAND SIX

(INTRODUCED JULY, 1919)
112" W.B. and 190.8 C.I.D.
(THROUGH '22)

MODEL 40
("41" = '22)

Cleveland Automobile Company
Cleveland, Ohio

BUILT BY

CHANDLER

CLEVELAND

19-22

FOR '21, GRAY AND DAVIS IGNITION IS REPLACED BY BOSCH (THROUGH '26)
4.45 GEAR RATIO (THROUGH '22)

1921 = OUTSIDE DOOR HANDLES ON OPEN CARS
1922 = DRUM HEADLIGHTS &

5-PASS. 2-DR. SEDAN
(INTRO. 1923)

23-24

MODEL 42
'24 HAS CHASSIS APRON PLATES (ALUMINUM KICK PADS,) BOSCH AUTOMATIC SPARK CONTROL, AND THIS NEW RADIATOR DESIGN →
('24 ONLY)

FISHER BODY

112 1/2" W.B., 4.9 GEAR RATIO

"ONE-SHOT" CHASSIS LUBRICATION

25-26

MODEL 31 (STANDARD)

"31"	"43"
108 1/2" W.B.	115" W.B.
30 × 4.75 TIRES	31 × 5.25 TIRES
165.5 C.I.D. ('25)	218.6 C.I.D.
180.1 " ('26)	60 H.P. @
45 H.P. @ 2800 ('26)	2800 RPM

MODEL 43 (SPECIAL 6) HAS ALUMINUM KICK PADS AND NICKEL TRIM

1926 MODEL HAS INTAKE MANIFOLD ABOVE EXHAUST MANIFOLD.

AUGUST, 1926 = BECAME CHANDLER STANDARD and SPECIAL SERIES.

CLIMBER

(K) = 4 CYLS., 192.4 C.I.D., 4.0 G.R., 33×4 TIRES, 117" W.B.
(S) = 6 CYLS., 248.9 C.I.D., 4.75 G.R. (THROUGH '22)
32×4½ TIRES, 125½" W.B. (230.1 C.I.D., 4.0 G.R. IN '23)

('20)   ('23)

(1919-1923)
CLIMBER MOTOR CORP.,
LITTLE ROCK, ARK.
4 OR 6-CYL.
HERSCHELL-SPILLMAN ENG.

COATS
(1922-1923)

COATS
STEAM
MOTORS,
SANDUSKY,
OHIO

COLE MOTOR CAR CO., INDIANAPOLIS (1909-1925)

Cole Aero-Eight

Tourster

NORTHWAY V-8 (346.3
C.I.D.) ENGINES
(THROUGH '25)

NEW FOR 1920: 1-PIECE
REAR AXLE HOUSING,
('20)   JOHNSON CARB.,
ADJUSTABLE
STORM-PROOF
WINDSHIELDS
ON MODELS
"884" + "885."

NEW BRAKE
ADJUSTER

127" W.B.
and 4.45 G.R. (TO '22)
33×5 TIRES (THROUGH '24)

20 "870" SERIES   21

"884"
TOUROSINE
(7-PASS.)

'22 IS 1ST YEAR WITH
SPLIT FRAME
ENDS, 4.1
G.R.

22   NEW "890" SERIES IN '22.

"SPORTOSINE"

'23 MODELS have DRUM-TYPE
HEADLIGHTS, COWL VENT,
and STATIONARY LOWER
HALF OF WINDSHIELD.

23

DISC WHEELS
ALSO
AVAILABLE.

127¼" W.B. (DURING '22,
and THROUGH '25.)

SOME '23
COLES have 3/4
RUNNING BOARDS
and SIDEMOUNTS.

"897"
BROUETTE

"MASTER"
SERIES

24

FULL-LENGTH
RUNNING BOARDS
FOUND ON ALL
COLES AGAIN,
IN 1924.

1925 MODEL SIMILAR TO
'24, BUT BALLOON TIRES
STANDARD INSTEAD OF
OPTIONAL (34×7.30)
76-80 H.P. @
2600 RPM
(3.5 TO 3.6 COMPR.)

"892-A"
5-PASSENGER
AERO-VOLANTE

'25 has 2-PC. REAR
"BUMPERETTES"

COLE
INDIANAPOLIS

65

(1916-1924) RADIATOR SHUTTERS WERE CONTROLLED BY A THERMOSTAT.

Columbia Six

COLUMBIA MOTORS COMPANY, DETROIT, U.S.A.

19-22

COLUMBIA SIX

115" W.B. (THROUGH '24)

The Columbia Six Five Passenger Touring Car

2-PASS. ROADSTER AND 4 PASS. COUPE ARE NEW MODELS FOR 1920. CHASSIS SPECS. GENERALLY SIMILAR TO 1919. 6 CYL., 224-C.I.D. CONTINENTAL ENGINE. (TO '22)

50 H.P. LIGHT 6 HAS 7-U CONTINENTAL 195.6 C.I.D. ENGINE. BIG 6 HAS 8-R CONT. 241.6 C.I.D. ENGINE

22½-24

1924

125" W.B.

6-CYL. CONTINENTAL ENGINE 303.1 C.I.D. (THROUGH '22) 4.66 GEAR RATIO

COMET
(1917—1922)

COMET AUTOMOBILE CO., DECATUR, ILL.

33 x 4½ TIRES ON '21 "C-53" MODEL AND '22 "C-53-2" MODEL.

20

"4-40"

117" W.B.

COMMONWEALTH

COMMONWEALTH MOTORS CO., JOLIET, ILLINOIS (1917-1922)

REPLACES PARTIN-PALMER CAR, 1917.

"4-45" ('21)

EVOLVED INTO THE CHECKER TAXI.

32 x 4

'20 HAS 4-CYL. LYCOMING 192.4 C.I.D. ENGINE INSTEAD OF 6-CYL. AS IN 1919.

MODEL "41" ('34) 4.33 G.R.

143.1 C.I.D. 4-CYL. 38 H.P. @ 2600 RPM

CONTINENTAL
(1933 - 1934)

CONT. AUTO. CO., DETROIT 1933 MODELS : "BEACON" 4, "FLYER" 6, and "ACE" 6 (V-WINDSHIELD ON "ACE")

CONTINENTAL ENGINES

101½" W.B.

MFD. 1929-1932; 1935-1937; BY AUBURN AUTOMOBILE CO., AUBURN, INDIANA

CORD FRONT DRIVE

"L-29" SERIES

(INTRODUCED LATE 1929)

STRAIGHT-8
298.6 C.I.D.
LYCOMING
"FDA"
ENGINE

125 H.P.
@ 3600 RPM

4.8 G.R.

DASH (L-29)

DELCO-REMY IGNITION (TO '32) FUEL PUMP

30 TO 32

137 1/2" W.B.

(NO 1933-1935 MODELS)

7.00 x 18 TIRES

1. Engine Heat Indicator.
2. Oil Pressure Gauge.
3. Spark Control.
4. Windshield Wiper Control, left.
5. Gasoline Throttle.
6. Glove Compartment.
7. Carburetor Choke.
8. Windshield Wiper Control, right.
9. Manifold Heat Control.
10. Gasoline Gauge.
11. Oil Level Gauge.
12. Speedometer.
13. Instrument Light Switch.
14. Ignition Lock.
15. Gear Shift Lever.
16. Starter Control.
17. Ammeter.

NEW CONCEALED HEADLIGHTS

SEDANS and CONVERT. MODELS.

HOOD EXH. PIPES ON SUPERCHARGED MODELS.

TACHOMETER

MACHINE-TURNED DASH (OCT., '35 = EARLIEST "810" has HEADLIGHT DOORS LOCATED CLOSER IN TOWARD GRILLE.)

NEW 288.6 C.I.D. V-8 ENGINE
125 H.P. @ 3500 RPM *
3.88 G.R.

"810"   "812"

36-37

* = 115 IN CERTAIN RATINGS

ONLY 2 COUPES BLT.

Auto-Lite IGNITION

COURIER
(1922-1924)

COURIER MOTOR CO., SANDUSKY, OHIO

(REPLACES MAIBOHM)

116" W.B.
5 TO 1 G.R.
32 × 4 TIRES

6-CYL., OVERHEAD-VALVE
195.6 C.I.D. FALLS ENGINE
ATWATER-KENT IGNITION

CRANE-SIMPLEX (1915-1924)

('22)

6 CYL.

SIMPLEX AUTOMOBILE CO.,
NEW BRUNSWICK, N.J.,
L.I. CITY, N.Y.

CRAWFORD
(CRAWFORD AUTOMOBILE CO., HAGERSTOWN, MD.)
(1905-1923)

SEE ALSO "DAGMAR"

('20)

MINOR CHANGES ONLY FOR '20.
6 CYL. CONTINENTAL ENG.
122½" W.B.

CROSLEY (1939-1952)

39

2 CYLINDERS

WEIGHT= ONLY 925 LBS.!
MECH. BRAKES
4.25 × 12" TIRES

5.14 GEAR RATIO

CROW-ELKHART
(1909-1924)
CROW ELKHART MOTOR CAR CO.

117" W.B.

21

4.25 G.R.

"L-55" ('19-20)
4 CYL. 192.4 C.I.D.
LYCOMING OR
HERSCHELL-SPILLMAN
ENGINE

19-20

6 CYL. RUTENB. ENGINE ALSO (H SERIES)

"S-67" 6 CYL.
7-PASS.

248.9 C.I.D.
HERSCH.-SP.
6-CYL.
ENGINE
ADOPTED
DURING '21
ON "S."

"L" CONT'D. AS 4-CYL. MODEL.

CUNNINGHAM
JAS. CUNNINGHAM SON + CO.,
ROCHESTER, N.Y.
(1907-1933)
V-8 ENGINES
441.7 C.I.D.
132"-142" W.B.

"V-4" **21**
4.08 G.R.

"82-A"
INSIDE-DRIVE 6-PASS.
LIMOUSINE

24

"125-A"

"LANDAULET" 7-PASS.

23

30

"V-9"

110 H.P. @ 2500 RPM

DAGMAR
(1922-1927)

CRAWFORD AUTOMOBILE CO.;
M.P. MÖLLER CAR CO.,
HAGERSTOWN, MD.
(EARLY "CRAWFORD-DAGMAR" has 138" W.B.)
6-CYL. CONTINENTAL OR LYCOMING ENGINES

LATER MODEL has 120" W.B.

DANIELS (1915-1924)

DANIELS MOTOR CAR CO., READING, PA.

NEW FOR 1920: DANIELS-BUILT V-8 (404.1 C.I.D.) ENGINE, IN MODEL "D-19" DANIELS EIGHT.

34 x 4½ TIRES (THROUGH '21)

"SUBMARINE SPEEDSTER"

TOURING

132" W.B.

6-PASS. TOURING SEDAN

33 x 5 TIRES, 1922-1924

NO SIGNIFICANT MODEL CHANGES 1920-1924, EXC. "23-28" SERIES STARTS '23

TOWN CAR

DASH

HEXAGON KNOB IN CENTER OF DASH IS VENT CONTROL. NEXT TO IT AT RIGHT IS HAND AIR PUMP.
(138" W.B. ALSO AVAIL. IN '24)

DAVIS (1908-1929)

"Built of the Best"

GEORGE W. DAVIS MOTOR CAR CO. RICHMOND, IND., U.S.A

FEW CHANGES on "51" FOR 1920. HAS 224 C.I.D. "7-R" CONTINENTAL 6-CYL. ENGINE, (THROUGH '22) STROMBERG CARB., 120" W.B. (THROUGH '23)

"71" SERIES ADDED DURING '22, with 115" W.B., 6-CYL., 195.6 C.I.D. "7-U" CONTINENTAL ENG. (THROUGH '24, KNOWN AS "90" IN '25) 5.1 G.R. (THROUGH '25)

"60," "70" SERIES ('23 SIMILAR)

"60" SERIES (63-65)
120" W.B. 241.5 C.I.D. 5.09 G.R.

The COUPÉ ("67")

"71"

(ALL 6 CYLS., 1916-1927)

"71" PHAETON

HYDR. BRAKES STARTING 1925

'25 "MOUNTAINEER 91" has 6-CYL. CONT. "8-R" (241.6) ENGINE (56 H.P. @ 2300)

(LARGER "92" has 115" W.B., 230.1 C.I.D. "11-U" CONT. ENG., 54 H.P. ('26) 68 H.P. ('27) 4.9 G.R.

"93" (W.B. lowered to 109") 169.2 C.I.D. "20-L" ENG. (185 C.I.D. 48 H.P. in '27)

"90" (115" W.B.) 49 H.P. @ 2500

1927="92-97" SIMILAR TO '26 "92." "SILVER ANNIVERSARY 94" REPLACES "93"
1928="99" has STR.-8 CONT. "14-S" ENGINE, 119" W.B., 84
1929="69" (6) and "89" (8)

DELLING STEAM CAR
(1923 - 1927) DELLING STEAM MOTOR CO.,
W. COLLINGWOOD,
N.J. and
PHILADELPHIA

132" W.B.
2.0
G.R.

2 CYLINDERS "126" has HYDR. BRKS., ALUM.
BODY, 32 × 6.20 TIRES ('26 SPECS.)

(1928 - 1961)

DE SOTO SIX
A CHRYSLER MOTORS PRODUCT

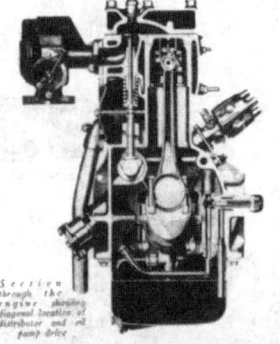

IGNITION :
DELCO : TO 2-1-29
NORTHEAST : AFTER
2-1-29

174.9 C.I.D.
6 CYLINDERS

Section through the engine showing diagonal location of distributor and oil pump drive

55 H.P. @ 3000 RPM
5.2 COMPR.

109"
WHEELBASE
STROM. CARB.

29

MODEL K
JULY, 1928
TO
MAY, 1930

Four-door, five-passenger de luxe sedan

(DE SOTO CARS
PRODUCED FROM
7-28 TO 12-60
FINAL CAR :
1961 V-8)

Business coupe with rear deck for luggage

(ALL DE SOTOS HAVE HYDRAULIC BRAKES,
'28-'61)

HAYES BODIES
ON SOME
"K" MODELS

has
VACUUM
TANK

SOME "K" MODELS HAVE
"De Soto Six" IN
CHROME - PLATED
SCRIPT, FASTENED
TO RADIATOR
CORE. (ALSO
IN '30)

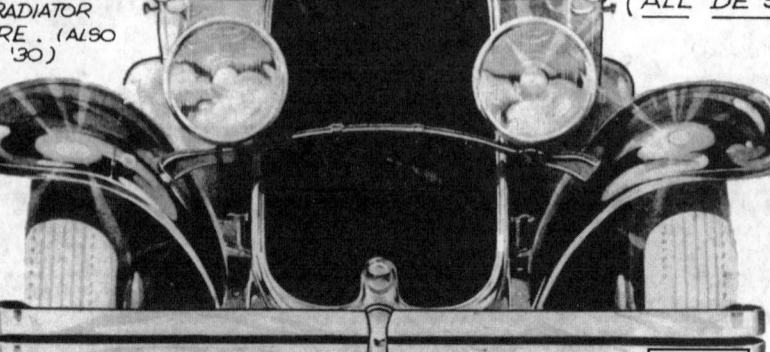

De luxe coupe with rumble-seat

Five-passenger, two-door sedan

EARLY '30 "K" LIKE '29, BUT HAS A FEW FALSE HOOD LOUVRES.

DE SOTO SIX

5.00 x 19

(DETAILS OF ROADSTER)

CARTER CARB. REPLACES STROMBERG.

Front Compartment

1—Windshield regulator handle
2—Ignition switch and lock
3—Throttle control hand lever
4—Horn push-button
5—Light control hand lever
6—Door remote control handle
7—Door window regulator handle
8—Gearshift lever
9—Windshield wiper control valve
10—Clutch pedal
11—Brake pedal
12—Rear view mirror

13—Fuel gauge
14—Choke control button
15—Oil gauge
16—Ammeter
17—Speedometer
18—Steering post support bracket
19—Release button
20—Transmission brake hand lever
21—Starter pedal
22—Accelerator pedal
23—Accelerator foot rest

Finer De Soto Six

(CK) STARTS 5-30
(AVAIL. TO 11-30)

NEW DISPL. OF 189.6 CU. IN.
60 H.P. @ 3400 RPM

$\frac{6}{8}$ **30** $\frac{6}{8}$

AFTER 11-30, "CF" has "NARROW PROFILE" RADIATOR SHELL. (SEE 1931)

De Soto STRAIGHT EIGHT

(CF) INTRO. 1-30

5.25 x 19

→ STYLE OF '30, with THICK RADIATOR SHELL.

207.7 C.I.D.

114 " W.B.
STROMBERG CARB. ON "CF"

DASH

70 H.P. @ 3400 RPM
FUEL PUMP ADDED

EIGHT SEDAN

EIGHT CONVERTIBLE COUPE

DE SOTO

NEW DASH ("SA") HAS GAUGES BEHIND OVAL GLASS PANEL.

6 "SA"

RUMBLE-SEAT DETAILS (8)

109 3/8" W.B.

205.3 C.I.D. 72 H.P. @ 3400 RPM (6)

8 "CF"

6 / 8

31

(STARTS 12-30)

(8) 114" W.B. 220.7 C.I.D. 77 H.P. @ 3400 RPM

FUEL PUMP

"CF" AVAIL. TO 2-32

31½ — EARLY **32**

("SA" and "CF" BLT. 7-23-31 and AFTER ARE SOMETIMES KNOWN AS "EARLY 1932.")

(SA)

"SA" OUTER VISOR RESTORED "Free-Wheeling" AVAIL., and

"SA" AVAIL. TO 3-32

"EASY-SHIFT" TRANSMISSION (SA OR CF)

(12-31 TO 10-32)

B+B CARB. (THROUGH '35)

CHROMED RADIATOR SHELL ON EARLY MODELS.

112 3/8" W.B.

211.4 C.I.D. 75 H.P. @ 3400 RPM NEW 5.25 × 18 AND OTHER TIRES.

32 "SC" 6 CYL. ONLY

Custom Roadster De Luxe

Custom 5 Passenger Sedan De Luxe

Custom Convertible Sedan De Luxe

Standard Coupe

Standard 2 Door Sedan

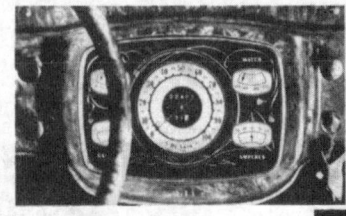

DE SOTO

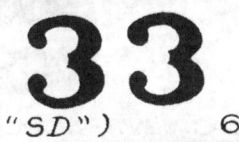

(11-32 to 10-33)

33
("SD") 6

114 3/8" W.B.   86 H.P. @ 3400 RPM

NEW 6 TO 1 COMPR.   NEW 5.50 x 17
217.8 C.I.D.   AND OTHER TIRES.

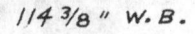

WHAT—NO HAND-STRAPS!   "WALK RIGHT IN" THESE DOORS

34
(SE) (1-34 TO 10-34)

THE WHEEL IS WHERE YOU WANT IT   RIDE INSIDE THE FRAME . . . NOT ON IT

ALL-NEW, STREAMLINED "AIRFLOW" (2 OR 4-DOOR)
IS ONLY MODEL OF DE SOTO AVAILABLE
FOR 1934.

115 1/2" W.B.
NEW 6.50 x 16 TIRES
(ON 1934 THROUGH 1936 "AIRFLOW")

241.5 C.I.D.   100 H.P. @ 3400 RPM   6.2 COMPR.

AIRSTREAM 6
(SF)

AIRFLOW 6 (SG)
6.5 COMP.
100 H.P. @ 3400

35
(STARTS 11-34)

116"
W.B.
6 TO 1
COMPR.
93 H.P.
@ 3400
RPM

115 1/2"
W.B.

6.25 x
16 TIRES (ON
1935 and 1936
"AIRSTREAM")

115 1/2
WB

(NEW CARTER CARB.)   118" W.B.
(BOTH SERIES)

AIRFLOW 6
(S-2)

AIRSTREAM CUSTOM 6
(S-1)

AIRSTREAM
ALSO AVAIL
WITH 1-PC.
WINDSHIELD

36
(STARTS 9-35)

73

SAME ENGINES AS 1935

DE SOTO

116" W.B.

All Seat Edges Padded.

Safety-height Instrument Panel.   All Panel Controls are Flush.

DISPLACEMENT REDUCED TO 228.1 CU. IN.
6.5 COMPR.   93 H.P. @ 3600 RPM
CARTER B + B CARBURETOR
(THROUGH '38)

37
(S-3)
(9-36 TO 8-37)

6.00 × 16 OR
6.50 × 16 TIRES
(THROUGH '40)

38   (S-5)
(9-37
TO
7-38)

DASH

('38 - 39 SPECIFICATIONS
SAME AS 1937)

CARTER CARB.

39 (S-6)

(8-38
TO
7-39)

SPEED INDICATOR
CHANGES COLORS

COLUMN SHIFT

DETROIT AIR-COOLED
(1923)

DETROIT AIR-COOLED CAR CO., DETROIT, MICH.
(ALSO KNOWN AS "D.A.C" CAR , 1922-1923)
V-6 AIR-COOLED ENGINE

DETROIT ELECTRIC
(1907-1938)
DETROIT ELECTRIC CAR CO., DETROIT

FALSE "RADIATOR" TRIED BRIEFLY

20

"88" 5-PASS. BROUGHAM

MOST LATER MODELS BUILT TO ORDER, AS IS THIS 1931 MODEL "99" →

21 100" W.B.

32 × 4½

ORIGINAL NAME : TRASK-DETROIT

DETROIT STEAM
(1922-1923)
DETROIT STEAM MOTORS CORP., DETROIT

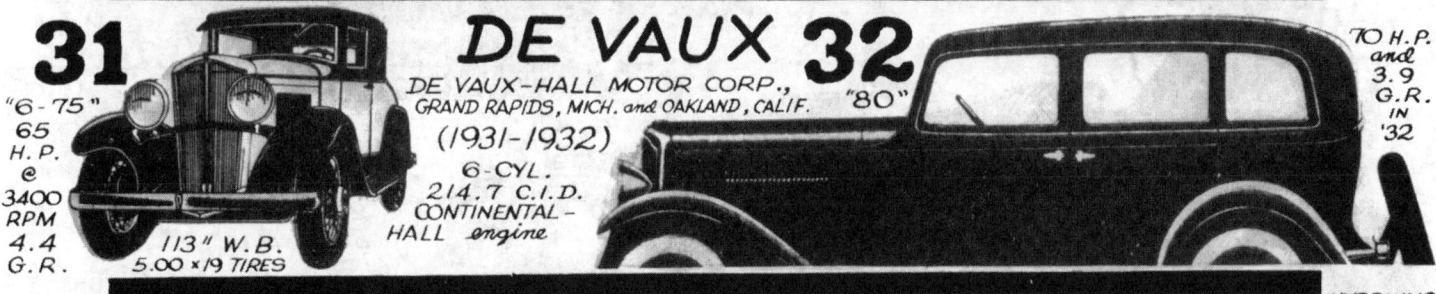

31

DE VAUX **32**

"6-75" 65 H.P. @ 3400 RPM 4.4 G.R.

DE VAUX-HALL MOTOR CORP.,
GRAND RAPIDS, MICH. and OAKLAND, CALIF.
(1931-1932)
6-CYL.
214.7 C.I.D.
CONTINENTAL-HALL *engine*

113" W.B.
5.00 ×19 TIRES

"80"

70 H.P. and 3.9 G.R. IN '32

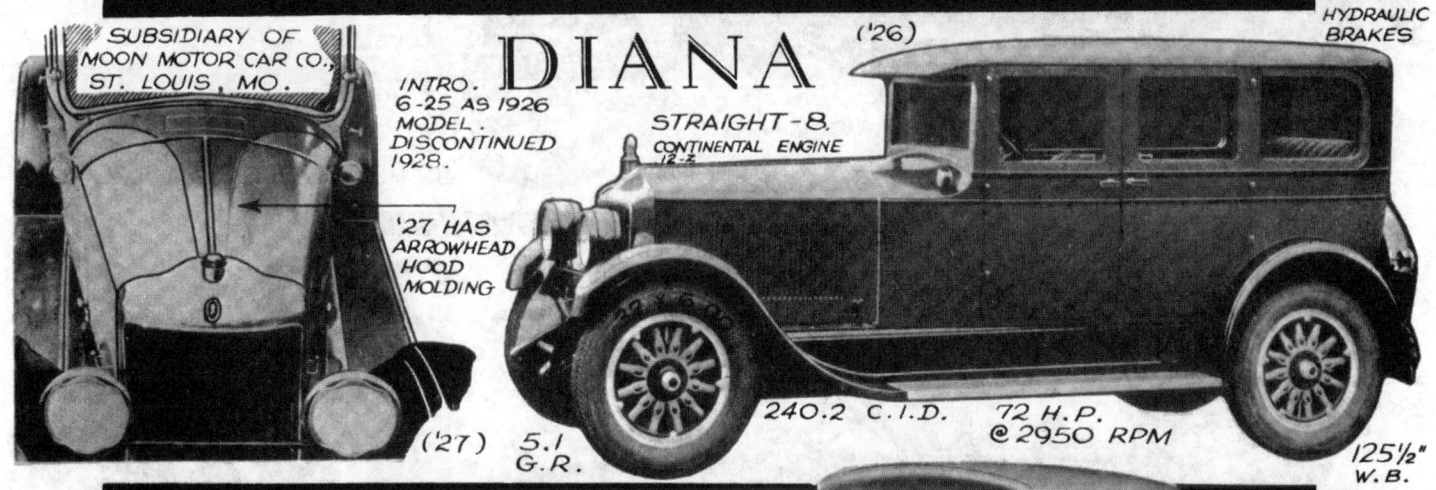

SUBSIDIARY OF MOON MOTOR CAR CO., ST. LOUIS, MO.

('26)

DIANA

INTRO. 6-25 AS 1926 MODEL. DISCONTINUED 1928.

STRAIGHT-8. CONTINENTAL ENGINE 12-5

'27 HAS ARROWHEAD HOOD MOLDING

HYDRAULIC BRAKES

('27) 5.1 G.R.

240.2 C.I.D.   72 H.P. @ 2950 RPM

125½" W.B.

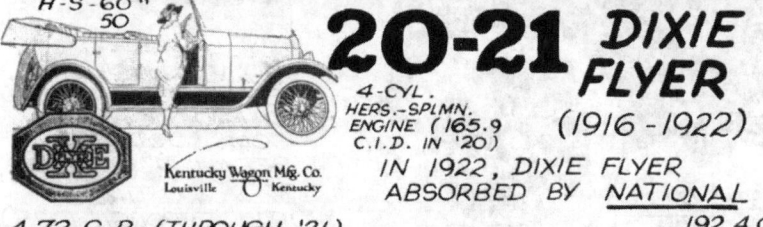

"H-S-60" 50

20-21 *DIXIE FLYER*

4-CYL. HERS.-SPLMN. ENGINE (165.9 C.I.D. IN '20)

(1916-1922)

IN 1922, DIXIE FLYER ABSORBED BY NATIONAL

22

4.75 G.R.

Kentucky Wagon Mfg. Co. Louisville Kentucky

4.72 G.R. (THROUGH '21)
32 × 4 TIRES

192.4 C.I.D. (SINCE '21)

112" W.B.
("HS-70" STARTS '21)

DOBLE STEAM

('25)

('29-32)

FORMERLY
"DOBLE-DETROIT"

('31-32)

EST. 1914,
DOBLE STEAM MOTORS
MOVED TO EMERYVILLE,
CALIF. IN 1924; IN
BUSINESS UNTIL 1932.

MURPHY BODY

DODGE BROTHERS

(SINCE NOV., 1914)
DODGE BROS., DETROIT
(A PRODUCT OF
CHRYSLER CORP. SINCE MID-1928.)

20

4-DOOR SEDAN

(2-19 TO 7-21)

7-19 TO 6-20

114" WHEELBASE (1916-1923)

4 CYLINDER,
212.3 C.I.D.
ENGINE
(1915 TO 1927)

35 H.P. @ 2000 RPM

(4 TO 1 COMPRESSION
(THROUGH 1926)

32 × 3½ TIRES (THROUGH 1921)

21-22

7-1-20 TO 5-23-22

JULY, 1921 ═══
BUDD-MICHELIN
STEEL DISC WHEELS
INTRODUCED ON
SOME DODGES;
SEDAN 4" LOWER.
32 × 4" TIRES
(1922 THROUGH 1925)

DODGE BROTHERS

32×4 STEEL DISC BUDD - MICHELIN WHEELS AVAIL.

5-24-22 TO 6-28-23

22½

TO

BUSINESS SEDAN
(ANNOUNCED 9-22)

SPEC. SUBURB. SEDAN

BUSINESS COUPE
(AVAILABLE SUMMER, 1922)

23

CANTRELL BODY

BABCOCK BODY

2-PASS. BUSINESS CPE.

(4-PASS. CPE. ALSO AVAILABLE)

7-1-23 TO 11-1-24

24

NEW 116" WHEELBASE

BUSINESS SEDAN

TYPE A

1924 Model Cantrell Suburban Body for Court Type Dodge Brothers Chassis

DODGE BROTHERS

TYPE-A SEDAN

25
NEW
COACH
26

JAN., '25

SPECIAL=
HAS NICKEL RADIATOR
SHELL

SPECIAL
TYPE-B SEDAN
(EARLY '26)
SEDANS

SPECIAL
TYPE-A SEDAN

I-PIECE WINDSHIELD
ON LATER MODELS.

SPECIAL

26½

DODGE BROTHERS

EARLY MODEL (TO FEB., '27) **MODEL 126**

31 × 5.25 TIRES

27

IN 1927, DODGE BROS. CARS ABANDON 12-VOLT ELECTRICAL SYSTEM IN FAVOR OF CONVENTIONAL 6-VOLT SYSTEM. ELECTRICAL SYSTEM CHANGED FROM ONE-UNIT TO 2-UNIT (STARTER + GENERATOR SEPERATED.)

"126"

SPARK and THROTTLE LEVERS MOVED TO TOP OF STEERING WHEEL. 40 H.P. @ 2400 RPM

FEB., '27 **ROOF-VISOR**

MODEL 124

NEW 4.1 TO 1 COMPR.

4 CYL.

MODEL 2249

SENIOR 6 224 C.I.D. 6 CYL. 60 H.P. @ 2800 RPM 5.3 COMPR. (FIRST 6-CYL. DODGE)

INTRO. 6-27

27½

(108" W.B.)

FAST 4 "128", INTRO. 7-27, CONT'D. TO 1928 SEASON 29 × 5.00 TIRES

6-CYLINDER DODGES FOR 1928

The VICTORY SIX
BY DODGE BROTHERS

(INTRO. 1-5-28) MODEL 130, 131

STD. 6 and VICTORY 6 HAVE 208 C.I.D., 5.2 COMPR. and 58 H.P. @ 3000 RPM with 29 × 5.00 TIRES

(MECHANICAL BRAKES) **STANDARD 6**

MODEL 140, 141

110" W.B.

112" W.B. 4.45 GEAR RATIO

HYDRAULIC BRAKES

VICTORY 6

The Deluxe Sedan

RT. HAND DRIVE - EXPORT MODEL

SENIOR 6 MODEL 2251

28

78 H.P. @ 3000 RPM 241.5 C.I.D. 5.2 COMPR.

31 × 6.00 TIRES

NEW 120" W.B.

DODGE BROTHERS

CHRYSLER MOTORS PRODUCT

6 (DA)

"DA" HAS SAME SPECS.
AS VICTORY 6. BUILT
1-29 TO 3-30
BUDD BODIES,
AS BEFORE

29

DA
VIC.

('29 MODEL STARTS
8-28)

HYDRAULIC BRAKES, INTRODUCED TO DODGE
ON '27-8 "SENIOR" and '28 "VICTORY 6," ARE
STANDARD ON ALL DODGES FROM 1929 ON.

DA
SR.

MURRAY
BODIES
ON
"SENIOR
6"
ONLY.

NEW VICTORY SIX

'29 "VICTORY 6" HAS HIGHER, LONGER BODY
THAN '28. SEDAN DOORS WIDENED 3".
SEAT CUSHIONS AND BACKS ARE DEEPER.

"FROSTED SILVER"
INST. PANEL

SENIOR
6

MODEL 2252 SR·6
BUILT 7-28 TO 6-29

(CONT'D. TO 6-30,
AS "DB" series)
COMPRESSION INCREASED TO 5.5

CHRYSLER PURCHASED
DODGE BROS. IN SPRING,
1928. 1929 AND LATER
DODGES ARE CHRYSLER PRODUCTS.

6.00 × 19" TIRES

80

DODGE   BROTHERS

SIX

(DA) TO 3-30

VACUUM TANK RETAINED ON "DA" SIX, AS ON LEFTOVER MODELS OF "SENIOR SIX."

NAME SHORTENED TO _DODGE_ DURING 1930.

NOTE NEW POSITION OF COWL LAMPS ON ABOVE MODEL.

30

NEW 8 (DC) HAS 114" W.B., 220.7 C.I.D., 5.4 COMPR., 75 H.P. @ 3400 RPM
4.6 GEAR RATIO
new FUEL PUMP

(DC)

EIGHT

60 H.P. @ 3400 RPM | 189.8 C.I.D.

DODGE SIX   (PRODUCTION STARTS 12-29)

109" W.B.

30½

TO MAY,

31

(DD)

new RADIATOR DESIGN

"DD" INTERIOR

224·928
MICHIGAN 1930

HAS FUEL PUMP

4.9 GEAR RATIO

DODGE SIX AND EIGHT

5.00 × 19 TIRES ON SIXES

New Dodge Six $815 to $845, New Dodge Eight $1095 to $1135, Standard Six $755 to $855, Standard Eight $995 to $1095. Prices f.o.b. factory

6 (DH)

211.5 C.I.D. 5.35 COMPR. 113 5/8" W.B. 4.66 G.R. 74 H.P. @ 3400 RPM

31

"Standard" MODELS ARE CONTINUATIONS OF 1930 "DD" 6 and "DC" 8.

THE LAST DODGE ROADSTER UNTIL 1949 →

8 (DG)

118" W.B. 240.3 C.I.D. 5.4 COMPR. 84 H.P. @ 3400 RPM 5.50 × 18 TIRES 4.60 GEAR RATIO

5.50 × 18 TIRES 4.6 GEAR RATIO (DL) 6

217.8 C.I.D. 79 H.P. @ 3400 RPM 6.35 COMPR. OPTIONAL

6 and 8 COUPES and CVT. CPES. HAVE 4.3 (6) and 3.91 (8) GEAR RATIOS

114 3/8" W.B.

32

4.1 GEAR RATIO 6.00 × 18 TIRES

282.1 C.I.D. 5.2 or 6.2 COMPR. 90 or 100 H.P. @ 3400 RPM

8 (DK)

CONVERTIBLE SEDAN (NEW)

122 3/8" W.B.

33

DODGE

REDUCED TO 201.3 C.I.D. 5.5 or 6.2 COMPR. 75 or 81 H.P. @ 3600 RPM

6
(DP)

REAR DETAILS

'33 DASH GAUGES IN CENTER

115" W.B.

The big new Dodge "6" Sedan—$675 f.o.b. factory, Detroit, special equipment extra

6
8

HOOD ON "8" DOES NOT CONCEAL COWL AS IT DOES ON "6"

DODGE "8"
WITH FLOATING POWER

An Aristocrat From Bumper to Bumper

"8" HAS COWL LAMPS

Dodge "8"
122" w.b.

OPTIONAL "RED HEAD" ON 8 GIVES 6.5 COMPRESSION.
'34 DASH GAUGES AT LEFT

92 or 100 H.P. @ 3400 RPM (8)

(DO) = (Final Dodge straight-8)

217.8 C.I.D. 5.6 or 6.5 COMPR.

82 or 87 H.P. @ 3600 RPM

117" W.B.

34
(DR)

LUGGAGE CARRIED BEHIND REAR SEAT-BACK.

83

DODGE

6.5 COMPRESSION ALUMINUM HEAD STANDARD ON "DS"

(DS) SPECIAL 121" WHEELBASE

6.25 × 16 TIRES

34½

(FEWER HOOD LOUVRES)

34 (CONT'D.)

"DRXX" MODEL WAS LOW-PRICED 1934½ SERIES, WITHOUT BUILT-IN VENT WINDOWS.

217.8 C.I.D. CONTINUED THROUGH 1941

The New Dodge Touring Sedan Four-Door—with Trunk

REAR DETAILS

Convertible Coupe

35 (DU)

Sedan

WITHOUT TRUNK

DASH

The New Dodge Touring Sedan Two-Door—with Trunk

SEDAN INTERIOR

WHEELBASE NOW 116" (AS ALSO IN 1936)

NEW HORN GRILLES BELOW LIGHTS

87 H.P. @ 3600 RPM (THROUGH 1940)

6.5 COMPRESSION (THROUGH 1941)

Two-Door Sedan

STEEL TIRE-COVER AVAILABLE

6.00 × 16 IS STANDARD TIRE SIZE UNTIL LATE 1940s.

Coupe with Rumble Seat

Coupe

DODGE

DODGE (D-2)

DASH

36

37
(D-5)

WESTCHESTER SUBURBAN WAGON

NEW "HIGH-SAFETY" INTERIOR

PULL-DRAWER KNOBS ON EARLY MODELS.

RECESSED

NEW HORIZONTAL GRILLE MOTIF

115" WHEELBASE IN 1937 and 1938

WINDSHIELDS DO NOT OPEN ON '38 CHRYSLER-BUILT CARS.

38
(D-8)

'39 ENGINE

INTERIOR

LIGHTED SPEED INDICATOR

FAST BACK

117" WHEELBASE

39 (D-11)

DORRIS
(1905-1926)

DORRIS MOTOR CAR CO.
ST. LOUIS, MO.

OWN 377 C.I.D., O.H.V.
6-CYL. ENG.

132" W.B.   WESTINGHOUSE IGNITION (THROUGH '21)

21 "6-80" 7-PASS. 33 x 5

22 NEW BOSCH IGNITION   "6-80"

(NO NEW PRODUCTION AFTER 1923.)

DORT
(1915-1924)

Dort Motor Car Company
Flint, Mich.

Quality Goes Clear Through

21 "17-A" OR "17-12" MODELS

NEW, ANGULAR STYLING FOR 1921, NEW 108" W.B.

Top and curtains up
When the storm beats down

20

(4) 4 CYL. 192.4 C.I.D. LYCOMING ENGINE

105½" W.B.

1922 "19-14" MODEL LIKE 1921.

MODEL "15" TOURING
FEW CHANGES FROM 1919.

23 "HARVARD SEDAN"

(6)

31 x 4 TIRES

NEW 1923
MODEL 18-23 HAS 108" W.B., LYCOMING ENGINE AS BEFORE,
4.60 GEAR RATIO
MODEL 25-20 HAS 115" W.B., NEW 195.6 C.I.D.,
6-CYL. FALLS ENGINE, 4.66 GEAR RATIO
45 HORSEPOWER   (INTRO. 11-22)

"27-C"
"3-DOOR COUPE" IS A
SEDAN WITH JUST ONE DOOR
ON LEFT SIDE.

FALLS ENGINE
(6 CYL., O.H.V.)
207.1 C.I.D. **24**
MODEL 27
NEW RADIATOR DESIGN
(THE FINAL DORT)

21 (97.4 CID) 4 CYLS.
104" W.B.
4.75 G.R.

DRIGGS (1921-1923)
DRIGGS ORDNANCE AND
MANUFACTURING CO.,
NEW HAVEN, CONN. AND N.Y.C.

22-23

OWN ENG.   30 x 3½ TIRES

DUESENBERG 8

(1920 – 1937)
DUESENBERG
MOTOR CO.,
INDIANAPOLIS, IND.

DASH

"A" SERIES
259.7 C.I.D.
STRAIGHT-8 ENGINE
100 H.P. @ 3600 RPM ('26 RATING)

HYDRAULIC BRAKES
STANDARD EQUIPMENT
90 MILES PER HOUR

PRESSURE FUEL FEED
IN '26.

134" W.B.

21-28

(JOINED AUBURN
IN 1926)

('27-'28 MODEL "X")

29 – 37

"J" SERIES
STRAIGHT-8
420 C.I.D.
265 H.P. @ 4200
RPM

AVAIL. WITH PRESSURE
FUEL FEED ('32)

HAS FUEL PUMP ('29)

MURPHY BODY

"SJ"
(SUPERCHARGED)
(NOTE THE
EXHAUST
PIPES
THROUGH
HOOD.)

BARKER
BODY

142½" – 153½"
WHEELBASES

DASH

RENOWNED
COACHBUILDERS SUPPLIED
MANY VARIETIES OF CUSTOM
BODIES.

"J"
(UN-SUPERCHARGED)

20 "A" MODEL — DUPONT

DUPONT MOTORS, INC. WILMINGTON, DEL. (ALSO MOORE, PA.)

(1920–1932)

124" W.B. (THROUGH '26)

16" BRAKE DRUMS, WATER TEMP. GAUGE ON DASH, CONCAVE BODY SIDES. OWN 4-CYL., 249.6 C.I.D. ENGINE (TO '23) 2-WH. MECH. BRAKES and 4.45 G.R. (THROUGH '24)

21

← 5-PASS. TOURING CAR

23

('24 HAS 6-CYL. HERSCHELL-SPILLMAN "90" ENGINE) (288.6 C.I.D.)

(6-CYL.) **24** MODEL C 57 H.P.

5-PASS. TOURING SEDAN

25 MODEL D (1925–1926) HAS NEW O.H.V. WISCONSIN 6-CYL. "Y" ENGINE (268.3 C.I.D. 75 H.P. @ 3000 RPM NEW HYDRAULIC BRAKES

4.7 GEAR RATIO 32 × 6.20 BALLOON TIRES (THROUGH '29)

MODEL E **28**

MODEL E RUNS FROM 1927 TO 1929. MODEL F ALSO, IN '28)

6-CYL. WISC. "Y" ENGINE 268.3 C.I.D., 75 H.P. @ 3000 RPM 32 × 6.20 TIRES MODEL E = 125" W.B., 4.7 GEAR RATIO MODEL F = 136" " 4.45 " "

140-H.P. SPEEDSTER **29-30** MODEL G

125" W.B.

→ NARROW "WOOD-LITES"

30-32 MODEL G (MERRIMAC BODY) 141" W.B.

MODEL G HAS STRAIGHT-8 CONTINENTAL "12-K" ENGINE (322 C.I.D.) WITH 114 H.P. @ 3200 RPM (GETS FUEL PUMP, '29) LEFTOVER CARS STILL AVAIL. IN 1933.

MODEL H ('31–32) HAS 146" W.B.

H.P. INCREASED IN 1932, TO 130 @ 3200 RPM

88

The DU PONT

6 - CYL. "B-22" HAS SQUARE-EDGED HOOD. 6 DISCONTINUED MID - 1924. (PHOTO AT UPPER RIGHT.)

('24)

DURANT
(1921 – 1932)
DURANT MOTORS, INC.
(OFFICES IN N.Y.C.)

"B-22" 6 CYL. ('22)

ANSTED ENG.

FOUR
"A-22"

21-25

('21-22 HAS WOOD WHEELS. DISC WHEELS ALSO, STARTING 1923.)

('25)

LATE '25 SOMETIMES CALLED "1926."

28
4 and 6 CYLS.

CONTINENTAL ENGINES USED (THROUGH '32) DURANT PRODUCTION SUSPENDED 1926-7, BUT STAR CAR CONTINUED.

(EARLY '28 4-CYL = " DURANT-STAR")

HAYES - HUNT BODIES

"4-40" ("M")

29

OTHER 6 - CYL. MODELS : "55," "60," "65," "6-60," "6-66"

("6-63" CONSIDERED AN EARLY '30 MODEL.)

(M SERIES (REPLACES STAR)

"6-70" DE LUXE SEDAN

119" W.B.

(65 H.P., 4-SPEED TRANS.)

BUDD ALL-STEEL BODIES ON SOME '30 DURANTS.
NOTE NEW EMBLEM

30

DURANT

EARLY '32 IS "619"

'30 "6-14" has NEW FUEL PUMP.

"6-17" GETS IT IN '31

"621," "622" also, IN '32 (71 H.P.)

31 "610," "612"
(4)   (6)
VERTICAL HOOD LOUVRES ; SOME MODELS HAVE RADIATOR SHUTTERS and SEATS THAT CONVERT TO A BED.

32 FINAL DURANT

"6-14" = 58 H.P., 199 CID
"6-17" = 70 H.P., 248 CID

('31)

SOME '30s HAVE VERTICAL HOOD LOUVRES.

DYMAXION 33-34

(ONLY 3 PILOT MODELS)
DESIGNED BY
BUCKMINSTER FULLER

SINGLE REAR WHEEL!

FORD V-8 REAR ENGINE

EAGLE 23-24

TOURING CARS ONLY

WITH 6-CYLINDER, 195.6 C.I.D. CONTINENTAL ENGINE (Auto-Lite IGN.)

BUILT, BRIEFLY, BY DURANT MOTORS

115" W.B.   4-WHEEL BRAKES
30 × 3½ TIRES   4.77 G.R.

The EARL 21-24

REPLACES BRISCOE

EARL MOTORS, INC.
JACKSON — MICHIGAN

"Cabriole"

4 CYL. 112" W.B.
('22 MODEL INTRO. 1921)

KNOWN AS
"BROUGHAM" UNTIL MID-'22

ELCAR

(1915-1931)

ELCAR MOTOR CO.,
ELKHART, INDIANA

116" W.B. IN '20

NEW STYLING FOR 1921
LYCOMING 4 CYL.
(192.4 cid) ('21)

(NEW STRAIGHT-LINE ROOF)

DRUM HEADLIGHTS ON 1922 MODELS, 118" W.B.

"4-40" ('23-24) 112" W.B.

(6 CYL MODELS w 224 cid CONT. ENG. ALSO)
117" W.B. IN '21 (4 + 6)

"6-60" IS 6-CYL., 118" W.B.

Three-Door Four Cylinder

NEW PEAKED RADIATOR FEATURED, MID-1924.

ELCAR
A WELL BUILT CAR

EMBLEM

'26 INTRODUCES LIGHT CONTROL ON STEERING WHEEL

26

MODEL "8-81"

25

"8-80" 7-PASS.

127" W.B.

FIRST YEAR FOR ELCAR STRAIGHT-8
(254.4 LYCOMING "H" ENG.)

63 H.P. @ 3000

27

"8-90"

(4 CYL. MODEL DISCONTINUED JAN., 1927)

FROM 1926 ON, LYCOMING ENGINES USED IN 6-CYL. MODELS also.

28

29

"PRINCESS"
NEW ROUNDED EDGE ON '29 RADIATOR

ELCAR-LEVER WAS AN ELCAR ENTRY IN 1930 AUTOMOBILE SHOW. IT HAD A POWELL-LEVER ENGINE WITH JOINTED CONNECTING RODS.

MODEL K
('20-21)

(1916 - 1924)
ELGIN MOTOR
CAR CORP.,
ELGIN and
ARGO,
ILL.

Elgin

(195.6 CID,
1922 ON)

4-WH.
BRKS.
ON
SOME
'24s

118" W.B.   NEW FOR 1920:
(THROUGH '24) COLUMBIA AXLES. 10"
        BORG + BECK CLUTCH REPLACES 8" TYPE.
(DISC WHEELS ON SPT. TOURING)   6-CYL., O.H.V.
        FALLS ENGINE

('24)
(NEW STYLING)

ERSKINE 6

CONTINENTAL "8-F" 6-CYL., L-HEAD
        ENGINE

(1927 TO 1930)
PRODUCT OF STUDEBAKER

146.1
C.I.D.
IN
1927

27

The Little
Aristocrat
40 H.P.
@ 3200

28 x 4.40

5.13
G.R.

107" W.B. (THROUGH '28)

4-WHEEL
BRAKES

STROM.
CARB.

'27 DASH

"AMERICAN 6"
SERIES

107" W.B.

new
SCHEBLER
CARB. (THROUGH
'30)

MODEL "51"
(STARTS
1-1-28)

28

29 x 4.75
TIRES

'28
(DASH GAUGES
GROUPED BEHIND
GLASS PANEL.)

CONT. "9-F" ENG.   (160.37 C.I.D.)
(THROUGH '29)   42 H.P.
DOES NOT HAVE FENDER BOXES,
AS SEEN ON '27 ERSKINE.   4.78 G.R.

20 x 4.75
TIRES

MODEL "52"

29

SOME SEDANS HAVE
BUDD BODIES.

DELCO-REMY IGNITION
(1927 THROUGH '30)

43 H.P. @ 3000 RPM

109" W.B.
new 109" W.B.

(STARTS 7-9-28. CARS
BUILT AFTER 8-5-29 CONSIDERED "EARLY 1930.")

"DYNAMIC NEW" SERIES
"53"

30

(STARTS
12-26-29)
70 H.P.

(OWN
ENGINE)

30½ STUDEBAKER 6
LOOKS THE
SAME
AS
THIS
MODEL.

HAS FUEL PUMP
(NEW ENGINE
SIZE:
205.3 C.I.D.)

NAME
CHANGED TO
STUDEBAKER 6

ERSKINE

STUDEBAKER BUILT

91

4.78 G.R. (SINCE '28)
new 114" W.B., 5.25 x 19 TIRES

ESSEX

INTRODUCED 1919,
BUILT BY HUDSON

1919-21

108½" WHEELBASE (THROUGH '23)

4 CYLINDERS
178.9 C.I.D.
55 H.P.
5.09 GEAR RATIO
(THROUGH '20)
4.66 GEAR RATIO
(THROUGH '23)

OIL CUPS INSTEAD OF GREASE CUPS

Coach (NEW)

new DRUM HEADLIGHTS and FLANGED CROWN FENDERS IN 1922.

22-23

(FINAL 4 CYLINDER ESSEX IN 1923)

(1924 NEW ENG., SIX RADIATOR SHELL)

NEW 6-CYL. 129.9 C.I.D. ENGINE OF 50 H.P. IN EARLY 1924.

144.7 C.I.D., 55 H.P. (THROUGH '27)

BALLOON 31 × 5.20 TIRES ('25) 30 × 4.95 TIRES ('26)

JUNE 23, 1924: BALLOON TIRES and LARGER ENGINE

NEW 5.6 G.R.

NEW 110½" W. B. (THROUGH '29)

24-25
(RECTANGULAR WINDSHIELD)

25½-26

ESSEX 26½

NEW STEEL BODIES WITH CURVED UPPER BACK.
LONG PIANO-TYPE DOOR HINGES = JULY, 1926

NICKEL-PLATED
RADIATOR = JULY, 1926

27

Speedabout

"SUPER 6"
(RESTYLED)

STARTER
CONTROL
ON DASH

JULY,
1927=
ENGINE STROKE 1/4"
LONGER. NEW 30 × 5
TIRES. REAR TIRE
CARRIER CHANGED FROM
BUCKET TYPE TO HOOP
TYPE (LIKE HUDSON.)

OR 31 × 5.00

5.4 O.R.

ALUMINUM
BODY PANELS OVER
HARDWOOD
FRAME

"POLISHED EBONY"
INSTRUMENT BOARD

28

BENDIX 4-WHEEL
MECHANICAL BRAKES

153.2 C.I.D.

160.4 C.I.D.   55 H.P. @
3600 RPM

"THE
CHALLENGER"

29

"CHASE SILVERED"
INSTRUMENT PANEL

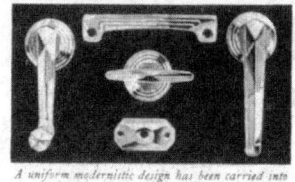

A uniform modernistic design has been carried into the details of Essex door handles, window lifts, lights and other appointments.

ESSEX

5.40 GEAR RATIO

ESSEX SUPER SIX

30

NEW 113" WHEELBASE
(THROUGH '32)

60 H.P. @ 3600 RPM

31

60 H.P. @ 3300 RPM

94

(NEW ENGINE SIZE
OF 175.3 C.I.D.)

5.1 OR 5.4
GEAR RATIOS

ESSEX

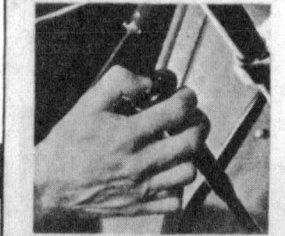

FREE-WHEELING CONTROL
IN CENTER OF
GEARSHIFT LEVER KNOB

WINDSHIELD
OPENER

New triple-sealed in a new-type housing that retains the oil intact over thousands of miles, the famous Hudson-Essex oil cushion clutch adds a new standard of saving and trouble-free operating to its long-established standard of durability and efficiency

1932 ESSEX SUPER-SIX COACH
Five Passengers . . . 114" Wheelbase

DIAMOND
UPHOLSTERY
PATTERN

NOTE NEW WARNING LIGHTS ON DASH

32

NEW "RIDE CONTROL" ADJUSTS SHOCK ABSORBERS
FROM INSIDE THE CAR.

5.25 × 18" TIRES
5.10 and 4.64 GEAR RATIOS

ESSEX 32 (CONT'D.)

REAR VIEW OF 1932 ESSEX

FOR 1932, ENGINE SIZE AGAIN INCREASED (TO 193.1 C.I.D.) 70 H.P. @ 3200 RPM

IN SUMMER OF 1932, THE ESSEX WAS REPLACED BY THE ESSEX-TERRAPLANE.

6 CYL. 106" W.B.
NEW 8 CYL. 113" W.B.

6

8

The New SEVENTY HORSEPOWER ENGINE *of the* 1932 ESSEX SUPER-SIX

TO 32½ 33

SEE ALSO "TERRAPLANE"

FALCON

115" W.B., 4.88 G.R.
32 × 4 TIRES
OWN 4 OR 6-CYL.
ENGINES —
LIGHT 4
192.4 C.I.D.
SIX
230.1 C.I.D.
(NOT IN FULL PROD.)

22

HALLADAY MOTORS
CORP.,
NEWARK, OHIO

BODY BY
HEALEY and CO.

REPLACES THE
HALLADAY CAR, 1922

ROOF-VISOR
ON 1927
CLOSED
MODELS

Falcon-Knight
(1927-1928)

27

6-CYL. SLEEVE-VALVE ENGINE

FALCON MOTORS CORP., ELYRIA, O.; DETROIT
(WILLYS-KNIGHT AFFILIATE)

1927 = 109½" W.B. (MODEL "10")
30 × 5.00 TIRES
5.11 GEAR RATIO ('28 ALSO)
156.6 C.I.D.   4.6 COMPRESSION
45 H.P. @ 3000 RPM ('28 ALSO)
DASH GAUGES UNDER SINGLE GLASS PANE

1928 = 109½" W.B. (MODEL "12")
29 × 5.50 TIRES
"FUMER" WARMS CARBURETOR
HARD-RUBBER-COVERED STEERING WHEEL
INDIVIDUAL DASH GAUGES (INCL. GAS
GAUGE)

28

FARGO

(1929 ON, BUILT BY
CHRYSLER CORP.)

29

(PRIMARILY COMMERCIAL
VEHICLES)

(6 CYL.)
HYDRAULIC BRAKES

FERRIS
20-22

OHIO MOTOR VEHICLE CO., CLEVELAND
(1920-1922)
130" W.B.
6-CYL. 303.1 C.I.D. CONTINENTAL ENG.
4.08 G.R.   32 × 4½ TIRES
BECOMES MODEL "60" IN 1922;
1922 MODEL "70" ALSO, with 325.1
C.I.D., 6-CYL. CONTINENTAL ENGINE.

BUILDERS OF HIGH GRADE MOTOR CARS

FLINT SIX

120"
W.B.

CONTINENTAL
ENGINES
6 CYLS.

FLINT MOTOR COMPANY
FLINT, MICHIGAN
(1923-1927)
AFFILIATED WITH
DURANT AND
LOCOMOBILE

23

268.4 C.I.D.

32
×
4½
TIRES

70 H.P. @ 2500 RPM
4.7 GEAR RATIO

FLINT SIX

24

4.78 G.R.
MODEL E

120" W.B.

(E) 55

120" W.B.

BROUGHAM

FLINT

MODEL "FIFTY-FIVE" 268.4 C.I.D., 64½ H.P. @ 2400 RPM

(E) 55

25

32 X 6.20

Model "55" Five Passenger Sedan

(MODEL "40" ALSO AVAIL.)'24-5
WITH 115" W.B., 196 C.I.D., 49 H.P. @ 2500)

"60" COUPE - ROADSTER ('27)

'27 "60" MODELS
BEGIN AT # 18776

The New Flint "SIXTY"
5-Passenger Sedan

60

FLINT

"60" HAS 230 C.I.D., 56 H.P. @ 2600

30 X 5.77

115" W.B.

The New Flint "EIGHTY" 268.4 C.I.D.
5-Passenger Sedan
65 H.P. @ 2400
120" W.B.

80

"Z-18"
"FLINT JUNIOR" COACH ('26-7) 110" W.B.

HAS 6-CYL.
169.3 C.I.D. ENGINE
40 H.P. @ 2300 RPM
2-WHEEL BRAKES
'26 == #100 - 1911
'27 == #1912 and up

'27 "80" MODELS BEGIN
AT # 20103

26-27

JR.

30 X 5.77

4.875 TO 1 GEAR RATIO

NOTE DIFFERENCES IN HOOD LOUVRE PANEL
AND PLACEMENT OF HOOD LATCH ON
'26 and '27 "60" MODELS ILLUSTRATED.

CENTER-DOOR
SEDAN

Ford
THE UNIVERSAL CAR

FORD MOTOR CO.,
DEARBORN, MICH.
(PRODUCTION
BEGINS 1903)

MODEL
"T"

(FIRST
INTRODUCED
LATE 1908,
REPLACING
MODEL "S.")

17-22

MINOR
IMPROVEMENTS
DURING COURSE OF
PRODUCTION

OWN IGN. SYSTEM

4 CYLINDERS, 176.7 C.I.D. ENGINE
20 HORSEPOWER (THROUGH '27)

100" WHEELBASE
30 × 3½" tires

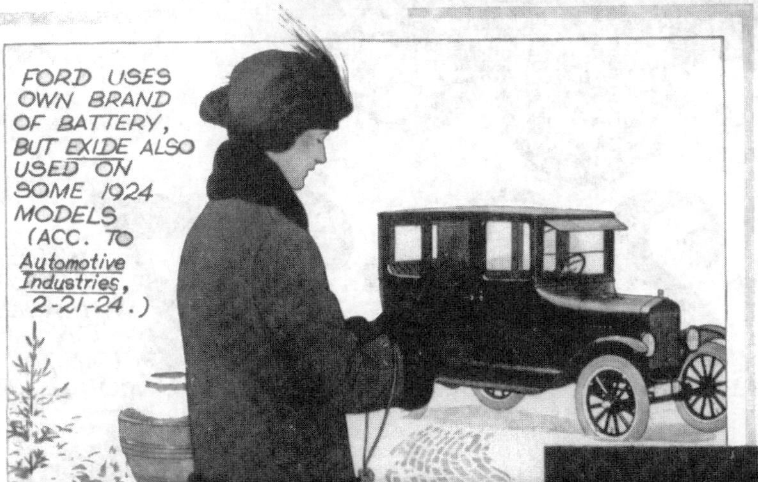

23-25

FORD USES
OWN BRAND
OF BATTERY,
BUT EXIDE ALSO
USED ON
SOME 1924
MODELS
(ACC. TO
Automotive
Industries,
2-21-24.)

RESTYLED '23 MODELS START
AUGUST, 1922.   CHOICE OF
2-DOOR OR 4-DOOR SEDANS.*
CLOSED CARS HAVE
RECTANGULAR REAR WINDOWS.

(BALLOON TIRES ON '25 MODELS.)

* = OTHER BODY TYPES ALSO.

99

Ford

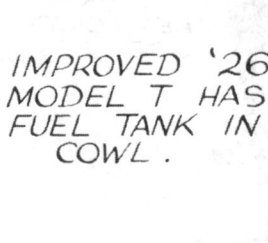

IMPROVED '26 MODEL T HAS FUEL TANK IN COWL.

PLANETARY TRANSMISSION A MODEL T CHARACTERISTIC.

THE RUNABOUT

TOURING

26-27

WIRE WHEELS AVAILABLE ON 1927 MODEL T.

COUPE

29 × 4.40 BALLOON TIRES STANDARD EQUIPMENT IN 1927; BALLOON TIRES OPTIONAL DURING 1926.

1927 = FINAL MODEL T

MODEL "A" 28-29

(INTRO. 12-2-27)

Ford

NEW 200.4 CUBIC-IN. DISPL., 4-CYL. ENGINE 40 H.P. @ 2200 RPM

EARLY '28 OPEN MODEL As HAVE NO OUTSIDE DOOR HANDLES.

MODEL "A" AN ALL-NEW CAR FOR 1928.

STANDARD TYPE SLIDING-GEAR TRANSMISSION ADOPTED.

new 4-WHEEL MECHANICAL BRAKES (THROUGH '38)

TAXI ('29)

SPORT COUPE (RIGID FABRIC TOP)

STATION WAGON ('29)

103½" W.B.

'28 HAS REDDISH-COLORED STEERING WHEEL.

21" (4.50 × 30) TIRES IN '28-29 3.7 GEAR RATIO

BRIGGS OR MURRAY BODIES

EARLIEST MODELS HAVE BRAKE LEVER AT LEFT.

TUDOR SEDAN

"LINCOLN" STYLING

"Ford" IN SCRIPT ON NEW BLUE-and-WHITE OVAL RADIATOR EMBL.

TOWN CAR ('29)

101

Ford

30

(INTRO. 12-28-29)

NEW, ENLARGED RADIATOR AND HOOD 3.77 GEAR RATIO

MODEL "A" (IMPROVED)

NEW STAINLESS STEEL BRIGHTWORK

LATE '30, '31 MODELS have HORIZONTAL RIBS ON INSTRUMENT PANEL.

4.75 × 19" TIRES ON 1930-31 MODEL As.

MODEL "A"

31

VICTORIA (PADDED TOP)

VICTORIA (METAL BACK)

"A-400" 2-DR. CONVT. SEDAN

SLANT-WINDSHIELD 31½

LEFTOVER MODEL As WERE SOLD EARLY IN 1932.

FORD

MODEL B- 4 CYL.
V8 - 8 CYL. (221 C.I.D.)
106" W.B.

new DASH WITH 3 CIRCULAR GAUGES SET ON AN OVAL PANEL.

HENRY FORD I with the FIRST FORD V-8 ENGINE

32 "18" SERIES

V-8 HAS EMBLEM ON TIE-BAR.

BOTH 3-WINDOW AND 5-WINDOW COUPES AVAILABLE FROM 1932 TO 1936.

(FIRST FORD V-8 ASSEMBLED MARCH 9, 1932.)

STARTING '32, BOTH 3-WINDOW (new) AND 5-WINDOW COUPES ARE AVAILABLE (THROUGH '36)

"40" SERIES **33** (4 and V-8) 3.77 G.R. (4) 4.33 (V-8)

(STARTS 2-33)

112" W.B.

5.50 x 17 TIRES (THR. '34)

WIRE WHEELS STD. (THROUGH '35)

(50-H.P. (MODEL "4-40" IS RARE 4-CYL. SERIES.) *

OPTIONAL-STYLE SM. WHEELS

* = OFFICIALLY, A CONTINUATION OF MODEL B, BUT WITH 1933 STYLING.

3-WINDOW COUPE

DASH

HEAVIER GRILLE FOR 1934

5-WINDOW COUPE

PHAETON (AVAIL. THROUGH '36)

1934 MODEL HAS 2 HANDLES ON EACH SIDE OF HOOD.

CONT'D. 112" W.B. (THROUGH '40) 4.11 G.R.

34 "40" SERIES (STARTS 12-33)

(V-8s EXCLUSIVELY)

Ford

FINAL YEAR WITH WIRE WHEELS. 4.11 G.R.

6.00 x 16

35 "48" SERIES (STARTS 12-34)

'35 DASH RESEMBLES ILLUSTRATED '36 VIEW, BUT CENTER VERTICAL CHROME STRIPS ON '35 ARE FARTHER APART.

"68" SERIES (STARTS OCT., 1935) new POINTED GRILLE and STEEL ARTILLERY WHEELS. 4.11 OR 3.54 G.R.

NOW 3 HORIZ. STRIPS ACROSS HOOD LOUVRES, (INSTEAD OF 4 AS IN '35.)

36

FORD'S FINAL ROADSTER

5-PASS. CLUB CABRIOLET (NEW)

new "60" KNOWN AS MODEL 74, has 4.44 G.R.

85-H.P. 221-C.I.D. V-8 CONT'D., AND A NEW ECONOMY "60" SERIES ADDED (WITH 135.9 C.I.D. 60-H.P. SMALL V-8 ENGINE.)

new ALL-STEEL TOP

37 (STARTS NOV., 1936)

DAD and ME (AGE 4) and OUR '37 FORD

104

"85" KNOWN AS MODEL 78, has 3.78 G.R.

FORD

60 H.P. = "82-A"
85 H.P. = "81-A"

STD.

DLX.

STANDARD 85 and 60 H.P.

DE LUXE 85 H.P.

38

(STARTS NOV., 1937)

FROM 1938 THROUGH 1940, FORD's STANDARD MODELS SOMEWHAT RESEMBLED (BUT WERE NOT IDENTICAL WITH) THE PREVIOUS YEAR'S DE LUXE MODEL.

112" W.B. (SINCE '33) SAME GEAR RATIOS SINCE '37.

DASH

STD. 85 and 60 H.P.

60 H.P. = "92-A"

85 H.P. = "91-A"

DE LUXE 85 H.P.

FORD BATTERIES and IGNITION ARE CHARACTERISTIC.

new HYDRAULIC BRAKES

39

(STARTS OCT., 1938)

FOX (1921-1923)

FOX MOTOR CO., PHILADELPHIA, PA.

6 CYLINDER, 50 H.P. AIR-COOLED, OVERHEAD VALVE, OVERHEAD CAM ENGINE

132" wheelbase
32 x 4½ TIRES
4.9 G.R.

"1924" MODEL (BUILT 1923)

DISPLACEMENT INCREASED FROM 248.9 TO 268.3 FOR 1923.

105

FRANKLIN
(1902-1934)

FRANKLIN
AUTOMOBILE COMPANY
SYRACUSE NEW YORK

17-20
SERIES 9

115" W.B.   4.33 GEAR RATIO

AIR-COOLED
6-CYL. OVERHEAD-VALVE
ENGINE (199.1 C.I.D.
THROUGH '27)

('21)   NEW "RADIATOR"

21-22

"DEMI-SEDAN"
(below, left) AVAILABLE EARLY 1922.
(SERIES 10-A STARTS
9-1-22)

23-25
SERIES 10

"10-B" (1923) DASH GAUGES IN 3 RECTANGULAR PANELS

"DEMI-SEDAN"
1924 "10-B" HAS SIROCCO FAN. BALLOON TIRES OPTIONAL.
EARLY 1925 "10-C" STARTS JULY, 1924, WITH ALEMITE
GASCOLATOR

STROMBERG
CARBURETOR. 60 MILES PER HOUR

FRANKLIN

INTRODUCING
NEW DESIGNS *by de Causse*

25½-26
SERIES 11
(INTRODUCED MARCH, 1925)

COUPÉ

'25½ TO '28 MODELS
FREQUENTLY KNOWN AS
"DE CAUSSE" FRANKLINS.

STARTING LATE 1926, CLOSED
FRANKLINS HAVE NARROW FRONT
CORNER POSTS WITH "CLEAR VISION"
WINDSHIELD.

VICTORIA
COUPE

26-STYLE
COUPÉ CONTINUED ALSO

27
SERIES 11-B
TIRE SIZE CHANGED
FROM 31 x 5.25 TO
32 x 6.
NEW SWAN
MANIFOLD WITH SQUARE CORNERS.

*(INTRODUCED JANUARY,
1927)*

SPORT SEDAN

The 25th
Anniversary
Franklin

FRANKLIN

AIRMAN "5" and "7" HAVE, RESPECTIVELY, 119" and 128" WHEELBASES. (32 × 6 and 31 × 6.20 TIRES)

AIRMAN SERIES

4-WHEEL LOCKHEED HYDRAULIC BRAKES WITH 14" DRUMS.

new 236.4 C.I.D. 46 H.P. @ 2500 RPM

28

SERIES 12-A (INTRODUCED OCT., 1927)

The new Franklin
AIRMAN LIMITED

SERIES 12-B
28½

WITH FENDER MIRRORS AND HEADLIGHT FOOT CONTROL

(INTRODUCED JULY, 1928)

WALKER BODIES, AS BEFORE

AC FUEL PUMP

FENDER PARKING LAMPS

29

"130," "135," "137" (120, 125 and 132-INCH WHEELBASES)

1929 has SMALLER CIRCLE ON "RADIATOR" TRIM

50 or 60-H.P. ENGINES

PRESSED STEEL CHASSIS FRAME

FRANKLIN

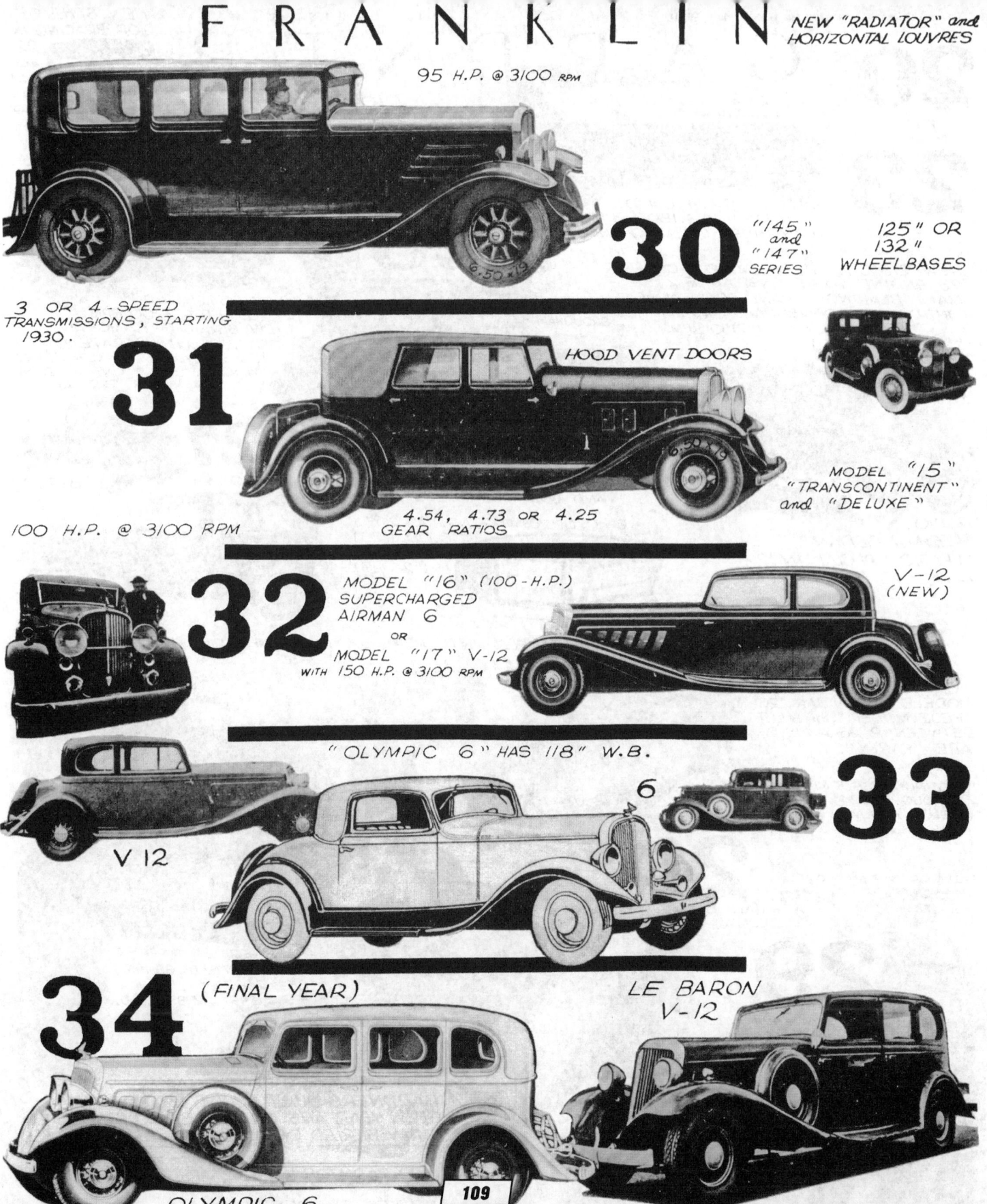

95 H.P. @ 3100 RPM

30 "145" and "147" SERIES

125" OR 132" WHEELBASES

3 OR 4 - SPEED TRANSMISSIONS, STARTING 1930.

31

HOOD VENT DOORS

MODEL "15" "TRANSCONTINENT" and "DELUXE"

100 H.P. @ 3100 RPM

4.54, 4.73 OR 4.25 GEAR RATIOS

32

MODEL "16" (100-H.P.) SUPERCHARGED AIRMAN 6 OR MODEL "17" V-12 WITH 150 H.P. @ 3100 RPM

V-12 (NEW)

"OLYMPIC 6" HAS 118" W.B.

V 12

6

33

34 (FINAL YEAR)

LE BARON V-12

OLYMPIC 6

109

GARDNER MOTOR CO., INC., ST. LOUIS, U. S. A.

GARDNER

(1919 - 1931)

NEW STYLE OF TOP BRACING IN '22, and 4.44 GEAR RATIO

20 TO 23

112" W.B. "LIGHT 4"

32 × 4 TIRES AND 4.8 GEAR RATIO ON 1923 MODEL "5."

192.4 C.I.D.
35 H.P. @ 1800 RPM
4-CYLINDER LYCOMING ENGINE

NEW 213.6 C.I.D. LYCOMING 4-CYL. '23 ENGINE HAS 5 (INSTEAD OF 2) MAIN BEARINGS. HAND BRAKE NOW CONTRACTS ON DRIVESHAFT. 43 H.P. @ 2150 RPM

25

"8-A"

2-DOOR BROUGHAM

254.4 C.I.D.
63 H.P. @ 3000 RPM
NEW STRAIGHT-8 MODELS FOR 1925 (ILLUSTRATED)
NEW 6-CYL. "6-A" ALSO (57 H.P.)
4-CYL. "5-C" CONTINUED WITH 44 H.P. @ 2200 RPM.

"5-C" (4 CYL.)

24

"RADIO SPECIAL" SEDAN
(RADIO SPECIAL IN '23 WAS SPORT TOURING CAR.)

CARS BUILT 8-25 OR LATER ARE CONSIDERED "1926" MODELS, AND HAVE HOOD SUPPORT ROD.

27

"8-80"   "8-90"

6-CYL. LYCOMING ENG. HAS 207.1 C.I.D. ('25)
223.8 C.I.D. ('26-27)

26

26 COUPE WINDSHIELD

NO MORE 6-CYL. GARDNERS UNTIL 1930 "136" MODEL.

"6-B" and "8-B" MODELS BEGIN JAN., '26 THESE MODELS, IF BUILT BETWEEN 8-26 and 12-26, ARE "EARLY '27s."

WESTINGHOUSE IGNITION THROUGH 1924 (DELCO) REMY IGNITION 1925 and on

RADIATOR CAP MASCOT

28

(ALL 8-CYL.) LYCOMING ENG.

29

(INTRO. 9-28)
"120," "125," "130" HAVE 65, 85, 115 H.P.

"75" 225.7 C.I.D., 65 H.P.
"85" 246.7 " , 74 "
"95" 298.6 C.I.D., 115 H.P.

GARDNERS BUILT DURING LATTER MONTHS OF A YEAR ARE USUALLY CONSIDERED TO BE EARLY SERIES OF FOLLOWING YEAR'S MODELS.

110 29 RADIATOR HIGHER, NARROWER THAN '28. BODIES BY CENTRAL

GARDNER

6-CYL.
80 H.P.

→ FRONT-WHEEL-
DRIVE MODEL
('30) WITH
SLOPING
FRONT END

"136" = 6 CYL., 185 C.I.D.
70 H.P. @ 3500 RPM
"140" = 8 CYL., 246.6 C.I.D.
90 H.P. @ 3300 RPM
"150" = 8 CYL., 298.6 C.I.D.
126 H.P. @ 3300 RPM

30

31

"136" = 122" W.B.
"140" = 125 "
"150" = 130 "

MODELS "136" "148" and "158"

ONLY THE
FRONT-WHEEL-DRIVE
MODEL
HAS THE ABOVE
UNIQUE RADIATOR DESIGN.

6 CYL. CONTINENTAL "11-E"
ENGINE (248 C.I.D.) USED. LYCOMING
"WR," "GR," "MDG" ENGINES IN 3 OTHER MODELS.

MECHANICAL
SPECIFICATIONS
AS BEFORE

"148"
HAS
100 H.P.

MESH-TYPE
CHROMED
STONE
GUARD
IN FRONT OF
RADIATOR.

GEARLESS STEAM CAR

(1921 - 1923)

GEARLESS MOTOR CORP.,
PITTSBURGH, PA.

GERONIMO

122" W.B.   (1917 - 1921)

TOURING CAR ("6-A-45")('20)
'20 MODEL BASICALLY UNCHANGED
GERONIMO BUILT OWN
BODIES STARTING 1919.

(6)

GERONIMO MOTOR CO.,
ENID, OKLA.
(LYCOMING ENGINE)('18)
(230.1 C.I.D. RUTENBER ENGINE ALSO) DELCO IGN.

GLOBE

MODEL "B-10"
115" W.B., 4.9 G.R.
32 × 4 TIRES

(1921 - 1922)
GLOBE MOTORS CO.,
CLEVELAND, OHIO

with "SUPREME" ENGINE
4 CYL., 178.9 C.I.D.
DELCO IGNITION

GRAHAM-PAIGE

(1928 TO 1941, INCLUDING GRAHAM)

THE 3 GRAHAM BROTHERS PICTURED ON EMBLEM. ↓

REPLACES *PAIGE*, JANUARY, 1928   HYDR. BRAKES NORTHEAST IGNITION SYSTEM

"610" IS LOWEST-PRICED SERIES, has 110½" W.B., 29 x 5.00 TIRES, 4.45 GEAR RATIO, 6 CYLS., 175 C.I.D., 52 H.P. @ 3100 RPM

"614" has 114" W.B., 29 x 5.25 TIRES, 3.9 G.R., 6 CYLS., 207 C.I.D., 71 H.P. @ 3200 RPM

"614" →

"619"

"619" has 119" W.B., 29 x 5.50 TIRES, 6 CYLS., 288 C.I.D., 97 H.P. @ 3200 RPM

28

(AUG., 1928 = "EARLY 1929s" SIMILAR, BUT NO LONGER HAVE VERTICAL SEAMS ON BACKS OF BODIES.)

← "629" →

"629" has 129" W.B., 3.65 G.R., 31 x 6.00 TIRES, SAME ENGINE AS "619."

"835" has 135" W.B., 31 x 6.20 TIRES, 3.65 G.R., STRAIGHT-8 ENGINE, 322 C.I.D.

ALL BUT "610" have 4-SPEED TRANSMISSION; (AVAIL. ON ALL BUT SMALL MODELS THROUGH '31.)

ALL MODELS HAVE FUEL PUMP.

"835"

GRAAAM-PAIGE

BODIES BY
GRAHAM-PAIGE
BRIGGS
ROBBINS
LE BARON (SPECIAL PHAETON)

"612" has
29 × 5.00 TIRES, 4.7
G.R., 190.8 C.I.D.,
62 H.P. @ 3200 RPM

BRIGGS BODY

"621"

VISOR BRACKETS
ON "612" and "615"

"615" has 5.50 × 19
TIRES, 3.9 G.R., 224 C.I.D.,
76 H.P. @ 3200 RPM

"621" has 6.00 × 19 TIRES,
3.6 G.R., 288.6 C.I.D.,
97 H.P. @ 3200 RPM

BEGINNING 1929,
DELCO-REMY
IGNITION ON ALL
GRAHAM-PAIGE
and GRAHAM CARS
TO FOLLOW.

AS IN '28,
MODEL NUMBERS
INDICATE NO. OF
CYLINDERS, and
WHEELBASE.

29

new THINNER
HOOD LOUVRES

"827" has
3.6 G.R.

"837" has
3.9 G.R.

"827" and "837"
have 6.50 × 19 TIRES,
STRAIGHT-8 ENGINES OF
322 C.I.D., 120 H.P. @ 3200
RPM

"827"

ROBBINS BODIES

(JULY 29, 1929, TO JANUARY, 1930)

EARLY **30**

3-SPOKE STEERING
WHEEL
NEW GLASS SUN VISOR

AFTER EARLY 1930,
"PAIGE" NAME RETAINED
ONLY FOR TAXIS AND
COMMERCIAL CARS.
JAN., 1930 = NEW STD. OR
SPEC. 6, STD. OR SPEC. 8, CUSTOM 8s

JAN., 1930 = 115, 122, 127, 137" W.B.,
66, 76, 96 (8-CYL.) OR 120 H.P. (8-CYL.)

STD. 6 (VISOR ON '31 MODEL)

GRAHAM **30½**

QUALITY IS THE BEST POLICY

GRAAAM

8 HAS DOOR-TYPE
HOOD VENTS, FENDER
PARKING LIGHTS.

GRAHAM

31

6

(CHROME - PLATED
WIRE WHEELS
AVAILABLE ON 6 and 8 CYL.
'31½ MODELS EXCEPT
"PROSPERITY 6 ," THE
'31½ ECONOMY MODEL OF
113" W.B., 207 C.I.D., 70 H.P.

(EARLY '32 MODELS
BEGIN JULY, 1931, RESEMBLE
'31 - 31½ GRAHAMS, BUT
Have OPTIONAL
FREE - WHEELING .)

1932 SIX
has 113" W.B.
5.50 × 17
TIRES ,
207.1 C.I.D.
70 H.P. @
3200 RPM
4.45 G.R.

DASH
(1932
Blue Streak)

The car is WIDER than it is high
('33)

224 C.I.D., 85-H.P. 6 IN 1933 ; 8-CYL. SPECS. LIKE '32.

32-33

'32 STD. and DLX. 8 SPECS. ALSO

'32 "BLUE STREAK" 8 (123" W.B.)
HAS 1-PIECE BUMPER, 245.4 C.I.D.,
90 H.P. @ 3400 RPM, 4.3 G.R.,
6.00 × 17 TIRES

4.27 GEAR RATIO
ON 1933 TO 1935
GRAHAMS .

8

34

6

6 = 116" W.B.,
6.25 × 16 TIRES,
224 C.I.D., 85 H.P.
@ 3400 RPM

123" W.B.,
6.50 × 16 TIRES, 245.4 C.I.D.,
95 H.P. @ 3400 RPM
CUSTOM 8 = 123" W.B., 7.00 × 16 TIRES ,
265.4 C.I.D., 135 H.P. @ 4000 RPM (Supercharger avail.)

F 968

STD. 6 "74" = 111" W.B.. 5.25 × 17 TIRES, 169.6 C.I.D., 70 H.P. @ 3500 RPM
SPECIAL 6 "73" = 116" W.B., 6.00 × 17 TIRES, 224 C.I.D., 85 H.P. @ 3400 RPM

35

6

(GRAHAM 8 HAS
2-PIECE
REAR WINDOW.)

8 "72" = 123" W.B.,
6.50 × 16 TIRES,
245.4 C.I.D., 95 H.P. @
3400 RPM
Supercharged 8 "75" =
123" W.B., 7.00 × 16 TIRES,
265.4 C.I.D., 140 H.P.
@ 4000 RPM

NO MORE
8-CYL. GRAHAMS
AFTER 1935.

ALL 1935 GRAHAMS HAVE
HORIZONTAL HOOD LOUVRES.

114

GRAHAM

6-CYLINDER MODELS ONLY (THROUGH '41)

36

"CRUSADER"

"80" CRUSADER" 111" W.B., 6.00 × 16 TIRES 4.55 G.R., 169.6 C.I.D., 70 H.P. @ 3500 RPM

"90 CAVALIER" 115" W.B., 6.00 × 16 TIRES, 4.2 G.R., 217.8 C.I.D., 85 H.P. @ 3300 RPM
("90-A" STARTS 3-36, has 4.45 G.R., 199.1 C.I.D.)

"110" Supercharged 115" W.B., 6.25 × 16 TIRES, 4.2 G.R., 217.8 C.I.D. 112 H.P. @ 4000 RPM

"85 CRUSADER" 111" W.B., 5.25 × 17 or 6.00 × 16 TIRES, 4.55 G.R., 169.6 C.I.D., 70 H.P. @ 3500 RPM (INDIVIDUAL HOOD PORTS with TRIANGLE CHROME GRILLES)*

(1936 - 1937 "CRUSADERS" RETAIN 1935 BODY STYLING.)

"95 CAVALIER" 116" W.B., 6.00 × 16 TIRES, 4.45 G.R., 199.1 C.I.D., 85 H.P. @ 3800 RPM

37

* '37 "CRUSADER" HOOD LOUVRES DO NOT EXTEND INTO GRILLE AS ON '36.

"116 SUPERCHARGER" 116" W.B., 6.25 × 16 TIRES, 4.27 G.R., 199.1 C.I.D., 106 H.P. @ 4000 RPM

"120 CUSTOM SUPERCHARGER" 120" W.B. (COUPES - 116") 4.27 G.R., 217.8 C.I.D. 116 H.P. @ 4000

6.25 × 16 TIRES (6.00 × 16 ON '39 "96" SERIES)

38-39

SUPERCHARGED CLUB SEDAN

STD. and SPEC. "96" have 90 H.P. @ 3600 RPM

('39)

('38)

RUNNING - BOARDS NOT FEATURED ON 1939 GRAHAMS.

FLOOR OR STEERING - COLUMN GEARSHIFT CONTROL IN '39.

6 CYLS., 217.8 C.I.D. 120" W.B., 4.27 G.R. (ALL '38s - 39s)

"SPIRIT OF MOTION" STYLING

SPEC. and CUSTOM "97" SUPERCHARGER have 116 H.P. @ 4000 RPM

GRANT 6

GRANT MOTOR CAR CORP., FINDLAY, OHIO (1913-1922)

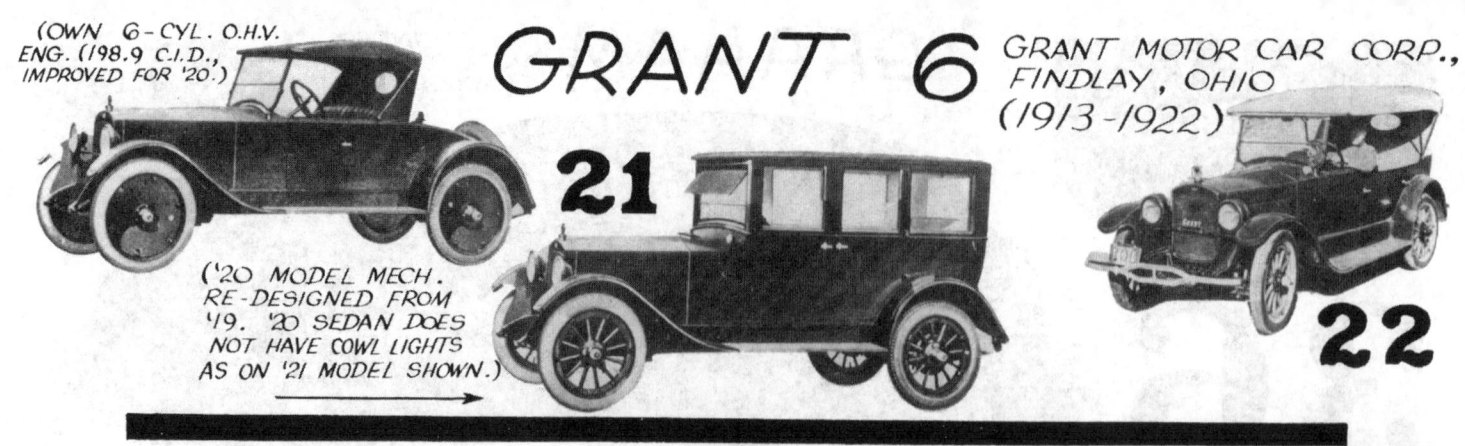

(OWN 6-CYL. O.H.V. ENG. (198.9 C.I.D., IMPROVED FOR '20.)

21

('20 MODEL MECH. RE-DESIGNED FROM '19. '20 SEDAN DOES NOT HAVE COWL LIGHTS AS ON '21 MODEL SHOWN.)

22

(1922–1926)

GRAY MOTOR CORP., DETROIT

Gray
Motor Corporation Detroit

4 CYLINDERS (OWN ENGINE)
165.1 C.I.D.
21 H.P. @ 1500 RPM ('25 RATING)

22

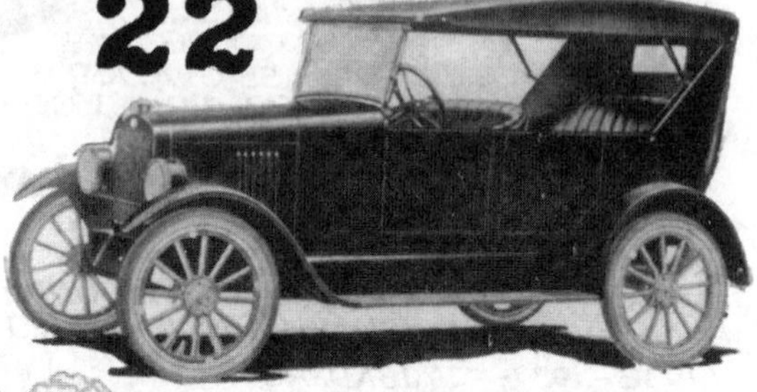

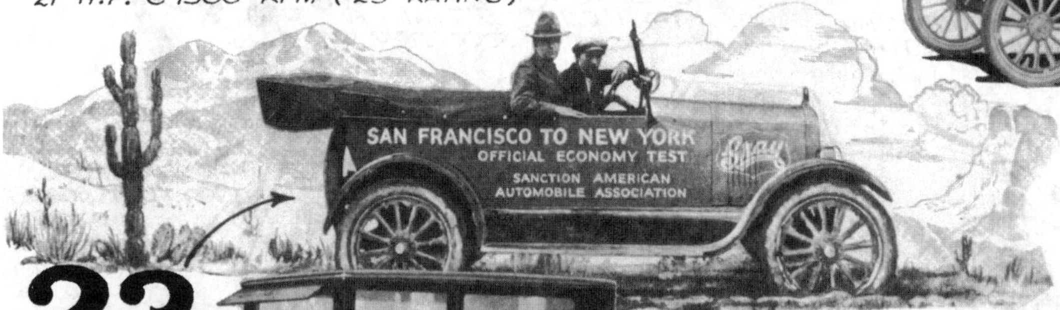
SAN FRANCISCO TO NEW YORK
OFFICIAL ECONOMY TEST
SANCTION AMERICAN AUTOMOBILE ASSOCIATION
Gray

100" WHEELBASE (THROUGH '23)
30 × 3½ TIRES (THROUGH '25)
3.9 GEAR RATIO
WESTINGHOUSE IGNITION (THROUGH '25)

23

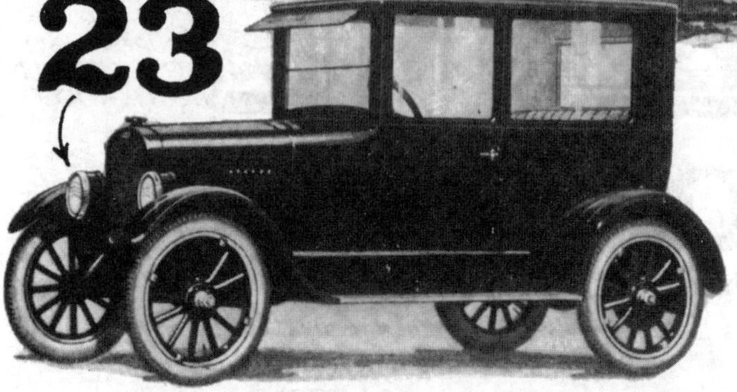

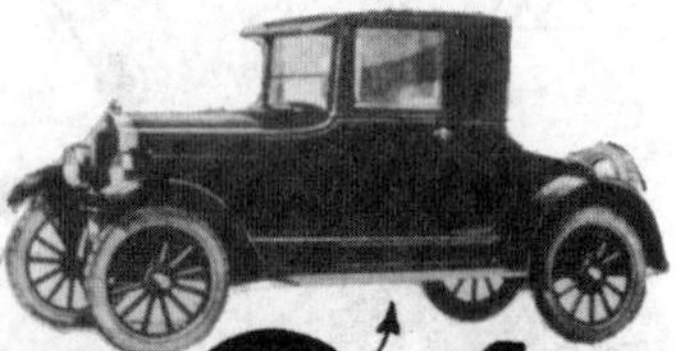

100" or 103½" W.B. IN '24
TOP SPEED ONLY 46 MILES PER HOUR

24

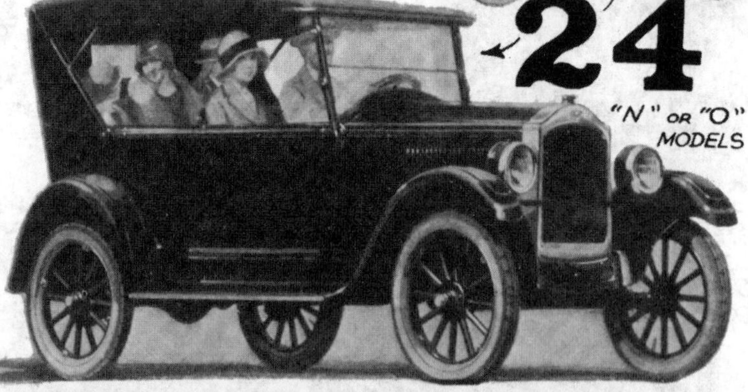

"N" or "O" MODELS

'25 and '26 SIMILAR-LOOKING TO '24, BUT LATE '24 GRAY HAS FUEL TANK AT REAR. BALLOON TIRES AVAIL. ON '25 MODEL, AND 104" W.B. (MODEL "O")

(105" WHEELBASE, 29 × 4.40 BALLOON TIRES, 4-WHEEL BRAKES ON '26 GRAY (MODEL "S" WITH Auto Lite IGN.)

GRAY LIGHT CAR

(NOT AFFILIATED WITH GRAY CAR ILLUSTRATED ABOVE.)

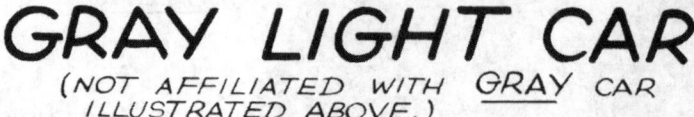

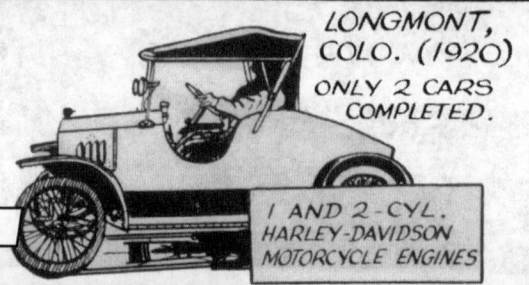

LONGMONT, COLO. (1920)
ONLY 2 CARS COMPLETED.

1 AND 2-CYL. HARLEY-DAVIDSON MOTORCYCLE ENGINES

HALLADAY

HALLADAY MOTORS CORPORATION
NEWARK, OHIO, U.S.A.

(1918 – 1922)

1921 = 116" W.B., 6 CYL. RUT. ENG.

1922 = 115" W.B., 4 + 6 CYLINDERS

4.9 G.R., 32 × 4½ TIRES ON ALL '21-'23 MODELS

Handley-Knight

**HANDLEY MOTORS, INC.,
KALAMAZOO, MICH.
(1921 – 1923)**

NAME SHORTENED TO HANDLEY DURING '23.

NEW MODEL →

EARLY '23 7-PASS.

125" W.B.

('22 = ALUMINUM REPL. LINOLEUM ON RUNNING BOARDS)

'23 "6-60" HAS 125" W.B., 268.4 MIDWEST ENG.

6 CYL. O.H.V. ('23)

240.6 C.I.D., 4-CYL. KNIGHT ENG. (THROUGH '22 "B" SERIES)

21-23

'23 "6-40" HAS 195.6 FALLS ENG., 115" W.B.

23½

HANSON 6

**HANSON MOTOR CO.,
ATLANTA, GA.
(1917 – 1923)**

1920 MODEL "54" *has* 119" W.B.

121" W.B., 1921 – 1924

EMBLEM →

('20)

('21)

MODEL "60" (1921 – 1922) HAS 224 C.I.D., 6-CYL. CONTINENTAL ENGINE.

(32 × 4 TIRES, 4.66 G.R.)

MODEL "66" (1923 – 1924) HAS CONTINENTAL "8-R" ENGINE (241.6 C.I.D.)

FINAL '24 MODEL (INTRO. 1923)

HARRIS 6

WISCONSIN AUTOMOTIVE CORP., MENASHA, WIS.

23 ONLY

HAYNES 20

THE HAYNES AUTOMOBILE COMPANY,

Kokomo, Indiana

IN PRODUCTION
1904 – 1925

ORIGINALLY "HAYNES-APPERSON"

1920 GEAR RATIOS :
4.42 ("45")   4.06 ("46")

'20 BATTERY UNDER FLOOR (INSTEAD OF UNDER SEAT AS IN 1919.)

127" W.B.

HAYNES-BUILT ENGINES :
"45" 6-CYL. 288.6 C.I.D. (L-HEAD) OR
"46" V-12 356.4 C.I.D. (O.H.V.)

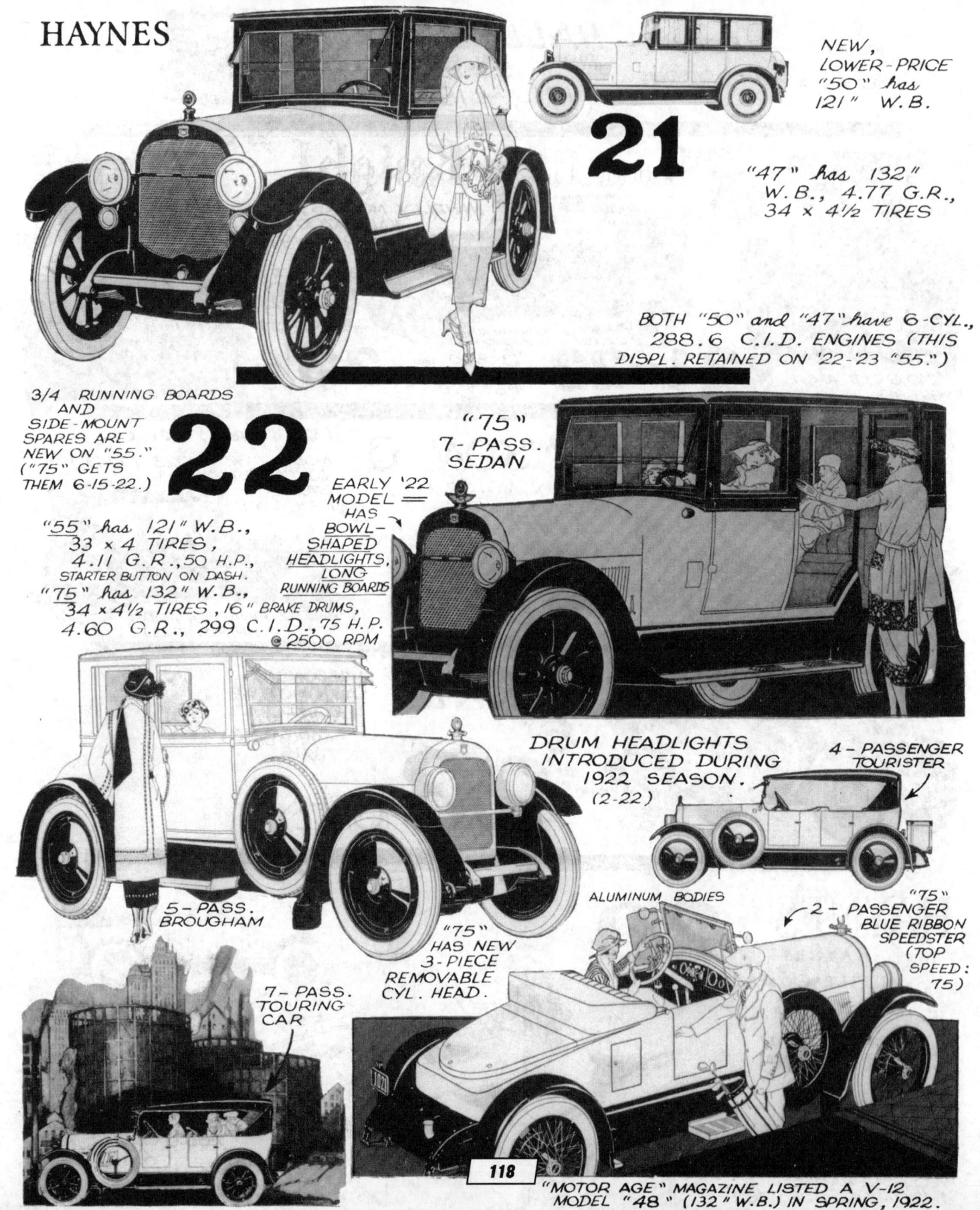

HAYNES

21

NEW, LOWER-PRICE "50" has 121" W.B.

"47" has 132" W.B., 4.77 G.R., 34 x 4½ TIRES

BOTH "50" and "47" have 6-CYL. 288.6 C.I.D. ENGINES (THIS DISPL. RETAINED ON '22-'23 "55.")

22

3/4 RUNNING BOARDS AND SIDE-MOUNT SPARES ARE NEW ON "55." ("75" GETS THEM 6-15-22.)

"55" has 121" W.B., 33 x 4 TIRES, 4.11 G.R., 50 H.P., STARTER BUTTON ON DASH.
"75" has 132" W.B., 34 x 4½ TIRES, 16" BRAKE DRUMS, 4.60 G.R., 299 C.I.D., 75 H.P. @ 2500 RPM

EARLY '22 MODEL = HAS BOWL-SHAPED HEADLIGHTS, LONG RUNNING BOARDS

"75" 7-PASS. SEDAN

5-PASS. BROUGHAM

DRUM HEADLIGHTS INTRODUCED DURING 1922 SEASON. (2-22)

4-PASSENGER TOURISTER

"75" HAS NEW 3-PIECE REMOVABLE CYL. HEAD.

7-PASS. TOURING CAR

ALUMINUM BODIES

"75" 2-PASSENGER BLUE RIBBON SPEEDSTER (TOP SPEED: 75)

118

"MOTOR AGE" MAGAZINE LISTED A V-12 MODEL "48" (132" W.B.) IN SPRING, 1922.

23

HAYNES ("55" and "75" REPLACED BY "57" and "77" DURING 1923.)

The New, 1923 Haynes 55 Sport Coupelet, 3 Pass

The New, 1923 Haynes 55 Sport Roadster, 2 Passengers

32 × 4½ TIRES CHANGED TO 33 × 5.77 DURING 1924.

"60" METROPOLITAN SEDAN

"60" IS ONLY SER. [F]OR 1924-1925.)

"60" TOURING (STARTS 8-23)

24

"W.B., 274.2 C.I.D. CYLS.

4.41 G.R.

50 H.P. @ 2400 RPM (MOST SPECS. AS IN '24)

25

[12]0" W.B. [and] 4-CYL. [BR]S

H.C.S. MOTOR CO., INDIANAPOLIS

H.C.S. (1920 – 1925)

126"-W.B. 288.6 C.I.D. 6-CYL. ALSO AVAIL., 1923-25 (MIDWEST ENG. IN EARLY MODELS.)

277.1 C.I.D., [4]- CYL., O.H.V. [W]EIDELY ENGINE [WI]TH LANCHESTER [VI]BRATION DAMPENER

SERIES 3 (1920-1922)

SERIES 6

SERIES 4 (1922-1925)

5-PASS. TOURING

HEINE-VELOX V-12 (SAN FRANCISCO, 1921)

148" W.B.

HERTZ

YELLOW CAB MFG. CO., CHICAGO (1925 – 1928)

BUILT FOR RENTAL USE

MODEL "D-1" has 114" W.B., 31 × 4 TIRES ('25) 30 × 5.77 ('26 ON) 4.72 GEAR RATIO 195.6 C.I.D. (230.1 C.I.D., '27) 6-CYLINDER CONTINENTAL ENGINE 49 H.P. @ 2500 (61 H.P. @ 2600 RPM, '27) DELCO IGNITION

('25)

[R]EPLACES 1924 [A]MBASSADOR "D-1")

HOLMES

CANTON, OHIO (1918 - 1923)

126" W.B. 4.9 G.R.

21-23

OWN AIR-COOLED ENGINE 6 CYLINDERS, O.H.V. (259.8 C.I.D.)

34 × 4½ TIRES

20

EISEMANN IGN. (THROUGH '23)

SERIES 4 (RESTYLED FOR 1921)

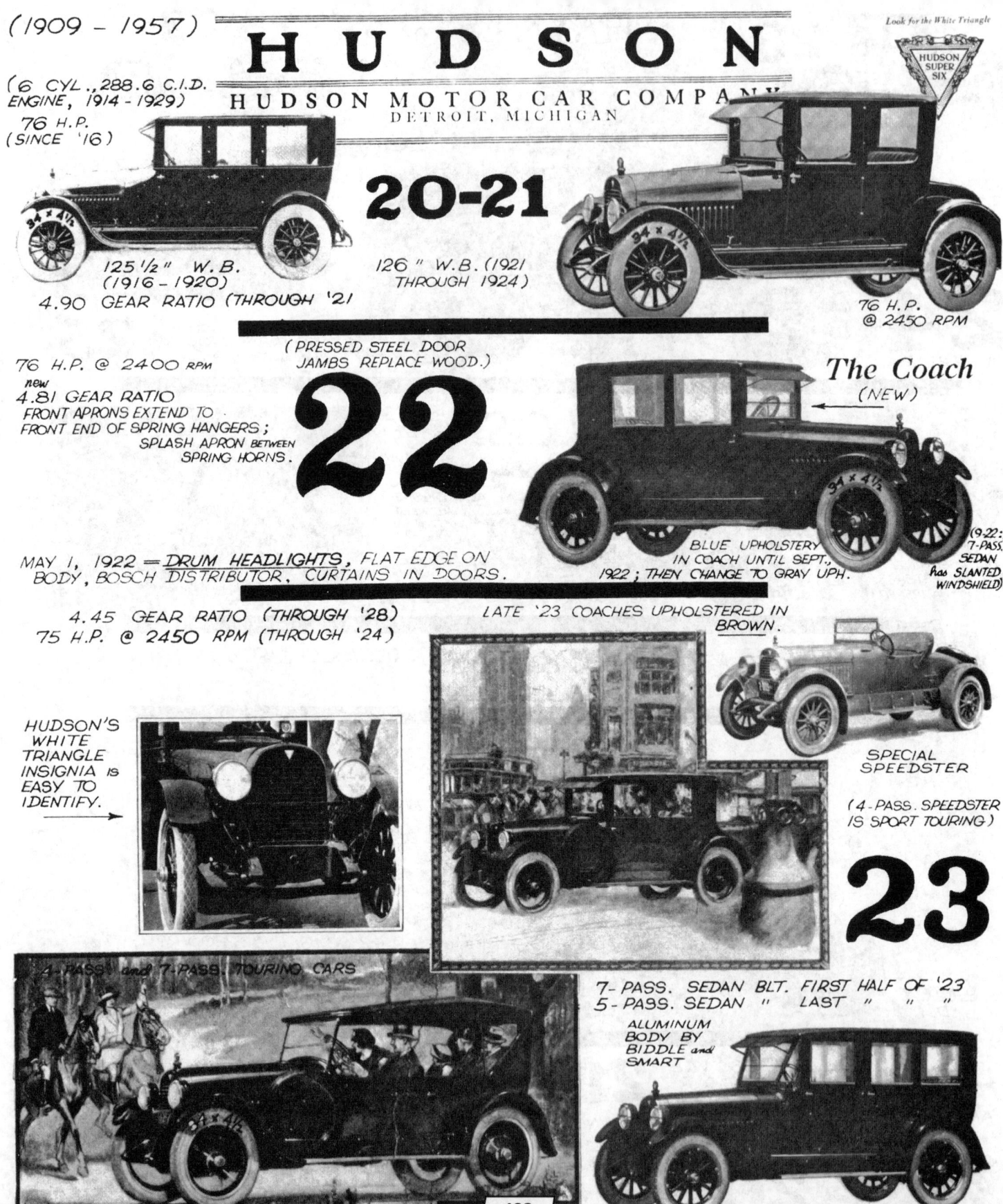

(1909 – 1957)

HUDSON
HUDSON MOTOR CAR COMPANY
DETROIT, MICHIGAN

Look for the White Triangle

HUDSON SUPER SIX

(6 CYL., 288.6 C.I.D. ENGINE, 1914 - 1929)

76 H.P. (SINCE '16)

20-21

125 ½" W.B. (1916 - 1920)
4.90 GEAR RATIO (THROUGH '21)

126" W.B. (1921 THROUGH 1924)

76 H.P. @ 2450 RPM

(PRESSED STEEL DOOR JAMBS REPLACE WOOD.)

76 H.P. @ 2400 RPM
new
4.81 GEAR RATIO
FRONT APRONS EXTEND TO FRONT END OF SPRING HANGERS;
SPLASH APRON BETWEEN SPRING HORNS.

22

The Coach (NEW)

BLUE UPHOLSTERY IN COACH UNTIL SEPT., 1922; THEN CHANGE TO GRAY UPH.

(9-22: 7-PASS. SEDAN has SLANTED WINDSHIELD)

MAY 1, 1922 = DRUM HEADLIGHTS, FLAT EDGE ON BODY, BOSCH DISTRIBUTOR, CURTAINS IN DOORS.

4.45 GEAR RATIO (THROUGH '28)
75 H.P. @ 2450 RPM (THROUGH '24)

LATE '23 COACHES UPHOLSTERED IN BROWN.

HUDSON'S WHITE TRIANGLE INSIGNIA IS EASY TO IDENTIFY.

SPECIAL SPEEDSTER

(4-PASS. SPEEDSTER IS SPORT TOURING)

23

4-PASS. and 7-PASS. TOURING CARS

7-PASS. SEDAN BLT. FIRST HALF OF '23
5-PASS. SEDAN " LAST " " "

ALUMINUM BODY BY BIDDLE and SMART

THE FINEST HUDSON EVER BUILT

HUDSON

INTERIOR
("CABRIOLET"
COUPE)

24

NEW RIDGED
FENDERS

LIMOUSINE

7-PASS.

25

33 × 6.20
(BALLOON
TIRES)

76 H.P. @ 2800 RPM
(THROUGH '26)

25½-26

(NEW WINDSHIELD)

The Brougham

(A NEW HUDSON MODEL)

HAS
ALUMINUM
BODY
PANELS,
LEATHER-
COVERED
REAR
QUARTER
SECTIONS.

26½ BROUGHAM
HAS ROOF-VISOR

33 × 6

HUDSON

COACH

27

F-HEAD ENGINE; 4-WHEEL BRAKES

95 H.P. @ 3100 RPM

BROUGHAM

WHEELBASES
118" = STANDARD; 127½" = CUSTOM

33 × 6 TIRES

RADIATOR SHUTTERS NOW VERTICAL.

JULY 1, 1927 = '27½ MODELS. REDESIGNED CYL. HEAD, ETC.

31 × 6.00 TIRES

CONVERTIBLE LANDAU SEDAN

ALL GAUGES UNDER ONE LONG PANEL, INDIRECTLY LIGHTED.

GEAR RATIOS
4.08 (S)
4.45 (O)

28

MODELS "S" and "O"

80-90 H.P.

31 × 6.00 TIRES

(MURPHY BODY)

(BRIGGS BODY)

WIRE WHEELS STANDARD ON LONG-WHEELBASE MODELS.

122½" OR 139" WHEELBASE
92 H.P. @ 3200 RPM

DASH

7-PASS. SEDAN

29

"THE GREATER HUDSON 6"

(BODY BY HUDSON)

4.08 GEAR RATIO
TOP SPEED = OVER 80

5-PASS. CLUB SEDAN
(BODY BY BIDDLE and SMART)

122

30 HUDSON

**8 CYLS., 213.8 C.I.D.
84 H.P. @ 3400 RPM**

(ALL MODELS HAD NEW
STRAIGHT-8 ENGINE.)

RADIATOR
FILLER
UNDER
HOOD

MODERNISTIC DASH

119" WHEELBASE

4.63 GEAR RATIO (THROUGH '32)
5.50 × 18 TIRES (THROUGH '31)

119" OR 126" W.B. (THROUGH '32)
233.7 C.I.D.

87 H.P. @ 3600 RPM

31

SOME 1931s
HAVE 1930-STYLE
HEADLIGHTS,
COWL LIGHTS and
WHEELS.

1931 7-PASS. PHAETON
HAS 1930-STYLE DASH.

DASH

CLUB SEDAN

31½

HUDSON

HUDSON EIGHT COACH
Five Passengers . . . . 119" Wheelbase
$1025 F.O.B. DETROIT

HUDSON EIGHT BUSINESS COUPE
Two Passengers . . . . 119" Wheelbase
$995 F.O.B. DETROIT

HUDSON EIGHT TOWN SEDAN
Five Passengers . . . . 119" Wheelbase
$1050 F.O.B. DETROIT

32

'32 INTERIOR

HUDSON EIGHT STANDARD SEDAN
Five Passengers . . . . 119" Wheelbase
$1095 F.O.B. DETROIT

HUDSON EIGHT SUBURBAN
Five Passengers . . . . 126" Wheelbase
$1275 F.O.B. DETROIT

HUDSON EIGHT SEDAN
Seven Passengers . . . . 132" Wheelbase
$1595 F.O.B. DETROIT

NEW GRILLE

PACEMAKER—Hudson Eight Standard Sedan for five passengers $1095 F.O.B. Detroit

254.4 C.I.D.   101 H.P. @ 3600 RPM   (THROUGH '33)

"STANDARD," "STERLING," and
"MAJOR" SERIES (119, 126, 132" W.B.)

Hudson bodies, strong, smart and luxuriously finished, are built in Hudson's own $15,000,000 body plant. They realise in full those qualities which make steel the modern material for all structural duty in this day of high-power engine capacities and improved highways inviting to speed and demanding safety. The entire front and framework of the Hudson-built body shown here is welded into a single rattle-proof unit of unusual strength.

124

17 x 6.00 TIRES (17 x 6.50 ON "MAJOR")

HUDSON

VACUUM CLUTCH
FREE WHEELING

SUPER 6 = ('33 ONLY) 193.1 C.I.D. 4.64 G.R.
73 H.P. @ 3200 RPM   (6 OR 8)
5.25 × 18 TIRES   113" W.B.

PACEMAKER
EIGHT = 119" OR 132" W.B.
6.00 × 17 TIRES
"MAJOR" HAS 6.50 × 17 TIRES

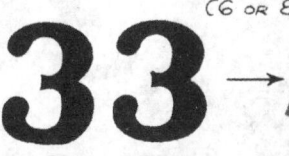
33 →

'34 DASH SIMILAR TO '35, BUT ASH TRAY IS ON GLOVE-BOX DOOR (PLUS OTHER MINOR DIFFERENCES)

"LTS" CHALLENGER ECONOMY MODEL STARTS JUNE, 1934, WITHOUT "AXLEFLEX" SPRINGING, DRAFTLESS VENTILATION, OR INSIDE SUN VISORS.

34

(8-CYL. ONLY;
NO HUDSON 6
IN 1934.)
108 H.P. @ 3800 RPM

6.25 OR 6.50 × 16
TIRES

116"   OR   123" WHEELBASE
"LT" = STD.   "LL" = STD.
"LU" = DLX.   "LLU" = DLX.

DELUXE MODELS HAVE RADIO

"GH" BIG 6 HAS 212 C.I.D., 93 H.P. @ 3800 RPM (THROUGH '36)

BIG 6 HAS
116" W.B.

4.11 GEAR
RATIO (THROUGH '38)

35

8 = 113 H.P. @ 3800
(THROUGH '36)   8

NEW,   OPTIONAL
"ELECTRIC HAND" GEARSHIFT ON STEERING COLUMN

"HT" SPECIAL 8
and
"HU" DELUXE 8
have 117" W.B.

"HHU"
CUSTOM 8
has 124" W.B.,
AS DO "HTL"
and "HUL"

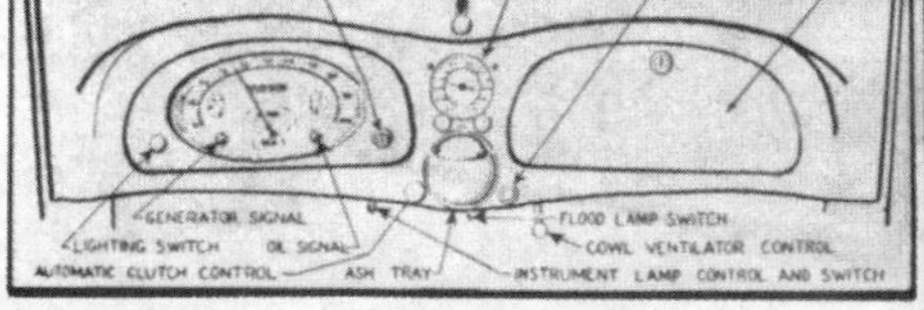

DASH

NEW BODY

HUDSON

6 HAS 120" W.B.

36

8 HAS 120" OR 127" W.B.

HYDRAULIC BRAKES

OVAL SPEEDOMETER
IN CENTER OF DASH

"CUSTOM" STEERING
WHEEL HAS 3 SETS OF
4 CHROME-PLATED SPOKES.

6 HAS 101 H.P.
@ 4000 RPM
(THROUGH '39)
122" W.B.
(THROUGH '39)

8 HAS 122 H.P.
@ 4200 RPM
(THROUGH '39)
122" OR 129"
8 W.B.
(THROUGH '39)

COUNTRY CLUB
8

37

New HUDSON Eight
122 AND 129-INCH WHEELBASE...122 HORSEPOWER

HUDSON TERRAPLANE

HUDSON SIX

'38 "112" HAS 83 H.P.

"112" HAS FRONT-HINGED HOOD.

38

OFFICIAL A.A. CAR
HUDSON 112

HUDSON

LOWER - PRICED "112" MODELS HAVE SEPERATE HEADLIGHTS AND DIFFERENT GRILLE.

"112" (112" W.B.) ("90" SERIES)

6 CYLS., 175 C.I.D.
86 H.P. @ 4000 RPM

"PACEMAKER 91" and "92"

6 = 118" W.B.
96 H.P. @
3900 RPM

COUNTRY CLUB 6 = ("93")
122" W.B.,
101 H.P. @
4000 RPM

39

NEW DASH AND STEERING COLUMN GEARSHIFT

NEW DASH-LOCKING SAFETY HOOD

HOOD HINGED AT FRONT... WIND CAN'T LIFT IT...

LOCKED BY LEVER INSIDE CAR: BATTERY AND ENGINE PARTS THEFT-PROOF

NEW CARRY-ALL LUGGAGE COMPARTMENT

DASH (IN "COUNTRY CLUB" model)

6

also

8 - CYLINDER
"95" COUNTRY CLUB
"97" CUSTOM
COUNTRY CLUB
122" OR 129" W.B.

4.1 GEAR RATIO

NEW AIRFOAM CUSHIONS

Airfoam is standard in new Hudson Country Club and Convertible models, optional at small cost in all other 1939 Hudsons.

6 - CYL., 224 C.I.D.
CONTINENTAL ENGINE

120" W.B.

$1895
f. o. b. Elkhart

1921 = MODEL "R"

1923 = 241.5
C.I.D., 4.5 G.R

Huffman 6

(1920-1925)

HUFFMAN BROS.
MOTOR CO.,
ELKHART, INDIANA

MODEL "W" ('20)

FINAL HUFFMANS HAVE HYDRAULIC BRAKES, DISC WHEELS.

HUPMOBILE

Hupp Motor Car Corporation
Detroit, Michigan

(1908 — 1940)

4 CYL.
182.5 C.I.D.
(THROUGH '25)

112" W.B. and
4.87 G.R. (THROUGH '24)

HIGHER RADIATOR AND
LOWER RUNNING-BOARDS
THAN ON 1919 MODEL.

20

"R-3"

32 x 4
TIRES
(THROUGH '24)

5 - PASSENGER
TOURING CAR

CLOSED CARS ADOPT SUN VISORS
WINDSHIELD WIPERS ADDED IN 1921

Hupmobile

OPEN CARS
NOW FEATURE
OUTSIDE DOOR HANDLES

21

2 - PASSENGER
ROADSTER

OLD-
STYLE
TAIL-LIGHT
RE-INTRODUCED.

FIRST YEAR WITH STEWART SPEEDOMETER.
EARLY MODELS HAVE TAN-LINED TOP AND
HAND ADJUSTMENT OF HEADLIGHT FOCUS.
LATER MODELS HAVE TWEED-LINED TOP
AND SCREWDRIVER
ADJUSTMENT OF
HEADLIGHT
FOCUS.

ROADSTER-COUPÉ

(INTRO.
DEC.,
1921)

22

FIRST YEAR FOR WINDOW
CRANKS IN CLOSED CAR DOORS.

COUPE TRUNK
DETAILS

23

"SPECIAL" MODELS HAVE NICKEL PLATING,
DRUM HEADLIGHTS, DELUXE EQUIPMENT

FRONT RIGHT SEAT FOLDS
UNDER
DASH
WHEN
NOT
IN USE.

Coupe Model RY · Two-Passenger

Special Roadster Model RRS

Coupe Model RK · Four-Passenger

HUPMOBILE

24

NEW 115" WHEELBASE

DRUM HEADLIGHTS ON **ALL** MODELS

3 DOOR CLUB SEDAN ('24 and '25)

(FINAL 4-CYL. MODEL (R-14) HAS 4.9 G.R.) 31 × 5.25 TIRES)

STRAIGHT-8 IS NEW FOR 1925.

"E-1" **8**

ONLY 1 DOOR ON LEFT SIDE.

"R-14" **4**

FOURS AND EIGHTS

25

118 1/4" W.B. 4.63 G.R. 246.7 C.I.D.

HYDRAULIC BRAKES ON NEW 8.

"A-1" **SIX**

114" W.B. (THROUGH '30)

195 C.I.D. 50 H.P. @ 3000 RPM

FRENCH-STYLE ROOF VISOR NOW AVAILABLE ON ALL CLOSED HUPMOBILES.

30 × 5.25 TIRES

30 × 5.25

26

"E-2" **EIGHT**

"E-2" 8 BERLINE SIMILAR TO ILLUS. SEDAN, BUT HAS LIMOUSINE-TYPE CLEAR GLASS (PARTITION) BACK OF DRIVER'S SEAT.

NEW 268.7 C.I.D. 63 H.P. @ 2700 RPM NEW 125" W.B.

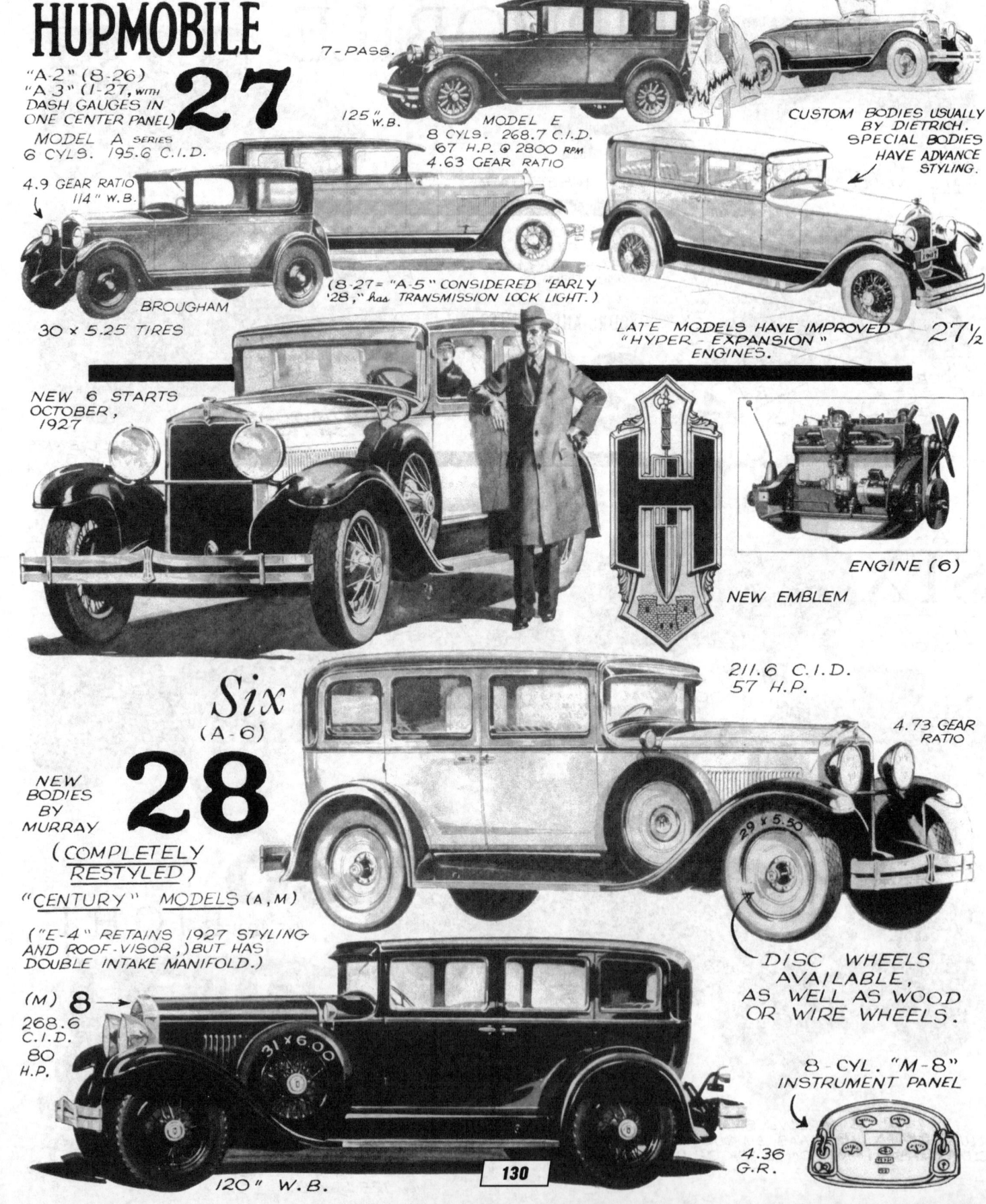

HUPMOBILE 27

"A-2" (8-26)
"A 3" (1-27, WITH
DASH GAUGES IN
ONE CENTER PANEL)

MODEL A SERIES
6 CYLS. 195.6 C.I.D.

4.9 GEAR RATIO
114" W.B.

7- PASS.

125" W.B.

MODEL E
8 CYLS. 268.7 C.I.D.
67 H.P. @ 2800 RPM
4.63 GEAR RATIO

CUSTOM BODIES USUALLY
BY DIETRICH. SPECIAL BODIES
HAVE ADVANCE
STYLING.

BROUGHAM

30 x 5.25 TIRES

(8-27= "A-5" CONSIDERED "EARLY
'28," has TRANSMISSION LOCK LIGHT.)

LATE MODELS HAVE IMPROVED
"HYPER - EXPANSION"
ENGINES.

27½

NEW 6 STARTS
OCTOBER,
1927

ENGINE (6)

NEW EMBLEM

Six (A-6)

211.6 C.I.D.
57 H.P.

4.73 GEAR
RATIO

28

NEW
BODIES
BY
MURRAY

(COMPLETELY
RESTYLED)

"CENTURY" MODELS (A, M)

("E-4" RETAINS 1927 STYLING
AND ROOF-VISOR,) BUT HAS
DOUBLE INTAKE MANIFOLD.)

29 X 5.50

DISC WHEELS
AVAILABLE,
AS WELL AS WOOD
OR WIRE WHEELS.

(M) 8
268.6
C.I.D.
80
H.P.

31 X 6.00

8 - CYL. "M-8"
INSTRUMENT PANEL

4.36
G.R.

120" W.B.

HUPMOBILE
1929 "CENTURY"
SIX & EIGHT

BODIES BY MURRAY,
EXCEPT FOR
BAKER-RAULANG
BODIES ON "M"
TOWN SEDAN, 7-PASS.
SEDAN, and LIMOUSINE.

29

CURVED AND
GROOVED FRONT SPLASH GUARD
EXTENDS OVER
SPRING HORNS.

SPECIFICATIONS SIMILAR
TO 1928, BUT 1929
SIX HAS 4.7 and other
GEAR RATIOS; "M" has 4.4

INSTRUMENT PANEL

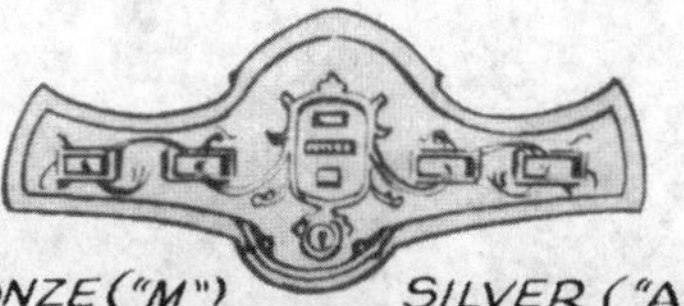

BRONZE ("M")   SILVER ("A")
OXIDIZED FINISH

HUPMOBILE

EXAGGERATED ARTIST'S RENDERING

6 WOOD, WIRE, OR DISC WHEELS AS BEFORE

The 1930 Hupmobile Eight Coupe showing new peaked deck and top

CENTURY · SIX

MODEL "S"
70 H.P. @ 3200
4.7 G.R.
211.6 C.I.D.
5.25 × 19 TIRES
(BEGINS 8-10-29)

EARLY "S" SIX, WITH DISC WHEELS, LOW-PLACED HOOD LOUVRES

8

Instrument Panel

Inside Light

30

MODEL "C"
8 CYL.
100 H.P. @
3200 RPM
268.6 C.I.D.
4.55 G.R.
6.00 × 19 TIRES
(SUPERSEDES "M," 9-18-29)

Radiator Cap   Outside Door-Handle

Inside Door Molding

137" - W.B. MODEL "U" HAS ENGINE LIKE MODEL "H."

MODEL "H"
8 CYL.
133 H.P. @
3400 RPM
365.6 C.I.D.
4.07 G.R.
125" W.B.
6.50 × 19 TIRES

Fender Parking Light   Smoking Set

Inside Door-Handles

NO VISOR

EIGHT

CENTURY 6

'31 SPECS. SIMILAR TO '30, BUT NEW "L" has 8-CYL., 240.2 C.I.D., 90 H.P. @ 3200 RPM

31

wheelbases:
"S-2" CENT. 6   113½
"L"   " 8   118
"C"   "   121
"H"   "   125
"U"   "   137

(FREE-WHEELING AVAIL. IN ALL MODELS AS OF 1-31.)

HUPMOBILE

STARTING '32, 1ST DIGIT OF MODEL NO. INDICATES YEAR ; OTHER 2 DIGITS ARE W.B.

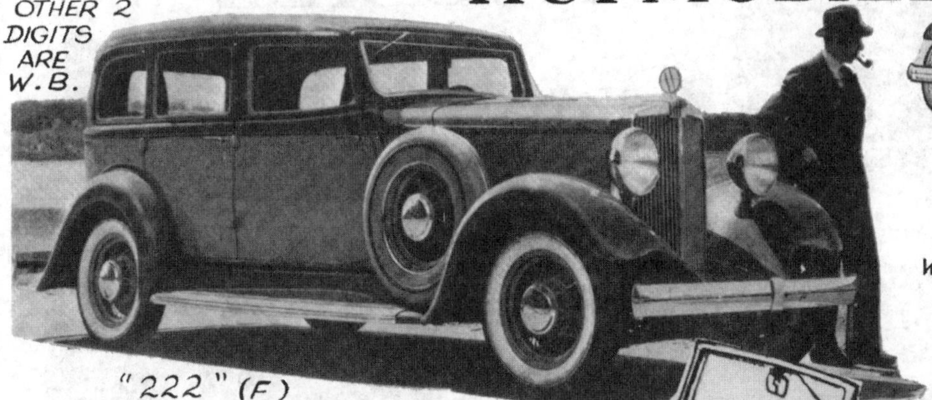

"222" (F)
8 CYL., 250.7 C.I.D.
93 H.P. @ 3200 RPM

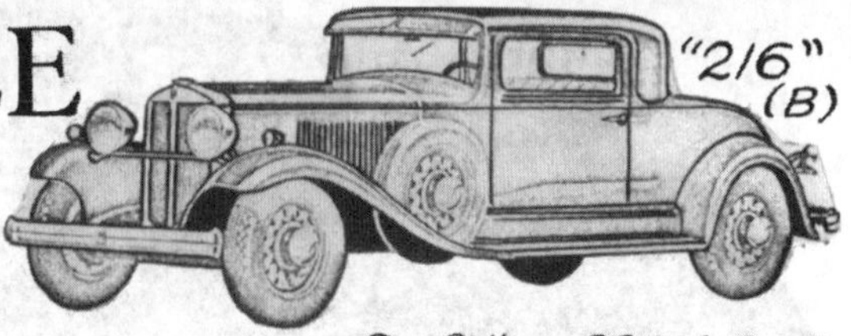

"216" (B)
6 CYL., 228.1 C.I.D.
75 H.P. @ 3200 RPM
4.54 G.R.

FREE-WHEELING AVAIL.

32

8 DIFFERENT MODEL SERIES!

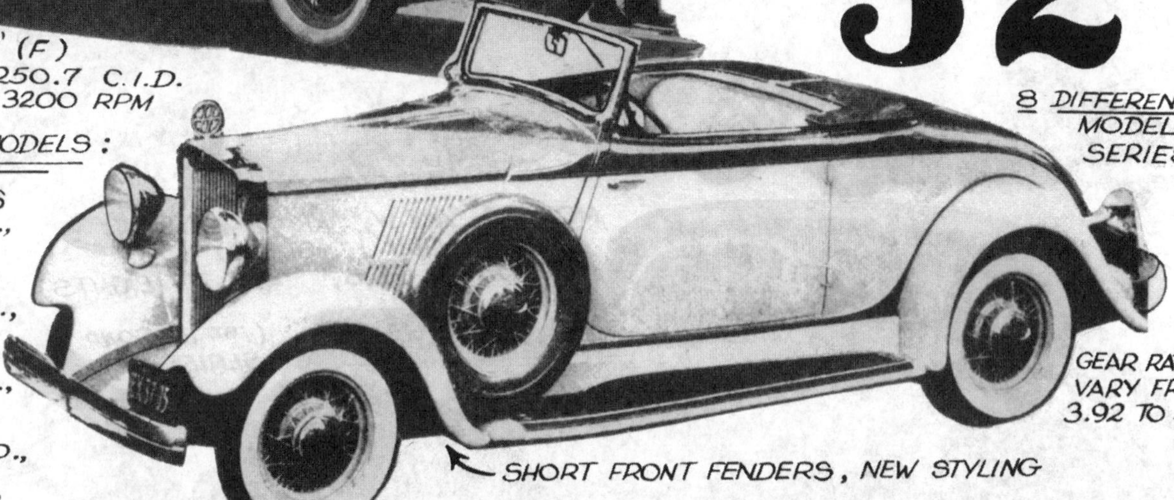

OTHER 1932 MODELS :

"214" (S) 6 (211.5 C.I.D., 70 H.P.)
"218" (L) 6 (240.2 C.I.D., 90 H.P.)
"221" (C) 8 (268.6 C.I.D., 100 H.P.)
"225" (H) 8 (365.6 C.I.D., 133 H.P.)
"226" (I) 8 (279.9 C.I.D., 103 H.P. ------- and "237" (U) 8 (SAME BIG ENGINE AS "225")

GEAR RATIOS VARY FROM 3.92 TO 4.7

SHORT FRONT FENDERS, NEW STYLING

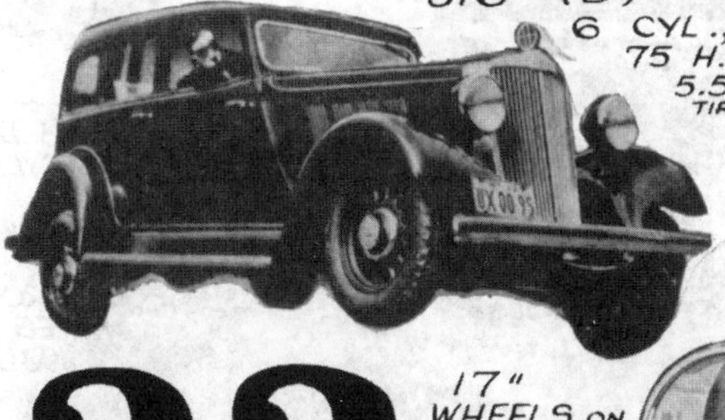

"316" (B)
6 CYL., 228.1 C.I.D.
75 H.P. @ 3200
5.50 x 18 TIRES

NON-OPENING WINDSHIELD ON "321-A" VARIATION

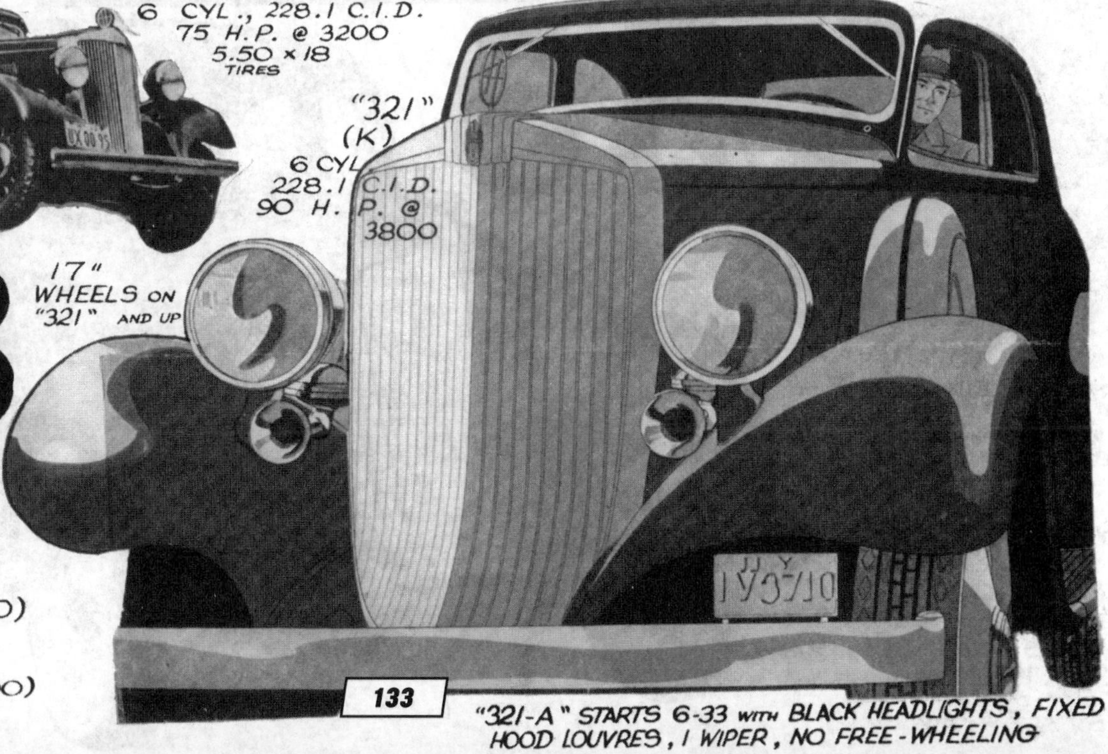

"321" (K)
6 CYL.
228.1 C.I.D.
90 H.P. @ 3800

33

17" WHEELS ON "321" AND UP

ALSO AVAILABLE :

"322" 8 (261.5 C.I.D., 96 H.P. @ 3200)
"326" 8 (303.2 C.I.D., 109 H.P. @ 3500)

"321-A" STARTS 6-33 WITH BLACK HEADLIGHTS, FIXED HOOD LOUVRES, 1 WIPER, NO FREE-WHEELING

HUPMOBILE

34

ACTUAL PHOTO →

← STANDARD 6

GLAMORIZED ADVERTISING ILLUSTRATION ←

ENGINES RANGE FROM 224 C.I.D. 6 (80 H.P.) TO 303.2 C.I.D. 8 (115 H.P.)

"421-J" →

MODELS "417-W," "KK-421-A," "K-421," "421-J," (SIXES) "422," "426," "427-T"(EIGHTS)

(1ST and 2ND SERIES)

NEW "AERODYNAMIC" MODELS ARE STREAMLINED.

35

"518-D" 6 CYLS.

118" W.B.

INTRO. FEB., 1935

REAR VIEW OF "518-D" (WITH HYDRAULIC BRAKES)

91 TO 120 H.P. 4.5 G.R. ON MOST

(MECHANICAL BRAKES ON (MODELS INTRO. OCT., 1934 : "517-W" (6) "521-J" (6) "527-T" (8)

8-CYL. "521-O" INTRO. MAY, 1935 (HYDR. BRAKES)

HUPMOBILE

35 (CONT'D.)

"527-T" COUPE
127½" W.B.

8 CYLS.
303.2 C.I.D.
120 H.P. @
3500 RPM

VACUUM MECH. BRAKES ON 527-T

36-37

6 - CYL.
SERIES
"618-G"
245.3
C.I.D.,
101 H.P. @
3600 RPM

4.27
G.R.

3 - PC. WINDSHIELD
RETAINED ON THIS
MODEL

8-CYL. SERIES
"621-N" 303.2 C.I.D.,120 H.P. @ 3500 RPM
4.09 OR 4.27 G.R.

121" W.B.

BECAUSE OF FINANCIAL PROBLEMS,
HUPMOBILE PRODUCTION
TEMPORARILY SUSPENDED 1936-1937
AND NO NEW "700" MODELS
ANNOUNCED FOR 1937.

38

SIX = "822-E"
245.3 C.I.D.
101 H.P. @ 3600 RPM
6.25 × 16
TIRES

4.54 G.R. (BOTH MODELS)

EIGHT=
"825-H"
303.2 C.I.D.
120 H.P. @
3500 RPM
6.50 × 16 TIRES

THIS "SENIOR" MODEL
CONTINUED INTO 1939,
WITHOUT CRANK HOLE
IN GRILLE.

39

OVERDRIVE
OPTIONAL

NEW
"R-915"
("SKYLARK")

CORD BODY DIES USED ON
"R-915," WITH NEW 115"
W.B. and
4.27 G.R.
6.00 ×
16
TIRES

"R-915"
JUNIOR 6
(INTRO. OCT., 1938.
REPLACED BY "SKYLARK")

("SENIOR" MODELS
"922-E" and "925-H" ARE CONTINUATIONS OF '38.)

(FINAL HUPMOBILE,
DISCONTINUED DURING 1940.)

"SKYLARK" 6 ONLY, IN 1940

INNES
(1921)

HENRY L. INNES,
JACKSONVILLE, FLORIDA
(COMPANY FORMED IN 1920, BUT
NO CARS ACTUALLY BUILT UNTIL
1921.)

with 4-CYLINDER
178.9 C.I.D.
SUPREME ENGINE
(3 3/8 " × 5")

ROADSTERS or 5-PASS.
TOURING CARS, *each with*
RIGID "PERMANENT TOP."

CHOICE OF
BATTERY OR MAGNETO
IGNITION.

SMALL TRUCK ALSO
(PLANNED)

JACKSON

JACKSON AUTOMOBILE CO.,
JACKSON, MICH. (1903-1923)

'20 "SPORT CAR" ("6-38")
HAS UNUSUAL TOP STYLE.

6-CYL., 3 1/4 " × 5" (248.9 C.I.D.)
HERSCHELL-SPILLMAN
ENGINE ALSO LISTED,
DURING SPRING, 1922.
("6-38" SERIES
CONTINUES)

20 "6-38"
6-CYLINDER,
224 C.I.D.
CONTINENTAL
ENGINE (TO '23)

121" W.B. (TO '23)
32 × 4 TIRES
REMY IGNITION
(AUTO-LITE LOCK)

'21 "6-38"
SEMI-SPORT →

21

32 × 4 1/2 TIRES, 4.75 GEAR RATIO (TO '23)

JAEGER
(1931 — 1933)

('32)

JAEGER MOTOR CAR CO.,
BELLEVILLE and CASS CITY,
MICHIGAN
(6-CYL. CONTINENTAL
ENGINE)

JEWETT

A Thrifty Six **JEWETT** *Built by Paige*

JEWETT'S 6-CYL. ENGINE IS A DEVELOPMENT FROM THE 1921 PAIGE "6-44" ENGINE, AND HAS THE ADDITION OF FORCE-FEED OILING.

22
"6-50"
12" BRAKE DRUMS

ATWATER KENT IGNITION

112" WHEELBASE (THROUGH '24)

248.9 C.I.D. (THROUGH '25)

50 HORSEPOWER (THROUGH '24)

FIRST YEAR WITH NO SECTOR ON SPARK OR THROTTLE HAND CONTROL.

23
"6-50"
14" BRAKE DRUMS

50 HORSEPOWER

24
"6-50"

De Luxe Sedan BODY COLOR = "LOTUS BLUE"

CARB. ON LEFT SIDE OF ENGINE. DISTRIBUTOR PUMP and GENERATOR ON RIGHT SIDE.

NICKEL TRIM ON DELUXE MODELS

3-PASS. BUSINESS MAN'S CPE. INTRO. ABOUT 2-24. DURING 1924, AND 4-PASS. CPE. DROPPED. NEW 2-DR. BROUGHAM SEATS CONVERT TO A BED.

AUTUMN, 1924 = 32 x 4.95 BALLOON TIRES, AND "AUTUMN GREEN" SATIN BODY COLOR (MOST MODELS)

JEWETT SIX
PAIGE BUILT

DE LUXE BROUGHAM

(STD. BROUGHAM has PAINTED RADIATOR, NO LANDAU IRONS.)

25

"6-50"
112" W.B.

STROMBERG CARB.
ATW. KENT IGNITION
LIGHT SWITCH
ON DASH

LOCKHEED
HYDRAULIC
4 WHEEL
BRAKES
AVAILABLE
(SINCE
1924)
($40
EXTRA)

HIGHER
HOOD
AND
LOWER
RUNNING-
BOARDS

new
"SATIN
LACQUER"
FINISH

LATER IN YEAR, EARLY
1926 "6-55" MODEL
HAS LOCKING STEERING
WHEEL. WHEELBASE
CHANGED FROM
112" TO
115", with LIGHT
SWITCH ON STEER. WH.

63 H.P.
@
2800 RPM
(ONLY 55 H.P.
CLAIMED EARLY
IN SEASON.)

CARB. MOVED
TO RIGHT SIDE
OF ENGINE,
FOR '25.

31 x 5.25   31 x 5.25

TOP SPEED = 65 MILES PER HOUR

COACH ($1260.)
(LOW-PRICED MODEL of CLOSED CAR. STARTS 4-25. HAS
DOORS 3' WIDE.)

INTERIOR

The New-Day JEWETT SIX
SERIES "6-40"

(STARTS DEC., 1925)
THE
ONLY JEWETT WITH
NEW, NARROW
CORNER POSTS

NICKELED RADIATOR SHELL
ON DE LUXE MODELS

NEW CONTINENTAL
ENGINE HAS 169.2 C.I.D.
and 40 H.P. @ 2400 RPM
JOHNSON CARB., REMY IGN.

26

"NEW-DAY"
MODEL HAS
SHORTENED
109"
W.B.

(A VERY SCARCE MODEL)

FINAL JEWETT (1927 MODEL)
WAS INTRODUCED SEPTEMBER, 1926.
ON JANUARY 3, 1927, ITS NAME WAS CHANGED TO
THE PAIGE "6-45," APPEARANCE WAS SAME.
(SEE PAIGE, 1927 FOR PICTURE.)

JONES 6

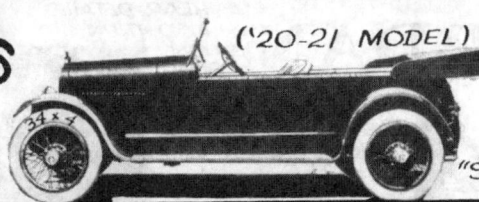

1920 MODEL 28 HAS IMPROVED RADIATOR, HIGH SHIFTING LEVER. CONTINENTAL ENGINE (303.1 C.I.D.!)

('20-21 MODEL)

(1915-1920) JONES MOTOR CAR CO., WICHITA, KANSAS

"SPEEDSTER" TOURING

126" W.B.
4.5 G.R.
AUTO-LITE
IGNITION

JORDAN MOTOR CAR COMPANY, Inc., Cleveland, Ohio

JORDAN

('21)

224 C.I.D., 120" W.B. (1916-1931)
1920 "M" FEATURES ONLY MINOR IMPROVEMENTS. NEW 4-DOOR SEDAN. LIGHTWEIGHT ALUMINUM BODIES

"F" SERIES HAS 303.1 C.I.D. ENGINE AND 127" W.B. (THROUGH '22) Delco IGNITION (THROUGH '24 and on 6-CYL. '25)

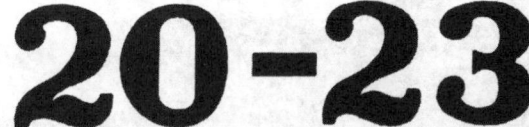

"Silhouette" TOURING

6-CYL. CONTINENTAL ENGINES
32 × 4 TIRES (M)
32 × 4½ " (F)

PRE-1922 JORDANS have SCREW-ON (THREADED) GAS TANK CAP, AND STARTER SWITCH ON FLOOR NEAR FRONT SEAT.

NEW INSTRUMENT BOARD IN 1922, with ALL GAUGES UNDER ONE GLASS.

4.66 GEAR RATIO (M)
4.08 " " (F)

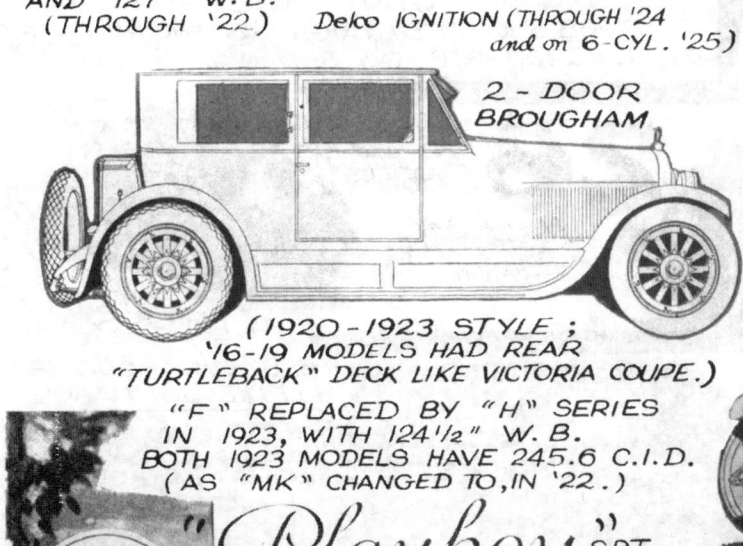

2-DOOR BROUGHAM

(1920-1923 STYLE; '16-19 MODELS HAD REAR "TURTLEBACK" DECK LIKE VICTORIA COUPE.)

"F" REPLACED BY "H" SERIES IN 1923, WITH 124½" W.B. BOTH 1923 MODELS HAVE 245.6 C.I.D. (AS "MK" CHANGED TO, IN '22.)

20-23

"M" and "F" SERIES ("M" BECOMES "MK" IN 1922)

4-DOOR BROUGHAM (INTRODUCED 1923)

JORDAN

"Playboy" SPT. ROADSTER

EARLY TYPE HAS DASH GAUGES AT RIGHT SIDE ←

DISC WHEELS AVAILABLE ON 1923 "PLAYBOY"

JORDAN

24

"MX-6" TOURING CAR (5-PASS.)

"MX," "H" "L" MODELS

120" W.B.

REAR DETAILS AND TRUNK ON "BLUE BOY" PHAETON (AS OF 11-24)

4.42 G.R.

(Am. Bosch IGN., 125½" W.B. ON 8)

25

"PLAYBOY"

4.45 G.R. (K)
4.64 G.R. (A,L)

"A," "K," "L" MODELS

BREWSTER-STYLE WINDSHIELD ON 1925 JORDAN CLOSED MODELS

SERIES A "Great Line 8" (new)
268.6 C.I.D. STRAIGHT-8 ENGINE (74 H.P. @ 3000)
56 H.P. @ 2400 RPM 6-CYL. STILL AVAIL.)(K or L)

26

8 CYL. ONLY "A" and "J" MODELS

(American-Bosch IGNITION ON 8s THROUGH '27)

NEW "J" HAS 116" W.B., 246.5 C.I.D. 64 H.P. @ 3000 RPM

27

8-CYL. MODEL "J" (J-1)

SAME SPECS. AS IN '26

SERIES "A" CONT'D. AS "AA"

new 6-CYL. MODEL "R" "LITTLE JORDAN"

199 C.I.D. 62 H.P. @ 3000 RPM Auto-Lite IGN.

107" W.B.   4.6 G.R.   The Sport Salon

28

"R" and "J-1" HAVE SAME SPECS. AS IN '27

FRONT END

SHORTER '28 HEADLIGHT SHELLS

NEW 268.7 C.I.D. MODEL "JE" "AIR LINE 8" HAS 4.45 G.R., CADET-TYPE VISOR, 116" W.B., 80 H.P. @ 3200 RPM

"LITTLE TOMBOY"

Auto-Lite IGNITION ON ALL BUT "J-1"

29

NEW 1929 RADIATOR SHUTTERS AND HORIZONTAL HOOD LOUVRES

Auto-Lite IGN. (THROUGH '32) new FUEL PUMP

"E" (6 CYL.) HAS 116" W.B., 248.3 C.I.D. 70 H.P. @ 3000 RPM

"G" (8-CYL.) HAS 125" W.B., 268.6 C.I.D., 85 H.P. @ 3200 RPM 4.45 G.R.

E

G

6

8

(NO 6-CYL. JORDAN AFTER 1929)

MURRAY or OHIO BODIES

140

JORDAN

31-32

8 - CYL. "SPEEDWAY ACE"

114 H.P. @ 3200
322.2 C.I.D.

MODEL "Z" 145" W.B.

OTHER 1930 JORDAN 8s:
"70-U" } 80 H.P.
"80" } 246.7 c.i.d.
"90" 85 H.P. 268.6 c.i.d.

SERIES "90" 125" W.B.

STREAMLINED SERIES WITH **BUILT-IN RADIO** !

30

"SPEEDBOY" PHAETON

(1929 TO 1932 TYPE ALSO AVAIL. DURING '30.)

SERIES "80" (120" W.B.) ALSO

JULIAN (1922)

JULIAN BROWN, SYRACUSE, N.Y.

RADIAL ENGINE AT REAR

KELSEY

FRICTION DRIVE

6 CYLS. (1921)
4 " (1922 ON)

KELSEY MOTOR CO., NEWARK and BELLEVILLE, N.J.

(1921 - 1924)

32 x 4 TIRES FOR '24, 206.4 CID LYCOMING REPLACES 192.4 CID G-B ENGINE.

EARLIEST KELSEYS HAVE "OWN ENGINE" (FALLS 195.6 CID)

116" W.B.

KENWORTHY

KENWORTHY MOTORS OF NEW ENGLAND; BOSTON, MASS.

(1920 - 1922)

(FACTORY IN MISHAWAKA, IND.)

NOTE PEAKED RADIATOR

"8-90" — OWN STRAIGHT-8
296.9 C.I.D. (3" x 5 1/4")
"LINE-O-EIGHT" ENGINE
130" W.B.   4.08 G.R.
32 x 4 1/2 TIRES

21

('22 SIMILAR)

(4-WHEEL BRAKES AVAILABLE.)

V-8 ENGINE
(INTRO. 2-15)

KING

KING MOTOR CAR CO., DETROIT
(1910-1923)

(PRODUCED IN BUFFALO, N.Y., 1923-1924)

('22)

20

21-23

SEDANETTE (4-PASS.)

KISSEL

KISSEL MOTOR CAR CO.
HARTFORD, WISCONSIN
(1906-1931)

The Custom **Built Car**

SPEEDSTER

4-DR. COACH-SEDAN
(INTRO. 1-8-21)

3.62 G.R. REPLACED
BY 4.25 G.R. IN '21.

BOSCH IGNITION ('20)
REMY IGNITION
('21 ON)

4-PASS. COUPE
4-PASS. TOURSTER

124" W.B.
(THROUGH '23)
OWN 6-CYL.,
284.4 C.I.D. ENGINE
(THROUGH '23)
32 × 4 TIRES
(THROUGH '23)

19-22

'22 IS FIRST YEAR WITH SELF-LUBRICATING BRONZE BUSHINGS
ON BRAKE MECHANISM.

POPULARLY KNOWN
AS "GOLD BUG"

DRUM HEADLIGHTS, 1-PC.
WINDSHIELDS

23-24

'24= OIL TEST
GAUGE
ROD ON
LEFT
SIDE
OF
ENG.

4.4 G.R.
IN '23

1923 "45" SERIES IS
JOINED BY
NEW "55" SERIES
NEW 121" W.B.,
SMALLER 6-CYL.
265 (264.8) C.I.D.
ENGINE (USED ON
6-CYL. CHASSIS
THROUGH '27)

BROUGHAM

6-CYL. 1925 "55" IS
FINAL KISSEL TO OFFER
2-WHEEL MECHANICAL
BRAKES.

70 M.P.H.
"6-55"

25-26

OIL TEST GAUGE ROD
IS ELIMINATED (1925)

"8-75"
STRAIGHT-8
MODEL INTRODUCED
JANUARY, 1925.
(HAS HYDR. BRAKES)
287.3 CID, 63 H.P. @ 2400 ('25)
310 CID, 71 H.P. @ 3100 ('26)

75 M.P.H. TOP SPEED

50
H.P.
@
2800 RPM
(53 @ 2300 IN '26)

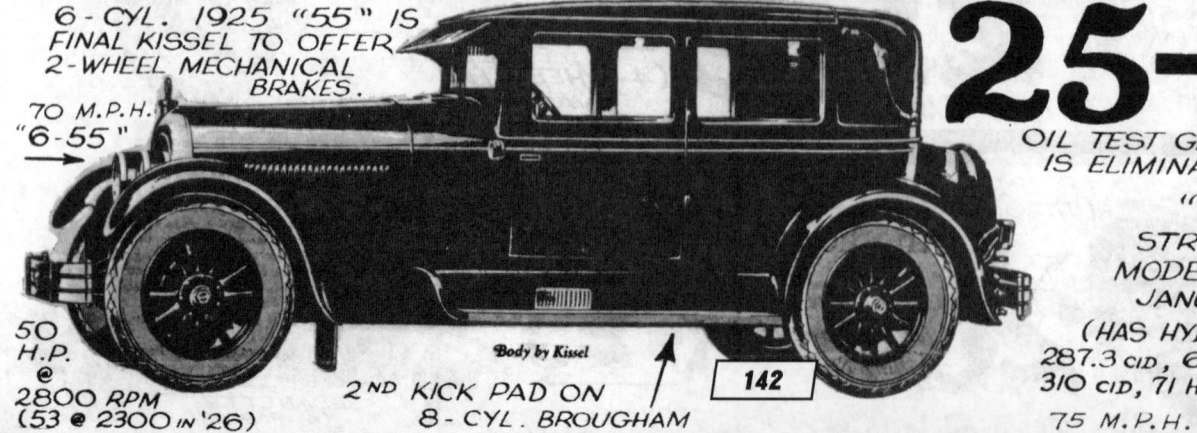

Body by Kissel

2ND KICK PAD ON
8-CYL. BROUGHAM

KISSEL

27

HYDRAULIC BRAKES ON ALL '26-'27 KISSELS.

4.6 G.R. ("8-65")   HEAVIER WHEEL SPOKES
'27 ENGINES CUSHIONED IN RUBBER

"6-55"   124-131" W.B.
264.8 C.I.D. 61 H.P. @ 2300

"8-65"   125-132"
W.B., NEW SMALL 8
(246.5 C.I.D.)(THROUGH '31)
65 H.P. @ 2000 RPM

8

"8-75" 131" W.B.
287.8 C.I.D., 71 H.P. @ 3000 RPM
(139" W.B. ALSO AVAIL.)

28

new, SMALL 185 C.I.D. 6
IN 117" W.B. "6-70"
52 H.P. @ 2900 RPM
(THROUGH '29)
4.63 G.R. 30 × 6.00 TIRES

(8-80) "SMALL 8" 4-DOOR
BROUGHAM
(REPLACES 8-65.
BUT HAS 70 H.P. @ 2900.
4.6 G.R. 31 × 6.20 TIRES)

HYDRAULIC BRAKES
CONTINUED
(THROUGH '31)

"8-80-S" has
125" W.B., 30 × 6.00 TIRES,
4.8 G.R.

1928 = NEW BODIES AND
ILCO-RYAN HEADLIGHTS; WATER
TEMP. GAUGE
ON DASH.

"8-90"

"8-75"
BECOMES "8-90" FOR '28,
WITH 85 H.P. @ 3100 RPM,
4.89 G.R., 30 × 6.75 TIRES
131" OR 139" W.B.

SPEEDSTER

VACUUM-
TANK FUEL FEED
CONTINUED
ON ALL MODELS
(TO '31)

125-132" W.B.

"95" COUPE-ROADSTER
(8 CYL.)
246.5 C.I.D.
95 H.P. @ 3200 RPM
4.8 G.R. (5.1 IN '30)
6.00 × 18 TIRES (ALSO
ON "6-73")

132-139" W.B.

30 × 6.75
TIRES
('29)

"126"
BROUGHAM
(8 CYL.)

298.6 C.I.D. 126 H.P.
4.89 G.R. (4.8 IN '30)
7.00 × 16 TIRES IN '30)

29-31

"WHITE EAGLE"
MODELS
(BEGIN AUG. 15, 1928)

1931
MODEL
IS FINAL
KISSEL.

MODEL "73" = 6 CYL. (185 C.I.D.)
52 H.P. @ 2900 ('29)   117" W.B.
75 H.P. @ 3500 ('30-31)
4.6 G.R. (5.3 IN '30)

STARTS 7-1-30

Kleiber

KLEIBER MOTOR CO.

(CARS = 1924-1929)
ALSO BUILT TRUCKS

11th and Folsom Sts.
SAN FRANCISCO

1800 E. 12th St.
OAKLAND

11th and San Pedro Sts.
LOS ANGELES

'27
(6)

'29
(8)

CONTINENTAL "8-R" 6-CYL. 241.6 C.I.D. ENGINE
55 H.P. @ 2300 RPM
122" W.B., 32 × 6.20 TIRES

'29 DASH →
(INSTRUMENTS SET IN BLACK WOOD
PANEL; OUTDATED STYLE FOR 1929!)

KLINE KAR

(1910 - 1923)

SINCE 1912, BLT. BY KLINE MOTOR CAR CORP., RICHMOND, VA.

20-22

"6-55" 121" W.B. 224 C.I.D.
6-CYL. CONTINENTAL ENGINE

"6-60" (1923) HAS 241.5 C.I.D.

LaFAYETTE

(1919 TO 1924)

LaFAYETTE MOTORS CORPORATION
Milwaukee, Wisconsin

20

132" W.B. V-8 ENGINE 348.4 C.I.D. (THROUGH '24) 100 H.P.

21
4.5 G.R.

The Four-Door Coupe (NEW)

(COMPANY ORIGINATED AT
INDIANAPOLIS, INDIANA)

22-23

THOUGH NEW BODY TYPES APPEARED, THE MODEL "134" DIDN'T FEATURE NOTEWORTHY CHANGES BETWEEN 1920 and 1924.

33 × 5 TIRES ON ALL

NEW ↑ 4.58 G.R.
PULL-TYPE HOOD FASTENERS and COWL BELT, LATE 1923

FRONT END, SHOWING RADIATOR SHUTTERS

CO. ABSORBED BY NASH. LA FAYETTE NAME APPEARS AGAIN IN 1934, ON LOW-PRICED CAR.

24

144

6 - CYLINDER
L - HEAD
ENGINE

LaFAYETTE

NASH BUILT

COUPE (ACTUAL PHOTO)

34

113" W.B. (THROUGH '36)

217.8 C.I.D. (THROUGH '36)
75 H.P. @ 3200 RPM
(THROUGH '35)
4.7 GEAR RATIO (THROUGH '35)

NEW 6.00 x 16 TIRES
AUTOMATIC STARTER WITH
CLUTCH PEDAL CONTROL.
3 HORIZONTAL LOUVRES
(INSTEAD OF VENT DOORS
ON HOOD)

CHASSIS

35

→

COUPE
(GROSSLY
EXAGGERATED
ARTIST'S
CONCEPTION
OF 1935.)

LaFAYETTE

ENGINE (7-BEARING)

NOTE HOW ENTIRE TRUNK BULGE OPENS, ON SEDAN

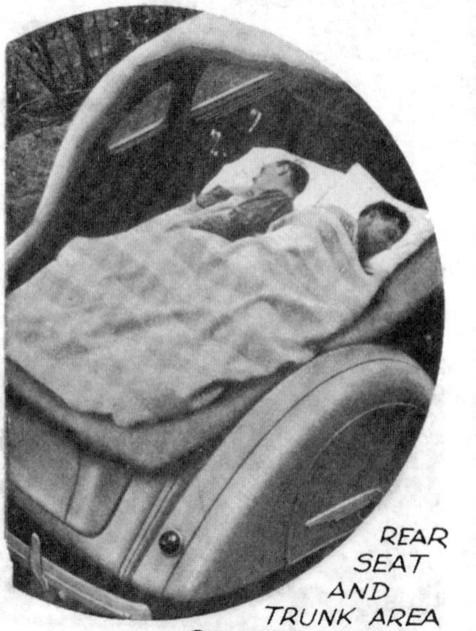

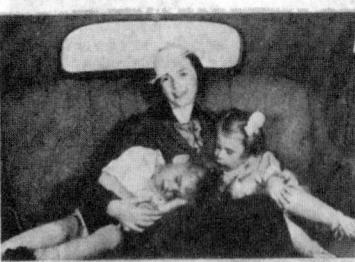

REAR SEAT, SHOWING UPHOLSTERY PATTERN

36

SEAMLESS ALL-STEEL TOP (ON LAFAYETTE OR NASH "400")

REAR SEAT AND TRUNK AREA CONVERTS TO A 6' DOUBLE BED (IN LAFAYETTE OR NASH "400" SEDANS)

NEW = HYDRAULIC BRAKES
4.4 GEAR RATIO

LATE MODELS HAVE DIE-CAST GRILLE.

FENDER SKIRTS AVAIL.

37

117" WHEELBASE AND SPECIFICATIONS SIMILAR TO '36 NASH "400."

4.11 GEAR RATIO

BECAME THE NASH-LAFAYETTE "400"

LaSalle

INTRO.
MARCH
1927

V-8
L-HEAD
ENGINE
(all years
except
'34 THROUGH
'36)

303 C.I.D.
(THROUGH '28)

27

MODEL
"303"

OPAQUED
GLASS VISOR

28

SEPT., 1927 = ELECTRO
LOCK ON DASHBOARD
REPLACES
TRANSMISSION
LOCK.

"303"
NEW,
NARROWER
HOOD LOUVRES

"HEAT ON AND OFF" CONTROL LEVER
ADDED ON LEFT SIDE OF DASH.

80 H.P. @ 3000 RPM
4.8 COMPRESSION

4.54 OR 4.91 GEAR RATIO
(THROUGH '29)

125 OR 134" WHEELBASE (THROUGH '29)

CHROME-PLATING ON ALL BRIGHTWORK
PARKING LAMPS MOVED TO
FRONT FENDERS

FISHER OR
FLEETWOOD
BODIES

327.7 C.I.D.
86 H.P. @ 3000 RPM
5.3 and other COMPRESSION RATIOS

INSTRUMENT PANEL DESIGN
SIMILAR TO CADILLAC'S.

SYNCHRO-MESH TRANSMISSION
(ALSO ON CADILLAC)

29

"328"

REAR SECTION OF
TOP FOLDS DOWN

(FUEL PUMP USED DURING '29)

147

LaSalle

30
"340"

340 C.I.D.
90 H.P. @
3000 RPM
5.18 COMPR.

THESE CARS
CARRIED INTO
EARLY '31.

VACUUM FUEL FEED RETURNS
(THROUGH '31)

DASH
(OPEN
MODELS)

6.50 × 19

134" W.B.
(THROUGH '31)

4.5 and other
GEAR RATIOS

ALL 1931 La SALLES
have 1-PIECE
BUMPERS.

(EARLIEST 1931 La SALLES have
VERTICAL HOOD LOUVRES
AS IN '30.)

MOST, BUT NOT ALL, have RADIATOR STONE GUARD.

31
"345"
(345-A)

353 C.I.D.
(THROUGH '33)

95 H.P. @
3000 RPM
5.35 COMPR.

6.50 × 19

4.5, 4.75
OR 4.91
GEAR RATIOS

LaSalle

FUEL PUMP RETURNS

4.6 GEAR RATIO (THROUGH '33)

7.00 x 17

32

"345-B"

115 H.P. @ 3000 RPM (THROUGH '33)

5.38 COMPR.

130" and 136" W.B. (THROUGH '33)

'33 DASH

"HERON" RADIATOR MASCOT with FILLER UNDER HOOD

33

"345-C"

BENDIX POWER BRAKES

5.40 COMPR.

GRACEFUL NEW STREAMLINING HYDRAULIC BRAKES 119" W.B.

34

MODEL "350"

7.00 x 16 TIRES (THROUGH '40)

STRAIGHT-8 ENGINE REPLACES V-8 (THROUGH '36)

240.3 C.I.D. 90 H.P. @ 3700 RPM

6.50 or 5.75 COMPR.

COUPE WITH BOTH RUMBLE-SEAT AND TRUNK

4.78 GEAR RATIO ('34 and '35)

35

"50" SERIES (CONT'D. TO '40)

(PUSH-BUTTON STARTER)

120" W.B. ('35 and '36)
105 H.P. @ 3600 RPM ('35 and '36)
6.50 or 5.75 COMPR.

V-WINDSHIELD, STEEL TOP

4.55 GEAR RATIO

36

HAND-BRAKE LEVER AT LEFT SIDE OF COWL.
6.25 or 5.75 COMPR. (THROUGH '40)

V-8 La Salle

LA SALLE V-8 PERFORMANCE COULD ONLY COME FROM CADILLAC—PIONEER AND LEADER IN FINE V-8 DESIGN SINCE 1914

CADILLAC MOTOR

NEW ENGINE has 322 C.I.D. (THROUGH '40) 125 H.P. @ 3400 RPM (THROUGH '39)

37

3.92 GEAR RATIO (THROUGH '40)

'38 INTERIOR

38

HOOD HINGED AT REAR, EXTENDS TO GRILLE WHICH IS 2" WIDER FOR 1938.

39

SLIDING "SUNSHINE ROOF" OPTIONAL (2-DR. and 4-DR. SEDANS)

NUVO CORD OR RIBBED BROADCLOTH UPHOLSTERY

LEACH
(1920-1923)
LEACH MOTOR CAR CO.,
LOS ANGELES, CALIF.

CONTINENTAL 6-CYL. 303.1 C.I.D. ENGINE IN '20 and '21

126½" W.B. ('20)
128" W.B. ('21)

32 × 4½ TIRES

BEAR RADIATOR EMBLEM
(LEACH-BILTWELL)

('22) 134" W.B.

OWN "POWER PLUS 6" O.H.C. engine (347.9 CID) DELCO IGN. IN '22-'23 MODEL "999"

(FEATURED NEW "CALIFORNIA TOP" WITH SLIDING WINDOWS.)

LEON RUBAY

118" W.B.
5.10 G.R.

(1922-1924)
RUBAY CO., CLEVELAND, OHIO

OWN 122 C.I.D. 4-CYL. O.H.C. engine

(4-WHEEL BRAKES)

BOSCH IGNITION

32 × 4

20 LEXINGTON (1909-1928)

6 CYL. L-HEAD 224 C.I.D. CONTINENTAL engine

"Minute Man Six" ("S")

LEXINGTON MOTOR CO., CONNERSVILLE, INDIANA (ORIGINATED IN LEXINGTON, KY.)

NO NEW MODEL LISTED AFTER 1926.

123" W.B. "U" SERIES STARTS 1-22

"20" W.B.

"MINUTE MAN" JOINED BY NEW "CONCORD" SERIES IN 1924, WITH 232.7 C.I.D. ANSTED O.H.V. 6-CYL. ENGINE

new '21 SERIES "T"
(NEW ANSTED 6 CYL. O.H.V. ENGINES) (MODEL "S" CONTINUED)

"Lark" MODEL 1921½-1922

128" W.B.

119" W.B., 32 × 4 TIRES

·FOLDED IN MID-20s, TAKEN OVER BY AUBURN

('23 =ABSORBED BY COLUMBIA)

117" W.B.

('21)

"10-C" OWN 6-CYL., 230.1 CID L-HEAD ENG. (Wagner IGN.)

LIBERTY SIX

('20) Liberty Motor Car Company, Detroit (1916-1924)

'22 SERIES "10-D"
4.66 G.R.

DRUM HEADLIGHTS IN 1922

LIBERTY

4.8 G.R. IN '23-'24

32 × 4 TIRES

151

Henry M. Leland
President
and
FOUNDER

LINCOLN
MOTOR CARS
LELAND–BUILT

LINCOLN MOTOR COMPANY
DETROIT, MICH.

Wilfred C. Leland
Vice-Pres. and Gen. Mgr.

V-8
(357.8 C.I.D.)
(THROUGH 1927)

OWN
CARBURETOR
FOR 1921

7-PASS.
TOURING CAR

33 x 5

Lincoln Intake Manifold with Carburetor and Electro-Fog Producer

*In the illustration, the intake manifold is
shown in section. The upper passage (A) is
for hot water; the lower passage (C) for hot
exhaust gases, and the passage between (B)
for intake gas mixture. The retort where
fuel is converted into fog is shown at "D"*

5-PASS.
TOURING
CAR

21
(STARTS AUTUMN,
1920)

130" WHEELBASE

(136" W.B. ON LIMOUSINE
AND TOWN CAR)
4.45 GEAR RATIO

DELCO IGNITION
(THROUGH '27)

33 x 5

152

70 MILES PER HOUR

LINCOLN

STANDARD WHEELBASE 136"
(THROUGH '30)

new STROMBERG
CARBURETOR
90 H.P.

SEVEN PASSENGER SEDAN

22

1-22 = FORD
MOTOR CO.
PURCHASES
LINCOLN MOTOR CO.

4-PASS.
SEDAN

DRUM HEADLIGHTS
ON MOST 1923
LINCOLNS.

7-PASS. TOURING CAR

33 × 5 TIRES CONT'D. (THROUGH '27)

23

JUDKINS COUPE
(A SIMILAR COUPE WITH 1921-STYLE
"REVERSED" REAR FENDERS ALSO AVAIL.)

95 H.P. @ 2800 RPM
(THROUGH '24)

7-PASS. SEDAN

LINCOLN

24

MODEL "124"

25

VERTICAL
RADIATOR SHUTTERS

MODEL "124"

LINCOLN

JUDKINS THREE-WINDOW BERLINE

90 H.P.
@ 2800 RPM
(THROUGH '27)

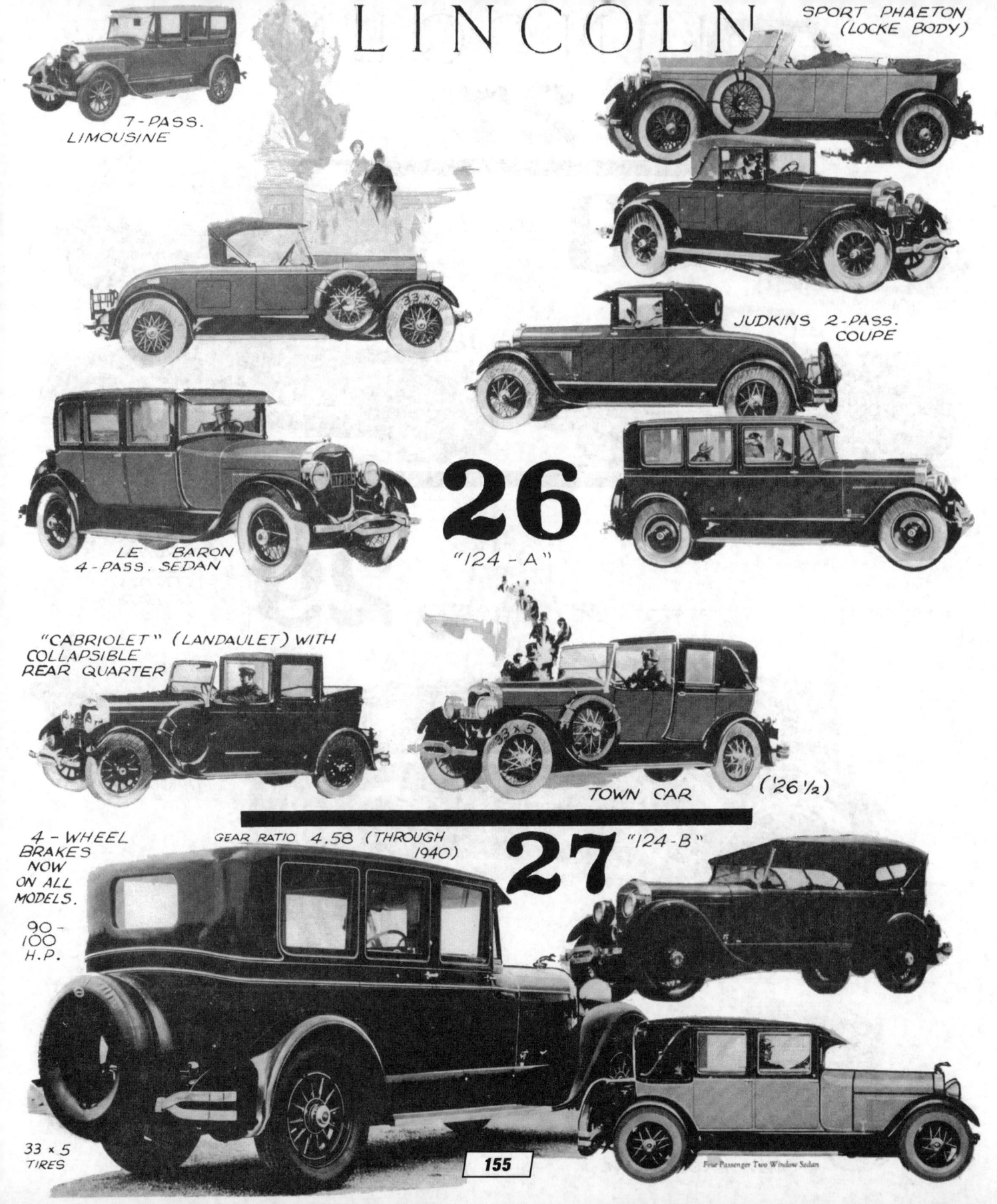

LINCOLN

SPORT PHAETON
(LOCKE BODY)

7-PASS.
LIMOUSINE

JUDKINS 2-PASS.
COUPE

LE BARON
4-PASS. SEDAN

26

"124-A"

"CABRIOLET" (LANDAULET) WITH
COLLAPSIBLE
REAR QUARTER

TOWN CAR   ('26½)

GEAR RATIO 4.58 (THROUGH 1940)   **27**   "124-B"

4-WHEEL
BRAKES
NOW
ON ALL
MODELS.

90-
100
H.P.

33 x 5
TIRES

Four Passenger Two Window Sedan

LINCOLN

27½

The Lincoln Four-Passenger Coupe

MODEL "152"

28

JUDKINS TWO-WINDOW BERLINE

33 x 5.50 TIRES

DELCO - REMY IGNITION (TO '31)

Club Roadster

29

BODIES BY
JUDKINS
DIETRICH
WILLOUGHBY
BRUNN
HOLBROOK
CENTRAL
LE BARON
ETC.

1929 — LE BARON AERO-PHAETON

90 H.P. @ 2800 RPM
(THROUGH '30)

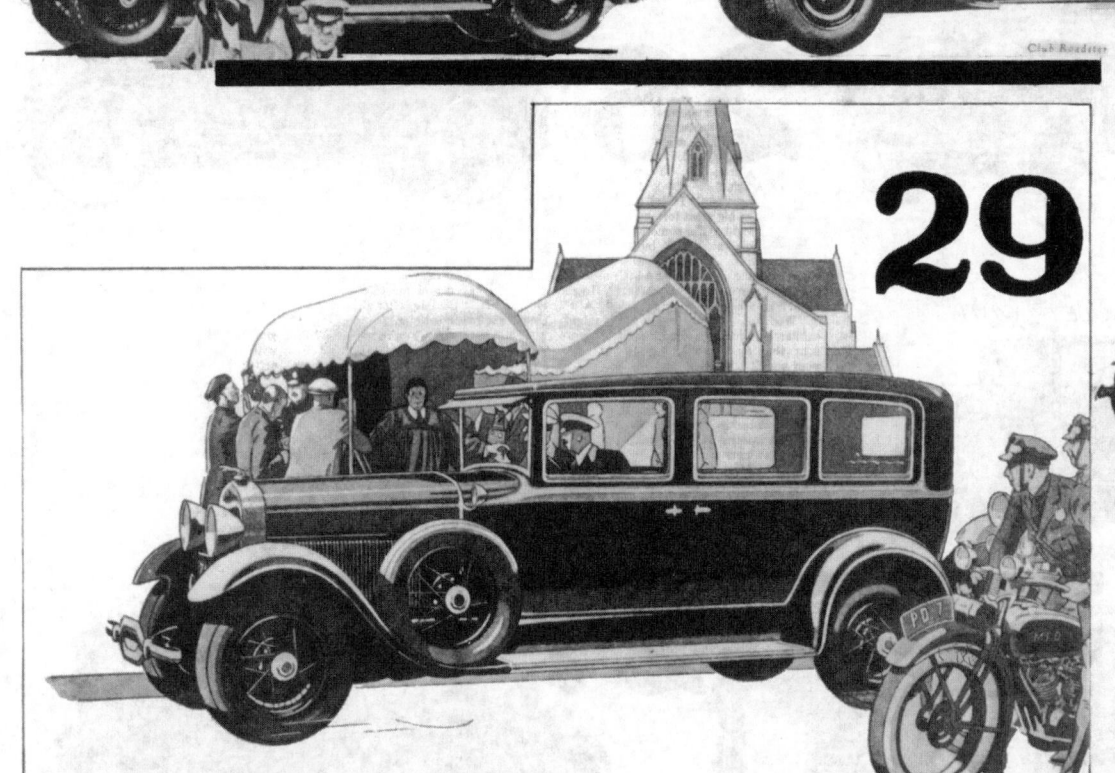

7.00 x 20" (32 x 6.75) TIRES

TOWN BROUGHAM

TOWN SEDAN

LINCOLN

1930 — BRUNN CABRIOLET

30

MODEL "169-B"
7.00 x 20
TIRES

SPORT TOURING
120 H.P. @
2900 RPM

7.00 x 19" TIRES

31

CONVERT.
VICTORIA

(BODY BY WATERHOUSE)

NEW 145" W.B.

INTERIOR

MODEL "204-A"

157

VACUUM FUEL FEED REPLACED BY
NEW FUEL PUMP

LINCOLN

4-PASSENGER PHAETON

V-8

120-125 H.P. @ 2900 RPM

7.00 × 18" TIRES ON V-8

"2-WINDOW TOWN SEDAN

136" W.B. ON V-8 "234-B"

V-12 (NEW)

32

V-12

WILLOUGHBY LIMOUSINE

145" W. B. ON V-12 "235"

V-12 HAS 447.9 C.I.D. ENGINE, WITH 150 H.P. @ 3400 RPM

7.50 × 18

TOWN CAR

(V-12) K-B

INT.

AUTO-LITE IGN.

DUAL-COWL PHAETON

158

LINCOLN

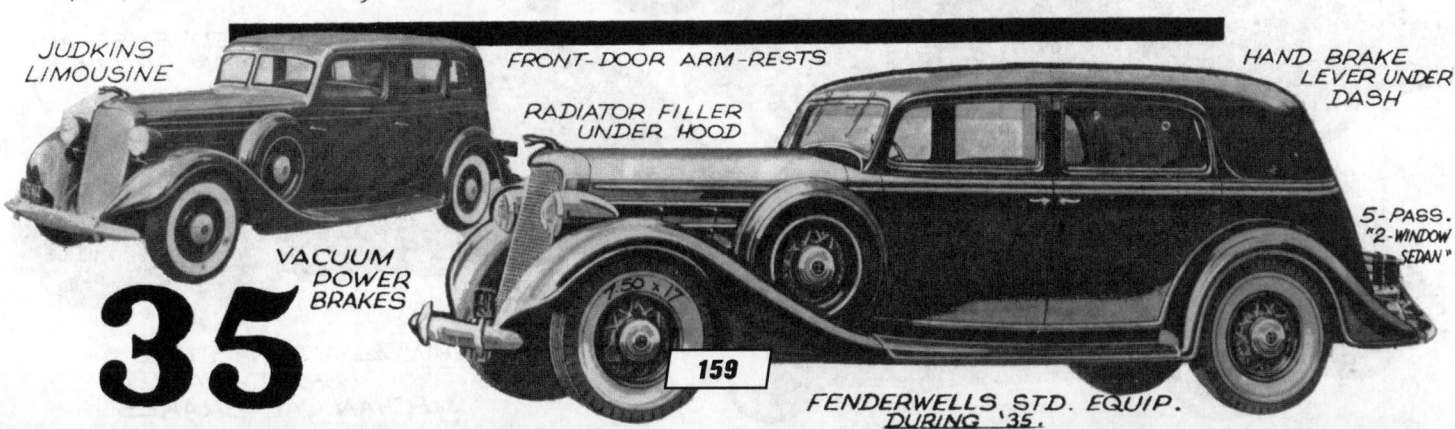

136" and 145" WHEELBASES

2-TONE
HORNS
BEHIND GRILLE

33

381.7-C.I.D. and 447-C.I.D. V-12 ENGINES (125 and 150 H.P. @ 3400 RPM)

ALL MODELS ADOPT SAME
TYPE OF 150-H.P. (@ 3400)
V-12 ENGINE.
(414 C.I.D.)
THIS ENGINE USED WITH
SAME SPECS. IN ALL LARGE ("K")
LINCOLNS FROM 1934 THROUGH
1940.)

HOOD VENT DOORS
THERMOSTATICALLY
CONTROLLED

LeBARON CONVERTIBLE ROADSTER

custom-built types by Judkins,
Brunn, Willoughby, Dietrich and Le Baron.

7.50 × 18 TIRES ON
145"-W.B. CUSTOM
200 SERIES

THE TWO-WINDOW TOWN SEDAN

136" and 145" W.B.
(THROUGH '40)
7.00/7.50 × 18 TIRES
(AS IN '33) (500 SER.)
4.58 GEAR RATIO
(THROUGH '40 "K")

34

MECHANICAL
VACUUM BOOSTER
BRAKES

THE FIVE-PASSENGER CONVERTIBLE SEDAN-PHAETON

JUDKINS
LIMOUSINE

FRONT-DOOR ARM-RESTS

RADIATOR FILLER
UNDER HOOD

HAND BRAKE
LEVER UNDER
DASH

35

VACUUM
POWER
BRAKES

5-PASS.
"2-WINDOW
SEDAN"

159

FENDERWELLS STD. EQUIP.
DURING '35.

LINCOLN

Lincoln Zephyr V-12 (NEW)

BLUE EMBLEM ON GRILLE

ZEPHYR OF 1936 THROUGH 1936 HAS 267.3 C.I.D. V-12 ENGINE (110 H.P. @ 3800-3900 RPM)

4.33 GEAR RATIO, 122" W.B. (THROUGH '37)
7.00 × 16" TIRES (THROUGH '41)

BRUNN "CABRIOLET"

BRUNN CVT. VICTORIA

36

MECHANICAL BRAKES (all)

BRIGHT METAL SPOKES ON STEERING WHEEL

37

ENTIRE LUGGAGE / TIRE COMPART. NOW ACCESSIBLE THROUGH THE TRUNK DOOR.

RED EMBLEM ON GRILLE

ZEPHYR

new QUIETER FAN has ALTERNATE LONG and SHORT BLADES.
MECHANICAL BRAKES

new V-SHAPED WINDSHIELD (K)

2-WINDOW BERLINE

LINCOLN

37 (CONT'D.)

BRUNN TOURING CABRIOLET

LIMOUSINE (WILLOUGHBY BODY)

HEADLIGHTS SUNKEN IN FENDERS →

VACUUM BOOSTER ON MODEL "K" BRAKES

ZEPHYR HAS NEW 125" W.B. AND 4.44 GEAR RATIO

38

LE BARON CONVERTIBLE SEDAN

ZEPHYR (RESTYLED)

The **LINCOLN**

STROMBERG CARB. (SINCE '22)

ZEPHYR HAS OWN IGNITION SYSTEM (SINCE '36)

ZEPHYR

CONTINUED USE OF AUTO-LITE IGNITION and 7.50 × 17" TIRES ON LARGE LINCOLNS

LARGE "K" TYPE DISCONTINUED AFTER '40

ZEPHYR GETS HYDRAULIC BRAKES

39

LOCOMOBILE

LOCOMOBILE CO.
OF AMERICA, INC.
BRIDGEPORT, CONN.
(1899 – 1929)

SPECIAL LOCOMOBILE SEDAN

"GUNBOAT" ROADSTER

17-29

(6 CYL.) MODEL "48"
OWN T-HEAD ENG.

TYPICAL HEADLIGHTS →

SPECIAL GROWLER COUPE
A type adapted from the old London Four Wheeler

524.8 C.I.D.
(THROUGH '29
103 H.P. @ 2100 RPM ('25-'26)
105 " ('27 ON)

NO DRASTIC MODEL CHANGES IN MODEL "48"
DURING MOST YEARS IT WAS AVAILABLE, BUT
GRADUAL REFINEMENTS WERE INCORPORATED.
THE "48" WAS LOCOMOBILE'S LARGEST CAR.
142" W.B.

AFTER EARLY 1920s, ('22)
DRUM HEADLIGHTS
USED FREQUENTLY →

('24) CUSTOM EXHAUST AND BRAKES

('23)

4-WHEEL
MECHANICAL BRAKES
ON ALL MODELS,
STARTING 1925.

3.5 GEAR RATIO ('24 ON)
BERLING IGN. REPLACED BY DELCO ('23 ON)
("48")

LATE "48s", LOWER-PRICED
MODELS ON
FOLLOWING PAGE.

('25)

Locomobile Junior Eight

OWN STRAIGHT - 8, L-HEAD
181.5 C.I.D. ENGINE   5.12 G.R.
63 H.P. @ 2800 RPM   124"
W.B.

25

"J-6" ALSO AVAIL.   6 CYL. OWN ENG.,
195.6 C.I.D.   4.77 G.R.
115" W.B.   30 × 5.77 TIRES

DE JON IGNITION USED ON
MOST '25-29 LOCOMOBILES (EXCEPT
"48")

26-27

JUNIOR 8 KNOWN
AS
"LOCOMOBILE
STRAIGHT 8"
IN 1927.

"90" has OWN
L-HEAD, 371.5 C.I.D.
ENGINE
86 to 90 H.P.
138" W.B.
4.5 and other G.R.s
(THROUGH '29)

33 × 6.75 TIRES
ON "90"

MODEL "90"
(INTRO. LATE 1925)
NOTE UNUSUAL STYLING
OF FRONT
PILLARS.

"48"
SPORTIF
(1927)

LYCOMING
STRAIGHT-8
ENGINES ON
'27-'29 "8-80"
AND '29 "8-88"

124" W.B.
"8-66 IS
AVAIL '27 (63 HP)
OWN O.H.V. ENG.

246.7 C.I.D., 4.77 G.R.
70
H.P.
@
3000

28

1928 "8-80" HAS WINDSHIELD
PILLARS AKIN TO MODEL 90.

130" W.B.
298.5 CID
90 H.P.
@ 3200
4.81 G.R.
32 × 6.00 TIRES
(THROUGH '29)

CONTINENTAL - ENGINED
1928 "8-70" HAS ROOF-VISOR, 122" W.B.
DRUM HEADLIGHTS, HOOD LOUVRES
LIKE 1927 "8," BUT RADIATOR SHAPED LIKE '29 (BUT WITH RADIMETER.)

LOCOMOBILE OR
CENTRAL
BODIES
"8-88"

130"
W.B.

115 H.P.
@ 3300 RPM

29 (FINAL YEAR)

"6-90"

SHOWN WITH OWNER:
GEO. BANCROFT (FILM STAR)

7-PASSENGER
SUBURBAN

SERIES 8
"48"

LORRAINE
(1920 –1922)

LORRAINE MOTORS CORP.,
GRAND RAPIDS, MICH.; DETROIT

114" W.B.

4-CYL., 192.4 C.I.D. HERSCHELL-SPILLMAN ENGINE

"21-R" ('21)

Maibohm

BUILT BY MAIBOHM, SANDUSKY, OHIO
(1916 to 1922)

6-CYL.
195.6 C.I.D.
FALLS ENGINE

20-22

MODEL "B"
116" W.B.

(REPLACED
BY
COURIER)

16-21

(1902 – 1933) MARMON

NORDYKE and MARMON, INDIANAPOLIS

136" W.B. (THROUGH '28)

MODEL "34"
(THROUGH '24)

('20)

DELCO IGNITION on ALL

6-CYL., O.H.V., 339.7 C.I.D.
(THROUGH '28)

3.75 G.R. and 32 x 4½ TIRES (THROUGH '23)

MODEL "34"
CONTINUES
FROM 1916.

EARLY '22 = DOES NOT
HAVE DRUM
HEADLIGHTS

22-23

HOOD LOUVRES
(INTRODUCED
DURING 1921.)

MARMON

7-PASS. PHAETON

24

4-WHEEL BRAKES OPTIONAL, IF DESIRED

NEW 4.10 GEAR RATIO (TO '26)
32 × 4½ OR 33 × 5 TIRES
(BALLOON TIRES AVAILABLE)

FINAL YEAR OF "34" SERIES

DURING LATE FEBRUARY, 1926, MANUFACTURER CHANGED NAME TO MARMON MOTOR CAR CO.

25-26

"74" SERIES

'25 HAS 82 H.P. @ 2650 RPM

" 4 DOOR BROUGHAM COUPE " ('25)

32 × 6.20 TIRES

'26 HAS 88 H.P. @ 2800 RPM, VARIOUS GEAR RATIOS

REAR DETAILS

← BROUGHAM ('26)

TOURING CAR

INTERIOR ('26) →

the little MARMON 8
AMERICA'S FIRST TRULY FINE SMALL CAR

(INTRO. JAN., 1927)

COUPE (WITH RUMBLE SEAT)

2-DOOR SEDAN

4-DOOR SEDAN

COLLAPSIBLE COUPE-ROADSTER (WITH R.S.)

4-PASS. SPEEDSTER (PHAETON)

new STRAIGHT-8, O.H.V.
190.1 C.I.D. ENGINE
64 H.P. @ 3200 RPM
116" W.B. 5.1 G.R.
70-75 MILES PER HOUR

2-PASS. SPEEDSTER (WITH RUMBLE SEAT)

HYPOID GEAR DRIVE

FEDCO I.D. NUMBERS

ELECTRIC CLOCK

27

4-WHEEL BRAKES ON BOTH SERIES

32 × 6.75 TIRES
4.1 G.R.

THIS 339.7 C.I.D. "E-75" 6-CYL. MODEL CONT'D. INTO 1928, BUT WITH LOWER H.P. RATING OF 75 @ 2800.

LATE '27s FEATURED UNUSUAL MARMON-VALENTINE "JEWEL COLORS."

84 H.P. @ 2700 RPM ('27)

COUPE-ROADSTER (NEW)

28

"68"
L-HEAD STR.-8
201.9 C.I.D.
72 H.P. @ 3200 RPM
114" W.B.
29 × 5.25 TIRES

4.9 GEAR RATIO

"78" O.H.V. STR.-8
216.8 C.I.D.
86 H.P. @ 3400 RPM

120" W.B., 29 × 5.50 TIRES

MARMON

THE NEW MARMON 68

THE NEW MARMON 78

"68" DASH

29

"68"

(STRAIGHT-8
ENGINES ONLY)
MOST SPECS.
AS IN 1928
HORIZONTAL HOOD LOUVRES
HAYES BODIES

"68" DISPLACEMENT UP TO 211.2, H.P. UP TO 76.
29 × 5.50
TIRES
(29 × 6.00
ON
"78")

"78" DASH
has CLOCK
AT LEFT
CENTER (BY
SPEED-
OMETER)

"8-69" = 118" W.B.
211.2 C.I.D.
84 H.P. @ 3400 RPM
4.9 G.R.   5.50 × 19 TIRES

"8-79" = 125" W.B.
303.2 C.I.D.
110 H.P. @ 3400 RPM
4.45 G.R.
6.00 × 19
TIRES

NEW HOOD VENT DOORS

30

ALL 1930 MARMONS HAVE
STRAIGHT-8, L-HEAD ENGINES.

"BIG 8" =
136" W.B.
315.2 C.I.D., 125 H.P.
@ 3400 RPM, 4.45 G.R.
6.50 × 19 TIRES

8
('31)

"8-69" BECOMES "70"
"8-79"
"BIG 8" BECOMES
"88" DURING 1931.

(8-CYL. SERIES DROPPED DURING 1932.)
'32 "8-125" has 130-136" W.B., 315.2 C.I.D., L-HEAD ENG. 125 H.P.
@ 3400
RPM

NOTE V-GRILLE
ON '32 "8-125"

31-33

167

7.00 ×
18 TIRES

200-H.P.
V-16
490.8 C.I.D., OHV, 145" W.B.

3.69 G.R.
IN '31;
3.78 ('32 ON)

"1934"
MODEL
AL90

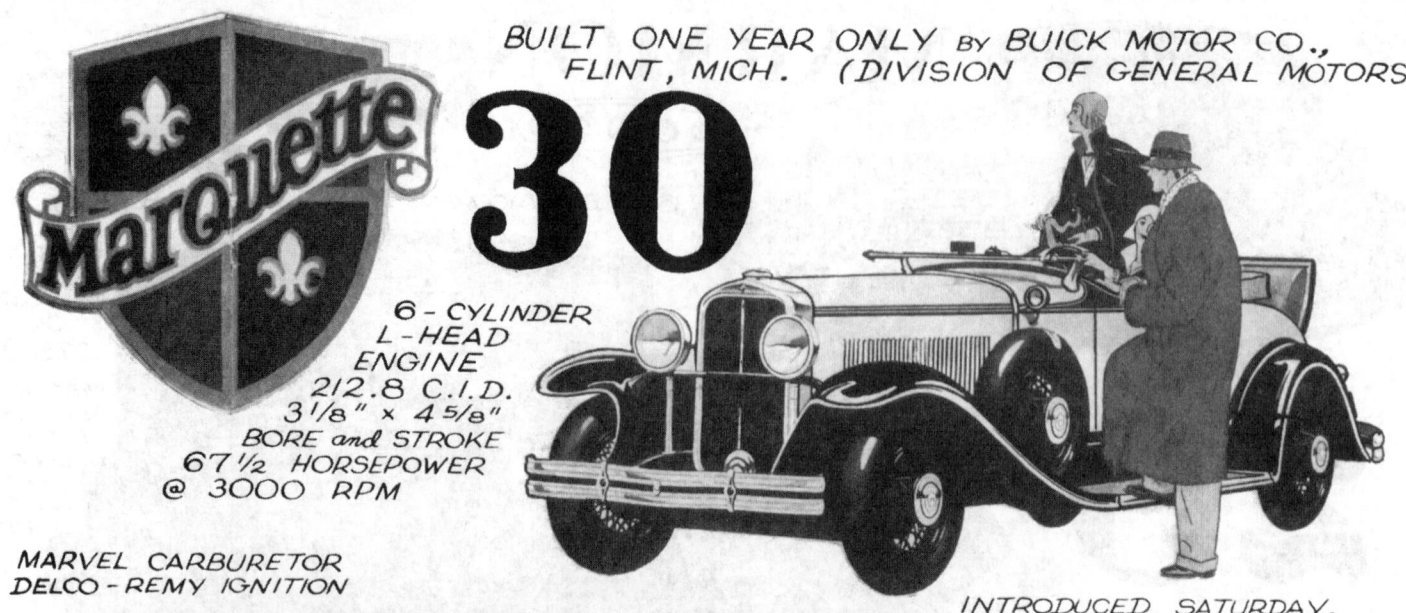

Marquette 30

BUILT ONE YEAR ONLY BY BUICK MOTOR CO., FLINT, MICH. (DIVISION OF GENERAL MOTORS)

6 - CYLINDER
L - HEAD
ENGINE
212.8 C.I.D.
3 1/8" × 4 5/8"
BORE and STROKE
67 1/2 HORSEPOWER
@ 3000 RPM

MARVEL CARBURETOR
DELCO - REMY IGNITION

INTRODUCED SATURDAY, JUNE 1, 1929.

114" WHEELBASE   4.54 GEAR RATIO
5.25 × 18 TIRES

BODY BY FISHER

MASTERBILT 6 (1926)
(AIR COOLED)

GOVRO - NELSON CO., DETROIT

ENGINEERED BY VICTOR GAVREAU, FORMERLY CHIEF ENGINEER OF THE PAN CAR.

MAINLY AN EXPERIMENT. NO DEALERSHIPS KNOWN TO HAVE EXISTED.

"RADIATOR" PLACED AHEAD OF FRONT AXLE

NO HOOD LOUVRES ON THIS PILOT MODEL.

MAXWELL

(1904 – 1925)

MAXWELL MOTOR COMPANY, INC.,

DETROIT, MICHIGAN

4 CYLS.
25 H.P.

(NEW CASTLE, INDIANA PLANT)

185.8 C.I.D. (THROUGH 1925)

109" WHEELBASE (THROUGH 1925)

30 x 3½

20-21

MODEL "25"

('21)

The Good Maxwell

NEW SERIES STARTS 11-21

22-24

CLUB COUPE

HORSEPOWER :
25 @ 1800 ('22)
30 @ 2150 ('23)
34 @ 2000 ('24)

EAGLE CARB. ('22)
STEWART CARB. ('23 THROUGH '25)

NEW EMBLEM

The CLUB SEDAN ('24)

PHANTOM VIEW, SHOWING WOODEN BODY FRAME

31 x 4

4.56 GEAR RATIO ('22)
4.6 ('23 -'25)

REMY IGNITION

58 MILES PER HOUR

NICKELED RADIATOR SHELL. ROOF-VISOR

25

GASOLINE

3.9 COMPRESSION

38 H.P. @ 2200 RPM
30 x 5.25 TIRES

REPLACED 6-25 BY CHRYSLER 4.

The New Good **MAXWELL**

MacDONALD (1923-1924) (STEAMER)

"BOBCAT" ROADSTER

MacDONALD STEAM AUTOMOTIVE CORP., GARFIELD, OHIO

McFARLAN (1910-1928)

McFARLAN MOTOR CAR CO., CONNERSVILLE, IND.

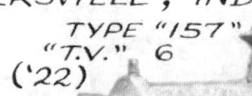

TYPE "157" "T.V." 6 ('22)

6-CYL. T-HEAD 572.5 C.I.D. ENGINE 140" W.B. 3.5 G.R.

7-PASS. SUBURBAN SEDAN

(SV)"LIGHT 6" ALSO AVAIL. IN 1924, WITH 127" W.B. 268.4 C.I.D. WISCONSIN ENG. 5.10 G.R.

'25 TOWN CAR

'26-7 8-IN-LINE "872" TOWN COUPE 131" W.B.

STRAIGHT-8 LYCOMING ENGINE 70 H.P. ('26) 79 H.P. ('27)

4-PASS. SPORTING

132" W.B. ('23)

MERCER (1910-1925)

MERCER AUTOMOBILE CO., TRENTON, N.J.

SERIES 5 = 4 CYLS. (298.2 C.I.D.) LARGER SERIES 6 (331.3 C.I.D., 6 CYL.) JOINS SERIES 5 IN '23

(2 1931 MERCER 8s BUILT BY ELCAR.)

RACEABOUT ('21)

SPORTS ROADSTER ('22)

MERCURY 8 (BEGINS WITH 1939 MODEL)

A PRODUCT OF THE [FORD MOTOR] R COMPANY
FORD MOTOR CO.

239 C.I.D. V-8

116" W.B.

39 95 H.P. @ 3600 RPM

REAR DETAILS (TRUNK OPEN)

MERCURY

MERCURY CARS, INC.
HOLLIS, N.Y.
(1918 – 1920) (4 CYL.)

METEOR

(1914 – 1930)
SHELBYVILLE, IND. and PIQUA, O.

('21)

METEOR MOTOR CAR CO.
Meteor
PIQUA, OHIO, U.S.A.

MILBURN
ELECTRIC

('21)

MODEL
"27-L"

(1914 – 1922) MILBURN WAGON CO.,
TOLEDO, OHIO

MILLER

(CUSTOM-BUILT)
V-8 OR
V-16

FRONT – WHEEL
DRIVE
SPEEDSTER

HARRY A. MILLER
(RELLIMAH, INC.)
LOS ANGELES,
CALIF.

31

"SPECIAL"

NEW, SLANTED
STYLING

MITCHELL
20-21

(1903 – 1923)

MITCHELL MOTORS CO.,
RACINE, WIS.
(MFR. NAME AS OF 1916 - 1923)

"F-40" 6-CYL., 248.9 CID
L-HEAD ENGINE 4.41 G.R.

FINAL "50" MODELS HAVE
CONVENTIONAL STYLING.

120" W.B.

MONITOR

(1915 - 1922)

MONITOR MOTOR CAR CO.,
COLUMBUS, OHIO

20

"B-50" and
"B-52" MODELS
IN 1921 (SAME
121" W.B.,
CONTINENTAL ENG.)

6-CYL. CONTINENTAL
"7-R" ENGINE
121" W.B. DISC WHEELS MODEL "M"

20

MONROE
FLINT, MICH.

(CONTROLLED BY
PREMIER,
1923-24)

(1914 – 1924)

(4 CYL.)

24

('24)

111" W.B.

('20)

"6-48" VICTORY
122" W.B.
224 C.I.D.
(THROUGH '22)
4.75 G.R.

32 × 4 TIRES   4.75 G.R.

"6-68"
125" W.B.
303.1 C.I.D.   33 × 5 TIRES
4.45 G.R.

MOON (1905-1929)
MOON HOOD
LOUVRES ARE
PUNCHED INWARD.
CHARACTERISTIC
PEAKED RADIATOR, 1919 THROUGH 1926

Built by
MOON MOTOR CAR COMPANY, St. LOUIS, U.S.A.

Moon's Ten Proven Units
1. Continental Red Seal Motor.   6. Borg & Beck Clutch.
2. Delco Starter and Ignition.   7. Rayfield Carburetor.
3. Timken Axles.   8. Exide Battery.
4. Spicer Universal Joints.   9. Fedders Radiator — Nickel-Silver.
5. Brown-Lipe Transmission.   10. Gemmer Steering Gear.

20
(6-CYL. ONLY,
UNTIL 1928)

"6-75"
('22 ONLY)
HAS 135" W.B.,
325.1 C.I.D.,
32 × 4½ TIRES
4.45 G.R.

('21 = DRUM HEADLIGHTS)

21-22

"6-48" →

(46 - H.P.
"6-40" STARTS 2-22)

(115" W.B.)
"6-40"

('24)

("6-58" STARTS
AUG., 1922
HAS
128" W.B.
241.6
C.I.D.
"8-R"
ENGINE
(TO '26)

D-27

115" W.B. "6-40" (U)
STARTING 8-23,
REPLACES
195.6 C.I.D.
"6-Y" ENG.
WITH 195.6
"7-U" ENG.
5.10 G.R.

23-24

("6-50" INTRO. DURING '24)

NEW "A"   113" W.B.
SERIES INTRODUCED 1924
LOCKHEED HYDRAULIC 4-WHEEL
BRAKES ALSO AVAILABLE (OPTIONAL).
("A" CONT'D. INTO '28)

60 M.P.H.

6-40 "NEWPORT" ('25)
50 H.P. @ 2600 RPM
6-50 "METROPOLITAN" ('25)
52 H.P. @ 2600 RPM
6-58 "LONDON"
56 H.P. @ 2300 RPM

25-26
(HYDRAULIC BRAKES,
NEW ROOF-VISOR)

('26 HAS HIGHER, NARROWER
RADIATOR, CROWN FENDERS.)

One of the Moon innovations of the year is this new Cabriolet roadster.
The deck lid opens up a fully upholstered rear seat "a deux." With the
lid down the car is a closed roadster. Concealed compartment for golf
bag and other luggage. Rear window may be lowered for communica-
tion between passengers.   (Patents applied for)

"A" HAS 113" W.B.
CONTINENTAL "7-Z" ENG.
50 H.P. @ 2600 RPM
30 × 5.25 TIRES

RADIATOR
DESIGN IS NEW.
USED 1
YEAR
ONLY.

27

NEW
"BULLET"
HEADLAMPS

"6-60" (new)
HAS
110" W.B.   185 C.I.D.
CONTINENTAL "26-L" ENG.
47 H.P. @ 2600 RPM
29 × 4.75 TIRES
(CONT'D. INTO 1928)

FINAL "A" ('28)
SOMETIMES KNOWN
AS 6-A.

new "6-72" (ROYAL)
HAS OLD-STYLE
BODY AND
ROOF-VISOR
BUT NEW
RADIATOR
DESIGN.

28

6 OR
8
CYL.

NEW STRAIGHT-8 "8-80"
HAS 125" W.B., 268.6 C.I.D.
CONTINENTAL ENG., 86 H.P.
@ 3200 RPM, 31 × 6.20 TIRES,
4.63 G.R.

STARTING AUGUST, 1928,
A RE-STYLED
"6-72" CONT'D. INTO
'29 WITH SAME 120" W.B.,
214.7 C.I.D. "11-E"
CONTINENTAL ENG., 66 H.P.
@ 3150 RPM, 29 × 5.50
TIRES, 4.9 G.R.

('29-'30 WINDSOR CARS ALSO)

"6-72"

"AEROTYPE" 8-80
(DISC. LATE '28)

PETITE
SEDAN

BODY BY
UNION CITY

29

FOR 1920, 8 HOOD LOUVRES ON EACH SIDE, LARGER RADIATOR

MOORE

(1916-1921)
MOORE MOTOR VEH. CO., DANVILLE, ILLINOIS

4-CYL. GOLDEN, BELKNAP and SCHWARTZ ENGINE *
3¾" × 4¼" B.+S. 22 H.P.
4.25 G.R.
*-NEW TURNER and MOORE ENGINE ALSO.

20

MODEL "F-30"
106" W.B.

30 × 3½

FOR EXPORT TO ENGLAND — BRITISH BODIES INSTALLED ON MOST.
114" W.B. 4 CYL.

MORRISS - LONDON (1919-1925)
CROW-ELKHART MOTOR CAR CO.; CENTURY MOTOR CO., ELKHART, IND.

NASH (1917-1957)

THE NASH SIX

THE NASH MOTORS COMPANY, KENOSHA, WISCONSIN

"681" SERIES = 261.3 C.I.D.
(MODELS 681-687)

("685" COUPE)
('20)

"SPORT"

('20)

19-20

(6 CYL.)

"681" 6 CYL. O.H.V.
248.9 C.I.D.
55 H.P. @ 2400 RPM
121" WHEELBASE
4.50 GEAR RATIO

33 × 4

7-PASS. SEDAN

(NOTE THINNER HOOD LOUVRES)

"41"

112" WHEELBASE

4-CYL. SERIES
(INTRODUCED LATE IN 1920, CONTINUED INTO 1924.)
'21 = 165.9 C.I.D., 35 H.P. @ 2200 RPM
LATER = 178.9 C.I.D., 37 H.P. @ 2800 RPM

22½ ('23)

21-22

(1922 6-CYL. SERIES BEGINS OCT., 1921, WITH MODELS "691" THROUGH "698;"
GAS GAUGE ON DASH; NEW, MORE POWERFUL EMERGENCY BRAKE ON TRANSMISSION.)

(NOTE NEW DRUM HEADLIGHTS)

The New Five Passenger Six Cylinder Sedan

NASH

Nash Leads the World in Motor Car Value

"CARRIOLE"
(INTRODUCED
1922)

← 4 CYL. →

23-24

NASH

(LARGER
BRAKE DRUMS.)

STEP-PLATES
IN 1924

6-CYL. 4 PASS.
VICTORIA (1924 STYLE)

The Nash Model 694 Sedan

(1924 MODELS END JULY 31, 1924.)

25

AJAX HAS 169.7 C.I.D.,
40 H.P. @ 2400 RPM
108" W.B.

21 × 4.75
TIRES

SPECIAL 6
112" W.B.

4.88
GEAR
RATIO

AJAX
SIX
NASH-BUILT

NEW
L-HEAD
ENGINE

(INTRODUCED
MAY 26, 1925)

(WITH 4-WHEEL
MECHANICAL BRAKES)

Coffee Shop

207.1 C.I.D.
46 H.P. @
2200 RPM

174

SPECIAL
SIX SEDAN

NASH

Leads the World in Motor Car Value

25 (CONT'D.)

"4-DOOR COUPE"

4-Wheel Brakes

ADVANCED SIX

OVERHEAD-VALVE, 6 CYLS.
248.9 C.I.D.
60 H.P. @ 2400 RPM

33 x 6

127-inch Wheelbase
Five Passengers

121" W.B. ON SOME BODY TYPES

4.50 GEAR RATIO

26

Light Six
4-Door Sedan

LIGHT 6
(REPLACES
AJAX)

The New
Special Six Series

112½" W.B.

31 x 5.25

New Special Six Sedan

(JULY, 1925)

The New
Advanced Six Series →

"4-DOOR COUPE"

NASH

Leads the World in Motor Car Value

27

108" W.B.
170 C.I.D.
40 H.P. @ 2400

LIGHT 6

4.77 GEAR RATIO

DELUXE LIGHT 6

(WITH BUMPERS)

LIGHT 6

SPEC. 6 WITH CONVENTIONAL ROOFLINE →

4.67 GEAR RATIO   112½" W.B.

SPECIAL 6

224 C.I.D. (THROUGH '29)
52 H.P. @ 2600

CAVALIER SEDAN (WIRE WH. AVAIL.)

"241"

New Nash Attractions

7-bearing crankshaft motor —world's smoothest type— powers all new Nash models.

New-type crankcase "breather" which prevents crankcase dilution.

Rubber insulated motor supports—(standard Nash practice for some time).

New-design motor muffler deepening operative quietness.

Motor heat control by new thermostatic water regulator.

Oil screen "agitator" preventing oil coagulation in coldest weather.

And many other new improvements.

A NEW Instrument Board

and Greater
Front Compartment Convenience

27
(CONT'D.)

69 H.P. @ 2500 RPM

ADVANCED 6
VICTORIA
127" W.B.

AMBASSADOR

AMBASSADOR

AMBASSADOR
(ADVANCED 6)
and
CAVALIER
(SPECIAL 6)
SEDANS INTRODUCED
AT CHICAGO AUTOMOBILE
SHOW, JANUARY 29, 1927.

NASH

EMBLEM AND MASCOT (ABOVE)

LIGHT 6 REPLACED BY
STANDARD 6 ("321")
108 1/4" W.B. 4.77 GEAR RATIO
184.1 C.I.D.   30 × 5.00
45 H.P. @ 2600   TIRES (THROUGH
                  '29)

"325" COUPE
SPECIAL 6   ("331")
HAS 224 C.I.D.
52 H.P. @ 2600 RPM
4.88 GEAR RATIO (THROUGH '29)
112 3/4" (TIRES = 30 × 5.25)
W.B.

28

ADVANCED 6 "SEDAN FOR 5"
(COACH) RESEMBLES ABOVE CAR (AND
ALSO HAS SAME FRENCH ROOF-LINE.)

32 × 6.00 TIRES' (THROUGH '29)
("361" SERIES)
ADVANCED 6 HAS 70 H.P.
@ 2400 RPM

"AMBASSADOR" →
("367")

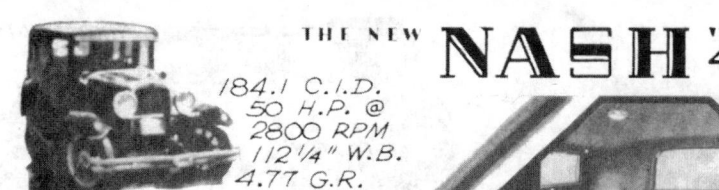

THE NEW NASH "400" SERIES

184.1 C.I.D.
50 H.P. @ 2800 RPM
112¼" W.B.
4.77 G.R.

STANDARD 6
(30 × 5.00 TIRES)

THE WORLD HAS A NEW AND FINER MOTOR CAR

Advanced Six Coupe

SPECIAL 6
(DUAL ROWS OF HOOD LOUVRES)
65 H.P. @ 2900 RPM
116" W.B.   29 × 5.50 TIRES

ADVANCED 6
78 H.P. @ 2900 RPM

29

ADVANCED 6   AMBASSADOR

NASH RADIATOR,
FITTED WITH USEFUL
ACCESSORY "ALLEN
VERTICAL SHUTTERS"
(SOLD SEPERATELY.)

BODIES BY NASH
OR SEAMAN

new = 2 SPARK PLUGS PER CYLINDER

Advanced Six Sedan

TWIN IGNITION MOTOR

29½ NASH

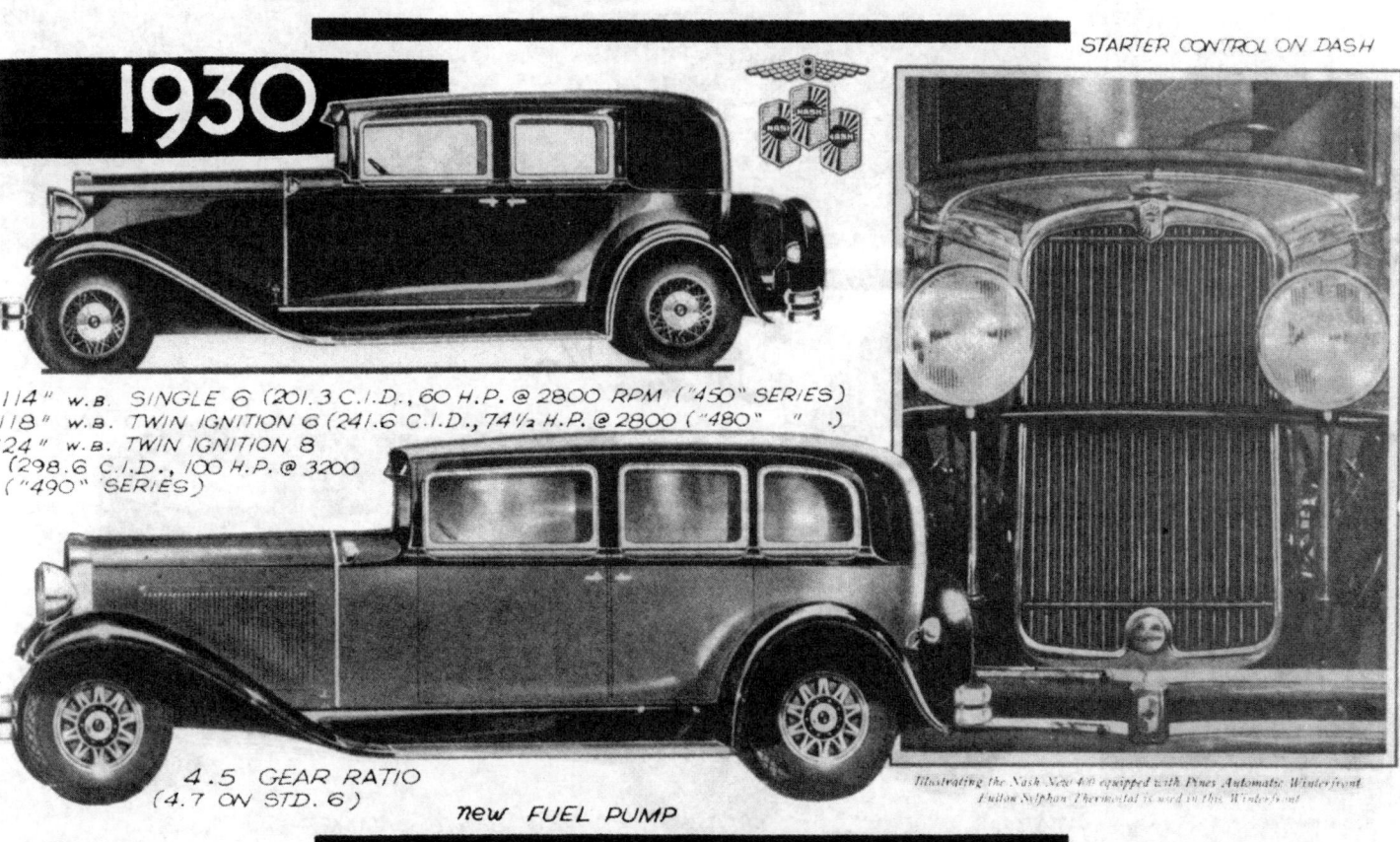

(MAY, 1929)

FINAL YEAR FOR VACUUM FUEL FEED.

FINAL YEAR OF 6-CYL. NASH CHOICES ONLY.

NEW "400" ROADSTER

1930

STARTER CONTROL ON DASH

114" W.B. SINGLE 6 (201.3 C.I.D., 60 H.P. @ 2800 RPM ("450" SERIES)
118" W.B. TWIN IGNITION 6 (241.6 C.I.D., 74½ H.P. @ 2800 ("480" " .)
124" W.B. TWIN IGNITION 8
(298.6 C.I.D., 100 H.P. @ 3200
("490" SERIES)

4.5 GEAR RATIO
(4.7 ON STD. 6)

new FUEL PUMP

Illustrating the Nash New 400 equipped with Pines Automatic Winterfront Fulton Sylphon Thermostat is used in this Winterfront

5.1, 5.1, 4.45, 4.5 RESPECTIVE GEAR RATIOS ON "6-60," "8-70," "8-80" and "8-90" SERIES

(INTRO. 10-30)

JAN., '31 = NEW "CONVERTIBLE SEDAN" (871 OR 881)

"8-70"

31

6-60 = 6 CYL., L-HEAD
201.3 CID   65 H.P.
114¼" WB, 5.00 × 19
TIRES (SPECS. THROUGH
EARLY '32 "960")

new
L-HEAD
STRAIGHT-8 "8-70"
227.2 CID   78 H.P.
(SPECS. THR. '32 "970")

116¼" WB
5.25 × 19
TIRES

8   TWIN IGN.
8-80 = STRAIGHT-8, O.H.V.
240.3 CID   87 H.P. @ 3400
121" WB,   5.50 × 18 TIRES
(94 H.P., 6.00 × 18 TIRES ON '32 "980")

TWIN IGN.
"8-90" = STRAIGHT-8, O.H.V.
298.6 CID   115 H.P. @ 3600 RPM
124-133" WB,   6.50 × 19 TIRES
(SPECS. THROUGH EARLY '32 "9 90")

NASH

NEW "V" GRILLE →

(INTRODUCED JUNE 28, 1931)

31½-32

EARLY '32s IN "900" MODEL SERIES

new SILENT-2ND SYNCHRO-SHIFT TRAN. and FREE-WHEELING

AMBASSADOR 8

32½

NEW BODY DESIGNS

STANDARD 8

INTRODUCED SATURDAY, FEB. 27, 1932

Beavertail Back of the new Nash Slip-Stream Body

RIDE CONTROL AVAIL.

5 NEW SERIES NAMES (AS IN '33)

EARLY '33 LOW-PRICED MODELS HAVE VERTICAL HOOD LOUVRES.

IN 5 SERIES :

BIG 6 === 116" WB, 75 H.P. @ 3200 RPM (217.8 CID)
STANDARD 8 === 116" WB, 80 H.P. @ 3200 RPM (247.4 CID)
SPECIAL 8 === 121" WB, 85 H.P. @ 3200 RPM   "   "
ADVANCED 8 === 128" WB, 100 H.P. @ 3400 RPM (260.8 CID)
AMBASSADOR 8 === 142" WB, 125 H.P. @ 3600 RPM (322 CID)
(OR 133")

33

MODEL "1194" AMB. 8 7-PASS.

142" W.B.

NASH

34

88-H.P. BIG 6 (234.8 CID)

IN ABOVE INTERIOR VIEW NOTE THE GROSS EXAGGERATION OF HOOD LENGTH (FROM AN ORIGINAL ADVERTISEMENT.)

AMBASSADOR

new HYDRAULIC BRAKES

35

BIG 6 BECOMES ADVANCED 6:

6.25 x 16 TIRES 120" W.B. (EARLY MODELS = 88 H.P. @ 3200 RPM) 4.4 G.R. (AS IN '34)

Super-Hydraulic Brakes
Automatic Cruising Gear
All-Steel, One-Piece Bodies
Synchronized Springing
Ball-Bearing Steering
Mid-Section Seating
Balanced Ride

Aeroform Design
Flying Power (Developed from Twin Ignition)

ADVANCED SIX VICTORIA **$895**
120" Wheelbase - 90 Horsepower

ADVANCED EIGHT VICTORIA **$1115**
125" Wheelbase - 102 Horsepower

AMBASSADOR EIGHT VICTORIA **$1240**
125" Wheelbase - 102 Horsepower

(EARLY MODELS OF ADV. 8, AMB. 8 100 H.P. @ 3400 RPM)

STARTING 1935, 1ST TWO DIGITS OF MODEL NO. INDICATES YEAR, BEGINNING WITH 3500 SERIES FOR 1935. SYSTEM USED ON NASH AND SUBSEQUENT AMERICAN MOTORS CARS.

181

NASH 36

ENGINE

EARLIEST "400" MODELS (STARTING AT # C-1001) ARE SOMETIMES LISTED AS LATE 1935 MODELS.

NASH 400 — MONITOR-SEALED MOTOR $675 *New!*

("400" (STARTS MAY, 1935)

"400" HAS 117" W.B., 6 CYL. 234.8 C.I.D., 90 H.P. @ 3400 RPM

4.1 GEAR RATIO

L-HEAD ENGINE ON "400"

"400" has 6.00 x 16 TIRES

"400" DELUXE

60½ IN.

SAME C.I.D. ON "400" and AMB. 6

ADVANCED 6 BECOMES AMBASSADOR 6

6.25 x 16 TIRES ON AMBASSADOR 6;

6.50 x 16 ON 8

NASH AUTOMATIC CRUISING GEAR! Available at slight extra cost. Reduces engine revolutions about ⅓ at high speeds. Gives you an entirely new ride sensation. Saves 15% to 25% in gasoline; as much as 50% in oil!

AMBASSADOR 6: 93 H.P. @ 3400 RPM

260.8 C.I.D. AMBASSADOR 8: 102 H.P. @ 3400 RPM

125" W.B. ON AMBASSADOR 6 OR 8

NASH

"LAFAYETTE" GRILLE MEMBERS ARE HORIZONTAL.

"37/3" 2-DOOR

"3788"

"3782"

37

AMBASSADOR

CHAS. W. NASH (FOUNDER)

"LAFAYETTE" BECOMES A 117"-W.B. SERIES OF NASH, (1937 THROUGH '40) (L-HEAD)

BABE RUTH

7.00 × 16 TIRES ON AMBASSADOR 8 (THROUGH '39)

"3781" CONVERTIBLE

"3815"

95 H.P. @ 3400 RPM (AS ON '37 AMB. 6)

117" W.B.

"LAFAYETTE"

AMBASSADOR 6

105 H.P. @ 3400 RPM (AS ON '37 AMB. 8) 4.11 G.R. (SINCE '37)

NASH World's FIRST CAR With CONDITIONED AIR For Winter Driving

38

JAN. 4, 1938: 1ST ANNIVERSARY OF 1937 NASH-KELVINATOR MERGER

OPTIONAL VACUUM SHIFT HAS CONTROL LEVER PROTRUDING FROM CENTER OF DASH.

← AMBASSADOR 8

115 H.P. @ 3400 RPM (4.1 G.R. (THROUGH FINAL STRAIGHT-8 SINCE '35)   NASH OF 1942)

LAFAYETTE has 99 H.P. @ 3400 RPM (THROUGH '40)

39

LAST STOP GAS

AMBASSADOR = 121" W.B. ON 6; 125" ON 8 (SINCE '37)

new 4.1 G.R. ON 6s, 4.4 ON AMBASSADOR 8.

183

The NATIONAL SEXTET

NATIONAL MOTOR CAR and VEHICLE CORP., INDIANAPOLIS

(1900-1924)

OVERHEAD-VALVE 6-CYLINDER ENGINE NEW FOR 1920; REPLACES THE FORMER L-HEAD 6-CYL. and V-12 TYPES. 301.3 C.I.D.

130" W.B., 32 × 4½ TIRES, 4.08 GEAR RATIO ON "SEXTET" (BB) (THROUGH '24)

FIVE CUSTOM BUILT BODY STYLES

DASH

FRONT END ('23)

20-24

WITH TOP DOWN

7-PASSENGER TOURING CAR

NOTE THE UNUSUALLY LONG REAR QUARTER WINDOWS →

7-PASSENGER SEDAN

IN '23, 112"-W.B. "6-31" and 121"-W.B. "6-51" MODELS ALSO, WITH 155 CID (OWN) and 241.6 CID (CONT.) ENG. "6-71" IS BB SERIES.

MODEL "D" UNCHANGED FROM 1919
104" W.B.
OWN 4-CYL., O.H.V.
145.7 C.I.D. ENGINE
4.25 G.R.
12-VOLT BOSCH IGNITION

32 × 4 TIRES

NELSON
(1917—1921)
E.A. NELSON MOTOR CAR CO., DETROIT

(WITH DOUBLE-DROP FRAME!)

NOMA 6 (1919-1923)

NOMA MOTORS CORP., N.Y.C.
224 CID CONTINENTAL OR BEAVER ENGINES
("3-C") (364.5 CID, "1-D")

('22)

32 × 4½ TIRES, 128" W.B.

Oakland Motor Car Company,
Pontiac, Michigan (1907-1931)

OAKLAND
SENSIBLE SIX
"34-C"

MARVEL
CARB.
(THROUGH '23)

20-21

6-CYL.
O.H.V.
177
C.I.D.
ENGINE

4.50
GEAR
RATIO

44 H.P. @ 2600 RPM
(THROUGH 1924)

"34-C"
SERIES
BOSCH IGN.('20) REMY ('21)

W.B. INCREASED FROM
112" TO 115" FOR 1920.
115" W.B. CONT'D.
THROUGH 1923.

22

DRUM-TYPE HEADLIGHTS.
WALNUT STEERING WHEEL.
WALNUT INSTRUMENT BOARD WITH
SILVER-FACED, GLASS-COVERED
INSTRUMENTS.

"34-D"
SERIES
(6-44)

32 × 4 TIRES
REMY IGNITION CONTINUED (THROUGH '26)

"6-44" SERIES

23

The New
Oakland
Six

NEW
4.66
GEAR
RATIO

1923 "6-44" IS THE
FINAL OAKLAND TO HAVE AN
OVERHEAD VALVE ENGINE.

185

OAKLAND

P R O D U C T   O F   G E N E R A L   M O T O R S

(STARTS 9-8-23)

113" W.B. (THROUGH 1927)

BLUE DUCO ON BODIES

The True Blue Six

24

"6-54" SERIES
(ADOPTS L-HEAD
VALVE ARRANGEMENT)

4-WHEEL BRAKES

STROMBERG CARB. (THROUGH '26)

'24 DASH GAUGES ON DARK
RECTANGULAR PANEL, BEHIND
GLASS PANE.

Oakland

PRODUCT OF GENERAL MOTORS

COUPE WITH LANDAU IRONS
AND OVAL QUARTER WINDOWS

25 "6-54"

HEADLIGHT
TIE-BAR
ELIMINATED

185 CU. IN. DISPL.
5 TO 1 COMPRESSION

4.7 GEAR RATIO

186

44 H.P. @ 2600 RPM
5 TO 1 COMPRESSION   60 M.P.H.

EARLIEST LANDAU SEDANS
HAVE OVAL REAR QUARTER
WINDOWS. IN AUTUMN,
1925, WINDOW STYLE IS
LIKE '27.

DASH
(RADIO,
WATER
TEMP.
GAUGE
NOT
ORIG.)

26 "OS"

(INTRO. 7-25)

45 H.P. @ 2600 RPM
(THROUGH '27)
new HARMONIC BALANCER
AIR CLEANER
5.0 COMPR.

4.8 COMPR.
MARVEL CARB.
(THROUGH '31)

27 "OS"

(INTRO. 7-26)

DELCO-
REMY
IGNITION
(THROUGH
'31)

FROM JULY 29, 1926 TO JAN. 9, 1927, THIS
'27 "GREATER OAKLAND 6" WAS RUN (IN DETROIT)
CONTINUOUSLY ON A TREADMILL, ON PUBLIC
DISPLAY, FOR A 100,000-MILE ENDURANCE
TEST. AVG. SPEED 25.49 M.P.H.,
AVG. 34.09 MILES PER GALLON.

COMPARE THE ACTUAL PHOTO ABOVE
WITH THE GLAMOURIZED ADVERTISING
ILLUSTRATION AT LEFT!

4.7 G.R.   FOOT-DIMMER FOR HEADLIGHTS   187   NATURAL-FINISH WOOD WHEELS
"RUBBER-SILENCED" CHASSIS

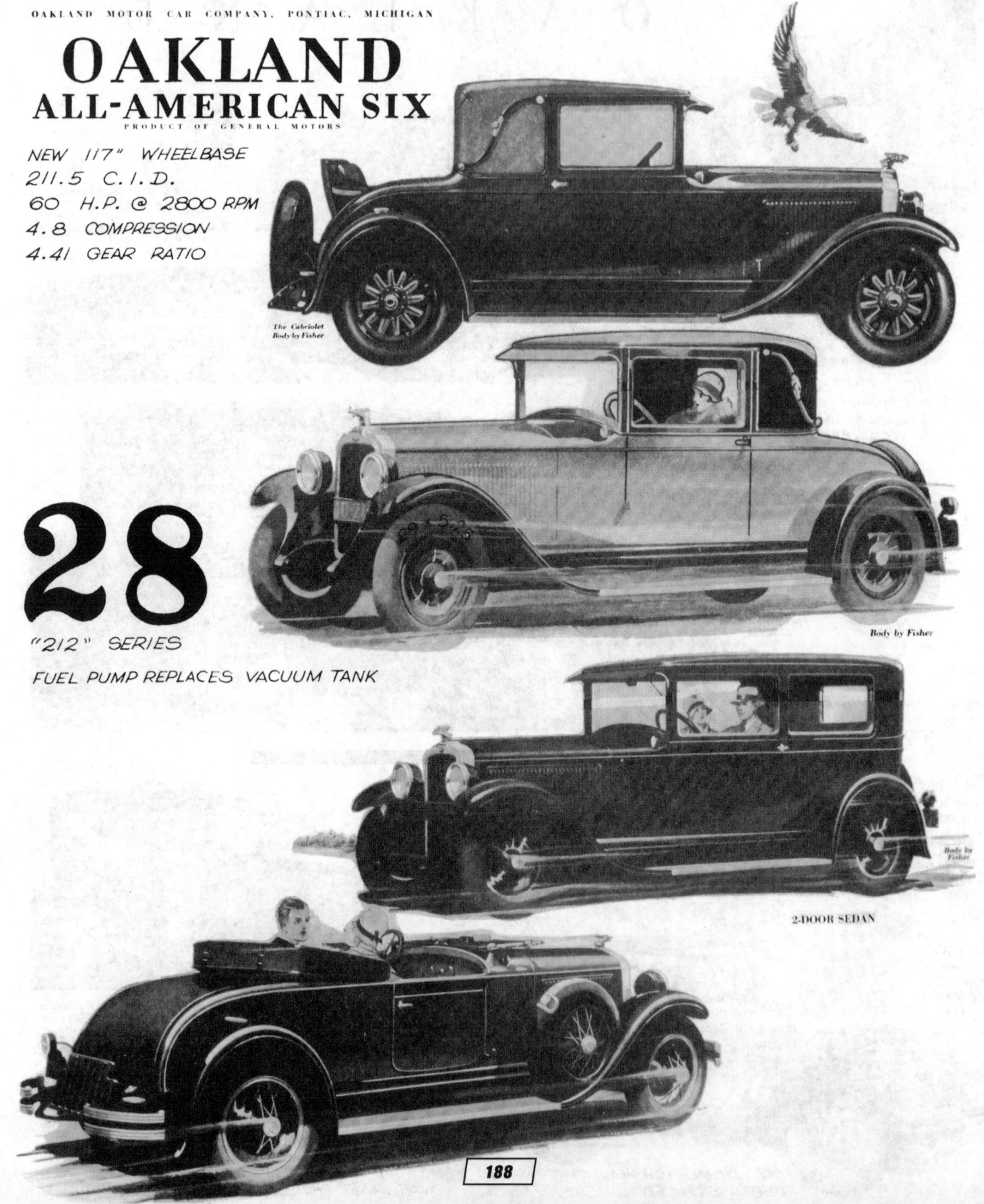

OAKLAND MOTOR CAR COMPANY, PONTIAC, MICHIGAN

OAKLAND
ALL-AMERICAN SIX
PRODUCT OF GENERAL MOTORS

NEW 117" WHEELBASE
211.5 C.I.D.
60 H.P. @ 2800 RPM
4.8 COMPRESSION
4.41 GEAR RATIO

28

"212" SERIES

FUEL PUMP REPLACES VACUUM TANK

The Cabriolet
Body by Fisher

Body by Fisher

Body by Fisher

2-DOOR SEDAN

188

OAKLAND

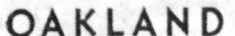

SMOOTH GLOSS-BLACK
INSTRUMENT PANEL WITH
SMALL, INDIVIDUAL CIRCULAR
BLACK-FACED GAUGES. DASH/MAP
LIGHTS

INDIRECT LIGHTING ALSO

ROADSTER and PHAETON
have BODY BY OAKLAND.
FISHER BODY ON
OTHERS.

117" W.B.

4.72 GEAR RATIO
228.1 C.I.D.   68 H.P. @ 3000 RPM

OAKLAND'S FINAL "ALL-AMERICAN SIX"

29

THE MOST RELIABLE AND
DURABLE OF OAKLANDS.
MORE 1929s HAVE SURVIVED
THAN ANY OTHER YEAR MODEL
OF THIS MAKE.

CONVERTIBLE
LANDAU SECTION

29 x 5.50 TIRES

NEW
MOLDINGS
ON
INSTRUMENT
PANEL

30

EIGHT
(V-8)

117" WHEELBASE,
251 C.I.D. (THROUGH
1931)

82 H.P. @ 3000 RPM
4.42 GEAR RATIO

5.50 x 18 TIRES
(1930 and 1931)

85 H.P. @ 3400 RPM
4.55 GEAR RATIO

31

(THE FINAL
OAKLAND)

MAKING NEW FRIENDS AND KEEPING THE OLD

OGREN (1915-1923)

OGREN MOTOR CAR CO., MILWAUKEE, WIS.

(NICKELED RADIATOR SHELL ON '22 MODEL.)

BOSCH IGNITION

6-CYL. CONTINENTAL ENGINE (325.1 C.I.D.) ('22-'23)

80-90 H.P.

TOP SPEED = 68 M.P.H. (ROADSTER, 90 MPH)

134" W.B.
33 × 5 TIRES

RAYFIELD CARB.

20 TO 23

OLDS MOTOR WORKS, LANSING, MICH. (EST. 1897)

Oldsmobile

Product of GENERAL MOTORS SINCE '09

6 ← MODEL "37-A"
112" W.B.
6 CYLS. (O.H.V.)
177 C.I.D.
4.58 GEAR RATIO
32 × 4" TIRES
44 H.P. @ 2600 RPM

JOHNSON CARB.

6-CYL. OR V-8 (SINCE '17) 8

20

MODEL "45-B"
122" W.B.
V-8 (T-HEAD)
246.7 C.I.D.
4.91 GEAR RATIO
33 × 4½" TIRES
58 H.P. @ 2600 RPM
BALL CARB.

4 (NEW)

"46" V-8 SIMILAR SPECS. AS '20 "45-B" BUT HAS 58 H.P. @ 2510 RPM

"43-A"
224.3 C.I.D., 43 H.P., 115" W.B.
REMY IGN.
4.66 GEAR RATIO
ZENITH CARB.

21

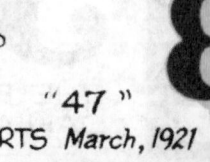

8

"47" STARTS March, 1921

OLDSMOBILE

REMY IGN. ON "43-A"
DELCO IGN. (OTHERS)

22

"46" V-8,
122" w.b., 4.93 GEAR RATIO

"43-A" = 4-CYL.,
115" w.b., 4.66 G.R.

"47" = V-8,
115" w.b., 5.10 G.R.
(THROUGH 1923)

4-CYL.
Semi-Sport
44 H.P. @ 2000 RPM

CARBURETORS:
"43-A" ZENITH
"47" JOHNSON
"46" BALL + BALL
(SAME IN '23)

"47" HAS 233.7 C.I.D.
V-8 ENGINE WITH
60 H.P. @ 2710 RPM

(FINAL YEAR
FOR 4 and
V-8)

The Four Cab—2 passengers—

The Four Sedan—5 passengers—

4-CYL. "43-A" HAS 4.70 GEAR RATIO, 40 H.P. @ 1800 RPM

"47"
(V-8) 63 H.P. @
2710 RPM

The Four Coupe—4 passengers—

23

PHANTOM VIEW
OF
"4" Brougham (AVAIL. 9-22)

4.92 G.R. ON
V-8 "46"

ALL MODELS have
DELCO IGN. (THROUGH '26)

PRODUCT OF GENERAL MOTORS

SPORT
TOURING

MODEL
"30"

SIX 24

(FROM '24 THROUGH '31,
6 CYL. ONLY)

42 H.P. @
2600 RPM

(3-WINDOW BUSINESS COUPE
KNOWN AS "CAB.")

STD. TOURING

110" W.B. (1924
and 1925)
ZENITH CARB. (THROUGH '25)

169.3 C.I.D. (THROUGH
'26)

191

31 x 4 TIRES IN
1924 and 1925, AS
WELL AS 5.10 GEAR RATIO

The Refined OLDSMOBILE SIX

PRODUCT OF GENERAL MOTORS

New Beauty outside — but same good chassis 40,000 owners know!

25

MODEL "30"

41 H.P. @ 2600 RPM (THROUGH '26)

DISC WHEELS AVAIL.

new RADIATOR DESIGN (THROUGH '27)

WALNUT-FINISH INSTRUMENT PANEL ('27)

DELCO-REMY IGN. ('27 ON)

26-27

30-D   30-E

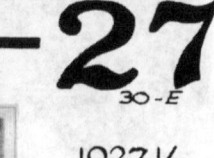

Chromium Plating (1927)

1927½ VISOR

110½" W.B.

'27 HAS 185 C.I.D., 40 H.P. @ 2600 RPM
30 × 5.25 TIRES,
4-WHEEL BRAKES (STARTING 1-27)
CARTER CARB. ('26) JOHNSON CARB. ('27)

4.73 GEAR RATIO

192

OLDSMOBILE

28

55 H.P. @ 2700 RPM
(THROUGH '29)

MODEL "F-28"

113½"
WHEELBASE and
197.5 C.I.D.
(THROUGH
1931)

28 × 5.25 TIRES IN 1928 and 1929
4.41 GEAR RATIO IN 1928 and 1929
SCHEBLER CARB. (THROUGH '29)

LATE MODEL —
NOTE LONGER ROW
OF HOOD LOUVRES

ON '28 OLDSMOBILES,
FUEL PUMP REPLACES VACUUM TANK

This emblem identifies
the new 1929 Oldsmobile

(ON RADIATOR)

29

MODEL
"F-29"

OLDSMOBILE
PRODUCT OF GENERAL MOTORS

62 H.P. @ 3000 RPM
JOHNSON CARB.

30
"F-30"

DASH
GAUGES, LEFT TO RT.:
AMMETER, WATER TEMP.,
SPEEDOMETER-ODOMETER,
OIL PRESSURE, GASOLINE

5.25 × 18 TIRES IN
1930 and 1931

4.54 GEAR RATIO

65 H.P. @ 3350 RPM

31
"F-31"

STROMB.
CARB.
(THROUGH
'35)

'31 DASH

4.56
GEAR RATIO
(THROUGH '33)

6.00 × 17 TIRES, 116½" W.B.

6 HAS 213.3 C.I.D.
and 71 H.P.
@ 3200 RPM

6 "F-32"

32

8
(NEW)
"L-32"

STRAIGHT-
8 HAS
240.3 C.I.D.
and 82
H.P. @
3200 RPM

194

DASH

OLDSMOBILE

33

4.56 GEAR RATIO

240.3 C.I.D. CONTINUED ON 8 (THROUGH '36)

8 HAS 90 H.P. @ 3350 RPM (THROUGH '34)

119" W.B. (THROUGH '34)

6 INCREASED TO 221.4 C.I.D. FOR '33 ONLY. 80 H.P. @ 3200 115" WHEELBASE

5.50 × 17 TIRES ON 6, 6.00 × 17 ON 8

THE NEW EIGHT . . . THE NEW SIX . . . TWO GENERAL MOTORS VALUES

34

6 HAS 5.50 × 17 TIRES, 8 HAS 7.00 × 16 TIRES, 4.56 GEAR RATIO 213.3 C.I.D., 84 H.P. @ 3250

4.78 GEAR RATIO

HYDRAULIC BRAKES

"F-34" (114" W.B.) 6

"L-34" 8

WOOD-GRAINED dash

'34 DASH

'35 DASH

8 HAS 100 H.P. @ 3400 RPM (THROUGH '36)

"L-35" 8

"F-35" 6

6 HAS 213.3 C.I.D. and 90 H.P. @ 3400 RPM (THROUGH '36)

7.00 × 16 TIRES (8) 121" W.B. (THROUGH '36)

6.25 × 16 TIRES ON 6

115" W.B. (THROUGH '36)

35

OLDSMOBILE

TOURING SEDAN (W. TRUNK)

INTERIOR

6 "F-36"

GAS FILLER LOCATED HIGHER ON RT. REAR FENDER.

FRONT DOORS NOW HINGED AT FRONT.

3-WINDOW SPORT COUPE

8 "L-36"

36

8 has FENDER PARKING LIGHTS, and 5 HORIZONTAL CROSS-MEMBERS VISIBLE IN GRILLE.

CARTER CARB. (BOTH MODELS, STARTING '36)

7.00 × 16 TIRES ON OLDSMOBILE 8 FOR 1936 and 1937

6 HAS 229.7 C.I.D. (THROUGH '40) and 95 H.P. @ 3400 (THROUGH '38)

TAIL-LIGHTS MOVED UP TO SIDES OF BODY

6 117" W.B. (THROUGH '38)

8 NOW USES 257.1 C.I.D.

110 H.P. @ 3600 RPM

8

37

196

124" W.B. (THROUGH '38)

OLDSMOBILE

THE SIX

6 HAS 6.50×16 TIRES

THE EIGHT

OPTIONAL ≡ AUTOMATIC TRANSMISSION!

38

OLDSMOBILE

6-CYL. "60" HAS 215.8 C.I.D. and 90 H.P. @ 3200 RPM

NEW "60" 4-DOOR SEDAN

39

"F-39" and "G-39" (6)
"L-39" (8)

1-PIECE REAR WINDOW →

6

6-CYL. "60" and "70" SERIES
115" and 120" W.B.

6-CYL. "70"
HAS 229.7 C.I.D. and
95 H.P. @ 3300 RPM

8

8-CYL.
"80"
HAS
257.1 C.I.D. and
110 H.P. @ 3500 RPM

Series 80   120" W.B.

Overland

(1903-1926) (1939 ALSO *)

* - SEE WILLYS

20-21

WILLYS-OVERLAND, INC., TOLEDO, OHIO
Sedans, Coupes, Touring Cars and Roadsters
Willys-Overland, Limited, Toronto, Canada
The John N. Willys Export Corporation, New York

(4 CYLS.,
143.1 C.I.D.)
27 H.P.
4.5 GEAR
RATIO

100" W.B. CONT'D.
THROUGH '26 (ON 4-CYL.)

with NEW, DIAGONALLY-MOUNTED
"TRIPLEX" SPRINGS

REAR
DETAILS

HOOD LOUVRES
NEW FOR
1920

Rides as if Every Bump Had Springs

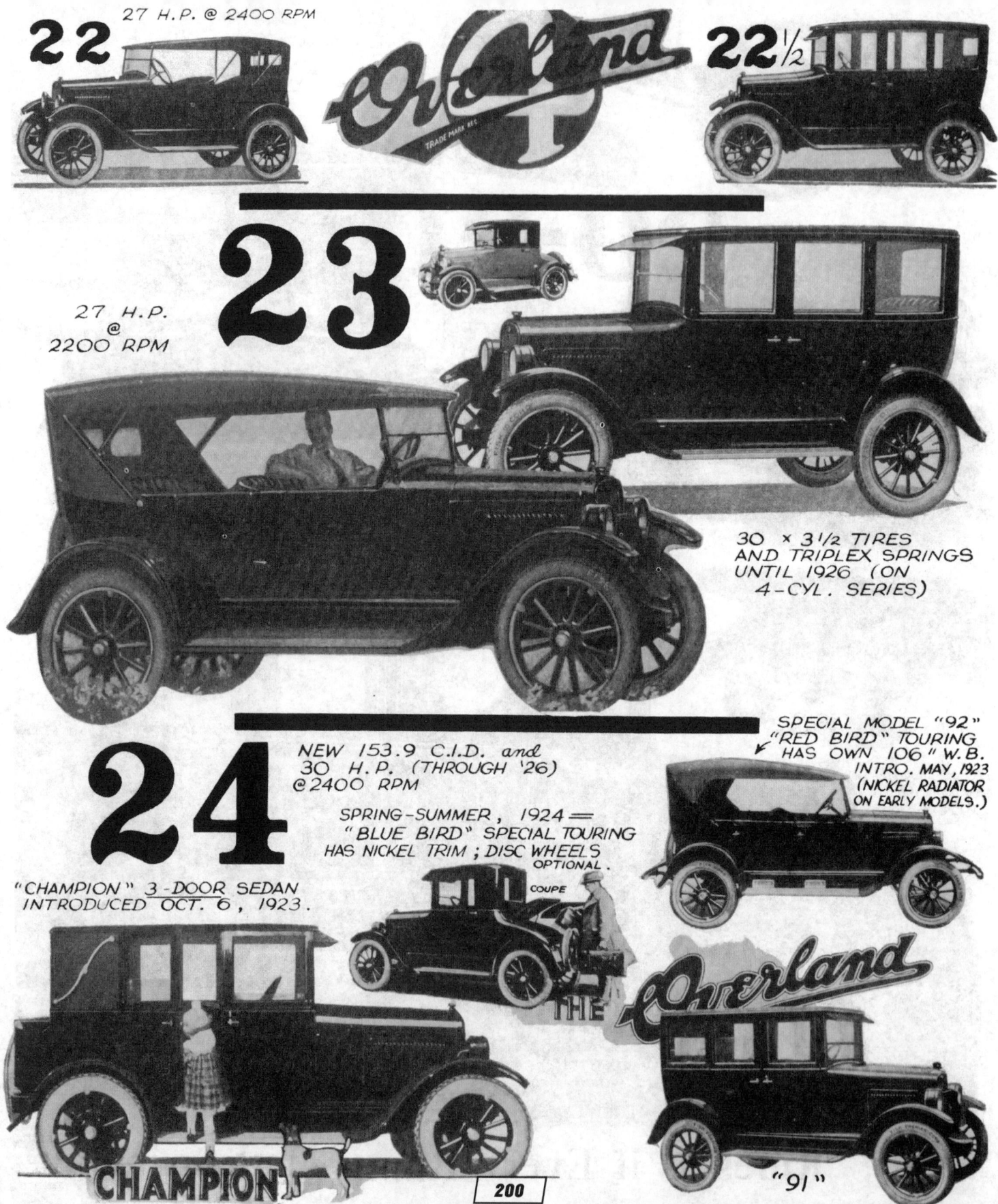

22 27 H.P. @ 2400 RPM

22½

Overland — TRADE MARK REG.

23

27 H.P. @ 2200 RPM

30 × 3½ TIRES AND TRIPLEX SPRINGS UNTIL 1926 (ON 4-CYL. SERIES)

24 NEW 153.9 C.I.D. and 30 H.P. (THROUGH '26) @2400 RPM

SPECIAL MODEL "92" "RED BIRD" TOURING HAS OWN 106" W.B. INTRO. MAY, 1923 (NICKEL RADIATOR ON EARLY MODELS.)

SPRING-SUMMER, 1924 = "BLUE BIRD" SPECIAL TOURING HAS NICKEL TRIM ; DISC WHEELS OPTIONAL.

"CHAMPION" 3-DOOR SEDAN INTRODUCED OCT. 6, 1923.

COUPE

THE *Overland*

CHAMPION

"91"

BUDD
(LIGHTWEIGHT, ALL-STEEL
BODIES ON 4-CYL.
MODELS, STARTING
AUGUST,
1924)

OVERLAND

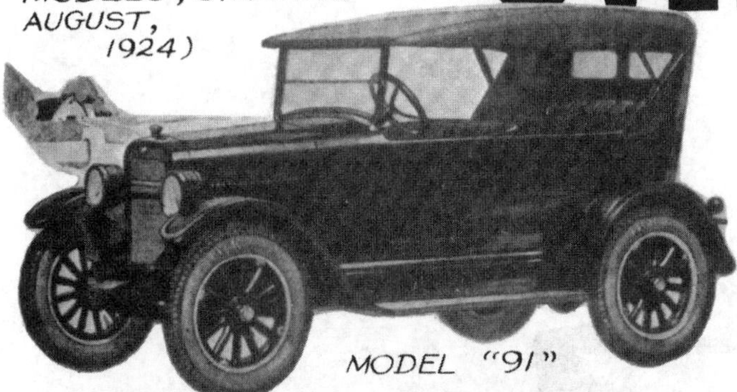

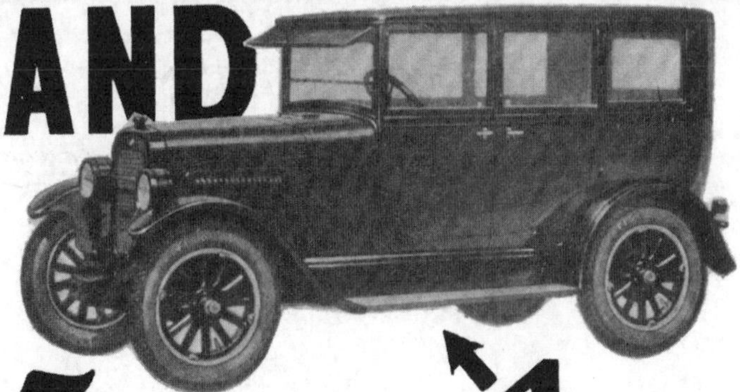

4

MODEL "91"

25

4 "91"

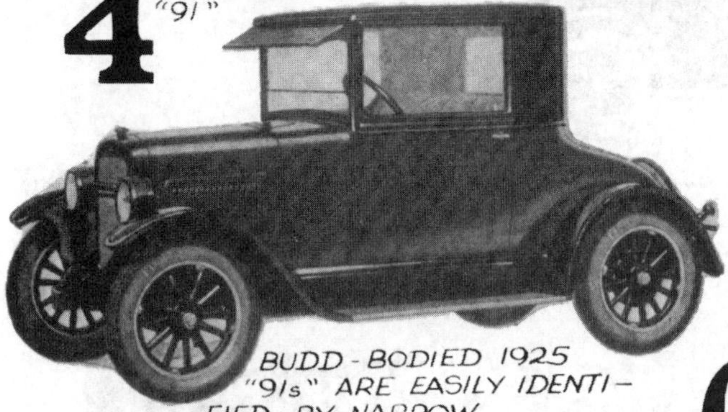

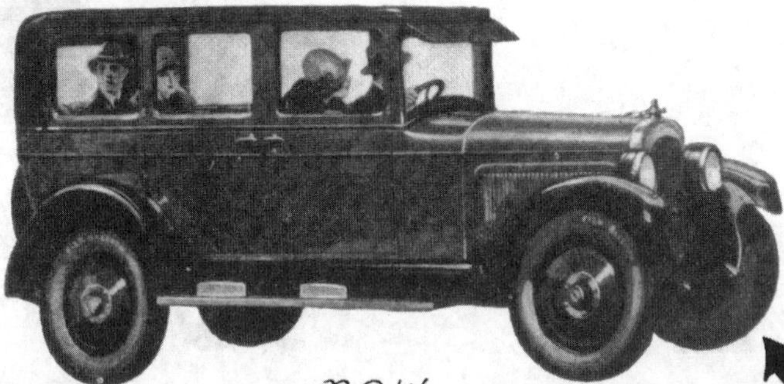

MODEL
"93"

BUDD-BODIED 1925
"91s" ARE EASILY IDENTI-
FIED BY NARROW
WINDSHIELD CORNER-POSTS.
(ON COUPES and SEDANS.)

new
OVERLAND SIX

NEW
'25 and '26 MODEL "93" 6-CYLINDER
OVERLANDS HAVE 169.6 C.I.D. ENGINE
WITH 38 H.P. @ 2800 RPM (30 × 5.25 TIRES)
and 112 3/4" W.B.

1926 4-CYL.
"91"
HAS BODY
SIMILAR TO 6.

26

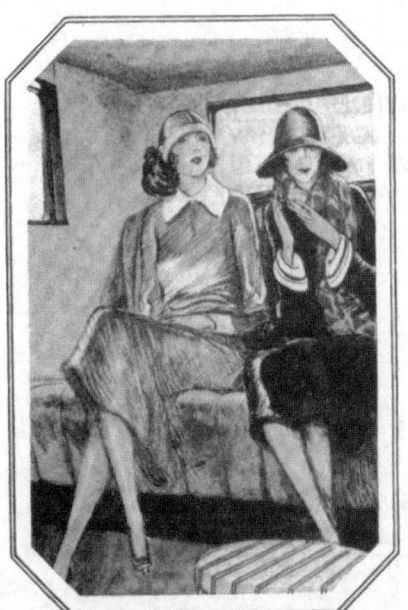

The seats are wider, the windows larger, the doors much broader than other cars of this size and price

REPLACED BY
WHIPPET

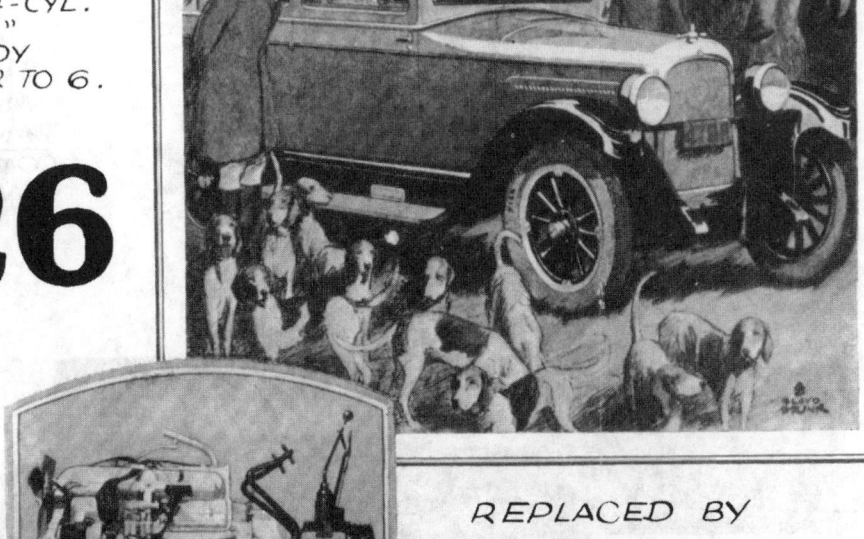

OWEN MAGNETIC —
(1914 – 1922)

THE CAR OF A
THOUSAND SPEEDS

OWEN MAGNETIC MOTOR CAR CORPORATION, BROADWAY AT 57th STREET, NEW YORK

(AND WILKES - BARRE, PA.)

19 — 21

142 " WHEELBASE
6 - CYL. WEIDELY ENGINE
(4 " x 5½ " BORE and STROKE)

CLOSE - COUPLED ('20)
(NOT LISTED EARLY IN SEASON.)

HAD A UNIQUE *ELECTRO -
MAGNETIC GEAR - SHIFT,*
CONTROLLED FROM QUADRANT
ON STEERING WHEEL.

(KNOWN AS THE
" CROWN MAGNETIC "
FOR 1922 SEASON)

202

PACKARD

PACKARD MOTOR CAR COMPANY, *Detroit*

"Ask the Man *Who Owns One"*

V-12
75 H.P. @ 2000 RPM
424.1 C.I.D.
136 " W.B.
4.36 GEAR RATIO
35 × 5" TIRES

DELCO IGN.
(THROUGH '27)
OWN CARB.
(THROUGH '29,
31-32)

(1899-1958)

("3-25" MODELS HAVE
128" W.B.)

18 TO 20

TWIN 6
(V-12)

SOME MODELS WITH 136" W.B.

21

TWIN 6
(85 H.P.)

SINGLE 6 (NEW)
(STARTS OCT., 1920)

NEW SINGLE SIX has
6-CYL., L-HEAD
241.6 C.I.D. ENGINE with
52 H.P. @ 2600 RPM (THROUGH '22)

SINGLE
6

116" W.B. ON 6,
AS IN 1921

22

TWIN 6
(DISCONTINUED
DURING
1923)
85 H.P.
@ 2600
RPM

THE
TWIN-SIX
SPECIAL

PACKARD

23

SINGLE 6

NEW 268.4 C.I.D. and 54 H.P. @ 2600 RPM (THROUGH '25)

"126" and "133" MODEL NUMBERS INDICATE WHEELBASE.

5-PASS. CPE.

6

6

24

PACKARD SIX FOUR-PASSENGER COUPE

STRAIGHT-8 HAS 357.8 C.I.D. and 84 H.P. @ 3000 RPM (THROUGH '26) 136" and 143" WHEELBASES

8 (NEW)

70 M.P.H. TOP SPEED OF 1925 "8" (4.7 GEAR RATIO)

ONLY PACKARD CAN BUILD A PACKARD

8

6

25

8 7-PASS.

204

75 M.P.H. 4.66 GEAR RATIO

PACKARD SIX and EIGHT

PACKARD

6

8

26

"426" and "433" are 6-CYL. MODELS
WITH
288.6 C.I.D., 82 H.P. @ 3200

27

"336" and "343" STRAIGHT-8
INCREASED TO 384.8 C.I.D.
and 106 H.P. @ 3200 RPM

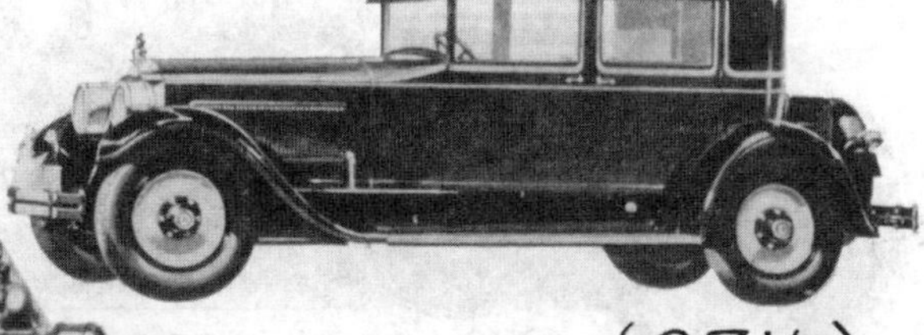

(27½)

PACKARD

6-CYL. "526" and "533" MODELS HAVE 126" and 133" W.B.

The New Packard Six Convertible Coupe

UNTIL 1937, THE "526" and "533" OF 1928 WERE PACKARD'S FINAL 6-CYL. MODELS. 288.6 C.I.D., 82 H.P. @ 3200 RPM

28

(FINAL YEAR FOR DRUM HEADLIGHTS.) DELCO-REMY IGN.

6

LIMOUSINE ·

1928 8-CYL. "443" HAS 143" WHEELBASE, VENT DOORS ON HOOD.

384.8 C.I.D. STRAIGHT-8 106 H.P. @ 3200 (THROUGH '30)

8

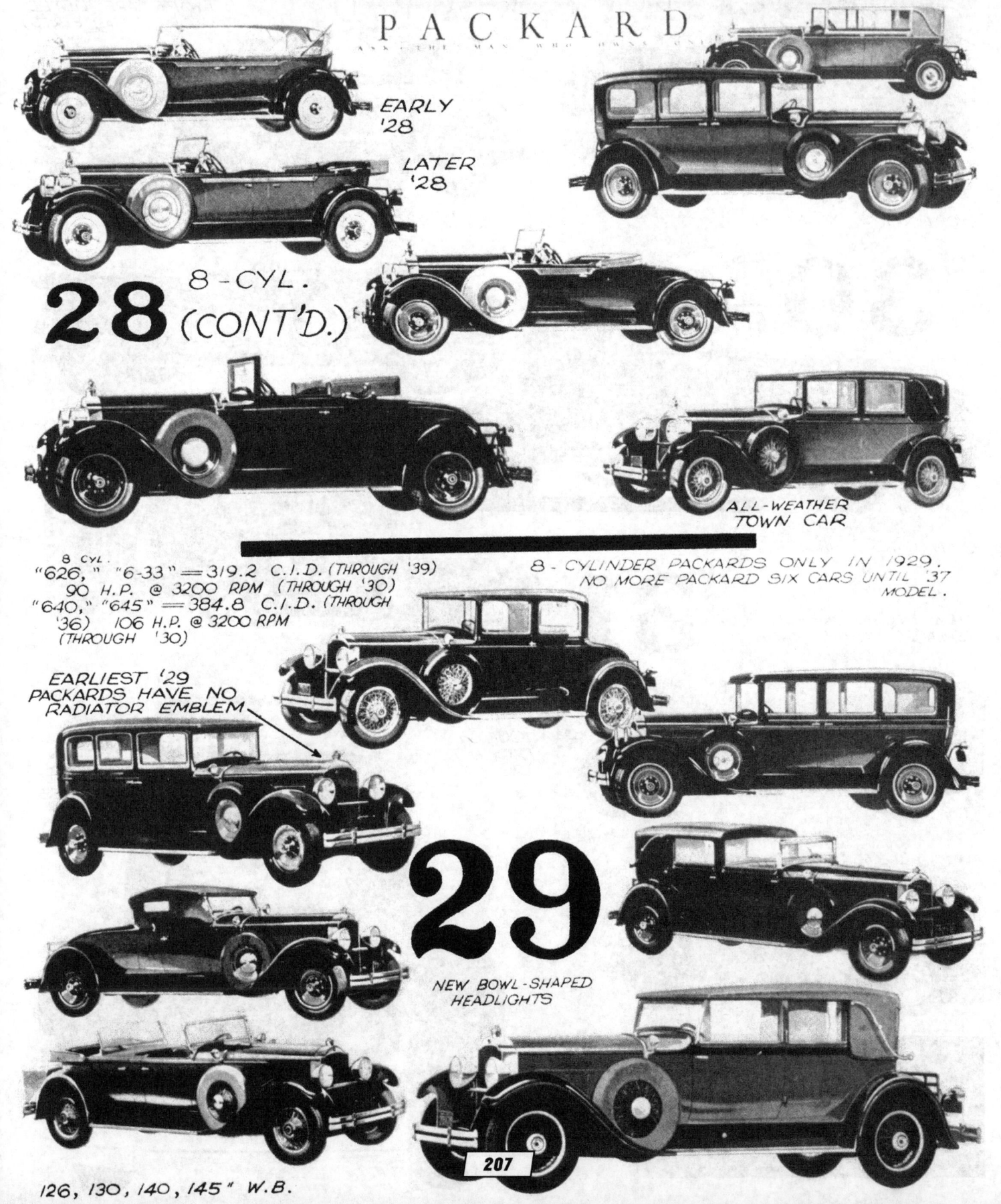

PACKARD
ASK THE MAN WHO OWNS ONE

EARLY '28

LATER '28

28 8-CYL. (CONT'D.)

ALL-WEATHER TOWN CAR

8 CYL.
"626," "6-33" = 319.2 C.I.D. (THROUGH '39)
90 H.P. @ 3200 RPM (THROUGH '30)
"640," "645" = 384.8 C.I.D. (THROUGH
'36) 106 H.P. @ 3200 RPM
(THROUGH '30)

8 - CYLINDER PACKARDS ONLY IN 1929.
NO MORE PACKARD SIX CARS UNTIL '37
MODEL.

EARLIEST '29
PACKARDS HAVE NO
RADIATOR EMBLEM

29

NEW BOWL-SHAPED
HEADLIGHTS

126, 130, 140, 145" W.B.

PACKARD

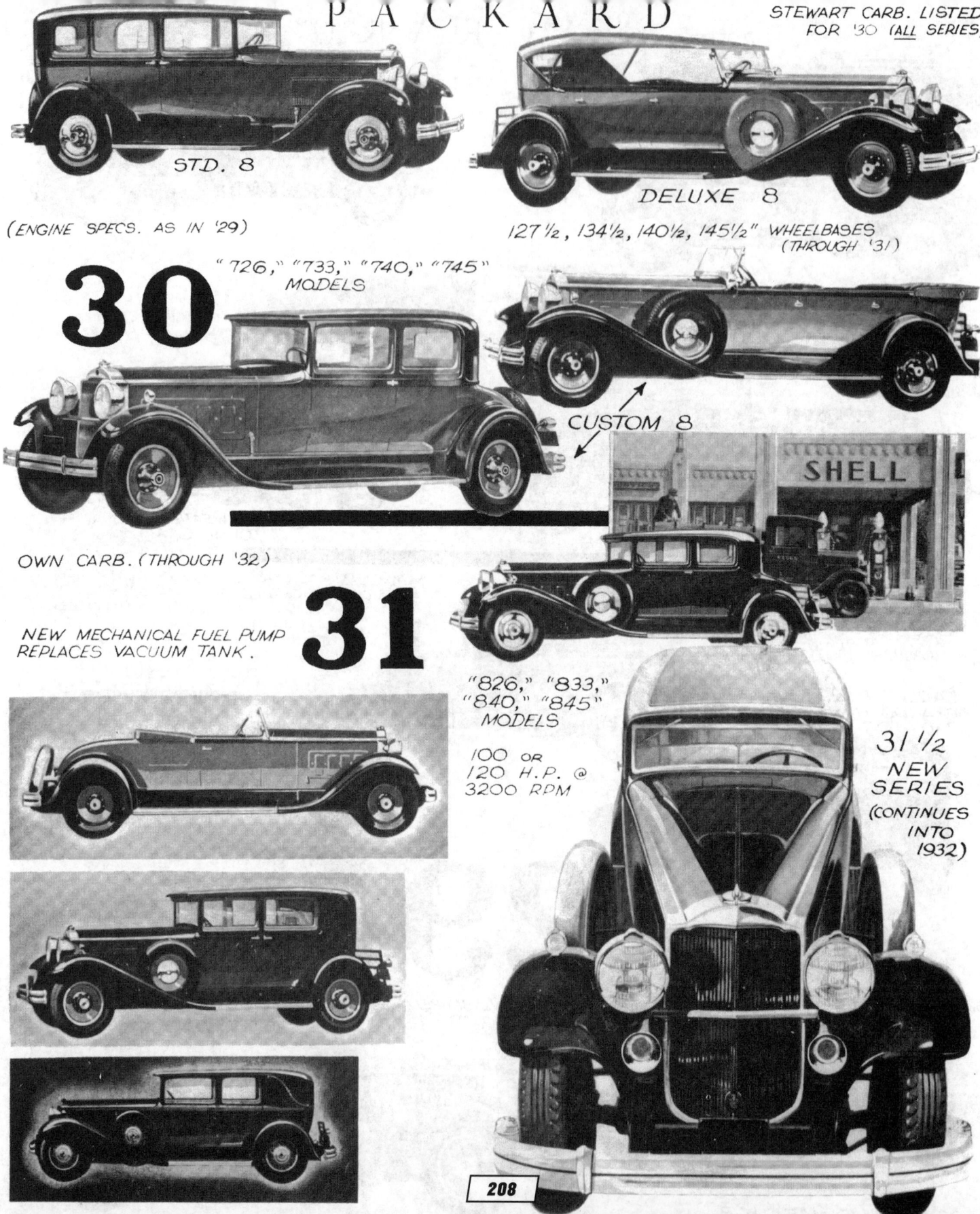

STD. 8

(ENGINE SPECS. AS IN '29)

DELUXE 8

127½, 134½, 140½, 145½" WHEELBASES
(THROUGH '31)

30

"726," "733," "740," "745" MODELS

CUSTOM 8

OWN CARB. (THROUGH '32)

31

NEW MECHANICAL FUEL PUMP REPLACES VACUUM TANK.

SHELL

"826," "833," "840," "845" MODELS

100 OR 120 H.P. @ 3200 RPM

31½ NEW SERIES (CONTINUES INTO 1932)

PACKARD

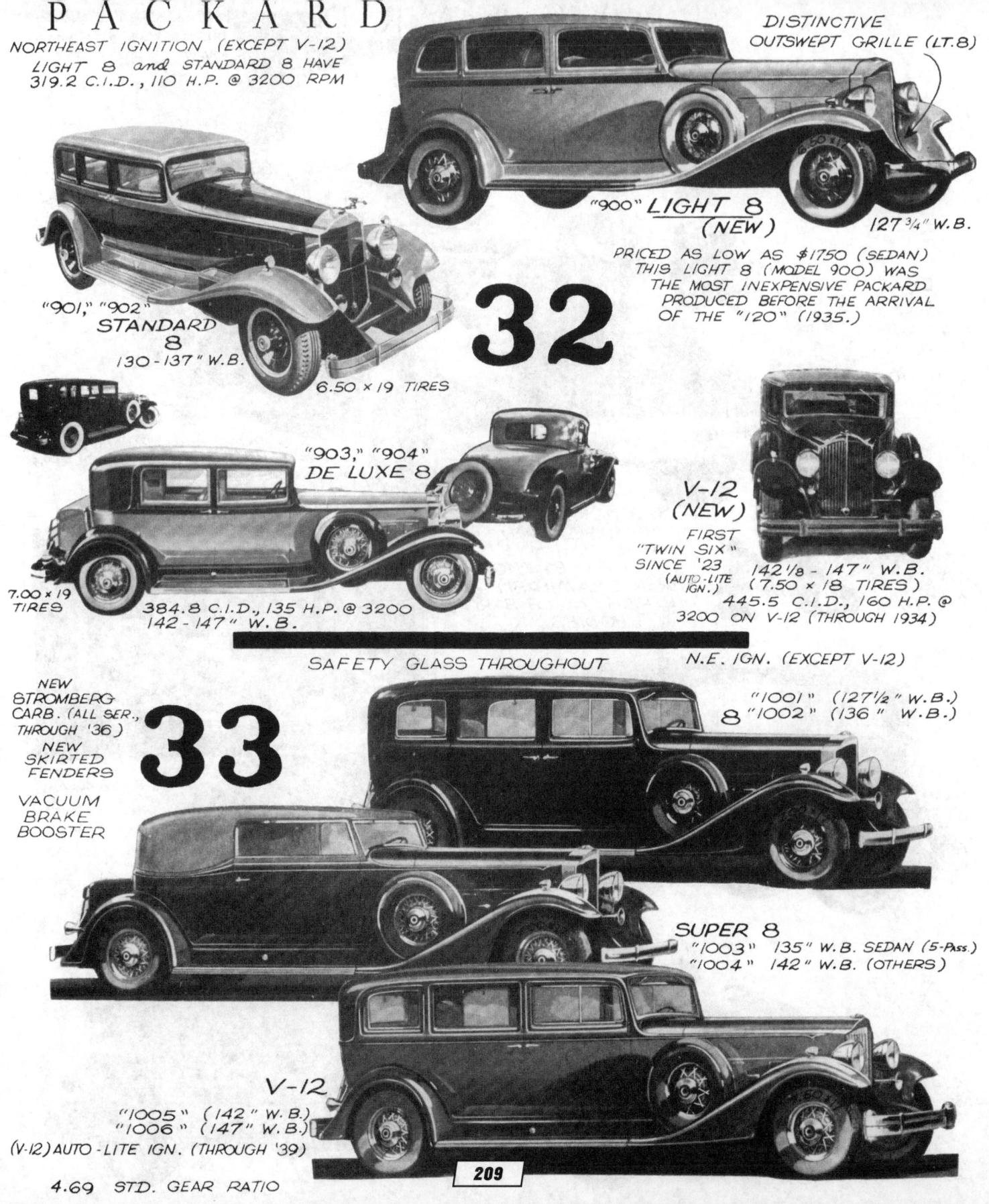

NORTHEAST IGNITION (EXCEPT V-12)
LIGHT 8 and STANDARD 8 HAVE
319.2 C.I.D., 110 H.P. @ 3200 RPM

DISTINCTIVE OUTSWEPT GRILLE (LT.8)

"900" LIGHT 8 (NEW) 127¾" W.B.

PRICED AS LOW AS $1750 (SEDAN)
THIS LIGHT 8 (MODEL 900) WAS
THE MOST INEXPENSIVE PACKARD
PRODUCED BEFORE THE ARRIVAL
OF THE "120" (1935.)

"901," "902" STANDARD 8
130-137" W.B.

6.50 × 19 TIRES

32

"903," "904" DE LUXE 8

7.00 × 19 TIRES

384.8 C.I.D., 135 H.P. @ 3200
142-147" W.B.

V-12 (NEW)
FIRST "TWIN SIX" SINCE '23
(AUTO-LITE IGN.)
142⅛ - 147" W.B.
(7.50 × 18 TIRES)
445.5 C.I.D., 160 H.P. @
3200 ON V-12 (THROUGH 1934)

SAFETY GLASS THROUGHOUT

N.E. IGN. (EXCEPT V-12)

NEW STROMBERG CARB. (ALL SER., THROUGH '36)
NEW SKIRTED FENDERS
VACUUM BRAKE BOOSTER

33

8 "1001" (127½" W.B.)
"1002" (136" W.B.)

SUPER 8
"1003" 135" W.B. SEDAN (5-PASS.)
"1004" 142" W.B. (OTHERS)

V-12
"1005" (142" W.B.)
"1006" (147" W.B.)
(V-12) AUTO-LITE IGN. (THROUGH '39)

4.69 STD. GEAR RATIO

P A C K A R D

4.69 STANDARD GEAR RATIO ON 8s

8
HAS CHROME-PLATING ON RADIATOR SHELL.

SUPER 8 "1103" and "1104" have 384.8 C.I.D. and 145 H.P. @ 3200 RPM

NORTHEAST IGN. (EXCEPT V-12)

34

135," 142", 147" WHEELBASES ON SUPER 8s. 147"-W.B. "1105" SUPER 8 AVAILABLE with DIETRICH or LE BARON BODIES.

DASH

V-12

4.41 OR 4.69 GEAR RATIOS ON V-12

142 OR 147" W.B. ON V-12

210

PACKARD

HYDRAULIC BRAKES ON "120" ONLY.

NEW LOW-COST 120

"120". HAS 8-CYL. 257.1 C.I.D. ENGINE,

110 H.P. @ 3850 RPM

120" W.B.

4.36 GEAR RATIO

"120" IS LOWEST-PRICED PACKARD EVER, AT ONLY

$980 to $1095

"120" SEDAN

35

"1203," "1204," "1205" HAVE 132, 139, 144" W.B.

SUPER 8

SUPER 8 HAS 384.8 C.I.D., 150 H.P. @ 3200 RPM 4.41 G.R.

EIGHT ("1200," "1201," "1202") HAS 127, 134, 139" W.B., 319.2 C.I.D., 130 H.P. @ 3200 RPM 4.69 GEAR RATIO

"1207" 139" W.B.
"1208" 144" W.B.

V-12

4.41 GEAR RATIO

V-12 has NEW 473.3 C.I.D. WITH 175 H.P. @ 3200 RPM

new AUTO-LITE IGN. ON "120" and "V-12" (THROUGH '39) OTHERS have NORTHEAST IGN. (FINAL YEAR)

PACKARD SKIPPED 1300 SERIES AND MOVED ON TO 1400 MODEL NUMBERS IN '36.

211

P A C K A R D

"120"
B

SUPER
8

SU. 8 has
DELCO-REMY IGN.
(THROUGH '37)

NEW 282 C.I.D.
120 H.P. @
3800 RPM
(THROUGH
'38
"1601")

36

V-12

MECHANICAL "POWER"
BRAKES ON LARGE 8s
AND V-12.

HYDRAULIC BRAKES ON ALL MODELS.

37

DE LUXE "120-CD"
and "138-CD" (138" W.B.)
HAVE AUTOMATIC RADIATOR SHUTTERS,
OTHER SPECIAL FEATURES.

NEW 6 HAS 236.7 C.I.D.
100 H.P. @ 3600 RPM

SIX

(NEW)
MODEL
115-C

115" W.B.
4.36 GEAR RATIO

6 has DELCO-REMY
IGN. (THROUGH '38)

120
C

120" W.B.
(CARTER CARB. ON
'37 "120")

"1500" (127"W.B.,)
"1501" (134" W.B.,) and
"1502" (139" W.B.) ARE SUPER 8
MODELS, WITH 319.2 C.I.D.
and 130 H.P. @ 3200 RPM
4.69 G.R., 7.50 × 16 TIRES
STROMBERG CARB.

212

V-12
STROMBERG CARB.

PACKARD
38

122" W.B.

MODEL
"1600"

NEW 245.3 C.I.D.,
STILL RATED AT 100 H.P.
@ 3600 RPM

6

8

"120" REPLACED
BY THIS "1601"
(127" W.B.) MODEL.

"1602" HAS 148"
W.B.

STROMBERG CARB. (ALL SERIES
EXCEPT 6)

SUPER 8

12

BODIES BY BRUNN

1938
MODEL NUMBERS
IN 1600 SERIES.

213

PACKARD

38 12 (CONT'D.)

AUTO-LITE IGN. ON ALL '38 MODELS EXCEPT 6.

SIX

6 has CHANDLER-GROVES CARB. (SINCE '37)

39 "CONTROLLED OVERDRIVE" OPTIONAL ON ALL MODELS.

1939 MODEL NUMBERS IN 1700 SERIES

120

EIGHT "1701" and "1702" (127" and 148" W.B.)

319.2 C.I.D. ENGINE (SINCE '29) 130 H.P. @ 3200 RPM (SINCE 1935 "EIGHT")

SUPER-8

AUTO-LITE IGN. ON ALL 1939 PACKARDS.

12

(FINAL V-12)

PAIGE (1909 – 1930)

The Most Beautiful Car in America

PAIGE-DETROIT MOTOR CAR COMPANY, DETROIT, *Michigan*

Manufacturers of Paige Motor Cars and Motor Trucks

19–20

PAIGE TRUCK →

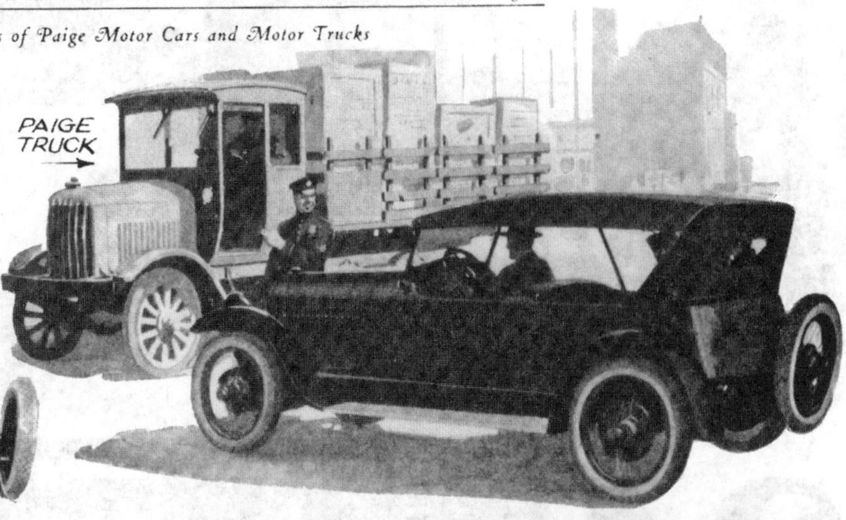

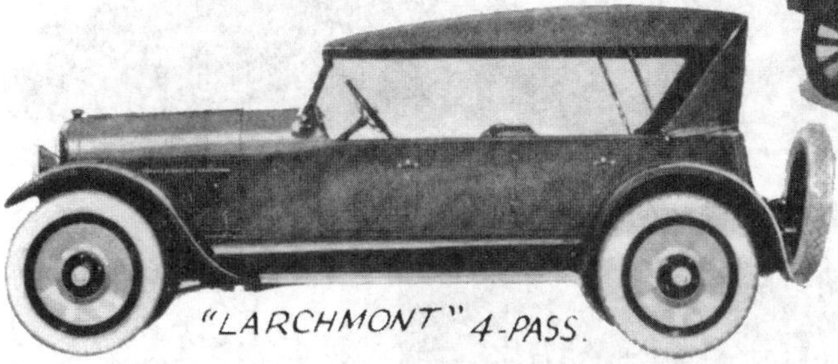

"LARCHMONT" 4-PASS.

"GLENBROOK" 5-PASS.

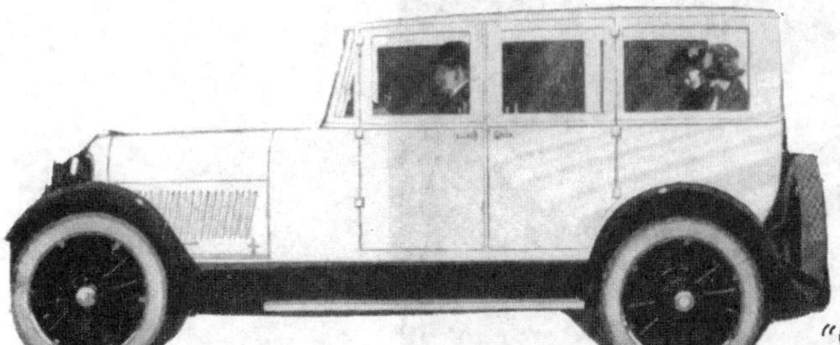

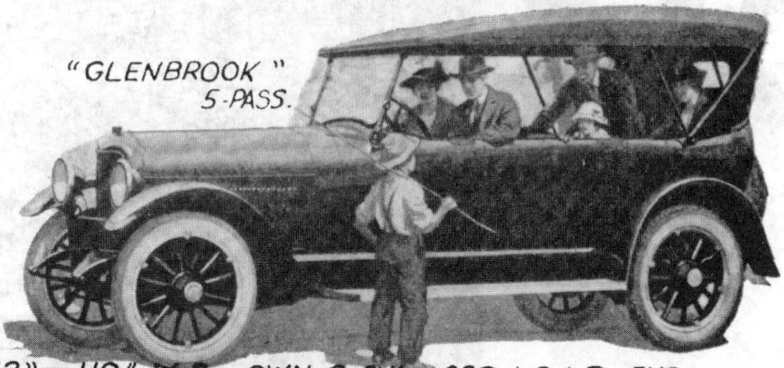

"6-42"=119" W.B.= OWN 6-CYL., 230.1 C.I.D. ENG.
"6-55"=127" W.B.= 303.1 C.I.D. 6-CYL. CONTINENTAL ENG.

"6-66" 7-PASS. SEDAN

On January 21st, the Paige, Daytona Model, 6-66 broke every stock car record for speed when it covered a measured mile in 35.01 seconds—a speed of 102.8 miles an hour.

119"-W.B. "6-42" CONTINUED IN 1921; IS "6-44" IN 1922.

21–22

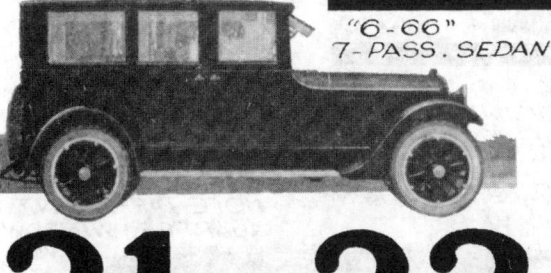

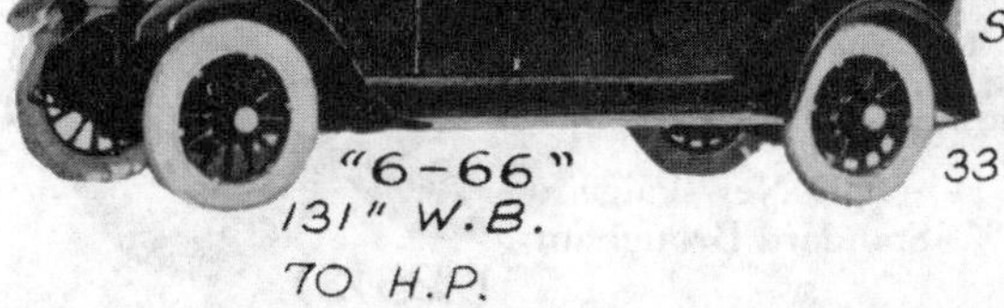

1922-STYLE TOP BOWS

"6-66" 131" W.B. 70 H.P.

331.4 C.I.D. CONT. ENG. (THROUGH '25)

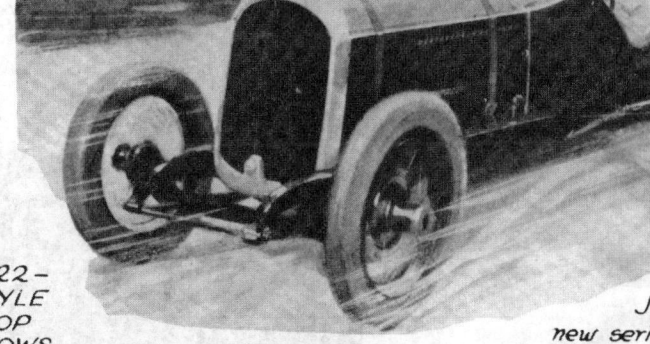

JULY, 1922 = new series "6-66" has NEW CLUTCH AND TRANSMISSION THAT PERMITS DOWN-SHIFTING FROM HIGH TO 2ND GEAR AT 35 M.P.H.

23

PAIGE

"6-66" BECOMES "6-70" IN 1923.

"6-70" DASH

131" WHEELBASE

"6-70"

24

NIGHT VIEW OF PAIGE FACTORY

4.6 GEAR RATIO

331.4 C.I.D.
6 - CYLINDER
CONTINENTAL
"10-A" ENGINE
73 H.P. @ 2400 RPM
131" W.B.

TOP SPEED = 75 M.P.H.

NOTE DIFFERENT QUARTER - WINDOW STYLE

MODEL "21-24"
4.9 G.R.

25

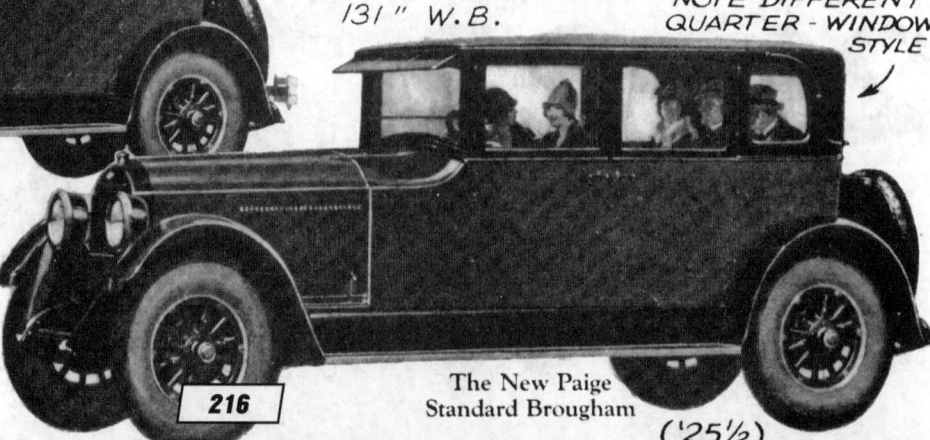

The New Paige
Standard Brougham

('25½)

PAIGE

26

MODEL
"24-26"
6 CYL.
248.8 C.I.D.
63 H.P. @
2800 RPM
HYDRAULIC BRAKES

125" W.B.

32 × 6.00 TIRES

The Most Beautiful Car in America

4.9 GEAR RATIO
109" W.B.

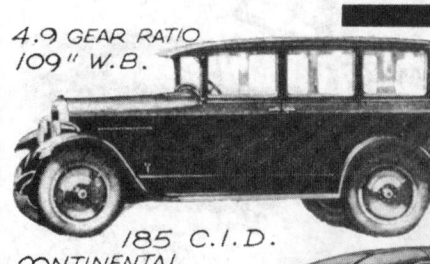

185 C.I.D.
CONTINENTAL
SPECIAL ENGINE
43 H.P.
@
2600
RPM

"6-45"
COUPE

4.45 GEAR RATIO
115" W.B.

HYDRAULIC BRAKES

MODEL
"6-45"
(FORMERLY
"JEWETT")

27

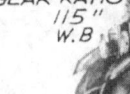

"6-65"
249 C.I.D., 63 H.P. @
2800 RPM

"6-75"
268 C.I.D., 68 H.P.
@ 3000 RPM
4.82 GEAR RATIO
125" W.B.

There are in the new Paige line 20 charming body types and color combinations on 4 chassis from $1095 to $2795 — all prices f. o. b. Detroit

STRAIGHT-8
"8-85"

4.82 G.R.

298.6
C.I.D. LYC.
ENG.
80 H.P.
@ 3000

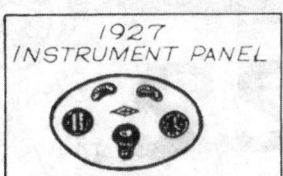

1927
INSTRUMENT PANEL

NEW NAME FOR
1928 :
GRAHAM-PAIGE

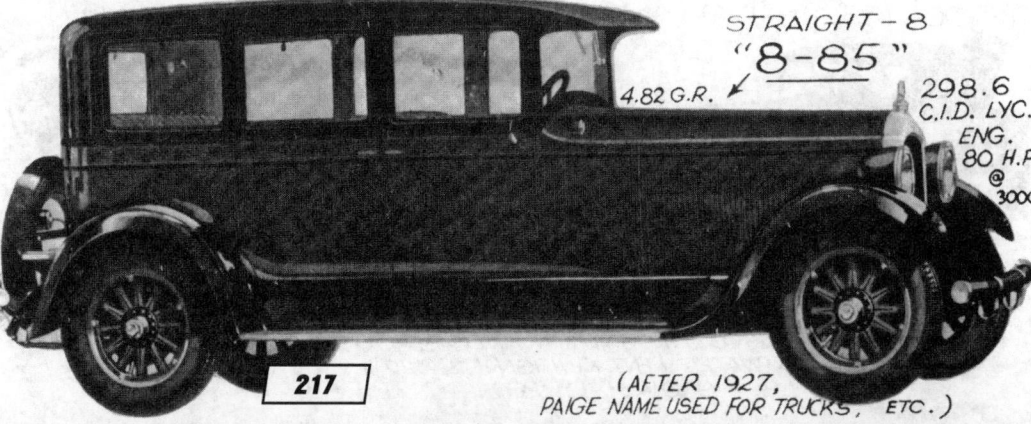

(AFTER 1927,
PAIGE NAME USED FOR TRUCKS, ETC.)

217

108" W.B.
MODEL "A"

PAN (1918-1922)

4 CYL., 165.9 C.I.D.
OWN O.H.V. ENGINE
33 x 4 TIRES
4.9 G.R.   (SEATS COULD BE
FOLDED, TO FORM
A BED.)

PAN MOTOR CO.,
ST. CLOUD, MINN.

125" W.B.
32 x 4 TIRES

PARENTI

(1920-1922)

OWN AIR COOLED V-8

PARENTI MOTORS CORP., BUFFALO, N.Y.

2 3/4" x 4 1/4" BORE and STROKE

PATERSON 6

22 "22-6-52"

W. A. PATERSON CO., FLINT, MICH.

(1908 — 1923)

('21)

('23)

32 x 4 1/2 TIRES
(THROUGH '23)
298.2 C.I.D.

4.5 G.R.
120" W.B.

21 "6-50"

6-CYL. CONTINENTAL ENGINE
(THROUGH '23)
224 C.I.D. (ALSO ON
'20 "6-47")

DELCO IGNITION (THROUGH
'23)

23 "23-6-52"
242 C.I.D.

7-PASS. SEDAN
SERIES 7
(V-8)
('21)

PEERLESS

(1900-1932) PEERLESS MOTOR CAR COMPANY, CLEVELAND, OHIO

Peerless Eight

MODEL "56"
('20)

19-22

"56-7"
CONT'D.
INTO 1922.

125" W.B. (THROUGH '22)
AUTO-LITE IGNITION AND 4.54 G.R. (THROUGH '20)
ATWATER-KENT IGNITION ('21-'22)
4.9 G.R. (TO '26)

OWN 331.8 C.I.D., V-8 L-HEAD ENGINE
(THROUGH '28)
34 x 4 1/2 TIRES (THROUGH '22)

PEERLESS

MODEL "66"

23

(INTRODUCED AUGUST, 1922)

NEW 128" W.B. (THROUGH '25, ON V-8)

TOWN COUPE (4-PASS.)

DELCO IGN. (ON 8s, THROUGH '29)

33 × 5 TIRES

PAINTED RADIATOR SHELL

24

6 CYL. "70"
V8 ══ "66"

new "70" has OWN 288.6 C.I.D. ENGINE (USED THROUGH '29) 126, 133" W. B. (THROUGH '26) 4.63 G.R., 32 × 4½ TIRES

("EQUIPOISED 8")
V-8 "67"

BALLOON TIRES, HYDRAULIC BRAKES

(INSTRUMENTS IN 3 OVALS, 2 GLASSED-IN)

70 H.P. @ 2500 RPM (THROUGH '26)

NEW RADIATOR DESIGN

25

(STYLE OF 6-CYL. "70" SIMILAR TO 1924) 70 H.P. @ 2500 RPM (THROUGH '29) 4.45 G.R. 33 × 6.20 TIRES

65 MILES PER HOUR

PEERLESS

6 - CYL., 230.2 C.I.D.
CONTINENTAL "8-U"
ENGINE ON NEW "6-80"
Auto-Lite IGNITION
30 × 5.77 TIRES ('26)
32 × 6.00 ('27)

26-27

FRENCH-STYLE
ROOF VISOR
(IN VOGUE ON
MANY AMERICAN
CARS OF 1925
TO 1928.)

The Remarkable
Six ~ 80
$1395 to $1795

116" W.B.
54 H.P. ('26)
63 " ('27)

288.5 C.I.D.
70 H.P. @ 2500
(120" W.B. "6-90"
7-WINDOW LANDAULET
SEDAN (WITH CONVERTIBLE
REAR QUARTERS) ALSO
AVAIL. IN 1927.

The Powerful
Six ~ 72
$1895 to $2995

126" W.B.
70 H.P.

DELCO IGN.
ON 6-72, 8-69

SMALL REAR QUARTER
WINDOWS ON MOST
PEERLESS COUPES
OF LATE 1920s.

133½" W.B. 70 H.P. ('26)
"80 " ('27)

The 90° V-type
Eight-69
$2995 to $3795

6 - 90
(NEW FOR 1927)

116"-W.B. "6-60" IS NEW FOR '27, has 199.1 C.I.D. CONTINENTAL ENG.,
52 H.P. @ 3000 RPM

EARLY 1928 MODELS : "6-60"   "6-80"
"6-90"   "8-69"(V-8)

28 (EARLY)

← MODEL   "6-60"
(INTRODUCED EARLY
SUMMER, 1927, WITH
ROOF-VISOR AS ON
'27 MODELS.)

62 H.P. @ 3000 RPM
(ALSO ON '29-30 "6-61")

PEERLESS
ALL THAT THE NAME IMPLIES

28

EARLIEST "6-91" MODELS HAVE PARKING LAMPS FARTHER BACK ON COWL.

120" W.B.

31 x 6.00

OWN 288.6 C.I.D. ENGINE 70 H.P. @ 2500

↗ *new Six-91*
('28 and '29)
(6-91 has VACUUM TANK.)

"6-91" HAD NO RADIATOR SHUTTERS, BUT ADD-ON ACCESSORY SHUTTERS (AS SHOWN) WERE SOLD SEPERATELY.

"6-61" has 116" W.B. 214.7 CID CONTINENTAL ENG. 62 H.P. @ 3000 4.88 G.R.

SIX .. 81
(INTRODUCED AUGUST 11, 1928)

116" W.B.

248.3 CID CONT'L. ENG. 66 H.P.

29

new FUEL PUMP on 6-61, 6-81, STD. 8

The new Six-61 Sedan

NEW STRAIGHT-8 "8-125" HAS 322 C.I.D. 114 H.P. @ 3300 RPM. RADIATOR SHUTTERS AND 3 SHIELDS ON FRONT BUMPER, ONE ON TIE BAR.

8-125

130" W.B.

30

"6-61-A" IS CONTINUATION OF '29 MODEL. (FINAL 6 AVAIL.)

STANDARD 8 HAS SINGLE GROUP OF VERTICAL HOOD LOUVRES AS ON "6-81" ABOVE, BUT PARKING LAMPS ON FENDERS.

AUTO-LITE IGNITION

MASTER 8 →

125" W.B., 4.45 G.R. 6.00 x 19 TIRES

MECH. BRKS. ON 8s

MASTER and CUSTOM 8 RATED 120 HP ('30)

138" W.B. CUSTOM 8 HAS VENT DOORS ON HOOD AND BEVELED LOWER DOOR EDGES ON SEDAN

31
TO
32

MECHANICAL BRAKES REPLACE HYDRAULICS ON ALL MODELS. 118"-W.B. STD. 8 ('31 ONLY) MASTER and CUSTOM 8s CONT'D.

MASTER 8 and CUSTOM 8 have 322 C.I.D. CONT. "13K" ENG. (115 H.P. @ 3200)

SAMPLE '32 V-16 ALSO BUILT.

221

The PETERS AUTOMOBILE
"Everybody's Car"

Peters Motor Corporation
Trenton   New Jersey
(1921—1922)

BUDDY MODEL   90" W. B.

IN 1919, PEAKED RADIATOR AND LOUVRELESS HOOD ADOPTED, IN ROLLS-ROYCE STYLE.

PHIANNA
NEW SERIES

(19-'21)

(1916-1922)
(PHIANNA MOTORS CO., NEWARK, N.J. — TO 1918

M. H. CARPENTER, LONG ISLAND CITY, N.Y. — 1919 ON)

"1922" PHIANNAS BUILT FROM 1921 PARTS ON HAND.

Piedmont
MOTOR CAR CO CO
LYNCHBURG VIRGINIA

(1917-1922) ## PIEDMONT
PIEDMONT MOTOR CAR CO., LYNCHBURG, VA.

MODEL E

THE PIERCE-ARROW MOTOR CAR COMPANY, Buffalo, N.Y.

PIERCE-ARROW
(1901 TO 1938)

"38" 134" W.B.

20
(RIGHT-HAND DRIVE)

"48" 142" W.B.

1921 — NEW MODEL "33" (138" W.B.) REPLACES 2 PREVIOUS MODELS

LEFT-HAND DRIVE

DUAL-VALVE ENGINE

4.28 G.R.

6 CYLS., 414.7 C.I.D.

21-23

('23)

PIERCE-ARROW

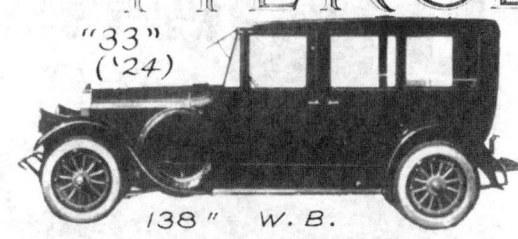

"33" ('24)

138" W. B.

"33" ('25)

100 H.P. @ 2600

24-26

LOWER-PRICED SERIES "80"
INTRODUCED
MID-1924.

Series 80

1925-6
"80"
HAS 288.6
C.I.D., 6 CYLS.,
70 H.P. @ 2600 RPM
130" W.B.

COACH
('25½)

27

"80"
(130" W.B.)

"36"
(138" W.B.)

223

PIERCE-ARROW

28

"81" REPLACES "80"

"36"
7-PASSENGER TOURING CAR
4.29 G.R.

"6-81" INSTRUMENT PANEL

75 H.P. @ 3200 RPM
130" W.B.
4.45 G.R.

29

"143"
(HOOD VENT DOORS)

NEW STRAIGHT-8 ENGINE
365 CU. IN. DISPL.
125 H.P. @ 3200 RPM
new FUEL PUMP

INSTRUMENT PANEL

143" W.B.

"133"
(7 GROUPS of VERTICAL HOOD LOUVRES)

133" W.B.

30

4.08 and 4.42 G.R.

"B"

340, 366
and 385 C.I.D. STRAIGHT-8s,
DEVELOPING 115, 125, 132 H.P.
@ 3000 RPM

132³/₈, 134, 139, 144" W.B.

31

"43" = 125 H.P.
134-7" W.B.
"42," "41" =
132 H.P.
142-7 W.B.

PIERCE ARROW

"54" STRAIGHT-8 HAS 366 C.I.D., 125 H.P. @ 3000

"53" V-12 = 140 H.P. @ 3100
"52," "51" V-12 = 150 H.P. @ 3100

4.42 GEAR RATIO

32

8

V-12 (NEW) 398 and 429 C.I.D.

7.00 × 17 TIRES
7.50 × 17 ON LARGE V-12.

"836"
136-9" W.B.

"SILVER ARROW" HAS SMALL REAR WINDOW

135-H.P. 8

POWER BRAKES
"1236" = 136" OR 139" W.B.
"1247," "1242" = 137" OR 142" W.B.

33

429 and 462-C.I.D. V-12s (160 and 175 H.P.)

"SILVER ARROW" AND ITS INTERIOR

34

"836-A"
DIFFERENT GRILLE, NO HOOD VENTS.*
(LOWER-PRICED MODEL,
STARTS APRIL, 1934.)

8 = 385 C.I.D.,
140 H.P. @ 3400

V-12 = 462 C.I.D.,
175 H.P. @ 3400

"836-A" DASH

* = HOOD VENTS OPTIONAL ON SOME "836-A" MODELS.

"1240-A"

MODIFIED "SILVER ARROW" OFFERED FOR 1934.

PIERCE-ARROW

35

CHOICE OF STR.8
V-12, CONT'D.
THROUGH '38.

"845," "1245," OR "1255"

17" WHEELS AS BEFORE,
CONT'D. THROUGH '38.

36

"1601"
STRAIGHT-8
HAS 139" OR 144" W.B.,
150 H.P. @ 3400 RPM

"1602," "1603" V-12s HAVE
139", 144", 147" W.B.,
185 H.P. @ 3400 RPM

← BACK SEAT OF
1936 MODEL

MECHANICAL BRAKES STILL RETAINED.

37-38

'37 = 1700 SER.

'38 = 1800 SER.

DISCONTINUED 1938

PILOT (1909-1924)

PILOT MOTOR CAR CO.,   120" W.B.
RICHMOND, IND.   (THROUGH '20)

"6-45" (SINCE '16)
HAS TEETER 6-CYL.
ENG. (230.1 CID)

('19-21)

126" W.B., 6-CYL.,
248.9 C.I.D.
HERSCH.-SPLM.
ENGINE (IN '21)

('22)

126" W.B.
('21 THROUGH '24)

('23)

('24)

"6-50"
CUSTOM SEDAN
6-CYL.
HERSCH.-SPLM.
"E" ENGINE
288.6 C.I.D.

"6-56"

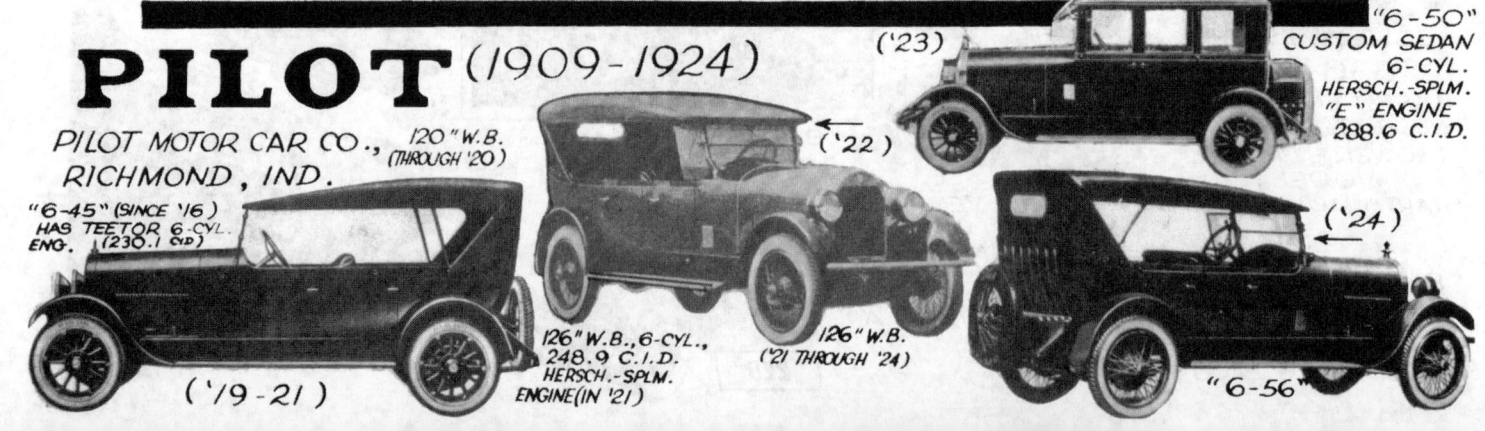

PLYMOUTH
A CHRYSLER
M O T O R S   P R O D U C T

"NARROW PROFILE" RADIATOR SHELL

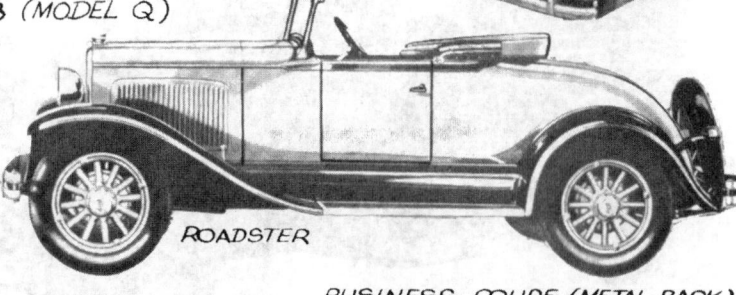

EARLY EMBLEM (CHRYSLER PLYMOUTH) MODEL "Q"

IN JAN, 1929, MODEL "U" BEGINS, WITH THE ABOVE EMBLEM

STARTS JUNE, 1928 (MODEL Q)

29

ROADSTER

REPLACES 1928 CHRYSLER "52" (4 CYLS.)

MODEL "Q"

(170.3 C.I.D.)

(4.6 COMPR.)

BUSINESS COUPE (METAL BACK)

45 H.P. @ 2800 RPM

GAS GAUGE ON TANK

109" WHEELBASE
4.3 GEAR RATIO

FEDCO I.D. PLATE

DASH

SOFT-TOP COUPE IS VERY SCARCE.

MODEL "U" STARTS 1-29, WITH IMPROVED 175.4 C.I.D. ENGINE (HAS NEW SQUARED-OFF CORNERS ON CYLINDER HEAD.)

SPORT COUPE

(EARLY '30 IS SIMILAR TO '29 MODEL.)

DELCO-REMY IGNITION (THROUGH '34)

30
LATE MODEL

STARTS APRIL, 1930 (EARLY '31 SIMILAR)

"NEW FINER" series

4.33 GEAR RATIO

EARLY TYPE WITH RECTANGULAR REAR WINDOW

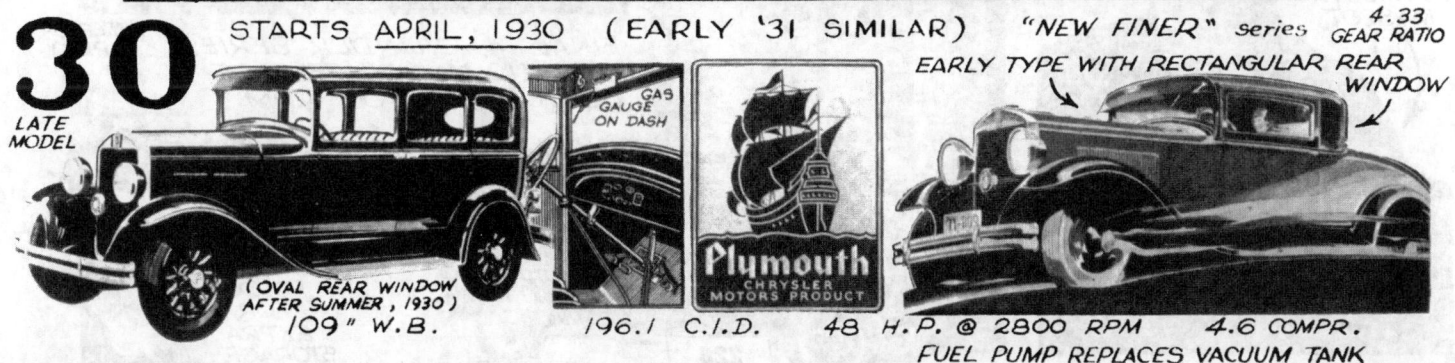

GAS GAUGE ON DASH

Plymouth
CHRYSLER MOTORS PRODUCT

(OVAL REAR WINDOW AFTER SUMMER, 1930)
109" W.B.

196.1 C.I.D.   48 H.P. @ 2800 RPM   4.6 COMPR.
FUEL PUMP REPLACES VACUUM TANK

PLYMOUTH

COWL VENTS ARE DELUXE EQUIPMENT

NEW GRILLE

31½ - 32

MODEL "PA"

STARTS JUNE, 1931

109 3/8" W.B.
56 H.P. @ 2800 RPM
NEW 4.9 COMPRESSION

"NEW Floating Power"

FLEXIBLE ENGINE MOUNTS, "EASY-SHIFT" CONSTANT-MESH TRANSMISSION, AND FREE WHEELING

SCREEN-TYPE STONE GUARD IS OPTIONAL

NEW SHIELD-SHAPED RADIATOR EMBLEM, NEW MASCOT, NEW HUB CAPS

NEW CIRCULAR DASH GAUGES (5 IN A ROW)

INTERIOR ("PA")

WIRE WHEELS STANDARD EQUIPMENT

"PA" "THRIFT" SEDANS (WITH ONLY 3 DASH GAUGES) AVAILABLE AFTER "PB" MODELS INTRODUCED.

WALTER P. CHRYSLER (FOUNDER OF CHRYSLER CORP.) SHOWING 1932 PLYMOUTH MASCOT

32½

MODEL "PB"

INTRODUCED APRIL, 1932

FINAL 4-CYLINDER SERIES
NEW 112 3/8" WHEELBASE
65 H.P. @ 3400 RPM

INTERIOR ("PB")

COUPE SEAT BACK FOLDS, FOR EXTRA STORAGE

(5.6 - COMPRESSION "Red Head" OPTIONAL)

228

NEW BODY DOORS HINGED AT REAR

PLYMOUTH

33
(FIRST 6-CYL. PLYMOUTH)

NEW 4.38 GEAR RATIO

"PC" MODEL (10-32 TO 3-33) CHROME ON RADIATOR SHELL 107" W.B.

189.8 C.I.D. 70 H.P. @ 3600 RPM WITH 5.5-COMPR. "SILVER DOME" HEAD, OR 76 H.P. @ 3600 RPM WITH 6.5-COMPRESSION "Red Head"

33½
(3-33 TO 12-33. PAINTED RADIATOR SHELL)

"PD"

STD. 107¾" W.B.
DE LUXE 113½" W.B.

34

"PF" "PG" MODELS 107¾" W.B.

"PE" DE LUXE has 113½" W.B.

4.11 GEAR RATIO

new 201.3 C.I.D. (THROUGH 1941)

NEW VENT WINDOWS ROLL DOWN INTO DOORS.

77 H.P. @ 3600 RPM WITH 5.8 COMPRESSION OR 82 H.P. @ 3600 WITH 6.5 ALUMINUM CYL. HEAD

DIP IN BUMPER

HOOD VENT DOORS NOT ON STD. MODELS.

35
"PJ"

4.13 GEAR RATIO

113" W.B. 85 H.P. @ 3600 RPM

6.7 COMPR. (THROUGH '41)

LATE '35 MODEL

(EARLY '35s [SHOWN AT LEFT] HAVE CHROMED HOOD "PORT-HOLES.")

AUTO-LITE IGNITION REPLACES DELCO-REMY.

229

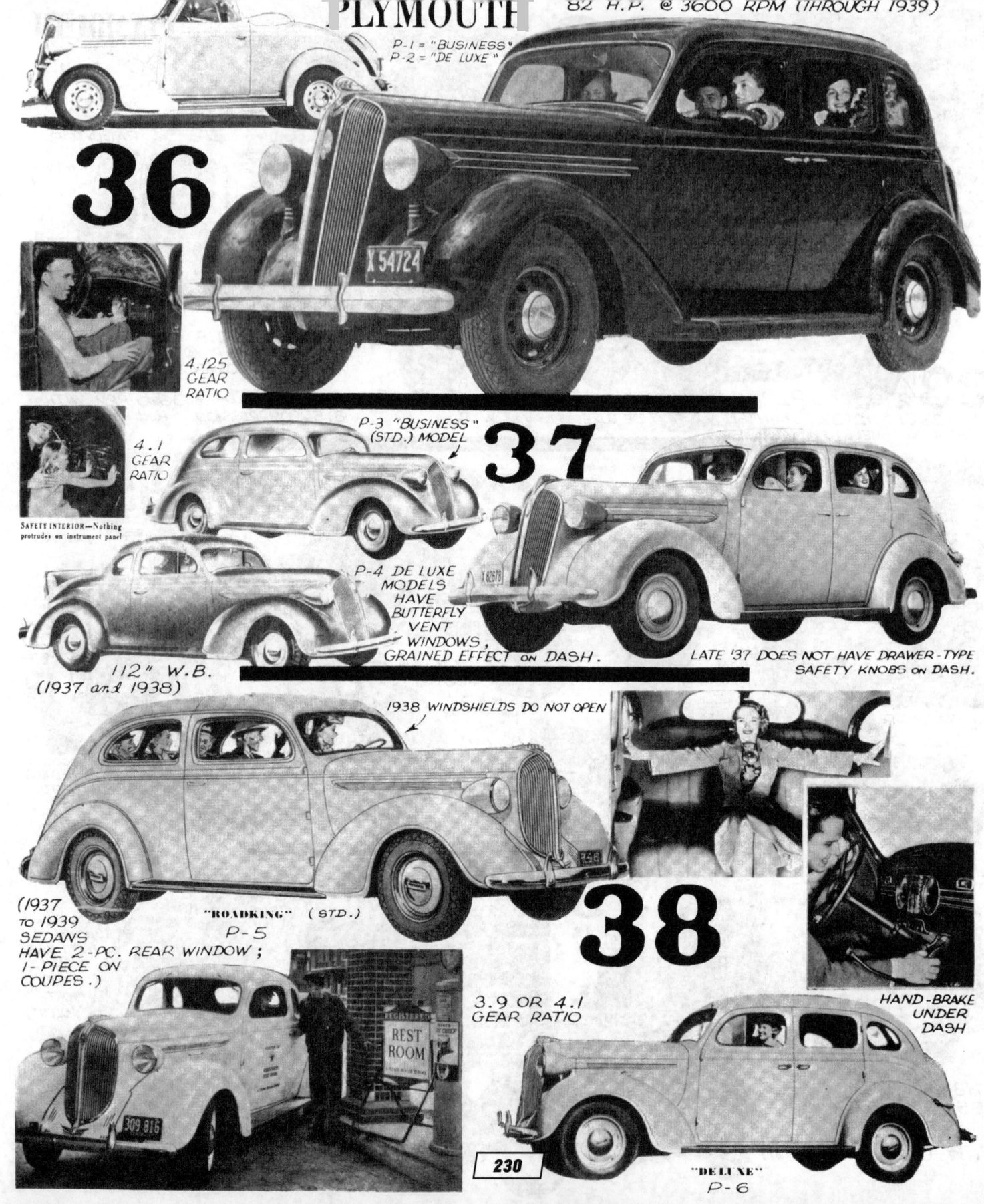

PLYMOUTH

82 H.P. @ 3600 RPM (THROUGH 1939)

P-1 = "BUSINESS"
P-2 = "DE LUXE"

36

4.125 GEAR RATIO

4.1 GEAR RATIO

SAFETY INTERIOR—Nothing protrudes on instrument panel

P-3 "BUSINESS" (STD.) MODEL

37

P-4 DE LUXE MODELS HAVE BUTTERFLY VENT WINDOWS, GRAINED EFFECT on DASH.

LATE '37 DOES NOT HAVE DRAWER-TYPE SAFETY KNOBS on DASH.

112" W.B.
(1937 and 1938)

1938 WINDSHIELDS DO NOT OPEN

(1937 to 1939 SEDANS HAVE 2-PC. REAR WINDOW; 1-PIECE ON COUPES.)

"ROADKING" (STD.)
P-5

38

HAND-BRAKE UNDER DASH

REGISTERED REST ROOM

3.9 OR 4.1 GEAR RATIO

"DELUXE"
P-6

PLYMOUTH

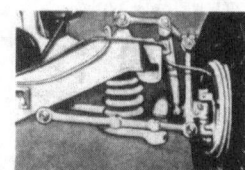

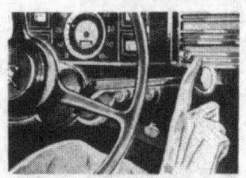

PERFECTED Remote Control Shifting with new All-Silent Auto-Mesh Transmission.

NEW "SAFETY SIGNAL" SPEEDOMETER

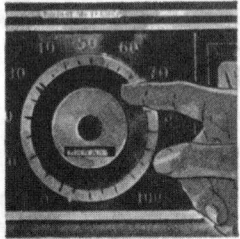

Indicator Light shows green up to 30 miles per hour...from 30 to 50, amber ...above 50, a warning red.

NEW AMOLA STEEL Coil Springs...

3.9, 4.1, OR 4.3 GEAR RATIO

NEW "ROADKING" (P-7)
NEW "DELUXE" (P-8)

NEW 114" W.B.

39

TURN A SWITCH AND THE TOP GOES UP OR DOWN—BY ITSELF!

AN "ECONOMY" ENGINE WITH 5.2 COMPR. and 65 H.P. WAS AVAIL. IF DESIRED, FROM 1935 THROUGH 1940.

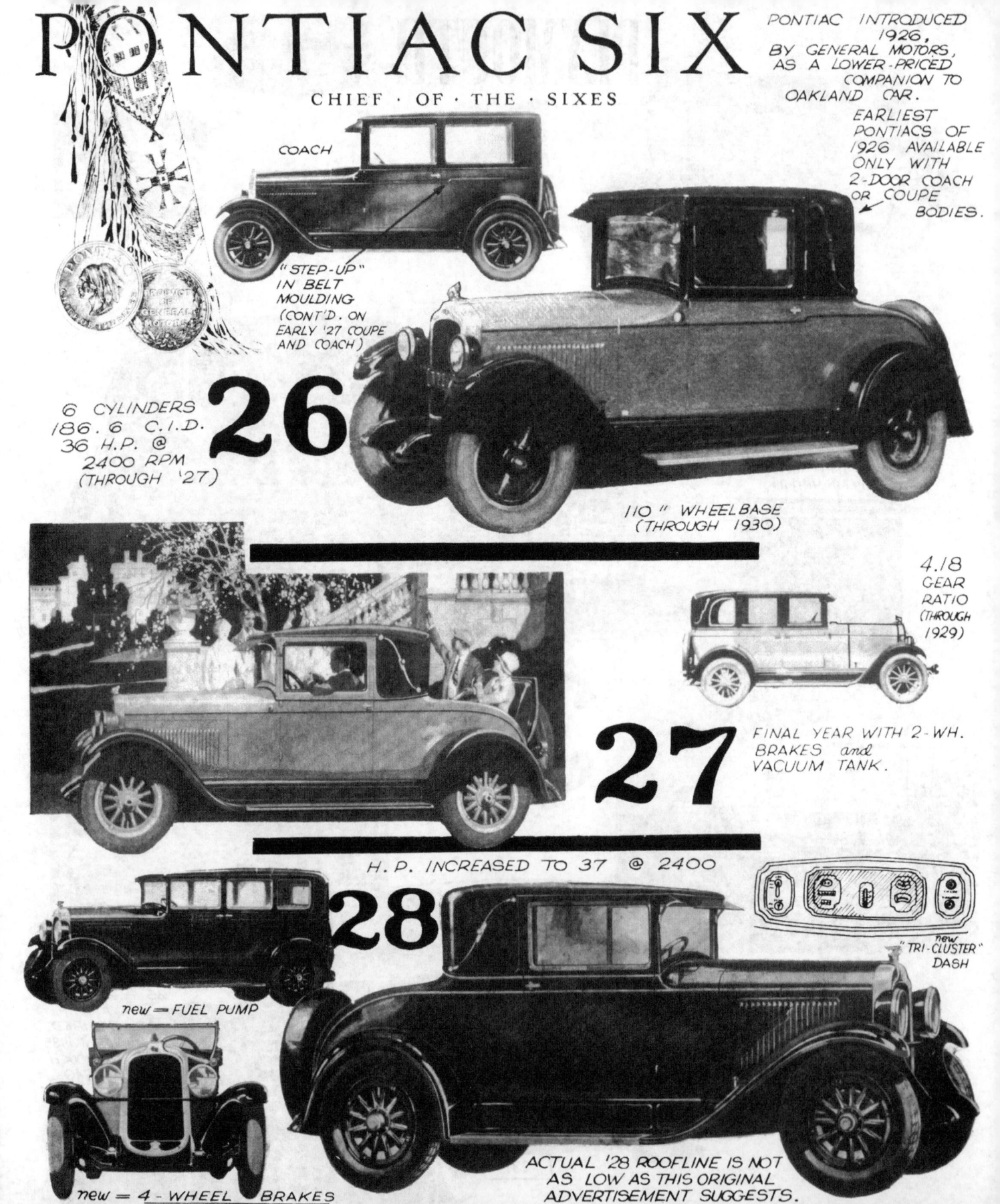

PONTIAC SIX

CHIEF · OF · THE · SIXES

PONTIAC INTRODUCED 1926, BY GENERAL MOTORS, AS A LOWER-PRICED COMPANION TO OAKLAND CAR.

EARLIEST PONTIACS OF 1926 AVAILABLE ONLY WITH 2-DOOR COACH OR COUPE BODIES.

COACH

"STEP-UP" IN BELT MOULDING (CONT'D. ON EARLY '27 COUPE AND COACH)

6 CYLINDERS 186.6 C.I.D. 36 H.P. @ 2400 RPM (THROUGH '27)

26

110" WHEELBASE (THROUGH 1930)

4.18 GEAR RATIO (THROUGH 1929)

27

FINAL YEAR WITH 2-WH. BRAKES and VACUUM TANK.

H.P. INCREASED TO 37 @ 2400

28

new "TRI-CLUSTER" DASH

new = FUEL PUMP

new = 4-WHEEL BRAKES

ACTUAL '28 ROOFLINE IS NOT AS LOW AS THIS ORIGINAL ADVERTISEMENT SUGGESTS.

PONTIAC

EARLY SERIES 29

(HORIZONTAL → HOOD LOUVRES)

RDSTR. *and* PHAETON *have* BODY BY OAKLAND-PONTIAC. FISHER BODY ON OTHERS.

200.4 C.I.D. (THROUGH '32)
57 H.P. @ 3000 RPM
OVAL REAR WINDOW

← **29½**

(VERTICAL HOOD LOUVRES)

29 x 5.00 TIRES

60 H.P. @ 3000 RPM (THROUGH '31)

4.42 GEAR RATIO

30

"6 - B"

SLIGHTLY SLANTED WINDSHIELD

5.00 x 19

4.55 GEAR RATIO

112" W. B.
5.00 x 19 TIRES

31

"6-401"

PONTIAC

32

(6 HAS INDIAN HEAD MASCOT, V-8 HAS BIRD.)

251 C.I.D. V-8 (1 YEAR ONLY)

· 65 H.P. @ 3200 (6)

85 H.P. @ 3400 (V-8)

"6-402" OR "8-302"

6 CYL. OR V-8

CHIEF OF VALUES

5.25 × 18 TIRES (6)
6.00 × 17 TIRES (V-8)

114" W.B. (6)
117" W.B. (V-8)

4.55 (6) OR 4.22 (8) GEAR RATIOS

(NO 6-CYLINDER PONTIACS FOR 1933 OR 1934)

MODEL "8-601"

33

(STRAIGHT-8)

223.4 C.I.D. (THROUGH 1935)

75 H.P. @ 3600 RPM

115" WHEELBASE
4.44 GEAR RATIO

5.50 × 17 TIRES ('33)

6.00 × 17 TIRES ('34)

34

(STRAIGHT-8)
"8-603"

84 H.P. @ 3600 RPM

117 1/4" W.B.
4.55 GEAR RATIO

PONTIAC

Silver Streak SIXES AND EIGHTS

8 HAS LEAPING FIGURE HOOD ORNAMENT; 6 HAS INDIAN HEAD IN CIRCLE.

(INTRODUCED DEC. 29, 1934)

STARTING 1935, 6 HAS 6.00 × 16 TIRES, 8 HAS 6.50 × 16

35

6-CYL. MODEL AVAILABLE ONCE AGAIN. STRAIGHT-8 CONTINUED.

HYDRAULIC BRAKES

8   6

TAIL/STOP LIGHT ON LEFT SIDE OF TRUNK DOOR.

1935 MODEL WAS FIRST TO USE FAMOUS "SILVER STREAK" BANDS OF CHROME ALONG CENTER OF HOOD (A PONTIAC TRADEMARK UNTIL MID-'50s.)

Pontiac's ridged Silver Streak and "V" windshield diffuse and deflect sun-glare.

"6-701" OR "6-AB" (6) 112" W.B. 208 C.I.D.* 80 H.P. @ 3600*

"8-605" OR "8-AA" (8) 116 5/8" W.B. 84 H.P. @ 3800

* – THROUGH '36

235

PONTIAC

6 = "BB" or "6-BA" DE LUXE
8 = "BA"

DE LUXE 8 COUPE

36
FRONT DOORS HINGED AT FRONT

SIMPLIFIED STARTING WITH AUTO-MATIC CHOKE

BUILT-IN LUGGAGE AND SPARE TIRE COMPARTMENT

6 SEDAN

THE MOST BEAUTIFUL THING ON WHEELS

236

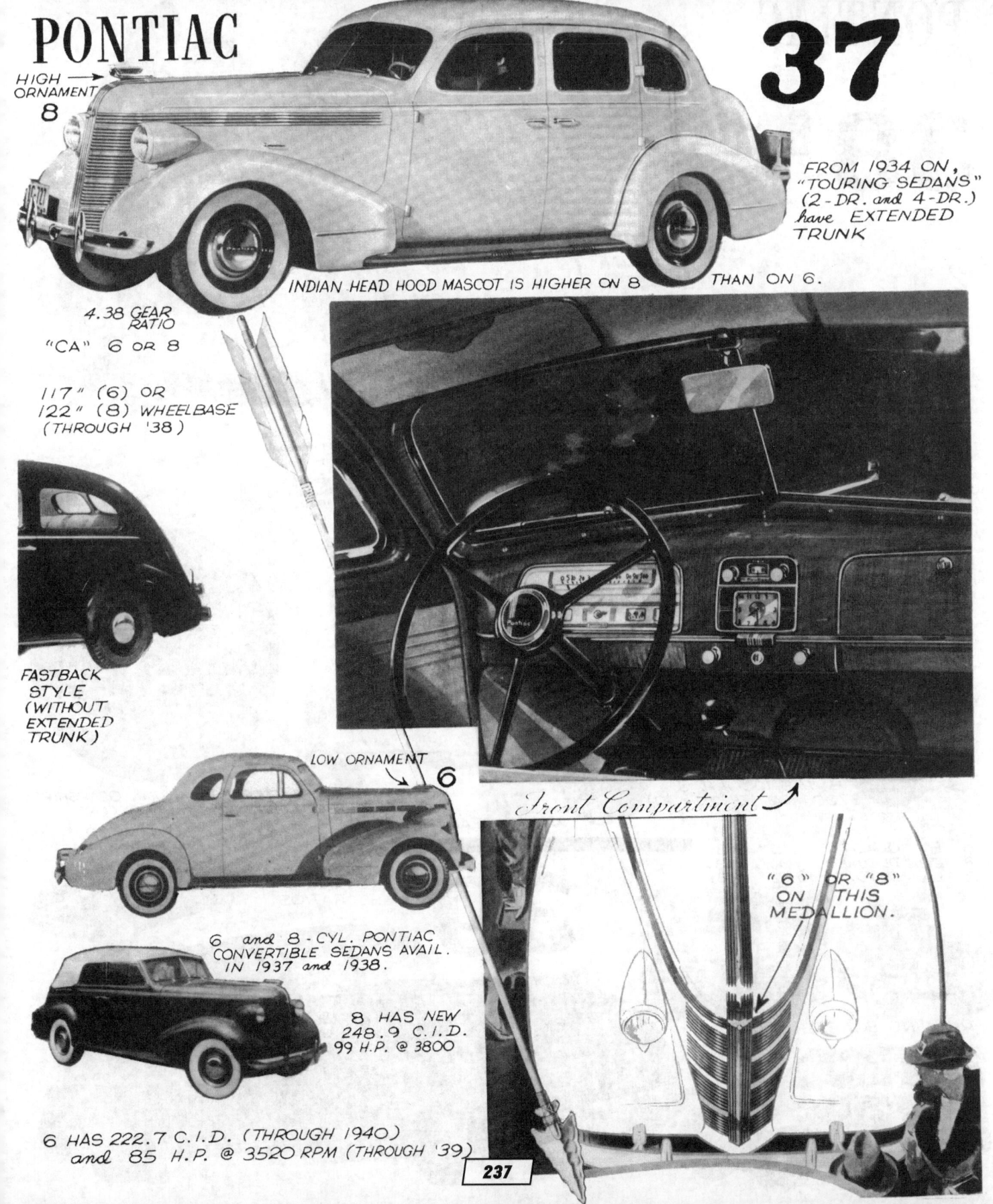

PONTIAC

37

HIGH →
ORNAMENT
8

FROM 1934 ON,
"TOURING SEDANS"
(2-DR. and 4-DR.)
have EXTENDED
TRUNK

INDIAN HEAD HOOD MASCOT IS HIGHER ON 8 THAN ON 6.

4.38 GEAR
RATIO

"CA" 6 OR 8

117" (6) OR
122" (8) WHEELBASE
(THROUGH '38)

FASTBACK
STYLE
(WITHOUT
EXTENDED
TRUNK)

LOW ORNAMENT
6

Front Compartment ↑

"6" OR "8"
ON THIS
MEDALLION.

6 and 8-CYL. PONTIAC
CONVERTIBLE SEDANS AVAIL.
IN 1937 and 1938.

8 HAS NEW
248.9 C.I.D.
99 H.P. @ 3800

6 HAS 222.7 C.I.D. (THROUGH 1940)
and 85 H.P. @ 3520 RPM (THROUGH '39)

PONTIAC

38⁶

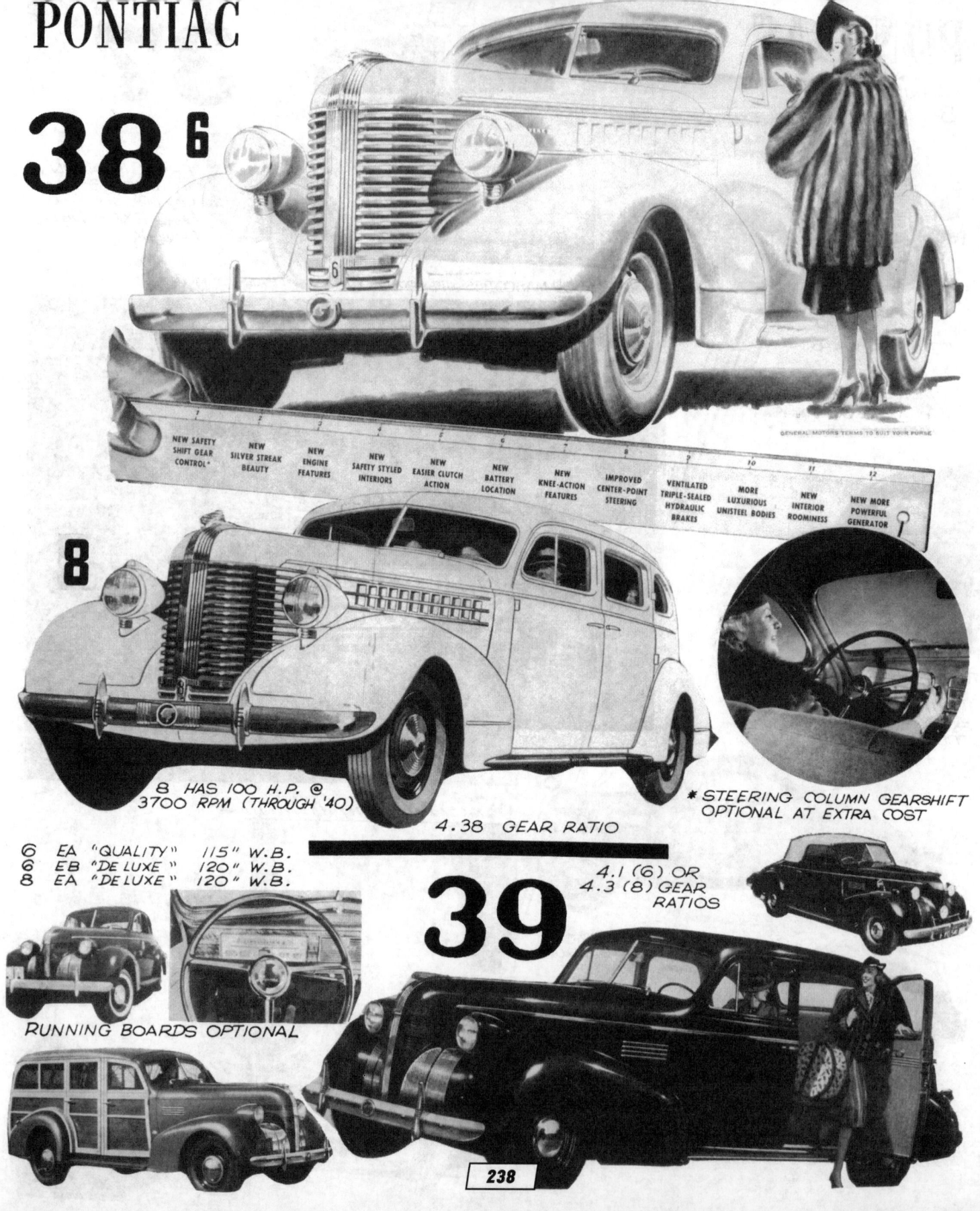

| NEW SAFETY SHIFT GEAR CONTROL* | NEW SILVER STREAK BEAUTY | NEW ENGINE FEATURES | NEW SAFETY STYLED INTERIORS | NEW EASIER CLUTCH ACTION | NEW BATTERY LOCATION | NEW KNEE-ACTION FEATURES | IMPROVED CENTER-POINT STEERING | VENTILATED TRIPLE-SEALED HYDRAULIC BRAKES | MORE LUXURIOUS UNISTEEL BODIES | NEW INTERIOR ROOMINESS | NEW MORE POWERFUL GENERATOR |

GENERAL MOTORS TERMS TO SUIT YOUR PURSE

8

8 HAS 100 H.P. @ 3700 RPM (THROUGH '40)

4.38 GEAR RATIO

* STEERING COLUMN GEARSHIFT OPTIONAL AT EXTRA COST

```
6   EA  "QUALITY"   115" W.B.
6   EB  "DE LUXE"   120" W.B.
8   EA  "DE LUXE"   120" W.B.
```

RUNNING BOARDS OPTIONAL

39

4.1 (6) OR 4.3 (8) GEAR RATIOS

PORTER
MODEL "45" ('20)

(1919 - 1922)
AMERICAN AND BRITISH MFG. CORP., BRIDGEPORT, CONN.

OWN 4-CYL.,
478.4 C.I.D. ENGINE
125 H.P.
12-VOLT ELECTRICAL SYS
3.0 GEAR RATIO
142"
WHEELBASE

MODEL "46"
(3.25 G.R.) ('21)

PREMIER (1903 - 1925)
M O T O R   C O R P
INDIANAPOLIS — USA
THE ALUMINUM SIX WITH MAGNETIC
GEAR SHIFT

EASILY IDENTIFIED BY V-SHAPED
RADIATOR AND STREAMLINED
COWL
LAMPS.

EXHAUST (RT.) SIDE
OF PREMIER'S OWN
ALUMINUM ENGINE (295.3 C.I.D.,
THROUGH 1925)

CUTLER-HAMMER MAGNETIC GEARSHIFT
CONTROLLED FROM STEERING WHEEL

('20)
"6-D"

126 ¾"
WHEELBASE
(THROUGH
1925)

STARTING 1922, CLOCK
and SPEEDOMETER ARE
COMBINED, AND C-H
MAGNETIC GEARSHIFT
BECOMES OPTIONAL,
AT $200. EXTRA.

('21)(6)

"6-D" 7-PASS.
CLOSED CAR

6 CYL.

"NEW SERIES"
"D-24"
('24)

7-PASSENGER SED.

239

R+V KNIGHT
(1920 - 1924)
R. + V. MOTOR CO., EAST MOLINE, ILLINOIS

SLEEVE - VALVE KNIGHT ENGINES

('21)

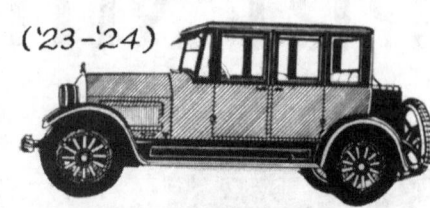

'21 MODEL R HAS NEW 116" W. B.

(LENGTH EXAGGERATED)

('20)

MODEL R = 4 CYL. (220.9 C.I.D.) 115" W.B.

MODEL J = 6 CYL. (259.8 C.I.D.) 127" W.B.

(FORMERLY KNOWN AS MOLINE KNIGHT and MOLINE DREADNOUGHT)

MODEL J SPORT CAR

('23-'24)

RAUCH + LANG ELECTRIC
(1905 - 1928)
BAKER, RAUCH and LANG, CLEVELAND, OHIO (UNTIL '22)
CHICOPEE FALLS, MASS. (TO '28)

also known as "R + L" OR "RAULANG"

('21) "C-55"

('20 MODEL IS SIMILAR)

('24-25)

6 - CYLINDER ENGINES (THROUGH '30)

"THE GOLD STANDARD OF VALUES"

REO

2 - WHEEL MECH. BRAKES (THROUGH '25)
4.66 G.R. (THROUGH '21)
33 x 4 TIRES (THROUGH '22)

(AUTOMOBILES = 1904 -1936)

REO MOTOR CAR COMPANY, Lansing, Mich.

SEDAN AND VICTORIA COUPE HAVE SLANTING WINDSHIELD.

20-21
"T-6" SERIES
6 CYL. F-HEAD ENGINE, 239.4 C.I.D., and 120" W. B. (THROUGH 1926)

NORTHEAST IGNITION (THROUGH '26)

REO22

"T-6" has 50 H.P. @ 2000 RPM, 33 x 4 TIRES

New 4-Passenger Coupe

"(B) T-6" and "U-6" MODELS LISTED DURING 1922.

4.7 G.R. (TO '26)

New Business Coupe

ALSO NEW: "LIGHT 7" SMALL 7-PASS. TOURING

"T-6" 23-24

33 x 4½ TIRES ALSO AVAILABLE IN 1924. (BALLOON TIRES OPTIONAL)

32 x 4

25

"T-6"

50 H.P. @ 2000 RPM (THROUGH '26)

32 x 6.20 BALLOON TIRES (THROUGH '26)

25½

Series G SEDAN

1-PC. WINDSHIELD, FULL-LENGTH BELT MOLDING

NEW ROOF-VISOR

50 H.P.

26

"T-6"

COUPE WITH WEDGE-SHAPED QUARTER WINDOWS AND DECORATIVE LANDAU IRONS

4-WHEEL MECHANICAL BRAKES

REO FLYING CLOUD

SEDAN · VICTORIA
BROUGHAM
SPORT COUPE

27

SPORT COUPE

VICTORIA

NEW "A" SERIES

6 CYLS. 121" WHEELBASE
249 CUBIC IN. DISPLACEMENT
65 H.P. @ 2800 RPM
4.58 GEAR RATIO

HYDRAULIC BRAKES
(THROUGH '36)

27½

COACH
DASH

INTRO. MAY 5, 1927

FINAL "1929" (Summer, '28)
MODELS HAVE MILITARY-STYLE PILLARS,
CADET VISOR.

WOLVERINE

114" W.B.
4.45 G.R.

28

"FLYING CLOUD" has 6-CYL., 249 C.I.D.
OWN ENGINE   DELCO-REMY IGNITION
73 H.P. @ 2800 RPM   121" W.B.
4.58 and other GEAR RATIOS

FLYING CLOUD

WOLVERINE has
6-CYL.   28 x 5.25 and other TIRES
199 C.I.D.
CONTINENTAL "15-E" ENGINE
NORTHEAST IGNITION   50 H.P. @ 2400 RPM

242

30 x 6.20 TIRES

REO

"MATE" EASILY IDENTIFIED BY THIS UNIQUE CURVED MOLDING.

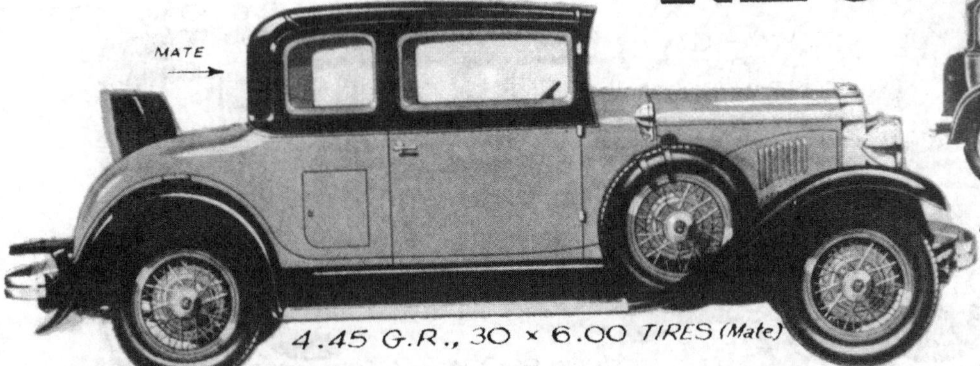

4.45 G.R., 30 × 6.00 TIRES (Mate)

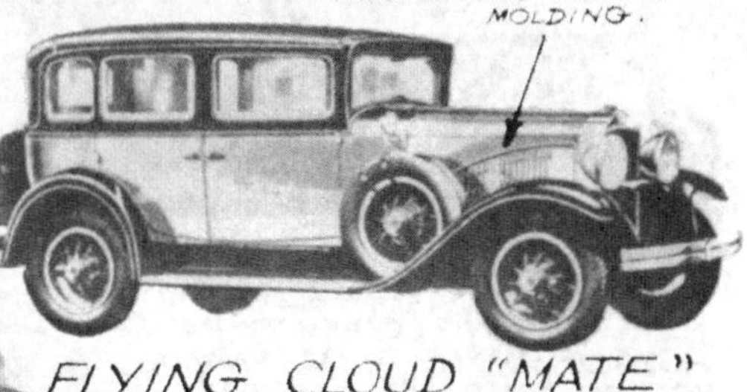

FLYING CLOUD "MATE"

(REPLACES "WOLVERINE" DECEMBER, 1928.)

"MATE" HAS MURRAY BODY, 115" W.B., 6-CYL., 214.7 C.I.D. CONTINENTAL "16-E" ENGINE 65 H.P. @ 2800 RPM new FUEL PUMP

1929 MASTER "FLYING CLOUD" RADIATOR, FITTED WITH OPTIONAL ALLEN SHUTTERFRONT

Delco-Remy IGNITION ON BOTH "MATE" and "MASTER" and on cars that follow.

29

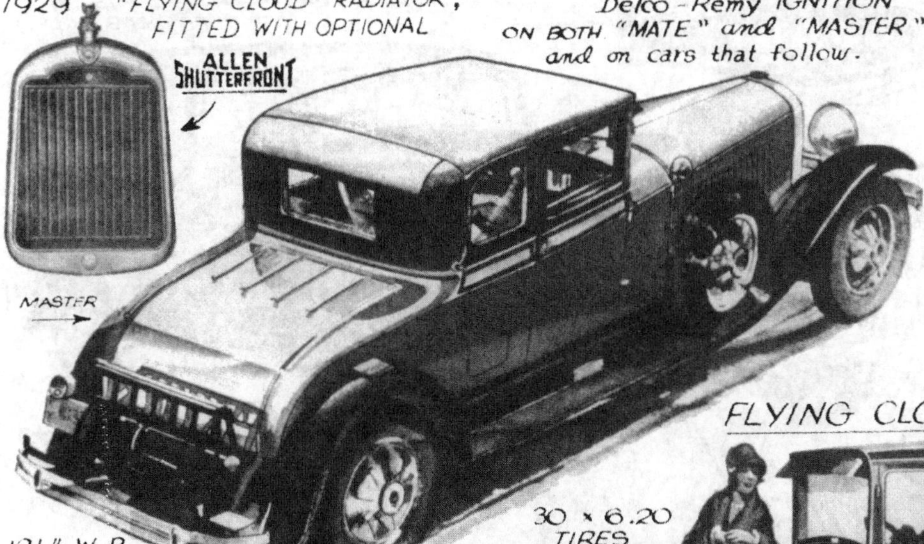

121" W.B.
OWN 6-CYL.
268.3 C.I.D. ENGINE
(USED ON CERTAIN MODELS THROUGH '35)
80 H.P. @ 3200 RPM

1929 ("MASTER") REO ANNOUNCED MARCH, 1928!

FLYING CLOUD ("MASTER" AS OF DEC., 1928.)

30 × 6.20 TIRES

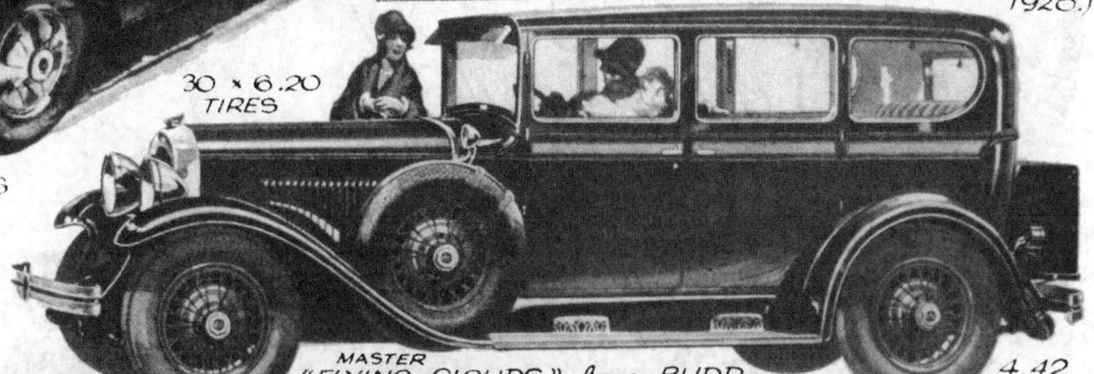

MASTER "FLYING CLOUDS" have BUDD OR HAYES-IONA BODIES.

"MASTER" RETAINS VACUUM TANK.

4.42 G.R.

30

"25" has 124" W.B., VACUUM TANK
OWN 6-CYL., 268.3 C.I.D. ENGINE
80 H.P. @ 3200 RPM
4.42 G.R., 6.50×18 TIRES

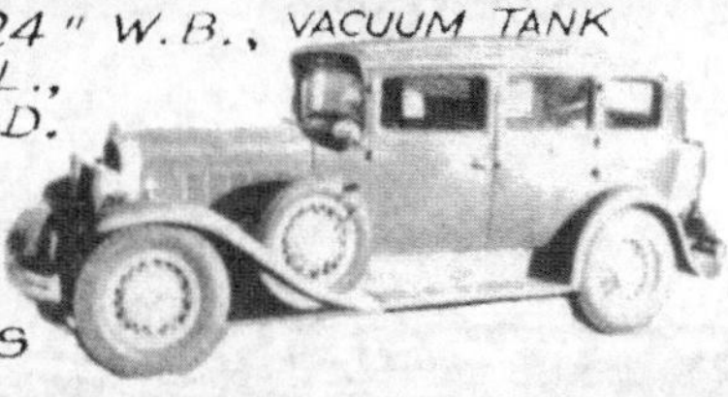

"15" has 115" W.B.
SAME 65-H.P. CONT. "16-E" ENG. AS '29 Mate
4.25 GEAR RATIO
6.00 × 18 TIRES
(SAME TIRES ON "20")
FUEL PUMP

MODEL "20" SPORT COUPE
(SAME ENGINE as "25")
120" W.B., 4.07 G.R.

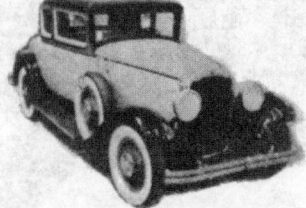

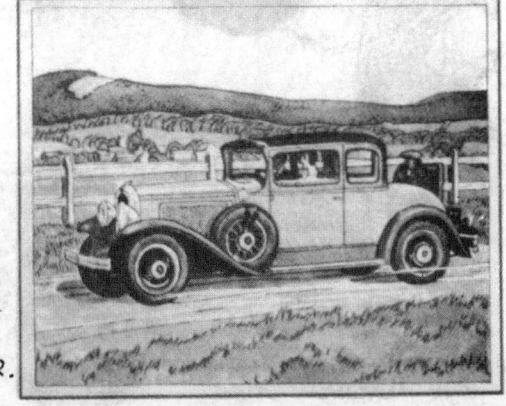

FLYING CLOUD 8

(6 ALSO) **REO**

6-CYL. "25-N" has 125" W.B., 268.3 C.I.D., 85 H.P. 4.42 G.R. 6.50×17 TIRES

FLYING CLOUD "8-21" CUSTOM SEDAN

(SOME FLYING CLOUDS HAVE ROYALE-STYLE AERODYNAMIC BODIES AND V-SHAPED GRILLES, BUT RETAIN EARLY '31 HOOD LOUVRES AS SHOWN ABOVE AND AT RIGHT.)

"8-21" SERIES CONT'D. INTO '32 (INSTRUMENT PANEL) (STD. MODEL HAS MESH V-GRILLE, PARK. LIGHTS ON FENDERS ONLY.)

1931½ "15" SERIES has 116" W.B., 4.27 G.R.

THE *Reo-Royale* EIGHT

1931 ROYALE 8 "N-35" (INTRODUCED OCTOBER, 1930.) has 135" W.B., STRAIGHT-8 357.8 C.I.D. ENG. 125 H.P. @ 3300 RPM (THROUGH '34) 4.07 G.R. 6.50×18 TIRES

31

ROYALE INTERIOR

ROYALE VICTORIA

"N-30" EIGHT has SAME ENGINE, TIRES, G.R. as "ROYALE," BUT has 130" W.B.

STRAIGHT-8 REO ENGINES AVAILABLE 1931 THROUGH 1934.

ROYALE CABRIOLET INTRODUCED APRIL, 1931.

244

REO

"6-21," "6-25" have 268.3 C.I.D., 85 H.P. @3200 RPM, 4.07 G.R. 6.00 × 17 TIRES

"8-21," "8-25" have 268.6 C.I.D., 90 H.P. @3300 RPM, 4.42 G.R. 6.00 × 17 TIRES

"8-31," "8-35 have 357.8 C.I.D., 125 H.P. @3300 RPM, 4.07 G.R. 6.50 × 18 TIRES

FLYING CLOUD MODEL "S"

32

(6 CYL "S" → HAS OUTSWEPT GRILLE)

REO FLYING CLOUD 8-25 COUPE

REO-ROYALE 8-35 SEDAN

REO-ROYALE 8-31 VICTORIA

1932 MODEL NUMBERS INDICATE NO. OF CYLINDERS, and WHEELBASE

1933 "S" has SAME ENGINE SPECS., SAME TIRE SIZE as '32 "6-21," but has 117½" W.B., 4.3 G.R. (STARTS 1-33, as "S-2;" FREE-WHEELING.) ("8-131" ALSO STARTS 1-33.)

"8-131" "ROYALE" 8 has SAME ENGINE SPECS., SAME TIRE SIZE as PREVIOUSLY. 131" W.B. 4.42 G.R. DELUXE MODELS KNOWN as "ELITE" SERIES

* "SELF-SHIFTER" AUTOMATIC TRANSMISSION INTRODUCED BY REO IN SPRING, 1933. (AVAIL. FOR BOTH 6 and 8.)

AN AMAZING NEW INVENTION*

?

33

34 REO

NO GEARSHIFT LEVER
33⅓ % easier to drive

2 LARGE, ROUND DASH INSTRUMENTS at CENTER

SIX (S-6) has 118" W.B., 268 C.I.D., 85 H.P. @ 3200 RPM, 4.3 G.R., 6.00 x 17 TIRES ("S-4" STARTS 12-33, HORIZONTAL LOUVRES.)

"ROYALE" 8 (N2-1) has SAME SPECS. as '33 MODEL; REO'S FINAL STRAIGHT-8.

131" W.B., but "CUSTOM" MODELS have 135" W.B.

MODELS ABOVE SERIAL NO. 5S-28677 START 7-34, CAN BE CONSIDERED "EARLY 1935."

NEW STREAMLINED MODELS START 2-35.

35

6 CYLINDER CARS ONLY ; NO MORE CONVERTIBLES.

REO SELF SHIFTER OPTIONAL IN 1935 REOS

DASH GAUGES MOVED TO LEFT.

FLYING CLOUD "6-A" 228 C.I.D. 90 H.P. @ 3400 RPM 115" W.B.

ROYALE "S-7" ("6-75") 268 C.I.D. 95 H.P. @ 3200 RPM 118" W.B. 6.50 x 16 TIRES BOTH SERIES have 4.3 G.R.

6.25 x 16 TIRES ON "FLYING CLOUD" (1935 and 1936)

COUPES AVAIL., BUT ONLY IN THE Royale '35 SERIES.

NO MORE COUPES , ONLY ONE REMAINING 1936 "FLYING CLOUD" SERIES

6 CYL. 228 C.I.D. 90 H.P. @ 3400

115" W.B. 4.27 G.R.

(STARTS 11-35)

36

AFTER 1936, REO TRUCKS

REVERE (1917-1926)

4-CYL. DUESENBERG ENGINE (TO '23)

131" W.B. (THROUGH '26)

REVERE MOTOR CAR CORP, LOGANSPORT IND

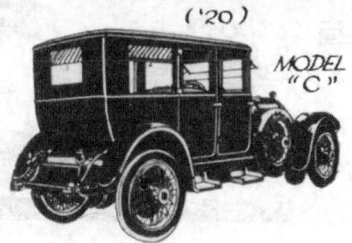
('20) MODEL "C"

32 × 4½ TIRES ON "C" AND "M" SERIES

"M" SERIES ('24-'26) HAS 4-CYL., 360.8 C.I.D. MONSEN/REVERE O.H.V. ENG., 2-WHEEL BRAKES

"25" SERIES ('25-'26) HAS 6-CYL., 331.4 C.I.D. CONT'L. "6-J" 70-H.P. ENG., AND 4-WHEEL BRAKES (32 × 6.20 BALLOON TIRES)   BOSCH IGNITION (ALL MODELS)

RICHELIEU (1922-1923)

(NOTE SIMILARITY TO REVERE CAR, ABOVE LEFT. RICHELIEU DESIGNED BY N. VAN ZANDT, FORMERLY WITH REVERE.)

RICHELIEU MOTOR CAR CORP., ASBURY PARK, N.J.
4-CYLINDER ROCHESTER-DUESENBERG 340.4 C.I.D. ENGINE
78 H.P. @ 2500 RPM   EISEMANN IGNITION

131" W.B.
32 × 4½ TIRES
2-WHEEL BRAKES

Rickenbacker
A · CAR · WORTHY · OF · ITS · NAME

Rickenbacker Motor Company
Detroit   Michigan   (FLYWHEEL AT EACH END OF CRANKSHAFT.)

(1922-1927)

('23) "HAT-IN-RING" EMBLEM

'22 HAS 6-CYL., 218 C.I.D. ENGINE, 58 H.P. @ 2800 RPM, 4.63 G.R., 32 × 4 TIRES, 4-WHEEL BRAKES, 117" W.B.

IGNITION:
AUTO LITE ('22)
ATW. KENT ('23)
BOSCH ('24-'27)
DELCO ('25-'27)

('23)
32 × 4

The only 4-door Coach-Brougham on the American Market

('25)

('25)

6-CYL. ONLY (THROUGH '24)

AM. BOSCH (6-70) OR DELCO-REMY ('27) IGNITION

"D" = 6 CYL., 236.4 CID 70 HP @ 3000
"8" = STRAIGHT-8 268.6 CID
BOTH HAVE 70 HP @ 3000, 117" WB

117"-WB "E-6" OR 121½"-WB "B-8" IN '26

'27 SPECS.
"6-70" = 118½"WB 236.4 CID 70 HP @ 3000
"8-80" = 119½"WB 268.5 CID 80 HP @ 3000
"8-90" = 136"WB

315.2 CID, 95 HP @ 3000

ROAMER (1916-1930)   BARLEY MOTOR CAR CO., KALAMAZOO, MICH.

4-CYL. ROCH.-DUES. ENG. ALSO

128"-WB "6-54" ('20)

6-CYLINDER, 303.1 CID CONT'L. ENGINE

('22) "6-54"

LYCOMING STRAIGHT-8 ENGINES
('27)

4-PASS. CLUB SEDAN "8-78" (120"WB) "8-88" (136"-WB)

ROCKNE 6
(1932-1933)
BY
(STUDEBAKER)

"6-10" IS 1933 MODEL.

"65" (110" W.B.)
189.9 C.I.D., 65
H.P. @ 3200 RPM
4.27 G.R.

"75" (114" W.B.)
205.3 C.I.D., 72
H.P. @ 3200 RPM
4.73 G.R.

(AUTO-LITE IGN. ON ALL)

('32)

5.25 × 18 TIRES (5.50 ON "75")

SPECS. AS '32 "65,"
BUT H.P. UP TO
70 @ 3200

ROLLIN (LATE '23 TO 1925)

ROLLIN MOTORS CO.,
CLEVELAND, OHIO
IGNITION = O.D. ('24) CONNECT. ('25)
31 × 5.20 TIRES   4-WHEEL BRKS.

COUPE DETAILS
('24)

W.B. = 112"   5.1 G.R.
149.3 C.I.D., 41 H.P. @ 2750 RPM (THROUGH '25)

('25)   6 CYL. ALSO

60 M.P.H.

'25 BELT MOLDING
RUNS FULL LENGTH OF CAR.

ROLLS-ROYCE

('23)   BEST CAR IN THE WORLD

6 CYL., 453 C.I.D.,
143½" W.B. ('25)

BUILT
IN
ENGLAND
SINCE 1904.

AMERICAN
FACTORY AT
SPRINGFIELD, MASS.
(1920-1931)

144¾" W.B.

('30)

"PHANTOM"
MODEL

'25 HAS
80 H.P. @
1800 R.P.M.,
3.25 GEAR RATIO,
73 M.P.H.
SPEED

"SILVER GHOST"
MODEL

("SILVER GHOST"
SUPERSEDED 1927
BY "PHANTOM")

7.00 × 20

THIS
1931 MODEL
"DERBY (BREWSTER)
SPEEDSTER" PHAETON
IS THE
FINAL AMERICAN-BUILT
ROLLS-ROYCE.

6 CYLINDERS (468 C.I.D.)
OVERHEAD VALVES (SINCE '29)
100 H.P. @ 2250 RPM

146½" WHEELBASE
3.72 GEAR RATIO
DE JON IGNITION

Roosevelt

MARMON-BUILT

(INTRODUCED MARCH, 1929)

NAMED FOR THEODORE ROOSEVELT, PRESIDENT OF U.S.A. FROM 1901 TO 1909.

A CAR FOR ALL

(1929 - 1930*)

DELCO-REMY IGN.

STRAIGHT 8 engine.

201.9 C.I.D.
77 H.P. @ 3400
5.50 × 19 TIRES
4.9 GEAR RATIO

* = LISTED AS MARMON, '30-'31

RUGBY (1927)

BUILT BY DURANT, PRIMARILY FOR EXPORT. COMPARABLE TO STAR.

NOTE THE RIGHT-HAND DRIVE

RUXTON (1929-1931)

(NEW ERA MOTORS, N.Y.C. "IN COOPERATION WITH" MOON AND KISSEL.)

RAINBOW-COLORED BANDS OF PAINT →

PHAETON, FITTED WITH TYPICAL "WOOD-LITES"

FRONT-WHEEL-DRIVE STRAIGHT-8 CONTINENTAL ENGINE (268.6 C.I.D. "18-S" WITH 100 H.P. @ 3400 RPM)
130" OR 140" W.B.   4.4 G.R.

SEDAN, FITTED WITH CONVENTIONAL-STYLE HEADLIGHTS

SEDAN has BUDD BODY
RDSTR." BAKER RAULANG BODY
PHAETON " KISSEL BODY →
CUSTOM MODELS ALSO

6.00 × 19 TIRES
HYDRAULIC BRAKES
Auto-Lite IGNITION

SAXON

(1913 - 1923)

SAXON MOTOR CAR CO., DETROIT, MICH. and YPSILANTI, MICH.

(6 CYLS. IN 1920)

FOR 1922, 178.9 C.I.D., O.H.V. 4-CYL. ROOT and VAN. ENG. REPLACED BY 192.3 C.I.D. GRAY ENGINE. WAGNER IGNITION

SAXON-DUPLEX 4 CYL. "BLACKSTONE" (5-PASS.) →

('21-23) "125" SERIES

32 × 4 TIRES

4.75 G.R.

SAYERS 6 (1917-1924)

DELCO IGNITION STROMBERG CARB. ('21)

"AVONDALE" 5-PASS.

118" W.B. (THROUGH '23)
6-CYL. 224 C.I.D. CONTINENTAL ENGINE (THROUGH '22)
241.6 C.I.D. IN '23

(SAYERS and SCOVILL CO., CINCINNATI, OHIO)

FOR 1924, NAME CHANGED TO

S. + S. (1924 - 1930)

'25 and '26 "ELMWOOD" SIMILAR TO '24, BUT HAS OVAL REAR QTR. WINDOWS, LANDAU IRONS (34 × 7.30 TIRES IN '26)

new 136" W.B. (TO '27)
new 33 × 5 TIRES (THROUGH '25)

('24)

('24) ← new 331.4 C.I.D. CONT'L. 6-CYL. "6-J" ENG. (TO '27)

S+S "BRIGHTON" 8 PASS. (6 CYL.)

MILITARY CADET VISOR and BOWL HEADLIGHTS for 1929

('29)

"42" SUPERLINE 8-PASS. "LAKEWOOD" SEDAN

STR.-8

FOR '28, "Washington 8" S.+S. HEARSE has 141" W.B., STR.-8 ENG. (3" × 4 3/4" B.+S.) ROOF-VISOR, DRUM ILCO-RYAN LITES, 33 × 6.20 TIRES

new 143" W.B.

new 3 7/8" × 4 1/2 B.+S.

SCHULER (1924)

(2 CYL.)

SCHULER MOTOR CAR CO. MILWAUKEE, WIS.

78" W.B.

6-CYL., 177 C.I.D. NORTHWAY F-HD. 40 H.P. ENGINE   Marvel CARB. 4.5 G.R. CHANGED TO 4.87 for '21.
SINCE '19, CHASSIS SIMILAR TO OAKLAND.

"B-39" TOURING
('20-'21) 115" W.B. 32 × 4 TIRES

SCRIPPS-BOOTH CO., DETROIT

SCRIPPS-BOOTH (1913-1922)

(BECAME A G.M. PRODUCT IN 1918.)

('20)

SEVERIN 6 (1920-1922)

TOURING-SPORTSTER

122" W.B., 6-CYL. CONTINENTAL 303.1 C.I.D. ENGINE

33 × 5 TIRES (33 × 4 on LOWEST-PRICED MODELS.)

SEVERIN MOTOR CAR CO., KANSAS CITY, MO.

SHAW (1920 - 1921)

('21) V-12

WALDEN W. SHAW LIVERY CO., CHICAGO (FORMERLY BUILT TAXIS)

WEIDELY V-12 ENGINE REPLACED 4-CYL. ROCHESTER-DUESENBERG ENGINE, 1921. LATER BECAME "AMBASSADOR."

A PROJECT BEGUN UNDER G.M., SHERIDAN WAS ACQUIRED BY WM. C. DURANT WHEN HE LEFT G.M., AND IT EVOLVED DURING '21 INTO THE 4-CYL. and 6-CYL. DURANT CARS.

SHERIDAN

SHERIDAN MOTOR CAR CO., MUNCIE, IND. (1920-1921)

116 OR 132" W.B., 4-CYL. OR V-8 NORTHWAY ENGINES

4 CYL. "B-41" 35 H.P.

B 41   4 CYL.

33 × 4 OR 33 × 5 TIRES

SINGER MOTOR CO., INC.,
MT. VERNON, N.Y.

SINGER
(1915 - 1920)
3.77 GEAR RATIO   33 x 5 TIRES

(REPLACED THE PALMER-SINGER CAR)

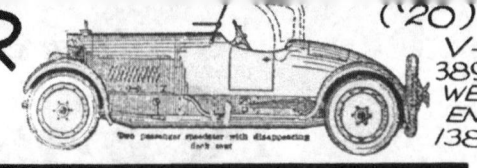
('20)
V-12
389.5 C.I.
WEIDELY ENGINE
138" W.B.

ROADSTER ALSO AVAIL.

"35" SERIES ('21)

SKELTON 4
SKELTON MOTOR CAR CO., ST. LOUIS, MO.
(1920 - 1922)
112" W.B.   192.4 C.I.D., L-HEAD LYCOMING ENGINE
32 x 3½ TIRES

CONNECTICUT IGN.
CARTER CARB.

4- CYLINDER

STANDARD EIGHT

STANDARD STEEL CAR COMPANY
Automotive Dept.   Pittsburgh, Pa

(1912 - 1923)

(V-8)
OWN L-HEAD, 331.8 C.I.D. ENGINE (THROUGH '23)

('20)

127" W.B.
4.45 G.R
ZENITH CARB
34 x 4½ TIRES
(THROUGH '23)

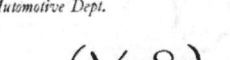

('22)

SPLITDORF IGNITION REPLACES CONNECTICUT FOR '22 and '23.

STANLEY
STEAM CAR
(1897 - 1927)
MANUFACTURER, IN 1924, CHANGED NAME FROM STANLEY MOTOR CARRIAGE CO. TO STANLEY VEHICLE CORP. OF AMERICA
NEWTON, MASS.

('21)
130" W.B.

32 x 4½ TIRES
1.50 GEAR RATIO ON '23 "740" SERIES;
32 x 5.77 TIRES, 122" W.B. and HYDRAULIC BRAKES ON FINAL "252" SERIES

34 x 4½ TIRES ('21)

2 CYL. STEAM ENGINE (4" x 5" CYLINDERS)

(1920 - 1922)
STANWOOD MOTOR CAR CO., ST. LOUIS, MO.

STANWOOD 6
6- CYLINDER CONTINENTAL ENGINE
224 C.I.D.

"A" TOURING CAR
118" W.B.   ('21)
ATW. KENT IGN.
STROMBERG CARB.
33 x 4 TIRES   4.5 G.R.

Low-cost Transportation
Star ⬟ Cars
DURANT MOTORS, Inc., NEW YORK CITY

(1922-1928)

(SHOWN WITH WM. C. DURANT, FOUNDER OF DURANT MOTORS')

22-23

(STARTS 6-22)

30 x 3½ TIRES

102" W. B. *and* 4 - CYLINDER CONTINENTAL 130.4 C.I.D. ENGINE (THROUGH '25)

WAGON ('23)

FOUR GREAT PLANTS AT ELIZABETH, N. J. ○ LANSING, MICH. ○ OAKLAND, CAL. ○ TORONTO, ONT.

24

For Your All-Weather Car Get a Sedan STAR

"SPECIAL" MODELS HAVE NICKEL TRIM *and* OPTIONAL DISC WHEELS.

Low-cost Transportation

Star Cars

The Coupster
TRADE MARK

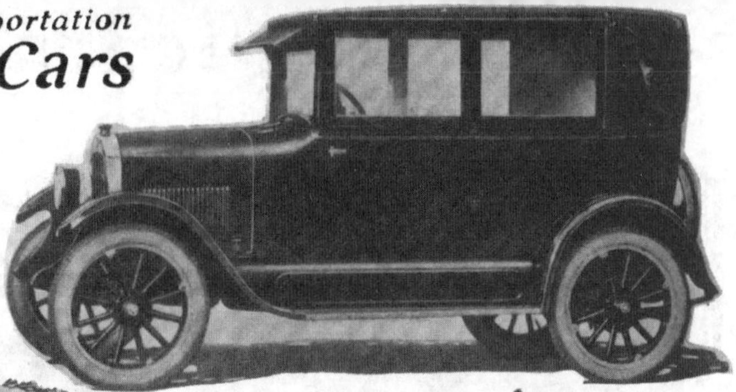

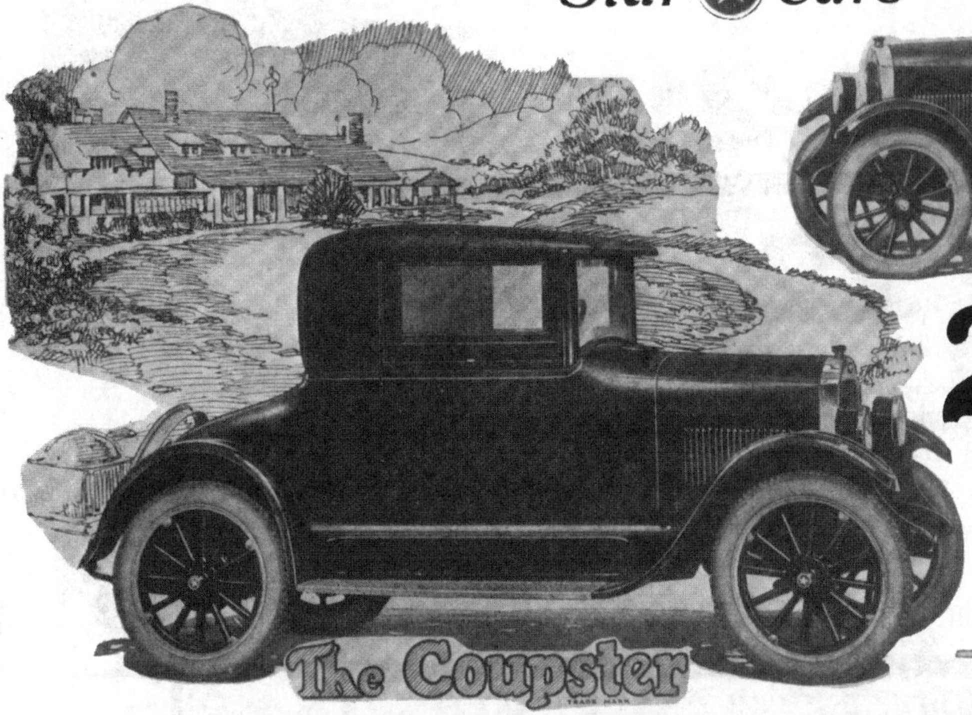

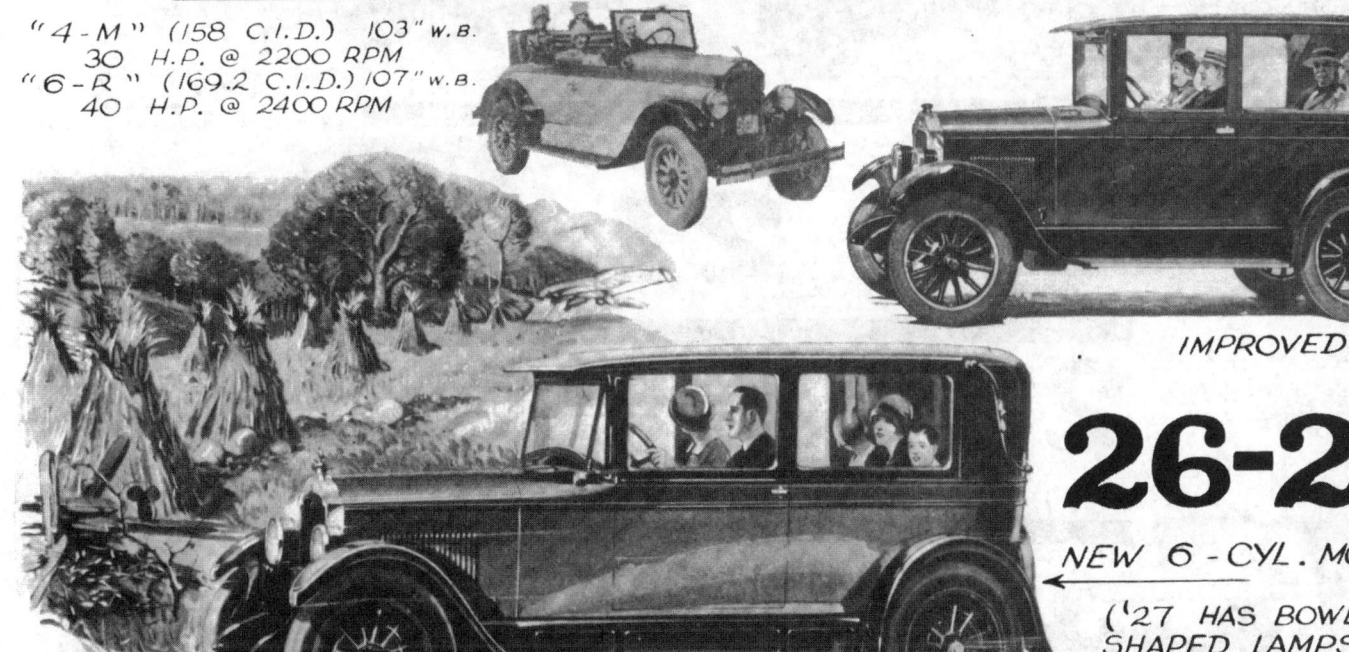

25

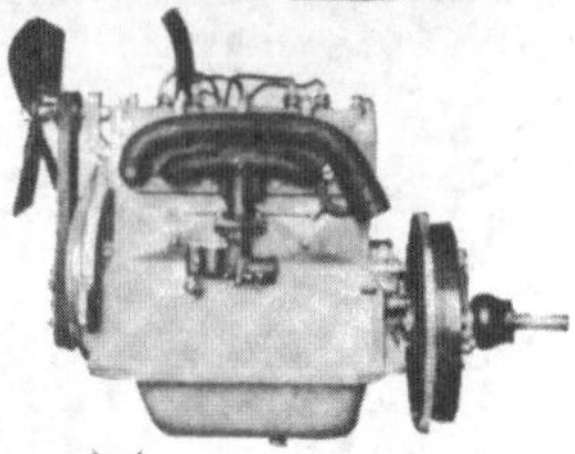

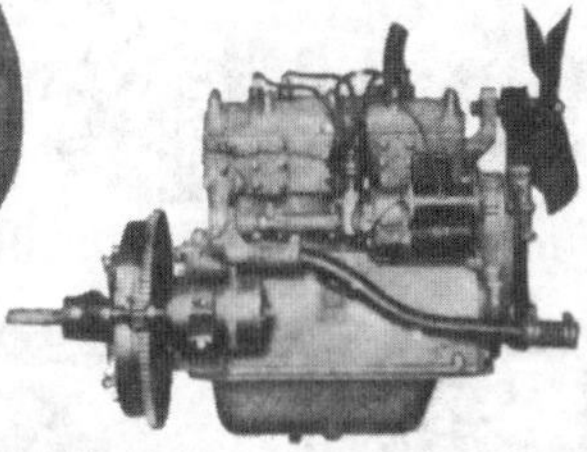

(LEFT SIDE)
ENGINE
(RIGHT SIDE)

"4-M" (158 C.I.D.) 103" W.B.
30 H.P. @ 2200 RPM
"6-R" (169.2 C.I.D.) 107" W.B.
40 H.P. @ 2400 RPM

IMPROVED 4

26-27

NEW 6-CYL. MODEL ←

('27 HAS BOWL-SHAPED LAMPS.)

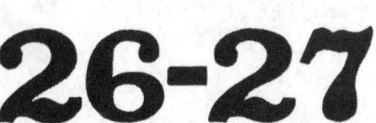

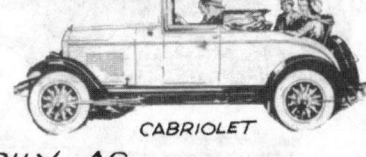

CABRIOLET

COUPE (6 CYL.)

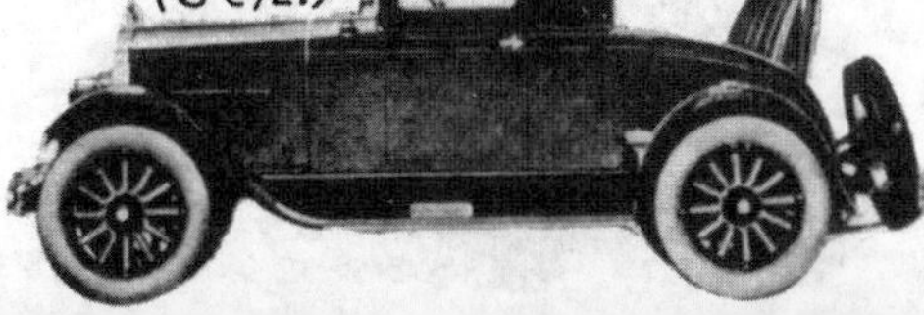

1928 MODEL KNOWN TEMPORARILY AS "DURANT-STAR," LATER AS DURANT 4.

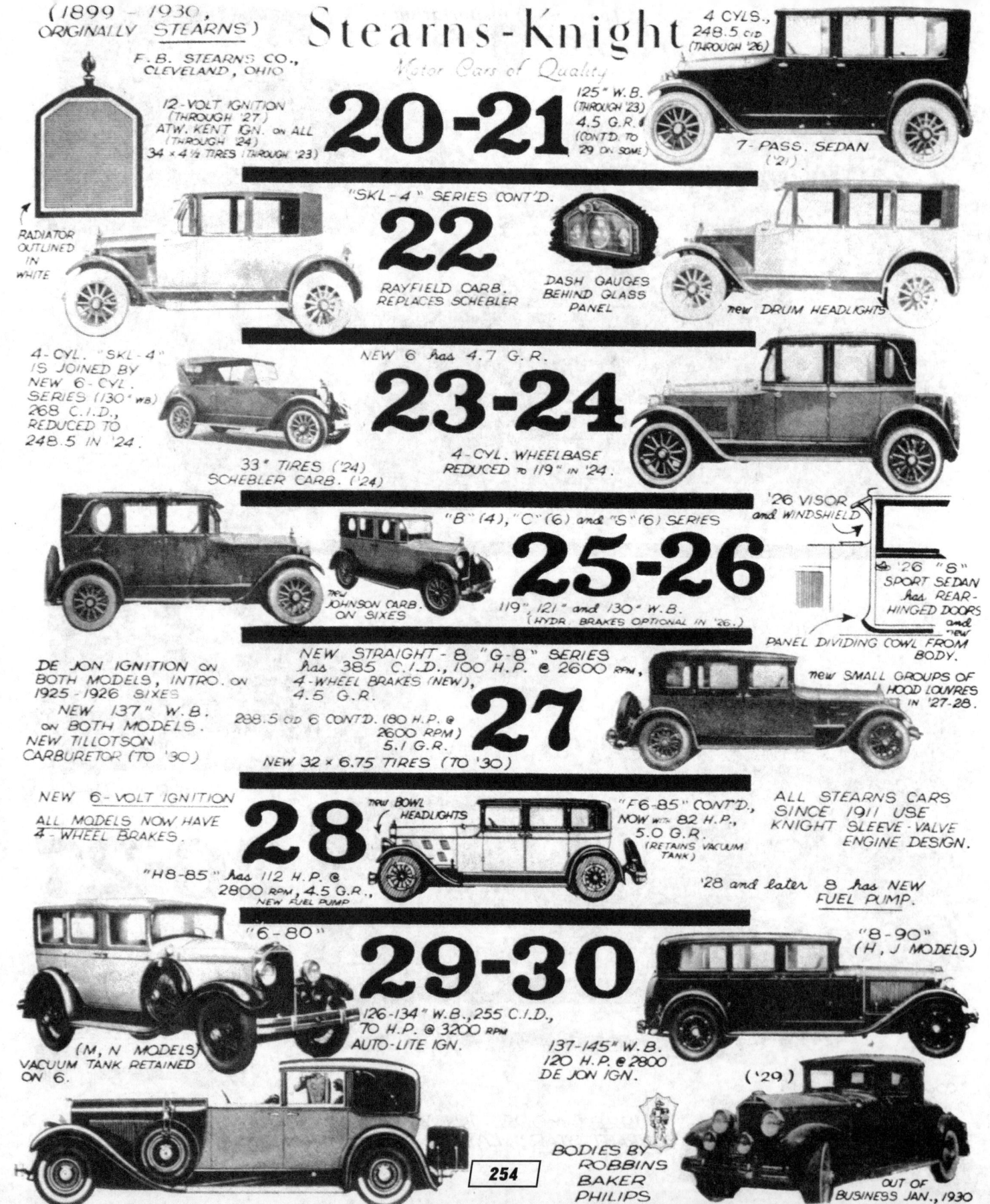

Stearns-Knight
Motor Cars of Quality

(1899 - 1930, ORIGINALLY STEARNS)

F. B. STEARNS CO., CLEVELAND, OHIO

4 CYLS., 248.5 CID (THROUGH '26)

12-VOLT IGNITION (THROUGH '27) ATW. KENT IGN. ON ALL (THROUGH '24) 34 x 4½ TIRES (THROUGH '23)

125" W.B. (THROUGH '23) 4.5 G.R. (CONT'D. TO '29 ON SOME)

20-21

7-PASS. SEDAN ('21)

RADIATOR OUTLINED IN WHITE

"SKL-4" SERIES CONT'D.

22

RAYFIELD CARB. REPLACES SCHEBLER

DASH GAUGES BEHIND GLASS PANEL

new DRUM HEADLIGHTS

4-CYL. "SKL-4" IS JOINED BY NEW 6-CYL. SERIES (130" wb) 268 C.I.D., REDUCED TO 248.5 IN '24.

NEW 6 has 4.7 G.R.

23-24

4-CYL. WHEELBASE REDUCED to 119" IN '24.

33" TIRES ('24) SCHEBLER CARB. ('24)

"B" (4), "C" (6) and "S" (6) SERIES

25-26

'26 VISOR and WINDSHIELD

new JOHNSON CARB. ON SIXES

119", 121" and 130" W.B. (HYDR. BRAKES OPTIONAL IN '26.)

'26 "S" SPORT SEDAN has REAR-HINGED DOORS and new PANEL DIVIDING COWL FROM BODY.

DE JON IGNITION on BOTH MODELS, INTRO. on 1925-1926 SIXES

NEW 137" W.B. ON BOTH MODELS. NEW TILLOTSON CARBURETOR (TO '30)

NEW STRAIGHT-8 "G-8" SERIES has 385 C.I.D., 100 H.P. @ 2600 RPM, 4-WHEEL BRAKES (NEW), 4.5 G.R.

288.5 CID 6 CONT'D. (80 H.P. @ 2600 RPM) 5.1 G.R.

27

NEW 32 x 6.75 TIRES (TO '30)

new SMALL GROUPS OF HOOD LOUVRES IN '27-28

NEW 6-VOLT IGNITION ALL MODELS NOW HAVE 4-WHEEL BRAKES.

new BOWL HEADLIGHTS

"F6-85" CONT'D., NOW with 82 H.P., 5.0 G.R. (RETAINS VACUUM TANK)

ALL STEARNS CARS SINCE 1911 USE KNIGHT SLEEVE-VALVE ENGINE DESIGN.

28

"H8-85" has 112 H.P. @ 2800 RPM, 4.5 G.R., NEW FUEL PUMP

'28 and later 8 has NEW FUEL PUMP.

"6-80"

"8-90" (H, J MODELS)

29-30

126-134" W.B., 255 C.I.D., 70 H.P. @ 3200 RPM AUTO-LITE IGN.

137-145" W.B. 120 H.P. @ 2800 DE JON IGN.

('29)

(M, N MODELS) VACUUM TANK RETAINED ON 6.

BODIES BY ROBBINS BAKER PHILIPS

OUT OF BUSINESS JAN., 1930

254

STEPHENS MOTOR WORKS *of Moline Plow Company* · Freeport, Illinois

STEPHENS *Salient Six*

(1916-1924)

17-22

Salient
"That which is strikingly manifest or catches the attention at once."
—Webster

6 CYL.
O.H.V.
224 C.I.D.
ENGINE
(THROUGH '24)

('21) CONNECTICUT IGNITION REPLACES Auto-Lite.

33 × 4½ TIRES (THROUGH '24, EXC. '23-'24 117" W.B. MODELS)

('22)

122" W.B.
(THROUGH '22)

('20)

with Artcraft Top

57 H.P. IN 1922

STEPHENS

NO MAJOR CHANGES BETWEEN 1917 and 1922.

'23 RESTYLED, WITH MODERN "LIGHTNING" INSIGNIA.

23-24

STEPHENS

FOR '23, DELCO IGN. REPLACES CONNECTICUT IGN., and STROMBERG CARB. REPLACES TILLOTSON.

NEW 117" and 124" W.B. "10," "20" models

32 × 4 TIRES, 4.66, 5.1 G.R. ON 117"-W.B. "10."

STERLING - KNIGHT 6

6-CYL., 230.2 C.I.D. SLEEVE-VALVE ENGINE

B-6   125" W.B.

(1923-1925)
STERLING-KNIGHT MOTORS CO., CLEVELAND and WARREN, OHIO

56 H.P. @ 2400 RPM and 5.09 G.R. ('25)

WESTINGHOUSE IGN.
32 × 4½ TIRES

STROMBERG CARB.
4.66 G.R. (TO '24)

138" W.B. (TO '27)

('21)

"E-6"
6-PASS.
3.94 G.R. (TO '24)

STEVENS - DURYEA

(1902-1927)

('22)

90 H.P. @ 2000 RPM

STEVENS-DURYEA (MOTORS) CO. CHICOPEE FALLS, MASS.

6-CYL., 510.4 CID, L-HEAD ENGINE (TO '27)

VESTIBULE LIMO.

BOSCH IGNITION REPLACES BERLING IGNITION (AFTER '24)

33 × 5 TIRES ('23 ON)

STOUT "SCARAB" *(1934-1939)*

WM. B. STOUT ENGINEERING CO., DEARBORN, MICH.

FORD V-8 ENGINE (AT REAR)

('35-'36)

255

STUDEBAKER

WAGNER IGNITION
STROM. CARB. ON MOST MODELS

Studebaker

CARS (1902-1966)

Detroit, Michigan   South Bend, Indiana   Walkerville, Canada
Address all Correspondence to South Bend

(CO. ORIGINATED 1852)

(EG) BIG 6
353.8 C.I.D. (THROUGH '27)
126" W.B. (THROUGH '24)

112" W.B.
32 × 4

(EH, EU) SPECIAL 6

(EJ) LIGHT 6 ('21)
207.1 C.I.D.
45 H.P. @ 2000 RPM
4.55 G.R. (THROUGH '24)

288.6 C.I.D. (THROUGH '27)
51 ('20) 55 ('21) H.P. @ 2000 RPM
4.33 G.R. (THROUGH '24)

32 × 4
119" W.B. (THROUGH '24)

33 × 4½
65 H.P. @ 2000

BIG 6 has BALL + BALL CARB. (THROUGH '27)

3.71 G.R. (THROUGH '24)

20-21

EARLY '22

('23) LIGHT 6
(has 31 × 4 TIRES, '23 - '24)

(WOOD WHEELS and PAINTED RADIATOR SHELL)

1-PC. WINDSHIELD ON SPECIAL 6 and BIG 6 TOURING CARS.

COUPE INTERIOR

SPECIAL 6 ('23½)

NEW "5-PASS. COUPE"

22-24

WAGNER, REMY IGNITION (THROUGH '25)

BIG 6
33 × 4½

TYPE OF '24

"EL" SPECIAL 6

"SPEEDSTER" PHAETON

STUDEBAKER

(STD. 6 REPLACES LIGHT 6)

new STANDARD 6
has 241.6 C.I.D.,
50 H.P. @ 2200 RPM
(TO '28) new 113" W.B. (THROUGH '29 "DICTATOR")
new 4.18 G.R.

STD. 6 "DUPLEX"

25

COMPLETELY
RESTYLED

(INTRO. FALL, '24)

STANDARD 6
FRONT VIEW

STD. 6

new *Duplex*

OPEN MODELS with
RIGID, STEEL-REINFORCED
TOPS.
("DUPLEX" MODELS avail. THROUGH '27.
1928 "DICTATOR" SERIES INCLUDES
"DUPLEX" PHAETON.)

2-WHEEL MECHANICAL
BRAKES ON ALL 3
SERIES, with 4-WH.
HYDRAULIC BRAKES
OPTIONAL
(THROUGH '26)

"DUPLEX"
ROADSTER,
with DETAILS of
PULL-DOWN
CURTAINS

SPECIAL 6 "DUPLEX"

WITH CURTAINS
OPEN

WITH
SIDE CURTAINS CLOSED

SPECIAL 6
has new 4.36 G.R. (THROUGH '27)
65 H.P. @ 2400 RPM
(THROUGH '27)
32 × 6.20 TIRES (THROUGH '26)
120" W.B. (THROUGH '28, '30
"COMMANDER")

SPECIAL 6 CONTINUES ITS UNIQUE
FLUTED RADIATOR SHELL

BIG 6
"5-PASS.
COUPE"
(COACH-STYLE,
UNLIKE
STUDEBAKER
4-PASS.
VICTORIA CPES.
WHICH HAVE
REAR DECK.)

BIG 6
has 75 H.P. @ 2400 RPM (THROUGH '27)
34 × 7.30 TIRES (THROUGH '26)
127" W.B. (THROUGH '27)   4.36 G.R.

STUDEBAKER

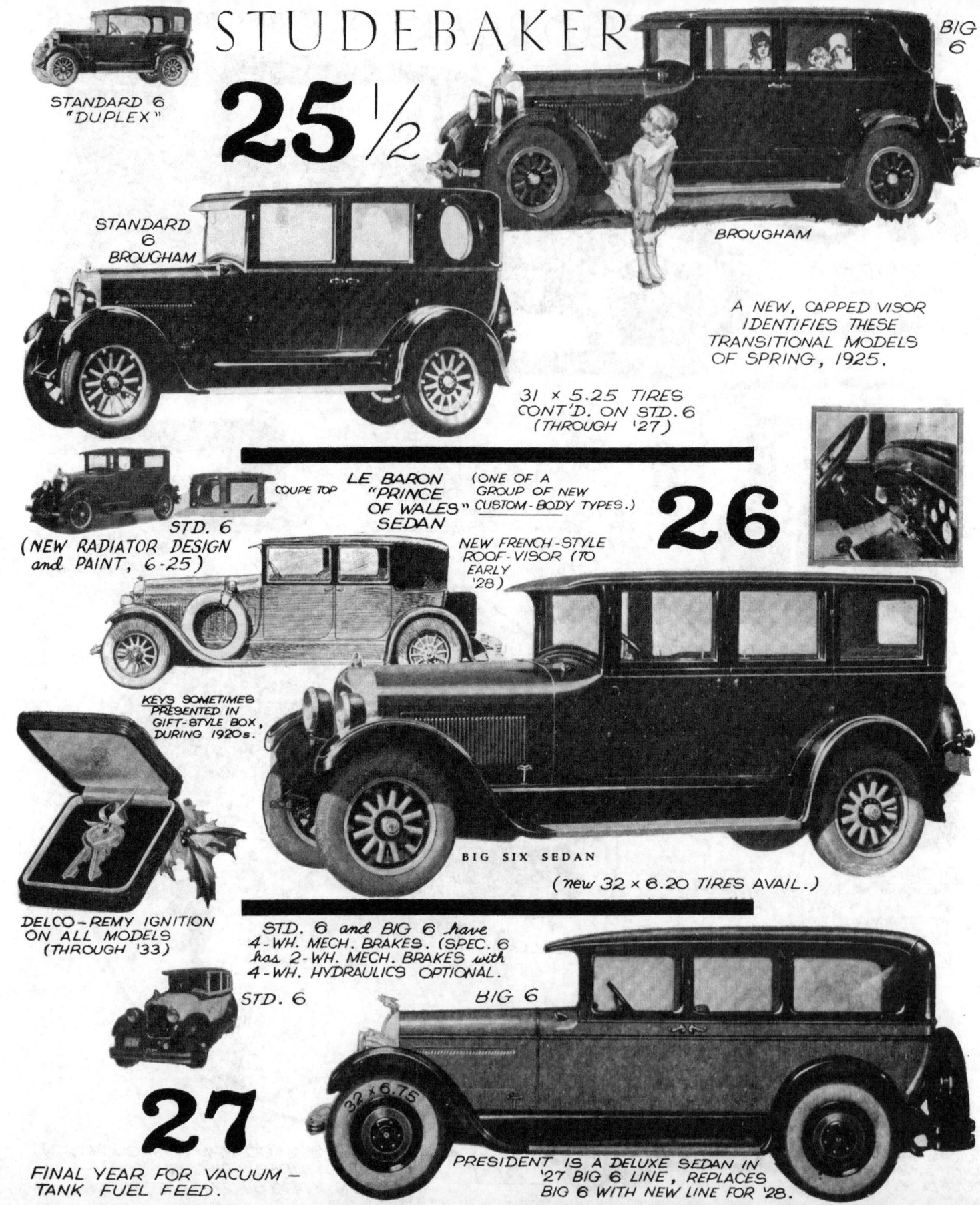

STANDARD 6 "DUPLEX"

BIG 6

25½

STANDARD 6 BROUGHAM

BROUGHAM

A NEW, CAPPED VISOR IDENTIFIES THESE TRANSITIONAL MODELS OF SPRING, 1925.

31 × 5.25 TIRES CONT'D. ON STD. 6 (THROUGH '27)

COUPE TOP

LE BARON "PRINCE OF WALES" SEDAN

(ONE OF A GROUP OF NEW CUSTOM-BODY TYPES.)

26

STD. 6

(NEW RADIATOR DESIGN and PAINT, 6-25)

NEW FRENCH-STYLE ROOF-VISOR (TO EARLY '28)

KEYS SOMETIMES PRESENTED IN GIFT-STYLE BOX, DURING 1920s.

BIG SIX SEDAN

(new 32 × 6.20 TIRES AVAIL.)

DELCO-REMY IGNITION ON ALL MODELS (THROUGH '33)

STD. 6 and BIG 6 have 4-WH. MECH. BRAKES. (SPEC. 6 has 2-WH. MECH. BRAKES with 4-WH. HYDRAULICS OPTIONAL.

STD. 6   BIG 6

27

32 × 6.75

FINAL YEAR FOR VACUUM-TANK FUEL FEED.

PRESIDENT IS A DELUXE SEDAN IN '27 BIG 6 LINE, REPLACES BIG 6 WITH NEW LINE FOR '28.

STUDEBAKER

NEW MODEL NAMES

NEW FUEL PUMP

50-H.P. DICTATOR 6 REPLACES STANDARD 6

75-H.P. COMMANDER 6 REPLACES SPEC. 6

SCHEBLER CARB. ON EARLY PRESIDENT 8 (313.1 CID) 131" W.B.

28

← PRESIDENT 8 FIRST 100-H.P. STUDEBAKER

28½

NEW SERIES HAS NEW RADIATOR DESIGN, NEW "MILITARY FRONT" WITH CADET STYLE VISOR.

4-WH. MECHANICAL BRAKES ON ALL (TO '34.)

DICTATOR 6 ('29) 67 H.P. @ 2800 RPM

NEW "6-53" STARTS DURING '30, WITH 114" W.B., 205.3 CID, 70 HP @ 3100 (THROUGH '31 "6-54")

7-WINDOW SEDANS ALSO AVAILABLE (AS SEEN ABOVE)

29-30

ROADSTER

70-H.P. DICTATOR 8 JOINS 68-H.P. DICTATOR 6 IN '30, BOTH WITH 115" WB

COMMANDER 6 and 8 IN '29 and '30. '29 6 = 74 HP (GJ) '30 " = 75 HP @ 3000, with 248.3 CID 8 = 80 HP @ 3600 with 250.4 CID BOTH WITH 119½" WB ('29) 120" WB ('30)

BROUGHAM

'30 MODEL has SMALL SETS OF VERTICAL HOOD LOUVRES, INSTEAD OF ONE LONG ROW.

COUPE

STROMBERG CARBURETOR STANDARD ON ALL (1929 THROUGH '36)

new '29 COMMANDER 8 (FD) has 5.50 × 19 TIRES, AS ON CMNDR. 6 and all '30 DICTATOR, COMMANDER MODELS.

'29 PRESIDENT 8 (FE, FH) has 114 H.P. @ 3200 RPM, new 336.7 C.I.D.

CONVERTIBLE CABRIOLET

TOURER ('30 ONLY)

VICTORIA COUPE

125-135" W.B. PRESIDENT 8 4.08, 4.31 G.R.

'29 HAS LANDAU IRONS

115 H.P. ('30)

STUDEBAKER

6 (6-54)

31

205.3 C.I.D. SIX (114" W.B.) HAS 70 H.P. @ 3200

114"-W.B. DICTATOR IS 8 ONLY, IN '31.

1931 MODELS HAVE NEW GRILLE, "OVALOID" HEADLIGHTS

new = "FREE WHEELING" (AVAIL. TO '35)

ROLL-UP WINDOWS

COMMANDER 8 BROUGHAM 124" W.B.

101 H.P.

PRESIDENT 8 CONVERTIBLE RDSTR.

122 H.P. @ 3200 RPM (THROUGH '32)

1932 MODELS : SIX
DICTATOR 8 (62)
COMMANDER 8 (71)
PRESIDENT 8 (91)

NEW CIRCULAR GAUGES IN OVAL PANEL (REPLACE FORMER UPRIGHT-RECTANGULAR GAUGES IN HORIZONTAL RECTANG. PANEL.

new ST. REGIS COUPE

'32 6 (6-55) has 117" W.B. (THROUGH '33) 230 C.I.D. (THROUGH '33) 80 H.P. @ 3200 RPM

DICT. 8 has 117" W.B. 81-85 H.P. @ 3200 (221 CID AS IN '31)

32

CMDR. 8 has new 125" WB BUT 101 HP @ 3200 and 250.4 CID AS BEFORE.

Studebaker Free Wheeling is controlled by a touch of a lever on the dash. There is no necessity for keeping your foot constantly on a button.

To start the Triumphant New Studebakers you simply switch on the ignition with a key. The engine instantly responds — and even should it stall at any time, it automatically starts again.

'32 tire sizes = 5.50 × 18 (6 and DICT. 8)   6.00 × 18 (CMNDR. 8)

6.50 × 18 (PRES. 8)

PRES. 8 has 135" WB 4.31 G.R.

MODELS : SIX, COMMANDER 8, (117" WB) PRESIDENT 8 and SPEEDWAY PRESIDENT 8 (125", 135" WB)

33

110-H.P. PRES. 8 (82) USES 250.4 CID STR.-8 ENGINE FORMERLY IN '32 CMNDR.

6 (56) has 85 HP @ 3200 RPM

CMR. 8 (73) has 236 CID, 100 HP @ 3800 RPM

"DICTATOR" MODEL SUSPENDED, RESUMED '34.

SPDWY. PRES. 8 (92) is FINAL USER OF THE 336.7 CID STR. 8 (132 HP @ 3400)

17" WHEELS ('33-'34)

117, 117, 125, 135" WHEELBASES, AS IN 1932.

34

STUDEBAKER

SEDAN REAR

BENDIX POWER BRAKES
(MECH. BRAKES ON DICTATOR 6)

CMNDR. 8 has 221 CID, 103 HP @ 4000 RPM 119" WB

'34 DICT. 6 has 205.3 CID (THROUGH '35) 87 H.P. @ 3600 RPM 113" W.B. 4.55 G.R.

new STREAM-LINED "LAND CRUISER" REAR ('34)

35

88-H.P. DICTATOR
new 6
114" WB

HYDRAULIC BRAKES (ALL)

"REGAL" has FENDERWELLS

120" W.B.
CMNDR. 8 has 107 HP @ 3800 RPM

NARROW GRILLE FOR 1935

PRESIDENT LAND CRUISER ('35)

36

DICTATOR 6

new 116" WB (THROUGH '37)

217.8 CID, 90 HP @ 3400 (THROUGH '40 CMNDR.)

(4.55 G.R. BECOMES STANDARD ON ALL.)

PRESIDENT 8

new 125" WB (THROUGH '37)
250.4 CID ('33 THROUGH '42)
115 H.P. @ 3600 (THROUGH '37)

'36-'37 COUPE REAR WINDOW.

STATE PRESIDENT 8

37

DICTATOR 6
USES CARTER CARB. DURING 1937.

new 1-PIECE HOOD is HINGED AT BACK.
VENT PANES IN FRONT DOORS.
EMERGENCY BRAKE LEVER HUNG AT LEFT.

261

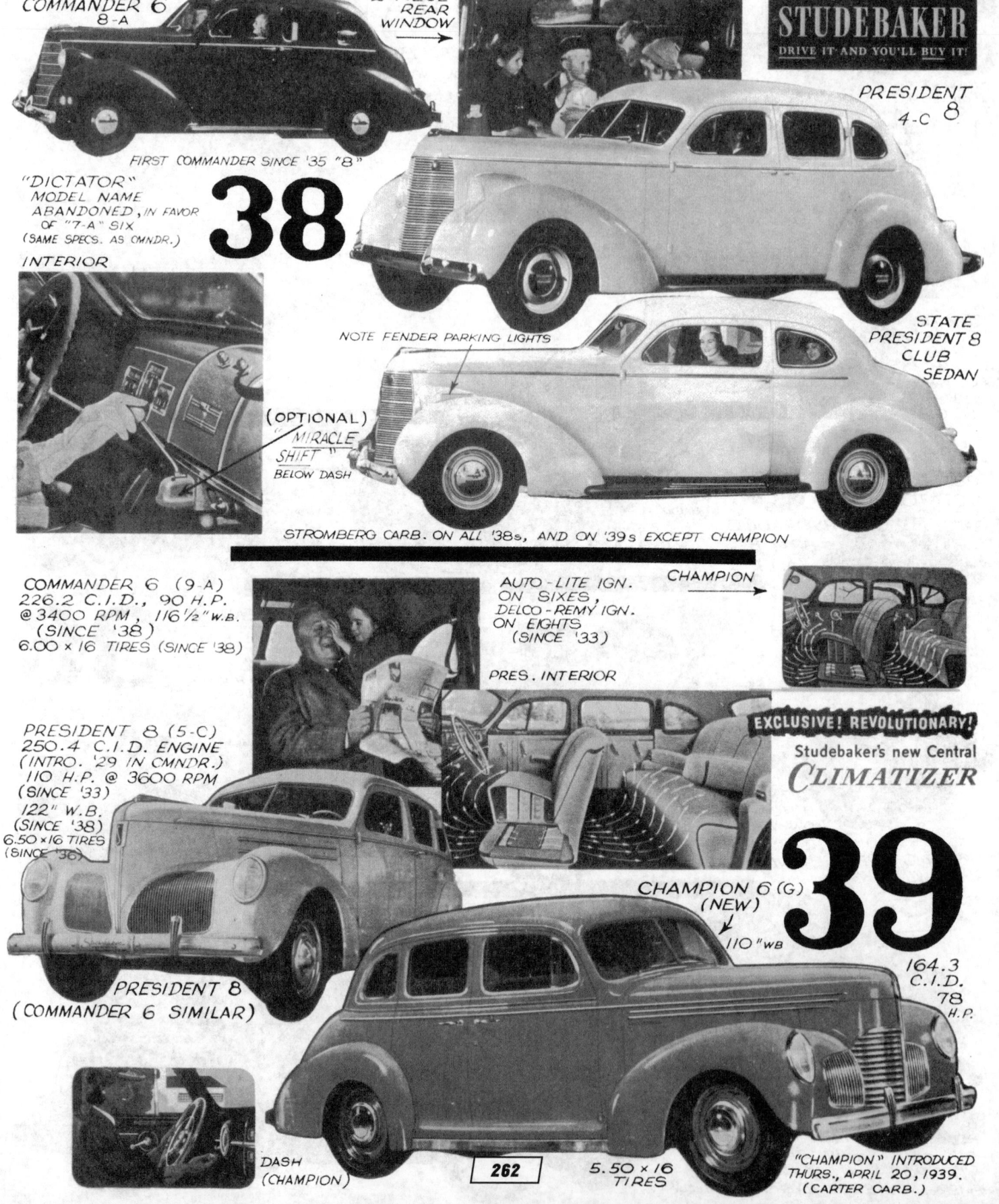

COMMANDER 6
8-A

2 PIECE REAR WINDOW →

STUDEBAKER
DRIVE IT AND YOU'LL BUY IT!

PRESIDENT 8
4-C

FIRST COMMANDER SINCE '35 "8"

"DICTATOR"
MODEL NAME ABANDONED, IN FAVOR OF "7-A" SIX
(SAME SPECS. AS CMNDR.)

38

STATE PRESIDENT 8
CLUB SEDAN

INTERIOR

NOTE FENDER PARKING LIGHTS

(OPTIONAL) "MIRACLE SHIFT" BELOW DASH

STROMBERG CARB. ON ALL '38s, AND ON '39s EXCEPT CHAMPION

COMMANDER 6 (9-A)
226.2 C.I.D., 90 H.P. @ 3400 RPM, 116½" W.B.
(SINCE '38)
6.00 × 16 TIRES (SINCE '38)

AUTO-LITE IGN. ON SIXES,
DELCO-REMY IGN. ON EIGHTS
(SINCE '33)

CHAMPION →

PRES. INTERIOR

EXCLUSIVE! REVOLUTIONARY!
Studebaker's new Central
CLIMATIZER

PRESIDENT 8 (5-C)
250.4 C.I.D. ENGINE
(INTRO. '29 IN CMNDR.)
110 H.P. @ 3600 RPM
(SINCE '33)
122" W.B.
(SINCE '38)
6.50 × 16 TIRES
(SINCE '36)

39

CHAMPION 6 (G)
(NEW)
110" WB

164.3
C.I.D.
78 H.P.

PRESIDENT 8
(COMMANDER 6 SIMILAR)

DASH (CHAMPION)

262

5.50 × 16 TIRES

"CHAMPION" INTRODUCED
THURS., APRIL 20, 1939.
(CARTER CARB.)

19-20

THE CAR THAT MADE STUTZ GOOD IN A DAY

(1912 - 1934)

STUTZ MOTOR CAR CO. OF AMERICA, INC., Indianapolis, U.S.A.

130" WHEELBASE (4-CYL. MODELS and '25 "6 95")

STROMBERG CARB. (THROUGH '25)

PRESSURE FUEL FEED (ON 4-CYL. MODELS THROUGH '24)

"H" SERIES AVAIL. IN VARIOUS BODY TYPES.

3.5 GEAR RATIO

"BEARCAT" STUTZ' MOST FAMOUS SPORTS MODEL.
(AVAIL. AS "SUPER BEARCAT" ON SHORT WHEELBASE, IN EARLY 1930s.)

STUTZ factory

IGNITION: DELCO (4-CYL.)
REMY (6-CYL., 23-25)
DELCO-REMY (AFTER '25)

4 CYL., 360.8 C.I.D. T-HEAD ENGINE (TO '24)

21-22

(LEFT-HAND DRIVE)

BEARCAT

FINER HOOD LOUVRES; HORN REMOVED FROM RT. SIDE

"K" and "H" MODELS

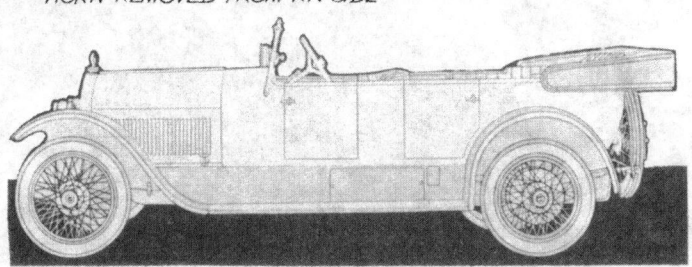

"KLDH" 1922 MODEL HAS NEW "DH" ENGINE and COMPENSATING SPRINGS.

23

KLDH "SPEEDWAY 4" 2-PASS. ROADSTER (3.75 G.R.)

268 C.I.D. NEW VACUUM FUEL FEED ON 6.

"690" 6 CYLINDER (NEW) 5-PASS. SEDAN

120" W.B.
(ALSO ON '24 "690" AND '25 "693," "694" "694-HB" SERIES

24-25

"SPEEDWAY 4" (FINAL YEAR FOR 4-CYL. MODEL WAS 1924.)

SPEEDWAY 6 "695"

1925 IS FINAL YEAR FOR STUTZ 6 (BOTH THE 130"-W.B. SPEEDWAY 6 AND 120"-W.B. SPECIAL 6 [694-HB] LATE MODELS AVAIL. WITH LOCKHEED HYD. BRAKE SYSTEM.])

SAFETY STUTZ

32 × 6.20 TIRES (THROUGH '28)
NEW HYDRAULIC BRAKES

Six body styles, designed and constructed under the supervision of Brewster of New York. All closed bodies automatically ventilated.

TOP
50"
70"
20"

131" W.B. (THROUGH '28)

The symbol of Safety

SAFETY *New* CHASSIS

NEW ZENITH CARB.
92 H.P. @
3200 RPM

The first and only automobile to provide safety-glass all around without extra charge to the buyer ✱

✱ = STUTZ' EARLY SAFETY GLASS RE-INFORCED BY FINE HORIZONTAL WIRES, VISIBLE TO THE EYE. ILCO-RYAN THICK-LENSED HEADLIGHTS ADOPTED, 1927 →

WORM DRIVE

287.3 C.I.D. STRAIGHT-8 (NEW)
(298.6 C.I.D. IN '27 and '28)

26-27

STUTZ
SAFETY 8 CHASSIS

5.0 G.R.
(THROUGH '28)

MODEL "AA"
"AA" SERIES

28

"BB"
115 H.P. @
3600 RPM

32 × 6.20
OR
32 × 6.75
TIRES

VACUUM and OTHER FUEL FEEDS AVAIL.

STUTZ

'29-30 BLACKHAWK L-8 has FUEL PUMP

WITH WEYMANN FABRIC-PANELED LIGHTWT. BODY

BODIES BY HALE KILBURN LE BARON WEYMANN

BLACKHAWK "L-6" HAS 6 CYLS., 241.5 C.I.D. 85 H.P. @ 3200

BLACKHAWK

"L-8" has STRAIGHT-8 ENG., 268.5 C.I.D. 88-90 H.P. @ 3100-3200 RPM

('29)

"MONACO"

SOME EARLY '29 BLACKHAWKS HAVE DART LOUVRES AT REAR OF HOOD. →

127½" W.B. ON ALL BLACKHAWKS. 4.75 G.R. ('29)

"M" SERIES

6.50 x 20

134½-145" W.B. (TO '34) STRAIGHT-8, 322 CID ENG. (TO '34)

115 H.P. @ 3600 RPM

All engines have overhead camshaft.

'29 FLEETWOOD TOWN CAR ALSO AVAIL.

4.5 G.R., EXCEPT ON '29 BLACKHAWK

29-30

FRONT DETAILS

BODIES BY LE BARON, WEYMANN, ROLLSTON, BRUNN, ETC.

STRAIGHT-8

6-CYL. "LA, LAA" SERIES (THROUGH '33) (CONTINUES BLACKHAWK 6 SPECS.)

VENT DOORS ON HOOD

DASH

('31)

31-34

NEW "CHALLENGER" SERIES JOINS "CUSTOM" IN 1933.

"SV-16", "DV-32"

SOME 1933-1934 STUTZES HAVE NEW STREAMLINING BUT RETAIN FLAT RADIATOR.

AUTO. CHOKE and CLUTCH, LARGER COWL VENTS IN 1933

TEMPLAR (1917-1924)

TEMPLAR MOTORS CORP., CLEVELAND, OHIO
with "VITALIC TOP-VALVE MOTOR"
(4 CYL., O.H.V.)
C.I.D.
43 H.P. @ 2100 RPM
118" W.B.

SPOTLIGHT MOVED LOWER DURING 1919.

ONLY 3 LUG-BOLTS BEFORE 1920.

TEMPLAR "SPORTETTE" ('21)

ROADSTER ('22)

6-CYL. AVAIL. BEFORE TEMPLAR DISCO

('24)

(THE FINAL TEMPLAR)

TERRAPLANE

(1933 — 1938)

BUILT BY HUDSON
(REPLACES THE 1932
ESSEX. TRANSITIONAL
MODELS OF 1932-1933 NAMED
"ESSEX-TERRAPLANE.")

33

106"(6) or 113"(8) W.B.

8 HAS HOOD VENT DOORS

6 CYL.
193.1 C.I.D.
70 H.P. @ 3200
8 CYL.
244 C.I.D.
94 H.P. @ 3200

TERRAPLANE

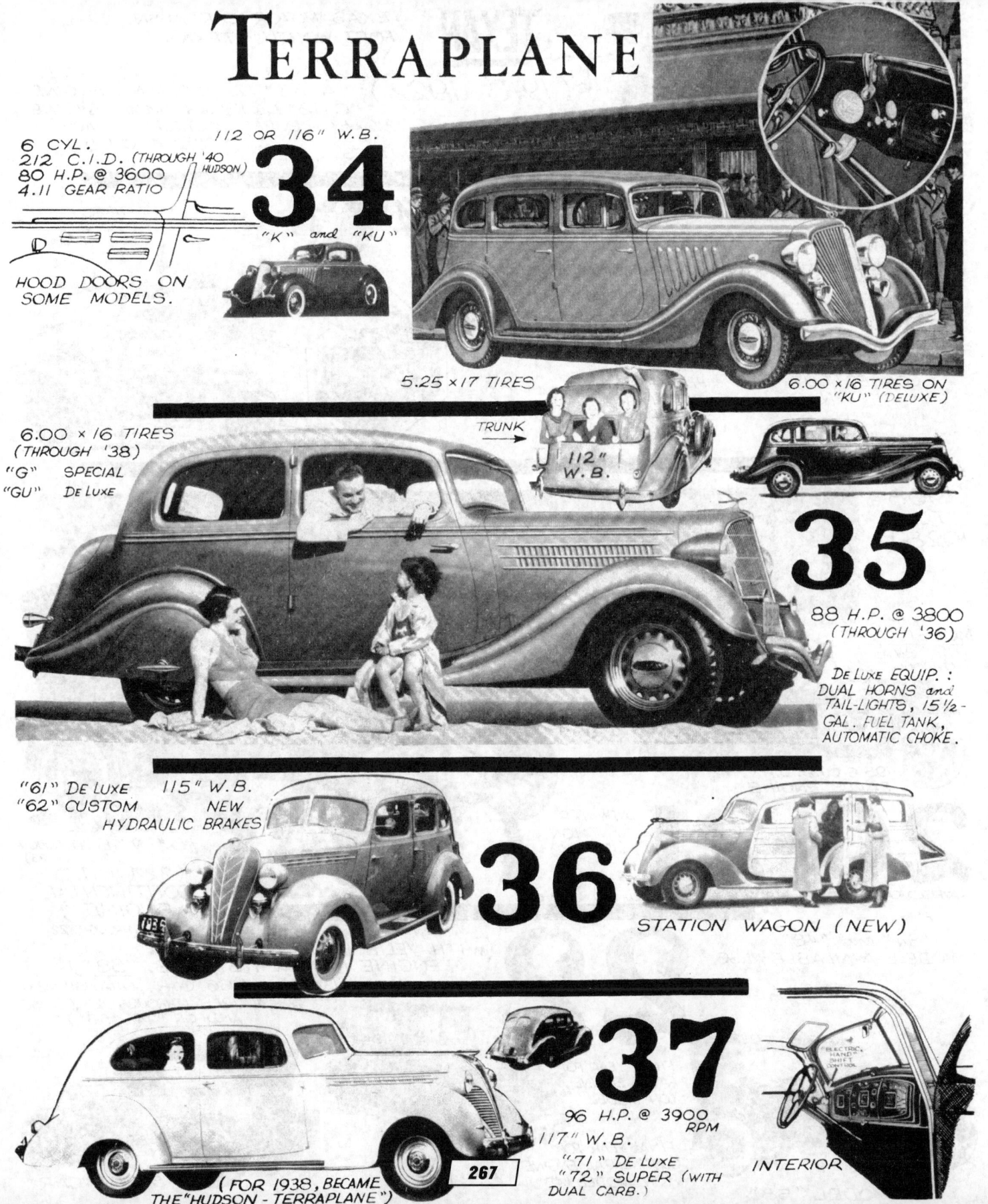

6 CYL.
212 C.I.D. (THROUGH '40 HUDSON)
80 H.P. @ 3600
4.11 GEAR RATIO

112 OR 116" W.B.

34
"K" and "KU"

HOOD DOORS ON SOME MODELS.

5.25 × 17 TIRES

6.00 × 16 TIRES ON "KU" (DELUXE)

6.00 × 16 TIRES (THROUGH '38)
"G" SPECIAL
"GU" DE LUXE

TRUNK

112" W.B.

35

88 H.P. @ 3800 (THROUGH '36)

DE LUXE EQUIP.: DUAL HORNS and TAIL-LIGHTS, 15½-GAL. FUEL TANK, AUTOMATIC CHOKE.

"61" DE LUXE
"62" CUSTOM
115" W.B.
NEW HYDRAULIC BRAKES

36

STATION WAGON (NEW)

37

96 H.P. @ 3900 RPM
117" W.B.
"71" DE LUXE
"72" SUPER (WITH DUAL CARB.)

(FOR 1938, BECAME THE "HUDSON-TERRAPLANE")

ELECTRIC HAND SHIFT CONTROL

INTERIOR

267

TEXAN

TEXAS MOTOR CAR ASSN., FORT WORTH, TEXAS

(1918-1922)

4 CYLS.   115" W.B.
"A-38" has LYCOMING ENGINE
"C-12" has HERSCH.-SPLMN. ENGINE
3½ x 5" is BORE and STROKE of EACH
(192.4 C.I.D.)

33 x 4 TIRES

TULSA 4   EMBLEM   33 x 4 TIRES ('20-22)

TULSA AUTO MFG. CO., TULSA, OKLA. (1917-1922)

MODEL "E"
('20-22)
117½" W.B.
4 CYL.
192.4 C.I.D.
HERSCHELL-
SPILLMAN
ENGINE
4.5 GEAR RATIO

ZENITH CARB.
CONNECTICUT
IGN.

VELIE

(1908 TO 1928)

VELIE MOTORS CORPORATION, Moline, Illinois

MODEL "34"
112" W.B.
(THROUGH '22)

MODEL "48"

6 CYLINDERS (ALL BUT '28 "8-88")

195.6 C.I.D. O.H.V. FALLS ENGINE

20-21

ATWATER KENT IGN. (TO '24)

RAYFIELD CARB. ('20)   STROMBERG CARB. ('21-'29)

115" W.B. (THROUGH '23)

(224 C.I.D. CONTINENTAL L-HEAD ENGINE) (THROUGH '22)

"34" and "48" MODELS AVAILABLE ALSO

22

(WITH VELIE-BUILT 195.6 C.I.D. ENGINE IN NEW 115"-W.B. "58")
(OVERHEAD VALVES) 4.66 G.R. (THROUGH '23)
32 x 4 TIRES (THROUGH '23, AND ON '24 "56")

FINAL YEAR FOR FALLS ENGINE (ON MODEL "34")

FINAL YEAR FOR CONTINENTAL ENGINE (ON MODEL "48")

new MODEL "58"

"SPORT CAR"

Velie

4.66 GEAR RATIO IN 1923

115" W.B.
(THROUGH '23)
118" W.B.
ON BOTH
"56" and
"58"
MODELS,
1924.

WESTINGHOUSE
IGNITION
(LATE '24
THROUGH '25)

2 - WHEEL
MECHANICAL
BRAKES

23-24

NEW 118" W.B. IN 1924 ; NEW ('24)
203.5 C.I.D.; 4.7 OR 5.1 GEAR RATIO

"60" IS ONLY SERIES
OF VELIE FOR 1925
and 1926.

25

MODEL "60"   6 CYLINDERS
OVERHEAD VALVES   204 C.I.D.
48 H.P. @ 2600 RPM

5.10 GEAR RATIO
118" WHEELBASE

new HYDRAULIC
4-WHEEL BRAKES
(TO '29)

THE SMARTEST CAR ON THE HIGHWAY

Four Door Coach

VELIE
ROADSTER

VELIE

'26 "60" has new 221.3 C.I.D., 58 H.P. @ 3000 RPM

new REMY IGNITION (DELCO-REMY ON '27 '60," '28 "77," "88")

30 × 5.25 TIRES

FOR 1927 and 1928, new "STANDARD 50" SERIES JOINS VELIE LINE, with Auto-Lite IGNITION, OWN 196 C.I.D., 6-CYL. O.H.V. ENGINE, 48 H.P. @ 2600 RPM

29 × 5.00 TIRES ('27) (30 × 5.25 ON '28 "STD. 50" and also "6-66,") also Auto Lite IGN.)

VELIE-BLT. ENGINES CONTINUE THERMO-SYPHON COOLING SYSTEM.

26-28

KNOWN IN '26 AS "SEDAN DE LUXE," AFTERWARDS AS THE "ROYAL SEDAN" (FRONT DOOR SLANTS TO ANGLE OF WINDSHIELD.)

('26)

DASH ('28)

VELIE O.H.V. ENGINE

BOWL-SHAPED HEADLAMPS APPEAR ON 1927 VELIES.

STRAIGHT-8 (298.6 CID) LYCOMING-ENGINED, 125"WB "8-88" VELIE ALSO, IN 1928 (FINAL YEAR.)

1928 "77" and "88" MODELS HAVE SURCINGLE PARKING LIGHTS; ON REAR OF COWL ON "66."

4.9 GEAR RATIO, EXCEPT 4.6 ON "8-88" (ONLY MODEL WITH SCHEBLER CARB.)

"1929" MODELS BUILT DURING 1928.

"6-66" ('28) 112"WB, 203.5 CID, 56 HP @ 2800 RPM
"6-77" ('28-9) 118"WB, 221 CID, 60 HP @ 2900 RPM, 32 × 6.00 TIRES

29

"6-77" ROYAL SEDAN (SAME AS '28 MODEL

AUTO PRODUCTION CEASED BY 1-29.

270

(LENGTH EXAGGERATED)

VIKING

1929 – 1930
BY GM's
OLDSMOBILE
DIVISION

PRODUCT OF GENERAL MOTORS

29

(INTRODUCED
APRIL, 1929)

EMBLEM

V-8 ENGINE
259.4 C.I.D.

80 H.P. @
3200 RPM

125" WHEELBASE
(THROUGH '30)

30 × 6.00 TIRES

30

81 H.P. @ 3200 RPM

6.00 × 18 TIRES

WALTHAM

6 CYLS.
45 H.P.

WALTHAM
MOTOR MFRS., INC.,
WALTHAM,
MASS.

22

REPLACES
"METZ" CAR
(1922 ONLY)

WASP

('20)

MARTIN-WASP CORP.,
BENNINGTON., VT. (1919-1925)
4 AND 6 CYL.

"2611" ('21) has 132" W.B., 4-CYL., 389.9 C.I.D.
WISCONSIN T-III AD ENGINE
BOSCH IGNITION   3.70 G.R.
STROMBERG CARB.   33 × 5 TIRES

WESTCOTT

The Car with a Longer Life

(1912 - 1925)

C-"38" (224 CID THROUGH '22)
LIGHTER 6 (5.09 G.R.)
(118" W.B.)

C-"48" (303.1 CID THROUGH '24)
LARGER 6 (4.45 OR)
(125" W.B.)

19-20

(A)   (C)

(38)   (48)
33 × 4 OR 32 × 4½
TIRES
(THROUGH '22)

THE WESTCOTT MOTOR CAR CO.
SPRINGFIELD, OHIO

TWIN OVAL REAR
WINDOWS IN TOP
CONTINENTAL ENGINES (ON
ALL BUT '24
"60")

"C-38"

'19 MODEL
SHOWN. '20 HAS FULL-LENGTH
BODY-HOOD BELT CREASE JUST
ABOVE DOOR HANDLES, ALSO A
NEW COWL VENT.

DELCO IGNITION ON ALL
RAYFIELD CARB.
(THROUGH '24)

"C-48"

21

1922 "A-44" LIKE '21 "C-38," BUT
HAS 120" W.B., 4.66 G.R.

NON-REMOVABLE CYLINDER-HEAD ON 303.1 CID ENG. → "D-48" for '23)
("C-44 and

23

The Closure $1795
Special Closure   1995
Brougham (including trunk)   2490
Sedan   2490
Special Sedan   2690

"CLOSURE" IS NEW ENCLOSED TOURING CAR
FOR 1923

32 × 4½
TIRES ON ALL
'23-'24
WESTCOTTS

C-44-241.5 CID, 4.9 GR
D-48-303.1 CID,
4.45 GR

The Car with a Longer Life

"6-60"
5-PASS.
SEDAN
('24)
("OWN"
ENGINE)

Interior of The New Westcott Model
The Closure

24

('25 has
4-W. BRKS.,

32 × 6.20 TIRES,
STROMBERG CARB., 56 H.P. @   2300 RPM)

OVERLAND

Whippet

FOURS   SIXES

4-CYL. "96" (INTRO. 7-26)
134.2 C.I.D.
(THROUGH '29)
30 H.P. @ 2800 RPM
4.5 G.R.
100¼" W.B. (THROUGH '28)

2.8 x 4.75 TIRES (19") (THROUGH 29)

27

6-CYL. "93-A"
169.6 C.I.D.
(THROUGH '28)
40 H.P. @ 2800 RPM

6-CYL. LANDAU →

109½" W.B. (THROUGH '28)

29 x 4.75 TIRES
(6 INTRO. 1-27)

VACUUM FUEL FEED, TILLOTSON CARB. and AUTO-LITE IGN. (THROUGH '30)

WHIPPET MASCOT ——→

BOTH SERIES have 4-WHEEL MECHANICAL BRAKES.

RAISED PANEL ON '27 FENDERS ↓

FISK

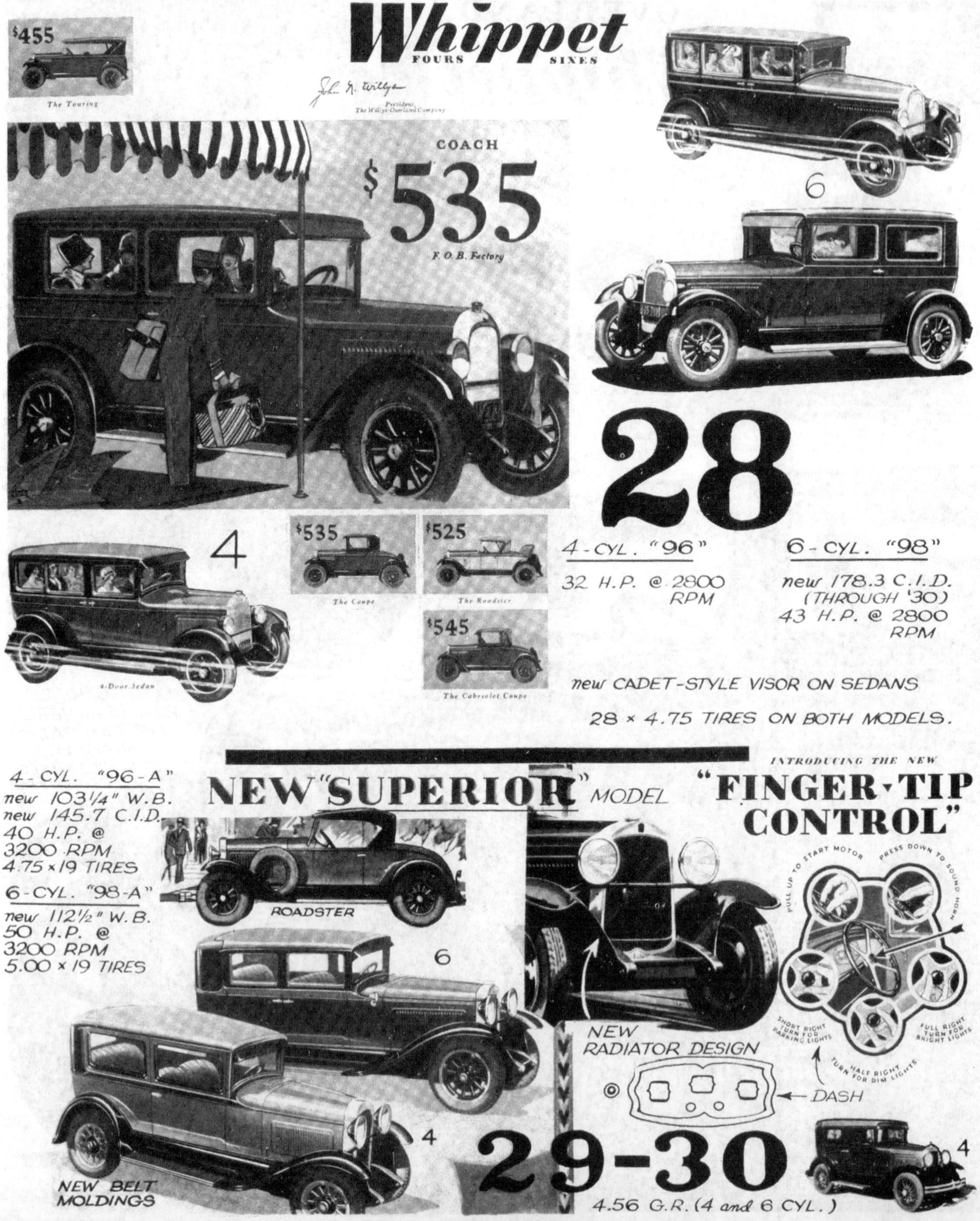

Whippet
FOURS SIXES
President, The Willys-Overland Company
$455
The Touring
COACH
$535
F. O. B. Factory
6
28
4
$535
The Coupe
$525
The Roadster
$545
The Cabriolet Coupe
4-Door Sedan
4-CYL. "96"
32 H.P. @ 2800 RPM
6-CYL. "98"
new 178.3 C.I.D. (THROUGH '30)
43 H.P. @ 2800 RPM
new CADET-STYLE VISOR ON SEDANS
28 × 4.75 TIRES ON BOTH MODELS.
4-CYL. "96-A"
new 103 1/4" W.B.
new 145.7 C.I.D.
40 H.P. @ 3200 RPM
4.75 × 19 TIRES
6-CYL. "98-A"
new 112 1/2" W.B.
50 H.P. @ 3200 RPM
5.00 × 19 TIRES
NEW "SUPERIOR" MODEL
ROADSTER
6
INTRODUCING THE NEW
"FINGER-TIP CONTROL"
PULL UP TO START MOTOR
PRESS DOWN TO SOUND HORN
SHORT RIGHT TURN FOR PARKING LIGHTS
FULL RIGHT TURN FOR BRIGHT LIGHTS
HALF RIGHT TURN FOR DIM LIGHTS
NEW RADIATOR DESIGN
DASH
4
NEW BELT MOLDINGS
29-30
4
4.56 G.R. (4 and 6 CYL.)

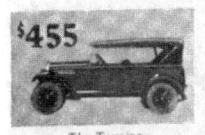

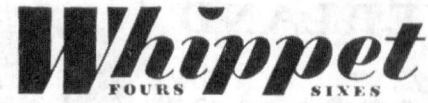

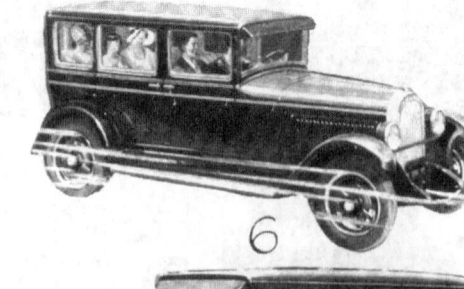

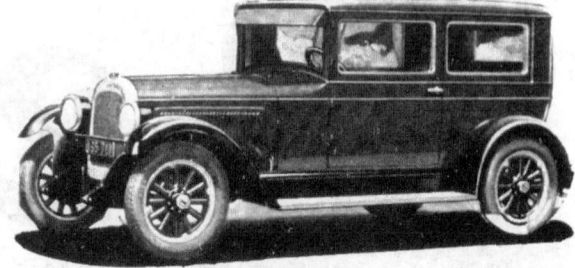

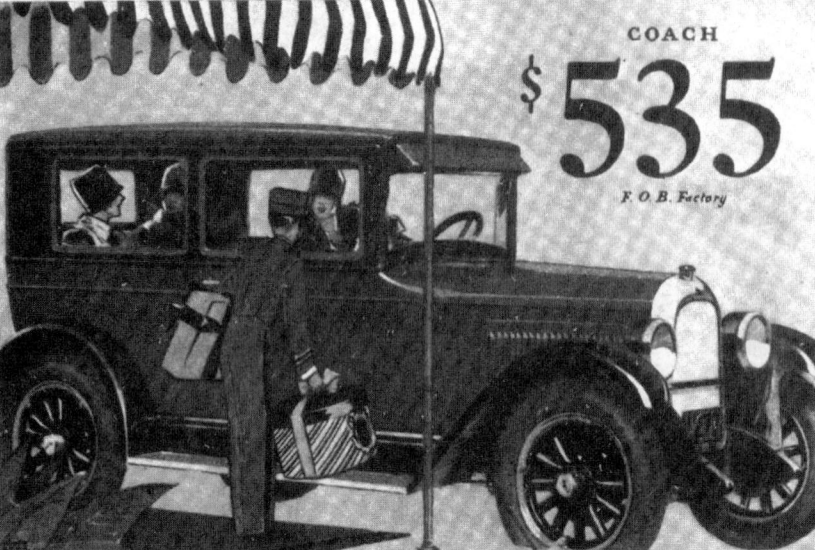

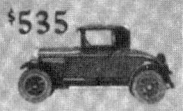

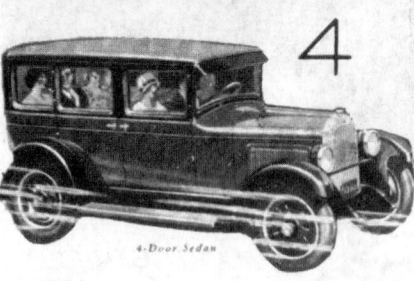

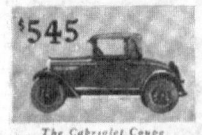

WHITE
CLEVELAND, OHIO
(SINCE 1900)

BETWEEN 1918 and 1936, CARS ON SPECIAL ORDER ONLY. TRUCK PRODUCTION CONTINUES.

1922 MODEL "15-A" 4 CYL.
"UTILITY" MODEL ("BUSINESS CAR," ANNOUNCED 11-21)

WILLS SAINTE CLAIRE
(1921-1927) DELCO IGN. (THROUGH '27) 65 H.P. @ 2700 RPM ('22) 4 TO 1 STD. GEAR RATIO

Motor Cars

WILLS SAINTE CLAIRE, INC.   MARYSVILLE, MICHIGAN

121" W.B. "A-68" with V-8 ENGINE 265.4 C.I.D. (THROUGH '26)

HOLLEY CARB. REPLACES ZENITH, 1923

('21)

(BUDD BODY)

('22)

('23)
121 or 127" W.B. ('23 THROUGH '25)

21-23

1925 = 6 CYL., 273.7 CID ("W-6") OVERHEAD CAM ENGINE ALSO AVAIL. (THROUGH '27) 65 H.P. @ 3200 RPM 128" W.B.

7-PASS. TOURING ('24)

4.9 G.R. ADOPTED DURING '24.

A+B-68 V-8 has SCHEBLER CARB., 65 H.P. @ 2700 RPM (TO '27)

24-25

HYDRAULIC BRAKES ('25)

"W-6" has 33 x 6.00 TIRES (THROUGH '26)

NEW 127" W.B. ON ALL MODELS

26-27

V-8 OR 6

THE NEW GRAY GOOSE TRAVELER

"B-68" OR "C-68" V-8

LANG BODY

T-6, W-6 6 CYLS. 66 H.P.

"NEW VOGUE" BROUGHAM

32 x 6.20 TIRES ON '27 "T-6" 4.9 G.R. ('27)

DISCONTINUED 1927

WILLYS

SIXES AND EIGHTS

WILLYS-OVERLAND, INC., TOLEDO, OHIO

WILLYS 8 SEDAN DE LUXE

Eight

8 HAS 120" W.B., 245.4 C.I.D., 80 H.P. @ 3200 RPM, 5.50 × 19 TIRES (THROUGH '31)

Six **30**

6 HAS 110" W.B., 192.9 C.I.D., 65 H.P. @ 3400 RPM, 5.00 × 19 TIRES (THROUGH '31)

REPLACES "WHIPPET" 6

"6-97" and 113"-wb "6-98-D" SHARE '30 "6" SPECS.

NEW NAME USED FOR 1931

HORIZONTAL HOOD LOUVRES ON SIX

"6-97," "6-98-D," and "8-80-D"

INSTRUMENT PANEL (6)

"8-80-D" SAME SPECS. AS '30, BUT 121" W.B.

HOOD VENT DOORS ON EIGHT

70-80 M.P.H.

WILLYS·OVERLAND

31

SIDE VIEW SIMILAR TO 1931-1932 WILLYS-KNIGHT "95." (SEE "WILLYS-KNIGHT.")

WILLYS 8 and WILLYS-KNIGHT INSTRUMENT PANEL →

WILLYS 6

1932 "SILVER ANNIVERSARY" MODELS with "SILVER STREAK" ENGINES

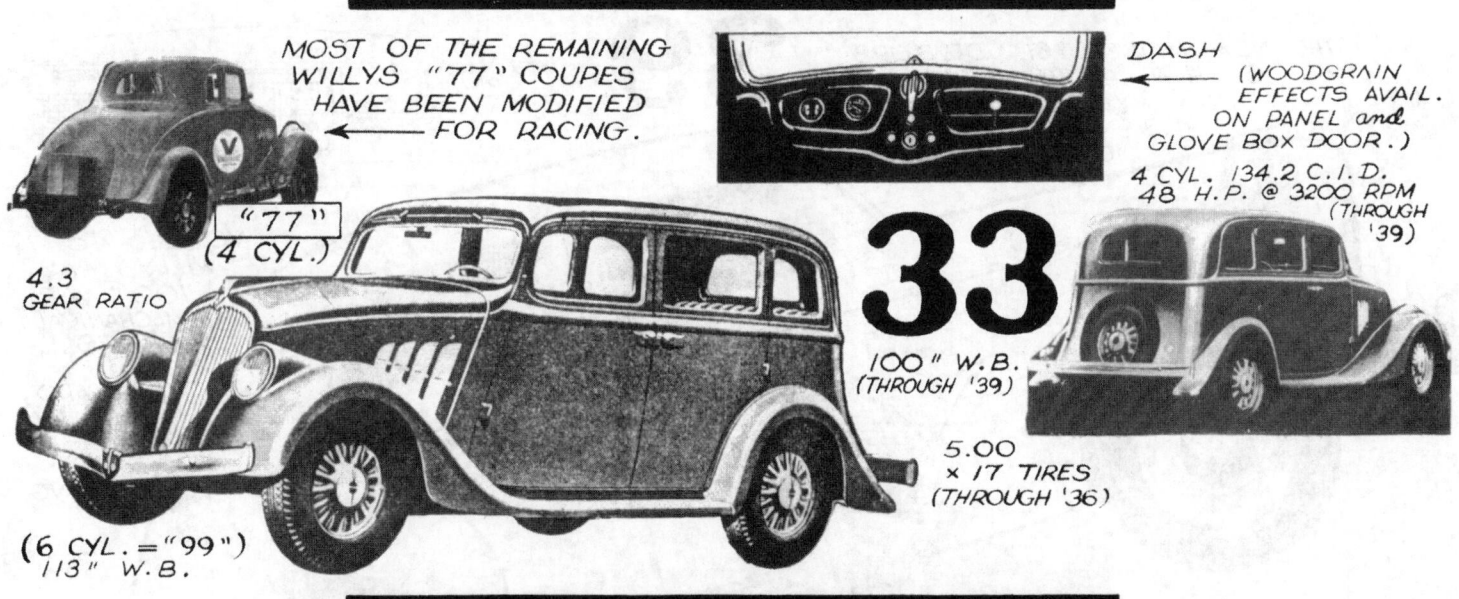

('32 6 DASH IS SAME DESIGN AS '31 6, BUT HAS WOOD-GRAIN EFFECTS)

32

('32 HAS RADIATOR FILLER UNDER 2" LONGER HOOD, AND TRUMPET HORN IN PLACE OF 1931 DISC-SHAPED VIBRATOR HORN.) "6-90-A" and "8-88-A"(AFTER 6-32) IS "1933" MODEL.

The Six Coach, $530

'32 "8-88" and "6-90" have SAME SPECS. AS CORRESPONDING '30-'31 MODELS, BUT 5.50×18 and 5.25×18 TIRES

MOST OF THE REMAINING WILLYS "77" COUPES HAVE BEEN MODIFIED ← FOR RACING.

DASH ← (WOODGRAIN EFFECTS AVAIL. ON PANEL and GLOVE BOX DOOR.)

4 CYL. 134.2 C.I.D. 48 H.P. @ 3200 RPM (THROUGH '39)

"77" (4 CYL.)

33

100" W.B. (THROUGH '39)

4.3 GEAR RATIO

5.00 × 17 TIRES (THROUGH '36)

(6 CYL.="99") 113" W.B.

NEW WIRE WHEELS

NEW SEMI-HORIZONTAL LOUVRES

34

277

WILLYS

(BUBBLE - SHAPED
HOOD VENT PORTS)
'35 HAS WIRE WHEELS.

35

36

'36 HAS STEEL-SPOKE
ARTILLERY WHEELS.

INTERIOR

EARLIEST '37
MODELS (BUILT
FALL, 1936,) HAVE NO
VERTICAL BUMPER GUARDS.

37-38

5.50 × 16 TIRES

39

THIS NEW MODEL "61" DEVELOPS
61 H.P. @ 3600 RPM,
HAS HYDRAULIC BRAKES,
4.3 - 4.55 GEAR RATIO,
102 " WHEELBASE.

DASH
(61)

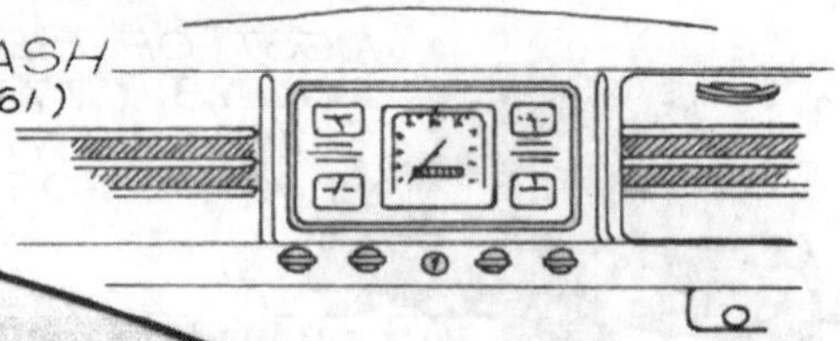

MODEL "48"
WILLYS HAS
100 " W.B.,
MECHANICAL
BRAKES,
4.1
GEAR RATIO,
5.00 × 16
TIRES,
1938
STYLING.

5.50 × 16 TIRES ON "61"

'Slip-stream'
A DESIGN OF SUPERB
BEAUTY

SHELL

278

DURING 1939, WILLYS "61"
KNOWN AS
OVERLAND   (4 CYL.)

WILLYS-KNIGHT

(1914 – 1932)

4-CYLINDER
SLEEVE-VALVE
ENGINE

185.8
C.I.D.
(THROUGH
'25)

40 H.P.
@
2600 RPM
('21-'22)

118" W.B.
(THROUGH '25)

WILLYS-OVERLAND, INC., *Toledo, Ohio*
WILLYS-OVERLAND, LIMITED, *Toronto, Canada*

Willys

20-21

5.00 GEAR RATIO
(THROUGH '22)

DIAGRAM OF A CYLINDER,
ILLUSTRATING
THE SLEEVE-
VALVE
MECHANISM

*No Other Motor Has Cost so
Little, Runs so Smoothly
at the 50,000th Mile.*

22

40 H.P. @ 2400 RPM
MODEL "64"   118" W.B.
and 32×4 TIRES

'23 MODEL
"67" HAS
124" W.B.
and
32×4½
TIRES

23-24

"COUNTRY
CLUB"
TOURING

4.44
GEAR
RATIO
('23)

4.44
and
5.12
('24)

Coupe-Sedan
Standard

WILLYS-KNIGHT

33 × 4.95

42 H.P. @
2200 RPM 4

4

25

"66"

126 " W.B. (UNTIL
'28)

6 (NEW)

NEW 6 HAS 236.4
C.I.D. (THROUGH '27)
and 60 H.P. @ 2800
RPM

280

WILLYS-KNIGHT

113¼" W.B. (THROUGH '28)

"70" (6 CYL.)
177.9 C.I.D. (THROUGH '32)
53 H.P. @ 3000 RPM

26

GREAT 6
60 H.P. @ 3000 RPM

27-28

ROADSTER

"70" SIX

The Only Motor-Car Engine That Improves With Use.

53 H.P. @
3100 RPM (3000 RPM, '28-9)

WITH TOP UP

TOP DOWN

CABRIOLET

1928 "70"
KNOWN AS
"SPECIAL 6"

WILLYS-KNIGHT

27-28
(CONT'D.)

MASCOT

109½" New
W.B. Standard Six
157.6 ("56")
C.I.D. ('28)

("56")

45 H.P. @ 3000 RPM

"GREAT 6"
"66" (1927)
"66-A" (1928)
NEW HORIZONTAL HOOD LOUVRES
('27½-'28)

DASH

One of the many new beautiful color combinations now available on the Willys-Knight Great Six. Upper body, black; lower body and wheels, spruce-green. Striping, ivory and red. Upholstered in fine quality gray-green mohair.

'28 "66-A" HAS
255 C.I.D.
(ENGINE SIZE RETAINED
THROUGH '32)

INSTR.
PANEL
('29)

29-30

"70-B"
6 CYLS., 177.9 C.I.D.
53 H.P. @
3000 RPM
4.89 G.R.
29 x 5.50
TIRES (5.50
x 19 in '30)

('29)

112½" W.B.

WILLYS-KNIGHT

29-30
(CONT'D.)

GREAT SIX
"66-B" 6 CYLS., 255 C.I.D.

72 ('29)
87 ('30)
H.P. @
3200 RPM

120" WHEELBASE
"GREAT 6" CAB. CPE., 7-PASS.
SEDAN AND LIMOUSINE *have*
ROBBINS BODIES.
WILLYS-OVERLAND BODIES
ON OTHERS.

GREAT SIX →

The artistically designed instrument panel, with instruments grouped in a setting of beauty and dignity.

('30)

"87" (1930)

The door interiors are upholstered in broadcloth, with a center strip of Bedford Cord, topped by an artistic panel in needlepoint.

31-32
(FINAL WILLYS-KNIGHT IS 1932 MODEL.)
"66-D"   87 H.P.
@ 3200

"95"
(1932)
177.9
C.I.D.
60 H.P. @ 3400
(SINCE '31)

283

(1929-1930) WINDSOR 8

MOON MOTOR CAR CO., ST. LOUIS, MO.

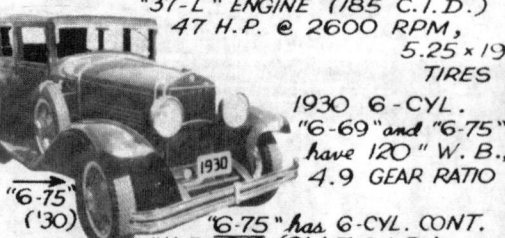

'29 DASH

6-CYL. '30 MODELS ALSO

1929 "WHITE PRINCE" has STRAIGHT-8 CONTINENTAL "15-S" ENGINE (268.6 C.I.D.) 88 H.P. @ 3100 RPM ('29) 125½" W.B.
* 4.8 and other GEAR RATIOS
31 × 6.00 TIRES ("8-82")
31 × 6.50 " ('8-92")
* 4.88 GEAR RATIO ("8-82")
3.93 " " ("8-92")

WINDSOR HAS MOON-STYLE RADIATOR (PAINTED, ON MOST TYPES) "8-82" BECOMES "8-85" FOR 1930, has 4.63 G.R., 6.00 × 19 TIRES

"8-92" CONT'D. 1930, with 6.50 × 19 TIRES, 3.9 G.R.

1930 "6-69" has 6-CYL. CONT. "37-L" ENGINE (185 C.I.D.) 47 H.P. @ 2600 RPM, 5.25 × 19 TIRES

1930 6-CYL. "6-69" and "6-75" have 120" W.B., 4.9 GEAR RATIO

"6-75" ('30)

"6-75" has 6-CYL. CONT. "11-E" ENG. (214.7 C.I.D.) 66 H.P. @ 3100 RPM, 5.50 × 19 TIRES

('29)

WINTHER 6 (1920-1923)

WINTHER MOTORS, INC., KENOSHA, WIS.
HERSCHELL-SPILLMAN ENGINE (248.9 C.I.D.)
(TRUCKS ALSO)

RADIATOR DESIGN

(DISC WHEELS ALSO AVAIL.

MODEL "61" ('21) has 120" W.B., 4.45 GEAR RATIO

WINTON SIX (1897 — 1924)

THE WINTON COMPANY   CLEVELAND

DURING 1922, MODEL "25" REPLACED BY MODEL "40"

has 132" W.B., OWN 6-CYL. L-HEAD ENGINE (347.9 C.I.D.)

4.90 G.R. (THROUGH '21)

('22)

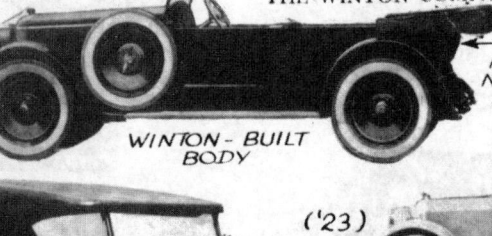

WINTON-BUILT BODY

NEW "40" 4-PASS. SPORT CAR

('23)

('23)

"40" 7-PASS. SEDAN

STROMBERG CARB. REPLACED BY RAYFIELD CARB., and NEW 4.58 G.R. FOR 1923 and 1924.

('24) 5-PASS. COUPE

YELLOW CAB (1921-1936)

Manufacturing Co.
Chicago, U. S. A.

'21

BUILT BY GENERAL MOTORS AFTER MID-1920s. KNOWN AS GENERAL CAB FROM 1936 TO 1938)

284

MY DAD HAD THAT CAR

HAD THAT CAR

PART TWO

1940–1965
AIRWAY TO WILLYS

CONTENTS

Airway.............................289
American Bantam...........289
Beech Plainsman 289
Bobbi Kar.......................289
Buick...............................290
Buick Special 310
Cadillac...........................314
Checker...........................337
Chevelle 338
Chevrolet 339
Chevy II 360
Chrysler 363
Comet..............................383
Cord (replicar) 385
Corvair............................386
Corvette 390

Crosley 392
Dart 394
Davis 397
Del Mar 397
De Soto 397
Dodge 408
Edsel 424
Fairlane 427
Falcon 429
Ford 432
Frazer 453
Gordon Diamond 455
Graham
(& Hupmobile)............455
Gregory 455
Hoppenstand 455

Henry J 456
Hudson 457
Imp 463
Imperial...........................464
International
Harvester.......................471
Jet 474
Kaiser 475
King Midget....................480
Kurtis 480
Lancer 481
Lark 482
Lincoln (& Lincoln
Continental).................484
Marlin 495
Mercury 496

Metropolitan 510
Mustang
(independent)...............511
Mustang (Ford) 511
Nash.................................513
Olds F-85 521
Oldsmobile 524
Packard (& Packard
Clipper)........................546
Playboy 555
Plymouth 556
Pontiac............................574
Pup 593
Rambler 593
Riviera.............................606
Studebaker 607

Tempest...........................622
Thunderbird....................626
Tasco 630
Town Shopper................630
Tucker 630
Valiant.............................631
Willys
(& Willys Jeep) 635

It is oddly unfortunate that yet another section of this book begins and ends with automobile brands that are no longer with us, as many makes didn't survive World War II. This chapter could be broken down differently, 1940–1942 and 1946–1965, because the automobile manufacturing business in the United States (indeed most of the world) was on hiatus during The Great War. There are many reasons for this, among them being that so many metals and other materials needed to produce an automobile were rationed by the government in order to preserve them for wartime needs, and because so many of the men that worked automotive production lines were drafted into military service. Also, carmakers were needed to produce the tools of war: tanks, ships, munitions, trucks and transport vehicles, plus what we now call jeeps.

Most American automotive designs were updated or all-new for 1940, and these models were little-changed until the United States entered the war in 1942. There was little to no civilian automotive production for model years 1943, 1944, and 1945. When the war was over, carmakers restarted production with what they had— the last 1942 designs were all quickly updated and freshened up for model year 1946, but few buyers really cared much. The cars in everyone's driveways had grown old by then, and the market was itching for new metal. Even knowing that most of the 1946 models were really warmed over and mildly updated '42s, hungry new car buyers lapped them up by the thousands. Some brands introduced much-updated, revised, or all-new vehicles for 1947 and 1948, but many of them, such as Ford, Cadillac, Oldsmobile and others, took a few years to get new cars designed, tested, and tooled up, not launching them until 1949.

Among the most exciting new car happenings in the immediate postwar era was the somewhat stillborn birth of Preston Tucker's car of the future, the landmark Tucker 48. This rear-engine marvel packed myriad safety features, high performance, luxury, and comfort into a dazzling four-door sedan. Unfortunately Tucker suffered countless teething problems in its infancy, and only about 50 or so of the cars were hand built in the company's sprawling Chicago factory. Did Tucker's dream drown in a sea of mismanagement, financial impropriety and Security and Exchange Commission lawsuits, or was he quietly put down by the Detroit Big Three because Ford, Chrysler, and GM were afraid of the competition by a car so revolutionary as the Tucker? Another one of those great stories "wrapped in a inside an enigma."

The 1940–1965 time period is dotted with so many great auto-motive achievements it's difficult to track them all:

- the all new Ford lineup for 1949,
- landmark overhead valve V-8 engines
  by Oldsmobile and Cadillac that same year,
- the new small-block Chevrolet V-8 for 1955,
- the birth of the Ford Thunderbird, the magic of the
  1955–1957 Chevrolet,
- the Continental Mk II, the "king of tailfins" 1959 Cadillac,
- an exciting new American sports car called "Corvette,"
- the Shelby Cobra in 1962,
- the 1963 Buick Riviera,
- the sublime elegance of the 1961–1963 Lincoln Continental,
- the first modern mid-sized muscle car—
  Pontiac's GTO— for 1964,
- and who could forget the new Ford Mustang launched in
  mid-1964 as a 1965 model (some of those early Mustangs
  are nicknamed 1964½, but they were really 1965s, as there
  officially was no 1964½ model).
- and of course, the ill-fated Edsel.

America in the1950s was generally filled with optimism, riding high on victory of WWII, and enjoying postwar booms in the economy, design, housing, and the jet age. Automobile design reflected all those things, growing ever-more flamboyant, feature-laden, and better performing with many "jet age" styling cues, such as taillights recalling glowing rocket engines and afterburners, chrome design touches and hood ornaments resembling aircraft, and even an Old-smobile model named "Jetfire."

The time between 1940–1965 stands among autodom's greatest eras. Enjoy your nostalgic tour of its many great automobiles in Part Two.

AIRWAY (1948-1949)

WT.= 775 lbs.
(PILOT MODELS)

T.P. HALL ENGINEERING, SAN DIEGO, CALIF.

AIR-COOLED ONAN REAR ENGINE
10.2 HP
ALUMINUM and PLASTIC BODY

(KNOWN AS [AMERICAN] AUSTIN, 1930-1934)   4 CYL., 75" WB

AMERICAN BANTAM

(1935-1941) AMERICAN BANTAM CAR CO., BUTLER, PA. (OTHER BODY TYPES ALSO)

MODEL
4-65
(1940-1941)
MECH. BRAKES

BEECH PLAINSMAN

(1948)

ALUMINUM
BODY
(1 PILOT
MODEL
ONLY)

BEECH AIRCRAFT CO., WICHITA, KAN.
4-CYL. air-cooled ENGINE
also,
ELECTRIC MOTOR
IN EA. WHEEL

BOBBI KAR

BOBBI MOTOR CAR
CO.,
SAN
DIEGO,
CALIF.

(1945-1947)

(REPL. BY 1948 KELLER)

4-CYL.
REAR
ENG.

92" WB

(ESTAB. 1903)

Buick

SPECIAL

SUPER

BUICK DIVISION OF **GENERAL MOTORS**

"Best buy's Buick!"

STRAIGHT-8 O.H.V. *engines* (SINCE '31)

1940

LIMITED

Not a six but an EIGHT for **$895** and up

SUPER 51

WHEN BETTER AUTOMOBILES ARE BUILT, BUICK WILL BUILD THEM

MODELS :
40 SPECIAL
50 SUPER
60 CENTURY
70 ROADMASTER
80, 90 LIMITED

248 or 320 CID
107 HP @ 3400 or 141 HP @ 3600
(SINCE '38)

with
Body by Fisher

40

RUBY KEELER JOLSON

Here she is with her Buick Estate Wagon, smart, comfortable, useful in no end of ways, and a bargain at $1242, plus $19.50 for white sidewall tires.★

Found **only** on CHEVROLET · PONTIAC ·

OLDSMOBILE · BUICK · CADILLAC

121, 126, 133 or 140" WB

new SAFETY-UNIT SEALED BEAM HEADLIGHTS — brighter, longer-lasting filament, in one weather-proof unit with lens and reflector — better lighting over a longer period.

SUPER 59

VARIOUS TIRE SIZES

EIGHT

ON DISPLAY FRIDAY
AT BUICK SHOWROOMS EVERYWHERE

BUICK

118, 121, 126 or 139" WB

Special 4-door Sedan,
Model 47, $1021.

USA 1941

41

115, 125 OR 165 HP

"Buy Buick's Best!" LIMITED

SPECIAL

('41 and EARLIER CONV'TS. HAVE NO REAR QUARTER WINDOWS)

DASH

118, 121, 124, 126, 129 or 139" WB
110, 118 or 165 HP

42-45

new "FADE-AWAY" FENDERS BLEND INTO DOORS

"Better Buy Buick"
EXEMPLAR OF GENERAL MOTORS VALUE

SPECIAL

CVT., 2-DR. ROADMASTER has FULL-LENGTH FRONT FENDERS

VERTICAL BARS IN new LOWER, BROADER GRILLE

11942

291

BUICK

PRICE RANGE: $1391. TO $2149.

CLOCK

DASH

CLOSE-UP OF
SPEEDOMETER

EASILY - RESETTABLE
2ND ODOMETER RECORDS TRIP
MILEAGE

ESTATE WAGON
(SUPER)

SUPER

new GRILLE

46

40 SPECIAL 121" WB
50 SUPER 124"
70 ROADMASTER 129"

SUPER

REAR VIEW   292

ROADMASTER

MODEL 51

SUPER

CONVERTIBLE *has* POWER-OPERATED TOP, SIDE WINDOWS *and* FRONT SEAT

When better automobiles are built **BUICK** will build them

47 $1497. TO $3030.

POSTWAR "BOMBSIGHT"-STYLE HOOD ORNAMENT (SINCE '46)

SPEC. *and* SUPER *have* 248 CID, 110 HP @ 3600 RPM

RDMSTR. *has* 320 CID, 144 HP @ 3600 RPM

MEDALLION MOVED LOWER; NOW *IN* TOP SECTION *OF* GRILLE.

USA 1947

Super

SUPER

SPEC.-SU.-RDMSTR. PRICES: $1735. TO $3433.

'48 SUPER *and* ROADMASTER NAMES ALSO APPEAR *ON* FRONT FENDERS.

48

ROADMASTER

SPECIAL (CONT'D. INTO '49)

OPTIONAL: *new* **Dynaflow** AUTO. TRANS.

7.00 x 15

MODEL NAME

BUICK

Super
has 3 "PORTHOLES"

49

TOTALLY RESTYLED
(EXCEPT SPECIAL)

ROADMASTER
has 4 "PORTHOLES"
150 HP

BACK SEAT
(SHOWING FOLDING
ARM REST)

ROADMASTER
with Dynaflow Drive

$1787. TO $3734.
PRICE RANGE

1949

new
DASH

"RIVIERA" (*new* H/T)

CVT.
TOP
REAR
DETAIL

LATE '49 CONVERTIBLES
and RIVIERAS *have*
new "SWEEP-SPEAR"
SIDE TRIM (AS ILLUSTRATED.)

BUICK

$1856.

115 HP SPECIAL

SPECIAL INTRODUCED EARLY (IN AUG., '49)

121½" WB EXCEPT ON "52" SUPER SEDAN (125½") and ON 126½" and 130¼" RDMSTRS.

SPECIAL RETAINS 2-PC. WINDSHIELD

STARTLING *new* "BUMPER-GRILLE"

50

THE ESTATE WAGON is yours on either SUPER or ROADMASTER chassis. Three power ranges to choose from.

128 HP **Super**

DASH (SPC.)

BACK SEAT (SEDAN)

152 HP **ROADMASTER** *RIVIERA*

130¼" WB ON "RIVIERA SEDAN"

ELONGATED "PORTHOLES"

BUICK

SPECIAL   SPECIAL DE LUXE

ESTATE WAGON

120 TO 128 HP

('51)

SUPER 128 HP

51-52

DASH ('52)

ROADMASTER

152 HP

170 HP

('51)   ROADMASTER ('52)

('51)   SUPER

'52 *has* BROADER HUBCAP MARGINS, FULL-HEIGHT VERT. BUMPER GUARDS, NO CHROME STRIPS ALONG REAR FENDERS.

Buick Eight

'51 BUMPER GUARDS DO NOT RUN DOWN FRONT OF BUMPER, BUT REST ON TOP.

Equipment, accessories, trim and models are subject to change without notice.

296

BUICK

FINAL STRAIGHT-8 IN SPECIAL

SPECIAL (125 HP @ 3800 RPM)

SPORT WIRE WH. AVAIL.

53

1903-1953

121½" WB (ALL MODELS EXC. 125½ WB RIVIERA SED.)

SUPER

new **V8**

322 CID ENGINE IN ALL BUT "SPECIAL"

164-170 HP

LIMITED-PRODUCTION "SKYLARK" CVT.

ROADMASTER RIVIERA

ROADMASTER (188 HP @ 4000)

BUICK

143 or 150 HP
SPECIAL

ALL V8s

195 or 200 HP
CENTURY

54

264 or 322 CID V8s
(THROUGH '55)

SKYLARK
$**4483.**

DASH

ROADMASTER

SUPER

177 or 182 HP
SUPER

ROADMASTER
200 HP @ 4100 RPM

BUICK

150 to 236 HP

ROADMASTER

TOP TO BOTTOM: SPECIAL, CENTURY, SUPER

55

DASH (SUPER)

MEDALLION GIVES 1956 DATE

SPECIAL

SPECIAL has 220 HP @ 4400 RPM
OTHERS, 255 HP @ 4400 RPM

CENTURY

SUPER

ROADMASTER

122 or 127" WB (SINCE '54)

56

322 CID V8s

new V-GRILLE (FINE HORIZ. PCS.)

BUICK

SPECIAL

WAGON

CVT.

4-DR. H/T

H/T

MODEL NAME ABOVE DIP IN SIDE CHROME TRIM (EXCEPT ON SPECIAL, WHICH HAS NO NAME HERE, OR ON SUPER (with 3 CURVED CHROME PCS. HERE.)

$3354.

CENTURY

new CENTURY CABALLERO WAGON (H/T STYLE)

ALL WITH new 364 CID ENGINE (CONT'D. IN SPECIAL and LE SABRE MODELS THROUGH 1961)

SUPER

CVT.

H/T

57

122" OR new 127½" WB (THROUGH '58)

4-DR. H/T

ROADMASTER

note UNUSUAL REAR DOOR TREATMENT ON THIS MODEL

300 HP @ 4600 RPM (EXCEPT SPECIAL, WHICH has 250 HP @ 4400) (THROUGH '58)

new CONVEX GRILLE with FINE VERTICAL PCS.

BUICK

SPECIAL

JUNE 1958

new BLOCK-STYLE GRILLE

HEAVY USE of CHROME TRIM

58

SIDE "PORTHOLES" DISCONTINUED (UNTIL '60)

250-HP SPECIAL

$2820.

SPECIAL

300 HP in CENTURY, SUPER, RDMSTR., LIMITED

SPECIAL CENTURY

CENTURY

THE AIR BORN B-58 BUICK

$2636.

$4557.

ROADMASTER

$5125.

new LIMITED (NAME REVIVED)

CVT.

BUICK

ALL-*new* MODEL NAMES FOR 1959:

LE SABRE, INVICTA, ELECTRA, ELECTRA 225

364 CID, 250 HP @ 4400 RPM

L⁰SABRE 123" WB

PACE CAR AT 1959 INDY 500 RACE

LE SABRE ALL BUT (SPEC.) have 325 HP @ 4400 RPM 401 CID

INVICTA 123" WB

59

(TOTALLY RESTYLED)

DASH

new SQUARED REAR ROOFLINE ON 4-DOOR H/T.

ELECTRA 126.3" WB

CANTED HEADLIGHTS

8.00 x 15

TOP-OF-LINE ELECTRA 225 IS ILLUSTRATED.

10.5 COMPR. IN 1959

BUICK

$3145.

$2915.

LE SABRE
has 210, 235, 250 or 300 HP

364 CID = LE S.
401 CID = OTHERS
(SAME CHOICES IN '61)

60

A RETURN
TO VARIOUS "PORTHOLE" TYPE SIDE
DECORATIONS AS USED ON
1949-1956 BUICKS

new
"Mirromagic"
INSTRUMENT
CLUSTER
LETS DRIVER SEE
GAUGES IN A
MIRROR THAT
CAN BE TILTED
TO SUIT DRIVER'S
OWN
EYE LEVEL.

INVICTA

123" WB = LE S., INVICTA
126.3" WB = EL., EL. 225

HEADLTS. PLACED HORIZONTALLY,
new GRILLE
with CONCAVE
VERTICAL
PIECES
and new
3-SHIELD
BADGE

INVICTA and
ELECTRAS have
325 HP @ 4400 RPM

INVICTA

1960 Buick Invicta 4-Door Hardtop in Magic-Mirror Tahiti Beige and Cordovan

ELECTRA

ELECTRA 225

$4300.

303

BUICK

(TOTALLY RESTYLED)

61

126" WB
ELECTRA 225

325 HP

(new ROOFLINE)

123" WB
250 HP
LE SABRE

La Sabre

SPECIAL-SIZE
BUICK SPECIAL
new COMPACT SERIES,
STARTING 1961
SEE SPECIAL BUICK

INVICTA

304

123" WB

325 HP

BUICK

2-DR.

4-DR. H/T

LE SABRE

62

$3567.

401 CID V8s (IN all FULL-SIZED MODELS)

ADVANCED THRUST

LE S. 265 HP @ 4400
INV. 280 HP @ 4400
ELEC. 325 HP @ 4400

H/T

4-DR. H/T

INVICTA

CVT.

$3815.

INVICTA ESTATE WAGON

$4034. (6-PASS.)

EL. 225 CVT.

ELECTRA 225

4-DR. H/T

H/T

ELECTRA has 126" WB (OTHERS 123")

SEDAN

Close-up of Wildcat shows you new medallions and unique fabric overlay (available in black or white).

new 325 HP **WILDCAT!** H/T

$4125.

BUICK

SEDAN

280 HP

63

LE SABRE
MODELS

$3298.

2-DR.

CVT.

WAGON
with
REAR-FACING
3RD SEAT

CLOSER VIEW OF
LE SABRE DASH
and ADDITIONAL '63
MODELS ILLUSTRATED
ON NEXT PAGE.

306

new V-SHAPED FRONT

BUICK

DASH

$4167.

INVICTA (FINAL YR.)
325 HP (ON ALL BUT LE SABRE)

note =
WILDCAT has
ITS OWN UNIQUE
GRILLE

WILDCAT

63 (CONT'D.)

$4047.

Electra 225

$4141.

ELECTRA TAIL-LIGHT
DETAIL

BUICK

ESTATE WAGON

LE SABRE

210 HP

64

$3458.

$3593.

WILDCAT
325 HP

THE WILDCAT CONVERTIBLE

THE WILDCAT 4-DOOR SEDAN

WILDCAT (CLOSE-UP)

$4357.

THE ELECTRA 225 CONVERTIBLE

ELECTRA
225

325 HP

THE ELECTRA 225 4-DOOR HARDTOP

BUICK

LE SABRE

H/T
(VINYL TOP)

123" WB
300 CID
210 HP
8.15×15 TIRES

LE SABRE
400

123 OR 126" WB
(SINCE '59)

65

$**3345.**
TO
$**4530.**

4-DR.
H/T

H/T

8.45×15
TIRES
126" WB
401 CID
325 HP

WILDCAT

CVT.

SEE ALSO:
RIVIERA

ELECTRA 225

H/T

8.85×15 TIRES

(INTRO. WED., OCT. 5, 1960, AS *SEPARATE COMPACT SERIES* OF BUICK)

SPECIAL-SIZE
BUICKSPECIAL
THE BEST OF BOTH WORLDS ⟶

(and **SKYLARK***)*

NEW!

BUICK'S REVOLUTIONARY ALUMINUM V-8. This hot 155 HP Fireball V-8 weighs just 318 pounds for a .487 horsepower to weight ratio — highest in the industry!

3 VIEWS OF SPECIAL (SEDAN)

61

WAGON *has* 1-PIECE SWING-UP REAR DOOR ↓

PRICES START AT
$**2659.**
(STD. CPE)

SPECIAL WAGON

$**3091.**

⟵ 112" WHEELBASE ⟶

THE CLEAN LOOK *of action*

BUICK skylark

SKYLARK is new LUXURY 185-HP MODEL *of* SPECIAL
↓

$**2949.**

SKYLARK IS AVAILABLE IN TWO-TONE OR SOLID COLORS (AS ILLUSTRATED)

note THAT SKYLARK *has* OWN REAR STYLING

112" WB *and* 6.50 × 13 TIRES (THROUGH '63)

BUICKSPECIAL

SPECIAL
2-DR. CPE.

4-DR. SEDAN

SPECIAL

SPECIAL DLX.

WAGON

3-SEAT
WAGON
$3136.

62

185-HP V8
OR *new* V6
ENGINE

SKYLARK

SPECIAL DE LUXE

SPECIAL
2-DR. SPORT COUPE

6.50 × 13 TIRES
(SINCE '61)

WAGON

SPECIAL
DE LUXE

SEDAN

$2682.

63

SKYLARK

H/T

CVT.

BUICK SPECIAL
DELUXE 4-DOOR SEDAN

SPEC.

Special 2-seat Station Wagon

SPEC. DLX.

210 HP

SKYLARK

SKYLARK

new 6.50 x 14 TIRES

new SPORTS WAGON

64

(9-PASS.)

$3562.

(CUST.)

new 115" WB

new RAISED PANORAMIC ROOF WINDOWS, AS ALSO FOUND IN new OLDS "VISTA-CRUISER" WAGON.

REAR FENDER TRIM (WAGON)

Skylark

INTERIOR VIEWS

This is the new Buick Skylark Sports Wagon. It has a raised roof so you can sit tall, and a new kind of shaded glass so you can look up and out, and a **forward**-facing third seat.

120" WB (WAGON)

300 CID "WILDCAT" V8

SPECIAL CVT.

SPECIAL SED.

BUICKSPECIAL

SKYLARK GRAN SPORT

SKYLARK GRAN SPORT

65

$2690. TO $3561.

SPECIAL 2-DR.

SKYROOF SPORTS WAG.

SKYLARK WITH new FULL-WIDTH TAIL-LIGHTS

H/T

Cadillac **40**

8 or 16 CYL.

COUPE

62

129" WB

V8 *has* 346 CID (SINCE '36) 135 or 140 HP @ 3400 RPM (SINCE '38)

DUAL DIVIDING STRIPS IN BACKLIGHT

127" WB

60 SPECIAL

V8 and V-16 PRICE RANGE OF $1685. TO $7175. V-16 PRICED FROM $5140.

INTERIOR

THE NEW *Seventy-Two*

Cadillac-Fleetwood

138" WB

FLEETWOOD 75 MODELS ALSO (141" WB)

Illustrated is the Touring Sedan for Five Passengers.

Cadillac
Standard of the World

40 (CONT'D.)

185 HP @ 3600

V-16 has 431 CID
(SINCE '38)

V-16
90
SERIES

FINAL 16-CYLINDER CAR
BUILT IN U.S.A.

$1240. and up
final
LA SALLE

LA SALLE
WAS A LOWER-PRICED
CADILLAC
SUBSIDIARY,
AVAILABLE
1927 TO 1940.

MODELS 50, 52 have
322 CID V8 (SINCE '37)
130 HP @ 3400 RPM
123" WB   7.00 × 16
TIRES

MODEL
61 (REPLACES LA SALLE)

$4230.
60 SPECIAL

FLEETWOOD
75

new
TAIL-LIGHTS

41

62 CONVERTIBLE CP.
$1645.

CONVERTIBLE
COUPE HAS
A BACK SEAT
INSIDE THE
CAB. →

new
FRONTAL
STYLING, with
BROAD, LOW
GRILLE

Cadillac Standard of the World

CADILLAC-FLEETWOOD

60-S

new HOOD RUNS TO WINDSHIELD

62

SMALL VERTICAL STRIPS ON FENDERS IDENTIFY 60-S.

ROUND GRILLE LIGHTS IN '42 ONLY

42-45

Fleetwood

MODEL "75" DOES NOT HAVE ↑ "FADE-AWAY" STYLE FENDERS (THROUGH '49.)

61

62

62

46

FLEETWOOD 60-S

(60-S *has* 5 SLOPING CHROME STRIPS ON REAR QUARTER PANEL.)

75

AS IN 1942, A TOTAL OF 6 HORIZONTAL GRILLE MEMBERS, BUT WITH *new* RECTANGULAR GRILLE LTS.

FRONT VIEW

Cadillac Standard of the World

TOTAL OF 5 HORIZONTAL MEMBERS IN 1947 GRILLE.

61
126" WB

62
129" WB

47 **$2060. TO $4590.** PRICE RANGE

Cadillac NAME ON FENDERS IS NOW IN SCRIPT STYLE.

CHROME STRIPS IDENTIFY 60-S
133" WB

346 CID 150 HP @ 3600 RPM

136" WB ON 75 (THROUGH '49)

new HEAVY FLANGES ON 1947 HUBCAPS.

TOTALLY RESTYLED (EXCEPT "75.")

62

61

has CHROME ROCKER PANEL STRIP

126" WB ON BOTH 61 and 62

$2357. TO $4590. PRICE RANGE

new "FISHTAIL" REAR FENDER FINS

PLAIN ROCKER PANEL ON "61."

48

FLEETWOOD 60-S
133" WB

60-S REAR FENDER HAS UNIQUE CHROME TRIM.

Cadillac
Standard of the World

61
$2840.
49

IMPROVED V-8
ENGINE NOW HAS
OVERHEAD
VALVES.

160 HP
(THROUGH '51)

...The worlds newest engine—for the worlds finest car!

$3103.

126" WB (61, 62)

62

$3549.

EXCEPT ON 75,
1949 GRILLE has
ONE LESS HORIZONTAL
PIECE THAN 1948.
new CHROME
WRAP-AROUNDS
EXTEND GRILLE AT
EITHER END.

62

new
"COUPE
DE VILLE"
HARDTOP
CONVERTIBLE

$5253.
75

133" WB
FLEETWOOD
60
SPECIAL

$3891.

"75" RETAINS
OLDER
STYLING.
136¼" WB

318

Cadillac — Standard of the World

61

122" WB

AS ILLUSTRATED, NO REAR QUARTER WINDOWS ON 61 SEDAN

50

62

126" WB

$2761.
TO
$4959.
PRICE RANGE

62 CVT. **$3654.**

new 1-PIECE WINDSHIELD

new GRILLE

Cadillac

60-S (130" WB)
60-S NOW has CHROME STRIPS (LOUVRES) HERE

ALL MODELS RESTYLED, INCLUDING "75."

75
(146 3/4" WB)

319

Cadillac
Standard of the World

FINAL "61" MODEL

61

62

PRICE RANGE:
$2917.
TO
$5405.

160 HP

60-S

75

51

new "WAFFLE" EXTENSIONS AT EITHER END OF 1951 GRILLE

320

GOLDEN ANNIVERSARY

Cadillac
Standard of the World

BEAUTIFUL NEW INTERIORS IN ALL MODELS

62 (NOW THE LOWEST-PRICED SERIES)

"V" INSIGNIA NOW COLORED GOLD, TO COMMEMORATE CADILLAC's 50TH ANNIVERSARY.

1902 52

52

PRICE RANGE : **$3452.** TO **$5572.**

THESE *new* DECORATIONS FOUND ON 1952 MODELS ONLY

STANDARD OF THE WORLD

147" WB 75

60-S

NEW 190-HORSEPOWER ENGINE
★ NEW HYDRA-MATIC DRIVE
★ NEW FRONT AND REAR END APPEARANCE
★ NEW CADILLAC POWER STEERING
★ NEW DUAL EXHAUST SYSTEM

321

Cadillac
Standard of the World

62

EL DORADO
CVT. (new)
(has WRAP-AROUND
WINDSHIELD)
$7750.

126" WB

60-S has
MORE CHROME
ALONG LOWER
EDGE, PLUS THE
CHARACTERISTIC
VERTICAL STRIPS.

<u>60-S</u> **$4341.**
130" WB

$4144.
62
CVT.

53

PRICE RANGE (EXC. EL D.)
$3571.
TO
$5621.

(THROUGH 1955)
331 CID
ENGINE
210 HP @
4150 RPM

LIMOUSINE

75

146.75" WB

322

Cadillac
Standard of the World

62

new 129" WB

$4261.

CPE. DE VILLE

DASH
(CONVERTIBLE)

60-S

new 133" WB

54

230 HP @
4400 RPM

new PANORAMIC
WINDSHIELD

75
LIMOUSINE
new 149.75" WB

EL DORADO
CONVERTIBLE

Cadillac
Standard of the World

129" WB

62

55

250 HP @ 4600 RPM

HIGHLIGHT FEATURE
of CADILLAC and OLDSMOBILE for '55!

AUTRONIC-EYE®

REAR VIEW

AUTOMATIC LIGHT 'TROL

1955

PADDED DASH DETAIL →

BRIGHT

DIM

BRIGHT

Automatically AT NIGHT!

60-S (133" WB)
('75 HAS VERTICAL CHROME STRIP RUNNING TO BOTTOM OF REAR FENDER.)

$**6286.**

EL DORADO

270 H.P. @ 4800 RPM

with IMPORTED, HANDCRAFTED LEATHER UPHOLSTERY

129" WB

Cadillac Standard of the World

CONVERT.

COUPE DE VILLE

62

60-S

PRICES START AT $4146.

(ACTUAL PHOTO)

LENGTH OFTEN EXAGGERATED IN ADVERTISING ART

new 365 CID (THROUGH '58) 285 HP @ 4600 RPM

56

FINER MEMBERS IN GRILLE

LIMOUSINE

75 $6773.

SEVILLE

Eldorado

BIARRITZ CVT.

$6501. FOR EITHER MODEL OF EL DORADO

305 H.P.

Cadillac Standard of the World

$4677. TO $13,074.
PRICE RANGE (new EL.D. BRGH. IS COSTLIEST MODEL.)

60-S

new SQUARED-OFF TAIL-FINS with LOW, ROUND TAIL-LIGHTS

REAR BRIGHTWORK PANELS on 60-S

57

EL DORADO BIARRITZ (325 HP)

62

300 HP

EL DORADO (BROUGHAM - 4 DR.) (SEVILLE - 2 DR.)

new GRILLE

ALL '58 MODELS have BACK-SLANTING FINS, AS SEEN ON '57 EL DORADO.

129½ WB

310 HP

58

FOUR HEADLIGHTS

new LOWER, BROADER GRILLE

1958

MORE 1958 MODELS ON NEXT PAGE

326

Cadillac
STANDARD OF THE WORLD

60-S CONTINUES LOWER BRIGHTWORK PANELS ON REAR FENDERS. 133" WB

AS IN 1957, EL DORADO BROUGHAM HAS ITS OWN UNIQUE FRONT END STYLING.

$13,074.

$7500.
FOR SEVILLE OR BIARR.

58
(CONT'D.)

note ROUNDED-DOWN REAR FENDER/DECK PANELS ONLY ON THESE 2 EL DORADO TYPES.

EL DORADO SEVILLE

(335 HP, 129½" WB ON EL DORADOS)

EL DORADO BIARRITZ

(149¾" WB ON 75)

327

Cadillac
STANDARD OF THE WORLD

ENORMOUS TAIL-FINS!

new "DOUBLE-DECK" GRILLE

DETAILS OF THE UNIQUE REAR END DESIGN IN 1959

CLOSER VIEW OF TRADITIONAL "V" ON REAR DECK

GRILLE MOTIF IS ALSO CARRIED ON AT REAR

59

325 HP   130" WB
(THROUGH '63)

2 DR. H/T

DE VILLE

NOTE THE ROOFLINE DIFFERENCES BETWEEN THESE 4-DOOR HARDTOPS

1959 PRICES START AT
$4892.

'59 HP FIGS. @ 4800 RPM
new 390 CID V8s

LIMOUSINE
$9748.
(CONT'D.)

FLEETWOOD 75 (149.87" WB)

328

Cadillac STANDARD OF THE WORLD

59
(CONT'D.)

FLEETWOOD 60 SPECIAL
(note ITS OWN UNIQUE SIDE and FENDER TRIM)

$6233.

note "FLEETWOOD" NAME ON FRONT FENDER PANEL. (60-S)

DASH

345-HP EL DORADO MODELS BELOW:

("ELDORADO" NAME on FRONT FENDER PANELS of BIARRITZ and SEVILLE ONLY.)
$7401. *(EITHER MODEL)*

BIARRITZ

BROUGHAM →

EL DORADO BROUGHAM STYLING DIFFERS FROM OTHER 1959 CADILLACS.
$13,075.

SEVILLE

329

Cadillac STANDARD OF THE WORLD

62

PICTURED AT
BOCA RATON HOTEL and CLUB,
FLORIDA

new 1-PC.
GRILLE

60

$**6233.**

60-S

PRICES START AT
$**4892.**

FOR 2-DR. 62
H/T (ILLUSTR.)

62

62

SEDAN
DE VILLE

62

TAIL-FINS REDUCED FOR '60,
IN STYLE OF '59 EL DORADO BROUGHAM.

330

(CONT'D.)

Cadillac STANDARD OF THE WORLD

FLEETWOOD 75
9-PASS. SEDAN
$9533.
$9748.
60 PRICE OF 75
LIMO. (ILLUSTR.
AT LEFT)
(CONT'D.)

FLEETWOOD
75 LIMOUSINE

EL DORADO
BROUGHAM

(SAME PRICES AS IN 1959
ON ALL 3 EL DORADOS)

EL DORADO
SEVILLE

FINAL H/T EL DORADOS UNTIL 1967,
AT WHICH TIME EL DORADO BECOMES A
SPECIAL FRONT-WHEEL-DRIVE 2-DR. H/T.

note
THAT THE
EL DORADO
BROUGHAM
has
SIDE TRIM
DIFFERENT
FROM
THAT OF THE
OTHER
EL DORADO
MODELS
OF
1960.

EL DORADO
BIARRITZ

(EL DO. CVT.
CONT'D. THROUGH '66)

331

375 HP

62

new
LOWER SIDE FIN,
TO BALANCE
EFFECT OF
UPPER TAIL FIN

61

new 129½" WB
RESTYLED, SLIGHTLY DOWNSIZED and
LIGHTENED

62

new
CONVEX
GRILLE

$4892.
TO
$9748.
PRICE
RANGE

CHROME BANDS NEAR
END OF REAR FENDER
IDENTIFY 60-S.

FLEETWOOD 60-S

$6233.

Cadillac
STANDARD OF THE WORLD

DASH

RADIO, CLOCK DETAIL

62

SEDAN DE VILLE

62

COUPE

$5189.

$5752.

Fog Lamps (OPT.)

$10,100.

FLEETWD. 60-S

FLEETWOOD 75 LIMO.

BACK SEAT

REAR COMPARTMENT (75)

$6529.

note CONVERTIBLE-TOP STYLING on HARDTOP.

62

PRICE RANGE: $5191. TO $10,104.

FLEETWOOD 75

FLEETWOOD 60-S

9-PASS.

62

DASH

"FLEETWOOD" on 60-S FENDER

REAR CLOSE-UP

EL DORADO BIARRITZ

63

HEAD-ON DETAIL of LIGHTS IN RELATION TO GRILLE

new 340 HP (62 SERIES ONLY)

new GRILLE EMPHASIZES "DOUBLE-DECK" STYLING.

Cadillac
STANDARD OF THE WORLD

DASH AND
INTERIOR
VIEWS

new
CONVEX
GRILLE

new "COMFORT CONTROL"

64

ALL MODELS NOW HAVE 340 HP @ 4600 RPM
and new 429 CID

75

"62" PRICES FROM
$5191.

Comfort Control
combines heating and air conditioning
in a single unit, the interior weather never
changes. Even humidity is under perfect
control. This system now available as an
extra-cost option.

Cadillac

CALAIS
(REPLACES 62 SER.)

DE VILLE

65

new TAIL-LIGHTS

PRICE RANGE:
$**5224.** TO $**10,125.**

new LARGE 1-PC. GRILLE

FLEETWOOD BROUGHAM

new VERTICALLY-PLACED HEADLIGHTS

1965

DASH

Cadillac

336

CHECKER

CHECKER MOTORS CORPORATION
Kalamazoo, Michigan

SINCE 1922

1947 TO 1955 STYLE →

1956 TO 1958 STYLE →

TAXIS, COMMERCIAL ONLY (THROUGH '58)

Checker Aerobus Limousine

CHRYSLER V8 ENGINE IN PRE-'64 AEROBUS

6-CYL. CONTINENTAL ENGINE USED (UNTIL '63.) STARTING 1964, CHEVROLET 6 OR V8.

DASH ('68)

Checker Marathon Deluxe Limousine

59 ON

NO YEARLY STYLE CHANGES. OCCASIONAL MINOR MODIFICATIONS.

120" WB

Checker Marathon 4-door sedan

SAFETY-BUMPERS (ENERGY-ABSORBING) ADDED IN MID-1970s.

INTERIOR ('69)

Checker Marathon 4-door station wagon

CHEVELLE
(NEW)
by Chevrolet

(2-DR. WAGON ALSO AVAIL.)

194 OR 230 CID 6 (120 OR 155 HP @ 4400 RPM)

64

ALSO 283 CID V8 (195 OR 220 HP @ 4800 RPM)

INTERIOR (MALIBU)

300

300 DELUXE

MALIBU →

115" W.B.

CHEVELLE

300 2-DR.

300 2-DR. 6-PASS. WAGON (MALIBU 4-DR. WAGON has CHROME STRIP ALONG SIDE.)

MALIBU SS

new HORIZONTALLY-SPLIT GRILLE

65

MALIBU SS

194 OR 230 CID 6 (120 OR 140 HP @ 4400 RPM)
ALSO:
(283 CID V8 AVAIL. ONLY WITH 195 HP @ 4800 RPM)
3 new 327 CID V8s (250, 300, OR 350 HP)

338

GM
BODY by FISHER

CHEVROLET

(EST. 1911)
SINCE 1912
6 CYL.
(SINCE '29)

note LIGHTS PARTIALLY SUNK INTO FENDERS

SPEC. DLX. DASH

MASTER 85 HAS STRAIGHT FRONT AXLE, OTHERS have "KNEE ACTION."

MINE FOR 1940

COUPE

MASTER DE LUXE

new 113" WB

The Special De Luxe Sport Sedan, $802

COACH

new "BANNER" TYPE WIDE GRILLE

SEDAN

(MASTER 85 ENDS '40)
MASTER DLX. and SPEC. DLX. ARE CONT'D. THROUGH '41

KB, KH, KA
40
(RESTYLED)

6.00 x 16 TIRES
(SINCE '37)

216.5 CID
85 HP @ 3200 RPM
(SINCE '37)

CVT.

Let This Power Cylinder Shift for You!

$659
MASTER 85 BUSINESS COUPE

Only Chevrolet has the New Exclusive Vacuum-Power Shift . . . the only steering column gearshift that does 80% of the work for you and requires only 20% driver effort!

CHEVROLET
EYE IT · · · TRY IT · · · BUY IT!

CHEVROLET

HEADLIGHTS SUNKEN FURTHER INTO FENDERS

INTERIOR

90 HP @ 3300 RPM

AG, AH

41

PARKING LIGHTS MOVED DOWN

new 116" WB (THROUGH '48)

COUPE

new 2-SPOKE STEERING WHEEL

| 90·H.P. ENGINE | YES | VACUUM-POWER SHIFT AT NO EXTRA COST | YES | UNITIZED KNEE-ACTION | YES | ORIGINAL FISHER NO DRAFT VENTILATION | YES |
| CONCEALED SAFETY-STEPS | YES | BODY BY FISHER WITH UNISTEEL TURRET TOP | YES | BOX-GIRDER FRAME | YES | TIPTOE-MATIC CLUTCH | YES |

"BLACKOUT" MODELS have PAINTED TRIM in place of CHROME.

BG, BH

42-45

PARK. LIGHTS in new GRILLE

FLEETMASTER (BH)

STYLEMASTER, FLEETMASTER, FLEETLINE ARE new MODEL NAMES (THROUGH '48)

USA No 1

'42 MEDALLION

new "FADEAWAY" FENDERS

CAR RATIONING RULES

recently announced by O.P.A. now make it much easier for eligible buyers to get delivery of new Chevrolets

(AS OF JUNE, 1942)

FLEETLINE MODELS ON NEXT PAGE

340

$880.

CHEVROLET

NEW CHEVROLET *Fleetline* AEROSEDAN

"FLEETLINE" (BH) MODELS
EASILY IDENTIFIED BY 3 HORIZONTAL CHROME STRIPS on each FENDER (THROUGH '48)

42-45
(CONT'D.)

NEW CHEVROLET *Fleetline* SPORTMASTER

SLOGAN: "THE FINEST CHEVROLET OF ALL TIME"

$920.

DK "FLEETMASTER" has CHROME TRIM AROUND WINDOW MOULDINGS

PRICE RANGE: $1022. TO $1614.

DJ, DK

46

new GRILLE

DJ "STYLEMASTER" (NO CHROME ON WINDOW or WINDSHIELD MOULDINGS.)

$1194.

SPORT SEDAN

'46 MEDALLION

STYLEMASTER

341

CHEVROLET

$1255.

216.5 CID
90 HP @ 3300 RPM

116" WB

EK FLEETMASTER

new GRILLE has PROTRUDING CENTER SECTION

EJ, EK

47

$1775.

FLEETMASTER CVT.

new MEDALLION

EK FLEETLINE AERO

EK FLEETLINE SPORTMASTER

$1525.

FJ STYLEMASTER

FK 1948 CHEVROLET "FLEETMASTER" Four Door Sedan

$1340.

FJ, FK

48

new "T"-SHAPED PIECE ADDED AT CENTER OF GRILLE

FK FLEETLINE

AERO

PRICE RANGE:
$1160. TO $1890.

PACE CAR AT 1948 INDY 500 RACE

342

CHEVROLET

2-DR. FLEETLINE 4-DR.

METAL-BODIED WAGON

PRICES START AT $1339.

GJ, GK

49

TOTALLY RESTYLED

GJ = SPECIAL
GK = DE LUXE

1949 TRUNK LID has SMALL "T" HANDLE WHICH TURNS.

2-DR. TOWN SEDAN

STYLELINE

4-DR. SPORT SEDAN

SPORT CPE.

VERTICAL PIECES IN LOWER HALF of GRILLE

new SHORTER 115" WB (THROUGH '57)

1949 HUBCAP has RED CENTER.

6.70 x 15

all-new INTERIOR (LEFT AND RIGHT VIEWS)

PONTOON-STYLE REAR FENDERS

DLX.
MODELS have CHROME AROUND WINDOWS and on FRONT FENDERS

CHROME (DLX.)
BLACK RUBBER (SPEC)

CHEVROLET

$1741.

new "Bel-Air" 2-DR. HARDTOP has WIDE BACKLIGHT →

1950 TRUNK LID has new RE-DESIGNED HANDLE.

DASH

STYLING SIMILAR TO 1949, EXCEPT FOR MINOR DIFFERENCES AS NOTED.

HJ = SPECIAL
HK = DE LUXE

new AUTOMATIC TRANSMISSION AVAILABLE

HJ, HK

50

new 1950 GRILLE WITHOUT VERTICAL LOWER CENTER PCS. SEEN IN '49.

PRICE RANGE:
$1329. TO $1994.

First low-priced car with **POWER**glide No-Shift driving ✱

✱ = POWERGLIDE SOMEWHAT LIKE BUICK'S "DYNAFLOW." (NOT INCLUDED IN ABOVE PRICES)

BACK SEAT (4-DR.)

The Styleline De Luxe 2-Door Sedan

1950 HUBCAP has YELLOW CENTER.

CHEVROLET

FLEETLINE

BEL-AIR $1914.

STYLELINE DE LUXE

STYLELINE PRICES START AT $1460.

JJ, JK

51

GRILLE CHANGED

NEW Safety-Sight Instrument Panel

INTERIOR VIEWS

NEW Modern-Mode Interiors

STYLELINE DE LUXE

new CHROME TRIM STYLE

CHEVROLET

$1696.

STYLELINE SPECIAL
(has MINIMUM of
CHROME TRIM)

FLEETLINE DLX
(NO MORE FLEETLN. SPECIAL.

NEW

26 Exterior Colors
and two-tone color
combinations to
choose from.

New Softer, Smoother
Ride with new and
improved shock
absorber action.

Improved Carbure-
tion with Auto-
matic Choke in
Powerglide models.

New Centerpoise
Power is smoother
— "screens out"
engine vibration.

Color-Matched Two-
Tone Interiors bring
new beauty to De
Luxe models.

52

KJ, KK

STYLELINE
DE LUXE 2-DR.

new 5 RIDGES RUN
DOWN CENTER HORIZ.
MEMBER of GRILLE.

new MEDALLION
$1519. TO $2281.
PRICE RANGE

(2 VIEWS)

STYLELINE DE LUXE
SPORT COUPE (ABOVE)

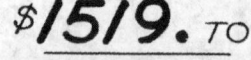

$1992.

BEL AIR (IN STYLELINE DLX. SERIES)
H/T

FINAL YEAR FOR STYLELINE and
FLEETLINE MODEL NAMES.

346

CHEVROLET

150

AT RIGHT: 210 SEDAN
(IN SAN FRANCISCO, CALIF.) →

210
2-DR.

BEL AIR SEDAN
(INTERIOR)

53
(TOTALLY
RESTYLED)

"Handyman"
(two of them)   6-PASS.   150
station wagons

210

BEL AIR
(note
EXTRA
TRIM and
CONTRASTING
COLOR STRIP on
REAR FENDER.)

BEL AIR now
TOP-OF-LINE SERIES
WHICH INCLUDES 2-DR. SEDAN,
4-DR. SEDAN, CONVERTIBLE (ILLUSTRATED)
and HIT SPORT COUPE (ILLUSTRATED)

235 CID ENGINE
(THROUGH '62, ON 6-CYL.)
108 OR 115 HP @ 3600 RPM)

WITH IMITATION
WOODGRAIN
TRIM

347

Townsman   8-PASS.

CHEVROLET

new MEDALLION
new TAIL-LIGHTS

54

Push Button Window Controls®
Push Button Door Latches
Push Button Door Locks (Keyless Locking)
Automatic Dome Light Switches
Pull Knob Light Switch
Pull Knob Ventilation Controls
Turn Knob Windshield Wiper Control (Push Button Washer®)
Push Button Headlight Dimmer

Top-Touch Power Brake Pedal®
Extra-Easy Power Steering®
Powerglide Automatic Transmission®
Push Lever Heater Controls®
Push Button Radio Controls-®
Push Button Glove Compartment Lock (Automatic Light†)
Finger-Touch Horn Blowing Ring®
Key-Turn Starter (Automatic Choke)
Top-Touch Accelerator Treadle
Push Button Automatic Seat Adjustment Control®
Lever Action Direction Signal Control (Automatic Return®)

Advanced Chevrolet Engineering brings

CYBERNETIC CHEVROLET
(Cybernetic = Automatic Control)

210 DELRAY COUPE

BEL AIR

115 HP @ 3700 RPM
OR 125 HP @ 4000 RPM

new OBLONG PARK. LIGHTS

new GRILLE has 5 VERTICAL PCS.
INSTEAD OF 3

348

CHEVROLET

_150_

$1593.

"ONE-FIFTY" HANDYMAN

2 VIEWS OF DASH

210 HANDYMAN

BEL AIR

THE "TWO-TEN" 4-DOOR SEDAN in Skyline Blue.

(TOTALLY RESTYLED)

55

new V-8

ALSO AVAIL. (265 CID, 162 HP @ 4400 RPM OR 180 HP @ 4600 RPM)
6 CYL. has 123 HP @ 3800 OR 136 HP @ 4200 RPM)

210 "TOWNSMAN" WAGON

THE BEL AIR BEAUVILLE

new "NOMAD" 2-DR. WAGON

(CHROME STRIPS RUNNING DOWN TAILGATE.)

CVT. IS PACE CAR AT 1955 INDY 500 RACE

$2472. (6)

CHEVROLET

56

THE "ONE-FIFTY" HANDYMAN
2 doors, 6 passengers, versatile and thrifty.

THE "TWO-TEN" HANDYMAN
2 doors, 6 passengers, all-vinyl interior.

THE "TWO-TEN" BEAUVILLE
4 doors, 9 passengers.

THE "TWO-TEN" TOWNSMAN
4 doors, 6 passengers, loads of cargo space.

BEL AIR 4-DOOR HARDTOP and interior

AIR COND. DETAIL

Now in the low price field...

$2329.

All components are located "up front" ... out of sight and out of the way! Harrison air conditioning is available on four great GM cars—Chevrolet, Pontiac, Oldsmobile and Buick.

AIR CONDITIONING!

BEL AIR BEAUVILLE 9-PASS. WAGON

new SMALL ROUND LENSES IN TAIL-LIGHTS →

210

AA·1956

CORVETTE

6.70 x 15 TIRES

BEL AIR SEDAN
140, 162, 170, 205 OR 225 HP

NOMAD

new FULL-WIDTH GRILLE

BEL AIR 2-DR.

350

CHEVROLET

new 7.50 × 14 TIRES

PRICES START AT $1885.

150

210

BEL AIR

1957 IS 3RD AND FINAL YEAR THAT THE NOMAD IS A SUPER-DELUXE 2-DOOR SPORT WAGON.

$2757. (6)

NEW TRIPLE-TURBINE TURBOGLIDE*
It's the last word in automatic drives. Super-smooth— and there's even a HILL RETARDER position on the selector, for safer control on the steepest down grades!

57

NOMAD and BEL AIR have new ANODIZED REAR FENDER PANEL.

4-DOOR WAGON

new GRILLE COMBINED with BUMPER

2-DR. H/T

BEL AIR

COMMAND POST CONTROL PANEL

HEADLIGHT-HOOD AIR VENTS

$2464.

4-DR. H/T

351

140, 162, 185, 220, 245, 250, 270 or 283 HP
(new 283 CID V8 JOINS 265 CID)

CHEVROLET

NOMAD
6-PASS.
4-DR.

DASH

BEL AIR

BISCAYNE

235 CID 6
has 145 HP
@ 4200
RPM

4-DR., 6 OR 9-PASS.
BROOKWOOD

new 117½" WB
(1958 ONLY)

58

2-DR.
6-PASS.
YEOMAN

CROSS-SECTION
OF "TURBO
THRUST"
V8 ENGINE

283 OR 348 CID V8s
(TO '62) (185 TO
280 HP)

new
IMPALA

$2693.

new
WAGON TAILGATE

IMPALAS
have 6
REAR LIGHTS,
AND EXTRA
"AIR SCOOP"
DECORATIONS.

352

CHEVROLET

1 – *Biscayne Utility Sedan.* Chevy's prices start right here—a handy, handsome 2-door with 31 cu. ft. of cargo space behind front seat.

2 – *Brookwood 2-Door,* Chevrolet's lowest priced wagon, is as dutiful as it is beautiful. Seats 6, holds up to 92 cu. ft. of cargo.

3 – *Impala 4-Door,* most elegant family sedan in the line, makes you wonder why anyone would want a car that costs more.

4 – *El Camino* combines stunning passenger car styling with the load space of a pickup. Good looks never carried so much weight!

5 – *Impala Convertible.* Chevy's got a special formula for carefree top-down fun.

6 – *Biscayne 2-Door.* This beauty's the lowest priced 6-passenger Chevy you can buy!

7 – *Nomad 4-Door,* 6-passenger station wagon—finest of Chevrolet's 5 wonderful wagons.

8 – *Bel Air 4-Door.* As luxurious as it looks, yet priced just above Chevy's thriftiest sedans.

9 – *Brookwood 4-Door.* Chevy's lowest priced 4-door wagon seats 6, holds 92 cu. ft. of cargo with rear seat down.

10 – *Bel Air 2-Door,* distinctively styled inside and out, carries a price tag just a notch above Chevy's thriftiest 2-door sedan.

11 – *Impala Sport Sedan.* Here's a 4-door hardtop with the kind of looks and luxury you'd expect only on the most expensive makes.

12 – *Kingswood 4-Door,* 9-passenger station wagon, offers rear-facing third seat and power-operated rear window at no extra cost.

13 – *Impala Sport Coupe.* It's one of Chevy's full series of elegant Impalas for '59. And you won't find a handsomer hardtop anywhere!

14 – *Parkwood 4-Door,* 6-passenger station wagon, distinctively trimmed inside and out, priced a shade above the thrifty Brookwoods.

15 – *Bel Air Sport Sedan.* It's Chevy's lowest priced hardtop—and it makes beautiful sense!

16 – *Corvette.* Take the wheel of America's only authentic sports car and treat yourself to the snappiest, happiest driving you've known.

17 – *Biscayne 4-Door,* thriftiest 4-door sedan in the line, is another big reason

BROOKWOOD

135 TO 315 HP

PRICE RANGE
$2160.
TO
$3009.

BEL AIR

NOMAD
4-DR., 6-PASS.

HUGE new TAIL-LIGHTS
59
(TOTALLY RESTYLED)
new 119" WB (THROUGH '70)

BIG "GULL WING" REAR DECK

353   IMPALA SPORT COUPE (H/T)

CHEVROLET

BISCAYNE

NOMAD

60

KINGSWOOD

PRICE RANGE: $2230. TO $2996.

BEL AIR

BEL AIR

new GRILLE

IMPALA SPORT CPE.

Impala 4-Door Sport Sedan

135 TO 335 HP

MODIFIED "GULL-WING" REAR STYLING, with new ROUND TAIL-LIGHTS

354

CHEVROLET

BROOKWOOD

BISCAYNE

NOMAD

135 TO 360 HP

1961

new ROOFLINE
(SPT. CPE.)

(HT)
SPT.
CPE.

BEL AIR

IMPALA

(RESTYLED)

61

$2230.
TO $3099.
PRICE RANGE
DASH

new
ROOFLINE →

BEL AIR
SPT. SED.

IMPALA

LIGHT CONTROL
SWITCH

CIGARETTE LIGHTER
AND ASH TRAY

RADIO CONTROLS

LEFT VENT
CONTROL

WIPER AND WASHER
CONTROL

HEATER
CONTROLS

RIGHT VENT
CONTROL

IGNITION
SWITCH

GLOVE BOX
AND LOCK

BISCAYNE

CHEVROLET

FINAL 235 CID
6 has
135 HP @
4000
RPM

BEL AIR SPT. CPE. ROOFLINE

DASH

BEL AIR

new GRILLE

M-1042

IMPALA

283, new 327 or
new 409 CID
V8s
(170
to
409
HP)

IMPALA
has
ALUMINIZED
PANELING
AROUND
TAIL-LIGHTS.

OUTER-EDGE TAIL-LTS.
DO NOT OPEN WITH
TRUNK.

IMPALA

62

(IMPALA I.D.)

JET-SMOOTH RIDE

BISCAYNE

DASH

IMPALA
SPORT SEDAN

BEL
AIR

1963

63

PRICE
RANGE:
$2558. TO **$3417.**

new 230 CID
6
(140 HP
@
4400 RPM.

IMPALA

note
CONVERTIBLE-STYLE
"CREASES" STAMPED
INTO STEEL ROOF
OF THIS IMPALA SPORT
COUPE.

V8s have
195 HP @ 4800
TO
425 HP @
6000

new
DIP IN MIDDLE OF
DECK LID ON 1963 MODELS.

1964 JET-SMOOTH CHEVROLET

BISCAYNE

BISCAYNE

BISCAYNE

new STRAIGHT-ACROSS DECK LID *with* CENTER RIDGE

2-DR. BISCAYNE $2590.

BEL AIR

64

283, 327, 409 cid V8 ENGINES, SAME SIZES AS IN '63   6 = 140 HP
V8s = 195, 250, 300, 340, 400 OR 425 HP

3.08 TO 4.56 GEAR RATIOS

9-PASS. WAGON

SPT. SEDAN 4-DR. H/T

IMPALA

IMPALA SS
H/T

ONE OF VARIOUS 1964 UPHOLSTERY PATTERNS

new IMPALA SS
$3185.

new GRILLE

358

DASH

CHEVROLET → **$2669.** 4 DOOR BISCAYNE

7.35 × 14 TIRES

BEL AIR

1965

IMPALA

IMPALA 3-SEAT WAGON

FY-1588

$3444. 8.25 × 14 TIRES ON WAGONS

IMPALA DASH

LIGHTS
VENT
WIPER WASHER
IGNITION SWITCH
LIGHTER
ASH TRAY
RADIO
HEATER
GLOVE BOX
VENT

POPULARLY REFERRED TO AS THE "COKE BOTTLE" PROFILE

H/T

65 (TOTALLY RESTYLED) AVAIL. with VINYL TOP

IMPALA SUPER SPORT

with SPORT WHEEL COVERS →

359

~ **$3210.**

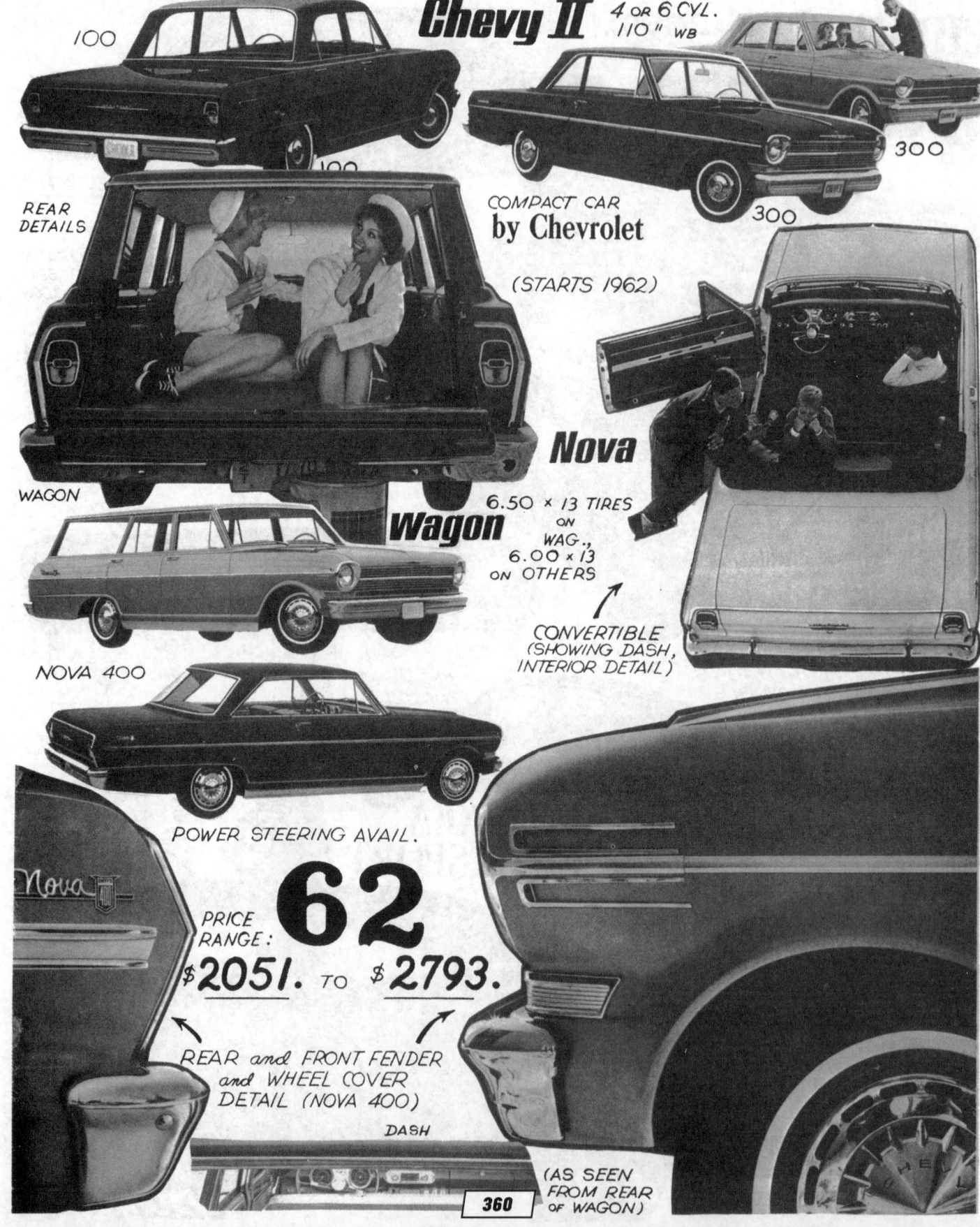

Chevy II 4 OR 6 CYL. 110" WB

100

100

300

300

REAR DETAILS

WAGON

NOVA 400

COMPACT CAR **by Chevrolet**

(STARTS 1962)

Nova

Wagon 6.50 × 13 TIRES ON WAG., 6.00 × 13 ON OTHERS

CONVERTIBLE (SHOWING DASH, INTERIOR DETAIL)

POWER STEERING AVAIL.

PRICE RANGE: **62** $2051. TO $2793.

Nova II

REAR and FRONT FENDER and WHEEL COVER DETAIL (NOVA 400)

DASH

(AS SEEN FROM REAR OF WAGON)

360

CHEVY II

100

$2313.

300

$2395.

$2710.

63

NOVA 400

120 HP
(6 CYL.)
(SINCE '62)

CHEVY II NOVA 400 SUPER SPORT CONVERTIBLE

new GRILLE

NEW V8 POWER
(OPTIONAL)

64

4, 6, OR V8

MORE '64s ON NEXT PAGE

CHEVY II

INTERIOR

64
(CONT'D.)

SPT.
CPE.

NOVA SS
(has THIS EMBLEM)

NOVA

SEDAN

CHEVY II

Super Sport

(TAILGATE OPEN)

NOVA

(TAILGATE CLOSED)

65

SEE ALSO: Chevrolet

CHRYSLER

CHRYSLER CORPORATION

(EST. 1924)

122½" WB (ROYAL + WND.)

DASH

FLUID DRIVE'S MAGIC

new GRILLE (9 HORIZ. PIECES)

ROYAL and WINDOR 6 have 241.5 CID (THROUGH '41) 108 HP @ 3600 RPM

ROYAL 6 (C-25 S)

C-25 (6-CYL.)

$895*
3-PASS. ROYAL COUPE

40

C-26 (8-CYL.)

Traveler 8 (C-26 K) (MADE IN 1940 ONLY)

AMERICA'S FIRST FLUID DRIVE! The vanes of the driving member force the fluid against those of the driven member, thus transmitting the power without a rigid metal connection. Incredibly smooth!

ONLY **$38** EXTRA

ALSO AVAILABLE ON THE NEW YORKER AND SARATOGA MODELS STANDARD ON CROWN IMPERIAL

HIGHLANDER (6 or 8) has SCOTTISH PLAID UPHOLSTERY

TRAVELER, SARATOGA and NEW YORKER 8   128½" WB 323.5 CID (THROUGH '50) 135 HP @ 3400 RPM (THR. '49)

Be Modern — Buy Chrysler!

ROYAL 6
(C-28-S)

CHRYSLER

3-WINDOW BUSINESS COUPE
$945.

41

new GRILLE (6 HORIZ. PCS.)

new (LARGER BODIES, BUT WHEELBASES 1" SHORTER.) AVAIL. with OR WITHOUT RUNNING BOARDS

SPECIAL "THUNDERBOLT" PHAETON IS PACE CAR AT 1941 INDY 500 RACE

Chrysler includes a Safety Clutch with Fluid Drive!

BE MODERN
Buy Chrysler!

1941 STEERING WHEEL and DASH

—WITH FLUID DRIVE AND VACAMATIC TRANSMISSION

$1096.

WINDSOR 6
(C-28-W)

SPITFIRE ENGINES!

Chrysler offers dozens of combinations in exterior colors and interior tailoring!

(SARATOGA 8 IS C-30-K)

CLUB COUPE INTERIOR (2-TONE)

364

CHRYSLER

TOWN and COUNTRY (NEW) 41 (CONT'D.)

$2795.

NEW YORKER HIGHLANDER 8 CONVT. (C-30-N)

PLAID UPHOLSTERY OPTIONAL @ EXTRA COST

WHEEL COVER

CROWN IMPERIAL 8 LIMOUSINE (C-33)

$1495.

42-45

C-34 (6)
C-36 (8)

ENGINE

TOWN and COUNTRY

DASH

New Yorker

new "WRAP-AROUND" GRILLE

(CROWN IMPERIAL is C-37.)

new "BEAUTY RINGS"

Fluid Drive and Vacamatic Transmission!

CHRYSLER

ROYAL 6 (C-38-S)
WINDSOR 6,
TOWN and COUNTRY 6
(C-38-W)
SARATOGA 8 (C-39-K)
NEW YORKER 8,
TOWN and COUNTRY 8
(C-39-N)
CROWN IMPERIAL 8
(C-40)

EMBLEM

Chrysler

CHRYSLER CARS CONTINUE USE OF ADD-ON
WHITE "BEAUTY RINGS," THUS
MAKING
UNNECESSARY
THE USE OF
HARD-TO-OBTAIN
WHITE SIDEWALL
TIRES.

PRICE RANGE :
$1415. TO $4767.
46-48
(new "HARMONICA" GRILLE)

6 CYL. *has* 250.6 CID
(1942 THROUGH 1951)
114 HP @ 3600 RPM (THROUGH '49)

8 CYL. *has* 323.5 CID
(1935 THROUGH 1950)
135 HP @ 3400 RPM (THROUGH '49)

(FINAL '48s SOLD AS "EARLY 1949" MODELS, UNTIL
RESTYLED MODELS AVAIL. FEB., 1949.)

121½" WB (6)
127½" WB (8)
145½" WB (CROWN
IMPERIAL 8, THROUGH '54)
139½" WB (6-CYL.
8-PASS., LIMO.)

CHRYSLER

TOWN + CNTRY. H/T (ONLY 7 BUILT)

CONVENTIONAL CONVERTIBLE INTERIOR →

(T+C FASTBACK SEDANS ONLY, 1941-1942)

TOWN and COUNTRY

$3123. ↑
('48)

ONE-OFF 2-DR. BROUGHAM (EXPERIMENTAL)

46-48
(CONT'D.)

'46-EARLY 1947 "TOWN and COUNTRY" MODELS have GENUINE WOODEN PANELS of ASH and MAHOGANY. (DK. PANELS ON LATER MODELS ARE DECALS)

CHRYSLER

WINDSOR 6

CLUB COUPE

NEW YORKER 8

(C-45) 125½" WB (THROUGH '54)

(LENGTH EXAGGERATED)

$3206.

NEW YORKER 8

ACTUAL LENGTH

NEW YORKER 8 (C-46) 131½" WB (THROUGH '52)

49 (TOTALLY RESTYLED)

CHRYSLER

PRESTOMATIC FLUID DRIVE TRANSMISSION
*gyrol Fluid Drive

PRICE RANGE: $2114. TO $5334.

$3970.

TOWN and COUNTRY 8 CONVERTIBLE (SAME SPECS. AS NEW YORKER)

CROWN IMPERIAL 8 LIMO. (C-47)

CHRYSLER

(FINAL YEAR FOR CHRYSLER STRAIGHT-8.)

ROYAL 6, WINDSOR 6
(C-48)

SARATOGA 8,
NEW YORKER 8,
TOWN and COUNTRY 8
(C-49)

50

PRICE RANGE
$2114. TO $5334.

TOWN and CNT. 8
AVAIL. ONLY AS H/T.

new GRILLE →

NY 8 ↗

NEW **LOW** LOOK!
NEW **LONG** LOOK!
NEW **LOVELY** LOOK!

$4003.

Crown Imperial

LIMOUSINE
(C-50)

CRN. IMP. REAR COMP. has QUARTER WINDOWS.

8 - CYL. MODELS NOW DEVELOP 135 HP @ 3200 RPM.

SARATOGA V8 (C-55)
125½" WB

NY V8
(C-52)
131½" WB

IMPERIAL V8
(C-54)
(CRN. IMP. IS C-53)

WINDSOR 6
(C-51-1)

new WIN. DLX. 6 IS C-51-2

new 331.1 CID O.H.V. V8 REPLACES STRAIGHT-8 (180 HP @ 4000 RPM) (THROUGH '53.)

51

(CVT.) IS PACE CAR AT 1951 INDY 500 RACE

K-310 CUSTOM-BUILT COUPE

CHRYSLER

CUSTM BLT.

125 ½" W.B.
(ITALIAN GHIA BODY)

(WINDSOR 6 ENG. CHANGES FROM 250.6 TO 264.5 CID, 116 TO 119 HP @ 3600.)

Imperial BY CHRYSLER

PHAETON   147½" W.B.
(FOR PARADE USE, ETC.)

A VARIETY OF ROSE WAS NAMED "CHRYSLER IMPERIAL."

IMPERIAL V8
(C-54)

52
(SIMILAR IN MOST RESPECTS TO 1951.)

(C-53)

$6994.

CROWN IMPERIAL LIMOUSINE

CHRYSLER

WINDSOR 6 (C-60-1) WINDSOR 6

WINDSOR DELUXE 6 (C-60-2)

ALL EXCEPT IMPERIAL *have* 125½"WB (THROUGH '54)

$**2555.** UP

NY

NEW YORKER V8 (C-56-1)

(NEW YORKER DELUXE V8 IS C-56-2) (new)

53 (new 1-PIECE WINDSHIELDS)

CUSTOM IMPERIAL V8 (C-58) new 133½"WB

CROWN IMPERIAL V8 (C-59)

Imperial BY CHRYSLER

IMPERIAL (STYLIZED EAGLE) HOOD ORNAMENT (new)

FOR 1954 TO 1965 IMPERIALS, SEE: IMPERIAL

371

CHRYSLER

WINDSOR DELUXE 6
(C-62)
264.5 CID
119 HP
@ 3600 RPM

NEWPORT H/T

↖ $2831.

NY 331.5 CID
V8s have
195
OR
235 HP
@ 4400 RPM

NEW YORKER
(C-63-1)

WINDSOR
DELUXE TOWN and
COUNTRY WAGON 6
$3321.

NEW
YORKER
DELUXE
(note
SMALL
EXTRA
HORIZONTAL
CHROME PIECE
ON REAR
FENDER)

54

(FINAL 6-CYL.)

DASH

NEW
YORKER
DELUXE V8 (C-63-2)

SEE ALSO "IMPERIAL" SECTION

WINDSOR DELUXE
(C-67)

ALL CHRYSLERS 126" WB,
NOW V8-POWERED.

WINDSOR DLX. V8
has 301 CID,
188 HP @ 4400 RPM.

55

(RESTYLED)

TOWN and
COUNTRY

NEW YORKER
DE LUXE (C-68)
(331 CID,
250 HP
@
4600 RPM)

300

← 300 HP @ 5200 RPM
126"
WB

$4109.

new **300** (C-300) 331 CID

CHRYSLER

New Pushbutton PowerFlite!
(Illustrated at right)

WINDSOR NEWPORT

DASH

(C-71)
WINDSOR

56

126" WB

(C-72)
NEW YORKER

N.Y.
TOWN and
COUNTRY

331 CID OR
new 354 CID V8
(225 HP @ 4400; 250 or 280 @ 4600)

NEW YORKER GRILLE
NOW DIFFERENT FROM
OTHERS.

New Yorker

NEW *"PowerStyle"* CHRYSLER FOR 1956

(C-72-300)
300-B

354 CID V8
(340 OR 355 HP
@ 5200)

NEW
YORKER
INTRODUCES
VERTICAL CHROME
STRIPS ON REAR
FENDER
(THROUGH '62.)

373

CHRYSLER

SEDAN $3088.

WINDSOR (C-75-1)

WINDSOR TOWN and COUNTRY WAGON

2-DR. H/T

57 (TOTALLY RESTYLED)

4 HEADLIGHTS ON MOST MODELS

4-DR. H/T

(C-75-2) **SARATOGA**

WND. and SAR. have 354 CID V8 (285 OR 295 HP @ 4600)

(C-76) **NEW YORKER** 2 DR. H/T

4-DR. H/T

SEDAN note ONLY 2 HEADLTS.

NEW YORKER has new 392 CID V8 (325 HP @ 4600 RPM) $4259.

H/T

300-C (C-76-300)

300-C has new HIGH and NARROWER GRILLE, ALSO new 392 CID V8 (9.25 OR 10 COMPR.) TWO 4-BBL. CARBS.

CVT. $5359.

THE MIGHTY CHRYSLER 300⚡C

America's Most Powerful Car!

300-C ENGINE 375 HP @ 5200 OR 390 HP @ 5400 RPM

374

CHRYSLER

300-D (LC3-S) →
380 OR 390 HP
@ 5200 RPM

58
126" WB
(new SHORTER 122" WB ON WINDSOR)

WINDSOR (LC1-L)

WINDSOR has 290 HP @ 4600 RPM (354 CID)

WINDSOR DARTLINE

note DIFFERENT SIDE TRIM on '58½ "DARTLINE" (ABOVE)

NEW YORKER

SARATOGA (LC2-M)
310 HP @ 4600 RPM (354 CID)

NEW YORKER (LC3-H)
345 HP @ 4600 RPM (SAME SIZE V8 [392 CID] as 300-D)

new ENGINES: 383 OR 413 CID

59
MC SERIES
305, 325, 350 HP @ 4600, OR 380 HP @ 5000 RPM

MORE 1959 CHRYSLERS ON NEXT PAGE

CHRYSLER

(MC2-M) SARATOGA

(MC1-L)
WINDSOR

LION-HEARTED
CHRYSLER '59

59
(CONT'D.)
(MC3-H)

NEW
YORKER

N.Y.
TOWN and COUNTRY
WAGON

CHRYSLER **300** (REAR FENDER BAND)

The international classic ... made in America

$5749.

300-E
(MC3-H)

300-E

CHRYSLER

60

4-DR. HIT

WINDSOR CVT.

SARATOGA
(PC2-M) *has*
383 CID V8
(325 HP @
4600 RPM)

has 383 CID V8
(305 HP @ 4600 RPM)

SAR. SEDAN

SARATOGA *has* GRILLE LIKE WINDSOR (ABOVE)

NEW YORKER (PC-3-H *has*
413 CID V8
(350 HP @
4600 RPM

NEW PUSHBUTTON DASH PUTS ALL THE CONTROLS AT YOUR FINGERTIPS

WINDSOR T+C

NEW YORKER TOWN and COUNTRY WAGON

WNDSR.

NY CVT.

300/F BY CHRYSLER

The 300F medallion is molded like a gear wheel to express the rugged spirit of the car.

The open grille gives the 300F a "Pure automobile" look.

413 CID V8
(375 HP @ 5000
OR
400 HP @ 5200 RPM)
→
(300-F)

(PC3-H)

CHRYSLER

wagon

(RC2-M) FINAL 1961 WINDSOR MODEL

$3303.

new NEWPORT LOW-PRICED SERIES 122" WB (RC1-L)

$3025. (NPT. H/T)

61

new GRILLES, CANTED HEADLIGHTS

NEWPORT *has new* 361 CID V8 (265 HP @ 4400 RPM) (OPTIONAL 413 CID V8 *has* 350 HP @ 4600 RPM)

1961

413 CID V8 *with* 350 HP @ 4600 RPM *in* RC3-H NEW YORKER

NY TOWN *and* COUNTRY

(FRONT END OF 300-G ILLUSTR. ON NEXT PAGE)

NY

$4133.

378

NEW YORKER SEDAN

CHRYSLER

300-G
new GRILLE
CLOSE-UP

300-G (RC4-P) has SAME ENGINES AS IN 1960

FINAL YR. OF 126" WB FOR 300 SERIES

61 →

(CONT'D.)

NEWPORT

(SCI-2) NEWPORT

361, 383, 413 OR new 426 CID V8 ENGINES

300

62

265 HP @ 4400 RPM TO 421 HP @ 5400 RPM

300-H (SC2-M)

N.Y.

N.Y. 4-DR. H/T

126" WB

NEW YORKER (SC3-H)

ALL 122" WB (EXCEPT NY)

CHRYSLER

PAINTED IN ACRYLIC ENAMELS

NEWPORT (TC1-L)

ALL MODELS NOW have 122" WB. (THROUGH '64)

ROUND TAIL-LIGHTS IN 1963.

63 TC SERIES

(RESTYLED IN new "KNIFE-EDGE" [CREASE] BODY DESIGN.)

SAME 4 V8 SIZES AS IN 1962, BUT TOP "300" HP FIGURE NOW IS 425 @ 5600, with new TOP 13.5 COMP.

PACE CAR AT 1963 INDY 500 RACE IS 300-J.

DASH

SALON (INTRO. 2-14-63)

NY TOWN and COUNTRY

(TC3-H) 1963 NEW YORKERS have VERTICAL LOUVRES ON FRONT FENDERS.

NEW YORKER

CHROME BANDS JOIN ENDS of GRILLE WITH EDGES of HOOD. (NY and 300)

300

NEW YORKER

(TC2-M) 300

380

CHRYSLER

6 or 9-PASS.

Chrysler Newport   Hardtop Town & Country Wagon

NEWPORT

Chrysler Newport Convertible

(VC1-L)

VC1 SERIES

64

COMPRESSION RATIOS NOW RUN FROM 9.0 to 10.1 to 1.

361, 383 or 413 CID V8s (265 HP @ 4400 RPM to 290 HP @ 4800)

NEW YORKER (VC1-H)

NY SALON

VINYL TRIM ON ROOF

note GRILLE and SIDE TRIM VARIATIONS BETWEEN "300" CVT. and H/T MODELS ILLUSTRATED

300 (K)

WAGON

300 (VC1-M)

INTERIOR 300

381

Chrysler Newport Convertible

(AC1-L) NEWPORT 7-W. SEDAN →

5-W. SEDAN

REAR INTERIOR (7-W. N.P. SEDAN)

N.Y.

NEWPORT CVT. (SHOWING DASH)

CHRYSLER
MOTORS CORPORATION
CHRYSLER DIVISION

NEW YORKER (AC1-H)

65 AC1 SERIES

300-L

'65's ONLY ENG. CHOICES ARE 383 OR 413 CID V8s (270 HP @ 4400 TO 360 @ 4800)

(AC1-M) 300-L's 413 CID V8 has SPECIAL CAM. **$47/6.** (CVT.)

NEWPT. PRICES START AT **$3442.**

300 has LARGE RED CROSS IN CENTER of GRILLE →

300 (AC1-M) **$4061.**

COMET (compact)

LINCOLN-MERCURY DIVISION *Ford Motor Company*

(INTRO. 3-60)

FROM $1998.

60

6 CYL. OHV 90 HP
114" WB

two- and four-door wagons
(109½" WB)

COMET

DASH SIMILAR TO 1960

new FRONT FENDER TRIM

61

new GRILLE

"Comet" NAME MOVED TO REAR FENDER

new ROUND TAIL-LIGHTS

NAME RETURNS TO FRONT FENDER

new GRILLE

CUSTOM

S-22

62

VILLAGER

383

Comet

63

COMET *SPORTSTER* hardtop

tach, bucket seats,

Vinyl covered roof optional.

DASH (CYCLONE)

THE COMET CYCLONE.
Super 289 cu. in. V-8,
chrome engine parts,
competition-type
wheel covers.

(MIDSEASON MODEL)

64

CALIENTE

Comet

CYCLONE H/T

404

CALIENTE H/T

65

VILLAGER

202

REAR FENDER DETAIL

40 days
from Cape Horn to Fairbanks

UP-9357

Cord

(SHORTER 100" WB REPLICA OF ORIGINAL 1936-1937 CORD)

DASH

150-180 HP CORVAIR 6 ENGINE

(STARTS 1963)

FIBERGLASS TYPE BODY OF "ROYALEX"

OTHERS SUBSEQUENTLY INVOLVED IN PRODUCING THESE REPLICARS.

MFD. BY GLENN PRAY, BROKEN ARROW, OKLA.

385

corvair

GENERAL MOTORS
(1960 – 1969)

COMPACT CAR
by Chevrolet

$1984. and up

DASH

569 SEDAN

500
(NO CHROME BELT TRIM)

WITH THE ENGINE IN THE REAR

60

CLUB COUPE and INTERIOR (727)

700

AIR- COOLED 6- CYL.
REAR ENGINE-TRANSAXLE UNIT
140 CID
80 HP @ 4400 RPM
6.50 x 13
TIRES 108" WB

SEDAN

BACK SEAT FOLDS, FOR CARGO.

$2103.
(769 SEDAN)

corvair

500

CLUB COUPE

spunkier 145-cu.-in. air-cooled rear engine

700

700 INTERIOR →

new OPTION. ELECTRIC HOT AIR HEATER

4-DOOR SEDANS

note UNIQUE WHEEL COVERS ON NEW MONZA →

new **CORVAIR MONZA CLUB COUPE** and INTERIOR →

61

2 new WAGON TYPES and **2** SUB-TYPES

CORVAIR GREENBRIER SPORTS WAGON

SWINGING SIDE DOORS 95" WB

$**2651.**

GREENBRIER (STD.)

$**2331.**

LAKEWOOD 500 (535)

700 (735)

LAKEWOOD STATION WAGONS

SMART, DURABLE INTERIORS—Shown here: the 700's rich fabric-vinyl upholstery, offered in three color-keyed choices. 500 all-vinyl interior also comes in three color-keyed blends. Check the push-button locks on rear doors. ▼

700

ENGINE UNDER REAR FLOOR.

corvair

500

GREENBRIER

62

MONZA

MONZA WAGON (ABOVE)
(FINAL YEAR FOR THIS
"LAKEWOOD" STYLE WAGON.
GREENBRIER VAN-TYPE
WAGON AVAIL. THROUGH
1965.)

DASH (ALL BUT SPYDER)

new
CORVAIR SPYDER
(150 HP)

63

MONZA

corvair

STD. ENGINE RAISED TO 95 HP.

DASH

64

MONZA

MONZA SPYDER (ABOVE) has 150 HP.

$3008.
(667 CVT.)

500

←DASH has CIRCULAR GAUGES.

MONZA

This year, all the coupes and sedans have hardtop styling

FROM $2281. **65**

new LARGER BODIES

(ONLY MAJOR CORVAIR RESTYLING)

MONZA SPORT SEDAN

140 HP (CORSA is new TOP OF LINE MODEL.)

New power choices, too. There's a new 140-hp engine that's standard in Corsa models and can be ordered for all others—and a 180-hp power plant that you can specify for your Corsa.

CORVETTE
Sports Car by CHEVROLET

6-CYL. CHEVROLET ENGINE (TO '55)

STARTS 1953 $3512.

53

FIBERGLASS BODIES (ON ALL)

('54)

SPEAR ON SIDE EMBLEM NOW POINTS UP.

54-55

FULL-LENGTH SIDE TRIM

V-8 ENGINE ALSO (1955)

ILLUSTRATED with DETACHABLE TOP

PRICE CUT 1955 ('55)

new TOP

56-57

new SIDE TRIM

V-8s ONLY

$2900. ('56)

$3437. ('57)

4 HEADLIGHTS

102" WB 230 HP

DASH

58

new VENT LOUVRE GROUP ON TOP OF HOOD (1958 ONLY)

$3631. new BUMPERS

59-60

$3872. (IN '60; $3 LESS THAN '59)

CORVETTE

61 $4272.

new GRILLE

62 $4375.
new SIDE-SCOOP DESIGN

new 250 HP

63 new "STINGRAY"
new SIDE-SCOOPS AGAIN
$4589.

new GRILLE, CONCEALED HEADLIGHTS, new 98"WB

64
new 1-PC. BACKLIGHT →
$4627.

Corvette Sting Ray Convertible in Saddle Tan
Corvette Sting Ray Sport Coupe in Riverside Red

$4723.

327 CID V-8 has 250, 300, 350, 365 or 375 HP @ 5500 RPM

65 $4508.

4-WHEEL DISC BRAKES

new VERTICAL LOUVRE DESIGN

425 HP 396 CID V8

1965½ CORVETTE "396"

CROSLEY

(1939 – 1952)

MFD. IN MARION, IND.

39-42

POWEL CROSLEY, JR.

FOUNDER OF CROSLEY CORP. (KNOWN AFTER WW 2 AS CROSLEY MOTORS)

2-CYL. AIR-COOLED WAUKESHA ENGINE (THROUGH '42)

12 HP

PRICE CUT TO **$299.** IN 1941.

$412. IN 1942

80" WB
4.25 × 12 TIRES

CVT. (OTHER MODELS ALSO AVAIL.)

"*a FINE car*" new 4-CYL. WATER-COOLED "COBRA" (COPPER-BRAZED) STAMPED-BLOCK 44 CID ENGINE (26½ HP @ 5400 RPM)

new BODY SIDES COMBINE with FULL-LENGTH FENDERS

WAGON

CVT.
$1035. ('47)

$931. = SEDAN

('47) *new GRILLE, BUILT-IN HEADLIGHTS ABOVE*

(TOTALLY RESTYLED)   80" WB

47-48

(POSTWAR PRODUCTION RESUMES DURING JUNE, 1946)

PICKUP

CROSLEY SPORTS-UTILITY

PANEL DELIVERY

 **CROSLEY**

NOW CROSLEY HAS THE **NEW LOOK**

48½

new GRILLE
ON MID-YEAR
"NEW LOOK" SERIES

FOR 1949, COPPER-BRAZED, 58-lb. STAMPED ENGINE
REPLACED BY IMPROVED CAST-IRON VERSION (CIBA.)

49-50

new GRILLE, "SPEEDLINE" STYLING

SEDAN

new "HOTSHOT" SPORTS ROADSTER ←

new HYDRAULIC DISC BRAKES (BY GOODYEAR-HAWLEY)

CVT.

WAGON

new BENDIX 9" HYDRAULIC BRAKES

Crosley Hotshot

SUPER

51-52

new 2-BLADED GRILLE *with* CENTER "SPINNER"

DISCONTINUED DURING 1952

DART

Dodge Division of Chrysler Corporation

FULL-SIZED
LOWER-PRICED
new COMPANION
TO DODGE

SENECA

(STARTS 1960)

PIONEER

$2283. UP

PHOENIX

118" WB (WAGONS 122")
(THROUGH '61)

60

PD3 (6 CYL.)
PD4 (V8)

225 CID SLANT 6 *has*
145 HP @ 4000 RPM
318, 361 *and* 383 CID V8 *have*
230, 255, 310, 325
OR 330 HP.

THE DODGE DART IS PRICED MODEL FOR
MODEL WITH OTHER LOW-PRICE CARS.

DODGE DART	CAR F	CAR P	CAR C
SENECA	Fairlane	Savoy	Biscayne
PIONEER	Fairlane 500	Belvedere	Bel Air
PHOENIX	Galaxie	Fury	Impala

WAGON
with
TAILGATE
OPEN

New Economy Slant "6" Uses
Exclusive Semi-Ram Intake Manifold!

New design
features
inclined block
with new
Equi-flow fuel
induction, over-
head valves,
for greater
fuel economy.

DART

145 HP 6-CYL.
CONTINUES

SENECA

SENECA STATION WAGON 6 OR V8,
6 PASSENGER

SENECA 4 DOOR SEDAN 6 OR V8

PIONEER STATION WAGON 6 OR V8,
6 OR 9 PASSENGER

PIONEER 4 DOOR SEDAN 6 OR V8

PIONEER

RD 3 (6 CYL.)
RD 4 (V8)

61

PHOENIX 4 DOOR HARDTOP 6 OR V8

PHOENIX

318, 361, 383 and
new 413 CID V8s
(230 TO 375 HP)

DART 330 2-DOOR HARDTOP 6 OR V8

DART 330 4-DOOR 6-PASSENGER WAGON 6 OR V8

DART 330 2-DOOR SEDAN 6 OR V8

DART 440 9-PASSENGER WAGON V8

new 116" WB
('62 ONLY)

SAME DISPL. AS '61
145 TO 380 HP

MODELS

DART 6 ═══ (SD1-L)
" " 300 (SD1-M)
" " 440 (SD1-H)
DART V8 ═══ (SD2-L)
" " 330 (SD2-M)
" " 440 (SD2-H)

62
(TOTALLY
RESTYLED)
SD SERIES

DART 440 CONVERTIBLE V8

1962 IS FINAL YEAR
THAT DART IS
DODGE-SIZED.

395

THE NEW LEAN BREED OF DODGE

DART
SEDAN

170

(RESTYLED)

63

TL1 SERIES

WAGON

2-DR.

WHEELBASE REDUCED AGAIN, TO 111"
(106" WB ON WAGONS)

$2288. UP

270

8.2 COMPR.

DASH

CVT.

GT

H/T

ALL 1963 DARTS ARE 6-CYL.
170 CID   101 HP @ 4400 RPM
OR 225 CID   145 HP @ 4000 RPM

TWO SLANT SIXES AS IN '63
new 273 CID V8
(180 HP @ 4200)

H/T

64 VL1 (6)
VL2 (V8)

GT

(270 STILL AVAIL.)

170

SEDAN

ENGINES AS IN 1964

65 AL1 (6)   AL2 (V8)

Dodge Dart 270 convertible. 6 and V8 power.

270

GT

Dodge Dart 4-door station wagon. 2-seat model only. 6 and V8 power.

$2310. UP

Dodge Dart 2-door sedan. 6 and V8 power.

Dart GT two-door hardtop.

DART, DART 270, DART GT MODELS

DAVIS

(1947-1949)

DAVIS MOTOR CO.,
VAN NUYS, CALIF.

4 CYL. 3-WHEELER

(NO CONNECTION *with the*
DAVIS CAR MFD. BEFORE 1930)

(17 BUILT)

(1949)

DEL MAR

DEL MAR MOTORS, INC.
SAN DIEGO, CALIF.

4 CYL.
CONTINENTAL
ENGINE

63 HP

(FEW BUILT)

100 HORSEPOWER
@ 3600 RPM
6 CYL.

DE SOTO

228.1 CID
(SINCE '37)

DASH

COACH

40
S-7

4-DOOR

DeSOTO
AMERICA'S FAMILY CAR
De Luxe Coupe De Luxe Sedan
$845 **$905**

A PRODUCT OF THE
CHRYSLER CORPORATION

6.00 × 16 TIRES
122½" WHEELBASE

397

DASH

new "ROCKET" BODIES

CUSTOM

1941 DeSoto

FLUID DRIVE
WITH
Simplimatic Transmission
(OPT.)

DLX.

41 S-8

121½" WB
(THROUGH '48)

100 HP (6.5 COMPR.)
105 HP (6.8 COMPR.)

DE LUXE COUPE
$**898**†

new 236.7 CID (THROUGH '50)
115 HP @ 3800 RPM

PERSONALIZED
INTERIORS

6.25 x 16
TIRES
(6.50 x 16
ON 139½" WB
MODELS)

DE SOTO
APPROVED
SERVICE
PLYMOUTH

42-

NEW AIRFOIL
LIGHTS

COLOR-MATCHED TO YOUR TASTE

45 S-10

CUSTOM

TOP
DISTORTED
"ARTIST'S
VIEW
↓

OUT OF SIGHT EXCEPT AT NIGHT

(AN
ACTUAL
PHOTO
ON
NEXT
PAGE)

(1942-45
(THIS IS ONLY SERIES *with* CONCEALED HEADLIGHTS.)

WARTIME DE SOTO
PRODUCTION of PARTS,
ASSEMBLIES FOR GEN.
SHERMAN TANKS
(ILLUSTRATED,) →
BOFORS ANTI-AIRCRAFT
CANNON, MILITARY
PLANES, ETC.

42-45
(CONT'D.)

"Styled to Stand Out
— Built to Stand Up!"

DeSoto

(ACTUAL PHOTO OF 1942 MODEL)

ONLY 24,771 1942 DE SOTOS
PRODUCED AUG., '41 TO JAN., '42.

ALL '48-STYLE
CHRYSLER CORP. CARS
CONT'D. to 2-49.

SINCE LATE 1935, LONG-WHEELBASE DE SOTO
7-PASS. or 8-PASS. SEDANS and LIMOUSINES
AVAIL., MANY SOLD IN FLEETS TO BIG-CITY
TAXICAB COMPANIES
139½" LONG W.B. AVAIL.
(FROM 1940 THROUGH 1954.)

9-PASS. SUBURBAN SED. ALSO

CUSTOM

S-11

46-48

109 HP @ 3600 RPM
TIRES : 6.50 × 15 , 6.50 × 16 L.W.B. ('46-47)
7.00 × 15, 7.50 × 15 L.W.B. ('48)

CONVENTIONAL
HEADLIGHTS
RESUMED

LARGER DIE-CAST
GRILLE

"8 out of 10
say DeSoto again*"

*=SLOGAN BASED ON POLL WHICH
INDICATED HOW MANY WOULD BUY ANOTHER DE SOTO.

399

DE SOTO

DE LUXE
(*has* NO EXTRA CHROME FENDER STRIPS.)

CUSTOM

S-13 **49** (TOTALLY RESTYLED)

new "25½" WB (THROUGH '54)

CARRY-ALL SEDAN

112 HP @ 3600 RPM (THROUGH '50)

CLOSER VIEW *of* 1949 GRILLE →

new SPORTSMAN H/T

RE-DESIGNED LIKENESS *of* HERNANDO DE SOTO, HISTORIC SPANISH EXPLORER FOR WHOM CAR WAS NAMED

1950 GRILLE *has* PAINTED SECTION IN CENTER, *with* *new* EMBLEM.

new ROUND PARKING LIGHTS

S-14 **50**

Drive a De Soto before you decide!

DE SOTO

SPORTSMAN   H/T

S-15-1 (DE LUXE)   S-15-2 (CUSTOM)

51

6-CYL. DISPLACEMENT RAISED TO 250.6 CID 116 HP @ 3600 RPM (THROUGH '54)

AS ON OTHER '51 CHRYSLER CORP. CARS, new "ORIFLOW" SHOCK ABSORBERS

new LOWER, SIMPLER GRILLE

1951 MODELS have SCRIPT LETTERING ABOVE GRILLE

new Full Power Steering

52

S-15 MODELS CONTINUE CUSTOM 6

1952 MODELS have BLOCK LETTERING ABOVE GRILLE

new FIRE DOME V8 (BELOW and RIGHT) (S-17)

S-17 CARS with AIR SCOOP HOOD ORNAMENT HAVE new "Fire Dome" 276.1 CID V8 ENGINE

Power Braking

160 h.p. @ 4000 RPM

V-8

DeSoto

new MODEL NAMES

POWERMASTER 6
(S-18)

FIREDOME V8
(S-16)

V8
CONTINUES 276.1 CID
(THROUGH '54)

160 HP @ 4400 RPM

new
POWER BRAKES
and OVERDRIVE
AVAILABLE

53

6 has a BROAD SHIELD
EMBLEM on HOOD;
V8 has "V"
BELOW a NARROWER
SHIELD (THROUGH '54)

SPORTSMAN

V8 has new
170 HP @ 4400 RPM

THE FINAL 6-CYL.
DE SOTO

POWERMASTER
6

(S-20)

"POWERFLITE" A.T. AVAIL.

CORONADO
SEDAN

FIREDOME V8
(S-19)

54

GRILLE MODIFIED
new SIDE TRIM
and TAIL-LIGHTS

DASH

402

De SOTO

The _Forward Look_

V8s ONLY (1955 ON)

new 126" WB

FLITE-CONTROL gear selector lever is mounted on De Soto's smart, new instrument panel—out of your way. Yet at your finger tips.

(TOTALLY RESTYLED)

55

new 291 CID
FIREDOME (S-22) 185 HP @ 4400 RPM
FIREFLITE (S-21) 200 HP @ 4400 RPM

DRIVE A DE SOTO BEFORE YOU DECIDE

(PUSH-BUTTON A.T.)

DASH (MINOR CHANGES FROM 1955)

230 HP @ 4400 RPM
FIREDOME (S-23)

new 341.4 CID
ADVENTURER (S-24)
320 HP @ 5200 RPM

"HIWAY HI-FI" BLT.-IN RECORD PLAYER AVAIL.

new MESH GRILLE

TRIPLE TAIL-LIGHTS with OVERLAPPING FIN

new 330 CID

56

255 HP @ 4400 RPM
FIREFLITE (S-24)

PACE CAR AT 1956 INDY 500 RACE

new 12-VOLT ELEC. SYS.

De Soto

new LOWER PRICE FIRESWEEP (S-27)
(has OWN FRONT END STYLING)

4-DR. H/T

(S-25) FIREDOME

SEDAN

(TOTALLY RESTYLED)

57

new 325, 341 OR 345 CID

245, 270, 295 OR 345 HP

2-DR. H/T

FIREFLITE (S-26)

ADVENTURER
(4 HEADLIGHTS, ANODIZED GOLD TRIM)
(S-26)

new 122" WB ON FIRESWEEP; 126" ON OTHERS (THROUGH '59)

4-DR. H/T

EXPLORER WAGON (3 SEATS)

SHOPPER (2 SEATS)

FIREFLITE SEDAN

404

DeSoto

(LS2-M) FIREDOME

(LS1-L) FIRESWEEP

16 MODELS, 4 SER.

new "TURBOFLASH" V8
(350 OR 361 CID)

280 TO 355 HP

FIREFLITE (LS3-H)

CLOSE-UP

58 LS SERIES

LARGE new "CONTROL TOWER" WINDSHIELD

DASH

GULFLEX   SERVICE   GULF

(LS3-S) ADVENTURER has ANODIZED SIDE TRIM

DE SOTO — the exciting look and feel of the future!

'59 DE SOTO

(MS1-L) FIRESWEEP

8.00 x 14 TIRES

361 OR *new* 383 CID V8
(THROUGH '60)
295 HP @ 4600 RPM
TO 350 HP @ 5000 RPM

(MS3-H)
FIREFLITE

FIREFLITE
SHOPPER

(ALL BUT FIRESWEEP HAVE
8.50 x 14 TIRES.)
(SINCE '57)

(MS2-M)
FIREDOME

ADVENTURER
(MS3-H)

DASH

1960 DE SOTO

DASH (*with* RAISED INSTRUMENT CLUSTER)

(PS1-L) FIREFLITE

BUILT-IN 45-RPM RECORD PLAYER OPTIONAL AGAIN (AS IN PLYMOUTH)

(PS3-M) ADVENTURER

H.P. CHOICES :
295 @ 4600 ; 305 @ 4600 ; 325 @ 4600 OR 330 @ 4800 RPM

10.0 TO 1 COMPRESSION

ALL 1960 and 1961 DE SOTOS ON 122" WB and 8.00 x 14 TIRES

1961 DE SOTO
ITS QUALITY SETS IT APART, ITS PRICE KEEPS IT WITHIN YOUR REACH

FROM $3102.

(THE FINAL DE SOTO CAR, AVAILABLE ONLY IN 2-DR. OR 4-DR. H/T BODIES)

ONLY THE 361 CID V8 IS AVAILABLE, *with* COMPRESSION REDUCED TO 9.0

265 HP @ 4400 RPM

ODD "SHARK-NOSE" TAIL-LIGHTS

4-DR. H/T

2-DR. H/T

PRODUCED 8-60 TO 12-60

DASH

The highly unusual instrument cluster, with the real type clock below the speedometer center. Not all options are shown.

2-TIERED GRILLE

DISCONTINUED

DODGE DIVISION **CHRYSLER** CORPORATION # DODGE (EST. LATE 1914)

LUXURY LINER DE LUXE **$825** and up

1940 Dodge 2-door Sedan $815, delivered in Detroit*

new 119½" WB (THROUGH '48)

DASH

40

D-17 = SPECIAL
D-14 = DE LUXE

87 HP @ 3600 RPM (SINCE '34)

3-WINDOW BUSNS. COUPE (new)

Slogan: "DODGE ENGINEERING COSTS NOTHING EXTRA" ('40)

FLUID DRIVE TRANSMISSION AVAIL.

6 CYL.

217.8 CID (SINCE '34)

91 HP @ 3800 RPM

D-19S = DELUXE
D-19C = CUSTOM

41 (RESTYLED)

DODGE SEDANS **$815** AND UP

COUPES, $755 and up

new LARGE, WIDE GRILLE

HOOD FOLDS "BUTTERFLY" STYLE

new Safety-Rim WHEELS

INTERIOR

DODGE

new 230.2 CID (TO '54)

new 6.7 COMPR. 105 HP @ 3600 RPM

new GRILLE with VEE CENTER SECTION

"THE NEW AND THE FINEST DODGE"

D-22 S = DELUXE
D-22 C = CUSTOM

42-45

7-WINDOW SEDAN

DASH and INTERIOR VIEWS

new 7.10 × 15 TIRES IN 1948

D-24 S = DE LUXE
D-24 C = CUSTOM

46-48

102 HP @ 3600 RPM

5-WINDOW SEDAN (ALL DOORS FRONT-HINGED)

"FADEAWAY" FENDERS

Dodge

SMOOTHEST CAR "AFLOAT"

409

ROADSTER (new)
(TOP UP)

2-DOOR

3-WINDOW COUPE

((ACTUAL PHOTO)
(TOP DOWN)

LOWER PRICED
NEW DODGE *WAYFARER*

The Daring New
DODGE
gyrol Fluid Drive plus GYRO-MATIC
Frees You from Shifting
OPTIONAL ON CORONET MODELS

49

D-29 = WAYFARER
(115" WB)

D-30 = MEADOWBROOK
and CORONET
(123½" WB)

(SAME WBs THROUGH '52)

(ABOVE) WAYFARER ROADSTER (ARTIST'S CONCEPTION)

New Dodge CORONET

CORONET WAGON

103 HP @ 3600 RPM
(TO '53)

new
SWITCH KEY STARTING

LONGER on the inside . . . SHORTER outside!
WIDER on the inside . . . NARROWER outside!
HIGHER on the inside . . . LOWER outside!

DODGE

new DIPLOMAT H/T

WAYFARER ROADSTER

INTERIOR

BACK SEAT

SUPER-SIZE LUGGAGE COMPARTMENT!

50

D-33 = WAYFARER
D-34 = MEADOWBROOK ; CORONET

new GRILLE with FEWER and HEAVIER PIECES

DODGE

WAYFARER

DASH

51

D-41 = WAYFARER

D-42   MEADOWBRK. ──────➤
       CORONET

SHOWN IN
SAN FRANCISCO,
LOOKING EAST
TOWARD OAKLAND.

CORONET

D-41 and D-42 SERIES
CONTINUE with LITTLE CHANGE

CORONET SIERRA
WAGON

new HUBCAPS

1952 SERIAL NOs. START AT:
WAYFARER   MEAD./CORONET

3717500l (Detroit)   3186760l
4800990l (San Leendro) 4509060l
4850760l (Los Angeles)
4552750l ═══
MD.,COR., (L.A.)

LOWER PART OF GRILLE is PAINTED.

52

FINAL YEAR FOR
WAYFARER MODEL ;
REPLACED
IN '53 BY
MEADOWBROOK SPECIAL

CORONET
"DIPLOMAT" H/T

DODGE

MEADOWBROOK 6
D-46

MEADOWBROOK SEDAN
MDBK. V8 is D-47

D-48 (114" WB)
D-44 (119")
CORONET V8

new 241.3 CID
V8 (THROUGH '54)

140 HP
@ 4400
RPM

Sensational New
140 Horsepower RED RAM V-8 ENGINE!

INTERIOR

CORONET SEDAN

6
OR V8

53

(RESTYLED)

WIRE WHEELS,
CONTINENTAL SPARE
AVAIL.

ABOUT 56%
OF 1953 DODGES
SOLD WERE
V8s.

CORONET
H/T

V8 MODELS
have

DODGE EIGHT

BELOW
RAM HOOD ORNAMENT

114" OR 119" WB
(THROUGH '54)

DODGE

CORONET 6

6-CYL. NOW HAS
110 HP @ 3600 RPM

D-51, D-52 (6 CYL.)

54 D-50,
D-53 (V8)

new GRILLE   ROYAL V8

ROYAL 500 CVT. IS PACE CAR AT 1954 INDY 500 RACE.

H/T

ROYAL V8
SEDAN

V8 has 140
OR 150 HP @ 4400 RPM
(7.1 OR 7.5 COMPR.)

VARIOUS INTERIORS
(JACQUARD FABRICS)

DEPENDABLE
NEW '54 **DODGE**
Elegance in Action

*Fully-automatic PowerFlite and full-time
Power Steering—yours at moderate extra cost.*

DODGE
FLASHES AHEAD IN '55

CORONET

REAR

CORONET V-8 2-DOOR SUBURBAN

ROYAL V-8 4-DOOR 8-PASSENGER SIERRA

V8 ENGINE NOW 270 CID

CUSTOM ROYAL V-8 4-DOOR SEDAN

new 3-TONE PAINT JOBS AVAIL.

55

D-56 (6 CYL.) (123 HP @ 3600 RPM)

new CUSTOM ROYAL LANCER

H/T

D-55 (V8) (175, 183 OR 193 HP @ 4400)

CUSTOM ROYAL LANCER SEDAN

THE *FORWARD LOOK*

new 120" WB (ON ALL, THROUGH '56)

6 CYL. NOW HAS 131 HP @ 3800 RPM (230 CID)
V8 has 189 TO 340 HP (270, 315 OR 354 CID)

D-62 (6 CYL.)
D-63 (V8)

56

The look, the feel, the power of success: New '56 Dodge Custom Royal Lancer 4-Door

new FINS and EMBLEM in GRILLE
new SIDE TRIM DIPS at REAR
new BUMPERS
HIGHER REAR FENDERS

In all the world no car like this
The New Dodge Lancer goes 4 door!

415

MORE 1956 DODGES ON NEXT PAGE

New '56 DODGE
(CONT'D.)
VALUE LEADER OF THE FORW.

SIERRA

CORONET LANCER

ROYAL

CORONET

DASH

8-PASS. CUSTOM SIERRA

CUSTOM ROYAL CONVERTIBLE

$2121. UP

PUSHBUTTON POWERFLITE, greatest advance in driving ease and control. Proven by years of successful testing!

new TYPES OF PUSH-BUTTON TRANSMISSION CONTROL

CUSTOM ROYAL LANCER

REAR CLOSE-UP

SWEPT·WING

'57 Dodge

(TOTALLY RESTYLED)
D-72 (6)   D-66, 67, 70 (V8)

2-DR. SUBURBAN (D-70)

new 325 or 354 CID V8s

4-DR. SIERRA (D-70) (D-71 IS CUSTOM SIERRA)

CORONET (6 or V8)
(D-72 or D-66)

ROYAL LANCER (D-67-1) 2-DR. H/T

CUSTOM ROYAL LANCER (D-67-2)

new 7.50 × 14 TIRES (8.00 × 14 WAGON, CVT.)

138 TO 340 HP

new 122" WB (ON ALL MODELS, THROUGH '59)

new COMPOUND-CURVED WINDSHIELD

ADDED LOWER "TEETH" IN GRILLE of ABOVE LATER MODEL.

REAR FINS "OVERLAP" FENDER

ROYAL

138 TO 333 HP

325, 350 or 361 CID V8s

CORONET

CUSTOM ROYAL LANCER

EARLY 1958 MODELS ABOVE

LD-1 (6)
LD-2, LD-3 (V8)

58

SPRING SWEPT·WING
by **Dodge**

58½ MODEL with IDENTIFYING CHARACTERISTICS

PAINTED HEADLIGHT AREA, also new GRILLE MEDALLION ON 58½

417

new colors

new interiors

'59 DODGE

Coronet 2-Door Sedan, V-8 or "6"

59½
Silver Challenger
two-door sedan

FINAL L-HEAD
230 CID 6
REDUCED TO 135 HP
@ 3600 RPM

326, 361 OR 383 CID V8s
have 255 HP @ 4400 RPM
TO 345 HP @ 5000 RPM

SIERRA

6 OR V8

CUSTOM ROYAL

new TAIL-LIGHTS

SWIVEL-
SEATS
AVAIL.
(new)

INTERIOR (CUSTOM
ROYAL CVT.)

59

MD1-L
(6)

MD2-L,
MD3-M,
MD3-L,
MD3-H (V8)

PUSH-
BUTTON
SHIFT
PLAN

DASH

418

⟨⟩ '60 DODGE

new
O.H.V.
SLANTED
6-CYL.
ENGINE
AVAIL. ONLY
in new
SUBSIDIARY
DART.

361 OR 383 CID V8s (THR.'61)
IN ALL DODGES EXCEPT
new DART OR '61-2 LANCER

(295 OR 330 HP)

122" WB ON LARGE DODGES
(THROUGH '61)

MATADOR·POLARA

POLARA has
BRIGHTWORK ON
LOWER REAR
FENDER.

PD1 and PD2
SERIES

new
DART

LISTED
SEPERATELY

60

POLARA has
HEAVY BAND
ATOP FENDER

UNIBODY
CONSTRUCTION

DODGE

265 TO 330 HP
122" WB

POLARA CONVERTIBLE VR

DASH

POLARA 2 DOOR HARDTOP V8

61

POLARA HARDTOP WAGON V8.
6 OR 9 PASSENGER

POLARA V8
IS
ONLY LARGE
SERIES

SEE ALSO DART,
OR
LANCER

Dodge Polara 500 - 2-dr Hardtop

Dodge Polara 500 - 4-dr Hardtop

POLARA 500

POLARA 500

361 OR
413 CID
V8
305
OR
380
HP

(SD2-P)
POLARA MODELS
TOTALLY RESTYLED
116" WB (AS ON
DART)

62

CUSTOM 880
(CONSERVATIVE
OLDER TYPE
STYLING) 122" WB

(SD3-L)

361 CID V8
265 HP @
4400 RPM

1963 DODGE

330 SERIES

440 SERIES

116" OR 119" WB

225 CID 6 (145 HP @ 4000)

318, 383 OR 426 CID V8 (230 TO 425 HP)

DASH

POLARA SERIES

POLARA 500 SERIES
BUCKET SEAT

TD SERIES

63

CUSTOM 880
361 OR 383 CID V8
(265 OR 305 HP)

122" WB

REAR VIEW OF CUSTOM 880 WAGON

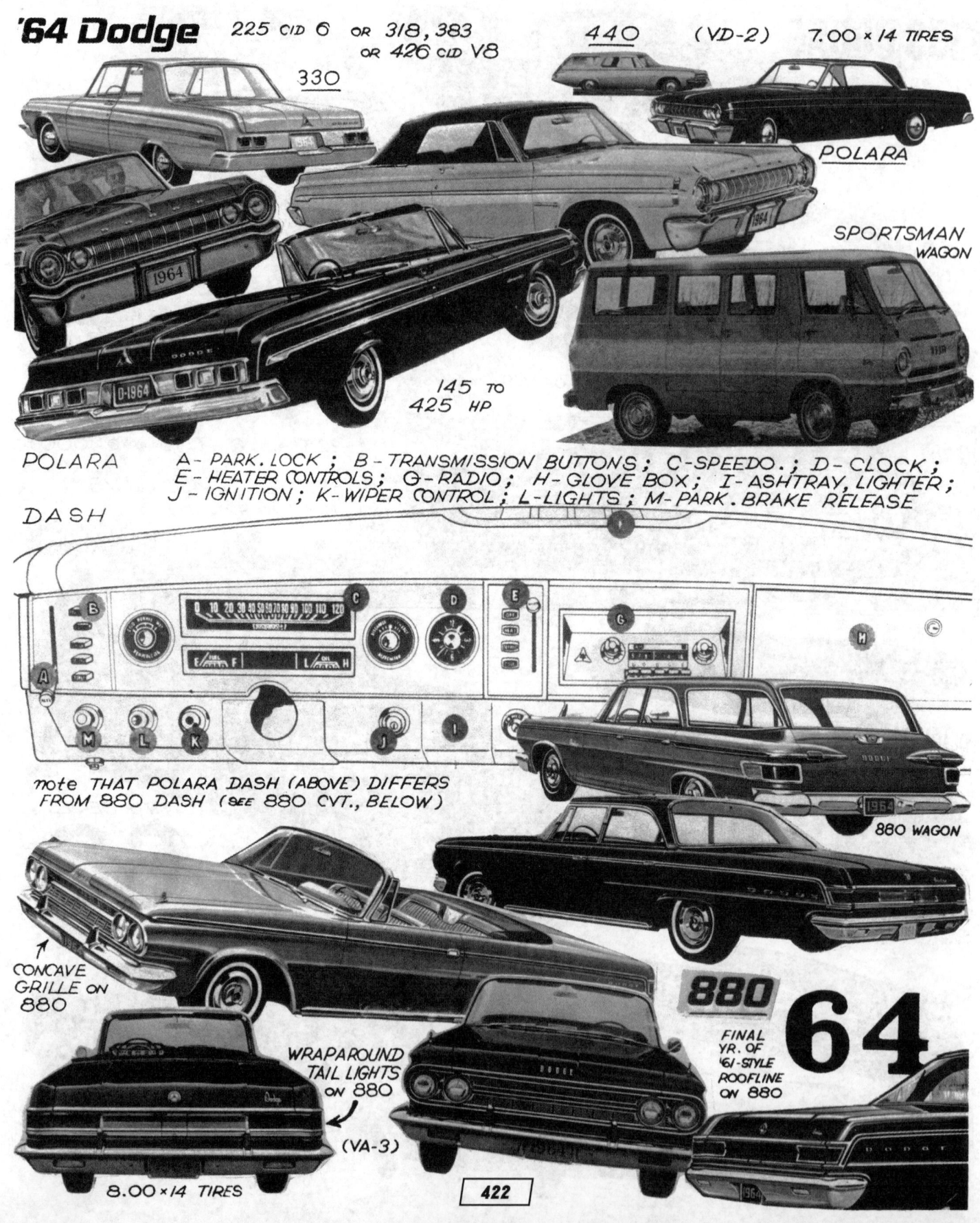

'64 Dodge

225 CID 6 OR 318, 383 OR 426 CID V8

330

440 (VD-2) 7.00 × 14 TIRES

POLARA

SPORTSMAN WAGON

1964

145 TO 425 HP

POLARA DASH

A - PARK. LOCK ; B - TRANSMISSION BUTTONS ; C - SPEEDO. ; D - CLOCK ;
E - HEATER CONTROLS ; G - RADIO ; H - GLOVE BOX ; I - ASHTRAY, LIGHTER ;
J - IGNITION ; K - WIPER CONTROL ; L - LIGHTS ; M - PARK. BRAKE RELEASE

note THAT POLARA DASH (ABOVE) DIFFERS
FROM 880 DASH (SEE 880 CVT., BELOW)

880 WAGON

CONCAVE GRILLE ON 880

WRAPAROUND TAIL LIGHTS on 880

(VA-3)

8.00 × 14 TIRES

880

64

FINAL YR. OF '61-STYLE ROOFLINE on 880

Dodge

116" and 117" WB

Coronet

AW1 (6)   AW2 (V8)

Dodge Coronet 440 2-door hardtop. 6 and V8 power.

Coronet

7.35 × 14 TIRES

CORONET DASH

Dodge Coronet 440 Station Wagon (3-seat model also offered)

7.75 × 14 TIRES

145, 180, 230, 265, 270, 315, 330 340, 365 or 425 HP.

Polara 4-door hardtop. V8 power. (AD2-L)

1965

V-8 CHOICES INCLUDE 273, 318, 361, 383, 413 or 426 CID

new 121" WB

Monaco two-door hardtop.

Dodge Monaco. Limited edition. 2-door hardtop. V8 power.

MONACO DASH

65 Monaco (AD2-P)

8.25 × 14 TIRES

Dodge Custom 880 4-Door Hardtop

Custom 880

880 (AD2-H)

423

Wagon has 8.50 × 14 TIRES

EDSEL

$2519.UP

MFD. BY FORD MOTOR CO. (1958, 1959, 1960 MODELS ONLY)

ROUNDUP 2-DR. WAGON

WAGONS HAVE SPECIAL TAIL-LIGHTS

note "HORSECOLLAR" CENTER GRILLE

SLOGAN: "THIS IS THE EDSEL" (OTHER SLOGANS ALSO)

"Teletouch" AUTO. TRANS. CONTROL BUTTONS IN STEERING-WHEEL HUB. (OPTIONAL) (1958 ONLY)

58

DASH → (with REVOLVING SPEEDOMETER)

VILLAGER 4-DR. WAGON

V-8s 361 CID, 303 HP OR 410 CID, 345 HP

BERMUDA 4-DR. (DELUXE WAGON with WOODGRAIN)

RANGER (LOWEST-PRICED)

(has MINIMUM of SIDE CHROME)

CITATION

PACER

CITATION (TOP of LINE) has INSET PANEL SET WITHIN REAR FENDER TRIM LOOP.

CORSAIR

W.B.s: 116" (WAGONS)

118" (RANGER, PACER)

124" (CORSAIR, CITATION)

EDSEL

RANGER

PACER, CITATION, ROUNDUP and BERMUDA MODELS NO LONGER AVAIL.

$2629. UP

223 CID 6-CYL. ENGINE ALSO AVAIL. STARTING 1959. (145 HP @ 4200 RPM)

3 V8 ENGINES:
Ranger 292 CID (200 HP @ 4500 RPM)
Express 332 CID (225 HP @ 4600)
OR Super Express 361 CID (303 HP @ 4600)

CORSAIR

new ROUND TAIL-LIGHTS

VILLAGER

new DASH

CORSAIR CHROME has VERTICAL STRIPS

59 (RESTYLED)

SLOGAN: "MAKES HISTORY BY MAKING SENSE"

INSET ANODIZED TRIM PANEL IDENTIFIES 1959 CORSAIR.

new 120" W.B. (ALL MODELS, THROUGH '60)

new GRILLE INCORPORATES HEADLIGHTS, with HORIZONTAL MEMBERS IN CENTER SECTION.

425

EDSEL

SLOGAN: "NEW! NIFTY! THRIFTY!"

CORSAIR NO LONGER AVAIL.

RANGER and VILLAGER ARE ONLY MODELS OFFERED FOR EDSEL'S BRIEF 1960 SEASON.

new TAIL-LIGHTS PICK UP VERTICAL OVAL THEME FORMERLY DISPLAYED IN EDSEL GRILLE.

FROM $2635.³⁰

RANGER

1960 MODEL PROD.:
WAGON, 6-PASS. (216)
WAGON, 9-PASS. (59)
2-DR. SEDAN (777)
4-DR. SEDAN (1,288)
2-DR. HARDTOP (295)
4-DR. HARDTOP (135)
CONVERTIBLE (76)
TOTAL = ONLY 2,846
1960 EDSELS BUILT!

60 (TOTALLY RESTYLED)

new SPLIT GRILLE

VILLAGER

new DASH

3 ENGINE CHOICES:
Economy 6 223 CID (145 HP @ 4000 RPM)

Ranger V8 292 CID (185 HP @ 4200 RPM)

Super Express V8 352 CID (300 HP @ 4600 RPM)

EDSELS DISCONTINUED NOV., 1959

426

FAIRLANE
BY
(FORD)

new COMPACT / INTERMEDIATE **6** OR **V-8** FOR 1962; FORMERLY A FULL-SIZED FORD SERIES

62

$2392. UP

500

new CONCAVE GRILLE

63

SQUIRE

63½ AVAIL. WITH new VINYL ROOF

H/T INTERIOR

FAIRLANE

"289" V-8 option

Fairlane wagons:

FAIRLANE CUSTOM RANCH WAGON

64

SEE ALSO:
FORD

optional features. 4-speed stick. Overdrive. Tachometer.

271 solid-lifter horsepower high-shift automatic!

$**2474**.UP

HEADLIGHTS PAIRED IN PLATES

NO MORE RAISED "AIR SCOOP" EFFECT ON HOOD

COBRA POWERED BY FORD

65

new OBLONG TAIL-LIGHTS

428

FALCON (compact) $1912. and up (1960–1970½ MODELS)

BY FORD

60

CHOICE OF 2-DR. OR 4-DR WAGONS

109½" WB
6.00 × 13 TIRES

6 CYL. 144 CID OVERHEAD VALVE ENGINE 90 HP

Ford
MOTOR COMPANY

A CHOICE OF TWO SURGING "SIXES"!
STD. 144 CID OR new 170 CID

2-DR.

4-DR.

85 HP (STD.)

4-DR. WAGON ALSO AVAIL.

FALCON TUDOR WAGON

1961

new FUTURA CONSOLE

FORD Falcon '61
WORLD'S MOST SUCCESSFUL NEW CAR

Futura

$2202. UP

FUTURA has 3 DARTS on REAR FENDERS, and SPECIAL HUBCAPS.

429

Falcon '62

BEST SHAPE ECONOMY'S EVER BEEN IN

FUTURA

FALCON SPORTS FUTURA

FUTURAS HAVE SPECIAL
FRONT FENDER TRIM,
AS ILLUSTRATED.

DELUXE

DELUXE

2-DR.

4-DR.

new
SQUIRE

STD. 2-DR.

STD.

new 164 HP V8
ALSO AVAIL.

63

DE LUXE

FUTURA

SQUIRE

new
CONVERTIBLE

FALCON

Lively new Sprint

THESE MODELS INTRODUCED IN MID-SEASON

63½

new scatback hardtop

Squire

new wider tread

64
(RESTYLED)

$2211. UP

new '260' cu. in. V-8 power option

new longer springs

Squire

New battery-saving alternator.

65

13" or 14" WHEELS

new 170 cu. in. standard Six with optional 3-speed Cruise-O-Matic transmission

new GRILLE

DASH

431

(SINCE 1903)

V8 L-HEAD ENGINE
(SINCE 1932)

STANDARD
has VERTICAL
BARS in
NARROW
GRILLE

Ford

FORD Division of FORD MOTOR COMPANY

DE LUXE

112" WB

1940 STANDARD GRILLE SOMEWHAT RESEMBLES THAT OF 1939 DE LUXE

4-PASS. COUPE has 2 FACING BACK SEATS

NEW BODY TYPE.

40 60 OR 85 HP (SINCE '37)

WITH 22 IMPORTANT IMPROVEMENTS

PRICES START AT $650. (STD. CPE.)

"STEP UP TO THE V·8 CLASS"

new GRILLE

FINGER-TIP GEARSHIFT on steering post. All models, no extra cost.

TRANSVERSE SPRINGS CONTINUE (THROUGH '48 MODEL)

new SEALED-BEAM LIGHTS

V·B 1940

DE LUXE

432

FORD "Get the facts and you'll get a FORD!"

TUDOR SEDAN

new 90 HP V8
new L-HEAD 6 also

41

(RESTYLED)

MODELS

SPECIAL (REPLACES STANDARD.

DELUXE

SUPER DELUXE

PRICES START AT
$665.
(V8 OR 6 SPECIAL CPE.)

NEW	Massive Beauty
NEW	Room Throughout
NEW	Vision All Around
NEW	Faster Acceleration
NEW	Stronger, Rigid Frame
NEW	Longer Wheelbase
NEW	Longer Springbase
NEW	Soft, Slower-action Springs
NEW	Soft Seat Cushions
NEW	Stabilizer Ride Control

CVT.

FORDOR SEDAN

new GRILLE

new 114" WB
6.00 x 16
TIRES.

SUPER DE LUXE

V8 or 6 $780.
(SPECIAL 6 CPE.)
new RECTANGULAR PARKING LIGHTS

Steel Stampings for Die-Castings

42-45

"America's Most Modern 6...America's Lowest-priced 8"

Plastics Replace Metal for Interior Trim

DASH

FORDOR SEDAN

new BROAD, LOW GRILLE with CURVED VERTICAL PCS.

"V8" OR "6" ON new EMBLEM

JM-547

$930.

433

FORD

PRICES START AT **$1003.** (6 CPE.)

V8 Six

NEW OVERSIZED BRAKES

CLUB COUPE

TUDOR

FORDOR

There's a *Ford* in your future

46

1946 MODEL STARTS JULY, 1945

new GRILLE

NEW 1946 FORD SPORTSMAN'S CONVERTIBLE (V8) (*with* GENUINE WOODEN BODY)

$1865.

Outside and inside, there never was a car like this before! The new Ford Sportsman's Convertible is really *two* cars in one! Ford designers have combined the paneled smartness of the station wagon and the touch-a-button convenience of the convertible!

ALL-METAL CVT. MORE COMMONLY SEEN (ILLUSTR. ON NEXT PAGE)

434

FORD

EARLY 47
(SIMILAR TO 1946)

Ford's out Front
(1947 SLOGAN)

CONVERTIBLE (METAL)

47½-48

1948 has new STEERING COLUMN LOCK.

... new stainless steel body molding newly fashioned door handles ...

... new body colors ...

$1517.*
V8 WAGON

FINER
There's a Ford in your future

A newly styled instrument panel with big new dials for easy reading

* = RAISED TO $1855 IN '48

new HOOD MEDALLION IDENTIFIES 6 OR V8

MODIFIED GRILLE NO LONGER has RED INDENTATIONS.

new ROUND PARKING LIGHTS PLACED BELOW HEADLIGHTS

new wheel rims and hub caps

new heavier bumper guards—And many other new features!

435

FORD

COUPE

TUDOR

PRICES START AT
$1333.
(DLX. COUPE)
(6 CYL.)

CVT.

FORDOR

NEW! '49
STARTS SPRING, '48
(TOTALLY RESTYLED)

Overdrive

Engine speed 42 m.p.h.   Car speed 60 m.p.h.

(OPTIONAL)

57% more luggage space.

Wagon

new "Hydra-Coil" FRONT SPRINGS

CHOICE OF COLOR

New "Flight Panel" dash . . .

(new CUSTOM SERIES REPLACES SUPER DE LUXE)

"6" OR "8" IN GRILLE "SPINNER" INDICATES NUMBER OF CYLINDERS.

FORD

"Country Squire"
STATION WAGON

(8-PASS.

CVT.

"Double Duty"

50

CHASSIS
(V8)

new
MID-SEASON 2-DR.
"CRESTLINER"

FORD

new
EMBLEM
ON
HOOD
(ALSO ON
DECK LID)

"TEST DRIVE" A '50 FORD   437

THERE'S A *Ford* IN YOUR FUTURE WITH A FUTURE BUILT IN!

FORD

CRESTLINE

51

DUAL SPINNERS IN GRILLE

new **VICTORIA**

VICTORIA INTERIOR

SQUIRE

new DASH

You can pay more, but you can't buy better!

VICTORIA H/T *with* WINDOWS OPEN

1951

REAR (SEDAN)

FORD

PRICES START AT $1526.

new MAINLINE *(has LEAST AMOUNT OF CHROME TRIM)*

COUNTRY SQUIRE 4-DOOR METAL WAGON *has* IMITATION MAHOGANY PANEL DECALS, FRAMED *with* REAL MAPLE *or* BIRCH TRIM.

new RANCH WAGON

Station Wagons

new COUNTRY SEDAN

52
(TOTALLY RESTYLED)

New Flight-Style Control Panel

Ford's new Center-Fill Fueling cuts down spillage.

DASH

new SUSPENDED PEDALS

CUSTOMLINE 2-DR.

"TEST DRIVE" A FORD TODAY YOU CAN PAY MORE BUT YOU CAN'T BUY BETTER

HUGE, curved, one-piece windshield and car-wide rear window to match. You can really see what's ahead and what's behind!

CRESTLINE SUNLINER V8 CRESTLINE VICTORIA

new GRILLE *has* APPEARANCE OF 3 "SPINNERS"

$2104.

Full-Circle Visibility

101 h.p. High-Compression

Mileage Maker Six

"Only V-8 in its field"!

110 h.p. High Compression

Strato-Star V-8

439

FORD

CVT. IS PACE CAR AT 1953 INDY 500 RACE

PRICES START AT
$1537.
(MAINLINE 6 CPE.)

MAINLINE 2-DR

DASH

FORD 50TH ANNIVERSARY

53

ONLY ONE "SPINNER" in new GRILLE.

SUNLINER

COUNTRY SQUIRE

FORD-O-MATIC (SINCE '51)

2-DOOR RANCH WAGON $2019. (6)

440

4-DOOR COUNTRY SEDAN

COUNTRY SQUIRE

NO SHIFTING...NO CLUTCHING

Ford Skyliner (CRESTLINE SERIES)

$2199.
(V8 $134 EXTRA)
with PLEXIGLASS
ROOF WINDOW

54

New 130-h.p.
Y-BLOCK V·8

MAINLINE

239 CID V8 ENDS '54

New Ball-Joint Front Suspension

New 115-h.p.
I-BLOCK SIX

223 CID (THR. '64)

4. Four-Way Power Seat.

CUSTOMLINE

5 optional power assists*

★ Master-Guide power steering does up to 75% of steering work . . . ★ Swift Sure Power Brakes do up to one-third of your stopping work . . . ★ Fordomatic Drive does *all* your shifting . . . ★ Power-Lift Windows open and close at a button's touch. And ★ 4-Way Power Seat adjusts up or down, forward or back, at a touch of the controls.   *At extra cost.

FORD

PRICES START AT **$1606.** (MAINLINE 6 CPE.)

SEDAN
MAINLINE

new GRILLE

RANCH WAGON

CUSTOM RANCH WAGON

COUNTRY SQUIRE

new FAIRLANE SUNLINER CVT. (ABOVE)

CUSTOMLINE

new "WRAP-AROUND" WINDSHIELD

120-H.P. 6 OR V8s with 162 OR 182 H.P.

55

6-PASS.

COUNTRY SEDANS

8-PASS. (with FAIRLANE SIDE TRIM)

FAIRLANE VICTORIA

"Y" SYMBOLIZES Y-BLOCK V8 new 272 CID

SIDE EMBLEM (ON FAIRLANE TYPES)

FAIRLANE CROWN VICTORIA (note BAND WRAPPED OVER ROOF)

new FAIRLANE MODELS IDENTIFIED BY SWEEP SIDE TRIM

FORD

MAINLINE

CUSTOM RANCH WAG.

6 NOW 137 HP @ 4200 RPM

V-8 h.p. upped

The 272-cubic inch Ford V-8, the standard eight for all Customline and Mainline Fords. Has modern dual carburetor, automatic choke, single exhaust.

FAIRLANE FORDOR

CTY. SQUIRE

The 292-cubic inch Thunderbird V-8, the standard eight for all Fairlanes and Station Wagons, is now available in all Customline and Mainline models, too. Has 4-barrel carburetor, dual exhausts.

202 H.P.

new 2-DR. LUXURY **PARKLANE** *WAGON (INTRO. TO COMPETE with CHEVY'S NOMAD.)*

CUSTOM COUNTRY SEDAN

56

CUSTOMLINE VICTORIA

SKYLINER   CROWN VICTORIA

The 312-cubic inch Thunderbird Special V-8.

225 h.p.

new 4-DR. H/T (FAIRLANE FORDOR VICTORIA)

1956 INTERIOR

FORD

6 CYL. INCREASED TO 144 HP

CNTRY. SED.

SQUIRE

LADDER-TYPE CONTOURED FRAME

4-way ball-joint front suspension

RANCH WAGON

CUSTOM TUDOR

CUSTOM (REPLACES MAINLINE)

CUSTOM 300 FORDOR

FAIRLANE (note UNIQUE SIDE TRIM)

New deep-offset hypoid axle

FAIRLANE 500 MODELS BELOW

UP TO 245 HP with "SILVER ANNIVERSARY" V8s."

57

FAIRLANE 500 4-DR. TOWN VICTORIA H/T

LOW-SILHOUETTE CARB.

new V8 SKYLINER has RETRACTABLE HARD TOP (POWER-OPERATED)

SUNLINER CVT.

$2942.↗

new FRONT END

REAR

444

FORD

6 CYL. NOW 145 HP (THROUGH '60)

CUSTOM 300

FAIRLANE 500 SKYLINER (SHOWN with TOP IN MOTION, and with TOP IN PLACE.)

NOTHING NEWER IN THE WORLD

RANCH WAGON (4-DR. ALSO AVAIL.)

DEL RIO RANCH WAGON

DASH

COUNTRY SEDAN

COUNTRY SQUIRE (2 VIEWS)

NEW INTERCEPTOR V-8

A TRUE AIR RIDE

FINE-CAR DETAIL

new ROOF GROOVES

58 (TOTALLY RESTYLED)

4 HEADLIGHTS

4 TAIL LIGHTS

F-1958

FAIRLANE 500

Versatile Cruise-O-Matic Drive! Set selector in D_1 position for brisk, solid-feeling take-off. Select D_2 for gentle, sure-footed starts. What's more, when new Cruise-O-Matic Drive is teamed with a new Interceptor V-8 engine it can give you up to 15 per cent more gasoline mileage.

V8s = 292, new 332 and new 352 CID (THROUGH '59)

Up to 300 h.p. with new Precision Fuel Induction.

445

FORD

CUSTOM 300

$**2132.** (6)

note "FORD" LETTERING ON HOOD

WINDSHIELD DOGLEG DETAILS

Fairlane 500

FAIRLANE 500 VICTORIA ROOFLINE (CLOSE-UP)

note EMBLEM ON HOOD

new GRILLE

(TOTALLY RESTYLED AGAIN)

59

145 TO 300 HP

FAIRLANE REAR FENDER

NEW FORD GALAXIE CLUB VICTORIA—THUNDERBIRD STYLING IN A 6-PASSENGER, 2-DOOR HARDTOP

new 1959½ TOP-OF-LINE GALAXIE MODELS ADDED, with T-BIRD ROOFLINE.

THE FINAL SKYLINER (GALAXIE)

446

FORD

wagons

ROOMY NEW FORD RANCH WAGON . . . LOWEST PRICED WAGON OF THE MOST POPULAR THREE

4-DOOR
and
2-DOOR
RANCH
WAGONS

FENDER
CHEVRONS
ON THIS '59½
RANCH WAGON

(INTERIOR VIEW EXAGGERATED)

59 (CONT'D.)

COUNTRY
SQUIRE
$3076
*

1959 DASH
(ILLUSTR. with
FACTORY-INSTALLED
AIR CONDITIONER
UNIT)

*WAGON PRICE
SHOWN APPLIES TO
V-8 9-PASSENGER
6 CYL. OR
6-PASS. MODELS
also avail.

COUNTRY
SEDAN
$2947. *

447

FORD

FAIRLANE 500

FAIRLANE PRICES START AT **$2170.** (6-CYL. 2-DR.)

GALAXIE TUDOR

(TOP UP)

SUNLINER CVT.

(TOP DOWN)

new STARLINER **$2723.** (V8; 6 ALSO AVAIL.)

ARCHED TAIL-LIGHTS ONLY ON 1960 MODELS →

GALAXIE FORDOR

NEW SLOPING HOOD GIVES INCREASED VISIBILITY

60 (TOTALLY RESTYLED FOR 3RD SUCCESSIVE YEAR!)

145 TO 300 HP

DASH

RANCH WAGON

COUNTRY SEDAN →

9-passenger Country Squire

Beautifully built to take care of itself...

2-DR.

FORD WHEEL COVER

4-DR.

FAIRLANE
FAIRLANE 500
(6 CUT TO 135 HP)

new GRILLE IS CONCAVE, BISECTED HORIZONTALLY

61

$2261.
(6)

GALAXIE 4-DR. TOWN VICTORIA H/T

(CLOSER VIEW OF GALAXIE WHEEL COVER AT UPPER RIGHT)

SQUIRE

RANCH WAGON

STATION WAGONS

CNTRY. SEDAN
292, 352 OR NEW 390 CID V8s (175 TO 401 HP)

1961

GALAXIE VICTORIA H/T → (CLOSE-UP and DASH)

STARLINER H/T

ROUND TAIL LIGHTS RETURN

449

1961

FORD

RANCH WAG.

COUNTRY SQUIRE

6-PASSENGER COUNTRY SEDAN
(9-pass. model also

SLOGAN:
live it up with a lively One from FORD

Galaxie
62

new BLUNTED REAR END

138 to 405 HP (THR. '63)

POWER STEERING

GALAXIE 500/XL.

DENOTES 405 HP THUNDERBIRD ENGINE

GALAXIE 500 and XL have GRILLE MEDALLION

Galaxie 500

1962

1962 TAIL LIGHTS

BUCKET SEATS and FLOOR CONSOLE IN new
Galaxie 500/XL!

new * SIDE TRIM

* = ON 500, XL

450

Galaxie 500
(SEDAN and CVT. ILLUSTR.)

FORD

GALAXIE

SQUIRE

63

note INDENTATION ALONG UPPER BORDER OF WOOD-LIKE "COUNTRY SQUIRE" SIDE TRIM.

new GRILLE with SHIELD EMBLEM, AND STEP-UP ALONG LOWER EDGE

new SIDE TRIM

DASH

BACKGROUND: MONACO, ON THE RIVIERA

PRICES START AT $2563. 6-CYL. "300" 2-DR.

UP TO 425 HP IN new '63½

new

Presenting the 63½ Super Torque Ford Sports Hardtop —brand new hardtop that looks like a convertible!

451

new SWING-AWAY STEERING WHEEL AVAILABLE

CLEAR GLASS BACKLIGHT IN CVT.

CUSTOM RANCH WAGON

FORD

SQUIRE

138 TO 425 HP

GALAXIE 500 4-DR. H/T

GALAXIE 500 XL

PRICES START AT $2586.

64

new GRILLE

($2600 IN '65)

(CUSTOM 6 2-DR.)

(RESTYLED) 150 TO 425 HP (THROUGH '67)

CUSTOM 500

65

P R N DRIVE L
CRUISE-O-MATIC

new VERTICAL STACKED HEADLIGHTS →

new DIP IN WAGON ROOF →

Convenient face-to-face rear seats and passenger space

SQUIRE

GALAXIE 500 XL

GALAXIE 500 LTD

TAIL LIGHT SHAPE 19 new

FRAZER

KAISER-FRAZER CORPORATION · **WILLOW RUN, MICHIGAN**

(1946–1951)

123½" W.B. (THROUGH '51)

(REPLACES PRE-WAR GRAHAM.)

47

F-47

EARLY FRAZERS (BLT. 1946) have PAINTED GRILLE.

LATER MODEL, with CHROME GRILLE →

EMBLEM

JE SUIS PRET

100 HP @ 3600 RPM   7.3 COMPRESS.

6 CYL., L-HEAD CONTINENTAL ENGINES   226.2 CID (USED in ALL FRAZERS)

3⁵⁄₁₆" × 4³⁄₈" BORE and STROKE (KAISER SPECS. SIMILAR)

SEE ALSO: **KAISER**

FRAZER REAR VIEW

47½-48

F-485 ; (MANHATTAN SEDAN IS NOW F-486)

$2152. OR $2550. (SINCE '47)

ILLUSTRATED ON FAMOUS "17-MILE-DRIVE," AT PEBBLE BEACH, CALIF.

ALL FRAZERS ARE 4-DOOR MODELS.

FRAZER

JOSEPH W. FRAZER (left) and HENRY J. KAISER (right,) STANDING BY THE 200,000 th CAR (A 1948 FRAZER) TO BE BUILT BY THE KAISER-FRAZER CORP.

200,000th

J.W. FRAZER

H.J. KAISER

112 HP

VAGABOND

PRICED FROM **$2321.**

F-505 and F-506 MANHATTAN are 1950 MODELS.

MANHATTAN SEDAN has HEAVY BAND of SIDE CHROME

49-50

1949 = F-495 OR F-496 MANHTN.

new LARGE GRILLE *and* PARKING LIGHTS

(1950 MODEL ENDS 2-50)

4-DOOR CVT.

new "MANHATTAN" LOOKS LIKE THE 4-DR. CVT., BUT *has* STEEL PAINTED OR NYLON-PADDED TOP SECTION.

VAGABOND

115 HP

DASH (SIMILAR TO 1949)

51
(RESTYLED)
F-515 OR F-516 MANHATTAN

STARTS 2-50

454

EXPERIMENTAL SAFETY CAR BLT. 1945 TO 1947 BY
H. GORDON HANSEN,
AT SAN LORENZO, CALIF.

GORDON DIAMOND

FORD V8 ENGINE

156" WB BETWEEN FRONT REAR
SINGLE WHEELS. ANOTHER PAIR OF
WHEELS "AMIDSHIPS."
PURCHASED BY HARRAH'S AUTOMOBILE COLLECTION

GRAHAM (and HUPMOBILE)

6 - CYL.
L - HEAD
ENGINES

115"
WB

FORMER CORD BODY DIES USED

40-41

'41 GRAHAM:
$895. and up
'40 HUPP:
$1145. and up

GRAHAM "HOLLYWOOD" and
HUPMOBILE "SKYLARK" LOOK ALMOST ALIKE!

(FURTHER DETAILS OF GRAHAM, HUPMOBILE INCLUDED IN "AMERICAN CAR SPOTTER'S GUIDE, 1920-1939")

GREGORY

(1949) (ANOTHER EXPER. MODEL, 1952)

BEN GREGORY, MFR.,
KANSAS CITY, MO.

4-CYL. Continental
REAR ENGINE
FRONT-WHEEL-
DRIVE

49

PRODUCTION ATTEMPTED

40 HP
94" WB

$1050. (PROPOSED PRICE)

(1948 -1949)

HOPPENSTAND

HOPPENSTAND MOTORS, INC., GREENVILLE, PA.

2-CYL. FLAT, AIR-COOLED, REAR ENG.

48-49

(1950-1954)

Henry J

PRICED FROM
$1299.
(WITH PERIODIC INCREASES)

4 OR 6-CYL.
"SUPERSONIC"
ENGINES

(2-DRS.
ONLY)

THIS
GRILLE
STYLE
RETAINED
ON 1952
HENRY J

513 = 4 CYL.
514 = DELUXE 6 CYL.

51

(INTRO. 1950)

KAISER-FRAZER CORPORATION, WILLOW RUN, MICHIGAN

GIVEN
THE
FASHION
ACADEMY
GOLD MEDAL
AWARD

ALLSTATE CAR = SPECIAL SERIES
OF HENRY J, SOLD EXCLUSIVELY
BY SEARS, ROEBUCK and CO.

('52)

52-54

CORSAIR
('53-
'54)

new
VAGABOND
has REAR
"CONTINENTAL" SPARE
TIRE/WHEEL

Henry J

new
GRILLE
ON
'53-54

Vagabond

('52)

456

HUDSON MOTOR CAR CO., DETROIT

HUDSON
SIX

(1909-1957)

$670 COUPE (6)

SERIES (6-CYL.)
40 = TRAVELER; DELUXE (113" WB)
41 = SUPER (118" WB)
43 = COUNTRY CLUB (125" WB)
48 = BIG BOY (125" WB)

92 HP @ 4000 (174.9 CID 6)
OR
102 HP @ 4000 (212 CID 6)

INTERIOR (6)

TOTAL OF 86,865 BLT.

new GRILLE

40

OVERDRIVE AVAIL.
4.11 STD. GEAR RATIO
6.50 × 16 TIRES

DASH →

SERIES (8-CYL.)
44 = SUPER
45 = DELUXE (118" WB)
47 = COUNTRY CLUB (125" WB)

H.P. RATINGS CONTINUE THROUGH '47

(CVT.) SUPER 8

128 HP @ 4200   **STRAIGHT 8**   (254.5 CID 8)

SHOULD HYDRAULIC BRAKES FAIL, EMERGENCY MECHANICAL SYSTEM TAKES OVER (SINCE '36)

"AUTO-POISE" FRONT WHEEL CONTROL WITH COIL SPRINGS

INTERIOR (8)

NEW HUDSON EIGHT PRICES START AT
$860

457

HUDSON
PRICES START AMONG AMERICA'S LOWEST

$695

79,529 BLT. 1941

SUPER 6 (SERIES 10)

"SYMPHONIC STYLING"

41

116," 121," OR 128" WB

"AMERICA'S SAFEST CAR"

new COMMODORE 8

• COMMODORE SERIES (Sixes and Eights)

ONLY 5,396 BLT. IN 1942

42-45

new EXTRA SIDE CHROME

COMMODORE 6 IS new

SUPER 6

6

CIVILIAN PROD. ENDS 2-5-42

SOME '42s NO LONGER have FRONT HOOD CHROME

1942

POSTWAR PRODUCTION RESUMES 8-30-45. 5,005 BLT. 1945; 93,870 BLT. 1946

46

SUPER 6

121" WB ON ALL (THROUGH '47) PRICED FROM

$1379.

COMM. has 2 VERT. STRIPS ON REAR WINDOW

COMMODORE (has **$1379.** UP

new GRILLE with RECESSED CENTER SECTION

HUDSON TRIANGLE EMBLEM AT FRONT END OF CHROME BELT STRIP)

PRICED FROM **$1421.**

SUPER 6

COMMODORE **$1421.** UP

47

103,310 BLT. 1947

SIMILAR TO 1946, BUT has HEAVIER CHROME MOULDING MARGIN AROUND MEDALLION OVER GRILLE.

HUDSON

CVTS. NOW HAVE MORE METAL ABOVE WINDSHIELD

142,454 BLT. 1948

new "Step Down" BODIES SURROUNDED BY FRAME

INTERIOR ('49.)

48-49

(TOTALLY RESTYLED)

new 124" WB ON ALL

"This time it's *Hudson*"

50

new PACEMAKER 6 IS LOWER-PRICED SERIES (119" WB)

COMMODORE 8

REAR SEAT VIEW

ROAD CLEARANCE

INVERTED "V" ON new GRILLE

143,586 BLT. 1950

51

92,859 BLT. 1951

PACEMAKER 6

$2642.

new HEAVIER, ARCHED GRILLE

$2568.

SUPER 6

COMM. 8

$2543.

new HORNET 6

PACEMAKER 6

COMMODORE 6

new **HUDSON WASP** with 6-CYL. "H-127" ENG.

Hollywood H/T (new)

HUDSON WASP TWO-DOOR BROUGHAM

CVT.

HOLLYWOOD WASP

CLUB CPE.

HORNET CLUB CPE.

new lower-priced running mate

52

HUDSON HORNET

SEDAN

HORNET

HUDSON

B-W ENGINEERING PRODUCTION

equipped with
B-W OVERDRIVE!
(OPTIONAL)

79,117 BLT. 1952

HYDRA-MATIC DRIVE
available for all '52 Hudsons
at extra cost.

Hudson-Aire Hardtop Styling
at standard sedan and coupe prices

COMMODORE 8

FINAL YEAR FOR STRAIGHT 8

HUDSON

SUPER WASP   1953 : 17,792 WASPS, 27,208 HORNETS   HORNET

53 new HOOD "AIR-SCOOP" and new GRILLE w/o INVERTED "V."

6-CYL. MODELS ONLY (THROUGH 1954)

(The *JETS* SHOWN ON "*JET*" PAGE)

The WASPS in the low-medium price field

SUPER WASP

new HIGH TAIL-LIGHTS

HUDSON DIVISION OF AMERICAN MOTORS
(RESULT OF MERGER WITH NASH, 5-1-54)

new 1-PC. WINDSHIELD

The **HORNET** in the medium price field

CLUB COUPES

new FRONT END DESIGN

54 (RESTYLED)

NEW HORNET SPECIAL
available in Four-Door Sedan, Club Sedan and Club Coupe—all at new low prices

2-DR. CLUB SEDAN

4-DR. SEDAN

HORNET *has* 160 HP

(170 HP with "Twin H" Power)

INTERIOR of HOLLYWOOD (CAR ILLUS. NEXT PAGE)

new CHROME PC. ON SIDE →

461

HUDSON
54
(CONT'D.)

HORNET
HOLLYWOOD
H/T

32,293 HUDSON CARS BLT. 1954

52,688 BLT. 1955 ("HUDSON"
NAME also USED on SOME Ramblers and
Metropolitans)

CUSTOM WASP
SEDAN

new ENGINE
CHOICES

V8
CHAMPIONSHIP
6

55

(TOTALLY
RESTYLED with
NASH BODY
DESIGN)

HOLLYWOOD H/T

PACKARD V8
USED

new
PEAKS OVER
HEADLIGHTS

22,588 BLT. 1956

HOLLYWOOD
H/T

BIG new
DIAMOND-SHAPED
GRILLE

56

SEDAN

DASH

462

HUDSON

DASH
with new Hydra-Matic

$2750.

new SIDE TRIM MOULDINGS

HORNET SUPER

Lower outside by 2 full inches

Hornet V-8

IS ONLY AVAIL. MODEL (SUPER OR CUSTOM)

327 CID
World's newest V-8 . . . 255 hp

57

new "V" EMBLEM ON GRILLE

ONLY 4,080 BLT. 1957

HORNET HOLLYWOOD H/T
(APPEARS LONGER IN
← PHOTO AT LEFT
THAN IN PHOTO ABOVE)

Slim outside for easy maneuvering

(DISCONTINUED JUNE 25, 1957)

. . . way up in power, way down in price!

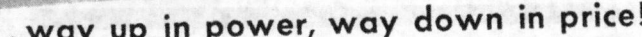

(1949 - 50)

IMP

INTERNATIONAL MOTOR PRODUCTS CO., GLENDALE, CALIF.

49-50

FIBERGLASS BODY
63" WB   APPR. 475 lbs.
1-CYL., 7-H.P. GLADDEN *engine*

SOME REPORTS LIST FINAL DATE AS 1955.

IMPERIAL

CUSTOM (C-64) 133½" WB

331.1 CID V8 (3¹³/₁₆ × 3⅝) 235 HP @ 4400 RPM

54

(EARLIER MODELS ILLUSTRATED WITH CHRYSLER.)

CROWN (C-66) 145½" WB

7.5 COMPR. (SINCE '51)

new 331 CID V8 (3.81 × 3.63) 250 HP @ 4600 RPM

55

IMPERIAL (C-69) 130" WB

CROWN IMPERIAL (C-70) 149½" WB (THROUGH '56)

(IMPERIAL CONSIDERED AN INDIVIDUAL MAKE, AS OF 1955.)

new 8.5 COMPRESSION

IMPERIAL (C-73) new 133" WB

354 CID; 280 HP @ 4600 RPM

56

CROWN IMPERIAL (C-70)

35 39

464

IMPERIAL

(IMI-1) $**5598.**

new 129" WB
(THROUGH '66)

new 392 CID (THROUGH '58)
325 HP @ 4600 RPM
new 9.25 COMPR.

57

new 129" WB
(THROUGH '66)

note DIFFERENCES IN
NUMBER OF HEADLIGHTS

CROWN
(IMI-2)

LE BARON
(IMI-4)
$**5743.**

LE BARON
SOUTHAMPTON

new 10.0 COMPRESSION
345 HP @ 4600 RPM

FENDER-GRILLE
DETAILS

LYI SERIES $**5969.**

58

IMPERIAL
NAME (NON-
LE BARONS)

465

IMPERIAL

CUSTOM SOUTHAMPTON (MYI-L)

LE BARON SOUTHAMPTON (MYI-H)

59

LE BARON

new CROWN (MYI-M)
413 CID, 10.1 COMPR. (THROUGH '65) 350 HP @ 4600 RPM (THROUGH 61) '65)

(PY2-M) CROWN

60

(PYI-L) CUSTOM SOUTHAMPTON

$**4933.**
TO
$**6318.**
PRICE RANGE

CUSTOM 4-DOOR SOUTHAMPTON

new 8.20 × 15 TIRES (THROUGH '64)

(PY3-H) LE BARON

466

IMPERIAL

CROWN
(RYI-M)

SOUTHAMPTON

new "FREE-STANDING HEADLIGHTS (THROUGH '63)

61

(RYI- SERIES)

America's Most Carefully Built Car

ORNAMENT at HOOD
FRONT ; *new*
SPLIT
GRILLE

IMPERIAL LE BARON 4-DR. SOUTHAMPTON (SYI-H)

(CUSTOM
IS SYI-L)

CROWN
(SYI-M)

62

RAISED
TAIL-LIGHTS

HP REDUCED TO
340 @ 4600 RPM
(THROUGH '65)

two-door Southampton

4-DR.
SOUTHAMPTON

IMPERIAL

CROWN
(TYI-M)

WHEEL COVER

HIGH, NARROW TAIL-LIGHTS

(FINAL YEAR FOR "CUSTOM" SERIES.)

DASH

(TYI-L) **CUSTOM**

63

(HAND-BUFFED ACRYLIC ENAMELS)

(TYI-H)

(TYI SERIES)

TL·1573

IMPERIAL LeBARON

The LeBaron cloisonné crest on the roof makes this the only car on which this federal jewelry excise tax is paid.

FREE-STANDING HEADLIGHTS FOR 3RD AND FINAL YEAR

IMPERIAL

CROWN COUPE (VYI-M)

(VYI-M)

Imperial Crown 4-Door Hardtop

LE BARON (VYI-H)

DASH

(VYI SERIES) **64**
$**5865**. TO $**6740**.
(TOTALLY RESTYLED; new DESIGN SOMEWHAT RESEMBLES LINCOLN CONTINENTAL.)

EAGLE CREST ON LE BARON VINYL TOP →

AUTO PILOT (left)
AM/FM RADIO (above)

HEADLIGHTS MOVED INTO new SPLIT GRILLE.

The Incomparable IMPERIAL

IMPERIAL

CROWN COUPE (AYI-M)

65

DASH

CHOICES
OF
UPH.
INCL.
REAL
LEATHER

LIGHT FLASHES IF FUEL, OIL,
TEMP. GAUGES NEED ATTENTION.

AIR COND. DUCTS (ON DASH)

HEADLIGHTS
PAIRED BEHIND
GLASS PANELS.

new GRILLE

(LE BARON
IS AYI-H)

INTERNATIONAL

(new "D" SERIES STARTS SPRING, 1937.)

INTERNATIONAL STATION WAGONS

Motor Truck Division
INTERNATIONAL HARVESTER COMPANY
180 North Michigan Avenue   Chicago 1, Illinois

39-40
"D" SERIES
6 CYL.

113" WB

INTERNATIONAL

See the New Green Diamond Engine

"K" LINE SERIES

41-46

47-49
"KB" SERIES

new OVERHEAD VALVE ENGINES (SILVER DIAMOND, SUPER BLUE DIAMOND, SUPER RED DIAMOND TYPES)

ALL-STEEL TRAVELALL WAGON

50-52

('52)

new GRILLE and 1-PIECE WINDSHIELD

471

INTERNATIONAL
53-55

⟶

56 "S" LINE

CONT'D. INTO EARLY '57; REPLACED BY "GOLDEN ANNIVERSARY" MODELS.

57-58

NEW **Golden Anniversary** MODEL

⟶

the TRAVELALL

59-60

GRILLE (TRUCK)

The Travelall

472

INTERNATIONAL 61-62

Scout

The Travelall

SCOUT is new for 1961.

63-64

(SCOUT ALSO CONTINUES)

THE TRAVELALL

65

THE Scout BY INTERNATIONAL

22,089 JETS BLT. 1953

53 $1858. and up

✈ **JET** BY HUDSON

6 CYLS.

(1953-1954)

104 HP

SUPER JET

DASH

105" WB

IN ALL THE WORLD NO OTHER CAR LIKE THIS!

JET

$1885.

54

SUPER-JET

$1933.

DASH

ITALIA

(ONLY 26 BUILT, ON SUPER-JET CHASSIS)

JET-LINER

$2057.

note THAT EACH SERIES IS QUICKLY IDENTIFIED IN '54 BY AMOUNT OF CHROME SIDE TRIM.

474

SEE ALSO: Hudson

KAISER

KAISER-FRAZER CORPORATION

• WILLOW RUN, MICHIGAN

(1946-1955)

EARLY MODEL, BUILT 1946

KAISER SPECIAL

with CORRUGATED BUMPER

SPECIAL = $1868.

CUSTOM = $2547.

AS IN FRAZER, 6-CYL., L-HEAD CONTINENTAL ENG. (ON ALL) 6.50 × 15" TIRES 123½" W.B.

EMBLEM

47

K-100 OR K-101 CUSTOM

KAISER 6

with PLAIN BUMPER

ALL OVER THE MAP — YOU'LL FIND EXPERT KAISER AND FRAZER SERVICE

K-F Distributors and parts warehouses   K-F Dealers, parts and service stations

KAISER

FACTORY-APPROVED PARTS AND

SERVICE

FRAZER

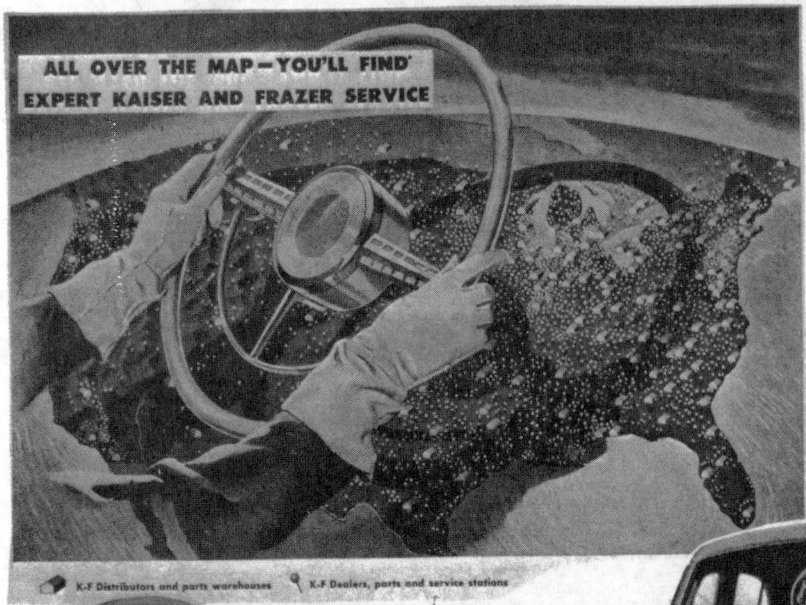

47½-48

K-481 OR K-482 CUSTOM

$1967.

$2557.

SEE ALSO: *FRAZER*

ILLUSTRATED AT CAPE COD, MASS.

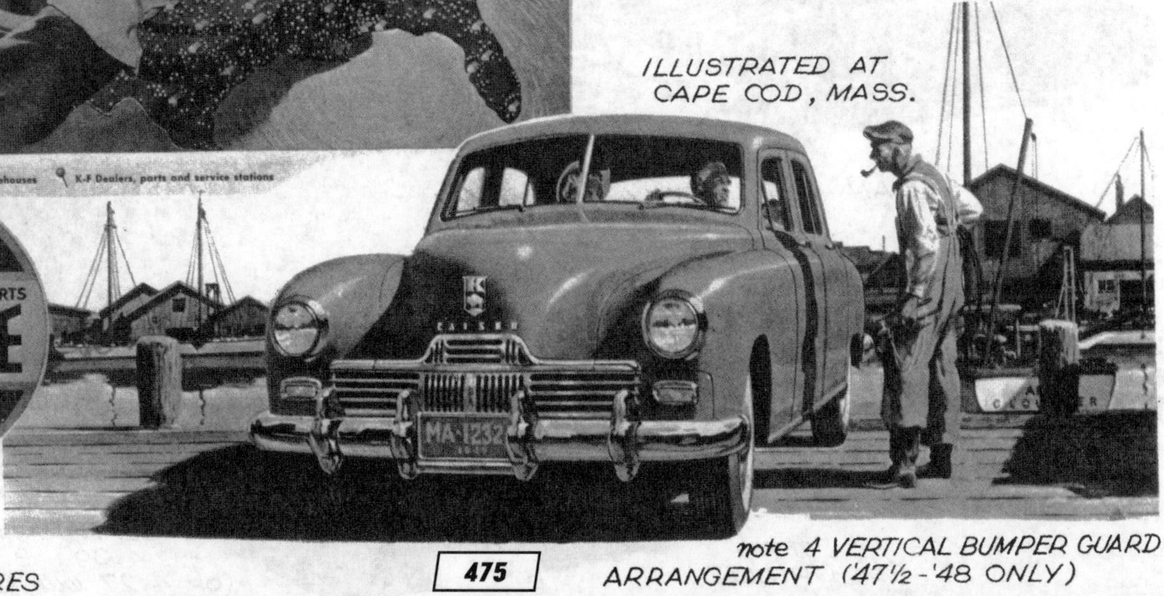

MA-1232

new 7.10 × 15" TIRES

note 4 VERTICAL BUMPER GUARD ARRANGEMENT ('47½-'48 ONLY)

TRAVELER
MODELS
FEATURE
FULL-OPENING
REAR
"HATCHBACK."

new
4-DOOR
CONVERTIBLE

49-50

new 112 HP

2-cars-in-one

$2088*

Kaiser Traveler

(new)

"TRAVELER"
MODEL NAME
IN SCRIPT

SEDAN

REAR 3/4 VIEW OF
VIRGINIAN

new
GRILLE

new
VIRGINIAN

4-DOOR
HARDTOP

GEAR RATIOS:
4.09; 3.91; 3.73
(OR 4.27 with OVERDRIVE)

Kaiser

SEE ALSO:
"HENRY J"

new 2-door sedan

new HORIZONTAL BLADE GRILLE →

K-511 = SPECIAL
K-512 = DE LUXE

1951

new HIGH, ARCHED TOP _with_ HUGE WINDOW AREA

(TOTALLY RESTYLED)

115 HP @ 3650 RPM

new 118½" WB

The newest car in America!

Anatomic Design*

↳ HOOD ORNAMENT ADDED (ON ALL)

new "GOLDEN DRAGON" (_with_ "ALLIGATOR" TYPE UPH., etc.)

HUBCAP VARIATION

Hydra-Matic AUTO. TRANS. OPTIONAL (THROUGH '55; also OPT. ON 1951 FRAZER)

Built to Better the Best on the Road!

MODELS
SPECIAL
VIRGINIAN
DE LUXE
MANHATTAN

'52 Kaiser Manhattan

new 1-PIECE WINDSHIELD

new BUMPER-BRIDGE PROTECTS 1952 GRILLE.

118 HP

PRICES
START AT
$1992.
(SPEC. COUPE)

Kaiser's Anatomic Engineering...

world's safest front seat!

1. Slant-back corner posts—narrower—no "blind spots"!
2. One-piece Safety-Mounted Windshield—designed to push outward upon severe impact!
3. Safety-Cushion Padded Instrument Panel!
4. Right hand emergency brake!
5. Recessed instruments—no protrusions!
6. Safety-level seat balances you more safely!
7. Extra front legroom—you sit in a safer position!

COMMENDED BY PARENTS

INTERIOR
DETAILS

New

478

K-521 = VIRGINIAN SPECIAL ; DE LUXE
K-522 = VIRGINIAN DE LUXE ; MANHATTAN

KAISER

PRICED FROM $**2313.**

new "V" FIGURE ADDED TO LOWER PART of FRONT and REAR EMBLEMS.

(new)

CAROLINA 2-DR. (K-538)

53

118 HP
118½" WB

REAR DETAILS

DE LUXE TRAVELER
(K-531 is DE LUXE SERIES)

MERGES with WILLYS-OVERLAND, TO FORM KAISER-WILLYS.

(LENGTH EXAGGERATED)

MANHATTAN (K-532)

(DRAGON is K-530)

KAISER-DARRIN DKF-161
WITH (fiberglass body)

OPTIONAL SUPERCHARGER GIVES 140 HP @ 3900 RPM (STD. HP 118)

'55

$**3668.**

new LIGHTS and CONCAVE GRILLE

W. 6 CYL.
161 CID
WILLYS F-head ENGINE

('54)

'55 SIMILAR, BUT with HIGHER CHROME FIN TIP on HOOD ORNAMENT (SEE ARROW)

54-55

1955 PRICES START AT $**2503.**

SIMILAR MODELS CONTINUED BY KAISER IN ARGENTINA (I.K.A.,) UNDER THE NAME of CARABELA. (1955 TO 1962.)

REAR ALSO RESTYLED

479

KING MIDGET

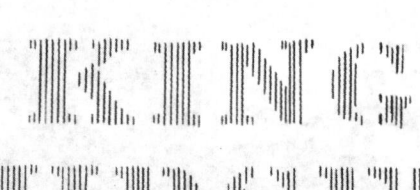

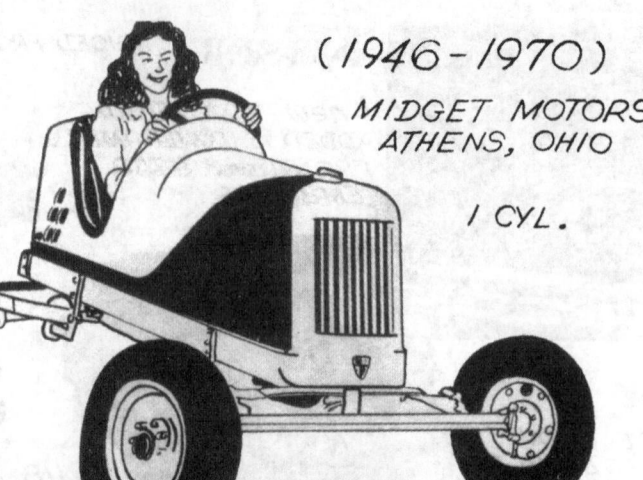

(1946-1970)

MIDGET MOTORS
ATHENS, OHIO

1 CYL.

46-50

('55)

EARLY

51-57

(TOTALLY RESTYLED
FOR 1951)

(RESTYLED EARLY '57)

LATER

57-70

30% HP INCREASE (to 12 HP) for 1966

KOHLER ENG.

DISCONTINUED
1970

$1095. IN '69

(1949-1950)

CHOICE OF V-8
ENGINES
100"
WB

KURTIS

KURTIS-KRAFT, INC.
LOS ANGELES and GLENDALE, CALIF.
(FRANK KURTIS, founder)

KURTIS
CONTINUED TO
BUILD OTHER TYPES OF
SPORTS and RACING CARS, AFTER
EARL MUNTZ BEGAN PRODUCING "JET"*

* BECOMES MUNTZ JET IN '51,
new 116" WB and ENLARGED to 4-PASS.

LANCER

[DODGE]

COMPACT

CHRYSLER CORPORATION

Lancer 170 Two-Door Sedan $2312.

WAGON

6 CYL. INCLINED O.H.V. ENGINE 170 CID with 101 HP @ 4400 RPM OR 148 HP @ 5200 RPM

LARGER 225 CID 6 ALSO AVAIL., with 145 HP @ 4000 RPM OR 196 HP @ 5200 RPM

61

RWI-L , RWI-H

INTERIOR

AIR COND., POWER STEERING and POWER BRAKES AVAIL.

1961

106½" WB

LANCERS BUILT 1961 and 1962 ONLY. UNITIZED BODY SIMILAR TO PLYMOUTH VALIANT.

H/T COMPACT DODGE LANCER

LANCER 170 2-DOOR SEDAN 6 $2256   (SLI-L)

ANCER 770 4-DOOR SEDAN 6 $2562.

LANCER 170 4-DOOR SEDAN 6

LANCER 170 6-PASSENGER WAGON 6   LANCER 770 2-DOOR SEDAN 6

new GT

62

SLI

770 (SLI-H)   1962   new GRILLE

(SLI-P)

DISCONTINUED AFTER 1962

481

LARK BY STUDEBAKER

COMPACT SERIES
(1959 - 1963)

2-DR. **PLAY WAGON**

59

6 - CYL. OR V8 ENGINES

note LOCATION of GRILLE MEDALLION ON 1959 MODEL

LUXURY Reclining seats that let all the way down are an optional touch of sublime comfort. Seats are pleated, appointments tasteful. Colors are harmoniously keyed to exteriors.

1959 LARK CARRIES "STUDEBAKER" NAME

60

GRILLE MEDALLION MOVED TO LOWER CENTER

31902

4-DR. WAGON and CONVERT. ARE new

"LARK" NAME AT REAR END OF FRONT FENDER

'LOVE THAT LARK BY STUDEBAKER"

LARK

4 HEADLIGHTS ON *new* 113" WB CRUISER

6 has 112 HP

180 TO 225 HP

61
GRILLE EMBLEM MOVED; *new* PARK. LIGHTS; "LARK" NAME MOVED TO FORWARD END OF FR. FENDERS

"You have to drive The Lark to believe it!"

6 has 112 HP

PACE CAR AT 1962 INDY 500 RACE

DAYTONA CVT.

"LARK" IN CAPITAL LETTERS

DETAILS OF *new* GRILLE

new ROUND TAIL-LIGHTS

62

VIEWS OF DASH

SUNROOF OPTIONAL ON *new* 225 HP **DAYTONA**

LARK NAME USED ONLY 1959-1963

SLIDING REAR ROOF SECTION ON *new* REGAL LARK WAGONAIRE

63

new GRILLE AGAIN

REGAL LARK

SEE ALSO
Studebaker

LINCOLN V·12

LINCOLN CARS INTRODUCED LATE '20 (FOR 1921.) PRODUCT OF FORD MOTOR COMPANY (LINCOLN MOTOR CAR DIV.) SINCE 1921.

$1360.

V-12 ENGINES (THROUGH '48)

40

new 292.1 CID (THROUGH '41)

-ZEPHYR

new 120 HP @ 3900 RPM

new 1-PIECE BACKLIGHT →

LINCOLN-ZEPHYR SERIES RUNS FROM 1936 THROUGH 1942 MODELS.

125" WB (SINCE '38)

$1400.

new SEALED BEAM HEADLIGHTS

LARGE, OLD-STYLE 150-HP "K" SERIES DISCONTINUED DURING 1940 SEASON, ALONG WITH ITS 414.1 CID ENGINE.

$2783.

CONTINENTAL COUPE

UNITIZED CONSTRUCTION OF BODY-AND-FRAME (IN CLOSED ZEPHYRS)

new CONTINENTAL

(FIRST FULL YEAR AVAIL. AS A REGULAR PRODUCTION MODEL)

CONTINENTAL has LOWER, BROADER BODY STYLING, AND SPARE TIRE IS MOUNTED OUTSIDE OF REAR DECK.

CONTINENTAL CABRIOLET $2840.

484

7.00 × 16 TIRES
(SINCE '36)

COUPE

CLUB COUPE

LINCOLN
41

SEDAN

4.44 G.R.
(SINCE '38)

new CHROMED BORDER AROUND GRILLE *and new* PARKING LTS. ATOP FRONT FENDERS

CONTINENTAL

$2700.

$2675.
(LIMO.)

CUSTOM
(SEDAN OR LIMO.)
SPECIAL 138" WB

new AUTOMATIC OVERDRIVE

BUTTON DOOR OPENERS *now* ON ALL

CONTINENTAL

new 305 CID
new 130 HP
@ 3800 RPM

new TALL HOOD MASCOT

42-45

new CHROME DECORATIONS AT EDGE OF REAR FENDERS (USED THROUGH '48)

new GRILLE

new 7.00 × 15 TIRES

"The Finest Lincolns Ever Built"

LINCOLN

CONTINENTAL (PACE CAR AT 1946 INDY 500 RACE)

HEAVIER NAMEPLATE ON SIDES OF 1946 HOOD

46

66-H

PRICE RANGE:

$2178.

TO

$4205.

new HEAVIER GRILLE has BOTH HORIZ. and VERT. PCS.

125" WB AS BEFORE, BUT "ZEPHYR" NAME NO LONGER USED.

RAISED HEXAGON AT CENTER OF 1946 HUB CAPS

new LARGER BUMPERS

CONVENTIONAL DOOR HANDLES RETURN, ON STD. TYPES

"Nothing could be finer"

"Lincoln" NAME IN CHROME ON SIDES OF HOOD and ON new PLAINER HUBCAPS

FINAL LINCOLNS with V-12 ENGINES (1948)

7-H   8-H

47-48

CONTINENTALS CONTINUE USE OF BUTTON DOOR OPENERS

CONTINENTAL

FINAL CONTINENTALS UNTIL 1956 MODEL

$4380. ('48)

($200. INCR. FROM '47)

486

new 2-PC. WINDSHIELD (ON STANDARD LINCOLNS ONLY) →

(EL) $2527.

$3948.

new COSMOPOLITAN (EH)

49 (TOTALLY RESTYLED)

BACK SEAT AREA (COSMO.)

The "custom touch" adds luxury to the 1949 Lincoln Cosmopolitan!

ALL WITH new V8 ENGINE (L-HEAD)

LINCOLN 1949

COSMOPOLITAN

new GRILLE IS LOWER

50

SOME MODELS PRICED ONLY $2 HIGHER THAN LAST YEAR'S

121" WB LINC. "LIDO" CPE. IS new

COSMO. "CAPRI" CPE. IS new

new FULL-LENGTH CHROME MOULDING ALONG BODY SIDES OF COSMOPOLITAN MODELS (AND CONT'D. ON STD. LINCOLNS) →

121" WB

final COSMOPOLITAN

125" WB

51

new GRILLE

COSMO. SPORT SEDAN $3182.

LINCOLN SPORT SEDAN

487

LINCOLN

new 123" WB

$3198.

H/T

CAPRI

COSMOPOLITAN

CVT. $3665.

52

COSMO. IS NOW LOWER-PRICED SERIES, BELOW CAPRI.

(TOTALLY RESTYLED)

"Lincoln" NAME IN SCRIPT LETTERING, ABOVE new GRILLE

$3226.

COSMOPOLITAN

COSMOPOLITAN LETTERING DETAILS

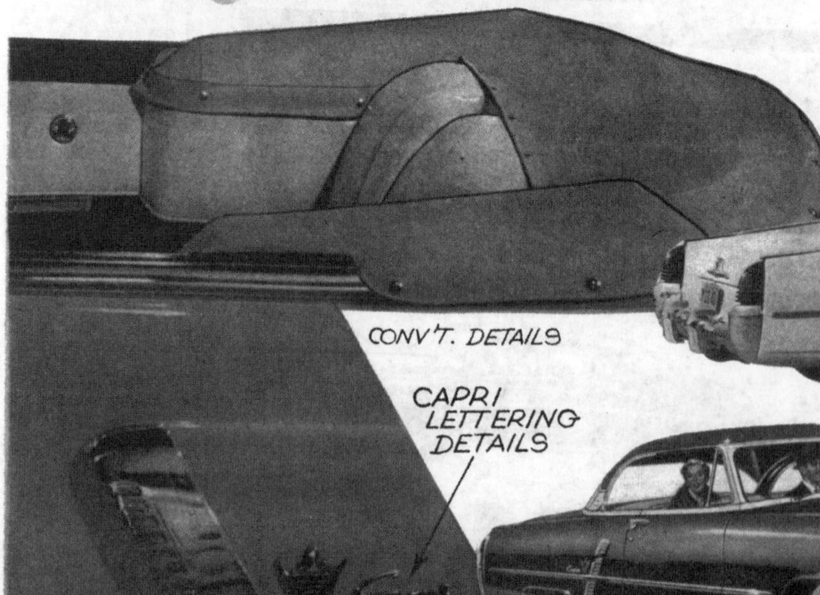

53

CONV'T. DETAILS

CAPRI LETTERING DETAILS

CAPRI $3549.

new BLOCK "LINCOLN" LETTERING, ABOVE GRILLE WHICH NOW CONTAINS STYLIZED "V" and SMALL EMBLEM

488

LINCOLN

new FENDER TRIM

54

new GRILLE

"LINCOLN" NAME NOW IN SCRIPT, and MOVED TO FRONT FENDER PANELS.

CONV'T.

CUSTOM IS LOWER-PRICED SERIES, PRICED from $3563.

CAPRI

225 HP

new GRILLE with ALL HORIZONTAL PIECES

55

new 126" WB, new 285 HP

56

new PREMIERE

new PANORAMIC WINDSHIELD

CAPRI H/T

FRENCHED HEADLIGHTS, and new PARK./DIRECTIONAL LIGHTS IN GRILLE

new CHROME SIDE SPEAR

ALSO, A REVIVED **Continental**

(SEE NEXT PAGE)

489

LINCOLN

Continental

Mark II

Continental Division · Ford Motor Company

$9538. ('56)

($157. MORE IN 1957.)

300 HP

126" WB

new
CONTINENTAL
STYLING
DIFFERS FROM
CAPRI, PREMIERE
MODELS (THROUGH '60)

56-57

NON-CONTINENTAL 1957 TYPES :   CAPRI PRICED FROM

$4649.

COUPE (H/T)

PREMIERE

CVT.

$5381.

LANDAU 4-DR. H/T

300 HP   **57**

490

CAPRI

new 131" WB (THROUGH '60)

PREMIERE

H/T $4803.

CONTINENTAL MARK III

Unmistakably . . . the finest in the fine car field

58 (TOTALLY RESTYLED)

new 375 HP

CONT'L. HAS *new* CRISS-CROSS GRILLE PATTERN

CONT'L. NO LONGER HAS "SPARE TIRE BULGE" IN REAR DECK

9.00 × 14 TIRES

$6283. (CVT.)

PREMIERE (CAPRI ALSO AVAIL.)

59 *new* GRILLE NOW ENCOMPASSES THE CANTED HEADLIGHTS

CUT TO 350 HP

CONTINENTAL MARK IV

9.50 × 14 TIRES

$7056.

491

LINCOLN

PREMIERE

2-DR. H/T

4-DR.

430 CID

HORSEPOWER CUT TO 315 @ 4100 RPM
(new CARBURETOR)
LEAF SPRINGS REPLACE
COILS AT REAR

new HOODED INSTRUMENTS

TYPICAL
UPHOLSTERY
(LEATHER
and
FABRICS)

60

DASH and
INSIDE
DOOR
HANDLE

CONTINENTAL MARK V

LANDAU
4-DR. H/T

2-DR. H/T

$5253. TO $10,230.
PRICE RANGE

FINAL YEAR FOR 2-DR.
CONVERTIBLE

TOWN CAR

LIMOUSINE

$9208.

9.50 × 14 TIRES

LINCOLN CONTINENTAL

61
(TOTALLY RESTYLED)

new DASH

$ 6067.

REDUCTION OF WHEELBASE TO 123" (THROUGH '63) and CUT IN H.P. TO 300 @ 4100 RPM (THROUGH '62)

DECK LID OPENS WHEN TOP MOVES

REAR

$ 6713.

new Four-Door Convertible

ALL MODELS NOW KNOWN AS *Lincoln Continental*

new GRILLE and REAR END OF HARMONIZING DESIGN

62

493

LINCOLN (CONTINENTAL)

63

DETAIL OF CENTER-OPENING DOORS

4-DR. CONV'T. with TOP UP

new 320 HP (THROUGH '65)

LIMOUSINE

The luggage compartment is larger.

greater

64

(SLIGHTLY ENLARGED)
new 126" WB (THROUGH '69)

3" LONGER THAN BEFORE

interior spaciousness

LIMO. ROOFLINE

DASH

CONV. (CONTINUES THROUGH '67)

$6938.

65

320 HP

430 CID

new GRILLE with HORIZONTAL MOTIF

494

⬡ LINCOLN Continental
America's most distinguished motorcar.

Marlin BY RAMBLER – Newest of the Sensible Spectaculars (1965-1967)
(ANNOUNCED 2-65)

116" WB
232 CID 6 (155 HP)
  OR
287 CID V8 (198 HP)
  OR
327 CID V8
270 HP @ 4700 RPM

65

POWER DISC BRAKES STANDARD

10,327 '65 MARLINS BLT.

WIRE WHEEL DETAIL

EASILY IDENTIFIED BY UNIQUE FASTBACK "KNIFE-EDGE" REAR STYLING

7.35 OR 7.75 × 14 TIRES

$3143. f.o.b. and up

Marlin GRILLE and SEATS (RECLINING)

Introducing excitement!
The swinging new man-size sports-fastback – MARLIN!

INTERIOR, THROUGH LONG SIDE WINDOW AREA

SEE ALSO:
495 RAMBLER

MERCURY DIVISION OF FORD MOTOR COMPANY

MERCURY 8

SEDAN-COUPE

STARTS with 1939 MODEL

116" WB (SINCE '39)

CVT. SEDAN ('40 ONLY)

40

DASH is BLUE and SILVER

L-HEAD V8 ENGINE

OVERDRIVE AVAIL.

$930.

new SEALED BEAM HEADLIGHTS

new VENT WINGS

CONTROLLED ALL-WEATHER VENTILATION

new 118" WB (THROUGH '51)

—THE AVIATION IDEA IN AN AUTOMOBILE

new GRILLE

RESTYLED

41

ENGINE

SPARE TIRE and WHEEL STOWED VERTICALLY AGAINST WALL

new 1-PC. BACKLIGHT

CONT'D. NEXT PAGE

MERCURY

41 (CONT'D.)

$920.

MORE ROOM—Wherever extra size contributes to comfort, Mercury is big. More head, leg and seat room enables passengers to relax and rest in perfect comfort as they ride.

SMART NEW STATION WAGON is a brand-new Mercury body type this year. Front end and driver's compartment follow the sedan styling. Body is of selected maple and birch. Choice of tan, blue or red hand-buffed leather upholstery. Large luggage capacity. White sidewall tires extra.

THE BIG CAR THAT STANDS ALONE IN ECONOMY

More Power Per Pound

new 6.50 × 15 TIRES

new 2-TIER GRILLE

42-45

NEW Liquamatic Drive (OPT.)

DOUBLE CHROME BANDS on FENDERS

$2078.

WOODEN BODY PANELS ON new SPORTSMAN

new GRILLE

new INTERIORS

46

$1412.

new GRILLE

CONT'D NEXT PAGE

MERCURY 46
(CONT'D.)

$1390.
"COUPE-
SEDAN"

"STEP OUT WITH MERCURY"

ALL-
STEEL
CONVERTIBLE
$1604.

INTERIORS ('47)

WAGON $1676.

BORDER OF
GRILLE IS NOW
CHROME-
PLATED

47-48

More OF EVERYTHING YOU WANT

WITH

Mercury

498

MERCURY

new 2-DR. WAGON

49

TOTALLY RESTYLED

110 HP

1949

Make your next car *Mercury*

FROM $*1997*.

new EMBLEMS AT EITHER END

"Better than ever"

50

PACE CAR AT 1950 INDY 500 RACE

LARGE PARK. LIGHTS AT ENDS OF GRILLE

1950

Nothing like it on the *Road!*

new GRILLE and new EMBLEMS

1951

51

new OPTIONAL MERC-O-MATIC

AUTO. TRANS. | 499 | LARGER BACKLIGHT

new VERT. TAIL-LIGHTS

for "the buy of your life!"

MERCURY
Merc-O-Matic Drive...or B-W Overdrive

CUSTOM

MONTEREY · hardtop · H/T

1952

new DASH

NEW 125 H.P. HIGH-COMPRESSION V-8

52 (TOTALLY RESTYLED)

FROM $1987.

new HOOD SCOOP

new BUMPER-GRILLE

new SHORTER 115" WB

new DECK-LID MEDALLION

POWER STEERING

DASH

POWER BRAKES

new HORIZ. REAR FENDER TRIM

53

3 new POWER OPTION CHOICES

new GRILLE, 118" WB

4-WAY POWER SEAT

(CONT'D.)

MERCURY $2057.

CUSTOM
(LOWER-PRICED than Monterey SER.)

53
(CONT'D.)

GET THE FACTS—
AND YOU'LL GO FOR
THE NEW 1953
MERCURY

CUSTOM

DASH

SEDANS

MONTEREY

new
**161-horsepower
engine**

"SUN VALLEY"
(new)

$2581. →

THE CAR THAT MAKES ANY DRIVING EASY

54

new
GRILLE

CUSTOM

new
REAR
STYLING →

MONTEREY

new
PANORAMIC
WINDSHIELD

new SIDE TRIM

new
188
HP

55 FROM
$2218.

new
GRILLE
and HOODED
HEADLIGHTS

new
119" WB

501

new
MONTCLAIR

SUN
VALLEY

MERCURY

MEDALIST (new)

For 1956 — the big move is to THE BIG MERCURY

MONTEREY

56

CUSTOM

VOYAGER
(IN Montclair SERIES)

"PHAETON" 4-DR. HARDTOP

$2507.

REAR 3/4 DETAIL

MONTCLAIR

new 210 HP

new GRILLE (CLOSE-UP)

502

interior

MERCURY

BIG M for '57

QUADRI-BEAM HEADLAMPS (LATER MODELS)

HIGH BEAM
LOW OR HIGH BEAM

(EARLY) MONTCLAIR

MONTEREY

PACE CAR AT 1957 INDY 500 RACE

with DREAM-CAR DESIGN

(LATER)

57 (TOTALLY RESTYLED)

new 122" WB 255 HP

FRONT ROOF VENTS ON TURNPIKE CR. (290 HP)

CONVENTIONAL STATION WAGON

NEW BIG M STATION WAGON

MERCURY ELIMINATES THE LIFT GATE, LOWERS THE TAIL GATE

new TURNPIKE CRUISER

THERE'S ONLY ONE SIDE PILLAR IN THE NEW MERCURY

COMMUTER

VOYAGER

2 and 4-DR. WAGONS

THE OPEN-AIR FEELING OF A HARDTOP

ONLY 2 HEADLIGHTS ON EARLY MODELS

COLONY PARK

$3677.

6 wagons

BIG new WEDGE TAIL-LIGHTS

CENTER OF BACKLIGHT OPENS, ON TURNPIKE CR.

5-7. NEW MONITOR CONTROL PANEL, TACHOMETER, AVERAGE SPEED COMPUTER

503

MERCURY

PRICED FROM $2547.

THE ALL-NEW PARK LANE

58

WHEEL COVER

122" WB (126" ON Park Lane)

20ᵗʰ ANNIVERSARY
'59 MERCURY

"BUILT TO LEAD
— BUILT TO LAST"

59

ENGINE

new GRILLE VARIES IN APPEARANCE, DEPENDING ON ANGLE FROM WHICH IT IS VIEWED (SEE ALSO NEXT PG.)

new ENLARGED WINDSHIELD AREA

504

(CONT'D.)

MERCURY

MONTEREY SEDAN

MONTCLAIR

59
(CONT'D.)

1959

FANCIER REAR STYLING
ON MONTCLAIR

PARK LANE
4-DR. H/T
CRUISER
(ABOVE)
has SPECIAL
REAR SIDE
TRIM

VOYAGER

COMMUTER

WHEEL
COVER

126" WB
(128"
ON
Park Lane)

COLONY PARK
$3932.
(6-PASS.)

SLIP THE THIRD SEAT UNDER THE FLOOR

$3330. (9-PASS.)

WAGON DETAILS

COMMUTER

MERCURY

FROM $2631.

2-DR. H/T (MONTEREY)

MONTCLAIR

MONTEREY

(RESTYLED) 60

4-DR H/T (MONTEREY)

9-PASS. COMMUTER $3240.

9-PASS. COLONY PARK $3950.

$3858.

PARK LANE 4-DR. H/T

$4018

PARK LANE CVT.

CHROME PCS. IDENTIFY MODEL SERIES

126" WB ON ALL MERCURYS (1960 ONLY)

MERCURY

the better low-price cars

METEOR 600

new series
V8 or new 6

METEOR 800

MODEL NAME at FRONT END of DOOR →

Meteor 800

61

MONTEREY

MONTEREY

COMMUTER

COLONY PARK

METEOR

62

S33 DASH

MONTEREY CUSTOM

METEOR

new GRILLES

S-33 WHEEL COVER

MONTEREY

new TAIL-LIGHTS AT TOP OF FENDERS

MERCURY

METEOR

FINAL METEOR. 6-CYL. MERC. ENG. ONLY IN COMET AFTER '63.

METEOR S-33

MONTEREY

new OPENING "BREEZEWAY" BACKLIGHT

H/T

4-DR H/T

CONSOLE (S-55)

63

S-55 and INTERIOR

MONTRY. CUSTOM MARAUDER ('63½)

METEOR CUSTOM

COUNTRY CRUISER

COLONY PARK and INTERIOR

MERCURY

V8s ONLY

No finer car in the medium-price field

Commuter station wagon

2-DR. H/T

COLONY PARK

MONTEREY

FROM **$3202.**

120" WB (ALL MOD.)

250 HP V8

64

4-DR. MARAUDER H/T
$3567.

↗ MONTCLAIR ↘

2-DR. H/T (BREEZEWAY ROOFLINE)

CLOSE-UP OF DOOR (PARK LANE) SHOWN ABOVE

$3799.
4-DR. MARAUDER H/T

PARK LANE (300 HP)
INTERIOR →

2-DR. H/T (BREEZEWAY ROOFLINE)

DASH

509

MERCURY

NOW IN THE LINCOLN CONTINENTAL TRADITION

TOTALLY RESTYLED

65

AMERICAN MOTORS IMPORTED

Metropolitan

(1954-1961)

"HOOD SCOOP"

ASSEMBLED IN ENGLAND BY AUSTIN, FOR U.S. MARKET

4 CYL., O.H.V. AUSTIN ENGINE

$1445. TO $1749.

(DURING '54 TO '61)

54-55

42 HP

TYPE CONT. TO EARLY 1956

OUTSIDE TRUNK DOOR ADDED DURING 1959 MODEL YEAR

56-61

new GRILLE and SIDE TRIM

CONVERTIBLE

52 HP

COUPE

AT YOUR **RAMBLER-METROPOLITAN** DEALER

510

MUSTANG

ROY C. McCARTHY,
MUSTANG ENGINEERING CO.,
SEATTLE AND RENTON, WASH.

(1947-1949)

4- CYL. HERCULES ENGINE
59 H.P.   65 M.P.H.
NO DEALERSHIPS ; _FACTORY ORDERS_ ONLY

49

ALUMINUM BODY
102" W.B.
5.50 × 15" TIRES

MUSTANG *Ford*

(STARTS APRIL, 1964)

65

6 OR V8
(170 CID)   (260 CID)

STD. TYPE w/o
GRILLE LIGHTS ➔

standard-equipment

(bucket seats, full carpeting, vinyl interior,
floor-mounted transmission)

Surprisingly spacious trunk

REAR

CVT. IS PACE CAR AT
1964 INDY 500
RACE.

WHEEL
COVER

STANDARD DASH (ABOVE)

$2368 *f.o.b.
Detroit

AND UP

ALL CIRCULAR GAUGES ON
DE LUXE DASH
(BELOW)

New luxury instrument panel

options _INCLUDE_ :

a 289 cu. in. V-8. Four-on-the-floor. Tachometer and clock
combo. Special handling package. Front disc brakes—

STANDARD
SIDE
EMBLEM
➔

NOTE
MESH
GRILLE
ON '65.

MUSTANG

Unique Ford GT stripe —
badge of America's greatest
total performance cars!

New integral arm rests — courtesy lights

INTERIOR VIEWS (ABOVE)

"2 + 2"
FASTBACK

NOTCHBACK HARDTOP

Mustang
GT

CONVERTIBLE

65
(CONT'D.)

EXTRA (FOG)
LIGHTS IN
GT GRILLE

IDENTIFYING
RACING STRIPES
ON GT →

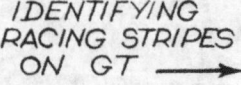

MUSTANG

(VINYL-COVERED ROOF AVAIL.)

NASH MOTORS—Division of Nash-Kelvinator Corporation, Detroit

Again... *IT'S THAT NEW* **NASH**

(1917 — 1957)

6 CYL. OR STRAIGHT-8

SEDAN

(ALSO BLT. LAFAYETTE LOWER-PRICED MODELS, 1934-1940)

$**795.** and up

1940 IS FINAL YEAR FOR 2-PIECE BACKLIGHT IN CLOSED NASH CARS

(THE FINAL) LAFAYETTE 6

117" WB
4.1 GR

OVERDRIVE AVAIL.

40

COACH

4013

AMBASSADOR 6 AVAIL. (121" WB)

"BUSTLE-BACK" SEDAN, SHOWING BACK SEAT BED AVAILABLE →

AMBASSADOR 8
125" WB

COUPE
4085

4081
CABRIOLET

"*Weather Eye*"
HEATER-COOLER AVAIL.
(SINCE '38)

63, 617 BLT. 1940

DASH

"SPECIAL" ROADSTER

513

NASH

600

80, 408
BLT. 1941

Now—coil springs on rear wheels, too!

4149
$745 BUYS

Nash
IN RED LETTERING
ON BUMPER and
HUBCAPS

"Go NASH
AND SAVE MONEY EVERY MILE"

41

AS BEFORE, FIRST 2
DIGITS IN MODEL NO.
SIGNIFY THE YEAR
(SINCE '35)
AMBASSADOR

4183 (8)

CLUB
COUPE
KNOWN AS
"BROUGHAM"

REAR

SINCE '41 "600s,"
UNITIZED
BODY-AND FRAME
CONSTRUCTION

31,700
BLT.

4240

42-
45

FINAL
STRAIGHT
8
NASH
MODELS

NASH

NOW 6-CYL. ONLY
(THROUGH '54)

600 DLX.

112" WB
L-HEAD
ENG.

4640

121" WB
112 HP OHV

4663

new MEDALLION and PK. LITES

new GRILLE

46

AMBASSADOR

PROD.
6148 (LATER '45)
98,769 (DURING '46)

MODEL 4664 AMB.
SUBURBAN SEDAN with
WOODEN PANELING

AMBASS. SEDAN
IS PACE CAR
AT 1947
INDY 500
RACE

4740 (600)

4760 (AMB.)

EL SEGUNDO, CALIF. and TORONTO, ONT. BRANCH PLANTS
PURCHASED THE PRECEDING YR.
MEXICO CITY
PLANT OPENS
6-18-47.

4748 (fastback)
4740 (bustle-back)

"You'll be Ahead with Nash"

47

new CHROMED EXTENSIONS AT EITHER SIDE
OF UPPER GRILLE PORTION

PROD.:
113,315

600

4842

COUPE

48

EXCEPT ON "600,"
new HIGHER BELT LINE
CHROME FOR 1948

SUPER

"FASTBACK"
SEDAN

4868

new CVT. (1,000 BLT.)
AMBASSADOR

4871

"BUSTLE BACK" SEDAN

4840

DASH
(MORE
DETAILS
NEXT
PAGE

MORE '48 DETAILS ON NEXT PAGE

4863
OR 4843

515

NASH

48 (CONT'D.)

118,621 BLT.

FULL VIEW OF INTERIOR

You'll be Ahead with **Nash**

Great Cars Since 1902

"SUPER" and "CUSTOM" are NEW

AMB.
SUPER (MODEL NAME ON SIDE OF HOOD.)

7.10 x 15

4860

EL SEGUNDO, CALIF. PLANT OPENS 10-48

600 82 HP

4949

has "600" IN CHROME, ON FRONT FENDER PANEL.

49

TOTALLY RESTYLED new *Airflyte*

PHANTOM VIEW

MODELS (NO CVTS.)

142,592 BLT.

ONE SINGLE WELDED UNIT!

with Girder-built Unitized Body and Frame
...Airliner-styled interiors...
Cockpit Control...Uniscope...
Matched Coil Springs on all
Four Wheels...Twin Beds...
Uniflo-Jet Carb

AMBASSADOR 112 HP

7.10 x 15

516

NASH
WITH *HYDRA-MATIC DRIVE*

BACKLIGHTS ENLARGED

191,865 BLT.

The Ambassador Custom 115 HP

50

... NEW SUPER-POWER ENGINES!

The Statesman 85 HP

(REPLACES 600)

new SLIDING GLOVE DRAWER THICKER BUMPER GUARDS

new **Rambler** *also avail.* AT NASH DEALERS

Airflytes for 1951

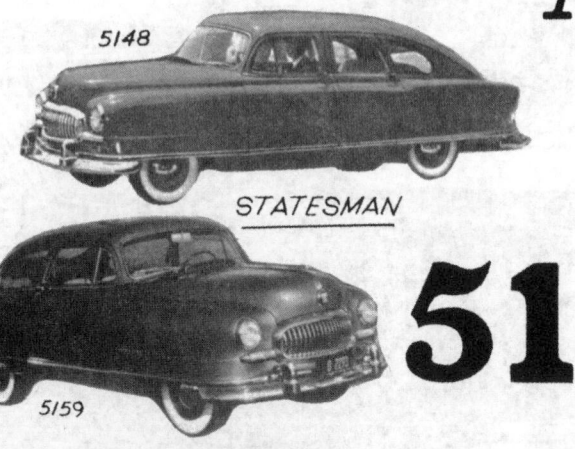

5148

STATESMAN

5159

New sky-flow fenders

TRUNK DETAILS

51

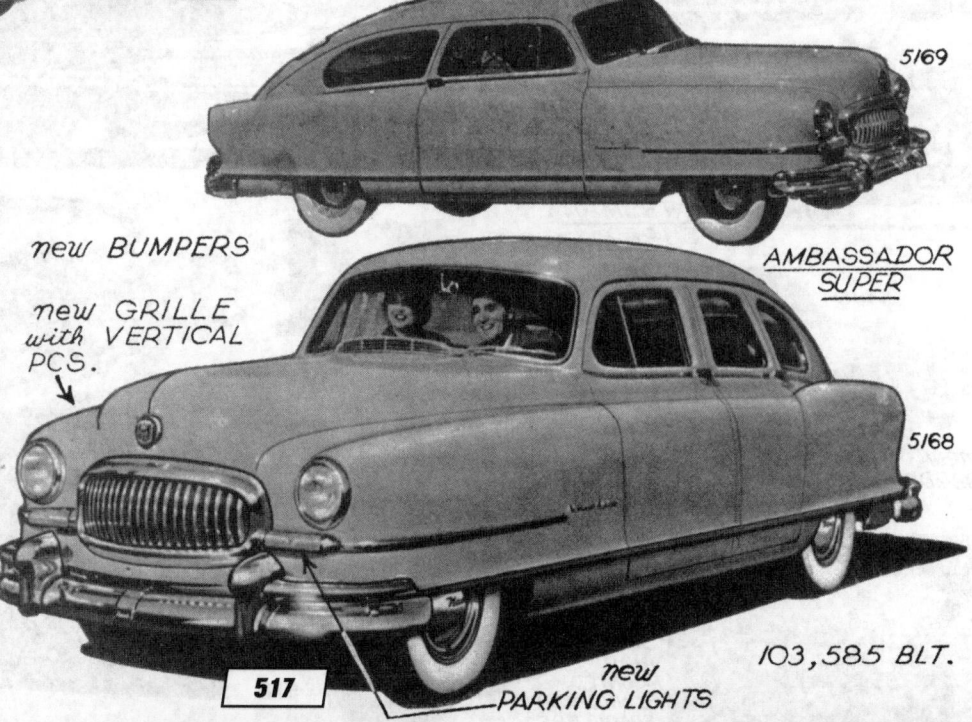

5169

new BUMPERS

new GRILLE with VERTICAL PCS.

AMBASSADOR SUPER

5168

new PARKING LIGHTS

103,585 BLT.

RECLINING SEATS
(with BODY CENTERPOST NOT SHOWN, IN ORDER THAT SEAT DETAIL CAN BE SEEN.)

NASH

Golden Airflytes 50TH ANNIVERSARY (OF RAMBLERS)

Pinin Farina, STYLIST

(TOTALLY RESTYLED FOR 1952)

('52)

5255

new 88 HP

new 114¼" WB
STATESMAN CUSTOM

AMBASSADOR CUSTOM
← 120 HP

5275

new 121¼" WB

5355

52-53

152,141 BLT.*   153,753 BLT.*   *= INCL. RMB.

('53)
100 HP

'53 with new STRIPS OF CHROME ON VENT

DASH ('53)

('53)
AMBASSADOR
COUNTRY CLUB
5377

Ambassador Country Club

110 HP
STATESMAN
SUPER

67,192 BLT.

54

130 HP
AMBASSADOR
SUPER
5465

5446

new BORDERS AROUND MODIFIED GRILLE

5475

AMERICAN MOTORS CORP. FORMED BY MAY 1, 1954 NASH-HUDSON MERGER.

ST. OR AM. CUST. MODELS have REAR-MOUNTED "CONTINENTAL" SPARE TIRE.

AMBASSADOR
CUSTOM

STATESMAN SUPER

5545-1

CNTRY. CLUB 5547-2

'55 NASH

5585-1

(RESTYLED)
Scena-Ramic WINDSH.

AMBASSADOR SUPER

new "INBOARD" HEADLIGHTS

5585-2

57,619 BLT.

AMB. CUSTOM
208-HP V8
PACKARD ENG. OPTIONAL

STATESMAN SUPER

5645-1

Ambassador Special

5665-1 (6)

AMBASSADOR SUPER 6

130 HP

56

AMBASSADOR CUSTOM V8

5657-1

5655-2

Torque-Flo V-8

THE NEW
Ambassador Special

WITH new A.M.C. - BUILT V8
190 HP
250 CID

(INTRO. 4-56)

519

NASH

AMBASSADOR COUNTRY CLUB

PHOTOGRAPHED IN DISNEYLAND

56
(CONT'D.)

DELUXE, SUPER, or CUSTOM 6
REPLACE
STATESMAN 6
MODELS

AMBASSADOR SUPER

V·8

5785-1

new GRILLE and SIDE TRIM

255 HP

57

THE
FINAL
NASH

5787-2

AMBASSADOR CUSTOM

121½"
WB

5785-2

• New wider front tread for surer footing
• New sharper, easier turning
• Airliner Reclining Seats
• All-Season Air Conditioning
• Choice of Hydramatic, Overdrive or Standard
• Twin Travel Beds

new
STACKED HEADLIGHTS

SUPERSEDED BY
RAMBLER

JOIN THE SWING TO THE TRAVEL KING
'57 *Nash*
World's Finest Travel Car

OLDS **F-85**→
BY
OLDSMOBILE
(COMPACT)

(STARTS 1961)

155 STD. HP

ENTIRE REAR DOOR
RAISES, ON WAGON

61

F-85 Cutlass

Above: F-85 Cutlass Sports Coupe. Also available: new F-85 Club Coupe . . .

112"
WB
6.50
× 13
TIRES
3.36
GEAR
RATIO

new
ROCKETTE **185** Engine
(ALUMINUM BLOCK)
185 HP
V8

10.25
COMPR.
4 BBL.
CARB.

OLDSMOBILE

F-85
SEDAN

$2713.

F-85-61

" ...it's every inch an
OLDSMOBILE "

OLDS F-85 →

F-85 COUPE

CUTLASS COUPE

CUTLASS

$2949.
(SAME PRICE AS
LAST YEAR)

62

F-85 COUPE

CUTLASS   H/T

CVT.

WAGON

JETFIRE H/T
(note HEAVIER SIDE TRIM)

new SHAPE OF
TAIL-LIGHT

TO 195 HP with
ALUMINUM V8

DELUXE
SEDAN

63

new GRILLE with
"OLDSMOBILE" NAME
ACROSS CENTER STRIP

OLDS F-85 →

522

There's 'Something Extra' about owning an OLDSMOBILE!

WAGON (DLX.)

OLDS F-85

CUTLASS

new 230 HP

F-85 V-6 SPORTS COUPE

VISTA-CRS. →

WHERE THE ACTION IS!

F-85-64

64 V8 OR V6

new VISTA-CRUISER WAGON *has* ROOF WINDOWS

WIRE WH. COVERS AVAIL.

OLDSMOBILE

OLDSMOBILE

CVT.

new ECON-O-WAY V-6

SEDAN PROFILE

an all-new transmission

JETAWAY DRIVE

JETFIRE ROCKET V-8

Vista-Cruiser

CUTLASS

65

4-4-2 *has* 400 CID V8

442

VISTA-CRUISER *has* FOLDING, FORWARD-FACING 3RD SEAT
Roomy cargo area—holds over 100 cubic feet!

1965

The Rocket Action Car!

CUTLASS

523

Product of GENERAL MOTORS **OLDSMOBILE** (SINCE 1897)

OLDS PRICES START AT **$807** up, FOR "60" BUSINESS COUPE

GM GENERAL MOTORS

(PAINTED HORIZ. PCS. IN GRILLE OF "60")

6 OR 8-CYL. L-HEAD ENGINES

40

new SEALED-BEAM HEADLAMPS

116" WB

6.00 × 16

"*Bigger and Better in Everything!*"

WITH *Hydra-Matic Drive*

AUTOMATIC TRANSMISSION (OPT.)

NO GEARS TO SHIFT!

124" WB

7.00 × 16

CUSTOM 8 CRUISER (90)

70

120" WB

229.7 CID 6 (SINCE '37) 95 HP @ 3400 RPM OR 257.1 CID 8 (SINCE '37) 110 HP @ 3600 RPM

"*BEST LOOKING CAR ON THE ROAD!*"

THE CAR *Ahead!*

STYLED TO LEAD BUILT TO LAST

new 238.1 CID 6 (100 HP @ 3400)

41

new 119" OR 125" WB

SPECIAL 60

new "SPECIAL 60" TOWN SEDAN (66 SER.)

6.00 × 16

$852., and up, f.o.b.

524

(CONT'D.)

41
(CONT'D.)

HYDRA-MATIC

ABOVE PLATE IDENTIFIES CARS *with* AUTO. TRANS.

STRAIGHT-8 ENGINE SPECS. AS IN '40.

PROVED AND IMPROVED FOR "42"!

HYDRA-MATIC DRIVE*

THE GENERAL MOTORS CONTRIBUTION TO SIMPLER, SAFER, MORE EFFICIENT DRIVING!

NO GEARS TO SHIFT! NO CLUTCH TO PRESS!

119", 125", OR 127" WB

"B-44" SERIES 42

(CONT'D.)

NEW 4U.4.42

525

OLDSMOBILE

SPECIAL 66

$960., f.o.b.

42 (CONT'D.)

ENGINE SPECS. AS BEFORE

INTERIOR

OLDSMOBILE IS TURNING OUT CANNON FOR FIGHTING PLANES - SHELL FOR THE ARTILLERY

DYNAMIC CRUISER

"YOU CAN ALWAYS COUNT ON OLDSMOBILE —

— IT'S QUALITY-BUILT TO LAST!"

CHROME TRIM ELIMINATED

WARTIME "BLACKOUT" MODEL →

42 ½ - 45

OLDSMOBILE

76

A NEW AND FINER

GM GENERAL MOTORS **HYDRA-MATIC DRIVE**

INTERIOR

66

98

125" WB

CLUB SEDAN   119" WB

46

$1290. and up, f.o.b. (66 CL. CPE.) ($95. MORE IN '47)

66

ENGINE SPECS. (6 and 8) AS SINCE '41

$2305. f.o.b.

66

STATION WAGON

98 CUSTOM CRUISER CVT. **$2160.**, f.o.b.

119", 125" OR 127" WB (THROUGH '48)

47

LONGER RED SECTION AROUND "OLDSMOBILE" NAME IN FRONT FENDER CHROME STRIP

It's *Smart* to own an Olds

CENTER SECTION OF BUMPER NO LONGER GROOVED AT TOP

527

OLDSMOBILE

76 (6-CYL.)

$1385. and up, f.o.b. (66 CL. CPE. or 2-DR.)

119" OR 125" WB ON OLD-STYLED 6 and 8

48

RETAINS 1947-STYLE BODY, BUT has "OLDSMOBILE" NAME and new CIRCLE EMBLEM ABOVE GRILLE, and NEW-STYLE CHROME SIDE TRIM.

new FUTURAMIC

"98" MODELS TOTALLY RESTYLED

127" WB

98 (OLDSMOBILE'S FINAL CARS with STRAIGHT-8 ENGINE)

"FUTURAMIC" NAME BEGINS WITH the 8-CYL. RESTYLED 1948 OLDSMOBILES, AND IS USED FOR A FEW YEARS AFTERWARDS.

$1740., f.o.b. 2-DR. CLUB SEDAN

98 CONVERTIBLE has new HYDRAULICALLY OPERATED POWER SIDE WINDOWS and AUTOMATIC FRONT SEAT ADJUSTER

$2160., f.o.b.

FUTURAMIC

528

OLDSMOBILE

$1732., and up, f.o.b.
(76 CL. CP.)

New

NEW *ROCKET* ENGINE!
(O.H.V V8)

135 HP
(TO '52)

76

105 HP
119½" WB
6

98
(125" WB)

49

new AIR SCOOPS
BELOW HEADLIGHTS

new "HOLIDAY" H/T $2973. f.o.b.,

You've got to <u>drive</u> it to believe it!

"88" DESIGNATION USUALLY
ON REAR
FENDER

UNLIKE "98," THE new '49½ "88" has
CURVED
LOWER
EDGES
OF
WINDSHIELD.

NEW "**88**" (49½.
INTRO.
AFTER SEASON
UNDER WAY)

119½" WB

LOWEST-PRICED CAR
WITH "ROCKET" ENGINE

$2375.,
f.o.b.
88 DLX. SEDAN

"88"

THIS
IDENTIFIES
V8 MODELS

CVT. IS PACE CAR AT
1949 INDY 500 RACE

"The New Thrill"

OLDSMOBILE ROCKETS AHEAD

FINAL 6-CYL. "76" has NO CHROME STRIP on FRONT FENDER

$1761., and up, f.o.b. (76 2-DR.)

"88"

OLDSMOBILE

50

88

88 CVT.

$2294., f.o.b.

98

Make a Date with a "Rocket 8"!

8.20 x 15 TIRES on 98 CVT.

V8s ONLY

(119½" WB ON 88 ONLY)

NEW! SUPER "88"

51

135 HP

7.60 x 15 TIRES (88, SU-88)

$1970., and up, f.o.b. (88 2-DR.)

530

(CONT'D.)

CVT. **$2673.**, f.o.b.

SUPER **"88"** 120" WB

2-DR. **$2265.**, f.o.b.

51 (CONT'D.)

"ROCKET" **98** 122" WB

New Room Inside!

DLX. HOLIDAY H/T **$2882.**, f.o.b.

$2610., f.o.b.

88

$2462., f.o.b.
SU-88
SEDAN

$2262., f.o.b. 2-DR.
120" WB

The "Rocket" Oldsmobile's
New Power Steering* makes
driving so easy you can...

Park with just 1 finger!

HORIZ.
GROOVES
ON SU-88 FENDER PAD;
VERTICAL GROOVES
ON 98.

SUPER

new VERTICAL
"TOOTH" AT
CENTER OF
GRILLE

52

new SIDE TRIM
(SEE DETAILS)

SU-88
H/T

98
TAIL-
LIGHT

Ninety-Eight
SEDAN
$2786.,
f.o.b.

1952

124" WB
160 HP
new "SUPER" RANGE IN Hydra-Matic

$3229.,
f.o.b.
CVT.

OLDSMOBILE

98

REAR QUARTER DETAILS (SEDAN)

Ninety
Eight

H/T

new
SIDE TRIM DESIGN
IDENTIFIES '52

OLDSMOBILE

88 2-DR.

88 has 150 HP @ 3600 RPM

$2262., f.o.b.

53

FINAL YR. FOR 303 CID V8s

DETAILS OF SUPER 88 HOLIDAY H/T

H/T

SUPER 88

DETAILS OF THE 1953 ENGINE

SEDAN

SU-88, 98 have 165 HP @ 3600 RPM

CVT. 3229., f.o.b.

AIR COND. AVAIL.

Holiday H/T

Ninety-Eight

$3022., f.o.b.

POWER BRAKES and POWER STEERING ORDERED with MOST UNITS.

OLDSMOBILE

$2237., and up, f.o.b.

88

new PANORAMIC WINDSHIELDS ON ALL

SUPER 88

HOLIDAY COUPÉ

170 HP @ 4000 (88)

185 HP @ 4000 (SU-88, 98)

ALL with *new* 324 CID V8s. (THROUGH '56)

54
(RESTYLED)

98

122" WB (88, SU-88)
126" WB (98)

98 STARFIRE CVT.

Ninety-Eight

REAR DETAILS (98)

$3248., f.o.b.

INTERIOR OF NEW *"Starfire"* 185 HP

LARGE, BOXY DECK AREA

1954

534

OLDSMOBILE
55

$2362., f.o.b.
SEDAN

88
185 HP
INT.

OLDSMOBILE'S
ENTIRELY NEW

SUPER 88

A HARDTOP...WITH 4 DOORS!

Holiday Sedan

IT'S A HOLIDAY... with Sedan convenience!
IT'S A SEDAN... with Holiday smartness!

Ninety Eight

NEW!
NEW!
NEW!

ALL-AROUND
new
202 HP
ENG.
(SU-88, 98)

56 88

FINAL
YR. FOR
324 CID V8
(230 OR 240 HP @ 4400 RPM)

INTERIOR

(CONT'D.
ON
NEXT
PAGE)

88
2-DR.
$2338., *and up,*
f.o.b.

"Holiday" new
BISECTED
GRILLE

535

$2484., *f.o.b.*
SU-88 2-DR.

OLDSMOBILE
SUPER 88

5 6
(CONT'D.)

98 4-DR. H/T
DLX. HOLIDAY
SEDAN

$3456., *f.o.b.*

GOLDEN
ROCKET

GOLDEN
ROCKET

f.o.b. PRICES START AT
$2691. (88 2-DR.)
277 HP @ 4400
RPM
WITH
new
371 CID
V8
(371 CID AVAIL.
THROUGH '60)

5 7
(RESTYLED)

SUPER 88

new
TAIL-LIGHTS *and*
SIDE TRIM

8.50 x 14
TIRES
(THROUGH '58)

new
SUPER 88 FIESTA

$3499., *f.o.b.*

new GRILLE

122" WB (126" ON 98)

SUPER

$3887., *f.o.b.*

note 3-PC.
BACKLIGHT ON
H/T (*new*)

new
Starfire 98

536

OLDSMOBILE

88

FIESTA
88

DYNAMIC 88
SUPER 88
NINETY-EIGHT
16 models to choose from!

(TOTALLY RESTYLED)

122½" OR 126½" WB

SUPER 88

265, 305 OR 312 HP

58

BADGE ON SU-88 and 98

98

for '58

New Rocket Engine is more powerful, gives greater performance than ever before. In addition, carburetion advances provide you with an opportunity for improved fuel savings, as much as 20%!

THE "CHROME KING" OF ALL CARS!

"OLDSmobility"

$2772., and up, f.o.b.

→ DASH DETAILS

New Trans-Portable®—a transistor radio that serves as your regular car radio, operating on car's built-in circuit, can also be unlocked and carried from car as a compact, lightweight portable.

New Safety-Vee Steering Wheel, with modern two-spoke, safety recessed design, allows unobstructed view of vital instrument panel gauges. New twin horn buttons are located within easy reach.

Dual-Range Power Heater® gives the exact amount of heat or ventilation exactly where you want it . . . when you want it. You merely touch a button . . . power does all the work for you!
*Optional at extra cost.

4 HEADLTS. ABOVE new GRILLE

new "LINEAR" LOOK

LTS. SEPERATED WITHIN new GRILLE

371 CID (270 HP @ 4600)
OR
new 394 CID (315 HP @ 4600)

59

(TOTALLY RESTYLED AGAIN)

$2837., and up, f.o.b.

(CONT'D.)

OLDSMOBILE

DYNAMIC 88

4-DR.

2-DR.

DY-88 HAS NO ROCKER PANEL CHROME

(LENGTH EXAGGERATED)

DYN. 88 HOLIDAY SCENICOUPE H/T

59 (CONT'D.)

FIESTA

SUPER 88

4-DR. H/T HOLIDAY SPORTSEDANS

new 9.00 x 14 TIRES on SU-88, 98

98

ninety-eight 4-door sedan

98 CVT.

$**4366.**,
f.o.b.

98 HOLIDAY SCENICOUPE H/T

DASH

1959

$2900., f.o.b.
88 CELEBRITY 4-DR. SEDAN

DYNAMIC 88

FIESTA WAGON

SUPER 88

OLDSMOBILE
60
PACE CAR AT 1960 INDY 500 RACE

98

with Roto-Matic Power Steering

240 OR 315 HP @ 4600 RPM
(FINAL YR. FOR SMALLER (371) V8)

GO OLDS '60!

DASH

SU-88 FIESTA WAGON

539

OLDSMOBILE

power features
and accessories
for your
driving pleasure

WINDOW SWITCHES

RADIO

WONDER BAR

POWER HEATER

MANUAL HEATER

Other Oldsmobile Options include such convenience features as: Guide-Matic Power Headlight Control, Safety Sentinel, Swivel Dome and Reading Lamp, Deck Lid Power Lock Release, Electric Ventipanes, De Luxe Wheel Discs, Trim Rings and Air Conditioning.

Starglo Moracceen interiors—optional at no extra cost in both Dynamic 88 Holiday Sedans and Holiday Coupes. And this long wearing, easy-to-clean all-vinyl trim is as handsome as it is durable.

THIS REAR-END STYLING IN 1961 ONLY

$ **3359.**, f.o.b.

DYNAMIC **88** 123" WB 250 HP

POWER ANTENNA

61 (TOTALLY RESTYLED)

DYNAMIC 88 FIESTA (AVAILABLE IN 2 AND 3-SEAT MODELS)

Super **88**

OLDSMOBILE 123" WB

Skyrocket PERFORMANCE!

DISTINGUISHED... DISTINCTIVE... DECIDEDLY NEW!

new *"Skyrocket"*
ENGINE (394 CID V8)
325 HP @ 4600 RPM
10 TO 1 COMPRESSION
(USED IN SU-88, 98;
OPTIONAL IN DY-88)

DASH

S-88-61

"OLDSMOBILE" NAME BELOW new GRILLE (ON 88s)

540

Foam-padded pattern cloth, handsomely accented with lustrous Jeweltone Moracceen, adds brilliant new sparkle to this Super 88 Holiday Sedan. Five harmonizing color choices are available.

(98 MODELS ON NEXT PAGE)

OLDSMOBILE

61 (CONT'D.)

V8

INTERIOR

CLASSIC 98 SPORT SEDAN

STARFIRE

(new)

CLASSIC 98

126" WB

98

CLASSIC 98 TOWN SEDAN

WHEEL COVER (98)

REAR QUARTER DETAIL

CLASSIC 98 HOLIDAY SEDAN

(LENGTH EXAGGERATED)

H/T

DYNAMIC 88

4-DR. H/T

WAGON has UNIQUE REAR FENDER DESIGN

62 (RESTYLED)

new SIDE SCULPTURING

$3404.. and up, f.o.b.

260 TO 345 HP (THROUGH '62)

new UPRIGHT GRILLE with "OLDSMOBILE" NAME ABOVE

(CONT'D.)

SUPER 88

98

HOLIDAY
SPORTS
SED.
(98)

62
(CONT'D.)

STARFIRE

98 WHEEL
COVERS

new HARDTOP CPE.
IN STARFIRE
SERIES

$**3423**.,
and up, f.o.b.

63

DYNAMIC 88

DYNAMIC 88 CONVERT. AVAIL.

542

(CONT'D.)

SU-88 GRILLE LIKE DYNAMIC 88

SUPER 88

SU-88 FIESTA

63 (CONT'D.)

98 TOWN SEDAN

98-LS (LUXURY SEDAN)

OLDSMOBILE

STARFIRE — REAR ROOFLINE

STARFIRE — REAR

STARFIRE — WHEEL COVER

(98 DETAILS)

4-DR. H/T $ **4238.**, f.o.b.

Ninety Eight

There's 'Something Extra' about owning an

OLDSMOBILE

NINETY-EIGHT · SUPER 88 · DYNAMIC 88 · F-85 · STARFIRE · JETFIRE

$3391.
f.o.b.

Jetstar 88   New full-size "88" series at a new lower price!

'64 OLDS →
WHERE THE ACTION IS!

new 330-cubic-inch Jetfire Rocket V-8

JETSTAR 88 CELEBRITY SEDAN

JETSTAR 88 HOLIDAY SEDAN

Jetstar 88

FIESTA STATION WAGON (2- or 3-seat)

DYNAMIC 88 HOLIDAY COUPE

CELEBRITY SEDAN

DYNAMIC 88

SUPER 88

394-cubic-inch
Starfire V-8 Engine

J 1964

Brilliant new sports coupe in the medium-price class!   Jetstar I

TOWN SEDAN

98

64

Starfire

S-1964

NINETY-EIGHT

1964

Ninety Eight

8-64

REAR
FENDER
(98)

544

65

330 CID V8   260 HP   123" WB
7.75 × 14 TIRES

Jetstar 88 **$3334.,**
f.o.b.

DYNAMIC 88 LINE
JOINED BY
new DELTA 88 →

$3504., f.o.b.
DYNAMIC
88
↓
H/T

Delta 88.

$3697., ↗
f.o.b.

8.25 × 14
TIRES

123"
WB

425 CID
SUPER
ROCKET
V8
360 HP
(TO 370 IN DELTA
88)

new GRILLE

DELTA 88 DASH

OLDSMOBILE

note THAT STARFIRE *and* 98
have OWN GRILLE
DESIGNS

CVT.

370 HP
STARFIRE →

H/T

$4761.,
f.o.b.

$4334.,
f.o.b.

98
LUXURY
SEDAN

98 (126" WB)

$4237.,
f.o.b.

WITH
VINYL
TOP

8.55 × 14 TIRES

HOLIDAY
SPORT
SEDAN

NINETY-EIGHT

545

98 DASH

'65 OLDSMOBILE
The Rocket Action Car!

PACKARD

(1899–1958)
PACKARD MOTOR CAR CO., DETROIT

SIX-CYL. OR STRAIGHT-8 L-HEAD ENGS.

DETAILS of COWL VENT, ETC.

INTERIOR DETAILS

110 SIX $975.

40
(1800 SERIES)

120 EIGHT $1095.

CVT.

$867 TO $6300

delivered in Detroit, State taxes extra. Prices subject to change without notice.

Air Cool-ditioning is available on closed models of the Packard 120, Super-Eight 160, and Custom Super-Eight 180 at extra cost, installed at the factory.

AIR CONDITIONING INTRODUCED FOR FIRST TIME!

OVERDRIVE OPTIONAL

ASK THE MAN WHO OWNS ONE

GRILLE GUARD ON 160 and LARGER MODELS

160 SUPER 8 and ENGINE

546

Model illustrated is Packard Super-8 One-Sixty Touring Sedan $1632* (white sidewall tires extra)

(CONTINUED)

DARRIN SEDAN

138" WB

THIS DARRIN MODEL (RARE) *has* TOP *and* BODY DESIGN ENTIRELY DIFFERENT *from* OTHER PACKARDS

PACKARD

$6100.

180 CUSTOM 8 BY DARRIN

4570.

127" WB

40
(CONT'D.)

DARRIN CONVERTIBLE

LIMOUSINE

180 CUSTOM 8

FORMAL SEDAN

$2825.

HEADLIGHTS SUNK DEEPER INTO FENDERS, *with* PARKING LIGHTS SET ON TOP

$1436. **$1024.**

110 SIX

120 WAGON

DLX. SEDAN INTERIOR (110)

DASH

new 1-PIECE BACKLIGHT

"the Class of '41"

41
(1900 SERIES)

6 lines of cars — 41 body styles
$907 TO **$5550**

261 AVAIL. TRIM COMBINATIONS!

120

547

180 DARRIN

PACKARD

new **CLIPPER** 8 CYL.

(STARTS 4-41)

41½ (1951 SERIES)

$1375.

OTHER 1941 MODELS CONTINUE ALSO

Clipper

←*new* 2-DR. CLIPPERS NOW ALSO AVAIL.

110

180

INTERIOR

LOOKING AHEAD?
SKIPPER THE CLIPPER

42-45 (2000 SERIES)

new CHOICE of 6 or 8-CYL. CLIPPERS

ELECTROMATIC DRIVE
SIMPLIFIED DRIVING WITH NO JERK·NO SLIP·NO CREEP

SUPER 8 *has* 148" WB

CUSTOM SUPER CLIPPER

$1746.
DELUXE CLIPPER

46-47 (2100 SERIES)

(BIG CITY PACKARD SHOWROOMS MORE LUXURIOUS THAN THIS RURAL OUTLET)

PM·1946

$3161.

EIGHT

STATION SEDAN
(new)

NEW SMOOTH
SIDE BODIES

SUPER-8 CVT.
IS FIRST OF
1948 PACKARDS
TO BE INTRODUCED

SUPER 8 130 HP

$2529.

$2990.

EARLY

48-49

(RESTYLED) (2200 SERIES)

$3461.

CUSTOM 8
160 HP

127" WB

$3866.

CUSTOM 8 has
CRISS-CROSS PIECES
IN GRILLE.

1948 - EARLY '49 DASH
ILLUSTR. ON NEXT PAGE

549

ASK THE MAN
WHO OWNS ONE

PACKARD

CLOSE-UP
VIEW OF
DASH

(2200 SERIES)

135 HP (8)
150 HP (SU.8)
160 HP (CUST. 8)

$2383. ('50)

DELUXE 8

EIGHT
(120" WB)

SUPER 8
new
127"
WB

DASH
and
BACKLIGHT
DETAILS

Ultramatic Drive

AVAIL.

"Golden Anniversary" new LARGER BACKLIGHTS
MODELS   ON 4-DOOR SEDANS

49½-50

(2300 SERIES)

CUSTOM 8
127" WB

77 MAJOR IMPROVEMENTS

"NEW, ALL-NEW"

PRICE RANGE
$2302.
TO
$3797.

200 (145 HP)

250 CVT.

Prestige car of the medium-priced field: Packard "200" Club Sedan—$2300*

—one of nine exciting new models for '51

122" WB

51-52

(TOTALLY RESTYLED 2400 SERIES)

(2500 SER.)

300

250 MAYFAIR

REAR SIDE DETAILS

1952 MODEL (left) SIMILAR, BUT has new HOOD ORNAMENT and MEDALLION ON GRILLE

Ultramatic

400 PATRICIAN

COSTLY MODELS CONTINUE CORMORANT FIGURE AS 1951 ORNAMENT

1951 MODELS have "PACKARD" NAME ABOVE GRILLE

PACKARD

New Armor-rib body construction!
New Tele-glance instrument panel!
New Safeti-set brake!

—the one for '51!

$2588.

CLIPPER DELUXE

New Packard CLIPPER

160 HP

new HOOD ORNAMENT and SMOOTH HORIZONTAL GRILLE PIECE (ON CLIPPER ONLY)

53 (2600 SERIES)

CLIPPER SERIES RETURNS (PREVIOUSLY AVAIL. 1941 – 1947)

new CAVALIER

127" WB

$3234.

MAYFAIR

MAYFAIR H/T ALSO, W/O 3 CHROME REAR FENDER PLAQUES SEEN ON ABOVE CVT.

400 PATRICIAN

new GROOVES IN HORIZONTAL GRILLE PIECE (EXCEPT ON CLIPPER)

new CARIBBEAN

$5209.

552

PANAMA

CLIPPER
DELUXE

SUPER CLIPPER

122," 127" OR 149" WB
150, 165, 185 OR 212 HP

54
(5400 SERIES)

DASH

CAVALIER

PATRICIAN

FINAL STRAIGHT-8 ENGINES
(288, 327 OR 359 CID)

STUDEBAKER-
PACKARD
MERGER

122" WB

CLIPPER

FIRST MAJOR
RESTYLING
SINCE 1951

new
V8
ENG.
with
O.H.V.
(320 OR 352 CID)

PATRICIAN

PRICE
RANGE:
$2586. TO $5932.

225, 245 OR 260
HP @ 4600 RPM

55
(5500
SERIES)

127" WB

400

CARIBBEAN

553

PACKARD

2731. CLIPPER DELUXE

CLIPPER SUPER *also avail.*

$3069.

CUSTOM CLIPPER

CUSTOM CLIPPER CONSTELLATION H/T

3164.

MEMBERS of CLIPPER GRILLE NOW HORIZONTAL.

122" WB (CLIPPERS) OTHERS, 127" WB

56
(5600 SERIES)

new DISPLACEMENT OF 374 CID ON ALL PACKARD V8 ENGINES. ALL BUT CARIBBEAN *have* 290 HP @ 4600 RPM.

3483.

EXECUTIVE

H/T
$3658.

WIDER-SPACED GRILLE PIECES *with* MESH BACKGROUND

$4160.

PATRICIAN

$4190.
400
H/T

"ASK THE MAN WHO OWNS *the New* ONE"

$5995.

CARIBBEAN
has 310 HP @ 4600 RPM

PACKARD (57-L SERIES)

57 new 120½" WB

$3212.

new SMALLER DISPLACEMENT of 289 CID

HP REDUCED TO 275 @ 4800 RPM

275 HP (THROUGH '58)

CLIPPER

SEDAN and WAGON are ONLY CHOICES LISTED DURING 1957.

new 116½" BODIES LIKE STUDEBAKER (THROUGH '58)

WAGON

$3384. (AS IN '57)

(58-L SERIES)

58

THE FINAL PACKARDS

ENG. SPECS. AS IN 1957.

SEDAN

FRONT END DETAILS

new HAWK H/T

4 HEADLIGHTS (EXCEPT ON HAWK)

$3995.

HAWK has 2 HEADLIGHTS, LOWER GRILLE

48 HP with 133 CID HERCULES ENGINE OR 40 HP with 91 CID CONT. ENG.

STEEL RETRACTABLE TOP

97 BLT. 4 CYL.

PLAYBOY

PLAYBOY MOTOR CAR CORP., BUFFALO, N.Y. (1946-1951)

48

3.73 OR 4.1 GEAR RATIO 90" W.B.

INTER.

$985.

555

PLYMOUTH DIVISION
CHRYSLER
CORPORATION

Plymouth (SINCE JUNE, 1928)

DASH

6 CYLINDERS (SINCE 1933)

new 117½" WB (THROUGH 1948)
6.00 × 16 TIRES (TO 1947)

new 1-PIECE REAR WINDOW ↓

2-DR.

COUPE

ROAD KING

WAGON

DE LUXE

201.3 cɪᴅ (SINCE '34)

new 84 HP @ 3600 RPM (87 HP with ALUMINUM CYL. HEAD)

new ROTARY DOOR LATCHES

WIPERS NOW FASTENED BELOW WINDSHIELD

40

CVT.

PLYMOUTH BUILDS GREAT CARS

P-9   ROAD KING
P-10 DE LUXE

ROAD KING MODELS DO NOT HAVE ADDITIONAL ROTATING VENT-WINDOWS IN FRONT DOORS.

COUPES START AT | SEDANS START AT
$645 | **$699**
DELIVERED IN DETROIT, MICH.

SEDAN

556

new GRILLE and SEALED-BEAM HEADLIGHTS

Plymouth

DE LUXE

SPEC. DLX.

$685.41 AND UP

'41

P-11 DE LUXE
P-12 SPECIAL DE LUXE

2 VIEWS OF DASH

87 OR 92 HP @ 3800 RPM

"BUY WISELY – BUY PLYMOUTH THE CAR THAT STANDS UP BEST"

new CLUB COUPE (5-PASS.)

4-DR., 5-WINDOW TOWN SEDAN ('42 ONLY)

95 HP @ 3400 RPM

(RESTYLED)

42

P-14C SPEC. DLX.

P-14S DE LUXE

FRONT DETAIL

Plymouth

SPECIAL DE LUXE *has* CHROME EFFECT on WINDSHIELD FRAME

1946 *has* FLAT BUTTON TYPE DOOR LOCK COVERS.

1948 *has new* 7.50 × 15 LOW-PRESSURE TIRES.

46-48 *

P-15S DLX. or P-15C SPECIAL DLX.

* = CONT'D. TO 2-49

95 HP @ 3600 RPM

CLUB COUPE

REAR (SEDAN)

$1075. TO $2068.
(PRICE RANGE, 1946 TO EARLY 1949)

CONVERTIBLE DASH IS PAINTED in BODY COLOR, INSTEAD of *being* WOODGRAINED.

SEDAN INTERIOR

558

SPECIAL DE LUXE *has* RADIO GRILLE

DE LUXE

Plymouth

new ALL-METAL 2-DR. SUBURBAN WAGON

P-17

SEDAN REAR DOORS NOW _FRONT-HINGED_

6.40×15 or 6.70×15 TIRES (THROUGH '52)

SPECIAL DELUXE 4-DOOR WAGON _has_ WOODEN PANELS.

P-18

97 HP @ 3600 RPM (THROUGH '52)

CLUB COUPE

new "Double-Size" CVT. BACKLIGHT _has_ REMOVABLE, ZIPPERED CENTER SECTION

49

P-17 (111" WB)
P-18 (118½" WB)

(TOTALLY RESTYLED)

HORIZONTAL CREASES ON BUMPERS ('49 ONLY)
new SWITCH-KEY STARTING

SLOGAN: "The car that likes to be compared"

Plymouth

DE LUXE

3-WINDOW BUSINESS COUPE

SPECIAL DE LUXE

PRICE RANGE: $1371. TO $2372.

50

P-19 DE LUXE (111" WB)

P-20 DE LUXE; SPEC. DLX. (118½" WB)

new EMBLEM

PLYMOUTH

DASH

new SMOOTH BUMPER SURFACE

new GRILLE has FEWER PIECES.

Plymouth

P-22 CONCORD

111" WB

1951 MODELS ILLUSTRATED UNLESS OTHERWISE NOTED.

1951 BELVEDERE is new H/T.

SHIELD BADGE REPLACED BY CIRCLE ON '52.

MODEL NAME IN SCRIPT ON 1952 FRONT FENDER

51-52

new CONCORD, CAMBRIDGE, CRANBROOK MODEL NAMES

('51)

DASH

P-23 CAMBRIDGE and CRANBRK. have 118½" WB

'50 PLYMOUTH TAXI

1952 BELVEDERE (BELOW) has new REAR COLOR SWEEP

('52)

561

Plymouth

100 HP @ 3600 RPM

SAVOY WAGON

new SPORT WIRE WHEELS OPTIONAL

CRANBROOK BELVEDERE

21769

CRANBROOK

53

(TOTALLY RESTYLED)
P-24-1 CAMBRIDGE
P-24-2 CRANBR.

new 114" WB (THROUGH '54)

6.70 × 15 TIRES (TO '56)

P-25-3 BELVEDERE

P-25-1 PLAZA

$1618. UP

LATE '54 has new 230.2 CID and 110 HP @ 3600 RPM

P-25-2 SAVOY

54

EARLY 1954 BELVEDERE H/T DOES NOT HAVE THIS COLOR BAND ON SIDE

BELVEDERE

Plymouth

230 CID 6 CYL. or new 241 CID or 260 CID V8s.

new AUTOMATIC TRANSMISSION CONTROL on DASH

PLAZA

SAVOY

PRICED FROM $1639.

55

(TOTALLY RESTYLED with new "FORWARD LOOK")

6 = 117 HP @ 4000 RPM

V8 = 157 or 167 HP @ 4400 RPM

CLUB COUPE

new PANORAMIC WINDSHIELD

BELVEDERE

new 115" WB (THROUGH '56)

H/T

6-CYL. has STRAIGHT EMBLEM ABOVE GRILLE →

V8 has ABOVE TYPE of EMBLEM

new FRENCHED HEADLIGHTS

Plymouth

SUBURBAN

6.70 × 15 TIRES
(ALL BUT *new* FURY)

CUSTOM SUBURBAN

SPORT SUBURBAN

PLAZA

BELVEDERE

SEDAN (ABOVE)

4-DR. H/T (BELOW)

PUSHBUTTON POWERFLITE:

SAVOY

56 P-28 (6)
P-29 (V8)

125, 180, 187, 200, 240 OR 270 HP

H/T

new **Fury** (WITH 303 CID V8)
7.10 × 15 TIRES)

new SHARPLY-PEAKED TAIL FINS

new MESH AT GRILLE CENTER

1956

Plymouth

PLAZA

EARLY '57 (6 OPEN SLOTS BELOW BUMPERS)

BELVEDERE

SAVOY

BELVEDERE

LATE '57 (EXTRA VERTICAL MEMBERS BELOW BUMPERS)

318 CID V8 IN FURY

new 8.00 x 14 TIRES ON FURY H/T

new 118" WB (122" WB ON WAGONS) (THROUGH '61)

SPORT SDN. (BELV.)

TAILGATE WINDOW DETAILS

SECRET LUGGAGE COMPARTMENT. Almost 10 cubic feet of locked space for safe, out-of-sight storage of luggage, cameras and other valuables. On all 6-pass. models.

132, 197, 215, 235 OR 290 HP

new 7.50 x 14 TIRES (ALL BUT FURY)

57

(TOTALLY RESTYLED)

P-30 (6)
P-31 (V8)

$1899. UP

DASH

565

Plymouth

58

LP-1 (6)
LP-2 (V8)

The De Luxe Suburban—2-door, 6-passenger

The Custom Suburban—2-door, 6-passenger

The Custom Suburban—4-door, 9- or 6-passenger

SPORT SUBURBAN

The Plaza 2-door Business Coupe

The Savoy 4-door Sedan

The Savoy 4-door Hardtop

The Belvedere 4-door Sedan

The Belvedere Convertible

Star of the Forward Look

INSTRUMENT CLUSTER

4 HEADLIGHTS

7.50 × 14 TIRES
BELVEDERE

(8.00 × 14 ON
9-PASS. WAGONS
and FURY H/T)

FURY

230 CID 6 (132 HP @ 3600)
318 CID V8
(225 or 250 HP @ 4400)
350 CID V8
(305 or 315 HP
@ 5000 RPM)

newest engine-"Golden Commando V-8"
(WITH ELECTRONIC FUEL INJECTION)

SILVER SPECIAL (RARE!)
(PLAZA)

Plymouth

CUSTOM SUBURBAN

SAVOY

4-door Sedan, V-8 or 6

BELVEDERE

2-door Sedan, V-8 or 6

OPTIONAL *new* SWIVEL SEATS (STD. IN SPORT FURY)

59

MP-1 (6)
MP-2 (V8)

7.50 × 14 TIRES

DASH

SPORT SUBURBAN

new SPORT FURY H/T

FINAL USE OF L-HEAD DESIGN IN PLYMOUTH SIX

new "CONTINENTAL BULGE" ON DECK LID

567 FURY

230 CID 6 (132 HP @ 3600)
318 CID V8 (230 or 260 HP @ 4400 RPM)
361 CID V8 (305 HP @ 4600 RPM)

Plymouth

SAVOY

BELVEDERE

new SLANTING O.H.V. 225 CID 6 (145 HP @ 4000 RPM) (TO '71)

V8s have 318, 361, OR 383 CID (230, 260, 305, 310, 325 OR 330 HP)

note THE REAR FENDER ORNAMENTS WHICH IDENTIFY EACH INDIVIDUAL MODEL SERIES.

CUSTOM SUBURBAN

FURY

4-DR. H/T

2-DR. H/T

WITH SEMI-RECTANGULAR STEERING WHEEL

WITHOUT GRILLE GUARD

WITH GRILLE GUARD

60

PP-1 (6 CYL.)
PP-2 (V8)

SHOWN with ROUND STEERING WHEEL

DASH

7.50 × 14 TIRES

568

CLOSER DETAILS OF WAGON

Plymouth

Battery-saving Alternator keeps battery charged when generators can't. Many police and taxi fleets pay extra to get special Alternator installations. Yet the amazing new Alternator is standard equipment on all 1961 Chrysler Corporation cars.

7.00 × 14 TIRES (6)
7.50 × 14 ON 6-CYL. WAGONS *and* V8s.
8.00 × 14 ON 9-PASS. V8 WAGON

ALTERNATOR TEST
DETROIT *to* CHICAGO

PLYMOUTH—This car traveled 328 miles without a battery. Alternator, standard on 1961 Chrysler Corporation cars, provided all necessary electrical energy.

61
RP-1 (6)
RP-2 (V8)

SPT. SBN.

145 TO 375 HP

$2260. UP   *FURY*

LARGEST OF 4 PLYMOUTH V8s is *new* 413 CID ENGINE (UP TO 375 HP @ 5200 RPM)

118" WB (WAGONS 122")

GRILLE GUARD AVAIL. ON SOME 1961 MODELS

new GRILLE

569

...SOLID BEAUTY

Plymouth

Look at Plymouth now!

SAVOY

PRICED FROM $2531.

SAVOY

6 = 6.50 × 14 TIRES
V8 = 7.00 × 14

BELVEDERE

Plymouth Belvedere 2-dr. Sedan

62 SP-1 (6)
SP-2 (V8)

(TOTALLY RESTYLED)

New Forward Flair Design

FURY

FURY

new 116" WB

145 TO 410 HP

FURY TURBO- (SPECIAL)

NEW SPORT FURY

Special red, white and blue insignia, new wheel covers and new rear deck design tell you that this one is the real thing! There is no mistaking a new Sport Fury—hardtop or convertible.

Action! Fly to 60 mph in 8.5 secs. with optional 305-hp Golden Commando V-8 engine.

Plymouth

7.00 × 14 TIRES

SAVOY

BELVEDERE

FURY

V8 OPTIONS

318 CID (230 HP @ 4400)
361 CID (265 HP @ 4400)
383 CID (320 to 330 HP)
426 CID (370 HP @
    4600 to 425 HP
    @ 5600 RPM)

FURY

FURY

1963 IS ONLY YEAR
with UNUSUAL
FRONT CORNER
PARK./DIRECTIONAL
LIGHTS

MB·2560

with a 5-year or 50,000-mile warranty

63

TP-1 (6 CYL.)
TP-2 (V8)

new GRILLE
new TAIL-LIGHTS
new FULL-LENGTH SIDE TRIM

Get up and go Plymouth!

new
426 CID V8 ENGINE
KNOWN AS
"Super Stock"

DASH

N·1558

A Transmission Drive Selector (optional)
B Transmission Parking Lock
C Clock (optional)
D Turn Signal Indicator
E Heater Controls (optional)
F Headlights and Panel Lights
G Defroster Outlets
H Windshield Wiper Control
I Ignition Switch
J Cigarette Lighter
K Ash Receiver
L Glove Compartment Lock
M Radio (optional)

SPORT FURY

PLYMOUTH'S ON 571 **THE MOVE**

Plymouth

7.00 × 14 TIRES

BELVEDERE

Savoy 2-Door Sedan

SAVOY

Savoy 6- or 9-Passenger Station Wagon

318, 361, 383 and 426 CID V8s

FURY

230 TO 425 HP

64

VP-1 (6 CYL.)
(V8)
VP-2

BELV..

FURY **wagon**

REAR OF FURY WAGON

$3/95.

SPORT FURY

1964

new CONVEX GRILLE

new H/T ROOFLINE

572

Plymouth

BELVEDERE II   116" WB

Belvedere Satellite

Belvedere I

new BELVEDERE SATELLITE
IS AVAIL. WITH TOP-OF-LINE
426 CID V8 WITH 425 HP @ 6000 RPM.

BELV. *has* 7.35 × 14 TIRES (EXC. WAGON)

EU-6778

Fury I

273 CID BARRACUDA V8 ENG. NOW AVAIL. IN BELVEDERE I (180 HP @ 4200 RPM)

PACE CAR AT 1965 INDY 500 RACE

SPORT FURY

Fury II

DASH

Fury III

7.75 × 14 TIRES
8.55 × 14 (FURY WAGON)

FURY III

145 TO 425 HP   **65**

AR-1 (6-CYL.)
AR-2 (V8)
ALL FURY TYPES GET *new* 119" WB (WAGONS 121")

Fury III 4-Door Hardtop

THE ROARING '65s

PONTIAC MOTOR DIVISION of
GENERAL MOTORS CORPORATION

Pontiac
AMERICA'S FINEST LOW-PRICED CAR

SINCE 1926

6.00 × 16 TIRES
(SINCE '35;
6-CYL.)

SPECIAL
6

AMERICA'S FINEST
LOW-PRICED CAR

Pontiac's sealed chassis is where Pontiac's amazing durability begins. Rugged, powerful, yet with micromatic precision in every vital unit, the Pontiac chassis is engineered to serve well long past the point when the average car is past its prime.

DELUXE 6

40

SPECIAL 6

DELUXE 8

TORPEDO 8

"HA" SPECIAL 6 MODEL 25
has 117" WB

"Silver Streak" CHROME STRIPS ALONG HOOD, REAR DECK,
A PONTIAC
CHARACTERISTIC
SINCE
1935.

ONLY
$783*
FOR THE
SPECIAL SIX
BUSINESS
COUPE
OTHER MODELS
SLIGHTLY HIGHER

"HB" DELUXE 6 MODEL 26
and "HA" DLX. 8 MODEL 28
have 120" WB

"HB" TORPEDO 8 MODEL 29
has 122" WB

TRIPLE-TIERED
BUMPER
GUARD
AVAIL.
ALSO

A-11214

574

Pontiac Torpedoes

CUSTOM TORPEDO

PONTIAC PRICES BEGIN AT
$828*
FOR DE LUXE "TORPEDO" SIX BUSINESS COUPE

STREAMLINER TORPEDO

DELUXE TORPEDO

CUSTOM TORPEDO

[ONLY $25 MORE FOR AN EIGHT IN ANY MODEL!]

41

NEW INTERIOR LUXURY is exemplified by this attractive new 1941 Pontiac instrument panel. Electric clock (except on some models) and radio at extra cost.

DETAILS OF *new* GRILLE *and* EMBLEM

THE FINE CAR
Pontiac
WITH THE <u>LOW</u> PRICE

Pontiac

Torpedo Business Coupe

Torpedo Sport Coupe

Torpedo Two-Door Sedan

Torpedo Metropolitan Four-Door Sedan

Torpedo Sedan Coupe

Torpedo Four-Door Sedan

Torpedo Convertible Sedan Coupe

Streamliner Four-Door Sedan

Streamliner Station Wagon

42-45

ONLY $25 MORE FOR AN EIGHT IN ANY MODEL

$895. *and up*

"with the things you're always liked - AND 15 NEW ONES TOO!*"*

THE **FINE** CAR WITH THE **LOW** PRICE

Streamliner Sedan Coupe

PX-1942

Pontiac offers ten new models superior in 15 ways to last year's

Full Speed Ahead on National Defense

To the production of a new type of heavy machine gun for the United States Navy, Pontiac is devoting two entire plants, totaling 10 acres of floor space and staffed with thousands of Pontiac production experts and skilled craftsmen working three shifts a day. In addition Pontiac has a total of 225 sub-contractors supplying machines and material to build this new gun which naval authorities describe as "the most effective weapon of its size ever produced." Defense comes first at Pontiac—and Pontiac is going full speed ahead!

Pontiac

Pontiac

Finest of the Famous "Silver Streaks"

TORPEDO

STREAMLINER

46

WHAT'S NEW AND IMPROVED IN THE 1946 PONTIAC

New, beautiful exterior appearance . . . New instrument panel . . . Heavier chrome finish . . . Improved, rust-resistant bodies . . . New interior trim . . . Improved clutch . . . New, wider wheel rims . . . Longer-life muffler and tail pipe . . . Improved cooling.

STREAMLINER

TORPEDO

47

NO VERTICAL PIECES IN 1947 GRILLE

TORPEDO

TORPEDO DELUXE

48

STREAMLINER DE LUXE

DE LUXE MODELS *have* CHROME STRIP *on* SIDE *of* FRONT FENDER, *and* CHROME REAR FENDER PADS

PONTIAC

49

(TOTALLY RESTYLED)

ALL-STEEL WAGON

50

VERTICAL "TEETH" NOW ADDED TO UPPER SECTION OF GRILLE

WHEEL COVER

REAR FENDER PAD DETAILS

51

L-HEAD 6 CYL. and STRAIGHT-8 ENGINES CONTINUE (THROUGH '54)

('52)

Dollar for Dollar you can't beat a
Pontiac

New High-Performance Economy Axle

1952 WHEEL COVER

52

SIDE VIEW OF MASCOT

More Power

new SIDE TRIM

New *Dual-Range*
Hydra-Matic Drive*

PONTIAC

CHIEFTAN SPECIAL

new "DUAL STREAK" RESTYLING
FEATURES TWIN GROUPS of
CHROME BANDS ALONG HOOD
and DECK, with new BODIES

CHIEFTAN DE LUXE

53

new
1-PIECE
WINDSHIELD

new 122" WB

$ **1956.**

$ **2774.**

PRICE
RANGE

WAGONS *with* GRAIN-DECORATED
UPPER PANELS (ABOVE) ARE PRICED
$80. ABOVE SIMILAR WAGONS
OF ONE SOLID COLOR ONLY.

The experimental Parisienne stands only
56 inches high. Inside and out it is a
designer's dream of how one "car of the
future" might be styled and equipped.

PARISIENNE

(SHOW CAR)
PUBLICLY DISPLAYED, BUT
NOT A PRODUCTION BODY
TYPE

De Luxe Catalina

Dollar for Dollar you can't beat a

Pontiac

PONTIAC

CHIEFTAN SPECIAL 6
(ALSO AVAIL. as 8)

CHIEFTAN DELUXE
(6 OR 8 CYL.)

A BRIEF (1 YR.) RETURN TO SINGLE GROUP OF CHROME STRIPS ON HOOD and DECK

54

new GRILLE with EMBLEM PLACED ABOVE

STAR CHIEF CUSTOM 8
(AT RIGHT and BELOW)

THE NEW *Star Chief*

8-CYL.
SERIES IDENTIFIED BY THESE "STARS" ON SIDE OF REAR FENDER

STAR CHIEF DE LUXE 8 (BELOW)
COSTS LESS THAN CUSTOM 8

CVT.

FRONT END and WHEEL COVER DETAILS

PONTIAC

CHIEFTAN 860

(TOTALLY RESTYLED)

55

new PANORAMIC WINDSHIELD →

CHIEFTAN 870

CHIEFTAN ═ 122" WB

STAR CHIEF ═ 124" WB

CHIEFTAN 870

CATALINA H/T (2 VIEWS)

new DASH

PRICE RANGE: $2105. TO $3128.

ALL MODELS
with new
"STRATO-
STREAK"
O.H.V. V8
ENGINE →
180 OR 200 HP

STAR CHIEF CUSTOM

CATALINA
(CVT. ALSO AVAIL.)

new
STAR CHIEF CUST.
SAFARI 2 DR.
LUXURY WAGON

BUMPER GUARDS
AVAILABLE
(RARE)

582

CHIEFTAN

SAFARI

STAR CHIEF

new 4-DR. H/

56 Pontiac

TO 227 HP

STAR CHIEF Custom Convertible

PLASTIC "JR. STAR CHIEF" CHILD'S ELECTRIC CARS ALSO, FOR DEALER PROMOTIONAL PURPOSES

REAR DETAILS

PONTIAC

CHIEFTAN
252 HP

SUPER CHIEF
270 HP

SU. CHIEF
WAGON
DOOR

STAR
CHIEF
270 HP

SAFARI WAGON

57

1957

BONNEVILLE
(new)

(LIMITED
PRODUCTION)

STAR CHIEF has
HEAVY CHROME BAND PLACED WITHIN
COLOR CONTRAST PANEL on
REAR FENDER

AMERICA'S NUMBER ① ROAD CAR!

new
FRONT END
(NO LONGER
USES
"Silver Streak"
CHROME BANDS)

STAR CH.
2-DR. H/T

584

PONTIAC

CHIEFTAN

3 STAR-LIKE FIGS. ON REAR FENDER OF CHIEFTAN; 4 ON SUPER CHIEF. (EACH MODEL CAN BE IDENTIFIED BY FENDER DECOR., AS ILLUS. BELOW)

USA1958

SUPER CHIEF

PONTIAC

USA-1958
AMERICA'S N°1 ROAD CAR

58
(RESTYLED)

STAR CHIEF

BOLDEST ADVANCE IN 50 YEARS

BOLD NEW Bonneville BY PONTIAC

PACE CAR AT 1958 INDY 500 RACE

BONNEVILLE

BONNEVILLE

PONTIAC

CATALINA

new "WIDE-TRACK"
59
(TOTALLY RESTYLED)

122" WB (CATALINA SERIES and on BONNEVL. WAGON)
124" WB ON OTHERS

new BONNEVILLE VISTA 4-DR. H/T

"BONNEVILLE" NAME ON BONNEVL. GRILLE

CATALINA SAFARI WAGON

(WIDTH EXAGGERATED)

"PONTIAC" NAME ON GRILLE OF CATALINA and STAR CHIEF. STAR CHIEF has STAR-LIKE FIGURES ALONG SIDE OF REAR FENDER.

DASH

8.00 × 14 TIRES

245 HP (280 w. Hydra Matic)
BONNEVL. has 260 HP (300 w. Hyd.)

PONTIAC 1960

STAR CHIEF

THE ONLY CAR WITH WIDE·TRACK WHEELS

WAGON AND VISTA DETAILS

BONNEVILLE

60

VENTURA H/T

CATALINA 2-DR.

SAFARI

61 (RESTYLED)

BONNEVILLE (STAR CHF. TAILLIGHTS SIMILAR)

PONTIAC

STAR CIHEF

61 CONT'D.

BONNEVILLE OFTEN *has* "BONNEVILLE" NAME ON GRILLE AS ILLUSTR.

VISTA 4 DOOR HARDTOPS

STAR CHIEF

STAR CHIEF VISTA

Wide-Track Pontiac
WIDEST STANCE ON THE ROAD

62

Bonneville

CATALINA

CATALINA 9-PASSENGER SAFARI

(CONTINUED)

STRATO - CHIEF
(SOLD ONLY IN CANADA)

WAGONS

LAURENTIAN
2 - DOOR

PONTIAC

LAURENTIAN
(SOLD ONLY IN CANADA)

62
(CONT'D.)

SPORT COUPE

SPORT COUPES

PARISIENNE
(SOLD ONLY IN CANADA)

SEDAN

GP

GRAND PRIX
New
DETAILS

MANUAL
SHIFT
CONSOLE

AUTO.
SHIFT
CONSOLE

BUCKET
SEATS

TACH.

303 HP

4 BBL. CARB.

$3917.

589

CATALINA

9-PASSENGER SAFARI

PONTIAC

STAR CHIEF 4-DOOR SEDAN

CATALINA SPORTS SEDAN

BONNEVILLE SPORTS COUPE

BONNEVILLE VISTA

CATALINA / ST. CHIEF

CATALINA

BONNEVILLE

63

2 VIEWS OF G.P.

GP
PONTIAC GRAND PRIX

590

'63 WIDE-TRACK PONTIAC

PONTIAC 120" WB — CATALINA

STAR CHIEF
(FRONT SIMILAR TO CATALINA)
123" WB
235 HP

64

CATALINA SEDAN

BONNEVILLE

WHEEL COVER

123" WB
BONN. BROUGHAM
w. VINYL TOP (BELOW)

INTERIOR

$3995.
(CVT.)

306 HP

PRESTON CLOTH-and-MORROKIDE INTERIOR

G.P.

120" WB

WAGON
(BONNEVILLE)

591

PONTIAC

CATALINA

CATALINA 2+2

note LOUVRES ON COWL OF 2+2

BON. BROUGHAM INTERIOR

BONNEVILLE

BONNEVILLE   (325 HP)
BROUGHAM 4-DR. H/T

65

G. P.

CAT. 2+2 INTERIOR

Pontiac for 1965
The year of the Quick Wide-Tracks

new GRILLE

Grand Prix

592

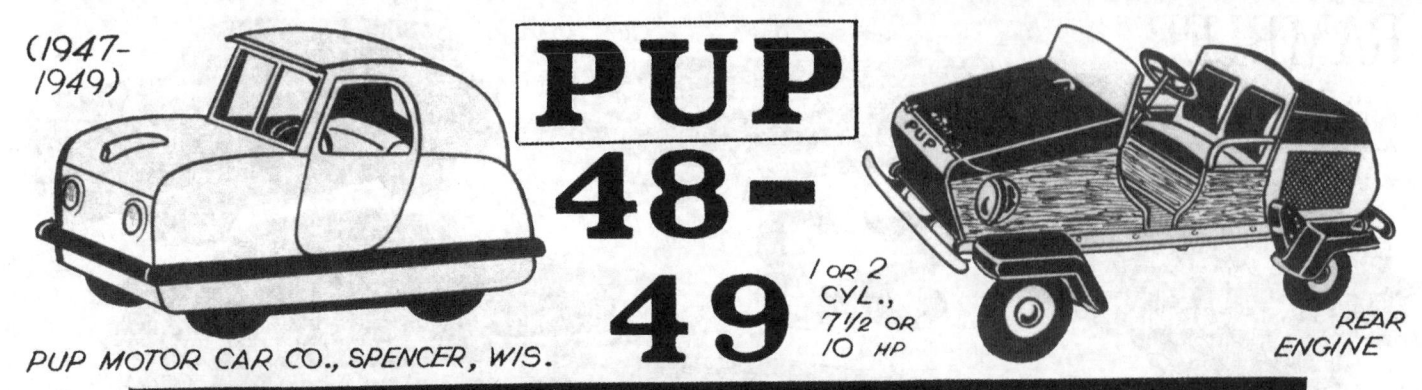

(1947-1949)

PUP MOTOR CAR CO., SPENCER, WIS.

PUP 48-49

1 OR 2 CYL., 7½ OR 10 HP

REAR ENGINE

AT NASH DEALERS

Rambler 6 CYL.

TOP DOWN
TOP UP

$1808., f.o.b. (CVT. OR WAGON)

100" WB

82 HP

MODEL 5021
New Rambler Convertible Landau
(CUSTOM SERIES)

50

"RAMBLER" NAME REVIVED BY NASH FOR THIS NEW COMPACT SERIES. CVT. INTRO. 3-50; WAGON 5-50

51-52

new "SUPER"

SUBURBAN MODEL 5114 (5214)

MODEL 5127 (5227)
"COUNTRY CLUB" HARDTOP INTRO. 6-51

57,555 RAMBLERS BLT. 1951; 53,055 RAMBLERS SOLD IN 1952

CONVERTIBLE CONTINUES

FIRST 2 DIGITS OF MODEL NUMBER INDICATE YEAR OF CAR

RAMBLER

85 HP
(90 with
Hydra-Matic)

5321
CVT.

CUSTOM

53

5327
COUNTRY
CLUB H/T

SUPER 2-DR.
SUBURBAN IS LOWEST-
PRICED: $**2003**., f.o.b.

GREENBRIER

5406
CLUB
SEDAN

new
DE LUXE

SUPER

5417

$**1550**., f.o.b.

5414

54

100" and
108" WB

Nash Motors, Division of
AMERICAN MOTORS CORP.
DETROIT, MICH.

5425

5427

CUSTOM

note LUGGAGE RACK
AND DIP IN REAR
ROOFLINE

REAR
DETAILS
(CROSS-
COUNTRY)

new 4-DR.
"CROSS-COUNTRY" WAGON (5428)

RAMBLER a Whole New Idea in Automobiles

5514

DELUXE 5515

SUPER

ALL-WEATHER-EYE

NEW IDEA! *Touch this knob—and it will always be springtime in your Rambler. No cold in winter! No heat in summer! No dust or traffic roar! You breathe only fresh, filtered air. It's American Motors' All-Season Air Conditioning*—greatest health, comfort, safety feature of fifty years. Needs no trunk space. And you buy a Rambler so equipped for less than the price of an ordinary car!*
Patents applied for

PRICES START AT
$1585.,
f.o.b.
(DLX. 2-DR.)

5517
COUNTRY
CLUB
CUSTOM

ON 9-22-55, FINAL AMC CAR ASSEMBLED AT EL SEGUNDO, CALIF. BRANCH FACTORY, *with* "DC-" SERIAL NUMBERS. KENOSHA, WIS. FACTORY CONTINUES *with* "D-" SERIAL NUMBERS AS USUAL.

new GRILLE
with
CRISS-
CROSS
PIECES

55

83,852
BLT.

CROSS-
COUNTRY   5518

INTERIOR
(H/T)

HUDSON
RAMBLER

NASH
RAMBLER

(DETERMINE BY NAME-PLATE ON GRILLE)

NOW AT *Nash* DEALERS AND HUDSON DEALERS EVERYWHERE

American Motors 595

RAMBLER

You'll make the Smart Switch for '56

Product of American Motors

AMERICAN MOTORS MEANS ⚙ MORE FOR AMERICANS

See Disneyland—great TV for all the family over ABC network.

DE LUXE
5615

SUPER
5618
-1

$2230

America's lowest-priced 4-door station wagon, delivered at the factory, including federal taxes. State and local taxes (if any), white wall tires and optional equipment (if desired), extra.

new 120-HP SIX with OVERHEAD VALVES

79,166 BLT.

new BROADER GRILLE ENCOMPASSES HEADLIGHTS

56

(RESTYLED)

108" WB ON ALL

Box-Girders All Around Passengers   Box-Sections Absorb Impact

The Old Way   SEE THE DIFFERENCE

Make the Smart Switch to Double Safe Single Unit Car Construction. All-welded, twice as rigid with "double lifetime" durability—means higher resale value.

NOTE VARIATIONS IN UPPER SIDE TRIM →

CUSTOM

Make the Smart Switch to the car that out-corners, out-parks them all. Entirely new ride—first low-priced car with Deep Coil Springs on all four wheels.

"Make the Smart Switch to Rambler!"

new COLOR SPEAR SIDE MOULDINGS ON CUSTOM

2 VIEWS OF new 4-DOOR H/T 5619-2

Make the Smart Switch to Airliner Reclining Seat luxury. You have a nap couch to keep children fidget-free on trips, relax grown-ups. Even a chaise longue!

new ROLL-DOWN REAR DOOR WINDOW →
5618-2

New Rambler Cross Country Station Wagon! Enjoy more fun per mile and per dollar in America's lowest-priced four-door Custom Station Wagon.

FLASH! RAMBLER TOPS MOBILGAS ECONOMY RUN FOR 2nd STRAIGHT YEAR! **24.35** m.p.g. with Hydra-Matic Drive!

OVERDRIVE AVAIL.

596

RAMBLER

CUSTOM

new 190 H.P. V·8 And Economy 6

5718-1 (6)
5728-1 (V8)

SUPER

5718-2 (6)
5728-2 (V8)
CROSS-COUNTRY

GEORGE ROMNEY
PRESIDENT, AMERICAN MOTORS
(UNTIL 2-62)

new REBEL V8

5739-2

255 HP
327 CID V8

AVAIL. AS REGULAR
OR HARDTOP
WAGON

5723-2 (V8)

SIDE MOULDINGS
CHANGED

Rambler Custom

6.70 x 15

57 20 MODELS

SMALL EXTRA PIECE
ADDED, IN TOP SECTION
OF GRILLE

114,084
RAMBLERS BLT.
1957

5729-2 (V8)

RAMBLER

5802 or 5806

DE LUXE

$1775., f.o.b. and up

127 HP 6 SUPER

new AMERICAN 6 (100" WB) 42,196 SOLD

new GRILLES

58

new TAIL-FINS (ON ALL BUT AMERICAN)

MORE THAN 100 IMPROVEMENTS! 22 MODELS

CUSTOM

215-HP REBEL V8

INTRODUCED FOR 1958, new AMERICAN and AMBASSADOR MODELS have OWN GRILLES, DIFFERENT FROM THOSE OF OTHER RAMBLERS.

REBEL V8

5829-2

DASH

5888-1 OR 2

new AMBASSADOR V8   117" WB

new = 4 HEADLIGHTS   270 HP (THROUGH '59)

5889-2

$2822., f.o.b.

598

186,227 RAMBLERS SOLD 1958

new "DEEP-DIP" RUSTPROOFING

RAMBLER

5902
5906

New 100 inch wheelbase
Rambler American

STATION WAGON

AMERICAN

$1835 Suggested delivered price at Kenosha, Wisconsin, for 2-door sedan at left. State and local taxes, if any, automatic transmission and optional equipment, extra.

SUPER

5915-1

5904-1
AMERICAN WAGON
IS new
90 HP

PUSH-BUTTON TRANS. AVAIL.

CUSTOM

5915-2

REBEL
108" WB

CROSS-
COUNTRY
5928-1 OR 2

REBEL

5929-2
COUNTRY
CLUB

5985-1 OR 2

AMBASSADOR

117" WB

270 HP V8

AMBASSADOR
CUSTOM

59

5989-2

DASH

$2822.·
f.o.b.

599

RAMBLER

90 HP   AMERICAN

6005

6004

DOORS NOW OPEN WIDER (75° INSTEAD OF 55°)

ROOF RACKS NOW ON ALL WAGONS

60

6002
$**1781.**, f.o.b. and up

S015
6 DELUXE
108" WB
127 HP

6018 WAGON

SUPER

6015-1 (6)
6025-1 (V8)

SEDAN

6015-2 (6)
6025-2 (V8)

CUSTOM COUNTRY CLUB
6019-2 (6)
6029-2 (V8)

REAR DETAILS

6018 or 6028 (-2 or 4)

CUSTOM

V8 = 200 HP

new REAR FENDERS

3 WIDE SEATS, 5 BIG DOORS. The tailgate is a fifth door with outside key lock so children can't open from inside. Rear seat passengers step in—no scrambling over seats or tailgate.

new "COMPOUND WRAP-AROUND" WINDSHIELD on AMBASSADOR

434,704 RAMBLERS SOLD 1960

WAGON (6 or 8-PASS.)
6088-1 to 4
2881., f.o.b., and up

AMB. CUSTOM COUNTRY CLUB
6089-2

AMBASSADOR V-8
BY RAMBLER
The New Standard of Basic Excellence in Luxury Cars

600

RAMBLER

6104

6105

6/08 4-DR. WAGONS *also*

6107-2
" -5

AMER. PRICES START AT **1831.,** f.o.b. (6/02)

$2369., f.o.b., *and up*

All New! A Convertible

"THE NEW WORLD STANDARD OF BASIC EXCELLENCE"

new Ceramic-Armored Muffler

AMERICAN 6
L-HEAD
90 OR
125 HP
OHV

AMERICAN WAGON REAR DETAILS

61
(RESTYLED)

CLASSIC 6 OR V8
127 OR 138 HP
6
OR
200 OR 215 HP
V8

CLASSIC DELUXE

CLOSE DETAIL OF CLASSIC FRONT END ↗

RAMBLER

CLASSIC CUSTOM
6/08-2 (6)
6/28-4 (V8)
(CLASSIC 2-DR. WAGONS *also*)

...New! First acoustical ceiling of molded fiber glass

6188-1,2 or 4

AMBASSADOR V8
↙ 250 OR 270 HP

CUSTOM 400 SEDAN JOINS AMBASSADOR LINE

6185-5

Rambler

World Standard of Compact Car Excellence

RAMBLER

62

6206

90 HP 6

1962 RAMBLER AMERICAN
DELUXE 4-DOOR SEDAN
(Also offered in Custom series)
6205

6208

RAMBLER AMERICAN DELUXE 4-DOOR STATION WAGON
(Also offered in Custom series)

1962 RAMBLER AMERICAN
DELUXE 2-DOOR CLUB SEDAN
(Also offered in Custom and "400" series)

6208

RAMBLER AMERICAN "400" 4-DOOR STATION WAGON
(Also offered in Deluxe and Custom series)

6216-2

new

1962 RAMBLER CLASSIC CUSTOM 2-DOOR CLUB SEDAN
(Also offered in Deluxe and "400" series)

6207-5

AMERICAN   **"400" CVT.**

new DOUBLE SAFETY BRAKES with TANDEM MASTER CYLINDER

6215-5

CLASSIC 400

6218-5

454,784
RAMBLERS BLT.
1962

RAMBLER CLASSIC 6 "400" CROSS COUNTRY STATION WAGON

6288-2

1962 RAMBLER AMBASSADOR
CUSTOM 4-DOOR STATION WAGON

WB CUT TO 108"

250 or 270 HP AMB. V8s

AMBASSADOR 400
AND INTERIOR

6285-5

RAMBLER

TOP QUALITY AT AMERICA'S LOWEST PRICE! **$1846**
Manufacturer's suggested retail price for the '63 Rambler American "220" Two-Door Sedan. Optional equipment, transportation, and state and local taxes, if any, extra. An award-winning Rambler value!

6302 220 ←

220 → 6304

6309-7

440-H H/T (with 138-HP OHV 6)

AMERICAN 6 100" WB

6305

440 CVT.

6306-5 440

6307-5

63

(CLASSICS and AMB. TOTALLY RESTYLED)

DASH

6315-2

660

CLASSIC 6 OR V8 new 112" WB

OPTIONAL 198-HP V8 (STARTING 3-1-63)

770

770

6315-5

6318-5

The New Shape Of Quality

New! Hidden storage compartment in wagon!

250 OR 270 HP AMBASSADOR V8 new 112" WB

880 CROSS COUNTRY

6388-2

990 WAGON SIMILAR

New! Curved glass side windows... for easier entry!

990

6386-5 2-DR.

6385-5 SEDAN

AMBASSADOR has LOWER BODY BAND

WINNER OF MOTOR TREND AWARD **CAR OF THE YEAR**

603

RAMBLER

new AMER. WAGON RESEMBLES A
SEDAN with GRAFTED-ON REAR SECTION

6406

220
6408

220

6407-5

AMERICAN

6.00 × 14
TIRES
(15" OPT.)

330

6405-2

440-H
6409-7

Y! TOP IN BLK., WHITE, GOLD or TURQ.

440

TO 138 HP

AMERICAN

TOTALLY RESTYLED
(new 106" WB)

6418

6418-5

770

660
2-DR.

6416-2

770

550

64

CLASSIC (6 has 127 or 138 HP)

393,863 RAMBLERS
BLT. 1964

4-DR.
6415-5

6489-5

990-H
(INTERIOR BELOW)

6488-5

990

990

FRESH NEW SPIRIT OF '64!

DASH (W/O AIR CONDITIONING)

DASH (WITH AIR CONDITIONING)

990
250 or 270 HP

AMBASSADOR

604

RAMBLER

6506 220

6508-2   6509-7   American 440-H

American 6

AMERICAN

330

6507-5

New! 3 different sizes of cars
New! 3 different wheelbases
New! 7 spectacular powerplants:
New Torque Command Sixes-
most advanced engines! Big V-8's

L-HEAD
195.6 CID
6 STILL
AVAIL. IN
AMERICAN
(90 HP @
3000 RPM)

65

CVTS. NOW IN ALL 3 LINES

DASH (AMERICAN)
412,736 RAMBLERS SOLD 1965

AMERICAN
GRILLE NOW
VERTICALLY
SPLIT INTO
4 HORIZ.
SECTIONS

440

195.6 OR 232 CID OHV 6s with
125 OR 155 HP

6518-5
Rambler Classic 770 Station Wagon

6517-5

770

CLASSIC

199 OR 232 CID 6
(128, 145, 155 HP)
198 HP
with 287 CID
V8

6519-5
Rambler Classic 770 Hardtop

SEE ALSO:
MARLIN

CLASSIC
DASH
770 SEDAN

6515-5

6587-5

CLAS.

GRILLE
CLOSE-
UPS

ALSO AVAIL. with
327 CID,
270-HP V8
ALSO USED IN
AMB.)

AMB.
(new HEADLIGHTS
VERTICALLY
STACKED)

CLASSIC 112" WB CONT'D.,
BUT AMBASSADOR WB
INCREASED TO 116".

6589-7

AMBASSADOR V8

990

SLOGAN:
THE SENSIBLE SPECTACULARS

DASH

AMBASSADOR   1965

RIVIERA

(STARTS 1963)

(by Buick)

401 CID
V8
325 HP @
4400 RPM

117" WB

7.10×15
TIRES

(DASH)

63

America's bid for a great new international classic car

64

'64 DASH

ADVENTURE IS A CAR CALLED RIVIERA AND IT'S A BUICK

(VINYL TOP ALSO AVAIL.)

new
TAIL-LIGHTS
IN BUMPER

65

new
CONCEALED
HEADLIGHTS

WIRE
WHEEL
OPTION

Wouldn't you really rather have a Buick?

606

(CARS = 1902-1966)

STUDEBAKER

STUDEBAKER CORP.,
SOUTH BEND, IND.
$660. *up*
(CHAMP.)

116½" WB (SINCE '38)

COMMANDER 6

226.2 CID
90 HP @ 3400 RPM

CLUB SEDAN

CHAMP. 2-DR. IS PACE CAR AT 1940 INDY 500 RACE.

CHAMP. 6 *has*
164.3 CID
78 HP @ 4000 RPM

250.4 CID   122" WB
PRESIDENT 8

40

110 HP @ 3600 RPM

Lowest priced CHAMPION

110" WB

new WIDER GRILLES

new 169.6 CID, 80 HP (CHAMP.)

You seldom use the clutch! That's due to Studebaker's famous gas-saving, engine-saving Economatic Shift with Overdrive—available on all Champion models at moderate extra cost.

PRICES BEGIN AT
$690

for a Champion Business Coupe
Champion Club Sedan with trunk .. $730
Champion Cruising Sedan with trunk .. $770

COMMANDER
94 HP @ 3600 RPM

41

new BAND TAPERS ALONG SIDES (EXCEPT ON SKYWAY)

Distinctively smart, new SKYWAY PRESIDENT 8

119" WB

Land Cruiser

AVAILABLE ON COMMANDER SIX OR PRESIDENT EIGHT CHASSIS

117 HP @ 4000 RPM
125" WB

STUDEBAKER

CHAMPION 6 has 170 CID (SINCE '41 and THROUGH '54)

HIGHEST QUALITY CAR IN LOWEST PRICE FIELD

PRICES BEGIN AT $810*

*for a Champion Business Coupe

4-G Champion 6

110" WB 5.50 × 16 TIRES

119" WB 6.25 × 16 TIRES

42-45

12-A

The Commander 6

Studebaker is building an unlimited quantity of airplane engines, military trucks and other matériel for national defense . . . and a limited number of passenger cars which are the finest Studebakers ever produced.
The Studebaker Corporation

CHAMPION . . . $810 and up
COMMANDER . . $1106 and up
PRESIDENT 8 . $1242 and up
f.o.b.

SKYWAY COMMANDER LAND CRUISER 6

PRESIDENT IS FINAL STRAIGHT-8 (FIRST PRES. 8 was 1928 MODEL)

124½" WB

8-C

World's first cars with Studebaker's new, perfected
Turbo-matic Drive
NO CLUTCH-PEDAL NO CREEP NO CLASH
Fluid coupling — with controlled gear selection — and automatic overdrive — available on President and Commander models at extra cost.

7.00×15

1942

The President 8

OVERDRIVE AVAIL.

SKYWAY CHAMPION IS ONLY SERIES AVAIL.

"DOUBLE DATER" COUPE

DASH

EARLY 46

RARE! (AVAIL. ONLY TO MAY, '46)

110" WB

$916. f.o.b.

Champion

BODIES AVAIL. = 3-PASS. COUPE;
5-PASS. "DOUBLE DATER" CPE.;
2-DR. CLUB SED.; 4-DR. CR. SEDAN

608

ALL-NEW 1947 MODELS START MAY, 1946

$1447.

First by far with a postwar car!

THE NEW 1947 STUDEBAKER

$1442. f.o.b.

new 112" WB ON 6-G CHAMPION

47

(TOTALLY RESTYLED)

Starlight COUPES

$1752.

CHAMPION STRLT. CPE. (ABOVE) has 1-PC. WINDSHIELD, UNLIKE OTHER CHAMPION MODELS

(SAME HP FIGS. SINCE '41)

14-A COMMANDER

119" WB

SEDAN

COMMANDER REGAL DE LUXE

$1910.

REGAL DE LUXE LAND CRUISER

DETAILS OF 2-DOOR SEDAN (CHAMP. REGAL DE LUXE)

123" WB

3-W. CPE.

CONVERTIBLE (new)

CHAMPION

new HORIZONTAL PIECE ACROSS EITHER END OF CHAMPION GRILLE

$1535., f.o.b.

New 1948 Studebaker

First in style

CHAMPION

SEDANS

$2077. COMMANDER

48

new HORIZ. CHROME ABOVE CMNDR. GRILLE

609

" First in style...first in vision...first by far with a postwar car "

$1762

CHAMPION (8-G)
NOW has 2
HORIZ. STRIPS
ACROSS
GRILLE

$1757.

$2135., f.o.b.

VERTICAL
CHROME CENTER
STRIP ADDED TO
CMNDR. GRILLE

STARLIGHT CPE.
and INTERIOR

STUDE. "STARLIGHT"
CLUB COUPES ARE AMONG
THE MOST UNUSUAL and
ATTRACTIVE BODY
STYLES EVER PRODUCED!

49

LAND CRUISER
INTERIOR

LAND CRUISER

REAR

new 113" WB (CHAMPIONS)   85 HP   **lowest price**

50

new
"BULLET-NOSE"
FRONT END
STYLING

CHAMPION
CUSTOM 6-PASS.
2-DOOR SEDAN
AS SHOWN

$ **1487** 50

"the "next look" in cars"   610   new 6.40 x 15
TIRES   (CONT'D.)

$1676.

CHAMPION
REGAL
DE LUXE 6

CHROME ALONG
ROCKER PANEL

Studebaker

2-DR.

$1566.

CHAMPION DLX. (9-G)
has RUBBER PAD ON REAR FENDER,
BUT NO CHROME ALONG ROCKER PANEL.

50
(CONT'D.)

CVT.

America likes Studebaker's new driving thrill—Every 1950 Studebaker handles with light-touch ease—rides so smoothly it almost completely abolishes travel fatigue. A new kind of coil spring front suspension.

COMMANDER (17-A)

$2024.

$2013.

LAND CRUISER

$2187.

America likes this "next look" in interiors —Fabulously fine nylon cord upholstery, introduced into motoring by Studebaker, is standard in the 1950 Land Cruiser and regal de luxe Commander. Land Cruiser is shown.

CHAMP. CUSTOM HAS NO HOOD ORNAMENT

SEDAN

Studebaker Champion

3-WINDOW BUSINESS COUPE $1643.

51

232.6 CID IN new O.H.V. V8 ENGINE ALSO AVAIL.

CHAMPION DE LUXE 6 (10-G) 85 HP

$1744.

(REGAL CHAMP. has LEATHER TRIM INSIDE DOORS.)

A brand new V-8 (233 CID) *Commander*

CVT.

has

120 h.p. @4000 (THROUGH '54)

STATE CMNDR. SEDAN

$2143.

"BULLET NOSE" GRILLE SOMEWHAT MODIFIED FROM '50.

new GRILLE IS FLUSH WITH FRONT END

COMMANDER LAND CRUISER $2289.

"STUDEBAKER...THE THRIFTY ONE FOR '51"

STUDEBAKER'S 100TH ANNIVERSARY
1852~1952

© 1952 The Studebaker Corporation
South Bend 27, Indiana, U.S.A.

CHAMPION PRICES START AT $**1735.**

REGAL COMMANDER

REGAL CHAMPION OR STATE COMMANDER CONVERTS. AVAIL.

PACE CAR AT 1952 INDY 500 RACE

LAND CRUISER

52
FRONT END RESTYLED

BODY DESIGN BASICALLY AS BEFORE, BUT CONTROVERSIAL "BULLET NOSE" DISCONTINUED IN FAVOR OF A MORE CONVENTIONAL (BUT EXTREMELY BROAD) GRILLE

"STARLINER" H/T IS new

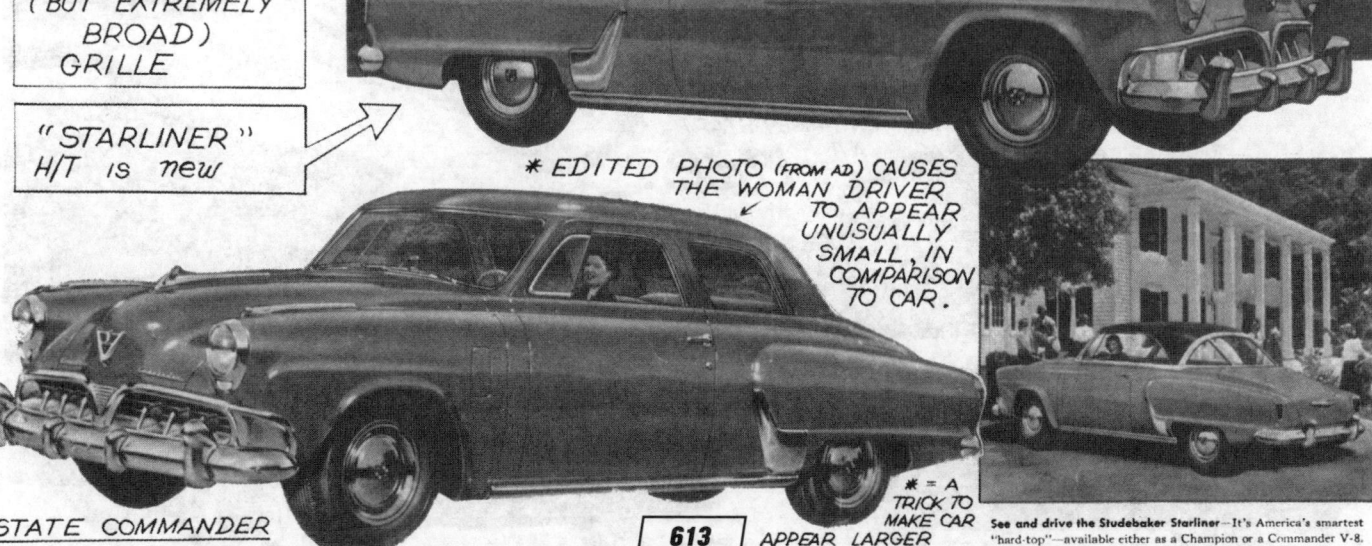

* EDITED PHOTO (FROM AD) CAUSES THE WOMAN DRIVER TO APPEAR UNUSUALLY SMALL, IN COMPARISON TO CAR.

STATE COMMANDER

*＝A TRICK TO MAKE CAR APPEAR LARGER

See and drive the Studebaker Starliner—It's America's smartest "hard-top"—available either as a Champion or a Commander V-8.

Studebaker

CHAMPION PRICES START AT $1735.

85 HP @ 4000 RPM

H/T

MEANS CHAMP. 6 H/T

170 CID 6 (THROUGH '54)

↑ new DESIGN WINS FASHION ACADEMY AWARD

53

(TOTALLY RESTYLED)

new 116½" WB (120½" ON CPE., H/T and LAND CRUISER)

MEANS CMNDR. V8

NO MORE CONVERTIBLES AVAILABLE (UNTIL '60 LARK)

VERTICAL PIECES ADDED TO GRILLE FOR 1954.

STUDEBAKERS, SINCE LATE 1930s, ARE Styled by *Raymond Loewy* →

CHAMPION PRICES START AT $1758.

54

CHAMPION CUSTOM

6 CYL. *has* 101 HP @ 4000 RPM (*new* 186 CID THROUGH '58)

A *BIG NEW* CHAMPION
America's No. 1 economy car!
Now more marvelous than ever!

CHAMPION PRICES START AT $ 1741.

55

CHAMPION DE LUXE

INTERIOR (CMNDR.)

COUPES

COMMANDER

(6-CYL. OR V8 WAGONS)

Now in the low price field!
A sensationally high-powered
NEW COMMANDER V-8

SPEEDSTER

CONESTOGA

STATE PRESIDENT

COMMANDER H/T DETAILS

NEW!
AMERICA'S SMARTEST TWO-TONING!

PRESIDENT

The first dynamic headliners of the
great Studebaker-Packard alliance!
Sensationally powered '55 Studebakers!
Amazingly low introductory prices!

224 OR
new 259 CID
V8s *have*
140, 162,
175 OR 185 HP

615

CHAMPION PRICES START AT $1841.

Studebaker

Craftsmanship with a Flair

PELHAM 6

CHAMPION 6

wagons

PARKVIEW V8

CMNDR. V8

FLIGHT HAWK 6

POWER HAWK V8

SKY HAWK V8

FRONT DETAILS OF COMMANDER V8

NEW DUAL EXHAUSTS·Built into the bumper for more style, more class than you've ever seen in a low price car. Ready for 4-barrel carburetion to boost mileage and power.

Hawks

GOLDEN HAWK V8 (275 HP)

The Golden Hawk

56

SEDAN

PRESIDENT V8

CLASSIC SEDAN *has* ROCKER PANEL TRIM

"CLASSIC" SEDAN

259, 289 OR 352 CID V8s

PRESIDENT V8 195 HP * @ 4500 RPM

new 12-VOLT ELECTRICAL SYSTEM

NEW CYCLOPS-EYE SPEEDOMETER

* 210 HP with 4-BBL. CARB.

PRESIDENT PINEHURST V8

616

Studebaker

CHAMP. SCOTSMAN IS A new BUDGET-PRICED MODEL with MINIMUM of CHROME and PLAINEST INTERIOR

101 HP

2-DR., 6-CYL. WAGONS
SCOTSMAN (116½" WB)
PELHAM (118½" WB)

W-1 SEDAN

57-G
CHAMPION SCOTSMAN 6 (new)
PRICES START AT
$1776. (2-DR.)

PLAIN, PAINTED HUB CAPS, 6.40 × 15 TIRES

57

(RESTYLED)

116½" WB ON MOST

57-G (6 CYL.)
57-H (8 CYL.)

CHAMPION DE LUXE 6

STUDEBAKER
1957

PROVINCIAL 4 DR. WAGON
P-4

D-4
PARKVIEW 2-DR. WAGON

COMMANDER
F-2 (CUSTOM)
F-4 (DELUXE)

$2561.

$2407.
PRESIDENT
W-6

$2246. (DLX.)

Studebaker-Packard

CORPORATION

Where pride of Workmanship comes first!

P-6

BROADMOOR 4-DR. WAGON

289 CID (275 HP @ 4800 RPM)
V8 GOLDEN HAWK

C-3 SILVER HAWK
186 CID 6 (101 HP)

K-7

$3185.

OR 210, 225 HP V8s (289 CID)

57 (CONT'D.)

Golden Hawk

58
4 HEADLIGHTS ON SOME MODELS

Studebaker Commanders and Champions

101 TO 275 HP

(SAME HP AS '57) THE FINAL GOLDEN HAWK

180-HP CMNDR.

" Studebaker cars take on a completely new luxury look for 1958!"

SCOTSMAN 6 PRICES START AT $1795.

NOTICE STRIKING DIFFERENCES IN APPEARANCE BETWEEN THE LT.-OVER-DK. AND DK.-OVER-LT. HARDTOPS

REAR DETAILS (SEDAN)

Studebaker President

The Hawk-inspired PRESIDENT STARLIGHT for 1958

Studebaker-Packard CORPORATION
Where pride of Workmanship comes first!

618

STUDEBAKER 59

HAWK 6 PRICES START AT **$2360.**

170 CID 6 (90 HP @ 4000) OR 259 CID V8s (180 or 195 HP @ 4500)

6 or V8
SILVER HAWK (C-6)

1959

120½" WB

SEE ALSO: **LARK** (STARTING 1959, LOWER-PRICED MODELS USE LARK NAME)

60

3 new STRIPS on SIDE of REAR FENDER

new 289 CID V8 RETURNS to HAWK AS ONLY AVAIL. ENG. (210 or 225 HP @ 4500 RPM)

$2650.

C-6 HAWK

6.70 x 15 TIRES

61

new TRIM DESIGN ALONG REAR FENDERS

HAWK

$2677.

(C-6)

62 (RESTYLED)

new HAWK GT

new ROOFLINE

new CLASSIC-STYLE GRILLE with HEAVY CHROME BORDERS

(K-6)

$3424. (UP $27. IN '63)

63

new GRILLE DESIGN with DECORATIVE CRISS-CROSS STRIPS ADDED

new AVANTI

HAWK GT

$4759.

AVANTI INTRO. DURING '62 109" WB 289 CID V8

STUDEBAKER

6.00, 6.50 or 6.70 × 15 TIRES

AVANTI V8

113" WB

109" WB

64

COMMANDER

109" WB

CHALLENGER (109" WB)

(AVAIL. 1964 ONLY)
112 HP 6 or
180 HP V8

113" WB ON
CRUISER V8

$2417.

120" WB

1964

FINAL
GRAN TURISMO HAWK

STUDE.
PRODUCTION
CONTINUES
ONLY AT THE
CANADIAN
BRANCH FACTORY,
FOR '65-66.

DETAILS
OF
WAGONAIRE
ILLUSTR.
AT RIGHT

TOPSIDE LUGGAGE RACK
(OPT.)

BRAKE RELEASE

Wagonaire

65

"the Common-Sense Car"

TAILGATE STEP

6 CYL.
OHV ENG.
(V8 ON NEXT PG.)
COMMANDER

(UNFOLDS
AND LOWERS)

$2581. (6 CYL.)

INTERIOR

620

(CONT'D.)

Studebaker

THE COMMON-SENSE CAR

Daytona Sports SEDAN

65 (CONT'D.)

CRUISER INTERIOR FEATURES

Exclusive Beauty Vanity in glove compartment —(opt.).

DAYTONA INTER.

CLOSER DETAIL OF DASH

V8 NOW has 195 HP

← FINAL YEAR OF 4 HEADLIGHTS

$2985.

→

Cruiser

S = 6
V = V8

PRICES START AT $2465. (COMMANDER 6 2-DR.)

194 CID, 120-HP 6 OR 283 CID, 195-HP V8

Studebaker
AUTOMOTIVE SALES CORPORATION

FINAL STUDEBAKERS HAVE THIS GRILLE.

LAST

Cars BY ST.-P.

66

109" OR 113" WB (SINCE 1962, ON LARK and LARK-BASED MODELS)

3-66 == DISCONTINUED

TEMPEST BY PONTIAC!

new COMPACT CAR

new 4-CYL. ENG. ADAPTED FROM THE RIGHT HALF OF A PONTIAC V8!

FROM $2329.

new FOR **61**

STD. and CUSTOM COUPES INTRO. IN MIDYEAR

(STD.)
4 (194.5 CID)
OR
V-8 (215 CID)

Independent suspension at all wheels

112" wheelbase
(THROUGH '63)

THE HOT TOPIC IS THE NEW TEMPEST BY PONTIAC

TROPHY 4 ENGINE

FOUR CYLINDERS

to *155 h.p.* (Or buy the 155 h.p. aluminum V-8 option.)

FRONT ENGINE ⟷ REAR TRANSMISSION

PERFECT BALANCE

PONTIAC'S TEMPEST
PICKED BY MOTOR TREND MAGAZINE AS
CAR OF THE YEAR

WITH
PONTIAC POWER STEERING (OPT.)

TEMPEST

62

STANDARD TEMPEST COUPE has BROAD BACKLIGHT, MINIMUM CHROME

CUSTOM COUPE has "TOWN CAR" BACKLIGHT

4 CYL. WITH 110, 115, 120, 140, OR 166 HP. 185-HP ALUMINUM V8 ALSO AVAIL.

new LE MANS

The gas-saving "4" with Pontiac Punch!

LE MANS

4 CYL. 195.4 CID (115-166 HP) TEMPEST (NAME RETURNS TO FRONT FENDER)

CVT. WITH TOP DOWN

LE MANS

326 CID V8 ALSO AVAILABLE (260 HP)

LE MANS has RECTANGULAR TAILLIGHTS, "LE MANS" ON FRONT FENDER.

63

LE MANS

WITH TOP UP

623

Wide-Track Pontiac Tempest

64
(RESTYLED)

Tempest

new 115" WB
new 215 CID
140-HP IN-LINE
O.H.V. 6

Tempest CUSTOM

SAFARI WAGON

326 CID V8 ALSO AVAIL.
(250 OR 280 HP)

LE MANS

GTO ("GTO"
APPEARS ON GRILLE)
(new)

LE MANS

TEMPEST

1965: The year of the Quick Wide-Tracks

TEMPEST

SAFARI WAGON

Tempest **65** FROM $2618.

140-HP 6 OR 250-285 HP V8

TEMPEST CUSTOM

H/T (new)

Le Mans

FRONT-END COMPARISON OF LE MANS (left) and GTO (right)

SEE ALSO: **Pontiac**

OFFICIAL PACE CAR–MOTOR TREND RIVERSIDE "500" COURTESY OF HURST

GTO

625

THUNDERBIRD

(INTRO. FALL, 1954, FOR 1955)

(Ford)

(MODEL 40) **55**

ALL with V-8 O.H.V. ENGINES

193 HP

"CLASSIC" T-BIRDS AVAIL. with REMOVABLE HARD TOP OR CVT. TOP (THROUGH '57)

102" WB (THROUGH '57)

$2944.

6.70 × 15 TIRES (THROUGH '56)

40-B H/T has new PORTHOLES (EXCEPT EARLY MODELS)

56

40-A

202 HP

new 7.50 × 14 TIRES

57

NAME MOVED TO FRONT-FENDERS

212 HP

GRILLE, BUMPERS, TAIL-LIGHTS MODIFIED

$3408.

new WHEEL COVERS

626

new DASH

THUNDERBIRD

DASH
63-A

58
(TOTALLY RESTYLED)

1958-T

Exclusive "Panel Console" 76-A

new 113" WB

300 HP (THROUGH '65)

The car *everyone* would love to own!

H/T 63-A

CVT. 76-A

new 8.00 x 14 TIRES

59

HORIZONTAL PCS. ON GRILLE and BETWEEN TAIL-LIGHTS

T-59

new SIDE TRIM EACH YEAR

6 TAIL-LIGHTS IN 1960

9 VERTICAL CHROME BANDS on EA. REAR FENDER (1960 ONLY)

60

$4222.

new GRILLE

sliding sun roof (*new*)

'60 THUNDERBIRD
THE WORLD'S MOST WANTED CAR

'61 THUNDERBIRD
UNIQUE IN ALL THE WORLD

PACE CAR AT 1961 INDY 500 RACE

$4637.

(OPTIONAL)

Swing-Away Steering Wheel glides out of your way for easier, more graceful entrances and exits—yet locks safely in place before you can drive.

61
(TOTALLY RESTYLED.)

$4170.

unmistakably New, unmistakably Thunderbird

new BODY TYPES and MODEL NUMBERS in 1962

HARDTOP

CVT.

LANDAU (new)

$5552.

$4511.

with VINYL TOP and DECORATIVE LANDAU IRONS

Thunderbird
Sports Roadster
(new)

new GRILLE

62

new SPTS. RDST. has TWIN TONNEAU CAPS (as illustrated)

H/Ts = MODEL 83
CVTS. = MODEL 85

unique in all the world

THUNDERBIRD

$4529. TO $5648.

H/T 83

INTERIOR (OFFERING WOOD-GRAIN EFFECTS)

63

LANDAU 87

CVT. 85

final SPORT ROADSTER 89

113.2" WB

64 (RESTYLED)

new 8.15 x 15 TIRES

new WIDE TAIL-LIGHTS with T-BIRD EMBLEM

new DASH

PRICED FROM $4486. (IN '64 and '65)

65 5 new VERTICAL STRIPS on EACH TAIL-LIGHT

INTERIOR with new WOOD-GRAIN EFFECTS

629

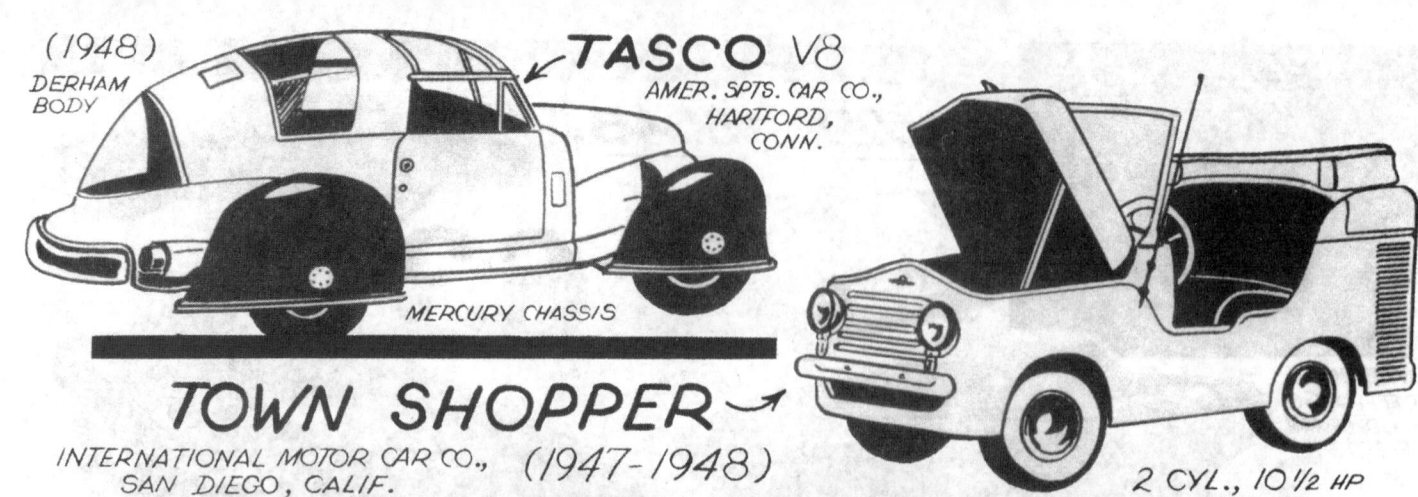

(1948)

DERHAM BODY

TASCO V8

AMER. SPTS. CAR CO., HARTFORD, CONN.

MERCURY CHASSIS

TOWN SHOPPER

INTERNATIONAL MOTOR CAR CO., SAN DIEGO, CALIF.

(1947-1948)

2 CYL., 10 1/2 HP

Tucker '48

THE TUCKER CORP., 7401 S. CICERO, CHICAGO, ILL. (1946-1949)

PRINCIPAL OUTPUT PRODUCED DURING 1947, BUT KNOWN AS 1948 MODELS.

TUCKER

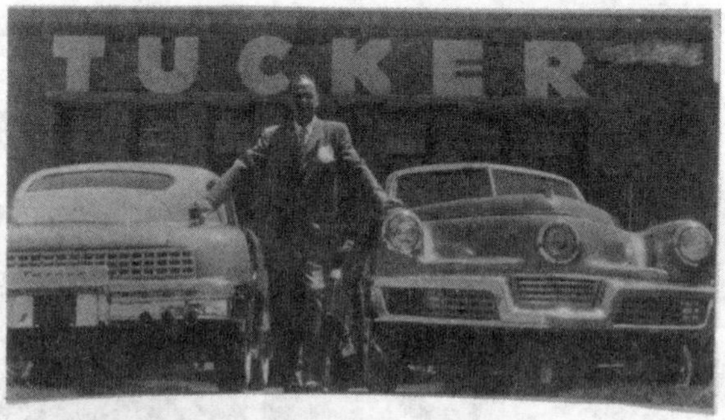

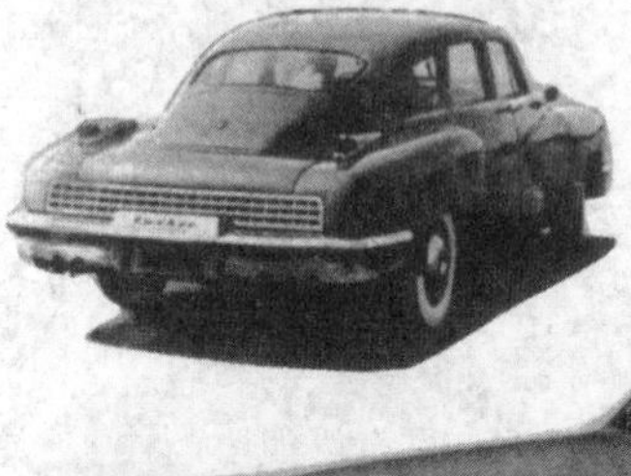

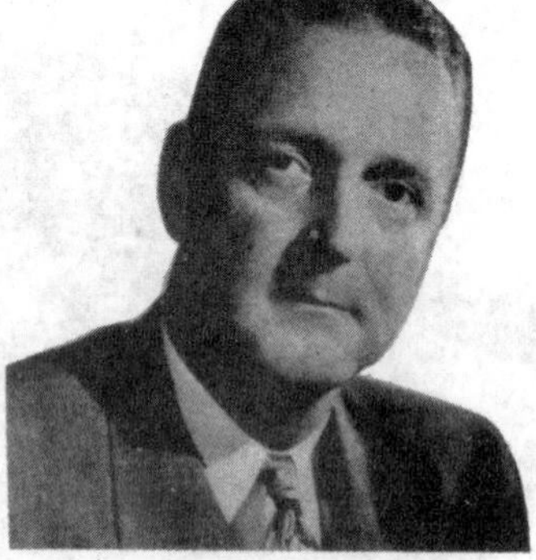

PRESTON TUCKER (FOUNDER) (1903-1956)

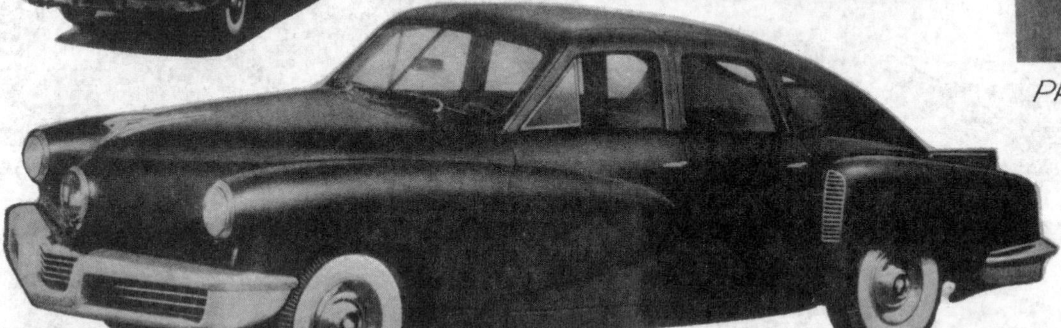

6 - CYL. HORIZ. OPPOSED FRANKLIN/TUCKER REAR ENGINE

TURNING (CENTER) "CYCLOPS EYE" HEADLIGHT

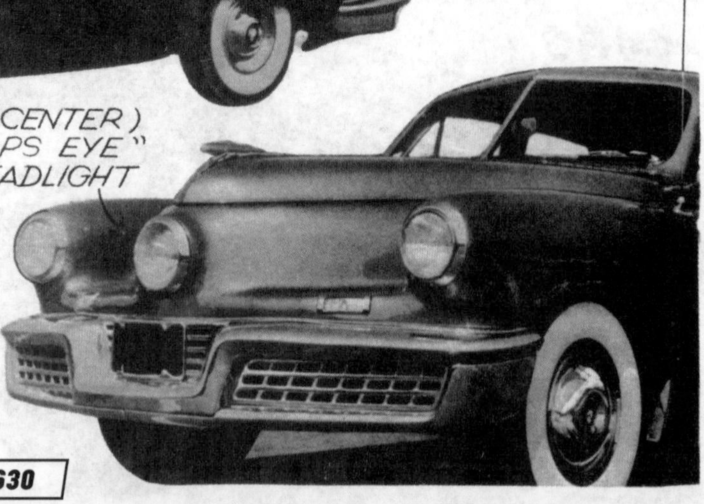

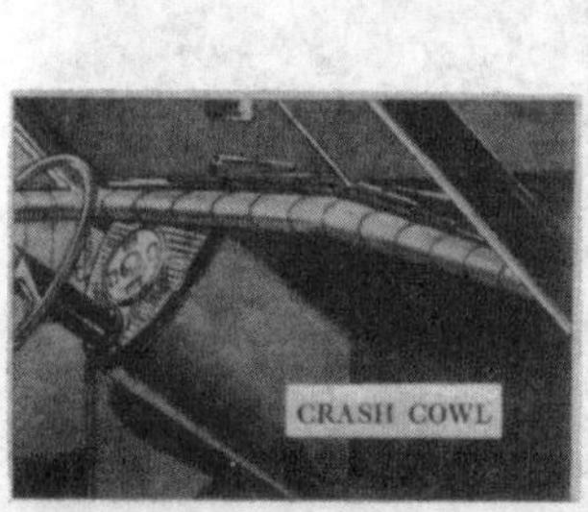

CRASH COWL

RARE! ONLY 53 BUILT, INCLUDING PILOT MODELS.

Tucker
SYMBOL OF SAFETY

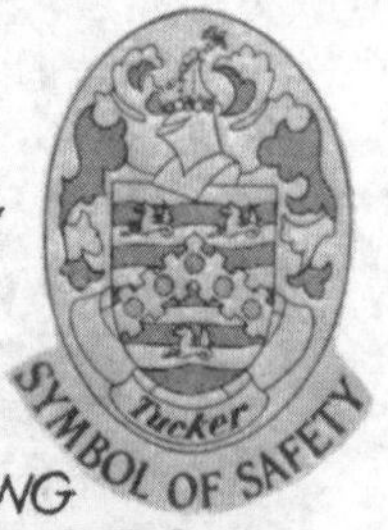

Valiant
NEW FROM CHRYSLER

V-100

$2053. and up
V-200

V-200s have EXTRA SIDE CHROME TRIM.

INCLINED 6-CYL. 170 CID O.H.V. ENGINE 101 HP @ 4400 RPM or 148 HP @ 5200 RPM

V-200

106½" WB (THROUGH '62)

1960

60

QXI-L OR QXI-H

V-100

225 CID PLYMOUTH 6 CYL. ENGINE ALSO AVAIL.) (145 HP @ 4000 RPM)

V-200

new H/T

V-200

1961

DASH

V-200

61

RVI-L OR RVI-H

note GRILLE CHANGE

FINAL YEAR FOR 148-HP VERSION OF SMALL ENGINE

V-200

VALIANT

$2590.

V-100

V-200

62

SVI

SVI-L (V-100)
SVI-H (V-200)
SVI-P (SIGNET)

new
SIGNET
(has
FRONT BUCKET SEATS)

$2538.

↑
SIGNET has ⑦
INSIGNIA on DARK GRILLE

(new 18-GALLON FUEL TANK)

Valiant V-100 2-door sedan metallic green

ENGINE ←

now
CONVTS.

TRANSMISSION
PUSHBUTTONS

106" WB

63 TVI

(TOTALLY
RESTYLED)

632

Valiant V-200 4-door station wagon/dark metallic blue

VALIANT

note THAT THIS LATER SERIES CONVERTIBLE has LESS REAR BRIGHTWORK and DIFFERENT DECK EMBLEM FROM "SIGNET" ILLUSTR. on PRECEDING PAGE

63 (CONT'D.)

Valiant presents

AMERICA'S LOWEST-PRICED CONVERTIBLE... $2340*

Barracuda (new) (INTRO. 4-2-64)

$2215.

V-100

$2670. (6)

6 CYL. OR V8

Valiant V-100 2-Door Sedan

64

V-200

VVI-L (V-100)
VVI-H (V-200)
VVI-P (SIGNET 200)
VVI-P29 (BARRACUDA)

new 273 CID V8 has 180 HP @ 4200 RPM

$2549.

SIGNET

new GRILLE with "PLYMOUTH" NAMEPLATE ABOVE

Valiant/64 style
Best all-around compact

633

$2766.

VALIANT

BARRACUDA

$2801. (V8)

65

6 and V8 ENGINE SPECS. AS BEFORE, EXCEPT THAT new OPTIONAL 10.5 COMPRESSION VERSION of V8 IS ALSO AVAIL., with 235 HP @ 5200 RPM

ALL-VINYL SEATS IN "100."

100

Plymouth Valiant 200 4-Door Station Wagon

200

6 CYL.:
AVI-L (100)
AVI-H (200)
AVI-P (SIGNET)
AVI-P29 (BARRACUDA)
(V8s have "AV2" PREFIXES)

200

DASH

Valiant Signet

The Roaring '65s*

new FLAT-PROFILE AIR CONDITIONER

$2234. TO $2932.

634   * = SLOGAN APPLIES TO PLYMOUTH ALSO.

COUPE

(WILLYS NAME SINCE 1917)
(ALSO WILLYS-KNIGHT, OVERLAND, WHIPPET)

WILLYS

WILLYS-OVERLAND
MOTORS, INC.
TOLEDO, O.
PRICED FROM $495.

DE LUXE

4 CYL. ONLY (SINCE '34 and THROUGH '47)

40
"4-40"

FLAT-BACKED
LOWER-PRICED "Speedway" MODEL
DOES NOT HAVE THE EXTRA STRIPS
(HORIZONTAL) ALONG FRONT END OF HOOD.

102" WB
4.3 GEAR RATIO

new = REAR QUARTER WINDOWS (SEDAN)

RED-LETTERED
"AMERICAR" NAME ON
HOOD STRIP

new 1-PC.
VERTICAL-
BARS
GRILLE
ON '41.

41
"4-41"

new 104" WB

new PLAINSMAN MODELS (AT TOP OF LINE) OFFER
OVERDRIVE and ALUMINUM HI-COMPR.
CYL. HEAD AS STD. EQUIP.

new 4.4 GEAR RATIO

AMERICAR

new
BISECTED
GRILLE

FROM $695.

42
"4-442"

ALSO

Jeep

(SEE FOLLOWING PAGES)

635

WILLYS 'Jeep'

UNIVERSAL JEEP (4-W-D)

MILITARY STYLE ('46)

← $1146.

EARLY MODEL ('46)

Station Wagon

All-Steel Station Wagon (new)

ENGINE →

MILITARY JEEPS INTRO.'41

46-
47

CJ-2A SERIES

('47)

$1565.

"Jeep Station Wagon" ON HOOD

104" WB

new 6-CYL STATION SEDAN ↘

has IMITATION WICKER PANELS

(PHOTOGRAPHED IN PORTLAND, ORE.)

4 CYL. (6 CYL. IN STA. SED.)

48

JEEP LT. TRUCKS ALSO AVAIL.

EXPORT MODEL (note PLAIN BUMPER SOMETIMES USED)

636

(CONT'D.)

WILLYS 48 (CONT'D.)

the Jeepster $1765.

JEEPSTER CVT. PRODUCED TO 1953; RE-INTRO. BY KAISER-JEEP, 1967.

4 OR 6 CYL.

New

JEEPSTER $1595. (FOR 4 CYL.)

THE 'Jeep' Station Wagon

6 - CYL. ENGINE NOW AVAIL. ALSO IN WAGON OR JEEPSTER. 4 - CYL. ALSO CONTINUES. 63 HP

49 'Jeep' Station Sedan
6 CYL. only

DEEP UPHOLSTERED SEATS, interior roominess and road-leveling wheel suspension add to the smooth, luxurious riding comfort of the 'Jeep' Station Sedan.

6.70 x 15

$1890.

WILLYS 'Jeep'

('50)

JEEPSTER

('51)

new GRILLE (EARLY '50 has '49-STYLE GRILLE.)

50-51

FIRST NON-JEEP WILLYS CAR PRODUCED SINCE 1942 MODELS:

The Revolutionary New *Aero Willys*

108" WB

AERO-WING ('52 ONLY)

MILITARY JEEP

AERO-ACE

52

AERO-LARK has 6-CYL. L-HEAD *engine*; WING, ACE, EAGLE *have* HURRICANE 6 F-HEAD. JEEP WAGONS, JEEPSTERS *also*

638

DETAILS OF F-HEAD COMBUSTION CHAMBER ➤

New Hurricane 6 Engine, F-head design with 7.6 compression, one of the world's most efficient power plants.

Willys Aero

AERO LARK

NO HOOD ORNAMENT ON LARK

2-DR.

AERO-LARK DELUXE ↗

4-DR.

AERO-FALCON

(REPLACES '52 AERO-WING) (AERO-FALCON 2-DR RESEMBLES LARK DLX.)

AERO-ACE

AERO-ACE 2-DR.

ACE H/T ALSO AVAIL. (ILLUSTR. AT LOWER RIGHT)

AERO-EAGLE H/T

AERO ACE H/T →

Station Wagon

JEEP 4 (4-W-D)

JEEP 6 DELUXE

Willys Aero

AERO FALCON NO LONGER AVAIL.

REAR SPARE TIRE

AERO EAGLE CUSTOM

LARK, ACE, EAGLE MODELS

54

H.P. INCREASED

Kaiser-Willys Sales Div.
Willys Motors, Inc.

90 OR 115 HP

WIDER OPENING TOP DOOR GIVES WIDEST OPENING OF ANY STATION WAGON IN ITS FIELD

WAGON has new GRILLE

CUSTOM

4 OR 6 CYL.

4-W-D

all-new GRILLE, TAIL-LIGHTS and TRIM

55

FINAL WILLYS CARS BUILT IN U.S.A., BUT JEEP PRODUCTION CONTINUES. KAISER JEEPS BLT. 1963 TO 1969. AMERICAN MOTORS CORP. BEGAN BUILDING JEEPS (SINCE START OF 1970 MODEL SEASON.)

BERMUDA H/T

640

MY DAD
HAD THAT CAR

PART THREE

1966–1980
AMERICAN MOTORS TO THUNDERBIRD

CONTENTS

American Motors 644

Buick............................677

Cadillac......................717

Chevelle 735

Chevette........................745

Chevrolet 747

Chrysler 800

Dodge 820

Ford 862

Imperial......................905

International
Harvester......................909

Jeep 915

Lincoln 922

Mercury 931

Oldsmobile 960

Plymouth 1000

Pontiac 1025

Thunderbird 1063

Miscellaneous 1069

This chapter contains an era that what some would describe as like Charles Dickens' *Tale of Two Cities*: "It was the best of times, it was the worst of times."

During the middle 1960s, the muscle car wars were thick with better performance, more cubic inches, more horsepower, and some of the best automotive styling and design ever to roll out of American car-making factories. The zenith of the muscle car era was 1970, with most cubes, compression, and power available in new car dealerships than at any time in previous history— race-car levels of performance, right off the showroom floor.

Equally, the end of this push for power was just around the corner. Government legislators began paying attention to the notions of air pollution, fuel economy, and vehicle safety, and effected legislation forcing automakers to pay attention as well. Nineteen seventy-one brought the birth of lower octane, unleaded gasolines . . . not the stuff performance was made of back then. Nineteen seventy-three forced the production of often ungainly five-mile-per-hour bumpers, and 1975 meant more stringent noxious emissions requirements, substantial losses in performance, and the implementation of catalytic converters as a means of meeting the new "smog laws." The big engines, like dinosaurs, were destined to extinction. Automakers were peddling double speed to keep up with ever more stringent safety and emissions legislation, as fuel prices began to rise from 1960s levels of around a quarter per gallon to fifty cents and ultimately a dollar per gallon (and more) for the new low-octane unleaded fuels. The late 1970s were famous for the first "gas crunch" fuel shortage. Government gas rationing was being considered for the first time since WWII.

Safety mandates, or carmakers' fear of them, nearly brought about the death of the convertible as a body style. Cars, were, however, becoming safer, and delivering better levels of fuel mileage. The American economy suffered several recessionary periods; smaller, more fuel efficient, and less-expensive-to-buy imported cars siphoned sales from America's long-standing brands. American Motors and Chrysler teetered on the brink of bankruptcy, unthinkable for a large automaker in the modern era.

American carmakers launched their own import fighters—the AMC Gremlin, Chevrolet's Vega, and the Ford Pinto—with relative levels of success and failure. In 1974, for the first time ever, the Ford Mustang, America's favorite "pony car" was offered with a four-cylinder engine, just a few years after the mighty Mustang Boss 302 claimed the SCCA Trans-Am Championship. The once sporty AMC AMX was reduced to a "badges, wheels, and racing stripes" kit on the lowly Hornet compact. For 1975, the base model Corvette put out a wheezing 165 horsepower.

What were real automotive enthusiasts to do? They, like the industry itself, persevered.

Carmakers soon realized that emissions, safety, and fuel economy legislation was here to stay, and would indeed become more restrictive in coming years, so the designers and engineers buckled down and began developing meaningful solutions to these issues that would allow new and future vehicles to meet or beat the requirements while offering acceptable drivability and performance. Fortunately, the technology required for computerized engine management systems was advancing at a rapid rate, so there was opportunity to gain ground there. Plus, many "imported" car brands were using electronic fuel injection as a means to improve or maintain performance while upping the game in terms of emissions and fuel economy; this during an era when most American cars still used carburetors, which opened another fertile territory of opportunity. A third way of getting smaller engines to perform like larger ones was turbocharging. There had been a few turbocharged American models in the past, but not many; the aforementioned Oldsmobile Jetfire, plus the Chevrolet Corvair Monza, of the early 1960s come to mind. Buick brought turbocharging back in a big way beginning in 1978 with their Regal Turbo.

As the 1970s progressed, American cars got incrementally better, via higher-tech ignition systems, more precise engine management "brains," increased development of fuel injection and turbos, and also less intrusive emissions and fuel economy measures. Big block V-8s— those 426 Hemis, 460 Lincolns, and 455 and 500 cubic inch GM engines—were done, but the increased focus on greater efficiency and performance, plus new attention being paid to the ways cars ride, handle, and stop, meant better days were ahead.

AMERICAN MOTORS

AMBASSADOR

232 CID (155 HP) 6 OR 3 V8s, UP TO 327 CID

*(TO 1974)

STD. V8 (287 CID)/98 HP)

990

66

CVT. $3337.

Six or V8

116" WB (THROUGH '66)

$3354.

wagon

* "AMBASSADOR" NAME ORIG. INTRO. 1927 BY NASH.

INTRO. 10-7-65

(880 MODELS PRICED FROM $2878.)

new **DPL.**

$3230.

H/T COUPE and DPL INTERIOR

(note THE UNIQUE BLACK- AND- WHITE CHECK PATTERN ON FABRIC SEAT AND DOOR SIDE COVER- ING)

American Motors....where quality is built in, not added on.

644

AMERICAN MOTORS *AMBASSADOR*

From $2515 to $3143.*

990

AMBASSADOR WAGONS

$3435.

880
2-DR.
$2971.

The Red Carpet Ride.

new
118"
WB

67

990 SEDAN
$3128.

DASH

HOOD
ORNAMENT
ADDED
↓

DPL
$3310.

1967

DPL GRILLE
BEARS 2
RALLY LIGHTS

AMBASSADOR DPL CONVERTIBLE AND HARDTOP
(DPL CVT. AVAIL.
ONLY IN 1967.)

**THE NOW CARS FROM THE
1967 AMERICAN MOTORS**

645

AMERICAN MOTORS **AMBASSADOR,**
DPL, OR SST
MODELS;
NO
MORE
880 OR
990
SERIES)

SEDAN
$3065.

DASH

new DOOR HANDLES

new SIDE SAFETY LIGHTS

new GRILLE

DPL (INTRO. 9-26-67) **68** AIR COND. NOW STD. EQUIP.

SST (ABOVE) has RALLY LIGHTS ON GRILLE.

WAGON (DPL) $3452.

DOOR OPENS SIDEWAYS OR SWINGS DOWN

68 DPL

NO MORE HOOD ORNAMENT UNTIL 1974.

AMERICAN MOTORS *AMBASSADOR*

69

AMBASSADOR SEDAN, DPL and SST SEDANS, WAGONS and H/Ts AVAILABLE. new 122" WB

"Ambassador" NAME ON new GRILLE; HORIZONTAL ROW OF HDLTS.

new HORIZONTAL SHAPE FOR FRONT SIDE SAFETY LIGHTS.

AMBER LTS. NOW IN NARROWER SLOTS.

$3,165 (SALE)

REAR

SST $3570.

(INTRO. 10-1-68)

To make an appointment for a test ride visit your American Motors Dealer. A number of them have chauffeurs available.

(INTRO. 9-25-69)

70

PLAINER GRILLE

FROM $3295.

'71 FROM $3706. (INTRO. 10-6-70)

BROUGHAM, SST WAGONS AVAIL.

STATION WAGON HAS **A V-8 ENGINE AIR-CONDITIONING, AUTOMATIC TRANS AS STANDARD EQUIP**

71 new GRILLE

DPL has new 258 CID, 150 HP 6 CYL. ENG. (STD.)

BROUGHAM SERIES ADDED

AMERICAN MOTORS *AMBASSADOR*

(DPL MODEL DISCONTINUED)
SST IS NOW LOWEST-PRICED, STARTING AT $3889. (4-DR.)

72

AMERICAN MOTORS 1972 BUYER PROTECTION PLAN.

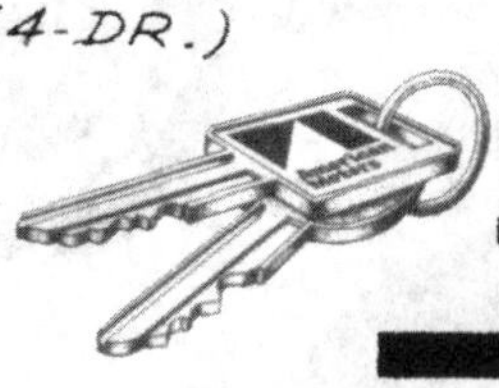

3 HEAVIER HORIZONTAL PIECES IN GRILLE.

⊿AMC
We back them better because we build them better.

WAGON $4645.

SEDAN, H/T or WAGON AVAIL.

new SAFETY BUMPERS

new HEAVIER VERTICAL PCS., AS WELL AS HORIZONTAL, IN GRILLE

73

SST DISCONTINUED; BROUGHAM IS ONLY REMAINING SERIES IN AMBASSADOR LINE (PRICED FROM $4245.

(FINAL H/T PRICED AT $4261.)

SEDAN $4245.

2-SEAT WAGON $4960.

3-SEAT, $5068.

HOOD ORNAMENT ADDED, (AGAIN) AND *all-new* GRILLE

DASH

The new Ambassador woodgrained instrument panel with AM-FM stereo radio, Adjust-O-Tilt wheel and Cruise-Command speed control.

74

FROM $4559. (SEDAN)

(THE FINAL AMBASSADOR)

GRAINED PANEL NOW GOES *HIGHER* UP BODY SIDES.

AMC American AMERICAN MOTORS CORPORATION

(TO 1969) **compact car**

ALSO KNOWN AS

Rambler

440

CVT.
$2704.

AMC
DEALERS
ADVERTISED AS
THE "FRIENDLY
GIANT
KILLERS"

$2588.

RACING STRIPES
ALONG HOOD
ARE NOT
INCLUDED
AS STD. EQUIPMENT.

new
Rogue H/T

106" WB
(THROUGH
'69)

66

GRILLE NOW SPLIT
INTO JUST 3
HORIZONTAL
SECTIONS.

199 CID 6
(128 HP) OR
ROGUE 290 CID V8
(200 HP)
6.45/6.95 x 14 TIRES

220

2-DR.
$2235.

(STANDARD MODEL)
DOES NOT HAVE
CHROME STRIP
ALONG SIDES.

649

American Motors...where quality is built in, not added on.

AMC American

DASH
$2306.

440

QUALITY BUILT IN — SO THE VALUE STAYS IN

$2591.

RAMBLER AMERICAN WAGON

$2665.

ROGUE

H/T

67

THIS '67 ROGUE IS THE FINAL CONVERTIBLE IN AMERICAN MODEL LINE.

new FRONT FENDER GROOVES ON ROGUE MATCH THE GRILLE.

$2489.

HORIZONTAL GRILLE PCS. ARE NOW UNBROKEN, (AS THEY WERE IN 1964.)

220

2-DR.

$2062.

THE NOW CARS

650

AMC American

440 → CHROME ALONG SIDE

220 ↓

220 4-DR. $2257.

ROGUE $2477.

68 ROGUE

68 440

ROGUE and 440 (ABOVE) have BRIGHT METAL BETWEEN TAIL-LTS.

2-DR. $2179.

68

(INTRO. 9-26-67)

new SINGLE HEAVY HORIZONTAL CHROME STRIP ACROSS GRILLE (OTHER HORIZ. PCS. ARE BLACK)

68-220

AMC American

STD. 199 CID 6 (128 HP)
290 CID V8
(200 HP)

(FINAL USE OF
"RAMBLER AMERICAN" NAME)

69

(INTRO. 10-1-68)

"RAMBLER"
NAME
NO LONGER
APPEARS ON
GRILLE. SOME
VERTICAL PCS.
NOW ALSO
VISIBLE.

THIS MODEL
REPLACED
BY :

new
TRI-COLOR HOOD EMBLEM

Rambler $1,998
(SALE PRICE)
(RAMBLER 220, 440
and ROGUE RANGE IS
$2231. TO $2710.

American Motors' Hornet
$1,994¹ to $3,589²

(NEW NAME ,
TOTALLY RESTYLED)
(INTRO. 9-25-69)

SLOGAN : "THE
LITTLE RICH
CAR "

70

new
ALUMINUM
GRILLE
new
19 - GAL.
FUEL
TANK

ENGINES :
199 CID 6, 128 HP
232 CID 6, 145 HP
232 CID 6, 155 HP
OR
304 CID V8,
210 HP

1970

S.S.T, WITH VINYL
TOP

new
108" WB

LOW-PRICE
HORNET has
LESS
TRIM,
PLAIN
SMALL
HUB-
CAPS

SEE ALSO
AMC "HORNET"

American Motors AMX (new)

(ASSOCIATED WITH JAVELIN SERIES THROUGH '74)

97" WB

(INTRO. 2-24-68)

$3485. ('68)
$3571. ('69)

EA. AMX CAR'S PRODUCTION NUMBER IS SET IN DASH.

1969 MODEL INTRO. 10-1-68.

V8 ENGINES 290 CID (225 HP) 343 CID OR 390 CID (315 HP)

READILY IDENTIFIED BY UNIQUE DUAL WEDGES ON HOOD, EACH BEARING 5 PARALLEL LOUVRES.

68-69

A-8 SERIAL # PREFIX

A-9 PREFIX FOR 1969, MORE STRIPE COMBINATIONS.

E70 x 14 TIRES

new STD. 360 CID V8 (290 HP)

70 $3677.

(INTRO. 9-25-69)

new ROCKER PANEL DECORATION

new E78 x 14 TIRES

new BODY STRIPE

new GRILLE and HOOD SCOOP

PRICES
$3861. ('71)
3505. ('72)
3555. ('73)
4073. ('74)

360 (OR 401 CID V8s OPTIONAL)

('72)

GRILLE SPOILER ('71)

JX 1971

71-74 (NO 1975-76 AMX)

BUMPER GUARDS

AMERICAN MOTORS AMX HORNET-AMX

108" WB

77

(AMX BECOMES OWN SERIES IN 1978.)

258 CID 6
(95 HP) OR
304 CID V8
(120 HP)
(V8 AVAIL. THROUGH '79)

WHEELBASE SHORTENED TO 96" ('79)

AMX-citement.

A higher level of excitement.

1979 MODELS ILLUSTRATED

78-80

6-CYL.
PRICES = $5624. ('78)
7019. ('79)
6766. ('80)

'78 V8 = $5391.
'79 V8 = 6769.

654

American Motors   **Classic**   *(1961 TO 1966)*

("RAMBLER CLASSIC")

intermediate size car   *112" WB*

WAGONS FROM $2888.

AVAILABLE IN "550," "770" OR "REBEL" SUB-MODELS.

770 CVT. $3065.

2 SIXES and 3 V8s AVAILABLE. STANDARD ENGS.: 287 CID V8 (198 HP) OR 232 CID 6 (145 HP) 6.95/7.35 × 14 TIRES

66

(THE FINAL "CLASSIC" LINE)

new GRILLE

(WHITE VINYL TOP ALSO AVAIL., 3-66)

new "CRISP-LINE" ROOF (Rebel/ H/T)

$2972.

(MARLIN ALSO IN CLASSIC LINE, '65 - '66.)

(SEE AMC MARLIN)

(INTRO. 10-7-65)

Rebel

(AVAIL. ONLY AS 2-DR. H/T)

(CLASSIC REPLACED BY THE

AMERICAN MOTORS 1967 Rebel *)*

AMC Concord

(REPLACES HORNET)

(SINCE 1978)

78
NEW

232 CID 6, (90 HP) OR 304 CID V8 (120 HP)

D/L. 2-DR.
SALE = $3949.
(REG. $4700.)

DASH

108" WB

(HATCHBACK, 4 DR. and WAGON AVAIL.)

121 CID 4-CYL. ENGINE and 258 CID 6-CYL. ENGINE ADDED; OTHER 6-CYL. and V8 STILL AVAIL. (FINAL CONCORD V8.)

D/L 4-DR. $5701.

D/L WAGON $5901.

4 new RECTANGULAR HEADLIGHTS

79

new GRILLE

$5701.

D/L HATCHBACK

LIMITED 4-DR. $6459.

1980 PRICES = $5868. TO $7323.

80

new WRAP-AROUND TAIL LTS.

151 CID 4 OR 258 CID 6

American Motors Gremlin

standard 6-cyl. engine.

(1970 TO 1978)

1970 SALE PRICES:

Gremlin	
$1,879	$1,959
2-Passenger.	4-Passenger.

INT. ('71)

96" WB

199 OR 232 CID 6 (128 OR 145 HP)

('70)

('70) "GREMLIN" FIGURE

('71)

HATCH WINDOW OPENS

"GREMLIN" FIGURE ON FENDER

(INTRO. WED., 4-1-70)

6.00 × 13 TIRES (THROUGH '72)

70-71

(INTRO. TUES., 9-15-70)

GREMLIN "X"

('71) has STRAIGHT-LINE BODY STRIPE

THIS HUBCAP STILL AVAIL. 1971.

BUMPER GUARD

657

AMC Gremlin
AMERICAN MOTORS
BUYER PROTECTION PLAN

(INTRO. WED., 9-22-71)
new V8 OPTIONAL

72

"THE BEST PUT-TOGETHER CARS OUT OF DETROIT THIS YEAR MAY COME OUT OF WISCONSIN.
THAT'S WHERE AMERICAN MOTORS MAKES THEM." —Popular Mechanics

FROM $2287.

Gremlin X

"5-LITRE V8" DESIGNATION INDICATES new 304 CID 304 CID V8.

new LEVI's UPHOLSTERY AVAILABLE (OPT.)

73

FROM $2325.

GREMLIN X
new CURVE IN BODY STRIPE. $2610.

new SAFETY BUMPERS
new 6.45 × 14 TIRES

AMC Gremlin
We back them better because we build them better.

FORMER HORIZONTAL MOULDINGS IN UPPER REAR QUARTER PANELS NOW ELIMINATED

new GRILLE, MINOR RESTYLING

74

FROM $2887.

GREMLIN X has new UP-CURVE AT REAR END of BODY STRIPE (AS ILLUSTRATED)

Six or V8

658

AMC Gremlin

FROM $3127.

(ADD $169. FOR BUCKET SEATS)

STD. 232 CID 6 (100 HP)

258 CID 6 OR 304 CID V8 OPTIONAL

VINYL INTERIOR

DASH

6-CYL. ENGINE

Levi's® Gremlin in H1 Deep Blue Metallic.

LEVI'S GREMLIN (ABOVE) and LEVI'S INTERIOR

See all the '75 economy cars from AMC and you'll see why people call AMC dealers

75 THE ECONOMY EXPERTS

X

Levi's

659

AMC Gremlin

232 CID 6 (100 HP)
304 CID V8 (150 HP)

6-CYL. PRICED FROM $3216.

(CUSTOM - $3325.)

6.45 × 14 TIRES

FINAL YEAR FOR "Gremlin" NAME AT FRONT OF RAISED CENTER SECTION OF HOOD

76

new GRILLE

" **Gremlin is America's lowest priced car.** " ($162. LESS FOR V8)

There's more to an AMC

INTRODUCING BUYER PROTECTION PLAN II
('77)

the only full 2 year, 24,000 mile warranty on engine and drive train.

note STRIPE PATTERN
('77)

6 CUT TO 90 HP

new 4 CYL. ENGINE ALSO AVAIL. (121 CID, 57 HP)

new GRILLE

77-78

THE FINAL GREMLIN

('78)

('78) LEVI'S INTERIOR STILL AVAIL.

X

SPECIAL NOTICE
All benefits of BPP II are also available on all new 1976 AMC models purchased on or after Sept. 1, 1976.

(REPLACED BY **SPIRIT**)

FROM $3499. ('78)

EPA MPG: 22 CITY, 35 HWY. (4 CYL.)

AMC ⧄ Hornet (FORMERLY American)

(1970 HORNET LISTED WITH AMERICAN)

232 CID 6 (135 HP @ 4000 RPM)
258 CID 6 (150 HP @ 3800 RPM)
304 CID V8 (210 HP @ 4400)

(INTRO. 10-6-70)

71

DASH

SC 360 (new)

WITH 360 CID V8 (245 HP @ 4400 OR 285 HP @ 4800)

$2853.

(new)
THE SPORTABOUT. STATION WAGON

ALSO AVAIL. WITH WOOD-GRAIN TRIM →

Spring Special

1971½

"SPECIALLY EQUIPPED" MODELS IN SPRING, 1971 INCLUDE

Free sunroofs

Hornet

new 3-SPOKE STEERING WHEEL AVAIL.

AMERICAN MOTORS BUYER PROTECTION PLAN ⧄

72

(INTRO. 9-22-71)

new IMPROVED "TORQUE-COMMAND AUTO. TRANS. AVAIL.

SPORTABOUT

FROM $2465.

HORNET

AMC Hornet AS ALSO USED IN GREMLIN, LEVI'S JEANS MATERIAL AVAIL. FOR INTERIOR (SPRING, 1973)

SPORTABOUT
station wagon

$2903. UNGRAINED SPORTABOUT ALSO AVAIL.

Introducing the Hornet Hatchback.

73

new GRILLE

AMC Hornet
We back them better because we build them better.

HATCHBACKS FROM $2715.

(new)

HORNET HATCHBACK $3665.

$3865. UNGRAINED

new 1974 ENERGY ABSORBING SAFETY BUMPERS

74

WITH GRAIN

HORNET SPORTABOUT

AMC 🔲 Hornet

1975 HORNETS PRICED FROM $3902.
1977 HORNETS FROM $4343.

FINAL 3 YEARS
FOR HORNET.
FEW VISIBLE
CHANGES FROM
1975 - 1977 EXCEPT
FOR BUMPER IMPROVEMENT
NOTED (1976.)

HORNET
Sportabout

Hometown **AMC**

Service

AMC BUYER PROTECTION PLAN.

new GRILLE

('75)

HORNET D/L
2-DR.

75-77

HATCHBACK "X"

('76)

('75)

1976 *has* THIN RUBBER STRIPS AT BUMPER EDGES

STD. AM RADIO

(AM/FM
ALSO AVAIL.)

(REPLACED BY
CONCORD,
1978)

663

('75) 4-DR.

AMERICAN MOTORS
Javelin
68

(1968 TO 1974)

(INTRO. 9-26-67)

(56,462 BLT.)

**brand new,
8 cylinder, 280 horsepower**

343 CID (290 CID V8 ALSO)

(232 CID 6 ALSO)

109" WB (THROUGH '70)

6.95/7.35 × 14 TIRES (THROUGH '69)

DASH HAS DEEPLY-RECESSED ROUND GAUGES and CONTROLS

$2743.

SST=$2848.

664

AMERICAN MOTORS *JAVELIN*

(INTRO. 10-1-68)

69

SCRIPT "JAVELIN" NAME NOW ABOVE GRILLE.

SPECIAL

Big Bad Javelin

IN "BIG BAD ORANGE," "BIG BAD BLUE" OR "BIG BAD GREEN," WITH PAINTED FRONT and REAR BUMPERS, OTHER OPTIONS.

new "BULL'S EYE"

new "MARK DONOHUE" REAR SPOILER AVAILABLE

WITH OPTIONAL DUAL EXHAUSTS and CHOICE OF 360 CID OR 390 CID V8s.

(INTRO. 9-25-69)

70

new GRILLE INCLUDES HEADLIGHTS UNDER A COMMON UPPER BORDER.

665

AMERICAN MOTORS *JAVELIN*

STD. JAVELIN $3386.

(INTRO. 10-6-70)

71

SST $3506.

(TOTALLY RESTYLED)

new 110" WB

IF YOU'RE GOING TO BUY A SPORTY CAR, BUY ONE THAT'S BEEN PLACES.

72

new GRILLE

$3296.

(INTRO. 9-22-71)

(1974 IS FINAL JAVELIN.)

$3347. ('73)

$3867. ('74)

73-74

new MESH GRILLE WITH RALLY LTS.

AMERICAN MOTORS (1965 - 1967)

MARLIN

IN 1965, 1966, A PART OF THE CLASSIC LINE

6 CYL. OR V8

112" WB (THROUGH '66)

66 (INTRO. 10-7-65)

(ONLY 4547 BLT.)

232 CID 6 (145 HP @ 4300 RPM) OR 287 CID V8 (198 HP @ 4700 RPM) 2 OTHER V8s AVAIL., TO 327 CID)

SALE $2601.

REG. $3051.

SOME WITH CORRUGATED ROCKER PANEL TRIM

NOW A PART OF AMBASSADOR LINE FOR '67.

new 118" WB

ROUND MEDALLION REMOVED FROM REAR DECK

6 CYL. has new 155 HP @ 4400 RPM; STD. V8 with new 290 CID (200 HP @ 4600 RPM) OR 2 new 343 CID V8s (TO 280 HP @ 4800 RPM)

67 (ONLY 2545 BLT.)

$3315.

new SIDE LT.

new SMOOTHER BODY SIDES, RECTANGULAR GAS FILLER DOOR

RALLY LTS. IN GRILLE

THE FINAL MARLIN

AMERICAN MOTORS Matador

(1971 TO 1978)

(INTRO. 10-6-70)

232 CID 6 (135 HP) OR STANDARD 304 CID V8 (210 HP)

(REPLACES **Rebel**)

If you were to compete against G.M., Ford and Chrysler, what would you do?

TAIL LIGHTS

71

118" WB
E78/G78 x 14
TIRES

H/T (ABOVE) $3306.

4 - DR. SEDAN $3277.

ROOF RACK and WITH WOODGRAIN

THE MATADOR STATION WAGON

2 - SEATS = $3680.
3 "   3798.

UNGRAINED WAGON AT LEFT, AS VIEWED FROM REAR INTERIOR OF WAGON.

AMERICAN MOTORS

A CAR YOU PROBABLY NEVER HEARD OF.
THE MATADOR.

(INTRO. 9-22-71)

72

WAGONS FROM $3652.

STD. 304 CID V8 HP CUT TO 150

new GRILLE

H/T = $3330.

The L.A. Police Department discovers the Matador.

POPULAR AS POLICE CARS IN VARIOUS WEST COAST CITIES and ELSEWHERE.

73

WAGONS = 2 SEAT $3652.
3 " 3760.

new GRILLE

SEDAN $3227.

FINAL MATADOR 2-DR. H/T PRICED AT $3261.

$3985.

WAGONS $4311. UP

SEDAN and WAGON = 118" WB
new COUPE (NEXT PG.) has 114" WB

(CONT'D NEXT PAGE)

74

AMERICAN MOTORS

PRESENTING THE
ONLY ALL-NEW MID-SIZE CAR FOR 1974

AMC ▼ Matador

REAR

ONLY COUPES
ARE TOTALLY
RESTYLED.

BLACK
TUFTED
NYLON-
KNIT FABRIC
WITH COPPER
BUTTONS IN ILLUSTRATED
"OLEG CASSINI" INTER. OPT.

OLEG CASSINI MODEL
BEARS A SIDE
MEDALLION.
$4428.
('74)

('75)

STRIPE, BLACK
GRILLE
ON
"X"

('74)

Matador X
$4289. ('74)

74-78

1974 COUPES PRICED
FROM $4029.
$5660.
IN 1978.

SEDAN $5302.
('77)

('75)

MATADOR
SERIES
ENDS 1978.

('76)

COUPE (ONLY)
GETS new GRILLE,
1976.

American Motors

AMC Pacer *(1975-1980)*
75-76

6 CYL.
232 CID

22-GAL.
FUEL TANK
100" WB

$3,299

AMERICAN MOTORS
$3,499
WITH A/C
('76)

The first wide small car.

2-DR. HATCHBACK CONTINUES

57.1"   60.7"

$4153. **Wagon** *(new)*

77

671

INTERIOR

There's more to an AMC

AMC ⫽ Pacer

78

304 CID V8
ALSO AVAIL.
('78-'79)

6 CYL.
90 HP
new
V8
120
HP

new
GRILLE

WAGON
$4519.

2 SERIES
NOW AVAIL.:
DL *and*
LIMITED

LIMITED
HATCHBACK
$6222. ('79)

(1979
EXAMPLES
ILLUSTR.)

DL INTERIOR (IN
CABERFAE CORDUROY)

6 HAS
new 258 CID
new WHEELS

LIMITED WAGON

$6372. ('79)
6974. ('80)

DL WAGON

(DL
HATCHBACK
ALSO
AVAIL.)

79-80

new UPRIGHT
HOOD ORNAMENT

(THE FINAL PACER)

$5456. ('79)
5980. ('80)

AMERICAN MOTORS

REBEL

(1967 TO 1970)

(FORMER CLASSIC MODEL)

DASH

$3049.
REBEL SST HARDTOP

$2863. SED.
770 WAG.

114" WB
232 CID 6
(145 HP)
OR
STD. 290 CID
V8 (200 HP) "550" FROM $2739.

67

UN-GRAINED
REBEL WAGONS $3155.

GRAINED

↑
new
"VENTURI"-STYLE
GRILLE

7.35/7.75 × 14
TIRES

SST CVT.
$3227.

new
SST
"INTAKE"
AHEAD OF
REAR
WHEELS
(ALSO IN '68)

1967

AMERICAN MOTORS Rebel

ANCHOR DECOR ON UPHOL.

VARIOUS UNIQUE WOODGRAINS and INTERIORS FOR REBEL WAGONS (SPRING, '67)

67½

MARINER WAGON

WITH "TYPHOON" V8 ENGINE

BLEACHED TEAKWOOD PLANK WOODGRAIN EFFECTS on BODY

550 (6 CYL.) WAGON

(550, SST ARE ONLY AMC CONVERTS. STILL AVAIL.)

SST (290 CID Typhoon V8)

6-CYL. 770

DASH

SST

(INTRO. 9-26-67)

68

SST "INTAKE" AHEAD OF REAR WHEELS

SQUARE, RECESSED DOOR HANDLES (new)

new SAFETY SIDE LIGHTS

68 SST

new 3-PIECE TAIL-LIGHTS

SST (OWN GRILLE)

AMERICAN MOTORS

An intermediate-sized car for the price of a compact.

Rebel $2,484 (SALE)

69

new GRILLE
new TAIL-LTS.,
WIDER TRACK

(INTRO. 10-1-68)

(REG. $2944.)

Rebel Wagon

(INTRO. 9-25-69)
(THE FINAL REBEL. REPLACED BY 1971 MATADOR)

70

new GRILLES

$2,766.* sale price

FRONT SAFETY LIGHTS NOW HORIZONTAL

(new)

the "Machine."

Up with The Rebel Machine

WITH 390 cid V8 (340 HP)

675

AMC SPIRIT

(REPLACES AMC Gremlin)

(STARTS 1979)

79 INTERIOR

4 CYL. (121 CID)
6 CYL. (232 OR 258 CID)
OR V-8 (304 CID)

LIFTBACK

G.T.

$5420.

96" WB

LIMITED

RELATIONSHIP TO FORMER GREMLIN CAN BE SEEN.

SEDAN

DL

$4504.

DASH

(V-8 NO LONGER AVAIL.)

80 $4687.

IN 1980, AMERICAN MOTORS WILL BE THE ONLY CAR MAKER IN AMERICA WITH...

ZIEBART
AMERICAN MOTORS BUYER PROTECTION PLAN
AMERICAN MOTORS 5-YEAR NO RUST-THRU WARRANTY

ALL THIS AT NO EXTRA COST.

BUILT FOR TODAY. BUILT TO LAST FOR TOMORROW.

LIFTBACK

GENERAL MOTORS

BUICK (full-sized)

(SINCE 1903)

(SEPARATE SECTION FOR
SPECIAL, SKYLARK, CENTURY, REGAL,
SPORT WAGON.)

LE SABRE (BELOW) 123" WB

WILDCAT (325 HP)
(GS - 340 HP)
126" WB

WILD.
CUSTOM
$ 4037.

WILDCAT has
UNIQUE GRILLE

$4421.

Electra 225

(and ELECT. 225
CUSTOM)

126" WB
401 CID V8
325 HP

ELECTRA
225 CUSTOM
SPT. CPE.
$ 4300.

66

(CUSTOM MODELS IN
EACH SERIES ARE
HIGHER-PRICED.)

**1966 Buick.
The tuned car.**

Electra 225 has 4 CHROME SEGMENTS,
LE SABRE has 3, and
WILDCAT has NONE

BUICK

LE SABRE 220 HP

CUST. H/T $3560.

DASH
(INTRO.
9-29-66)

67

new
SLANTING SCULPTURED
LINES RUNNING LENGTH
OF BODY SIDES

WILDCAT

430 CID
360 HP V8
(THROUGH '69)

Electra 225

430 CID V8

ELECTRA 225
LIMITED

WILDCAT

68

(INTRO.
9-21-67)

H/T
$3951.

WILDCAT CUSTOM
H/T $4172.

(CONT'D.
NEXT PAGE)

BUICK

LE SABRE

(SHOWN WITH and WITHOUT VINYL TOP)

Le Sabre. $3771.

68 (CONT'D.)

INTERIOR

(ELEC. 225 LTD.)

ELECTRA 225 LIMITED

$4597.

ELECTRA 225

SEDANS FROM $4288.

...feeling in an ... your living room. My ... me that feeling. The interior ... t a bit gaudy!"

... like a puff of wind. And it takes a hill like a ... solutely devoted to the Electra Limited!"

...ents get in the car and say,'I didn't ...'re building a car like this today!'"

Wouldn't you really rather have a Buick?

GM

BUICK

No wonder Buick owners keep selling Buicks for us.
Wouldn't you really rather have a Buick?

350 CID
V8

LE SABRE
4-DR. H/T FROM $3740.

69

(INTRO. 9-26-68)

LE SABRE
GRILLE has 5
HORIZONTAL PCS.;
(ILLUSTR. WILDCAT
GRILLE has
JUST ONE.)

WILDCAT

430 CID V8

ELECTRA 225

(ELECTRA
GRILLE AT
LOWER
LEFT)

430 CID
V8

LEs. CUSTOM 455 $4570.

1970 BUICK
SOMETHING TO BELIEVE IN.

HUB OF LE SABRE STEER. WH. DIFF. FR. OTHERS

LeSABRE

new 124" WB (THROUGH '76)

LeSabre 4-door Sedan.
FROM $4169.

LeSabre Custom Convertible.

$4532.

LeSabre Custom 4-door Hardtop.
FROM $4403.

LE SABRE CUSTOM 455 IS ADDED, TOPPING 3 LE SABRE LINES.

(INTRO. 9-18-69)

70

WILDCAT CUSTOM IS NOW ONLY WILDCAT LINE.

(CONT'D. NEXT PAGE)

$4892.

Wildcat Custom 4-door Hardtop.

681

BUICK

$4974.

WILDCAT CUSTOM
(CONT'D.)

Wildcat Custom Convertible

Something to believe in.

DASH
(Elec. 225)
(EST. WAG.,
WILDCAT,
LE SABRE.
SIMILAR)

70 (CONT'D.)

$5272.

124" WB

ESTATE WAGON
(new)

ELECTRA
225
CUSTOM
SPT. CPE.
(H/T)

(new
127" WB
ON ELECT.)
(THROUGH '76)

$5709.

Electra 225 Custom Convertible

Electra 225 Custom Limited 4-door Hardtop

new 455 CID V8
(370 HP)
(SAME
ENG. IN
ESTATE
WAGON)

$5312.

682

BUICK

LE SABRE SPT. CPE (2-DR. H/T) $4592.
CUSTOM LE SABRE 4680.

LE s. CUSTOM 4-DR. H/T $4744.

WILL RUN ON UNLEADED GAS, BECAUSE OF 1971 ENG. MODIFICATIONS

new LOW OBLONG REAR SIDE LTS. (THROUGH '73)

LE SABRE

"Something to believe in."

71 (INTRO. 10-3-70)

124" WB (127" ON ELECTRAS, ESTATE WAGON)

CENTURION (new)

455 CID V8 3/5 HP

FROM $5170.

"BUICK"

GRILLE

CENTURION REPLACES WILDCAT (CVT. ALSO AVAIL.)

FROM $5465.

ELECTRA 225

(ELECTRA 225 CUSTOM, LTD. also)

BUICK

Something to believe in.

$4596.

1972 Buick LeSabre.

350 CID V8
150 HP

LE.S. CUSTOM
SPT. CPE.
$4624.

CENTURION
GRILLE IS
SIMILAR, BUT
has ALL-
VERTICAL
PCS.

LeSabre.

72
(INTRO. 9-23-71)

FROM
$5427.

1972 Buick Electra 225.

455 CID V8
STD.
225 HP
(SAME V8 AS IN
CENTURION)

$4624. (CUST. SPT. CPE.)

1973 LeSabre.

73

new
SAFETY
BUMPERS

LeSABRE

(CONT'D.
NEXT
PAGE)

1973 Centurion.

BUICK.
The solid feeling.

DASH

REAR END DETAIL

Centurion

CVT. $4993.

$4803.

(FINAL YEAR FOR CENTURION)

73 (CONT'D.)

Electra 225

Electra 225
FROM $5428.

Estate Wagon
$5551.

DASH CLOSE-UP

685

BUICK

LeSabre Luxus Convertible

$5256.

LeSabre FROM $4915.

GRAINED 3-SEAT WAG. $6043.

Estate Wagon

74

new STYLE OF REAR QUARTER WINDOWS ON COUPES

Electra 225 FROM $5428.

$6425.

1974 Electra Limited

HIGHER BUMPER GUARDS ON SOME CARS

Low-fuel indicator. Available on all Electras. The red light warns you when the fuel level drops to approximately 4½ gallons.

686

BUICK

75

BUICK ELECTRA PARK AVENUE.
$7584.

LeSabre.

SPT. CPE.
$5413.
LUXUS SPT. CPE.
$5634.

FINAL
BUICK
CVT.
(LE SABRE
LUXUS)
AVAILABLE,
AT
$5706.

BUICK Dedicated to the *Free Spirit* in just about *everyone*.

LeSabre
231 CID V8
105 HP
$5350.

LeSabre CUSTOM.
350 CID V8
155 HP

76

new GRILLES

Electra 225
INTERIOR

$7874.

PARK AVE.
Electra 225

455 CID
V8
205 HP

EL. 225 CUST. PRICED
FROM $6970.

BUICK

SPT. CPE. $6449.

LeSabres.

new SHORTER 116" WB

REAR (WRAP-AROUND TAIL-LTS.)

'77 Le SABRE CUSTOM.

$6122.

DASH (LE S.)

VARIOUS ENGINES:
231 CID BUICK V6 (105 HP @ 3400 RPM)
350 CID V8s (2)
CHEVROLET = 160 HP @ 3800
OLDS = 170 HP @ 3800
403 CID V8 (OLDS) 185 HP @ 3600

ELECTRA 225

'77

BUICK SALESMEN'S 1977 SALES CAMPAIGN BADGE →

I'M OPEN TO OFFERS

ELCTR. WITH new SHORTER 119" WB

Electra 225

new SMALLER 350 CID V8 IN ELECTRA

FROM $7303.

688

BUICK Dedicated to the Free Spirit in just about everyone.

BUICK
A little science.
A little magic.

America's only turbocharged production automobile engine.

OTHER ENGS.
231 CID STD. V6
301 CID V8
305 CID V8
350 CID V8
403 CID V8

TURBO.
V6 (231 CID)
(151/175 HP) AVAIL. IN
SPT. CPE.
$6890.

There are four turbocharged production cars in the entire world.
Two of them are Buicks.

The other two cars are the Porsche Turbo Carrera and the Turbo Saab.

Buick LeSabre. Under $5800.

SALE PRICE ABOVE ; REG. PRICED FROM $6259.

ESTATE WAG.
$7399. w. GRAIN

78 new GRILLES

THE NEW ELECTRA:

22 HIGHWAY **15** CITY **18** COMBINED*

ELECTRA SEDANS $7996. UP

ELECTRA 225 ; ELECTRA LTD. OR
ELECTRA PARK AVE. MODELS
WITH 350 CID V8 (153 HP)
(405 CID V8
ALSO AVAIL.)

ELECT. CPES. PRICED FROM $7821.

ELECTRA

FRONT DETAILS

ELECTRA INTERIOR

689

BUICK

SPT. CPE. $7657. LE SABRE

Buick LeSabre 4-door $6110, 18 EPA-estimated mpg,

79

BUICK
After all, life is to enjoy.

Electra

FROM $8877.

(EST. WAG. (NOW *has* ONLY 3 HOOD PORTS, LIKE LE SABRE) ('79 ONLY)

3-SEAT WAGON W. GRAIN $8360.

ESTATE WAGON

690

BUICK

Buick Diesels AVAIL.

LE SABRE MODELS NO LONGER BEAR IDENTIFYING HOOD PORTS.

LeSabre

$8530.

LeSabre

80

The new 4.1 Liter Electra. America's first and only traditional luxury car powered by a V-6 engine.

AS BEFORE, LE SABRE SPT. CPE. has DIFFERENT GRILLE.

ELECTRA PARK AVE. has WIRE WHEELS, FULL-LENGTH CHROME BELT

F.C. LTD. CPE.

Electra
LIMITED SEDAN $9816.

ELECTRA EPA EST. MPG=17 HWY=23

$10,717.

LeSabre and Electra Estate Wagons

691

$10,513.

BUICK COMPACTS

(COMPACT LINE OF BUICKS STARTS 1961)

(SPECIAL IS LOWEST-PRICED MODEL, FROM $2783.)

(GS)

Buick Sportwagon FROM $3390.

DASH (GS)

225 CID 6 (155 HP) OR 300 CID V8 (210 HP)

115" WB

66

GS WITH 401 CID, 325-HP WILDCAT V8 ENG.

SKYLARK GS (GRAN SPORT) H/T $3384.

1966 Buick. The tuned car.

new GS-340.

GS-400. $3563.

SPECIALS FROM $2844.

67 new GRILLES

Skylark

BUICK COMPACTS

SPORT WAGON FR. $3711.

Skylark (SKYLARK CUSTOM)

WAGON and SEDAN have 115" WB; CPE. and CVT. have 112" WB.

$3326.

2-DR. W.B. SHORTENED TO 112"

GS-400 WITH 400 CID V8 (340 HP) $3528.

(RESTYLED)

68

7.75 × 14 TIRES

350 CID V8 (280 HP @ 4600 RPM)

GS-350

(GS-400 LOOKS SIMILAR)

$3295.

new 230-HP V8 (STD. IN SKYLARK CUST.) RUNS ON REGULAR GAS

693

BUICK Sportwagon
COMPACTS

WITH *new* "DUAL ACTION" TAILGATE →

FROM $4195.

350 C/D V8
3 SIDE PORTS LIKE SPECIAL (DLX.)

"350"

GS-350
350 C/D V8
(280 HP)

$3810.

GS-400
400 C/D V8 (340 HP)

H/T $3954.

"400 LETTERING

MODIFIED STAGE I GS-400 has "STAGE I" LETTERING INSTEAD, ALSO HI-LIFT CAM, 3.64 GEAR RATIO, ETC.

69
new GRILLES

SKYLARK
H/T FR. $3739.

350 C/D V8 STD. ON SKYLARK CUSTOM; AVAIL. ON OTHER SKYLARKS.

No wonder Buick owners keep selling Buicks for us.

Wouldn't you really rather have a Buick?

694

BUICK
COMPACTS

$3737.
SKYLARK
350

Skylark

WITH 350 CID
V8 (260 HP)

"SPECIAL"
MODEL NAME
DISCONTINUED

70

SPORTWAGON.
FROM $3977.

4-door Sedan.
$3614.

(SKYLARK
CUSTOM
4-DR. SED.
IS SIMILAR)

SKYLARK

$3563.

(VINYL
TOP
EXTRA)

1970

(CONT'D.
NEXT
PAGE)

2-door Sedan.

695

BUICK COMPACTS

$3899.

$3868.

SKYLARK CUSTOM

CVT. $3987.

70
(CONT'D.)

GS-455 STAGE I H/T

(360 HP)

Introducing automobiles
to light your fire.

(GS H/T
$3865.)

GS-455

GS 455 Convertible.

$4257.

455 C/D V8
(350 HP)

BUICK
COMPACTS

1971 Buick. Something to believe in.

GS

71

$4259.

SKYLARK CUSTOM →

$4100.

WILL RUN LOW-LEAD OR UNLEADED FUELS.

(SKYLARK CUSTOM, GS ARE FINAL CONVERTIBLES IN COMPACT SERIES.)

Skylark 350.

72

(FINAL USE OF SKYLARK NAME UNTIL 1975)

Buick Bargain Days.

1972 Buick Skylark. Something to believe in.

73 new NAME = **CENTURY**
(TOTALLY RESTYLED)

(CONT'D. NEXT PAGE)

$4073.

Century Luxus Colonnade Hardtop Coupe

BUICK COMPACTS

Century 350 Colonnade Hardtop Coupe

Wouldn't you really rather have a Buick?

PRICE OF $3811. FOR EITHER BODY TYPE

Century 350 Colonnade Hardtop Sedan.

Gran Sport Colonnade Hardtop Coupe.

Century **73** (CONT'D.)

"BUICK" NAME ABOVE GRILLE ON **CENTURY 350**

(WAGONS ON NEXT PAGE)

Regal instrument panel.

REGAL IS new TOP MODEL IN new CENT. LINE.

CENTURY **REGAL**

VERTICAL PCS. IN REGAL GRILLE

Regal Colonnade Hardtop Coupe.

$4210.

698

BUICK
COMPACTS

Century Station Wagon.

$4222. UP

73
(CONT'D.)

WOODGRAIN
OPTIONAL
AT EXTRA
COST

Century *LUXUS*

$4385. UP

Introducing Apollo. By Buick.

4-DR.
$2883.

111" WB
250 CID 6 (100 HP) OR
350 CID V8 (150 HP)

instrument panel with wood-grain vinyl accents.

73½

(INTRO.
APRIL,
1973)

2-DR.
CPE.
$2860.

2-DR.
HATCHBACK
$3009.

E78 × 14
TIRES

Custom interior available.

BUICK COMPACTS

Apollo

GRILLE MODIFIED

FROM $3877.

Apollo $3900.

1974 Apollo INTERIOR

Century Regal *new SEDAN (JOINS CPE)* $4734.

Gran Sport

74

Century 350

DASH

$4622.

Century Luxus

$4303.

new TAIL-LIGHTS

1974 Buick Station Wagons *also* $4602.

REAR BUMPER *of* Station Wagon

FROM $4160.

BUICK
COMPACTS

HATCHBACK
(REGULAR
OR "S"
MODELS)
97" WB

Skyhawk

(new) 231 CID V-6
(110 HP)

BUICK Dedicated to the Free Spirit in just about everyone.

BR 78 x 13
TIRES

SKYLARK S/R

SKYLARK

RETURNS TO
JOIN (AND THEN REPLACE)
APOLLO SERIES.

$5122.

75 (CENTURY
LUXUS
REPLACED BY
CENTURY
CUSTOM.)

V-6 Buick Century
SPECIAL
$4665.

REGAL
$5098.

According to E.P.A. figures,

Century Wagons

In dynamometer tests recently conducted
by the Environmental Protection Agency,
a Buick Century equipped with a 3.8-litre
V-6 got 24 miles per gallon in the highway
tests. (And 16 mpg in the city test.)

701

BUICK COMPACTS

UNUSUAL ROOF OF REGAL TYPE (SINCE '73)

76 (CONT'D.)

CENTURY

CENTURY SPECIAL PRICED AT $4836.

note GRILLE DIFFERENCES

$5366.

REGAL

coupes

A LIMITED NUMBER of "INDIANAPOLIS 500" CENTURY V-6 PACE CAR REPLICAS (IN SPECIAL SILVER, RED and BLACK PAINT COMBINATION) AVAIL. at BUICK DEALERS.

PACE CAR REPLICA (RARE)

BUICK
COMPACTS

SKYHAWK FROM $4299.

SKYHAWK

(NIGHTHAWK → has SPECIAL PAINT)

Nighthawk.

SKYLARK
V-6

2.56 GEAR RATIO

MPG. 27 HWY., 17 CITY

77

REGAL

OPT. SUN ROOF

SALE $5115.05
(REG. $5739.)

Century

4-DR. FROM $5390.

CENTURY

REGAL

W/O GUARDS

W/ GUARDS

CENTURY **SPECIAL** $5/97.

new BUMPERS

704

BUICK
COMPACTS

A little science. A little magic.

Wagon Century

231 CID V-6

CENTURY SPECIAL PRICED FROM $5754.

$6461.

MPG = 27 HWY. 19 CITY

CENTURY

new FASTBACK REAR

new 2-door or 4-door

note DIFF. BETWEEN ROCKER PANEL/LOWER DOOR TRIM ON CENTURY → and CENT. CUSTOM →

$6098. (4-DR.)

Century Custom

"3.2 Litre" on COWL

(TOTALLY RESTYLED)

"CENTURY CUSTOM" on REAR FENDERS

196 OR 231 CID V6 (86/102 HP)

305 CID V8 (145 HP)

78

all-new BODY SHAPES 108" WB

231 CID V6 TURBO (151/175 HP)

TURBO REGAL

$6480.

STD. WH. CVR.

REGAL

CLOSE VIEW OF REGAL FRONT END

BUICK

Regal

REGAL FROM $6197.

REGAL DASH has GRAINED STRIP

BUICK
COMPACTS

Skyhawk. FROM $4855.

79

Skylark.

HATCHBACK $5543.

SEDAN $5493.

turbocharged

Regal. $7144.

Century Special.

Century Limited and Century Custom.

$6497.

Century Sport Coupe $6928.

$7154.

BUICK
After all, life is to enjoy.

Century Wagons.
(UNGRAINED CENT. SPEC. ALSO)

706

BUICK COMPACTS

Skyhawk
WITH
ROAD HAWK
OPTION
PACKAGE

EPA EST MPG	EST. HWY	EST DRIVING RANGE	EST HWY RANGE
15	24	277	444

FROM $5313.
FINAL
SKYHAWK
(DISCONT'D.
1-80)

80

SKYLARK
FROM
$6525.
(2-DR.)

(SOME 1980 MODELS
AVAIL. SPRING, 1979)

Skylark is equipped with GM-built
engines produced by various divisions.
See your dealer for details.

Skylark

DASH

new
104.9"
WB
4 CYL. OR V6

EPA EST MPG	EST HWY	EST DRIVING RANGE	EST HWY RANGE
24	38	336	532

(CONT'D.
NEXT PAGE)

new
SPORT
COUPE
$7140.

(SPORT
SEDAN ALSO

707

BUICK *RIVIERA* (OWN SEPARATE SERIES SINCE 1963)

425 c.i.d V8 (360 HP)
8.45 × 15 TIRES

luxury cars.

new 119" WB FROM $4513.

new GRILLE

66

Riviera GS

GS MODEL

1966 Buick. The tuned car.

TAIL LIGHTS

HAZARD FLASHERS AT ALL CORNERS, and ENERGY-ABSORBING STEERING COLUMN

new 430 C.I.D V8 (360 HP)

(INTRO. 9-29-66)

67

CENTER CONSOLE AVAIL.

$4557.

BUICK
RIVIERA

(INTRO. 9-21-67) $4703.

VINYL TOP

68

PLAIN TOP

new SPLIT GRILLE

new SIDE SAFETY LIGHTS

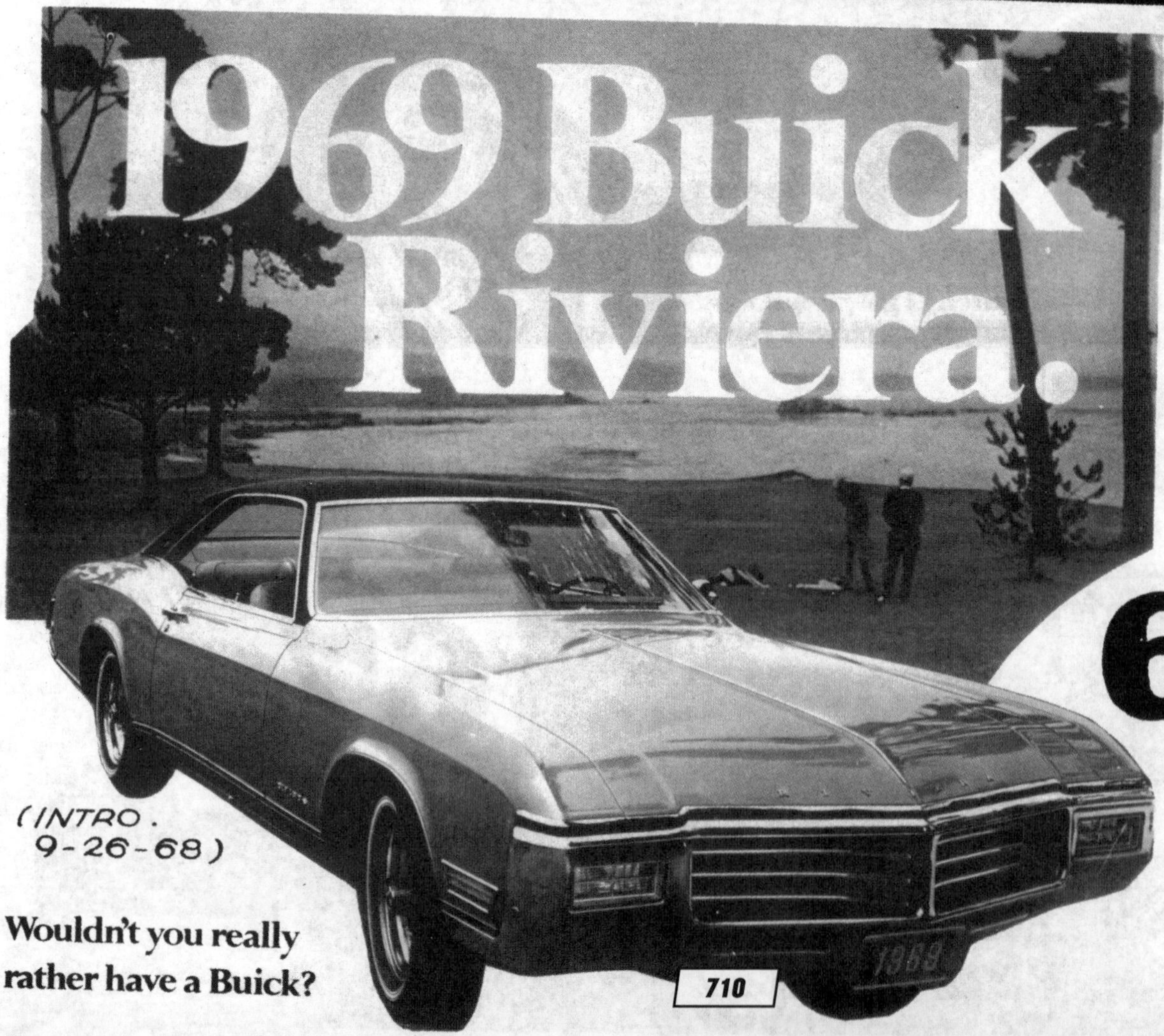

1969 Buick Riviera.

BACKGROUND SCENE: PEBBLE BEACH, CALIF.

$5321.

new 8.55 x 15 TIRES

69

new GRILLE

(INTRO. 9-26-68)

Wouldn't you really rather have a Buick?

BUICK *RIVIERA*

VINYL TOP

new H78 x 15 TIRES

note:
1970 IS
THE ONLY
MODEL
WITH THIS
UNIQUE
new
DECORATIVE
MID-SIDE TRIM
WITH DIP

70

new
RED
ROUND
SIDE SAFETY LT.
AT REAR, WITH
RIVIERA "R" SYMBOL
IN CHROME,
ACROSS
LENS.

PLAIN TOP

new GRILLE
WIDER
REAR WINDOW
new TAIL LIGHTS

new 455 CID V8
(370 HP)

Something to believe in.

$5474.

DASH

(INTRO. 9-18-69)

GS

"GS"
LETTERING

BUICK RIVIERA

(INTRO. 10-3-70)

GS

1971 Buick Riviera GS.

(TOTALLY RESTYLED)

71

new 122" WB

ANOTHER VIEW OF TAIL ↓

$5917.

3.42 GEAR RATIO

315 HP WITH 455 CID V8

EMPHASIS ON *all-new* POINTED BOAT-TAIL REAR END STYLING.

Something to believe in.

HP CUT AGAIN TO 250 (455 CID V8)

$5790.

new SIDE CHROME

72

new TAIL-LIGHTS

(INTRO. 9-23-71)

712

AccuDrive, variable ratio power steering, power front disc brakes, new durable stamped steel rocker arms, new computer-selected chassis springs for superb ride and handling, new windshield washer and radiator overflow coolant reservoirs integrated with the fan shroud, solenoid actuated throttle stop, new Exhaust Gas Recirculation (EGR) and Air Injection Reactor (AIR) emission control systems, evaporative emission control system, integral voltage regulator and Delcotron, brake proportioning valve

BUICK RIVIERA

$5795.

new GRILLE

73

DASH

new THICKER ROCKER PANEL TRIM COVERS PART OF DOOR

Engine, standard: 455 C.I.D. V-8. Carburetion: 4-barrel.

Engine, available: Stage 1 modified 4-barrel 455 C.I.D. V-8 engine with performance ratio, positive traction axle and special ornamentation.

Transmission, standard: Turbo Hydra-matic 400 automatic.

Axle Ratios: with standard engine: 2.93:1; with Stage 1 engine: 3.23:1 with positive traction.

STD. HP 250

REAR LIC. PLATE NOW IN CENTER

FINAL YR. FOR POINTED REAR

Bravo Cloth and Madrid-grain Vinyl 60/40 Notchback seat available in Riviera in Blue, Sandalwood or Saddle.

Newport Knit Vinyl and Madrid-grain Vinyl 40/40 seats standard in Riviera in Sandalwood or Black.
ALSO:
Oxen-grain Expanded Vinyl and Madrid-grain Vinyl 60/40 Notchback seat available in Riviera in Green, Sandalwood, Saddle, Black or Burgundy.

Oxen-grain Expanded Vinyl and Madrid-grain Vinyl 40/40 seats available in Riviera in White, Saddle or Black.

INTERIORS 713

$6308.
PLAIN TOP

BUICK *RIVIERA*

74

PARTIAL VINYL TOP

RESTYLED (ALL-*new* ROOFLINE and REAR) HP CUT TO 230 (455 CID V8)

new J78 x 15 TIRES

OPT. LEATHER UPHOLSTERY

new DASH

HOOD ORNAMENT ADDED →

new VERTICAL GRILLE WITH "RIVIERA" NAME ABOVE GRILLE, 1974.

new RECTANGULAR HEADLIGHTS

75

JR 78 x 15 TIRES (THROUGH '76)

$6993.

new GRILLE
new CORNER LTS.
"BUICK" NAME ABOVE GRILLE.
"RIVIERA" ON GRILLE, IN SCRIPT.

BUICK *RIVIERA*

PLAIN TOP

HP CUT TO 205
(FINAL 455 CID BIG V8)

76

$7401.

new
GRILLE

VINYL
TOP

BUICK Dedicated to
the *Free Spirit* in just about everyone.

(SLOGAN 1975 TO 1977)

$7988.

new UPSWEPT REAR
QUARTER MOLDING   (DOWNSIZED)

77

SMALLER
350 CID V8
(170 HP)

new GRILLE
new FRONT and
CORNER LIGHT
DESIGN

new 116" WB (THROUGH '78)   GR 78 x 15
TIRES
(THROUGH '78)

The Riviera LXXV.

(OPT. SILVER-and-BLACK
BUICK 75TH ANNIVERSARY
COLOR SCHEME)

78

$8763.

350 OR
403 CID V8

BUICK
LXXV

**A little science.
A little magic.**

BUICK RIVIERA
After all, life is to enjoy.
('79)

$10,960.⁰⁰ (S) ('79)
11,822.⁰⁰ (S) ('80)

DASH

new 114" WB

79-80

"S" (TOP, LEFT) ('79)
(has BLACK GRILLE and SIDE MIRRORS, OWN WHEEL CVRS.)

RESTYLED and DOWN SIZED

new FRONT-WHEEL-DRIVE

V6 OR V8

$10,683.⁰⁰ ('79)
11,491.⁰⁰ ('80)

1980 has new INTERIORS and REAR VIEW MIRRORS PLACED FURTHER FORWARD ON DOORS (arrow)

S

('80)

716

(SINCE 1902)

Cadillac

Standard of the World

New elegance,
new excellence,
new excitement!

Interior
(FLEETWOOD)

9.00 x 15 TIRES
129.5" WB
(CALAIS, DE VILLE)
133" WB
(FLTWD. 60 SP.)
149.75" WB
(FLTWD. 75)

SEDAN de VILLE

$6303.

V-8 ENGINES
(SINCE 1915 MODEL)
(OVERHEAD VALVES
SINCE 1949)
129½" WB
(FLEETWOODS have
133" or 149¾" WB)

429 CID V8 (340 HP)

66

EMBLEM

FLEETWOOD
60 SPECIAL

BROUGHAM

$7417.

717

Cadillac

new GRILLE
67

H/T COUPE $5718.

CALAIS

SEDAN $5893.

DE VILLE

SEDAN $6303. (SAME PRICE) ↓

$6286. CVT.

4-DR. H/T

4-DR. H/T

H/T COUPE DE VILLE $6070.

FRONT DETAIL

(CONT'D. NEXT PAGE)

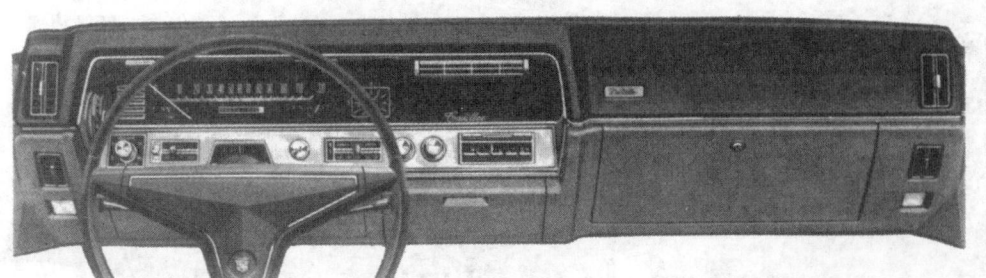

new DASH

EL DORADO BECOMES SEPARATE SERIES, 1967 ON. SEE "CADILLAC EL DORADO" SECTION.

VINYL PADDED TOP ON THE BROUGHAM

FLEETWOOD 60 SPECIAL

BROUGHAM $7417.

67
(CONT'D.)

SEDAN WITH PLAIN TOP

$7101.

FLEETWOOD 75

(has 8.20 × 15 TIRES)

SEDAN = $10,522.
LIMOUSINE = 10,733.

75 INTERIOR (7-PASS.) IN LIGHT GRAY DEVONSHIRE CLOTH

Cadillac

Brilliant new styling • Dramatic new interiors • Totally new instrument panel • Concealed windshield wipers • Improved variable-ratio power steering • New disc brakes available • Wide choice of eleven luxurious body styles

new 472 CID V8 (375 HP)

DE VILLE
CVT.
$6101.

4-DR. H/T
DE VILLE = $6463.
CALAIS = 6169.

CALAIS CPE. (H/T)
$5993.

Elegance in action

68

(RESTYLED)
(INTRO. 9-21-67)

DE VILLE
$6463.

new DASH

CPE. DE VILLE (H/T)
$6230.

TWILIGHT SENTINEL
AUTO. HDLT. CONTROL (LTS.
WILL STAY ON 90 SEC.
AFTER IGNITION
SHUT OFF)

$7577.

FLEETWOOD (60
SPECIAL)
BROUGHAM

FLEETWOOD 75
LIMOUSINE
(PADDED
ROOF OPT.)

$10,930.

Cadillac

$7788.

FLEETWOOD 60 SPECIAL

(INTRO. 9-26-68)

4 HEADLTS. NOW IN HORIZONTAL PAIRS

69

new GRILLE

new REAR STYLING

BROUGHAM

DE VILLE $6399.

$6632.

-a masterpiece from the master craftsmen.

Cadillac presents the **Spirit** of the **Seventies**

FINAL DE VILLE

CVT. $6772.

4-DR. H/T $6822.

DE VILLE

The elegantly spirited 1970 Cadillac

(INTRO. 9-18-69)

H/T $6588.

70

new GRILLE

new CORNERING LTS.

new L78 x 15 TIRES (all models)

Fleetwood 75.

$11,227. UP

721

Cadillac

HORSEPOWER CUT TO 345 @ 4400 RPM (GROSS) OR 220 @ 4000 RPM (NET)

$ 6983.

DASH

2.93 GEAR RATIO (3.15 ON 75)

CPE. DE VILLE H/T

DE VILLE *new* 130" WB

new 1-PC. TAIL-LIGHTS

4-DR. H/T

$ 7177.

AM/FM STEREO RADIO *and* 8-TRACK TAPE PLAYER AVAIL.

new RUBBER-TIPPED BUMPER GUARDS (ON ALL MODELS)

71 (INTRO. 9-29-70)

new GRILLE *new* WIDELY-SPACED HEADLTS.

SIDE VIEW (60-S)

(CONVERTIBLE MOVED TO EL DORADO LINE, 1971-76)

One of the most appreciated new Cadillac luxuries available is the lamp monitoring system that tells you whether your headlights, rear lights and turn signals are functioning properly. Coupled with the lamp monitoring system is a warning light that tells you when your windshield washer fluid is low.

DETAILS OF REAR QUARTER OUTSIDE COURTESY LIGHT

133" WB FLEETWOOD 60 SPECIAL BROUGHAM

(*note* ARCHED WINDOWS)

$8502.

(FLTWD. 75 GETS *new* 151½" WB)

(27-GAL. FUEL TANK) CAN RUN ON REGULAR *or* UNLEADED FUEL

Cadillac

FLEETWOOD BROUGHAM

HP CUT AGAIN, TO 220 (THROUGH '73) (INTRO. 9-23-71)

$8843.

72

new GRILLE

AUX. LTS. MOVED UP FROM BUMPER and PLACED BETWEEN HEADLTS.

H/T DE VILLE $6874.
CALAIS $6477.

$6477.

CALAIS

DASH

DE VILLE 4-DR. H/T $7096.

73

new GRILLE

Fleetwood Seventy-Five

AS BEFORE, A WREATH AROUND EMBLEM IDENTIFIES THE FLEETWOOD.

INTER. (75)

723

LIMO. $12,063

Cadillac

$7752.

new REAR QUARTER
WINDOWS

CPE. DEVILLE

← HOOD ORNAMENT
ADDED DURING '74,
BUT AVAIL. ON EARLY
"SPECIAL MODELS."

MOST
EARLY '74s
BEAR CRESTS ABOVE GRILLE,
AS ILLUSTRATED.

AVG.
MPG
12 CITY
15.8
HWY.

HP
CUT TO
205

74

new
GRILLE

new
2-TIER CORNER LTS.;
HDLTS. CLOSER TOGETHER
(ROUND, IN SQUARE FRAMES)

CPE.

$9422. UP

FLEETWOOD

BROUGHAM
$10,414.

$9184. TO $14,557. PRICE RANGE

ELDORADO 500 CID V8
NOW USED,
BUT HP CUT
TO 190
(THROUGH '76)

W. ORNAMENT ON
HOOD
↓

75

new
GRILLE,
RECTANGULAR
HEADLIGHTS

FINAL YEAR FOR CALAIS MODELS

Cadillac

H/T $8629

DE VILLE $9265.

$9067.

FLTWD. BROUGHAM TALISMAN SEDAN $12,748

76 new FINER "CROSSHATCH" GRILLE PCS.

new WHEELBASES:
DE VILLE, BROUGHAM = 121½"
"75" = 144½"

$11,546.

SEDAN DE VILLE $10,020.

(FLEETWOOD) BROUGHAM

new 425 CID V8 (180 HP)

new 77
"DOWNSIZED" MODELS (TOTALLY RESTYLED)

COUPE DE VILLE
(2 VIEWS)
$9810.

TYPICAL MODERN SHOWROOM

Cadillac

FLEETWOOD BROUGHAM
$12,292.

78

"Cadillac" NAME NOW ABOVE GRILLE, IN CHROME SCRIPT.
(SEE ARROW)

Behind the great name...
...a great car.

EMBLEM
(HOOD)

(new)

DE VILLE
CPE.
(IN SHOWROOM, TOP SCENE) PRICED
AT $10,444.

(75 FORMAL LIMO.
PRICED AT
$ 20,363.)

new GRILLE has MORE VERTICAL and FEWER HORIZONTAL PCS.

Cadillac

(DIESEL ENG. AVAIL.)

new GRILLE *has* SMALLER and MORE CRISS-CROSS PCS., *with* "*Cadillac*" NAME RETURNED TO UPPER BORDER of GRILLE.

79

DASH → **new** OPERA LIGHT ON FLTWD. BRGHM.

CPE. DE VILLE $12,401.

AVAIL. ←

$14,927.

The Fleetwood Brougham

$23,388.

The Fleetwood Limousine

SIMULATED TEAKWOOD TRIM ON DASH

new SMALLER 368 CID V8 (150 HP)

80

new GRILLE *has* MOSTLY VERTICAL PIECES. **new** WIDE AMBER AUX. LTS. BELOW HEADLTS. and CORNER LTS. →

120" WB *Cadillac Eldorado* (OWN SERIES SINCE 1967)

with front-wheel drive.

67 New

FLEETWOOD CREST ON REAR QUARTER PANEL

429 CID V8 (340 HP)

$6955.

ELDORADO ... world's finest personal car

Elegance in action!

CONCEALED HDLT. DETAIL

68

new 472 CID V8 (375 HP)

new FRONT CORNER LT. IN FENDER TIP

new REAR SAFETY LIGHT

DIAMOND PATTERN CLOTH AND VINYL

CHOICES OF UPHOLSTERY (LEATHER ALSO AVAIL.)

$7283. (VINYL LANDAU TOP $137 EXTRA)

DEAUVILLE CLOTH WITH VINYL BOLSTERS (CHOICE OF 4 COLORS)

FRONT ST. BACK ST.

728

Cadillac Eldorado

PLAIN TOP

$ 7389.

69
new GRILLE WITH FINER PCS.
new UNCONCEALED HEADLIGHTS

VINYL TOP

WITH OPT. SUNROOF

DASH

70
new GRILLE and SIDE TRIM
new 500 CID V8 (400 HP)

new L78 × 15 TIRES

FROM $7607.

1971 DASH

(FIRST EL DORADO CVT. AVAIL. SINCE 1966)

REAR QUARTER WINDOWS ARE *new*

71
new GRILLE
new 126.3" WB

$ 8468.

NAME JUST BELOW CHROME STRIP

$ 8098.

729

Cadillac Eldorado

$8252.

HP CUT TO 235 (THROUGH '73)

72 new GRILLE

$7936.

(SAME PRICES AS '72)

REAR

CORNER LTS. NOW LOWER AT FRONT END

new GRILLE

73

new ENERGY-ABSORBING SAFETY BUMPERS

Cadillac Eldorado

CONVERTIBLE
$9322.

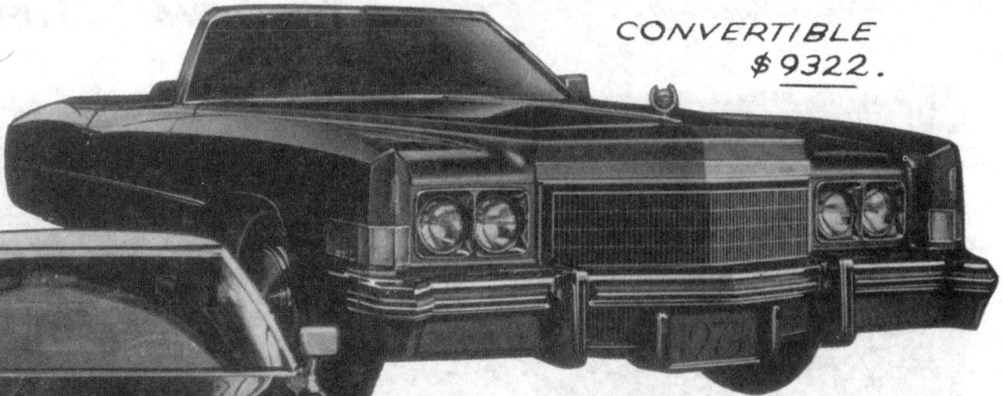

CPE.
$8995.

19M 506

74

new GRILLE *has*
MORE VERTICAL PCS.

HP CUT TO
210

$9935.

HP CUT
AGAIN,
TO
190

INTERIOR
(CVT.)

new GRILLE

new
↙
$10,354

NAME
NO
LONGER APPEARS
ON
SIDE
OF
COWL **75** SIDE
SAFETY
LT.
NOW
MOVED /
BACK FROM FRONT CORNER

Cadillac Eldorado

Eldorado Convertible (BELOW) $11,049.

Last of a magnificent breed.

THE FINAL CONVERTIBLE MFD. BY A MAJOR AMERICAN FACTORY!

"Cadillac" NAME NOW ABOVE GRILLE.

76 (CPE. PRICE = $10,586.)

It is the only convertible now built in America. And it will be our last. The very last. Because the Eldorado Convertible will not be offered in 1977.

new SMALLER 425 CID V8 (180 HP)

new GRILLE WITH MORE, FINER VERTICAL PCS. and "ELDORADO" NAME ABOVE.

77

PHANTOM VIEW

Automatic Level Control. Adjusts for changing loads automatically

Four-Wheel Disc Brakes. Ventilated discs have cooling fins for rapid heat dissipation.

Automatic Climate Control. Redesigned for 1977. Compressor works only when necessary

COUPE = $11,187.

BIARRITZ CPE. = $12,947)

(CPE. PRICED FROM $11,921.)

QUARTER PANEL LIGHT

Eldorado Custom Biarritz

78

new GRILLE WITH HEAVIER HORIZONTAL PCS.

$13,786.

Cadillac Eldorado

$17,043.

BIARRITZ

$14,693.

new BOXY REAR QUARTERS →

DOWNSIZED, with new SHORT 113.9" WB

79
(RESTYLED)

FUEL-INJECTED 350 CID V8 (170 HP)

CPE. PRICED FROM $15,509.

368 CID V8 (350 CID V8 IN CALIFORNIA)

(160 OR 145 HP)

80

Available for Eldorado

Astroroof Shown with Biarritz

Eldorado Wire Wheel Covers

AS BEFORE, note SPECIAL REAR QUARTER PANEL DECOR WHICH IDENTIFIES *Eldorado Biarritz*

← $18,003.

20.6-GAL. FUEL TANK

P205/75R15 TIRES 2.19 GEAR RATIO

1980 GRILLE

Digital Electronic Fuel Injection and on-board diagnostics for servicing.

Standard for Eldorado...Available at no extra cost for Seville

FUEL INJECTION

new AMBER LIGHTS BELOW HEADLAMPS

Cadillac **Seville**

International size *luxury car.*

114.3" WB
350 CID V8 (180 HP)

Coordinating Lights

Tilt and Telescope Steering Wheel

$12,479.   (INTRO. SPRING, 1975)

new **76**

77

$13,359.

Elegante

$16,867.

$14,267.

78

$16,249.

(ELEGANTE, $18,984.)

79

HP CUT TO 170

Simulated Teak Woodgrain Panel inlaid with the appearance of Butterfly Walnut

DASH

Standard for Seville...Available for Eldorado, DeVilles and Fleetwood Brougham.

DIESEL
350 CID DIESEL V8 ENG.
(105 HP)

80

(RESTYLED)

New Grille with Stand-Up Wreath and Crest.

$19,662.

(ELEGANTE, $22,596.)

new CLASSIC ROLLS-ROYCE STYLE REAR DECK 114" WB

Seville

(SINCE 1964) **CHEVELLE BY CHEVROLET** MID-SIZE

FULL COIL SUSPENSION

115" WB

(300 IS LOWEST-
PRICED, LITTLE CHROME, $2607 UP.
300 DLX. has CHROME STRIP
ALONG SIDE .)

Malibu Wagon
2-SEAT

MALIBU CVT. = $3030.

MALIBU

$3093.

H/T SPT. CPE.
$2821.

194 CID 6 (120 HP)
230 CID 6 (140 HP)
283 CID **TURBO-FIRE V8**
(195 OR 220 HP)
327 CID V8 (275 HP)
396 CID V8s
(325 OR 360 HP)

**FLUSH-AND-DRY
ROCKER PANELS**

CHEVELLE

(300 TYPES
have PLAINER
REAR DECKS
WITHOUT CHROME
ORNAMENTATION)

66

DASH

CHEVELLE

OPTIONAL
TACH.

SS 396 $3219.

SS
has
Turbo-Jet V8's

(396 CID)

6.95/7.35
×14 TIRES
(OPT. RED-STRIPE
NYLON TIRE and
MAG.-STYLE WHEEL COVER)

(SS CVT. ALSO
AVAIL.)

CHEVELLE

$3079.

MALIBU

7.35 × 14 TIRES

H/T $2877.

DASH and CONSOLE

new GRILLES and TAIL-LIGHTS

67 SS 396

Turbo-Jet V8

new safety features standard — GM-developed energy-absorbing steering column, four-way hazard warning flasher, dual master cylinder brake system with warning light, folding front seat back latches.

SS 396.

SS 396

(F.70 × 14 TIRES ON SS-396)

H/T $3083.

SS 396

note "SS 396" IN GRILLE CENTER

2-SEAT **CONCOURS**

new TOP-OF-LINE WAGON (300 DLX. and MALIBU WAGONS ALSO AVAIL.)

$3269

LARGER STD. 307 CID V8
(200 HP) USES REG. GAS
230 CID STD. 6
(140 HP)

CHEVELLE BY CHEVROLET

MALIBU

68 (RESTYLED)

AT CENTER:
Chevelle Nomad Custom
WAGON
(new)
$3303.
(3-ST.)

new WB
112" 2 DR.
116" 4 DR.
(THROUGH '77)

WITH
OPT.
VINYL TOP

SS-396

H/T = $3249.

FRONT VENT WINDOWS ELIMINATED

STD.
230 CID 6
(140 HP)
307 CID V8
(200 HP)

69

new
GRILLES

new
LOCKING STEERING COLUMN
and TRANS. LEVER

MALIBU H/T
$3025.
$3372 WITH
OPTIONAL ILLUS.
SS-396
PACKAGE

(also NOMAD,
GREENBRIER,
CONCOURS,
CONCOURS EST.
WAGONS AVAIL.)

737

WAGONS FROM $3655.

CHEVELLE BY CHEVROLET
WITH OPTIONAL Chevelle SS 396 PACKAGE

TOP TO BOTTOM: NOMAD, GREENBRIER, CONCOURS, CONCOURS ESTATE WAGONS

CHEVROLET
On The Move.

new 2-TIER GRILLE

70

new 250 CID STD. 6 (155 HP)

UP TO 400 CID TURBO-JET V8 (330 HP)

MALIBU

H/T $3534.

SS PKG.

new TAIL-LIGHTS RECESSED IN REAR BUMPER

MALIBU

11M875

STD 250 CID 6 (145 HP)

71

STD 307 CID V8 (200 HP)

new GRILLE and BUMPERS. new CORNER LTS. new SINGLE HEADLTS.

H/T $3719.

1971. You've changed. We've changed.

CHEVELLE

SCENE: 6 FLAGS AMUSEMT. PK., ATLANTA, GA.

250 CID 6 (110 HP)
307 CID V8 (130 HP)
350 CID V8 (165 OR 175 HP)
400 CID V8 (240 HP)
454 CID V8 (SS) (270 HP)

72 *new* GRILLE

Building a better way to see the U.S.A.

4-DR. SEDAN FROM $3486.

H/T ILLUSTR. WITH and W/O VINYL TOP

H/T $3683.

MALIBU

"HEAVY CHEVY" SPT. CPE. has BLACK GRILLE, SPECIAL STRIPING (INTRO. MID-'71)

DLX. CPE. $3599.

DLX. 4-DR. = $3566.

COLONNADE 4-DR.

Malibu $3711.

100 TO 245 HP (400 CID V8 DISCONTINUED '73 ONLY)

(CONT'D. NEXT PAGE)

73 *new* TOTALLY RESTYLED **DELUXE** COLONNADE CPE. and 4-DR. (ABOVE)
ENERGY-ABSORBING SAFETY BUMPERS

Chevrolet. Building a better way to see the U.S.A.

CHEVELLE

OPT. WHEEL COVERS

LAGUNA FRONT END IS ENTIRE BUMPER. OTHER *new TYPE* BUMPER AT TOP (GUARDS OPT.)

MALIBU

DLX. WAGON $3909. UP

MALIBU FR. $3997.

wagon

CPE. $3743.

MALIBU

OPTION. SWING-OUT (90°) BUCKET SEATS

(MALIBU SS *has* "SS" IN CENTER OF BLACK GRILLE *and* ON COWL.)

DASH (LAGUNA)

REAR

New Laguna

$4373.

CPE. $3932.

Laguna Estate

740

CHEVELLE BY CHEVROLET

(CHEVELLE DELUXE DISCONTINUED)

$2878* MALIBU 6 COUPE

$2873* MALIBU 6 SEDAN

(MALIBU, CLASSIC and CLASSIC EST. WAGONS AVAIL.)

Engines	Power Rating*
Turbo-Thrift 250 Six	100-hp
Turbo-Fire 350 V8	145-hp
Turbo-Fire 350 V8	160-hp
Turbo-Fire 400 V8	150-hp
Turbo-Fire 400 V8	180-hp
Turbo-Jet 454 V8	235-hp

74

new GRILLES

(DURING 1974, MALIBU 6 CPE. PRICE INCREASED TO $3954.!)

Malibu Classic

Malibu Classic

$4590.

LANDAU CPE.

Malibu Classic: (NEW)

new HOOD ORNAMENT (MAL.CLASSIC ONLY)

Malibu Classic Sedan

Chevrolet makes sense for America.

$4376.

Chevelle Laguna Type S-3.

(note 2 AVAILABLE TOP STYLES)

NEW

LAGUNA TYPE S-3

S-3 GRILLE

$4504.

S-3

(GR70 x 15 TIRES ON Laguna)

CHEVELLE coupe. **$3407.***

MALIBU The lowest-priced sedan. **$3402.***

Malibu Wagon

$4989.

MALIBU CLASSIC

CPE.

Malibu Classic instrument panel, with new speedometer calibrated in both miles per hour (mph) and kilometers per hour (kph).

$5412. WAGON (MAL. CLASSIC ESTATE) → (3-ST.)

22% higher gas mileage with standard V8

(ALSO AVAIL W/O GRAIN)

SEDAN $4744.

250 CID 6 (105 HP)
350 CID V8 (145 OR 155 HP)
400 CID V8 (175 HP)
454 CID V8 (215 HP)

NEW 75

catalytic converter.

(RESTYLED FRONT and REAR ENDS)

new SLOPING FRONT ON
LAGUNA TYPE S-3

$4867.

LAGUNA TYPE S-3

(ALSO AVAIL. INTO 1976)

DASH

'76 Chevelle.
A size whose time has come.

Two roomy Chevelles priced under $3671. (SALE)
26 MPG Highway, 18 MPG City, EPA.*

REG. $4711.

$5185. (LANDAU)

MALIBU CLASSIC

76

new GRILLES (MAL. CLASSIC *has* OWN 4 HEADLIGHTS, MESH-TYPE GRILLE) →

MALIBU

← REG. $4746.

* = WITH 250 CID 6 (105 HP) 20 HWY., 14 CITY WITH 305 CID V8 (new, 140 HP)

(454 CID V8 DISCONT'D.)

Smart, complete, mid-size Chevelle.

(NO MORE TYPE 9-3)

MALIBU WAGON

$5466.

SALE: $3885.

77

new GRILLES, FEWER ENG. CHOICES

MALIBU

250 CID 6 (110 HP)
305 CID V8 (145 HP)
350 CID V8 (170 HP)

MALIBU CLASSIC

$5651.

DASH (MALIBU CLASSIC)

$5327.

(illustr. LARGE SIDE MIRROR IS OPTIONAL.)

TAIL-LT. DETAILS

CHEVELLE

NOW KNOWN AS **CHEVY MALIBU**

MALIBU WAGON CLASSIC

$6025.

MPG 29 HWY. 21 EPA WITH 200 CID V6

23 HWY., 16 EPA 231 CID V6

Malibu.

$5543.

EST. $6221.

95 TO 170 HP

NEW-SIZE 78 new SHORTER 108" WB

(RESTYLED)

DASH (MALIBU CLASSIC)

MALIBU, MALIBU CLASSIC

now SHARE GRILLE, BUT MAL. CLASSIC has CHROME TRIM AROUND WINDOWS, ETC.

(SPEC. INSTRUMENTATION PKG. has SMALL ROUND GAUGES.)

new 200, 231 CID V6s (305, 350 CID V8s ALSO)

" SEE WHAT'S NEW TODAY IN A CHEVROLET. "

5902.

(22) EPA estimated MPG / (28) Highway estimate

"A FRESH NEW SLICE OF APPLE PIE"

$6512.

MALIBU CLASSIC

(DASH LIKE '78, BUT WITH "Malibu Classic" LETTERING AT RT.)
(new 267 CID V8 ADDED)

79 new GRILLE

MALIBU 4-D SEDAN

$4915. (SALE)

VALUE IS WHAT MAKES A MALIBU A CHEVROLET.

MPG: 20 EPA 26 HWY.

new GRILLE

MAL. PRICED FROM $6543.

80 Malibu CLASSIC

$7063.

744

Chevette

STANDARD: Deluxe grille.

78

new 4-DR. $3805. (97.3" WB)

MANY new STANDARD FEATURES (ILLUSTR.)

STANDARD: AM radio. STANDARD: Console. STANDARD: Swing-out rear windows. STANDARD: Wheel trim rings. STANDARD: Cigarette lighter. STANDARD: Color-keyed instrument panel. STANDARD: Glove compartment lock.

STANDARD: Carpeting.

$3695. 2-Door

STANDARD: Fully synchronized 4-Speed transmission.

97.6 CID 4 (63 HP) NOW STANDARD

STANDARD: Bumper rub strips. STANDARD: Sport steering wheel. STANDARD: Body side moldings.

'78 Chevette. A lot more car for a lot less money.*

SCOOTER $3340. WITH FEWER FEATURES

BEST-SELLING SMALL CAR IN AMERICA.

79

new GRILLE

70 HP

SCOOTER (NO SIDE TRIM) $3724.

('79)

$4220.

1979 and 1980 DASH SIMILAR EXCEPT FOR MINOR CHANGES IN SPEC. INSTRUMENTATION PKG. (illustrated)

$4100.

74 HP AVAIL.

2-TONE PAINT AVAIL.

70 HP

('80)

80

new 4-PIECE WRAP-AROUND TAIL-LIGHTS

TACHOMETER. Constantly monitors engine speed

A lot of car for the money. 1980

$4756. (2-DR. and SCOOTER AVAIL.)

100377

SINCE 1918, MFD. BY **General Motors**

CHEVROLET

(EST. 1911) FROM $2832. (BISCAYNE 2-DR.)

Caprice DASH

IMPALA HUB CAP

IMPALA

66

new GRILLE, BUMPER and TAIL-LIGHT

(INTRO. THURSDAY 10-7-65)

119" WB
7.75/8.25 x 14 TIRES

STD. ENGINES
250 CID 6 (155 HP)
283 CID V8 (195 HP)

NEW

← REAR VIEW

$3800. (3-SEAT)

Caprice Custom Wagon

✱ CAPRICE
Custom Series

note HORIZONTAL BANDS ACROSS CAPRICE TAILLIGHTS (UNLIKE TAILLIGHTS OF BISCAYNE, BEL AIR OR IMPALA MODELS)

CUSTOM SEDAN $35/6.

✱-(CAPRICE INTRO. 1965, AS A $242 OPT. PKG.)

$3453.
CAPR. CUST. CPE. ROOFLINE (New)

DENOTES A 327 CID V8

747

'67 Chevrolet gives you that sure feeling

Biscayne
$3036.

$3469. UP

(INTRO. 9-29 66)

Impala

STANDARD ENGINES
155-hp Turbo-Thrift 250 Six
195-hp Turbo-Fire 283 V8
EXTRA-COST OPTIONAL ENGINES
275-hp Turbo-Fire 327 V8
325-hp Turbo-Jet 396 V8
385-hp Turbo-Jet 427 V8

'67 IMPALA

Impala SS
$3350.

67

new GRILLE

$3192.

1967

Impala Sport Coupe

Caprice Custom Sedan

$3477.

new GRILLE IS HORIZONTALLY BISECTED BY BUMPER CROSS BAR

68

new ROUND TAIL LTS. IN BUMPER

$3809. UP

CAPRICE

CUSTOM SEDAN $3621.

CUSTOM CPE.

formal

STD. 250 CID 6 (155 HP)
307 CID V8 (200 HP)

$3371.

Impala coupes

note SMALL new SIDE LIGHTS

Fastback
SPORT CPE.

1968

$3318.

748

(INTRO. 9-21-67)

BE SMART! BE SURE! BUY NOW AT YOUR CHEVROLET DEALER'S.

CHEVROLET

ALL ENGINES
EXCEPT 427 CID V8s
USE REGULAR
GAS.

Impala

$3427.

new
PLASTIC
GRILLE

$3426.

(INTRO. 9-26-68)

ENGINES : 250 CID 6 (155 HP)
327 CID V8 (235 HP)
350 CID V8 (255 OR 300 HP)
396 CID V8
(265 HP)
427 CID V8
(335 OR 390 HP)

69

(RESTYLED)

new
KINGSWOOD
ESTATE
(3-SEAT)
$4019.

new CONCEALED
HEADLIGHTS

Caprice

wagon
new
BROOKWOOD,
TOWNSMAN, KINGSWOOD
and KINGSWOOD ESTATE
WAGONS

Putting you first, keeps us first.

note FLARED
REAR FENDERS

(INTRO. 9-26-68)

BROOKWOOD, TOWNSMAN, KINGSWOOD
KINGSWOOD ESTATE WAGONS
(FROM TOP, DOWN)
(119" WB)

2-ST. $4088.

70 Wagons (7 MODELS)

new V-GRILLE

$3812.

(INTRO. 9-18-69)
3-ST. $4201.

KINGS. EST.

Impala

Right Car. Right Price. Right Now.

← IMPALA CUSTOM H/T $3607.

Chevrolet

350

2-DR. CUST. H/T

← Caprice $3815.

(new MONTE CARLO in SEPARATE SECTION.)

On the move: The Chevrolet '70.

BROOKWD.

Impala

(BISCAYNE 4-DR. SED. FR. $3885.)

(INTRO. 9-29-70)
STD. HP CUT (6-145) (V8 -245)

$4239.

new GRILLES

71

new 121½" WB

Caprice. ↗

CAPR. CUSTOM SED. 4-DR. H/T $4545.

Caprice TYPE WITH MID-SIDE TRIM SPEAR (TYPE W/O, ABOVE RT.)

1971. You've changed. We've changed.

Impala $4257.

72

1972 SLOGAN: "CHEVROLET. BUILDING A BETTER WAY TO SEE THE U.S.A."

(FINAL BISCAYNE 4-DR. PRICED AT $3878.)

FINE HORIZ PCS. IN IMPALA GRILLE ↗

350 CID V8 HP CUT AGAIN, (TO 165)

$4479.

Caprice 4-Door Sedan.
(new)

WITH 400 CID V8 (170 HP) CAPRICE

FINAL 127" WB

CAPRICE GRILLE DETAIL

SUBURBAN (CARRYALL) FR. $3640.

(INTRO. 9-23-71)

WITH DISAPPEARING TAILGATE

WAGON

WHEEL COVER TYPE USED ON 2-DR. H/T

CHEVROLET

LOWEST-PRICED IS NOW THE **BELAIR**

73

4-DR. SEDAN AT $4018. → new GRILLES

$4196.

IMPALA

Impala

350 CID V8 CUT TO 145 HP
G78 × 15 TIRES
(L78 × 15, WAGONS)

New improved front bumper system that retracts on minor impact and hydraulically cushions the shock. **CAPRICE**

DASH

IMPALA CUSTOM CPE. has INDENTED REAR WINDOW.

CAPRICE ESTATE WAGON FROM $4784.

OPTIONAL WIRE WHEEL COVERS

$4755.

$4496.

CAPRICE

AGAIN, CAPRICE has OWN GRILLE.

CAPRICE 400 CID V8 CUT TO 150 HP

1973 Chevrolet. Building a better way to see the U.S.A.

CHEVROLET

IMPALA

(BEL-AIR 4-DR. SED. PRICED AT $4473.)

IMPALA SPT. CPE. $4675. CUSTOM CPE. $4742.

74

IMPALA SPT. SED. $4728.

DASH (CAPRICE)

new GRILLE TOTALLY ABOVE BUMPER. new FRONT CORNER LIGHTS ADDED.

CAPRICE MODELS FR. $4978. (4-DR.)

Caprice Estate wagon

FROM $5313.

New Flip-Down seats (wagon)

Caprice Classic

note GIANT new RR. QUARTER WINDOW ON **Caprice Classic**

CUST. CPE. $4996.

REAR

CVT. $5258.

Caprice

CHEVROLET

↖ FINAL BEL-AIR

BEL AIR 4-DOOR SEDAN

IMPALA

(FINAL CVT.)

IMPALA 4-DOOR

NEW CATALYTIC CONVERTER
(Standard, all '75 Chevrolet cars, and trucks 6,000 GVW and below.)

LANDAU CPE. WITH LARGE QUARTER WINDOWS STILL AVAILABLE

CAPRICE CLASSIC SPORT SEDAN

75

Caprice Classic

(new)

CATALYTIC CONVERTER (SINCE 1975)

CHEVROLET MAKES SENSE FOR AMERICA

Chevy Suburban

$4707. UP 129" WB

FROM $5758.

Now that makes sense

CAPRICE ESTATE

IMPALA TAIL-LTS.

$5068.

4190 ED

EPA M.P.G. 13 CITY, 18 HWY. (w. STD. 350-2 V8)

IMPALA 76

↖ NO MID-SIDE CHROME STRIP.

Impala S

SEDAN

$5323.

(CONT'D. NEXT PAGE)

754

INTERIOR

CHEVROLET 76
(CONT'D.)

$5638.

(FINAL 4-DR. H/T)

$5603.

Caprice Classic

note
DIFFERENCES IN
WHEEL COVERS

1976. Chevrolet makes room for America.

(TOTALLY RESTYLED)

Now that's more like it.

Impala

IMPALA RR.

The 1977 Caprice Classic Sedan

New

$5967.

116" WB

SIZE

CAPRICE CLASSIC CPE. $5917.

77

Caprice Classic.

22 mpg. hwy.   17 mpg. city

REAR

CID 6 (110 HP)
STD. 305 CID V8
(145 HP)

DASH
(CAPRICE)

20.2-cubic-foot trunk

SUBURBAN $5087. UP

FROM $6427.   CAPR. ESTATE
WAGON

CHEVROLET

$ 6042.

SEE WHAT'S NEW TODAY IN A CHEVROLET.

(INTRO. THURS., 10-8-77)

IMPALA

78

new GRILLES

WAGON

EPA M.P.G. 17 CITY, 24 HWY. with 250 CID 6 (110 HP)

305 CID V8 (145 HP)

POWER SKY ROOF AVAIL. (above)

CAPRICE CLASSIC

$ 6460.

Impala ←

CAPR. CLSSC. (REAR) ('79)

new HORIZ. STRIPS ACROSS CORNER LTS.

Impala

new GRILLES **79**

Caprice Classic

$ 7324.   America has driven it to the top.

$ 6829. UP

305 CID V8 CUT TO 130 HP

350 CID V8 (170 HP)

$ 7754. UP

CHEVROLET

EST. RANGE
450 CITY   650 HWY

WITH 25-GAL. FUEL TANK

18 | 26
EPA EST MPG · HWY ESTIMATE
WITH STD. 229 V6 ENG.
(115 HP)

IMPALA WAGON FR. $7526.

IMPALA

IMPALA SPT. CPE.

$7105.

IMPALA SEDAN $7214.

new P205/75R×15 TIRES (P225 ON WAGONS)

80

CAPRICE CLASSIC LANDAU CPE. has BRIGHTWORK BAR EXTENDING UP OVER ROOF $7954.

STD. 267 CID V8 (120 HP) 305 OR 350 CID AVAIL.

DASH (CAPRICE CLASSIC)

RICH WOODGRAIN EFFECTS

CAPRICE CLASSIC

SEDAN $7635.

CAPR. $8125. UP ESTATE WAGON

BOTH IMPALA AND CAPRICE CLASSIC GRILLES ARE **NEW**

New engines.

757

CHEVROLET **Camaro** (1967-1981)
(INTRO. 9-29-66)

6 CYL. OR V8
(140 TO 325 HP)
108" WB

NEW

67

STOCK
CAMARO 6
COUPE
(FROM $2792.)

RS (RALLY SPORT)
WITH CONCEALED HEADLTS.
AVAIL.

SS-350 CPE.
W. CONCEALED LTS.

"SS 350" ON GRILLE

SS - 350
WITH 350 CID V-8 ENG.
(295 HP) OR 396 CID (325 HP)

SS-350
Interior

Command Performance
"The Hugger"

Camaro SS

CHEVROLET

(SEE DATA AT LOWER LEFT)

new GRILLE
new "FLOW-THROUGH" VENTILATION
ELIMINATES VENT PANES

68

new
DASH

DUAL ROWS of SQUARE PORTS
ATOP HOOD (SS MODELS)

SS

(STD. CAMARO
H/T FROM
$ 2917.)

230 CID 6
(140 HP)
OR
327 CID V8
(210 HP)
STD.

NOTE new
FRONT and
REAR SIDE
(RECTANGULAR)
SAFETY LIGHTS,
AS REQUIRED BY
LAW

7.35 × 14 TIRES

REAR FENDER

Chevrolet **Camaro** (FINAL CONVERTIBLE AVAILABLE)

SS SPT. CPE. WITH RALLY SPORT EQUIP.

69 (CONTINUES TO FEB., 1970)

140 HP 6 TO 396 CID 325 HP V8

(EARLY 327 CID, 210 HP V8 REPL. BY NEW STD. 307 CID, 200 HP)

Step on the gas and it steps up performance.

V-SHAPE and CRISS-CROSS PCS. IN new GRILLE → (BLK.)

SIDE LOUVRE DETAIL

new E78 x 14 TIRES

(AVAILABLE FOR EITHER SS OR Z-28)

Camaro's new Super Scoop

(IT OPENS ON ACCELERATION, PROVIDING COOL AIR TO CARBURETOR, ETC.)

SS has BIG V8 ENG., POWER DISC BRAKES, WIDE OVAL TIRES, and 3-SPEED FLOOR SHIFT.

350

Camaro SS

CHEVROLET
Putting you first, keeps us first.

Camaro
Chevrolet

The instrument panel wraps around you. A new invisible resilient bumper surrounds the grille of RS models.
There are four transmissions available. And six power plants up to the 360-hp 396.

'70 FROM $3089.

DASH

Super Hugger.

RS

RS (RALLY SPORT) CPE.) (note ROUND INBOARD PARK./DIR. LTS., PROTRUDING GRILLE)

REAR DETAIL

(RESTYLED)

70 -71

(1970 (SOMETIMES REFERRED TO AS THE 1970½ CAMARO, BY REASON OF ITS LATE DEBUT.)

New Camaro. Feb. 26th.

We've never announced a car at this time before.
But then nobody's ever announced a car like this before.

STD. 250 CID 6 (155 HP) OR 307 CID V8 (200 HP)

(BLUE OR BROWN VINYL TOPS NOT AVAIL. UNTIL '71)

Z-28 PKG.: $573. EXTRA

FRONT DISC BRAKES NOW STD.

360 HP V8 AVAIL.

(Z-28 has BROAD DUAL STRIPES on HOOD and DECK)

SPORT CPE. WITH DELUXE BUMPER

See it. At your Chevrolet Sports Dept.

Chevrolet
Building a better way
to see the U.S.A.

Camaro **Sport Coupe**

Sport Coupe / Rally Sport / SS / Z28

DASH

STD. 307 CID V8 (130 HP) (6 ALSO AVAIL.)

72

FEWER PCS. IN *new* STD. GRILLE

FROM $3580. (V8)

Rally Sport

Super Sport

"SS 350"

4-SPOKE STEER. WHEEL

new STD. EQUIP.

"Z28"

Z28

note "Z-28" ON GRILLE

762

(REAR)

JVL-710

307 CID V8 CUT TO 115 HP
(6 CYL. AVAIL.)

Z-28

V8
SPORT
COUPE
$3608.

(NOT
AVAIL.
ON
Z-28)
TURBINE
I WHEEL

UNIROYAL

73

new
FRONT BUMPER

LT DASH
(LT "LUXURY
TOURING")
$3884.
(V8)

↑
AVAIL.
ONLY
FOR
SPT.
CPE.
OR
RS

LT (new)

RALLY
SPORT ($90. LESS
FOR 6-CYL.)

(SS
NOT
AVAIL.)

Chevrolet **Camaro**

STD. $4091. (LT=$4438.)

TOTALLY RESTYLED

74

Z-28

(6 CYL. $212. LESS)

250 CID (100 HP) 6 CYL. STILL AVAIL.; STANDARD V8 IS 350 CID, (WITH *new* 145 HP)

DASH

TAIL-LT. DETAIL

$4424. Sport Coupe or Type LT. ($4796.)
(105 HP 6 CYL. $145 LESS)

SPORT COUPE

2-TONE
WITH RALLY SPORT TRIM

('75)

75 -76

new RECTANGULAR EMBLEM, NOW ON HOOD *and* REAR DECK

Camaro

('75) **TYPE LT**   LT WOODGRAINED

Chevrolet Camaro

Z28

Z-28 SPOILER

$5767.

STD. 305 CID V8 (145 HP) OR 250 CID 6 (100 HP)

SPT. CPE. $5082.

STD. E/FR78 × 14/B TIRES

(Z-28 = GR70 × 15)

SPECIAL PAINT JOB ON Z-28

Z28 **77**

RETURNS!

Z-28 350 CID V8 has 170 HP (ENG. AVAIL. FOR "LT" also)

SEE WHAT'S NEW TODAY IN A CHEVROLET.

OVERHEAD VIEW OF new T-BAR ROOF AVAIL.

new ALL-MOLDED FRONT APPEARS "BUMPERLESS"

78

(6-CYL. has new 110 HP)

Camaro Z28 has new SLANTING LOUVRES ON SIDE OF COWL.

$6236.

(STD. $5562. UP)

new T-BAR AVAIL.

DASH

LT FR. $5962.

765

STD. 250 CID 6 (115 HP) OR 305 CID V8 (130 HP)

Camaro Sport Coupe

$ 6252.

Camaro Rally Sport

(FULL LINE ILLUSTR.)

79

RS FROM $6661.

WITH T-TOP (OPTIONAL)

Z-28 DASH ILLUSTR. AT TOP OF PAGE

"Z-28" SIDE DECAL NOW ON DOOR

Z-28 GRILLE

new Camaro Berlinetta

Z-28 has 350 CID V8 (170 HP)

1979 Camaro Z28

$ 7167.

$ 6995.

CAMARO. THE HUGGER.

766

Camaro Chevrolet

SPORT COUPE. $6699.

AVAILABLE OPTION

TAIL-LT. DETAILS

80

BERLINETTA

$7462.

new STD. ENGINES 229 CID 6 (115 HP) 267 CID V8 (120 HP) (305 CID V8 AVAIL.)

RALLY SPORT FROM $7116.

AVAIL. FOR RALLY SPT. OR SPT. CPE.

NOT TO BE CONFUSED WITH WIRE WHEELS SHOWN ON BERLINETTA

Z28 DASH

EPA MPG: 20 CITY 26 HWY. (6)

Z 28 FOR 1980. THE MAXIMUM CAMARO. WITH 350 CID V8 (new 190 HP)

(STARTS WITH 1980 MODEL) **CHEVROLET** Citation (FRONT WHEEL DRIVE)

A whole new kind of compact car.

TRANSVERSE ENGINE
104.9" WB
P185/80R x 13 TIRES

STD. DASH

Club Coupe. →
$6300.

2-DR. HATCHBACK
$6427.
(STD. CPE = $5965.)

(ALSO KNOWN AS "CHEVY" CITATION.)

4-DR. HATCHBACK
$6293.

Custom Interior DASH
(ROUND GAUGES)

(NEW) 80

(INTRO. 4-19-79)

SLIP STREAM STYLING

Full Wheel Covers.

EPA MPG 24 CITY, 38 HWY. WITH 151 CID 4 (90 HP)

173 CID V6 (110 OR 115 HP) ALSO AVAIL.

SPORT PACKAGE - $500.

X-11
WITH SPECIAL PAINT JOB, P205/70R-13 TIRES

X-11 STEERING WHEEL

(X-11 CL. CPE. ALSO AVAIL.)

"THE FIRST CHEVY OF THE '80s"

768

(1960-1969) MONZA

CHEVROLET CORVAIR

rear-engine design with Independent suspension at all four wheels

A most unusual car for people who enjoy the unusual!

H/T $2556.

$2630. SPT. SEDAN (4-DR. H/T)

MONZA CVT. $2699.

(FINAL) CORSA 66

$2666. (H/T)

$2809.

1966 SALES: 88,951 ("500" IS LOWEST-PRICED MODEL, FROM $2289.)

108" WB   6 CYL., 164 CID
7.00 × 13 TIRES   95-140 HP

500

$2339.

CORSA SERIES NO LONGER AVAILABLE 1967

1967 SALES: 24,736

67

THIS BEST IDENTIFIES A 1967 MODEL.

95 OR 110 HP ENGINES ONLY, DURING 1967.

New oval steering wheel — This easy-to-grip wheel sits atop the GM-developed energy-absorbing steering column — one of many new standard safety features. Others include 4-way hazard warning flasher and a lane-change feature incorporated in direction signal control.

'67 Corvair
The rear-engine road car

MONZA CVT. $2770.

769

Chevrolet CORVAIR

$2457.

a true hardtop.
And it's Chevrolet's
lowest priced hardtop.

Corvair 500

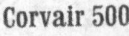

"500" INTERIOR

Corvair Power Teams

ENGINES	TRANS-MISSIONS	AXLE RATIOS
95-HP TURBO-AIR 164 (Standard)	3-Speed (Standard)	3.55:1
	4-Speed (Extra-cost)	3.55:1
	Powerglide (Extra-cost)	3.27:1 *
110-HP TURBO-AIR 164 (Extra-cost)	3-Speed (Standard)	3.27:1 *
	4-Speed (Extra-cost)	3.27:1 *
	Powerglide (Extra-cost)	3.55:1
140-HP TURBO-AIR 164 (Extra-cost)	3-Speed (Standard)	3.55:1
	4-Speed (Extra-cost)	3.55:1
	Powerglide (Extra-cost)	3.55:1

Positraction available for all ratios.
*3.55:1 may be specified

1968 PRICES SHOWN. $10 INCREASE, 1969.
SALES:
1968 = 12,977
1969 = 3,102

$2840.

MONZA CONVERTIBLE

new DASH

new SIDE SAFETY LTS.

(DISCONTINUED 5-14-69)

68-69

(FULL 1968-1969 LINE ILLUSTR.)

(NO 4-DR. HARDTOPS AFTER 1967)

OPT. WIRE WHEEL COVERS ←

MONZA SPT. CPE.

OPT. LUGGAGE CARRIER

MONZA INTERIOR

$2721.

'68 Standard Safety Features

☐ Energy-absorbing steering column ☐ Seat belts with pushbutton buckles for all passenger positions. ☐ Shoulder belts for driver and right front passenger with pushbutton buckles and convenient stowage provision on all models except convertibles ☐ Passenger-guard door locks with deflecting lock buttons — all doors ☐ Four-way hazard warning flasher ☐ Dual master cylinder brake system with warning light and corrosion-resistant brake lines ☐ Latches on front seat backs ☐ Dual-speed windshield wipers and washers ☐ Outside rearview mirror ☐ Back-up lights. ☐ New side marker lights and parking lights that illuminate with headlights ☐ Padded instrument panel, sun visors, windshield pillars ☐ Reduced-glare instrument panel top, inside windshield moldings, horn button, steering wheel hub, and windshield wiper arms and blades ☐ Inside day-night mirror with deflecting base ☐ Lane-change feature in direction-signal control ☐ Safety armrests ☐ Thick-laminate windshield ☐ Soft, low-profile window control knobs and coat hooks ☐ Energy-absorbing seat backs ☐ Yielding door and window control handles ☐ Energy-absorbing instrument panel with smooth contoured knobs and levers ☐ Tire safety rim ☐ Safety door latches and hinges ☐ Uniform shift quadrant ☐ Snag-resistant steering wheel hardware ☐ Fuel tank and filler pipe security.

770

Chevrolet **CORVETTE** *(SINCE 1953)*

STINGRAY CPE.

OPT. 427 CID (425 HP)

*98" WB (ALL) V8 ENGINES   STD. 327 CID (300 HP)

66-67

7.75×14 TIRES

('66) $4784.

FR. $4573.   FR. $4604.

(CVT. and H/T CVT. ALSO)

(* - SINCE 1963)

327 CID (300 - 350 HP) OR 427 CID (390, 400 OR 435 HP)

(TOTALLY RESTYLED)

68

OPT. HARD TOP ↓

$5157. CPE.

new F70 × 15 TIRES

CVT. $4814.

new T-TOP (INTERIOR)

Corvette simulated-wood steering wheel and instrumentation

'69 Corvette ~CHEVROLET~ a true American sports car.

note "STINGRAY" NAME ADDED, ON FRONT FENDERS 327 CID REPL. BY new 350 CID V8 (300 HP)
427 CID CONT'D. (390, 400, 430 OR 435 HP)

69

EU·9262

STINGRAY COUPE WITH ROOF SECTIONS REMOVED

(350 CID OR new 454 CID V8)

new VENTS

70-72

(300, 350, 370, 390 OR 460 HP '70)
('71 270, 330, 365, 425 HP OR 210, 275, 285, 325 SAE NET HP)
('72 200, 255 OR 270 HP)

new CRISS-CROSS PCS. IN GRILLE; SQUARE PK. LTS.

('71)

('71)

FROM $ 5126. ('70)
5548. ('71)
5532. ('72)
(CVT. PRICES)

(1972 CARRIES LIC. PLATE IN GRILLE CENTER, AS DO MANY PREV. MODELS.)

Chevrolet Corvette

Building a better way to see the U.S.A.

$5847.

$5621.

73

new GRILLE and PARKING LIGHTS
new RESILIENT BODY-COLORED BUILT-IN FRONT BUMPER

new DOMED HOOD

350 CID (190 HP @ 4400 RPM OR 250 HP @ 5200)

454 CID (275 HP @ 4400 RPM)

GR 70 × 15 TIRES

We gave it radials, a quieter ride, guard beams and a nose job.

CVT.

(350 OR 454 CID)

DASH

74

RESTYLED (sloping) REAR END

195,250 OR 270 HP

1974

773

Chevrolet

Corvette
75-76

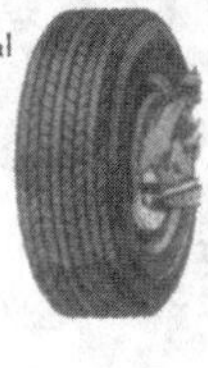

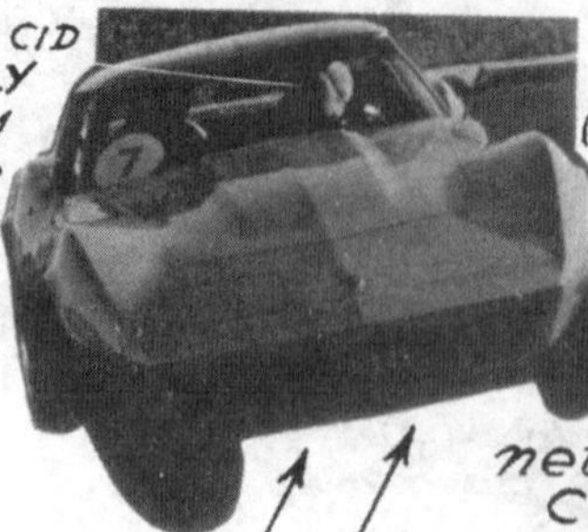

(350 CID ONLY FROM 165 HP ('75) 180 HP ('76)

('75)

IMPROVED BUMPER SYSTEM ('75)

INTRODUCING A MORE EFFICIENT CORVETTE.

new HIGH ENERGY IGNITION

new CATALYTIC CONVERTER

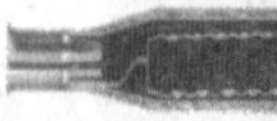

(1975 IS FINAL CONVERT.)

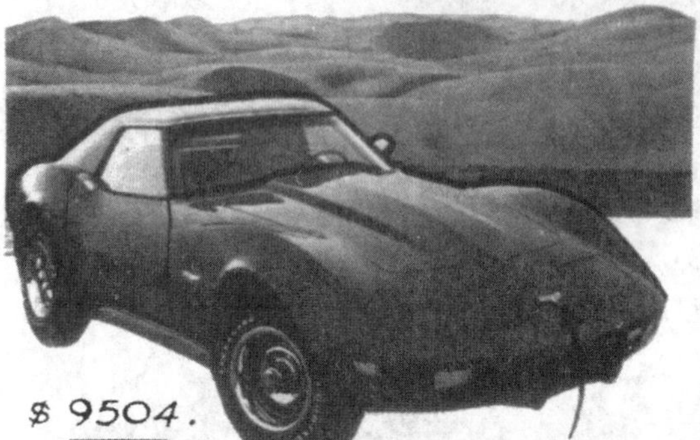

$ 9504.

new EMBLEM

DASH

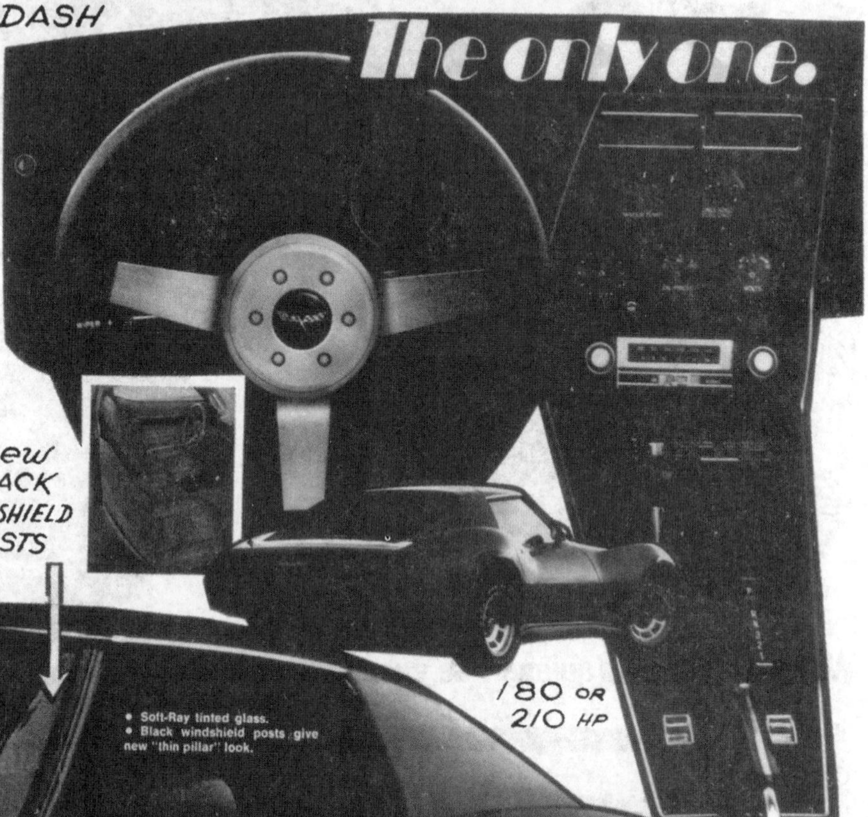

The only one.

77
new BLACK WINDSHIELD POSTS

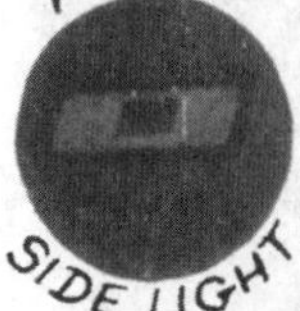

FRONT

SIDE LIGHT LENS

- Soft-Ray tinted glass.
- Black windshield posts give new "thin pillar" look.

180 OR 210 HP

FIRESTONE

500

774

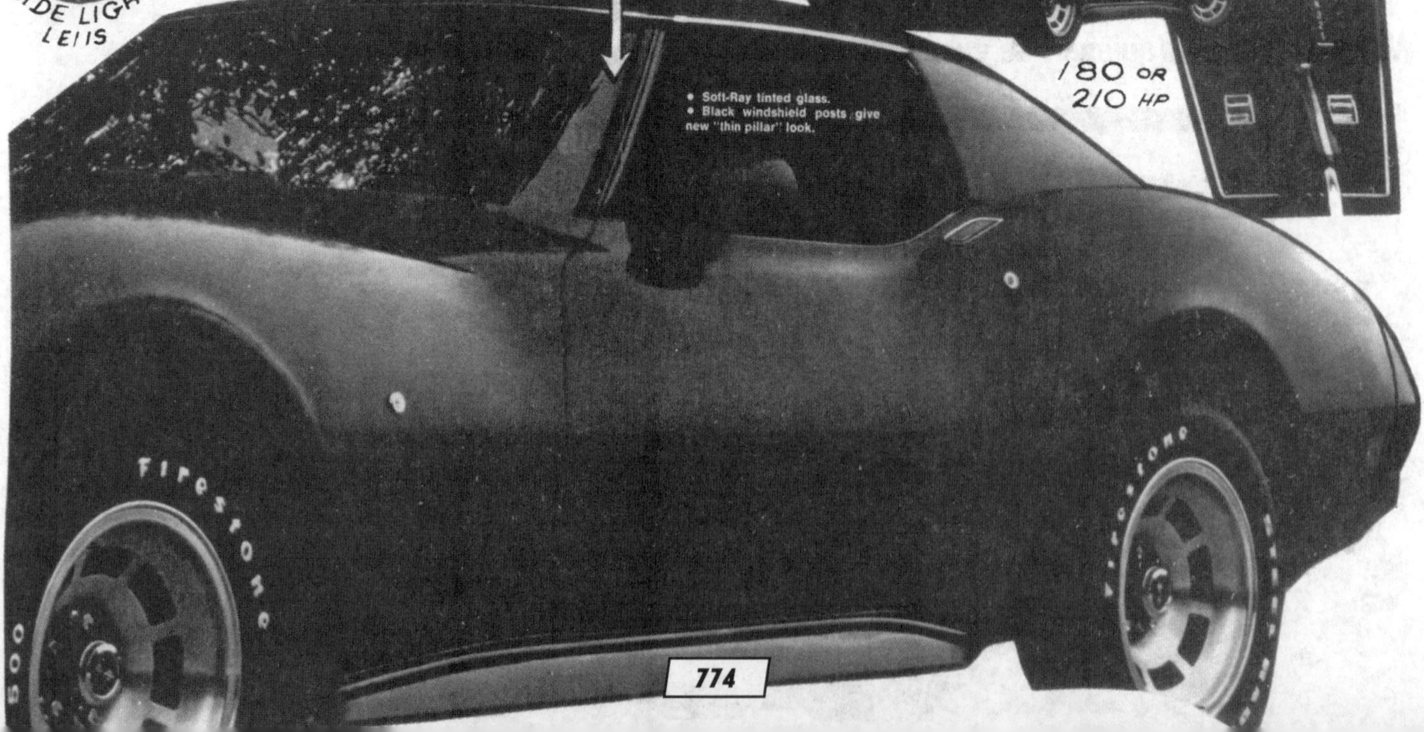

Chevrolet Corvette

350 CID V8 (175, 185 OR 220 HP)

SEE WHAT'S NEW TODAY IN A CHEVROLET.

Silver Anniversary Corvette.

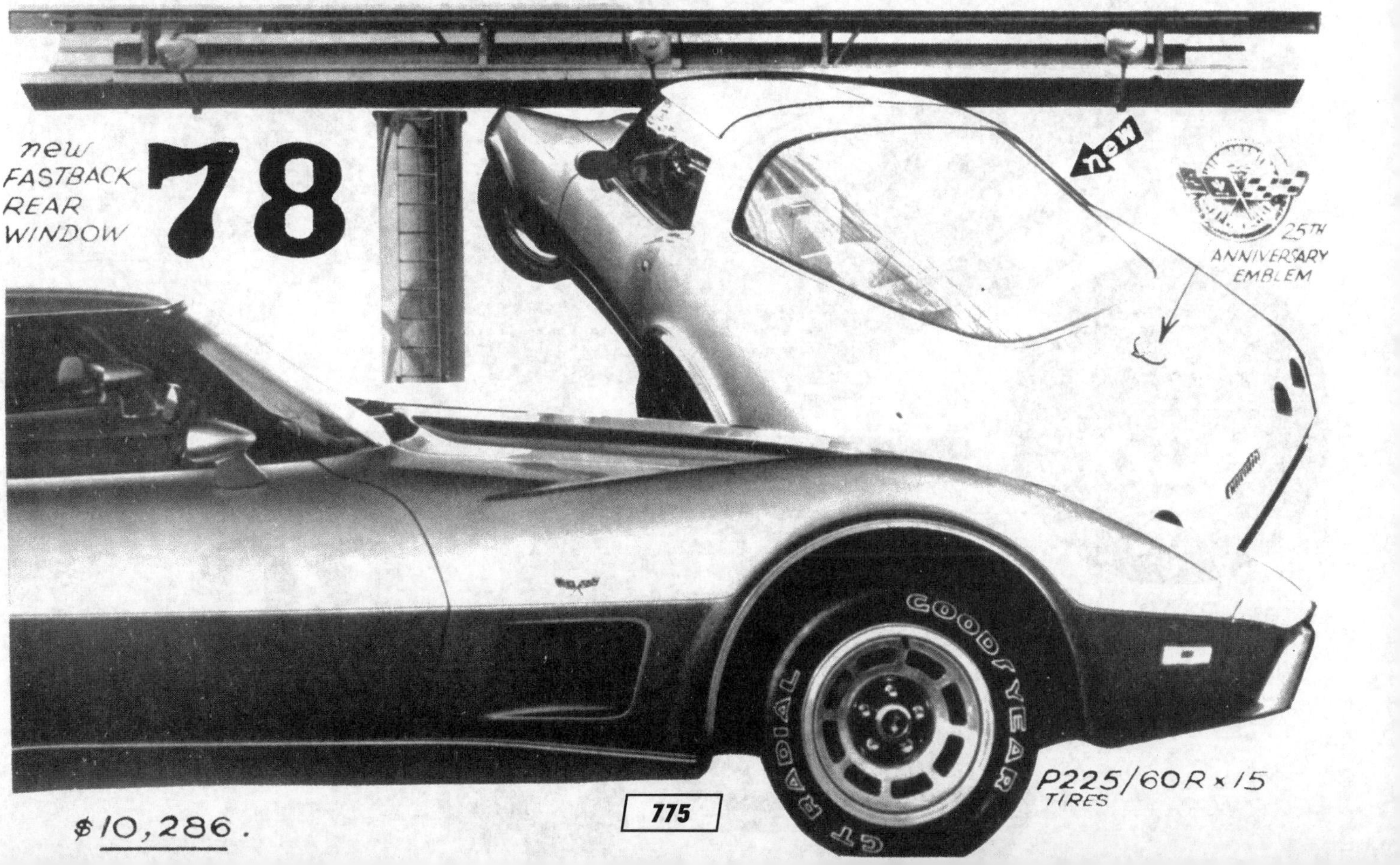

new FASTBACK REAR WINDOW

78

new

25TH ANNIVERSARY EMBLEM

GOODYEAR GT RADIAL

P225/60R x 15 TIRES

$10,286.

775

Chevrolet CORVETTE

79

DASH AND CONS.

FIBERGLASS BODIES ON ALL CORVETTES (1953 ON)

P225/70R x15 OR P255/60R x15 TIRES

$11,536.

350 CID V8 STD. (195-225 HP)

new REAR SPOILER

(GDYR. GT TIRES, 1980)

$13,104.

new 2-PC. CORNERING LTS.

(RESTYLED)

80

(new 305 CID V8 ALSO AVAIL.) 180-190 HP

new FRONT END WITH AIR DAM; LOW-PROFILE HOOD

776

CHEVROLET Monte Carlo

(2-DR. H/Ts ONLY)

70

(INTRO. 9-18-69)

$3123. (NEW)

$3464. (REG.)

116" WB

V-8 ENGINES:
350 CID (250 HP)
350 CID (300
400   265
400   330
454 CID (360 HP) (IN SS MODEL)

G78×15/B TIRES

IMITATION (VINYL) CARPATHIAN BURLED ELM GRAIN ON INSTRUMENT PANEL

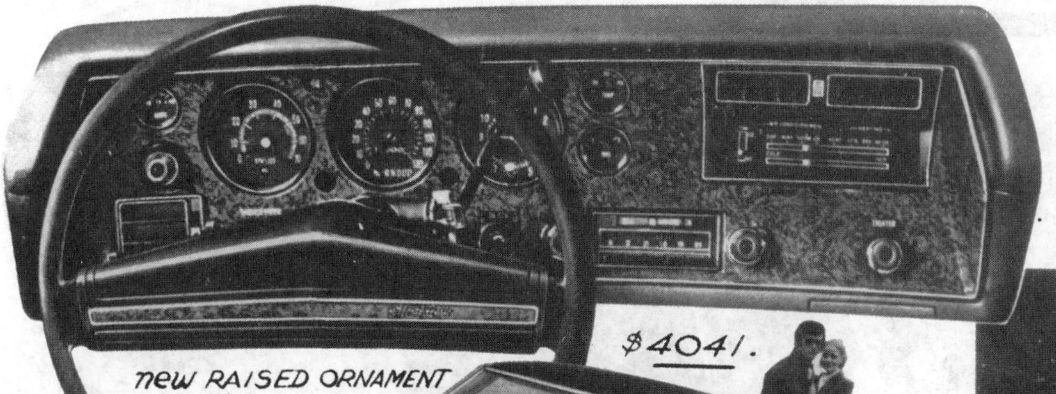

71

new GRILLE

new RAISED ORNAMENT

$4041.

245, 270, 300 OR 365 HP

1971. You've changed.
We've changed.

DASH

CHEVROLET MONTE CARLO

new GRILLE

72

$4009.

STD. 350 CID V8 CUT TO 165 HP

CUT TO 145 HP

new DASH (RESTYLED)

73

new OPERA WINDOWS

3 CPE. MODELS AVAIL., FR. $3827.

STD., S, LANDAU MODELS

778

CHEVROLET Monte Carlo

Landau

TURBINE II WHEEL

DASH

$4858.

S OR LANDAU TYPES (BOTH ILLUSTR.)

new TAIL-LTS.

74

new GRILLE

$46/4.

Monte Carlo S

SIMULATED WIRE WHEEL COVER →

new GR70 × 15/B TIRES

CHEVROLET MAKES SENSE FOR AMERICA

LANDAU OPE. $5273.

new TAIL-LTS.

75 *new* GRILLE

S COUPE $5003.

RALLY WHEEL

DASH

new DLX. WHEEL COVER

Monte Carlo

When a car makes you feel good about its looks, that's style. When it makes you feel good about yourself, that's character.

76

DASH

new GRILLE

w/o VINYL TOP $5218.

DELUXE WH. COVER

WITH VINYL TOP → $5511.

Wire wheel covers.

Rally wheels.

Turbine II wheels. Std. on Landau.

new TAIL-LIGHTS
new 305 CID V8 (140 HP)

LANDAU CPE.

305 CID (145 HP) V8, OR 350 CID (170 HP) V8

Like you, it's an original.

w/o VINYL TOP $5539.

LANDAU CPE. W/VINYL TOP

new TAIL-LIGHTS

RALLY WHEELS

$5869.

77

DELUXE WHEEL CVR.

1977 DASH IS SIMILAR IN MOST RESPECTS TO 1976 TYPE ILLUSTR.

GR 70 × 15 TIRES

new SPORT WHEEL COVER

new GRILLE

780

new 108" WB

CHEVROLET Monte Carlo

78
RESTYLED

SPORT CPE.
$6086.

LANDAU
CPE.
$6451.

new
205
/70R×14
TIRES

DASH

105 HP,
231 CID
V-6 IS
new
STANDARD
ENGINE.
305 CID
V8 ALSO
AVAIL.
(145 HP)

The Third Generation Monte Carlo.
A new dimension in affordable luxury.

DASH
SIMILAR
TO 1978

T - TOP
(OPT.)

200/231
CID V6s
(94/115 HP)
267/305 CID V8s STD.
(125/160 HP) (350 CID V8 AVAIL.)

79
new
FRONT
and REAR CORNER LIGHT
LENSES
(w. HORIZONTAL
STRIPS)

RALLY
WHEEL

SPORT
CPE. $6711.
(LANDAU
CPE. $7561.)

CHEVROLET MONTE CARLO

80

WITH *T-TOP* AND **2-TONE PAINT OPTION**

new GRILLE has FEWER PIECES. 4 new RECTANGULAR HEAD-LIGHTS

SPORT CPE. $7040.

LOW SIDE LIGHT REPLACES CORNER TYPE.

new DASH

new STYLE OF RALLY WHEEL

LANDAU CPE. $7288.

P-205/70R-14 TIRES STANDARD

115 HP, 229 CID V-6 IS new STD. ENG. (231 CID IN CALIFORNIA) (110 HP.)

(TURBO V6 AVAIL.)

267/305 CID V8s AVAIL. (120/155 HP)

(SINCE 1975)

Chevrolet
Chevrolet makes sense for America

Monza

97" WB 87 HP
4 · CYL. (140 CID)
OR
2 V-8s)

THE NEW MONZA "S"
HATCHBACK COUPE
$3946.

Monza 2+2

COWL LETTERING

18½ - GAL. FUEL TANK

75-76

POWER VENT SLOTS

TROMPE L'OEIL WHEEL COVERS. That's
French for "fool the eye." Which is what
these standard wheel covers do beautifully.
They look like expensive metal wheels but
they're tough molded polycast.

BR 78 × 13 TIRES

$4250.

2+2

"V8 4.3 LITRE" PLAQUE DESIGNATES A 262½ CID V8 (110 HP) (125 HP, 305 CID V8 AVAIL. ALSO)

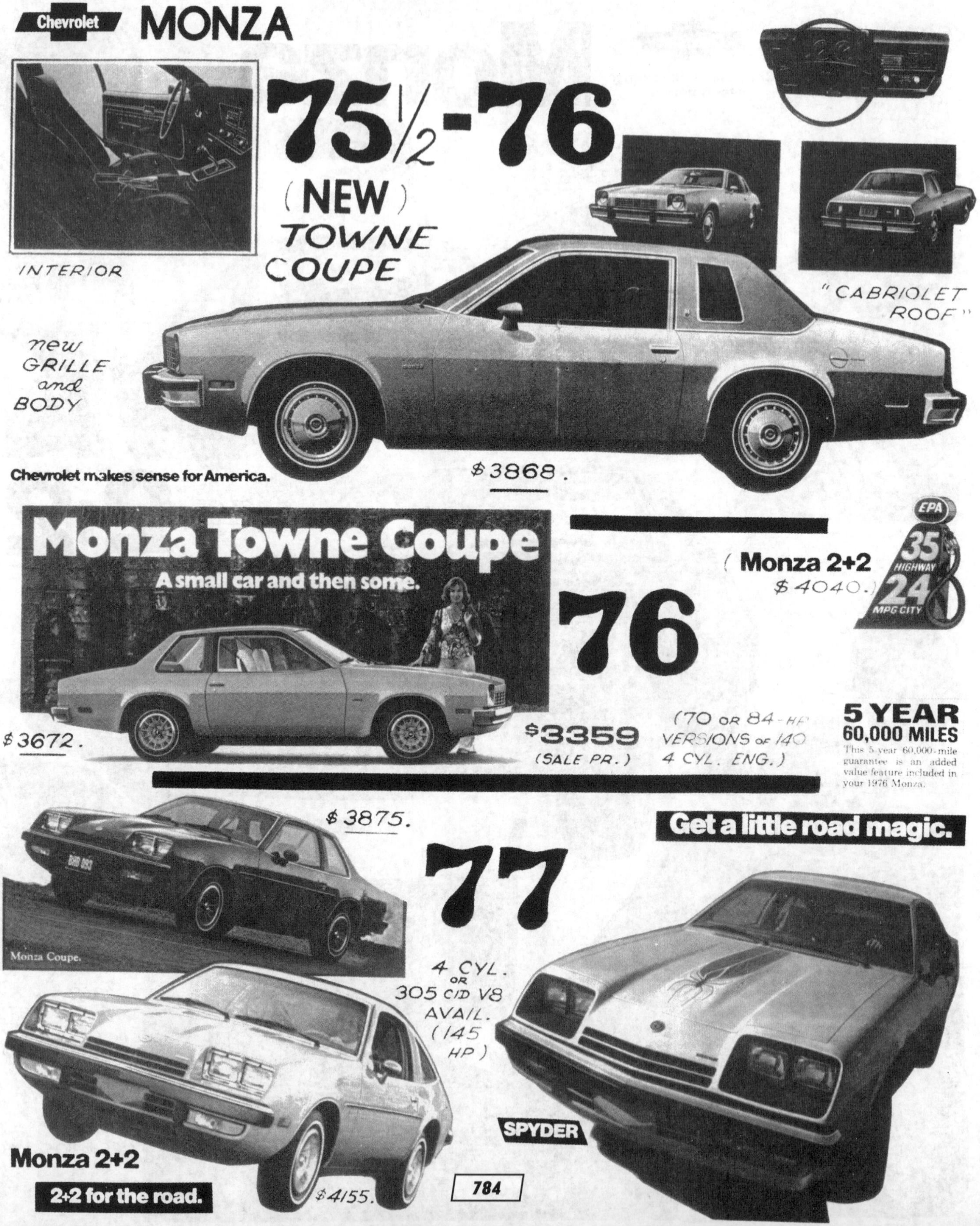
Chevrolet MONZA
75½-76
(NEW) TOWNE COUPE
INTERIOR
"CABRIOLET ROOF"
new GRILLE and BODY
Chevrolet makes sense for America.
$3868.
Monza Towne Coupe
A small car and then some.
$3672.
(Monza 2+2 $4040.)
EPA
35 HIGHWAY
24 MPG CITY
76
$3359 (SALE PR.)
(70 OR 84-HP VERSIONS OF 140 4 CYL. ENG.)
5 YEAR
60,000 MILES
This 5 year 60,000-mile guarantee is an added value feature included in your 1976 Monza.
$3875.
Get a little road magic.
77
Monza Coupe.
4 CYL. OR 305 C/D V8 AVAIL. (145 HP)
SPYDER
Monza 2+2
2+2 for the road.
$4155.

Chevrolet MONZA

4 CYL. OR **V6** (V8 AVAIL. ALSO)

('78)

WAGON (1979 FINAL YR., AT $4646.)

NEW ('78)

SALE $3698

(ESTATE WAG. ALSO, '78 ONLY)

EPA ESTIMATES
34/24
HWY CITY

WAGON **78-80**

new GRILLES

BODY SIDE MOULDINGS BECOME STD. EQUIPMENT IN 1979.

COUPE

$4080. ('78)
4517. ('79)
5041. ('80)
(4497. SALE)

Monza 2+2

DASH

('80)

(1979 MODELS ILLUSTRATED, UNLESS OTHERWISE INDICATED.)

WITH OPT. "SPYDER" PACKAGE

2+2 Sport

785

(1971 – 1977) **Chevrolet** VEGA

PANEL EXPRESS

KAMMBACK WAGON

HATCHBACK

97" WHEELBASE

4 CYL. OVERHEAD CAM 140 CID 90 HP @ 4800 RPM

KNOWN AS 2300 SERIES (BECAUSE ENG. IS IN 2300-cc CLASS)

new aluminum engine

71

(NEW)

FROM $2320.

2.53, 2.92 OR 3.36 GEAR RATIOS

RO-3468

(GTs ON NEXT PAGE)

STD. 2-DR.

NAMEPLATE READS: "CHEVROLET VEGA 2300" (ON 1971 and 1972 MODELS ONLY)

25 MPG. 786 **CHEVY'S NEW LITTLE VEGA.**

VEGA CHEVROLET

WAGON

GT.

2-DR.
HATCH-
BACK

(NEW)

BLACK GRILLE
A-70 × 13 TIRES
110 HP

(OTHER MODELS
CONTINUE FROM '71)

"GT"

71 - 72

INTRODUCING THE VEGA GT.

The Custom Interior

We can show you only so much here. Available GT equipment includes special instrumentation: tach, amp and temp gauges, electric clock, and sport steering wheel.

GT
DASH
(ABOVE)
has ROUND
GAUGES

CUSTOM INTERIOR

Swing-out rear side window.

SWING-OUT
REAR
SIDE
WINDOW
(OPT.)

NO STYLING CHANGE, BUT
SOME IMPROVEMENTS:
EASIER-SHIFTING 3 and
4-SPEED TRANSMISSIONS.
new WINDSHIELD WASHER CONTROL.
NAMEPLATE NOW READS
"VEGA BY CHEVROLET."

73

Better belts and jack.

STRONGER
BUMPERS

new
ESTATE
WAGON
$2850.

**Chevrolet
introduces a
neat little
woody.**

787

The Vega LX.
It's a deluxe version of the Notchback Coupe, with a vinyl roof cover.

(1975)

VEGA

DASH

GT DASH

VEGA GT.

new
TAIL-
LIGHTS

FROM $2788.
('74)

new
GRILLE

Introducing the Cosworth Vega. ('75)

It's the special Vega with a number of hand-assembled, very expensive components.

The Cosworth engine comes out of Cosworth Engineering of England and makes use of sophisticated developments like twin camshafts and electronic fuel injection. It develops 120 horsepower at 5600 rpm and a torque of 115 lb. ft. at 5200 rpm.

The Cosworth interior has special instrumentation

The only exterior color available is the one shown here black, highlighted by gold decals, pinstriping and wheels.

Vega GT. To stripe or not to stripe?
That's up to you. GT sport stripes can be ordered in black or white.

CHROME "GT" (ON COWLS OF UNSTRIPED GTs)

"COSWORTH TWIN CAM" DECAL

('75)

TWIN CAMS.
$5979.

74-75

$ 3031. ('74)
$ 3314. ('75)

VEGA WAGONS

STD. WAGON

GT →

Vega Estate Wagon.
$ 3259. ('74)

(Vega Estate GT.
ALSO AVAIL.)

PANEL
EXPRESS
(NOT IN VEGA LINE
AFTER 1975)

788

VEGA
CHEVROLET

OPTIONAL SUN-ROOF

SPORT CPE.

new GRILLE

• 40 mph in white numbers with metric equivalents in blue

• Soft-rim steering wheel with cushioned center

• Inside hood release.

1976 SLOGAN: "built to take it."

• Available AM/FM radio and accessory electric clock

DASH

• Function symbols in head-lights, cigarette lighter and radio control knobs.

new LARGER TAIL-LTS.

HATCHBACK

wagon
$3540. ('76)
$3836. ('77)

The 1976 Vega Dura-Built 140 engine is so good it's backed up by a 5-year or 60,000-mile guarantee.

ALSO AVAIL.:
GT WAGON, GRAINED ESTATE, ESTATE GT WAGONS

76-77

(FINAL '76 COSWORTH PRICED AT $6135.)

• Tachometer, temperature gauge and voltmeter.

• Wood-grain vinyl accents.

• Electric clock

• 40 mph in white numbers with metric equivalents in blue.

• Assist handle built into instrument panel pad.

• Inside hood release.

• Four-spoke sport steering wheel.

• Available Four-Season air conditioning and AM/FM radio.

• Cigarette lighter.

1977 GT

vega gt

"Today's Vega"

(1977 SLOGAN)

33 mpg highway/24 mpg city (EPA).

789

GT DASH

(1962-1979)

CHEVY II by CHEVROLET

DELUXE MODELS KNOWN AS

Nova

153 CID 4 (93 HP)
194 CID 6 (120 HP)
283 CID V8 (195 HP)
6.50 × 13 TIRES
(WAG. = 6.95 × 14)

Station Wagon

110" WB (1962-1967)

NOVA H/ SUPER SPORT H/T $2652.

66 new GRILLE; new TALLER TAIL-LTS.

LOWEST-PRICED "100" 2-DR. IS $2250.)

STATION WAGON AVAIL. THROUGH '67. (FROM $2709.)

NOVA SS H/T $2708.

4-CYL = 90 HP
6-CYL = 140 HP
V8 = 195 HP

67

1967 GRILLE DIFFERENCE ILLUSTR. AT LOWER LEFT

NOVA 4-DR. $2519.

'67 Chevy II
The stylish economy car

790

DASH

Chevy II **NOVA**: The not-too-small car *CHEVROLET*

(WAGONS NO LONGER AVAIL.)

STD. 4-DR. (w/o SIDE CHROME)

SS

68

(TOTALLY RESTYLED)
new 111" WB
(THROUGH '79)

SS
OPTION
$210.
EXTRA

SALE PR.

all-new Nova at only **$2261.00***
(STD. CPE.)

153 CID 4 (90 HP)
230 CID 6 (140 HP)
307 CID V8 (200 HP)

UP TO 295 HP
AVAIL.
7.35 × 14
TIRES

1968 EASILY
IDENTIFIED BY
"CHEVY II" NAME ON
TOP BORDER OF GRILLE.

SPORT
WHEELS

OPTIONAL
BUMPER
GUARDS

RALLY WHEEL

791

CHEVY Nova

(NOVA REPLACES CHEVY II NAME)

new COWL LOUVRES

CHEVROLET EMBLEM NOW APPEARS ON TOP BORDER OF GRILLE.

69

153 CID 4 (90 HP)
230 CID 6 (140 HP)
307 CID V8 (200 HP)
SS OPTION : 350 CID V8 (300 HP)

"307" CID NUMBER ABOVE SIDE LIGHTS

PRICED FROM $2446.
(4-CYL. CPE.)

V8 CPE. $2624.

SS GRILLE

7.35 x 14 TIRES

CHEVY Nova 70

·SANDWICHES · FRIES · MALTS·

FROM $2554.
4-CYL.
CPE.

1970 IS FINAL YR. FOR COWL LOUVRES.

new E78 × 14/B TIRES

new SQUARER SHAPE TO PARK./DIRECTIONAL LTS.

The Nova Coupe.
You didn't want it changed for the sake of change.

So we improved it for the sake of improvement.

$2637. ('71-6) 2613. ('72-6)
$2732. ('71-V8) 2703. ('72-V8)
Nova Sedan

CPES. FROM
$2607. ('71) 2585. ('72)

250 CID 6
(145 HP)
(110 HP, '72)

307 CID V8
(200 HP)
(130 HP, '72)

RATED HP and PRICE CUTS, 1972

STD. CPE. W/O SIDE TRIM

71-72

1972 NOVAS ILLUSTRATED

DASH

793

CHEVY Nova

(RESTYLED)

73

CPE. FR. $2589.
4-DR. FR. $2617.

BACKGROUND SCENE: HISTORIC PLYMOUTH, MASS.

250 CID 6 (100 HP)
307 CID V8 (115 HP)

Hatchback (New)

FROM $2738.

new 2-TONE ROOF ACCENT TRIM AVAILABLE (ON CAR ILLUSTR. ABOVE, CENTER)

4 TAIL-LIGHTS (new)

Chevrolet. Building a better way to see the U.S.A.

1973 DASH (BELOW)
(1974 DASH SIMILAR)

new GRILLE WITH PARK./DIRECTIONAL LIGHTS BUILT IN

CHEVY Nova
74

250 CID
6
(100 HP)

new
350 CID V8
(145 HP)

DASH

CPE.
FROM
$3101.

Nova Hatchback Hutch. This handy camping tent attaches quickly and easily to Nova Hatchback models, transforming them into economy two-sleeper campers.

CHEVROLET EMBLEM
ADDED TO 1974 GRILLE

SEDAN FROM $3131.

new
BRIGHT
ANODIZED ALUMINUM HUBCAPS

Full wheel covers. Shown left. Rally wheels with bright trim rings (included with SS). Shown right.

CUSTOM
SS

SS
has OWN
GRILLE.

new
"NOVA BY CHEVROLET"
ON DECK
(ALSO
ON
HOOD
ON
DRIVER'S
SIDE)

HATCHBACK
FROM
$3225.

NOVA SIX.

$3218.*
* REG. $3966.

(RESTYLED)
75

EPA mileage:
16 city,
21 highway.

HATCHBACK
CPE. $4214.

NOVA

FR78 × 14
TIRES
(EXCEPT ON
$3966. "S"
CPE. AT TOP,
LEFT)

NOVA CUSTOM
$4270.

So we've distinguished the exterior of our '75 Nova LN—front, rear and sides—with this classic LN emblem.

It appears inside, too (on the steering wheel), along with some of the nicest things that ever happened to a compact.

250 CID 6 (105 HP)
new 262 CID V8
(110 HP)

$4650.

LN (new)

DASH (LN)

LN 4-DR.
$4663.

CHEVROLET
MAKES SENSE
FOR AMERICA

796

HATCHBACK $4366.

$3283*
Nova 4-Door Sedan
(REG. $4232.)

Nova

E78 × 14/B TIRES ON STD. NOVA

Nova SS Coupe.

250 CID 6 (105 HP)
305 CID V8 (140 HP)

(Introducing Concours.)

76

note THAT GRILLE OF NEW CONCOURS has HEAVY PANEL OF BRIGHTWORK ABOVE

Concours Coupe

Concours

(new)

4-Door Sedan
$4780.

$4745.

CONCOURS has HOOD ORNAMENT and FULL-LENGTH SIDE TRIM. (CONCOURS TIRE SIZE = FR 78 × 14/B) CONCOURS HATCHBACK AVAIL., AT $4922.

NOVA DASH RESEMBLES ILLUSTRATED CONCOURS DASH, BUT DOES NOT have WOOD GRAIN.

• Instrument cluster with rosewood vinyl accents, smoked lenses, bright framing.

• Available electric clock.

• Built-in heater and defroster system.

• Concours identification on steering wheel.

• Available Four-Season air conditioning and AM/FM stereo radio.

• Cigarette lighter.

• Glove compartment light and lock.

• Soft-rim steering wheel with cushioned center.

• Color keyed steering wheel with wood-grain vinyl accent.

Concours

797

CHEVY NOVA

EXTRA-LG. BUMPER GUARDS ONLY ON POLICE CARS.

SEDAN $4539.

CPE. FR. $4489.

77 new GRILLES

UNIQUE MESH GRILLE ON

NOVA RALLY

(BECOMES THE NOVA CUSTOM RALLY IN '78, WITH SIMILAR STYLING)

new 110 HP (6) 145 HP (V8)

CONCOURS GRILLE

THE FINAL CONCOURS

TRIPLE TAIL LTS. (new)

$5073.

Concours: A world class luxury compact from Chevrolet.

SEE WHAT'S NEW TODAY IN A CHEVROLET

26 MPG. HWY., 19 CITY

CHEVY NOVA 4-DR. * (REG. $4852.)

$3823.*

2-DR.
$3702.
* (REG. $4777.)

EMBLEM ADDED ABOVE GRILLE, new BUMPERS (STD. NOVA)

78

HOOD ORNAMENT NOT INCL. ON new CUSTOM

NOVA CUSTOM (FORMERLY THE CONCOURS)

Nova

HATCHBACK $5260.

NOVA

Nova Models.

RALLY WHEELS

RALLY →

(note RALLY INSIGNIA and BODY STRIPES

79

250 CID 6 (115 HP)
305 CID V8 (130 HP) OR 350 CID V8 (170 HP)

new GRILLE WITH ALL-HORIZONTAL PCS.

BUMPER RUB STRIP and GUARDS OPTION.

DASH (NOVA CUSTOM)

Nova Custom Models. $5406.

FINAL NOVA. REPLACED BY CHEVY CITATION FOR 1980.

WIRE WHEEL COVER

CABRIOLET ROOF COVER (OPT.)

$5306.

GRILLE TOP BORDER BEARS "Chevrolet" NAME.

POL

CHRYSLER MOTORS CORPORATION

Chrysler

(SINCE 1924)

H/T $3534.

Move up to Chrysler

6-PASS. $4177.
9-PASS. $4283.

Town & Country Wagon

NEWPORT

383 CID V8 (270 HP)

NEW YORKER

440 CID V8 (350 HP)

NY H/T $4248.

NY 4-DR. H/T $4324.

1966

new GRILLES

66

DASH (NY)

V8s 383 OR 440 CID 124" WB (WAGONS = 121")

"300" has 383 CID V8 (325 HP)

2-DR. H/T $4005.

300

300 has 3 CHROME STRIPS ACROSS TAIL-LIGHTS (AS ILLUSTRATED)

GRILLE →

800

4-DR. H/T

$4081.

CHRYSLER

Take Charge...Move up to Chrysler '67

H/T $3639.

NEWPORT

DASH (N.P. CUST.)

NEWPORT CUSTOM 2-DR. H/T $3827.

67

(NEWPORT) TOWN and COUNTRY WAGON FROM $4286.

4-DR. H/T

$4430.

NEW YORKER

new TAIL-LIGHTS WRAP AROUND REAR FENDER.

$4299.

SEDAN

(CONT'D. NEXT PAGE)

CHRYSLER

300

67
(CONT'D.)

You can tell a 300 by its dash.

SLOT-TYPE TAIL LIGHTS (new)

2-DR. H/T $4134.

Three Hundred.

4-DR. H/T $4210.

WHEEL COVER

OPTIONAL ROAD WHEEL

FLOOR CONSOLE WITH PERFORMANCE INDICATOR

DISC BRAKE WHEEL COVER

new BULGING GRILLE

CVT. $4487.

CHRYSLER CONVERTIBLES DISCONTINUED AFTER 1970.

802

make your move

MOVE UP TO CHRYSLER '68

CREASE PATTERN ON REAR FENDER

9 PASS. $5022.

4-DR. H/T $4271.

NEWPORT

TOWN and COUNTRY WAGON

NEW YORKER

68

EASILY RECOGNIZED AS 1968 MODELS BY THE SMALL SIDE SAFETY LIGHTS REQUIRED BY LAW IN '68.

4-DR. H/T $4999.

1968 REAR SAFETY LIGHTS ARE TINY and ROUND (300)

H/T

300

note 5 "LOUVRES"

CONVERTIBLE

300 has new CONCEALED HEADLIGHTS WITH CHRYSLER NAME ABOVE HEADLIGHT DOOR

803

CHRYSLER

NEWPORT H/T
$4323.

4-DR.
H/T
$4568.
NEWPORT CUSTOM

WIND
DEFLECTOR
ON WAGON
ROOF

wagon

Announcing your next car:

The great new Chrysler.

TOWN and
COUNTRY
NOW IN NEW YORKER LINE.
6-PASS. $5193.

NEW
YORKER **69** (RESTYLED)

N.Y.
4-DR. H/T
$5225.

1969

REAR

300

H/T
$4714.

note
VERT.
PCS. IN
300 GRILLE

CHRYSLER

NEWPORT CUSTOM

STANDARD-TYPE NEWPORT DOES NOT HAVE SIDE TRIM AS SEEN ON THESE MODELS.

4-DR. H/T $4705.

Your next car: 1970 Chrysler.

(WITH ANTIQUE GOLD VINYL TOP COVERING, AZTEC EAGLE HOOD MEDALLION)

(ABOVE)
The new Chrysler Cordoba.

(SPECIAL-EDITION H/T)

70

6-PASS. $5349.

TOWN and COUNTRY WAGON

NEW YORKER GRILLE IS SIMILAR, BUT has UPRIGHT RECTANGULAR MEDALLION AT CENTER.

300 (3 VIEWS)

4-DR. H/T $4928.

H/T $4849.

DDA-70

REAR DETAIL (300

CHRYSLER

$4672.

ROYAL
(REAR)

NEWPORT
CUSTOM

(NEWPORT)
ROYAL
(new)

71
new
GRILLES

"ROYAL"
NAME
BELOW
"NEWPORT,"
ON COWL
PANEL

ROYAL

DIFFERING
DETAILS

(CONT'D.
NEXT PAGE)

Chrysler New Yorker & Town & Country

FROM $5596.

DASH →

SUN ROOF OPT.

NEW YORKER

$5686.

1971

71 (CONT'D.)

↑ HEAVY CHROME SIDE STRIP ON NEW YORKER 4-DOOR HARDTOP

4-DR. H/T $5205.

2-DR. H/T $5126.

Chrysler 300

1971

(CHRYSLER CONVERTS. NO LONGER AVAIL.)

CHRYSLER
Plymouth
Coming Through.

CHRYSLER

$4863.

Newport Custom

new OUTBOARD TAIL-LIGHTS

Newport Royal

$4630.

new GRILLES

72

NEW YORKER H/T $5552.

Town & Country

FROM $5692.

(300 DISCONTINUED UNTIL '79)

(*new*)

New Yorker Brougham

2-DR. N.Y. BRGHM. $5777.

73

new GRILLE, *new* FRONT END STYLING. "CHRYSLER" NAME ABOVE GRILLE

Chrysler Newport
Extra care in engineering...it makes a difference.

new ENERGY-ABSORBING SAFETY BUMPERS

CHRYSLER

Town & Country Wagon
FROM $5885.

73
(CONT'D.)

4 - DR.
H/T
FROM $5769.

Chrysler New Yorker
Extra care in engineering...it makes a difference.

For generations, an automobile advanced in engineering.
For 1974, a totally new expression of that idea.

(RESTYLED)

new NARROW "CLASSIC" STYLE GRILLE.
NEWPORT TYPES have DIFFERENT
ARRANGEMENT of GRILLE PCS. and VERTICAL
OUTBOARD TAIL-LIGHTS.

74

Chrysler New Yorker

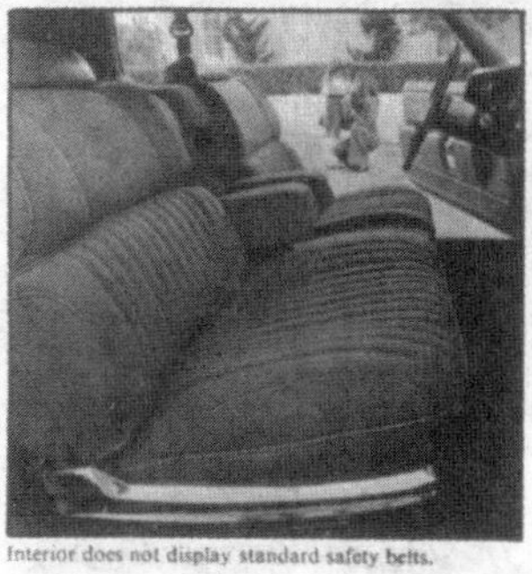

AVAILABLE
FEB.,
1974,
NEW
YORKER
ST. REGIS COUPE has
new OPERA WINDOWS.

Interior does not display standard safety belts.

ILLUSTR. 2-DR. H/T : $6288.

CHRYSLER

note TUBULAR COURTESY LTS. JUST FORWARD OF OPERA WINDOWS

MEDALLION (BELOW) IS FEATURED IN CENTER OF CORDOBA HOOD ORNAMENT

CORDOBA CPE.

318 CID
V8
150

CORDOBA IS ENTIRELY

Cordoba

The New Small Chrysler

NEW! 75

WITH SMALL (115") WB
WITH VINYL-COVERED TOP

$5581.

(TOWN and COUNTRY, NEWPORT, NEWPORT CUSTOM MODELS ALSO AVAIL.)

FINAL 4-DR. SEDAN N.Y. BROUGH. IN 1975, PRICED AT $6851.

ALSO 2-DR. H/T $6908.

← ILLUSTR. 4-DR. H/T $6998.

Chrysler New Yorker Brougham

new DUAL SLOTS IN BUMPER, new BUMPER GUARDS

new CRISS-CROSS PCS. IN GRILLE

CHRYSLER

76

$5959.

Chrysler Cordoba

new GRILLE WITH
ALL-VERTICAL PCS.

new ELECTRONIC IGNITION "LEAN BURN" ENGINE AVAILABLE EVERYWHERE EXCEPT IN CALIFORNIA.

THE FINAL NEWPORT CUSTOM

TOWN and COUNTRY WAGON has GRILLE LIKE ILLUSTRATED NEWPORT CUSTOM, BUT STD. NEWPORT DOES NOT HAVE THE HEAVY VERTICAL STRIP NOR 2 HEAVY HORIZONTAL STRIPS ACROSS GRILLE.

$6207.

THE LARGE SIDE MIRRORS ARE OPTIONAL, IN TRAILER TOWING ACCESSORY PACKAGE.

$7368.

(NEW YORKER'S new "WATERFALL" GRILLE IS SIMILAR TO TYPE LAST USED ON DISCONTINUED 1975 IMPERIAL.)

The 1976 Chrysler New Yorker Brougham

CHRYSLER

$6012.

NEW T-BAR ROOF OPTION

Chrysler Cordoba

(NEW STEEL-TOP CORDOBA "S": $5962.)

FINE CROSS-PCS. ADDED TO CORDOBA GRILLE.

INTRODUCING CHRYSLER LEBARON.

$5,741. AS SHOWN.

WITH 318 CID V8, 145 HP
112.7" WB

$5,758.

NEW SIZE

LEATHER SEATS OPT. IN LE BARON MEDALLION SERIES.

77

LE BARON GRILLE CLOSE-UP

(N.Y. 2-DR. ALSO AVAIL.)

1977 Newport. $5374.

1977 Chrysler New Yorker.

$7873.

812

CHRYSLER

(W. PAINTED STEEL TOP)

CHRYSLER CORDOBA 'S'. $5550.

1978 Chrysler Cordoba
"The picture of style and taste."

DON'T SETTLE FOR ANYTHING LESS.

new 2-TIER RECTANGULAR CORDOBA HDLTS.

LeBARON
TOWN & COUNTRY.

TAIL-LIGHT DETAIL

T+C REAR

$5761.
(new)

Le BARON

(WAGON ADDED)

SWING-UP STEERING WHEEL

$5270.

'S COUPE
$5.14

78

25 MPG HWY / 17* MPG CITY

MODELS. 4 DR ONLY AFTER 1978.

FINAL NP 2 DR $6432.

NEWPORT

NEW YORKER

NEW GRILLE

NY 4-DR. $8420.

CHRYSLER

CHRYSLER 300.

(FIRST new "300 SINCE 1971)

note UNIQUE GRILLE

79

DASH

WITH 360 CID V8

("300" SHARES CORDOBA CHASSIS)

DASH

CORDOBA

PRICED FROM $6666.

REAR DETAIL

new GRILLE

CORDOBA

2-TONE HOOD PAINT VARIATION

T-TOP

THE CONTEMPORARY CLASSIC.

CHRYSLER

LeBARON. $6124.

$6835.

LeBARON MEDALLION 2-DOOR

$6361.

LeBARON SALON.
NEWEST NAME IN THE LeBARON LINEUP.

LeBARON TOWN & COUNTRY

T-TOP 2-DR.
AVAIL., ALSO
SUNROOFS

$7055.

79 (CONT'D.)

DASH

28 MPG HWY. | 18 MPG CITY

REAR
DETAILS

new GRILLE

LeBARON MEDALLION 4-DOOR SEDAN.
$7063.

CHRYSLER

225 CID 6
OR
318 CID V8

NEWPORT

23 MPG HWY 17 MPG* CITY

NEWPORT EMBLEM

CHRYSLER NEWPORT. $6,089.†
NOW YOU CAN HAVE IT ALL...NOW.

79 (CONT'D.)

Chrysler New Yorker
Fifth Avenue EDITION

$10,596.

note LOUVRES

DASH (FIFTH AVENUE)

NEW YORKER
$9096.

CHRYSLER

Cordoba.

IMITATION CABRIOLET ROOF AVAIL.

new GRILLE and SINGLE HEADLIGHTS

80

DASH

CORDOBA PRICED FROM $7454.

"Cordoba. An American Classic."

REAR DETAILS

GRILLE UNLIKE OTHER 1980 LE BARONS

(CONT'D NEXT PAGE)

LeBaron Salon Two-Door LS Limited.

817

CHRYSLER

COUPES PRICED FROM $6801.

LeBaron

new PLAIN-SIDED WAGON $7158.

SEDANS ALSO AVAIL.

new GRILLE is CLASSIC STYLE, has ALL-VERT. PCS. *new* DIRECTIONAL LTS.

LeBaron Town & Country Wagon. $7747.

80 (CONT'D.)

new PENTASTAR EMBLEM

NEWPORT $7858.

1980 N.P. SLOGAN: "FRIEND OF THE FAMILY."

new LT. ADDED

818

CHRYSLER

THE INCOMPARABLE NEW YORKER

ALUMINUM ROAD WHEELS O.P.T. (NEWPORT OR NEW YORKER)

$10,459

new WHEEL COVERS

NEW YORKER

80
(CONT'D.)

LITTLE DIFFERENCE BETWEEN '79/'80 N.Y. DASH

FIFTH AVENUE

CHRYSLER

FIFTH AVENUE

$11,759

"THE ONE AND ONLY."

2 new HORIZONTAL STRIPS ON 1980 5TH AVE. FENDER LIGHT

CHRYSLER
MOTORS CORPORATION

DODGE

(SINCE 1915 MODEL)

(MFD. BY CHRYSLER CORP. SINCE 1928)

JOIN THE DODGE REBELLION

...ONET SERIES (lowest priced Coronets ...DE CHROME)

Coronet DELUXE

$3065.

$2737.

(440 WAGONS ALSO)

66

(6 CYL. OR V8)

117" WB

Coronet 440

$2891.

Signal when ready. Hidden behind the handsome grille are Coronet's turn signals and parking lights.

CORONET 440

440 H/T INTERIOR (ABOVE)

$3045.

Coronet 500

$3261.

Coronet 500.

500 DASH

(CONT'D. NEXT PAGE)

820

DODGE

POLARA

66 (CONT'D.)

FROM $3555.

Polara

$3533.

(121" WB and V8 ENGINES IN POLARA, MONACO)

$3405.

Monaco

Polara

$3320.

("POLARA 500" MODELS ALSO)

Slip gracefully and frugally out of the low-price field. It's never been so easy. See what Dodge Monaco and Polara cars offer you as standard equipment. Then slip behind the wheel—and get a kick out of driving!

MONACO FROM $3808 *wagons*

$3759.

REAR DECK BEARS "MONACO" NAME, INSTEAD OF "DODGE"

A-60

90" WB

$2884.

CUSTOM SPORTSMAN

($2567. STD. SPORTSMAN ALSO)

Monaco 500 2-door hardtop. 383 4-barrel V8 power, standard.

MONACO 500—THE VERY FINEST DODGE OF ALL FOR '66!

821

Coronet

Dodge Coronet 2-seat station wagon.

Dodge Coronet Deluxe 2-seat station wagon.

3141. **440** **DLX.**

FRONT CLOSE-UP

COR. DLX.

440

(INTRO.
9-29-66)
67
new GRILLES

$3352.

CORONET R/T

(w. 440 CID V8)

FROM $3666.

Dodge Coronet 500 SE (Special Edition)

Coronet 500

The Dodge Rebellion wants you!

COR. 500
TAIL-LTS. A
APPEAR INVISIBLE
BY DAY.

MONACO

Dodge Polara station wagon, available in 2-seat and 3-seat models.

· POLARA STATION WAGON
(POL. 500 *has* VERTICAL
TRIM STRIPS NEAR FRONT
TIP OF FRONT FENDER.)

POLARA REAR
LIKE MONACO

$3676.

Monaco 500

BEARS
"DODGE" NAME
AT REAR

"MONACO"
NAME
AT REAR,
(EXCEPT ON
MONACO 500)

$3896.

822

CORRUGATED

$3072.

440 H/T $3521.

69 (INTRO. 9-19-68)

White Hat Special Coronet.

The Dodge Coronet White Hat Special comes in a 2-door hardtop or 4-door sedan—with the features listed below—at a special low package price.
■ Vinyl roof in black, white, tan, green—or standard top
■ Whitewall tires ■ Front, rear bumper guards ■ Deep-dish wheel covers ■ Light group ■ Outside, remote-control rearview mirror ■ Bright trim package.

Coronet. 500

$3655.

Coronet 500

note DUAL HOOD SCOOPS ON

CORONET SUPER BEE

STANDARD SUPER BEE EQUIPMENT
• Special 4-bbl. 383-cid Magnum V8 (440 Magnum V8 heads, valve gear, hot cam and manifolds), 335 hp @ 5,200 rpm • Dual exhaust
• Hurst 4-speed with HD clutch • HD suspension
• HD shocks • HD brakes • Dodge Charger Rallye instrument panel
OPTIONAL
• 426 Hemi—two 4-bbl. carbs—425 hp @ 5,000 rpm
REAR AXLE RATIOS
• 383 Magnum V8—standard 3.23:1; optional: 3.55:1, 3.91:1
• Hemi—standard: 3.23:1; optional: 3.54 (with 4-speed manual), 3.55:1 (with automatic), 4.10:1 (with manual or automatic)

H/T $3697. (note BEE FIGURE ON GRILLE)

THIS DECAL and POPULAR ADVERTISING FIGURE IS WELL KNOWN, BUT DIFFERS FROM BEE ON GRILLE.

824

DODGE

Polara.

a 230-hp V8. Not to mention an all-new instrument panel and concealed windsh... wipe...

4-DR. H/T
$3996.

69
(CONT'D.)

FINAL YEAR
FOR POLARA
500

This year,
DODGE
is turning up the *fever*

Monaco.

MONACO
GRILLE
(left)
DIFFERS
ONLY SLIGHTLY
FROM
POLARA's.

wagon **Dodge** CHRYSLER MOTORS CORPORATION

In a test of acceleration, economy, and braking ability, a 1969 Monaco was overall winner, Class II, in the Union/Pure Oil Performance Trials.

FROM $4707.

$4381.

all-new
aircraft-type instrument panel. And ahead
of it all—a big 383-cu.-in. V8. 1969 Monaco.

H/T $3670.

MORE TOPS...MORE MODELS
Three tops available. Standard (shown), a Special Edition (SE) with vinyl-covered formal roof hardtop, and convertible. All nine models feature concealed wipers, locking steering-wheel column, deep-pile carpeting, dual headlights, and more.

Challenger hardtop, showing deluxe wheel covers.

SE ↗ WITH FORMAL ROOF, SMALL REAR WINDOW $3902.

Challenger (NEW)

...you could be **DODGE MATERIAL.** **70**

(INTRO. 9-23-69)

110" WB
225 CID 6
(145 HP) OR
318 CID V8
(230 HP)
D78/E78 × 14 TIRES

$4249.

DODGE CHALLENGER R/T CONVERTIBLE

Challenger R/T, showing bumblebee stripe (12 colors available).

Challenger R/T

FROM $4007.

note HOOD VARIATIONS ON THESE 2 R/T HARDTOPS. CAR ABOVE has 2 LG. VENT SLOTS; CAR AT RIGHT has SHAKER TYPE AIR SCOOP.

1970

(CONT'D. NEXT PAGE)

"R/T" EMBLEM ON GRILLE

F70 × 14 TIRES ON R/T

826

DODGE

Coronet Deluxe station wagon. 2-seat model only—Six or V8 power.

440 **$36/6.**

Coronet 440 station wagon, 2-seat models—Six or V8 power; 3-seat model V8 power only.

Coronet 440 4-door sedan.

CORONET

Coronet R/T 2-door hardtop. (Convertible also available.)

$3826.

Coronet 500 station wagon, 2-seat and 3-seat models. 318 V8, std.

Coronet 500 2-door hardtop.

Super Bee

1970

$3919.

Coronet 500

70 (CONT'D.)

Polara

GRILLE CLOSE UP

1970

Polara

$4022.

Polara 2-door hardtop, with optional Gator Grain roof.

Polara station wagon, 2-seat and 3-seat models. 318 V8, std.

Polara convertible.

$4221.

Polara Custom 4-door sedan. Polara 4-door sedan also available.

$4305.

FROM $4905.

MONACO

A-100 SPORTSMAN

FROM $3207.

4-DR. H/T $4538.

1970

827

Challenger.

PRICED FROM $3569.

CHALLENGER T/A

(note STRIPES and SPEC. PAINT)

R/T 383 CID V8 (300 HP) $4009.

(INTRO. 10-6-70) CHALLENGER R T

71

RESTYLED *SPORTSMAN*

(ILLUSTRATED WITH OPTIONAL TRAVCO CAMPER TOP)

new SPORTSMAN B-100, B-200 OR B-300 new 109" OR 127" WB

Coronet wagons FROM $3947.

CRESTWOOD $4352. UP

CORONET

(CONT'D NEXT PAGE)

SEDANS FROM $3649.

DODGE

DASH

$4538 AND UP

POLARA

WIRE WHEEL COVER

71 (CONT'D.)

POLARA CUSTOM 4-DR. H/T $4376.

DODGE POLARA

FROM $5105.

DLX. WHEEL COVER

MONACO

DODGE MONACO

H/T $4631.

DODGE MONACO

DODGE

DASH

CHALLENGER.
100" WB

150 HP, 318 CID V8 (225 CID 6 AVAIL.)

$3634.

7.35 × 14 TIRES

CHALLENGER RALLYE

340 CID V8 AVAIL.

F70×14 TIRES

72 (INTRO. 9-28-71)

new GRILLES

SPORTSMAN (B-100, B-200, B-300)

$3615. AND UP

CORONET CRESTWOOD

9-PASS. $4451.

E78×14 TIRES on all CORONETS (H78×14, WAGONS)

Coronet

CORONET CUSTOM

SEDAN $3766.

(CONT'D. NEXT PAGE)

118" WB

830

DODGE

SED.
$4096

POL. CST.
WAG.
$4849.

DASH

POLARA

PROTECTIVE VINYL-FACED RUB MOLDING ALONG
BODY SIDES

POLARA
CUSTOM
H/T $4308.

72 (CONT'D.)

$5105.
TO 5566.

note UNUSUALLY
HIGH PLACEMENT
OF GRAINED
PANELING ON
MONACO
WAGON.

Monaco.

H/T
$4631.

ATTRACTIVE
MONACO
DOOR PANEL

4-DR.
H/T
$4694.

WITH
BUMPER GUARDS
(THAT ALSO SERVE AS
GRILLE GUARDS)

DODGE

73

new GRILLES

$3752.

Challenger Rallye

(FINAL 1974 CHALLENGER *has* SHORT SIDE PORTS IN COWL, BUT NO STRIPS ACROSS DOOR AS SEEN ON 1973 MODEL ILLUSTR. ABOVE.)

Coronet '73

CORONET SEDAN

STD. CORONET SEDAN $3757.

SEDAN $3907.

Coronet Wagons

wagons $4358. (ABOVE)

Coronet Custom

Coronet CUSTOM

CORONET CRESTWOOD WAGON, 6-PASS.: $4449.; 9-PASS.: $4569.

(FINAL POLARA TYPES IN 1973)

Polara

SPORTSMAN. THE LARGEST SELLING COMPACT WAGON BUILT IN AMERICA.

POLARA 4-DR. SEDAN

Polara 2 Dr. Hardtop

H/T

Sportsman.

(CONT'D. NEXT PAGE)

DODGE

Polara Custom 2-Dr. Hardtop.

Polara Custom Wagon

Polara Custom

73
(CONT'D.)

new
ELECTRONIC
IGNITION
STD. EQUIP.

Polara Custom 4-Door Hardtop

Extra care in engineering makes a difference in Dodge...depend on it.

Monaco

Monaco Brougham 4-Dr. Sedan.

DASH

SHIFT
INDICATOR
ON
SPEEDOMETER

P R N D 2 1

833

Monaco Wagon

DODGE

(CHALLENGER DISCONTINUED DURING 1974; NAME RETURNS 1978 ON JAPANESE IMPORT VERSION.)

CORONET CUSTOM $4333.

(CORONET and CORO. CUST. SEDANS ONLY)

DODGE MONACO BROUGHAM WAGONS (tow up to 7,000 lbs.).

CHRYSLER

WAGON AT LEFT, FROM $5860.

(NO POLARA SERIES; DISCONTINUED)

74

new GRILLES WITH "DODGE" NAME ABOVE, CENTER.

H/Ts FROM $4783.

MONACO

1974

4-DR. H/Ts FROM $5039.

MONACO, CUSTOM and BROUGHAM

EXTRA CARE IN ENGINEERING MAKES A DIFFERENCE IN **DODGE... DEPEND ON IT.**

DIVISIONS WITHIN MONACO SERIES

SPORTSMAN

DODGE SPORTSMAN WAGONS (tow up to 6,000 lbs.).

B-100, B-200 OR B-300 SERIES

note SIDE DOOR VARIATIONS

new GRILLE, WITH DODGE NAME ABOVE

$5011. - 6155.

DODGE

Coronet Two-Door Hardtop

2-DR. $5977. ('75)

('75) FINAL '76 CORONET has HOOD ORNAMENT.

75-76

Introducing the Royal Monaco Brougham

SINCE 1975, MOST 6-CYL. MODELS COST MORE THAN COMPARABLE V8s.

DODGE SPORTSMAN WAGON
Extra care in engineering makes a difference.

SEATING ARRANGEMENT

No wonder we're number one.

MONACO NOW has FORMER CORONET WHEELBASE: (2-DR., 115"; 4-DR., 117½")

77

MONACO

REAR

2-DRS. FROM $5061.

(CONT'D. NEXT PAGE)

DODGE

BROUGHAM 2-DR. $5297.

PLAID INTERIOR AVAIL.

MONACO

$5818.

MONACO CRESTWOOD WAGON

MONACO WHEEL WITH HOLES

77 (CONT'D.)

$5619.

CPE. ROOFLINE VARIETIES

Royal Monaco Brougham Hardtop

LOW SIDE LIGHTS ON ROYAL MONACO

ROYAL MONACO

BROUGHAM SEDAN

WITH DIPLOMAT ROOF PKG.

$5634.

wagon

REAR DETAILS

$6353.

836

DODGE

standard Diplomat or
DELUXE MEDALLION MODELS
112.7" WB

77½

"DIPLOMAT. THAT FIENDISHLY SEDUCTIVE NEW CAR BY DODGE." **NEW**

$5569 as shown. More seductive luxury than you ever dreamed of... in a manageable new size from Dodge.

The look is classic. Sculptured.   The smooth V8 is standard.

2-DR. MEDALLION
$5522.10 AS SHOWN (SALE)

REG. $5907.

318 CID V8 (145 HP)

FR 78 × 15 TIRES

VELOUR STD. IN MEDALLION INTERIOR (4-DR. ILLUSTR.)

DIPLOMAT

(6TH DIGIT IN SERIAL # PREFIX IS NOW 8 ··· SIGNIFYING 1978 MODEL.)

25/17
MPG HWY   MPG CITY

WITH T-BAR ROOF

$5969, AS SHOWN. (SALE)

WAGON ADDED TO LINE (FROM $6471.)

MODELS DRESSED LIKE SHERLOCK HOLMES and DR. WATSON CONTINUE APPEARING IN DODGE DIPLOMAT ADVERTISING. (RIGHT, TOP RIGHT)

LOWER-COST DIPLOMAT "S" ADDED: (CPE., $5726. SED., $5882.)

78

(new MODELS ADDED)

(CONT'D. NEXT PAGE)

SALE

PRICED AS SHOWN: $5195*

1978 DODGE DIPLOMAT FOUR-DOOR

Base price	$ 5147
Six-cylinder engine	Standard
Power front disc brakes	Standard
4-speed manual transmission†	Standard
Deluxe wheel covers	Standard
Power steering	Standard
Transverse torsion-bar suspension	Standard
Vinyl roof	Standard
White sidewall radial tires	$ 48
Total	$ 5195*

(REG. $6132.)

837

DODGE

78 (CONT'D.)

LOTS MORE VISIBILITY.
We've put more glass area in the side windows behind the front doors. And rear quarter windows in the Maxiwagon wrap right around the corners to make backing up a snap.

Maxiwagon has eight inches more loadspace length this year. Room for more cargo and more fun.

(NEW)

BLT. 1978-1979 ONLY

SPORTSMAN WAGON
FROM AMERICA'S NO.1 SELLER OF VAN-WAGONS.

8. NEW ANTITHEFT MEASURES.
The steering column now locks when you shut off the ignition. And the door vent windows have new latches that click shut for extra security.

ALL-NEW SEATS.

23 MPG HWY/ 17 MPG CITY.
EPA estimates for Dodge Sportsman B100 wagon, with standard 225-cubic-inch six-cylinder engine and manual transmission.

ALL-NEW INSTRUMENT PANEL.
Sedan-type luxury combined with servicing convenience. The combined starter and ignition switch is now on the locking steering column.

DIPLOMAT WAGON 28 MPG HWY/18 MPG CITY *

(WAGON INTERIOR ILLUSTR. ON NEXT PAGE)

79

SPORTSMAN →

FR. $6869.

new GRILLE, new FRONT BUMPER, STACKED RECT. HEADLTS. OPT. (SPTSMN.)

"HEY, THAT'S MY DODGE."

838

FROM $7343.

(CONT'D. NEXT PAGE)

DODGE *Diplomat*

28 MPG HWY/18 MPG CITY

PRICED FROM $6001.

T-BAR ROOFS OPTIONAL

"HEY, THAT'S MY DODGE."

Re-introducing the full-size car. The totally new St. Regis by Dodge.

(REAR) ST. REGIS

79 (CONT'D.)

$7190. (V8) $7429. (6)

FINAL *MAGNUM XE* $6380.

NEW

ST. REGIS DASH

118½" WB

St.Regis

318 CID V8 (140 HP) AVAIL.

A standard two-barrel Super Six provides exceptional mileage. (225 CID) 23 mpg highway/17 mpg city

DODGE

DIPLOMAT FOUR-DOOR.

$6485.

$6334.

DIPLOMAT TWO-DOOR.

Introducing Diplomat S-Type Coupe. A new level of driving

DIPLOMAT 80

new GRILLE
new 108.7" WB ON 2-DRS.

(S-TYPE DASH ILLUS. AT LOWER LEFT)

(112.7" WB CONT'D. ON 4-DRS.)

CLOTH-and-VINYL SEATS IN SALON INTERIOR

$6621.

DIPLOMAT WAGON.

$7311.

WITH WOODGRAIN

STD. 225 CID 6 (100/110 HP)
STD. 318 CID V8 (140 HP)

$6772.

OPT. WIRE WH. COVERS

Protective rub strips front and rear (std)

Power brakes—front disc, rear drum (std)

DIPLOMAT DASH (S)

SALON 4-DR.

(CONT'D. NEXT PAGE)

1980 DODGE MIRADA
(REPLACES MAGNUM)

new 112.7" WB

"CABRIOLET" H/T AVAIL.

FROM $7217.

GRILLE

Working Gauges
Brushed-Metal Instrument Panel

17 EPA EST. MPG. 25 EST. HWY. MPG.

18-GAL. FUEL TANK

225 CID 6 (100/110 HP)
318 CID V8 (140 HP) OR
360 CID V8

FR.

REAR

MIRADA

P195/7R15 TIRES

80 (CONT'D.)

new SIDE TRIM, BODY STRIPING ADDED

Touring Edition Instrument Cluster.

ST. REGIS

$7733.

new
St. Regis Touring Edition.

new W. VINYL ROOF

ST. REGIS

ST. REGIS

Test drive total performance in a full-size car.

841

ST. REGIS. THE SUBJECT IS LUXURY.

225 CID 6 (100 HP) OR 318 CID V8 (140-150 HP)

DODGE ASPEN

(REPLACES DART, 1976)
(REPL. BY ARIES FOR 1981)
"Unbelievable."
(ONE-WORD SLOGAN)

76-77

108½" WB (2-DR.)
112½" WB (4-DR.)

Winner of the 1976 Motor Trend Magazine Car of the Year Award.

Aspen R/T has a bold look. With a blacked-out grille, wide rallye wheels, distinctive stripes.

R/T

$4872. ('76)

6-passenger only

EPA MPG: 30 HWY. 18 CITY

('77)

1976 FROM $4155. TO $4916. 1977 FROM $4515. TO $5216.

(ASPEN, CUSTOM and SPECIAL EDITION MODELS)

(HOOD ORN. ON SPEC. E.D.)

new T-TOP AVAIL. ('77)

('76 MODELS SHOWN, EXCEPT WHERE INDICATED OTHERWISE)

SMALLER FEELS BIGGER IN AN ASPEN.

Dodge ASPEN

$ 5684.

SPECIAL EDITION

CUSTOM $5513.

CUSTOM 5087.

SPECIAL EDITION $5410.

Aspen Wagon $4294. (REG. $5203.)

25/18 MPG HWY MPG CITY

78 new GRILLE and TAIL-LTS.

DASH

FULL-LENGTH SIDE STRIPE ON CPE. WITH R/T SPORT PAK

AS BEFORE, NO SIDE CHROME ON STD. ASPEN MODELS; SPEC. ED. MODELS have HOOD ORNAMENTS.

the R/T Sport Pak.

SUPER COUPE (BLACKED-GRILLE, SPOILER, ETC.)

SPECIAL EDITION $5262.

NARROWER new GRILLE, WITH FLANKING AMBER AUX. LTS. MOVED UP FROM BUMPER.

(ILLUSTRATED T-TOP IS OPTIONAL AT EXTRA COST)

Dodge **ASPEN**

WITH
SUNRISE →
PACKAGE

WITH
2-TONE PAINT and
DECOR PACKAGE

Aspen coupe

STANDARD ASPEN SEDAN

$5201.
(COUPES FROM
$5100.)

79

WITH **Aspen R.T.** PKG.

DASH

ASPEN SED.
WITH 2-TONE PAINT
and DECOR PACKAGE

$5675. →

Aspen Special Edition Coupe

Aspen Special Edition Wagon

$6061.

SPECIAL
EDITION
EXT. and
INTERIOR
PKG.

REAR

$5808.

Dodge ASPEN

INTER. and EXT. OF ASPEN CPE. WITH SUNRISE OPTION PACKAGE

Special.

Test drive Total Performance from Dodge.

SALE $4994.

SPECIAL has MINIMUM OF CHROME TRIM.

Optional T-Bar roof
The next best thing to a convertible. Tinted glass panels lift out and store in the trunk to give that fresh air feeling to any Aspen coupe.

ENGINES & TRANSMISSIONS
Federal
☐ 3.7-liter (225 CID) 1V Slant Six (std)
☐ 5.2-liter (318 CID) 2V V-8 (opt)
High Altitude
☐ 5.2-liter (318 CID) 4V V-8 (opt)
California
☐ 3.7-liter (225 CID) 1V Slant Six (std)

☐ 5.2-liter (318 CID) 4V V-8 (opt)
☐ Three-speed manual (std) (N A Calif or V-8)
☐ Four-speed manual (opt) (N A Calif or V-8)
☐ TorqueFlite automatic (opt)

SEDAN, CPE., WAGON SHOWN WITH SPECIAL EDITION PACKAGE

(STD. UNGRAINED WAGONS FROM $6141.)

SEDAN WITH CUSTOM PACKAGE

new GRILLE; RECTANGULAR HEADLIGHTS

(FINAL ASPEN)

80

Optional cast aluminum road wheels
Add that sporty road car image to any Aspen with the addition of these great looking optional wheels

DASH

3-SP. MANUAL TRANS. (3.2 GEAR RATIO) BUT CALIFORNIA-SOLD CARS have 2.9 GEAR RATIO WITH TorqueFlite AUTO. TRANS.

(REPLACED BY 1981 ARIES)

⑰ EPA EST MPG · 25 EST HWY MPG

845

(1966–1978) Dodge CHARGER

66 (new)

$3469.

HDLTS. DISAPPEAR INTO GRILLE

BUCKET SEATS, FRONT and BACK

V8s: 318 CID (230 HP)
361 (265 HP)
383 (325 HP)
426 CID Hemi (425 HP)

... new leader of the Dodge Rebellion.

117" WB (LIKE Coronet) (THROUGH '70)

7.35 x 14 TIRES

FASTBACK STYLING (THROUGH '67)

VINYL TOP OPT.

new 440 MAGNUM V8 AVAIL.

$3482.

67

XP-29 MODEL CONTINUES WITH FEW CHANGES

the Dodge Rebellion.

846

$3184. UP

Dodge Charger

new SIDE SAFETY LTS. (ROUND)

68
(RESTYLED)
NO LONGER
A FASTBACK

Join the fun ... catch
Dodge fever

FROM $3371.

R/T SE

STANDARD CHARGER R/T EQUIPMENT
• 440-cid Magnum (4-bbl.) V8, 375 hp
• Choice of 3-speed automatic or Hurst
 4-speed manual • Dual exhausts
• HD suspension • HD shocks • HD brakes
• Dodge Charger Rallye instrument
 panel • F70x14 wide-treads
OPTIONAL
• 426 Hemi

69
new SPLIT GRILLE

Success Car of the Year

69½-70

Totally new

UNIQUE REAR "TAIL" (RARE)

Charger Daytona:

(1970 PLYMOUTH ROAD-RUNNER "SUPERBIRD" SIMILAR)

847

Dodge Charger

SE (SPECIAL EDITION) AVAIL. IN 500 OR R/T SERIES

500 WITH FRONT BUCKET SEATS FROM $3496.

R/T (WITH LONGITUDINAL TAPE STRIPE, RALLYE WHEELS)

$3878. (AVAIL. WITH BUMBLEBEE STRIPE)

CHARGER $3358. UP

70 FOR 1970 DODGE INTRODUCES A NEW MODEL CHARGER AT A NEW LOWER PRICE

$3001. (226 C/D 6 NOW AVAIL.) (145 HP)

(REG. $3358.)

(STD.) CHARGER (WITH FULL-WIDTH FRONT SEAT)

If you don't want another same old brand-new car...

you could be DODGE MATERIAL.

(6 OR V8) (440 CID V8 [375 HP] IN R/T)

LEFT DECK-SIDE SPORT TYPE GAS FILLER CAP

RACK OPTIONAL

DASH

FUEL

CHARGER R/T

Dodge CHARGER

dash

CHARGER

FROM $3527.

ROOF DETAILS

72

new GRILLES

Charger Topper
landau vinyl roof.

WITH CONCEALED HEADLIGHTS, RALLYE DASH, BUMPER GUARDS and SPECIAL TRIM. (note CONVENTIONAL TYPE STEERING WHEEL USED) (arrow)

CHARGER RALLYE

REAR

BULGE ON RALLYE HOOD is PAINTED BLACK.

DOOR SLOTS

(ON RALLYE ONLY)

RALLYE has OWN GRILLE (HORIZONTAL PCS.) and OPEN HDLTS.

SE GRILLE DETAIL

"Special Edition"

SE

DASH

$4017.

Dodge. Depend on it.

Dodge Charger

COUPE FROM $3700.

CHARGER COUPE WITH LANDAU TOP

SE.

4/53.

new GRILLE

"HALO" TOP

73

"LANDAU" TOP

CHARGER H/T $3949.

new SAFETY BUMPERS; ELECTRONIC IGNITION STD.

225 CID 6
318 CID V8
340, 400 OR 440 CID V8s ALSO
(105 TO 260 HP)

E78×14
4 P/R
TIRES

SE with new 3-PC. LOUVRED QUARTER WINDOWS

SE

OPT. SUNROOF AVAIL. WITH VINYL TOP

SE INT.

CHARGER RALLYE
The Rallye Package is available on V8 Charger hardtops and coupes, and includes the following items: Rallye Instrument Cluster • Power bulged hood • Body side tape stripes • Hood pins • Front and rear sway bars • E70 x 14 tires with raised white letters.

Charger Rallye.

Rallye Hardtop

Rallye Coupe

Extra care in engineering makes a difference in Dodge...depend on it.

Dodge Charger

$4171.

CHARGER COUPE

This year, go Charger style.

(FULL 1974 LINE ILLUSTR.)

74

CHARGER H/T $4370.

SE has HOOD ORNAMENT

E78 or F78 × 14 TIRES

CHARGER **SE** $4584.

EXTRA CARE IN ENGINEERING MAKES A DIFFERENCE IN DODGE ...DEPEND ON IT.

Introducing Dodge Charger Special Edition '75

HORIZ.- LOUVRED OPERA WINDOWS ARE *new* AND OPT.

2.45 GEAR RATIO

SE $5412.

318, 360 OR 400 CID V8s (150 TO 235 HP)

"You'll love the change we made."

75

(RESTYLED) (RESEMBLES CHRYSLER'S *new* CORDOBA)

DASH

GR78 × 15 TIRES, OTHERS

852

Dodge Charger

CHARGER DAYTONA
(new)

75½

(DAYTONA ADDED
IN MID-SEASON)

"CHARGER
DAYTONA"
NAME ON SIDE

Once you've looked, you're hooked.

4 MODELS,
SALE PRICED
FROM

$3736.

(BASIC
CHARGER
REG.
$4744.)

new
SPORT=
$5033.

23 MPG. HWY., 16 CITY
WITH 6-CYL. 225 CID (100 HP)

76

SE $5334.

'76
DAYTONA

SE
$5692.

(MOVES TO MONACO LINE)

FINAL CHARGER SE A PART OF 1978
MONACO LINE AT $5951.

new
GRILLE

77

318 CID V8
(145 HP) STD.
6-CYL. STILL
AVAIL.

1977½
T-TOP

Dodge Dart

(SINCE 1960; COMPACT-SIZE SINCE 1963)

170 CID 6 (101 HP)
225 CID 6 (145 HP) OR
273 CID V8 (235 HP)

DART

2-DR. $2319.

Dart 4-door sedan. Six or 273 V8 power.
$2383.

WAGONS

$2661.

6.50 × 13 TIRES

66

JOIN THE DODGE REBELLION

111" WB (106," WAGONS)

270 WAGON $2758.

270 CVT. $2795.

DART 270 SERIES

2-DR. $2439.

270 H/T $2532.

270 4-DR. $2505.

GT

GT HAS CHROME ATOP FR. FENDERS AND ON ROCKER PANELS

GT H/T $2642.
PARTIAL VINYL TOP AVAIL.

GT CVT. $2925.

FULL 1966 LINE ILLUSTRATED

854

$2453. DART

$2416.

DART
WAGONS
DISCONTINUED

(INTRO
9-29-
66)

67

(RESTYLED)

new SUNKEN-IN
REAR WINDOW

$2591.

DART
270

$2617.

The Dodge Rebellion:
Operation '67

Go '67 Dart!"

GT

$2961.

REDESIGNED
RECESSED
INSTRUMENT
PANEL

note "GT"
TAGS

$2728.

FULL
1967 LINE
ILLUSTRATED

Dodge Dart

2-DR.
$2556.

4-DR.
$2593.

270 4-DR.
$2732.

270

(INTRO. 9-14-67)

Dodge fever 68 new GRILLES

270 H/T
$2758.

TAIL-LT. DETAIL

PLAIN TOP

GT

GT CVT.
$3064.

GTS CVT.
$3445.

GT H/T
$2860.

VINYL TOP (OPT.)

GT SPORT
(GTS)
340 C/D V8

340 C/D V8

FULL 1968 LINE ILLUSTRATED

H/T
$3251.

This year, **DODGE**
(270 BECOMES **CUSTOM**)

is turning up the *fever*

DASH

69 new GRILLES

Announcing Dart Swinger.

(INTRO. 9-19-68)

$2637.

856

Dodge Dart

you could be **DODGE MATERIAL.**

DART CUSTOM 4-DR. SEDAN $2972.

4-DR. **DART**

$2807.

1970

CUSTOM

CUSTOM H/T $2999.

OPT. WH. CVRS.

60 DAY SWINGER AUTOMATIC SALE!

(NO DART 2-DR. SEDAN AVAIL. 1969 OR 1970)

INCLUDES EXTRAS LISTED AT BOTTOM OF PAGE.

70

(INTRO. 9-23-69) (BUCKET STS. OPT. IN CUST., SW. 340 H/Ts)

SWINGER 340 H/T $3171.

$2790.

SWINGER H/T

SWINGER

Dart Swinger 2-door hardtop. Our lowest priced hardtop.

1970

SHOWING ALL-STEEL RALLYE WHEELS

SWINGER 340 (ABOVE)

SHOWN w.th LIGHT COLORED VINYL ROOF

FULL 1970 LINE ILLUSTRATED

DART "Swinger"

* SALE PACKAGE INCLUDES

- VINYL ROOF
- D78 X 14 WHITEWALL TIRES
- DELUXE WHEEL COVERS
- DELUXE VINYL INTERIOR TRIM
- "RIM-BLOW" STEERING WHEEL

DART SWINGER 2-DOOR HARDTOP

- LEFT, REMOTE-CONTROL MIRROR
- CARPETS
- VINYL BODY-SIDE MOULDINGS
- BUMPER GUARDS (Frt. & Rr.)
- WHEEL-LIP/BELT MOULDINGS

automatic trans.

857

Dodge
Dart

SWINGER
$2808.

Dart CUSTOM
$2856.

(INTRO. 9-15-70)

new GRILLE **71** new BODY (ONLY ON NEW DEMON CPES.)

$3000.

340 CID V8 (275 HP)

DEMON 340

(new) **DEMON**

(108" WB) FROM $2590.

198 CID 6 (125 HP) OR 3/8 CID V8 (230 HP)

Demon

DODGE DEMON

ALSO AVAIL. SWINGER SPEC. H/T ($2649.) and DART SEDAN ($2697.)

$2665.

72 new GRILLE

(INTRO. 9-28-71)

DODGE DART

DART

DART SWINGER H/T $2773.

DART DEMON

DART DEMON

$2561.

Dodge. Depend on it.

858

DART

1972 DEMON REAR STYLING SIMILAR TO 1971.

Dodge Dart

$2898.

NO SIDE CHROME ON **DART SWINGER SPECIAL** H/T

$2702.

$2857.

Dart Custom Sedan & Swinger Hardtop

73 new GRILLE and BUMPERS

Dart Sport.

$2664.

DASH

$3124.

SPORT (108" WB) MODELS REPLACE DART DEMONS.

REAR CLOSE-UP (DART)

SPORT 340

Dodge invents the Convertriple. Three cars for the price of one.

DODGE DART

SWINGER
$3873.

CUSTOM
$3915.

TODAY—more than ever—
Dart is right on target.

(SPORT TOPPER, SPORT HANG 10, SPORT RALLYE DELS ALSO)

74

$3674.

Extra care in engineering
makes a difference in Dodge
...depend on it.

DART SPORT CONVERTRIPLE '74.

Dart Special Edition.
new

1 IT'S A FIVE-PASSENGER COUPE. With the size and features you wouldn't expect from a compact. Features such as torsion-bar suspension, Unibody construction, and the Electronic Ignition System...Dart Sport 1 makes 2 and 3 that much better.

2 IT'S A SUN ROOF CONVERTIBLE. What an option! You get a secure metal sun roof that slides open to give you the sun in the morning and the moon at night. With Dart Sport, the sky's the limit. So sit back, relax, and start to follow the sun.

3 IT'S AN ECONOMY WAGON. With the optional fold-down rear seat, you can flip yourself into a wagon in seconds and have a fully carpeted cargo space that's six-and-a-half-feet long. Dart Sport Convertriple '74. Pack it up and get going.

The new Dart Special Edition is based on the premise that a small car can be a very luxurious car. High-backed seats covered in crushed velour

1974

$4349.

Dart Special Edition.

$4565.

Dart "Hang 10."

DASH

new GRILLE

(EARLY)

75-76
Dodge is right on target

1975

(REPLACED BY DODGE ASPEN)

860

DODGE OMNI

4-DR. ('78) $3981.

SINCE 1978

GRAINED SIDE TRIM OPTIONAL

('78) REAR (OMNI has HORIZONTAL STRIPS ACROSS TAIL-LIGHTS; HORIZON DOES NOT.)

O-24 2+2 FASTBACK (HATCHBACK) STARTS 1979. DE TOMASO VERSION ALSO AVAIL. 1980.

IT DOES IT ALL.

4-DR. 99.2" WB

2-DR. ('79 ON) 96.7" WB

78-80

WITH VOLKSWAGEN 4-CYL. ENGINE 104.7 CID

155/80 × 13 TIRES

(LENGTH EXAGGERATED)

2+2 ('79)-new 2-DR. = $4801.
" " 5611. ('80)

OPTIONAL SUNROOF WITH GLASS DOOR

('79)

OMNI GRILLE has ALL HORIZONTAL PCS.

PLYMOUTH HORIZON SPECS. SIMILAR

861

119" WB (THROUGH '68)
(6 CYL. OR V8)
painting all
our engines blue

Ford Motor Company
(SINCE 1903)
FROM $2825.
(CUSTOM 2-DR.)
CUSTOM 500
$2977.

STD.
289 CID V8
(200 HP)

STD. 240 CID 6 (150 HP)

66
new
2-TIERED GRILLE

H/T
$3130.

GALAXIE 500

new 2-WAY
"Magic
Doorgate"
ON WAGONS

COUNTRY
SQUIRE
WAGON

new Stereo-Sonic TAPE SYSTEM

4-SEAT:
$3710.

note UNIQUE
HOOD ORNAMENTS
ON THESE CARS

$3431.

7.35/7.75
× 15
TIRES

GALAXIE
500
LTD

note 7 LITRE
SIGN ON
THIS GRILLE

In the Greatest Year Yet
For Total Performance,
There Are...
**49 NEW WAYS
TO GO FORD!**

862

FORD

YOU'RE AHEAD IN A FORD

$2898.

IMPACT ABSORBING STEERING WHEEL WITH PADDED HUB

Custom and Custom 500

$3052.

new GRILLE and TAIL-LIGHTS

67

(INTRO. 9-30-66)

(SINCE 1952, RANCH WAGON and COUNTRY SEDAN ARE UN-GRAINED FORD WAGONS.)

GALAXIE 500

$3212.

LTD
$3677.

COUNTRY SQUIRE
$3816.

SelectShift transmission you can use automatically or manually.

863

XL

$3558.

FORD
$3048.

CUSTOM (CUST. 500, GAL. 500 ALSO USE THIS GRILLE) ↙

DUAL-FACING REAR SEATS AVAIL.

COUNTRY SQUIRE (LTD) $3977.

(INTRO. 9-22-67)

68

new GRILLES
new 302 CID V8
(210 HP)
6 ALSO CONT'D.

INTERIOR (XL)

$3450.
XL

new CONCEALED HEADLIGHTS (LTD, XL)

OPEN

CLOSED

See the light!
FORD
Ford has a better idea.

(INTRO. 9-27-68)

new Ford Club Wagon

69

new GRILLES
new 121" WB (THROUGH '78)
(C.W. 105½" OR 123½" WB)
(CONT'D. NEXT PAGE)

COUNTRY SEDAN
FR. ↙ $3741.

standard wagon
RANCH WAGON IS LOWEST-PRICED

FR. $2900.

C.W. SINCE '65

FORD

new 150 HP IN 6

$3257.

DASH

CUSTOM 500

SIDE CHROME STRIP NOT SEEN ON CUSTOM.)

69
(CONT'D.)

$3514.

LTD

LTD INSIGNIA ABOVE GRILLE

XL

SPRTSRF. H/T $3536

It's the going thing!

GALAXIE, XL, LTD WITH 351 CID V8 (250 HP)

SPECIAL GALAXIE 500 2-DOOR HARDTOP

70

new GRILLES new F/G/H 78 x 15 TIRES

$3522.

FORD GALAXIE 500 SPORTSROOF

COUNTRY SQUIRE

$3573.

Take a Quiet Break in a FORD.

(INTRO. 9-19-69)

LTD

AND INTERIOR

$4199. UP

$3724.

865

FORD $4530 2-DR. LTD BROUGHAM **LTD**

COUNTRY SQUIRE

(INTRO. 9-18-70)

FROM $4809.

STD 240 CID 6 (140 HP) OR 302 CID V8 (210 HP)

Take a Quiet Break... '71 Ford.

71 new

new GRILLE

BUMPER DIPS, TO FOLLOW CONTOUR OF POINTED GRILLE.

DASH

LTD FINAL CVT. CVT. $4517.

COUNTRY SQUIRE FROM $4792.

(INTRO. 9-24-71)

72

2 SLIGHTLY DIFFERING new GRILLES

302 CID V8 (140 HP)
351 CID V8 (153 HP)

Quiet Plus.

GALAXIE 500

H/T $4161.

new

LTD STRAIGHT-ACROSS POINTED BUMPER

FORD

The closer you look, the better we look.

FROM $4550.

$4206.

G78 ×15 TIRES

COUNTRY SEDAN

(RANCH WAGON LOOKS SIMILAR)

GALAXIE 500

(6 and 302 CID V8 NOT AVAIL. IN FULL-SIZED LINE)

(CUSTOM 500 4-DR. SEDAN HAS NO CHROME SIDE STRIP.) ($4014.)

351, 400, 429 OR 460 CID V8s, J78 ×15 TIRES ON WAGONS

73 (RESTYLED)

DASH

✓ AVAIL. POWER-OPERATED SUN ROOF

FROM $4356.

new INSIDE HOOD LOCK, and FRONT DISC BRAKES STANDARD

LTD

LTD BROUGHAM PILLARLESS 4-DOOR H/T also available, AND 2-DR. H/T, 4-DR. PILLARED H/T

PILLARED 4-DR. H/T FR. $4364.

CLOSER REAR DETAILS (LTD)

FORD

FROM $5399.
LTD Country Squire

DASH

LTD
BROUGHAM 2-DR. $5170.

74 *new* GRILLE; LTD *has* HOOD ORNAMENT
($4483 CUSTOM 500 4-DR. *is* LOWEST-PRICED LARGE FORD.)
(FINAL YR. FOR GALAXIE 500)

LTD REAR

new

LTD
AND LTD BROUGHAM

$5649.

DASH
3-SEAT $6115.

COUNTRY SQUIRE

CONCEALED HDLTS. RETURN

75
HOOD ORNAMENT
FRONT RESTYLED

$6003.

LTD. LANDAU
(new)
(FINAL YEAR FOR CUSTOM 500)

FORD wagon

4-SEAT COUNTRY SQUIRE WAGON $6213.

(4-DR. STD. LTD IS LOWEST-PRICED, AT $5316.)

LTD

(ABOVE) '76½ COUNTRY SQUIRE

NO LONGER SHOWN WITH CHROME STRIP WHICH FORMERLY RAN ALONG GRAINED PANEL

351, 400 OR 460 C/D V8s

76

FEW NOTICEABLE CHANGES FROM 1975

note new WHEEL COVERS

$6177.

LTD LANDAU

NO LONGER HAS BODY-PAINTED SECTIONS BETWEEN THE 3 AMBER LENSES.

LTD Wagon

LTD. The full-size car

(LTD GENERALLY SIMILAR TO 1976 MODEL)

WITH STD. 351 C/D V8 (161 HP)

77

LTD LANDAU 4-DR. $6340.

FR. $6464.

FR. $6012.

new LTD II has 302 C/D V8 (130 HP) and HR78 × 14 TIRES

BROUGH. 5698.

Now, in addition to the full-size Ford LTD, Ford also offers LTD's kind of quality and luxury in a sportier, trimmer car that's priced and handles like a mid-size.

the new trimmer, sportier LTD II

(REPLACES TORINO)

FROM $5156. (S)

114"/118" WB 2-DR. 4-DR.

$5362. UP (STD. 2-DR.)

(RANCHERO NOW IN LTD II SERIES)

FORD
(E-100
124" WB)
138" WB
CLUB
WAGON
TYPES:
E-150,
250
OR
350

Built Ford Tough

SUPER WAGON

CL. W. INT.

FROM $6756.

LTD DASH

FORD LTD
LANDAU
(REAR)

FINAL
LARGE
(121" WB)
LTD

78

LTD, LTD II
NOW SHARE STD. 302 CID V8
(134 HP)

LTD

FORD LTD
FORD DIVISION
75th ANNIVERSARY

2-SEAT:
$6848.

Ford LTD Country Squire

LTD
LANDAU $6614.

LTD
(REAR)

$6127.

LTD II

LTD II
DASH

NOW 2
LTD II
COUPE
STYLES

$6027.

new WHEELS

870

LTD II
LTD BROUGHAM *has*
MID-SIDE TRIM.

FORD

CAPTAIN'S CLUB

Wagon

300 CID 6
OR 302, 351, 460 CID
V8s IN CLUB WAGONS
(FR. $7086.)

LTD II

"It's like they made it for me... sporty and practical"

LTD II 2-door Brougham in Pastel Chamois

(FINAL LTD II = ABOVE)

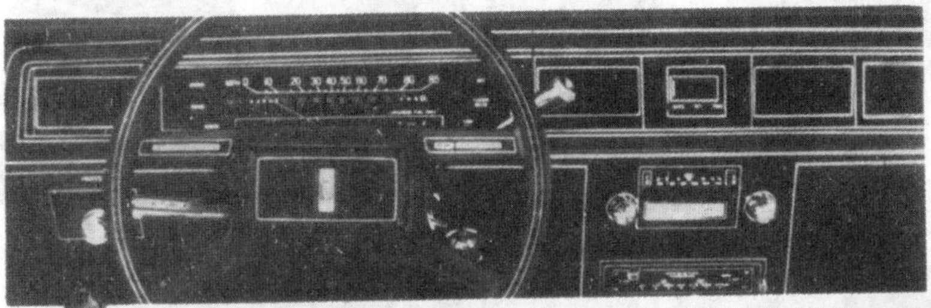

1979 NEW AMERICAN ROAD CAR

↖ STD. LTD

LTD DASH
CNTRY. SQ.
FR. $7291.

FORD LTD

LANDAU ↙

302 CID V8
(134 HP)
351 CID V8
(144 HP)

LTDs DOWNSIZED, WITH new 114.4" WB

(TOTALLY RESTYLED LTD, LANDAU)

79

note: 1979 has TALL, NARROW HOOD ORNAMENT ↙

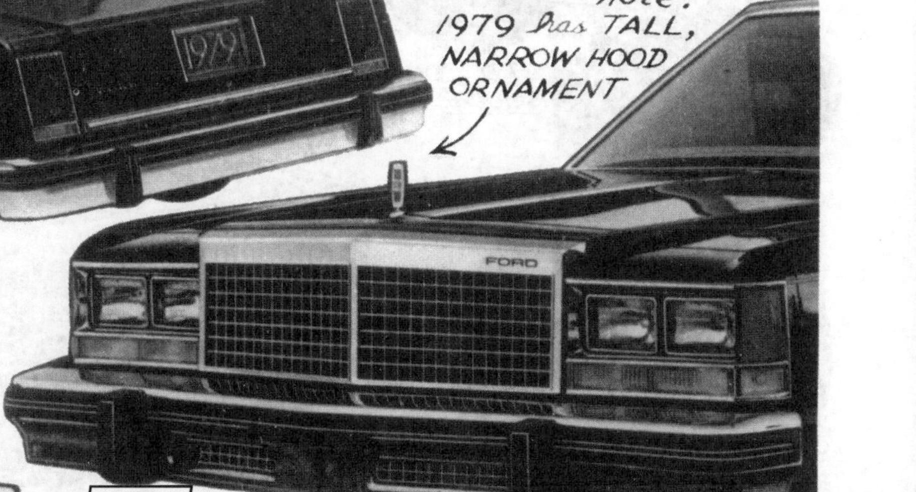

DETAILS OF STD. LTD 2-DR.

FORD

FORD
DIFF. GRILLE ON LOW-PRICED LTD "S" →

$7019.

DASH

new HIGHER BELT STRIPING FOR 1980

80

(LTD "S" WAGON ALSO)
new P205, P215 75R x 14 TIRES

$7769.

(new)

FORD LTD CROWN VICTORIA
SEDAN DETAILS IN CIRCLE AT LOWER LEFT)

2-DR. $7248.

LTD.

$7706.

new WIDER HOOD ORN. (CNTRY. SQ. and CRN. VICT.)

$8125.
(6-PASS.)
LTD COUNTRY SQUIRE

NO HOOD ORNAMENT on STD. LTDs

$7900.

CROWN VICTORIA SEDAN

(new)

Ford *FAIRLANE / TORINO*

(A SEPARATE COMPACT/INTERMEDIATE SERIES SINCE 1962)

(TORINO INTRO. 1968; FINAL FAIRLANE, 1970.)

116" WB
200 CID 6 (120 HP)
289 CID V8
(200 HP)
OR 390 CID
V8 (335 HP)
(IN GT)

500 - XL

Fairlane re-invented...for 1966

The Wizard of Aah's 1966 Fairlane

H/T $3201.

Fairlane GT —

(GTA *has* AUTO. TRANS.)

Special GT and GTA identification

NAME ON REAR FENDER

convertible

$3426.

GT
DASH

66

new GRILLE, *new* VERTICALLY-STACKED HEADLIGHTS, *new* TAIL-LTS.

new GRAINED SQUIRE WAGON (113" WB)
$3229.

new "MAGIC DOORGATE" SWINGS OUT OR DOWN.

FAIRLANE 500

FAIRLANE 500
H/T $2976.

FORD *Fairlane* / TORINO

FAIRLANE CLUB CPE. $2741.

500

Fairlane

CLUB CPE. $2821.

CVT. $3289.

SQUIRE $3347.

500/XL

H/T $3063.

Fairlane 500 Wagon

$3163.

67 *new GRILLE*

INTERIOR (500/XL)

Fairlane 500/XL Interior

390 ▼ INDICATES A 390 CID V8 IN CAR.

GT H/T $3178.

(note SIDE PAINT STRIPING ON GT)

That GT feeling is contagious: every Fairlane has it.

SHOW YOUR STRIPES!

(INTRO. 9-30-66)

FORD *Fairlane* / TORINO

TORINO. GT

(new)

FORMAL H/T
$3156

CVT.
$3359.

TORINO
INT.

TORINO
GT

302 CID V8
(210 HP) OR
390 CID V8

FASTBACK
$3105.

Torino Squire

FAIRLANE
500

$3011.

68

(INTRO. 9-22-67)

ALSO 289 CID V8
(195 HP) OR 200 CID 6 (115 HP)

FAIRLANE

FAIRLANE
SEDAN

H/T $2909.

$2962.

FORD *Fairlane* / TORINO

note: REAR SIDE SAFETY LIGHTS SMALLER, MOVED FORWARD AND DOWN.

FAIRLANE

$2941.

(INTRO. 9-27-68)

$2952.

69 *new* GRILLES

The 1969 winning streak rolls on. The Ford victory at Martinsville makes it six big wins for Torino over all the other specially modified stock cars.

DATE	EVENT	DRIVER
February 1	Riverside 500	Richard Petty
February 16	ARCA 300	Benny Parsons
February 23	Daytona 500	Lee Roy Yarbrough
March 9	Carolina 500	David Pearson
April 13	Richmond 250	David Pearson
April 27	Virginia 500	Richard Petty

With a roaring start like this the Torinos are well on their way to a repeat of last season's Grand Slam when Torino took the NASCAR, USAC and ARCA championships.

302 CID V8
4 OTHER V8s,
OR 428 CID 4V
COBRA JET V8 (335 HP)

Torino Talladega

IS '69½ SUPER STOCK SPORTSROOF MODEL. HAS SMALL RECTANGULAR SAFETY LTS. AT LOWER SIDE OF FRONT FENDER.

TORINO GT

SPORTSROOF (FASTBACK) $3203.

428

HOOD SCOOP

TORINO SEDAN
(ALSO AVAIL: CONVERTIBLE) $3186.

(CONT'D. IN FORD TORINO SECTION)

Ford Fairmont

Ford Motor Co. (SINCE 1978)

105½" WB
$4754. ('78)
5773. ('80)

2-DR.

(new) $5474. ('78)
6577. ('80)

Squire Wagon

REAR

78-80

140 CID 4 (88 HP); 200 CID 6 (85 HP)
302 CID V8 (139 HP) (THROUGH '79)
255 CID V8 (1980)

CR78×14 TIRES
(PLAIN-SIDED
WAGONS ALSO,
FROM $5109. ('78) TO
$6059. ('80)

FUTURA

SPECIAL
COUPE *has*
OWN GRILLE

$5209. ('78) 6/78.
('80)
BR78×14 TIRES

1978 CARS
ILLUSTRATED,
UNLESS NOTED
OTHERWISE

('80)

4-DR.

$4754.
('78)
5157.
('79)
5890.
('80)

DLX. WOOD-TONED
DASH ('80)

2-TONE COLOR BANDS
AVAILABLE ON
1980 MODELS

877

Ford *Falcon*

(1960–1970)

$2669.
($2781., FUTURA)

FUTURA

new THINNER SIDE TRIM

66

new GRILLE

SPT. CPE. WITH VINYL TOP $2555.

DASH

(FALCON RANCHERO PICKUP ALSO AVAIL.)

FORD

1966

111" WB
170 CID 6
(105 HP)
200 CID 6
(120 HP) IN
SPT. CPE., WAGON
289 CID V8
(180 - 200 HP)

6 CYL.
OR V8
(SINCE '63)

2-DR. $2284.

FUTURA
SPTS. CPE.

$2663.

2 new COWL INDENTATION
('67 ONLY)

67

REAR (STD.)

(INTRO. 9-30-66)

new GRILLE

Ford FALCON WAGON ('69)

('68)

EARLY **68-70**

170 CID 6 (100 HP)
289 CID V8 (195 HP)
200 CID 6 AVAIL. '69-
'70 (115-120 HP)
302 CID V8 (220 HP) '69-70

FALCON. 7 MODELS. MORE THAN ANY OTHER COMPACT.

('70)

FUTURA SEDAN

111" WB (WAGONS 113")

FALCON PRODUCTION SUSPENDED BECAUSE OF HIGH COST OF ADDING LOCKING STEERING COLUMNS, IN COMPLIANCE WITH GOVT. SAFETY REGULATIONS.

INTERIOR ('69)

('69)

new E78/G78 × 14 TIRES

FALCON TEMPORARILY REVIVED, AS A BUDGET-PRICED MODEL OF TORINO.

2-DR.

70½ NEW

LARGER 117"-WB TORINO SERIES (WAGON- 114")

3 FINAL FALCONS =
2-DR. $2827.
4-DR. $2867.
4-DR. WAGON $3163.

(DISCONTINUED SUMMER, 1970)

STD. ENGINES:

new 250 CID 6 (155 HP)
302 CID V8 (220 HP)

AVAILABLE
51 CID V8 (250 OR 300 HP)
429 CID V8 (360 OR 370 HP)

879

FORD Granada

(INTRO. 1975)

...elegance in a new efficient size

109.9" WB

$3698*...2-Door
($4860., '77)

STANDARD GRANADA

200 CID 6

250 CID 6 IN CALIF.-
SOLD CARS and GHIA

ENGINE

$3756*...4-Door

GRILLE

DR 78 × 14 TIRES

14-18' mpg: city / 18-26' mpg: highway

75-77

(302, 351 CID V8 ALSO AVAIL.)

2-DR. $5025.

On the Inside, Ghia
Offers More Luxury

$5083. '75
5232. '76
5368. '77

GRANADA GHIA

(MORE SIDE TRIM and
VINYL TOP)

(1975 EXAMPLES, UNLESS
OTHERWISE INDICATED)

REAR DETAIL

■ Odense Vinyl Trim High-
lights — appear in the 'roof
center pillars — the
bodyside moldings which are
both protective and decorative — and on the distinctive
lower back panel applique.

DASH

SPORT COUPE
('76)

SALE:
$4189.

note
SPECIAL WHEELS

880

■ Steering Wheel with Downswept Spokes —
permits excellent driver visibility of the
instrument panel controls and gauges.

Ford Granada

$5390.

**STD.
GRANADA**
250 CID 6 (97 HP)
302 CID V8 (139 HP)
new 255 CID V8 also, 1980

new
2-TONE PAINT AVAIL. on
1979 GHIA

('79)

2 DR.

GHIA

$5556.
('78)

4 DR. $5635.
            ('78)

note HEAVY
SIDE TRIM on
GRANADA GHIA

$5878.

('80)

('78)

('80)

DASH ('79)

1980 WHEEL
COVERS

78-80

new GRILLE and
ESS MODEL
INTRO. 1978

('80)

note UNIQUE RR.
QUARTER WINDOW
on **ESS** CPES.

ESS SEDAN
('78) $5821.

$5936.
('79)

('79) TYPE of ESS COWL LETTERING
DETERMINES YEAR.

1980 GAS
MILEAGE →

19	EPA EST. MPG	28	EST. HWY. MPG
342	EST. RANGE	504	EST. HWY. RANGE

Ford Motor Company

FORD MAVERICK

(compact)

(1970 - 1977 MODELS)

For $1995...
it's a little gas.

(2-DR. ONLY)

70
(new)

(REG. $2257.)

INITIAL (1970) MAVERICK INTRO. APRIL 17, 1969.

(SEE NOTE AT LOWER LEFT)

← STANDARD DASH

```
103" WB
6 CYL.
170 CID
105 HP @
4200 RPM
    OR
200 CID
120 HP @
4000 RPM
16-GAL. FUEL TANK
```

6.00 × 13 TIRES (14" OPT.)

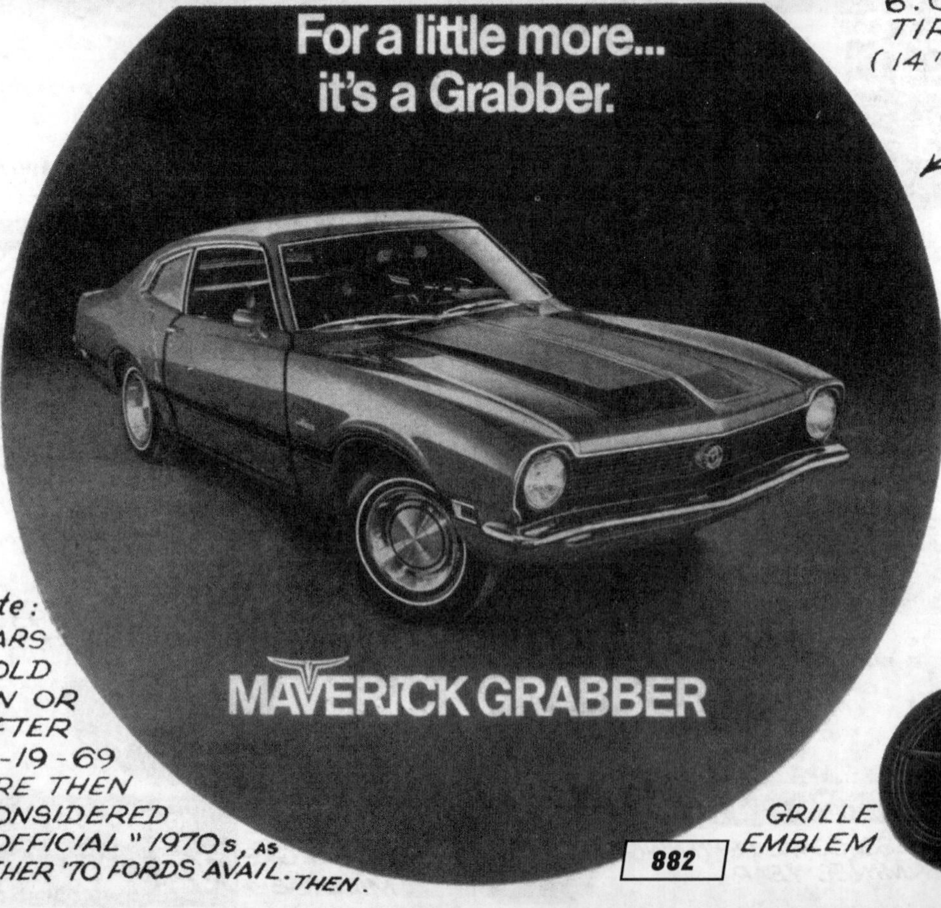

For a little more...
it's a Grabber.

Here's what you get:
- 200-cubic-inch Six
- Bodyside tape stripes, black-painted hood and grille
- White sidewalls, 14" wheels and trim rings
- Deck lid spoiler, dual racing mirrors
- 3-spoke woodtone steering wheel, black all-vinyl seat trim
- Choice of five hot Grabber colors

GRABBER MODEL ADDED FEB., 1970

MAVERICK GRABBER

note: CARS SOLD ON OR AFTER 9-19-69 ARE THEN CONSIDERED "OFFICIAL" 1970s, AS OTHER '70 FORDS AVAIL. THEN.

GRILLE EMBLEM

GAS CAP

882

FORD MAVERICK

new 6.45 × 14 TIRES (THROUGH '74)

MAVERICK
The Simple Machine

Grabber $2598. ('71)
2583. ('72)

STD. 2-DR.
$2419. ('71)
2414. ('72)

CHOICE OF 3 SIXES OR V8 ENGINE SINCE MID-1971 SEASON. (1971 MODELS INTRO. 9-11-70; 1972 MODELS INTRO. 9-24-71)

new GRILLE and HOOD SCOOPS on GRABBER

71-72

new 4-DR. $2479. ('71)
ADDED 2469. ('72)

DASH (LUXURY DECOR TYPE)

73

Maverick is available now with optional 250-six automatic or 302-V8 engines.

new GRILLE

$2,695.*
WITH new VINYL TOP

FORD MAVERICK
FORD DIVISION Ford

MAVERICK

new BUMPERS

FORD MAVERICK

WITH SHOULDER HARNESSES

74

Energy absorbing bumper for '74.

2-DR. $3063.
4-DR. 3097.
GRABBER 3196.

note
MAVERICK NAME ON
DELUXE REAR QUARTER
VINYL PANELS

MAVERICK
Grained vinyl roof.

cushioned bench seats trimmed in random stripe cloth and Vinyl.

2-DR.

GRABBER

2-DR. === 103" WB
4-DR. === 109.9" WB

interior is available in a choice of blue, black, tan or a new light green.

In order to achieve the emisssion standards established for 1975, catalytic converters will be installed on all 200 CID engines. On the optional 250 and 302 CID engines, it will not be required.

4-DR.

DASH

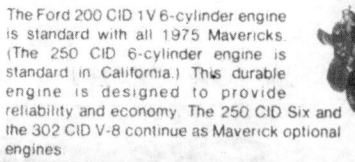

new RADIAL-PLY TIRES BR/CR 78×14 (DR 70×14 - GRABBER)

75

The Ford 200 CID 1V 6-cylinder engine is standard with all 1975 Mavericks. (The 250 CID 6-cylinder engine is standard in California.) This durable engine is designed to provide reliability and economy. The 250 CID Six and the 302 CID V-8 continue as Maverick optional engines.

new
1975
OPTION

DECK LID-MOUNTED LUGGAGE RACK.

76-77

new FLOOR-OPERATED PARKING BRAKE

MAVERICK DISCONTINUED 1977

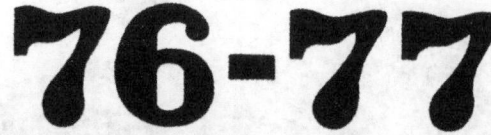

OPTIONAL
ALPINE PLAID
ON SEATS

EPA MPG:
30 HWY.
22 CITY

new
SPLIT
GRILLE

('76)

'77 4-DR.
$3719.

FENDER BADGE ON GT

(FORD) Mustang **Ford Motor Co.**

(INTRO. 4-64, FOR '65)

108" WB
200 CID 6 (120 HP)
289 CID V8 (200 HP)

2+2
$2924.

66

SIDE EMBLEM: CHROMED HORSE WITH RED, WHITE and BLUE VERTICAL BARS

MESH IN GRILLE REPLACED BY HORIZONTAL STRIPS FOR 1966.

DASH

Mustang's new instrument panel groups five easy-to-read dials

$2970.

CVT.

VARIATION

MUSTANG! MUSTANG! MUSTANG!

(SLOGAN)

REAR 6.95 x 14 TIRES

$2734.

DASH

FROM $2791.

TYPE WITH PLAIN REAR PANEL 2+2

new GRILLE

67

$2921.

SPORTS SPRINT

GT 2+2 $3242.

SLOGAN:
Take the Mustang Pledge.

885

FORD MUSTANG

Carroll Shelby Presents _The Road Cars..._
G.T. 350 and G.T. 500 **for 1967**

500

67

SHELBY G.T.

MODIFIED
(SHELBY TYPES)

350

SHELBY
COBRA
DASH

68 new GRILLES

Shelby Cobra

$3312.

new
SIDE
TRIM

GT
2+2

STD.
2-DR.
H/T
PRICED
FROM $2938.

STD. 6 and
V8 REDUCED 5 HP

FORD MUSTANG

FORD DIVISION *Ford*

GT H/T $3129.

69

new GRILLE

1969

MACH 1

Ford's Exclusive "Shaker" scoop actually protrudes through the hood—rams air directly into the carburetor under full throttle.

MACH 1

1969

$3480.

MACH 1

SPORTSROOF

(MUSTANG "E" SPORTSROOF IS $3078 WITH 250 CID 6, 155 HP)

MACH 1 ENGINE: 351 CID V8 (250 HP)

GT SPORTSROOF (FASTBACK)

GRANDE

$3329 GRANDE has LOW REAR-FACING "SCOOP" LIKE GT MODELS.

STD. ENGINES :
200 CID **6** (115 HP)
302 CID **V8** (220 HP)

SHELBY CARS STILL CUSTOM-CRAFTED WITH FORD PARTS, BUT NO LONGER BEAR A CLOSE RESEMBLANCE TO MUSTANG.

MUSTANG

GT CVT. $3343.

FORD MUSTANG

GRANDE

$3628.

$3283.

$3876.

70

Boss 302

MACH I

WITH 428
COBRA JET
V-8 (E70×14
TIRES)

new GRILLE

6 OR V8,
9 ENGINE
CHOICES FOR 1970.

BOSS 302
USES 302 CID,
290-H.P. V-8,
F60 × 15 TIRES.
(new E78×14, MOST OTHER
MODELS)

$4046.

MACH I

MACH I
WHEEL
DETAIL

7 ENGINE CHOICES FOR
1971
STD. 250 CID 6 (145 HP)
STD.
302 CID
V8
(210 HP)
H/T
$3783.

new
109" WB

(RESTYLED)

71

MACH I
GRILLE

GRANDE SIMILAR,
BUT has
VINYL-COVERED
TOP
($3989.)

FORD MUSTANG

For Spring Only. A Mustang of a New Stripe.

A New Mustang Hardtop. It's a Special Spring Value at your Ford Dealer's. Now.

REAR WINDOW

71½

STYLED LIKE MACH I, BUT has BLACK VINYL-COVERED TOP, BLACK SIDE STRIPES; BODY and BUMPERS ARE RED.

FORD MUSTANG *

72

SPORTSROOF
$3557.

H/T
$3500.

HP CUTS
250 CID 6 (99 HP)
302 CID V8 (141 HP)

*= FORD PREFIX ADDED IN MUSTANG ADVERTISING, 1972.

MACH I
$3737.

CVT. $3785.

GRANDE

DASH

$3686.

Control and balance

FORD MUSTANG

DASH
STD. 302 CID V8 (141 HP)
(6 CYL. AVAIL.)

$3557.

$3500.

Convertible

Hardtop

SportsRoof

5 MODELS IN 1973
(ALL ILLUSTRATED HERE

*LAST OF THE "BIG" MUSTANGS

MACH 1

$3737.
E70 × 14
TIRES

new GRILLE

73

*FINAL
109" WB
TYPES

FRONT DETAILS

(new)
CRISS-CROSS
GRILLE

new BUMPERS,
COLOR-KEYED TO
BODY COLOR

CLOSER DETAIL
of GRILLE CENTER

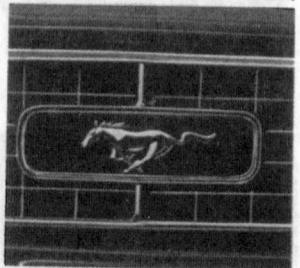

NOTE new
SHOULDER
HARNESSES IN
ABOVE CAR

GRANDE
$3686. E78 × 14 TIRES
(EXC. MACH 1)

890

Ford Mustang II. A new class of small car: First Class.

DASH

Mustang II

HATCH-BACK

B78/BR78/BR70 × 13 TIRES (new)

Mach I.
$4444.

$4327.

3-Door 2+2.

FRONT CLOSE-UP (GHIA)

WINDOW DEFR.

74

139 CID
4-CYL.
OR
V-6
(169 CID)

ALL-NEW

SMALLER THAN
PREVIOUS
MUSTANGS
(96.2" WB)

Ghia
$4479.

$4133.
Hardtop.

THIS MEDALLION USUALLY SEEN ON GHIA
(FULL LINE ILLUSTRATED)

FORD MUSTANG II

The closer you look, the better we look.

GHIA '75 MODELS have new ROOFLINE and new UPRIGHT RADIATOR ORNAMENT

Silver Ghia. (new)

GHIA FR. $4514.

new 1975 STEERING WHEEL WITH DOWNWARD-CURVED SPOKE

STD. TYPE H/T

75

$4105.

new HUB CAPS

BR 78 × 13 TIRES
139 CID 4 (83 HP)
169 CID 6 (97 HP)

3-Door 2+2.
$4394.

CARS WITH new CATALYTIC CONVERTER HAVE UNLEADED FUEL WARNING DECAL OVER GAS FILLER CAP.

Mach 1. $4492.

302 CID V-8 JOINS 4-CYL. and V-6.

LATE IN 1975 MODEL YEAR, SIMPLIFIED MPG MODELS JOIN OTHERS, AS LOW-PRICED ECONOMY LEADERS. $3529. (SALE PRICE)

Official U.S. Government Environmental Protection Agency tests:
28mpg (4-speed manual) highway...18mpg city.
26mpg (automatic) highway...18mpg city.
New Mustang II MPG

GHIA MPG

75½

NO HOOD ORNAMENT, new HUB CAPS, FEWER "FRILLS."

892

Mustang II MPG $3,529*

FORD MUSTANG II

MPG

STALLION (new)

AVAIL. AS 2+2 OR H/T, with BLACK GRILLE and WINDOW MOLDINGS. STALLION DECAL ON COWL →

EPA estimates:
Mustang II MPG.
34 mpg highway **24** mpg city

FROM $4101.

$4519.   MACH I

DASH

(INCLUDES TACHOMETER)

new AIR-SCOOP UNDERNEATH FRONT BUMPER.

76

COBRA II

140 CID 4 (new 92 HP)
new 171 CID V6 (100 HP)
302 CID V8 (134 HP)

The score for '76: **Mustang II. Boredom Zero.**

MACH I

↗ $4645.

16½-GAL. FUEL TANK

H/T (SPECIAL PAINT or DECALS OPTIONAL)

3.18 GEAR RATIO WITH 4 CYL.; OTHERWISE 3.0

$4496.

3-DOOR
2+2

77

(HP CUTS)

ENGINES =

4-CYL. (140 CID)
V-6 (170.8 CID)(93 HP)
V-8 (302 CID)(139 HP)

COBRA II

SuperCoupe

893

GHIA 2-DR. $4538.

DASH

140 CID 4 (88 HP)
171 CID V6 (90 HP)
302 CID V8 (139 HP)

FORD MUSTANG II

78 STD. H/T FROM $4121.

COBRA
(COBRA FIG. ON GRILLE)

3-DR. SPORT

MUSTANG
1979: The New Breed.

$5158.

new 100.4" WB

DASH

2-DR. SPORT

79 STYLING ALL-NEW

$5364.

GHIA
(GHIA. SPT. FASTBK. AVAIL.)

$4793.

FR. $5846. 3-DR.

$5536.

2-DR.

140 CID 4
200 CID 6
225 or new
255 CID V8s
(TURBO 4 AVAIL.)

80

HOOD SCOOP WITH TURBO ENG.

(23) EPA EST MPG (38) EST HWY MPG

894

($7474. COBRA 3-DR. SPT. FASTBACK ALSO AVAIL.)

(1971-1980)

Pinto
Ford Motor Co.

94" WB, 4 CYL.

Hello world.

$2298.

3-DOOR HATCHBACK

97.6 CID (75 HP @ 5000 RPM) OR 122 CID (100 HP @ 5600)

2-DR. $2155.

new **71**

(INTRO. 9-11-70)

Put a little kick in your life.

BLACK OR WHITE VINYL TOP AVAIL.

MULTI-PURPOSE KEY

Do it yourself and save. Pinto is designed to be so simple you can do most servicing yourself. The owner's manual shows you how. And the free Do-It-Yourself Key (above) helps you do everything from gauge the spark-plug gap to adjust the headlight beam.

6.00 x 13 TIRES

$2494.

ALSO AVAIL. W/O GRAIN PANELS

new SPORTS ACCENT TRIM

122 CID 4 CUT TO 86 HP

new **Wagon**

$2708.

72

(INTRO. 9-24-71)

DASH

3-DOOR HATCHBACK

new SPRINT DECOR IN WHITE and BLUE, WITH RED STRIPING

new SUNROOF AVAIL.

$2355.

When you get back to basics, you get back to Ford.

895

FORD PINTO

FORD DIVISION Ford

73

UNGRAINED WAGON : $2572.

SQR. WAG. $2809.

3-DR. $2422.

DELUXE BUMPER HAS VERTICAL GUARDS and PROTECTIVE BLACK VINYL STRIP

(PLAIN BUMPERS CONTINUED ALSO)

2-DR. $2299.

6.00 x 13 / A 78 x 13 TIRES

122 OR 139 CID 4

SQUIRE $3337. ('74)

new BR 78 x 13 TIRES IN 1975

2-DR. $2852. ('74)

new ENERGY-ABSORBING BUMPERS

74-75

$3700.

(1975 139 CID 4 RATED AT 83 HP)

75½

MPG WITH DLX. BUMPERS EXTERIOR DECOR TRIM STRIP

New Ford Pinto MPG 28mpg. $2,769. (SALE)

896

REG. FR. $3329.

FORD PINTO
(VARIOUS MODELS CONTINUE)

38 MPG highway, 25 city).

Pinto Pony MPG. More car for the money.

76 new GRILLE WITH CRISS-CROSS PCS.

new PONY MPG (ABOVE) has A MINIMUM OF CHROME TRIM, AND PLAIN HUBCAPS (LOWEST-PRICED MODEL)

Pinto Pony MPG $2,895 (REG. $2966.)

2-DR. PONY $3164. ('77); $3341. ('78)

$3861. ('77)

WITH PLAIN SIDES

$4075. ('78)

the best sellers in their class

1977:
140 CID 4 (89 HP)
171 CID V6 (93 HP)
RESPECTIVE HP CUT TO 88 AND 90 IN 1978.

77-78

new "ALL-GLASS" HATCHBACK DOOR VARIATION ('77)

Wagons ('78)

$3666. ('77)

A 78 × 13 TIRES

mileage.	
39 mpg highway	27 mpg city
HWY.	CITY

6. Woodgrain vinyl paneling
7. Roomy cargo area (cargo volume index 67.2 cubic feet)
8. Flipper rear side windows
9. Low sticker price
10. Electro-dip corrosion protection
11. Sporty suspension system
12. 4-speed floor-mounted transmission (standard; SelectShift automatic (optional)
13. Precise rack and pinion steering.
14. Power front disc brakes
15. Larger standard engine (2.3 litre, 4-cylinder cast iron) than Datsun F-10 to Sportswagon Toyota Corolla and Corona.

DuraSpark ignition No points or condenser to replace
Critical areas around lights and grille are dent chip and scratch resistant and absolutely rustproof.

SQUIRE WAGON (ABOVE) $4204. ('77)	WAGON	
	33 mpg highway	23 mpg city
	HWY.	CITY

new SLOPING GRILLE, new FRONT-END STYLING ('77)

2-DR. $3550. ('77) 3617. ('78)

897

FORD PINTO *PONY* **wagon**

CRUISING
(PANEL/VAN)
WAGON

THIS
TYPE INTRO.
1977

NEW Design in here

NEW Design up here

FRONT, REAR CHANGES

1979
NEW Design back here

OLD-
STYLE
DUAL-
CLUSTER
ALSO
CONT'D.

SQUIRE

(1)

A78×13 ('79) TIRES   BR 78 × 13 ('80)

79-80

PONY
FROM
$3571.
('79)
$4121.
('80)

new FRONT END, new
TAIL-LIGHTS

note 3 STYLES
OF REAR
WINDOW

1980

**NEW
UP FRONT**

FINAL
PINTO,
1980

RALLYE

WITH
RALLYE
TRIM

898

1980

2-DR.
$4643. ('80)

FORD TORINO
(REPLACES FAIRLANE)

Torino. 14 models

TORINO SPORTSROOF

$3506. (FINAL FAIRLANE)

250 CID 6 (150 HP) OR 302 CID V8 (220 HP)

FAIRLANE 500 2-DOOR HARDTOP

new 117" WB (114" ON WAGONS and RANCHEROS)

OFFIAL PACE CAR

GT CVT. $3968.

Torino GT Convertible. The Pace Car for all America.

HOOD SCOOP ON GT

(INTRO. 9-19-69)   Torino GT-

(TOTALLY RESTYLED)   **70**

(CONT'D. NEXT PAGE)

GT has 302, 351 OR 429 CID V8 E78/G78 × 14 TIRES (F70 × 14, COBRA)

new PROFILE FOR SPORTSROOF →

TORINO BROUGHAM (new) $3762.

(FORMAL ROOFLINE)

VINYL TOP

SPOILER DECK ↓

$3861.

(351 CID V8 USES REGULAR GAS)

MOTOR TREND "Car of the Year!"

899

FORD TORINO

LIGHTS CLOSED (BY DAY)

WITH LIGHTS OPEN

FROM $3568.

TORINO 4-DOOR SEDAN

2 COBRA REAR DECK PAINT VARIATIONS

360 HP COBRA (429 CID V8) $3843. (note DUAL PIPES)

RECTANGULAR INSTRUMENTS ON 1970 DASH

70 (CONT'D.)

TORINO COBRA

PLAIN TOP, FORMAL ROOFLINE

TORINO 2-DOOR HARDTOP

$3655.

DELUXE WHEEL COVER

WITH CHROME SIDE TRIM

WITH NON-DISAPPEARING HEADLIGHTS

FORD TORINO

$4333.

SQUIRE WAGON

$3812.

1971 Torino 500 SportsRoof

71

new SPLIT GRILLE; EXPOSED HEADLTS.

BROUGHAM 4-DR. HARDTOP

250 CID 6 (145 HP) OR 302 CID V8 (210 HP)

(INTRO. 9-18-70)

$4022.

The first Gran Torino.

SPORT H/T

HP RATINGS REDUCED
250 CID 6 (95 HP)
302 CID V8 (140 HP)

4-DR. PILLARED H/T
$3736.

$3883.
(note HOOD SCOOP ON SPORT)

FORD GRAN TORINO

WITH VINYL TOP

(RESTYLED)

(INTRO. 9-24-71)

72

(CONT'D. NEXT PAGE)

REAR

GRAN TOR. 2-DR. H/T $3756. UP

WITH PLAIN TOP

new GRAN TORINO has THIS new NARROW GRILLE.

901

More car than you expected.

FORD TORINO

new SHORTER 114" WB
(new 118" WB ON
RANCHERO, WAGONS)

(Standard)
TORINO
has
THIS BROAD GRILLE

FROM
$3834.

72
(CONT'D.)

FROM
$4275.

DASH
(CIRCULAR
INSTRUMENTS
CONTINUE, AS
IS USUAL
TORINO STYLE.)

VIEWS
OF
WOODGRAINED
Gran Torino Wagon

INTERIOR

902

The solid mid-size car.

FORD TORINO

3-SEAT SQUIRE $4339.

GRAN TORINO

STD. TORINO *has* OWN WIDER GRILLE

114" WB (2-DR.)
118" WB (4-DR.)

73

FINAL TORINO 6 (250 CID)

302 CID V8 STD.

new GRILLES (INTRO. FRIDAY, 9-22-72)

The closer you look, the better we look.

DASH

new GRILLES
new OPERA WINDOWS *in* COUPES

V8s ONLY 302, 351 CID

74

Gran Torino Squire
$5021.
(3-SEAT)

$3797. UP

GRAN TORINO ELITE
(*new,* '74½)

$4752.

DASH

DUAL OPERA WINDOWS

903

Ford Torino. Under $4,000.*

(* = REG. $4499.)

with automatic transmission,
power front disc brakes, power steering,
V-8, steel-belted radials

$5347.

('76)

GRAN 2-DR.
TORINO BROUGHAM

TORINO
The solid mid-size.

75-76

*(1975 EXAMPLES SHOWN,
UNLESS OTHERWISE INDICATED)*

351 CID V8 (148 HP)
G78 x14 TIRES

(400 OR 460 CID
V8s OPT. IN ELITE)

INTERIOR DECOR GR.
DASH

▲ The Beautiful Standard Elite Interior.

ELITE WHEEL COVERS

▲Full Wheel Covers. Standard at no extra cost.   ▲Luxury Wheel Covers. Thunderbird inspired, add a nice dress-up touch.   ▲Wire Wheel Covers. Classic styling in the finest European tradition.   ▲Deep-Dish Aluminum Wheels. A sporty look, with bright chrome lugs.

*(ELITES AFTER JAN., 1975 DO NOT
HAVE SEAT-BELT INTERLOCK SYSTEM.)*

Torino
('76)

ELITE HR78 x15 TIRES

a lot of car for about $4200.*

For about the same kind of money as a little 4-passenger foreign car
you can choose a 6-passenger '76 Torino with a standard V-8,
automatic transmission, power front disc brakes, power steering,
steel belted radials, solid state ignition, and more.

(* = REG. $4728.)

(REPL. BY
1977 LTD II)

$5309.
($5435.-'76)

IMPERIAL

(1926-1975; 1981-)

BY **CHRYSLER** CORPORATION

129" WB

$6505. CROWN CPE. (H/T)

V8 ENGINE (SINCE '55)
new 440 CID
(350 HP)
9.15×15 TIRES

66

CROWN SERIES *and*
$7158. LE BARON
4-DR. H/T

new GRILLE

CONVERT. AVAIL. AT $6764.

FR. $6351. (4-DR. H/T)

THE INCOMPARABLE **IMPERIAL**
Finest of the fine cars built by Chrysler Corporation

IMPERIAL NAME SET IN *new* ALL-HORIZONTAL GRILLE

new CORNER LTS. IN FENDERS

Imperial '67... the newest prestige automobile in a decade.

← *new* 4-DR. SEDAN ADDED $5991.

new SHORTER 127" WB

67

(INTRO. 9-29-66)

$6861.

IMPERIAL CONVERTIBLE DISCONTINUED AFTER 1968

REAR DETAILS

IMPERIAL

CROWN
COUPE $6381.

68

LE BARON
$7599.

(INTRO. 9-14-67)

CROWN
4-DR.
H/T
$6774.

new GRILLE

FINAL CVT. ($7156.)

"Imperial" NAME ON
new GRILLE, AND
CREST ON HOOD,
REAR DECK.

LE BARON
4-DR.
H/T $6793.

(new LE BARON 2-DR. H/T
ADDED)

BLOCK-LETTER
"IMPERIAL" NAME
IN CENTER OF
REAR BUMPER

HEADLIGHTS
CONCEALED
IN
new
GRILLE

69 (INTRO.
9-19-68)

TOTALLY
RESTYLED WITH
BULGE-SIDED "FUSELAGE" STYLING

(CONT'D. NEXT PAGE)

906

IMPERIAL

$6564. LE BARON 2-DR. H/T (*new*)

note TRIPLE OPENINGS FOR SAFETY LT.

VINYL-COVERED TOP BEARS TRADITIONAL IMPERIAL EAGLE MEDALLION

69

(CONT'D.)

('70)

"THE NEW CHOICE"   FROM $6419. ('70)

FR. $6745. ('71)

LE BARON 4-DR. H/T

(INTRO. 9-23-69)   *new* GRILLE   (INTRO. 10-6-70)

70-71

FINAL CROWN MODELS IN 1970.   LE BARON MODELS ONLY, IN 1971.

HP CUT TO 335, '71.

$6977.   *new* HEADLIGHT PLAQUES ADDED TO GRILLE OF '71.

IMPERIAL *(SINCE 1971, REDUCED TO A TOP-LINE MODEL of CHRYSLER, RATHER THAN A SEPARATE MAKE AS SINCE 1955.*

"BUTTERFLY" VENT WINDOWS ELIMINATED

72 *(INTRO. 9-28-71)*

CHRYSLER
Coming through with the kind of car America wants.

new GRILLE

2-DR. H/T $6795.

HP CUT TO 225

L84 × 15 TIRES (SINCE '71)

73

HP CUT TO 215

4-DR. H/T $7305.

2-DR. H/T $7077.

new GRILLE with FINER PCS.; IMPROVED BUMPERS with VERTICAL GUARDS

IMP'L. PRODUCTION LIMITED ONLY TO LE BARON 2-DR. OR 4-DR. H/Ts, 1971 THROUGH 1975.

RESTYLED FOR 1974. (1975 SIMILAR) FEATURING DRAMATIC new NARROW "WATERFALL" GRILLE; new HEADLIGHT DOORS ARE PLAIN METAL.

74-75

new LR78 × 15 TIRES

HP UP TO 230 (215, 1975)

HOOD ORNAMENT ADDED '74

FR. $8900. ('75)

(NO 1976 TO 1980 IMPERIALS)

$7258.('74)

new ENERGY-ABSORBING BUMPERS

INTERNATIONAL HARVESTER COMPANY
CHICAGO, ILLINOIS

SCOUT INTRO '61.

4 - CYL.
(SOME WITH
4-WHEEL DRIVE)

66

100" WB

(SUMMER, '66)
New International Scout Sportop

WITH SLANTING
SOFT TOP OR
HARD TOP ←

DASH

New Scout 800 by International

SALE PRICE
$1777.16   (REG. $2280.)

ROADSTER
OR
PICKUP
STYLE ALSO
AVAILABLE

The home of
McMILLEN PARK
Little League

The Travelall

↓ 119"
WB

(THROUGH
'73)
(6 CYL.
OR V8)

FROM
$2841.

SCOUT SIMILAR TO
——— 1966, BUT new V8
ENGINE IS NOW OPTIONAL.

67

The new
top-powered
V-8 SCOUT!

4-CYL.
$2406.
and up

TRAVELALL
has new
GRILLE

AB-711

68

International *Scout*

FROM
$2660.

EMBLEM REMOVED
FROM ABOVE GRILLE
(TRAVELALL)

Travelall
FROM
$3146.

**Travelall. The big-family wagon
from International.**

new
GRILLES
and SIDE
SAFETY LIGHTS ('69)

FROM
$3272. ('69)
3502. ('70)

new 800-A SCOUT SERIES

69-70

2
TOP
STYLES
AVAIL.
FOR
SCOUT

2-TONE
SCOUT
"ARISTOCRAT"

(INTRO.
SUMMER, '69)

Scout

FROM
$2940.
('69)

4, 6, OR V8
SCOUT
ENGINES
('70 UP)

---

71 $3350.

WITH
SPECIAL
PAINT AND
STRIPING

new 800-B
SCOUT

NEXT
PAGE:
1971
TRAVELALL

The new Scout Comanche.

INTERNATIONAL HARVESTER

DASH

REAR

2 SETS OF VENT SLOTS ATOP COWL

71
(CONT'D.)

| STD. $3610. | CUSTOM |
| DLX. 3631. | $3740. → |

1971

Travelall

new GRILLE

International Travelall
The wagon built to tow.

FROM $3656.

new STD.
6-258
ENGINE

72

new GRILLES;
new DASH

ENGINES:
196 CID SLANT-4 (111 HP)
232 CID 6 (135 HP)
304 CID V8 (193 HP)
345 CID V8 (197 HP)

new
Scout II (INTRO. SPRING, '71)

(POWER BRAKES and STEER. OPT.)

DELUXE INTERIOR (Scout II)

$3344.

International Harvester

SCOUT

$3426.

GEAR RATIOS

3.31
3.73
OR
4.27

1973

new GRILLE

19 - GAL.
FUEL
TANK

ENGINES : (SCOUT, TRAVELALL)
258 CID 6 (113 HP)
304 CID V8 (137 HP)
345 CID V8 (144 HP)

ALSO AVAIL. (IN
TRAVELALL ONLY 392 CID V8
(179 HP)

73

TRAVELALL

FROM
$3662.

GEAR RATIOS

3.73
4.09
OR
4.56

20 - GALLON
FUEL TANK
(15 - GAL.
RESERVE AVAIL.)

CUSTOM (ILLUSTR.) = $3790.

912

INTERNATIONAL HARVESTER

SCOUT® II

$3943. ('74)
$4712. ('75)

74-

75

AFTER 1975, ALL PASSENGER MODELS ARE IN

SCOUT

LINE.

It leads a double life

(FINAL TRAVELALL OF 1974-1975 has 120" WB)

new GRILLE ('74)

(new DIESELS AVAIL.)*

76

new TERRA, TRAVELER have 118" WB

$5394. (new)   Scout Terra

$5438. Scout II

new GRILLE

Scout Traveler
$5844.

INTERNATIONAL SCOUT

(100" WB CONTINUES ON SCOUT II)

* - 198 CID 6

SCOUT THE AMERICA OTHERS PASS BY.

TRAVELTOP $5834.
TRAVELER $6205.

77

new GRILLE

new SS II
$5251.

TERRA PICKUP $5720.

913

INTERNATIONAL SCOUT

REAR

('79)

SS II has OWN GRILLE

EXTRA CHARGE FOR OPTIONAL 6-CYL. DIESEL ENGINE: $2581.('78) 2495.('79)

note VARIOUS '79 STRIPING PATTERN TYPES

Scout leads the way.
('78)

78-79

new GRILLE ('78)

1979 PRICES	
SS II	$ 6187.
TRAVELTOP	6993.
TERRA PCKP.	7044.
TRAVELER V8	7657.

SCOUT. ('79)
Anything less is just a car.

TURBOCHARGED DIESEL
AVAIL.

DIESEL ENGINES OPTIONAL (SINCE 1976)

NISSAN (DATSUN) ENG.

80

new GRILLE, VARIOUS STRIPING COMBINATIONS

914

100,000-MILE, 5-YEAR ENGINE AND BODY WARRANTY

FIGHT BACK WITH SCOUT.
Anything less is just a car.

Our new Turbo-Diesel engine.

Scout Turbo-Diesel fuel economy: 22 EPA EST MPG 24 EST HWY MPG

KAISER Jeep CORPORATION

Toledo, OHIO

'Jeep'

The Flying 'Jeep' Universal

with 4-wheel drive

4-CYL. "HURRICANE" OR V6 160 HP

(V8 AVAIL.)

66

DJ-5 DJ-6 (2WD)
81" OR 101" WB
CJ-5 CJ-6 (4WD)

You've got to drive it to believe it! See your 'Jeep' dealer.

Wagoneer

REAR

110" WB
6 CYL. or V8

NOW! THESE 10 SAFETY FEATURES ARE STANDARD:
☐ Seat belts front and rear
☐ Padded sun visors
☐ Padded dashboard
☐ High-impact windshield
☐ Outside rear-view mirror
☐ Dual brake system
☐ Self adjusting brakes
☐ 4-way warning flashers
☐ Back-up lights
☐ Windshield washer and dual-speed wipers

"Holy Toledo, what a car!"

$2748.

Jeepster

4-CYL. STD.;
101" WB

REAR DETAILS (JEEPSTER)

67

JEEPSTER REVIVED; OTHER MODELS CONT'D.

JEEPSTER AVAIL. THROUGH '72.

4-wheel drive

RDSTR. FROM $2466.

There's a whole family of Jeepsters to choose from...Convertible; Jeepster Commando Station Wagon; Jeepster Commando Pick-up; Jeepster Commando Roadster.

Jeep

UNIVERSAL JEEPS PRICED FROM $2011.

4-wheel drive. **Jeep Wagoneer**

Flip one simple lever for the extra safety of 'Jeep' 4-wheel drive.

68

4-DR. FROM $3702. (2-DR. ALSO AVAIL.) FOR FINAL TIME IN WAGONEER LINE.)

'Jeep'
4-wheel drive
The 2-Car Cars.

CAMPER EASILY REMOVABLE

Away from the camper.

$3112.
Jeepster Commando

69

WITH V-6 ENG.

New family camper for your Jeep' Universal.

FROM $4145.
WAGONEER

NOW MFD. BY
AMERICAN MOTORS

'Jeep'
The 2-Car Car.

Jeepster
COMMANDO
4 CYL. OR V6
$3207.

FROM $4284.

232 CID HI-TORQUE (145 HP @ 4300 RPM) 6 CYL.

CJ-5

70

OPT. DAUNTLESS 350 CID V8 (230 HP @ 4400)

FORMER GRILLE STYLE RETAINED ON **Gladiator** PICKUPS.

Wagoneer

new GRILLE

916

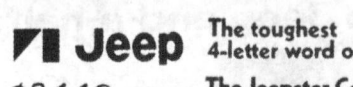
Jeep The toughest 4-letter word on wheels.

$3446.

The Jeepster Commando- it hasn't found a place it can't conquer.

('71)

NOW KNOWN AS **Jeep Commando.** 1973

$3506.
('73)

new COMMANDO GRILLE, 1972

1973 = new DASH, IMPROVED FRONT AXLE-AND-PROP-SHAFT JOINTS. IMPROVED EXH. VALVE SEATS.

1971-72 SLOGAN : " **Jeep guts.** " ('72)

The most famous 4-wheel drive vehicle of them all is now tougher and longer-lasting...believe it or not!

(4-W-D ILLUSTR. ABOVE)

232 CID 6,
258 CID 6,
OR
304
CID V8

CJ FROM $3086

IMPROVED DRIVE TRAIN, CLUTCH LINKAGE, 1973
ALSO FUEL TANK SKID PLATE.

new 84" OR 104" WB ON 1972 UNIVERSAL

Jeep Introduces Automatic 4-Wheel Drive. ('73)

71-73

The Jeep Wagoneer- the first 4-wheel drive family wagon.

FROM $4447.

REAR ('72)

Jeep Wagoneer.

('71)

QUADRA-TRAC—Someday all 4-wheel drive vehicles may have a system like it...Jeep Wagoneer has it now.

WITH GRAINED STRIP

W/O GRAIN note EMBLEM ON FRONT FENDER ('73) 279

1973 = new FULLY-PADDED DASH, new ARM RESTS (FR. and REAR DOORS) FROM $4501.

6 CYL. OR V8

Jeep

"It's a Jeep and-a-half"

New FROM $4211. 6 CYL. 109" WB

LATE MODEL

Jeep CJ-5 "RENEGADE" WITH ROLL BAR

6 OR V8 UNIVERSAL

Cherokee. EARLY MODEL, W. BUMPER GUARDS and LARGE SIDE MIRRORS.

(REPLACES COMMANDO)

74

$3574. STD. CJ-5

standard equipment: • Automatic Transmission P R N D 2 1

Wagoneer: 4-wheel drive (V8 ENGINE)

FROM $5466.

FROM $4099.

FROM $6013. **Wagoneer** V8 (BROADER GRAIN PANEL)

FROM $4851.

Cherokee

DECORATION new on FRONT END OF SIDE TRIM STRIP ON THE **Cherokee™**

75

PHANTOM VIEW OF REAR SECTION (SHOWING LUGGAGE SPACE PROVIDED BEHIND BACK SEAT)

Slogan: "JEEP WROTE THE BOOK ON 4-WHEEL DRIVE."

918

How to tell Jeep's New CJ-7 from the CJ-5

Jeep wrote the book on 4-wheel drive.

Not by driving! CJ-7 and CJ-5 both take on the toughest trails with traditional rugged JEEP® vehicle performance. To tell a CJ-7, look for:

Automatic transmission: Now available for the first time in a CJ vehicle.

Quadra-Trac®: Our optional automatic 4-wheel drive system that gives you exceptional control—without shifting.

Longer wheelbase: A 93.5" wheelbase gives you a smoother, more comfortable ride on-road or off.

New doors: All metal with roll-down windows, and vinyl door trim panels that give added insulation and extra protection from the weather.

Extra room: Enough extra room to take along 2 sleeping bags, a cook stove, water can, lanterns and a few other good things. Plus CJ-7 has a steel liftgate that allows easy access to cargo.

— 93.5 —

CJ 'Jeep'

One piece injection molded top: A CJ-7 can be topped off with this sturdy removable hard top that is as good looking as it is durable (Choose black or white.)

AVAIL. AS CJ-5 OR CJ-7

(SAME DECORATION STILL AVAIL. ON 1979 GOLD. EAGLE.)

76 - 77

('76) **Wagoneer**
STANDARD $6399.
CUSTOM 6572.

Cherokee "CHIEF"

Jeep Cherokee Chief

Cherokee Chief

"Wagoneer" NAME

('77)

Wagoneer

$7695.

('77)

The golden eagle Limited Edition Jeep CJ's

(new in 1977)

Jeep
we wrote the book on 4-wheel drive

Jeep

$ 6675.

Introducing the Jeep Wagoneer Limited

Jeep Wrote the Book on 4-Wheel Drive

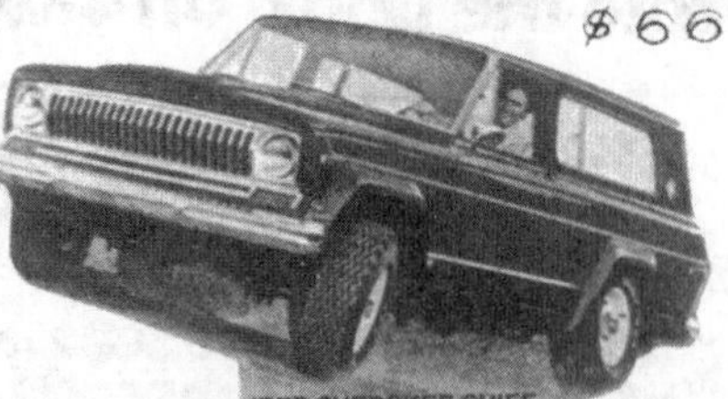

CHEROKEE
4-DR.
ALSO AVAIL.
(SINCE '77)

JEEP CHEROKEE CHIEF
Bold black accent striping, featuring "Cherokee Chief"; big all-terrain tires and flared fenders set this beauty apart.

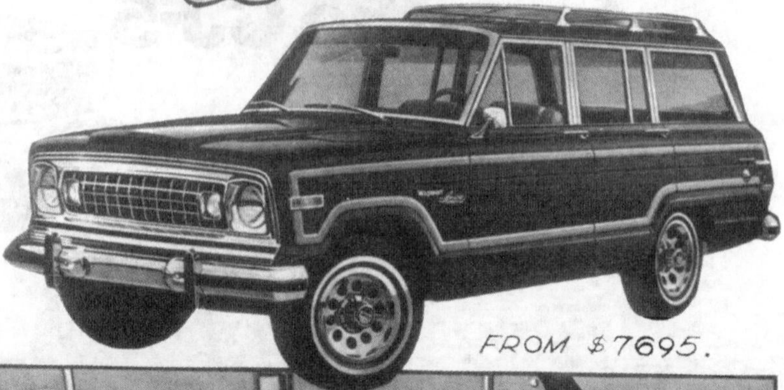

FROM $ 7695.

JEEP CJ-7 RENEGADE
Racy "Renegade" hood striping; styled steel wheels; big all-terrain tires. Available on both CJ-5 and CJ-7.

6 CYL.
(V8 = $ 186. EXTRA)

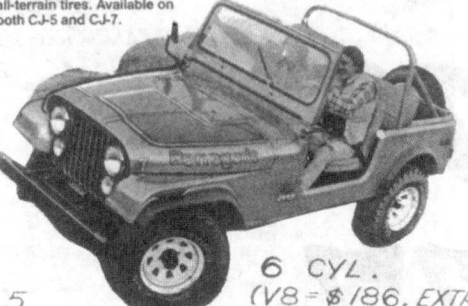

CJ-5
BASIC
$ 4995.

CJ-7
BASIC SOFT-TOP
$ 5095.
BASIC HARDTOP
$ 5705.

78

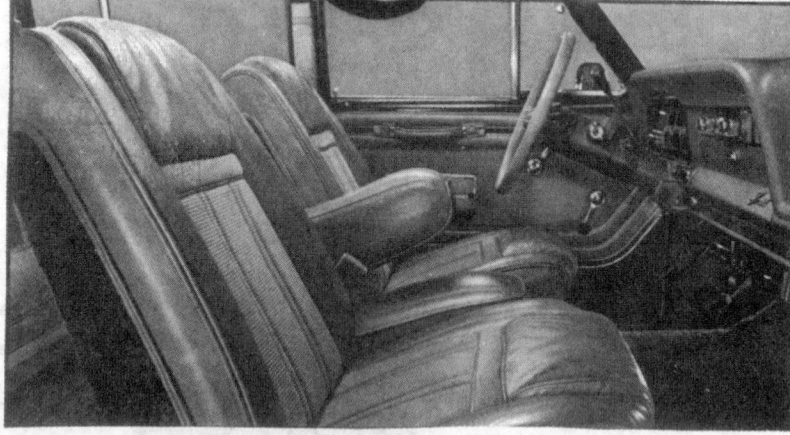

CJ-5 UNIVERSAL
PRICED FROM $ 5858.

79

new GRILLES
ON
CHEROKEE, WAGONEER

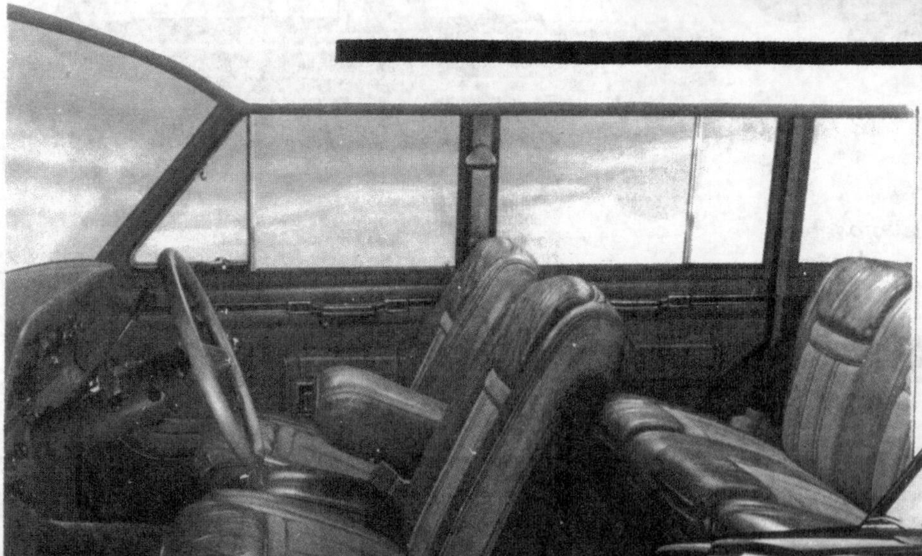

INTERIOR

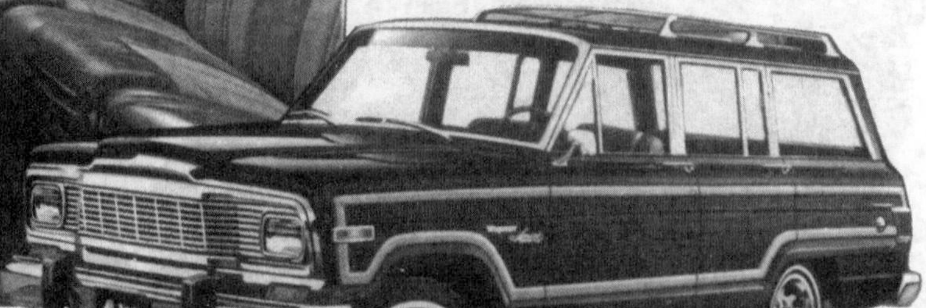

$ 9156.

Jeep Wagoneer Limited

Jeep
We wrote the book on 4-wheel drive

Jeep

Jeep CJ

Who says economy has to be dull?

UNIVERSAL JEEP (RENEGADE MODEL)

NEW HIGH EFFICIENCY GEAR RATIOS
Redesigned for 1980 for greater fuel efficiency without sacrificing the Jeep CJ's high-power performance capabilities.

note THAT RENEGADE STRIPING PATTERNS CHANGE FROM YEAR TO YEAR.

80

15 EPA EST MPG 20 HWY EST MPG

Introducing a feisty, new 4-cylinder engine and power train that deliver an EPA estimated MPG of 21 and a highway estimate of 25.*

(4 CYL. PREVIOUSLY AVAIL. UNTIL 1971)

CJ FEATURES

NEW UPGRADED 4-SPEED TRANSMISSION
Now standard! Four speeds mean greater versatility on-road and off! And greater fuel economy, too!

FREE WHEELING HUBS
Standard for 1980! Lets you disengage front wheels when 4-wheel drive is not needed — one more way to save gas!

Cherokee

We wrote the book on 4-wheel drive.

19 HWY EST MPG 15 EPA EST MPG

Jeep Wagoneer *Limited*
The ultimate wagon

new WHEELS; POSITION OF COWL LETTERING CHANGED

921

Lincoln
Continental

(LINCOLN EST. 1920 : '21 MODEL)

Ford | **MERCURY LINCOLN**

BY **Ford Motor Company.** SINCE 1922

HOOD ORNAMENT

126" WB
new 462 CID V8
(340 HP)
9.15 × 15 TIRES

4-DR.

$ 6383.

$ 6118.

H/T (new)

66

FENDER-TIP LTS. DISCONTINUED UNTIL 1968

FRONT END DETAILS

4-DR. CVT. $ 7016.

Lincoln Continental for 1966: unmistakably new, yet unmistakably Continental

(LEATHER UPH. STD. IN CVT., $111 EXTRA IN OTHERS)

(INTRO. 9-30-66)

2-DR. H/T
(WITHOUT VINYL TOP)
$ 6185.

67

GRILLE SLIGHTLY CHANGED, and EMBLEM REMOVED FROM SIDE OF FRONT FENDER

4-DR.
(WITH VINYL TOP)

4-DR., STD. TOP
$ 6427.
(VINYL LANDAU TOP $132. EXTRA)

1967 IS FINAL YEAR FOR THE 4-DOOR CONVERTIBLE.

2-DR. H/T, BELOW $6400. (STD.) ($6537. w. LANDAU TOP)

A VARIETY OF HUB CAP

new AM/FM STEREO ($244 EXTRA)

Wraparound parking lights and taillights

new coupe roof line.

$6634.

DETAILS OF new GRILLE

RAISED HOOD ORNAMENT ELIMINATED (UNTIL 1972)

EMBLEM REPLACES NAME ABOVE GRILLE, DURING 1968

new SAFETY SIDE LIGHTS

68 (INTRO. 9-22-67)

new BROAD STEER. WH. HUB, DARKER-COLORED DASH

new REAR STYLING

2 SERIES NOW AVAIL.

69

(INTRO. 9-27-68)
new GRILLE WITH CONTINENTAL NAME ABOVE. (126" WB)

new "COMPUTER DESIGNED" 460 C/D V8 (365 HP)

(NO 4-DR. MK. TYPES UNTIL 1980 MK. VI)

$ 7423.

4-DR.: $6876.

Continental

(2-DR. $6495.)

(NEW)

The Continental Mark III.

(INTRODUCED 4-5-68)
(COMPLETELY new AND UNIQUE FRONT STYLING, and 117.2" WB

(INTRO. 9-19-69)

STD. CONTINENTAL GETS new 127" WB, new GRILLE

2-DR.

4-DR.

Mark III CONTINUES WITH 1969 STYLING, THROUGH '71.

FRONT SIDE LIGHTS NOW MOVED DOWN TO ENDS OF BUMPER (ON STD. SERIES, THROUGH 1973)

new 225 x 15 TIRES

70

new BROAD GRILLE WITH HORIZONTAL PCS.; new CONCEALED HEADLIGHTS

924

LINCOLN CONTINENTAL

Continental: the final step up.

The Town Car.
(new)

TOWN CAR

TOWN CAR MODEL
CARRIES DESIGNATION
ON
SIDE

GOLDEN
ANNIV.
MODELS

71

(INTRO.
9-18-
70)
FR. $7016.

new NARROWER GRILLE

STD. CONTINENTAL STYLING
SIMILAR TO ABOVE "TOWN CAR"

new CRISS-CROSS
GRILLE PCS.

Continental

$7068 (2 DR.)
7302 (4-DR.)

new GRILLE

72

(INTRO. 9-17-71)

HP CUT
TO 224

MK. IV
$8640

(MK.
IV
REPLACES
MK. III)
new 120.4" WB

(new) CONTINENTAL MARK IV

WITH BIG *new* GRILLE THAT DIPS
INTO BUMPER (1972 ONLY)

HP RATING BACK TO
365 AGAIN

CONTINENTAL MARK IV

LINCOLN CONTINENTAL

NOTE *new*
SAFETY
BUMPERS
(ON *BOTH*
MODEL SERIES)

73

8832.

$7474.

CONT. NAME ABOVE GRILLE
(FIRST TIME SINCE 1969)

MK.IV
$9574.
(10,265.
LATER IN
YR.)

LINCOLN CONTINENTAL

REAR

74

new GRILLE (CONTINTL.)

230 R 15
TIRES

MARK IV

DASH

FROM
$7727.
($8309.
LATER IN
YR.)

CONTINENTAL

235 x 15
TIRES

CONTINENTAL TOWN COUPÉ

DASH

CONTINENTAL NAME ON
REAR FENDER

75

460 CID V8
NOW RATED
AT 206 HP

CONTINENTAL TOWN CAR

new
GRILLE

FROM
$9214.

LINCOLN CONTINENTAL
CONTINENTAL MARK IV

DASH

new WHEEL COVERS

MARK IV

$11,082.

75 (CONT'D)

new MID-SIDE PROTECTIVE TRIM MOLDING (CONT. and MK. IV)

230R15 TIRES (all MODELS)

new BAND OVER ROOF (CONTINENTAL TOWN MODELS)

CONTINENTAL

76

127.2" WB

STD. 2-DR. $9142. (4-DR. $9293.)

TOWN CAR

CLOSER DETAIL OF COACH LAMPS AND TRIM

230R15 TIRES

927 (CONT'D. NEXT PAGE)

LINCOLN CONTINENTAL
CONTINENTAL MARK IV

(new MK. IV DESIGNER SER. w. SPEC. PAINT and INT. by DESIGNER FOR WHICH NAMED)

GIVENCHY (BELOW)

(TURQUOISE and WHITE)

76 (CONT'D)

PUCCI
(BURGUNDY and SILVER)

The Givenchy Edition Mark IV

CARTIER
(PEARL GRAY)

BILL BLASS
(BLUE and CREAM)

(USUAL $11,060 MK. TYPES CONTINUE ALSO)

FR. $12,560.

Introducing the Mark IV Designer Series

new MARK V

new 400 CID V8 *(173 HP)*

PUCCI
(BLACK and WHITE)

GIVENCHY
(DARK JADE and CHAMOIS)

(DES. = $12,996. UP)
(STD. = 11,396.)

BILL BLASS
(MIDNIGHT BLUE and PIGSKIN)

77
(RESTYLED)

CARTIER
(DOVE GRAY)

new TRIPLE COWL LOUVRES

928

LINCOLN VERSAILLES
(new) 110" WB

(VERSAILLES AVAIL. 1977-1980)

('79)
('80 VERS. SIMILAR)

$14,169 in 1980

('77)
302 CID V8 IN VERSAILLES (351 CID AVAIL. OUTSIDE CALIF. IN '77)

VERSAILLES INTERIOR ('77) →

An investment in engineering.

77-79

400 CID V8 CONT.

LINCOLN CONTINENTAL

('78)
FROM $9974. ('78) 10,985. ('79)

(FINAL LARGE-SIZED MODELS IN 1979)

('78)
STD. CONT'L. NOW USES MARK V-TYPE UPRIGHT GRILLE.

78-79

4 "DESIGNER EDITIONS" CONTINUE, WITH *new* COLORS. $13,899. ('78) 14,592. ('79)

MARK V

SOME CONT. and MK. V 1979s KNOWN AS "COLLECTOR'S SERIES"

('79)

('78)

$20,099.

1978 DIAMOND JUBILEE EDITION

CONTINENTAL WITH EXPOSED HEADLIGHTS 117.4" WB

TOWN COUPÉ

TOWN CAR

302 CID V8

$13,840.

17 **EPA EST. MPG 24 EST. HWY MPG

ELECTRONIC DASH

117.4" WB 4-PA.

SIGNATURE SERIES

R. $21,424.

80 new SIZE 114" WB (2-DR.)

MARK VI

DESIGNER SERIES CONTINUES; BLASS MODEL RESEMBLES A CONVERTIBLE IN 1979 and 1980

FR. $15,236.

(SINCE 1939)

Mercury

390 CID V8 (265 or 275 HP)
410 CID V8 (330 HP)
428 CID V8 (345 HP)

MERCURY
LINCOLN
Ford

LINCOLN-MERCURY
DIVISION OF
Ford Motor Co

123" WB
(119", WAGONS)

PARK
LANE
CVT.

$4039.

Dual-Action Tailgate. Swings down like a regular tailgate
for cargo. Or swings aside like a door for people.

COLONY
PARK
WAGON

walnut-toned paneling.

2-SEAT=$3893.; 3-9SEAT=$3988.
(UNGRAINED COMMUTER
WAGONS
ALSO
AVAIL.)

VINYL TOP
AVAIL.

66

MONTEREY, MONTCLAIR,
PARK LANE, S-55
MODELS

PARK LANE 4-DR. H/T
$3892.

MONTEREY
2-DR.
$3217.

Move ahead with

Mercury

in the Lincoln Continental tradition

2.8
TO 3.5
GEAR RATIOS
8.15 × 15 TIRES

931

Mercury

Mercury, the Man's Car.

(INTRO. 9-30-66)

STD. 390 CID V8 has new 270 HP.

wagon

67

new PROTRUDING CENTER SECTION OF FRONT END

new BROUGHAM and MARQUIS MODELS. S-55 DISCONTINUED.

FRONT END DETAILS

PRICES START AT $3297.

(uncommon)

PREMIERE CPE.

First hardtop with yacht-deck vinyl paneling.

PARK LANE

new FRONT CORNERING and REAR SIDE LTS.

68 (INTRO. 9-22-67)

new GRILLE

(FINAL YR. FOR COMMUTER WAGON)

1968

Mercury

new 124" WB
(121" ON MARAUDER, WAGONS)

STD. 390 CID V8
(265/280 HP)

COLONY PARK

(new MONTEREY, MONTEREY CUSTOM WAGONS ALSO AVAIL.)

the new MARQUIS. (now INCLUDES ADDITIONAL BODY TYPES)

MARQUIS
429 CID V8
(320 HP)

2-DR. H/T
$4098.

69
(INTRO. 9-27-68)

(new MARQUIS BROUGHAM ALSO AVAIL.)

new CONCEALED HEADLIGHTS ON MARQUIS, MARAUDER

8.25/8.55 × 15 TIRES

note OWN REAR STYLING ON new MARAUDER (X-100)

2-DR. H/T
429 CID V8
(360 HP)

Lincoln-Mercury leads the way

$4270.

933

(MONTEREY and MTY. CUSTOM have ONE-TIER HORIZ. GRILLE and 4 EXPOSED HDLTS.)

Mercury

Marquis Colony Park

(FINAL FULL-SIZED MERCURY CONVERTIBLES)

70 (INTRO. 9-19-69)

VERTICAL PCS ADDED TO GRILLE

Marquis

DETAILS

4-DR. H/T

G78 × 15 TIRES
H78 × 15, WAGONS

new 351 CID V8 (240 HP)
new 400 CID V8 (260 HP)
429 CID V8 (320 HP)

Marquis

FRONT END CLOSE-UP

GRILLE NOW ENTIRELY ABOVE BUMPER

71

Better ideas make better cars.

(INTRO. 9-18-70)

934

Mercury

DASH (MONTEREY CUSTOM)

MONTEREY $4391.

note SMALL HUB CAPS

REAR (MONTEREY)

MONTEREY CUSTOM **H/T** $4530. (*has* CHROME STRIP ALONG MID-SIDE)

VARIOUS MONTEREY TYPES *have* EXPOSED HEADLIGHTS

H.P. CUT:
351 CID V8 (163 HP)
400 CID V8 (172 HP)
429 CID V8 (208 HP)

72
new "WAFFLE" GRILLE PATTERN

(INTRO. 9-17-71)

COLONY PARK ($5045. (2-SEAT) 5167. (4-SEAT)

Better ideas make better cars:

Marquis
4-DR. H/T $5132.

Mercury's **ride rated better than a $34,000 limousine by 36 out of 50 professional chauffeurs.**

MARQUIS BROUGHAM PILLARED 4-DR. H/T $5400.

DASH (MARQUIS BROUGHAM)

3-SPOKE STEERING WHEEL

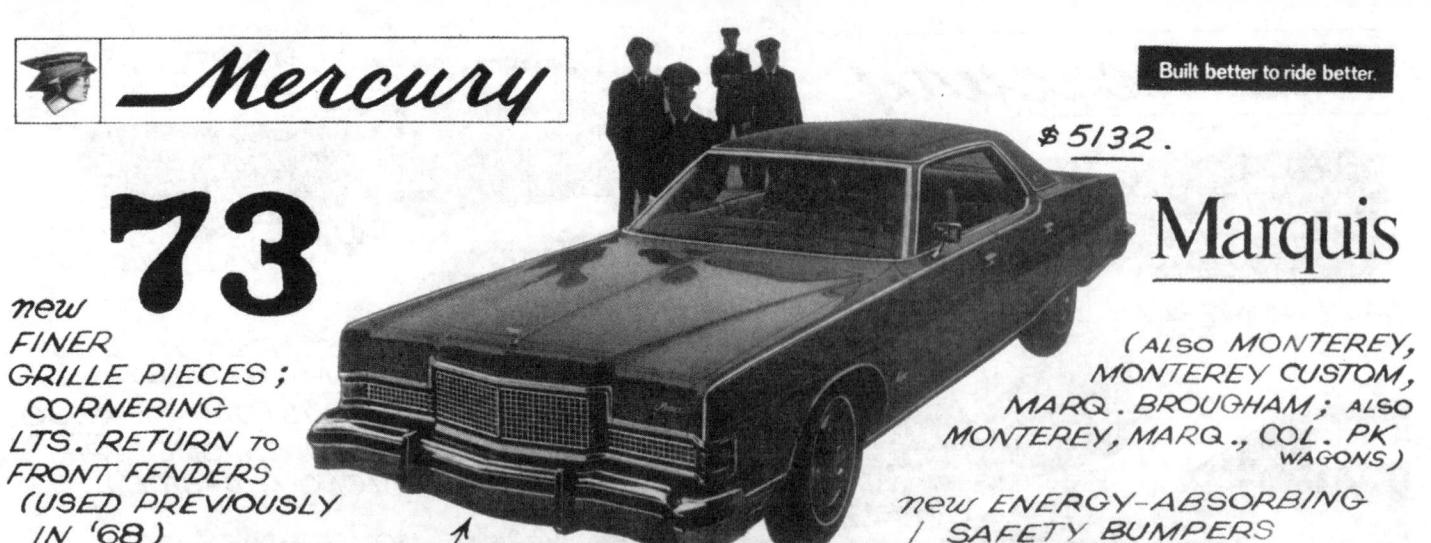

Mercury

Built better to ride better.

73

new FINER GRILLE PIECES; CORNERING LTS. RETURN TO FRONT FENDERS (USED PREVIOUSLY IN '68)

$ 5132.

Marquis

(ALSO MONTEREY, MONTEREY CUSTOM, MARQ. BROUGHAM; ALSO MONTEREY, MARQ., COL. PK WAGONS)

new ENERGY-ABSORBING SAFETY BUMPERS

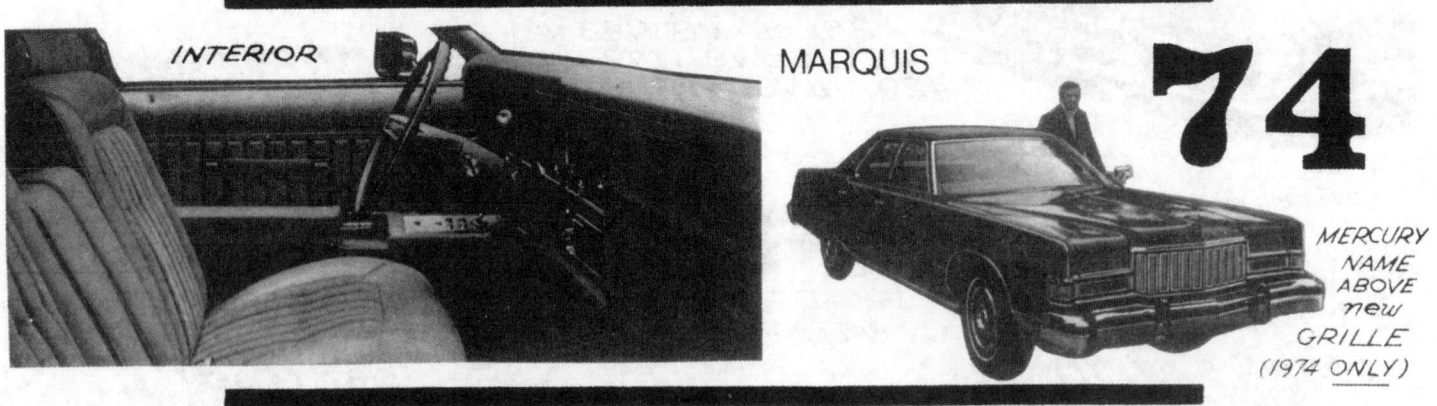

INTERIOR

MARQUIS

74

MERCURY NAME ABOVE new GRILLE (1974 ONLY)

---

new HEADLIGHT COVERS, new GRILLE, HIGHER CORNER LIGHTS

MARQUIS

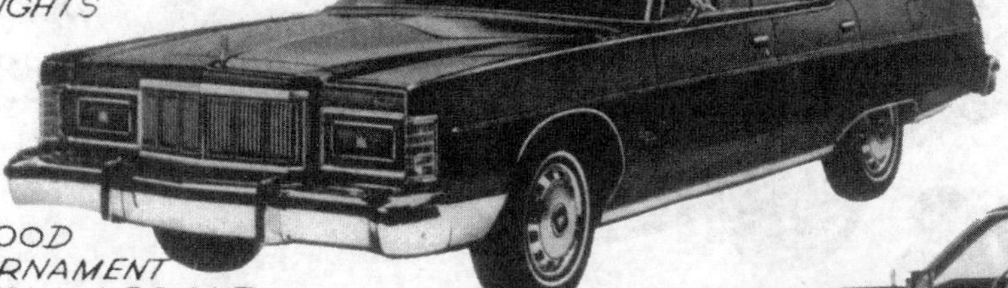

HOOD ORNAMENT NOW UPRIGHT

MARQUIS WAGON

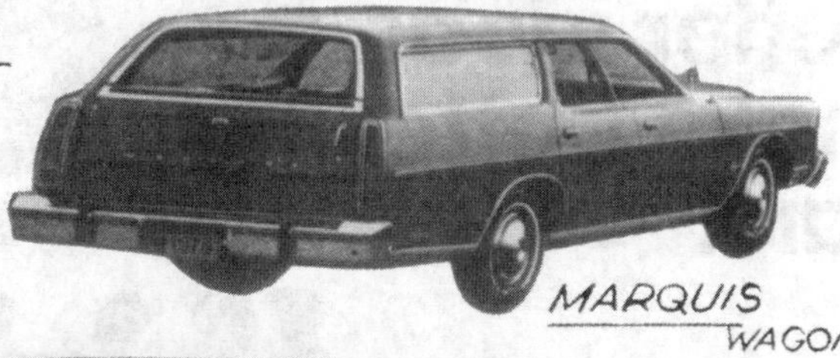

75-78

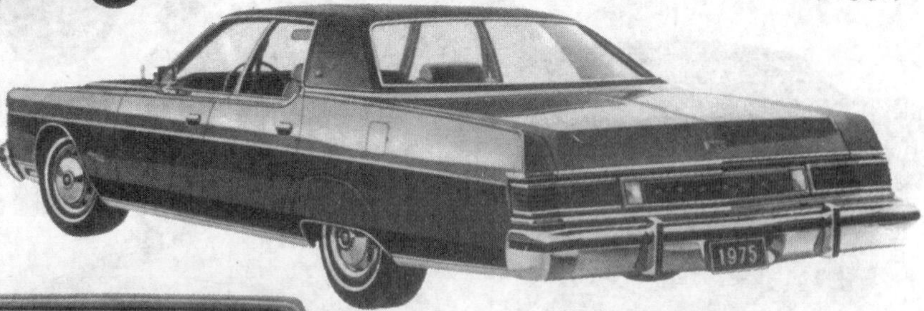

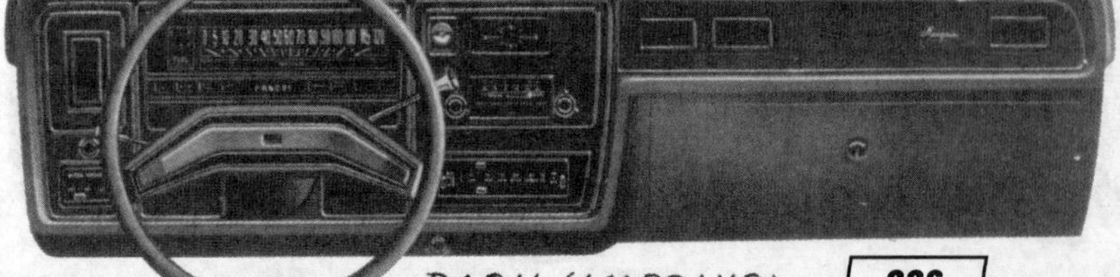

1978 MARQUIS has SIDE TRIM LIKE GRAND MARQUIS

(CONT'D. NEXT PAGE)

DASH (MARQUIS)

Mercury GRAND MARQUIS

GRAND MARQUIS DASH *has* SWIRLED WOOD-GRAIN VINYL TRIM

75-78 (CONT'D.)

COLONY PARK

GRAND MARQUIS

DASH PLAQUE ('77)

'RIDE-ENGINEERED by LINCOLN MERCURY

DETAILS OF *new* UPRIGHT HOOD ORNAMENT INTRO. 1975

1979 MARQUIS *has* EXTRA CHROME STRIP ALONG MID-SIDE

all-new 1979 Mercury Marquis $6755.

79

RESTYLED AND DOWN-SIZED

302 OR 351 CID V8   new 114.4" WB

new RECTANGULAR EXPOSED HEADLIGHTS

INTERIOR

MARQ., COL. PK. WAGONS AVAIL.

GRAND MARQUIS $8186.

Mercury

$7328. MARQUIS $8129. (MR. BROUGH.)

LUXURY WHEEL COVER

15" FULL WHEEL COVER

P205/75R×14 TIRES (P215/75R×14, WAGONS)

80

MINOR TRIM CHANGES IN SOME TYPES, *new* AUTOMATIC OVERDRIVE TRANS. AVAIL.

COLONY PARK

FROM $8408.

UNGRAINED MARQUIS STATION WAGON ALSO AVAIL.

GRAND MARQUIS TWO-DOOR.

$8658.

4-DR. $8846.

WIRE WHEEL COVERS

RED CENTER ON '79 TYPE, BLACK ON '80 (PERTAINS TO WIRE ONLY)

GRAND MARQUIS.

DASH

note COURTESY LT. and BAND OVER ROOF

CAST ALUMINUM TURBINE SPOKE WHEELS

"RESUME" SWITCH AVAIL. SINCE 1979

FRONT DETAILS

938

MERCURY Bobcat (1975 – 1980)

140 CID 4 (92 HP) (ALSO AVAIL., STARTING '76 171 CID V6, 100 HP)

94½" WB

3-DOOR RUNABOUT

3-DR. FROM $3456. ('75)

('75)

DASH

24 TO 29 MPG HWY. 17 TO 19 MPG CITY ('75)

(QUITE SIMILAR TO FORD PINTO)

('75)

FROM $3748. ('75)

VILLAGER WAGON

75-78

1976 = IMITATION CHERRY WOODGRAIN OPT. ON RUNABOUT, AT $3809.

1977 = new EXTRUDED ALUMINUM BUMPERS; new ALL-GLASS HATCHBACK DOOR, MOON-ROOF, 4-WAY ADJUSTABLE DRIVER'S SEAT ARE OPTIONAL

REAR

1978 is the year to LOVE THAT BOBCAT. More standard features than last year for a lower sticker price.*

a. Steel-belted radials now standard.
b. Styled-steel wheels with trim rings now standard.
c. Power front-disc brakes now standard.
d. Tinted glass now standard.
e. Front stabilizer bar now standard.

('78)

UNGRAINED WAGON also AVAIL. SINCE 1977.

Bobcat wagons come with all the same standard features.

939

MERCURY BOBCAT

WHEEL and WHEEL COVER CHOICES →

('79)
$4104.
UP

3-DOOR RUNABOUT

1980

w. SPORTS ACCENT GROUP ('80)

WITH SPORTS PACKAGE OPTION ('79)

new GRILLE **79-80**

WITH SPORT OPTION ('80)

140 CID 4 OR 171 CID V6
BR 78 × 13 TIRES

OPTIONAL SPORTS INSTRUMENTATION DASH

STD. VINYL INT. ('80)

RECTANGLE DASH CLUSTER ←

('80)

BOBCAT AND VILLAGER WAGONS

('79)

VILLAGER
$4519. ('79)
4950. ('80)
(REPLACED BY 1981 LYNX)

ROSEWOOD-TONE and WOODTONE GRAIN

MERCURY COMET

Custom Sports-Coupe

(1960 – 1977)
(COMET NAME NOT USED IN 1970)

There are 13 models convertibles, wagons, hardtops, sedans.

new 116" WB (WAGONS 113")

MERCURY — Ford — LINCOLN

Completely equipped with white-walls, deluxe wheel covers, vinyl interiors, wall-to-wall carpeting, heater-defroster, seat belts (front and rear), emergency flasher, lots more.

$2908.   Comet Caliente

$3168.

'Performance Car of the Year' Named Pace Car For Memorial Day 500

Official PACE CAR   Mercury COMET CYCLONE GT   INDIANAPOLIS 500

6.95/7.35/7.75 × 14 TIRES

66

new GRILLES

OPT. DUAL HOOD SCOOPS

CYCLONE H/T $3028.

"Performance Car of the Year"

$3510.

200 CID 6 (120 HP)
289 CID V8 (200 HP)
390 CID V8s
(265, 275 OR 335 HP) OR
427 CID V8

Cyclone GT

has BODY STRIPES

$3250.

Mercury COMET

Mercury COMET

HORIZ.-GROOVED DASH →

CALIENTE

$2994.

7.35/ × 7.75 × 14 TIRES

Caliente Grandé interior has blue Gossamer nylon or Chambrey nylon in black or parchment. Both framed with crinkle vinyl.

Mercury, the Man's Car.

67
(INTRO. 9-30-66)

202, CAPRI, CALIENTE, CYCLONE, CYCLONE GT

CYCLONE GT

$3386.

$3290.

CYCLONE GT (INTRO. 9-22-67)

(RESTYLED)

68

NOTE new SIDE SAFETY LTS.

new MONTEGO

MONTEGO MX

$3135.

116" WB
200 CID 6 (115 HP) OR
289 CID V8 (195 HP)

Mercury COMET

STD. ENGINES : *new* 250 CID 6 (155 HP) OR 302 CID V8 (220 HP)

69

V8s UP TO 428 CID (INTRO. 9-27-68)

MONTEGO

H/T $3070. UP

(STD. COMET H/T $2997.)

1969 COMET and MONTEGO SHARE THIS GRILLE.

COMET NAME UNUSED IN '70.

MONTEGO, MONTEGO MX, MONTEGO MX BROUGHAM, CYCLONE, CYCL. GT *and* CYCL. SPOILER MODELS AVAIL. (INTRO. 9-19-69)

70 *new* PROTRUDING-CENTER FRONT END WITH ODD *new* GRILLE

Password for action

(SPOILER GRILLE LIKE GT, BUT has EXPOSED HEADLIGHTS.)

(New)

WITH CJ 429 CID V8 (370 HP) $4365.

Cyclone Spoiler.

351 CID OR 429 CID V8 (360 HP) $3996.

'70 Mercury Cyclone GT.
with the accent on action.

(MONTEGO ON NEXT PAGE)

943

STD. ENG. IS 250 CID 6 (155 HP @ 4000 RPM) OR 302 CID V8

H/Ts FROM $3511.

Mercury presents Montego 1970. The action intermediate with the accent on luxury.

70 (CONT'D.)

Montego

2 or 4 doors, "6" or V-8

COMET

170 CID OR 250 CID 6 (100, 115 OR 145 HP) 302 CID V8 (210 HP)

103" WB (2-DR.) 109.9" (4-DR.)

SALE $2276.

SALE $2217.

Comet RETURNS

COMET DASH

71 (INTRO. 9-11-70)

VINYL TOP OPTIONAL

Comet GT. SALE $2395.80

(MONTEGO ON NEXT PAGE)

Better ideas make better cars. The better small car.

22 MPG (6 CYL., CITY/HWY.)

Mercury COMET

Better ideas make better cars:

Printed electrical circuits in instrument cluster

Energy-absorbing steering column with locking features

Woodgrain vinyl paneling on the dash

Head restraints

Flow-thru ventilation

$2798

Dual brake system, self-adjusting brakes

Front tread 60.5"

Overall length 209.9"

Exhaust emission control system

Bias-belted tires

Rear tread 60.0"

(STD. CPE. NO SIDE CHROME) **Montego**

71
(CONT'D.)

(REGULAR PRICE, 2-DR. 3694. UP)

117" WB (114" ON WAGONS)

250 CID 6 (145 HP)
302 CID V8 (210 HP)
F78 × 14 TIRES
(G78 × 14, WAGONS)

INTERIOR

REAR

ALL MODEL SERIES AVAIL. IN 1970 ARE CONTINUED. 1971 IS FINAL YR. FOR CYCLONE TYPES.

CENTER OF HOOD PROTRUDES AS BEFORE, BUT MONTEGO _has new_ STANDARD GRILLE WITH CRISS-CROSS PIECES _and_ EXPOSED HEADLIGHTS.

MONTEGO CYCLONE GT

STANDARD CYCLONE ENGINE: 351 CID V8 (285 HP @ 5400 RPM)

GT GRILLE QUITE SIMILAR TO 1970 GT, BUT _has_ new "GT" LETTERING IN CENTER CIRCLE.

1971

Mercury Comet

COMET DASH

A BETTER IDEA FOR SAFETY: BUCKLE UP.

4-DR. (STD.) $2474.
6.45 x 14 TIRES

COMET

Comet GT
$2595.

4-DR. WITH EXTERIOR DECOR GROUP OPTION

72 FRONT RESTYLED ON MONTEGOS

(INTRO. 9-17-71)

MONTEGO
Mercury Montego 2-Door Hardtop

Better ideas make better cars.

note GT HOOD SCOOPS

MONTEGOS: new 114" WB (118" 4-DR.)   H/T $3639.

302 CID V8 (140 HP) STD. ENG.

MONTEGO GT FASTBACK 2-DR. H/T $4137.

note GT LOUVRES (3)

Mercury Montego MX Brougham

MX DASH
MX 4-DR. PILLARED H/T

$3918.

$3742.

946

Mercury COMET

MX WAGON
(UNGRAINED)
Montego MX

2-SEAT
$4055.

3-SEAT
$4131.

72(CONT'D.)

302 CID V8 STD. ON WAGONS
(ROOF RACK OPTIONAL)

MX
VILLAGER

2-SEAT $4229.
3-SEAT 4305.

F 78 × 14 TIRES

Built better to ride better.
MERCURY MONTEGO

MONTEGO MX
BROUGHAM 4-DR.
$3928.

73

(FINAL YR. FOR MONT.
GT FASTBACK)

LARGE new ENERGY-ABSORBING
SAFETY BUMPERS.

2-DR.
H/Ts:
MONTEGO
$3649.
MONTEGO MX
$3772.
MONTEGO MX
BROUGHAM
$3938.

(COMET PRICES FROM
$3122.)

74

Mercury Montego

GRILLE MOTIF
NO LONGER CONT'D.
AROUND
HEADLIGHTS.

MONTEGO TIRE SIZES:
G/H/HR 78 × 14

MONTEGO 2-DRS.
PRICED FROM $4162.

new
REAR QUARTER
OPERA
WINDOWS ON
MX BROUGHAM
2-DR
$4481.

(INTERIOR ALSO
ILLUSTRATED)

Montego MX Brougham with optional
Custom Trim, radio, remote control mirror,
opera windows, white sidewall tires
and bumper protection group.

Mercury COMET

4-DR. $3453.

Mercury Comet with Custom Option

Mercury Comet

200 CID 6 (78 HP)

new BUMPER SLOTS

COMET 2-DRS. FROM $3419. (GT PKG. $277.)

Mercury Comet standard interior in cloth-and-vinyl

75

new DUAL SLOTS IN FRONT BUMPERS

MX VILLAGER WAGON (FROM $5450.)

MX BRGHM. INT.

Mercury Montego MX

MX H/T $4845.

REAR

351 CID V8 (150 HP) IN MONTEGOS

2-DR. H/Ts (4-DR. AVAIL. ALSO)

$4994.

Custom Trim Option instrument panel for Montego MX Brougham

Mercury Montego MX Brougham—Custom Trim Option

Mercury COMET

4-DR. $3633.

2-DR. WITH OPTIONAL SPORTS ACCENT GROUP and SPORTS VINYL ROOF

200 CID 6 (78 HP) (250 CID 6 OR 302 CID V8 AVAIL.)

C 78 × 14 TIRES

(BASIC 2-DR. PRICE: $3566.)

76

SLIGHT CHANGE IN COMET GRILLE and AUX. LTS.

Comet Custom interior option

COMET WITH CUSTOM OPTION

FINAL COMETS AVAIL. INTO 1977 SEASON.

IMITATION CHERRY WOODGRAIN ON MONTEGO MX VILLAGER

2-SEAT = $5626.
3-SEAT = 5734.

MONTEGO

4-DR. $4904.

351 CID V8 (154 HP) (400 OR 460 CID V8 OPT.)

MONTEGO DISCONTINUED AT END OF 1976 MODEL RUN.

MX Villager standard interior

A distinctive note: Opera window

(MX BROUGHAM 2-DR.)

MONTEGO MX 2-DR. H/T $5026.

Mercury Cougar (STARTS 1967)

$ 3213.

New

111" WB
289 CID V8
(200 HP)
7.35 × 14 TIRES
390 CID V8
(320 HP) IN "GT
PERFORMANCE GRP."

67

COUGAR ADVERTISING
MASCOT

WITH *TRIP*
ODOMETER

XR-7 $ 3443.

has GRAINED DASH
and BEARS
THIS SYMBOL

XR7

note EMBLEM
ON HEADLIGHT
COVER SECTION

COUGAR

950

MERCURY COUGAR

E 70 × 14 TIRES
289 CID V8 STD.
427 CID V8 (390 HP)
IN GT.E

(GT MODEL ALSO)

electric sunroof

$3296.

68

$3594.

XR-7-G has SPORT-STYLE HOOD and RALLYE LIGHTS (GT.E has HORIZ. BAND ACROSS GRILLE)

new SAFETY SIDE LIGHTS

FROM $3383.

1969½ "ELIMINATOR" (not illustr.) has new FRONT and REAR SPOILERS.

VARIOUS V8s AVAIL., INCLUDING new 351 CID V8 (250 HP @ 4600 RPM)
E 78 × 14 TIRES

69

new DOWNSWEPT SIDE SCULPTURE

new GRILLE

(new STD. or XR-7 CONVERTIBLES ALSO AVAIL.)

MERCURY COUGAR XR-7

$4170.

A RETURN OF DOWNWARD EXTENSION OF HOOD AT CENTER, AS IN 1968.

note THAT XR-7 GRILLE DIFFERS FROM STANDARD 1970 COUGAR GRILLE SEEN ON "HOUNDSTOOTH" MODEL BELOW

FROM $3871.

'70

new GRILLES.
"ELIMINATOR" has HOOD SCOOP and STRIPES, BODY STRIPES and BLACK GRILLE)

CLOSER VIEW OF HOUNDSTOOTH TOP COVERING

It's wild. It's sophisticated. It's elegant. The sporty look of houndstooth for spring. Cougar sets the trend with houndstooth check vinyl roof and hi-back cloth-and-vinyl buckets. Designer Pauline Trigère comes up with a swaggering houndstooth cape to match. Cougar... far more than just a sporty car. It's styled with European flair. Lean and sculptured, with concealed headlamps and sequential rear turn signals. Powered by a restless 351 cubic-inch V-8. It's the best

INTERIOR

Introducing the Houndstooth Cougar...

"HOUNDSTOOTH" MODEL STARTS SPRING, 1970

with a little something to match by Pauline Trigère.

952

MERCURY COUGAR

DASH

351 CID V8
CUT FR. 240
TO 164 HP FOR
1972.
CONVERTIBLE
('72)

new 112" WB

XR-7

('71)

(RESTYLED)

71-72

XR-7 ROUND EMBLEM
(OTHERWISE,
EMBLEM IS UPRIGHT
RECTANGULAR.)

953

MERCURY COUGAR

(PRICED FROM $3821., AFTER 1972 PRICE CUTS)

SUNROOF DETAILS

new GRILLE STYLED LIKE A "RADIATOR"

(FINAL COUGAR CONVERTS.)

DASH

XR-7

73

$4152.

It's not like anybody else's car.

INT.

1974 DASH (1975 has new 2-SPOKE STEERING WHEEL.)

1975 and 1976 have 2 OPENINGS IN LOWER CENTER SECTION OF FRONT BUMPER

XR-7

new REAR QUARTER OPERA WINDOWS

74-76

('74)

new UPHOLSTERY PATTERN XR-7, '74

new ORNAMENT

1974, WITHOUT BUMPER OPENINGS
new GRILLE

new AND ENLARGED SERIES

MERCURY COUGAR

PRICED FROM
$5284. ('77)

$5631.
('78)

2 New Hardtops

FOR
1977
ONLY,
2 New Wagons

77-78

(351 CID V8, 161 HP IN
WAGONS)

2 New Sedans

2-DRS.
114" WB
4-DRS.
118" WB
302 CID V8
(130 HP)

(RESTYLED)

('77)

**Introducing a new symbol of driving excitement.
The 1977 Cougar XR-7 unleashes 6 new running mates.**

XR-7

FINAL COUGAR DASH
WITH ROUND GAUGES

302 OR 351 CID V8

79

STD.
H/T
$6165.

BODY-COLOR TAPE
STRIPS IN XR-7
GRILLE

NEW TAILLIGHTS
WITH HORIZONTAL
CHROME STRIPS

955

$6635. **XR-7**

MERCURY COUGAR

 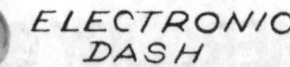 ELECTRONIC DASH

new STANDARD DASH

255 OR 302 CID V8s

new KEYLESS (OPTIONAL) DOOR ENTRY (PUSH-BUTTON) COMBINATION LOCK

80
FROM $7271.

(DOWNSIZED) (*new* 104.8" WB)

XR-7

new REAR STYLING

P185/75R×14 TIRES

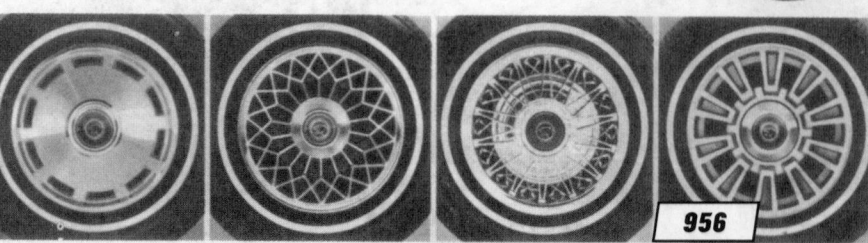

WHEEL CHOICES (left to right) STANDARD COVER; DECOR GROUP COVER; WIRE WHEEL COVER; CAST ALUMINUM WHEEL.

MERCURY **MONARCH** (1975 TO 1980)

REAR ('75)

LINCOLN-MERCURY INTRODUCES
A NEW PRECISION SIZE LUXURY CAR

109.9" WB

STD. MONARCH CPE. FROM $3764. ('75)

HOOD ORNAMENT

GHIA DASH, INTERIOR

Mercury Monarch Ghia instrument panel with optional AM/FM/Multiplex stereo radio and tape player.

ENGINES:
200 CID 6 (78 HP);
250 CID 6; 302 CID V8
(130 HP); 351 CID V8

GHIA

GHIA "GRAND MONARCH" SPEC. DELUXE 4-DR. ALSO AVAIL. 1975-1976 (IN ADDITION TO GHIA 4-DR. and CPE.)

$5149. ('75)

75-77

(1975 = GHIA MEDALLION ON SEDAN DOOR POST)

(1976 = GHIA MEDALLION MOVED)

('75) $5207.

('76) $5299.

MERCURY
MONARCH

RIDE-ENGINEERED

250 C/D 6 OR
302 C/D V8

$5996.
('80)
STD. MONARCH CPE.

CPE. INTERIOR (RECLINING
BUCKET SEATS OPT.)

STEER. WHEEL WITH OPTIONAL
FINGERTIP SPEED CONTROL

$6552.
('80)

"ESS" INTERIOR (ESS INTRO. 1978)

WITH GHIA OPTION

(1980 EXAMPLES, UNLESS
OTHERWISE INDICATED

new **78-80** (FINAL
HEAD-   MONARCH)
LTS.;
new
BUMPERS; "Mercury" NAME IN SCRIPT, LOWER ON
GRILLE; CORNERING LTS. MOVED BACK FR. FRONT
AVAIL. WHEEL COVERS ('78-80)   OF FENDER

SEDAN

('79) ('80)
MONARCH ESS

COWL
LETTERING
READS:
"MONARCH   "ESS
ESS" ('78)   MONARCH"('79)   OR "ESS" ('80)

$6505.
('80)

MERCURY ZEPHYR (STARTS 1978)

(QUITE SIMILAR TO FORD FAIRMONT)

WAGONS

STD. ROUND-HUB STEER. WH.

REAR WIPER AVAIL. FOR WAGON

1978 WHEEL CVR. →

1979-1980 WHEELS and COVERS ←

LOWER DASH IS OPTIONAL SPORTS INSTRU-MENTATION GROUP

2-DR.

AVAIL. WITH GHIA OPTION

4-DR.

78-80

ENERGY ENGINEERED FOR MILEAGE: EPA EST. **33** HWY. **23** CITY

140.3 CID 4 (89 HP), 200 CID 6 (96 HP), 302 CID V8 (130 HP) (255 CID V8 AVAIL. '80)

SPECIAL HOOD and WHEELS with TURBO OPTION

Z-7 SPORT COUPE.

(105½" WB)

1980 EXAMPLES ILLUSTRATED

"ES" OPTION ('78-79) has BLACK AREAS AROUND SIDE WINDOWS

'RIDE-ENGINEERED

ORIG. 1978 PRICES $4700. and UP

$5944. ('80)

(SINCE 1897)
CUTLASS, STARFIRE ('75 ON) and TORONADO MODELS ILLUSTRATED SEPARATELY

Oldsmobile

JETSTAR 88 FROM $3314.
DYNAMIC 88 FROM $3442.

123" WB

88

4-DR. H/T HOLIDAY SEDAN $3757.

DELTA **88**

2-DR. H/T HOLIDAY CPE. $3682.

66

425 CID V8 (310 HP) STD.
(JETSTAR 88 has 330 CID V8 (260 HP)

123" WB
425 CID V8 (365 HP)

Starfire:

(STARFIRE IS LUXURY H/T WITH BIG V8. NOT TO BE CONFUSED WITH SMALL CAR OF 1975 ON, WITH SAME NAME.)

Ninety-Eight:

126" WB (THROUGH '68)

98 SEDANS FROM $4592.

98 has CRISS-CROSS GRILLE PCS.

STEP OUT FRONT IN 66 ...in a Rocket Action Olds!

365 HP (98)

Oldsmobile

330 or 425 CID V8s

(new DELMONT 88 REPLACES FORMER JETSTAR 88)

TOWN SED. 3543.

4-DR. H/T $3675.

has DELMONT 88 NAME OVER COWL

DELMONT 88
Brand-new 88 series! Goes to show what Olds can do with a modest price tag... and a lot of Toronado inspiration.

DELMONT 88 DASH

$3912.

The Rocket Action Cars are out front again!

(INTRO. 9-29-66)

67 new GRILLES

Engineered for excitement... Toronado-style!
'67 OLDSMOBILE

DELTA 88 CVT.

DELTA 88 4-DR. H/T HOLIDAY SEDAN $3954.

DELTA 88 $3786.

REAR

TOWN SEDAN

(CONT'D. NEXT PAGE)

DELTA 88 HOLIDAY COUPE (2-DR. H/T) $3878.

Oldsmobile

$3951.
HOLIDAY CPE.

↗ CLOSE
VIEW
OF
SIDE
TRIM LOUVRES

425 CID V8

DELTA 88 CUSTOM

Two all-new Custom hardtops highlight the Delta 88 line.

1967

67 (CONT'D.)

$4011.

$4736.

Ninety-Eight:

HOLIDAY CPE. (H/T)

98 LUXURY SEDAN

$4873.

98

365 HP

note VERTICAL TAIL LTS.

CLOSE-UP (REAR)

Oldsmobile Ninety Eight

(98)

$5020.

$4798.

8.85 × 14 TIRES

98 DASH

Oldsmobile

(INTRO. 9-21-67)

Drive a youngmobile from Oldsmobile

V8s UP TO 455 CID

68

new SPLIT GRILLES

98

DELMONT **88**

(DELTA GRILLE SAME)

LUXURY SEDAN

Tilt & Telescope steering wheel"

(310 HP) 455 CID V8

REAR

Escape from the ordinary in Olds

DELTA 88 *has* 350 CID V8 (250 HP)

Delta 88 Royale

(new 124" WB) →

(INTRO. 9-26-68)

69

new GRILLES

8.55 x 15 TIRES

Delta 88 Royale

note SIDE LOUVRES

98 REAR

Olds Ninety-Eight

(new 127" WB)

963

Delta 88 Royale

STD. DELTA 88 USES 350 CID V8 (250 HP) $3969. UP

Oldsmobile: Escape from the ordinary.

$5215.

$4350.

88

ROYALE 455 CID V8 (310 HP)

98

455 CID V8 (365 HP) J78×15 TIRES

ROYALE GRILLE DETAILS

new GRILLES

70 (INTRO. 9-18-69)

H78×15 TIRES

Oldsmobile

ROYALE COWL LOUVRES

Wouldn't it be nice to have an Escape Machine?

71

(INTRO. 9-29-70)

(CONT'D. NEXT PAGE)

FROM $5440.

The new Glide-Away Tailgate!

127" WB

Just turn the key...watch it disappear...out of sight!

Introducing a totally new luxury station wagon for 1971: The Oldsmobile Custom Cruiser.

964

Oldsmobile

DELTA 88 TOWN SED. $4516.

THIS TOWN SEDAN IS ONLY DELTA 88 CSTM. WITH CHROME STRIP SHOWN HERE

DELTA 88 CUSTOM

DELTA 88 and DELTA 88 CUSTOM GRILLE →

DELTA 88 DASH

DELTA (4-DR.) H/T ROOFLINES

ROYALE (2-DR.)

Bumper Guards, Front and Rear—Feature rubber inserts to reduce dings, dents and help protect your investment.

(OPT.)

H/T $4953.

DELTA 88 ROYALE

← ROYALE GRILLE ROYALE CVT. $5088.

98 DASH

NINETY-EIGHT 127" WB

71 (CONT'D.)

98s PRICED FROM $5454. 455 CID V8 (320 HP)

Oldsmobile ALWAYS A STEP AHEAD

98 TAIL-LIGHT DETAIL

$5690.

965

Oldsmobile

350 CID V8 (160 HP)

Delta 88

$4517.

$4754.

DELTA 88 ROYALE HARDTOP COUPE — 4695.

DELTA 88 ROYALE TOWN SEDAN — 4617.

DELTA 88 ROYALE CONVERTIBLE — 4903.

Delta 88 Royale
Not just another pretty car.

72

An exceptional new bumper

It gives a little.
Mounted on steel springs, it flexes, then returns to position, to help absorb minor impacts.

new GRILLES

(INTRO. 9-23-71)

98 REAR

Ninety-Eight

A responsive 455-cubic-inch Rocket V-8 engine that runs efficiently on regular, no-lead or low-lead gasolines.

TIFFANY CLOCK

The Limited-Edition Regency.
A very special Ninety-Eight with the Tiffany touch to mark Oldsmobile's 75th Anniversary.

$5393.

(225 HP)

98 REGENCY INTERIOR

FROM $5391.

Custom Cruiser

OLDSMOBILE
ALWAYS A STEP AHEAD

Oldsmobile

$4517.

Delta 88 Royale.

88 REAR

98 REAR

Not just another pretty car.

73 (RESTYLED)

$5452.

Custom-Cruiser.
FROM $5356.

127" WB
455 CID V8
(225 HP)

Ninety-Eight

DASH

98

DELTA 88 $4988

$5049.

new COUPE STYLING

DELTA 88 GRILLE

74 new GRILLES

CUSTOM CRUISER

(CONT'D. NEXT PAGE)

FROM $5683.

Front and rear bumpers are mounted on hydraulic cylinders which cushion minor impacts. '74 Oldsmobile Delta 88.

Oldsmobile

98 s FROM $6003.

instrument panel is now redesigned to provide a new message center which monitors the car and signals you when something is wrong.

NINETY-EIGHT

HOOD ORNAMENT ADDED ←

$6334.

98 REGENCY.

455 CID V8 (210 HP)
J/L 78 × 15 TIRES

74 (CONT'D.)

DELTA 88 ROYALE

FINAL CVT. (DELTA 88 ROYALE) $5772.

98 REGENCY

124" WB
350 CID V8 (170 HP)

$6925.

$5623.

Delta 88 Royale

75 new GRILLES

98 REGENCY $6784.

CUSTOM CRUISER

98:
127" WB
455 CID V8 (190 HP)

98 GRILLE DETAILS

FROM $6134.

It's a good feeling to have an Olds around you.

968

Oldsmobile
Can we build one for you?

DELTA 88

4-DR. H/T $5641.

TOWN SEDAN $5521.

"MESSAGE CENTER"

TOWN SEDAN $5681.

DELTA 88 ROYALE

WITH CROWN LANDAU OPTION →

DASH

350 CID V8
170 HP
HR 78×15 TIRES

H/T $5749.

DELTA 88 ROYALE (REAR)

(98 ON NEXT PAGE)

(UNGRAINED)

76 new GRILLES

127" WB

455 CID V8
190 HP
FROM $6326.

CUSTOM CRUISER

(WITH GRAIN)

Oldsmobile
Can we build one for you?

98

LS COUPE

$7294.

$7147.

REGENCY SEDAN

98 REGENCY CPE.

76 (CONT'D.)

Delta 88 Can we build one for you?

EPA MPG 22 HWY. 17 CITY WITH AVAIL. 260 CID V8 (110 HP)

DASH

Delta 88

The 1977 Delta 88.

98 Regency Coupé new 119" WB

new 116" WB

$6109. 231 CID V6 (105 HP) ALSO AVAIL.

DELTA 88

98 REG.

98 (REAR)

DOWNSIZED, new GRILLES

REAR QUARTERS

77

← 98 Regency →
Can we build one for you?

$7764.
(WAGON ON NEXT PAGE)

KMN 204

Oldsmobile

CUSTOM CRUISER

77 (CONT'D.)

NOW *has* GRILLE LIKE 88

FROM $6725.

NOW ON 116" WB, LIKE 88 SERIES

(new REAR-FACING 3RD SEAT AVAIL.)

OLDSMOBILE NAME MOVED LOWER

There's a lot of News in Olds today.

Introducing the world's first passenger cars with a diesel V8.

78

$7918.

Custom Cruiser

27 mpg HWY 19 mpg CITY 22 mpg Composite

FROM $7191.

Ninety-Eight

30 mpg HWY 21 mpg CITY 24 mpg Composite

Delta 88

30 mpg HWY 21 mpg CITY 24 mpg Composite

HOOD EMBLEM ON DIESELS

(new)

Oldsmobile
Holiday 88 Coupe
Can we build one for you?

"OLDSMOBILE" NAME MOVED TO LOWER PORTION OF GRILLES IN 1978.

$6311.

DELTA 88
Can we build one for you?

note: CUSTOM CRUISER *has* OWN UNIQUE GRILLE IN 1979

Custom Cruiser
Have one built for you.

FROM $7651.

79

(CONT'D. NEXT PAGE)

Oldsmobile

88 Holiday Coupe
Have one built for you.

$ 6626.

$6726.

DELTA 88

DIESEL HOOD EMBLEM

Royale

Delta 88 Royale

DELTA 88 ROYALE (REAR)

79
(CONT'D.)

$6998.

Have one built for you.

98 DASH

98 LS

98 REGENCY SEDAN REAR QUARTER PANEL

$8377.

98 Regency
Have one built for you.

$8579.

350 CID V8 ENGS.
GAS 160 HP
DIESEL 125 HP

EPA MPG:
GAS 21 HWY.
15 CITY
DIESEL 29 HWY.
21 CITY

GRILLE EMBLEM

Oldsmobile
WE'VE HAD ONE BUILT FOR YOU.

diesel Delta 88.

22	594
EPA EST MPG	EST DRIVING RANGE
34	918
HWY EST	EST HIGHWAY RANGE

DELTA 88 (GAS) PRICES START AT $7382.

HOLIDAY COUPE

DELTA 88

ROYALE

$7641.

DELTA 88 DASH AND STEERING WHEEL

98 REGENCY

$9741.

$9619.

98 MILEAGE

17	425
EPA EST MPG	EST DRIVING RANGE
25	625
HWY EST SMG	EST HIGHWAY RANGE

80 (RESTYLED)

Custom Cruiser Diesel			
21	462	31	682
EPA MPG	EPA Est Range	Hwy Est	Hwy Range

UNGRAINED
WOODGRAINED

Custom Cruiser. FROM $8410.

98 STEERING WHEEL

88-STYLE GRILLE RESUMES

973

Oldsmobile **CUTLASS** (and F-85) (SINCE 1961)

with 12 windows.

(F-85 SIMILAR, BUT W/O SIDE CHROME; FROM $2783.)

VISTA-CRUISER (FROM $3300.)

new REAR

120" WB

330 CID V8 UP TO 320 HP

SPT. CPE. FROM $2998.

66

new GRILLE, WITH "OLDSMOBILE" NAME NOW ON UPPER BORDER

$3211.

CUTLASS SUPREME

4-DR. H/T (new)

STEP OUT FRONT IN '66 ...in a Rocket Action Olds!

115" WB (EXCEPT ON VISTA-CR.)

4-4-2

4 bbl. 400 CID 350 HP

442

442

Oldsmobile

CUTLASS

new 250 CID 6 AVAIL. (155 HP)

330 CID V8 STD. (250 HP)

67

new GRILLE; AUX. LTS. BETWEEN EA. PAIR OF HEADLIGHTS

F-85 $3183.

Olds 4-4-2

DASH

VISTA-CRUISER

(CUSTOM 3-SEAT: $3734.)

4-4-2 CVT.

CUTLASS SUPREME

$3265.

320 HP

Engineered for excitement . . . Toronado-style!
'67 OLDSMOBILE

CUTLASS "S"

new 112" WB (2-DR.) 116" WB (4-DR.)

68

(RESTYLED)

F-85 FROM $2988.

NOTE new SIDE SAFETY LTS.

new 350 CID V8 (250 HP)
4-4-2 has AVAILABLE
400 CID V8 (325/350 HP)
155-HP, 250 CID 6 ALSO AVAIL.

VISTA-CRUISER

$3910. (3-SEAT)

WAGON has 121" WB WITH 350 OR 400 CID V8

975

Drive a youngmobile from Oldsmobile

Oldsmobile **CUTLASS**

CUTLASS SUPREME
4-DR. H/T $3486.
310 HP

350 CID V8

ESCAPE FROM THE ORDINARY.

W-31

Vista-Cruiser:

$3854. (2-SEAT)
$3997. (3-SEAT)

69

GRILLES NOW SPLIT; AUX. LTS. NOW IN BMPR. ←

250 CID 6 OR 350 CID V8

Cutlass S.

NOW SHOWING YOUNGMOBILE THINKING 1969

DR. OLDSMOBILE

1969 W·MACHINES W·30/W·31

OLDS "MUSCLE CARS" PROMOTE IN COMICAL "DR. OLDSMOBILE" ADS (AS ABOVE AND ON NEXT PG.)

4·4·2

W TYPES have LOW AIR SCOOPS

Cutlass

350 CID V8 (250-310 HP) IN **OLDS W·31.**

OLDS 4·4·2 W·30

400 CID V8 (360 HP @ 5400 RPM)

W-31 Models. Available in Cutlass S and F-85 V-8 models.
Wheelbase .... 112"

Oldsmobile

CUTLASS

Olds Vista-Cruiser: The all-family Escape Machine. $4095. (3-ST.)

$3953. (2-SEAT)

CUTLASS "S"

CUTLASS SUPREME (FRONT)

70

(RESTYLED)

150 CID 6 (155 HP)
350 CID V8 (250 HP)

"DR. OLDSMOBILE" and HIS ODDBALL ASSISTANT CREW

Cutlass Supreme—

Wouldn't it be nice to have an Escape Machine?

new 2-DR.H/T $3532.

4-4-2
W-30 H/T
455 CID V8
370 HP @
5200 RPM
3.42 G.R.
G70 x 14 TIRES

RALLYE 350

note "442" AT CENTER

977

SPLIT GRILLE

F-85 SEDAN $3789.

$4291. CUTLASS SUPREME.

Oldsmobile CUTLASS

250 CID 6 (145 HP)

71

350 CID V8s (240/260 HP)

Oldsmobile ALWAYS A STEP AHEAD

112" WB (2-DR.)
116" (4-DR.)

CUTLASS CRUISER $4358.

$4922. (3-SEAT) VISTA-CRUISER

CUTLASS "S" $3862.

REAR ROOFLINE (CUTLASS SUPR.)

4-4-2 and DASH

SUPER STOCK WHEELS AVAIL. IN 15 COLORS

455 CID V8 (340 HP)

Oldsmobile

WAGONS FOR 1972
CUTLASS

GM

VISTA CRUISER
(3-SEAT) $4706.

FINAL 121" WB V.C. WITH RAISED ROOF WINDOW SECT. (GRILLE LIKE CUTL. SUPR.)

CUTLASS CRUISER
$4296.

CUTLASS 350 CID V8 (160 HP)

new GRILLES

F-85 DASH

F 85
TOWN SEDAN
$3756.

new 6-SEGMENT TAIL LTS. (ON ALL BUT WAGONS)

72

Cutlass Supreme
350 CID V8 (180 HP) H/T

Cutlass Supreme Hardtop Coupe

$4046.

4-4-2 DASH

4-4-2 *has* DUAL EXHAUST PIPES

4-4-2

CUTLASS S

$3825.

4-4-2

now in 4 types: 4-4-2 AVAIL. w. 350 CID OR 455 CID V8

1972 OLDSMOBILE
ALWAYS A STEP AHEAD

Meet the 1972 Olds 4·4·2, 4·4·2, 4·4·2, 4·4·2!

Oldsmobile CUTLASS

The brand-new '73 Olds Vista-Cruiser.
If you don't see the 9th window right away...

new 116" WB

3-SEAT: $4634.

Cutlass.
$3885.

'73

(RESTYLED)

new "COLONNADE" ROOFS
new SINGLE HEADLTS.

350 CID V8 (180 HP)
(THROUGH '74)

look in the roof.

DASH

Cutlass Salon. A new Olds in the grand touring tradition.

$4496.

Cutlass Salon

new OPERA WINDOWS

Cutlass Supreme
H/T
$4064.

4-4-2 PACKAGE

(W-29)

"SOFT-SELL" SALES CAMPAIGN BY

The Quiet Men of Olds
We give you a great deal more than just a great deal.

Cutlass S.

980

Oldsmobile **CUTLASS**

H78 × 14 TIRES

SUPREME CRUISER

(NO WOOD-GRAIN)

3-SEAT: $4481.

Whatever happens with gasoline, the important thing to you is the car you put the gasoline in.

OLDSMOBILE

CUTLASS "S" COUPE

Recent Proving Ground tests show 17.6 mpg average at 55 mph.

SUPREME

FROM $4143.

VISTA-CRUISER

3-SEAT: $4691.

DASH (CUTL. SALON)

74

4-4-2 PACKAGE

CPE. is new

CUTLASS SALON

Built in the Grand Touring tradition.

new AUX. LTS. QUICKLY IDENTIFY A 1974 MODEL (EXCEPT 4-4-2)

It's a good feeling to have an Olds around you.

Oldsmobile CUTLASS

new TAIL-LTS.

$3756. Cutlass
16 MPG CITY
21 MPG HWY.

* REG. PRICES START AT $4583.

75

new GRILLES

250 CID 6 (105 HP) 260 CID V8 (110 HP)
350 CID V8 (170 HP)
FR78 × 15 TIRES

SUPREME

Cutlass S:
(4-4-2 has HOOD STRIPES and SLOTS; CHROME IN PLACE OF AUX. LIGHTS)

CUTLASS S

442

4-4-2 (S)

Can we build one for you?

new "WATERFALL" GRILLES

76

FROM $4905.

VISTA-CRUISER

3-SEAT: $5728.

CUTLASS SUPREME CRUISER

OLDSMOBILE CUTLASS - 9

3-SEAT: $5610.

(CONT'D. NEXT PAGE)

982

Oldsmobile

CUTLASS

$5519.

Cutlass Salon

ROCKET 260 V8 STD.

5-SP. TRANS. AVAIL.

76 (CONT'D.)

New

Cutlass S Sedan

(ABOVE)

DASH

T-TOP AVAIL. (SUPR. and SALON)

$5486.

Cutlass Supreme Brougham

FINAL VISTA-CRUISER

$5821 - 5973.

S

25 MPG HWY. 17 CITY STD. 231 CID V6

$5256. (SALE = $4811.)

77

new GRILLES

4-4-2

231 CID V6 (105 HP)
260 CID V8 (110 HP)

Cutlass Supreme

$5575.

DASH (S)   Can we build one for you?

983

Oldsmobile CUTLASS

THE NEW CUTLASS SALON.
A CARFULL OF NEW IDEAS.

FROM $5663.

All new bi-level instrument panel

CUTLASS S

23	MPG HIGHWAY
16	MPG CITY
18	MPG COMBINED

Cutlass Cruiser
$6356
(REPLACES VISTA-CR.)
(new 2-PIECE TAILGATE)

Color-coordinated dual mirrors add eye-catching sportiness.

Special paint scheme: White w. choice of metallic Carmine, Camel Tan, Blue or Green.
Super-stock wheels to give an added flash of color.

$6502.
Supreme Brougham

27 MPG HWY., 19 CITY WITH AVAIL. 260 CID V8

(DOWNSIZED) 108" WB

CUTLASS SUPREME
78

new Cutlass Calais V-6

$6451.

T-TOP AVAIL.

Cutlass Supreme

Can we build one for you?

5-SP. TRANS. AVAIL. IN SALON, CALAIS

$6097.
(T-TOP EXTRA)

Cutlass Supreme

Oldsmobile **CUTLASS** 2-DR. SALON $5985.

$6085.

Cutlass Salon Have one built for you.

There's a lot of news in Olds today.

$6269.

SALON BROUGHAM

new 90 HP DIESEL V8 (260 CID) AVAIL., 32 MPG HWY., 24 MPG CITY
ALSO 231 CID V6 (115 HP) OR 260 CID V8 (105 HP)

$6394.

5.7-litre, 350 CID V8s ALSO AVAIL. (GAS OR DIESEL, 125 HP)

CALAIS DASH

$6853.

$6425. CUTLASS **CALAIS**

CUTLASS SUPREME CPE.

DASH

T-TOP AVAIL.

SUPREME BROUGHAM $6854.

79 *new* GRILLES

4-4-2

CUTLASS CRUISERS (2-SEAT ONLY)

MOJAVE INTERIOR AVAIL. IN BROUGH.

CUTLASS CRUISER $6266.
CRUISER BROUGHAM $6468.
(WOODGRAIN OPT.)

350 CID DIESEL AVAIL.

985

Oldsmobile CUTLASS

SALON BROUGH. $7168.

DASH

80 *new* GRILLES

ENGINE CHOICES:
231 CID V6 (110 HP)
260 CID V8 (105 HP)
305 CID V8
350 CID DIESEL V8 (105 HP)

CUTLASS 4-DOOR

CUTLASS LS SEDAN: $7327.

Cutlass Brougham Sedan. $7653.

AVAIL. PADDED-GRIP CUSTOM SPORT STEER. WHEEL

(STD. EQUIP. ON CALAIS)

| 20 | 360 |
| 27 | 486 |

Available instrumentation — with voltmeter, temperature and oil pressure gages, plus trip odometer. Standard on Calais.

CALAIS $7690.

(CONT'D. NEXT PAGE)

Oldsmobile
WE'VE HAD ONE BUILT FOR YOU.

Oldsmobile CUTLASS

T-TOP AVAIL. ON CPES.

REAR DETAILS

CUTLASS SUPREME

$7226.

20 EPA EST MPG	360 EST DRIVING RANGE
27 HWY EST MPG	486 EST HIGHWAY RANGE

SUNROOF OPT.

80 (CONT'D.)

CUTLASS CRUISER

$7029.

(V-6 OR DIESEL V8 OPT.)

(BELOW) SUPREME BROUGHAM

AVAIL. 5.7-litre (350 CID) DIESEL V8 ENG. ($960. EXTRA)

$7568.

Cutlass Cruiser Diesel

22 EPA Est MPG	400 EPA Est. Range	34 Hwy Est	618 Hwy Range

wagon

N. KANARIS

CRUISER BROUGHAM

$7254.

20 EPA EST MPG	362 EST DRIVING RANGE
27 HWY	488 EST HIGHWAY RANGE

GM

987

Olds Omega

Omega F-85 (INTRO. DURING 1975 SEASON) $4314. Can we build one for you?

76

new GRILLE (SIMPLER, 4-SECTION ALL-VERTICAL)

(LITTLE CHROME ON F-85)

F-85 INTERIOR IN "RACINE FABRIC" →

$4409.

Omega SX

OMEGA

BROUGHAM

(4-DR. BROUGHAM ALSO)

$4599.

SX

(F-85 CONT'D. WITH FEW CHANGES)

BROUGHAM $4913.

OMEGA

$4776.

77 new GRILLE (CRISS-CROSS PCS.)

BROUGHAM 4-DR. $4973.

new DASH

989

Olds Omega

78

HATCHBACK WITH SX SPORT TRIM

Oldsmobile Omega Hatchback '78 Can we build one for you?

ON SALE $4482. (REG. $5300.)

(INTERIOR)

Oldsmobile Omega Brougham Can we build one for you?

new GRILLE WITH MOSTLY HORIZONTAL PCS.

28 MPG HWY. 16 MPG CITY (V6)

(4-DR. BRGM.)

231 CID V6 (115 HP) OR 305 CID V8 (130 HP) (OMEGA'S FINAL V8)

BROUGHAM CPE.

HATCHBACK

79

Oldsmobile Omega Have one built for you.

BROUGHAM 4-DR. $5672.

new GRILLE WITH ALL-VERTICAL PCS.

BROUGHAM CPE.

new 4 CYL. (151 CID, 90 HP) OR V6 (173 CID, 115 HP) new 105" WB

80

new DASH

OMEGA

SX

$6455.

(TOTALLY RESTYLED)

BROUGHAM 4-DR.

(SX GRILLE ALL-BLACK)

Oldsmobile Omega.

Oldsmobile Starfire (1975-1980)

INTERIOR

FROM $4171. ('75)

1975 DASH

1975 DASH

FULL INSTRUMENTS STD. 97" WB
231 CID V6 OR 140 CID 4
2.56 GEAR RATIO

STD. TYPE ('76)

('75)

B78 x13 TIRES 18½-GAL. FUEL TANK

75-76

GT ('76)

(SX MODEL *has* THINNER SIDE STRIPE THAN GT)

Starfire GT

new DASH, 1976, LOOKS SAME AS '77 and FOLLOWING YRS.

JERRY'S ORANGE BURGERS

FROM $4261. ('77)

('77)

140 CID 4 (84 HP) OR 231 CID V6 (105 HP) (145 HP, 305 CID V8 AVAIL. '78)

new GRILLE

77-78

('77) GT

Oldsmobile Starfire

$4095⁰⁰

FIRENZA

GT

NO SIDE-STRIPING ON STD. STARFIRE

SPT. STEER. WH.

79

new GRILLE and SINGLE HEAD-LIGHTS

151 CID 4, 231 CID V6, OR 305 CID V8 (130 HP)

REAR VIEW

There's a lot of news in Olds today.

INTERIOR

WHEEL

TYPICAL 1980 STARFIRE INTERIOR SAME AS 1979 SHOWN ABOVE

STD. STARFIRE $5294.

151 CID 4 (90 HP)

231 CID V6 (110 HP; DOWN FROM 115)

FIRENZA $5721.

(ORIG. INTRO. DURING '78 MODEL YEAR) (has REAR SPOILER)

STARFIRE
Nifty little road machines built for the long and winding

GT

$5495. (SX)

(THE FINAL STARFIRE)

80

new GRILLE WITH MOSTLY HORIZONTAL PCS.

Oldsmobile TORONADO

(SINCE 1966)

Front-wheel drive

NEW

66

FROM $5125.

Step out front in '66...in a Rocket Action Olds!
TORONADO

119" WB (THROUGH '70)

V8 ENGINE (ON ALL)
425 CID
385 HP

new GRILLE

new WHEEL COVERS

67

FROM $5182.

(STD. OR DLX. 2-DR HT, 1966 and 1967)

new SPLIT GRILLE

68

new 455 CID V8
375 HP

$5258.

(ONLY 1 MODEL OF 2-DR. H/T AVAIL.)

Toronado.
Test drive the front-wheel-drive "youngmobile" from Oldsmobile.

Escape from the ordinary

OLDSMOBILE NOW SHOWING YOUNGMOBILE THINKING 1969

$5344.

69

new REAR DECK

new GRILLE

12-hour day. Meetings. Memos. The midnight oil. Wouldn't it be nice to have an Escape Machine?

Oldsmobile Toronado

REAR 3/4 VIEW

3 2-DR. H/Ts AVAIL.
STD.= $5531.
CUSTOM = $5724.

new FRONT STYLING

70

GRILLE DETAIL

Oldsmobile ALWAYS A STEP AHEAD

new WRAP-AROUND "CONTROL CENTER" DASH →

new ROOFLINE

CUSTOM H/T $5988.

new TWO-LEVEL TAIL LTS.

(RESTYLED)
71
new 122.3" WB

new GRILLE OPENINGS BELOW LTS.

new DOOR HANDLES

1971 Toronado The Unmistakable One, from Oldsmobile.

994

1972 TORONADO.
THERE'S NOTHING COMMON ABOUT IT.

DASH

2-LEVEL
TAIL-LIGHTS
CONTINUE

HP CUT
TO 250

72

CUSTOM
$5986.
BROUGHAM
$6140.

WILL RUN ON
EITHER LEADED
OR UNLEADED GAS
(SINCE '71)

ALL-VERTICAL
GRILLE OPENINGS →

OLDSMOBILE
ALWAYS A STEP AHEAD

INTERIOR

73

REAR

new
GRILLE SLOTS ATOP
FR. BUMPER

PRICES AS IN 1972

995

Oldsmobile Toronado

new DASH (new "MESSAGE CENTER" WARNING LTS.)

HOOD ORNAMENT ADDED

74

HP CUT TO 230

CUSTOM $6634.

BROUGHAM $6798.

WITH OPERA ROOF

CUSTOM $7095.

BROUGHAM $7325.

new SQUARE LTS.

75

HP CUT TO 215

A new touch of distinction. Toronado's T-crest hood ornament. Another, the opera roof you can order. (seen below).

ORNAMENT

note TOP COVER VARIATIONS

It's a good feeling to have an Olds around you.

REAR DETAILS

DETAILS of "MESSAGE CENTER" SECTIONS BELOW SPEEDO.

new STRIP ON REAR FENDER, and HEAVIER SIDE TRIM STRIPS, ARE THE MOST OBVIOUS MEANS OF DISTINGUISHING THE 1976 FROM PREVIOUS TORONADO.

CUSTOM $7494.

BROUGHAM $7740.

76

BACK SEAT

OTHER UPH. STYLES ALSO AVAIL.

FRONT COMPARTMENT

Oldsmobile Toronado

77

BROUGHAM $ 8287.

DASH

WRAPAROUND REAR WINDOW (XSR) WITH CREASED CORNERS EA. SIDE

← NEW

NEW Toronado XSR
Can we build one for you?

CID CUT TO 403
HP CUT TO 200

<u>XSR</u> AVAIL. WITH OR WITHOUT T-TOP

new GRILLE

XS = $10,837.
XSR = $11,285.

TORONADO
HP CUT TO 185

new GRILLE WITH ALL VERTICAL PCS.

78

"CAN WE BUILD ONE FOR YOU?" SLOGAN CONTINUES

FINAL TORONADO WITH THIS TYPE BODY, BEFORE MAJOR RESTYLING

BROUGHAM $8899.

XS $11,599.

Oldsmobile
Toronado
Have one built for you.

Announcing the all-new 1979 Toronado...

CID CUT TO 350
HP CUT TO 165

new DASH

ROOF-LINE

79

(TOTALLY RESTYLED and DOWNSIZED)

$10,112.

new 114" WB

"Oldsmobile"
(IN LOWER-CASE LETTERS)

new STEERING WHEEL DESIGN

XSC SPORT COUPE

(with SPECIAL DECOR)

BROUGHAM

$11,360.

80.

GAS OR DIESEL V8s

GAS = 307 CID
150 HP
DIESEL = 350 CID
105 HP
2.41 GEAR RATIO

new GRILLE

999

(SINCE 6-28 INTRO. OF 1929 MODEL "Q")

Plymouth

PLYMOUTH DIVISION **CHRYSLER** MOTORS CORPORATION
by Chrysler Corp.

6.95/7.35/7.75 × 14 TIRES

$ 3045.

Satellite / Belvedere 116" WB

Let yourself go... *Plymouth*
VIP FURY BELVEDERE VALIANT BARRACUDA

STD.
225 CID 6 (145 HP)
OR
273 CID V8 (180 HP)
OR 318 CID V8 (230 HP)

66 new GRILLES

SPT. **Fury** 119" WB

VIP(new)

(117" OR 121"-WB WAGONS AVAIL.)

4-door VIP

FURY WHEEL COVER
$ 3365.

$ 3492.

The new 2-d hardtop VIP. **Plymouth**

(INTRO. 1-66

DASH

66½ 2-DR. VIP $3429.

$3101. **Belvedere** (SATELLITE)

67 new GRILLES

(INTRO. 9-29-66)

REAR DECK DETAILS (GTX)

Belvedere GTX (new) WITH 440 CID V8 (375 HP)

1001

GTX H/T $3330.

(CONT'D. NEXT PAGE)

'67 Plymouth VIP

FRONT DETAIL

2-DR. VIP H/T $3476.

Plymouth is out to win you ♥ over this year.

67 (CONT'D.)

FURY I, FURY II, FURY III and SPORT FURY MODELS (SINCE '65)

FURY TOP DETAIL

SPT. FURY $3638. CVT.

Fury

2-DR. HARDTOP

4-DR. H/T

SPORT FURY SIDE SCRIPT

SPORT Fury

new "FAST TOP" $3392.

engine, drive tr. 5-year/50,000-mile warranty

FURY III $3604. (3-SEAT)

Fury wagon

REAR DETAILS, WITH REAR FACING SEAT

Fury

DASH (FURY) WHEEL CVR.

1002

Plymouth

new 190 HP FOR 273 CID V8

SATELLITE

H/T $3047.

3-SEAT $3602.

Satellite Sport Wagon

SPT. SATELLITE SERIES has 318 CID V8 (230 HP)

(INTRO. 9-14-67)

68

new CIRCULAR SIDE SAFETY LIGHTS AT EITHER END

$3229.

ROAD-RUNNER (new) with 383 CID V8 (335 HP)

FROM $3805.

(FURY) SPORT SUBURBAN

FURY III 4-DR. H/T $3430.

SATELLITE WAGON (FRONT)

Fury

$3623.

SPORT FURY FROM $3569.

Belvedere

Plymouth

CPE. $2967.

BELVEDERE
SPORT SATELLITE

$3251.

(RESTYLED)

69

(INTRO.
9-19-68)

new
AIR VANE VENTILATION
FOR WAGON

Road Runner

$3284.

SPORT FURY

$3671.

**A completely new Fury
for 1969.**

Sport Suburban

(OTHER
VIEW
ABOVE)

$4086.
(3-SEAT)

DASH
(FURY)

STARTING
1969,
PLYMOUTH
SIDE
LIGHTS
ARE
RECTANGULAR.

VIP
GRILLE

VIP FROM
$3750.

Look what Plymouth's up to now: 1004

Plymouth

FROM $3066
(BELV. CPE.)

NOBODY MAKES IT LIKE **Plymouth makes it** ♥

(SLOGAN)

ROAD RUNNER FROM $3290.

ROAD RUNNER BIRD FIGURE NOT AVAILABLE.

(USED ONLY IN ADVERTISING TO IDENTIFY ROAD RUNNER)

BELVEDERE GRILLES SIMILAR, BUT WITHOUT BRIGHT VERTICAL PCS.

70

(INTRO. 9-23-69)

ANTI-THEFT LOCK ON STEERING COLUMN.

FURY II 2 DR. $3381

Fury I SEDAN $3303.

FURY GRAN COUPE

new FULL-LOOP FURY BUMPERS ENCIRCLE LTS. FRONT and REAR.

NOTE new CONCEALED HEADLIGHT FEATURE (ALSO ON SPORT FURY)

(new DUSTER IN VALIANT SECTION.)

FURY III CONVERTIBLE $3788.

Plymouth

$ 3535.

SATELLITE TYPES WITH new 3-PC. SIDE LTS.

Satellite Coming Through.

new 115" WB (2-DR.)
117" WB (4-DR.)

SAT. CUSTOM, BROUGHAM have EXTRA LTS. IN GRILLE.

new **Sebring** (CPE., DASH BELOW)

(RESTYLED)

new GRILLES, ETC **71** (INTRO. 10-6-70)

$4268.

GTX ↗

WITH 440 CID V8 (370 HP)

(note UNIQUE STRIPING, TRIM ON THESE SPECIALTY CPES.)

ROAD RUNNER ↘

$ 3930.
SEBRING PLUS

DASH (GTX, ROAD RUNNER)

SOME ROAD RUNNERS ADVERTISED WITH CHROME AROUND GRILLE

(RR 383 CID V8 has 300 HP)

(FURY ON NEXT PAGE)

$3918.

Plymouth

FURY I HAS LESS SIDE CHROME
$3676.

Fury II
$3824.

FURY II and III GRILLE

Fury III Interior

Fury III

$4030.

$3998.

71
(CONT'D.)

ALTERNATOR, TEMP.
GAS GAUGES SET
ABOVE

120-MPH
SPEEDO.

2-DR. FORMAL HARDTOPS

FURY III

$4086.

Sport Fury

Sport Fury

$4140.

(FROM $4494.)
SPORT SUBURBAN

GRAN CPE.

3 CHROME TABS ATOP
FR. FENDERS OF
Sport Fury GT

1007

Plymouth

Coming through with the kind of car America wants.

SATELLITE

$3484.

$3553.

SATELLITE CUSTOM
$3723.

(INTRO. 9-28-71)

72

SEBRING has CHROME TRIM HERE
STANDARD 318 CID V8
CUT TO 150 HP
(6 AVAIL.)

ROAD RUNNER

$3863.

THIS GRILLE ALSO USED BY SATELLITE REGENT WAGON

RR 400 CID V8 (255 HP)

FURY I
$3915.

FURY III
$4214.

FURY GRAN SEDAN CPE.

$4438.

$4425.

ALL-NEW FURY GRILLE

FURY SPORT SUBURBAN
FR. $4840.

1008

Plymouth STD. 225 CID 6 (105 HP) 3/8 CID V8 (150 HP)

Satellite Wagon FROM $4050.

SATELLITE, CUSTOM, REGENT WAGONS IN SAT. SERIES

73

Satellite

FRONT RESTYLED $3714.

SEDAN

DIFFERING TAIL LIGHT DESIGNS

SATELLITE REGENT WAGON (SAME GRILLE AS SATELLITE CUSTOM)

E/F/H78; F70×14 TIRES (ON VARIOUS SAT. TYPES)

Satellite Coupe $3645.

DASH

SATELLITE SEBRING

$3893.

$3887.

Road Runner (2 VIEWS)

(FURY ON NEXT PAGE)

Plymouth

FURY

$4323.

F 78 × 15 TIRES

Fury I 4-Door Sedan
$4032.

Fury III

Fury II

360 CID
V8
(170 HP)
ENGINE IN
SUBURBAN,
CUSTOM SUBURBAN,
and SPT. SUB.
WAGONS have
(FURY SERIES)

four-door
73
(CONT'D.)

PLYMOUTH
1973

SPORT SUBURBAN
has GRAB
IRONS
$5056.
(3-SEAT)

FR.
$4521.

FURY
GRAN
note EMBLEMS

wagon

DASH

FR. $4703.
CUSTOM SUBURBAN

Plymouth

(FINAL)
SATELLITE

(SATELLITE SERIES ENDS DURING '1974)   FR. $3890.

SATELLITE WAGONS
FR. $4042

SATELLITE CUSTOM $4220. UP

new Voyager

↙ WITH SATELLITE TYPE OF 225 CID 6 (105 HP)

FROM $4060.   109" WB   B100, B200, B300

REGENT FR. $4441.

DASH (FURY)

SATELLITE REGENT
(SATELLITE CUSTOM SED. has SAME new GRILLE DESIGN)

74

PLYMOUTH FURY WAGONS

CUSTOM SUB.

CST. SUB. FROM $4814.

360 CID V8 (180 HP) IN FURY

FURY III H/T $4474.

Fury

SPT. SUBURBAN FR. $5065.

SLOGAN: "EXTRA CARE IN ENGINEERING ... IT MAKES A DIFFERENCE"

400 CID V8 (185/205 HP) IN GRAN FURY, WAGONS.

WAGONS INCLUDE:
Fury Sport Suburban • Custom Suburban • Suburban
Satellite Regent • Satellite Custom • Satellite

1011

Plymouth

('75)

The Small Fury.
(new 115"/117½" WB)

75-76

Plymouth Fury

$3699.
(SALE)

GOOD GAS MILEAGE.
EVEN WITH AN
AUTOMATIC TRANSMISSION
23 mpg. 16 mpg.
hwy. city
EPA estimates

(ROAD-RUNNER MOVED TO FURY SERIES, 1975)

(RESTYLED)

('76)

FURY

('76) $6344. Gran Fury Sport Suburban.
(124" WB)

FURY

SINCE 1975,
NUMBER OF
FULL-SIZE
PLYMOUTH
MODELS
REDUCED

(ROAD-RUNNER RE-APPEARS AS A 1977 VOLARE MODEL.)

77-78

('78)

('77)
new GRILLE

(NO 121½", 124"WB GRAN FURY TYPES AFTER 1977.)

1980 GR. FY. RETURNS WITH 118½" WB)

1980 PLYMOUTH GRAN FURY.
A MATTER OF FAMILY PRIDE.

(NO 1979 MODEL OF PLYMOUTH FURY)

225 CID 6
(100 HP)
TOTALLY RESTYLED
AND DOWNSIZED

80

FROM $6823.

V8s ALSO
AVAIL.
318 CID
(140
OR
155 HP)
OR
360 CID

DASH

P195/75 R15 TIRES
and OTHERS

1012

PLYMOUTH HORIZON (SINCE 1978)

WITH VOLKSWAGEN 4 CYL. 104.7 CID ENGINE

99.2" WB
FROM $3981.

155/80 × 13 TIRES

$3706*	
38 / 25†	
HWY / CITY	

GRAIN TRIM (ABOVE)

WHEN YOU WANT TO GO ANYWHERE IN COMFORT AND CONFIDENCE.

RELAX. PLYMOUTH HORIZON CAN HANDLE IT.

new **78**

DODGE OMNI SPECS. SIMILAR

THAT'S IMAGINATION. THAT'S PLYMOUTH.

new TC-3 2-DR.
2+2 FASTBACK (HATCHBACK) $4801. ('79)

79-80

96.7" WB ON 2-DR.

1980 PRICES:
$5265. (4-DR.)
5611. (2-DR.)

ORIG. TYPE CONT'D. with VARIED TRIM and OPTIONS

2-DR. has BODY and GRILLE STYLE UNLIKE 4-DR.

DASH (TC-3, 1979)

"SPORT APPEARANCE" TRIM with TC-3

SIDE DECAL, and CAST ALUMINUM WHEELS.

1013

Plymouth **Valiant** 66

(VALIANT = 1960-1976)
(VOLARE = 1976-1980)

PLYMOUTH DIVISION ◆ CHRYSLER MOTORS CORPORATION

SIGNET H/T $2487.

100, 200 OR SIGNET MODELS

106" WB

6-CYL. OR V8 FROM $2862.

Barracuda (SINCE 1964)

DASH ('67 BARRACUDA INTRO. 11-25-66)

new 108" WB

('67 VALIANT INTRO. 9-29-66)

TAIL-LT.

67

new GRILLE

100 2-DR. $2346.

100 (WITH 200 DECOR OPTION) (NOTE SIDE CHROME)

100 REAR

4-DR. $2537.

SIGNET

2-DR. $2491.

TURN SIGNAL INDICATOR IS VISIBLE TO DRIVER

(200 ELIMINATED AS A MODEL SERIES)

'67

1014

Plymouth Valiant

BARRACUDA

FR. $2936.

**Barracuda.
4 new engines.**

225 CID 6 (145 HP)

318, 340, 383 CID
V8s
(FROM 230 HP)

6.95 x 14
TIRES (ON
BARRACUDA
SINCE 1967)

(INTRO. 9-14-67)

VALIANT SIGNET
2-DR. $2633.

68

new
GRILLES

(FINAL YR. FOR
SPLIT GRILLE ON
VALIANT)

6.50/7.00
x 13 TIRES

VALIANT

new GRILLES

69

SIGNET 4-DR.
$2737.

(INTRO. 9-19-68)

'CUDA
340

('CUDA 383 AVAIL.)

Barracuda Coupe,
Convertible and 'Cuda

1015

Plymouth Valiant

Barracuda

$3219.

Barracuda is America's lowest priced sporty car.

Barracuda is so popular that sales are up 53%.

$3543.
(CUDA)

(new GRAN COUPE ALSO)

new HEMI-'CUDA
WITH "AIR GRABBER" and 426 CID V8

2-DR. RESTYLED VALIANT NOW KNOWN AS

Duster

PLYMOUTH "HEART" NECKTIE USED IN ADVERTISING

(INTRO. 9-23-69)

70

VALIANT/ DUSTER DASH

new MODELS (RESTYLED)

FROM $2172.

NOBODY MAKES IT LIKE *Plymouth makes it* ♥

(new DUSTER 340 ALSO AVAIL., WITH 340 CID V8 ENGINE, 275 HP)

DUSTER CARTOON DECALS

SLOT-LIKE TAIL LTS.

THE GOLD DUSTER

The Gold Duster—Special Version of The Popular Duster

It includes:
- 225 CID ENGINE OR 318 CID ENGINE
- WHITE SIDEWALL TIRES
- UNIQUE DELUXE WHEEL COVERS
- BUCKET-SEAT STYLE TRIM
- DUAL HORNS
- CHROME DRIP MOLDING
- ARGENT PAINTED GRILL
- GOLD DUSTER EMBLEM
- GOLD SIDE TAPE STRIPES
- GOLD REAR STRIPES
- CIGAR LIGHTER

Plymouth Valiant **Barra*cuda***

$3583.
(H/T)

6-PORT
GRILLE

$3840.

(THE FINAL
BARRACUDA
CVT.)

('71
BARRA-
CUDA
INTRO.
10-6
-70)

VALIANT
(below)

$3891.

$2639.

DUSTER 340 (below)

$2982.

340
SPOILER OPT. →

'cuda

71
new
GRILLES

('71 VAL.
INTRO.
9-15-
70)

SCAMP
2-DR. H/T
(new)
(SCAMP has
111" WB. $2808.

ALL
OTHER
MODELS
RETAIN
108"
WB.) $2560.

DUSTER

Plymouth Valiant 'CUDA
BARRACUDA

$3761.

$3554.

'Cuda 2-Door Hardtop

Rallye Instrument Cluster. What you see is what you get on Barracuda and 'Cuda.

Barracuda & 'Cuda

STD. VINYL SEATS

Interiors

Duster 72

(BELOW, and NEXT PAGE) (new GRILLES)
(INTRO. 9-28-71)

DUSTER 340

OPT. VALIANT BENCH SEAT IN VINYL and CLOTH

OPT. DUSTER, DUSTER 340, VALIANT BENCH SEAT

$2987.

DUSTER HAS SLIGHTLY ALTERED REAR (DUSTER NAME AT VERY CENTER, PLY. NAME OFF LID.)

SPECIAL TOP ON Gold Duster.

Plymouth Valiant

WITH SIDE STRIPE and "DUSTER" DECAL AT FRONT END OF STRIPE

1972

VALIANT
$2608.

Valiant 4-Door Sedan

Twister Package. A lot of extras for your Duster including rear quarter panel designation and hood paint treatment.

WITH SIDE TRIM STRIP and CHROME "DUSTER" LETTERING ON COWL

Twister

Valiant Scamp

72 (CONT'D.)

SCAMP CLOTH-AND-VINYL SEAT (OPT.)

$2773.

STD. SCAMP VINYL SPLIT-BACK BENCH SEAT

BUMPER GUARDS

NAME ADDED

1972

PLYMOUTH Scamp

1019

new WH. COVERS

Plymouth Valiant

Barracuda $3675.

'CUDA $3860.

SCAMP'S GRAINED DASH OPTIONAL IN VALIANT/DUSTER MODELS.

73

vinyl roof **Gold Duster.**

new GRILLE

VALIANT 4-DR. $2687.

new SAFETY BUMPERS

DUSTER $2616.

Duster 340

$3093.

SCAMP $2857.

Plymouth Duster 340
Extra care in engineering...it makes a difference.

1020

Plymouth Valiant

$3352.

DUSTER 360 (below) REPLACES FORMER DUSTER 340. has new 360 CID V8 ENG., BUT HP CUT TO 190.

Duster 360

Space Duster

Gold Duster

Plymouth Duster
Extra care in engineering...it makes a difference.
CHRYSLER Plymouth

FINAL YR. FOR BARRACUDA, 'CUDA (FEW CHANGES FROM 1973.)

74

new
Valiant Brougham
INTERIOR

Introducing Plymouth Valiant Brougham.

$4014.

WITH new BEIGE CRUSHED VELOUR UPHOLSTERY (SEE ILLUSTR. AT RIGHT, CENTER)

REAR OF SCAMP RESTYLED

$3361.

Plymouth Scamp.

(automatic transmission INCL.)

Plymouth Valiant

America's **No.1** selling small car comes from Plymouth.

(SCAMP H/T STILL AVAIL.)

**The style of a European sedan.
At the price of an American compact.
Valiant Brougham.**

More car in a small car. That's par for Duster.

75-76

FINAL VALIANTS and DUSTERS.
(REPLACED BY new VOLARE AFTER 1976.)

Plymouth

Volaré

The new small car from Plymouth.

RESTYLED, and ½" LONGER WHEELBASES :
2-DR.= 108½"
4-DR.= 112½"

76

225 OID, 100 HP 6
OR
318 OID, 150 HP V8

PREMIER WAGON = $4859.

The accent is on comfort... and space.

LG. MIRRORS OPTIONAL, USED WHEN HAULING TRAILERS

VOLARE, CUSTOM OR PREMIER MODELS

PREMIER 4-DR.= $4892.

Plymouth Volaré

PREMIER 4-DR. →

Volaré Premier 4-Door Sedan

Volaré. The small car with the accent on comfort.

← PREMIER WAGON

SPT. CPE WITH OPERA WINDOWS

ROAD RUNNER

The new Volaré T-Bar Roof:
(T TOP)

77

VOLARÉS 3

NOTE THAT SOME 1977 VOLARES DON'T HAVE HOOD ORNAMENTS, IF NOT IN PREMIER SERIES

new SPORT COUPES ADDED ("FUN-RUNNERS") PLUS new T-TOP OPTION

SUN RUNNER
(WITH SUN ROOF OR T-TOP)

FRONT RUNNER

Don't Give Up.
Get a New Plymouth Volaré

19/14 *
MPG HWY MPG CITY
$4427 **
Price includes optional automatic transmission.

DUSTER CPE. RETURNS, 1979.

78-79

4-DR. ('78)

new GRILLE WITH "WAFFLE" PATTERN

(CONT'D. NEXT PAGE)

1023

Plymouth Volaré

78-79 (CONT'D.)

('78) **25/18*** MPG HWY MPG CITY
$4362**

** = SALE PRICE

Volaré. America's first choice in wagons.

PREMIER WAGON $5672.

COUPE WITH "PREMIER" PACKAGE

ROAD-RUNNER

WAGON (CUSTOM PKG.)

(GRAINED PREMIER WAGON AVAIL.)

4-DR. WITH "CUSTOM" PKG.

(LOWEST-PRICED VOLARE IS SPECIAL CPE., AT $5610.)

80 new GRILLE (FINAL VOLARE)

DUSTER CPE.

(REPLACED BY 1981 RELIANT)

*DASH

FRONT SIDE SAFETY LIGHTS NOW VERTICAL, and AT FENDER CORNER.

GM MARK OF EXCELLENCE **PONTIAC** (SINCE 1926)

full-sized cars.

V-8 ENGINES (SINCE 1955)

CATALINA SCRIPT; COWL LETTERING IN OTHER MODELS WITH NAMES IN BLOCK LETTERS

$3628.

Catalina
389 CID V8
(290 HP)
121" WB

↖ $3240.

new GRILLES **66**

$4011.

"2+2" LETTERING

CATALINA WAGONS FROM $4164.

DASH

2+2
421 CID V8
(338 HP) (356 OR 376 HP AVAIL.)
121" WB

Ventura

Star Chief Executive
389 CID V8 (290 HP)
124" WB

REAR FENDER TRIM

H/T (new) $3590.

(CONT'D. NEXT PAGE)

INTERIOR (EXEC.)

PONTIAC

$4385.

WAGONS : 121" WB

Wide-Track Pontiac/'66

"BONNEVILLE" NAME ALSO SEEN ON GRILLE OF

Bonneville

124" WB

BONNEVILLE WAGON $4704.

$4543.

STAINLESS STEEL LOWER SIDE TRIM (BNVL., GP)

66 (CONT'D.)

389 C/D V8 IN BON., GP (333 HP)

BONNEVILLE BROUGHAM OPTION

GRAND PRIX has OWN REAR STYLING, 121" WB

Grand Prix

$4449.

AVAIL. ONLY AS A 2-DR. H/T

GRAND PRIX has "GP" and RALLY LTS. ON GRILLE

GRAND PRIX has OWN GRILLE

SIDE DETAILS

UP TO 376 HP AVAIL. (GP)

WOOD-GRAIN ON GRAND PRIX DASH

PONTIAC

400 CID V8 (265 OR 290 HP)

CATALINA H/T $3518.

FROM $4723.

EXECUTIVE SAFARI WAGON

"MORROKIDE" (IMITATION LEATHER) and CLOTH UPHOLSTERY AVAIL.

(INTRO. 9-21-67)

68

METAL "NOSE" MORE PRONOUNCED THAN BEFORE.

new GRILLES, TAIL LTS.

VENTURA 4-DR. H/T

$4571.

DASH (BONNEVILLE BROUGHAM) 400 CID V8 (340 HP)

124" WB BONNEVILLE H/T (WITH TAIL LIGHT DETAILS ABOVE)

GP 400 CID V8 (350 HP)

WAGONS have 400 CID V8 (265, 290 or 340 HP)

GRAND PRIX H/T $4676.

Pontiac announces the great break away!

Pontiac Station Wagons

CATALINA FROM $4496.

$5081. BONNEVILLE

EXECUTIVE SAFARI

FROM $4849.

CATALINA, VENTURA, EXECUTIVE have THIS GRILLE

new GRILLES

69

(INTRO. 9-26-68)

TYPICAL PONTIAC MEDALLION

RECTANGULAR-CLUSTER NON-GP DASH

BONNEVILLE $4733.
428 CID V8 (360 HP)

new 125" WB

GRAND PRIX

new 118" WB

GP NOW has UN-SHROUDED INDIVIDUALLY-SET HEADLIGHTS

GP new "WRAP-AROUND" DASH

$4853.

1029

400 CID V8 (350 HP)

PONTIAC

EXECUTIVE
3-SEAT WAGON
$5178.

70

new GRILLES (INTRO. 9-18-69)

$4034.

122" WB (SINCE '69)

CATALINA CONVT. (EXECUTIVE has SAME GRILLE)

DASH (BNV.)

(NO MORE VENTURA MODELS, BUT AVAIL. AS $106. OPTION IN CATALINA LINE.)

BONNEVILLE

BONNEVILLE
4-DR. SEDAN $4746.
(DASH ABOVE)

new 455 CID V8 (360 HP) IS PONTIAC'S LARGEST ENGINE.

$4876.

$4961.

GRAND PRIX AND INTERIOR

This is the way it's going to be.

PONTIAC

The First Catalina Brougham

H/T $4614.

CATALINA new 123" WB

350 OR 400 CID V8 (250 OR 265 HP)

G/H 78 x 15 TIRES $5236.

Catalina
H/T $4400.

71 new GRILLES
(INTRO. 9-29-70)

The first

Grand Ville ← (new)

GR. VILLE

$5096.

126" WB
455 CID V8
(280 OR 325 HP) IN
BNNVLLE., GR. VILLE

Bonneville RESEMBLES GRAND VILLE, BUT BEARS THESE MARKS

Pure Pontiac!

GP H/T $5087.

71 115   REAR

Grand Prix

118" WB 400 CID V8 (300 HP)

note ONLY 2 HEADLTS. ON GP

G 78 x 14 TIRES

1031

PONTIAC SAFARI WAGON (3-SEAT)

Safari

$4992.

$5320. (3-SEAT)

(UNGRAINED) GRAND SAFARI

SAFARI GRILLE (ABOVE) IS LIKE THAT OF CATALINA. GRAND SAFARI has CRISS-CROSS GRILLE PCS. (AS BONNEVILLE and GRAND VILLE.)

WAGONS WITH 127" WB 400 OR 425 CID V8s (265 OR 280 HP)

Grand Safari

3 VIEWS OF TAILGATE, SHOWING HOW WINDOW RETRACTS INTO ROOF, AND DOOR LOWERS UNDER FLOOR.

71 (CONT'D.)

L78 × 15 TIRES

GR. SAFARI 2-SEAT: $5170. 3-SEAT: $5320.

Pontiac

350 OR 400 CID V8 (160 OR 175 HP) IN CATALINA

400 OR 455 CID V8s (175 OR 185 HP) IN WAGONS

new ENERGY-ABSORBING SAFETY BUMPER

CONVERTIBLE $4596.

'72 Pontiac ...a cut above!

Catalina

123½" WB SEDAN $4229.

G78 × 15 TIRES

CVT. $5156.

Grand Ville

OWN TAIL-LTS., BUT GRILLE LIKE BONNEVILLE

126" WB

new GRILLES

72 HP CUTS

H78 × 15 TIRES, 455 CID V8 (185 OR 220 HP) IN BNVL., GR.VIL.

(INTRO. 9-23-71)

Bonneville

SEDAN $4685.

BONNE. 4-DR. H/T $4809.

GP (BELOW) WITH 400 CID V8 (200 HP)

Grand Prix

$4988.

G78 × 14 TIRES (GP)

REAR

118" WB FRONT

PONTIAC 124" WB

CATALINA FROM $4209.

REAR (BNVLLE.)

new WIDE GRILLES ON 1973 MODELS ONLY. (ON ALL BUT GP)

new OPERA WINDOW → $4974.

(new 116" WB) GRAND PRIX (RESTYLED)

124" WB BONNEVILLE (GRANDVILLE GRILLE SIMILAR)

4 DR. H/T $4716.

LG. SIDE MIRRORS NOT STD. EQUIPMENT.

73

350, 400 OR 455 CID V8s (150 TO 215 HP)

new "COLONNADE" H/T CPE. $4837.

$4794. CATALINA

CATALINA SAFARI (GRAND SAFARI ON NEXT PAGE)

400 OR 455 CID V8s (175-225 HP)

BONNEVILLE

74 (RESTYLED)

new WRAPAROUND PARK./DIR. LIGHTS, ONLY ON GRANDVILLE.

$5498.

GRANDVILLE H/T

REAR

(CONT'D.)

$5198.

$5495.

GRAND PRIX and DASH

Grand Prix instrument panel. Shown with available rally gauge cluster and Custom Sport wheel.

PONTIAC

BONNEVILLE BLOCK TWEED UPHOLSTERY ←

74
(CONT'D.)

3-SEAT WAGON WITH WOODGRAIN $5969.

Grand Safari
Pontiac's full-sized station wagon

Catalina

$5867.

Catalina
Pontiac's lowest priced full-sized car.

CATALINA (3-SEAT) SAFARI

$5272.

ROUND HEAD-LIGHTS

new
RECTANGULAR HEADLIGHTS

$6306. **Grand Safari**

Beautiful things are happening at your Pontiac dealer's!

Grand Ville Brougham
Pontiac's most luxurious full-sized car.

$6430.

G/H/LR78×15 TIRES
$6468.

75
new GRILLES

123.4" WB

400 CID V8s (170-185 HP)

DASH

Bonneville

Grand Prix
Pontiac's classic personal car.

GP

"SJ" $6128.

$5657.

R|T|S Radial Tuned Suspension

1035

PONTIAC
Bonneville

Bonneville: 19 mpg Highway / 13 mpg City (EPA)

CATALINA SIMILAR TO ABOVE CAR, BUT HAS 5 HVY. HORIZONTAL STRIPS ACROSS GRILLE.

CATALINA 4-DR. SEDAN ($5370.) IS LOWEST-PRICED FULL-SIZED PONTIAC.

76
new GRILLES

SJ

400 AND 450 CID V8s (170, 185, 200 HP)

STANDARD GP COUPE $5377.
SJ = $5802.
LJ = $6138.

DASH

STANDARD
Grand Prix. $4798.*

(* = REGULARLY PRICED AT $5377.)

GP 350 CID (160 HP)

116" WB

new "WATERFALL" GRILLE

(UNILLUSTRATED "LJ" has 2-TONE PAINT WITH SPECIAL STRIPING.)

OTHER MODELS RESTYLED, DOWNSIZED (SEE NEXT PG.)

77

(ON GP, LARGE CORNER LTS. REPL. BY new EXTRA LT. BETWEEN EACH PAIR OF HEADLIGHTS, AS SHOWN)

GRAND PRIX

new GRILLE, WITH PCS. SPACED FURTHER APART.

new WHEELS

new 180 HP (SJ)

$5,109.*
(SALE)

PONTIAC ▼ THE MARK OF GREAT CARS

GRAND PRIX

REG. $5701. (LJ = $6064.)
(SJ = $6334.)

(CONT'D. NEXT PAGE)

PONTIAC

This is the newest Bonneville since Wide-Track.

BONNEVILLE SEDAN $6089. new 116" WB

new DASH (GAUGES PLACED HIGH)

BONNEVILLE BROUGHAM (VINYL TOP)

$6624.

ALL-METAL TOP

PONTIAC NAME ABOVE LTS.

new 231 CID V6 (105 HP)

77 (CONT'D.)

new 301 CID V8 (135 HP)

WITH WOODGRAIN

3-SEAT GRAND SAFARI $6569.

PHANTOM VIEW, SHOWING HOW REAR DOOR OPENS SIDEWAYS OR SWINGS DOWN.

Pontiac

GRAND **Safari wagon**

$7079.

CATALINA SAFARI FROM $6601.

DASH

Bonneville

$5931.

(REG. $6608.)

1978 ▼ Pontiac's best year yet!

(GP RESTYLED)

$7354.

Bonneville Brougham

301 CID V8 INCREASED TO 140 HP (V6 UNCHANGED)

FR/HR 78 × 15 TIRES

Grand Prix

new GRILLES

new DASH

78

$5772.*

(REG. $6185.)

108" WB ON GRAND PRIX

GRAND PRIX HOOD ORNAMENT

GP

Grand Prix.

25 mpg Highway, 18 City!

1038

PONTIAC

$6645.

CATALINA and DASH

18 EPA ESTIMATE MPG **27** HWY ESTIMATE

2-DR. $6909. UP

SAFARI

GP "LJ" (STRIPED) with DE LUXE VINYL TOP

BONNEVILLE AND BNV. BROUGH.

79 new GRILLES

V6 INCR. TO 115 HP (V8 UNCHANGED)

CLOSE-UP OF BONNEVILLE GRILLE, FRONT END

LJ $6840.

195/75R14 205/70R14 (SJ) TIRES

GRAND PRIX

FROM $6530.

231 CID V6 (115 HP) EPA:

19 EPA EST MPG **25** HWY EST

ALSO AVAIL: 301 CID V8 (140/150 CID)

THE 1979 PONTIACS ▽ OUR BEST GET BETTER

PONTIAC

CATALINA

GAS MILEAGE

231 CID V6 (115 HP)

80

OR *new* 265 CID V8 (120 HP)

SEDAN $7322.

BONNEVILLE INTERIOR

ALL NEW STYLING FOR COUPE →

BONNEVILLE *and* CATALINA NOW SHARE SAME GRILLE DESIGN.

BONNEVILLE CPE. = $7837.

GRAND (BONNEVILLE)

SAFARI WAGON

$8570.

GRAND PRIX

GP DASH

LJ WITH OPTIONAL T-TOP →

GP PRICES START AT $7096.

MORE PONTIAC EXCITEMENT TO THE GALLON

V6 OR *new* 265 OR 301 CID V8 (120 OR 140 HP)

LJ = $7475.
SJ = $7993.

Pontiac COMPACTS

(1961 TEMPEST 4 WAS FIRST PONT. COMPACT)

medium-priced

TEMPEST OHC SPRINT

(SPRINT PKG.)

(230 CID OHC 6, 165 HP)
207 HP @ 5200 RPM, SPRINT
OR 326 CID V8 (250 HP)
115" WB

LE MANS

$3006. (H/T)

CVT. FROM $3093.

(REAR) GTO

66

(TEMPEST, CUSTOM, LE MANS OR GTO MODELS)

GTO

GTO HAS RALLY LTS., "GTO" ON GRILLE.

GTO HAS 389 CID V8 (335 HP)

"GTO" MEANS "GRAN TURISMO OMOLOGATO"

CVT. $3425.

The tiger scores again! Wide-Track Pontiac/'66

Wide-Track Pontiac/67

7.75 × 14 TIRES

LE MANS

GTO CVT. $3547.

SAME HP AS 1966, EXCEPT NEW 215 HP IN SPRINT

HOOD SCOOP DETAIL

H/T $3317. **Pontiac GTO**

67

GTO HAS F 70 × 14 TIRES

new GRILLES (TEMPEST FROM $2787.)

RALLY I

RALLY II

H/T $3094.

PONTIAC
COMPACTS
LE MANS

(RESTYLED)

68

We've just received our 4th Car of the Year award.

new GRILLES. HEADLTS. NOW HORIZONTALLY PAIRED.
112" WB = 2-DR., 116" = 4-DR.

Wide-Track '68 Pontiacs

GTO HEADLTS. CONCEALED

HAS 400 CID V8 265 OR 350 HP

GTO

400 CID V8 (366 - 370 HP)

ALL RISE FOR

The Judge

SPOILER

The Judge: a special GTO by Pontiac

H/T $3544.

69

new GRILLES

250 CID 6 (175 HP) STD. 350 CID V8 (265 HP)

DASH (JUDGE)

LE MANS

H/T $3292.

The year of the great Pontiac break away

$3634. (CVT.)

70

New T-37 Hardtop. (TEMPEST)

This is the way fun is going to be.

(CONT'D. NEXT PAGE)

new LeMans Sport

new NARROW GRILLES

250 CID 6 (155 HP)
350/400 CID V8s
255-350 HP

LE MANS

PONTIAC
COMPACTS

CPE.
$3187.

70 (CONT'D.)

(FINAL USE OF
TEMPEST MODEL
NAME)

F78/G78
× 14
TIRES

GTO

H/T $3661.

**"This is
the way it's
going to be."**

GTO HEADLTS.
NO LONGER CONCEALED

400 OR 455 CID V8
(350 TO 370 HP)

H/T = $3690.

GTO

$4235.

(CVT. = $4465.)

LE
MANS
T-37

71

(CONT'D.
NEXT PAGE)

250 CID 6 (145 HP)
TO
455 CID V8 (335 HP;
310 NET HP)

PONTIAC COMPACTS

LE MANS WAGON

Le Mans

new 2-WAY TAIL-GATE SWINGS ASIDE OR DOWN.

$4216. (2-ST.) $4329. (3-ST.)

71 (CONT'D.)

GRILLE ↓

DASH

4-DR. $2684.

Ventura II

(new)

(INTRO. SUMMER, 1971)

250 CID 6 (145 HP) OR 307 CID V8 (200 HP)

SPRINT CPE. (DISTINGUISHED BY HEAVY SIDE STRIPE)

71½ -72

new LOWEST-PRICED PONTIAC SERIES 111" WB

CPE. $2654.

E78 × 14 TIRES

note DISTINCTIVE 4-PC. GRILLE, SINGLE HEADLTS.

PONTIAC COMPACTS

LeMans $3690.

72

GTO

GTO HARDTOP COUPE

"GTO" ON LOWER REAR FENDER

$3598.

LeMANS 4-DR. SEDAN

LeMANS COUPE

AVAIL. LeMans

GT H/T CPE. (note SIDE TRIM)

LE MANS (WITH ENDURA FRONT END OPTION)

GTO has SAME FRONT AS ABOVE, EXCEPT FOR "GTO" INSTEAD OF "PONTIAC" ON GRILLE.

$4147.

LeMANS 3-SEAT STATION WAGON

2-SEAT GRAND LE M. (GRAINED)

$4104.

LeMans Station Wagons

(FINAL LeM. CVT.) *LeMANS SPORT CONVERTIBLE*

LeMans Sport

Luxury LeMans (new)

(note THE DIFFERENCES AMONG GRILLES OF VARIOUS LE MANS TYPES ON THIS PAGE)

LuXURY LeMANS 4-DOOR HARDTOP

4-DR. H/T $4077.

STD. 350 CID V8 CUT TO 160 HP.

400 OR 455 CID V8s ALSO AVAIL.

VINYL ROOF and CREST DETAIL ABOVE

2-DR. H/T $3954.

1045

PONTIAC
COMPACTS

250 CID 6 (100 HP)
new 350 CID V8
(150 HP)

FROM
$2660.

'73 Ventura.

(VENTURA
CUSTOM
ALSO)

DASH

VENTURA
NO
LONGER
KNOWN AS
"VENTURA II"

new
BUMPERS

new GRILLES

73
Introducing
LeMans
Sport Cpe.

new
LOUVRED
REAR
QUARTER
WINDOW
DETAIL

$3867.

Le Mans.
(LUXURY
LE MANS has 8
HEAVY
VERT.
GRILLE
PCS.)
→

LUXURY LE
MANS

$4129. (CONT'D.
NEXT PAGE)

PONTIAC COMPACTS
73 (CONT'D.)

GRAND AM

CPE.
112" WB

(new)

2-DR.
$4969.

4 DR. $5058.

Introducing
the first Grand Am.

400 CID
V8
(170 HP)
GR 70 ×15
TIRES

Grand Am
(SIDE INSIGNIA)

The Wide-Track people have a way with cars.

GRAND (NOTE THICK, PADDED
AM MERCEDES-TYPE HUB ON
DASH STEERING WHEEL) (arrow)

Ventura

Pontiac's low-priced
compact car.

250 CID 6 (100 HP)
350 CID V8
← (150 HP OR
155 HP) →

LE MANS
2-DR. COLONNADE
H/T

Ventura Custom Sprint in Sunstorm Yellow

$3176.

Ventura Custom Hatchback Coupe
in Carmel Beige

**VENTURA
CUSTOM**

74
new
GRILLES

$3869.

$3055.

VENTURA **GTO**
(CONT'D. NEXT PAGE)

1047

PONTIAC COMPACTS

RTS Radial Tuned Suspension

74 (CONT'D.)

$4114.

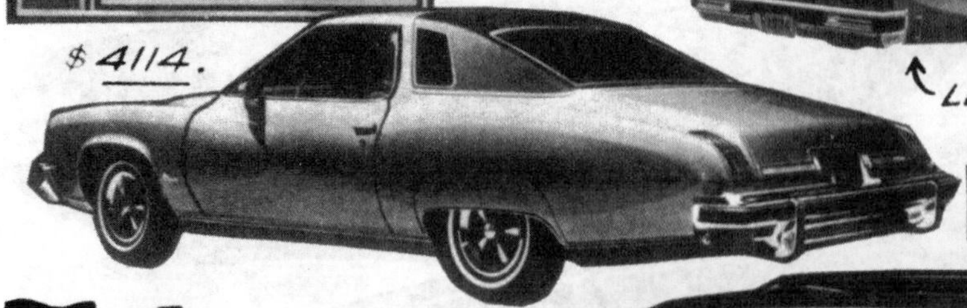

$4373.

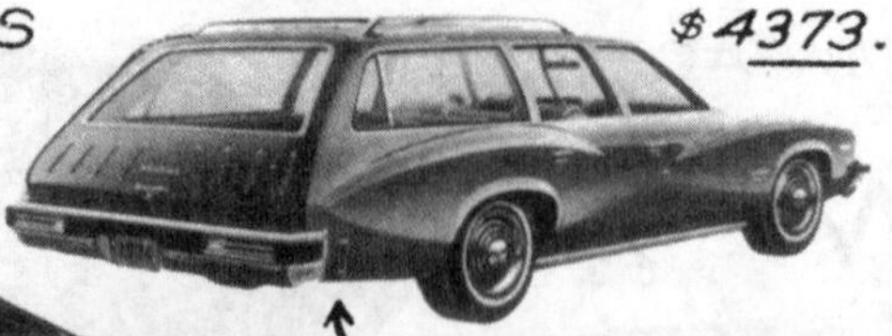

LE MANS SAFARI (3-SEAT)

Luxury LeMan's

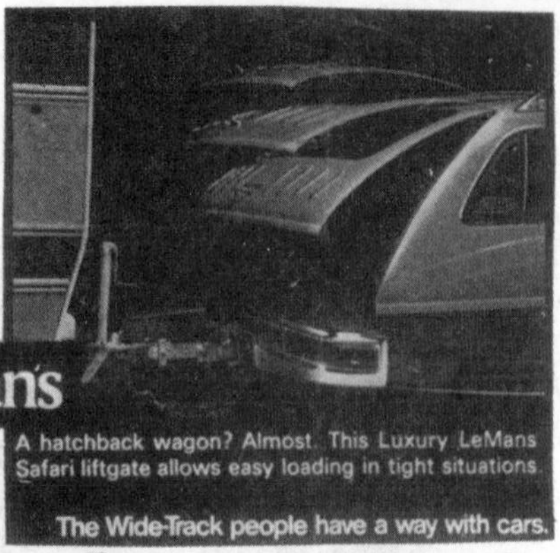

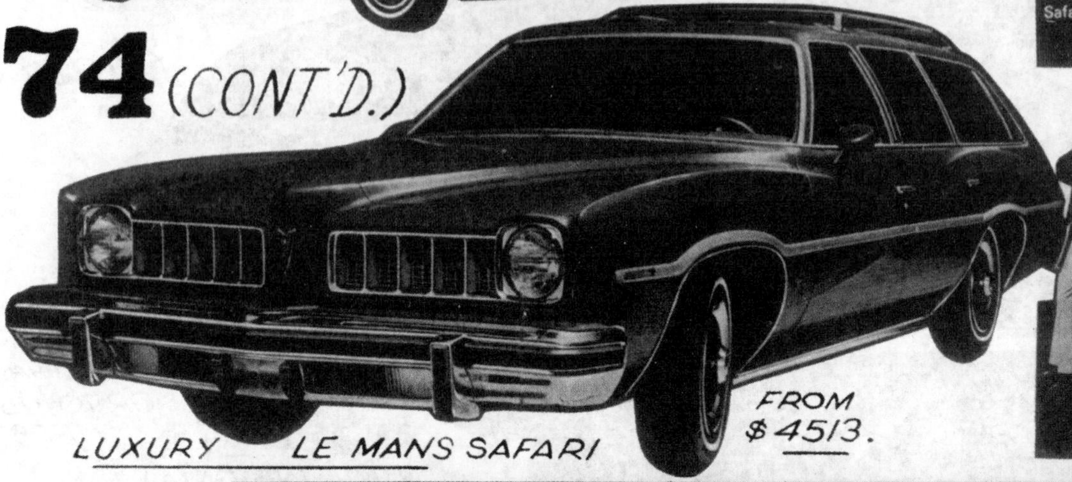

LUXURY LE MANS SAFARI

FROM $4513.

FROM $4806.

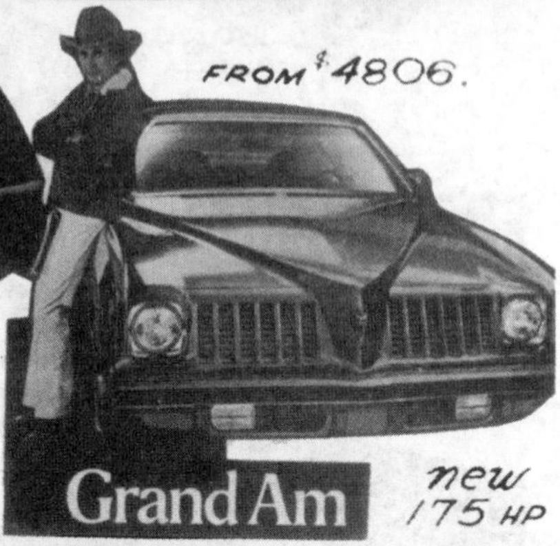

Grand Am

new 175 HP

Introducing the first subcompact Pontiac Astre.

37 MPG

140 CID 4 (78 HP) (87 HP IN "SJ" MODELS) 97" WB

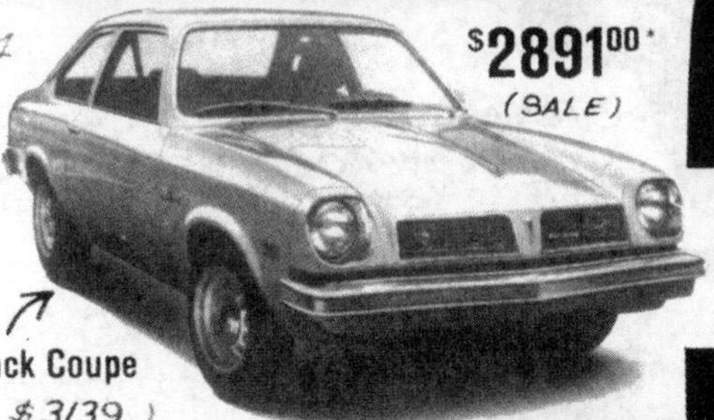

$2891.00* (SALE)

Astre S Notchback Coupe (REG. $3139.)

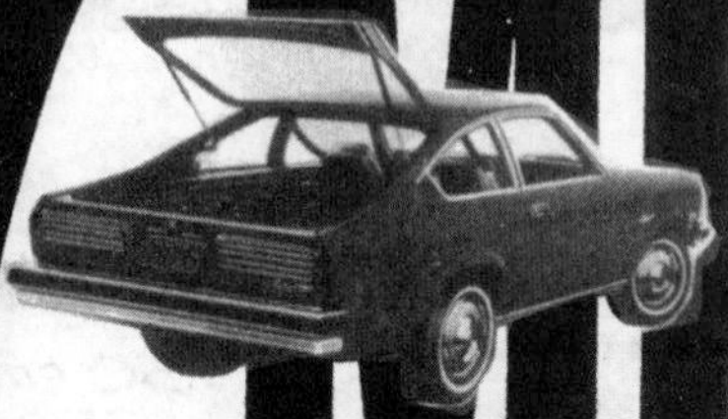

A78 x 13 TIRES

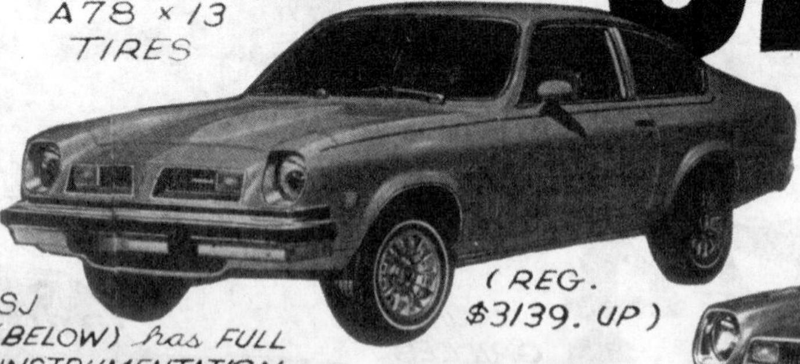

SJ $3851.

(REG. $3139. UP)

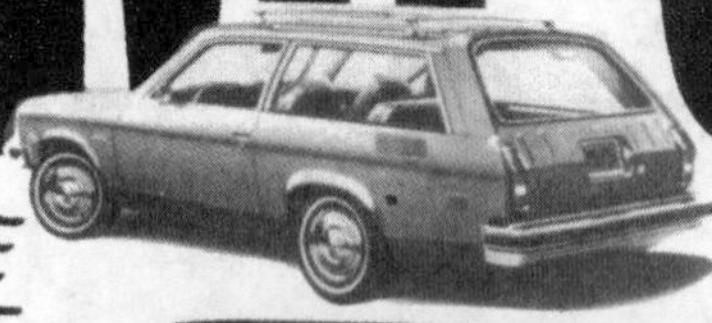

$3369.

ASTRE (new)

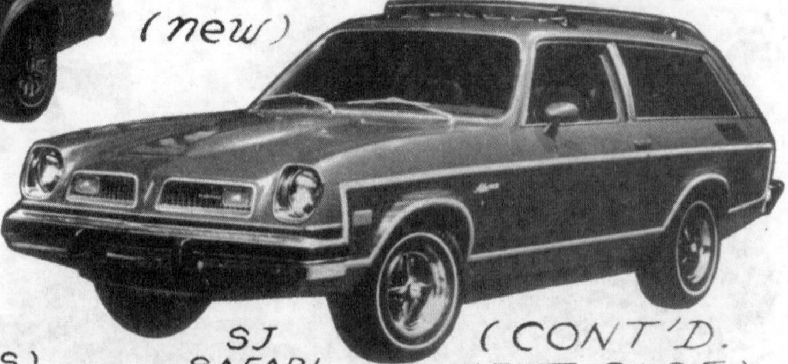

SJ SAFARI $3927.

ASTRE SJ DASH (BELOW) has FULL RALLY INSTRUMENTATION

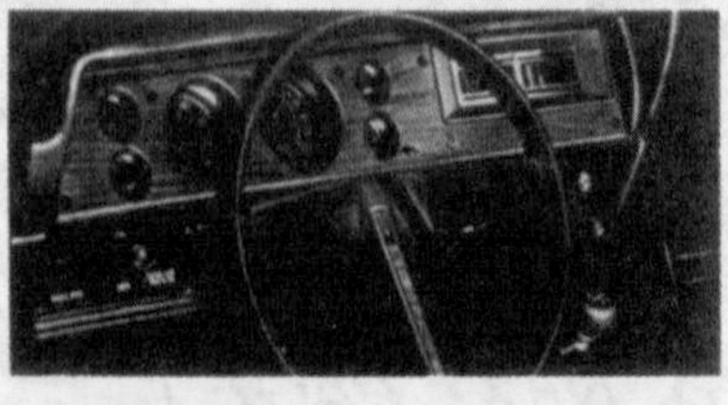

75 (new GRILLES)

(CONT'D. NEXT PAGE)

PONTIAC

COMPACTS VENTURA CUSTOM 4-DR. $4334

Pontiac strikes again.

DASH

HATCHBACK $4302.

VENTURA
250 CID 6 (105 HP)

Ventura's standard instrument panel. The custom cushion steering wheel is standard on Ventura Custom, Sprint and SJ. It's available on Ventura.

Ventura SJ.
→
$4699. (CPE.)
4716. (HATCH.)
4824. (4-DR.)

75
(CONT'D.)
2-DR. COLONNADE

$4749.

Grand LeMans

H/T CPE.

LeMans Safari
(3-SEAT)
$5207.

350 CID V8 (155 HP)

LeMans

Grand LeMans Safari

$4605.

$4627.

CPE. ROOF LINE

Grand Am.

$5401. (3-SEAT)

$5495.

DASH ↗

Grand Am
(NO MORE GRAND AMS UNTIL 1978)

400 CID V8 (170 HP)

PONTIAC

COMPACTS

The Mark of Great Cars.

subcompact Astre

FR. $3377.

VENTURA
250 CID 6
260 CID V8
(BOTH 110 HP)
IN VENT. OR
LE M., GR. LE M.

DASH

FROM $5106.

1976 PONTIAC GRAND LeMANS.

Sunbird
(new)
97" WB
$3921.

BASIC 140 CID 4 IN SUNBIRD OR ASTRE (70 HP)

76

(new GRILLES)

LeMans toppings are available in four flavors. This landau, full vinyl, canopy or padded landau.

ASTRE SAFARI WAGON

ASTRE HATCHBACK

37 26
MPG/HIGHWAY   MPG/CITY

37 26
MPG/HIGHWAY   MPG/CITY

SUNBIRD SPORT HATCH

SUNBIRD

$4226
4101.

"IRON DUKE"
151 CID 87 HP 4-CYL. ENG. (STD. 140 CID has 84 HP)

77

new GRILLES

SPT. CPE.

PHOENIX FROM $5060.
(2-DR.)

PHOENIX
(111.1" WB)

(NEW)
WITH
151 CID 4 (87 HP)
231 CID V6 (105 HP) OR
301 CID V8 (135 HP)

PONTIAC ▼ THE MARK OF GREAT CARS

PONTIAC
COMPACTS
77
(CONT'D.)

THE FINAL **Ventura**

4-CYL., 231 CID V6 (105 HP), OR 301 CID V8 (135 HP)

$4635.

GRAND LE MANS and DASH

$5520.

Grand Le Mans

$6186.

new 231 CID V-6

new 108" WB

85 HP 4 OR 105 HP V6

Sunbird $3541

78
(Resized)
Pontiac's best year yet!

LE MANS DASH

27 mpg Hwy. 19 mpg City! These are EPA estimates for LeMans with its std. 3.8 litre (231 CID) 2-bbl. V-6 and available auto. trans.

REAR

$5866. UP

LE MANS SAFARI WAGON

GRAND AM

301 CID V8 (140 HP)

$6091. UP

LEMANS $4481.

PONTIAC
COMPACTS

A78×13 TIRES (SINCE '76)

FROM $4276.

SUNBIRD

DASH

SUNBIRD "FORMULA" PACKAGE INCLUDES EXTRAS SHOWN (REAR SPOILER ALSO)

SUNBIRD SPORT SAFARI $4633. (INTRO. '78 @ $4181.)

note AVAIL. VINYL-COVERED LANDAU TOP on PHOENIX CPE.

SOME MODELS have new GRILLES

79

(CONT'D. NEXT PAGE)

CPE. $5274.

PHOENIX

PHOENIX DASH

LJ GRILLE

LJ $5874.

PONTIAC COMPACTS

GRAND LE MANS $6410.

231 CID V6 (115 HP)
301 CID V8 (140 HP)

79 (CONT'D.)

LE MANS $6085.

$6222. UP

SAFARI WAGON

REAR

CPE. $6338.

GRAND AM

GRAND AM 1980 GRILLE →

80 (new GRILLES) WITH STD. SIDE MIRROR AND WHEEL COVERS

151 CID 4 (86 HP)
231 CID V6 (115 HP)

SUNBIRD STD. CPE. $4915.

A78 x 13 TIRES (SINCE '76)

SUNBIRD

You'll recognize this 'Bird by its distinctive tail feathers. Sunbird Sport Hatch, shown with available Formula Package.

$5274. PLUS FORM. PKG.

(CONT'D. NEXT PAGE)

SUNBIRD SPT. CPE. $5164.

4-DR. HATCHBK.

COMPACTS PONTIAC

PHOENIX

with *new* FRONT-WHEEL DRIVE

new 104.9" WB

LJ WHEEL →

REAR DETAIL (4-DR. HTBK.)

PHOENIX

PHOENIX

ROUND HUB STEER. WHEEL *also*

(22)(33)
EPA ESTIMATE MPG   HW'Y ESTIMATE

MORE PONTIAC TO THE GALLON

151 CID 4 (90 HP)
173 CID V6 (115 HP)

80 (CONT'D.)

LE MANS

CPE. $6799

$8371. UP

GRAND LE MANS

23/ CID V6 (115 HP) OR 265 CID V8 (120 HP)

4-DR. $7523.

GRAND LE MANS SAFARI

FROM $8371.

GRAND LE MANS/GRAND LE MANS SAFARI:
(19)(26)(343)(470)

(FINAL GRAND AM)

MORE PONTIAC EXCITEMENT TO THE GALLON

1054

(SINCE 1967) **PONTIAC** Firebird

The Magnificent Five are here!

$3127.

(215-HP) SPRINT

108" WB

230 CID OHC 6

STD. FIREBIRD
230 CID OHC 6
(165 HP)

E70 × 14 W.O. TIRES

400 **67** (new)

(INTRO. 2-23-67)

Firebird HO.

HO (note STRIPE, "HO" LETTERING on SIDES.
(HO MEANS "HIGH OUTPUT")

V8 326 CID (285 HP)

400 CID V8 (325 HP)

326 326 CID V8 (250 HP)

Firebird 326

$3705. (INTRO. 9-21-67)

Firebird 400.

new 250 CID FOR OHC 6 (175 HP)
(SPRINT 6 = 215 HP)
350 CID V8 (265 HP)
400 CID V8 (335 HP)

68 new SIDE SAFETY LIGHTS

(VARIOUS MODELS CONT'D.)

H/Ts FROM $3238 ; CVTS. FR. $3453

400 H/T $3490.
400 CID V8 (330 OR 335 HP)

1055

PONTIAC
Firebird

(INTRO. 9-26-68)

69 *new* NARROW GRILLE

HOOD-
MOUNTED TACH.
STILL AVAILABLE
(SINCE '67)

Firebird 400 by Pontiac

$3588.

400
CVT.
$3772.

REAR
SPOILER
DETAILS

TRANS.-AM
DASH

Firebird Trans Am.
(new)

69½

LONG HOOD SCOOPS

400 C.I.D.
V8
(335 HP)
3.55 TO /
GEAR
RATIO

$4366.
('70 SEASON)

1056

PONTIAC FIREBIRD

TRANS-AM (345 HP)
400 CID V8

$4149.

FORMULA 400

FORMULA 400
400 CID V8 (330 HP)
(note HOOD SCOOPS)

DENT-PROOF PLASTIC "ENDURA" FRONT END

FIREBIRD SYMBOL

DASH

(RESTYLED)
70+
new GRILLE
SINGLE HEADLTS.
new RECTANGULAR-SPLIT SIDE LIGHTS

E78 × 14 TIRES

TRANS-AM has STRIPE, SPOILER, and AIR DAM BELOW GRILLE

T.A. $4752.

all two-door hardtops — $3999.

ESPRIT
(has BIRD EMBLEM ABOVE GRILLE)

(KNOWN OFFICIALLY AS "1970½" MODELS. INTRO. 2-26-70)

The all-new Firebirds are here.

STD. CPE has NO SPECIAL TRIM.
$3743.

Pontiac announces the beginning of tomorrow.
New, even for Pontiac.

1057

PONTIAC FIREBIRD

STD. CPE. FROM $3910.

71 (INTRO. 9-29-70)

335-HP TRANS-AM has F60 × 15 TIRES; FORMULA has E70 × 14 (OTHERS, E78 × 14)

"Pure Pontiac!"

A bumper you can knock. And a price you can't.

250 CID 6 (145 HP) OR 350 CID V8 (250 HP) STD.

Esprit $4155.

new WHEEL COVERS →

FROM 3716.

STD. WH. CVR.

STD. H/T

STD. REAR

DASH

(STD. 350 CID V8 CUT TO 160 HP)

Formula 400

$3981.

(FORM. 350 and 455 ALSO AVAIL.) (350 CID V8 CUT TO 175 HP)

ESPRIT $3954.

new MESH PATTERN IN GRILLE →

72 (INTRO. 9-23-71)

Trans Am

$4718

T.A. (455 CID H.O. V8 CUT TO 300 HP)

PONTIAC FIREBIRD

73

$3716. STD. CPE.

(OTHER MODELS CONT'D. TRANS-AM OFFERS GIANT "FIREBIRD" DECAL FIGURE ATOP HOOD.)

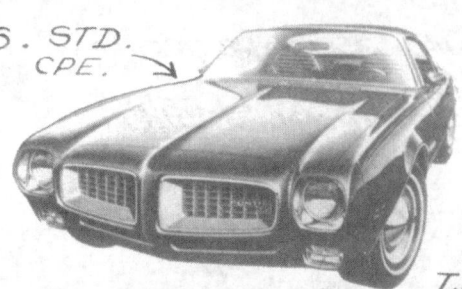

new CRISS-CROSS PCS. IN GRILLE.

350 CID V8 CUT TO 150 HP
T.A. 455 CID V8 CUT TO 215 HP

$ 3865. (STD.)

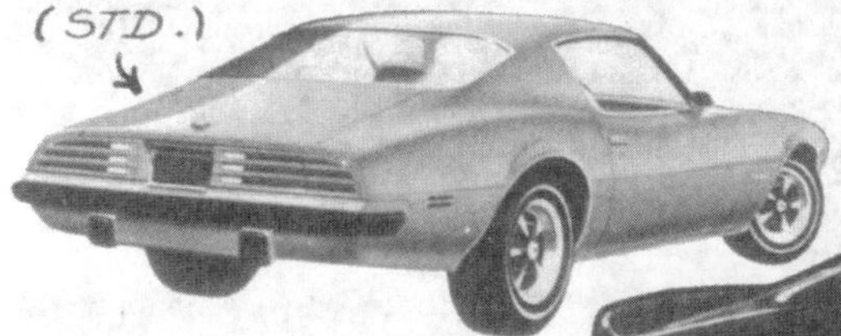

TRANS-AM

$ 4708.

The Wide-Track people have a way with cars.

FIREBIRD DECAL

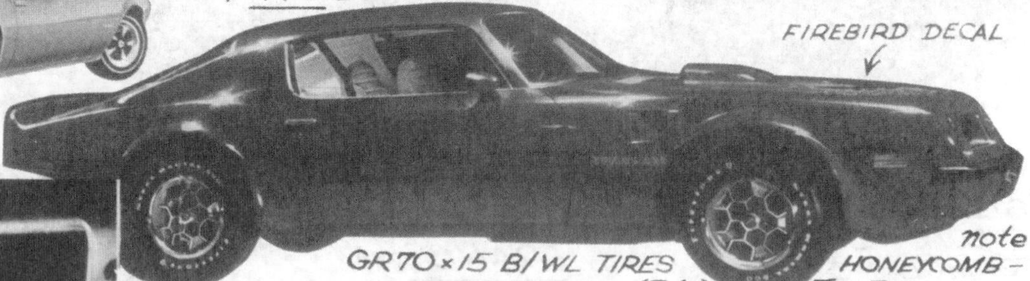

GR70 x 15 B/WL TIRES (T.A.)

note HONEYCOMB-TYPE WHEELS

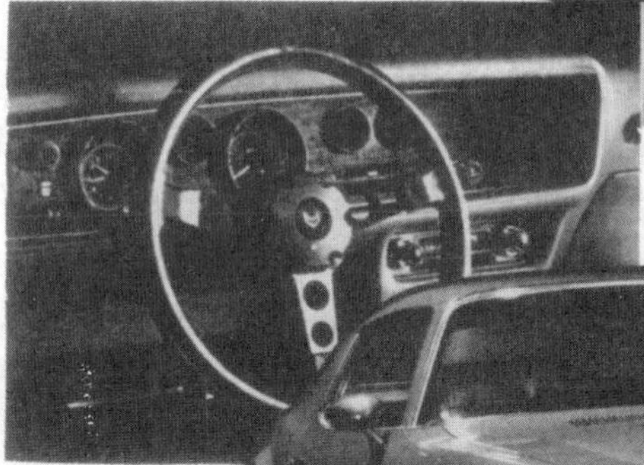

DASH

74

RESTYLED, SLOPING FRONT END WITH VERTICAL PCS. IN GRILLE

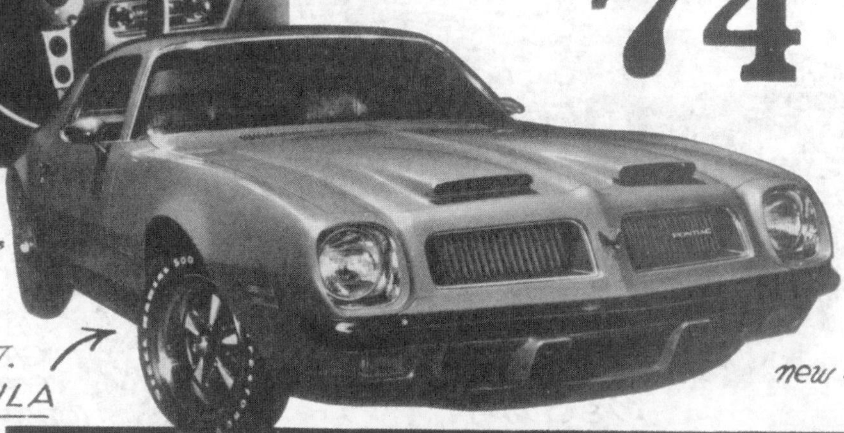

Part engineering. Part soul.

FORMULA HAS GR70 x 14 TIRES

$ 4207. FORMULA

250 CID 6 (100 HP)
350 CID V8 (155 HP)
170 HP IN FORMULA)
new 400 CID TRANS AM V8 (225 HP) (185 HP IN '75)

$ 4853.

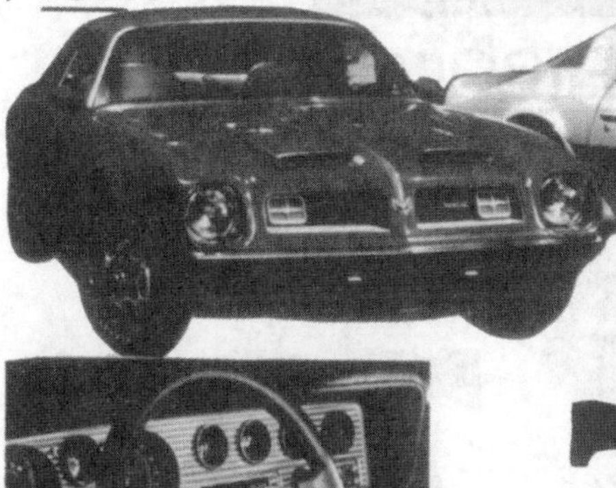

TRANS-AM

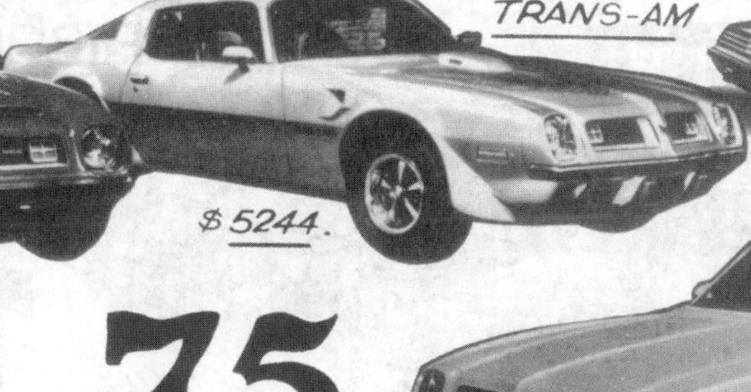

$ 5244.

STD.

$ 4584.

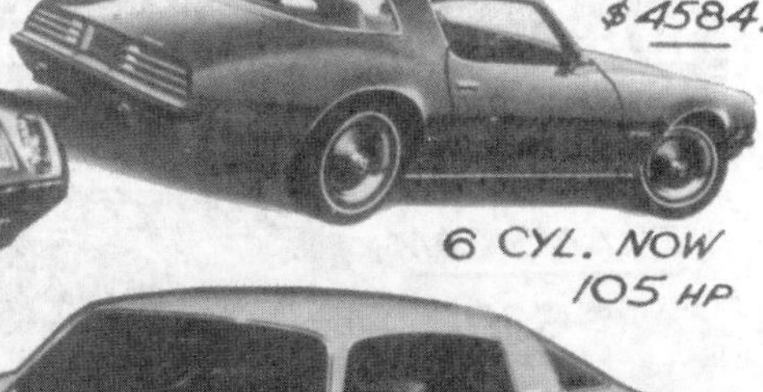

6 CYL. NOW 105 HP

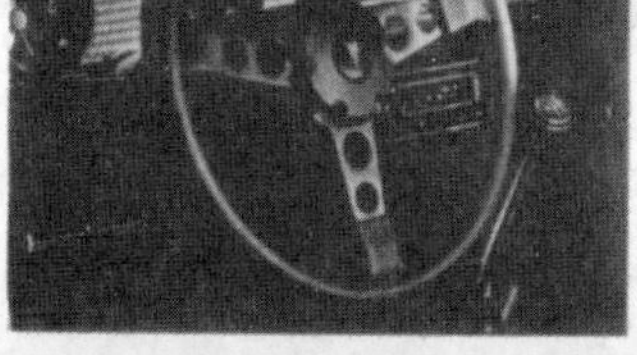

T.A. DASH

75

(new AUX. LTS. and HORIZ. PCS. IN GRILLE)

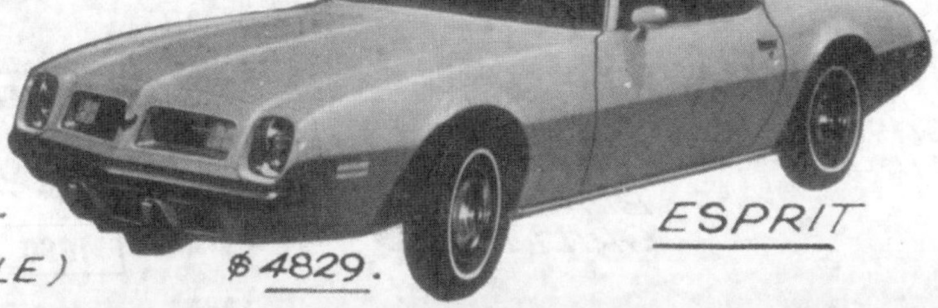

ESPRIT

$ 4829.

PONTIAC FIREBIRD

250 CID 6 (110 HP)   350 CID V8 (160 HP)
STD. = $4834.
ESPIRIT = $5090.   TR. AM. = $5514.

76   new GRILLE WITH MESH PCS.

FORMULA $5092.

PONTIAC ▾ The Mark of Great Cars

STD. = $5174.
ESPRIT = 5455.
FORMULA = 5534.

TRANS-AM $6013.

(SE OR SKYBIRD PKG. AVAIL.)

77

new GRILLE WITH new QUADRUPLE RECTANGULAR HEADLIGHTS

231 CID V6 (105 HP)
301 CID V8 (135 HP)

TR. AM 400 CID V8 (180 HP)

GR 70 × 15 TIRES (TR. AM)
(OTHERS = FR78 × 15)

1978 ▾ Pontiac's best year yet!

STD. Firebird has 231 CID V6 (105 HP)
$5662.

OPTIONAL T-BAR ROOF
TRANS-AM $6390.

ESPRIT $5959.

400 CID V8 (403 CID, CALIF.)

GR 70 × 15 TIRES

new BLACK GRILLE

FORMULA
305 CID V8 (145 HP) NOT AVAIL. IN CALIF. $6039.

78

(SE, SKYBIRD OR new REDBIRD PKG. AVAIL.)

1060

PONTIAC FIREBIRD

231 CID V6
(115 HP)
301 CID V8
(140 HP)
(305, 350 CID AV.)
403 CID V8 (TR. AM.)
(185 HP)

A NEW BREED OF WOW.

(Pontiac, Buick, Chev. and
Oldsmobile ENGINES
USED)

(225/70R14
TIRES ON TR. AM. OR FORMULA;
FR 78×15 ON OTHERS)

79

(RESTYLED
FRONT and
REAR)

new
SEPARATELY-
PORTED
HEAD
LIGHTS

2.41 TO 3.23
GEAR
RATIOS
AVAIL.

STD.
FIREBIRD $6046.
(ESPRIT = $6414.)

FORMULA

YHL 633

$6633.

400 CID V8
(220 HP)
ALSO
AVAIL.

TRANS-AM
DASH

Trans Am.

$6914.

As exciting going as it is coming.

↖ CLOSER
DETAILS OF
TRANS-

1061

(SINCE 1955)

Thunderbird

Ford Motor Company

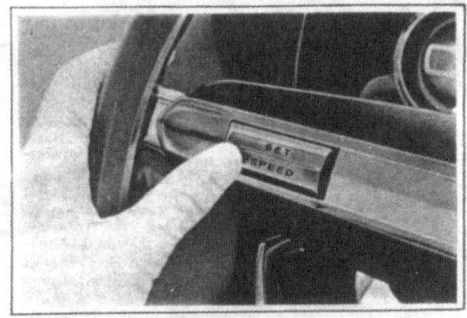

Highway Pilot Control...

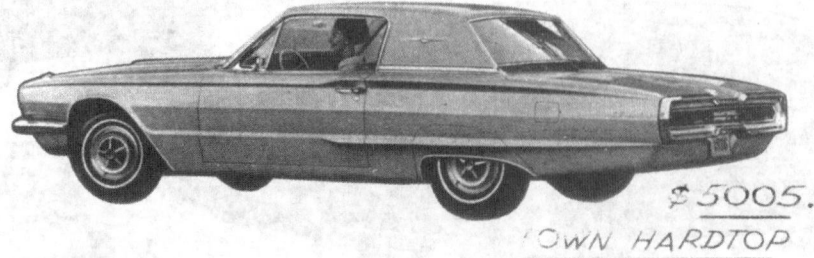

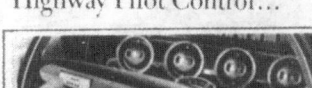

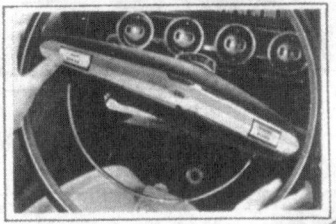

THROTTLE-SET CONTROLS BUILT INTO SPOKE OF STEERING WHEEL (ABOVE)

$5005.

TOWN HARDTOP

TOWN LANDAU

$5105.

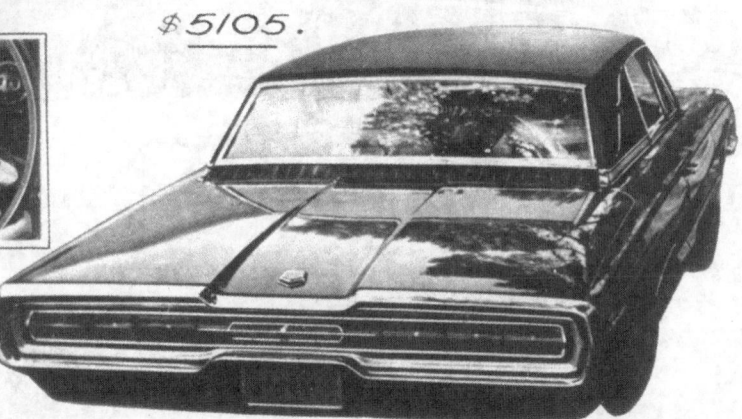

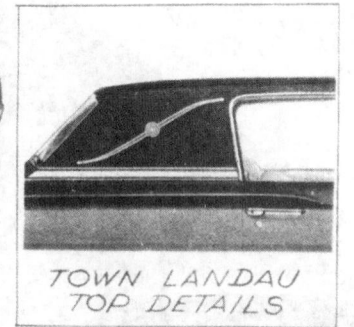

TOWN LANDAU TOP DETAILS

SEQUENTIAL TURN SIGNALS IN FULL-WIDTH TAIL-LIGHTS

new GRILLE; new TAIL-LTS.

66

113" WB

FINAL THUNDERBIRD CONVERTIBLE AVAIL. 1966, AT $5400.

390 CID V8 (315 HP)

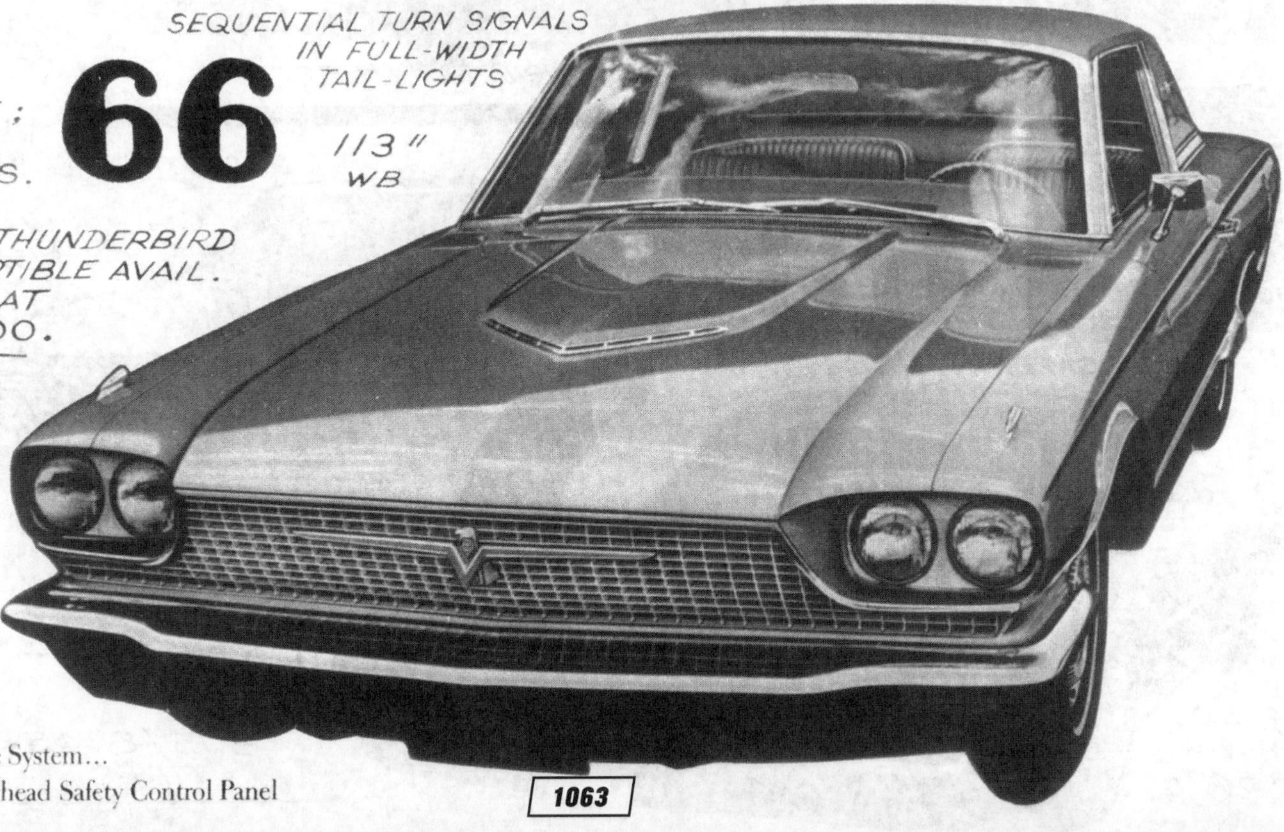

Stereo-Tape System...
Overhead Safety Control Panel

THUNDERBIRD **67**
(RESTYLED)
(INTRO. 9-30-66)

2-DR. FR. $5144.

DASH

note HOW A SIDE SECTION OF TOP OPENS WITH REAR DOOR

new CONCEALED HEADLIGHTS IN new GRILLE

new 115" WB (2-DR.) 117" WB (4-DR.)

LANDAU 4-DOOR IS new $5366.

INTERIOR

68

(INTRO. 9-22-67)

2-DR. FROM $5263.

new SIDE SAFETY LIGHTS

new GRILLE

new 429 CID V8 (360 HP)

8.15/8.45 × 15 TIRES

4-DR. LANDAU $5471.

THUNDERBIRD

OPTIONAL SUN ROOF

2-DR. $5359.
2-DR. LANDAU 5499.
4-DR. LANDAU 5578.

2-DR. (FORMAL ROOFLINE) LANDAU (INTRO. 9-27-68)

new 8.55×15 TIRES

STD. 2-DR. ROOFLINE

4-DR.

69

new GRILLE

INTERIOR

new 215R15 TIRES

FROM $5498.

70

(RESTYLED) (INTRO. 9-19-69)

new POINTED FRONT END STYLING, WITH HEADLIGHTS NO LONGER CONCEALED

FINAL 4-DR. ($5920.)

EVERY 3RD HORIZONTAL STRIP IN GRILLE APPEARS HEAVIER

WITH LANDAU ROOFLINE $5841.

new H78×15 TIRES

71

THUNDERBIRD NAME OVER REAR SIDE LIGHT (INTRO. 9-18-70)

HARDTOP ROOFLINE $5698.

THUNDERBIRD

'72

HP CUT TO 212

new 120.4" WB

215 R15 TIRES

FRONT END TOTALLY RESTYLED

(INTRO. 9-24-71)

2-DR. H/T is ONLY TYPE NOW AVAIL. = $5730.

INTERIOR

PAINTED DISC WHEEL COVERS ALSO

ALL-HORIZONTAL GRILLE PCS.

new OPERA WINDOWS

new ORNAMENT ATOP HOOD

1975 WHEEL CHOICES

Deluxe Wheel Covers

Simulated Wire Wheel Covers

Deep-Dish Aluminum Wheels Standard with Copper Luxury Group

Wide White Sidewall Tires (new)

20TH ANNIV. "SILVER" OR "COPPER" '75 MODELS AVAIL.

('75)

INSTR. PANEL ('73)

new 460 CID V8 IN '74

194 HP ('75)

$6170. ('73)
7790. ('76)

CRISS-CROSS GRILLE PCS.

73-76

('73)

1066

Base sticker price: $5,063*

THUNDERBIRD

new SHORTER 114" WB

STD. new 302 CID V8 (130 HP, '77)
(134 HP, '78)

('77)

'77 FROM $5568.

NOT ALL MODELS HAVE THIS LOWER LIGHT

A new look...

a new size... a new price...

but unmistakably Thunderbird

'77 LANDAU has 400 CID V8 (173 HP) ($7990.)

77-78

Among the new Thunderbird's fine appointments is this handsome instrument panel.

('77)

INSTRUMENT PANEL

T-TOP AVAIL.

NOTE new PLACEMENT OF SIDE WINDOWS

302 OR 351 CID V8 (134 OR 144 HP)

Heritage

79

new GRILLE

STD. $6439.
TOWN LANDAU = $8866.
HERITAGE = $10,687.

THUNDERBIRD

new 255 CID V8, OR 302 CID V8

DASH

New-Size
SILVER ANNIVERSARY MODELS

(RESTYLED) **80** WB SHORTER = now 108.4"

WIRE
WHEEL
COVERS
(OPT.)

P185/75R × 14
TIRES

$7003. TO
$11,679., PLUS
EXTRAS

ALUMINUM
WHEELS
(OPT.)

LUXURY
WHEEL COVER

SLOGAN:
Spread your wings

1980

MISCELLANEOUS RARITIES

INCLUDING REPLICARS (MODERN COPIES OF FAMOUS CLASSICS) KIT CARS (TO BE ASSEMBLED BY OWNER, ON CHASSIS OF VW, ETC.)

THESE ARE BUT A FEW EXAMPLES OF THE MANY EXCLUSIVE, LIMITED-PRODUCTION AUTOMOBILES AVAILABLE ON SPECIAL ORDER SINCE 1966. (SOME ARE IN CURRENT PROD.) AN ENTIRE BOOK COULD BE WRITTEN ON SUCH RARE CARS, AS THE CURRENT FIELD IS QUITE EXTENSIVE!

AUBURN ('74)

BRADLEY GT ('76)

AZTEC 7 ('76)

BRICKLIN ('74)

CLENET ('77)

(DATE IN PARENTHESES REFERS ONLY TO YEAR OF SPECIFIC EXAMPLE ILLUSTR., AND DOES NOT MEAN THAT PRODUCTION IS, OR WAS, LIMITED TO A SINGLE YEAR.)

CORD ('66)

LIBERTY ('76)

EXCALIBUR ('79)

GLASSIC ('71)

MIGI ('76)

MOHS ('67)

FASCINATION ('72) (PILOT MOD.)

MY DAD HAD THAT CAR

PART FOUR

1981–1990
AMERICAN CAR SPOTTER'S GUIDE

CONTENTS

AMC 1075

Buick 1084

Cadillac 1106

Chevrolet 1127

Chrysler 1148

Dodge 1165

Eagle 1185

Ford 1187

Geo 1229

Horizon and Omni 1231

Lincoln 1238

Mercury 1246

Merkur/Scorpio 1276

Oldsmobile 1277

Plymouth 1313

Pontiac 1323

If any two concepts most clearly mark this decade, its "front-wheel drive" and "rebirth of performance," although these notions didn't always walk hand in hand.

General Motors went big on new front wheel drive body/chassis architecture in 1980 called the "X Platform." X yielded similar Buick, Chevrolet, Pontiac, and Oldsmobile models. The design goals were a car line that could be sold throughout the world and was flexible enough to be produced under four different nameplates on the same assembly lines, exceptional interior roominess for a compact/mid-sized car, front-wheel drive, and four- and six-cylinder engines aimed at balancing good drivability, emissions compliance, and high fuel economy. Chrysler followed suit with its "K-car" front-wheel drive platform, also offered across all of its nameplates (Chrysler, Dodge, and Plymouth) as a two-door sedan, four-door sedan, or station wagon, plus more compact two- and four-door hatchback models. Ford bet most of its small car marbles on the "world car" front-wheel drive Ford Escort. Front-wheel drive was viewed as a more efficient way of packaging a car's power train (with neither a heavy rear axle out back nor a driveshaft needed to transmit power from the front of the car to the back axle), meaning potentially less vehicle weight, and a roomier interior without the need for a "driveshaft hump" running down the middle of the passenger compartment.

GM's X-cars were strong sellers and lived a long life in the marketplace. Recall that financially teetering Chrysler needed a big win to avoid bankruptcy, and got it with the K-cars, which turned out to be the Swiss army knife of vehicle platforms. It was ultimately built in a near-countless variety of bodystyles, including a convertible and a long wheelbase mini limo, and spawned the birth of the modern minivan in 1984. The Ford Escort was also particularly long-lived, only finally being replaced by the Focus model in 2000.

Horsepower hounds suffered a long dry spell during most of the mid-to-late 1970s, and things began to turn around on this front for the new decade as well. General Motors brought out a new, better handling, much improved, and faster Camaro Z/28 and Pontiac Firebird TransAm for 1982, which perked up the performance scene considerably. Ford met them pony for pony with a revitalized and reborn Mustang GT 5.0-V8 the same year. In looking to add some sales sizzle and performance sparkle to its compact front-drive models, Chrysler formed a partnership with Carroll Shelby, who so dazzled the sports and muscle car scene in the 1960s with the Shelby Cobra and his take on the Mustang GT 350 and GT500. Shelby developed affordable performance and style packages for several of the compact Chryslers, and while they didn't offer the straight line acceleration of the GM and Ford V-8 powered muscle cars, they were quick enough, handled well, looked sporty, and didn't cost a lot. Performance—with emissions compliance, safety, and good fuel economy this time around—was back in the mid-1980s. The 5.0-liter Mustang GT performed so well that many state highway patrol departments brought them online as "interceptor" vehicles needed to run down speeding Porsches, Lamborghinis, and Ferraris.

You'll find many other interesting pearls in this 1981–1990 section. For example, the most affordable domestic car you could buy in 1987 was the stripped down, ultra fuel-efficient Dodge Omni America model with a base price of just $5499. Don't look for a 1983 Corvette—there wasn't one. The Corvette was in continuous production from 1953 through 1982, going on hiatus for 1983 to have sufficient time to properly develop the radically new and improved "C4" Corvette of 1984. For a time mid-decade, Lincoln offered a smorgasbord of luxury models: a Lincoln Mark VI (coupe or sedan), the Continental sedan, a mildly reconstituted Ford Granada called the Versailles, and the larger-than-large Town Car. For the first time in its long history as one of America's favorite "personal luxury" cars, the Ford Thunderbird was offered with a turbocharged, four-cylinder engine.

This decade represented great change, most of it for the better. Funny that the last car mentioned in the book is the Pontiac Phoenix. With Pontiac gone from the GM roster of brands since 2009, we can only wonder if this last entry portends that Pontiac, a brand beloved by many, will some day "rise like the Phoenix from the ashes." Or maybe it was just a curious coincidence?

Alliance DL.
956
4-DR.
$8067.

American Motors
ALLIANCE

Renault Alliance. Born in Europe... Raised in America.

NEW
Convertible

4 CYL. ENGINE

AS BEFORE, THE DIAMOND-SHAPED RENAULT EMBLEM APPEARS ON GRILLE.

V.I.N.=1XMDC9—XFX #

CVT.
IS
new,
AVAIL. IN
2 SERIES:
973 L =
$11,001.
976 DL =
12,001.

"DL" has 5-SP. TRANS. and FUEL INJECTED 1.4-LIT. 4 CYL. ENG.

Renault Alliance Limited fully adjustable rocker/recliner bucket seats are trimmed in luxury Pin Dot fabric in Almond or Garnet. Honey leather trim is available.

105 CID 4 has 77 HP @ 5000 RPM

3.56 GEAR RATIO

INTERIOR (LTD.)

"L" 2 DR.
$7317.
963

(ENCORE HATCHBACKS ALSO AVAIL. $6386. 8293.)

LTD.
$8567.
958

STD.
WHEEL

LIMITED (LTD.) ONLY AVAILABLE AS A 4 DR. SEDAN.

The new more powerful 1.7L engine, standard on Alliance Limited and Convertibles and available on all other models, except base, utilizes closed loop, electronic fuel injection

Renault Alliance Limited.
The Most Elegant Alliance.

AMC

Alliance

Fog lamps are available on all Alliance models.

SUNROOF (OPT.)

DL 4 DR.
DC956
$7360. →
SPEC. PRICE, 7-86
(REG. $7927 ~ 8645.)

('86 ½)

ENCORE DISCONTINUED DURING 1986 MODEL YEAR (REPLACED BY 1987 GTA)

2 DR. SED. $9364. CONVERTIBLE $13264.)

IMPROVED MPG IN 1986
41 MPG HWY 35 CITY
12½ GALLON FUEL TANK

3 SPEED AUTO. TRANS. AVAIL.
(W. 3.56 TO 1 GEAR RATIO)

RPM X 100

TACH. STD. ON DL and LTD. OPTIONAL ON L SERIES.

A Keyless Entry System uses coded infrared lightwaves to remotely operate door lock mechanisms. It's available on Alliance L, DL and Limited models.

86-87

CHRYSLER CORP. BUYS CONTROLLING INTEREST IN AMC FROM RENAULT, AS OF MARCH, 1987.

Encore

3 DR. OR 5 DR. AVAIL.

5/50 PROTECTION

1987 ALLIANCE MPG (W. AUTO. TRANS.):
27/31 (85 CID 4)
24/29 (105 CID 4)

V.I.N. =
1XM (DC930) - F - # (1985)
1XM (DC933) - G - # (1986)
1XM (DC960) H # (1987)
GTA, ALLIANCE BOTH DISCONT'D. DURING 1987.

ALLIANCE PRICE RANGES:
7058. - 12001. ('85)
6759. - 12284. ('86)
7219. - 12844. ('87)

BLACK LEATHER WRAP. STEERING WHEEL (OPT.; STD. ON DL CVT.)

('86)

$7377 - 8535.
(FINAL 1986 ENCORE)

Electronic
DASH WITH
LCD (LIQUID CRYSTAL DISPLAY) INSTRUMENTATION

Power door locks and windows (front windows only on sedans) may be ordered on Alliance DL, Limited and Convertibles.

ALLIANCE DL

AMERICAN MOTORS CORPORATION

Concord

(SINCE 1978)

EPA MILEAGE VARIES FROM 19 CITY, 26 HWY. TO 23 CITY, 34 HWY., DEPENDING ON ENG. AND TRANS. USED.

VEHICLE I.D. NUMBERS START with
STD. = 1AMBM 060 —
DL. = 1AMBA 0650B —
LTD. = 1AMBA 0670B —

Custom wheel cover standard base

Full styled wheel cover (stainless steel) standard Concord DL.

INTERIOR

Turbocast II aluminum wheels optional all models

Wire wheel cover standard Concord Limited

81 new GRILLE

06-7

LTD. 2 DR. (LIMITED) **8347.**

WITH
Ziebart Factory Rust Protection and Full Five (5) Year Perforation from Corrosion Warranty

151 CID 4 OR 258 CID 6

108" WB

3.08 GR w. 4 CYL.; 2.37, 2.53 OR 2.73 w. 6. CYL. 22-G. FUEL TANK

CONCORD SEDAN

DL

05-5

DL 4 DR. $ **8025.**

(LOWEST-PRICED MODEL IS STD. 2-DR. CONCORD, AT $7501.)

REAR HATCH OF WAGON

LFP-717

P195/75R14 TIRES

08-5

DL WAGON $ **8242.**

1078

WAGON INTERIOR

Concord

24 MPG (EPA) WAGON

DL WAGONS FROM $9466.
(GRAINED AVAIL. ALSO)

25 MPG (EPA) SEDAN

22 GAL. FUEL TANK

LTD. 2-DR. $9217.
06-7

DL

TILT STEERING WHEEL

Custom Wheel Cover
— Std. Spirit/ Concord Base.

Full Styled Wheel Cover
— Std. Concord DL. Opt. Concord Base.

Styled Wheel Cover (Noryl)
— Std. Spirit DL. Opt. Concord Base; Concord DL.

Spoke Style Wheels
— Std. Spirit G.T. Pkg. Opt. other Spirit/ Concord.

Turbocast II Aluminum Wheels
— Opt. all Spirit/Concord.

Wire Wheel Cover
— Std. Concord Limited. Opt. all other Spirit/ Concord.

AVAIL. WHEEL and COVER STYLES

82

STARTING V.I.N.
STD. -0
1ACBM060-

DL -5
1AMBM065-

LTD. -7
1AMBM067-

FULL VINYL ROOF	STANDARD
4.2-LITER 6-CYLINDER ENGINE	STANDARD
INDIVIDUAL RECLINING SEATS	STANDARD
QUARTZ DIGITAL CLOCK	STANDARD
DELUXE BODYSIDE MOLDING	STANDARD
WHITE SIDEWALL RADIAL TIRES	STANDARD
WIRE WHEELCOVERS	STANDARD
DELUXE EXTERIOR TRIM	STANDARD
FRONT AND REAR BUMPER GUARDS	STANDARD
REMOTE CONTROL EXTERIOR MIRROR	STANDARD
EXTRA-QUIET SOUND INSULATION PACKAGE	STANDARD
WOODGRAIN INSTRUMENT PANEL	STANDARD
EXCLUSIVE BUYER PROTECTION PLAN®	STANDARD
FULL 5-YEAR NO RUST-THRU WARRANTY™	STANDARD
ZIEBART® FACTORY RUST PROTECTION	STANDARD
PRICE	$6995

AVAILABLE AT OVER 1500 AMERICAN MOTORS DEALERS NATIONWIDE.

*LIST PRICE EXCLUDING TAX, LICENSE, DESTINATION CHARGES, AND OTHER OPTIONAL OR REGIONAL EQUIPMENT EXTRA. SEE YOUR DEALER FOR WARRANTY AND RUST PROGRAM DETAILS.
Ziebart is a registered trademark of Ziebart International Corporation.

258 CID 6 CYL. 19 ONLY ENGINE AVAILABLE IN 1983 CONCORDS. NO 2-DR. MODELS.

CONCORD DL
$6995.*
(REG. $8823.)

*=SPECIAL PRICE

83

FINAL CONCORD MODELS
(WAGON IS ONLY LTD MODEL FOR 1983.)

TRUST THE TOUGH AMERICANS TO BUILD IN VALUE.
AMERICAN MOTORS

(1983 V.I.N. START W. 1AMCA)

AMC

EAGLE
FROM AMERICAN·MOTORS

$ **10388.**
UP
'82
2
DR.

1982 V.I.N. = 1AMBH (360) (-) CK000001 UP

1982 SX/4
FR. $ **9030.**

22 GAL. GAS TANK

4-DR.
(AVAIL.
UNTIL
1987)
FINAL USE OF GM·BLT.
2.5L 4 IN 1983

2-DR. SEDAN DISCONTINUED
AFTER 1982; SX/4 DISC. AFTER '83.

(1982 EXAMPLES ILLUSTRATED)

21 GAL.
GAS TANK
(SX/4 OR
KAMMBACK)

SX/4

1983
V.I.N. = 1AMCA (350) XD (-) 000001

82-84
UP

4 OR 6 CYL.

new AMC·BLT. 2.5L 4

INTERIOR

1984 V.I.N. = 1ACCK
(355) XEX
000001 UP

KAMMBACK (ABOVE) DISCONTINUED
AFTER 1982.   FROM $ **8378.**

32 MPG / 23 MPG
(ALL EAGLES)
2.73 GEAR RATIO
('85)

2-WHEEL/4-WHEEL DRIVE

WAGON ADOPTS THE
STRAIGHT-ACROSS GRILLE
(AS ILLUSTRATED BELOW)

1982
WAG.
FROM

22 GAL. GAS
TANK

23 MPG (EPA)

$ **11235.**

258 CID 6 IS ONLY
AVAIL. ENGINE
(115 HP @ 3200 RPM)

EARLY
85-88

P195/
75R15
TIRES

1985 WAGON
$ **12,872.**

EARLY '88 WAGON
$ **13,417.**

V.I.N. INCLUDES F (1985)
G (1986)
H (1987)
J (EARLY '88)

22 GAL.
FUEL TK.   ('85)

WAGON IS THE ONLY MODEL IN
EARLY '88 LINE. CHRYSLER CORP.
BUYS AMC FROM RENAULT. FOR
'88-90 CHRYSLER BLT. MODELS,
SEE "EAGLE."

AMERICAN MOTORS

SPIRIT

(1979 TO 1983)

REPLACES GREMLIN

V.I.N.
STD.= 1 (A) M (B) M 4 (5) 0 (-) B (-) —
DL = 1 AMBM 455 XB (-) 000001 UP

DL LIFTBACK
$6079.

DASH (WITH OPTIONAL EQUIPMENT)

23/33 EPA EST MPG / EST HWY*

43-5

Standard

81

new GRILLE

Full styled wheel cover (Noryl) standard Spirit DL

"DELUXE GRAIN" VINYL SEAT (DL)

Spoke styled wheels standard Spirit G.T.

43-0

XAF 135

STD. SPIRIT LIFTBACK
$5772.

← COVENTRY CHECK VINYL-AND-FABRIC UPHOLST. PATTERN

ONLY CAR BUILT IN AMERICA WITH 100% EXTERIOR BODY PANELS OF GALVANIZED STEEL.

96" WB
151 CID 4
OR
258 CID 6

G.T. LIFTBACK (WITH BLACKED-OUT CENTER PILLARS, ETC.)

21-GALLON FUEL TANK

P185/75 R14 TIRES

Inside Spirit

STD. DASH

DL SEDAN
$5979.↓

46-5

GREMLIN ANCESTRY EVIDENT, IN THIS BODY TYPE.

BUILT TO LAST

1082

$6648.
DL
43-5

AMERICAN MOTORS SPIRIT

SPIRIT LIFTBACK

note "SPOILER" WITH GT PACKAGE (new)

46-0

STD. SPIRIT SEDAN $6165.

V.I.N. STARTS WITH IACBM

82

GRILLE CLOSE-UP →

37 HWY EST. | 25 EPA EST MPG

5-SP. TRANS., GAUGE PACKAGE OPTION ←

POP-UP SUNROOF (OPT.)

21 MPG EPA

DL LIFTBACK IS ONLY OTHER 1983 MODEL ($6765.) 43-5

AND STANDARD FEATURES.

4.2-LITER 6-CYLINDER ENGINE	STANDARD
HALOGEN FOG LAMPS	STANDARD
TURBOCAST II ALUMINUM WHEELS	STANDARD
ARRIVA *STEEL* BELTED RADIALS	STANDARD
TACHOMETER	STANDARD
RALLY GAUGES—OIL PRESSURE, AMPERE, VACUUM	STANDARD
LEFT AND RIGHT REMOTE SPORT MIRRORS	STANDARD
FRONT AND REAR SWAY BARS	STANDARD
SPORT LEATHER-WRAPPED STEERING WHEEL	STANDARD
ELECTRIC CLOCK	STANDARD
FULL CENTER SHIFT CONSOLE WITH ARMREST	STANDARD
RECLINING BUCKET SEATS	STANDARD
SPLIT FOLDING REAR SEAT	STANDARD
FRONT AND REAR BUMPER GUARDS AND NERF STRIPS	STANDARD
BLACKOUT G.T. APPEARANCE PACKAGE	STANDARD
EXCLUSIVE BUYER PROTECTION PLAN®	STANDARD
FULL 5-YEAR NO RUST-THRU WARRANTY™	STANDARD
ZIEBART® FACTORY RUST PROTECTION	STANDARD
PRICE	$6495

AVAILABLE AT OVER 1500 AMERICAN MOTORS DEALERS NATIONWIDE.

*LIST PRICE EXCLUDING TAX, LICENSE, DESTINATION CHARGES, AND OTHER OPTIONAL OR REGIONAL EQUIPMENT EXTRA. SEE YOUR DEALER FOR WARRANTY AND RUST PROGRAM DETAILS.
Ziebart is a registered trademark of Ziebart International Corporation.

GT DASH (GT NOW A SERIES)

V.I.N. STARTS WITH IAMCA ENDS WITH XD(-) 000001 UP

83

NEW

GT IS

258 CID 6 IS ONLY ENGINE OFFERED IN 1983.

(SPIRIT DISCONTINUED 1983

1083

43-9 LIFTBACK

SPIRIT G.T.

TRUST THE TOUGH AMERICANS TO BUILD IN VALUE.

AMERICAN MOTORS

$6495.* *REG. $7347.

(SINCE 1903)
A GM PRODUCT SINCE 1908

GM MARK OF EXCELLENCE

BUICK

WOULDN'T YOU REALLY RATHER HAVE A BUICK?

(SKYHAWK NOT AVAIL. 1981)
SKYLARK SEDANS
$7958. UP

SKYLARK CPES. $7812. UP

SKYLARK

SKYLARK HAS 104.9" WB, FRONT-WHEEL DRIVE, 151 CID 4 (90 HP) OR 173 CID V6 (115 HP) P185/80R13 TIRES (P205/70R13 ON SPT.)

SPORT COUPE 4D37 $8446.

V.I.N. STARTS WITH 1G4(-) — ENDS WITH -B-#

81

note SPORT MODEL HAS DIFFERENT GRILLE.

REAR DOOR POWER VENT WINDOW OPT.

SPT. SEDAN ALSO AVAIL.

CENTURY DASH

CENTURY HAS 231 CID V6 (110 HP) OR 265 CID V8 (119 HP)

108.1" WB CENTURY

AVAIL. IN RIVIERA = TRIP MONITOR

CENTURY LIMITED

CENTURY WAGONS AVAIL.

4L69 $9037.

1084

BUICK

Wouldn't you really rather have a Buick?

T-BAR ROOF OPTION

VOLTMETER OPT.

81

3.8 L (231 CID) TURBO V6 (170 HP) AVAIL. IN REGAL SPT. CPE.

108.1" WB **REGAL** (COUPES ONLY)
231 CID V6 (110 HP) OR 265 CID V8 (119 HP)

REGAL DASH

4J47 REGAL CPE. $8593.
4M47 LTD. CPE. 9062.
4K47 TURBO SPT. COUPE 9565.

REGAL

AVAILABLE COACH LAMPS AND LANDAU TOP

REGAL LTD.

LE SABRE 4N37 CPE. **$8864.**

4P37 LTD CPE. $9115.
4P69 LTD. SED. **$9250.**

IN BACKGROUND = 1878 VICTORIAN GREENHOUSES IN GOLDEN GATE PARK, SAN FRANCISCO

LE SABRE

115.9" WB (ALSO 307 CID V8, 150 HP) OR 350 CID DIESEL V8 (105 HP)

231 CID V6 (110 HP) 28/19 MPG
252 " (125 HP, NEW AUTO. O.D. TRANS.) 29/18 MPG

4N69 SEDAN **$8954.**

The 1981 Buick LeSabre.

LE SABRE DASH

P205/75R15 TIRES (LE SABRE)

ELECTRA

4W69 ELECT. PARK AVENUE SEDAN **$12,203.**

4X69 ELECTRA LTD. **$11,353.**

ELECTRA

118.9" WB

105 HP, 350 CID DIESEL V8 AVAIL.; STD. 307 CID V8 (150 HP)

LTD. and PK. AVE. COUPES AVAILABLE

1085

P225/75R × 15 TIRES

BUICK 81

WAGON HAS OWN 116" WB

$12,441. UP

4V35
ELECTRA ESTATE WAGON

TAIL-GATE SWINGS SIDE-WAYS OR DOWN.

ELECTRA WAGON V.I.N. = 1G4AV35YOB (-)10001 UP

T TYPE ROOF

RIVIERA

V.I.N. = 1G4AZ5730 B (-)10001 UP

RIVIERA ROOFLINES

114" WB
105-180 HP

LANDAU ROOF OPTION FORMAL

RIVIERA DASH

Engine Riviera: • Standard 4.1 liter V-6 • Available 3.8 liter turbocharged V-6 (N.A. California) • Available 5.0 liter V-8 • Available 5.7 liter diesel V-8   T TYPE: • Standard 3.8 liter turbo-charged V-6 (N.A. California) • Available 4.1 liter V-6 • Available 5.0 liter V-8 (Buicks are equipped with GM-built engines supplied by various divisions. See your dealer for details.) • **Chassis** Standard: • Front-wheel drive • Power steering • Power front disc/rear drum brakes • Four-wheel independent suspension • Front torsion bars, rear coil springs • Automatic level control • Gran Touring suspension (T TYPE) Available: • Four-wheel disc brakes • Firm ride-and-handling (Riviera) • Gran Touring suspension (Riviera) • **Comfort and Convenience** Standard: • 45/45 notchback seats with fold-down center armrest on driver's side (Riviera) • Cloth bucket seats (T TYPE) • 6-way power seat, driver's side • Door courtesy and warning lights • Storage console (T TYPE) • Side-window defroster outlets • Quartz-crystal-controlled digital clock • Soft-Ray tinted glass • Power windows • AM-FM stereo radio (delete radio option available) • Lights: front ashtray, under-dash, courtesy, glove compartment, engine compartment, luggage compartment • Electric door locks • Automatic power antenna • Air conditioner • Trip odometer • Remote-control, outside left- and right-hand rearview mirrors • Headlamps "on" indicator • Cornering lights • Tungsten-halogen, high-beam headlights (T TYPE)   Available: • Luggage compart-ment protective floor mat • Front and rear carpet savers with inserts • Exterior coach lamps (included with vinyl tops) • Door-edge guards • Color-coordinated, protective body-side moldings • Sunroof—electric operation • Astroroof—electric sliding glass (Headroom is reduced slightly with either option) • Heavily padded Landau top with coach lamps • Electric fuel cap lock (not available with diesel engine) • Custom locking wire wheel covers • Chrome-plated road wheels (4) • Theft-deterrent system with starter interrupt • Leather-trimmed seats (in seatbacks and seating areas) • 6-way power seat, passenger side • Reclining electric seatback, passenger side • Reclining electric seatback, driver's side • Reclining manual seatback, passenger side (T TYPE) • Tilt steering column • Tilt and telescoping steering column (Riviera) • Automatic electric door locks • Electric trunk lock release • Electric trunk lock • Front and rear light monitors • Lighted visor vanity mirrors • Rear quarter courtesy and reading lamps • Two-speed wiper with low-speed delay feature • Tungsten-halogen, high-beam headlights (Riviera) • Extended-range speakers • Concert Sound speaker system • ETR AM-FM stereo radio • 8-track tape player with AM-FM stereo radio • 8-track tape player with ETR AM-FM stereo radio • Cassette tape player and ETR AM-FM stereo radio • Cassette tape player with AM-FM stereo radio • CB and AM-FM stereo radio with Triband power antenna • CB, 8-track tape player and ETR AM-FM stereo radio with Triband power antenna • Full-feature AM-FM stereo radio • Cassette tape player and Full-feature AM-FM stereo radio • 8-track tape player and Full-feature AM-FM stereo radio • Electronic Touch Climate Control air conditioner • Electric rear-window defogger • Cruise-Master speed control with resume-speed feature • Fuel usage light • Low fuel indicator • Trip monitor • Illuminated door lock and interior light control • Twilight Sentinel headlamp control • Electrically operated, outside rearview mirrors — **Appearance and Protection** Standard: • A fluid indicator (T TYPE) • Front and rear bumper guards • Bumper prote. wipers • Sport steering wheel (T TYPE) • L designers' Sport wh belts • Dual n and re wheel (Rivier

RIVIERA FEATURES AND OPTIONS LISTED ABOVE.

$12,821.   **The 1981 Riviera.**

T TYPE = $13,765.

T TYPE V.I.N. = 1G4A Y5730B(-)10001 UP

1086

1982   Buick   Skyhawk.

$8817. UP

New
SKYHAWK

RETURNS.
(PREVIOUSLY
AVAILABLE
1975 — 1980.)

SKYHAWK DASH

101.2" WB
112, 122
CID 4

CUSTOM
OR LTD
CPES.,
SEDANS

AVAILABLE
SUNROOF

23 MPG
(EPA)

CENTER BACK-UP LTS.   P175/80R13 TIRES

13.6 GAL.
FUEL TK.

82

V.I.N. =
1G4A ( )
- C - 000001
UP

T27 SKYHAWK LTD. CPE.

$9259.

173 CID V6 (115 HP)

SKYLARK

(ALSO A
151 CID
4 (90 HP)

41 EST HWY	26 EPA EST MPG

14½ GALLON
FUEL TANK

2.8 liter High Output V-6

104.9" WB

SKYLARK,
SPT., LTD.
COUPES and
SEDANS,
FROM
$9028.
TO 9769.

Skylark Limited notchback seat

TUNE-UP
BRAKES
MUFFLERS

VXG-185

Buick Skylark.

Buick

2.5 Liter L4
40 Hwy. Est. | 25 EPA Est. mpg

New CENTURY CUSTOM COUPE 4H27

CENTURY

15½ GAL. FUEL TK. 25 MPG (EPA)

V6 (3.8L)

82

$10054.

new OPT.

4.3 liter diesel V-6

Regal Estate Wagon instrument panel with available equipment.

REGAL DASH

1982 Regal Sedan HAS OWN GRILLE

18.1 GAL. FUEL TK.

NEW

REGAL

108.1" WB

FROM $9885.

30 EST. HWY | 21 EPA EST. MPG

LeSabre Limited Coupe

4P37 LE SABRE LIMITED CPE. $10431.

(REGAL ESTATE WAGON AVAIL., AT $10,231. 4J35)

LE SABRE

115.9" WB

ELEC. LTD. $12,738.

$14,044.

4W69

25 GAL. FUEL TANK

ELECTRA

118.9" WB

4N69

CUSTOM SED. $10,130.

28 EST. HWY | 19 EPA EST. MPG

ELECT. PK. AVE. CPE $13,893. 4W37

ELECTRA PARK AVE. SEDAN

RIVIERA (now CVT. ALSO)

Coupe

Electra Estate Wagon

ELECTRA DASH (LESAB. SIMILAR, BUT WITH BOOMERANG-SHAPED STEERING-WHEEL HUB.)

16 MPG (EPA) 22 GAL. FUEL TK. (WAGON)

21 GAL. FUEL TANK

(GRILLE SIMILAR TO THAT OF 1981 MODEL)

RIVIERA 15,868. UP

Z67 RIVIERA CVT. $ 25590. ←

BUICK
Wouldn't you really rather have a 'Buick'?

ELECTRA $13,973. UP 18/29 MPG (V6)

LESABRE $10,604. UP

		EST HWY?	EPA EST MPG	EST HWY RANGE	EST DRIVING RANGE	FUEL TANK CAPACITY
BUICK SKYHAWK	1.8 Liter L-4#	46	28	625	381	13.6
BUICK SKYLARK	2.5 Liter L-4	42	27	613	394	14.6
BUICK CENTURY	2.5 Liter L-4	39	24	612	377	15.7
	4.3 Liter Diesel V-6#†	44	27	730	448	16.6
BUICK REGAL	3.8 Liter V-6*	30	21	543	380	18.1
	3.8 Liter Turbo V-6	29	18	525	326	18.1
	4.3 Liter Diesel V-6	36	25	712	495	19.8
BUICK LESABRE	3.8 Liter V-6*	27	19	675	475	25.0
	5.7 Liter Diesel V-8#†	34	23	884	598	26.0
BUICK ELECTRA	4.1 Liter V-6*	29	18	725	450	25.0
	5.7 Liter Diesel V-8#†	36	22	936	572	26.0
RIVIERA	4.1 Liter V-6*	29	17	612	357	21.1
	3.8 Liter Turbo V-6#†	27	19	569	337	21.1
	5.7 Liter Diesel V-8#†	36	21	821	479	22.8

REGAL $10,351. UP 21/30 MPG

1983 BUICK V.I.N. 1G4A (S69P) -D-#

CENTURY $9980. UP 24/39 MPG

83

SKYLARK T TYPE DASH

27/42 MPG **SKYLARK** $9068. UP

28/46 MPG

SKYHAWK $8547. UP

SKYLARK T TYPE

TAIL-LIGHT DETAIL

FOR 1983, RIVIERA T TYPE IS JOINED BY HIGH-PEFORM. T TYPE MODELS IN REGAL, CENTURY, SKYLARK (ILLUSTR.) AND SKYHAWK LINES.

MORE T-TYPE DETAILS ON NEXT PAGE.

note THE DIFFERENCE FROM REGULAR SKLK. GRILLE.

THE SKYLARK TYPE. new 1089 D372 $10,857.

NEW SKYHAWK
WAGON T35 LTD.
(LEFT FOREGROUND)
$9523.

T-TYPES

BUICK
Wouldn't you really rather have a Buick?

RIV.   REGAL   SKYLARK

SKYHAWK

NEW

CENTURY T TYPE

$10,564.

83

CENTURY T TYPE

CENTURY
T-TYPE INTER.

SKYHAWK TYPE
DASH

103 MPH (RIVIERA
T-TYPE)

THE T TYPE POWERTEAMS.

	Horsepower @ RPM	Torque @ RPM	5-speed Manual Overdrive Transmission (standard)	4-speed Manual Transmission (standard)	Automatic Transmission (standard)	Automatic Transmission (available)	Automatic Transmission with Overdrive (standard)
Skyhawk T TYPE Powerteam							
1.8 liter (112 CID) OHC L-4 (LH8) [O] (Standard)	84@ 5200	102@ 2800	3.83			3.18 (3.33)	
Skylark T TYPE Powerteam							
2.8 liter (173 CID) H.O. 2-bbl. V-6 (LH7) [Z] (Standard)	135@ 5400	145@ 2400		3.65		3.06	
Century T TYPE Powerteam							
3.0 liter (181 CID) 2-bbl. V-6 (LK9) [E] (Standard)	110@ 4800	145@ 2000			2.97		
Regal T TYPE Powerteam							
3.8 liter (231 CID) 4-bbl. Turbocharged V-6 (LC8) [8] (Standard)	180@ 4000	290@ 2400					3.42
Riviera T TYPE Powerteam							
3.8 liter (231 CID) 4-bbl. Turbocharged V-6 (LC8) [8] (Standard)	180@ 4000	290@ 2400					3.36

[O]—Produced by GM-Brazil [Z]—Produced by GM-Chevrolet [E]—Produced by GM-Buick [8]—Produced by GM-Buick

MODELS AVAIL.

Skyhawk Custom Coupe
Skyhawk Custom Sedan
Skyhawk T TYPE Coupe
Skyhawk Limited Coupe
Skyhawk Limited Sedan
Skyhawk Custom Wagon
Skyhawk Limited Wagon

SKYHAWK

Skylark Custom Coupe
Skylark Custom Sedan
Skylark T TYPE Coupe

Skylark Limited Coupe
Skylark Limited Sedan

SKYLARK
FROM $9079.

Official Car of the XXIIIrd Olympiad
Los Angeles 1984

BUICK
84

CENTURY

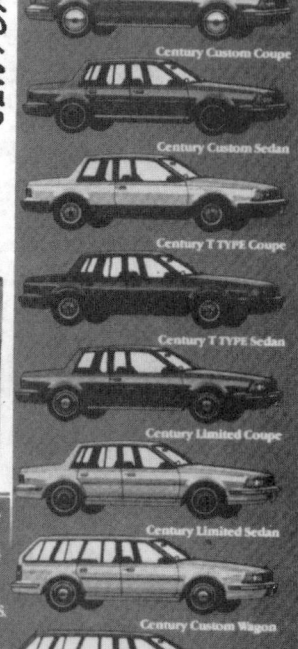

Century Custom Coupe
Century Custom Sedan
Century T TYPE Coupe
Century T TYPE Sedan
Century Limited Coupe
Century Limited Sedan
Century Custom Wagon
Century Estate Wagon

SKYHAWK DASH

SKYHAWK DASH and REAR
$8964. UP

SKYLARK DASH

Selected 1984 Features
1. The 1984 Buick Century Olympia Sedan. A limited number of these specially equipped and appointed Century Sedans are being produced to commemorate Buick's sponsorship of both the 1984 Olympics and the 1984 U.S. Olympic Team.

The Century Olympia is well-equipped for its assignment. Beyond its gleaming white exterior, gold accented aluminum wheels, deck lid luggage rack, gold accent striping, and special ornamentation is an interior that's pure Century, but with plenty of its own commemorative touches. Like rich brown interior trim with handsome tan cloth covering either the standard 55/45 notchback seating or the available 45/45 seating with console. And front seat headrests we embroidered with official U.S. Olympic Team symbols.
2. Tilt steering column. Facilitates driver entry and exit while offering a wide range of driving positions

$10753
Regal Coupe
Regal Sedan
Regal T TYPE Coupe
Regal Limited Coupe
Regal Limited Sedan

REGAL
1/6 MPH (T-TYPE)

new

CENTURY OLYMPIA

CENTURY DASH

LE SABRE

1984 V.I.N.
1GA4 (569P)
- E - #

CENTURY T-TYPE
HAS OWN GRILLE

REGAL DASH

OFF AUTO LIGHTS
MAX DELAY

LeSabre Custom Coupe
LeSabre Custom Sedan
LeSabre Limited Coupe
LeSabre Limited Sedan

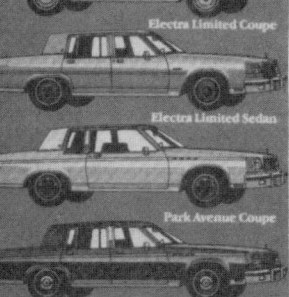

Electra Limited Coupe
Electra Limited Sedan
Park Avenue Coupe
Park Avenue Sedan

LE SABRE/ELECTRA DASH

"TWILIGHT SENTINEL"
(OPT.)
LEAVES HEADLTS. ON UNTIL DRIVER IS INDOORS.

ELECTRA
FROM
$14952.

(AT LEFT)
V35 ESTATE WAGON
$15633. UP

Riviera Coupe
Riviera T TYPE
Riviera Convertible

RIVIERA

RIVIERA DASH

Skyhawk Limited Sedan.   JT69P $9682.   121 CID 4   (86 HP @ 4900 RPM)   (110 CID + TURBO 4 AVAIL.)

BUICK
Wouldn't you really rather have a 'Buick'

Skyhawk Wagon

P175/80R13 TIRES
3.65 GEAR RATIO

13.6 GAL. FUEL TANK

JE270 T-TYPE $9961.

Skyhawk Limited Wagon interior.

Skyhawk Custom Wagon.

Skyhawk Custom Wagon cargo area.

SKYHAWK
101.2" WB

1985 BUICK V.I.N. = 1G4 (J369P) —F—#

85

SKYLARK

104.9"   151 CID 4
2.53 GEAR RATIO   OR 173 CID V6
(112 HP @ 5100 RPM)

15.1 GAL. FUEL TK.

$9667.

P185/80R13 TIRES

XB69R
SKYLARK CUSTOM SED.
(XC69R LTD. " $10,243.)

J935P CUSTOM = $9518.
JT35P LIMITED = 9978.
(SKYHAWK WAGONS)

note MEDALLION ON CENTURY T-TYPE GRILLE VARIATION

Deck lid luggage rack

AL 353

Century

CENTURY LIMITED COUPE   AL273

$11580.

231 CID V6 (125 HP @ 4400 RPM)
181 CID V6 AVAIL.

High-mounted center stop lamp

Rear facing third seat

2.84 GEAR RATIO
P195/70R14 TIRES

AH 353

Century Custom Wagon.

SEDAN (AH193) $11,284. (CUSTOM)   15.1 GAL. FUEL TK. $11,680.

(IN UPPER VIEW, WITH BOY ON BIKE = CENTURY EST. WAGON : $12,118.)

P185/80R13 TIRES
13.6 GAL. FUEL TK.

INSTR. PANEL

SOMERSET
2.84 GEAR RATIO

4 CYL. OR 181 CID V6 (125 HP @ 4900 RPM)

Buick

$10,252.
NJ27U
SOMERSET REGAL

N M27U SOMERSET LIMITED $10,861.

103.4" WB

(V6 FOR $485. EXTRA)

New SOMERSET

(ALSO KNOWN AS "SOMERSET REGAL" IN 1985.) COUPES ONLY

REAR DECK SPOILER ON REGAL T-TYPE

GM47A

Buick Regal Limited $10,861.

REGAL

121 MPH

BUICK REGAL

Regal Grand National.

85 NEW

REGAL GRAND NATIONAL 231 CID V6 (200 HP @ 4000 RPM) 4-SP. TRANS.

Cast aluminum wheel

LE SABRE COLLECTORS EDITION INTERIOR

LeSabre Estate Wagon
BR35Y

LE SABRE

$13179.

$13121.

$11658.

SED.

LE SABRE CUSTOM CPE. BN37A

Buick LeSabre Collectors Edition.

BP69A

Park Avenue Sedan.

231 CID V6 (125 HP @ 4400 RPM) (V6 DIESEL ALSO AVAIL.) 2.84 GEAR RATIO

Electra 380 Coupe.

18-GAL. FUEL TANK

307 CID V8 IN WAGON, WITH DIESEL V8 ALSO AVAIL.

P205/75R x 14 TIRES

Buick

Electra Estate Wagon interior.

CW693 $16,740.

ELECTRA

SEDANS AND COUPES TOTALLY RESTYLED **NEW** 110.8" WB

Electra Estate Wagon cargo area.

PARK AVE. INT.

Electra Estate Wagon   (WAGON NOT RESTYLED)

CF693
ELECTRA T-TYPE SED.
$16,528. **NEW**   108 MPH

BV35Y

$16,078. 2 SEAT
16,298. 3 SEAT

WAGON RETAINS 115.9" WB

RIVIERA **85**   114" WB

307 CID V8 (140 HP)
350 CID DIESEL V8 (105 HP)

$27,297.

Z57 COUPE
17,210.

Riviera Coupe interior.

ASTROROOF (OPT.)

Riviera Convertible.

Leather-wrapped sport steering wheel (T Type)

TURBO 231 CID V6 (200 HP) IN T-TYPE

Y57
T-TYPE V6
TURBO CPE.

$18,154.

Z67

1094

BUICK **SKYLARK**
FR. $11100.

4 OR V6

SOMERSET
DASH

T-TYPE $10591.
JE270

SKYHAWK
4 OR TURBO 4
101.2" WB
FR. $9539.

SKYHAWK

SKYHAWK DASH

Somerset S/E.

4 OR V6

SOMERSET

$10905. UP

SKYHAWK LTD.
$10293.
JT69P.

V6 OR 4

CENTURY
$12136. UP

86

V.I.N. =
1G4 ( )
-C-#

$14128.
REGAL T TYPE

GK477

REGAL
DASH

REGAL

24 MPH
REGAL OR
NATIONAL

(STD. GRILLE) $11818.

(LE SABRE DASH SIMILAR)

V6 TURBO,
V6, OR
V8
FROM

new 110.8" WB
FRONT WH. DRIVE
LE SABRE
V6
(V8
WAGON)

RIVIERA ELECTRONIC DASH (BELOW) (V6)

ELECTRA
DASH

V6 **ELECTRA**
$16316. UP

V8 WAGON
(AVAIL.)

T TYPE
SEDAN
CF69B

COUPE

55

110
MPH
(RIVIERA
T-TYPE)

RIVIERA
Touch the screen of the
Graphic Control Center to tell it
what you want and it responds
with information, it provides
control of audio and climate
control systems, it even tells you
specifically about systems that
need your attention. And tells

Buick

SKYHAWK CPES. FROM $10,282. →

25/31 MPG w. 122 cid 4
21/27 " w. 121 cid TURBO 4

"J" BODY

SKYHAWK

INT.

87

JS811 CUSTOM WAGON $11,009.

JT 811 LTD. WAGON $11,601.

SKYHAWK WAGON MPG: 24/31 (121 cid 4)

1987 BUICK V.I.N.
1G4 (JS51K) - H - #

AVAIL. ON SKYLK.

SKYLARK $11,450. UP

OR SOMRST.

SKYHAWK WHEEL CHOICES
"N" BODY

SKYLARK

(SEDANS ONLY)

SKYLARK DASH

SOMERSET DASH

AVAIL. ON SKYLARK OR SOMERSET

WITH DECK RACK

MPG: 22/32 (151 cid 4 SKYLK. and SOMRST.)

NM14U SOMERSET LTD. $12,538.

INTERIOR

(THE FINAL SOMERSET) "N" BODY

SOMERSET

(COUPES ONLY)

NJ14U SOMERSET CUSTOM $11,492.

WITH BLACKOUT "T" PKG. ↑

Where better really matters.

W. EXTERIOR SPORT PKG.

CENTURY DASH

CENT. LTD. INTERIOR

"A" BODY
CENTURY

V6 OR 4

PRICED FROM
$12,643.

22/32 MPG
W. 151 CID 4;
20/26
W. 173 CID V6

AL51W LIMITED SEDAN
$13,392.

CENTURY WAGON

AL81W

(UNGRAINED AH81W
CENTURY CUSTOM WAG.
$13,277.)

CENTURY WAGON MPG:
21/28 (151 CID 4)

ESTATE WAGON
$13,797.

87

"G" BODY
REGAL

V6 OR V8 OR V6 TURBO

(FINAL) GRAND NATIONAL

REGAL MPG:
19/24 (231 CID V6)
17/23 (307 CID V8)

REGAL DASH

$13,492.

GM11A LIMITED COUPE
115 MPH

"T" PKG. (W. TURBO)

Buick

BR81Y

LeSABRE
new GRILLE
FROM
$13,913.
"H" BODY

3.8 L V6

LeSABRE ESTATE WAGON
"B" BODY

$15,199.

W. T-TYPE PKG. 117 MPH
(new for LeS.)

87
"C" BODY
ELECTRA
PRICED FROM
$18,269.

CW513
$19,641.

BV81Y
ELECTRA ESTATE WAGON
$18,744.   "B" BODY
ELECTRA DASH

WAGON
MPG:
16/24
(307 CID V8, IN
LE SAB. or ELECT.)

WHEEL CHOICES

ELECTRA/PARK AVENUE

"E" BODY
RIVIERA
EZ113

RIVIERA DASH (new OIL PRESSURE GA.)

IMPROVED
3.8 L V6

$21,229.

JS511 SEDAN $10,800.

26/36 MPG (5 SP. MAN.)
25/32 MPG (AUTO. TR.)

JS811 WAGON $11,745.

FRONT DETAIL

POWER STEERING, POWER FRONT DISC BRAKES, AM/FM STEREO RADIO, CLOCK ARE STD. EQUIPMENT. MPG: 36 HWY, 26 CITY (5-SP.)

2.0 L 4 (90 HP @ 5600 RPM)

SKYHAWK

(LEFT, and ABOVE)

25/36 MPG

(THE FINAL SKYHAWK)

89

1989 BUICK V.I.N. = 1G4 (JS511) -K- #

JS111 SKYHAWK CPE. $10,800.

SKYLARK INTERIOR

Skylark

REAR QUARTER VIEW OF SKYLARK SEDAN

(SKYLARK COUPE ON NEXT PAGE)

NC54U CUSTOM SEDAN $12,116.

ND54U LIMITED SEDAN $13,376.

23/32 MPG (4 CYL.) 20/27 MPG (V6)

1100

BUICK

SKYLARK
(CONT'D.)

3300 MFI V6
(160 HP @ 5200 RPM)

27/20 MPG

NJ14U CUSTOM COUPE $12,116.

2.5 L TECH 4
(115 HP @ 5200 RPM)
DOHC 2.3 L
QUAD 4
(150 HP @ 5200)

NM14U LIMITED COUPE $13,376.

89

MPG
(SKYLARK)
32/23 2.3 4
30/23 2.5 4

19/30 MPG

AH81N CENTURY CUSTOM WAGON $13,606.

AL81N CENTURY ESTATE WAGON

$14,406.

Century offers a wealth of premium features: New optional 160-horsepower 3300 V-6 engine   Automatic transmission, power steering and power front disc brakes   6-passenger roominess and 16.2-cubic-foot trunk   AM-FM stereo radio and clock, and extended-range speakers   Whitewall tires with deluxe wheelcovers   And more.

Century.

2.5 L TECH 4
(98 HP @ 4800 RPM)

MPG:
30 HWY,
23 CITY
(4 CYL.)

AH11N CUSTOM COUPE $12,649.

$12,879.

AH51N CUSTOM SEDAN

20/29 MPG
(6 CYL.)

CENTURY RESTYLED

AL51N LIMITED SEDAN

$13,806.

1101

WB14W CUSTOM CP.
$14,669.

BUICK Regal.

20/29 MPG

Regal features: a 2.8-litre V-6 engine 4-wheel independent DynaRide suspension 4-wheel power disc brakes Front-wheel drive Air conditioning Automatic transmission with overdrive Reclining front seats AM-FM stereo with seek and scan.

The Great American Road belongs to BUICK

BUICK LeSABRE

WD14W LIMITED COUPE
$15,194.

FINAL LE SABRE T-TYPE in 1989

(UNGRAINED)

17/24 MPG
LeSabre Estate Wagon.

T-TYPE COUPE 3800 V6 (165 HP @ 4800 RPM) MPG: 28/19

89

19/28 MPG (LE SAB.)

HR14C LIMITED CPE.
$17,135.

BR81Y LE SABRE ESTATE WAG. (GRAINED)

$17,275.

LE SABRE
HP54C CUSTOM SEDAN $15,835.
HR54C LIMITED " 17,235.

Electra and LeSabre Estate Wagons
RETAIN OLD STYLING, V8s

FINAL YR. FOR SEPARATE LESABRE and ELECTRA ESTATE WAGONS.

WAGON MPG: 24 HWY., 17 CITY

WAGON 5.0 L V8 has 140 HP @ 3200

$21,440.
BV81Y ELECTRA ESTATE WAGON

ELECTRA ESTATE WAGON

Buick CF54C T TYPE
$22597.

ELECTRA

Electra/Park Avenue. $21142.

(9AME V6,
MPG AS LeS.)

CU54C

new Buick Ultra.

RIVIERA

Riviera
$23,525 EC11C

RIVIERA GRILLE

RIVIERA FRONT END CLOSE-UP

19/28 MPG

REATTA INT.

89

The distinctive Reatta combines the exhilaration of a sports car with the luxury of a Buick.

Crafted in limited numbers to exacting quality standards, its long list of premium features includes: 165-horsepower 3800 V-6 · 4-wheel anti-lock disc braking system · 4-wheel independent suspension · 6-way power seats · Hand-buffed finish.

Reatta

EC11C
$27,250.

19/28 MPG

BUICK

(SKYHAWK MODELS DISCONTINUED)

SKYLARKS FROM $11811.

13.6 GAL. FUEL TANK 20/31 MPG

NJ14U

New
DASH and INTERIOR (SKYLARK)

SKYLARK 4 OR V6 (110 OR 160 HP)

$13063.

SKYLARK CUSTOM COUPE

new SKYLARK LUXURY EDIT. SEDAN HAS UNIQUE REAR DOOR and REAR QUARTER PANELS

New GRILLE

ND54U SKYLARK LUXURY EDITION

103.4" WB

$14585.

90

V.I.N. = 1G4 (NV54U) - L - #

$16615.

$15730. CENTURY CUSTOM WAG.

CENTURY LIMITED WAGON

AL84N

CENTURY A SERIES
104.8" WB
HAS 2.5 L 4 (110 HP)
OR 3.3 L V6 (160 HP)

CENTURY SED. REAR QUARTERS

REGAL HAS 3.1L, 191 CID V6 OR 3.8L, 231 CID V6 (135 OR 170 HP)

new REGAL SEDAN HAS ITS OWN GRILLE DESIGN

W SERIES
V6 REGAL

REGAL COUPE $15655. UP

REGAL CUSTOM OR LIMITED SEDANS

NEW

16.5 GALLON FUEL TANK 19/30 MPG

REGAL

107½" WB

1104

BUICK

CUSTOM or LIMITED TYPES IN MOST BUICK MODEL SERIES.

LE SABRE SEDAN **$16555.** and up

LE SABRE COUPE

LeSabre V6

H SERIES

90

LE SABRE GRILLE →

110.8" WB ON LE SABRE or ELECTRA

ELECTRA/PARK AVENUE
← ULTRA CU54C

C SERIES
ELECTRA/
CF54C T TYPE

$21784. UP (LTD. SEDAN)

ELECTRA PARK AVENUE FRONT END →

ULTRA WHEEL DESIGN

3.8L V6 231 CID (165 HP @ 4800 RPM) 19/28 MPG 18 GAL. FUEL TK.

PARK AVE
CW54C $23/25.

2 DIFF. RIVIERA ROOFS

108" WB

$28375.

$24455.
new RIVIERA DASH LIKE REATTA's BUT GRAINED.

RIVIERA V6

EC14C

$28885.

REATTA V6 LIKE ELECT.

DASH (REATTA)

NEW

RIVIERA GRILLE

REATTA CONV'T. EC34C

REATTA FRONT END

18/27 MPG(EPA)

98½" WB

$18445.

WITH 307 CID 5.0L V8 140 HP @ 3200 RPM) 17/24 MPG

BR84Y
ESTATE WAGON
(1 TYPE ONLY)
REPLACES SEPARATE LE SABRE / ELECTRA WAGONS

WAGON INT.

FR. END

115.9" WB

22 GAL. FUEL TK.

$14,999.

Cadillac

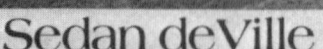
Sedan deVille

Cabriolet

81
121.4" WB

The Cabriolet roof treatment shown is available for Coupe deVille with gleaming crossover roof molding. A similar treatment is standard with Fleetwood Brougham Coupe.

Coupe deVille

$14,997.

GM Cadillac

New for 1981... V8-6-4 Fuel Injection is standard equipment.

V8 (GAS) 368 CID

V.I.N. =
1G6A (   )B(-)
000001 UP

NEW GRILLE

252 CID V6

New 24.6 Gallon Fuel Tank. Standard with V8-6-4 engine. 25 gallon fuel tank standard with V6. 27 gallon fuel tank standard with Diesel.

New Underhood Light. Provides nighttime illumination of oil dipstick, belts and other engine components.

Available V6 engine. (With overdrive for Fleetwood Broughams and DeVilles.)

1981 Cadillac Radios
including new Symphonic Sound System.

New Symphonic Sound System with Cassette Player and Electronically Tuned AM/FM Stereo Radio

Diesel Power available across the line.

350 CID 105 HP

Cadillac announces V8-6-4 Fuel Injection

New
As you drive, the 1981 Cadillac automatically goes from 8 to 6 to 4 cylinders.

Fleetwood Brougham

(4 OTHER RADIO/TAPE SETS SHOWN W. 1981 SEVILLE.)

$16,552.

Is V8-6-4 Fuel Injection standard equipment?
Yes, the V8-6-4 fuel-injected engine is the standard gasoline engine for all 1981 Cadillacs.

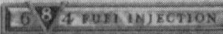
6 8 4 FUEL INJECTION

How does it operate?
As you leave your driveway, all 8 cylinders in your gasoline-powered 1981 Cadillac are in operation. Then, as you reach intermediate speeds on a street or avenue and your power requirements lessen, the car automatically switches to 6 cylinders. And then, when you reach cruising speeds and your power needs decrease further, the car automatically switches to 4-cylinder operation.

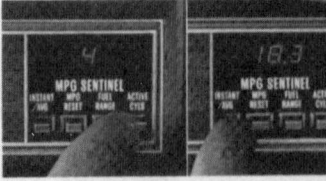

Active cylinder display shown left   one function of new MPG Sentinel

Can I tell how many cylinders are active at any given time?

Yes. Push a button and Cadillac's MPG Sentinel on the instrument panel shows a digital display of the number of cylinders active at that moment. The MPG Sentinel will also show instantaneous mpg and average mpg.

SPECIAL 144.5" WB
$25,933.

Cadillac Limousine

Cadillac
It's a new power system

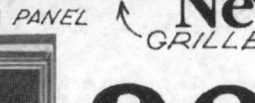
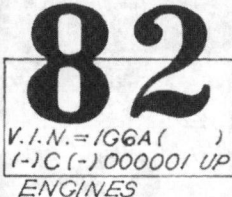

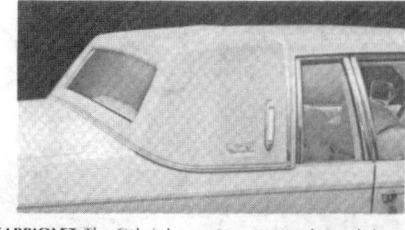

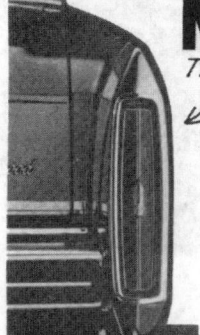

Cadillac

THE FLEETWOOD LIMOUSINES
$32,197. (FORMAL)

LIMO. SED.
$31,323.

144 1/2" WB

PARTIAL VIEW OF DASH

17 MPG EPA 22 DIESEL

252 CID V8 (135 HP) 350 CID DIES. V8 (105 HP) OR 368 CID V8-6-4 (140 HP) '83

SEDAN DE VILLE $18,494.

"Cadillac" NAME MOVED DOWN ONTO GRILLE, 1983.

new 1983
HT 4100 ALUMINUM-BLOCK EFI ENG. STD. IN ALL BUT CIMARRON + FLEETWD. LIMO.

83-84

(DETAIL AT LOWER LEFT OF DIFFERENCE BETW. 1983 and 1984.)

$18,009.

DE VILLES

COUPE DE VL.

Standard De Ville Wheel Disc.

note new 1984 WINGED EMBLEM ON TURN SIGNAL GLASS.

V.I.N. INCLUDES
– XD (1983)
– XE (1984)

Front Cornering Lights and Lamp Monitors.

WINGED EMBLEM NOT ON 1983 GLASS.

105 MPH

1984 EXAMPS. ILLUSTR.

FLEETWOOD BROUGHAM

CPE. $20,811.

1108

REAR QUARTER EMBLEM ON FLTWD. BR. 4-DR.

Standard Fleetwood Brougham Wheel Disc.

New 1985 Coupe de Ville $16,999**

Cadillac

TOTALLY RESTYLED DE VILLE and STD. FLEETWOOD NOW WITH FRONT-WHEEL-DRIVE **New** →

* REGULARLY $18,859.

FRONT-WH-DR. FLEETWOOD $21,909.

SEDAN DE VILLE

105 MPH

249 CID V8
(135 HP @ 4400 RPM)
2.97 GEAR RATIO
P205/75R14 TIRES
18-GAL. FUEL TK.

$19,440.

FLEETWOOD BROUGHAM

FRONT DETAILS OF FRONT-WHEEL-DRIVE FLEETWOOD

V.I.N.=
1G6
( )
XF
(-)
#

85

SOME MODELS DOWNSIZED TO 110.8" WB, WITH FRONT-WHEEL-DRIVE

Some Cadillacs are equipped with engines produced by other GM divisions, subsidiaries or affiliated companies worldwide.

(REAR WHEEL DR.)
121½" WB

— HIGH MOUNTED CENTER STOP LAMP **New** BECOMES MANDATORY ON ALL NEW CARS SOLD IN U.S.A. STARTING FALL, 1985.

"STRETCH LIMOUSINE"
(BY MOLONEY)
CHICAGO

(NEW 134.4" WB LIMO. ALSO AVAIL. IN FRONT-WH.-DR. FLEETWOOD SER.)

Cadillac Fleetwood with center high-mounted

CADILLAC'S NEW 4-YEAR/50,000-MILE LIMITED WARRANTY!
The 1985 front-wheel drive Fleetwood and De Villes are backed by Cadillac's special new limited warranty. In some cases, a deductible applies. See your dealer for details.

BEST OF ALL...IT'S A CADILLAC

CADILLAC

FLEETWOOD
BROUGHAM
CONTINUES
(w. NEW 5.0-LITRE
V8 (140 HP @
3200 RPM)
307 CID

TOURING COUPE
TOURING SEDAN
106 MPH

NEW
(w. 4.1 LITRE V8)
130 HP @ 4200 RPM
249 CID

DEVILLE PRICES START AT $20,559.
(new TOURING COUPE
OR TOURING SEDAN PKG. OPT.)

BACKGROUND:
SAN FRANCISCO, CA.

SEDAN DE VILLE

86 new
MODELS
ADDED

DIESEL
ENGINES
NOT LISTED
IN 1986.

FLEETWOOD

(FLEETWOOD
BROUGHAM
$22,155.
(DW698)

V.I.N. = 106 (DW698)
- G - #

Limousine

FLEETWD.
75
NEW

CLOSE-UP OF
FORMAL ROOFLINE
REAR QUARTERS

1110   CH33B   FORMAL LIMOUSINE $36,590.
134.4" WB

1987 (DEVILLE) MPG: 17/25 (w. 302 cid V8) (SAME FOR FLEETWOOD)

Cadillac

1987 (BROUGHAM) MPG: 18/25 (w. 307 cid V8)

1987 (LIMOUSINE) MPG: 17/24 (w. 249 cid V8)

"C" BODY

('87)

DE VILLE
(ABOVE)

1987 V.I.N. = 1G6 ( ) - H - #
(new COMPOSITE HDLTS.)

(DEVILLE TOURING OPTION PACKAGE $2880. EXTRA IN 1987. ALSO AVAIL. '88)

87-88

new GRILLE WITH "WAFFLE" CRISS-CROSS PCS.

1988 V.I.N. = 1G8 ( ) - J - #

AVAILABLE 1987~1988
MODELS =   (PRICES)

			MODEL ID #
DEVILLE 4-DR. —	$23,138.	('87)	CD518
	24,834.	('88)	CD515
DEVILLE 2-DR. —	22,795.	('87)	CD118
	24,479.	('88)	CD115
BROUGHAM ———	24,096.	('87)	DW518
	25,072.	('88)	DW51Y
FLEETWOOD D'ELEGANCE —	27,333.	('87)	CB518
new	29,454.	('88)	CB515
FLEETWOOD 60 SPECIAL —	36,079.	('87)	C9518
(115.8" WB)	36,180.	('88)	C9515
FLEETWOOD 75 LIMOUSINE —	37,739.	('87)	CH518
PRESIDENTIAL LIMO. (LWB)		('88)	

INTERIOR (BR.)

Cadillac 5.0 LITER

1988

CADILLAC BROUGHAM
"D" BODY

('88)

THIS 121½" WB BRGHM. WAS AMERICA'S LONGEST REGULAR PRODUCTION CAR, AT THE TIME (EXCEPT FOR LIMOUSINES)

Cadillac Brougham, America's longest production car.

THE ONLY WAY TO TRAVEL IS   CADILLAC STYLE.

CADILLAC

DEVILLE

$26,309.

$28,446. ('90)

DEVILLE DASH

89-90
longer

WB ON SEDANS (113.8")

(2 DR., 110.8")

Sedan de Ville

DE VILLE

17/25 MPG

Cadillac
4.5 LITER V8

4.5 LITRE, 273 CID
V8 ENGINE (155 HP)
(180 HP IN 1990)

CADILLAC STYLE

18/25 MPG
18 GAL. FUEL TK.

(1989 EXAMPLES ILLUSTR., UNLESS OTHERWISE INDICATED)

FLTWD. SEDAN
$30,850.
$33,530. ('90)

FLEETWOOD

60 S. INT.

Sixty Special

('90)

17/24 MPG ('89)

60-SPECIAL SEDAN has EXCLUSIVE 22-WAY-ADJUSTABLE POWER SEAT! →

$34,780. 37,530. ('90)

■ Standard full padded roof w Sedan and Fleetwood Sixty Special)

■ Standard formal cabriolet roof-Fleetw

1990 DASH W. AIR BAG IN STEER. WH. HUB

← 1989 DASH

■ Available painted metal roof shown with available Astroroof (reduces headroom slightly)

FLEETWOOD

$26,968. ('89)
28,718. ('90)

CADILLAC

CHROME PILLAR ON 1990

QUILTED UPHOLSTERY (PLEATED ALSO AVAIL.) ('89)

BROUGHAM MODELS WITH OWN GRILLE DESIGN.

OWN GRILLE DESIGN.

NEW

(BOLDER)

BROUGHAM

BROUGHAM FUEL TK. 25 GAL.
17/24 MPG (307 CID)
14/21 " (350 CID)

new 175 HP 5.7 L V8 AVAIL. 1990 (350 CID) (307 CID ALSO)

1990 has COMPOSITE HDLTS. + new CRNR. LIGHTS.

89-90
STRETCH
LIMOUSINES

LIMOUSINE
NINETEEN HUNDRED NINETY

1989 V.I.N. = 1G6 (   ) -K- #

24K GOLD-FINISH KEYS

LIMO. INTERIOR

The only way to travel is Cadillac style.

1990 V.I.N. = 1G6 (   ) -L- #

1113

CADILLAC ALLANTÉ

"V" BODY

ALUMINUM OR FABRIC TOPS

ROADSTER
123 MPH ('87)
119 MPH ('88)

BUCKET RECARO LEATHER SEATS

* V.I.N. = VR 3/8 ('87) – H – #
  VR 3/7 ('88) – J – #
  " " ON
  ('89) – K – #;
  CVT. VR 338 ('90)
  CVT./HT VR 338 ('90)
  – L – #

87-90

New
FOR 1987

* ALL V.I.N.s
  BEGIN WITH 1G6

22 GAL. FUEL TANK
15/22 MPG (EPA)

STD. EQUIPMENT
DRIVER AIRBAG and
new ANTI-SPIN
TRACTION CONTROL
IN 1990

PININFARINA
DESIGN

PRICES =
$55,200. ('87)
56,533. ('88)
57,183. ('89)
CVT.
51,550. ('90)
1990
CVT./HT
57,183.

TRUNK

ALLANTÉ

TRUNK LOCK
DETAIL

REAR

(1989
EXAMPLES
ILLUSTRATED)

99.4" W.B.
V8 ENGINE
249 CID
170 HP @ 4300 RPM
(1989 = new 200 HP)
@ 4400 RPM)   273 CID ('90)

ANALOG OR DIGITAL GAUGES

DIGITAL   15/22 MPG, 1990   ANALOG

Cadillac Cimarron
THIS IS THE NEW

CADILLAC'S FIRST AND ONLY COMPACT CAR! (4 DR. SEDANS ONLY)

P195/70R13 TIRES

REG. PRICE $12,906.

($12,131. SPECIAL PRICE)

FRONT-WHEEL-DRIVE

DASH →

6JG69

ANNOUNCING  BY CADILLAC

Quick-handling. Road-hugging. And fun to drive. This is Cimarron. An efficient new kind of Cadillac. With the traction of front-wheel drive. MacPherson strut front suspension and power-assisted rack and pinion steering with responsive 14:1 steering gear ratio. Plus it has Cadillac refinements such as genuine leather seating areas for five, body-contoured front bucket seats, air conditioning and more. All standard. Test drive Cimarron by Cadillac. Now available at all Cadillac dealers.

42 [26]*

*Use estimated mpg for comparison. Your mileage may differ depending on speed, distance, weather. Actual highway mileage lower. Some Cadillacs are equipped with engines produced by other GM divisions, subsidiaries, or affiliated companies worldwide. See your dealer for details.

A NEW KIND OF CADILLAC FOR A NEW KIND OF CADILLAC OWNER.

X-RAY VIEW BELOW

Front-wheel drive.

Leather-wrapped steering wheel.

Genuine leather seating areas for five.

Power-assisted rack and pinion steering with responsive 14:1 steering gear ratio.

Semi-independent rear suspension with variable rate springs.

Fully independent MacPherson strut front suspension.

Stabilizer bars — front and rear.

Same front legroom as some full-size cars.

42 highway estimate... [26] EPA estimated mpg*... with manual transmission.

Body-contoured front bucket seats with lumbar support.

Four-speed manual overdrive transmission. (Three-speed automatic available at extra cost.)

Aluminum alloy wheels... with computer-matched tires.

$12,131**

V.I.N. = 1G6A G69G (-) C (-)

82 new

101.2" WB
4 CYLINDER, 112.4 CID ENG.
85 HP
14 GALLON FUEL TANK

	CIMARRON
EPA MILEAGE RATINGS WITH STD. TRANS. HWY EST. EPA EST. MPG*	42 / [26]
FRONT-WHEEL DRIVE	STANDARD
POWER-ASSISTED RACK AND PINION STEERING	STANDARD
FOUR-SPEED MANUAL INCLUDING OVERDRIVE	STANDARD
TACHOMETER	STANDARD
EPA PASSENGER COMPARTMENT VOLUME	89 CU. FT.
ALUMINUM ALLOY WHEELS	STANDARD
AIR CONDITIONING	STANDARD
LEATHER WRAPPED STEERING WHEEL	STANDARD
LEATHER SEATING AREAS	STANDARD
MSRP**	$12,131 (F.O.B.)

V.I.N. 1G6A-G69(-)XD(-)000001 up

new 121 CID 4
88 HP   25 MPG, EPA

$12,905.

"Cadillac" NAME IN SCRIPT, ON GRILLE

6JG69

83

new GRILLE

new HOOD MEDALLION

new FOG LAMPS (TUNGSTEN HALOGEN)

1115   new ALUMINUM ALLOY WHEELS

2.83 G.R. (5 SP. MANUAL TR.)
3.18 G.R. (3 SP. A/T)

1984
DASH →

"D'ORO" PKG.
BLACK w. GILT TRIM   LEATHER UPHOLSTERY

(LEATHER FACED
FRONT BUCKET
SEATS STD.)

84

new GRILLE
IN 1984

CIMARRON '84
THIS ONE'S GOT THE TOUCH.

new TAIL LIGHTS and EXTERIOR TRIM $13,304.

V.I.N. = 1G6A G69 PXE (-) 000001 UP

G69P
(6JG69)

6JG69P

V.I.N. = 1G6A G69 PXF (-) 000001 UP

85

New SIDE TRIM
and MOLDINGS

CADILLAC CIMARRON

new STEERING
WHEEL
WITH SQUARED
CENTER PC.

$14,242.
("D'ORO" PKG.
$934. EXTRA)

A NEW BREED OF AGILE, MOBILE,
NEW STYLE CADILLAC

CLOSE-UP VIEW OF
HOOD MEDALLION

THE LUXURY OF LEATHER IN THE
CADILLAC OF SMALLER CARS

101.2" WB

3.18 GEAR RATIO
P195/70R13
TIRES
13.6 GAL. FUEL
TANK

TAIL LIGHT
DETAILS

1985 Cimarron
The Cadillac of smaller cars

Best of all...it's a Cadillac.

new
173 CID *
V6 AVAIL.,
IN ADDITION
TO 4-CYL.
121 CID. 88 HP ENG.

110 MPH WITH V6
* 129 HP @ 4800 RPM

CHOOSE V6 POWER AND GAS-CHARGED SHOCKS
IN CIMARRON... CADILLAC CIMARRON

1986 CIMARRON
BEST OF ALL...
IT'S A CADILLAC.
Let's Get It Together... Buckle Up.

new HIGH-UP EXTRA BRAKE LIGHT IN REAR WINDOW

Cadillac CIMARRON

86

2.8 Liter V6

BUCKET SEATS

V.I.N.=1G6 (JG69P)-G-#

FRONT   REAR

4 = 88 HP @ 4800 RPM
V6 = 129 " @ 4800

$15,004.

new DASH

JG69P

PERHAPS THE MOST SURPRISING NEW CAR YOU'LL DRIVE THIS YEAR.

V.I.N. (1987)=1G6 (JG51W)-H-#

SHEDS NEW LIGHT ON LUXURY AND PERFORMANCE.

(1986½ SLOGAN)

$15,817.

($16,886. IN 1988)

THIS new FRONT STYLING FIRST AVAIL. ON SPECIAL "D'ORO" EARLY '86 MODEL.

JG51W (1987-1988)

new COMPOSITE HEADLIGHTS, WITH WRAP-AROUND TURN INDICATORS and PARKING LAMPS

CONTROL STALK OF THE IMPROVED

CUSTOM CRUISE III

(AVAIL. ON MOST GM-BLT. CARS)

(86½)

"J" BODY

('87)

(1986½ STARTS SPRING, 1986 ; SOME MAY CONSIDER IT "EARLY 1987.")

86½-88

The Sporty Spirit of Cadillac.

(1987)

1987 MPG 23/30 (121 CID 4) 20/26 (173 CID V6)

CIMARRON DISCONTINUED 1988.

V.I.N. (1988)=1G6 (JG51W)-J-#

EL DORADO
A MODEL
SERIES
SINCE '53.

Cadillac ELDORADO

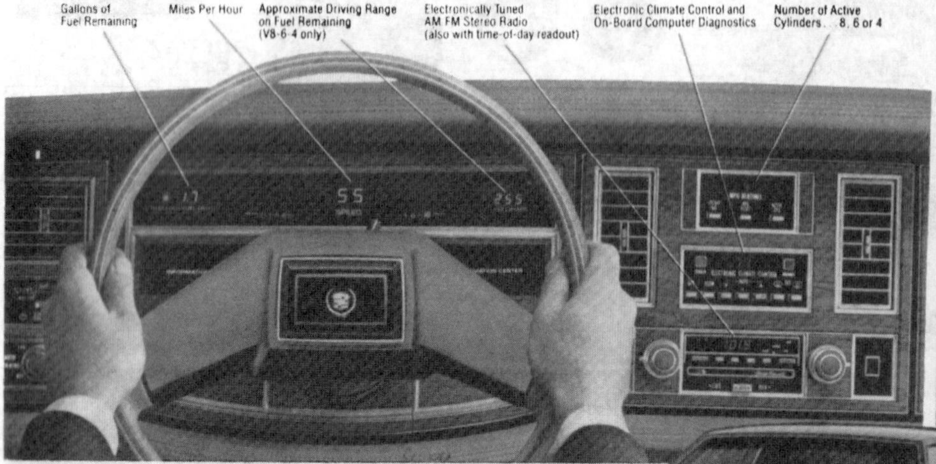

Gallons of Fuel Remaining
Miles Per Hour
Approximate Driving Range on Fuel Remaining (V8-6-4 only)
Electronically Tuned AM FM Stereo Radio (also with time-of-day readout)
Electronic Climate Control and On-Board Computer Diagnostics
Number of Active Cylinders... 8, 6 or 4

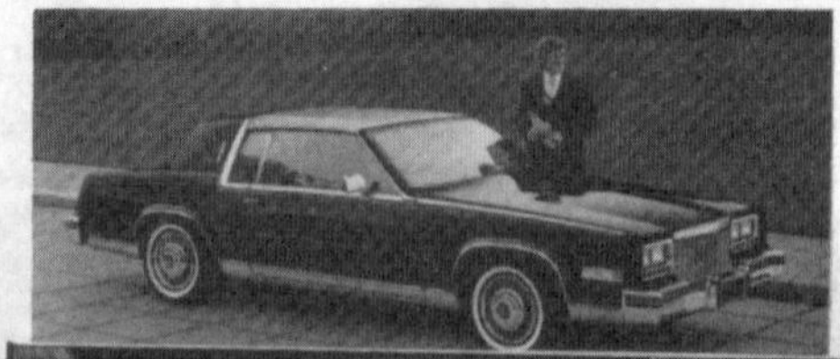

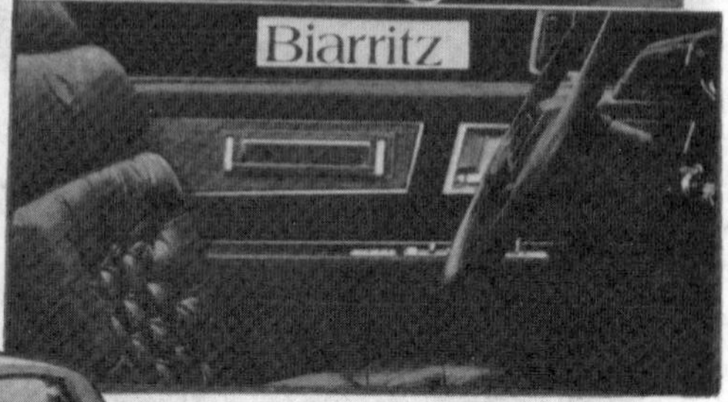

Biarritz

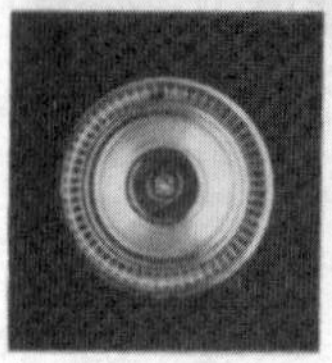

Standard Eldorado Wheel Covers

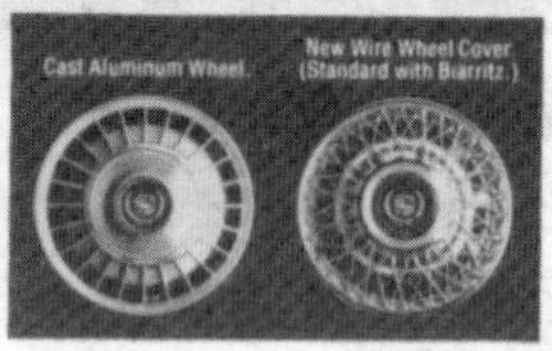

Cast Aluminum Wheel.
New Wire Wheel Cover (Standard with Biarritz.)

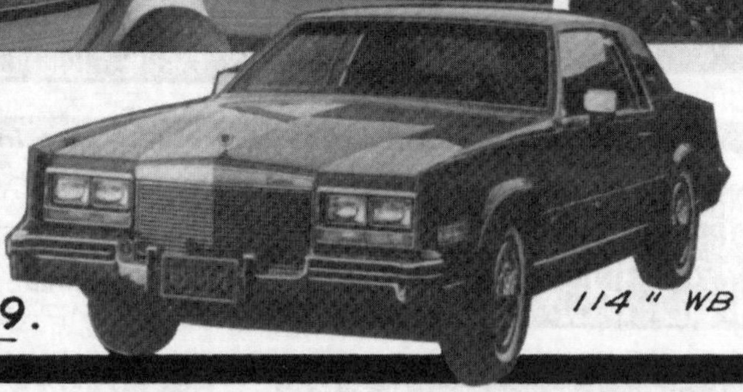

$20,186.
(BIARRITZ)

81

"V8 - 6 - 4" ENGINE AVAIL. (368 CID)

FRONT-WHEEL-DR. (SINCE 1967)

$17,249.

114" WB

V.I.N.=1G6AL5740B(-)#

CHOICE OF 5 COLORS OF LEATHER UPHOLSTERY IN BIARRITZ, $22880.

(NOT ILLUSTR.)

$19,545.

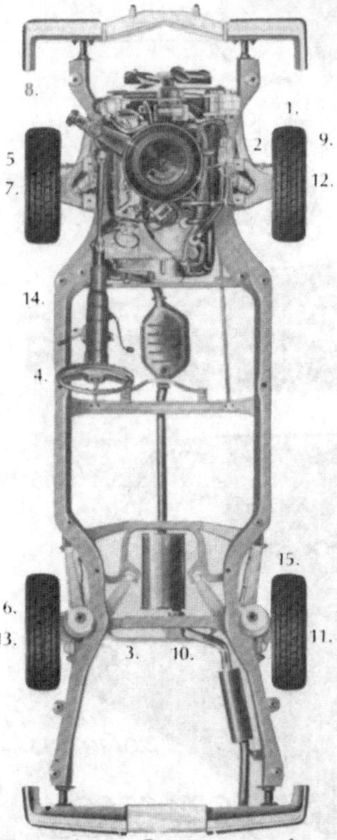

8.
1.
2
9.
5
7.
12.
14.
4.
15.
6.
13.
3.
10.
11.

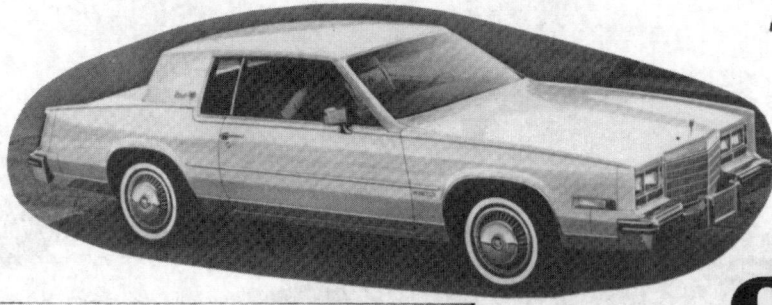

new GRILLE WITH ONLY 4 HORIZONTAL PCS.

V.I.N.=1G6AL578(-)C(-)000001 UP

82

TOURING COUPE HAS CAP-LIKE FLAT HOOD ORNAMENT, AS ILLUSTR.

20.3 GAL. FUEL TK. 17 MPG (EPA)

TOURING CPE. INTERIOR

Special Edition... Eldorado Touring Coupe

note GROOVED BRIGHTWORK, LOWER SIDES.

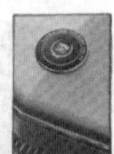

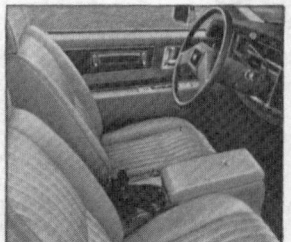

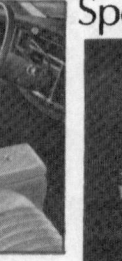

Touring Suspension...
Available for Eldorado and Seville.

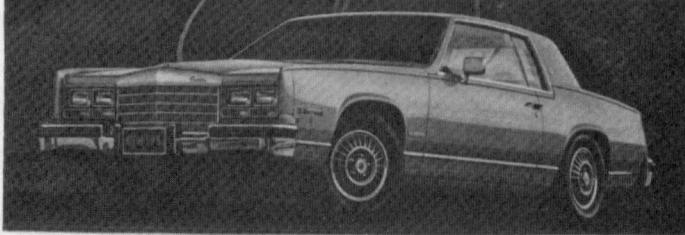

CADILLAC
ELDORADO

BIARRITZ
$23,593.

OPT. FULL CABR. ROOF ↓

Eldorado Biarritz
Outside, this Eldorado "dream machine" for 1983 features a brushed stainless steel roof cap, wire wheel covers, opera lamps and "Biarritz" script on the sail panels. Inside, tufted pillow-style seating and steering wheel are tailored in rich Sierra Grain leather. Eldorado Biarritz is shown in Cotillion White with a matching Elk Grain Cabriolet vinyl roof.

Eldorado Touring Coupe
Created for the person who loves to drive, Eldorado TC has a firm "feel the road" responsiveness. Large diameter stabilizer bars. Reclining leather faced bucket seats with lumbar and lateral support. Large P225/70R15 steel belted blackwall radial tires. (Tire chains should not be used with these tires. Their use may cause damage to your car.) And more. Including a special cloisonne medallion on the hood. Available in two colors: Sonora Saddle Firemist and Sable Black, shown.

17 MPG EPA
21 MPG, DIESEL EPA

83

V.I.N. = 1G6AL578 XD (-)00000/ UP

STD. ELDORADO FROM **$20,198.**

four-wheel disc brakes, Digital Fuel Injection and more. Including the available Full Cabriolet roof shown.

20.3 GAL. FUEL TANK (22.9 " " WITH DIESEL V8)

BEST OF ALL...IT'S A CADILLAC.
Let's Get It Together...Buckle Up.

COUPE

the Eldorado Biarritz for 1984.

135 HP @ 4400 RPM (105 @ 3200 IN DIESEL V8)

$32,155.
(CONVT.)
↓
(STD. ELDORADO COUPE FROM **$21,211.**)

2.10 G.R. (1.95 " WITH DIESEL)

CADILLAC'S FIRST STOCK CONVERT-IBLE AVAIL. SINCE '76!

84
NEW!

THE CADILLAC OF CONVERTIBLES IS BACK!

1119

V.I.N.= 1G6AL 578 XE (-) 00000/ UP

C A D I L L A C
E L D O R A D O

BIARRITZ COUPE
EL 578
$25,195.

COUPE

EL 678

FINAL
BIARRITZ CVT. $32,974.

85

V.I.N.=1G6A
L578 XF (-)
00000/ UP

COUPES FROM
$21,800.

EL 578
$24,751. ('86)
$24,819. ('87)
EL 118

↑
STD.
EL DORADO COUPE (has CADILLAC
CREST ON REAR QUARTER PANEL)

CONVT. NOT
LISTED 1986 ON

V.I.N. (1986)=1G6 (EL 578)
—G— #

(CABRIOLET-STYLE ROOF OPTION
AVAIL. 1987.)

SUSPENSION
RE-TUNED 1987
FOR A SOFTER
RIDE.

1986 EXAMPLES
SHOWN

86-87

TOTALLY RESTYLED,
AND
WHEELBASE
SHORTENED TO
108," IN 1986.

"E" BODY

INTERIOR
(BIARRITZ)

1987 MPG: 17/25
(249 cid V8)

note "Biarritz" NAME
ON RT. SIDE OF
DECK LID
and ON
PADDED
REAR
QUARTER
PANEL.

↑
BIARRITZ (CPE. ONLY)
$27,846. ('86) EL 578
27,664. ('87) EL 118

V.I.N. (1987)=1G6 (EL 118)
—H— #

FRONT END
(ELDORADO)

1120

CADILLAC

Eldorado

DRIVER AIRBAG STD IN 1990

108" WB

■ Available gold ornamentation
- rear script (shown)

RESTYLED

LONGER AMBER SIDE LIGHT, new GRILLE

88—90

17/25 MPG ('89)

EL 115 ('88)
EL 118 ('89)
EL 133 ('90)

273 cu
new 180 HP (4.5 L) EFI V8 in 1990,
new BUMPER MOLDINGS

STD. "SNOWFLAKE LOOK" ALUMINUM ALLOY WHEEL new IN 1988.
WIRE WHEEL DISC ON BIARRITZ, OPT. OTHERWISE.

DASH

RESHAPED REAR WINDOW TREATMENT, 1988

Standard painted metal roof (not available on Eldorado Biarritz)

Available full cabriolet roof for Eldorado (not available on Eldorado Biarritz)

Standard formal cabriolet padded roof with opera lamps for Eldorado Biarritz

■ Available full padded roof for Eldorado (not available on Biarritz). Shown with available Astroroof (reduces headroom slightly)

16/25 MPG, 1990
18.8 GALLON FUEL TANK

FROM
$26,321.
('88)
$27,288.
('89)

(1989 EXAMPLES ILLUSTRATED)

V.I.N. ENDS WITH -J-# (1988);
-K-# (1989); -L-# (1990)

Cast aluminum wheel.
Available at no extra cost.

Standard cross-laced wire
wheel cover.

Cadillac SEVILLE (SINCE 1976)

BRITISH-STYLE CLASSIC "KNIFE-EDGE" BODY SINCE 1980

TRUNK
DETAILS

Cadillac-size trunk has over 14 cubic feet of usable space.

Seville.

$21547.

V.I.N. =
1G6 (-)
S69 (N)
(-) B
(-)
00000l
UP

81

350 CID (105 HP) DIESEL V8
(CADILLAC V6 OR V8 GAS
ENGINES AVAIL.) 114" WB

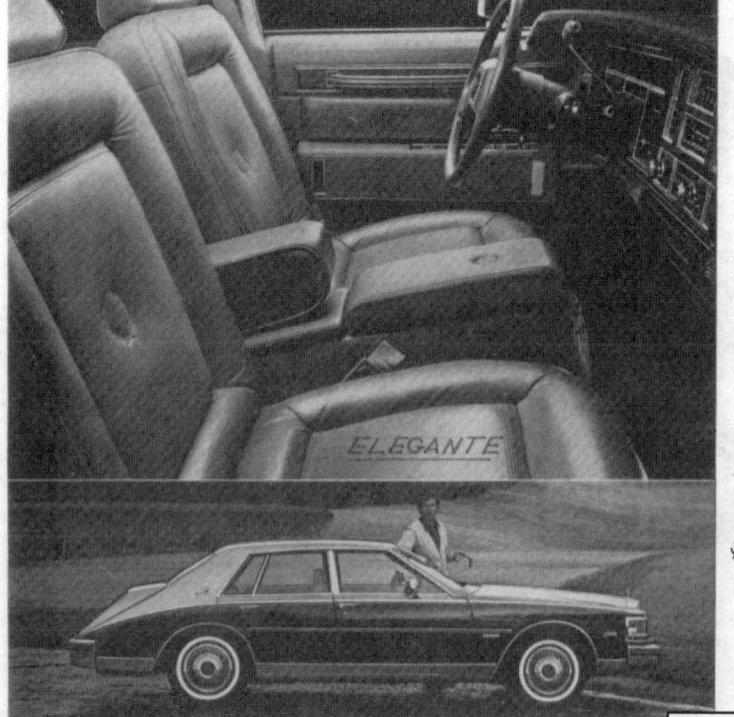

ELEGANTE

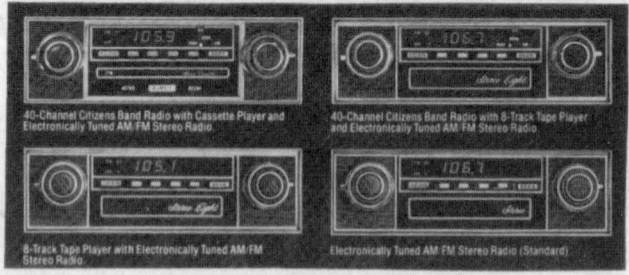

40-Channel Citizens Band Radio with Cassette Player and
Electronically Tuned AM/FM Stereo Radio.

40-Channel Citizens Band Radio with 8-Track Tape Player
and Electronically Tuned AM/FM Stereo Radio.

8-Track Tape Player with Electronically Tuned AM/FM
Stereo Radio.

Electronically Tuned AM/FM Stereo Radio (Standard)

Seville
Elegante
$24446.

(ABOVE) VARIOUS
RADIO/STEREO/TAPE
COMBINATIONS AVAILABLE
(IN ADDITION TO TYPE ILLUSTR.
WITH 1981 CADILLAC DEVILLE/
FLTWD.

ELECTRONIC
CLIMATE
CONTROL →

1122

The HT 4100 DFI Power System ...only Cadillac has it.

For 80 years, Americans have trusted Cadillac to lead the way. And their confidence has been rewarded. The first American production car with a V8 engine. The first V16. The first Diesel V8 as standard equipment. And now another first...the remarkable new

HT 4100 DIGITAL FUEL INJECTION

HT 4100 Power System. With everything from Digital Fuel Injection and automatic overdrive to a smooth new V8. From a Fuel Data Panel that can help you become a more efficient driver...to On-Board Computer Diagnostics to help take the guesswork out of servicing.

There's an HT 4100 DFI Power System standard for DeVilles, Fleetwood Broughams, Eldorado and Seville.

Cadillac

Seville
BY CADILLAC

V.I.N. IG6AS698 (-) C (-) 00000I UP

("HT-4100 DFI" V8 [GAS] IS STD., BUT OTHER ENGINES OPT.)

82

with automatic overdrive.

Seville...

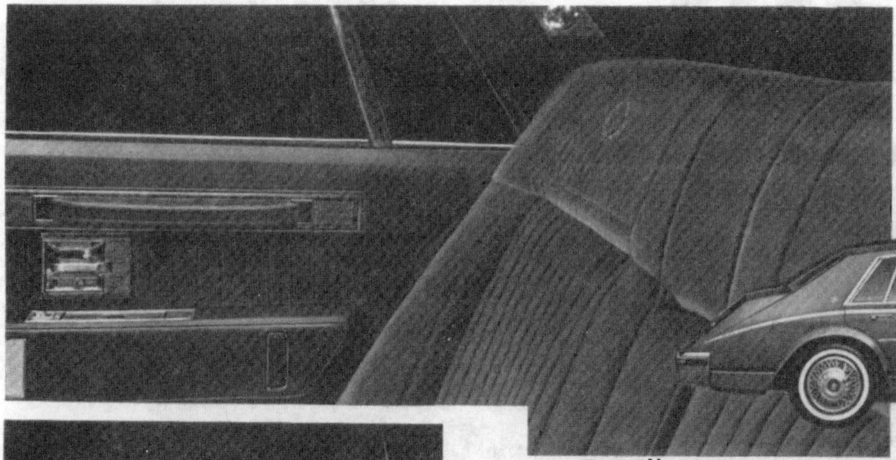

$24,093.

Seville Interiors

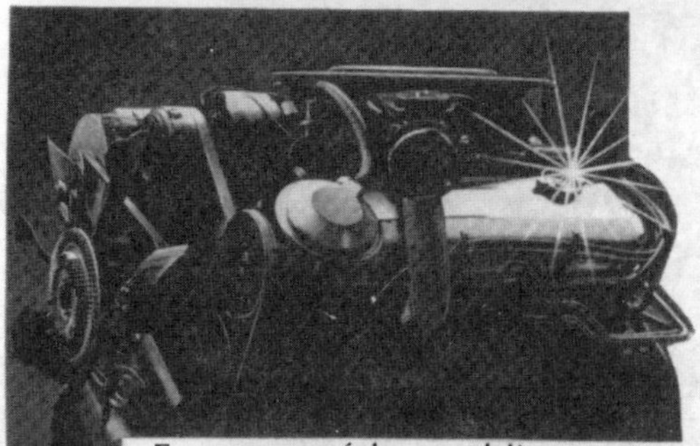

From one of the world's most advanced engine plants...

At the heart of the HT 4100 Power System is a smooth new V8. Its chrome-plated valve covers are just one indication of the painstaking attention to detail.

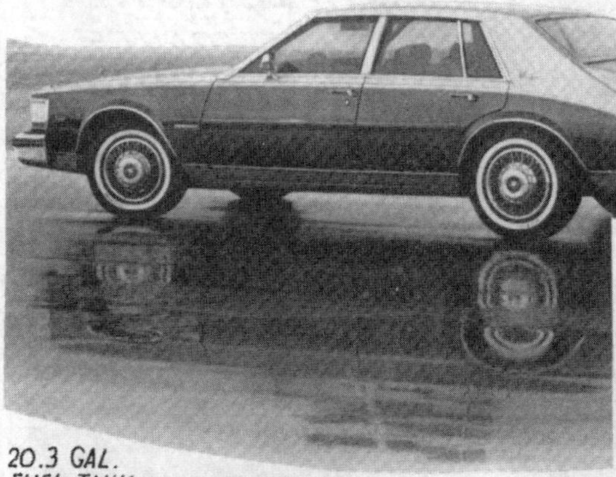

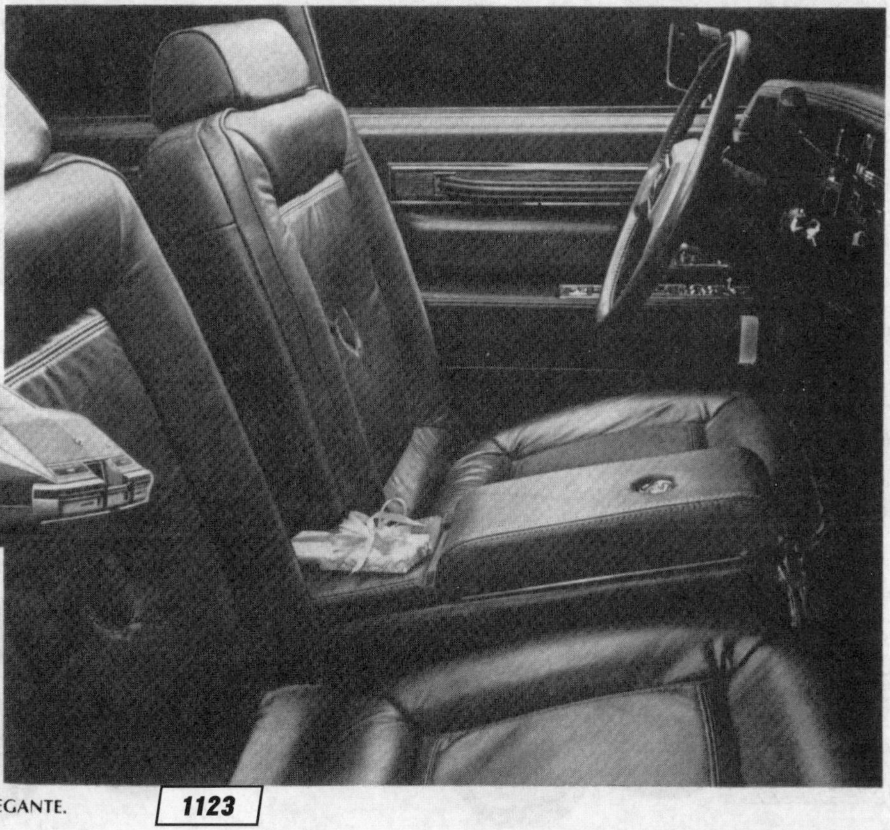

20.3 GAL. FUEL TANK 17 MPG (EPA)

$27,188.

SEVILLE ELEGANTE.

1123

Cadillac

Seville
BEST OF ALL...IT'S A CADILLAC

WITH CABRIOLET ROOF OPTION →

WITH STANDARD ROOF

Full Cabriolet Roofs for Seville and Eldorado.
This dramatic treatment recaptures the dash and flair of the classic Cadillac convertibles. The simulated convertible roof design appears authentic in virtually every detail—from the canvas-look fabric to the welted seams. It is available in four colors: Black, Dark Blue, Dark Briar Brown (shown on Seville with Woodland Haze exterior) and White (shown on Eldorado with Balboa Blue exterior).

ELEGANTE $26,183.

2 TONE PAINT, LEATHER SEATS and TRIM IN ELEGANTE

6KS69

83

$22,304. and up

17 MPG EPA
21 MPG, DIESEL EPA

V.I.N.= 1G6A S698 XD (-) 000001 UP

V.I.N.= 1G6A S698 XE (-) 000001 UP

NEW BLACK ACCENT TRIM ON DASH

Seville's Instrument Panel with elegant new Black Accent Interior Trim Moldings. (Available features also shown.)

GAS OR DIESEL V8s (135 OR 105 HP)
3.15 OR 3.36 GEAR RATIO (2.93 w. DIESEL)

84

Seville Aluminum Alloy Wheel

WITH CABRIOLET ROOF OPTION

V.I.N.= 1G6A S698 XE (-) 000001 UP

Standard Seville Wheel Disc.

SEDAN = $23,337.
ELEGANTE = $27,216.

Standard Seville Elegante Wire Wheel Disc

FUEL CAP'Y.
20.3 GAS
22.8 DIESEL

Cadillac
249 cid V8

DIESEL V8 AVAIL.

SEVILLE

85

114" WB

V.I.N. =
1G6AS698
XF (-)
000001 UP

SEDAN $24,128.

ELEGANTE
SEDAN $28,007.
6KS69

"K" BODY

TOTALLY
RESTYLED
1986
110 MPH
new SHORTER 108" WB

K9 698

K9 518

MPG:
17/25
(249 cid V8)
1987

86-87 NEW

CASHMERE CLOTH —
and LEATHER COMBINATION
SEATING AREAS and new
REAR DOOR LOCK SWITCHES
IN 1987.

PRICED FROM
$27,256. ('86)
$27,405. ('87)

INTERIOR ('86)

(1986 EXAMPLES ILLUSTR.)

ELEGANTE
INTERIOR
←

ELEGANTE
$30,851. ('86)
$101.
LESS
IN
'87!

SUSPENSION SOFTENED IN 1987.

Announcing the 1986 Seville.
The new essence of elegance

108" WB
18.8 GAL. FUEL TK.

17/25 MPG ('89)

Cadillac SEVILLE

COMPACT DISC PLAYER OPTION → (STD. IN 1990)

16/25 MPG, 1990

OPTIONAL

SEDANS PRICED FROM
$29,057. ('88)
$30,300. ('89)
$32,380. ('90)

Cadillac Seville, America's ultimate luxury sedan

Available Phaeton roof

■ Available Astroroof (now available with Phaeton roof), shown with standard painted metal roof. (Astroroof reduces headroom slightly.)

ROOF TREATMENTS

DASH

KS 515

88-90

new 155 HP V8

180 HP 4.5 L EFI V8 IN 1990

2.97 : 1 GEAR RATIO

■ Available gold ornamentation– available wheel cover wreath and crest (shown)*

"STS" INTRO. MID-1988 (TOUR. SEDAN IN 1990)

Seville STS

REAR (STS)

WHEEL TREATMENTS

STS has DIFFERENT GRILLE OF ITS OWN.

■ Standard 15"x6" lace-look aluminum alloy wheels –Seville

■ Available 15" wire wheel discs–Seville (not avail w/touring suspension)

■ Standard 15" x 7" exclusive fine-finish alloy wheels–Seville STS

■ Available 15"x6" aluminum alloy wheels–Seville (standard with touring suspension)

'89 "STS" $36,054.

1989 EXAMPLES ILLUSTR.

CHEVROLET (SINCE 1911)

Chevrolet GM

1XX68

151 CID 4 (90 HP) OR 173 CID V6 (115, 135 HP)

1XX08 W. X11 PKG.

P185/80 × 13/B TIRES
CITATION HAS FRONT-WHEEL DR.
(FIRST INTRO. SPRING, '79 AS
1980 MODEL)

1981 CHEVY CITATION
104.9" WB

X-11 at a glance.
Vehicle type: front-engine, front-wheel-drive, 5-passenger, 3-door hatchback.
Engine type: V6, water-cooled, cast-iron block and heads, 1x2-bbl carburetor.
Displacement ... 173 cu in, 2830 cc
Power (SAE net) ... 135 bhp
@ 5400 rpm
Transmission ... 4-speed, manual
Wheelbase ... 104.9 in.
Length ... 176.7 in.
Curb weight ... 2650 lbs.

$9264.
CITATION X-11

MPG : 26/19 (V6)

$8377. UP

P195 75R14 TIRES

(NO MONTE CARLO DIESEL LISTED)

V.I.N. =
IGIA ( )OB - #

1AZ37

Monte Carlo 108.1" WB. V6, V8 ENGINES LIKE IMPALA, CAPR.

643-291

81

IMPALA

CAPRICE CLASSIC DASH

MOST IMPALA SPECS. SIMILAR TO **CAPRICE**
116" WB
229, 231 CID V6
115, 110 HP
267, 305 CID V8

Caprice Diesel.
33 HWY EST / 21 EPA EST MPG*
WITH AVAIL. 350 CID DIESEL V8 (105 HP)
P205 (225) 7R15 TIRES

$7852. UP (WAGON)

54.4"

66.3"

CAVALIER WAGON

USA-1 IS TAKING CHARGE

Chevrolet

CAPRICE · CELEBRITY · CAVALIER · CHEVETTE · CAMARO · CITATION · MALIBU · MONTE CARLO · CORVETTE

24 MPG EPA, 27 DIESEL

CELEBRITY

1AW27 COUPE
$9198.
(1AW19 SEDAN,
$9348.)

CITATION

MPG: 42/27
(1.5l CID 4)

new CS LUXURY SERIES OF CAVALIER; CADET DISCONT'D.

$7589. UP

CAVALIER

26 MPG, EPA

new CAVALIER CONVERT. AVAIL., AT $12,380.

83

120 MPH (MONTE CARLO SS)

V.I.N. ENDS WITH —D—#

Citation 4-Door Hatchback $8664. V6 AVAIL.

CAPRICE CLASSIC DASH

UNLEADED FUEL ONLY

40

IMPALA GRILLE

(IMPALA WAGONS DISCONT'D.; IMPALA SEDAN ONLY,

AVAIL. CRUISE CONTROL $9643.)

(1BL69)

SET COAST CRUISE OFF ON RESUME

18 MPG EPA
23 MPG, DIESEL EPA

1BN69 CAPRICE SEDAN (CLASSIC) $10,114.

(NO 2-DR. CAPRICE IN '83)

CAPRICE CLASSIC

USA1

1129

CAVALIER, TYPE 10, and CS MODELS

OFFICIAL U.S. CARS AND TRUCKS OF THE XIV OLYMPIC WINTER GAMES

CHEVROLET
taking charge

LET'S GET IT TOGETHER...BUCKLE UP

$7933.⁷⁰ $12,694.

Cavalier

new GRILLE

V.I.N. ENDS WITH -E-#

84

IJD35

CS WAGON $8420.

CAVALIER INTERIOR

CITATION RE-NAMED AS

Citation II.

WITH 16 MECHANICAL IMPROVE-MENTS.

CITATION II SEDAN CONTINUES FASTBACK STYLING

151 CID 4 (92 HP) 104.9" WB
173 CID V6 (112 HP)
173 CID H.O. V6 (135 HP)

1XX68 $8786. (CITATION II)

New

965 BCR

← CELEBRITY
Our new Celebrity Wagon. It can put 8 people in space. →

CELEB. EUROSPORT ↓

112 MPH

IAW35 CELEBRITY WAGON $9358.

IBL69 IMPALA V6 SEDAN $10212.

W. BLACK TRIM

STD. CELEBRITY GRILLE FOR 1984

MPG: 39/25 (2-DR. CAPRICE RETURNS)

SS (RESTYLED)

MONTE CARLO SS V8
$11,956. Z37G

(Z37A V6 COUPE RETAINS FORMER STYLE.)

305 CID V8 (150 HP) (OPT. 350 CID DIESEL V8) $11,834.

(CAPRICE) **CLASSIC ESTATE** 116" WB

Cavalier

TODAY'S CHEVROLET

CITATION II DETAILS

CITATION II

$8344
(C9 WAG., $8665)

101.2" WB

121 cid 4 (88 HP)
173 cid 6 (125 HP)

CAVALIER
CS SEDAN
(JD69P) $8499.

114 MPH
(Z24)

V.I.N. ENDS WITH - F-#

CELEBRITY 104.9 WB

AW19W
$10367.

X68R
$8830. FINAL
CITATION II

151 cid 4 (V6 AVAIL.)
14.6 GAL. FUEL TANK
3.65 G.R.

104.9" WB
P215/60R14 TIRES

85

new ENG. DAMPENER ON ALL GAS ENGINES (SILENCER)

173 cid V6 112, 130 HP

2.84 GEAR RATIO

(AVAIL. 262 cid V6 DIESEL HAS 85 HP.) (88 HP w. 151 cid 4)

P195/75R14 TIRES
15.7 GAL. FUEL TANK

CELEBR. DASH
$10558.

new "ESTATE" GRAINING AVAIL. ON CEL. WAG.

Monte Carlo

SS (GZ37G) $12524.
V8

SPORT CPE. $10684.
V6

117 MPH

(COUPE RETURNED TO CAPRICE CLASSIC LINE IN 1984.)

CELEBRITY

$11919.
BN35H WAGON

CAPRICE CLASSIC

262 cid V6 (130 HP)
305 cid V8 (165 HP)
OR 350 cid DIES. V8 (105 HP)

NEW

CAPR. CLAS. DASH

1131

Chevrolet ('86)

$14010
JE67P
"R9"
CAVALIER
CVT.
115 MPH
(Z24)

"A" BODY

TODAY'S CHEVROLET

CELEBRITY

$11195
AW19W

MOST MODELS CONTINUE WITH FEW CHANGES FR. 1985.

86 -87

IMPALA DISCONT'D.
CITATION II "

118 MPH

"J" BODY
$10358.
Z24
COUPE

CAVALIER
CONVERTIBLE AVAIL.
SINCE 1983

CAVALIER MPG:
24/31
(121 CID 4, 1987)

CELEBRITY MPG:
20/28 (173 CID V6)
(1987)

new CELEBRITY GRILLE ('86)
(COMPOSITE HEADLTS., 1987)

new BROUGHAM ADDED TO 1986 CAPRICE LINE
$12654.

('86)

CAVALIER
R9
WAGON

"G" BODY
108"
WB
305 CID
V8

Monte Carlo.
SS
SPORT CPE.
$13630. ('86) GZ37H
14652. UP ('87)
GZ11H

BN69Z

new FOR 1986
CAPRICE CLASSIC BROUGHAM

('86)

('86)

MONTE CARLO **LS** LUXURY SPT. CPE (GZ37Z)
← HAS DIFFERENT FRONT.
262 CID V6 (new FASTBACK AEROCOUPE ALSO, '87.)

new
1986
GRILLE

CAPRICE CLASSIC
DASH
('87)

BU5IZ
LS

new 1987 "LS"
HAS LANDAU TOP
$15055.

1987 CAPRICE CLASSIC
WAGON
('86)

$12642.

('87)
SPORT
COUPE
BN11Z "B" BODY

CAPRICE CLASSIC

1987
HAS
new 2-IN-ONE
"COMPOSITE" WIDE
HEADLIGHTS

V.I.N. ENDS WITH –G–# ('86)
" " " –H–# ('87)

1987 CAPRICE MPG : 18/27 (262 CID V6); 18/25 (307 CID V8)

Chevrolet Cavalier Z.24 Coupe   Chevrolet Celebrity Eurosport Coupe   Chevrolet Caprice Classic Brougham Sedan

V6 OR V8

CAVALIER Z24 $12,215.   4 OR V6 $14,900.

CAVALIER
(RESTYLED)

Cavaliers: the coupe, sedan and wagon; very stylish RS coupe and sedan; aggressive Z24 coupe and posh convertible.

You'll love the surprising new look that extends from Cavalier's new grille and hood, along its body-side molding, around its wheels, all the way to its new rear bumper.

$10,665.   CAVALIER RS CPE.   JE111

2.0 L 4 OR
QUICK 2.8 LITER MULTI-PORT V6.

V.I.N. ENDS WITH -J-# (IN BAR. OR CORS.)

88

BERETTA DASH

LV111

Grand Touring Beretta GT $11,656.00*
New

BERETTA
(COUPES ONLY)

115-120 MPH   103.4" WB
1988
BERETTA AND CORSICA ("L" BODY)
INTRODUCED EARLY
(SPRING, 1987)

(CORSICA AVAIL. ONLY AS 4 DR.)

Touring Grand Corsica LT $10,991.00**
(** REG. $11195.)
LT 511

110 MPH

New

103.4" WB

Corsica LT Hatchback Sedan.

Corsica LT 2.5 L 4 $11,640.
5 SP. ISUZU TRANS. (OPT. 3-SP A/T)

CORSICA DASH

Corsica LT Sedan.

BERETTA CVT.
4 OR ('90½)
V6

Beretta GTZ → HAS ITS OWN BLANKED-OUT GRILLE 180 HP QUAD 4 (138 CID)

BERETTA DASH

LUMINA **New**

CAVALIER R9 DASH

Cavalier Wagon.

$10,382.

CHEVROLET

CAVALIER VL CPE.
$9794

↑
CAVALIER

New

$14715.

90

107½" WB

V.I.N. ENDS WITH —L—#
(CELEBRITY WAGONS CONT'D.
BUT NO SEDAN)

Lumina Euro GRILLE and DASH

LUMINA DASH ↑
151 CID 4 (110 HP)
191 CID V6 (135 HP)
27/21 MPG (4)
27/19 " (6)

Lumina $14260.

Caprice Classic Sedan.

Caprice Classic Brougham Sedan.

Caprice Classic Brougham LS Sedan.

Caprice Classic Wagon.

new ↓ 120 HP V6
$15300.
Lumina APV

CHEVROLET CAMARO

(SINCE 1967)

BERLINETTA DASH and CUSTOM CLOTH INTER.

28 Est. Hwy   20 EPA Est. MPG   (V6)

1981 CHEVY CAMARO THE HUGGER

SPORT COUPE $8142.

IFP87 (J)

DELCO AM/FM STEREO

15 x 7" BODY-COLORED SPT. WHEEL ←

108" WHEELBASE

115 OR 110 HP V6s,
120 - 190 HP V8s
229 CID V6, 267 CID,
305 CID OR 350
CID V8s.
(231 CID V6
IN CALIFORNIA
ONLY)

81

STD. SPT. CPE INTERIOR

IFP87 (L)

Z-28

P205/75R×14 OR P225/70R×15 TIRES

ALUMINUM WHEEL ↑

WITH OPTIONAL CLOTH

V.I.N.=1G1(-)( )(-)B(-)10000I UP

Z-28 $9337.

Z28 SPOILER DETAILS ↓

825 DQI

BERLINETTA $8938.
IFS87

CAMARO

CAMAROS PRICED FR.

Ø 9336.	'82
9862.	83
10,026.	84
10,237.	85
10,914.	86
11,674.	87
12,674.	88
13,199.	89
12,754.	90

(V6 PRICES;
V8s AT EXTRA COST)

V6 SPT. CPE. ↗

Z-28

1982 Z28
$10,957. (V8)

DASH ↗

16 GAL. FUEL TANK
24 MPG (EPA)
('82)

New Z28 Camaro.

82 New ON
FRONTAL STYLING

V6 OR V8 ENGINES *
new SHORTER
101" WHEELBASE

* 4 CYL. ENG.
ALSO AVAIL.
1982-1986.

5 SPEED,
5 LITR.
V8 Z28
INTRO.
'83

Z28
134 MPH,
1983

BERLINETTA
HAS OWN
FRONTAL
STYLING

114 MPH,
1984

116 MPH,
1985

VEH. I.D. #s INCLUDE:
1982 = 1G1AP87 (2)(-)(C)(-)
1982 BERLIN. = AS87 (1)
1983 = 1G1AP87 (-)XD (-)
1983 BERLINETTA = 1G1A987 (-) XD (-)
1984 = 1G1AP87HXE (-)
1984 BERLINETTA = 1G1A987HXE (-)
1985 = HXF IN I.D. # or
FP87S, FS87S, or FP87H IN I.D. #
(1986 SAME, BUT CHEV. I.D. #s
(F)(-)87 (-) - G -)
INCLUDE

(1982 EXAMPLES ILLUSTR.)
ABOVE)

1986 HAS 3RD BRAKE LT. (REAR WNDW.)

1987
MPG : 16/25 (V8)

1987 = (FP()-H-#)   1988 = (FP()-J-#)   1989 =
(GENERAL CHEV. KEY NUMBERS)   FP- K -
1990 =
FP
-L-

RS SERIES REPLACES
BERLINETTA, 1987
(V6 OR V8)

RS CONVT. STARTS 1987,
PRICED FROM
$16,073.
FP31S

CPE. ALSO
AVAIL.

('89)

RS

1987 =
3RD BRAKE
LIGHT MOVED
DOWN TO
BACK OF DECK,
ABOVE LIC. PLATE.

NEW IROC Z28
1985
FP87H
140 MPH
('85)

135-150
MPH
('87)

(IROC = INTERNATIONAL
RACE OF CHAMPIONS)

DRIVER AIRBAG IN 1990

"F"
BODY

26/16 MPG ('90)

DELUXE DASH

1981 V.I.N.= 1G1A B089 (-)
B (-) 000001 UP
SCOOTER = 1G1A J089
(-) B (-) 100001 UP

COLUMN —
MOUNTED
"SMART
SWITCH"

97.3"
WHEEL-
BASE
ON
THE
4-
DR.

81-82

151 CID 4 OR 173 CID V8   98 CID 4
90 HP   115 HP   70 HP
                12½ GAL. FUEL TK.

lower price!

$4595.⁰⁰

REG. #5308.

"SCOOTER" 1TJ08

FROM
$5730.
('82)

1981
MODELS
ILLUSTR.

39 / 30
HWY. EST.   EPA EST. MPG

2-DR. (94.3"
WHEELBASE)

P175/70 R13 TIRES
(ROOF RACK
OPTIONAL)

AM RADIO (BELOW)

New
DIESEL
MODELS
ALSO
AVAIL. '82.
(116 CID
4 CYL.)

1982 V.I.N. =
1G1AB08C(-)C
(-) 000001 UP
(SCOOTER=1G1AJ08C(-)
C(-) 000001 UP)

COMPUTER
COMMAND
CONTROL

Every 1981 gasoline-
engined Chevrolet
passenger car includes a
sophisticated, thoroughly
tested on-board computer
as standard equipment.

(AM/FM ALSO AVAIL.)

FILLER DOOR

60 EST. HWY. 43 EPA EST. MPG*

(WITH OPT. 4-CYL. DIESEL ENG. AVAIL. TO 1986.)

CHEVETTE

98 CID 4 (65 HP @ 5200 RPM) (1985)

3.38 GEAR RATIO (1985)

12½ GAL. FUEL TANK (1985)

('83)

...CS ...SER. ...ONLY, ...'985 ...ON

DIESEL

('83)

P155/80R13 TIRES (1985)

DASH

('83)

83-87

BLACK GRILLE

(FINAL CHEVETTE)

1987 MPG: 25/30 (w. 98 CID 4)

('86)

'83 DIESEL CHEVETTE FROM $6535.

FINAL "SCOOTER" $5765. ('83)

(2-DR. FROM $5735. IN 1987.)

"T" BODY

VEH I.D. #s INCLUDE:
'83 and
'84 — J or B08C or 68C
'85 — TB08A or TB68A
(D SUFFIX = DIESEL)
'86 — TB08C or TB68C
'87 — TB21C or TB61C

('84)

CHEVROLET CORVETTE.

(SINCE 1953)

(V8-POWERED SINCE 1955)

(ALL CORVETTES WITH FIBERGLASS BODIES)

98" WHEELBASE

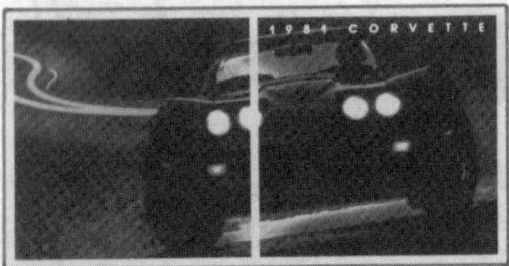

P225/70R x 15 B TIRES

new AUXILIARY ELECTRIC FAN CUTS IN WHEN EXTRA ENGINE COOLING NEEDED. IMPROVED BATTERY.
24-GAL. FUEL TANK

1981
V.I.N. =
1G1AY8760
B (-)100001
UP

1YZ87

81

new FIBERGLASS-REINFORCED "MONOLEAF" REAR SPRINGS. new STAINLESS STEEL, FREE-FLOW EXHAUST MANIFOLDS.

4-SPEED MANUAL TRANSMISSION, OR AUTOMATIC.
350 cid V8 (190 HP)*
$16,141.

* CALIFORNIA 305 V8 ALSO (SINCE 1980)

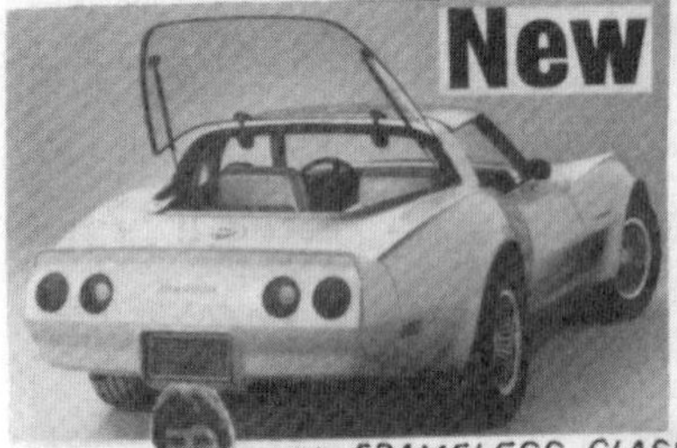

New

STD. COUPE (1YZ87)
$19368.
(P225/70R x 15/B TIRES)

V.I.N. =
1G1AY 878 (-) C (-) 000001 UP

w. FRAMELESS GLASS HATCHBACK

COLLECT. ED. INTER AND EXTER. IN SILVER/BEIGE (METALLIC)

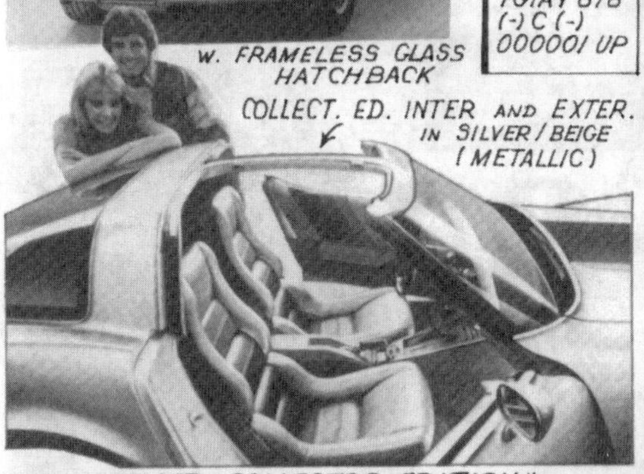

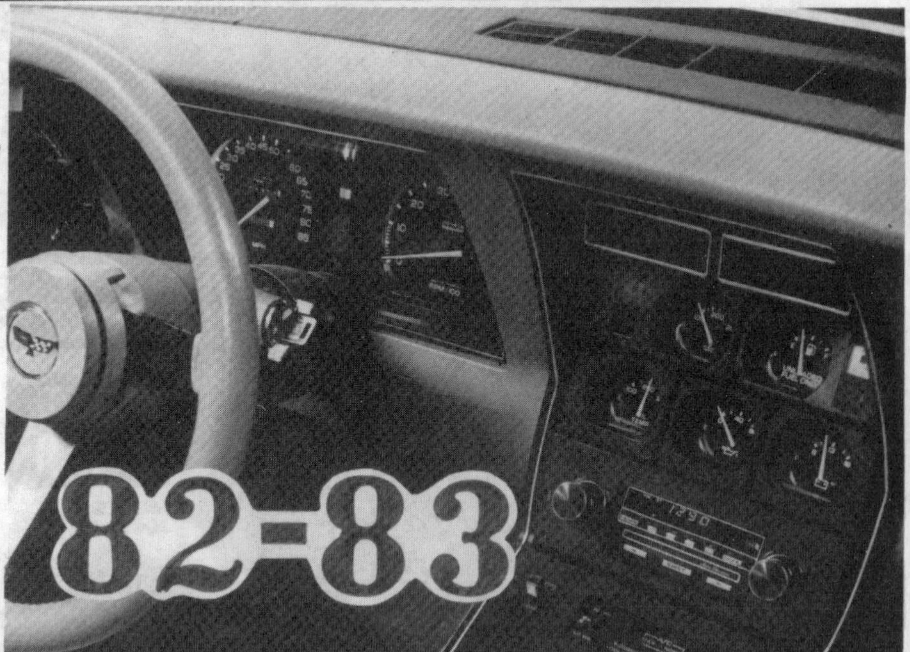

NEW "COLLECTOR EDITION" HATCHBACK COUPE
(1YY07)

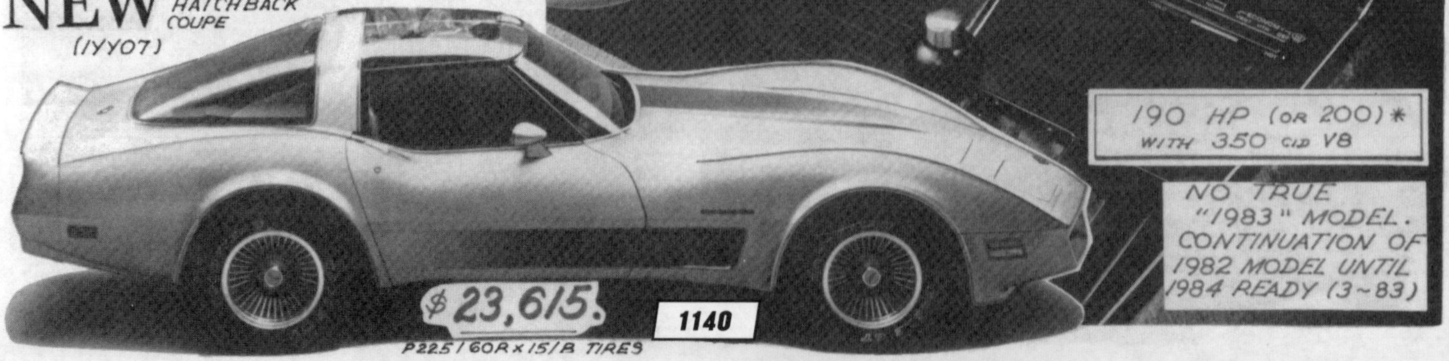

82-83

190 HP (OR 200)*
WITH 350 cid V8

NO TRUE "1983" MODEL. CONTINUATION OF 1982 MODEL UNTIL 1984 READY (3~83)

$23,615.

P225/60R x 15/B TIRES

CHEVROLET CORVETTE

V.I.N.=1G1AY078
XE (-)
000001 UP

3.07 OR 3.31 TO 1 GEAR RATIO

142 MPH

2-CHOICE AIRCRAFT-TYPE BUCKET SEATS (INCL. LEATHER)

EMBLEM

INSIDE AND OUT, **TOTALLY NEW!**

1YY07

84

(AVAILABLE AT DEALERS SPRING, 1983.)

new SHORTER 96.2" WB

350 CID V8 (205 NET HP @ 4300 RPM)

BIGGEST CHANGE IN CORVETTE SINCE THE 1960s

The optional Delco-GM/Bose Music System ETR™ AM/FM Stereo with Seek and Scan, Cassette Tape and Clock.

$895. EXTRA

P215/65R15 TIRES

$24,405.
(LATER $24,972.)

ENGINE and FRONT AXLE

New Dash SOPHISTICATED DASH HAS DUAL ANALOG AND DIGITAL READOUT OF SPEEDO. and TACHOMETER! SWITCH CONTROL OF OTHER GA. READOUTS.

WE'RE TAKING CHARGE.

CHEVROLET CORVETTE

(SHOWN WITH HEADLTS. OPEN)

(YY 078)

$ 26,501. *

96.2" WB

P255/50 VR 16 TIRES
20 GAL. FUEL TANK

DASHBOARD GRAPHICS IMPROVED, FOR CLARITY

Z 51 SUSPENSION AVAILABLE

* BASE PRICE = $24,891., EARLY IN YEAR

85

350 CID V8 IMPROVED
new 230 HP @ 4000 RPM
2.87, 2.73 OR 3.07 GR

NUMEROUS MECHANICAL IMPROVEMENTS!

TOP SPEED INCREASED TO 150 MPH
16 MPG AVG. (EPA)

V.I.N. = 1G1AYO78XF (-) 000001 UP

YY78

144 MPH

COUPE 29,055

(COUPES ONLY, IN EARLIEST WEEKS OF MODEL YEAR)
OPT. GLASS ROOF PANEL, $615.
DUAL ROOF PANELS, $ 915.
MANUAL TRANS. DELCO BOSE STEREO and LEATHER UPHOL. AVAIL.

HIGH-UP 3RD BRAKELIGHT MANDATORY ON ALL 1986 and LATER CARS.

V.I.N. ENDS WITH (YY67) OR (YY78) - G - #

DASH

86

NEW

OFFICIAL PACE CAR

(YY67) ROADSTER (CONVERTIBLE) $ 34,130.

new COMPUTERIZED BOSCH ABS II

Anti-lock braking power

CHEVROLET ⟨⟩ CORVETTE

"Y" BODY

"TURBO PORT INJECTION" INSCRIBED ON BELT TRIM STRIP

178 MPH WITH CALLAWAY TURBO ($50,865.)

STOCK TOP SPEED 152 MPH *

*133-158 MPH IN VARIOUS OTHER TESTS, DEPENDING ON OPTIONS.

16 MPG (EPA)

87

NOW OFFERING 3 CHOICES OF SUSPENSION: BASE; Z51; and new Z52

240 HP @ 4000 RPM

REAR DETAILS (SHOWN WITH OPTIONAL BRIDGESTONE TIRES)

(YY 3/8) CONVERTIBLE $35,062.

V.I.N. ENDS WITH -H- #

DETAILS OF ENGINE COMPARTMENT

(YY 2/8) COUPE $29,889.

CHEVROLET ✦ CORVETTE

20.5 MPG (EPA)

new 245 HP
TOP SPEED = 159 MPH

88

V.I.N. ENDS WITH -J-#

new OPTIONAL REAR SPOILER and FRONT AIR DAM ("BODY KIT")

new WHEELS (6 OPENINGS)

COUPE (YY 218) **$30,435.**

HANDLING PKG. and 17" WHEELS AVAILABLE

(YY318) CONVERTIBLE **35,775.**

TOP DETAILS

HIGH-PERFORMANCE, 190 MPH (380 HP)
NEW ZR1 OPT.
FOR 1990 HAS 17" WHEELS.

16/25 MPG

IN 1990, GLOVE BOX RETURNS ON *new* ANALOG/ DIGITAL INSTR. PANEL. DRIVER AIRBAG IN 1990

COUPE (YY 218) **$32,525.**
CVT. (YY318) **37,765.**

1989 V.I.N. ENDS WITH -K-# (1990-L-#)

New WHEELS (MORE OPENINGS)

15/24 MPG (EPA) w. 4 SP. AUTO. TR.

245 - 250 HP STD. *in 1990*

89-90

NEW 6-SPEED MANUAL AVAILABLE 16/25 MPG (EPA)

new OPTIONAL TIRE MONITOR WARNS OF AIR PRESSURE DEFICIENCY. (SIMILAR OPTION REPORTEDLY AVAIL. 1987)

NEW

1990 DASH

1990 PRICES
3 DR. $32479.
CVT. $37764.
3 DR. ZR-1 = $58,995.

1144

CHEVROLET MALIBU
(1964 – 1983)
(ORIGINALLY CHEVELLE)

New Dash.

V.I.N.s START w. 1G1, END w.-B-#
WAGON V.I.N.=1G1AW35K0B(-)100001 UP
1AT35 — MALIBU WAGON $8178.

INTERIOR

with optional vinyl roof.
SPT. SED. $8001.
1AT69

SPT. CPE $7885.

1AT27

108.1" WB
18.2 GAL.
FUEL TANK

229 CID V6
(115 HP) OR
267 CID V8
(120 HP)

81 new GRILLE, TAIL-LIGHTS and DASH

Malibu Classic

LANDAU COUPE $8479.
1AW27
($8215. CLASSIC SPT. CPE AVAIL.)

$8348.
CLASSIC SEDAN
1AW69

W. HEATED REAR WINDOW

"CLASSIC" WAGON LEFT REAR PANEL ↓

WOODGRAIN AVAIL. (CLASSIC ESTATE WAGON)
$8726. UP
1AW35

P185/75R x 14 TIRES (P195 ON WAGON)

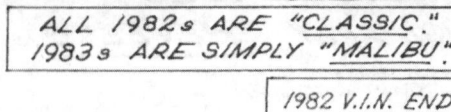

MALIBU CLASSIC

ALL 1982s ARE "CLASSIC."
1983s ARE SIMPLY "MALIBU"

1982 V.I.N. ENDS WITH
–C–# ; 1983 "   "
–AXD–#

NEW GRILLE WITH
CRISS-CROSS PCS.

82-83

NO MORE
2 DR. MODELS

'83 HAS "MALIBU"
NAME ON SIDE.

SPORT SEDAN
$ 9321. ('82) 9335. ('83)

GAS OR *DIESEL*
V6s and V8s
NOW AVAIL.

WAGON
$ 9450.
9468. ('83)

("ESTATE WAGON" STILL AVAIL. ALSO)

INTERIOR

Malibu Classic instrument panel.

1982 EXAMPLES ILLUSTRATED
21 GAL. FUEL TK.
(18.2 GAL. WAGON)

21 MPG (EPA)
23 MPG
DIESEL EPA

1983 HAS "MALIBU"
NAME ON SIDE,
JUST BEYOND FR.
WHEEL OPENING.

DISCONTINUED
1983

Malibu Classic standard notchback bench seat with folding center armrest.

CHEVROLET NOVA - SPECTRUM - SPRINT

JAPANESE - AMERICAN

(AVAIL. 1985-1988)

Nova Hatchback Sedan.

New Chevy Nova. Imported from America.

Nova

93 MPH

NOVA NAME RETURNS 1985, FOR NEW GM/ TOYOTA CARS BLT. IN FREMONT, CAL.

"S" BODY

$9105. ('88)

1988 Chevy Nova

← NOVA

95.7" WB 97 CID 4 $7485. ('85)

NOVA 24/46 MPG

1986 MODELS ILLUSTRATED, UNLESS OTHERWISE INDICATED.

NOVA SK194 4 DR. JOINED BY SK684 HATCHBACK IN 1986. (AS SHOWN, UPPER LEFT) NEW TWIN CAM SEDAN ADDED 88, AT $11705. (110 MPH)

EARLY SPECTRUMS IMPORTED TO EASTERN USA ONLY. "R" BODY

(BLT. BY ISUZU, JAPAN)

SPECTRUM →

94½" WB

SPECTRUM

90 CID 4 31/33 MPG

$6575. ('85) 8450. ('88)

1988 SPRINT TURBO GRILLE

1988 MR212

TURBO

$8470. 104 MPH

SPRINT.

$6026. ('86)

89 MPH

$6295. ('85) $6785. ('88) (EXPRESS)

(THESE CARS ALL REPLACED BY CHEVY'S NEW 1989

GEO

LINE.)

NEW SPRINT 5 DR. IN 1986

SPRINT 31/58 MPG

EARLY SPRINTS IMPORTED TO WESTERN USA ONLY.

'85 FROM $4949.

SPRINT 3 DR.

88.4" WB 3 CYL. 61 CID 48 HP 85 MPH.

MFD. BY SUZUKI, JAPAN "M" BODY

P145/80 SR12 TIRES

CHRYSLER

(SINCE 1924)

(SEE ALSO = CHRYSLER CORDOBA and IMPERIAL)

V.I.N. =
1C3BM (   )
EOB (-) 000001 UP

81

(NY = 318 CID V8 STD., INSTEAD OF 360 CID)

NEW YORKER (5 AVE. PKG.)
$13,526.

1981 Chrysler LeBaron

M SERIES LE BARON
$7840.

Chrysler LeBaron Town and Country. 26 est hwy, 17 EPA est mpg.
$9176. M49

118½" WB   R57

MINOR CHANGES ONLY, BETWEEN THESE FULL-SIZED, RWD CHRYSLERS, FOR 1980 and 1981. MAJOR 1981 CHANGES FOR CHRYSLER CORP. INVOLVED ITS ALL-NEW FWD DODGE ARIES and PLYMOUTH RELIANT "K CARS."

sedan

← NEW YORKER
$11,704.

R47
NEWPORT
$9092.   118½" WB
(FINAL YEAR)

C SERIES

LeBaron

SEDANS FROM
$9664.

(MEDALLION SEDAN $9929.)
C 56

new SHORTER 99.9" WB
13 GAL. FUEL TK.

THE FIRST 4-CYL. CHRYSLER SINCE THE 1928 "52" SERIES!
new 4 CYL. ENGINE (135 or 158 CID)

82

TOTALLY RESTYLED AND DOWNSIZED

40 est hwy 26 est mpg

PART OF REAR QUARTER PANEL INCORPORATED INTO REAR DOORS.

CHRYSLER

V.I.N.=IC3B
(C or F) ( )
(B or E)-C-
000001 UP

LE BARON SERIES

(CONT'D.)

$10,852.
('82½)

WAGON V.I.N.=IC3BC59D(-)C
(-) #

31 · 23

INTER.

COUPE C42
$9570.
MEDALLION COUPE
$9835. C52

C59

IMITATION
WOODGRAINED
WAGONS ONLY.
(1981 UN-
GRAINED
CHRYSLER WAGON
DISCONT'D.)

New TOWN & COUNTRY.

WAGON (NOT AVAIL.
UNTIL MID-SEASON)
AM/FM w. 8-TRACK TAPE

17 MPG (EPA)

40 · 26

A CONVERTIBLE
For 1982

Le BARON

NEW

31 · 23 $14,900

(AVAIL.
SPRING, 1982)

W. MARK CROSS
LEATHER INTER.

82

NEW YORKER

$12,152.

AM/FM + CASSETTE

NEW YORKER
has 112.7" WB
225 CID 6
(90 HP @
3600 RPM)
OR
318 CID V8 (130 HP @
4000 RPM, 2 BBL CARB.)
(IN CALIFORNIA,
4 BBL. CARB.
165 HP @
4000
RPM)

18-GAL. GAS TANK
2.9 G.R. (6)
2.2 G.R. (V8)
P205/75R
× 15
TIRES

F66

18 GAL. FUEL TK.
18 MPG (EPA)

F66

REAR
DETAIL

$13,799.
NEW YORKER
FIFTH AVENUE

5 AVE.

W. VINYL/
LEATHER
UPH.

LeBARON

It starts with great looks and it goes on to make great sense.

$12,097. UP
CVT. (C55)

C51

CPE.
$10,055.

$10,833.
WAGON

C59

24 MPG, EPA

$9892.
SED.
C56

CHRYSLER TOWN & COUNTRY

ORIGINAL 1946 T+C CVT. SHOWN ABOVE. (NO T+C CONVERTIBLES BLT. SINCE 1949.)

26 MPG EPA

C55

NEW

TOWN & COUNTRY CONVERTIBLE

CVT.
$15,965.

WE'VE RE-ENGINEERED THE AMERICAN LUXURY CAR
THE NEW CHRYSLER CORPORATION QUALITY ENGINEERED TO BE THE BEST

83 New

$10,487.
E CLASS

T46

E CLASS EXECUTIVE SEDAN (BELOW) NOT AVAILABLE DURING EARLY MONTHS OF 1983.

124" OR 131" WB

CHRYSLER EXECUTIVE SEDAN
Available for order this spring

CHRYSLER E CLASS

WITH new ELECTRONIC VOICE ALERT SYSTEM (ALSO IN LE BARON)

24 MPG EPA

$12,355.
T56

CHRYSLER NEW YORKER

new 4 CYL., 103" WB

NEW YORKER INT.

V.I.N.=
1C3B (   )
_ XD (-)
000001 UP

5TH AVE.

$13,862.
F66
18 MPG EPA

5TH AVE. RETAINS REAR WHEEL DRIVE.

112.7" WB (5TH AVE.)

NY 5 AVE.
225 CID 6 (90 HP) OR 318 CID V8 (130 HP)

NEW YORKER FIFTH AVENUE

CHRYSLER $16,893.

TOWN + COUNTRY CONVERTIBLE KCP27

LeBARON

CVT. $12,730. KCP27

NEW
REAR QUARTER WINDOWS and IMPROVED TOPS ON CVTS.

84

V.I.N.= IC3B ( ) -XE (-) 000001 UP

19,475.
EXECUTIVE 124" WB

new

KCP48

CHRYSLER EXECUTIVE SEDAN

$15,893.
(MARK CROSS) LEATHER UPH.

$10,202. SED. KCP41

COUPE $10,357. KCP22

41 HWY. 27 EPA

MPG 31 HWY 23 EPA new LARGER FUEL TANK

TOWN and COUNTRY WAGON KCP45
$10,991.

ETH41
$10,716.

CHRYSLER E CLASS
(FINAL YEAR FOR E CLASS)

NEW

AJL LIMOUSINE 131" WB $22,475.

4 CYL.

THRIFTY

In A Chrysler Limousine

KCP48/AJL

Chrysler

(BELOW, LEFT): T + C CVT. $17,404.
CVT. KCP27 " WAGON $11,510.
KCP45

The turbocharged Chrysler Town & Country. the power of a V-8 with the efficiency of a 4.

TOWN and CTRY. V.I.N.=
1C3BC59GXF (-)
000001 UP

AVAIL. TURBO
P185/70R14 TIRES

LE BARON V.I.N.=
1C3BC56
DXF (-)
000001
UP
100.3"
WB

COUPE
135 OR 158 CID 4 (96 OR 101 HP) $10,607.
KCP22

LE BARON

14 GAL. FUEL TANK
3.02 GEAR RAT.

$10,456.
SEDAN
KCP41

WAGON 23 HWY, 20 EPA

LE BARON GTS

NEW

(STYLING DIFF. FR. OTHER CHRYSLERS)

REAR VIEW OF GTS

P185/70R14 TIRES

$13,036.
CVT.

LE BARON   KCP27

Chrysler LeBaron GTS four-door sedan.

3.56 GEAR RATIO

14 GAL. FUEL TANK

HCH44
$10,701.

103.1" WB

GTS GRAPHIC INSTR. PANEL

(LS $11,597.)
HCP44

85

new GTS has 135 CID 4
99 HP (OR 146 HP
WITH TURBO) (115 MPH)

GTS

GTS
V.I.N.=
1C3BH48
DXF (-) 000001 UP
P185/70R14 TIRES

TURBO

MORE GTS DETAILS

LeBaron GTS.

SEATS

VIEW THRU GTS HATCHBACK

THE·NEW·CHRYSLER·TECHNOLOGY

5 AVE. AGAIN FEATURES TUFTED CUSHION-STYLE CLOTH UPHOL. SEATS

(1985 LASER SIM. TO 1984)
$10456.
(XE $12378.)
117 MPH

85

131.3" WB

EXECUTIVE **limousine.** KCP49

$**26,830.**

(FINAL YR.) 156 CID 4

MPG 23 HWY, 20 CITY

V.I.N.=1C3B C52 GXF (-) 000001 UP

P185/75R14 TIRES

1985 CHRYSLER FIFTH AVENUE

112.7" WB, 318 CID V8
(130 HP)

$**15,496.**

MFS41

P205/75R15 TIRES

V.I.N.=
1C3BF64
PXF (-)
000001 UP

1985 Turbo New Yorker.

ADDITIONAL LOUVRES ATOP HOOD

($610. LESS w. TURBO)

158 CID, 101 HP (OR 135 CID 140 HP TURBO 4)

4 CYL.
103.1" WB
P185/75R14 TIRES

$**13,967.**

ETP41

NEW YORKER V.I.N.=1C3BT56GXF(-)000001/UP

CHRYSLER

V.I.N.= IC3B ( )( )
—G— #

(C59D) T+C WAGON
12,537.

new...

86

HIGH-MOUNTED 3RD BRAKE LIGHT ADDED

CHRYSLER **LASER**
$11051. UP

LE BARON (EXCEPT GTS) has **NEW** AMBER CORNER LIGHTS NEXT TO HEADLIGHTS.

C56D

$11144. L.B. COUPE
C51D

A64E

$11294.

XT IS TURBO 4

H58D

CHRYSLER LASER XE

A54K   LASER XE

GTS

H48D
GTS HIGHLINE
$11441.

GTS PREMIUM (H58D) (ILLUSTR. ABOVE) **$12367.**

LE BARON

TURBO

new WIDER 50/50 SEATS IN NEW YORKER

T56K

103.3" WB

New Yorker.
$14,796.

153 CID FUEL INJ. 4 CYL.

101 MPH

C55D
LE BARON
CONVERTIBLE
$13862.
(W. MARK CROSS LEATHER INTER., $17005.)
(FINAL 1986 WOODGRAINED TRIM TOWN and COUNTRY CVT. $18005.)

CHRYSLER FIFTH AVENUE
F66P $16241.

NY REAR CLOSE DETAIL

(EXECUTIVE LIMO. DISCONTINUED.)

1155

112.7" WB   318 CID V8

(LASER DISCONTINUED ;
RETURNS in
PLYMOUTH
1990
LINE.)

CHRYSLER

"H"
BODY

LE BARON GTS
HIGHLINE $11,889.
PREMIUM   12,722.

H48D HIGHLINE, H58D PREMIUM
(E SUFFIX W. TURBO 4 ENG.)

new
WHEELS

$15,808.

"E" BODY   T56K

NEW
YORKER
and ITS INTERIOR

(TOWN and COUNTRY CONVERT.
DISCONTINUED)

LE
BARON
COUPE
HIGHLINE C41K

$13,020.
PREMIUM C51K
$14,156.

LE BARON CPE.
and CVT.
TOTALLY
RESTYLED
("CV" BODY)

87

MPG : 22 27 (135 CID 4)
(19/24 " " " w. A/T)

LE BAR.

**New
DESIGN**

135 CID 4
TURBO
140 HP
@
5200
RPM

109-120
MPH

C55E

LE
BARON
PREMIUM
CONVERTIBLE
3.02 GEAR
RATIO

new WHEELS

2.51 GEAR RATIO
14 GAL. FUEL TANK
P205/60 HR15
TIRES

(5TH AVE.,
LE BARON
SEDAN,
T + C WAGON
STILL AVAIL.)

new LTS.
CONCEALED

**FRONTAL
NEW LOOK**

5TH AVE. ON
NEXT PAGE

1156

CHRYSLER

5TH AVE. MPG: 16/21 (318 CID V8)
TWN. + CTRY. WAGON " 19/24 (135 CID 4, A/T)

"M" BODY
CONSERVATIVE
STYLING
RETAINED
ON

5TH AVENUE

(4 DR. IS
ONLY BODY
TYPE.)

REAR DETAILS

F66P

DASH

87

TILT STEERING WHEEL

18-GAL. FUEL TANK

V.I.N. =
- 1C3B
(C46D)-
H- #

OPT. AUTO. SPEED CONTROL

LIGHT-COLORED CAR GIVES ILLUSION OF APPEARING LARGER THAN DARK CARS.

318 CID V8 (140 HP @ 3600 RPM)

$17,831.
F66P

OPT. ILLUMINATED VISOR VANITY MIRROR

P205/75R15 TIRES

OPTIONAL AM/FM STEREO/TAPE and DIGITAL CLOCK

5TH AVENUE BACK SEAT

INTERIOR TRIM

Standard Chrysler Fifth Avenue. Kimberly cloth 60/40 individually adjustable front seats with adjustable head restraints. folding center armrest, and passenger side seatback recliner. Available in Dark Blue, Red, Silver, Almond.

Optional Chrysler Fifth Avenue. Corinthian leather with vinyl trim 60/40 individually adjustable front seats with adjustable head restraints. folding center armrest, and passenger side seatback recliner. Available in Dark Blue, Red, Silver, Almond.

CHIMES REMINDER WHEN HEADLIGHTS LEFT ON, KEY IN IGN., OR SEAT BELTS UNFSTND. (AIR CONDITIONING STD.)

1157

CHRYSLER LE BARON

$9495. (SPECIAL PRICE.)

CHRYSLER INTRODUCES THE CRYSTAL KEY PROGRAM. BETTER OWNER CARE THAN EVEN ROLLS ROYCE OR MERCEDES.

J41D HIGHLINE OR J51K PREMIUM

LE BARON

COUPE, REG. $13,266. UP

CONVERTIBLE $15,752. UP

2.5-LITER EFI, OR A 2.2-LITER EFI TURBOCHARGED 4 CYL. ENG.

LE B. TURBO WHEEL

MODELS:

| New Yorker Landau |
| New Yorker |
| New Yorker Turbo |
| Fifth Avenue |
| LeBaron Convertible |
| LeBaron Coupe |
| LeBaron Four-Door Sedan |
| Town & Country Wagon |
| LeBaron GTS |
| Conquest TSi |

88 A

new RESTYLED N.Y. / LANDAU

J45D HIGHLINE OR J55K PREM. (TURBO, — E SUFFIX)

New safety

Air bags work quicker than you can blink your eye.

Air bags and seat belts.

H48D HIGHLINE OR H58K PREMIUM (TURBO, — E)

LE BARON GTS

PERFORMANCE SEDAN

(LITTLE CHANGE FROM 1987) $12,591. UP

LE BARON 4 DR.

C 56 D

NEW STARTING 5-15-88,

air bags standard equipment *

ON LE BARON CPE. and CVT.; 5TH AVE.; DODGE DAYTONA and DIPLO.; PLY. GRAN FURY

(* ON DRIVER'S SIDE)

$12,522.

LE BARON

C59K

$14,125.

TOWN and COUNTRY WAGON

STRIPE ALONG SIDE OF TURBO →

(T + C IS DISCONTINUED DURING 1988, RESUMES AS 1990 MINI VAN.)

When you think about it, the air bag is a truly remarkable device. It is made of nylon, with a neoprene coating to seal it. A coating of talcum powder covers the inside of the bag to help it expand fully when activated. It is neatly folded inside the steering wheel trim cover.

When sensors detect a front-end collision of sufficient force to trigger it, the air bag inflates to help protect the driver's head and chest. It all happens in about 50 milliseconds, just half the time it takes to blink your eye. Then, the bag partially deflates.

STEERING COLUMN ATTACHMENT · FOLDED AIR BAG · COVER · INFLATOR · STEERING WHEEL

CHRYSLER

4 CYL. NEW YORKER TURBO POWER.

THESE MODELS NOT RESTYLED.

F66P

V8-ENGINED FIFTH AVENUE

new 1988½ 5TH AVE. HAS DRIVER AIRBAG AS STD. EQUIP. $18,815.

U463

$17,868.

NEW YORKER LANDAU

U663 New

$19,949.

New V6 ENGINE IN THESE 2 MODELS

INTERIOR DETAILS

new Chrysler New Yorker.

$17,856.

• Advanced front-wheel drive • Powerful new V-6 engine
• Electronic fuel injection • Four-wheel disc anti-lock braking system
• Self-leveling suspension • Crystal Clear paint
• Adjustable front and rear seat headrests • Power rack-and-pinion steering
• Automatic temperature control air conditioning
• Power six-way driver's seat • Mark Cross leather seating
• Rear-seat stereo headphone controls
• Electronic instrument panel • Electronic speed control
• On-board travel computer • Crystal Key owner care

V.I.N. = -(1C OR JJ)
3B (C54N) -J-#

88

ALTERNATE WHEEL CHOICE

"Landau" NAME ON PADDED REAR QTR. PANEL

CLOSER DETAILS OF NEW YORKER LANDAU

CHRYSLER. DRIVING TO BE THE BEST.

Chrysler 7/70

The New Chrysler Corporation

CHRYSLER CORDOBA

(1975 TO 1983)

DASH

INTER. →

SPECIAL PACKAGE:

Corinthian Edition

(1980 and 1981 ONLY)

$9047.

J52

Cordoba shown in Baron Red.

CORDOBA

V.I.N.=1C3BJ (-) 2E0B (-) 000001 UP

P195/75R15 TIRES

J62
LS
$7765.

(REG. $8277.)

LS has DIFFERENT GRILLE, WITH "LS" IN CENTER DISC. (6 CYL. STD.)

W. CABRIOLET ROOF PACKAGE (ABOVE)

81

112.7" WHEELBASE

225 CID 6
3/8 CID V8
(140 OR 155 HP)

AIR COND. CONTROLS

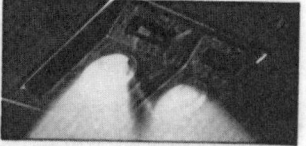

READING LIGHTS

2.7 GEAR RAT. (2.9 w. A/C)

LIGHTED VISOR MIRRORS

TURBINE WHEEL TRIM

17 EPA
26 HWY.
MPG (V8)

1161

CHRYSLER CORDOBA

DASH

82
ALL NOW HAVE
PADDED TOPS

S52

$10,397.

2.9 GEAR RATIO

CHRYSLER
NAME NOW ON
LEFT SIDE OF DECK
LID →

S62 **LS** $9458.

225 CID 6 (90 HP @ 3600)
318 CID V8 (130 @ 4000;
165 HP IN CALIFORNIA)

V.I.N. = 1C3BS52
EOC (-) 000001 UP

18 GAL. FUEL TANK 18 MPG (EPA)

LS
SHOWN WITH OPTIONAL
CABRIOLET ROOF TREATMENT

FINAL YEAR
FOR LS
MODEL

24 EST. MPG 18 EST. MPG
We've re-engineered the American luxury car.
THE NEW CHRYSLER CORPORATION. QUALITY ENGINEERED TO BE THE BEST

DASH

83

• Automatic Transmission • Power Front Disc Brakes • Dual
Remote Mirrors • Glass Belted Radials • Halogen Headlamps
• Electronic Digital Clock • Leather Wrapped Steering Wheel
• Padded Landau Vinyl Roof • and 12 additional luxury features.

225 CID 6 (90 HP)
OR
318 CID V8
(140 HP)

INTERIOR

V.I.N. = 1C3BS52HXD (-) 000001 UP

$11,006.

S52

Chrysler

(CORDOBA DISCONTINUED
DURING 1983)

Chrysler Imperial.

(1926 – 1975; 1981 – 1983; RETURNS 1990)

MARK CROSS INTERIOR ('81)

KNOWN SIMPLY AS "IMPERIAL," 1954 – 1975 and 1981 – 1983.

112.7" WB
318 CID V8
140 HP @ 4000 RPM

"Every luxury is standard. And there are more luxuries standard than any car in America."

('81) DASH

The New Chrysler Corporation

CORPORATE SYMBOL

2-DR. ONLY

18 GALLON FUEL TANK
16 MPG (EPA) ('82)

it's time for Imperial.

$18,822. ('81)
21,513. ('82)
19,228. ('83)

NEW MODEL Y-62

81-83

LITTLE CHANGE FROM 1981 TO 1983.
P205/75R x 15 TIRES
2.24 GEAR RATIO

NO IMPERIALS AVAILABLE 1984 TO 1989.

LEE IACOCCA, CHAIRMAN OF THE "NEW CHRYSLER CORP."
FRANK SINATRA, MOVIE AND RECORDING STAR

('83) V.I.N. ENDS WITH
—B-# (1981) —C-# (1982) —D-# (1983)

THEY APPEARED (AND WERE QUOTED) IN VARIOUS IMPERIAL ADS.

RETURNS 1990 AS "CHRYSLER IMPERIAL."

3.3L (201 CID) V6 (147 HP @ 4800 RPM) 17/25 MPG
16 GALLON FUEL TANK

90 New $25545.

109.3" WB

4 DR. ONLY

V.I.N. ENDS WITH —L-#

195/75R x 14 TIRES

Mark Cross Ultrasoft leather.

(1989-1990)

CHRYSLER MASERATI "TC"

ASSEMBLED IN ITALY BY
MASERATI-INNOCENTI
IMPORTED BY CHRYSLER

1990 MPG. FIGS.
18/25 EPA w.
4 CYL. and 5 SP.
MANUAL TRANS.
17/24 w. V6 and A/T

WITH ITALIAN LEATHER UPH.

$30,000. UP
$33,000 IN 1990

convertible
soft or removable hard top.

('89)   FP-10

160 HP 4 ALSO
AVAIL. 1989

18/22
MPG ('89)

CLOSER
REAR
DETAILS

4 CYL. DOHC
16-VALVE ENGINE
135 CID   7.3 COMPR.
200 HP @ 5500 RPM
3.47 G.R.   5 SP. TRANS.
(new 181 CID MITSUBISHI V6 (141 HP) ALSO
FOR 1990)

93" WHEELBASE

"Q" BODY

89
-90

DRIVER'S
AIRBAG IN
NEW GRAINED
STEERING WHEEL FOR 1990

135 M.P.H.

14 GAL. FUEL TK.

MASERATI EMBLEM
AT CONSOLE

V.I.N.
ENDS
WITH
—K
—#
(1989)

—L
—#
(1990)

('89)

205/60 VR 15 TIRES

New

1164

Imported for Dodge and Plymouth, built by Mitsubishi Motors Corp. in Japan.

COLT

(SINCE 1971)

4 CYL. (86 OR 98 CID, 64 OR 72 HP @ 5000 RPM)
90.6" WB

- Room for five
- MCA-JET engine
- 3-Door hatchback
- Front-wheel drive • Built by Mitsubishi Motors Corp., of Japan.

*Sticker prices higher: CA, LA, MA, MD, MS, NE, NJ, WI, AK, CO, TX, WA.

DE LUXE
$5300. ('81)
$5889. ('82)

note RUB RAIL ON SIDE OF DE LUXE (ABOVE)

(1982 EXAMPLES ILLUSTRATED)

THE LOWEST-PRICED HIGH-MILEAGE JAPANESE IMPORTS... DODGE COLT & PLYMOUTH CHAMP...

1981
V.I.N. =
3B3BE (-) 4 (-) OB100001 UP

COLT STANDARD
$5075. ('81)

INTERIORS

$4995 *BASE STICKER PRICE LOWEST PRICED OF ALL CARS OVER 37 EPA ESTIMATED MPG.

-400 FACTORY REBATE AT PARTICIPATING DEALERS

$4595 *SUGGESTED RETAIL PRICE WITH REBATE

*EXCLUDING TAX, TITLE, LICENSE, DESTINATION CHARGE AND OPTIONAL EQUIPMENT NOT AVAILABLE IN AREAS WHERE HIGH ALTITUDE EMISSION PACKAGE IS REQUIRED.

DASH

MPG
39 EPA
51 HWY

COLT CUSTOM
$5606 $6211.
('81)   ('82)

51 EST HWY MPG 39 EPA EST MPG
Use EPA estimate for comparison only. Your mileage may vary. Actual highway mileage will probably be less. CA mileage lower.

81-82

DODGE COLT ("IDL" BODY)

$5532.

PLYMOUTH CHAMP
(FINAL CHAMP)

('82½)
SIMILAR PLYMOUTH "CHAMP" AVAIL. '79~'82

$5632.

'82 V.I.N. JB3BE242(-)C(-)000001 UP

RS (ABOVE)
Dodge Colt RS
Our fun to drive, economical to run, top of the line Colt RS has a touch of class and a whole lot of sportiness and value almost everywhere you look.

RS WITH 2 TONE PAINT AND "RS" DECAL

These good-looking cast aluminum road wheels and P175/70R13 radial tires are part of the RS Package and Road Wheel Package, both available as options on Colt Custom. (Raised white letter—RS only.)

COLT

HIGH-TECH IMPORTS

STARTING 1983, MITSUBISHI ALSO BEGINS IMPORTING OTHER MODELS UNDER ITS OWN NAME.

35 EPA* EST MPG   **45** EST HWY

REGULARLY **$5084.** (2 DR.)

COLT GTS *new*

51 HWY EST MPG   **38** EPA** EST MPG

4 DR. FROM **$5688.**

DELUXE 2-DR. HATCHBACK **$5809.**

CUSTOM 2-DR. HATCHBACK **$6148.**

CUSTOM 4-DR. HATCHBACK **$6268**

83

V.I.N. = JP3 BE 242 (-) D (-) 000001 UP

Enter Colt GTS, imported only for Dodge and Plymouth. With black matte accents all around, rakish spoiler, side-glass louvres, wide tires, GTS badges and racing stripes, this Colt looks the part

V.I.N. = J (B) 3BE 24 AXE (-) 000001 UP

3.DPM45

TURBO COLT:

IMPORTS WITH A PURPOSE

new

VISTA WAGON 103.3" WB 4 CYL.

REG. **$8205.**

84

Vista is the wagon re-invented for today. Vista seats 7 passengers and those seats flip up or down, to handle just about any combination of people and things.

36 EST HWY   **28** EPA* EST MPG*

TURBO COLT (w. 1.6L TURBOCHARGED 4 102 HP @ 5500 RPM) WITH MICHELIN XVS 165/70 HR 13 TIRES

53 EST HWY   **41** EPA* EST MPG*

VISTA

WITH VARIOUS SEATING ARRANGEMENTS

TALLER and WITH MORE HEADROOM THAN OTHER COLT MODELS

$8,115 ADV. SPEC. PRICE

HATCHBACKS ARE NOW CALLED "3 DOOR" OR "5 DOOR" MODELS.

SPECIAL AD. PRICE **$4,995**

1987 MPG : 29/33 (90 CID 4); 24/28 (98 CID 4);
23/24 (VISTA WAGON w. 122 CID 4)
1987 V.I.N. = 1B3B (A24K)—H—#

(DODGE = "1DL" BODY)
(PLYMOUTH = "1PL" BODY)

Dodge Plymouth
IMPORTS

Colt

Four-wheel drive

(OPT.)

4WD INTRO.
ON VISTA
DURING '85.

4WD $12108. H39D
('87)
$10864.
2WD G39D

Colts are built by Mitsubishi and sold exclusively at Chrysler-Ply.

Dodge

Colt Premier $8926.

4-DR.
A46K (SHOWN ABOVE)
('87)

BELOW: E
3 DR. HATCHBACK
$6169.

TURBO DL HATCHBK.
A34F
(A34K W/O TURBO)

VISTA : DODGE "3DM" BODY
PLYMOUTH "3PM" "

EXCEPT ON VISTA ABOVE,
"COLT" NAME MOVED TO CENTER
OF GRILLE.

87—

NEW WHEEL DESIGNS

88

1988 V.I.N. =
JB3B
(A24K)
—J—#

TURBOCHARGED
ENGINE,
$748. EXTRA
AUTO. TRANS.
455.
AIR COND.. $717.
POWER STEERING $236.

"DL"
wagon ('88)

INTRODUCED 1988

A24K E

25/46 MPG

$8859.
SPECIAL PRICE

A39P

1988
COLTS
PRICED FROM
$6134.
(DOWN $35.)

New

(REG.
$8898.)

優秀 Colt
It's all the Japanese you need to know.

1168

Buckle up for safety.

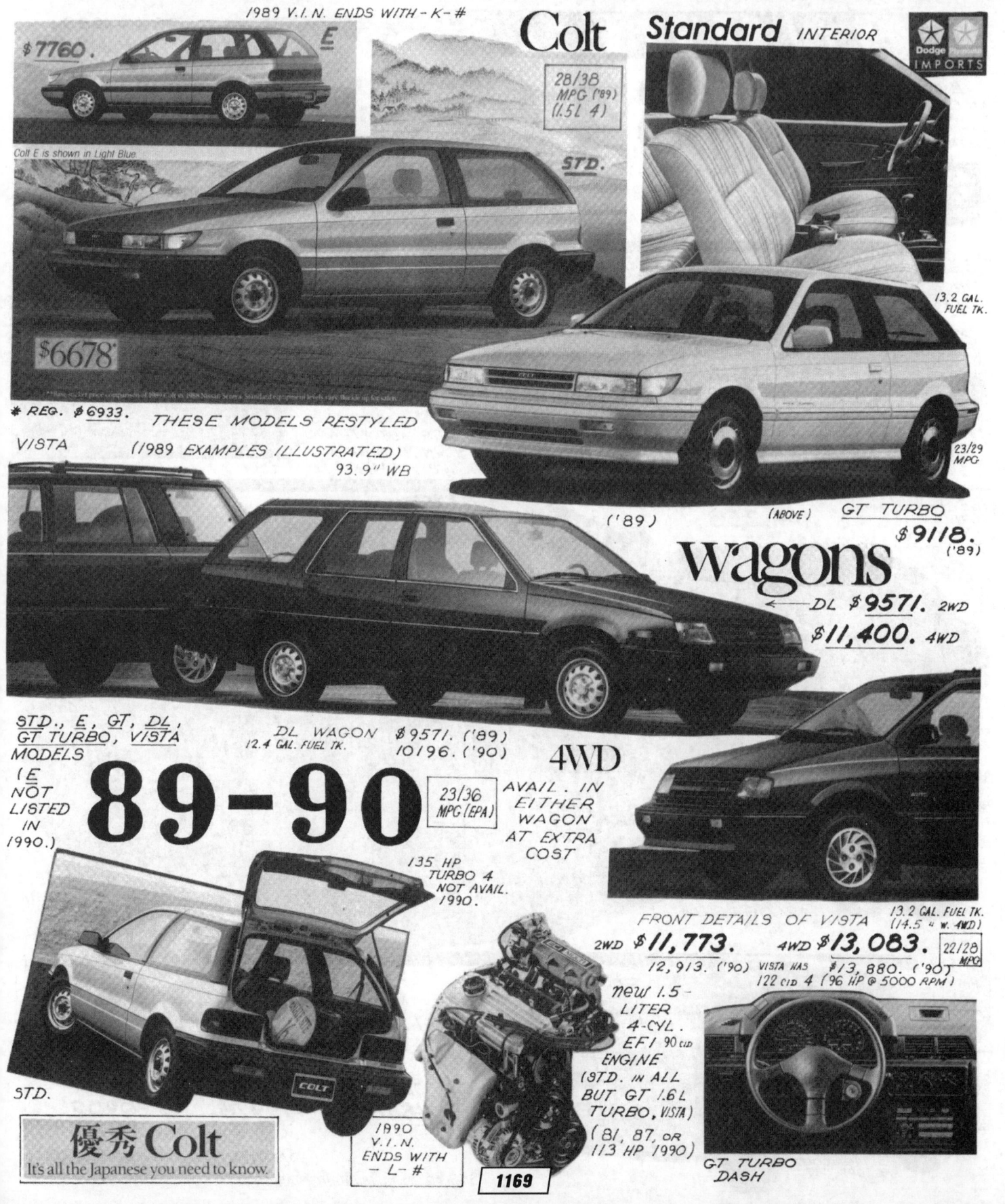

1989 V.I.N. ENDS WITH - K - #

$7760.

E

Colt E is shown in Light Blue.

$6678*

* REG. $6933

*Base sticker price comparison of 1989 Colt vs 1988 Nissan Sentra. Standard equipment levels vary. Buckle up for safety.

Colt Standard INTERIOR

28/38 MPG ('89) (1.5L 4)

STD.

13.2 GAL. FUEL TK.

23/29 MPG

('89)   (ABOVE)   GT TURBO
$9118. ('89)

wagons

← DL $9571. 2WD
$11,400. 4WD

VISTA

THESE MODELS RESTYLED
(1989 EXAMPLES ILLUSTRATED)
93.9" WB

STD., E, GT, DL,
GT TURBO, VISTA
MODELS
(E NOT LISTED IN 1990.)

DL WAGON $9571. ('89)
12.4 GAL. FUEL TK.   10196. ('90)

89-90

23/36 MPG (EPA)

4WD

AVAIL. IN EITHER WAGON AT EXTRA COST

135 HP TURBO 4 NOT AVAIL. 1990.

FRONT DETAILS OF VISTA
13.2 GAL. FUEL TK. (14.5 w. 4WD)

2WD $11,773.   4WD $13,083.
12,913. ('90)   VISTA HAS $13,880. ('90)
122 CID 4 ('96 HP @ 5000 RPM)   22/28 MPG

NEW 1.5-
LITER
4-CYL.
EFI 90 CID
ENGINE
(STD. IN ALL
BUT GT 1.6L
TURBO, VISTA)
(81, 87, OR
113 HP 1990)

STD.

1990 V.I.N. ENDS WITH - L - #

GT TURBO DASH

1169

優秀 Colt
It's all the Japanese you need to know.

CONQUEST

(1984-1989)

MADE IN JAPAN BY MITSUBISHI and EXCLUSIVELY DISTRIBUTED BY **Dodge** **Plymouth**

new **84** C41E
95.9" WB
156 CID TURBO 4 (145 HP @ 5000 RPM)
$13,464.
P195/70R14 TIRES (15" AVAIL.)
WHEEL DETAIL

INTERIOR ('84)

DISC BRAKES (SINCE 1984)
$13,902.   123 MPH

"TECHNICA" PKG. AVAIL. (SINCE 1984)

85 C54H
5 SP. MANUAL OR 2 SP. AUTO TRANS. (SINCE 1984)
V.I.N.=J(B)3BC44HXF(-)#

('84 V.I.N.=HXE INSTEAD OF HXF)

155.9 CID TURBO 4 176 HP @ 5000 RPM 3.54 G.R. 19.8 GAL. FUEL TANK

$14,756.

Dodge **Plymouth**

V.I.N. ENDS WITH —G—#

5 SP. TRANS.

3.54 GEAR RATIO

C54H **86** *new* INTERCOOLED ENGINE PKG.= $2200. EXTRA

TSi ILLUSTR.

18/24 MPG ('89)

DISTRIBUTED BY CHRYSLER, 1987 TO 1989.

C54H   C54N (1988 and 1989)

87-89

V.I.N. ENDS WITH —H—# (1987) —J—# (1988) —K—# (1989)

1987 $16365. C54H
1988 TSi $19976. C54N
1989 TSi $20902. C54N

('88)

TSi INTERCOOLER PKG. OPT. '87

(DISCONT'D. DURING 1989)

SIMILAR TO MITSUBISHI STARION)

ARIES DASH

ARIES FROM $7690.

ST. REGIS DISCONT'D.

Dodge

ARIES

America's Driving Machines

1982 ARIES HAS "D" MODEL DESIGNATION ("K" IN 1981)

13 GALLON FUEL TANK

26 MPG (EPA)

ARIES INTERIOR

D21

D49 CUSTOM $8956.

Aries K 4-door—America's highest mileage 6-passenger sedan.

V.I.N. = 1B3B ( ) - C - #

82

new "PENTASTAR" HOOD and DECK ORNAMENTS

D89 SE $9528.

Aries K wagon—America's highest mileage 6-passenger wagon.

NEW

V46 (LS) V56

400 SEDAN (REAR DOORS EXTEND INTO QUARTER PANEL)

New

400 CONVERTIBLE V45

13 GAL. FUEL TANK 26 MPG (EPA)

$13,727.

400 "LS" V51 COUPE $9735.

99.9" WB 135 OR 156 CID 4

225 CID V6 OR 318 CID V8

(18 GAL. FUEL TANK 18 MPG EPA, MIRADA AND DIPLOMAT)

Dodge 400's. NEW

6 OR V8 (DIPLOMAT, DIPLOMAT MEDALLION SEDANS STILL AVAIL., FROM $8950.)

1172

Mirada CMX

$9819. UP (CMX PKG. EXTRA COST)

X62

WITH A LOW PRICE: $6577.***

(REG. $8410. AND UP)

26 MPG EPA

$8551. UP

$9391. UP

Dodge

AMERICA'S DRIVING MACHINES

ARIES

(ABOVE, AND AT LEFT)

V51 COUPE $9592.

1983 DODGE V.I.N. = (1 OR J) 83B (E242)-D-#

V56 SEDAN $9555.

FINAL "400" MODELS IN 1983

DODGE 400

26 MPG EPA

new 5-SP. MANUAL TRANSAXLE AVAIL.

CONVERTIBLE

V55 CVT. $13,602.

LOTS OF MPGS: 41 EST. HWY. 29 EPA EST. MPG**

INTRODUCING DODGE 600.

New

E46 SED. $9987.

MANY DODGE DIPLOMAT SEDANS USED IN TAXI SERVICE.

Yellow

G26 18 MPG EPA

24 MPG EPA

102.9" WB 4 CYL.

135' OR 158 CID

94 OR 93 HP

TRANSVERSE MOUNTED 2.2 LITER ENGINE 32 EST. HWY., 24 EPA EST. MPG**

DIPLOMAT FROM $9674.

CONTINUES GRILLE STYLE INTRODUCED 1980.

83

Dodge MIRADA $10,689* (AS EQUIPPED)

112.7" WB 225 CID 6 OR 318 CID V8 (100 HP) (140 HP)

DASH

new "TALKING CAR" RECORDED VOICE WARNING SYSTEM

600 ES $9472*

(REG. $10,518.) 98 MPH

INCLUDES: (600 ES)

FRONT-WHEEL DRIVE

38 EST. HWY., 23 EPA EST. MPG**

5/50 PROTECTION PLAN†

FIVE-PASSENGER SEATING

TRANSVERSE-MOUNTED 2.2 LITER ENGINE

ALUMINUM ROAD WHEELS

FIRM-FEEL POWER STEERING (WITH QUICKER RATIO)

POWER BRA... (FRONT DISC, RE...

SPORT SUSPENSION (LARGER SWAY BARS, FRONT & REAR, HIGHER-CONTROL SHOCKS, FRONT & REAR)

5-SPEED MANUAL TRANSMISSION

STEEL-BELTED RADIALS

ELECTRONIC VOICE ALERT (MONITORS 10 FUNCTIONS)

DUAL OUTSIDE POWER MIRRORS

AM RADIO

RECLINING BUCKET SEATS

DIGITAL CLOCK

PADDED DOOR TRIM PANELS

CARPETED TRUNK

SPORT STEERING WHEEL

POWER TRUNK RELEASE

ELECTRIC FUEL-FILLER DOOR RELEASE

BUMPER RUB STRIPS

FR...

X62 (FINAL MIRADA H/T AVAIL., $10437.)

600 ES

Dodge

84

400 SERIES IS DISCONTINUED

DODGE ARIES K.

INTERIOR

$**8743.** AND UP

Highest mileage: 41 est. hwy., [29] EPA

new 100.3" WB

ARIES SE INTERIOR

ARIES FRONT END, WITH CLOSE VIEW OF new WHEEL

1984 V.I.N. = 1B3B (E24A) - E - #

600 E9 $11115.

108 MPH

600 SERIES.

4 CYL. OR TURBO 4

new 600 CONV'TS.

$**11949.** UP WITH new POWER QUARTER WINDOWS

600 DASH

CARAVAN WAGON IS

NEW "S" BODY

MPG 41 DIPLOMAT SE (RESTYLED FRONT) $**11432.**

REAR WHEEL DR.

Diplomat

DIPLOMAT 112.7" WB 318 CID V8 (130 HP)

600 MODELS:
V56D SEDAN
E31D COUPE
V55D CVT.
E46D
"SE"
SED.

new HIGH-MOUNTED 3RD BRAKE LT.

note LOUVRES ON THE HOOD

Dodge 5/50
DIVISION OF CHRYSLER MOTORS

↑ THIS ES (CVT. ONLY) HAS 135 CID TURBO 4

(V8 DIPLOMAT SALON AND SE SEDAN AVAIL., FROM $11385.)

(SIMILAR TO 1984 ILLUSTRATED)

AN AMERICAN REVOLUTION

DODGE

(2 VIEWS)

DODGE 600 ES TURBO

86

V55E $15266.

"P" BODY 924D SHADOW COUPE $9104.

DODGE SHADOW
4 CYL. OR TURBO 4

97" WB
111 MPH

New

928D SHADOW SED. AVAIL., AT $9304.

MPG: 23/27 25/33 (5 SP.) 135 CID 4)

87

SHADOW (REAR)

V.I.N. 1B3B (Z18C) → H-#

SALON OR SE DIPLOMAT MPG: 16/21 (W. 318 CID V8) $11922 SALON G26P $13002 SE G56P (ILLUSTR. AT LOWER LEFT)

ARIES LE $9988.

"K" BODY D41D CPE.

STD. AND LE ARIES ONLY; SE DISCONT'D.

ARIES MPG: 23/28 (135 CID 4, A/T) 22/27 (152 CID 4)

600 MPG 19/26 w. 135 CID 4 and A/T 22/27 (152 CID 4)

1987 DODGE LANCER.

LANCER MPG: 23/26 (135 CID 4, A/T) 22/27 (152 CID 4)

X48D SPT. SED. OR X68D ES SPT. SED. "H" BODY

"E" BODY

↑ 600 E36D SEDAN $11218. E46D SE SEDAN $11880.

1987 DODGE DIPLOMAT. SE "M" BODY

REG. $11589. UP ($9852. ADV. SPECIAL)

COUPE P24D

SHADOW

SED. P28D

19/34 MPG

SHADOW →

SHADOW

THE NEW SPIRIT OF DODGE

Dodge
DIVISION OF CHRYSLER CORPORATION

SPIRIT DASH

SHADOW

$10050. (CPE.)
$10250. (SEDAN)

89

V.I.N. = (1 OR J) B3 →
(P24D) — K — #

A46G OR "LE" A56G SPIRIT

SPIRIT
FROM $11489.

18/34 MPG

SPIRIT REPLACES 600

New

IN 1989
103.3" WB 2.5 L.
4 OR TURBO 4

ES

Spirit. ES

3.0 L V6 AVAIL. ALSO

SPIRIT ES INTERIOR and REAR DETAILS

A76J SPIRIT ES $14310.

SPIRIT SEDANS ONLY

ES HAS ADDITN'L. LOWER GRILLE AND LTS.

ES
TURBO 4

LANCER SHELBY
$17670.

H78A
19/24 MPG

Lancer Shelby is shown above in Bright White Pearl Coat

16/22 MPG

DYNASTY FROM $13575.

ARIES AMERICA
FINAL 1989 MODEL K41D

$9600.

23/34 MPG

(ARIES, LANCER, DIPLOMAT DISCONTINUED 1990.)

DIPLOMAT

DYNASTY

DODGE

SHADOW
P24D
LIFTBACK COUPE
$10525.
(SHADOW P48D
4 DR. AVAILABLE,
$10725.)
93 HP UP

SPIRIT INTER.

97" WB

SHADOW INTERIOR

2.2 or 2.5 L 4 or
TURBO 4.
2.5 L 4 or 150 HP
TURBO 4 or 3.0L V6
AVAIL. IN
SPIRIT.

$14956.
SPIRIT
ES

DODGE SPIRIT
ES
TURBO

SPIRITS FROM
$12418.

103.3" WB

(ARIES, LANCER, DIPLOMAT
ARE DISCONTINUED.)

Spirit

A76J **ES**
2.5 L TURBO
4 or 3.0L
OHC MPI V6
103.3" WB

(SPIRIT and SPIRIT LE
have 2.5 L 4 ENG.,
with ES ENGINES
OPTIONAL.)

3.3-liter OHV
MPI V-6

NEW 3.3 L OHV MPI
V6 ENGINE AVAIL. ON
DYNASTY
LE (3.0 V6,
4 CYL. 2.5 L
ALSO)

90

V.I.N. ENDS
WITH — L — #

(ALL 4 DRS.
EXC. SHADOW)

MONACO ES INTERIOR
(LEATHER SEATS and POWER SEAT
CONTROLS OPT.)

100 or 141 HP
or 147 HP **DODGE DYNASTY.** 104.3" WB
$15034. UP

MONACO INTRO. FOR
1990 ½ SEASON

NEW **MONACO**
LE or ES
106" WB

MONACO
SIMILAR TO
EAGLE
PREMIER

MONACO SERIES RETURNS
(FIRST SINCE 1978)

3.0 L OHC
MPI V6
4 SP. A/T   26 MPG EPA

(MADE IN JAPAN)

V.I.N.=
3B3B
D437
0B
10001
UP

Dodge Challenger

From Mitsubishi high technology

(1978–1983)

99" WB
155.9 CID 4
105 HP
5-SP. TRANS.

$7516. UP *

195/70 HR × 14 TIRES
* (ILLUSTR. ALUMINUM WHEELS OPTIONAL.)

(PLYMOUTH SAPPORO IS SIMILAR)

D 43 **81**

INTERIOR

D 43 **82**

V.I.N. =
JB3BD437
(-) C (-)
00000I UP

$8036.

HP CUT TO 100

AVAIL. UPH.

NEW

"TECHNICA" INSTRUMENT PANEL

STANDARD DASH

45 MPH

$8323.

The Anti-Shock Sticker

D 43 **83**

OPT. "TECHNICA" PKG. INCLUDES new GRAPHIC INSTR. PANEL, BLACK and SILVER BODY PAINT, ETC.

CHALLENGER & SAPPORO: MORE STANDARD EQUIPMENT

PRICES START AT ONLY $8323.

V.I.N. =
JP3BD437(-)D
(-)00000I UP

HIGH-TECH IMPORTS
Built by Mitsubishi Motors Corp.
Master Car Builders of Japan.

1180

Dodge CHARGER

(RE-INTRO. 1981)
(ORIG. 1966 TO 1978)

4 CYL.
104.7 or 133 CID
(63 or 94 HP)
96.6" WB

REG. $ 7721. ('82)
8054. ('83)

P175 75R x13 TIRES
FRONT WHEEL DRIVE

THE 2.2 VERSION. $7438

41 | 26 mph
MPG : 46 / 28

1982
1983

Z54

BASE MODEL
HATCHBACK
34/51 MPG

$ 7213.
('83)

Z44 ('83)

1981 MODEL
DOES NOT
HAVE EMBLEM
ON HOOD.

81 -83

SUNROOF
OPTIONAL

EACH OF THE 3 BASIC
CHARGER TYPES HAS ITS OWN
UNIQUE REAR QUARTER
PANEL and WINDOW STYLING
AS SHOWN. (SIMILAR TO PLY.
HORIZON TC-3 and TURISMO.)

1983 MODELS ILLUSTRATED

V.I.N.	1981 ENDS WITH	B #
	1982 " "	C #
	1983 " "	D #

THE SHELBY VERSION. $8290*
(BELOW)

Dodge
AMERICA'S DRIVING MACHINES

CARROLL SHELBY

SPECIAL SHELBY COLORS:

RADIANT SILVER with SANTA FE BLUE TAPE, OR
SANTA FE BLUE with RADIANT SILVER TAPE.

1983 ½ SHELBY HAS OWN
GRILLE DESIGN,
LESS WINDOW
SPACE, AND IS

NEW
IN MID 1983

MPG 40/25

117 MPH

P195/50 R x15 TIRES
GOODYEAR

Z64 SHELBY
REG. $ 8602.

107 HP
@ 5600 RPM

CHARGER

Dodge

CHARGER 2+2

LZP24
$8101.
(SPECIAL PRICE $7288.)

↑ SHELBY CHARGER REG. $9534.

EXCEPT FOR SHELBY LZS24 CHARGER, NOW WITH 4 HEADLIGHTS

LZH24

LZS24

BASE CHARGER SG494

REG. $7420.

LZS24

FRONT-WHEEL-DRIVE SPORT COUPE.

96.6" WB
97.1 or 133 CID 4 (94, 110 HP)
133 CID H.O. 4 AVAIL.

24/37 MPG

2+2 INTER.

2+2 BASE CHARGER FRONT END

OPTIONAL CHARGER 2+2 INTERIOR

SHELBY CHARGER S85-11

INTRO. new DODGE DAYTONA (BELOW)

84

97" WB
97.1 or 135 CID 4 (99 HP)
135 CID TURBO 4 (142 HP)
(140 HP WITH A/T)

DAYTONA TURBO

GVH24

DAYTONA

GVS24

$9898.

$11817.

↑ 1984½

122 MPH

SPECIAL MID YEAR PRICE: $9232.*

NOTE DIFFERING WHEELS AS WELL AS OTHER VARIATIONS ILLUSTR.

V.I.N. ENDS WITH — E — #

MPG: 24/43

DAYTONA DASH

01 GAL CONSUMED

DAYTONA INT.*

P195/60VR x 15 GOODYEAR EAGLE GT TIRES STD. ON TURBO Z PKG.

2.2 LITER ENGINE DAYTONA TURBO Z. PACKAGE

CHARGER, DAYTONA

32% NASTIER.

Dodge's incredible Shelby Charger now boasts an unfair advantage. Turbocharging.

V.I.N. ENDS WITH — F — #

85

LZS24 $9391.

P205/50 VR 15 TIRES (SHELBY)

CHARGER 97.1 CID 4 (64 HP); 135 CID 4 (101 HP)

3.56 GEAR RATIO
13 GAL. FUEL TANK

Dodge
AN AMERICAN REVOLUTION

124 MPH

DAYTONA INTER. →

MPG (EPA)
34 HWY. /
23 CITY

DAYTONA

GVH24 ADV. SPEC. PRICE,
(REG. $10107.) $8505.
5-SP. TRANS. ; FUEL INJECT.

135 CID TURBO 4 (146 HP)

DAYTONA TURBO Z

ALUMINUM WHEELS, $322.

GV-924 TURBO DAYTONA (W. "Z" PKG.)

$11,888., PLUS COST OF "Z" PKG.

NEW WHEELS

BASE MODEL CHARGER, 2.2, and SHELBY CHARGER TURBO CONTINUE ($7790. TO $9747.)

130 MPH (SHELBY GLHS)

A44D

DAYTONA HATCHBACK $10,700.

DAYTONA Z TURBO HATCHBACK

$12,988.
(T-BAR ROOF OPTIONAL AT EXTRA COST)
146 HP

V.I.N. ENDS WITH — G — #

86

A64E

Dodge
DIVISION OF CHRYSLER CORPORATION
AN AMERICAN REVOLUTION

1183

CHARGER, DAYTONA

Dodge

DAYTONA MPG 22/27 (w. 152 cu 4)

$14,474. "L" BODY
A64E

('87)

FINAL CHARGER AND SHELBY CHARGER ('87)

Z44C CHARGER, $7585. 134 MPH
Z64E SHELBY CHR., $10,226.

(SEE DODGE VEH. I.D. NUMBERS)

DAYTONA SHELBY Z

AG4A, $15176. IN 1988

DAYTONA TURBO Z

CHARGER DASH

Dodge IT'S GOTTA BE A DODGE.

('87)

new

$15 637.
('87) A54E

DAYTONA PACIFICA

($15 488., 1988)

A44K

DODGE DAYTONA

$8995.* ('88)

SPECIAL PRICE

* REG. $11,807.

2 VIEWS ('88)

"G" BODY

DAYTONA PACIFICA

87-88

WHEELS SHOWN, $310. EXTRA

Daytona, shown in Daytona Blue Clear Coat

DASH ('89)

Dodge THE NEW SPIRIT OF DODGE
THE PERFORMANCE DIVISION OF CHRYSLER MOTORS

$14634. ('89)
16066. ('90)

G74A SHELBY ('90)
(LEFT and BELOW)
(G74C in 1990)

('89) 174 HP 4 (TURBO)

89-

90 19/32 MPG (EPA)

DRIVER AIRBAG STD.

G24K $11,045. ('89)
G44K (ES) 12,145. "
G64J (turbo) 13,870. "
A44K $11,808. ('90)
ES 13,008. "
ES TURBO 15,218. "

DAYTONA

SHELBY

Daytona Shelby and ES Turbo instrument panel ('90)

G74A

DODGE DAYTONA SHELBY

EAGLE

MFD BY **CHRYSLER CORPORATION** (1988 ON)

CHRYSLER · PLYMOUTH · DODGE
DODGE TRUCKS · JEEP · EAGLE

MEDALLION

DL WAGON 12,317.

(FF48E)

DL SEDAN (FF45B) $11,589.
LX SEDAN (FF45C) 12,103.

V.I.N. = (VF1 OR 2XM)(FF45B) — J — #

NEW 88

MEDALLION HAS 2.2 L 4-CYL. ENGINE

102.3" WB
(108.2" ON WAGON)

Designed by Giugiaro in Turin, Italy, Premier is distinguished by its beautiful styling. But it is more than a dramatic look that makes Premier unique. Under the hood of the Premier ES is a highly advanced, multi-port fuel-injected 3.0 litre overhead cam aluminum V6 engine. The only aluminum V6 you'll find on a North American-built car.

Premier's admirable European qualities, including a four-wheel independent suspension for wonderful agility and precise handling, are artfully combined with its more traditional American advantages.

1988 Eagle Premier

Jeep Eagle
Expect the Best.

PREMIER

3.0 L V6 OR 2.5 L 4 106" WB

REAR DETAILS

LX SEDAN (JT559) 13,729.
LS SEDAN (JP557) 15,334.

V6 ENGINE (PREMIER)

PRE-1988 EAGLES IN AMC SECTION

1185

EAGLE

SUMMIT MADE ('89) IN JAPAN BY MITSUBISHI

1989 SUMMIT DL $11,536.
SUMMIT LX 11,872.

SUMMIT

*113 HP @ 6500 RPM

new SUMMIT has 96.7" WB, 1.5 or 1.6 L 4 CYL. ENG. (SIMILAR TO MITSUBISHI MIRAGE.)

PREMIER ES LEATHER SEATING!

THE NEXT STEP. THE ALL-NEW EAGLE SUMMIT.

A word about confidence. Every Eagle carries Chrysler's exclusive 7-year/70,000-mile Protection Plan!† **770**

1989 V.I.N. ENDS WITH —K-# ; —L-# in 1990

1990 STD. SEDAN $11,139 ; DL $11,625. LX $12,309. ES $13,347.

23/35 MPG SUMMIT '89

89-90

4-CYL. PREMIER ENG. NOT AVAIL. 1990.

PREMIER LX $14,556. ('89); $16,691. ('90)
"   ES 16,539. ('89); 18,310. ('90)

106" WB 3.0 L V6 or 2.5 L 4

LX ('90)

LX WAGON ADDED TO 1989 MEDALLION LINE. (NO 1990 MODEL)

PREMIER ES.

('89)

22/31 MPG ('89) PREMIER 4 CYL.

PREMIER BUILT AT FORMER AMC FACTORY IN ONTARIO, CANADA. (150 HP RENAULT 180 CID V6) 18/27 MPG

PRESENTING PREMIER ES LIMITED.

NEW

(SPECS. AS OTHER PREMIERS)

PREMIER ES LTD. (CB 66 U) $19,181. ('89)

20,737. ('90)

Eagle Premier Limited

The ES Limited has independent suspension at all four wheels. And an advanced torsion-bar rear suspension. A major reason for its world-class ride and handling.
Inside: roomy, comfortable, and generously fitted with genuine leather. With functionally positioned instruments and controls.

Jeep Eagle
Expect the Best.

JAPANESE-AMERICAN
TALON COUPE (4 CYL.) $13,449.
TALON TSi (4 CYL. TURBO) 15,207.
TALON TSi ALL-WHEEL DR. $16,891.

('90)

EAGLE TALON

Talon TSi's ergonomically designed cockpit features easy-to-read analog instrumentation, leather-wrapped steering wheel, and ideally positioned leather knob shifter grip.

New Eagle Talon With All-Wheel Dr

(STARTS 1990)
TALON BUILT IN NORMAL, ILLINOIS BY CHRYSLER-AND-MITSUBISHI "DIAMOND STAR MOTORS."

122 CID 4   (135 OR 195 HP)   22/29 MPG (EPA) (20/25, 4WD)

(SINCE 1903) **FORD**

SELECTAIRE CONDITIONER

Wagon

LTD Wagon, Light Pine Glow (4I)

WOOD-GRAINED COUNTRY SQUIRE $9714.

GRILLE

DIGITAL CLOCK

11:53
DATE E/T TIME

UNGRAINED LTD WAGONS PRICED FROM $9016.

2 DR. $8681.

3-Way Magic Doorgate.

CROWN VICTORIA INTERIOR

114.4" WB

81

V.I.N.= 1FAB (P31) ( )(-)60000/ UP

V8 OR 6

4 DR. $9458.

Crown Victoria

CROWN VICT. HAS WRAP-OVER BRIGHTWORK BAND WHICH DIVIDES FRONT PORTION OF ROOF FROM REAR PORTION, "TOWN CAR" STYLE.

2 DR. $9325.

20-GAL. FUEL TANK

1981 LTD DOES NOT HAVE DUAL LOWER GRILLE OPENINGS IN THE BUMPER, AS 1980 HAD.

FORD

OPTIONAL "TRIP MINDER" COMPUTER ON DASH

(LTD "S" WAGONS AVAIL. FR. $9953.)

TRIP MINDER — S E M R / 07:51 / 58 ET / TIME TRIP ECON FUEL

LTD — 18 MPG

$9744.

85 MPH SPEEDOMETER

LTD WAGON

$10,243.

$10,750.

LTD COUNTRY SQUIRE

CROWN VICTORIA 2-DR.

POWER SEAT CONTROLS

FORD 82

V.I.N. = 1FABP ( ) DOC (-)000001 UP

82

255 OR 302 CID V8 s 114.3" WB

GAS MILEAGE ESTIMATES 26 18

17 MPG (WAGON)

20 GAL. FUEL TANK (ON ALL)

Ford — TRADITIONAL OVAL EMBLEM RETURNS (FRONT AND REAR)

CROWN VICTORIA HAS REAR CHROME STRIP (new)

1188

FORD

LTD V.I.N. =
1FAB P31 BXD (-) 000001 UP
LTD WAGON V.I.N. =
1FABP37BXD (-) #

CROWN VICTORIA V.I.N. =
1FABP34FXD (-) #
CROWN VICTORIA WAGON V.I.N.
1FAB P38FXD (-) #
P215/75R x14 TIRES
302 CID V8 IN
CROWN VICTORIA

CROWN VICT.
"S" 4-DR.
P43/41 K
$10334.
2-DR. SEDAN
P42
11298.
4 DR. SED
P43
11298.
(S, STD.,
CNTRY SQ.
WAGONS ALSO)

114.3" WB
LTD Crown Victoria
has NEW GRILLE

83

STANDARD LTD SERIES TOTALLY RESTYLED AND DOWNSIZED, WITH NEW 105.6" WB

UN-GRAINED

GRAINED

FORD LTD

19 MPG EPA
P40

LTD Wagon

$9727. (GRAIN TRIM OPT.)

16 MPG EPA

LTD Country Squire in Pastel Vanilla.
P44

$11457.

Ford
OVAL EMBLEM

LTD DASH

103 MPH

55 MPH

105½" WB

NEW DOWNSIZED LTD.

NEW LOOK

140 CID 4
OR
LPG 4,
200 CID 6,
232 CID V6
(112 HP)

P185/75R14 TIRES

P39 SEDAN $9605.

P39 60H BROUGHAM SEDAN $9993.

24 MPG EPA (4 CYL.)
19 MPG EPA (6)

HAVE YOU DRIVEN A FORD...LATELY?

P185/75R x14 TIRES

Ford LTD
$10,271.

140 CID 4 (88 HP) OR 232 CID V6 (120 HP) ON LTD

NEW LTD/LX SEDAN has BLACK WINDOW PILLARS, V8 ENG. 115 MPH V.I.N. ENDS w. —E—#

Ford LTD 84

W. COUNTRY SQUIRE GRAIN OPTION ↓

$12,084.

Ford LTD Crown Victoria Wagons

Ford LTD
FROM $10,183.

LEATHER UPH. AVAIL. IN "INTERIOR LUXURY GROUP" PKG.

CTRY. SQUIRE $12,501. (WITH DUAL FACING RR. STS.)

$12,334. (6-PASS.)

WITH TAILGATE DOWN

302 OR 351 CID V8s IN CRN. VICT./SQUIRE (140 OR 180 HP)

Have you driven a Ford... lately? Ford

P215/75R x14 TIRES

VELOUR INTERIOR OF **Crown Victoria**

FORD LTD CROWN VICTORIA

CR. VICT. 2 DR. OR CROWN VICTORIA 4-DR.

$12,177. VENT WINDOW OPT.

E M
S R
24 IN MPG
TIME TRIP ECON FUEL

1190

FORD

FROM
$10461. ('85)
11220. ('86)

LTD →

('85)

105½" WB
232 CID V6

THIS 302 CID V8-POWERED LTD/LX NOT AVAIL. AFTER 1985.
V6 LTD. NOT AVAIL. AFTER 1986.

('85)

$12,590 **Ford LTD/LX high-performance**

85-87

FORD EMBLEM MOVED TO CENTER OF GRILLE (ON LTD)

CRWN. VICT. and SQUIRE 302 CID V8

17/27 EPA MPG

('85)

LTD. AVAIL. W. 4, V6 OR V8

"S" CROWN VIC. FROM
$11832. ('85)
13430. ('86)
14340. ('87)

('87)

LTD Crown Victoria

302 OR 351 CID V8
"PANTHER" BODY

V.I.N. ENDS WITH
— F-# (1985)
— G-# (1986)
— H-# (1987)

WAGON INTERIOR

LTD

13032. ('85)
13897. ('86)
15047. ('87)
"LX" SQUIRE WAGON ALSO, 1986 ON.

('87) **Country Squire Wagon**

V8 ENGINES ONLY

88

RESTYLED FRONT END

V.I.N. ENDS WITH —J-#

CROWN VICT. SEDANS and WAGONS ONLY, SINCE 1987. NO MORE SEPARATE LTD SERIES.

P73F

Ford LTD Crown Victoria.

$15,721.

P72F "S": $15155.)

1191

Ford LTD CROWN VICTORIA

DASH →

17/24 MPG

SEDAN = $16,356. ('89)
17,767. ('90)

LX SEDAN $17,272. ('89); $18,404. ('90)

89-90

AVAIL. WHEELS ('90)
1990 has NEW DASH,
COOLANT TEMP. GA.

BP SERIES ('89)   CP SERIES ('90)

LX SEDAN
CENTER PILLAR

DRIVER AIR BAG

**CROWN VICTORIA
WAGONS**

UNGRAINED →

GRAINED
BP79F
COUNTRY
SQUIRE
LX
WAGON
$18,061.
('89)
$19,181.
CP79F ('90)

(1990
EXAMPLES
ILLUSTR.)

V.I.N. =
1989
ENDS
WITH
– K –
#,
1990
WITH
– L –
#.

UNGRAINED WAGONS FROM
$16,714. ('89); $18,178. ('90)

302 CID V8 (150 HP
@ 3200 RPM)

1192

17/24
MPG

Best-Built American Cars.

FORD ESCORT

BUILT IN AMERICA

THE NEW WORLD CAR

Built to take on the world... and doing it!

V.I.N. =
IFA (-) PO5
(-) XBY
60000I UP

81 new

6723.

94.2" WHEELBASE

HATCHBACKS + WAGONS

STD.	FROM	$5742.
L	"	6078.
GL	"	6422.
GLX	"	7060.
SS	"	6723.

ESCORT SS

OPT. INSTR. GROUP 19 STANDARD EQUIP. IN SS

INTERIOR

SS WAGON $7048.

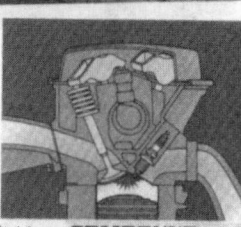

4 CYL. 98 CID

COMPOUND-VALVE HEMISPHERICAL HEAD ENGINE

GLX $7060

44	30
EPA EST HWY	EPA EST MPG

FORD ESCORT

DASH

SUNROOF AVAIL.

4 DR.

2 DR.

New

HATCHBACK 4-DR. SEDAN ADDED

47	31
EST HWY	EST EPA MPG

10 GALLON FUEL TANK

STD. —— $6387.
"L" —— 6919.
"GL" —— 7181.
"GLX" —— 7832.

GLX

WAGON
$8004.

WAGON INTERIOR

(GRAINED WAGON WAS ALSO AVAIL. IN '81.)

"GT" HATCHBACK 2DR. REPLACES "SS" SERIES

WAGON MPG:

44 EST HWY	28 EPA EST MPG

"L" WAGON $7116.
"GL" WAGON 7400.

At the heart of the World Car Wagon, the CVH engine.

82

OVAL "FORD" EMBLEM ADDED TO GRILLE

PRICED FROM $6180.

NEW The Ford

V.I.N. = 1FAB P0520C (-) 000001 UP

FORD ESCORT

Escort GT has the functional good looks of a serious road machine: rear spoiler, front air-dam, racing mirrors, TR-type steel wheels and a sporty blackout treatment.

P07

GT
$8010.
100 MPH

4-DRS. FROM $6654.

"L" IS NOW LOWEST-PRICED ESCORT, AT $6447. and up.

optional FS engine with improved mileage ratings

fuel injected. Escort GT comes equipped with a 1.6 liter electronically fuel injected engine, hooked up to a 5-speed transaxle.

GRAINED "GLX" WAGON $7897.

over 90 new improvements, ranging from a new luxury sound insulation package to a new fuel-conscious shift indicator light.

V.I.N. =
1FAB P052
XD (-)
000001 UP

UNGRAINED GLX WAGON ←

P11

43 EST HWY	29 EPA EST MPG

ESCORT WAGON

(GL 2 DR., $7131.)
(GLX, $7518.)

GL $7348.
P14

new 84 HP AVAIL. W. 5 SP. OR A/T

83

For comparison. Applicable only to sedans without power steering or A/C. Requires FS engine. Your mileage may vary depending on speed, distance and weather. Actual highway mileage lower. Not available in California.

47 EST HWY	33 EPA EST MPG

NEW
GRILLE, WITH ADDED VERTICAL PIECES →

ESCORT 1983 FORD ESCORT

FORD ESCORT

LX
$8412.

('84)

Escort Diesel:
('84)
NEW FOR 1984

46 EPA EST. MPG.
68 EST. HWY.

ALSO NEW DASH

(LX NOT AVAIL. IN LATER (1985))

STANDARD MODEL has PLAIN SIDES (above)
$5906. ('84)
5898. ('85)

Escort LX
$8322.

STEEL WHEEL

TR TYPE ALUMINUM WHEEL

84-85

new choice of GAS or DIESEL ENGINES

Escort L
$6377.

V.I.N. ENDS WITH
— E — # (1984)
— F — # (1985)

Turbo GT
$8799.

1985 MODELS ILLUSTRATED (UNLESS OTHERWISE NOTED)

Escort GL
4 DR. 7343.

Escort GT
$8066.

1196

BLACK GT DASH

(SIMILAR TO NEW 1986 MERCURY LYNX "XR-3")

GT has AERO-DYNAMIC FRONT STYLING, FRONT and REAR STABILIZER BARS, 15" ALUMINUM WHEELS with P195/60HR15 TIRES

V.I.N. = 1FABP (319) — G - #

FORD ESCORT

Escort GT
$8620.

HAS OWN "GT" ASYMMETRICAL GRILLE, new 4-CYL. HIGH-OUTPUT 1.9 LITER ENG.

UP TO 108 HP @ 5200 RPM

86

new "PONY" 2-DR. HATCHBACK IS LOWEST-PRICED 1986 ESCORT, AT $6229.

"L" and "LX" MODELS AVAIL. IN 3 BODY TYPES, and ALSO A new "SELECT L".

GT has REAR SPOILER

"GL" SERIES DISCONTINUED *

* FOR 1986 ONLY

Ford Escort. The world's best-selling car.

FORD ESCORT
WORLD'S BEST-SELLING CAR FOUR YEARS RUNNING.

(259) V.I.N. ENDS WITH — H — #

HATCHBK. 4 DR.
$7962.

(GL 2-DR.
HATCHBK.
$7748.)
(219)

GL →

(289) WAGON
$8243.

1.9 L 4 EFI ENG. w. "EEC IV"
ELECTRONIC ENG.
CONTROL SYSTEM
(DIESEL 4
AVAIL.)

ESCORT GL

"ERIKA"
BODY

87

"GL" SERIES
RETURNS,
REPLACES ALL
OTHER SERIES
EXCEPT FOR
"GT," 2-DR.
"PONY"
HATCHBACK,
ESCORT-
RELATED
"EXP."

CLOSE
DETAILS OF
HEADLIGHTS
AND
TAILLIGHTS

109 MPH (GT)

PONY = $6807.   (209)
GT = 9/69.   (23J)
(EA. AVAIL. AS 2-DR. HTCHBK. ONLY)

(PRICED FR. $7297. =
P209 PONY 2-DR.
HATCHBK.)

88 GL   P259

1988 V.I.N.
ENDS WITH
— J — #

$8078.

1198

Ford Escort

LX 4 DR. HATCHBK.
$8256.
P959

(FINAL EXP:
P889 2 DR.
LUXURY COUPE
$8510.)

Ford Escort. The world's best-selling car six years running.

1988½ Ford Escort.

MIDSEASON MODEL CHANGE OFFICIALLY LABELED 1988½ BY FORD MOTOR CO.

FRONT END

OTHER MODELS:			
PONY 2-DR. HTCHBK.	$7472.	P909	
LX " " "	7926.	P919	
GT " " "	9402.	P93J	
LX WAGON	8782.	P989	

1988½ LX NO LONGER INCLDS. (AS STD. EQUIPMENT) STYLED ROAD WHEELS OR BUMPER GUARDS (STD. ON 1988 GL)

('89)

GT

1989 LX INCL. A/T, AM/FM and CASSETTE PLAYER, DIGITAL CLOCK, A/C, POWER STEER., and OTHER EXTRAS AT N/C.

('89) $9030. ('89) LX **Escort Wagon.**

114 CID 4
90 HP
(110 HP, GT)

1989 LX SEDAN AND DASH (BELOW)

('89)

LX 2-DR.
HATCHBACK
$8174. ('89)

114 CID 4
(90 OR 110 HP)

1989 V.I.N. ENDS WITH -K-#

89-90

1990 V.I.N. ENDS WITH -L-#

	1989		1990	
PONY PP909	$7661.	P209	$8360.	
LX PP919	8174.	P219	8837.	
LX SED. PP959	8504.	P259	9167.	
LX WAG. PP989	9030.	P289	9692.	
GT P93J	9650.	P23J	10184.	

(ALL MODELS ARE HATCHBACKS; 2-DR. UNLESS OTHERWISE INDICATED.)

REAR SHOULD. BELTS STD. FOR 1990.

27/36 MPG (5 SP.)

1199

FORD EXP

Brand-new

(1982 TO 1988)

ONE MODEL ONLY IN 1982

$8812. ('82)

11.3 GALLON FUEL TK.

45 EPA EST. HWY. 28 EPA EST. MPG

INTERIOR

w. FRONT-WH. DRIVE

1982 V.I.N. = 1FAB PO120 C (-) 000001 UP

94.2" WB

('82)

82-83

1983 V.I.N. = 1FAB PO12 XD (-) 000001 UP

STORAGE SPACE BEHIND THE 2 FRONT SEATS

4 CYL., 98 CID (70 HP)
←CVH ENGINE

$7145. - 10004. ('83)

4 ADDITIONAL MODELS IN 1983 ONLY (COUPES)

TWIN-SLOT GRILLE

DASH

1984 V.I.N. = 1FABPO14XE (-) 100001 UP
MPG: 42 HWY / 26 EPA

(FINAL TURBO CPE. 19 1985 O/8)
1985 V.I.N. = 1FAB PO14XF (-) 10000I UP

EXP Turbo.

84-86

PRICE RANGES

$6931. - 10863. ('84)
6975. - 10918. ('85)
7465. or 8514. ('86)

1986 V.I.N. = 1FABP (019) or (01J) - G - #

PRODUCTION SUSPENDED APRIL, 1985.

('84)

DASH

MID-1986, EXP BECOMES A PART OF **ESCORT** LINE

86 HP (108, GT)

86½-88

1987 V.I.N. = 1FA DD (179) or ('8J) - H - #

109 MPH

1987 = 179 LUXURY CPE. $8100.
18J SPORT CPE. 9274.
ONLY REMAINING 1988½ ESCORT EXP IS P889 LUXURY CPE., AT $8510.

1988 (FINAL YR.) V.I.N. = (1FA) or (KNJ) B (P/79) - J - # (1988 ½ SUBSITUTE [P179] WITH [P889] IN V.I.N.)

25/33 MPG

1200

Escort EXP

FORD FAIRMONT —MERCURY ZEPHYR

FAIRMONT V.I.N.=1FA(-)(P20)AXB(-) 600001 UP

ZEPHYR V.I.N.=1ME(-)(P70)(A)XB(-) 600001 UP

(AVAIL. 1978-1983)

FAIRMONT DASH

FAIRMONT
FUTURA INTERIOR

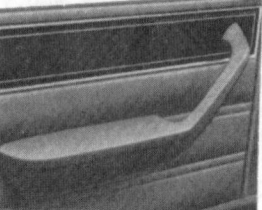

Integral door pull handles and armrests

THIS UNIQUE REAR QUARTER WINDOW TREATMENT EXCLUSIVE TO FAIRMONT FUTURA and MERCURY ZEPHYR Z-7.

P23

↑ FAIRMONT
WAGONS
$8019.
and up

'81

FUTURA

105 ½" WB
140 CID 4
OR 200 CID 6
(225 CID V8
AVAIL. ALSO)

34 EPA EST. HWY   23 EPA EST. MPG

FUTURA HAS ITS OWN GRILLE DESIGN

$7667.

Fairmont 2-Door

P23

FUTURA   COUPE
$7982.

P21 SEDAN
OR P21/605
FUTURA
SEDAN

$7786.

ZEPHYR
PRICES
$7738.
and up ↓

ZEPHYR has ALL VERTICAL PCS. IN GRILLE (AS ILLUSTR. AT LOWER RIGHT)

14-GAL FUEL TANK
P175/75 R x 14 TIRES

MERCURY **ZEPHYR**

SPECS. SIMILAR TO FAIRMONT

23 EPA EST. MPG, 34 ES

Z-7

ZEPHYR

EST. HWY.

4 DR. ALSO AVAIL.

FORD FAIRMONT FUTURA and MERCURY ZEPHYR

14 GAL. FUEL TK.

SEATS IN MEDIUM FAWN CLOTH/VINYL (OPT.)

1982 FAIRMONT P22 COUPE

A/C CONTROLS (OPT.)

DASH (FAIRMONT)

('83)

$8382.

1982 V.I.N. 1FABP22A0C (-) 000001 UP

AM/FM STEREO w. CASSETTE TAPE PLAYER (OPT.)

WAGONS NOT AVAILABLE. REMAINING FAIRMONTS NOW IN "FUTURA" SERIES.

FUTURA

1983 FAIRMONT V.I.N.: "S" FUTURA = 1FABP 37 AXD (-) # FUTURA = 1FABP37BXD (-) 000001 UP

22 MPG (EPA)

STD. 2 DR. ROOFLINE

STD. 140 CID OHC 4 ENGINE (88 HP)

(200 CID 87 HP 6 AVAIL.)

82-83

MERCURY ZEPHYR

ZEPHYR MPG: 36 HWY/24 EPA ('82)

impressive fuel economy.
33 EST HWY **22** EST EPA MPG

ZEPHYR HAS DECORATIVE FLAPS AS BEFORE. 16 GAL. FUEL TK. (NEW 20 GAL. FUEL TK. OPT.)

$8184. UP ('82)
8460. " ('83)
STD. and "GS" SEDANS, Z-7 CPES.

1982 ZEPHYR V.I.N. 1MEBP71A0C (-) #
1983 ZEPHYR V.I.N. 1MEBP71BXD (-) #

FAIRMONT SEDANS FROM $8284. ('82) $8608. ('83)

FORD FAIRMONT

FRONT END

BODY CONSTRUCTION DETAILS

LOW-COST "S" MODELS ADDED TO '83 FAIRMONT LINE: 2 DR., $7825. (P35/41 K) 4 DR., 7965. (P36/41 K)

FRONT CLOSE-UP

$6419.* SPECIAL PRICE IN 1982

FORD FAIRMONT 82-83

1202

FORD FESTIVA

(1988 ON) (MFD. BY KIA MOTORS SEOUL, S. KOREA)

INTERIOR ('88)

90.2" WB
87 CID
OHC 4
(58 HP @ 5000 RPM)
5-SP. TRANS. +
2.61 G.R.
(LX)

10-GAL. GAS TANK

FESTIVA. THE FUN STARTS AT

$5765. (L)

(ADV. BASE PRICE)

1988	L =	$5882.
"	L PLUS	6302.
"	LX	7031.
1989	L	5954.
"	L PLUS	6627.
"	LX	7356.
1990	L	6824.
"	L PLUS	7371.
"	LX	8010.

35 / 41 MPG , 1990
(31/33 w. AUTO. TR.)

LX
91-95 MPH

165/70 SR12 TIRES

5 SP. TRANS. and FUEL INJECTION STD. FOR 1990, 63 HP @ 5000)

NEW
28 / 47 MPG
88-90

V.I.N. ENDS WITH —J—# (1988) —K—# (1989) —L—# (1990)

new 1990 GRILLE

1990 INTERIOR and "L" (BELOW)

REAR VIEW
19 M352
('90)   **L PLUS**

OPT. AIR COND.

POP-OUT QUARTER WINDOWS

DASH

('90)

FORD GRANADA

(1975 TO 1982)

A/C CONTROLS

DASH (GLX)

V.I.N. = IFABPZ 6B (-)
B (-) 600001 UP

STD. "L" INTERIOR

L

L
2 DR.
$8167.

4, 6 OR V8

new SHORTER 105½" WB

RESTYLED

81

CLOSE-UP OF new FRONT END

FORD

GLX has BLACK AROUND HEADLIGHTS.

L
4 DR.
$8326.

GL

GLX 4 DR.
$8841.

GL
2 DR.
8568.

new MODEL SERIES

1204

FORD **GRANADA GLX** INTERIOR

L SERIES

new 232 CID 112 HP V6 REPLACES V8. (4, L6 STILL AVAIL.)

← L

$9029.

22 MPG (EPA)

GL SERIES

GL WAGON $9678. ↓

new "DEEP WELL" TRUNK INTERIOR

OPTIONAL GRAPHIC DISPLAY WARNS OF PROBLEMS. (LTS., WASHER FLUID, LOW FUEL SUPPLY)

LAMP · WASHER FLUID · LOW FUEL · BRAKE LAMP · HEADLAMP

82

OVAL FORD BADGE RETURNS

GLX 2 DR.

16 GAL. FUEL TK. $9569.

↑ A 4TH NEW WHEEL COVER "SUNBURST"-TYPE DESIGN IS AVAIL. IN MID-SEASON.)

33 EST. HWY 22 EST. MPG

MPG

GRANADA WAGON

OPTIONAL 2-WAY LIFTGATE ↓→

1982

(140 CID 4, 200 CID 6 HAVE 88 HP)

UN-GRAINED L WAGON $9262. ↓

new "TOT-GUARD" RESTRAINT FOR SMALL CHILDREN AVAIL. IN MID-SEASON.

GRANADA WAGONS ARE

New BADGE (Ford)

19 MPG (EPA)

NEW

WARNING CHIMES OPTIONAL

1205

V.I.N. ENDS WITH — C — #

1982 MODEL IS FINAL GRANADA. (BUT NAME COULD RETURN IN FUTURE)

Ford Mustang
(SINCE APRIL, 1964)

81

Ford

AVAIL. LEATHER WRAPPED STEERING WHEEL

CONSOLE

V.I.N. ENDS w. B (-) 600001 UP

POWER SIDE WINDOWS *new*

INTERIOR

VARIOUS WHEELS AVAIL., AS SHOWN

100.4" WB 12½ GAL. FUEL TANK

P-10 2 DR. $7581.

P-12 GHIA

IMITATION CABRIOLET ROOF IS NOT CONVERTIBLE.

$7896. *and up*

(P-13 GHIA 3-DR. FASTBACK ALSO AVAIL. AT $8040.)

P-15 COBRA TURBO $9057.

(w. 4 SP. TRANS. OPTIONAL)

AVAILABLE SUNROOF OR T-BAR TOP

3-DR.

COBRA REAR

cobra

COBRA

140 CID 4 OR TURBO 4 200 CID 6 OR 255 CID V8 (115 HP)

OPT. BLACK LIFTGATE LOUVRES

HOOD DECAL

(C)

COBRA INTERIOR

37 EST HWY • 22 EPA EST MPG
5-SPEED OVERDRIVE OPTION

GLX SERIES   GLX INTER.   **Ford Mustang**

GLX
$8631. UP

ENGINES:
140 CID 4 (86 HP)
(ALSO 140 CID 4
"FS" ENG. AVAIL.)
200 CID 6 (87 HP) 255 CID V8 (111 HP)
302 CID HO V8 (157 HP)

CLOSER VIEW OF
GLX DASH WITH GRAINED TRIM

new
302 CID V8
(5.0 L)

157
HP

P16

NEW

$9678.
GT HAS OWN GRILLE
and HOOD.

Mustang GT
(AVAIL. w. T-BAR ROOF)

AUTOMATIC
OR
MANUAL
TRANSMISSION

V.I.N. ENDS WITH
- C (-) 000001 UP

82

P185/75R
x14 TIRES (GT)

P175/75R14
TIRES STD.

33 | 22
EST HWY | EPA EST MPG
(WITH 140 CID 4)

GT DASH and INTERIOR

MUSTANG GL

WITH
T-BAR
ROOF
OPTION

MPG:
32 HWY
22 EPA
WITH
STD.
4-
CYL.

GRAPHIC DISPLAY WARNING MODULE

TAIL LAMP   WASHER FLUID
LOW FUEL
BRAKE LAMP   HEADLAMP

RECARO SEATS
AVAILABLE

GL
$8495.

Ford Mustang

24 MPG EPA (4 CYL. W. MANUAL TR.)

19 MPG EPA (V6)

15.4 GAL. FUEL TANK

L SERIES $8466. (2 DR.) P26

T-BAR

new 232 CID V6 AVAIL., WITH 112 HP (4 CYL. OR V8 ALSO AVAIL.)

3 DR. HATCHBACK FROM $9178. (GL) P28/60C

P27/602 GLX CONVERTIBLE $13,767.

100½" WB

RESTYLED

New CONVERTIBLE!

83

302 CID V8

V.I.N. ENDS WITH —XD (-) 000001 UP

OPENING QTR. WINDOWS

New for '83—Sport Performance Bucket Seats. These special bucket seats are optional equipment in GL, GLX and GT.

GT PRICES =
CONV'T. $14,602.
3-DR. HTCH. 10,426.
TURBO 2-DR. 10,712.
(MODEL NO. P27/932; P28/932)
GT PERFORMANCE-STYLE HOOD TREATMENT

125 MPH (GT)

1983½ MPG (4 CYL.)

49-States		California	
40 EST. HWY	26 EPA EST MPG	36 EST. HWY	24 EPA EST MPG

VARIOUS WHEELS AVAILABLE

Ford Mustang

USED BY POLICE FORCES IN 15 DIFF. STATES !

P185/75R × 14 STD. TIRE SIZE

L 2-DR. $8856.
L 3-DR. (new) 9027.
LX (new)
2-DR. $9048.
3-DR. 9254.
CVT. 13,168.

GL, GLX DISCONTINUED

SVO

INTERIOR (SVO)

The 20th Anniversary Mustang

84 (SPRING, 1984)

Have you driven a Ford... lately? Ford

ENGINES:
140 CID 4 (88 HP)
(145 OR 175 HP WITH TURBO)
232 CID V6 (120 HP)
302 CID V8 (HO) 175, 165 HP
AUTOMATIC OVERDRIVE AVAIL.

REAR VIEWS OF SVO

V.I.N. ENDS WITH -XE (-) 100001 UP

Mustang GT

GT 3-DR. $ **10,695.**
GT CONV'T. $ **14,168.**

175 HP V8

GT, TURBO GT WITH P205/70 HR × 14 TIRES

Get it together — Buckle up.

SVO 3 DR. TURBO $**16,713.**

SVO

WITH P225/50 VR 16 TIRES

TURBO GT CVT. $14,362. (3 DR., $10,879.)
("SVO" MEANS "SPECIAL VEHICLE OPERATIONS")

SVO

NEW

128 MPH

Get it together—Buckle up.

Ford Mustang

('85)
P26/602

ADVERTISED
SPECIAL, LX
$6885. ('85)

P27/602
LX CVT. $13,102. ('85)
232 CID V6
(V8 AVAIL.)

(L SERIES
DISCONTINUED)

302 CID
GT V8
has
210 HP
135
MPH

4 CYL. LX ↑
REG. ('85) $ **8441** UP

NEW HIGH BRAKE LT. IN 1986

GT CONVERTIBLE
$ **16,281.**
('86)

GT

OTHER 1986 MODELS :

LX 2 DR. (4 CYL.)	$ 8325.	
LX HATCHBK.	"	8880.
SVO " (TURBO 4)	15,646.	
LX CVT. (V6)	13,957.	
GT HATCHBK. (V8)	12,449.	

Mustang GT. (V8) ('85)

85-86

1985 V.I.N.=1FABP (28M)-F-#

3 DR. $11,553. (P28/932)
GT CVT. 15,253. (P27/932)

new GRILLE
(SLOT TYPE)

1986 V.I.N.=1FABP
(26A)-G-#

1985 MUSTANG ENGINES = 140 CID 4
(88 HP); 140 CID TURBO 4 (175 HP);
232 CID V6 (120 HP); 302 CID V8 (165, 210 HP)

LX CVT.
has PLAIN
REAR DECK
↘

SVO
('85)

100½" WB
ON
ALL
MODELS

3-DR.
$ **14,895.**
P28/939

SVO
140 CID
4 CYL. W.
TURBO
(175 HP)

SVO INCREASED TO
205 HP @ 5000 RPM,
new 3:73 TO 1 GEAR RATIO

(FINAL V6 ENGINE AND SVO IN 1986)

1210

('87)

Have you driven a Ford...lately?

RESTYLED 1987

1987 MODELS
LX 2 DR. $ 9948.
LX 3 DR.   10367.
LX CVT.   14729.
GT "   17529.
GT 3 DR.   13783.

18/27 MPG, 1987
(302 cid 5.0L V8)

GT

Ford Mustang

BP45E $ 18914.   (1989)

REAR SPOILER
(LX)

(GT HAS
HORIZONTAL
SLOTTED
TAILLIGHTS.)

2-DR.

100.5" WHEELBASE

FRONT

LX VIEWS   **LX**

100.5"

179.6"

89.1"

52.1"

3 DR. REAR

56.6"   57.0"

V.I.N. ENDS WITH
—H—# (1987)
—J—# (1988)
—K—# (1989)
—L—# (1990)

4 CYL.
EFI has
90 HP @
3800 RPM

('87)

87-

90

3
DR.

"FOX"
BODY
USED

LX 5.0L

DASH (GT)

136 MPH
MODIFIED
SALEEN MUSTANG
AVAILABLE

5 0

ON COWL
IDENTIFIES A
V-8 POWERED CAR.

4 OR V8 IN
MUSTANG LX

$ 11341. - 20297.

1990 PRICE RANGE
(DRIVER'S AIR-
BAG STD.
IN 1990)

GT
5.0 L
V8

142
MPH

50

17/29
MPG
('90)

NO
GRILLE
ABOVE
ON GT

GT

1989 MODELS ILLUSTRATED,
UNLESS OTHERWISE NOTED.

1211

FORD PROBE

Probe GT instrument panel in Titanium with Preferred Equipment Package 261A. Some equipment shown is optional.

V.I.N. ENDS WITH – L – #

GT DASH w. ANALOG GAUGES

FORD PROBE LX

LX

GT WHEEL (ABOVE)

GT AND DASH (ABOVE)
$16,570. (new GRILLE)

133 cid 2.2 L TURBO 4
(145 HP @ 4300 RPM)
(STD. 2.2 L 4 has 110 HP @ 4700 RPM)
182 cid 3.0 L V6 has 140 HP @ 4800 RPM (new)

90

(RIGHT, and BELOW)

LX   LX

ELECTRONIC CONTROLS

FORD PROBE GL w. 2.2 L 4 (110 HP @ 4700)
$13,434.

15.1 GAL. FUEL TANK
19/31 MPG

REAR DETAILS (new TAILLIGHTS)

1213 L V6 (@ 4800) LX **$14,852.**

(SINCE 1986) # FORD TAURUS

MFD. BY
Ford Motor Company

NEW

$10,833. UP
(L SEDAN) 29D

MPH
km/h
ODO
SEL
TRIP
RESET
SPEED
ALARM
FUEL
ECON
DTE
ECON
RESET

"TAURUS"
BODY

1986
SEDANS
FROM
$11,464.
(MT5
29D)

1987 MODELS, PRICES
MT5 SED. 51D $12543.   GL SEDAN 52D $12836.
"   WAG. 56D - 13104.   "   WAGON 57U - 14016.
L SEDAN 50D - 11864.   LX SED. 53U - 15059.
"   WAGON 55U - 13084.   LX WAG. 58U - 15669.

86-87

106" WB   182 CID V6 (140 HP)   INTERIOR
OR 153 CID 4 (90 HP)   24-27 MPG (EPA, CITY)

114 MPH

OFF
LIGHTS

MECHANICALLY
SIMILAR TO
new
MERCURY
SABLE

SEDAN (29U)
$13,777.
(LX)

1986
EXAMPLES
ILLUSTR.

CLOSER
VIEW OF
ELECTRONIC
INSTR.
PANEL

WAGONS FROM
$11,929.

MT5, L, GL
and LX
SERIES

113 MPH

1214

1986 V.I.N. ENDS WITH
-G-#   1987 w. -H-#

FORD TAURUS

Quality is Job 1.

3.0 OR 3.8 LITER V6
(2.5 L. 4 AVAIL.)

88

*115 MPH WITH
3.8 L V6*

Dealer Service:

ELECTRONIC
DIAGNOSIS
(TAURUS ENGINE
COMPARTMENT ILLSTR.)

*1988 FORD V.I.N. =
(IFA OR KNJ) B (P51D)
—J—#*

LX SED. (P53U)
$15,392.

*MT5 SED. (4 CYL.) (P51D)
          $12,926.
L SED. (P50U) $13,266.
   WAG. (P55U)   13,898.
GL SED. (P52U)   13,773.
   WAG. (P57U)   14,381.
   (MODEL NUMBERS
        END IN "D," IF 2.5 L
   4-CYL. ENGINE USED)*

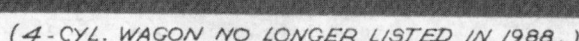

(4-CYL. WAGON NO LONGER LISTED IN 1988.)

LX WAGON (P58U)
$16,124.

wagon

*WITH
REAR
DETAIL*

LX

GL WAGON and SEDAN (BELOW)
1989 V.I.N. ENDS WITH —K—#; 1990 WITH —L—#

FORD TAURUS

19/29 MPG ('89)

ELECTRONIC DASH

L →

ANALOG DASH

TAURUS L, GL, LX

(1990 EXAMPLES ILLUSTRATED)
L = $13688. up ('89)
    13912. up ('90)
GL = 14112. up ('89)
     14385. up ('90)
LX = 15732. up ('89)
     16635. up ('90)

LX ↗

TAURUS

19 M 359

SHO $20189. ('89)
22088. ('90)

BP—U SERIES

P—U SER.

89-90

FORD TAURUS SHO (new) IN 1989

(1990 POLICE SPEC. HAS 4 HORIZ. COOLING SLOTS ON EA. SIDE OF EMBLEM.)

(1990 DASH SLIGHTLY CHANGED)

SHO

TAURUS SHO

(REPLACES *FAIRMONT*)

Ford

TEMPO

Front-wheel drive.

L 4-DR. (P21) $**7557.**

Tempo L 4-Door Sedan

L 2-DR. (P18) $**7557.**

GL 2-DR. (P19) $**8962.**

(GL 4-DR., P22 $8962.)

Tempo GL 2-Door Coupe

(OPT.)

NEW

"HIGH SWIRL COMBUSTION" ENGINE

84

SUNROOF AVAIL.

GLX 2-DR. (P20) $**9424.**

140 CID 4 (HSC FS = 84 HP, HSC = 90 HP)

99.9" WB P175/80R×13 TIRES

L, GL, GLX MODELS (2 DR. or 4 DR.)

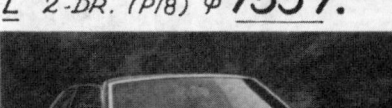

MECHANICALLY SIMILAR TO *new* MERCURY *TOPAZ*.

Tempo's new tach. (OPT.)

Tempo GLX 4-Door Sedan

GLX 4 DR. (P23) $**9424.**

V.I.N. 1FAB P18RXE (-) 100001 UP

100 MPH

THE ALL-NEW 1984 FORD TEMPO
STYLE AND TECHNOLOGY IN TOTAL HARMONY

New diesel option.
121 CID, 4-CYL, 52-HP *DIESEL* ENG. AVAIL. LATER *in* 1984.

41 EPA EST. MPG	56 EST. HWY.

Get it together—Buckle up.

INTERIOR

1217

Ford Tempo

V.I.N.=IFA (-) P
(-)I(-)(-) XF (-)
000001 UP

The forward thinking car.

DASH

L

7415.
(2 or 4 DR.)

85

GLX 4 DR. $9771.
(2 DR. 9723.) NEW WHEELS
P175/80 R13 TIRES

GL

$8629.

140 CID 4 IN
86 HP EFI OR
100 HP EFI
VERSIONS. (121 CID, 52 HP DIESEL 4
CONT'D.)
3.73/2.73 GEAR
RATIO

GL NOW AVAIL.
IN STANDARD,
SELECT,
LUXURY
OR SPORT
PACKAGES.

GLX IN
STANDARD
OR
LUXURY
PACKAGES.

14 GALLON
FUEL
TANK

New

Sport GL.

Electronically fuel-injected
2300 HSC engine

Ford Tempo

"TOPAZ" BODY

L SERIES DISCONTINUED.
GL and LX ONLY.

OPTIONAL DIESEL ENG.
(H) STILL AVAIL.
1986, NOT
LISTED 1987.

('86)

new
4-W-D
LX MODELS
(1987) ↓
34 9 2-DR.
$11,215.

39 9 4-DR.
11,365.

1987 MPG:
22/27
140 cid 4
w. A/T

('86)

1986 MODELS
GL : 19X 2-DR. $9128.
     22 X 4 DR.   9278.
LX : 20 X 2 DR. 10,119.
     23 X 4 DR.   10,318.
  1987 = 31X GL 2-DR. $9813.
     36X GL 4 DR. 9963.
     33 9 SPT. GL 2 DR.
        $ 10,589
     38 9 SPT. GL 4 DR. 10,739.
     32X LX 2 DR. 10,974.
     37X LX 4 DR.
        11,173.

new 2-SLOT GRILLE w.
FORD EMBLEM ABOVE IT.

GL
Sport

86-
87

V.I.N. ENDS WITH
—G— # (1986)
—H— # (1987)

SINCE MID-'86,
AIR-BAG
RESTRAINT SYST.
AVAIL. (1987 MODEL)

TEMPO
ALL WHEEL DRIVE

NEW FOR 1987

ALL WHEEL DRIVE
OFF ON

There's something new about this
Ford Tempo. Four wheel power at
your finger tips. It comes into play
through a simple switch and it's
a move you can make while on
the move.

1987
DASH

TEMPO GL

29 M172

GL

4 DR. (ILLUSTR.)

(22X) $ **9278.** ('86)

(36X) **9963.** ('87)   104 MPH
                        (1987, 4WD)

1988 MODELS =
GL : P31X 2 DR. $10,311.
P36X 4 DR. 10,461.
GLS : P33S 2 DR. 10,902.
P38S 4 DR. 11,053.
LX : P37X 4 DR. 11,390.
4WD : P39S 4 DR. 11,584.

Ford Tempo

(SAME MODELS
and NUMBERS
IN 1989
$10,785. TO 12,073.)

GL →

('88)

1989 GLS
INTERIOR →

GLS
$11053. ('88)
$11576. ('89)

PP38S
$12258.
(1990)
GLS

('89)

1989
GLS
ILLUSTR.

88-90
RESTYLED

141 CID 2.3 L 4
(98 OR 100 HP @ 4400 RPM)
21/32 MPG (VARIABLE AS TO
TRANSMISSION 5 SP. O/D,
3 SP. AUTO., 4WD)
15.9 GAL. FUEL TANK
(14.2 " " " w. 4WD)

V.I.N. ENDS WITH
— J — # (1988)
— K — # (1989)
— L — # (1990)

(LX 2 DR.
DISCONT'D.
1988)

Buckle-up–together we can save lives.

LX

('88)

$11390. ('88)
11884. ('89)
12415. ('90)

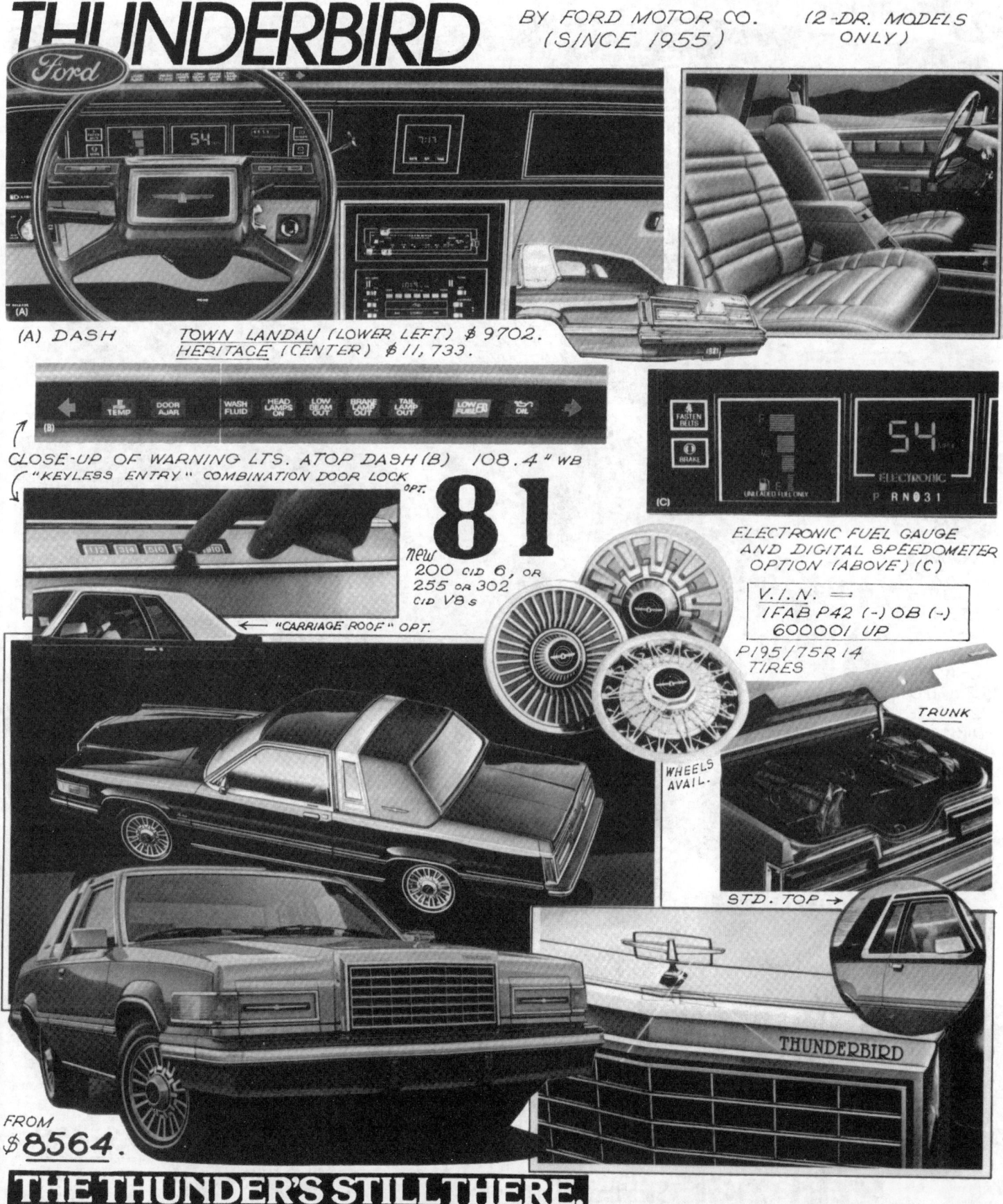

THUNDERBIRD

BY FORD MOTOR CO. (SINCE 1955)

(2-DR. MODELS ONLY)

(A) DASH. TOWN LANDAU (LOWER LEFT) $9702. HERITAGE (CENTER) $11,733.

CLOSE-UP OF WARNING LTS. ATOP DASH (B) 108.4" WB

"KEYLESS ENTRY" COMBINATION DOOR LOCK

OPT. new 81
200 CID 6, OR
255 OR 302
CID V8s

← "CARRIAGE ROOF" OPT.

ELECTRONIC FUEL GAUGE AND DIGITAL SPEEDOMETER OPTION (ABOVE) (C)

V.I.N. =
1FAB P42 (-) OB (-)
600001 UP

P195/75R14 TIRES

WHEELS AVAIL.

TRUNK

STD. TOP →

THUNDERBIRD

FROM $8564.

THE THUNDER'S STILL THERE.

THUNDERBIRD
Ford

W. "CARRIAGE TOP"

THUNDERBIRD SERIES

$9823.

ENGINES
200 CID 6
(88 HP)
255 CID V8
(111 HP)
OR
NEW
232 CID V6
(112 HP)
SHOWN
BELOW, LEFT

21 GAL. FUEL TANK

MPG : 24 HWY, 18 EPA EST.
30 HWY, 18 EPA (V6, O/D)
CALIF. : 30 HWY, 19 EPA

"TRIPMINDER" COMPUTER

new (OPT.)

S E M
07 51
58 ET
TIME TRIP ECON FUEL

82 TOWN LANDAU

$11,034.

V.I.N. = 1FAB (P42) BOC (-)000001 UP

V6 is **New**

VENT WINDOWS OPT.

$13,156.

HERITAGE SERIES

1982

THUNDERBIRD

V.I.N. = IFABP463XD UP ; TURBO = IFAB P46WXD UP

TURBO 4, 2.32 c/d V6 or 302 c/d V8

New The turbocharger.

NEW
4-CYL. TURBO ENG. (145 HP)

5-speed transmission.

83 new shape new 104" WB

new SEATS

HERITAGE MODEL HAS THIS EMBLEM

PRICED FROM **$10,401.** 20 MPG EPA (V6)

AM/FM STEREO w. CASSETTE PLAYER

HERITAGE COUPE **$13,432.**

HERITAGE

NEW TURBO COUPE

123 MPH ↓ **$13,170.**

33 MPG HWY, 22 EPA EST. (4)

STD. and HERITAGE MODELS HAVE SILVER AREA AROUND HEADLTS.

HA9 P 205/70HR x 14 GOODYEAR EAGLE GT TIRES

18-GALLON FUEL TANK (20.7 w. V8)

Thunderbird

Ford

V.I.N. = 1FABP46TXE (-) 10001 UP (SAME FOR TURBO)
STD. COUPE
$10,808.

↑
TRX
ALUM.
WHEEL

4 CYL. TURBO
(145 HP)
232 CID V6
(120 HP)
302 CID V8
(140 HP)

New ELAN
$13,836.
(REPLACES HERITAGE)

P195/75R
× 14 TIRES
STD. *

84

FRONT END

The FILA Thunderbird.

FILA
FILA = $15,646.

New

* note:
FILA HAS
P205/
70 HR
× 14
TIRES,
COLOR-
COORDINATED
WHEELS

FILA

FILA INTERIOR

CAST ALUMINUM WHEEL

Turbo Coupe
$13,820.

P R N D 2 1

AVAIL. W.
AUTOMATIC **shift**

Thunderbird

Ford

30th Anniversary
Thunderbird
STD. $11,424.

ELAN
$13,091.

85

1225

Thunderbird

85

EVERY 1985 FILA INCLUDES A FILA CANVAS SPORT BAG w. LEATHER PORTFOLIO, BEACH TOWEL, OTHER MISC. ITEMS.

FILA

FILA

V6

(FINAL FILA)

$16,149.

6 WAY POW. SEAT IN GRAY SUEDE CLOTH or WHITE LEATH. 1985 FILA has NEWLY-DESIGNED DIGITAL INST. PANEL.

FILA IN EITHER BLACK, RED MEDIUM CHARCOAL, or THE UNIQUE "PASTEL CHARCOAL" WITH DARK CHARCOAL LOWER ACCENT TREATMENT. PINSTRIPING and FILA EMBLEM ALSO.

note BLACK GRILLE, "BLACKED-OUT" FRONT END TREATMENT.

V.I.N. = 1FAB (P46) TXF (-) 10001 UP

$14,540.

Turbo Coupe
140 CID TURBO 4

TURBO COUPE DASH

Thunderbird 86
Ford

137 MPH

140 CID TURBO 4
has
155 HP @ 4600 RPM
and P225VR60/15 GOODYEAR
"GATORBACK"
TIRES
18/23 MPG (302 CID V8)
(1987)

STD. CPE. $12,214.
(463)
ELAN CPE. 13,748.
(463)
TURBO CPE. 15,652.
(46W)

V.I.N. =
1FABP
(46 W)
—G—#

(FILA DISCONTINUED)

Have you driven a Ford... lately? *Ford*

V.I.N. ENDS WITH —H—# (1987); —J—# (1988)

LX ('87)
↓ (REPLACES ELAN)

LX

x 623 ('87)
P624 ('88)

"S" BODY

1987/1988
MODELS =
COUPE (V6)
$13460. / 13927.
LX (V6)
$15789. / 16214.
SPORT COUPE
(5.0L V8)
(61F) $15497. /
(P61F) 16359.

87-88

new FRONT

('87)

TURBO COUPE 12.3 L TURBO 4
$17547. / 17578. (FINAL 1988,
P64T)
TURBO HAS ABS BRAKING,
COMPUTERIZED SUSPENSION
and INTERCOOLED
TURBOCHARGER

64W (1987)

Turbo Coupe.

TURBO INCREASED
TO 185~190 HP
IN 1987
(190 HP IN
1988)

'31 MPH

('87)
REAR →
INT.
(TURB.) →

1227

SC.*
$ 20278. ('89)
P64R
$ 21413. ('90)

(* "SUPER COUPE")
SUPER-CHARG. INTER-COOLED 210 HP V6

Ford **Thunderbird**
TURBO 4 and V8 SPT. CPE. DISCONTD.

"SC" ON FRONT BUMPER

V.I.N. ENDS WITH –K–# ('89) "–L–# ('90)

Have you driven a Ford...lately?

17 TO 23 MPG

NEW

('89)

19 GALLON GAS TANK

COUPE (P604) $15067. (15440.;'90)

3.8 L, 232 cid V6 (140 HP @ 3800 RPM ON STD., LX) (19/27 MPG)

REAR-WHEEL DRIVE RETAINED

LX INTERIOR ('89)

89-90

new WHEELS

new SHEET METAL new 113" WHEELBASE, BUT BODY LENGTH 4" SHORTER

new POWER EQUIP. OR LUXURY GROUP OPTIONS FOR 1990

LX

('90)
LX CPE. (P624) $17272. ('89) 17723. ('90)

3-Year/50,000 Mile Bumper-to-Bumper Backing by General Motors.

(INCL. SPECTRUM, SPRINT) REPLACES

MPG 58 HWY 53 CITY

GEO NEW 89

(STARTS 1989)
(DISTRIBUTED BY CHEVROLET DEALERS)

Japanese

3 CYL. METRO LSi 5 SP. MPG 46 CITY / 50 HWY. (38 /40 w. AUTO TRANS.)

METRO (FORMERLY SPRINT) MFD. BY SUZUKI, JAPAN

FRONT VIEW

DASH

MS 212 BASE METRO $5995. (REG. $6250.) (ABOVE)

GEO METRO LSi

note DIFFERENCES IN WHEELS OF EACH OF THESE TWO MODELS.

"BRAIN-POWERED"

PERFORMANCE QUALITY VALUE

THINKING MAN SYMBOLIC FIGURE SEEN IN 1989 GEO ADVERTISE-MENTS.

THE LOGIC OF GEO-LOGIC

METRO LSi 2-DR. $6895. (4 DR., $7195.) (REG. $7150. and $7450.)

'89 Geo Spectrum

BLT. BY ISUZU, JAPAN

EARLY 1989 4-CYLINDER **SPECTRUM** 4 DR. NOTCHBACK $8110. (2-DR. HTCHBK., $7610.)

GEO KNOWN AS "PASSPORT" IN CANADA.

V.I.N. ENDS WITH — K - #

TRACKER BLT. BY SUZUKI, JAPAN, OR BY GM/SUZUKI, CANADA

GEO TRACKER

(JAPANESE-AMERICAN NOVA REPLACED BY 1990 GEO PRIZM, INTRO. IN EARLY 1989.)

12,495. LSi MODEL

10,495. HARDTOP 10,195. CONV'T.

TRACKER DASH

WITH 4-WHEEL DRIVE MPG = 28 CITY, 29 HWY (5 SP.); 25 CITY/HWY (AUTO TR.)

1229

METRO DASH

GEO

METRO LSi

$8351.

93.1" WB (SEDANS)
89.2" WB (COUPES)

3 CYLINDERS

58/53 MPG (40/38 w. A/T)

61 CID
55 HP @ 5700 RPM

Geo Metro XFi.
$6551.

1990 GEO V.I.N. ENDS WITH - L - #

Geo Tracker.
97 CID 4

86.6" WB (80 HP @ 5500)

GRILLE

SIMILAR TO SUZUKI SIDEKICK

Geo Storm

96½" WB
4 CYL. (95, 130 HP)

BLT. BY ISUZU, JAPAN

New

$10,705. UP

24 TO 36 MPG, DEPENDING ON ENG. + TR.

$11,297. UP

90

Geo Tracker Convertible's 2-position soft top is available in black or white, depending on exterior color selected.

DASH

STORM DASH

STORM (REAR)

TRACKER

GEO PRIZM
HATCHBACK SEDAN

Geo Prizm.
= BLT. IN USA BY GM/TOYOTA

4 CYL. (102, 130 HP) 98 CID
95.7" WB

$11,369. UP **new**

34/28 MPG

PRIZM DASH

GEO PRIZM LSi
4-DOOR SEDAN

Get to know
Geo

SILHOUETTES

STD.

MISER

HORIZON *and* OMNI

Plymouth

Dodge

The New Chrysler Corporation

Trans-4 engine
front-wheel-drive

4 CYL., 104.7 CID
OR 133 CID

(1978 - 1990)

HORIZON V.I.N.= IP3BL18
AOB (-) 00001 UP

TC3 V.I.N.=
IP3B L24
AOB — #

PLYMOUTH HORIZON MISER
L18 **$5,299**
50 30 EST.HWY. EPA EST.MPG

MISER HAS NO CHROME TRIM ON ROCKER PANEL.)

REG. 6002.

96.6" WB

('81)

"MISER" MODELS AVAILABLE IN 1981 and 1982 ONLY.

TRANVERSE ENGINE PLACEMENT

PLYMOUTH TC 3 HATCHBACK
L24 **$6,149**
41 27 EST.HWY. EPA EST.MPG

Dodge Omni Miser
as shown $5499.**

L18

99.1" WB

OMNI V.I.N.=
33BL24
OB (-) 10000I UP

EURO SIDE-TRIM

Omni Euro-Sedan: as low as $6722.**
41 est. hwy. 25 EPA est. mpg.
Fuel efficiency enhanced by
advanced computer technology.

with Premium Exterior Package.

DASH DETAILS

L SERIES
81

PREMIUM TRIM

L28

with Custom Exterior Package.

CUSTOM TRIM

Horizon

HORIZON GRILLE has ALL VERTICAL PIECES.

OFF ON RESUME
LO HI SET WASH

L28

HORIZON and OMNI
M SERIES
Z SERIES

82

Horizon Custom 47 30 M48

"PENTASTAR"
new EMBLEM ON GRILLE
TURISMO 2 + 2 (BELOW)

MODEL		Prices Start of	Prices as shown
Horizon Miser	M18	$5499	$5639
Turismo 2.2	M54	$7345	$7345

HORIZON MISER:
35 EPA EST MPG, 52 ESTIMATED HIGHWAY.*

Horizon Miser 52 35

HORIZON

Plymouth

TRI-COUNTY RALLY
CHECKPOINT

$7,345*

Turismo 2.2 41 26

DASH

0 to 50 in 6.4 seconds*
41 26 mpg**

13 GAL. FUEL TK.

OMNI

HORIZON
new GRILLE EMBLEMS

OMNI
50 30 mpg*
EST. HWY. EPA EST. MPG

V.I.N. ENDS WITH AOC (-) #

Z18
Omni Miser

HORIZON
E-TYPE:

1982
OMNIS
and HORIZONS
REGULARLY PRICED FROM
$6103.

NOTICE THAT 024 MISER (RT.)
HAS MORE WINDOW AREA
THAN 024 CUSTOM (BELOW)

024 MISER

HORIZON
DASH
(E)

Z14
$6486.

34* EPA EST MPG, 51 EST. HIGHWAY.

DODGE 024...

024 CUSTOM
$7027.

Z44

FINAL YR. FOR
Euro-Sedan

1232

RALLYE CLUSTER (OPT.)

("MISER" MODELS DISCONTINUED)

HORIZON and OMNI
M SERIES   Z SERIES

AND WE'VE ADDED 13 NEW FEATURES FOR $626 LESS.

DASH

NEW TAILLIGHTS

83

HORIZON — $6809. UP
OMNI — 6675. UP

HORIZON CUSTOM

CONTROL STALK
(W. "SPEED CONTROL" DESIGNATION SINCE '82)

HORIZON CUSTOM INTERIOR
$7039.

NEW
5-SPEED TRANS-AXLE OPT.

ENGINE IMPROVED FOR 8% BETTER HWY. MPG

REAR DETAILS

HORIZON V.I.N. =1P3BM18 BXD (-) 000001 UP

DODGE OMNI

(1982 "024" REPLACED BY 1983 CHARGER)

OMNI V.I.N.= 1B3BZ48 BXD (-) 000001 UP

EXTRAORDINARY MILEAGE: 51 EST. HWY., 34 EPA EST.

important new standard features such as power brakes, reclining bucket seats, and halogen head lamps.

PRICE: $5841.

HORIZON and OMNI

OMNI GRILLE

LM SERIES

LZ SERIES

MPG:
43 EST. HWY,
27 EPA
EST.

LZE44 /
AGB

OMNI
(SAME PRICES
AS HORIZON)

new GLH
(OMNI ONLY) $ **7658.**
106 MPH
110 HP 2.2 L ENG.

Plymouth Turismo 2.2 for 1984. ↑ 0 ~ 50 IN 5.85 SECONDS

new GRAPHICS, 2-TONE PAINT,
SPOILER, 14" RALLYE ROAD WHEELS,
GOODYEAR EAGLE GT TIRES, ETC.

TURISMO 2.2 - $ **8101.**
STD. TURISMO - **7420.**

HORIZON DASH and INT.

84 new GRILLES

1984 V.I.N. ENDS WITH
AXE (-) #

HORIZON
SE
$ **6895.**

HORIZON
$ **6690.**

REAR DETAILS

109 MPH

PLYMOUTH
TURISMO'S DODGE
COUNTERPART
IS CHARGER. (SEE
DODGE CHARGER / DAYTONA
PAGES)

1234

DASH

HORIZON and OMNI
M SERIES   Z SERIES
"L" BODY

STD. WHEEL

(STD., SE, or GLH OMNIS,
  1985-1986 ;
  "AMERICA" ONLY,
  STARTING
  1987.)

HI-PERFORMANCE
OMNI
GLH
('85)

(STD.)
M18A
HORIZON

$6871. ('85)
7146.
('86)

$7940.
LZE44/AGB

Horizon SE

$7101.
('85)
7382.
('86)

$872. EXTRA FOR
TURBO 4
ENG.

('86)

HORIZON

M48A

HORIZON

OPT. AUTOMATIC
SPEED
CONTROL

COOL   TEMPERATURE   WARM   HI
OFF MAX A/C A/C   VENT HEAT   LO

AIR COND. CONTROLS

TURISMO
DASH

2+2:
M54F
('85)
M54A
('86)

85-
87

OPT. SUNROOF AND REAR
WINDOW SUNSHD.

2+2
$8622. ('86)

(CONT'D.
NEXT
PAGE)

TURISMO

FINAL TURISMO and DUSTER ARE 1987 MODELS.

('87)

HORIZON and OMNI

55.7

TURISMO... "L" BODY

Turismo Duster $8894. ('86)

DUSTER CONSIDERED AN OPT. "PACKAGE" IN 1985 -1986

1987 MPG: (TURISMO) 23/27 (135 CID 4 w. A/T)

V.I.N. ENDS WITH
- F → # 1985
- G → " 1986
- H → " 1987

(1987 MODEL YEAR BEGINS JUNE, 1986) ("AMERICA" SERIES, 1987 ON)

85-87

9:40 AM/FM SET VOL BASS TREBLE TUNE SPKR BALANCE 1 2 3 4 5

CLOCK / RADIO

20/43 MPG

1987 OMNI "AMERICA" NOW HAS 2.2-LITER ENG. + 5 SP. TR. AS STD EQUIP.

OMNI "AMERICA."
← REG. $6895.
('87)

('86)

4 CYLINDER ENGINES:
(STD.)   (OPT.)

TURISMO/ DUSTER DASH

106 MPH (HORIZON AMERICA, 1987)

1.6-liter (97.1 CID) four-cylinder engine 64 hp @ 4,800 rpm; 87 lb-ft torque @ 2,800 rpm.

2.2-liter (135 CID) Trans-4 engine; 96 hp @ 5,200 rpm; 119 lb-ft torque @ 3,200 rpm.

Dodge
AN AMERICAN REVOLUTION

DODGE OMNI "AMERICA"

GET MORE IN AMERICA, WITH DODGE OMNI "AMERICA"

THE LOWEST PRICED AMERICAN CAR YOU CAN BUY.
SPECIAL PRICE: $5499.

LEASE
Zero down. $99 month.

LINCOLN (SINCE 1921)

OPTIONAL "KEYLESS ENTRY SYSTEM"
4 SP. AUTO. OVERDRIVE TRANS.

$14,560. 2 DR.

(new MODEL NAME)
TOWN CAR
$14,958. 4 DR.

V.I.N.=
ILN (-)
P93FXB (-)
600001 UP
(MK. VI, P95)

$23,144.

HOOD ORNAMENT

CONTINENTAL
MARK VI 2-DR.
"SIGNATURE"
(OVAL OPERA
WINDOWS)(4 DR. ALSO)

"INSTANT
FUEL ECONOMY"
READOUT
ON
DASH
IS new

81

302 CID (5.0 LITRE) EFI
V8 ENGINE

117.3" WB
(114.3" ON
2-DR. MODEL
OF MK VI)

18-GAL.
FUEL
TANK

MARK
VI
DESIGNER
SERIES
(FROM
$20,554.
"BILL BLASS" EDITION
(GIVENCHY, PUCCI, and
CARTIER EDITIONS ALSO
AVAIL.)

MARK VI
HAS
HEADLIGHT
COVERS

16 EPA EST. MPG   24 HWY EST

CONTINENTAL MARK VI

LINCOLN

18 GAL. FUEL TANK
17 MPG
(EPA)

Lincoln Town Car

P94
TOWN CAR
$16,880.

V.I.N. ENDS WITH
— OC (—)
000001 UP

82

MARK VI FRONT
FENDER DETAIL,
SHOWING CONTINENTAL
EMBLEM ON CORNER
LIGHT

TOWN CAR FRONT DETAILS

new DOWNSIZED CONT'L.
WITH 108½" WB

C · O · N

"CONTINENTAL"
NAME ON IMITATION
TIRE COVER

CONTINENTAL
REAR DECK DETAILS
20 GAL. FUEL TK.
18 MPG
(EPA)

1982 CONTINENTAL

REAR
EMBLEM

New

(ALL 3 SERIES AVAIL. IN
SIGNATURE OR
DESIGNERS MODELS
ALSO.)

CONTINENTAL $21,808.
UP
P98

18
GAL.
FUEL
TK.

17
MPG
(EPA)

1982 MARK VI

MARK VI COUPE
$19,958. UP
P95

LINCOLN

16 MPG EPA

TOWN CAR $17,916. (P96)

(SIGNATURE $19,258; CARTIER DESIGNER $20594.)
60 U   605

83

302 CID V8 has 134 HP

new ANTI-THEFT ALARM (OPT.)

CLOSE-UP FRONT DETAIL OF MK. VI

TOWN CAR REAR

V.I.N. ENDS WITH — FXD (-) #

1983 MARK VI

("SIGNATURE" and "PUCCI" MK. VIS ALSO)

60 N BLASS

BILL BLASS ED. w. CABRIOLET ROOF $25,242.

$23,285.
60 R

TYPICAL MK. VI OPERA WINDOW

MK. VI PRICES = $20,939. and up

CONTINENTAL

New

"VALENTINO" ADDED TO THE DESIGNER" ED. LINE (WALNUT MOON-DUST OVER GOLDEN MIST COLOR SCHEME)

O.P.T. AUTOMATIC DIMMING DAY/NIGHT MIRROR 15

New

P97 $21,694.

AP10240

(60 M "GIVENCHY" MODEL ALSO)

1240

LINCOLN

TOWN CAR
19,069.

117.3" WB
P96

302 CID V8
OR 6 CYL. new
DIESEL (BMW)
TURBO AVAIL.

DESIGNER
CONTINENTAL
HAS 2-TONE
COLORS

VALENTINO
$24926.

CLOSE
VIEW OF
HOOD
ORNAMENT

SIGNATURE,
$21039.
DESIGNER, $22516.

84
P97

(new MK. VII STARTS)

new CONT'L. INTERIOR w. REAL WOOD TRIM,
new OVERHEAD CONSOLE w. WARNING LTS.
and READING LAMPS.

CONTINENTAL
$22478.

GIVENCHY INTERIOR
IN ADMIRAL BLUE
(EXTERIOR IN
SLATE BLUE
METALLIC OVER
MIDNIGHT BLUE
METALLIC

$24,951.

New

FRONT STYLING

V.I.N. ENDS WITH
FXE (-) 000001/ UP

CONTINENTAL and
new MK. VII w. 108½" WB, 302 CID V8
(130 HP @ 3200 RPM)

111
MPH

BILL BLASS, VERSACE
MK. VIIs ALSO, AS
WELL AS STD., LSC.

REAR DETAILS OF
Mark VII P98

MARK VII INT.
(ABOVE) HAS
NO WOODGRAIN
TRIM, LSC
MODEL, $24415.

$22416.

1241

NEW

CONTINENTAL MARK VII.

MPG:
26 HWY,
17 EPA

LINCOLN

NEW GRILLE ON **Town Car.** $19,756.

(CVT.-STYLE "CARRIAGE" ROOF ALSO AVAIL.)

TOWN CAR SIGNATURE SERIES $22,991.
TOWN CAR DESIGNER EDIT. $24,229.

P96/705A

P96/700A

P96/710A

V.I.N. = 1LNBP96FXF UP (TOWN CAR)

302 CID V8 (140 HP) (180 @ 4200 IN MK.7)

CONT'L. V.I.N. 1MRB P97FXF UP

P97/860A

GIVENCHY DESIGNER SERIES CONTINENTAL $26,430. (VALENTINO, $26725.) P97/865A

P215/70R15

P97/850A **CONTINENTAL** $23,683.

146 CID 6 CYL. TURBO DIESEL ENG. AVAILABLE (115 HP)

GOODYEAR EAGLE GT

STD. EQUIPMT. TIRE ON MK.VII. (P215/65R × 15 ON LSC)

85

P98/800A **MARK VII** $23,571.

(MK.VII LSC, BILL BLASS, and VERSACE ALSO AVAIL.)

MK.VII OVERHEAD CONSOLE AND DASH

(note: MOST LSCs HAVE AUX. LTS. BELOW FRONT BUMPER, AS SEEN ON 1984 EXAMPLE.)

AVAIL. ANTI-LOCK BRAKE SYSTEM

V.I.N.=1MRB P98FXF UP (MK.VII)

1242

LINCOLN

('87)

COMPACT DISC PLAYER OPT. IN 1987 TOWN CAR.

V.I.N. (1986) ILNBP (96F) -F-#
(1987) ILNBM (81F) -H-#

('86) "PANTHER" BODY

('87)

STD. SIGNATURE, or DESIGNER

TOWN CAR 1987 MPG: 17/27 (V8)

('87)

TOWN CAR.

TOWN CAR

1986 PRICES FR. $21,473.
1987 " " 23,361.

CONTINENTAL WHEEL DETAIL

86-87

302 cid V8 (17/27 MPG) 1987

"LS" BODY CONTINENTAL FRONT DETAIL ↘

Lincoln Continental.

110 MPH

('86)

Lincoln-Mercury Div

120 MPH

MARK VII (LSC)

STD. MK.VII, LSC OR BILL BLASS

"FOX" BODY

1987 FINAL YR. FOR CONT'L. W. V8

CONT'L. SED. OR "GIVENCHY" SEDAN, FROM $24556. ('86) 26008 ('87)

MK. VII FROM $22399. ('86) 23770. ('87)

LINCOLN. What a luxury car should be.

1243

LINCOLN

1988 V.I.N. = 1LN8M (8/F)-J-# 8/F SEDAN, 82F SIGNATURE ", OR 83F DESIGNER / CARTIER SED.

('88)

$25,591. UP ('88)
26,806. UP ('89)

1988 TOWN CAR HAS "LINCOLN" NAME ABOVE LT.

88-89 NEW

1989 V.I.N. = 1LN-M (8/F) -K-#

STYLING FOR 1988

Continental

new 109" WB 3.8 L V6 (new)

TOWN CAR 5.0 L V8
117.3" WB

17/24 MPG ('89)

1989 GRILLE HAS RELOCATED "LINCOLN" NAME

New

V6 ENG. IN CONTINENTAL ONLY

CONTINENTAL

974 SEDAN $26,602. ('88)
28,852. ('89)

SIGNATURE SEDAN $28,468.
984
30,460. ('89)

108½" WB 5.0 L V8
17/24 MPG ('89)

MARK VII
93E BILL BLASS or LSC 92E

EACH $26,904.
$28,119 ('89)

new GRILLE on MARK VII

LINCOLN. What a luxury car should be.

LINCOLN

MK.VII

TOWN CAR SEDAN 81F $29156.
" " SIGNATURE 82F 31276.
" " CARTIER 83F 33364.

TOTALLY RESTYLED **TOWN CAR**

117.4 " WB
302 CID V8 (150 HP @ 3200 RPM)
18 GAL. FUEL TANK
17/24 MPG

TOWN CAR IS MOTOR TREND'S 1990 "CAR OF THE YEAR."

CELLULAR TELEPHONE OPTIONAL

V.I.N. = 1LN-M (81F) - L - #

90

(MK. VII HAS 22.1 GAL. FUEL TANK.)

V8 MARK VII BILL BLASS (93E, $29801.) and LSC (92E, $30023.) 2-DR. SEDANS CONTINUE (WITH LITTLE CHANGE.) new DASH.

DRIVER AND RT. FRONT PASSENGER AIR BAGS ON ALL 1990 LINCOLN CARS.

CONTINENTAL new GRILLE DASH

V6 **CONTINENTAL**
SEDAN $30796. 974
SIGNATURE SED. 3/901. 984
232 CID V6 (140 HP @ 3800 RPM) 19/28 MPG 18.6 GAL. FUEL TANK

LINCOLN. What a luxury car should be.

1245   REAR DETAILS

MERCURY

(SINCE 1939)
(BY LINCOLN-MERCURY DIVISION *Ford*)

A/C CONTROLS

INTERIOR (C.P.)

DASH DETAIL

P87

MERCURY MARQUIS WAGON in Dark Cordovan Metallic.

$10,182.

8891.

RADIO (AM/FM)

MARQUIS → P81

81

18 EPA EST. MPG 26 HWY EST

114.3" WB
255, 302, OR
351 CID V8 s
AUTO. OVERDRIVE AVAIL.

P82

MARQUIS BROUGHAM

$10,418.

P 205 / 75R x 14 TIRES

V.I.N.= 1MEB
P820 B (-)
60000/ UP

- POWER ANTENNA
- POWER DOOR LOCKS
- POWER SEATS
- POWER WINDOWS*

OPT.

GRAND MARQUIS

$11,315.

P85

MARQUIS COLONY PARK
WAGON

P88

$11,177.

SEAT (WAGON)

ORNAMENT

1246

VEHICLE IDENTIFICATION NOS. =
IMEBP81 DOC (–) (MARQUIS)
IMEBP98 DOC (–) (MARQ. BROUGHAM)
IMEBP84 DOC (–) (GRAND MARQUIS)
IMEBP88 DOC (–) (WAGONS)
NUMBERS FOLLOWED BY
000001 UP

MARQUIS, 53 CUBIC FEET | 17 EST MPG CITY | 26 EST HWY

(WAGON)

MERCURY

COLONY PARK WAGON
↙ P88

82

255 OR 302 CID V8s

$12,071.
($12,238.,
W. DUAL-FACING
THIRD
REAR SEATS)

P85 4 DR.
GRAND MARQUIS
$12,520.

20 GAL.
FUEL TANK

18 MPG (SED.)
EPA

An advanced Automatic Overdrive Transmission
cuts engine speed on the highway by 30%. And options
run the gamut from luxury cloth or leather seats to a
formal roof (shown), digital electronic sound

SIDE-LT.
DETAIL

NEW ENGINES

140 CID 4
200 CID 6
OR
232 CID V6
(112 HP)
WITH 4-SP.
O.D. TRANS.

(RESTYLED
1983 MARQUIS
↙ P89

NEW SHORTER
105 1/2" WB
$9939.

MARQUIS V.I.N. =
IMEBP81, ETC.
"TRIPMINDER" COMPUTER OPTIONAL

83

MARQUIS
WAGON V.I.N. =
IMEBP87BXD
(–) 000001 UP

24 MPG EPA
(MARQUIS 4)
19 MPG EPA
(MARQ. 6, V6)
16 MPG EPA
(GRAND M. V8)

GRAND
MARQUIS   P93

GRAND MARQUIS

NEW WHEELS →

SEATBELT WARNING CHIMES
V.I.N. IMEBP84 FXD (–) 000001 UP
GRAND MARQUIS
LS

MORE HORIZONTAL
BANDS ADDED TO
TAIL-LIGHTS.

$13,172.

MERCURY. THE SUBSTANCE SHOWS.

1247

MERCURY

OPTIONAL ELECTRONIC INSTRUMENT CLUSTER is IMPROVED.

P90

MARQUIS WAGON
$**10,393.**
2-WAY LIFTGATE is OPTIONAL.

MARQ. WAGON V.I.N. =
IMEBP903XE (-)
000001 UP

INTERIOR

P89

MARQUIS 4 DR.
$**10,305.**
MARQ. BROUGHAM
4 DR.
10,608.

MARQUIS V.I.N. =
IMEBP893XE (-)
000001 UP

MARQUIS
BROUGHAM
WAGON (P90/60H)
$**10,667.**

GR. MQ. LS 4-DR.
$**14,159.**

GRAND MARQUIS 2 DR. $13492.
"   "   4 DR. 13604.
"   " LS 2 DR. 14047.

P95/60H

GRAND MARQUIS LS INTERIOR

GRAND MARQUIS COLONY PARK
LS WAGON $**13790.** UP

84

V.I.N. = IMEBP93FXE (-)
000001 UP (GR. MARQ.)
P94FXE (-)(COL. PK.)

P94

1248

903 MARQUIS WAGON $10,675.

MERCURY

← MARQ. BROUGH. WAGON $10,974.

903

V8 (GRAND MARQUIS and COLONY PK. SER. CONT'D WITH FEW CHANGES)

85

V.I.N. = IMEBP893 XF (-)000001 UP

105½" WB $10,583. UP

↓ new TAIL LTS.

AVAILABLE WHEEL STYLES

893

MARQUIS

CLOSE DETAILS OF new GRILLE (MARQUIS)

"MERCURY" NAME MOVED →

MERCURY

MERCURY MARQUIS

LINCOLN-MERCURY DIVISION Ford

MERCURY

FROM $11,342. ('86)   114.3" WB   GRAND MARQUIS LS 2-DR. $15,917. ('86)

FROM $16,588. ('87)
17/27 MPG (302 cu.in V8)
"PANTHER" BODY
1986 EXAMPLES ILLUSTRATED

MERCURY. The shape you want to be in.

1986 MARQUIS RESEMBLES 1985 MODELS
1986 IS FINAL YR.
FOR MARQUIS V6 or 4
(NOT SHOWN)

COLONY PARK LS

GRAND MARQUIS

1986
V.I.N.=
1MEBP
(93F TO 903)
-G-#

86-
87

HIGH-MOUNTED
3RD BRAKE LT.
ON ALL
1986 and
LATER
MODELS

1987 V.I.N.=1MEBM
(M72F TO 79F)-H-#

CHILD RESTRAINT

Mercury
NAME AT TOP
CORNER OF
GRILLE

WHEEL TYPES

1250

COLONY PARK
LS

MERCURY

(2 - DR. MODELS
DISCONTINUED)

GRAND MARQUIS
ROOFLINE

GS or
LS
MODELS
AVAIL.

1990
DASH IS **NEW**

CLIMATE CONTROL
AIR CONDITIONING
SYSTEM OPTIONAL

REAR

1988 V.I.N.= (1ME or 3MA)
BM (74F)-J - #

88-90

79F
COLONY PARK
WAGON, LS
$18939. ('88)
19309. ('89)
20782. ('90)

GS SEDAN   LS SEDAN
WAGON   WAGON

1989 V.I.N. =
1ME-M (74F)-K-#
-L-# IN 1990 V.I.N.

RESTYLED,
1988
114.3" WB
5.0 L V8
302 CID
150 HP @
3200
RPM

74 F
COLONY PARK
WAGON, GS
$18355. ('88) 18727 ('89)
20210 ('90)

1990 AUDIO SPEAKERS NOW
IN DOOR PANELS INSTEAD
OF ON DASH.

GRAND MARQUIS
SEDAN
$19475.
UP ('90)

18 GAL.
FUEL TANK

1990 EXAMPLES
ILLUSTRATED

17/24
MPG,
EPA

OTHER WHEELS AVAILABLE

(1969-1986)
(NAME TO RETURN IN 1991)

MERCURY CAPRI

(MFD. BY FORD OF GERMANY UNTIL 1978; MFD. IN U.S.A. 1979 TO 1986.)

100.4" WB
140 CID 4 OR TURBO 4, 200 CID 6, OR 255 CID V8 IN 1981.

P175/80R × 13 TIRES

STD. $8095.

"GS" $8277.

"RS" 8329.

"RS" WITH T-BAR ROOF OPT.

1981 EXAMPLES ILLUSTR., UNLESS OTHERWISE INDICATED.

"BLACK MAGIC" 3-DR. HATCHBACK is new, PRICED AT $8739.

"RS" TURBO* 8937.

CAPRI
LINCOLN-MERCURY DIVISION

81-82

V.I.N. = IME (-) P67 (A) XB 60000/ UP

V.I.N. = IMEB P67 B0C (-) 000001 UP ("RS" has -P67FOC- V.I.N.)

"BLACK MAGIC" CPE. and INTERIOR (T-BAR ROOF OPT.)

"TR" PERFORM. PKG. OPT.

new 1982 H.O. (HIGH OUTPUT) CAPRI w. new 157 HP 302 CID V8 (RS)

For power, you've got choices ranging from a 2.3-liter overhead cam four to a 5.0-liter V-8 that still remembers it's a V-8.

A five-speed overdrive transmission is standard. There are four different sound systems available, a flashy T-roof, special wheels, special paint, even a choice of steering wheels.

FROM $8362 ('82)

MPG: 21 EPA CITY, 34 36 HWY. (WEST COAST) 2.3 L, 5-SPEED

('82)

('82)

1252

4 CYL. CAPRI V.I.N.= IMEBP79AXD (-)000001 UP
R9 (V8) V.I.N.= IMEBP67FXD
(-)000001 UP

CAPRI

$8895. TO $10368.

83

NEW "BUBBLEBACK" DESIGN, WITH UNIQUE WRAPAROUND BODYSIDE MOLDING 100.4" WB CONTINUES

STD. L, GS, BLACK MAGIC CRIMSON CAT OR RS MODELS, ALL 3-DOOR HATCHBACKS

GS INTERIOR P79/602 $9653.

5.0 LITER (302 CID) 4 BBL. V8 has 178 HP (232 CID V6 has 112 HP) 19 MPG EPA

(140 CID 4 and TURBO 4 ALSO AVAIL.) TO 24 MPG EPA

AVAILABLE WHEELS

84

GS (4 CYL.) V.I.N. = IMEBP793 XE (-)000001 UP

RS (V8) V.I.N. = IMEBP79MXE (-)000001 UP.

DASH

TURBO RS INTERIOR

TURBO RS $11,443.

140 CID 4 CYL. TURBO ENG. 145 HP @ 4600 RPM

TURBO V.I.N. = IMEBP79WXE (-)000001 UP

New

(FRONT VIEW OF TURBO RS ON NEXT PAGE)

1253

1984 IS FINAL YR. FOR RS MODELS.

1984 Capri Turbo RS, FRONT VIEW

RS REPLACED BY 5.0 L (V8) IN 1985.
(1985 V.I.N. ENDS w. — F - # ; 1986 " " — G - #)

Mercury CAPRI

Options

AM/FM RADIO w. CASSETTE

↓ SUN ROOF   1986 DASH   T-ROOF

1984 EXAMPLES ILLUSTR.

84-86

GS or 5.0 L 3 DR. HATCHBKS. ONLY, IN 1985 and 1986.

A/C OPT.

1985 $9500. OR 11891.
     GS (79A)   5.0 L (79M)
1986 9977. OR 12708.

ENDS 1986

84 V8 RS $11,306. ↑ (IN SAN FRANCISCO, CALIF.)

MERCURY COUGAR

(SINCE 1967)

new

Introducing the Cougar 4-door.

INTERIOR

Premium Sound Systems. And many other options. With the standard engine and automatic transmission required on Cougar with LS option (shown below), the new Cougar is rated at 22* EPA EST. MPG, 31 EST HWY. The 1981 Cougar 4-door. A 4-door car is one thing. But a Cougar is another.

4 DR. RETURNS, AFTER BEING OMITTED FROM 1980 SERIES.

$ 8387. P77 4 DR.

($8228. P76 2 DR.)

105 1/2" WB

139 CID 4,
200 CID 6,
OR
255 CID V8

81

PARTIALLY RESTYLED

V.I.N. =
IME (-)
P76 (A)
XB (-)
60000/ UP
XR-7 =
IME (-)
P90 (-) XB
60000/
UP

Notice the new two-tone paint treatment, the electronic instrument cluster, and the unique convertible-like carriage roof options.

COUGAR XR-7
LINCOLN-MERCURY DIVISION

CABRIOLET OPTION, XR-7

COUGAR XR-7

108.4" WB
(XR-7)
255 OR 302 CID
V8 s
OR
200 CID 6

$ 8762. (P90 CPE.)

GS OPTION
$ 320.

LS OPTION
$ 715.

ROARO SEATS,
KEYLESS
ENTRY "
OCKS
VAILABLE
LSO.

FRONT
DETAIL

STD.
XR-7
CAB
DETAIL

options like the TR-type tires, cast aluminum wheels, and a special suspension. AM/FM cassette stereo with Dolby® NR. And your choice of three engines: the 3.3 liter 6, or the optional 4.2 and 5.0 liter V-8's...both available with Automatic Overdrive Transmission.

The standard engine drive train is rated 18 EPA EST. MPG, 24 EST. HWY. Compare to estimated MPG of other cars. Your mileage may differ, depending on speed, weather, and trip length. Actual highway mileage probably lower.

GS
4 DR.
WAGON
9495.
78)

New

COUGAR WAGON

82

(WAGON AVAIL. 1982 ONLY)
6, new V6, OR V8
(4 CYL. DISCONT'D.)
OTHER MODELS (GS, LS, XR-7) CONT'D., $9262. UP
(2 DR. and 4 DR. AVAIL.)

"MERCURY"
INSCRIPTION
ON new
1982 GRILLE

V.I.N. = IMEBP76BOC UP
XR-7 = " P9ODOC UP

MERCURY COUGAR

LINCOLN-MERCURY DIVISION **Ford**

(4 DR. SEDAN and WAGON DISCONTINUED)

ALL-NEW SHAPE

20 MPG EPA (V6)

83

TOTALLY RESTYLED

new 104" W.B.
2.47 GEAR RATIO

(ILLUSTRATED)
LS COUPE
(P92/603)
$12,054.

MERCURY. THE SUBSTANCE SHOWS.

V.I.N. = IMEBP923XD(-) 000001/ UP

232 CID V6
5 LITER EFI
(V8 AVAILABLE)

STD. COUPE
(P92)
$10,725.

note UNIQUE new ROOFLINE

UPRIGHT COUGAR-HEAD DISC HOOD ORNAMENT ON 1983 COUGAR

2.73 GEAR RATIO IS **New**

XR-7 RETURNS AS TURBO 4.
(next pg.)

84

New FLAT RADIATOR BADGE (ROUND) (INSTEAD OF UPRIGHT ORNAMENT)

MERCURY COUGAR

LINCOLN-MERCURY DIVISION **Ford**

84

V.I.N.= 1MEBP923XE (-) 000001 UP
XR-7 = 1MEBP92WXE (-) 000001 UP

INTERIOR (XR-7)

ELECTRONIC FUEL INJ. NOW ON ALL COUGAR ENGINES.

XR-7

XR-7 TURBO

104" WB

$14,240.

XR-7 TURBO-CHARGER →

WHEELS

new "CHECK OIL" LIGHT ON DASH

21 GAL. FUEL TANK (18 ON XR7)

POWER TRAIN COMBINATIONS		REAR AXLE RATIO		
ENGINE	TRANSMISSION	49-STATES	HIGH ALTITUDE	CALIF.
3.8L EFI V-6 (STD.)	3-speed SelectShift Automatic with lock up torque converter (STD.)	2.73(a)	NA	2.73(a)
2.3L EFI Turbo I-4 (XR-7 Only)	3-speed SelectShift Automatic (STD.)	3.45(b)	3.45(b)	3.45(b)
2.3L EFI Turbo I-4 (XR-7 Only)	Manual 5-speed Overdrive (OPT.)	3.45(b)	3.45(b)	3.45(b)
5.0L OPT. EFI V-8	Automatic Overdrive (OPT.)	3.08(a)	3.08(a)	3.08(a)

STD. P92 COUGAR →

$11,153.

1257

MERCURY COUGAR

OPT. "KEYLESS ENTRY" DOOR LOCK

GRAINED LS DASH

new CRISSCROSS PCS. IN GRILLE

new TAILLIGHTS

ELECTRONIC (DIGITAL) INSTRUMENT CLUSTER OPTIONAL, BUT NOT AVAIL. ON XR-7.

(XR-7 HAS BLACK DASH, CIRCULAR ANALOG GAUGES)

$15,089. XR-7 (P92/934)

STD. CPE (P92) $11,825. (P92/ LS CPE. 603) $13,025.

P205/70R × 14 TIRES ON STD. OR LS. (P215 OPT.)

P225/60 VR15 TIRES ON XR-7 ONLY.

V.I.N. ENDS WITH —XF (—) #

85

new GRILLE
new TAIL LIGHTS
new 20.6 GAL. FUEL TANK

232 CID V6 (120 HP)
302 CID V8 (140 HP)

2.73 GR w. V6 OR V8.
3.45 WITH TURBO 4 (XR-7)

140 C/D TURBO 4 145 HP

XR-7 HAS DIFF. SIDE TRIM

STANDARD ON XR-7. PERFORM. ALUMINUM

TR ALUMINUM WHEEL

WIRE LOCKING WH. CVR.

POLYCAST ROAD WHEEL

LUXURY WHEEL CVR.

STANDARD ON LS

WHEEL CHOICES

1258

MERCURY COUGAR

XR-7 / 92W $15886.

232 CID V6 (V8 AVAIL.) IN GS OR LS (20.6 GAL. FUEL TANK)

XR-7 has 140 CID TURBO 4. 18.2 GAL. FUEL TANK

86 New MERCURY TRADEMARK →

(GS CPE. [923] $12615.)

V.I.N. = 1MEBP (92W) - G - #

1986 CARS HAVE HIGH-UP 3RD BRAKE LT.

$13951. LS

104.0" WB

WT. = 3033 LBS. ('87)

MERCURY. The shape you want to be in.
LINCOLN-MERCURY DIVISION Ford

"S" BODY

new 104.2" WB

RESTYLED

LS has 3.8 L. V6 OR 5.0 L. V8. (120 HP) (150 HP)
XR7 has 5.0 L. V8 (150 HP) and 4-SP. AUTOMATIC OVERDRIVE TRANS.

1987 LS CPE. $14,062. (603)
" XR7 CPE. 16,092. (62F)

1987 V.I.N. 1MEBM (62F) -- H -- #

('87)

87- 88

1987 MPG: 18/27 (302 CID V8)

new 22.1 GAL. FUEL TK.

1988 V.I.N. ENDS WITH -- J -#

1988 GRILLE and DASH →

1988 LS INTERIOR

1988 LS CPE. (604) $14,458. XR7 CPE. 16,589. (62F)

POWER MIRRORS STD. EQUIPMENT

Cougar XR-7 instrument panel.
Some features shown may be optional.

1259

1988 WEIGHTS: 3137 LBS. (LS) 3385 " (XR-7)

PULSE-QUICKENING COMFORT.

MERCURY COUGAR

V.I.N. =
1ME-M
(62R)
— K-#

"KEYLESS
ENTRY"
DOOR LOCK
OPTION ↓

LS and DASH

89

new
113"
WB

BODY RESTYLED

new 19-GAL. GAS TANK

LS
$15,903.
(60)

XR-7 and DASH (BELOW) $20,105. (62)
(PAINTED GRILLE on XR-7)

MERCURY

SUPERCHARGED COUGAR XR7.

MERCURY COUGAR

new CONTOURED HEAD RESTRAINTS

V.I.N. ENDS WITH — L - #

19 / 27 MPG 19-GAL. GAS TANK

(604) *LS*

$16,276.

90

XR-7 has 3.8 L. V6 (210 HP, 232 cid SUPERCHARGED)

LS has 140 HP VERSION OF 3.8 L V6.

XR-7 CONTINUES PAINTED GRILLE.

XR-7 WHEEL

XR-7 (62-F)

$21,236.

AVAIL. WITH 15" OR 16" WHEELS. P205/70R15 TIRES STANDARD ON LS. P225/60R16 STD. ON XR-7.

note new WARNING LTS. BELOW GAUGES ON XR-7 DASH

Cougar XR7 instrument panel. Some features shown may be optional.

XR-7 DASH 17/23 MPG WITH SUPERCH.

ELECTRONIC DASH (OPT.)

1261

MERCURY LN7 (SPECIAL SPORT VARIATION OF *LYNX*.)

(1982-1983)

11.3 GAL. FUEL TK.

NEW

1982
MPG: 29 EPA
46 HWY.
STD.
3-DR. HATCHBACK IS ONLY MODEL FOR 1982.

94.2" WB

1982 V.I.N.= IMEBP6I20 C(-)000001 UP

DASH

WHEEL STYLE ON CAR ABOVE

(1982 EXAMPLES ILLUSTR.)

DETAIL OF SIDE

$9258. ('82)

4 MODELS IN 1983:
3 DR. - $8875.
SPT. HTCHBK. COUPE -
$9559.
GR. SPT. HTCHBK.
CPE.- $9940.
"RS"
$10,240.

82-83

98 CID 4 70 HP

"HO "('83)
80 HP

FRONT

MULTI-
PORT
E.F.I.
AVAIL.
'83

(WIDTH EXAGGERATED)

1983 V.I.N.=IMEBP612XD (-)000001 UP

MERCURY LYNX

(1981–1987)

(MECHANICALLY SIMILAR TO FORD ESCORT)

(REPLACES BOBCAT)

made in America.
26 EPA EST. MPG **36** HWY EST.

27 EPA EST. MPG **42** EST. HWY

WAGON

WAGONS FR. $**6515.**

Full-door trim panels. And such tailored optional touches as woodtone bodyside treatment, liftgate wiper and washer, roof rack, even speed control.

INTERIORS

WAGON

81 NEW

2 DR.

94.2" WHEELBASE

TRANSVERSE ENGINE

HALOGEN HDLTS.

FRONT WHEEL DRIVE

FRONT DISC BRAKES

30 *EPA EST. MPG **44** HWY. EST.

STD., L, GL, RS, GS or LS SERIES

2-DR. HATCHBACKS FR. $**5783.**

V.I.N.
IME (-)
P63 (-) XB
(-) 600001 UP

MADE IN AMERICA

2-DR. HTCHBK. PRICES :
STD. =
$6212.
L =
6860.
GL =
6871.
GS =
7658.
LS =
8163.
RS =
7220.

V.I.N. = !MEBP 6320 C
(-) 000001 UP

LYNX

2-DR.

WAGONS :
L = $7282.
GL = 7298.
GS =
$7995.
LS =
8500.

the Lynx wagon has the best gas-mileage rating of any American-built wagon— either manual transaxle or optional automatic transaxle.

| MANUAL | 28 EPA EST. MPG | 44 EST. HWY. |
| AUTOMATIC | 29 EPA EST. MPG | 41 EST. HWY. |

P165/80R13 TIRES

GS INTERIOR

10 GAL. FUEL TANK

31 MPG (EPA)
2-DR.

4-DR.

31 EPA EST. MPG | 47 EST. HWY.

82

STD.
$6419.
L 7077.
GL 7088.
GS 7875.
LS 8379.

(ABOVE PRICES
FOR NEW
5 DR. MODELS)

NEW LYNX 5-DOOR

1264

MERCURY **L Y N X R S**

LINCOLN-MERCURY DIVISION *Ford*

P165/70R
365 TIRES
ON
RS.

98 CID 4 CYL.
ENGINES

CVH   70 HP
HO   80 HP
EFI   88 HP
FEC ENG.
ALSO
AVAIL.

RS
3 DR.

GROUND CONTROL: The standard TR performance package of Michelin TRX tires, TR sport steel wheels, and a TR sport suspension lets you hug corners and straighten out sharp curves.
POWER EQUIPMENT: The standard 1.6 liter multi-port electronic fuel-injected engine* gives you a clean, crisp, fast start. One touch of the accelerator and you're off!
MAXIMUM EFFICIENCY: The standard five-speed manual transmission gives you all the excitement of close-ratio shifting, while maximizing the power of the engine.

$7996.
P57

V.I.N. =
IMEBP632XD (-)
00000/ UP

83
NEW GRILLE

"EFI
5-SPEED"

MPG:
44 HWY.
25 EPA
w. 1.6 -LITRE HO ENG.
and 5-SP. MANUAL O.D. TRANS.

LYNX LTS

LTS 5 DR.
$8055.
P65/934

P165/
80R13 TIRES

MERCURY. THE SUBSTANCE SHOWS.

P54	L 3 DR.	$6516.	
P65	L 5 DR.	6818.	
P60	L WAGON	6931.	
P55	GS 3 DR.	7178.	
P66	GS 5 DR.	7489.	
	GS WAGON	7574.	P61
	LTS 5 DR.	8055.	P65/934
	RS 3 DR.	7996.	P57
	LS 3 DR.	8231.	P58
	LS 5 DR.	8543.	P68
	LS WAGON	8611.	P63

1265

MERCURY LYNX

OPTIONAL 7-BAND GRAPHIC AUDIO EQUALIZER →

196 IMPROVEMENTS IN LYNX SINCE THE FIRST MODEL OF 1981!

DASH

LTS 5 DR. $8725.

"EFI" MEANS ELECTRONIC FUEL INJECTION

EFI

70, 80 OR 88 HP WITH 98 CID 4

84

GS VILLAGER $7551. UP

LYNX GS 3-DOOR
LYNX GS 5-DOOR
LYNX GS STATION WAGON

L WAGON $7110.

V.I.N.
IMEB P.542 XE (-) 000001 UP
new 4 CYL. DIESEL ENG. OPT.

(STD. 3-DOOR FROM $5790.)

L $6772.

TAILLIGHT DETAIL

LYNX

MPG: 56 HWY 37 EPA

TR SPORT CAST ALUMINUM WHEEL

LYNX L 3-DOOR
LYNX L 5-DOOR
LYNX L STATION WAGON

MERCURY LYNX

(1984 EXAMPLES ILLUSTRATED)

TAILGATE (WAGON) →

LIFETIME SERVICE GUARANTEE

L, GS, LTS INTERIOR COLORS
Charcoal
Canyon Red
Academy Blue
Desert Tan

Perhaps the most intelligently designed 102 cu. ft. you've ever seen. With 85 cu. ft. of passenger space and approximately 26 cu. ft. of cargo space with the rear seat down," it will never make you wish you bought something bigger.

OPT. CHILD RESTRAINT

SPEED CONTROL STEER. WHEEL AVAIL. ↑

DIESEL MPG. = 68 HWY, 46 EPA

GS INTERIOR

New
(AVAIL. THROUGH '87)

OPT. 4-CYL. DIESEL ENGINE

84

NEW INTERIORS

ELECTRONIC AM/FM STEREO w. CASSETTE

13 GAL. FUEL TANK (10-GAL. ON 5-DR. w. "FUEL SAVER" OPTION)

GS CONSOLE

RS INTERIOR IN "DESERT TAN"
RS = (FINAL '84)
$8652.
(RS TURBO ALSO AVAIL.) ↓

RS DASH →

MERCURY

RS AND RS TURBO INTERIOR COLORS
Charcoal
Desert Tan

VENT WINDOWS OPT. →

RS HAS 165/70R365 TRX MICHELIN TIRES

MERCURY. A MORE ENLIGHTENED APPROACH.
LINCOLN MERCURY DIVISION — Ford

Mercury Lynx

$5986†

† ADVERTISED 1985½ STARTING PRICE
REG. $6057. UP

EARLY 1985 SIMILAR TO 1984 BUT w. FOLLOWING MODELS and PRICES:

NEW 113 cid 4 CYL. ENGINE

STD. 3 DR. HTCHBK.	$	5930.
L " "		6796.
L 5 DR. "		7010.
L WAGON		7133.
GS 3 DR. HTCHBK.		7243.
GS 5 DR. "		7457.
GS WAGON		7507.

1985 V.I.N.   1MEPP (-)(-) XF (-)000001 UP
1986 "   1MEBP ——— G-#
1987 "   1MEBM ——— H-#

SPRING, 1985 ("1985½") MODELS with "EURO STYLE" HDLTS. and STYLIZED EMBLEM

XR3 113 cid 4 (108 HP @ 5200 RPM)

$ **8243.**
(9251., 1987)

MPG:
33 CITY,
43 HWY.

GASOLINE

85 **NEW** -87

XR3 HAS OWN GRILLE
(STARTS 1986)

GS GRILLE

1986 DASH

FINAL 1987 MODELS $6870. UP

L 3 DR. $**7034.** ('86)

LYNX

RPM x 1000   FUEL   TEMP   UNLEADED FUEL ONLY   TRIP RESET ▶   MPH

FRONT WHEEL DRIVE

Mercury Sable. (SINCE 1986)

LS SEDAN (87U)
$13,762.

115 MPH

GAS FILLER ON RIGHT

INTERIOR

MECHANICALLY SIMILAR TO new FORD TAURUS

86 **New**

106" WHEELBASE new type 182 CID V6 ENGINE

V.I.N. = IMEBP (87D) — G — #

UNIQUE "LASER" LIGHTBAR EXTENDING BETWEEN HEADLTS.

Mercury Sable LS Sedan

X-RAY VIEW, WITH DETAILS OF FRONT WHEEL DRIVE, TRANSVERSE V6 ENG., ETC.

(GS HAS PLAINER LOWER SIDE TRIM
87-D SED.=$11,888.
88U WAGON = 12,964.)

Sophisticated new shape. The 1986 Mercury Sable.

ROOF RACK DETAIL

LS **wagon.** (88U) $14,256.

1269

Mercury Sable.

GS WAGON

"TAURUS" BODY $13,554. ('87)

$14,198. ('88)

$14,118. ('87)
$14,839. ('88)

GS **New** SERIES MODEL NUMBERS (50 U)

SABLE WAGON **87-**

1987 V.I.N. ENDS WITH
-H-# (-J-# 1988)

88 ('88)

(55 U)

Sable's optional digital instrumentation.
Some features shown may be optional.

Sable LS instrument panel.
Some features shown may be optional.

$15,515. ('87)
15,858. ('88)
LS WAGON
(58 U)

UPHOLSTERY (SEDAN)

1987
EXAMPLES
ILLUSTR.
(UNLESS OTHERWISE
NOTED.) **LS**

SEDAN
(53 U)

$14,970. ('87)
15,191. ('88)

1270

Mercury Sable.

('89)

GS SEDAN
(50U)
$14,551.('89) 15,520.('90)

GS SEDAN INTERIOR

GS
SABLE WAGON. (55U)
$15,254. ('89)
16,465. ('90)

16-GALLON FUEL TANK
19 TO 21 MPG, EPA (CITY)

MERCURY
LINCOLN
Quality is Job 1.

('90)

89-90

1990 has new DASH,
DRIVER'S AIR BAG,
and new OPTIONAL
ANTI-LOCK BRAKING.

LS SEDAN
(53U)
$15,544. ('89)
16,522. ('90)

3.0L, 182 cid V6   OPT. 3.8L, 232 cid V6
(140 HP @ 4800 RPM)   (140 HP @ 3800 RPM)
21/29 MPG   19/28 MPG

LS WAGON
(58U)
$16322. ('89)
17493. ('90)

Sable LS interior in leather.
Some features shown may be optional.

1271

MERCURY TOPAZ

LINCOLN-MERCURY DIVISION — Ford

(P73) LS 2 DR. $10638.

(SAME PRICE FOR LS 4 DR.) (P76)

(REPLACES MERCURY ZEPHYR.) FRONT WHEEL DRIVE

STARTS WITH 1984 MODEL.

('84)

GS 9144. P72 2.DR. OR 4.DR. P75

43 EST. HWY. 28 EPA

90 HP, 140 CID 4 "2300 HSC" ENGINE IS new WITH HIGH SWIRL COMBUSTION CHAMBER DESIGN. →

121 CID 4 CYL. DIESEL (52 HP) ALSO AVAIL.

(INTRO. MAY 26, 1983 AS EARLY 1984 MODEL.)

CROSS SECTION VIEW OF A CYLINDER

note THAT GS HAS THINNER RUB STRIP ON SIDE THAN LS. (GS ADVERTISED SPECIAL PRICE OF $7991.)

15.2 GAL. FUEL TANK (14 GAL. ON EARLY MODELS)

1984 V.I.N.= IMEB (P72) RXE (-) 000001 UP

1985 V.I.N.= IMEPP7 (-) (-) XF (-) 000001 UP

99 MPH

Ford's EEC-IV* is the most advanced on-board automotive computer in the world.

1985 PRICES : GS 2DR. OR 4-DR. $9013.
LS 2 DR. (P73) $10619.
LS 4 DR. (P76) 10668.

(MECHANICALLY SIMILAR TO FORD TEMPO.)

NEW 84-85

LS INTERIOR ('84)

EMBLEM

ACCORD. TO VAR. SOURCES 1984-1985 TOPAZ MODEL NUMBERS HAVE "P" PREFIX OR "R" SUFFIX. (H SUFFIX IF EQUIPPED WITH DIESEL ENGINE.)

P76(R)

('85)

TOPAZ GS

$9465. UP ('86) = GS 2 DR. ('86) (72X)
10,206 UP ('87) = " " " ('87) (31X)
" 4 DR. ('86) (75X)
$9615.
" " " ('87) (36X)
$10 356.
1987 GS SPORT
2 DR. (33S) $10850.
4 DR.
(38S)
$11000.

"TOPAZ" BODY

SPORT DASH

Mercury Topaz

1986 V.I.N. =
IMEBP (72X)
- G - #
1987 V.I.N. =
IMEBM (M31X)
- H - #

22-27 MPG (w. A/T)

(GS SPORT PACKAGE AVAIL. 1986)
(1987 EXAMPLES ILLUSTRATED)

33S

GS SPORT
(new in 1987)

140 CID
(2.3 L) 4 CYL.
ENGINES
HSC =
86 HP @ 4000
HSO =
100 HP @ 4600
(4 CYL. DIESEL ALSO
AVAIL. 1986)

new
GRILLE

37X
LS
4 DR.
$11830.
('87)

AVAIL. IN 1987:
DRIVER AIRBAG

LS DASH

86-87

(LS 2 DR. NOT
AVAILABLE 1987)

4WD
CONTROL

ALL WHEEL DRIVE
OFF ON

1986 LS
2 DR. (73X)
$10621.
4 DR. (76X) $10891.

NEW TOPAZ ALL-WHEEL-DRIVE OPTION, 1987

Mercury Topaz

ALL-WHEEL DRIVE
OPTIONAL

new LTS SEDAN (38S)
$12,421. ('88)
('88)

XR5 SPT. SED. (2-DR.)
ALSO new IN 1988
(33S) $11,711.

DRIVER'S AIRBAG OPTIONAL

LTS INTERIOR

new DASH IN 1988 WITH ALL ANALOG GAUGES IN FIELD OF DRIVER'S VISION

88-90
RESTYLED

XR-5 INTERIOR ('88)

1988 V.I.N. = (1ME OR 3MA) BM (31X)- J- # 1989 V.I.N. ENDS WITH K #; 1990 WITH L #

GRILLE
('88)

← BLACK — PAINTED SIDE PILLARS CREATE THE APPEARANCE OF A 4-DR H/T.

Topaz LTS instrument panel. Some features shown may be optional.

MODELS = GS (2+4 DOOR) LS (4 DR.) XR5 (2 DR.) LTS (4 DR.)

XR5 ('88)

15.9 - GALLON FUEL TANK

MERCURY SYMBOL ON WHEEL (1989)

$11462. ('89) GS

NEW SHAPE
OF REAR UPPER BODY

('89)

REAR DETAILS

The Shape You Want To Be In.
MERCURY

1990 FROM $11817. (GS 2-DR.)

141 CID (2.3 L) 4 (98 OR 100 HP @ 4400 RPM) 23/31 MPG (22-26 w. A/T)

TOPAZ

ASSEMBLED BY FORD OF MEXICO; SOME MAZDA COMPONENTS (JAPAN)

MERCURY TRACER (1988 ON)
(REPLACES LYNX)

28/35 MPG (MANUAL 5 SP.)
26/29 (A/T)
('89)

$9592. ('88)

#135 WAGON

104-105 MPH

SPORT HATCHBACK #115

small car

88-90

UPHOLSTERY

(EXCEPT FOR WAGON, 1990 EXAMPLES ILLUSTRATED)

PRICED FROM
$8409. ('88)
8891. ('89)

1.6 L OHC
4 CYL.
82 HP @
5000
RPM

94.7" WB
11.9 GAL.
GAS TANK

P175/70R13
TIRES

V.I.N.
ENDS
WITH
-J-#
(1988)
-K-#
(1989)
-L-#
(1990)

TRACER

#125 4-DR. HATCHBACK

EMBLEM

MERKUR

New **MERKUR** (INCL. SCORPIO)

NEW

1 Fog lamp switch
2 Rear window defroster switch
3 Rear window wiper washer switch
4 Flash to pass high beam control
5 Instrument panel illumination control
6 Low oil pressure indicator
7 Discharge indicator
8 Low brake fluid level indicator
9 Ice alert warning indicator
10 Door ajar/exterior bulb failure graphic warning display
11 Disc brake pad wear indicator
12 Low coolant level indicator
13 Low washer fluid level indicator
14 Low oil level indicator
15 Low fuel level indicator
16 Seat belt indicator
17 Right/left remote electric mirror control
18 Easy access fuse panel
19 Parking headlamp control
20 Windshield wiper washer control
21 Interval wiper control
22 Heated front seat switch (optional)
23 Grundig AM/FM stereo cassette
24 Power window control
25 Cassette storage trays

(STARTS 1985)

15 GAL. FUEL TK.

Merkur XR4Ti from Germany.

(3 DOOR HATCHBACKS ONLY, UNTIL 1987.)

1985 V.I.N. = WF11P (80W) - F - #
1986 " = " - G - #
1987 " = "1PT " - H - #

note DUAL REAR SPOILERS ON XR4Ti (ALSO, DUAL PAIRS OF REAR QUARTER WINDOWS ARE AN IDENTIFYING FEATURE.)

85- 87

129 MPH ("SIERRA" BODY)

$16965. ('85)
16788. ('86)
XR4Ti 18401. ('87)

102.7" WB 2.3L TURBO 4 (170 HP) MFD. BY FORD MOTOR CO. OF GERMANY, IMPORTED BY LINCOLN-MERCURY

New ('88)

81V "GRANADA" BODY **SCORPIO** INTERIOR

5 DOOR SED.

$19,711. ('88)

117-130 MPH (SCORPIO)

MERKUR INT.

X4Ti ('88)

$20,408. ('89)

(INTRO. SUMMER, 1987) 108.7" WB 2.9L V6

$24,782. ('88)
25,772. ('89)

SCORPIO

('89)

V.I.N. = 1988: WF1PT (80T) - J - #
1989: WF1-T (80W) - K - #
1990: _ L _ #

88-90

144 HP new 145 HP
ONLY SCORPIO IMPORTED IN 1990.
17/23 MPG

80W

MERKUR XR4Ti

AVAIL. T-BAR TOP

Oldsmobile
Cutlass

INTERMEDIATE-SIZED
108.1" WB (ESTABL. 1897)

V.I.N. = 1G3A
( )OB 100001/ UP

2 VIEWS OF CUTLASS SEDAN

STANDARD V6
21 / 30
EPA Est. Hwy Est. mpg

3K47
CALAIS
$9042.
(CALAIS COUPE ONLY)

81

231 CID V6 (110 HP)
260 OR 305 CID V8s (105, 155 HP)
350 CID DIESEL V8 (105 HP)

diesel

"DIESEL" HOOD ORNAMENT IDENTIFIES DIESEL CARS.

THIS OPTIONAL GAUGE PACKAGE IS STANDARD EQUIPMENT ON "CALAIS" MODEL.

$8342.

P195 (185)/75R x 14 TIRES

UN-GRAINED "CUTLASS CRUISER" WAGON HAS GRILLE LIKE CUTLASS SEDAN (ABOVE, RT.)

AVAIL. WHEEL STYLES

Cutlass Cruiser Brougham.
wagon with luxury touches.

WITH GRAINED SIDES

3J35
$8763.

(STD. CUTL. CRUISER, #3G35, $8454.)

DASH (W/O OPT. GAUGE PKG.)

SUPREME
HAS OWN OUTSWEPT GRILLE WITH ALL VERTICAL PCS. $8522.
3R47 COUPE

CUTLASS SUPREME BROUGHAM

(BROUGHAMS HAVE GRILLE LIKE ILLUSTRATED WAGON.)

CPE. 3M47 $9007.

$8674.

Delta 88

116" WB
P20575R x15
TIRES

3L69

GM

Oldsmobile

We've had one built for you.

FULL-SIZE
MODELS

DELTA 88 DASH

V6, V8 OR
DIESEL
V8

STANDARD V6		DIESEL V8	
19	28	23	34
EPA Est. mpg	Hwy. Est.	EPA Est. mpg	Hwy. Est.

REMEMBER. *Compare* the "estimated mpg" to the "estimated mpg" of other cars. You may get different mileage, depending on how fast you drive, weather conditions and trip length. Actual highway mileage will probably be less than the estimated highway fuel economy. Diesel estimates lower in California. Oldsmobiles are equipped with GM-built engines produced by various divisions. See your dealer for details.
IMPORTANT: Computer Command Control is on all standard 1981 gasoline engines. It helps reduce exhaust emissions while allowing good fuel efficiency.

(3L37 STD. DELTA CPE. AVAIL. AT $8578.)

$11,208.

98
REGENCY
COUPE

3X37

119" WB

DELTA 88
"ROYALE" CPE.
$8842. 116" WB

3N37

81

Buying a luxury car need not mean giving up economy.
Oldsmobile Ninety-Eight Regency's standard V6 engine offers an EPA estimated 18 mpg, estimated highway 29. With available diesel engine, an EPA estimated 21 mpg, estimated highway 33.

98
DASH

3P35

98 INTERIOR
WITH TUFTED SEATS

98 GRILLE

NINETY-EIGHT REG.

CUSTOM CRUISER
Functional utility? It takes on luxurious forms.

FROM $9602. P225/75R15 TIRES ON WAGON

3X69
$11,365.
(3X37 CPE: 11,208.)

The new Ninety-Eight Regency.

NEW *CIERA SERIES*

Oldsmobile We've had one built for you.

A new diesel V6 for 1982.

CUTLASS CIERA BROUGHAM SEDAN

$10,673.

DASH

AVAILABLE RALLYE WHEEL

$10,471.

CUTLASS CIERA BROUGHAM COUPE

↙ note GRILLE IS DIFFERENT FROM STD. CIERA GRILLE ON SEDAN ILLUSTR. BELOW.

CLOSER DETAIL OF DASH

40 | 25
Hwy Est. | EPA Est. mpg

CUTLASS CIERA

82

104.9" WB

42 | 28
Hwy Est. | EPA Est. mpg

CIERA IS *new* FRONT-WHEEL DRIVE SERIES

$9921.

151 CID 4 CYL. ENGINE (173 CID V6 AVAIL.)

$10,071.

DIESEL 260 CID V6 ENG. AVAIL. (V8 ALSO, IN LARGER OLDSMOBILES.)

$10,231.

1279

CUTLASS CIERA LS SEDAN

Oldsmobile

CUTLASS SUPREME

108.1" WB

Cutlass Supreme.

CUTLASS CRUISER WAGON INTERIOR

3R47 COUPE $9761.

V.I.N. ENDS WITH — OC — #

DIESEL V6	
36 HwyEst	25 EPA Est.mpg

STANDARD V6	
30 HwyEst	21 EPA Est.mpg

$10,078.

CUTLASS CRUISER

3H35

82

Split-tailgate. Top swings up. Bottom drops down for a loading platform on Cruiser.

CUTLASS CALAIS

(COUPE ONLY)

3K47

231 CID V6 (110 HP)

260 CID V8 (105 HP)

307 CID V8 (155 HP)

263 CID DIESEL V6 OR 350 CID DIESEL V8 (105 HP)

$10,552.

(T-BAR TOP OPT. AT EXTRA COST)

BROUGH. SEDAN INTER.

$10,333.

$10,428.

CUTLASS SUPREME BROUGHAM SEDAN

CUTLASS SUPREME BROUGHAM COUPE

We've had one built for you.

1280

Oldsmobile

25 GALLON FUEL TANK (GAS)
19 MPG (EPA)

INTERIOR

STANDARD V6
28 | **19**

Diesel mileage estimates.

MODELS		Fuel Tank Cap.	Est. Hwy.	Est. Hwy. Range	EPA Est. MPG	Est. Range
Cutlass Supreme	(V6)	19.8	36	712	25	495
Cutlass Supreme	(V8)	19.8	34	673	23	455
Cutlass Cruiser	(V8)	18.2	34	618	23	418
Delta 88	(V8)	26.0	34	884	23	598
Ninety-Eight	(V8)	26.0	33	858	22	572
Custom Cruiser	(V8)	22.0	33	726	22	484
Toronado	(V8)	22.8	36	820	21	478

INTERIOR

82

DELTA 88 ROYALE
$10,456.

$9857. **DELTA 88**

88 DASH

Custom Cruiser facts, figures and features.

CUSTOM CRUISER
WAGON
22 GAL. FUEL TANK
16 MPG (EPA)
$10,867.
(11,082. WITH 3RD SEAT)

REAR-FACING 3RD SEAT OPT.

$13,167.

2.5 GALLON FUEL TANK
18 MPG (EPA)

98 DASH
252 CID V6,
307 CID V8
(150 HP) OR
350 CID DIES. V8

119" WB

NINETY-EIGHT REGENCY

COUPE
$12,990.

Oldsmobile

GRILLE

LS

15.7 GAL. GAS TANK
20/39 MPG

← CUTLASS CIERA LS SEDAN

24 MPG
EPA (4)
19 MPG
EPA (V6)

CUTLASS CIERA ES

AJ19
$10,031.

104.9" WB

$9842.

COUPE AJ27

CUTLASS CIERA DASH

V.I.N. = 1G3A
(IJ19)(E) XD (-) #

$10,524.

"SUPER STOCK" WHEEL DESIGN

4 CYL. ENGINE BY PONTIAC →

83

151 CID EFI 4 (92 HP)
181 CID V6 (110 HP)
263 CID DIESEL V6 (85 HP) 28/43 MPG
(16.4 GAL. FUEL TK. w. DIESEL)

P185/80R x 13 TIRES

BROUGHAM INTERIOR

AM19 CUTLASS CIERA BROUGHAM
(GRILLE LIKE L9)

Cutlass Ciera

Brougham

Oldsmobile Diesel

AVAILABLE w. 19.8 GAL. FUEL TANK
(18.1 GAL. TANK w. GAS ENGINES)

Oldsmobile

CUTLASS SUPREME SEDAN

GR69

BUICK
231 CID
V6
(110 HP)
263 CID
V6 DIESEL
(85 HP)
307 CID V8s
(155 OR 180 HP)
350 CID
DIESEL V8
(105 HP)

$10,354.
10,201.

83

GM47

CUTLASS SUPREME BROUGHAM
(GM69 SEDAN AVAIL. AT 10970)
$10,840.

GR47

CUTLASS SUPREME COUPE

WRAP-OVER TAIL LIGHTS

108.1" WB

P195/75R x 14 TIRES

17/37 MPG (DEPENDING ON TYPE OF ENGINE)

CALAIS INSTRUMENT GROUP

CUTLASS CALAIS

GK47

$10,599.

T-BAR ROOF OPTIONAL

CALAIS HAS SAME OUTSWEPT GRILLE AS CUTL. SUPR. BROUGHAM.

21/30 MPG (V6)   17/24 MPG (V8)   23/35 MPG (DIESEL V8)

CUTLASS CRUISER
$10,632.
GH35

Oldsmobile

18.2 GAL. FUEL TANK (GAS OR DIESEL)

STOW-AWAY COMPARTMENT IN REAR SECTION OF CRUISER ←

BL69

DELTA 88 $10,396.

DELTA 88 DASH

231 CID V6 BUICK-BUILT; 307 CID V8 and DIESEL 350 CID V8 and DIESEL 262½ CID V6 are OLDSMOBILE-BUILT.

DELTA 88 ROYALE BROUGHAM COUPE

BY37
$10,983.

25 GAL. GAS TANK (28 GAL. DIESEL)

83

17/27 MPG (V6, V8) 22/37 MPG (DIESEL V8)

NINETY-EIGHT REGENCY COUPE

IN "98", 252 CID V6 is BUICK-BUILT. 307 CID V8 and 350 CID DIESEL V8 ARE OLDSMOBILE-BUILT.

CRUISE-CONTROL STALK

CX37
$13,793.

16/26 MPG (V8) 22/38 (DIESEL V8)

GRILLE and DASH = 98 REGENCY

22 GAL. FUEL TANK (GAS OR DIES.)

$11,395. UP
(11615. w. 3RD SEAT)

1284

BP35

CUSTOM CRUISER

Oldsmobile

AVAILABLE ELECTRONIC INSTRUMENT PANEL

ON-BOARD COMPUTER CHECKS VARIOUS ENGINE FUNCTIONS CONTINUOUSLY.

AJ19

$10,347. LS

Cutlass Ciera.

AVAIL. 181 CID V6 ENGINE (110 HP)

AM19 CUTLASS CIERA BROUGHAM 4 DR. SEDAN

$10,865. ↗

MPG:
43 HWY., 28 EPA w.
263 CID (85 HP)
V6 DIESEL.
39 HWY., 25 EPA w.
151 CID (92 HP)
4 CYL. GAS ENG.

V.I.N. = 1G3A (C35P) — E — #

84

Cutlass Ciera Holiday Coupe.

new Cutlass Cruiser.

$10,695. ⊛

Introducing the first mid-size, front-wheel-drive Olds wagon ever—the new Cutlass Cruiser.

J35E

$10,910. (WITH 3RD SEAT)

Room for 8

CUTLASS CIERA HAS 104.9" WB

V6 diesel

AVAIL. WITH "TRAVELING PACKAGE" (AM/FM STEREO RADIO, WIRE WHEEL DISCS, POWER DOOR LOCKS and CRUISE CONTROL OR REAR WINDOW DEFOGGER)

CUTLASS CRUISER WAGON IS NOW A PART OF CIERA SERIES.
⊛ BASE PRICE RAISED TO $10945. DURING 1985.

Limited Edition Hurst/Olds

307 CID V8 (180 HP) "MUSCLE CAR!"

There is a special feel in an Oldsmobile

1285

Oldsmobile

$11,271. $10,632. →

W/O VINYL ROOF

Cutlass Supreme

108.1" WB

$11,401.

$11,368.

MPG : 31 HWY, 21 EPA (STD. 231 CID, 110 HP V6) 41 HWY, 25 EPA (AVAIL. 263 CID, 85 HP DIESEL V6)

84

Delta 88

Let's get it together... buckle up.

DELTA 88 LS 4 DR. SED. INT.

$11,816. (BELOW)

AVAIL. 350 CID DIESEL V8 (105 HP)   116" WB
35 HWY, 23 EPA
OR STD. 231 CID V6 (110 HP) OR 307 CID V8

Delta 88 LS

Ninety-Eight Regency. 119" WB

252 CID V6 (125 HP), 307 CID V8 (140 HP), OR 350 CID V8 DIESEL (105 HP)

$15,876.

1286

CALAIS COUPES ONLY, IN FIRST (1985) MODEL YR.

Oldsmobile

CALAIS IS NOW A SEPARATE, SMALLER SERIES, NO LONGER A COUPE IN THE CUTLASS SERIES.

Calais

NF27U COUPE $9824.

SUPREME CPE. $10,239. NT27U

109 MPH

New

4 CYL. OR V6
(151 CID 92 HP) (183 CID 120 HP)

Calais

103.4" WHEELBASE

INDIANAPOLIS 500 PACE CAR

OFFICIAL PACE CAR

(CUSTOM BUILT ONLY)

DASH

13.6 GALLON FUEL TANK

P185/80R x13 TIRES

2.84 GEAR RATIO

CALAIS 500

V.I.N.
1G3 (AJ19E)
— F—#

85

CUTLASS CRUISER WAGON IS A PART OF CUTLASS CIERA SERIES.

OPTIONAL V6

CALAIS INTERIOR

AJ35E
CUTLASS CRUISER $11,337. ↓

CUTLASS CRUISER WAGON

CALAIS REAR

CUTLASS CRUISER   Cutlass Cruiser

There is a special feel in an *Oldsmobile*

1287

Oldsmobile

CIERA DASH

ELECTRONIC DASH

Electronic instrument cluster, available. Offers easy-to-understand digital speedometer, bar graph fuel level and engine temperature gages, low-fuel warning indicator, trip odometer, English/metric conversion switch and turn signal indicators.

CONSOLE

TRUNK-TOP LUGGAGE RACK OPTIONAL

CUTLASS CIERA BROUGHAM COUPE

AM27E
$11,266.

85

(CIERA PRICES START AT $10786. FOR AJ27E "L9" CPE.)
4, V6 OR DIESEL V6

A = DELUXE DISCS; B = WIRE WH. DISCS;
C = SUPER STOCK WHEELS (BODY COLOR);
D = DELUXE STYLED
   DISCS (STD. ON E9);
E = ALUMINUM-STYLED

CUTLASS CIERA HOLIDAY COUPE

ES 4

GT PKG. (BELOW) AVAIL. LATE IN SEASON, ALSO IN 1986 and 1987.

HOLIDAY COUPE INTERIOR

(AVAIL. IN CIERA, new DIGITAL AUTO CALCU-LATOR

COMPUTES M.P.G., DRIVING TIME, OTHER TRIP INFO.)

THERE IS A SPECIAL FEEL IN AN OLDSMOBILE

Cutlass Ciera GT.

Cutlass Ciera GT

CUTLASS SUPREME

Oldsmobile
CUTLASS SUPREME

$10,941. AND UP

BROUGHAM SEDAN $11,746.

COUPES ONLY HAVE THE OUTSWEPT GRILLE.

Rallye gage cluster available. Gages galore help you to stay informed.

85

CUSTOM SPORT STEERING WHEEL

OPT.

NEW

Cutlass 442.

CUTLASS SUPR. BROUGHAM CPE. has SIMILAR FRONT

442 Oldsmobile

4-4-2 HAS A 5.0-LITER V8 →

Delta 88.

CUSTOM CRUISER $12,832.

88 FROM $11,801. (WITH 231 cid V6)

$16,539. 98 REGENCY BROUGHAM

Ninety-Eight Regency

OPT.

V6 diesel

CRUISE CONTROL III

ES

(GT RESEMBLES ES)

1986 V.I.N. = 1G3 (AJ19W)
— G — #

Oldsmobile

NF27U
CALAIS
COUPE
$10,763.

There is a special feel in an Oldsmobile

Olds CALAIS

CALAIS SEDAN
(DETAILS)

4-DOOR CALAIS IS
New

86

NF69U
$10,958.

151 CID 4
(V6 ALSO AVAIL.)

NT27U
CALAIS
SUPREME
COUPE (RT.)

$11,148. →

CALAIS SUPREME COUPE

CALAIS SUPREME
SEDAN
↓$11,343.
NT69U

New

California Calais

LIMITED EDITION (300 CARS)
FOR CALIF.   CUSTOM PAINT,
FUEL-INJECTED V6
CUSTOM AIR SCOOPS, ALLOY WHEELS
(HAS SPECIAL MEDALLION) →

1290

Oldsmobile

CUTLASS CIERAS FROM **$11,927.**
AJ27W (*L* COUPE)

SL COUPE **$12,945.** AM37W

W. CIERA ES PACKAGE →

CUTLASS CIERA

111 MPH

CUTLASS

SED. **$12,036.** GR69A

$12,715.

CUTLASS SUPREME BROUGHAM SEDAN GM69A

CUTLASS SUPREME COUPE AND SEDAN

$11,862. GR47A CPE.

86

DELTA 88 BROUGHAM COUPE WHEEL

CUTLASS SALON AND CUTLASS 442

REAR DETAILS

DELTA 88 ROYALE COUPE

DELTA 88 ROYALE COUPE (HN37L) **$13,235.**

111 MPH

DELTA 88

DELTA ↙88↗

110.8" WB WB

$17,727. CW11B

WHEEL STYLE

NINETY-EIGHT REGENCY BROUGHAM COUPE

ABOVE: HY69L DELTA 88 ROYAL BRGHM. SEDAN **$13936.**

REGENCY
Ninety-Eight

GRILLE ←

BROUGHAM SEDAN **$17,654.** CW69B

1291

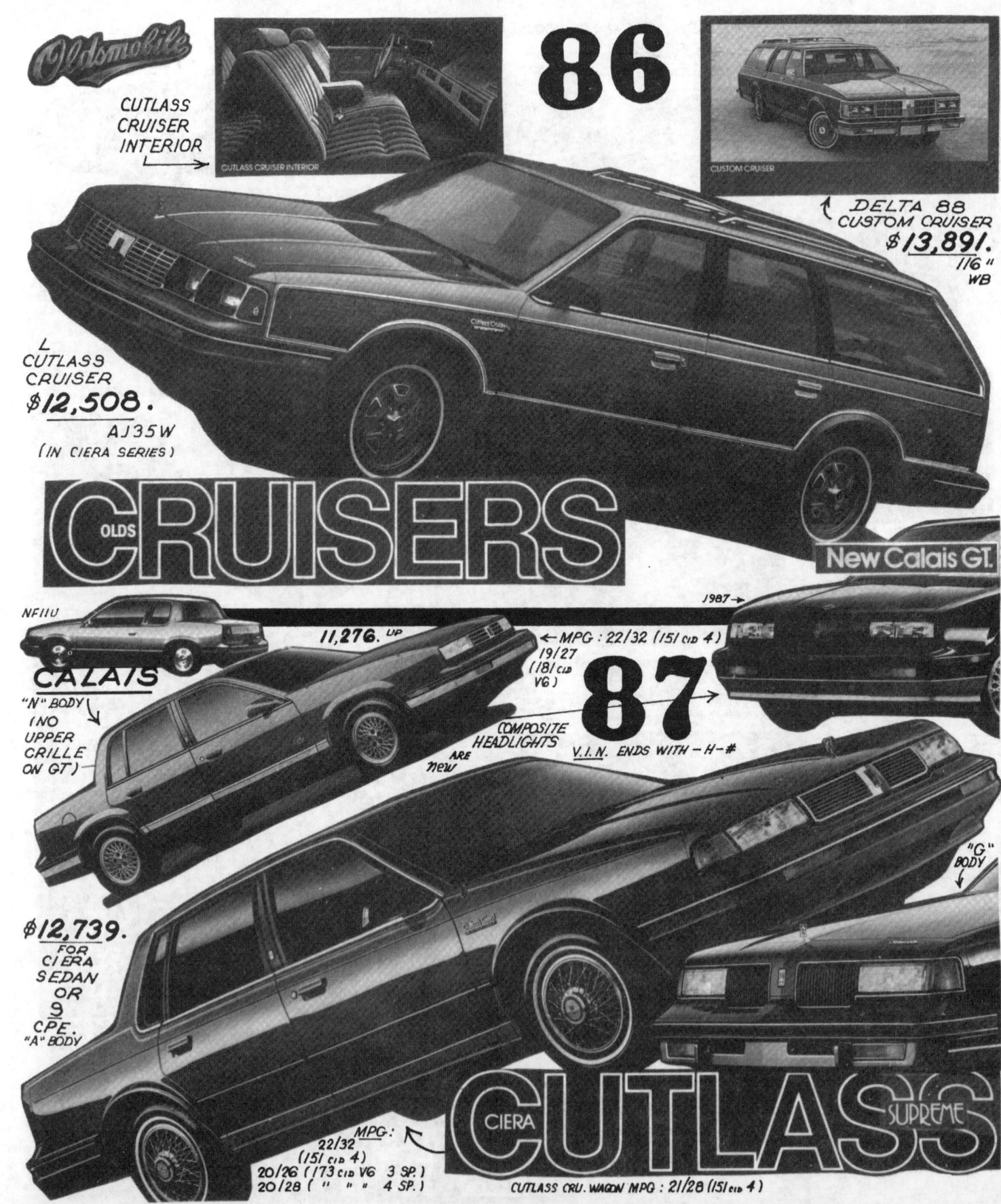

Oldsmobile

86

CUTLASS CRUISER INTERIOR

CUTLASS CRUISER INTERIOR

CUSTOM CRUISER

DELTA 88 CUSTOM CRUISER $13,891.
116" WB

L CUTLASS CRUISER $12,508.
AJ35W
(IN CIERA SERIES)

OLDS CRUISERS

New Calais GT.

NF11U

1987→

CALAIS
"N" BODY
(NO UPPER GRILLE ON GT)

11,276. UP

←MPG: 22/32 (151 CID 4)
19/27 (181 CID V6)

COMPOSITE HEADLIGHTS ARE new

87→

V.I.N. ENDS WITH -H-#

"G" BODY

$12,739.
FOR CIERA SEDAN OR 9 CPE.
"A" BODY

CIERA CUTLASS SUPREME

MPG:
22/32 (151 CID 4)
20/26 (173 CID V6 3 SP.)
20/28 (" " "   4 SP.)

CUTLASS CRU. WAGON MPG: 21/28 (151 CID 4)

Oldsmobile

$11885. *and up* (SED. OR COUPÉ)

CUTLASS CALAIS.

103.4" W.B

4 OR V6 (3.0 L) (2.3 OR 2.5L)

INT'L. COUPE

W. 150 HP "QUAD 4" ENG. (3.0 L V6 AVAIL. ALSO)

CUTLASS CALAIS

NK/ID INT'L. COUPE TOP $14585.

CUTLASS CIERA INTERNATIONAL SERIES

$16995. AS513

CIERA INTERNATIONAL COUPE $16,165. (AS113)

104.9" WB

SYMBOL OF INTERNATIONAL SERIES

CUTLASS CIERA.

OLDSMOBILE QUALITY. FEEL IT.

88

V.I.N. = 1G3 (AJ113) — J — #

$13601. UP (SEDANS)

CIERA has 2.5 L 4 OR 2.8 OR 3.8 L V6.

CIERA SERIES INCLUDES THE CUTLASS CRUISER $14265. AJ813

CUTLASS SUPR. CLASSIC COUPE (GR11Y) $14,368.

BROUGHAM CPE. (GM11Y) 15,200.

5.0 L V8 108.1" WB

AM813

$14940. BROUGHAM CRUISER

GRAINED

UNGRAINED

$16074.

CUTLASS SUPREME CLASSIC.

1294 New

CUTLASS SUPREME INTERNATIONAL COUPE (WR11W)

2.8 L V6 ENG. 107½" WB

OLDSMOBILE

Oldsmobile **DELTA 88**

110.8" WB

MODELS

ROYALE SEDAN	$14,978.
" COUPE	"
ROYALE BROUGH. SEDAN	$15,931.
ROYALE BROUGH. COUPE	"
CUST. CRUISER V8	$16,135.*

DRIVER'S AIRBAG OPTIONAL ON DELTA 88.

88

"The new 3.8 SFI 3800 V6, built at GM's powertrain facility in Flint, Michigan, offers impressive performance. But not at the expense of fuel efficiency."

new
NEW 3.8 SFI 3800 V6 PROVIDES PREMIUM PERFORMANCE FOR DELTA 88, NINETY-EIGHT AND TORONADO!

NINETY-EIGHT REGENCY

Ninety Eight Regency

BELOW:
98 TOURING SEDAN
$24,995. CY5/C

"Seating areas are leather. Front buckets adjust 14 ways—not only for comfort, but also for front, side, and lumbar support."

"During hard braking, brake pressure corrects as conditions require, providing smooth, anti-lock braking power."

CX5/C SEDAN
$19,192.
BRGH. SED.
$20,268.
CW5/C

* CUST. CRUISER WAGON IN DELTA 88 LINE, BUT HAS 116" WB and 5.0L V8.

BP81Y
CUSTOM CRUISER

Limited Edition Touring Sedan

OLDSMOBILE QUALITY. FEEL IT.

Oldsmobile

STD. ENG.
2.5 L
4-CYL.
FUEL-
INJ.
"TECH
IV"
(33 HWY,
23 CITY)

$13,443.
SL NT14U

23/35 MPG
(4)

20/27 MPG
(V6)

16v QUAD 4 DOHC

150
HP

S, SL AVAILABLE
WITH THE
new 3300
V6, OR

16-valve Quad 4 engine

CALAIS
ADVERTISED
SPECIAL PRICES of
$9995.
UP

Cutlass Calais

NK14D
INT'L.
COUPE
$15,310.

S ↗
NF14U $12,294.

(CALAIS SEDANS
ALSO AVAILABLE)

V.I.N.
ENDS
WITH
-K-#
89

(CRUISER WAGON
AJ81W, $15,218;
SL CRUISER
WAGON
AM81N,
$16,645.)

AS51N
INTERNATIONAL SEDAN
$17,245.

Cutlass Ciera

4
CYL.
2.8
OR 3.3 L V6 ENGINES

MODIFIED
GRILLE
↙

new
TAIL-
LIGHTS, REAR
WINDOW

23/30 MPG (4)
20/29 MPG (V6)

The New Generation of
OLDSMOBILE

Oldsmobile

Cutlass Supreme

18/30 MPG

DISC BRAKES

Custom Cutlass Supreme
Limited Edition

Available only in the Western U.S., only for a limited time.
• Front and rear air dams
• Rear spoiler
• Side skirts
• 15" wheels with color-keyed covers
• Special numbered dash plaque
• Many more custom features

89

STD. ENGINE: 173 C.I.D. (2.8 L) V6 (130 HP @ 4500 RPM) 2.33 TO 1 GEAR RATIO

WR14W INTERNATIONAL COUPE $18,065.

WS14W SL COUPE $15,650.

(WH14W COUPE $14,750.)

107½" WB
4-9P. AUTO.
TRANSAXLE
P195/75R14
TIRES *

CUTLASS Supreme

INTERIOR

The New Generation of OLDSMOBILE

AVIS

1297

* WITH EXCEPTIONS

Oldsmobile

19/28 MPG

Eighty-Eight

3800 V6 ENGINE

ROYALE SED. $15,800.

HN51C

ROYALE COUPE HN11C
$15,700.
ROYALE BROUGH.
COUPE HY11C
$16,800.

CHROME GRILLE OF THIS DESIGN ON CUSTOM CRUISER WAGON (V8) BP 81Y
$19,793.

89

new
98 REGENCY GRILLE RESEMBLES TOURING SEDAN GRILLE, BUT CHROMED.

18/28 MPG

CV54C

TOUR. SED. $26,545.

98 REGENCY

CX51C SEDAN $21,566.
CW51C BROUGHAM   22,535.

Ninety-Eight
Touring Sedan

new GRILLE   1298

Oldsmobile **CUTLASS CALAIS**

W. QUAD 4-4-2 PKG.

$11680.
(SAME PRICE FOR STD. NL14U CPE.)

NL 54U
STD. CALAIS SEDAN

151 OR 140 CID 4
(110, 160 OR 180 HP)
AVAIL. 204 CID V6
(160 HP @ 5200 RPM)

90

DASH (INT'L)
w. (COMPACT DISC PLAYER OPTIONAL)

SL COUPE *NT14D*
$14340.

$12680.

20/33 MPG
(VARIES ACCORD. TO TYPE OF POWERTRAIN)

V.I.N. = 1G3(AJ14N)
— L-#

NF54U S SEDAN (SAME PRICE FOR NF14U S CPE.)

13.6 GALLON
FUEL TANK
103.4" WB
P185/75R14
TIRES

NK54A
INTERNATIONAL
SEDAN SL
$15960.

NEW "SILHOUETTE" USED MINIVAN AVAIL.
191 CID V6 $17695.

THESE WHEELS STD. OR OPT. ON VARIOUS
CUTLASS SERIES (DETAILS AT LOWER LEFT)

WHEELS:

1 - ALUM. 16" (CUT. SP. INTL.)
2 - ALUM. 15" (CUTLASS SUPREME)
3 - DLX. 14" DISC " "
4 - ALUM. 14" (CUTLASS CIERA)
5 - SIMULATED WIRE 14" (CIERA, CRUIS.)
6 - DLX. 14" DISC (" , ")
7 - ALUM. 16" (CUTLASS CALAIS INT'L.)
8 - ALUM. 14" (CUTL. CALAIS SL)
9 - " " (" " S)
10 - 5 SPOKE CAST ALUMINUM 14"
   (CUTL. CALAIS S w. QUAD 4 PKG.)
11 - SPT. WHEEL w. STAINLESS STEEL
   TRIM RINGS, 14" (CALAIS S)
12 - DLX. DISC 14" (CUTL. CALAIS)

1299

CUTLASS **CIERA**

Oldsmobile

CIERA DASH, GRILLE

$14,360.
S
CPE.
AJ113

CIERA MPG 23/31 (4) 20/29 (V6)

1.5l CID 4 (110 HP @ 5200 RPM) OR 204 CID V6 (160 HP @ 5200)

CUTLASS **CRUISER**

WAGON (ENTIRE TAILGATE CAN BE SWUNG UP)

FROM $15,360.

21/27 MPG (4)

20/29 MPG (V6)

INTERNATIONAL SERIES DASH

The New Generation of OLDSMOBILE

CUTLASS **SUPREME**

SEDAN

191 CID V6 (135 HP) 140 CID QUAD 4 160 HP (HO 180 HP)

16½ GAL. FUEL TK.

V6 19/32 MPG 22/29 " (4)

WS11W SL CPE. $16,550.

4 DR. **NEW** **90**

107½" WB

SAFETY ROLL BAR

FRONT END DETAILS

New

CUTLASS SUPREME WT14T CONVERTIBLE

w. 135 HP 3.1L V6

1300

CUSTOM CRUISER (w. 5.0 L V8)

Oldsmobile REAR

88 ROYALE

88 ROYALE

88 ROYALE

NEW GRILLE (88 ROYALE)

REMOTE CONTROL KEY RING

18/27 MPG (88 and 98 SERIES)

98 REGENCY DASH

90

98 REG.

98 REGENCY GRILLE CLOSE-UP

88 and 98 have 3800 cc V6 (165 HP @ 4800 RPM) 18-GAL. FUEL TANK

TOURING SEDAN INSTRUMENT PANEL

98 TOURING SEDAN

Oldsmobile

FIRENZA (1982-1988)

NEW 82

101.2" WB
4 CYL.
(112 OR 121 C.I.D)

SX HATCHBACK $9509.

Introducing Firenza.

P175 / 80 R13 TIRES

Firenza SX Hatchback

The newest, smallest Oldsmobile.
Front-wheel drive
A 4-cylinder engine
Oldsmobile Firenza.

INTERIOR

OTHER MODELS
4-DR. SEDAN $8978.
S COUPE 8943.
LX SED. (4 DR.) 9430.

V.I.N.=1G3A C69 GOC (-) 000001 UP

110 CID 4 BLT. BY GM OF BRAZIL!
121 CID 4 BLT. BY CHEVROLET (USA)

SUNROOF OPT.

WHEELS
A-SUPER STOCK
B-SIMULATED WIRE DISC
C-RALLYE
D-DELUXE WHEEL DISC. STD.

25/46 MPG

LX SEDAN

NEW FIRENZA CRUISER

WAGON $8903. ($9256. FOR CRUISER BROUGHAM)

23/43 MPG (WAGON)

PADDED CUSTOM SPT. STEER. WH. and RALLYE INSTRUMENTS STD. on SX CPE.

FROM $8596. ("S" CPE.)

83

INTERIOR

DASH

14 GAL. FUEL TANK

V.I.N. = 1G3A C69 (-) XD (-) 000001 UP

Olds Firenza

SEDAN	$8900.
S COUPE	8813.
LX SEDAN	9248.
SX COUPE	9352.
CRUISER WAGON	9120.
LX CRUIS. "	9468.

84 WITH **GT.** PKG.

V.I.N.
1G3A (C69)
PXE (-)
000001 UP

ES PKG.
INTERIOR

V.I.N.
1G3JC69PXF UP

FROM
$9038.
(S COUPE)

$9352. Cruiser

ES PKG.
$700.
(GT PKG.
$1360.)

85

FROM 9477.('86) 10301.('87)

MPG: 25/31 (122 CID 4)
1987
"J" BODY

COUPE,
SEDAN, S HATCHBACK CPE.

86-87

JC27P COUPE
('86)

1986 EXAMPLES ILLUSTR.

1986 V.I.N. ENDS
with
-G-#
1987 w.
-H-#

FIRENZA
CRUISER
WAGON

"BLACKOUT"
TRIM, 1987

('86)

LC and
FINAL LX MODELS

1987 LC COUPE WHEEL

new
GT (JD77W)
HATCHBACK
COUPE (V6)
$11,254.
$12569. ('87) JD21W
(NO 1988 GT)

JC5II SEDAN
$11075.
(CPE. SAME
PRICE)

REDUCED TO 1 BASIC
SERIES

JC1II
CPE.

V.I.N.= 1G3 (JC1II)
—J-#

RECLINING BUCKET
SEATS
$11775. →
JC811 FIRENZA
CRUISER WAGON

88

new GRILLE
and
new
COMPOSITE
HEADLIGHTS

(DISCONT'D. 1988)

1303

Oldsmobile **Omega**

(1973-1984)

REAR DETAIL

$ 7750. and up

STANDARD L4
Equipped with
Automatic Trans

| 23 | 33 |
EPA Est. | Hwy. Est
mpg |

81
new GRILLE
(STD. / BRGHM.)

V.I.N.= IG3AB37 UP (STD.)
IG3AE37 UP (BROUGH.)

BROUGHAM COUPE
(VINYL-COVERED REAR QTRS.)

$ 8107.

ES-2500

DASH

VARIOUS WHEEL TYPES =

A - POLYCAST
B - WIRE (SIMULATED)
C - DELUXE WITH BODY COLOR
D - RALLYE
E - DELUXE CHROME
F - BRIGHT WHEEL WITH TRIM RING

A B
C D
E F

SX

SPORT OMEGA

sportOmega

105" WHEELBASE

151 CID 4	90 HP
173 CID V6	115 HP
P185/80R13 TIRES	

Front-wheel-dr.

Oldsmobile
We've had one built for you.

OMEGA

14 GALLON FUEL TANK

Standard 4-Cyl. Engine
41 | **26**
Hwy. Est | EPA Est. mpg

OMEGA

4-DR.
$9000.

2-DR.
$8814.

SEDAN
("ES")
$10,338.

V.I.N. =
1G3AB37ROC UP (STD.)
1GAE37RXOC UP (BR.)

(BLACKED-
OUT SIDE-
PILLARS)
ON ES)

"ES" HAS OWN GRILLE

82

("ES" PKG.
PART OF
BROUGHAM SER.)

A B C

BROUGHAM
SEDAN
DETAIL

To you we present
OMEGA ES

"VISTA VENT"

OMEGA
BROUGHAM
SEDAN

OPT. SUNROOF
$9317.

$9148.

OMEGA
BROUGHAM
COUPE

1305

Olds Omega

V.I.N. (1983) = IG3AB69 UP (STD.)
IG3AE69 UP (BROUGHAM)

(1984) = IG3AB69ZXE UP (STD.)
IG3AE69ZXE UP (BROUGHAM)

DASH ('83)

PRICED FROM
$8998. ('83)
9159. ('84)

FUEL TANK
14.6 GAL. (4)
15.1 GAL. (V6)

OMEGA COUPE & SEDAN

ES 2800.

$1046. EXTRA FOR '83 "ES" PKG.

SEDAN

151 CID PONTIAC 4 (24/42 MPG) OR 173 CID CHEVROLET V6 (21/34 MPG)

new GRILLES (EXCEPT ES)

83-84

WHEEL STYLES

A   B   C   D

COUPE

(1983 EXAMPLES ILLUSTRATED)

ON 1984 STD./ BROUGHAM, EACH HALF OF GRILLE HAS THIS DESIGN. (1984 "ES" IS LITTLE CHANGED.)

BROUGHAM ('83)

ALL '84s BUT ES have HOOD ORNAMENT.

BROUGHAM

PRICED FROM
$9287. ('83)
9448. ('84)

1984 IS FINAL OMEGA.

Oldsmobile TORONADO

We've had one built for you.

(SINCE 1966)

Have a Toronado built for you. For you alone.

(ALL TORONADOS HAVE FEATURED FRONT-WHEEL-DRIVE, STARTING WITH THEIR VERY FIRST 1966 MODEL.)

$12,995 → ALL 1981 MODELS ARE COUPES.

LONG "TORONADO" NAME ABOVE GRILLE.

EXTRA CONTROLS BUILT INTO ARM REST ↓

DASH

V.I.N. 1G3AZ5740B(-)10000/ UP

"XSC" HAS XSC DESIGNATION ON REAR QUARTER PANEL.

4 WHEEL TYPES
A — STANDARD WHEEL DISC
B — XSC PAINTED DISC
C — LOCKING SIMULATED WIRE DISCS
D — ALUMINUM SPORT WHEEL

← ·AVAILABLE DIESEL V8 ENGINE (5.7-LITER) 350 CID (105 HP)

81

3Z 57 SERIES

AVAIL. LEATHER AND DOESKIN UPHOLST.

114" W.B.
252 CID V6

OR

307 CID V8
(150 HP)

P 205/75R × 15 TIRES
(P225/70R×15 ON "XSC")

15.2 CU. FT. TRUNK IS LINED AND CARPETED.

Oldsmobile TORONADO

V.I.N.
1G3AZ57YOC (-) 000001 UP

3Z 57

252 CID V6 STD.
OR
307 CID V8 (150 HP)

82

OPT.
350 CID
DIESEL V8
(105 HP)

NAME MOVED TO ONE SIDE FOR 1982

$15,125.

TORONADO BROUGHAM

INTERIOR

AM/FM STEREO WITH CASSETTE PLAYER (OPT.)

DIESEL V8	
36 Hwy Est.	21 EPA Est.mpg

EARLY-1980s "AUSTERITY SPEEDOMETER" ONLY REGISTERS TO 85 MPH! (CLOSE VIEW ABOVE)

DASH

Tempmatic air conditioning.

SUNROOF AVAIL.

REMINDER-LIGHT PACKAGE (OPT.)

21.1 GAL. FUEL TANK 16 MPG (EPA) (W. GASOLINE V8 ENG.)

THE OPTIONAL FEATURES ILLUSTRATED ARE ALSO AVAILABLE ON **OTHER** OLDSMOBILES.

FLOURESCENT DIGITAL CLOCK (OPT.)

STANDARD V6	
29 Hwy Est.	17 EPA Est.mpg

CRUISE CONTROL (OPT.)

"XSC" PACKAGE NO LONGER LISTED

Oldsmobile **TORONADO**

V.I.N. = 1G3A 257 YXD (-) 000001 UP

EZ 57
83
NO HOOD ORNAMENT IN 1983

EMBLEM ON HOOD (new).

DASH

"TORONADO" NAME NOW MOVED DOWN, ONTO GRILLE

BUICK-BUILT V6 STD. (252 CID, 125 HP) 17/29 MPG

16/27 MPG (V8)

OLDSMOBILE 307 CID V8 AVAIL. (140 HP) OLDSMOBILE (350 CID, 105 HP DIESEL V8 ALSO AVAIL.) 22/38 MPG

POWER CONTROLS IN DOOR

A   B

A = STD. WHEEL DISC B = AVAIL. WIRE WHEEL DISC WITH LOCK.

15.2 CU. FT. LINED and CARPETED TRUNK

OPTIONAL ELECTRIC SLIDING ASTRO ROOF

$15,827. **BROUGHAM COUPE** →

WITH OPT.

Caliente
PACKAGE

V.I.N. = 1G3AZ57 YXE (-) 000001 UP

new GRILLE. HOOD ORNAMENT RETURNS.

ELECTRONIC SYNTHESIZED VOICE INFORMATION SYSTEM AVAIL., or REMINDER LIGHTS.

84
EZ 57

Let's get it together... buckle up.

$16,832. UP (BROUGHAM has LOWER ROCKER PANEL TRIM, PLUS A SEPARATE RUB STRIP FURTHER UP.)

There is a special feel in an *Oldsmobile*

INTERIOR

1309

Oldsmobile TORONADO

110 MPH

SHOWN WITH OPT. **CALIENTE** PACKAGE (WITH HEAVY BRIGHTWK. UPPER BORDER OF GRILLE, PADDED TOP, ETC.)

new
LOWER SIDE TRIM

EZ57Y

85

GRILLE MODIFIED

ELECTRONIC VOICE INFORMATION SYSTEM STILL OPTIONAL

There is a special feel in an *Oldsmobile*

BROUGHAM COUPE

$ 17,353.

V.I.N.=1G3 - EZ57YXFX000001 UP

FINAL 114"-WB MODEL

ELECTRONIC INSTRUMENT PANEL

V.I.N.=1G3 EZ57B - G - #

CLOSE DETAIL OF NEW BUILT-ON SIDE MIRROR

GM

INTERIOR

"20TH ANNIVERSARY PACKAGE" OPTIONAL

EZ57B

86

TOTALLY RESTYLED AND DOWNSIZED

new 108" WB

BUICK-BASED 231 CID V6 (140 HP @ 4400 RPM) 4 SP. AT 2.97 GEAR RATIO

P215/ 60R15 TIRES

BROUGHAM COUPE

$ 19,918.

new FRONT PROFILE DETAIL

CONCEALED HEADLIGHTS RETURN

18 GAL. FUEL TANK

There is a special feel in an *Oldsmobile*

1310

V.I.N. ENDS WITH —H—#

Oldsmobile
Oldsmobile Quality. Feel it.

TORONADO
"E" BODY

EZ113

87

DETAILS of CONCEALED
HEADLTS., CORNER LTS.

BROUGHAM
$20438.

TROFÉO
$22433.

New

INTRODUCING TORONADO TROFÉO.

EZ11C COUPE
$21,363.

STD. TORONADO WHEEL
(NOT AVAIL. ON TROFEO)

88

TEVES ELECTRONIC
ANTI-LOCK BRAKING
SYSTEM OPTIONAL

new 3.8-LITRE
SFI 3800
V6 ENGINE

OLDSMOBILE QUALITY
FEEL IT

REAR DETAILS

Toronado
Troféo

EV11C TROFEO $23220.   V.I.N. ENDS WITH —J—#

The New Generation of
OLDSMOBILE

TROFÉO

89

V.I.N. = 1G3
EV (or EZ) 11C—K—#

WHEEL
DETAIL
215/60R15
TIRES

EZ11C
COUPE $23,132.

EV11C
TROFEO $25,545.

19/28 MPG

note MINUTE VARIATIONS IN 1987~1989
LOWER LTS.

Oldsmobile TORONADO

INTERIOR, WITH OPTIONAL CELLULAR TELEPHONE.

CD PLAYER AVAIL.

90

LONGER BODY

108" WB

18 GAL. FUEL TANK 17/26 MPG

3.8L 231 CID (3800) V6 ENG. has 165 HP @ 5200 RPM

TORONADO new 215/60R 16 TIRES

VISUAL INFO. CENTER (OPT.)

$25545. TROFEO EV14C

V.I.N. ENDS WITH — L — #

EZ14C $23284. (STD. TORONADO)

1312

PLYMOUTH and NEW RELIANT-K

99.6" WHEELBASE
4 CYLS. (135 OR 156 CID)

K59 SE WAGON $8736.

$5880* is the surprising price of the base model Reliant K Coupe.

($7552., WEST COAST)

FRONT-WHEEL-DRIVE PLYMOUTH RELIANT-K AMERICA'S HIGHEST GASOLINE MILEAGE SIX-PASSENGER CAR.

FRONT-WHEEL-DRIVE AND HIGH MILEAGE

STD., CUSTOM, and "SE" MODELS, TO $8736.

25 CITY **41** HWY

(CUSTOM WAGON K49 $8203.)

V.I.N. = IP3B ( ) (-)OB (-) 000001 UP

SEDAN

81 RELIANT IS **new**

4-DRS. $100. MORE THAN CPES.

The Chrysler 2.2 litre "Trans 4" with Electronic Fuel Control. A significant step forward in automotive engineering.

SIMILAR TO new DODGE ARIES K-CAR.

SLOGAN: "THE AMERICAN WAY TO BEAT THE PUMP."

P175/75 R13 TIRES

$6865.

($8610. R27 GRAN FURY IS AVAIL. = SEE 1982 PAGE)

STD. DASH   W. 2-SPOKE STEER. WH.

PLYMOUTH

P26 **RELIANT FOUR-DOOR**

$7831.

Reliant's standard instrument panel and two spoke luxury steer.

front-wheel-drive

41 EST HWY 26 EPA EST MPG

RELIANT CUSTOM 2-DR.

P41

CUSTOM $8520.

RELIANT TWO-DOOR

COUPE

AVAIL. CONSOLE SHIFT

WITH CABRIOLET ROOF OPT.

13 GAL. FUEL TANK
26 MPG (EPA)

P49 CUSTOM $8956.

RELIANT WAGONS

SE (GRAINED) $9528.

40 EST HWY 26 EPA EST MPG

P59

V.I.N. = (P3B ( )
(-) OC (-) 00000I UP

GRAN FURY REAR

B26 **GRAN FURY**

82

(AVAIL. ONLY AS A 4-DR.)

WT. LIGHTENED TO 3364 LBS. FOR 1982. $8880.

SIDE DETAILS

Premium Turbine Wheel Covers.

9:28 Chronometer

Electronic Digital Clock.

Tilt Steering Column.

WB SHORTENED FROM 118½ TO 112.7"

Rear Window Defroster.

18 GAL. FUEL TANK
18 MPG (EPA)

225 CID 6 (90 HP) OR
318 CID V8 (140 HP)

246

1982 PLYMOUTH ... THE AMERICAN WAY TO GET YOUR MONEY'S WORTH.

IP3B   P49   CUSTOM WAGON
$9391.
(REG. PRICE)

Plymouth Reliant Wagon $7,636* 41 est. hwy. 28 EPA est MPG*

(P59 SE WAGON = $9727.)

RELIANT S.E. WAGON $8,756*
(equipped as shown)

New

83

GRAN FURY
18 MPG (6)
16 MPG (V8)
EPA AVERAGES

Plymouth Scamp GT $7,255* 47 est. hwy. 28 EPA est MPG*

Plymouth Reliant K Sedan $6,718*
41 est. hwy. 29 EPA est MPG*

V.I.N. =
IP3B (M18B)
—D—#

Introducing the SCAMP

Reliant   STD., CUSTOM (WAGON) OR SE SERIES

GRAN FURY ENGINES =
225 CID 6 (90 HP)
OR 318 CID V8
(140 HP)

GRAN FURY
B26 4-DR.
$9449.

P195/75R15 TIRES

PICKUP CAR (ABOVE)
LISTED ONLY FOR
1983 MODEL YR.
M44 — $7517.
M64 GT—8006.
104.2" WB
135 CID 4
P175/75R13 TIRES
(P195/60R14 = GT)

P21C COUPE
$8743.
P41C SE COUPE
$9256.

5/50 Plymouth Reliant K. Match it! (If you can.)

P49C CUSTOM WAGON
$9529.

P59C SE WAGON $9769.

29/41 EPA MPG

84

V.I.N. = IP3B (P26)
· CXE — #

112" WB

RELIANT K

NEW

GRILLE WITH CENTER
CHRYSLER CORP.
PENTASTAR
MEDALLION

NEW

Plymouth Voyager
135 OR 156 CID 4
(99 OR 101 HP)

The Magic Wagon

$10252.
UP (STD., SE OR LE)

P46C SE SED.
$9382.
5/50   (GRAN FURY = $10447.)

A five-year or 50,000-mile Protection Plan.

P26C SEDAN
$8855.

24/37 MPG, EPA

Plymouth-the best built, best backed American cars-

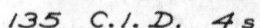

P42D RELIANT
LE WAGON
$10,607.

P39D
RELIANT SE
WAGON
$10,476.

PLYMOUTH

PLYMOUTH RELIANT

SE WAGON INTERIOR

LE

86

(NO WAGON
IN STD.
SERIES)

GRAINED BODY
PANELS STD. ON
LE WAGON, BUT
COULD BE DEDUCTED
FOR CREDIT.

CARAVELLE
Options → WIRE
WHEEL COVER W.
LOCK

Caravelle

68.0"

53.1"

103.3"
187.2"

57.6"

57.2"

*Including optional bumper guards

A/C   RECIRC   TEMP
HI   PANEL   BI-LEV   FLOOR

AIR COND.

1986 MODELS INCLUDE
THE NEW, MANDATORY
HIGH 3RD BRAKE LT. AT REAR.

CARAVELLE...
J36D SEDAN
$10,424.

GRAN FURY
B26P SALON SED.
$11,385.

MPG:
16/27 (318 CID V8)*

VERY FEW
CHANGES IN
GRAN FURY
(DURING THE 1982
-1989 ERA.)

MPG: 22/27 (152 CID
4)*

*1987
FIGURE
(EPA)

PLYMOUTH

114 MPH (SUNDANCE TURBO)

541D

4 OR TURBO 4

546D
"P" BODY

New **SUNDANCE**

← 97" WB

REAR DETAILS

"E" BODY **CARAVELLE**

$11021.
and up

100.4" WB ON WAGON; 100.3" ON OTHER RELIANTS

MPG: 23/28 (135 CID 4) SUNDANCE OR RELIANT

Reliant $10,769.
P39D LE WAGON ↓

LE WAGON WITH GRAINED TRIM OPT. →

RELIANT LE INTERIOR

87
New
119" WB GRAND VOYAGER WAGON ADDED TO " LINE. (98 MPH) $14203.

COUPE $9204.

$9404.

J36D SE = J46D

RELIANT LE ↗

P36D

CARAVELLE DASH

$11922.

"THE PRIDE IS BACK."

K BODY 10325.

7/70 (LIMITED WARRANTY)

"M" BODY **GRAN FURY** 826P

NEW STEER. WHEEL

SUNDANCE DASH

88

SUNROOF OPT. ↓

Sundance

LIFTBACK REAR DETAILS

4 OR TURBO 4

541D LIFTBACK COUPE (ILLUSTR.) $9652.

PLYMOUTH

BUCKET SEATS (SUNDANCE)

SUNDANCE (CONT'D.)

$9852. S46D SED.

SUNDANCE INT.

SUNDANCE DASH

America

$10282

LE

$9888. UP
RELIANT LE INTERIOR

Plymouth Reliant America
$6995

SPECIAL PRICE =
88

GRAN FURY STEREO and INTERIOR

note "V6" EMBLEM JUST BEHIND HDLTS. OF GRAND VOYAGER MITSUBISHI V6 ENG. STD. IN GRAND VOYAGER LE.

Grand Voyager, like all Voyagers, is designed for easy garageability and handling

1988½ GRAN FURY has DRIVER'S AIRBAG.

Voyager

Gran Fury

B16P SEDAN = $12622.
B26P SALON " = 12766.

PLYMOUTH
SATISFY THE CUSTOMER

1989 PLYMOUTH SUNDANCE

4 CYL.
OR
TURBO 4

BASE M.S.R.P.	$8,395*
OPTION PACKAGE	+$791
	$9,186

(P28D LIFTBACK SED. REG. $10250.)

P24D LIFTBACK CPE. REG. $10050.

SUNROOF AVAIL.

Full instrumentation

"RS" PACKAGE OPTIONAL

5-speed overdrive

19/34 MPG

Sundance RS interior

PLYMOUTH SUNDANCE. STARTING AT $8,395.

4.9%† A.P.R. OR **$600** FACTORY CASH BACK

89

FINAL YEAR FOR RELIANT AND GRAN FURY.

18/23 MPG (V6)
18/28 MPG (4)

*112" OR 119" WB

PLYMOUTH ACCLAIM LX. $14,395. (6)   A76U

A46K ACCLAIM = $11,656.
A56K   "   LE = 13,031.
(19/34 MPG)

NEW

103.3" WB
4, TURBO 4, OR 6

PLYMOUTH VOYAGER. $13,095. UP

1320

SUNDANCE DASH

$10585 COUPE — (RELIANT DISCONT'D.) SUNDANCE $10785. SEDAN

93, 100 OR 150 HP.

PLYMOUTH
SATISFY THE CUSTOMER

XP28D

Sundance

135 OR 153 CID 4 OR 4 TURBO

20/32 MPG (EPA)

LASER WITH 92, 135 OR 190 HP. (107 OR 122 CID 4 OR TRB 4)

4-CYL. LASER ENGINE

THE NEW 1990 PLYMOUTH LASER

AVAIL. WHEEL

LASERS
LIFTBACK CS34T $11309.
RS LIFTBK. CS44T $12354.
RS TURBO $14359. CS44J

LASER IS MADE IN JAPAN BY MITSUBISHI

90

LASER has 15.9 GAL. TANK, 97.2" WB 22/32 MPG (EPA)

LASER DASH

IN CHRYSLER LINE FROM 1984 TO 1986 LASER RETURNS IN 1990 PLYMOUTH LINE.

ACCLAIM LX DASH

GRAND VOYAGER w. LONG 119" WB

VOYAGER 2WD
18/28 MPG EPA (4)
18/24 MPG EPA (V6)

UNEXPECTED PRICE:
The new Plymouth Laser.
$10,397 starting price.

PERFORMANCE:
Plymouth Laser RS Turbo.
16-valve intercooled turbo.
190 horsepower.
0-60 in 6.6 seconds.
$13,394 as shown.

(4-DR. ONLY)

ACCLAIM STD.= $12,318.
LE = 13,626.
(4 CYL., TURBO 4, OR V6)
LX= $15,064. (V6)

SE (K413) $15536.
LE (K513) 16862. (ILLUSTR.)
112" WB VOYAGER (4 OR V6)
AVAIL., FROM $13095.

21/32 MPG (EPA)

1321

The New Chrysler Corporation.
Plymouth

SAPORO (MADE IN JAPAN)

BUILT BY MITSUBISHI — IMPORTED ONLY FOR PLYMOUTH

(1978 – 1983)

MPG:
30 HWY,
20 EPA
EST.

156 CID
4 CYL.
105 HP
P195/70
R14 TIRES

D - 43

81

LUX COUPE
$7249.

(NO OTHER BODY TYPE AVAIL.)

99" WB

DASH →

V.I.N.=3P3BD437
(-) B 10000I UP
5 SP. TRANS.

Sapporo. From Mitsubishi, Master Car Builders of Japan.

82

V.I.N.=JP3BD437
(-) C (-) 000001

36 HWY, 24 EPA EST.
(SAME IN 1983,
WITH 34 HWY and
22 EPA EST.
IN
CALIFORNIA.)

HP REDUCED
TO 100, MPG INCREASED

$8036.
UP

V.I.N.=JP3BD437 (-) D (-)
000001 UP

83

note "BLACKOUT"
SIDE-
PILLARS

new OPTIONAL "TECHNICA" ELECTRONIC
INSTR. PANEL and VOICE ALERT
SYSTEM

$8323.

(DODGE "CHALLEN-GER" is SIMILAR.)

MCA-Jet engine, with a third valve in each cylinder

22 MPG
EPA
CALIFORNIA

1322

all new

1981 PONTIAC T1000

2M08

3 DR. $5793.
5 DR. 5939.

PONTIAC (SINCE 1926)

94.3" WB
98 CID
4
70 HP

2M68

155/80R × 13 B TIRES

81

T1000 interior featuring available cloth seating.

Sport wheel and available auto trans

Cargo area with rear seat down.

More PONTIAC to the Gallon

LE MANS $8076.

30 HWY EST 21 EPA EST MPG

2F69

$8540.

GRAND LE MANS

LeM., Gr. Le M. w. 108.1" WB, 231 CID V6 (115HP) 265 or 301 CID V8 (120 or 140 HP) 185/75R × 14 TIRES

$8763.
2F35

Wagon.

PLUS PONTIAC'S NEW EFFICIENCY SYSTEM, INCLUDING GM'S COMPUTER COMMAND CONTROL

PONTIAC'S '81 GRAND LE MANS SAFARI
(195/75R × 14 TIRES)

LE MANS DASH

new TAILLIGHTS

formal

V-6

30 HWY EST 21 EPA EST MPG

1323

108.1" WB
231 CID V6 (115 HP)
265 CID V8 (120 HP)
(AVAIL.= 350 CID DIESEL V8)

$8462.=STD. (2J37) $8841.=LJ (2K37)
$9974.=BROUGHAM (2P37)

29 HWY EST 20 EPA EST MPG

GRAND PRIX

(NEW BROUGHAM REPLACES SJ MODEL)

PONTIAC

GRAND PRIX DASH

GRAND PRIX
V.I.N.= 1G2AJ37AOB (-)
10000/ UP
(ALL PONTIAC V.I.N.s BEGIN WITH 1G2A)

81

(THE FINAL CATALINA)

CATALINA 116" WB
2L69 SED.
$8620.

(2L37 COUPE $8516.)

28 HWY EST 19 EPA EST MPG

V-6 BONNEVILLE 116" WB

$8798. UP

2R37
BONVL. BRGH.
CPE.
$9729.

2L35
SAFARI

↑ $9730.
(NEW AUTO. O.D.
TRANS.; OPT. ON
BONNEVILLE)

BONNEVILLE SAFARI 2N35

↑ GRAND LE MANS

'82 PONTIAC

L68C T1000
5 DR. SED.
$6478.

T1000

12.5 GAL.
FUEL
TANK

26
MPG
(EPA)

T1000's sporty instrument panel and steering wheel.

J-2000 COUPES FROM
$8406.

T-1000 DASH
(ABOVE)

82

L08C CPE.
$6315.

J2000
is
New

101.2"
WB
112 CID
4
85 HP

14 GAL.
FUEL
TK.

P175/
80R 13
TIRES

THE NEW J GENERATION

J
2000
PRICE
RANGE =
$8406.
TO
9306.

J2000
mpg rating

42 HWY.
26 EPA
(OR 30 EPA)

DASH

INTER.

NOW THE EXCITEMENT BEGINS

15.9 GAL.
FUEL TK.
26 MPG
(EPA)

PONTIAC

4 VERTICAL
PCS. IN
EA. ½
OF GRILLE
(NOT
VISIBLE
IN
PICTURE)

6000
DASH

$9803.
UP

104.8"
WB

PONTIAC 6000

NEW

(DESIGNED LIKE
QUALITY IMPORT
CARS,
TO MEET THE IMPORT
COMPETITION)

GRAND PRIX

40 | 25
Hwy. Est. EPA Est. mpg

GRAND PRIX

108.1" WB

23/34 MPG
EPA w.
DIESEL
V8

LJ

82

GRAND PRIX LJ $**9961.**
(K37C)

'82 BONNEVILLE MODEL G

$**9700.**
N69C SEDAN

231 CID V6 (115 HP)

NEW SHORTER
108.1"
WB

N35C
WAGON
$**9867.**

Coming or going, the Model G Wagon looks
impressive.

CATALINA
SERIES IS
DISCONTINUED.

OPT.
350 CID
DIESEL
V8
(105 HP)
(R69C BROUGHAM $10,158.)

18.1 GAL.
FUEL TANK
21 MPG (EPA)
(23/34" w. V8 DIESEL)

BONNEVILLE
REAR

PONTIAC 1000

(3-DR. L08
$6146.
98 CID 4
(70 HP)
94.3" WB

L68
5 DR.
$6349.
97.3" WB

1000 INSTR. PANEL

1000
27 MPG EPA
42 MPG EPA (DIESEL) MANUAL TR.

2000 INSTR. PANEL

2000
101.2" WB

28 MPG EPA

109 CID 4 (85 HP)
122 CID 4 (90 HP)
P175/80R13 TIRES

P195/70R13 ON SE

C27

C67 2000 SUNBIRD CVT.

$12,614. **NEW**

C69
$8708.

2000 LE 4 DR. SEDAN

5-SPEED

83

2000 SE HATCHBACK
$9708. (D77)

G27

6000 LE
$9976.
10,123.
G19

6000 AVAIL. W. EFI 151 CID 4 (90 HP), OR
173 CID V8 (108 HP), H.O. V6,
260 CID V6 DIESEL (85 HP)

P185/80R13 TIRES

6000 STE
$14,711.
H19

6000
(DASH ILLUSTR. ON FOLLOWING PAGE)
104.8" WB

New

105 MPH

P195/70R14 TIRES (STE)

STE SPECIAL TOURING EDITION

1000 DASH

PONTIAC

Pontiac 1000's instrument panel features optically soothing orange lighting and new graphics.

1000 HAS
1.6 L OHC
98 CID 4
65 HP

1000

V.I.N. —
1G2A L08
CXE (-) 00001 UP

84

$6184. 3 DR. L08E
5 DR. L68E $6384.

2000 DASH

All 2000 Sunbirds feature instrument panels with optically soothing orange lighting and distinctive graphics.

$13,069. C67E

TURBO

DOHC

NEW

2000 Sunbird LE Convertible comes equipped with a power vinyl top

2000 SUNBIRD
V.I.N. STARTS w.
1G2ABG690XE (-)
(LE: C690XE)
(TURBO SE: D690XE)

120 HP TURBO 4

2000 SUNBIRD TURBO

114 MPH

1329

2000 SUNBIRD TURBO 10,580.
D69E SED.

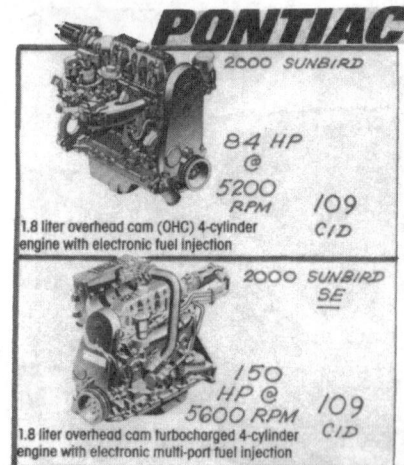

PONTIAC

2000 SUNBIRD

84 HP @ 5200 RPM — 109 CID

1.8 liter overhead cam (OHC) 4-cylinder engine with electronic fuel injection

2000 SUNBIRD SE

150 HP @ 5600 RPM — 109 CID

1.8 liter overhead cam turbocharged 4-cylinder engine with electronic multi-port fuel injection

FIERO FIREBD. PHOENIX 6000 (OPT. IN FIREBIRD SE)

92 HP @ 4400 — 151 CID

2.5 liter 4-cylinder engine with electronic fuel injection

6000 STE PHOENIX S/E FIREBIRD S/E

5400 RPM / 125 OR 130 HP @ 5400 RPM — 173 CID

2.8 liter High Output V-6 engine

G.P. BONNEVL. PARISIENNE

110 HP @ 3800 RPM — 231 CID

3.8 liter V-6 engine

PARISIENNE WAGON (OPT. IN G.P., TRANS AM, BONNEVILLE, FIREBIRD S/E)

150 HP @ 4000 RPM — 305 CID

5.0 liter V-8 engine with 4-bbl.

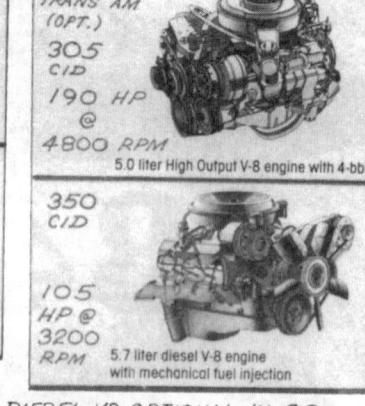

TRANS AM (OPT.)

305 CID — 190 HP @ 4800 RPM

5.0 liter High Output V-8 engine with 4-bbl.

350 CID — 105 HP @ 3200 RPM

5.7 liter diesel V-8 engine with mechanical fuel injection

ENGINES AVAILABLE

DIESEL V8 OPTIONAL IN GP, BONNEVILLE, PARISIENNE

FUEL INJECTION

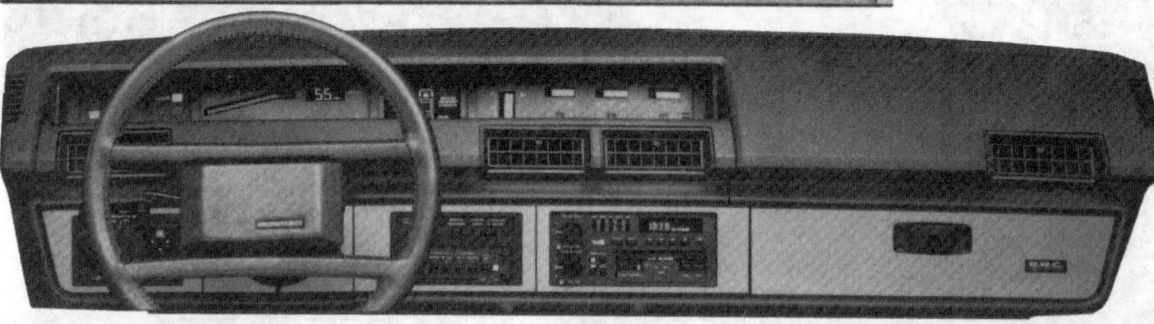

The 6000 STE's new fluorescent instrumentation reveals key operational functions in a manner that's easily seen and understood.

NEW!

A digital speedometer and analog tachometer are new features on the STE's all-electronic instrument panel.

104.9" WB

6000 STE

$14,851.

H19E

INFLATOR MOUNTED IN TRUNK, WORKING OFF AIR PRESSURE SYSTEM, FOR ELECT. RIDE CONTROL (STE)

ON / OFF — INFLATOR

84

$10365. UP

6000 SERIES WAGONS ARE **New**

6000 STE has P195/70R x 14 TIRES (P185/75 x 14 ON OTHER 6000 SERIES MODELS)

STD. 6000 SERIES DASH

New

The STE's new neutral-density taillight includes amber lens turn signals.

The Pontiac 6000's slim, easy-to-read instrument panel is bathed in an optically soothing orange light. A new tachometer and rally gages are available.

PONTIAC 6000

PONTIAC

G27E

6000 LE CPE. $10,286.

84

G19E 6000 LE SED. $10,436.

$10,401. UP (GP)

DASH (GP)

LE REPLACES LJ SERIES $10880.

GRAND PRIX

The new electronic tri-mode cruise control, available on all Grand Prix models has accelerate, resume and tap-up/tap-down features.

108.7 WB

231 CID V6 (110 HP) V8 (150 HP) OR 350 CID DIESEL V8 (105 HP)

195/ 75R x 14 TIRES

BROUGHAM CONTINUES AS TOP OF LINE GRAND PRIX MODEL. $11555.

106 MPH

PARISIENNE L69E SED. $11,198.

T69E BROUGHAM $11,598.

10,387. UP

REAR DETAIL OF BONNEVILLE LE

PARISIENNE

BONNEVILLE

6000

PONTIAC ▼ WE BUILD EXCITEMENT

NEW PONTIAC 6000 SPORT WAGON

F35E

$10,365

SHOWN WITH TAILGATE LOWERED

PONTIAC

Parisienne's available gage package includes a trip odometer, temperature gage and fuel economy gage, all

NEW

PARISIENNE WAGON
$11,711. (8 PASS.)
L35E
225/75 R x 15 TIRES
(205/75 R x 15 on SEDANS)

84

WAGON V.I.N. =
1G2AL35HXE
(-) 000001 UP

115.9" WB
150 HP V8
(350 CID, 105 HP
DIESEL V8 AVAIL.)

PONTIAC SUNBIRD

WAGON $8971. UP

IN 1985, KNOWN AS "SUNBIRD" (INSTEAD OF "SUNBIRD 2000")

$6130. 2 DR. **1000**

$6380. 4 DR.

LE 4-DR. C69F
$9249.

$11,160.

PONTIAC 1000

TAIL-LIGHT DETAIL (4 DR. SEDAN)

D77F 3 DR.
9E TURBO

85

1000 INTERIOR

SUNBIRD TURBO 4 ENGINE

SUNBIRD DASH

D69F
$10,850.

SUNBIRD S/E TURBO

note AIR SLOTS ON HOOD (ARROW)

PONTIAC

GRAND AM MODEL RETURNS

(COUPES ONLY)

LE

AVAILABLE GRAND AM WHEELS

P185/80R13 TIRES

103.4" WB

GRAND AM

New

E27F STD. = $9390.

LE = 9880.

V27F

85

SYS CHK — SYSTEMS OK

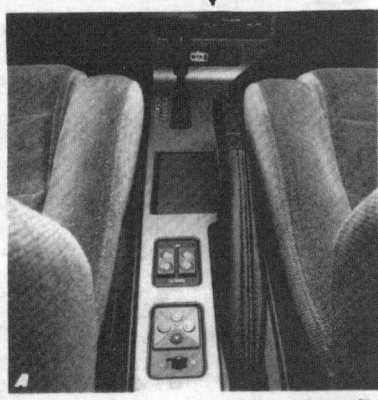

CONSOLE

PONTIAC
AUTOMATIC LIGHT SENSOR
RPM X1000
0 1 2 3 4 5 6 7

0 MPH

F GALS
UNLEADED FUEL ONLY

CLOSER VIEW OF PANEL

WE BUILD EXCITEMENT

ELECTRONIC INSTR. PANEL DETAILS

AM/FM STEREO + CASSETTE CONTROLS

151 CID 4 (92 HP) OR 181 CID V6 (125 HP)

ADVERTISED SPECIAL PRICE $7995. UP
LE = $9158.

PONTIAC

1333

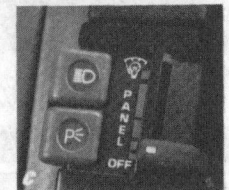

LIGHT SWITCHES (SEE ARROW AT LEFT SIDE OF DASH)

WIPER CONTROLS

PONTIAC 6000

104.8" WB
151 CID 4
(92 HP)
173 CID V6
(112 HP)

P185/75R14 TIRES

With multi-port fuel injection, **(New)**

262 CID DIESEL V8 (85 HP) AVAIL.

F19F SED. $10,223.
F27F COUPE 10,043.
F35F WAGON 10,579.
LE: G19F SED. 10,683.
G27F CPE. 10,529.
G35F WAGON 11,013.

6000 DASH

6000 STE

FUNCTION MONITOR
WASHER FLUID
LOW COOLANT
LOW FUEL

LAMP CHECK
HEAD · HI BEAM
TURN SIGNAL
BRAKE · TAIL
LIGHT

SERVICE REMINDER
CHANGE OIL
OIL FILTER
ROTATE TIRES
TUNE UP
MILES

$15,243. H19F

← GRAND PRIX DASH

6000 STE

112 MPH

P195/70R14 TIRES (STE)

85

GRAND PRIX

108.1" WB
(GP or BNVL.)

231 CID V6 (110 HP)
or 305 CID V8 (150 HP)

G37A $10713. and up
GRAND PRIX, LE and BROUGHAM AVAIL. (GP37A)

GJ37A GK37A (LE)

1985 V.I.N. ENDS WITH -F-#

WITH REAR DETAILS

PARISIENNE

116" WB   L69F SEDAN $11,600. ↓

4 DRS. ONLY

BONNEVILLE

N69F STD., S69F LE, or R69F BROUGHAM

NEW → FENDER SKIRTS (Parisienne)

T69F BROUGHAM $12,330.

L35F PARISIENNE WAGON $12,150.

$10,693. UP

WE BUILD EXCITEMENT

$6684.

$6464.

PONTIAC

TL 68C 5 DR. 1000
97.3" WB

86

V.I.N. =
1G2
(TL08C)
- G - #

1000

TL 08C
3 DR. 1000
94.3" WB

1000 DASH

(3-DR. and 5-DR.
HATCHBACKS ONLY in 1000
LINE.)

JD270 SUNBIRD SE COUPE $9201.

4 DR.
ROOFLINE
(SUNBIRD)

JB350
WAGON
$9611.

SUNBIRD
101.2" WB

STD., SE, new GT
MODELS (LE PKG.
AVAIL.)

TURBO GT CVT.
$15879.
JU67J

JU77J TURBO GT 3-DR.
HATCHBACK
$11299.

1.8 L
OHC 4
(84 HP
@ 5200
RPM)

STD.
ENG.
IN
SUNBIRD

STD. ENG. IN
SUNBIRD GT
110 CID (1.8 L)
OHC
TURBO 4
(150 HP @
5600 RPM)

TURBO GT
FRONT
END

(OPT.
IN OTHER
SUNB.
MODELS.
NOT AVAIL. IN WAGON)

NEW

PONTIAC

$10,229.

GRAND AM

NE69 U STD. 4 DR.,
NE27U " CPE.,
NV69 U LE 4 DR.,
NV27U LE CPE.
3.0 L V6 → OPT.
125 HP @ 4900 RPM)

New
4 DR. GRAND AM

NEW !

GRAND AM SE
CPE. 111 MPH

NW27L 181 CID V6

NW27L 2-DR. **$12,514.**
(NW69L 4 DR., 12,764.)

6000
STD., LE, SE OR STE

LE

GRILLE

TAIL LTS.

WITH T-BAR ROOF OPTION

AVAILABLE 5.0 L V8 (150 TO 170 HP)

GRAND PRIX
$11,423. UP
(STD., LE OR BROUGHAM)

GRILLE →

86

2.8 L V6 (130 TO 140 HP)

6000 STE
AH19W
$16,363.
(FINAL PARISN.)

$13,174.

PARISIENNE
BROUGHAM SEDAN BT69Z

GN69A $ 11,413.
GS69A (LE) 11,693.
GR69A (BROUGHAM) 12,243.

DASH LIKE 1985 GP DASH ILLUSTR.

BONNEVILLE
(FINAL YR. THAT BNVL. USES GM "G" BODY)

BL35H

PARISIENNE WAGON
$13,004.
305 CID V8 (5.0 L)

1336

WE BUILD EXCITEMENT

PONTIAC

GM "T" BODY

1000 DASH ▾

(1987 IS FINAL 1000 MODEL.)

87

1000
TL21C 3 DR. $6699.
TL61C 5 DR. 6839.

SUNBIRD S/E
AVAIL. W. TURBO 4

GM "J" BODY

SUNBIRD $17,029.

JU31M GT CVT.

SUNBIRD
new 122 cid 2.0 L 4
25/31 MPG (96 HP)
SUNBIRDS $9561. UP

SUNBIRD MODELS
STD. OR GT
4 DR. SEDANS;
SE OR GT CPES.;
SE OR GT 3-DR. HTCHBKS.;
SE OR GT CONVERTIBLES (120 MPH, GT)

GRAND AM DASH

GRAND AM AUTOMATIC BELT SYSTEM STD. AFTER JAN., 1987. →

GRAND AM
20/27 MPG
22/32 "

GRAND AM 4 DR. SED.
$11,034. UP
COUPE $10,609.
LE SED. = 11,734.
LE CPE. = 11,534.
SE SED. = 13,944.
SE CPE. = 13,704.
(GM "N" BODY)

PONTIAC 6000
22/32 MPG (151 cid 4)
FROM
$12,298.
(GM "A" BODY)

6000 DASH

WAGON
AE81W SE
$14,238

21/28 MPG

New LARGEST PONTIAC WAGON (FORMERLY PARISIENNE) IS NOW KNOWN AS **SAFARI** (NOT TO BE CONFUSED W. GMC "SAFARI" MINI-VAN.)

$14,434.

new 4.3 L V6 AVAIL. (GP)

PONTIAC

119 MPH

87

BL 81 H (GM "B" BODY) 116" WB 5.0 L V8 (307 CID) 16/24 MPG

GRAND PRIX

GJ11A STD. $12,258.
GK11A (LE) 12,988.
GP11A (BRGM.) 13,708.
(GM "G" BODY)
19/24 MPG (V6)

NEW PONTIAC BONNEVILLE ➝
WE BUILD EXCITEMENT

WITH FRONT-WHEEL DRIVE

3.8 L V6
110-120 MPH

BONNEVILLE TOTALLY RESTYLED

HZ513

USES GM "H" BODY

new 110.8" WB

new AUTOMATIC SAFETY BELT SYSTEM FOR DRIVER AND RT. FRONT PASSENGER STD. ON BONNEVILLE AFTER. NOV., 1986 (AND ON GR. AM AFTER JAN., 1987)

BONNEVILLE LE
$15,341.

AIR CONDITIONING IS STD. EQUIPMENT ON BONNEVILLE.

PONTIAC

GRAND AM = 16/36 MPG WITH 2.5 L 4 and AUTO. TR.

4 DR.
$11,634.
NE51U

NW11M
$14,434.

GRAND AM SE

(SE HAS TURBO 4, POWER DOOR LOCKS, P215/60R14 GOODYEAR EAGLE GT+4 TIRES)

GRAND PRIX

(TOTALLY RESTYLED)
173 CID V6 (130 HP @ 4800 RPM)

WP11W
SE COUPE $15,679.
(ILLUSTRATED)

DASH
WJ11W
COUPE $13,744.

WK11W
LE COUPE $14,444.

RETURN OF THE **LE MANS**
NOW MFD. IN KOREA BY DAEWOO. (REPLACES 1000)

SEDAN
$8215.
TN516

AEROCOUPE TN116
$7615.

(LE MANS IS ONLY FOREIGN-MADE MODEL OF PONTIAC)

BRAND NEW

88

99.2" WB
98 CID 4
(74 HP @ 5200 RPM)
5 SP. TRANS.
(A/T AVAIL.)
13-GAL. FUEL TANK

(SUNBIRD, 6000, BONNEVILLE SERIES AND SAFARI WAGON ALSO AVAIL.)

INTERIOR VIEWS

new 107.6" WB

P215/65R15
GOODYEAR TIRES
(EAGLE GT+4)

MOTOR TREND'S CAR OF THE YEAR

We Build Excitement

PONTIAC

TR51K SE 4 DR.
$**9744**.

99.2" WB **LE MANS**

1.6 L 4 (74 HP)
2.0L 4 (95 HP)

SE

FRONT DETAILS

22/40 MPG

(LOWEST-PRICED MODEL IS TX216
"VALUE LEADER" 2 DR.
AEROCOUPE = $6714.)

STANDARD WHEELS:

$**9464**.

TS 21 K "AERO COUPE" (FASTBACK) LE MANS **GSE** →

New

G9E

89

LeMans' semi-independent rear suspension is simple, sturdy, and leaves a low load floor. The transverse beam "twists" to glide over bumps and through potholes, while the 18 mm stabilizer bar resists body roll.

SUNBIRD

20/36 MPG

SE

JB51K SED.
$11,072.

LE
←

JB11K LE CPE.

$**10,972**.

SUNBIRD LE

JD11K SE CPE.
$**11,222**.

FRONT END OF **GT** CVT. JU31M
$**18,414**.

SUNBIRD GT INTERIOR

PONTIAC

89

2.3 L (150 HP) "QUAD 4" ENGINE GRAND AM →

2.5 L (112 HP) "TECH 4" and 2.0 L (165 HP) TURBO 4 ENGS. ALSO AVAIL. IN G.A. _SE_

GRAND AM

NE 51U
Grand Am LE Sedan

GRAND AM

21/35 MPG

NWIIM SE CPE.
$15,189.

_LE_

103.4" WB
13.6 GAL. GAS TANK

$12,259.

6000 LE WAGON $14994.

6000 SE SEDAN (AE5IW) $16624.

← 6000 →

6000 WAGON MPG: 24/30 (4) 20/29 (V6)

We Build Excitement

WJ14W

$14,354.

GRAND PRIX (STD.)

Grand Prix LE moves out smartly and smoothly with this 2.8L V6 with MFI. The single belt drive never needs maintenance. Check-and-fill points are clearly marked, too.

GRAND PRIX 18/30 MPG

LE INT ← _LE_

The optional Grand Prix Sport Package includes a special front fascia and grilles, fog lamps, red-accented body side moldings, styled steel wheels, Eagle GT tires, Rally gauges, an AM/FM cassette deck, a 60-40 split front seat, and more. The cast aluminum wheels shown, and bucket seats, are also available at extra cost.

$15,304.

WK 14 W

Bonneville LE HX51C

$15,334.

LE

PONTIAC

18/28 MPG

3.8 L "3800 SFI" V6 (165 HP)

$17,704.

BONNEVILLE SERIES

SE HZ51C

SSE

(SSE INTRO. IN 1988 MODEL YR.)

HY51C

Choose the available UT4 Delco sound system and Pontiac reinvents the wheel. Not only are function controls duplicated on the hub, but so are heating and air conditioning adjustments.

A gear-driven balance shaft in the LE's 3800 SFI V6 rotates at crank speed, but in the opposite direction to help eliminate unbalance before it happens. When it comes to engines, there are no "good vibrations."

BONNEVILLE WHEELS

89

STANDARD AND AVAILABLE WHEELS:

BONNEVILLE SSE AND INTERIOR

ANTI-LOCK BRAKES STD. ON SSE

$23,404.

SAFARI INTERIOR

STD. WHEEL COVER (L.) (WIRE OPT.)

WAGON

BL 81 Y (FINAL PONTIAC SAFARI WAG.)

"Understressed" is an understatement for Safari's 5.0L 4-bbl V8 and its 255 lbs-ft of torque. It makes cargo a going proposition.

SAFARI WAGON 17/24 MPG

KEY TO BONNEVILLE WHLS.

(L to R):
Aero-Torque 14" wheel covers on 6"-wide wheels. Standard on LE.
Diamond-Spoke 15" x 6" aluminum sport wheels. Available on LE and SE.
Tri-Port 15" x 6" cast aluminum wheels. Standard on SE.
SSE-Specific Aero-Lite 16" x 7" cast aluminum wheels. Standard on SSE.

1342

$16,164.

LE SEDAN (FRONT END)

22/40 MPG (VARIES WITH POWERTRAIN USED)

PONTIAC
LE MANS
4 CYL.
98 or 121 CID
(1.6 or 2.0 L)
74 or 96 HP

← LE MANS DASH (OTHER GAUGE CHOICES AVAIL., BUT STD. DASHBOARDS SHOWN)
↙ SUNBIRD DASH

TN516

LE MANS LE AEROCOUPE TN116 (ABOVE)

21/36 MPG
SUNBIRD
4 or TURBO 4

SUNBIRD LE CONV'T. ALSO AVAIL. 21/33 MPG

SUNBIRD SE $11230.

JDII K

NEW TRANS SPORT MINIVAN AVAIL. $16300. UP

↑ SUNBIRD LE JB51K

$10825.
($15534., CONV'T.)

NVII U

GRAND AM LE NVII U

$12229.

GRAND AM LE

$12229.
13.6 GAL. FUEL TANK
23/37 MPG (VARIES WITH POWERTRAIN USED)

GRAND AM
3 DIFF. 4 CYL. ENGS. AVAIL.
AEB1W

6000 DASH (OPT. GAUGES ABOVE)

6000 V6 SE

6000 LE
$14064.

$18959. ↑

AEB1W

AG51W
19/31 MPG

GRAND PRIX DASH

90
LIGHT-BAR GRILLE ON G.P. STE →

GRAND PRIX V6
SE

GRAND PRIX LE SEDAN

$15019.

NEW SPOILER REPL. LUGGAGE RACK ON 1990 BONNEVILLE SE →

BONNEVILLE DASH

BONNEVILLE SSE $24499.

19649.

BONNEVILLE
110.8" WB
18/27 MPG
3.8L 231 CID V6
(165 HP @ 5200 RPM)

HZ513

HY513

PONTIAC FIERO *(1984-1988)*

"ENDURAFLEX" FIBERGLASS BODY PANELS ATTACHED TO STEEL FRAME

ALTERNATE WHEEL CHOICES

DISC BRAKES

TRUNK IS IN BACK OF MID → ENGINE CMPT.

93.4" WHEELBASE

MID 4 CYL. ENGINE MOUNTED IN BACK OF FRONT SEAT.

151 CID

2.5 L

POP-UP CONCEALED HEADLIGHTS

Fiero

EMBLEM

NEW 84

V.I.N. = 1G2A
- - -
RXE UP

COUPES ONLY

10.2 GAL. FUEL TANK
MPG : 40 HWY, 26-27 CITY, EPA

E37 — $8431.
M37 SPORT - 9244.
F37 "SE" — $10,344.

INSTR. PANEL →

10.5 MPH

PONTIAC ▽ WE BUILD EXCITEMENT

PONTIAC FIERO

Fiero

SE DASH ('86)

SPORT COUPE $9740. ('85)

PM37R

(ONLY CAR TO USE GM "P" BODY)

SE ('85)

GT IS **NEW** FOR 1985.

GT
125 MPH (1985)
123 " (1986)

Fiero GT

G·T EMBLEM

('85)

PG379

$12,590. ('85)

GT SPOILER REAR ↘

V.I.N.
(1985) 1G2( )-F-#
(1986) 1G2( )-G-#
(1987) 1G2( )-H-#
(1988) (1G or KL)2 ( )-J-#
(INDIVIDUAL BODY MODEL NUMBERS APPEAR IN BLANK PARENTHESES)

85-88 **GT**

(LARGER 12-GAL. FUEL TANKS STD. IN 1987)

OTHER
1985 MODELS = PE37R CPE. $8927.
PM37R SPT. CPE. 9740.
PF37R SE CPE. 10,740.

1986	PE37R CPE.	$9381.
	PM37R SPT. CPE	10,234.
	PF37R SE CPE.	11,380.
	PG979 GT CPE.	13,710.
1987	PE11R CPE.	9231.
	PM11R SPT. CPE.	10,749.
	PF11R SE CPE.	12,049.
	PG119 GT CPE.	14,299.
1988	PE11R CPE. (4)	9809.
	PE119 FORMULA CPE. (V6) (125 MPH)	11,809.
	PG119 GT CPE. (V6)	$14,809.

INTERIOR VIEWS (GT, '85)

V6 ENGINE ('85)

FIERO GT
$14,809. ('88)

WITH 2.8 L V6 HP INCREASED TO 135 FOR 1988.

FINAL 1988 MODEL

An all-new suspension, a whole new feel for the road!

(DISCONTINUED AUG., 1988)

Wide, light, rugged Diamond-Spoke cast aluminum wheels carry meaty 15" Eagle GT+4 radials. The rear rubber is even wider than the front.

5-SP. TRANS. AVAIL. 1987 and 1988

WE BUILD EXCITEMENT

(MECHANICALLY SIMILAR TO CHEVROLET CAMARO)

Pontiac

FIREBIRD (SINCE 1967)

2T87 **ESPRIT** (FINAL YEAR) $8657.

108.2" WB

81

V.I.N. STARTS WITH 1G2A, INCLUDES —OB (-)—

2V87 **FORMULA** $8867.

231 CID V6 (115 HP)

2987 STD. COUPE $8262.

OR 305 CID V8 (301, 265 CID AVAIL.) (120-210 HP)

2W87 **TRANS AM** $9335.↓

INSTRUMENT PANEL

205 OR 225/70R × 15 TIRES

PONTIAC ▼ NOW THE EXCITEMENT REALLY BEGINS

W87 **TRANS AM** $10,906.

82 RESTYLED

new. SHORTER 101" WB

new HATCHBACK BODIES

new 4 CYL. (151 CID) ENG. AVAIL. ALSO.

REAR SPOILER

15 MPG (EPA, CITY)

Bandit

COWL

P205/70R 14 TIRES

1346

FIREBIRD

S87 STD. COUPE
$9692.

PONTIAC
new 151 CID 4 OR
173 CID V6,
305 CID V8

LEATHER
SEATS
(W. VINYL
BOLSTERS)
AVAIL.

New

One grip of the standard Formula steering wheel and you'll feel the excitement of Pontiac's new Trans Am for 1982. (Available Viscount seats shown.)

X87 **S/E →**
$11,196.

24 MPG (EPA)

14 GALLON FUEL TANK

TRANS AM w. OPT. T-BAR ROOF

82

V.I.N. INCLUDES 877 (-) C (-)

TRANS AM

4 CYL 24 MPG (EPA)

W87 **TRANS AM** **$11,942.**

RECARO SEATS AVAIL.
14 GAL. FUEL TANK

DASH

V.I.N. INCLUDES -87 (-) XD (-)-

EFI 151 CID 4 (90 HP)
173 CID V6 (105 HP)
(H.O. V6 AVAIL.)
305 CID V8
(105 HP IN CFI VERSION)

83

REAR

S87 STD. COUPE
$10,225.

X87 S/E COUPE
$11,768.

195/75R14 TIRES
(205/70 R 14, S/E, TA)

V8 15 MPG (EPA)

1347

PONTIAC FIREBIRD

When you're out making night moves, new orange lighted instrument graphics will help you keep track of your Firebird's vital statistics.

This sophisticated 2.8 liter High Output V-6 charges Firebird S/E with 125 eager horses.

(107 OR 125 HP 173 CID V6 ALSO AVAIL.)

WE BUILD EXCITEMENT — S87E) STD.

$10,380. (V6)
($8795.
ADV. PRICE W. 151 CID 4)

S/E X87E
$12,200.

151 CID 4 HAS 92 HP.

84
V.I.N. INCLUDES -87HXE-

195/75 R 14 OR 205/70 R 14 TIRES

W87E
TRANS AM
$12,250.

5.0 L (305 CID) V8 (150 OR 190 HP)

1348

W87 TRANS AM
$12,874.

TRANS AM HAS AVAIL.
P245/50 VR16
UNIDIRECTIONAL
TIRES.

PONTIAC FIREBIRD

987
STD. COUPE
$10,553.

135 MPH
TRANS AM

$12,874.

195/75R14, P205 70R14,
P215/65 R15 TIRES ALSO

85 S/E $12,618.
(X87)

151 CID 4 (88 HP),
173 CID V6,
305 CID V8
(150 HP)
(205 HP w. EFI)

V.I.N.=
1G2
(FS87S)
-F- #

FLOOR CONSOLE

TRANS AM

305 CID V8
(210 HP @ 4400 RPM)

PANEL

INTERIOR (TRANS AM)

WE BUILD EXCITEMENT

FINAL S/E $13,624.
FX87S

STD. COUPE $11,258.
FS872

PONTIAC FIREBIRD

2.5 L "TECH 4" ENG. AVAIL. (88 or 92 HP)

190 HP V8

86 new HIGH-UP 3RD BRAKE LIGHT (see arrow)

ENGINES AVAIL.

2.5 L "TECH 4" (ILLUSTR.)
4 CYL. (88 HP @ 4400 RPM)
2.8 L V6 (130 - 140 HP)
5.0 L V8 (150 - 170 HP)
(ALSO "HO" HIGH OUTPUT VERSIONS OF 5.0 L V8 WITH 190 HP @ 4400 OR 205 @ 4200 RPM)

FW87H

TRANS AM
14,024.

SHOWN WITH OPTIONAL (EXTRA COST) T-BAR ROOF

V.I.N.=1G2 (FS872)-G-#

INTERIOR

2 BASIC MODELS IN 1987. (S/E DISCONTINUED)

87 2.8 L V6 (135 HP)
5.0 L V8 (205 HP)
OR Corvette
5.7 L V8 (210 HP) (ALL WITH MULTI-PORT FUEL INJECTION)

FS21S   STD. CPE.
$12,038.

FW21H TRANS AM
$14,938.
(145-MPH GTA PKG. AVAIL.; ALSO 305 OR 350 CID EFI V8s)

205 HP EFI HI-OUTPUT V8

FORMULA RETURNS AS OPTION PKG.

note "FORMULA 350" ON LOWER EDGE OF DOOR

134 MPH (GM "F" BODY)

V.I.N.=1G2 (FS21S)-H-#

1350

88-90

STD. CPE. (w. 2.8 L V6)   STD. INTERIOR →
$12,798. ('88) FS21S
$13,703. ('89) "
$13,079. ('90)
FS 239

V.I.N. (1988) (1G or KL) 2 (FS21S)-J-#
(1989) (1G2 or KL2)(FS21S)-K-#
(1990)(1G or KL) 2 (FS23S)- L- #

FORMULA $13,798. ('88) FS21E
$14,878. ('89) "

FS23H 15564. ('90)

5.0 L V8 (IN FORMULA, TRANS AM) AVAIL. WITH 170, 190, 215 OR 225 HP.

1989 EXAMPLES SHOWN, UNLESS OTHERWISE INDICATED.

$17464. ('90)

TRANS AM
$15,798. ('88) FW21E
$16,928. ('89) "

STANDARD AND AVAILABLE WHEELS:

(L to R).
Diamond-Spoke 16"x 8" aluminum wheels. Standard on GTA. Available on Trans Am.
Deep-Dish 15" x 7" Hi-Tech Turbo aluminum wheels. Standard on Coupe and Trans Am.
Deep-Dish 16" x 8" Hi-Tech Turbo aluminum wheels. Standard on Formula.

2.8 L V6 ENG. (18/27 MPG EPA, 1990)

(16/26 MPG EPA, 1990 WITH V8)

DISC BRAKE DETAIL

('88)

TRANS AM GTA

$19,713. ('88) FW21F $20,778. ('89)
(w. 5.7 L V8, 225 HP)
$23,759. ('90) FW23J

1351

PONTIAC PHOENIX

(1977—1984)

ENGINEERED WITH FRONT-WHEEL DRIVE
Phoenix offers a choice of L4 or V-6

GM

SUNROOF OPT.

2Y37 COUPE $7714.

BUMPER GUARDS AVAIL.

2Y68 5-DR. SEDAN $7905.

STD. SERIES V.I.N. = 1G2AY3750B (-)10000/ UP

104.9" WB

81

151 CID 4 (90 HP) OR 173 CID V6 (115 HP)

PLUS PONTIAC'S NEW EFFICIENCY SYSTEM, INCLUDING GM'S COMPUTER COMMAND CONTROL
A computer adjusts the air/fuel mixture in the carburetor.

INTERIOR

LJ 2Z68 5-DR. SEDAN $8376.
(2Z37 CPE. 8185.)
LJ V.I.N. = 1G2AZ350B(-)10000/ UP

ALL SEDANS ARE HATCH-BACKS.

MORE PONTIAC PERFORMANCE TO THE GALLON

SEDAN and COUPE WITH $449. "SJ" OPTION = (BLACKED-OUT SIDE-PILLARS, SPECIAL TRIM PKG., ETC.

AVAILABLE

P185/80 R x 13 TIRES

32 HWY. EST. / 22 EPA EST. MPG

1352

PHOENIX: PONTIAC'S 1981 "X" CAR

PONTIAC *PHOENIX*

V.I.N. (STD.) IG2AY37ROC (-)000001 up
(LJ) IG2AZ37ROC " "
(SJ) IG2AT37ROC " "

V6

1982 PHOENIX SJ Pontiac puts some punch into front-wheel drive! A new High Output 2.8 liter V-6 with cold air induction and free-flow exhaust puts some real excitement into your driving! A standard four-on-the-floor keeps you on top of the action.

LJ
$9097.

PADDED REAR QUARTERS

26 MPG (EPA) 14 GAL. FUEL TK.
P185/80R13 TIRES (STD., LJ)

Available luxury notchback seats (standard on Phoenix LJ) add an extra touch of richness that helps make Phoenix as comfortable as it is beautiful.

4 CYL. and V6 AS IN '81

82

Phoenix Hatchback is ready to play when you are!

$8793. (ABOVE)

STD.	Y37C	COUPE	$8585
	Y68C	HATCHBACK	8793
LJ	Z37C	COUPE	9097
	Z68C	HATCHBACK	9279
SJ	T37C	COUPE	10,148
	T68C	HATCHBACK	10,309

DASH

BLACK WINDOW TRIM, 2-TONE PAINT ON SJ →

SJ

SJ
$10,148.

2 VIEWS OF SJ COUPE

SJ DASH and SPORT* STEERING WHEEL
205/70R13 TIRES ON SJ
*FORMULA

High output excitement characterizes this road-ready street machine! With an available rear deck spoiler to complete the SJ Coupe scene!

Slick up your Phoenix with available Delco-GM AM/FM stereo radio and cassette tape, electric rear window defogger and rally gages (standard on Phoenix SJ).

NOW THE EXCITEMENT BEGINS

1353

To personalize your Phoenix, order available rally gages with tach, Delco-GM AM/FM stereo cassette and air conditioning, all operating out of the tracy instrument panel.

151 CID EFI 4 (90 HP) OR 173 CID V6 (115 HP; H.O. 135 HP)

PONTIAC

PHOENIX

Z37 LJ CPE. $9219. (STD., $8672.)

1983 PHOENIX LJ

SJ and WHEEL

83

new GRILLE

SJ CPE. $10,381.

V.I.N. (STD.) 1G2AY37 (-) XD (-) 000001 UP (LJ) 1G2AZ37 (-) XD (-) 000001 UP (SJ) 1G2AT37 " " " "

Z68 LJ HTCHBK. $9428.

27 MPG EPA (4) 22 MPG EPA (V6)

▼ WE BUILD EXCITEMENT

(STD. CPE. FROM $8830.) (LE REPLACES LJ)

FORMULA STEER. WHEEL (OPT.) → LE $9556.

151 CID 4 (92 HP) OR 173 CID V6 (112 OR 130 HP)

new INTERIOR TRIM, SEATS and HEADRESTS

84

FINAL YEAR

V.I.N. FROM = 1G2AY37ZXE (STD.) 1G2AZ37ZE (LE)

1G2AT37ZE (SE)

After dark, the Phoenix instrument panel glows bright with new optically soothing orange lighting.

SE (REPLACES SJ)

2.8 L H.O. V6

(DISCONTINUED AFTER 1984)

INDEX

A

A-100 Sportsman (Dodge). *See* Sportsman
Acclaim (Plymouth), 1320, 1321
Ace, 5
Advanced Eight (Nash), 181
Advanced Six (Nash), 175, 177, 178, 181
Adventurer (De Soto), 403–407
Aero (Willys), 638–640
Aero-Eight (Cole), 65
Aerobus (Checker), 337
Airflow (Chrysler), 61–63
Airflow (DeSoto), 73
Airflyte (Nash), 516, 517
Airman (Franklin), 108
Airstream (Chrysler), 62
Airstream (DeSoto), 73
Airway, 289
Ajax Six (Nash), 174
Allanté (Cadillac), 1114
Allen, 5
Alliance (American Motors), 1075–1077
Allstate (Henry J), 456
Ambassador (American Motors/Rambler)
  1958-1965, 598, 600–605
  1966-1968, 644–648, 667
Ambassador (Nash)
  1927-1939, 177, 180–183
  1940-1957, 513–520
AMCO, 5
American (independent), 5
American (American Motors/Rambler)
  1958-1965, 598–605
  1966-1969, 649, 651, 652
American Bantam, 289
American Motors (AMC). *See also* Rambler
  1966-1980, 644–676
  1981-1988, 1075–1083
  Alliance, 1075–1077
  Ambassador, 598, 600–605, 644–648, 667
  American, 598–605, 649, 651, 652
  AMX, 653, 654
  Classic, 601–605, 655
  Concord, 656, 1078–1079
  Eagle, 1080–1081
  Encore, 1075, 1077
  Gremlin, 657–660
  Hornet, 652, 661–663
  Javelin, 664–666
  Kammback, 1080
  Marlin, 495, 655, 667
  Matador, 668–670
  Metropolitan (import), 510
  Pacer, 671–672
  Rambler, 517, 593–605, 649, 650, 652, 655
  Rebel, 597–599, 655, 673–675
  Renault (import), 1075
  Rogue, 649–651
  Spirit, 676, 1082–1083
American Steamer, 6
AMX (American Motors), 653, 654
Anderson, 6
Apollo (Buick), 699, 700
Apperson, 7
Argonne Four, 7
Aries (Dodge), 1171–1178
Aspen (Dodge), 842–845
Astre (Pontiac), 1048, 1050
Auburn, 8–12, 1069
  Beauty-Six, 8
  SC-852, 12
Austin Four, 13. *See also* American Bantam
Avanti (Studebaker), 619, 620
Aztec, 1069

B

B-44 (Oldsmobile), 525
Balboa, 13
Barracuda (Plymouth), 633, 634, 1014–1018, 1020
Bay State, 13
Bearcat (Stutz), 263
Beauty-Six (Auburn), 8
Beech Plainsman, 289
Beggs, 13
Bel Air (Chevrolet), 344–348, 350, 351, 353, 355, 356, 358, 359
Bell, 14
Belvedere (Plymouth)
  1951-1959, 561–567
  1960-1965, 568, 570–573
  1966-1969, 1000, 1001, 1004
Beretta (Chevrolet), 1133–1135
Bermuda (Edsel), 424
Bermuda (Willys), 640
Biddle, 14
Big Six (Nash), 181
Big Six (Studebaker), 256–258
Birch, 14
Birmingham, 14
Biscayne (Chevrolet), 352, 354–359
Blue Streak (Graham), 114
Bobbi Kar, 289
Bobcat (Mercury), 939, 940
Body Key (chart), 4
Bonneville (Pontiac)
  1957-1965, 584–588, 590–592
  1966-1980, 1026–1031, 1033–1040
  1981-1990, 1324, 1326, 1328, 1330, 1334, 1336, 1338, 1342, 1343
Bour-Davis, 14
Bradley, 1069
Brewster, 15
Brewster-Ford, 15
Bricklin, 1069
Briggs & Stratton, 15
Briscoe, 15. *See also* Earl
Broadmoor (Studebaker), 617
Brooke-Spacke, 15
Brooks Steamer, 15
Brookwood (Chevrolet), 352, 353, 355
Brougham (Cadillac), 1111, 1113
Brougham (Hudson), 121
Bryan Steamer, 16
Buick
  1919-1939, 16–25
  1940-1965, 290–309
  1966-1980, 677–716
  1981-1990, 1084–1105
  Apollo, 699, 700
  Centurion, 683, 685
  Century, 25, 298–301, 697–701, 703–706, 708, 1088–1092, 1097, 1099, 1101, 1104
  Electra, 302–305, 307–309, 677–680, 682–691, 1085, 1086, 1088, 1089, 1091, 1094, 1095, 1097, 1099, 1102, 1103, 1105
  Estate Wagon, 290, 292, 296, 308, 682, 685, 686, 689–691
  Invicta, 302–305, 307

Buick (*cont.*)

Le Sabre, 302–306, 308, 309, 677–681, 683,
684, 686–691, 1085, 1089, 1093, 1095, 1098,
1099, 1102, 1105

Limited, 25, 290, 291, 301

Master 6, 18, 19

Reatta, 1099, 1103, 1105

Regal, 701, 703–705, 708, 1085, 1088, 1089,
1091, 1093, 1097, 1099, 1102, 1104

Riviera, 294, 295, 297, 606, 709–716, 1086,
1088, 1089, 1091, 1094, 1095, 1097, 1103,
1105

Roadmaster, 25, 291–301

Silver Anniversary, 21

Skyhawk, 701, 702, 704, 706, 707, 1087, 1089,
1090, 1092, 1095, 1096, 1099, 1100

Skylark, 297, 298, 310–313, 692–697, 701, 702,
704, 706–708, 1084, 1087, 1089, 1091, 1092,
1095, 1096, 1099–1101, 1104

Somerset, 1093, 1096

Special, 25, 290, 291, 295–301, 310–313

Sport Wagon, 313, 692–695

Standard Six, 18, 19

Super, 290, 292–300

Ultra, 1103

Wildcat, 305, 307–309, 677, 678, 680, 682

Buick Special (*1961-1965*), 310–313

Bush, 25

C

Cadillac

1920-1939, 26–34

1940-1965, 314–336

1966-1980, 717–734

1981-1990, 1106–1126

Allanté, 1114

Brougham, 1111, 1113

Calais, 336, 718, 720, 723, 725

Cimarron, 1115–1117

Coupe de Ville, 318, 323, 325, 725

de Ville, 318, 323, 325, 328, 330, 333, 336, 718,
720–727, 1106–1112

Eldorado, 322–327, 329, 331, 334, 724,
728–733, 1118–1121

Fleetwood, 33, 34, 314–318, 328, 329, 331–334,
336, 717, 719–727, 1106–1112

Seventy-Two, 314

Seville, 327, 329, 331, 734, 1122–1126

Calais (Cadillac), 336, 718, 720, 723, 725

Calais (Oldsmobile), 1277, 1287, 1290, 1292

Caliente (Mercury), 384, 385, 942

Camaro (Chevrolet), 758–767, 1136–1137

Cambridge (Plymouth), 562

Capitol (Chevrolet), 41

Capri (Lincoln), 488–491

Capri (Mercury), 1252–1254

Caprice (Chevrolet)

1966-1980, 747–757

1981-1989, 1127, 1129–1132, 1134

Caravan Wagon (Dodge), 1174

Caravelle (Plymouth), 1316–1318

Cardway, 35

Caribbean (Packard), 552–554

Carolina (Kaiser), 479

Carriole (Nash), 174

Case, 35

Catalina (Pontiac)

1955-1965, 582, 586–588, 590–592

1966-1980, 1025, 1027–1031, 1033–1036, 1039,
1040

1981, 1324

Cavalier (Chevrolet), 1128–1135

Cavalier (Graham), 115

Cavalier (Packard), 552, 553

Celebrity (Chevrolet), 1128–1132, 1134, 1135

Centurion (Buick), 683, 685

Century (Buick)

1937, 25

1954-1958, 298–301

1973-1980, 697–701, 703–706, 708

1982-1990, 1088–1092, 1097, 1099, 1101,
1104

Century (Hupmobile), 131, 132

Challenger (Dodge), 826, 828, 830, 832, 1180

Challenger (Studebaker), 620

Chalmers, 35

Champ (Plymouth), 1165

Champion (Studebaker), 262, 607–612,
614–617

Chandler, 36–38. *See also* Cleveland Six

Chummy, 37

Coach Imperial, 37

Dispatch, 36

Metropolitan, 36, 38

Royal, 36, 38

Special, 38

Standard Six, 38

Charger (Dodge), 846–853, 1181–1184

Checker, 39, 337

Aerobus, 337

Marathon, 337

Cherokee (Jeep), 918–921

Chevelle (Chevrolet), 338, 735–744. *See also*
Malibu (Chevrolet)

Chevette (Chevrolet), 745–746, 1138–1139

Chevrolet

1920-1939, 39–49

1940-1965, 339–359

1966-1980, 735–799

1981-1990, 1127–1147

Bel Air, 344–348, 350, 351, 353, 355, 356, 358,
359

Beretta, 1133–1135

Biscayne, 352, 354–359

Brookwood, 352, 353, 355

Camaro, 758–767, 1136–1137

Capitol, 41

Caprice, 747–757, 1127, 1129–1132, 1134

Cavalier, 1128–1135

Celebrity, 1128–1132, 1134, 1135

Chevelle, 338, 735–744

Chevette, 745–746, 1138–1139

Chevy II, 360–362, 790–799

Citation, 768, 1127–1131

Concours, 797–798

Confederate, 46

Corsica, 1133–1135

Corvair, 386–389, 769–770

Corvette, 350, 390–391, 771–776, 1140–1144

Deluxe, 343–346

Eagle, 47

FB, 39

Fleetline, 341–343, 345, 346

Fleetmaster, 340–342

Geo (distributed by Chevrolet), 1229–1230

Handyman, 347, 349, 350

Impala, 352–359, 747–757, 1127, 1129, 1132

Independence, 46

International, 43

Kingswood, 354

Lumina, 1135

Malibu, 338, 735–744, 1145–1146

Master, 47–49, 339

Monte Carlo, 777–782, 1127, 1130–1132

Monza, 783–785

National, 42

Nomad, 349–355

Nova, 1147

Spectrum, 1147

Sprint, 1147

Standard, 46–48

Styleline, 343, 345, 346

Stylemaster, 341, 342

Superior, 40

Townsman, 347, 349, 350

Universal, 45

Vega, 786–789

Yeoman, 352

Chevy II (Chevrolet)

   1962-1965, 360–362

   1966-1979, 790–799

   Nova, 360–362, 790–799

Chieftain (Pontiac), 580–585

Chrysler. See also Dodge; Jeep; Plymouth

   1924-1939, 50–63

   1940-1965, 363–382

   1966-1980, 800–819

   1981-1990, 1148–1164

   Airflow, 61–63

   Airstream, 62

   Conquest, 1170

   Cordoba, 805, 810–814, 817, 1161–1162

   Crown Imperial, 365, 368–370, 464, 466–470

   Deluxe Eight, 59, 62

   Eagle, 1185–1186

   Eight, 59, 60

   Executive, 1154

   Fifth Avenue, 816, 819, 1149, 1150, 1154, 1155, 1157, 1159, 1160

   Four, 51

   Imperial, 50, 52, 53, 55, 56, 60, 61, 63, 369–371, 464–470, 905–908, 1148, 1163

   K car, 1171

   Laser, 1151, 1155

   Le Baron, 812, 813, 815, 817, 818, 906, 907, 1148–1150, 1152–1156, 1158, 1160

   Model B, 50

   New Yorker, 63, 365, 368, 371–382, 800, 801, 803, 807–813, 816, 819, 1148–1151, 1154–1156, 1158–1160

   Newport, 378–382, 800, 801, 803–804, 806, 808, 809, 811–813, 816, 818, 1148

   Royal, 363, 364

   Royal 6, 63

   Royal 8, 61

   Saratoga, 369, 374–377

Six, 50, 58–62

TC by Maserati (import), 1164

300, 372, 374–377, 379–382, 800, 802–805, 807, 814

Thunderbolt, 364

Town & Country, 365, 367–369, 372, 374, 376–378, 380, 381, 800, 801, 804, 805, 807–809, 815, 818, 1149, 1150, 1152, 1153, 1155, 1157, 1158, 1160

Traveler, 363

Windsor, 363, 364, 368, 370–378

Chummy (Chandler), 37

Cimarron (Cadillac), 1115–1117

Citation (Chevrolet), 768, 1127–1131

Citation (Edsel), 424

CJ (Jeep), 918–921

Classic (American Motors/Rambler), 601–605, 655

Clenet, 1069

Cleveland Six, 64

Climber, 65

Clipper (Packard), 548, 552–555

Club Coupe (Corvair), 387

Club Coupe (Ford), 434

Club Wagon (Ford), 864, 871

Coach Imperial (Chandler), 37

Coats, 65

Cole Aero-Eight, 65

Colony Park (Mercury)

   1957-1964, 503, 505–509

   1966-1980, 931, 933–935, 938

   1981-1990, 1246–1251

Colt (Dodge/Plymouth), 1165–1169

Columbia Six, 66

Comet (independent), 66

Comet (Mercury)

   1960-1965, 383–385

   1966-1976, 941–949

Commander (Studebaker)

   1928-1939, 259–262

   1940-1947, 607–609

   1950-1965, 611–613, 615–618, 620

Commodore (Hudson), 458–460

Commonwealth, 66

Commuter (Mercury), 503, 505–507

Concord (American Motors), 656, 1078–1079

Concord (Plymouth), 561

Concours (Chevrolet), 797–798

Conestoga (Studebaker), 615

Confederate (Chevrolet), 46

Conquest (Dodge/Chrysler), 1170

Continental (independent), 66

Continental (Lincoln)

   1940-1948, 484–486

   1954-1965, 489–494

   1966-1980, 922–930

   1981-1990, 1238–1245

Cord (Auburn Automobile Co.)

   1930-1932, 1936-1937, 67

   1963, 385

Cord (replicar), 385, 1069

Cordoba (Chrysler), 805, 810–814, 817, 1161–1162

Coronado (De Soto), 402

Coronet (Dodge)

   1949-1958, 410, 412–417

   1965, 423

   1966-1969, 820, 822–824

   1970-1976, 827, 828, 830, 832, 834, 835

Corsa (Corvair), 769

Corsair (Edsel), 424, 425

Corsica (Chevrolet), 1133–1135

Corvair (Chevrolet)

   1960-1965, 386–389

   1966-1969, 769–770

   Club Coupe, 387

   Corsa, 769

   Greenbrier, 387, 388

   Lakewood, 387

   Monza, 387–389, 769

Corvette (Chevrolet)

   1953-1965, 350, 390–391

   1966-1980, 771–776

   1981-1990, 1140–1144

   Stingray, 391

Cosmopolitan (Lincoln), 487, 488

Cougar (Mercury)

   1967-1980, 950–956

   1981-1990, 1255–1261

Country Club (Hudson), 126

Country Club (Rambler), 593, 599

Country Sedan (Ford)

   1952-1961, 439, 440, 443–445, 447–449

   1969-1973, 864, 867

Country Squire (Ford)

   1950-1959, 437, 439–442, 445, 447

   1966-1980, 862–866, 868, 869, 871, 872

   1981-1987, 1187, 1188, 1191

Coupe de Ville (Cadillac), 318, 323, 325, 725

Courier, 68

Cranbrook (Plymouth), 562

Crane-Simplex, 68

Crawford, 68

Crestline (Ford), 438, 439, 441

Crestliner (Ford), 437

Crosley, 68, 392–393

Cross-Country (Rambler), 594, 597

Crow-Elkhart, 68

Crown Imperial (Chrysler)

1941, 365

1949-1952, 368–370

1954, 464

1959-1965, 466–470

Crown Victoria (Ford)

1980, 872

1981-1990, 1187, 1188, 1190–1192

Cruiser (Studebaker), 620

Crusader (Graham), 115

Cunningham, 68

Custom (De Soto), 398–401

Custom (Dodge), 408, 409, 418

Custom (Ford), 436

Custom (Imperial), 464, 466, 468

Custom (Lincoln), 489

Custom (Mercury), 501, 502

Custom (Rambler), 593–595, 597–600

Custom (Willys), 640

Custom 8 (Peerless), 221

Custom 300 (Ford), 444–446, 862–865

Custom 500 (Ford), 452

Custom 880 (Dodge), 420–423

Custom Cruiser (Oldsmobile)

1940, 524

1971-1980, 964, 966–969, 971, 973

1981-1990, 1278, 1281, 1284, 1289, 1292, 1295, 1301

Custom Royal (Dodge), 415, 416

Custom Sportsman (Dodge), 821, 823

Customline (Ford), 441, 443

Cutlass (Oldsmobile)

1961-1965, 521–523

1966-1980, 974–987

1981-1990, 1277, 1279, 1280, 1282–1289, 1291, 1292, 1294, 1296, 1297, 1299, 1300

Cyclone (Mercury), 384, 385, 941–943, 945

D

Dagmar, 69

Daniels, 69

Dart (Dodge)

1960-1965, 394–396

1966-1976, 854–860

GT, 396

Phoenix, 394, 395

Pioneer, 394, 395

Seneca, 394, 395

Davis, 69, 397

Daytona (Dodge), 853, 1182–1184

Daytona (Studebaker/Lark), 483, 621

De Soto

1929-1939, 70–74

1940-1961, 397–407

Adventurer, 403–407

Airflow, 73

Airstream, 73

Coronado, 402

Custom, 398–401

Deluxe, 398, 400, 401

Firedome, 401–406

Fireflite, 403–407

Firesweep, 404–406

Model K, 70

Powermaster, 402

Six, 70, 71

Sportsman, 400, 402

Suburban, 399

de Ville (Cadillac)

1949, 318

1954-1959, 323, 325, 328

1960-1965, 330, 333, 336

1967-1980, 718, 720–727

1981-1990, 1106–1112

Del Mar, 397

Delling Steam, 70

Delmont 88 (Oldsmobile), 961, 963

Delta 88 (Oldsmobile). *See* Eighty Eight
   (Oldsmobile) for model years
   1989-1991

1965, 545

1966-1980, 960–973

1981-1988, 1278, 1281, 1284, 1286, 1289, 1291, 1293, 1295

Deluxe (Chevrolet), 343–346

Deluxe (De Soto), 398, 400, 401

Deluxe (Dodge), 408, 409

Deluxe (Falcon), 430

Deluxe (Ford), 105, 432, 433

Deluxe (Plymouth), 231, 556–558, 560

Deluxe (Pontiac), 574

Deluxe (Rambler), 594–596, 598, 600

Deluxe Eight (Chrysler), 59, 62

Deluxe Eight (Packard), 208

Detroit Air-Cooled, 75

Detroit Electric, 75

Detroit Steam, 75

DeVaux, 75

Diana, 75

Dictator (Studebaker), 259–261

Diplomat (Dodge)

1950, 411

1977-1980, 837, 839, 840

1981-1989, 1171, 1173, 1174, 1176–1178

Dispatch (Chandler), 36

Dixie Flyer, 75

Doble Steam, 76

Dodge

1920-1939, 76–85

1940-1965, 408–423

1966-1980, 820–861

1981-1990, 1165–1184

Aries, 1171–1178

Aspen, 842–845

Caravan Wagon, 1174

Challenger, 826, 828, 830, 832, 1180

Charger, 846–853, 1181–1184

Colt, 1165–1169

Conquest, 1170

Coronet, 410, 412–417, 423, 820, 822–824, 827, 828, 830, 832, 834, 835

Custom, 408, 409, 418

Custom 880, 420–423

Custom Royal, 415, 416

Custom Sportsman, 821, 823

Dart, 394–396, 854–860

Daytona, 853, 1182–1184

Deluxe, 408, 409

Diplomat, 411, 837, 839, 840, 1171, 1173, 1174, 1176–1178

Dynasty, 1177–1179

Eight, 81–83

400, 1172

Lancer, 415, 416, 481, 1175–1178

Magnum, 838, 839

Matador, 419

Meadowbrook, 410, 412, 413

Mirada, 841, 1171–1173

Monaco, 423, 821–823, 825, 827, 829, 831, 833, 835, 836, 1179

Omni, 861, 1231–1237

Polara, 419–423, 821–823, 825, 827, 829, 831–833

Royal, 414, 416, 417

St. Regis, 839, 841, 1171

Senior 6, 79, 80

Shadow, 1176–1179

Sierra, 416–418

Silver Challenger, 418

Six, 80–83

Spirit, 1178, 1179

Sportsman, 422, 827, 828, 830, 832, 834, 835, 838

Standard Six, 79

Suburban, 417

Victory Six, 79, 80

Wayfarer, 410–412

Westchester Suburban, 85

Dodge Brothers, 76–81

Dorris, 86

Dort, 86

Driggs, 86

Duesenberg, 87

Duplex (Studebaker), 257

Dupont, 88

Durant, 89

Duster (Plymouth), 1016–1018, 1020–1022, 1024

Dymaxion, 90

Dynamic 88 (Oldsmobile), 538–542, 544, 545

Dynamic Cruiser (Oldsmobile), 526

Dynasty (Dodge), 1177–1179

E

Eagle (independent), 90

Eagle (American Motors), 1080–1081

Eagle (Chevrolet), 47

Eagle (Chrysler), 1185–1186

Earl, 90

Edsel (Ford), 424–426

Bermuda, 424

Citation, 424

Corsair, 424, 425

Pacer, 424

Ranger, 424–426

Roundup, 424

Villager, 424–426

Eight (Chrysler), 59, 60

Eight (Dodge), 81–83

Eight (Packard), 549, 550

880 (Dodge). *See* Custom 880 (Dodge)

Eighty Eight (Oldsmobile). *See also* Dynamic 88 (Oldsmobile); Super 88 (Oldsmobile)

1949-1960, 529–535, 537, 539

1966-1970, 960, 961, 964

1989-1990, 1298, 1301

Elcar, 90

Eldorado (Cadillac)

1953-1963, 322–327, 329, 331, 334

1975-1980, 724, 728–733

1981-1990, 1118–1121

Electra (Buick)

1959-1965, 302–305, 307–309

1966-1980, 677–680, 682–691

1981-1990, 1085, 1086, 1088, 1089, 1091, 1094, 1095, 1097, 1099, 1102, 1103, 1105

Elgin, 91

Encore (American Motors), 1075, 1077

Erskine, 91

Escort (Ford), 1193–1200

Essex, 92–96. *See also* Terraplane

Estate Wagon (Buick)

1940-1951, 290, 292, 296

1964, 308

1970-1980, 682, 685, 686, 689–691

Excalibur, 1069

Executive (Chrysler), 1154

Executive (Packard), 554

Executive (Pontiac), 1027–1030

EXP (Ford), 1200

F

Fairlane (Ford)

1955-1961, 442–446, 448, 449

1962-1965, 427–428

1966-1969, 873–876

Fairmont (Ford), 877, 1201, 1202

Falcon (independent), 97

Falcon (Ford)

1960-1965, 429–431

1966-1970, 878, 879

Deluxe, 430

Futura, 429, 430

Scatback, 431

Sprint, 431

Squire, 430, 431

Falcon-Knight, 97

Fargo, 97

Fascination, 1069

FB (Chevrolet), 39

Ferris, 97

Festiva (Ford), 1203

Fiero (Pontiac), 1344–1345

Fifth Avenue (Chrysler)

1979-1980, 816, 819

1982-1990, 1149, 1150, 1154, 1155, 1157, 1159, 1160

Firebird (Pontiac)

1967-1980, 1055–1062

1981-1990, 1346–1351

Trans Am, 1056–1062, 1330, 1346–1351

Firedome (De Soto), 401–406

Fireflite (De Soto), 403–407

Firenza (Oldsmobile), 992, 1302–1303

Firesweep (De Soto), 404–406

Fleetline (Chevrolet), 341–343, 345, 346

Fleetmaster (Chevrolet), 340–342

Fleetwood (Cadillac)

1937-1939, 33, 34

1940-1949, 314–318

1959-1965, 328, 329, 331–334, 336

1966-1980, 717, 719–727

1981-1990, 1106–1112

Flint, 97–98

Flying Cloud (Reo), 242–246

Ford. *See also* Lincoln; Mercury

1917-1939, 99–105

1940-1965, 432–452

1966-1980, 862–904

1981-1990, 1187–1228

Club Coupe, 434

Club Wagon, 864, 871

Country Sedan, 439, 440, 443–445, 447–449, 864, 867

Country Squire, 437, 439–442, 445, 447, 862–866, 868, 869, 871, 872, 1187, 1188, 1191

Crestline, 438, 439, 441

Crestliner, 437

Crown Victoria, 872, 1187, 1188, 1190–1192

Custom, 436

Custom 300, 444–446, 862–865

Custom 500, 452

Customline, 441, 443

Deluxe, 105, 432, 433

Edsel, 424–426

Escort, 1193–1200

EXP, 1200

Fairlane, 427–428, 442–446, 448, 449, 873–876

Fairmont, 877, 1201, 1202

Ford (*cont.*)

  Falcon, 429–431, 878, 879

  Festiva, 1203

  Fordor, 434, 436

  Galaxie, 446, 448–452, 862, 863, 865–867

  Granada, 880–881, 1204–1205

  LTD, 865–872, 1187–1191

  Mainline, 439–443

  Maverick, 882–884

  Model 40, 103

  Model A, 101–102

  Model B, 103

  Model T, 99–100

  Mustang, 511–512, 885–894, 1206–1212

  Parklane, 443

  Pinto, 895–898

  Probe, 1212–1213

  Ranch Wagon, 439, 440, 442–445, 447, 448,
    450, 452

  Skyliner, 443, 444

  Sportsman, 434

  Squire, 438, 444, 449, 451, 452

  Standard, 105

  Starliner, 448, 449

  Sunliner, 439, 440, 442, 444

  Super Wagon, 870

  Taurus, 1214–1216

  Tempo, 1217–1220

  Thunderbird, 626–629, 1063–1068, 1221–1228

  Torino, 873–876, 899–904

  Tudor, 433, 434, 436

  Victoria, 438

  XL, 864, 865

Fordor (Ford), 434, 436

Four (Chrysler), 51

4-4-2 (Oldsmobile), 523, 974–979

400 (Dodge), 1172

Fox, 105

Franklin, 106–109

  Airman, 108

  Le Baron, 109

  Olympic, 109

Frazer, 453–454. *See also* Kaiser

  Manhattan, 454

  Vagabond, 454

Fury (Plymouth)

  1956-1965, 564–573

  1966-1980, 1000–1003, 1005, 1007, 1008,
    1010–1012

Futura (Falcon), 429, 430

Futurmatic (Oldsmobile), 528

G

Galaxie (Ford), 446, 448–452, 862, 863, 865–867

Gardner, 110–111

Gearless Steam, 111

General Motors. *See* Buick; Cadillac; Chevrolet;
    Oldsmobile; Pontiac

Geo (distributed by Chevrolet), 1229–1230

Geronimo, 111

Gladiator (Jeep), 916

Glenbrook (Paige), 215

Globe, 111

Golden Rocket (Oldsmobile), 536

Gordon Diamond, 455

Graham, 113–115, 455

  Blue Streak, 114

  Cavalier, 115

  Crusader, 115

Graham-Paige, 112–113

Gran Fury (Plymouth), 1314, 1315, 1317, 1319

Granada (Ford), 880–881, 1204–1205

Grand Am (Pontiac)

  1973-1980, 1047–1049, 1051, 1053

  1985-1990, 1333, 1336, 1337, 1339, 1341,
    1343

Grand Le Mans (Pontiac), 1049–1051, 1053, 1054,
    1323

Grand Marquis (Mercury)

  1975-1980, 937, 938

  1981-1990, 1246–1248, 1251

Grand Prix (Pontiac)

  1962-1965, 589, 591, 592

  1966-1980, 1026–1031, 1033–1036,
    1038–1040

  1981-1990, 1324, 1326, 1328, 1331, 1334, 1336,
    1338, 1339, 1341, 1343

Grand Safari (Pontiac), 1037–1040, 1049, 1054

Grand Ville (Pontiac), 1031, 1033, 1035

Grand Voyager (Plymouth), 1321

Grant Six, 116

Gray (Detroit, Michigan), 116

Gray Light Car (Longmont, Colorado), 116

Greenbrier (Corvair), 387, 388

Greenbrier (Rambler), 594

Gregory, 455

Gremlin (American Motors), 657–660

GT (Dart), 396

GTO (Pontiac)

  1964-1965, 624, 625

  1966-1975, 1041–1043, 1045, 1047

H

Halladay, 117

Handley-Knight, 117

Handyman (Chevrolet), 347, 349, 350

Hanson Six, 117

Harris Six, 117

Hawk (Packard), 555

Hawk (Studebaker), 616, 618–620

Haynes, 117–119

H.C.S., 119

Heine-Velox, 119

Henry J, 456

  Allstate, 456

  Vagabond, 456

Hertz, 119

Holiday (Oldsmobile), 533, 535, 538, 542,
    545

Hollywood (Hudson), 460, 462, 463

Holmes, 119

Hoppenstand, 455

Horizon (Plymouth), 1013, 1231–1237

Hornet (American Motors), 652,
    661–663

Hornet (Hudson), 459–463

Hudson. *See also* Essex

  1920-1939, 120–127

  1940-1957, 457–463

  Brougham, 121

  Commodore, 458–460

  Country Club, 126

  Hollywood, 460, 462, 463

  Hornet, 459–463

  Pacemaker, 124, 127, 459

  Speedster, 120

  Super 6, 458, 459

  Wasp, 460–462

Huffman, 127

Hupmobile

  1920-1939, 128–135

  1940-1941, 455

  Century, 131, 132

  Junior Six, 135

  Skylark, 135

  Standard Six, 134

Hurst/Olds (Oldsmobile), 1285

I

Imp, 463

Impala (Chevrolet), 352–359, 747–757, 1127, 1129, 1132

Imperial (Chrysler)
  1925-1938, 50, 52, 53, 55, 56, 60, 61, 63
  1951-1953, 369–371
  1954-1965, 464–470
  1966-1975, 905–908
  1968-1975, 906–908
  1981-1990, 1148, 1163
  Custom, 464, 466, 468
  Le Baron, 465–469

Independence (Chevrolet), 46

Innes, 136

International (Chevrolet), 43

International (International Harvester)
  1939-1965, 471–473
  1966-1980, 909–914
  Scout, 473, 909–914
  Travelall, 471–473, 909–912

Invicta (Buick), 302–305, 307

J

J2000 (Pontiac), 1325

Jackson, 136

Jaeger, 136

Javelin (American Motors), 664–666

Jeep
  1966-1980, 915–921
  Cherokee, 918–921
  CJ, 918–921
  Gladiator, 916
  Jeepster, 915–917
  Wagoneer, 915–921

Jeep (Willys)
  1946-1954, 636–640

Jeepster (Jeep), 915–917

Jeepster (Willys), 637

Jet, 474

Jetstar 88 (Oldsmobile), 544, 545

Jewett, 137–138

Jones Six, 139

Jordan, 139–141

Judkins (Lincoln), 153, 155, 159

Julian, 141

Junior Eight (Locomobile), 163

Junior Six (Hupmobile), 135

K

K car (Chrysler), 1171. *See also* Aries (Dodge); 400 (Dodge); Le Baron (Chrysler, 1981-1988 only); Reliant (Plymouth)

Kaiser. *See also* Frazer; Henry J
  1947-1955, 475–479
  Carolina, 479
  Manhattan, 478, 479
  Traveler, 476, 479
  Virginian, 476

Kammback (American Motors), 1080

Kelsey, 141

Kenworthy, 141

King, 141

King Midget, 480

Kingswood (Chevrolet), 354

Kissel, 142–143

Kleiber, 144

Kline Kar, 144

Kurtis, 480

L

La Salle
  1927-1939, 147–150
  1940, 315

Lafayette (Nash), 183, 513

Lafayette Motors, 144–146

Lakewood (Corvair), 387

Lancer (Dodge), 415, 416, 481, 1175–1178

Land Cruiser (Studebaker), 607, 611–613

Larchmont (Paige), 215

Lark, 482–483

Laser (Chrysler), 1151, 1155

Laser (Plymouth), 1321

Laurentian (Pontiac), 589

Le Baron (Chrysler)
  1968-1971, 906, 907
  1977-1980, 812, 813, 815, 817, 818
  1981-1990, 1148–1150, 1152–1156, 1158, 1160

Le Baron (Franklin), 109

Le Baron (Imperial), 465–469

Le Baron (Lincoln), 155, 161

Le Mans (Pontiac)
  1962-1965, 623–625
  1966-1980, 1041–1051, 1053, 1054
  1981-1990, 1323, 1339, 1340, 1343

Le Sabre (Buick)
  1959-1965, 302–306, 308, 309
  1966-1969, 677–680
  1970-1980, 681, 683, 684, 686–691
  1981-1990, 1085, 1089, 1093, 1095, 1098, 1099, 1102, 1105

Leach, 151

Leon Rubay, 151

Lexington, 151

Liberty, 1069

Liberty Six, 151

Light Eight (Packard), 209

Light Six (Nash), 175, 176

Light Six (Studebaker), 256

Limited (Buick), 25, 290, 291, 301

Lincoln
  1921-1939, 152–161
  1940-1965, 484–494
  1966-1980, 922–930
  1981-1990, 1238–1245
  Capri, 488–491
  Continental, 484–486, 489–494, 922–930, 1238–1245
  Cosmopolitan, 487, 488
  Custom, 489
  Judkins, 153, 155, 159
  Le Baron, 155, 161
  Premiere, 489, 491, 492
  Town Car, 492, 1238–1245
  Zephyr, 160, 161, 484

LN7 (Mercury), 1262

Locomobile, 162–163

Lorraine, 164

LTD (Ford), 865–872, 1187–1191

LTD Crown Victoria (Ford). *See* Crown Victoria (Ford)

Lumina (Chevrolet), 1135

Lynx (Mercury), 1262–1268

M

MacDonald, 170

Magnum (Dodge), 838, 839

Maibohm, 164

Mainline (Ford), 439–443

Malibu (Chevrolet), 338, 735–744, 1145–1146

Manhattan (Frazer), 454

Manhattan (Kaiser), 478, 479

Marathon (Checker), 337

Marauder (Mercury), 933

Marlin (American Motors/Rambler), 495, 655, 667

Marmon, 164–167

Marquette, 168

Marquis (Mercury), 932–938, 1246–1249

Master (Chevrolet), 47–49, 339

Master (Rio), 243

Master 6 (Buick), 18, 19

Master 8 (Peerless), 221

Masterbilt Six, 168

Matador (American Motors), 668–670

Matador (Dodge), 419

Maverick (Ford), 882–884

Maxwell, 169

Mayfair (Packard), 551, 552

McFarlan, 170

Meadowbrook (Dodge), 410, 412, 413

Medalist (Mercury), 502

Mercer, 170

Mercury

   1939, 170

   1940-1965, 496–510

   1966-1980, 931–959

   1981-1990, 1246–1275

   Bobcat, 939, 940

   Caliente, 384, 385, 942

   Capri, 1252–1254

   Colony Park, 503, 505–509, 931, 933–935, 938,
     1246–1251

   Comet, 383–385, 941–949

   Commuter, 503, 505–507

   Cougar, 950–956, 1255–1261

   Custom, 501, 502

   Cyclone, 384, 385, 941–943, 945

   Grand Marquis, 937, 938, 1246–1248, 1251

   LN7, 1262

   Lynx, 1262–1268

   Marauder, 933

   Marquis, 932–938, 1246–1249

   Medalist, 502

   Merkur/Scorpio (import), 1276

   Meteor, 507, 508

   Monarch, 957, 958

   Montclair, 501–503, 505, 506, 509

   Montego, 942–949

   Monterey, 501–503, 505–509, 931, 935

   Park Lane, 504–506, 509, 931, 932

   Premiere, 932

   Sable, 1269–1271

   Sportsman, 497

   Topaz, 1272–1274

   Tracer, 1272–1274

   Turnpike Cruiser, 503

   Voyager, 502, 503

   Zephyr, 959, 1201

Mercury Cars, Inc., 171

Merkur/Scorpio (dist. by Mercury), 1276

Meteor (independent), 171

Meteor (Mercury), 507, 508

Metropolitan (American Motors import), 510

Metropolitan (Chandler), 36, 38

Milburn, 171

Miller, 171

Mirada (Dodge), 841, 1171–1173

Mitchell, 171

Model 40 (Ford), 103

Model A (Ford), 101–102

Model B (Chrysler), 50

Model B (Ford), 103

Model K (DeSoto), 70

Model T (Ford), 99–100

Mohs, 1069

Monaco (Dodge)

   1965, 423

   1966-1969, 821–823, 825

   1970-1977, 827, 829, 831, 833, 835, 836

   1990, 1179

Monarch (Mercury), 957, 958

Monitor, 171

Monroe, 171

Montclair (Mercury), 501–503, 505, 506, 509

Monte Carlo (Chevrolet), 777–782, 1127,
   1130–1132

Montego (Mercury), 942–949

Monterey (Mercury), 501–503, 505–509, 931,
   935

Monza (Chevrolet), 783–785

Monza (Corvair), 387–389, 769

Moon, 172

Moon Motor Car Windsor Eight, 284

Moore, 173

Morriss-London, 173

Mustang (independent), 511

Mustang (Ford)

   1965, 511–512

   1966-1980, 885–894

   1981-1989, 1206–1212

N

Nash. *See also* Rambler

   1919-1939, 173–183

   1940-1957, 513–520

   Advanced Eight, 181

   Advanced Six, 175, 177, 178, 181

   Airflyte, 516, 517

   Ajax Six, 174

   Ambassador, 177, 180–183, 513–520

   Big Six, 181

   Carriole, 174

   Lafayette, 183, 513

   Light Six, 175, 176

   Rambler, 517

   Special 6, 174–178

   Standard Eight, 180

   Standard Six, 177, 178

   Statesman, 517–519

   Super, 515, 516

   Victoria, 174

National (independent), 184

National (Chevrolet), 42

Nelson, 184

New Yorker (Chrysler)

   1939, 63

   1941, 365

   1949-1959, 368, 371–376

   1960-1965, 377–382

   1966-1968, 800, 801, 803

   1971-1980, 807–813, 816, 819

   1981-1989, 1148–1151, 1154–1156, 1158–1160

Newport (Chrysler)

   1961-1965, 378–382

   1966-1969, 800, 801, 803–804

   1971-1980, 806, 808, 809, 811–813, 816, 818

   1981, 1148

Ninety-Eight (98) (Oldsmobile)

   1947-1948, 527, 528

   1950-, 530–535, 538, 541, 543–545

   1966-1980, 960, 962, 963, 965, 966, 968,
     970–973

   1981-1990, 1278, 1281, 1284, 1286, 1289, 1291,
     1293, 1295, 1298, 1301

Noma Six, 184

Nomad (Chevrolet), 349–355

Nova (Chevrolet), 1147

Nova (Chevy II), 360–362, 790–799

O

Oakland, 185–189

Ogren, 190

Olds F-85 (1961-1965), 521–523

Oldsmobile
1920-1939, 190–198
1940-1965, 524–545
1961-1965, 521–523
1966-1980, 960–999
1981-1990, 1277–1312
B-44, 525
Calais, 1277, 1287, 1290, 1292
Custom Cruiser, 524, 964, 966–969, 971, 973, 1278, 1281, 1284, 1289, 1292, 1295, 1301
Cutlass, 521–523, 974–987, 1277, 1279, 1280, 1282–1289, 1291, 1292, 1294, 1296, 1297, 1299, 1300
Delmont 88, 961, 963
Delta 88, 545, 960–973, 1278, 1281, 1284, 1286, 1289, 1291, 1293, 1295
Dynamic 88, 538–542, 544, 545
Dynamic Cruiser, 526
Eighty Eight, 529–535, 537, 539, 960, 961, 964, 1298, 1301
F-85, 521–523
Firenza, 992, 1302–1303
4-4-2, 523, 974–979
Futurmatic, 528
Golden Rocket, 536
Holiday, 533, 535, 538, 542, 545
Hurst/Olds, 1285
Jetstar 88, 544, 545
Ninety-Eight (98), 527, 528, 530–535, 538, 541, 543–545, 960, 962, 963, 965, 966, 968, 970–973, 1278, 1281, 1284, 1286, 1289, 1291, 1293, 1295, 1298, 1301
Omega, 988–990, 1304–1306
Special 60, 524
Special 66, 526
Starfire, 534, 536, 542–545, 960, 991, 992
Super 88, 531–540, 542–544
Toronado, 993–999, 1307–1312
Vista-Cruiser, 523, 974–983
Olympic (Franklin), 109
Omega (Oldsmobile), 988–990, 1304–1306
Omni (Dodge), 861, 1231–1237
1000 (Pontiac), 1327, 1329, 1335, 1337
Overland, 199–201. *See also* Whippet; Willys
Owen Magnetic, 202

P

Pacemaker (Hudson), 124, 127, 459
Pacer (American Motors), 671–672

Pacer (Edsel), 424
Packard
1918-1939, 203–214
1940-1958, 546–555
Caribbean, 552–554
Cavalier, 552, 553
Clipper, 548, 552–555
Deluxe Eight, 208
Eight, 549, 550
Executive, 554
Hawk, 555
Light Eight, 209
Mayfair, 551, 552
Panama, 553
Patrician, 551, 553, 554
Single Six, 203, 204
Standard Eight, 208, 209
Super Eight, 209, 211–214
Twin Six, 203
Paige, 215–217
Glenbrook, 215
Larchmont, 215
Pan, 218
Panama (Packard), 553
Parenti, 218
Parisienne (Pontiac)
1953, 580
1962, 589
1983-1986, 1328, 1330–1332, 1334, 1336
Park Lane (Mercury), 504–506, 509, 931, 932
Parklane (Ford), 443
Parkview (Studebaker), 616, 617
Paterson Six, 218
Patrician (Packard), 551, 553, 554
Peerless, 218–221
Custom 8, 221
Master 8, 221
Pelham (Studebaker), 616
Peters, 222
Phianna, 222
Phoenix (Dart), 394, 395
Phoenix (Pontiac), 1050, 1052, 1054, 1352–1354
Piedmont, 222
Pierce-Arrow, 222–226
Pilot, 226
Pinto (Ford), 895–898
Pioneer (Dart), 394, 395
Plainsman (Willys), 635
Playboy (independent), 555

Playboy (Jordan), 139, 140
Plaza (Plymouth), 563, 565, 566
Plymouth
1929-1939, 227–231
1940-1965, 556–573
1966-1980, 1000–1024
1981-1983, 1313–1322
Acclaim, 1320, 1321
Barracuda, 633, 634, 1014–1018, 1020
Belvedere, 561–568, 570–573, 1000, 1001, 1004
Cambridge, 562
Caravelle, 1316–1318
Champ, 1165
Colt, 1165–1169
Concord, 561
Cranbrook, 562
Deluxe, 231, 556–558, 560
Duster, 1016–1018, 1020–1022, 1024
Fury, 564–573, 1000–1003, 1005, 1007, 1008, 1010–1012
Gran Fury, 1314, 1315, 1317, 1319
Grand Voyager, 1321
Horizon, 1013, 1231–1237
Laser, 1321
Plaza, 563, 565, 566
Reliant, 1313–1319
Road King, 231, 556
Road Runner, 1003–1006, 1008, 1009, 1023, 1024
Sapporo, 1180, 1322
Satellite, 1000–1003, 1006, 1008, 1009, 1011
Savoy, 562–566, 568, 570–572
Scamp, 1017, 1019, 1021, 1315
Sebring, 1006
Special Deluxe, 557–560
Sport Fury, 567, 570–572
Sport Suburban, 565–567, 569, 1004, 1007, 1008, 1010, 1011
Suburban, 559, 564, 566–569
Sundance, 1318–1321
Turismo, 1234–1236
Valiant, 631–634, 1014–1022
Volaré, 1022–1024
Voyager, 1011, 1315, 1318–1320
Polara (Dodge)
1960-1965, 419–423
1966-1973, 821–823, 825, 827, 829, 831–833
Pontiac
1926-1939, 232–238
1940-1954, 574–592

Pontiac (*cont.*)

1966-1980, 1025–1062

1981-1990, 1323–1354

Astre, 1048, 1050

Bonneville, 584–588, 590–592, 1026–1031, 1033–1040, 1324, 1326, 1328, 1330, 1334, 1336, 1338, 1342, 1343

Catalina, 582, 586–588, 590–592, 1025, 1027–1031, 1033–1036, 1039, 1040, 1324

Chieftain, 580–585

Deluxe, 574

Executive, 1027–1030

Fiero, 1344–1345

Firebird, 1055–1062, 1346–1351

Grand Am, 1047–1049, 1051, 1053, 1333, 1336, 1337, 1339, 1341, 1343

Grand Le Mans, 1049–1051, 1053, 1054, 1323

Grand Prix, 589, 591, 592, 1026–1031, 1033–1036, 1038–1040, 1324, 1326, 1328, 1331, 1334, 1336, 1338, 1339, 1341, 1343

Grand Safari, 1037–1040, 1049, 1054

Grand Ville, 1031, 1033, 1035

GTO, 624, 625, 1041–1043, 1045, 1047

J2000, 1325

Laurentian, 589

Le Mans, 623–625, 1041–1051, 1053, 1054, 1323, 1339, 1340, 1343

1000, 1327, 1329, 1335, 1337

Parisienne, 580, 589, 1328, 1330–1332, 1334, 1336

Phoenix, 1050, 1052, 1054, 1352–1354

Safari, 582, 583, 587, 624, 625, 1053, 1324, 1338, 1342

6000, 1327, 1328, 1330, 1331, 1334, 1336, 1337, 1341, 1343

Special, 574

Star Chief, 581, 583–585, 587, 588, 590, 591, 1025

Strato-Chief, 589

Streamliner, 576, 577

Sunbird, 1050–1053, 1332, 1335, 1337, 1340, 1343

Super Chief, 584, 585

T1000, 1323

Tempest, 622–625, 1041, 1042

Torpedo, 574–577

Trans Am, 1056–1062, 1330, 1346–1351

2000, 1327, 1329

2000 Sunbird, 1330

Ventura, 587, 1025, 1028, 1044, 1046, 1047, 1049–1051

Porter, 239

Powermaster (De Soto), 402

Premier, 239

Premiere (Lincoln), 489, 491, 492

Premiere (Mercury), 932

President (Studebaker), 259–262, 607, 608, 615–618

Probe (Ford), 1212–1213

Provincial (Studebaker), 617

Pup, 593

R

Radio Special (Gardner), 110

Rambler. *See also* American Motors

1950, 517

1950-1965, 593–605

1966-1969, 649, 650, 652, 655

Country Club, 593, 599

Cross-Country, 594, 597

Custom, 593–595, 597–600

Deluxe, 594–596, 598, 600

Greenbrier, 594

Super, 594, 596, 597, 599, 600

Ranch Wagon (Ford), 439, 440, 442–445, 447, 448, 450, 452

Ranger (Edsel), 424–426

Rauch & Lang, 240

Reatta (Buick), 1099, 1103, 1105

Rebel (American Motors/Rambler), 597–599, 655, 673–675

Regal (Buick)

1975-1980, 701, 703–705, 708

1981-1990, 1085, 1088, 1089, 1091, 1093, 1097, 1099, 1102, 1104

Reliant (Plymouth), 1313–1319

Renault (American Motors import), 1075

Reo, 240–246

Flying Cloud, 242–246

Master, 243

Royale, 244, 246

Wolverine, 242

Revere, 247

Richelieu, 247

Rickenbacker, 247

Riviera (Buick)

1949-1953, 294, 295, 297

1963-1965, 606

1966-1980, 709–716

1981-1990, 1086, 1088, 1089, 1091, 1094, 1095, 1097, 1103, 1105

Road King (Plymouth), 231, 556

Road Runner (Plymouth), 1003–1006, 1008, 1009, 1023, 1024

Roadmaster (Buick), 25, 291–301

Roamer, 247

Rockne Six, 248

Rogue (American Motors), 649–651

Rollin, 248

Rolls-Royce, 248

Roosevelt, 249

Roundup (Edsel), 424

Royal (Chandler), 36, 38

Royal (Chrysler), 61, 63, 363, 364

Royal (Dodge), 414, 416, 417

Royale (Rio), 244, 246

Rugby, 249

Ruxton, 249

R&V Knight, 240

S

Sable (Mercury), 1269–1271

Safari (Pontiac)

1955-1960, 582, 583, 587

1964-1965, 624, 625

1979, 1053

1981-1990, 1324, 1338, 1342

St. Regis (Dodge), 839, 841, 1171

Sapporo (Plymouth), 1180, 1322

Saratoga (Chrysler), 369, 374–377

Satellite (Plymouth), 1000–1003, 1006, 1008, 1009, 1011

Savoy (Plymouth), 562–566, 568, 570–572

Saxon, 249

Sayers (S&S), 250

SC-852 (Auburn), 12

Scamp (Plymouth), 1017, 1019, 1021, 1315

Scatback (Falcon), 431

Schuler, 250

Scout (International Harvester), 473, 909–914

Scripps-Booth, 250

Sebring (Plymouth), 1006

Seneca (Dart), 394, 395

Senior 6 (Dodge), 79, 80

Seventy-Two (Cadillac), 314

Severin, 250

Seville (Cadillac)
   1958-1960, 327, 329, 331
   1976-1980, 734
   1981-1990, 1122–1126
Shadow (Dodge), 1176–1179
Shaw, 250
Sheridan, 250
Sierra (Dodge), 416–418
Signet (Plymouth/Valiant), 632–634
Silver Anniversary (Buick), 21
Silver Challenger (Dodge), 418
Silver Ghost (Rolls-Royce), 248
Singer, 251
Single Six (Packard), 203, 204
Six (Chrysler), 50, 58–62
Six (DeSoto), 70, 71
Six (Dodge), 80–83
6000 (Pontiac), 1327, 1328, 1330, 1331, 1334,
   1336, 1337, 1341, 1343
Skelton Four, 251
Skyhawk (Buick)
   1975-1980, 701, 702, 704, 706, 707
   1982-1989, 1087, 1089, 1090, 1092, 1095, 1096,
   1099, 1100
Skylark (Buick)
   1953-1954, 297, 298
   1961-1965, 310–313
   1966-1969, 692–694
   1970-1980, 695–697, 701, 702, 704,
   706–708
   1981-1990, 1084, 1087, 1089, 1091, 1092, 1095,
   1096, 1099–1101, 1104
Skylark (Hupmobile), 135
Skyliner (Ford), 443, 444
Skyway Champion (Studebaker), 607, 608
Somerset (Buick), 1093, 1096
Special (Buick), 25, 290, 291, 295–301, 310–313
Special (Pontiac), 574
Special 6 (Chandler), 38
Special 6 (Nash), 174–178
Special 6 (Studebaker), 256
Special 60 (Oldsmobile), 524
Special 66 (Oldsmobile), 526
Special Deluxe (Plymouth), 557–560
Spectrum (Chevrolet), 1147
Speedster (Hudson), 120
Speedster (Studebaker), 615
Speedway (Stutz), 263
Spirit (American Motors), 676, 1082–1083

Spirit (Dodge), 1178, 1179
Sport Fury (Plymouth), 567, 570–572
Sport Suburban (Plymouth)
   1957-1961, 565–567, 569
   1969-1980, 1004, 1007, 1008, 1010, 1011
Sport Wagon (Buick), 313, 692–695
Sportsman (De Soto), 400, 402
Sportsman (Dodge), 422, 827, 828, 830, 832, 834,
   835, 838
Sportsman (Ford), 434
Sportsman (Mercury), 497
Sprint (Chevrolet), 1147
Sprint (Falcon), 431
Squire (Falcon), 430, 431
Squire (Ford), 438, 444, 449, 451, 452
Standard (Chevrolet), 46–48
Standard (Ford), 105
Standard Eight (Nash), 180
Standard Eight (Packard), 208, 209
Standard Eight (Standard Steel Car Company),
   251
Standard Six (Buick), 18, 19
Standard Six (Chandler), 38
Standard Six (Dodge), 79
Standard Six (Hupmobile), 134
Standard Six (Nash), 177, 178
Standard Six (Studebaker), 257, 258
Standard Steel Car Company, 251
Stanley, 251
Stanwood Six, 251
Star, 252–253
Star Chief (Pontiac)
   1954-1958, 581, 583–585
   1960-1964, 587, 588, 590, 591
   1966, 1025
Starfire (Oldsmobile)
   1954-1965, 534, 536, 542–545
   1966-1980, 960, 991, 992
Starlight (Studebaker), 609, 610
Starliner (Ford), 448, 449
Statesman (Nash), 517–519
Stearns-Knight, 254
Stephens, 255
Sterling-Knight, 255
Stevens-Duryea, 255
Stingray (Corvette), 391
Stout Scarab, 255
Strato-Chief (Pontiac), 589
Streamliner (Pontiac), 576, 577

Studebaker. *See also* Erskine
   1920-1939, 256–262
   1940-1966, 607–621
   Avanti, 619, 620
   Big Six, 256–258
   Broadmoor, 617
   Challenger, 620
   Champion, 262, 607–612, 614–617
   Commander, 259–262, 607–609, 611–613,
   615–618, 620
   Conestoga, 615
   Cruiser, 620
   Daytona, 483, 620
   Dictator, 259–261
   Duplex, 257
   Hawk, 616, 618–620
   Land Cruiser, 607, 611–613
   Lark, 482–483
   Light Six, 256
   Parkview, 616, 617
   Pelham, 616
   President, 259–262, 607, 608, 615–618
   Provincial, 617
   Skyway Champion, 607, 608
   Special 6, 256
   Speedster, 615
   Standard Six, 257, 258
   Starlight, 609, 610
   Wagonaire, 620
Stutz, 263–265
   Bearcat, 263
   Speedway, 263
Styleline (Chevrolet), 343, 345, 346
Stylemaster (Chevrolet), 341, 342
Suburban (De Soto), 399
Suburban (Dodge), 417
Suburban (Plymouth), 559, 564, 566–569
Sunbird (Pontiac)
   1976-1980, 1050–1053
   1985-1990, 1332, 1335, 1337, 1340,
   1343
Sundance (Plymouth), 1318–1321
Sunliner (Ford), 439, 440, 442, 444
Super (Buick), 290, 292–300
Super (Nash), 515, 516
Super (Rambler), 594, 596, 597, 599, 600
Super 6 (Hudson), 458, 459
Super 88 (Oldsmobile), 531–540,
   542–544

Super Chief (Pontiac), 584, 585
Super Eight (Packard), 209, 211–214
Super Wagon (Ford), 870
Superior (Chevrolet), 40

T

T1000 (Pontiac), 1323
Tasco, 630
Taurus (Ford), 1214–1216
TC by Maserati (dist. by Chrysler), 1164
Tempest (Pontiac)
    1961-1965, 622–625
    1966-1970, 1041, 1042
Templar, 266
Tempo (Ford), 1217–1220
Terraplane, 266–267
Texan, 268
300 (Chrysler)
    1954-1959, 372, 374–376
    1960-1965, 377, 379–382
    1966-1979, 800, 802–805, 807, 814
Thunderbird (Ford), 1221–1228
    1955-1965, 626–629
    1966-1980, 1063–1068
Thunderbolt (Chrysler), 364
Tire Key (chart), 4
Topaz (Mercury), 1272–1274
Torino (Ford), 873–876, 899–904
Toronado (Oldsmobile), 993–999, 1307–1312
Torpedo (Pontiac), 574–577
Town Car (Lincoln)
    1960, 492
    1981-1990, 1238–1245
Town & Country (Chrysler)
    1942-1949, 365, 367, 368
    1950-1959, 369, 372, 374, 376
    1960-1964, 377, 378, 380, 381
    1966-1980, 800, 801, 804, 805, 807–809, 815, 818
    1982-1990, 1149, 1150, 1152, 1153, 1155, 1157, 1158, 1160
Town Shopper, 630
Townsman (Chevrolet), 347, 349, 350

Tracer (Mercury), 1272–1274
Trans Am (Pontiac Firebird)
    1969-1980, 1056–1062
    1984-1990, 1330, 1346–1351
Travelall (International Harvester), 471–473, 909–912
Traveler (Chrysler), 363
Traveler (Kaiser), 476, 479
Tucker, 630
Tudor (Ford), 433, 434, 436
Tulsa Four, 268
Turismo (Plymouth), 1234–1236
Turnpike Cruiser (Mercury), 503
Twin Six (Packard), 203
2000 (Pontiac), 1327, 1329
2000 Sunbird (Pontiac), 1330

U

Ultra (Buick), 1103
Universal (Chevrolet), 45

V

Vagabond (Frazer), 454
Vagabond (Henry J), 456
Valiant (Plymouth)
    1960-1965, 631–634
    1966-1976, 1014–1022
Vega (Chevrolet), 786–789
Velie, 268–270
Ventura (Pontiac), 587, 1025, 1028, 1044, 1046, 1047, 1049–1051
Victoria (Ford), 438
Victoria (Nash), 174
Victory Six (Dodge), 79, 80
Viking, 271
Villager (Edsel), 424–426
Virginian (Kaiser), 476
Vista-Cruiser (Oldsmobile), 523, 974–983
Volaré (Plymouth), 1022–1024
Voyager (Mercury), 502, 503
Voyager (Plymouth), 1011, 1315, 1318–1320

W

Wagonaire (Studebaker), 620
Wagoneer (Jeep), 915–921
Waltham, 272
Wasp (Hudson), 460–462
Wasp (Martin-Wasp Corp.), 272
Wayfarer (Dodge), 410–412
Westchester Suburban (Dodge), 85
Westcott, 272
Whippet, 273–274
White, 275
Wildcat (Buick)
    1962-1965, 305, 307–309
    1966-1970, 677, 678, 680, 682
Wills Sainte Claire, 275
Willys
    1930-1939, 276–278
    1940-1955, 635–640
    Aero, 638–640
    Bermuda, 640
    Custom, 640
    Jeep, 636–640
    Jeepster, 637
    Plainsman, 635
Willys-Knight, 279–283
Willys-Overland, 276
Windsor (Chrysler), 363, 364, 368, 370–378
Windsor Eight (Moon Motor Car), 284
Winther Six, 284
Winton Six, 284
Wolverine (Rio), 242

X

XL (Ford), 864, 865

Y

Yellow Cab, 284
Yeoman (Chevrolet), 352

Z

Zephyr (Lincoln), 160, 161, 484
Zephyr (Mercury), 959, 1201